EDEXCEL FOR A LEVEL I

PSYCHOLOGY

CHRISTINE BRAIN

In order to ensure that this resource offers high-quality support for the associated Pearson qualification, it has been through a review process by the awarding body. This process confirms that this resource fully covers the teaching and learning content of the specification or part of a specification at which it is aimed. It also confirms that it demonstrates an appropriate balance between the development of subject skills, knowledge and understanding, in addition to preparation for assessment.

Endorsement does not cover any guidance on assessment activities or processes (e.g. practice questions or advice on how to answer assessment questions) included in the resource, nor does it prescribe any particular approach to the teaching or delivery of a related course.

While the publishers have made every attempt to ensure that advice on the qualification and its assessment is accurate, the official specification and associated assessment guidance materials are the only authoritative source of information and should always be referred to for definitive guidance.

Pearson examiners have not contributed to any sections in this resource relevant to examination papers for which they have responsibility.

Examiners will not use endorsed resources as a source of material for any assessment set by Pearson.

Endorsement of a resource does not mean that the resource is required to achieve this Pearson qualification, nor does it mean that it is the only suitable material available to support the qualification, and any resource lists produced by the awarding body shall include this and other appropriate resources.

Hachette UK's policy is to use papers that are natural, renewable and recyclable products and made from wood grown in sustainable forests. The logging and manufacturing processes are expected to conform to the environmental regulations of the country of origin.

Orders: please contact Bookpoint Ltd, 130 Milton Park, Abingdon, Oxon OX14 4SB. Telephone: (44) 01235 827720. Fax: (44) 01235 400454. Email education@bookpoint.co.uk Lines are open from 9 a.m. to 5 p.m., Monday to Saturday, with a 24-hour message answering service. You can also order through our website: www.hoddereducation.co.uk

ISBN: 978 1 4718 3545 2

© Christine Brain 2016

First published in 2016 by

Hodder Education,

An Hachette UK Company

Carmelite House

50 Victoria Embankment

London EC4Y 0DZ

www.hoddereducation.co.uk

Impression number   10 9 8 7 6 5 4 3 2

Year   2019 2018 2017 2016

Cover image © puckillustrations-Fotolia

Illustrations by Barking Dog

Typeset in 10/12.5 pts. BemboStd, by Aptara inc.

Printed in Dubai

A catalogue record for this title is available from the British Library.

CONTENTS

Additional material on website

Additional key questions and worked-through practical investigations for clinical, criminological, child and health psychology

Appendix: Psychological skills – methods

Answers to progress checks

Introduction

This textbook is written specifically for students following the Edexcel GCE 2015 A level Psychology specification. This book focuses on Year Two of the A level course, with Book One covering Year One and the AS level course.

The A level course

Features of the A level course include:

- All exams are at the end of the course.
- There are three exam papers – covering Paper One: four topic areas, Paper Two: two applications, and Paper Three: a psychological skills element.
- Year One focuses on four topic areas – social, cognitive and biological psychology, and learning theories (in Book One).
- Year Two focuses on two applications – clinical and one from criminological, child and health psychology, as well as on psychological skills (this is the focus of Book Two).
- Each topic area and application has some content, method, studies, a key question and a practical investigation.
- 'Psychological skills' is a 'revision' paper, covering three sections: the methodology in the whole course; a review of studies in psychology; and issues and debates in psychology.

Year Two of the A level course – a brief summary of the applications (Paper Two)

Year Two of the A level covers clinical psychology and other applications. You have to choose one application to go with clinical psychology. The choice is from criminological, child or health psychology. Each application is called a 'topic area' in this book. The two applications you cover are examined in Paper Two of the A level. Year Two also covers a synoptic section called 'Psychological skills', which is summarised separately and is examined in Paper Three of the A level.

Clinical psychology in your course looks at issues around diagnosing mental health disorders and then focuses on symptoms and features, explanations and treatments for schizophrenia, as well as for one other mental disorder you choose. The choice is from unipolar depression, anorexia nervosa or obsessive-compulsive disorder. The methods covered are interview and case study, as well as cross-cultural, cross-sectional and longitudinal designs, meta-analysis and primary and secondary data. There is also focus on the Health and Care Professions Council guidelines for clinical practitioners. In all the applications, specific learning from Year One is reviewed, relating to analysis of quantitative data, including the use of descriptive and inferential statistics, and analysis of qualitative data. Grounded theory as a way of analysing qualitative data is added to your Year One learning about analysing data. In clinical psychology, there is one classic study as in Year One topic areas, but there is also a compulsory study focusing on schizophrenia. Then the contemporary study is a choice of two, depending on which 'other' disorder you choose. There is one key question to examine, and one practical investigation to carry out. As in Year One topic areas, the key question must focus on content covered in the application. The practical application must be a content analysis looking at attitudes to mental health.

Criminological psychology in your course covers explanations of crime and anti-social behaviour, understanding the offender, including case formulation and cognitive and ethical interviewing, and treatments for offenders. There is also coverage of eyewitness unreliability and issues affecting juror decision-making. The methods covered are field and laboratory experiments as they relate to research into eyewitness testimony, as well as the case study research method. In method sections, it is important to be able to evaluate using issues of reliability, validity, generalisability, credibility, subjectivity/objectivity and ethics. In criminological psychology, there is an emphasis on reliability, validity, objectivity, credibility and ethics. Sampling is reviewed from Year One and, as in clinical psychology, there is a review of Year One material around the analysis of both qualitative and quantitative data. Meta-analysis and correlation are added to requirements regarding analysis of quantitative data and grounded theory is required alongside thematic analysis with regard to analysis of qualitative data. There is one classic study, and one contemporary study from a choice of three, one key question to examine, and one practical investigation to carry out. Studies, key question and practical are all linked to the content.

Child psychology in your course covers Bowlby's and Ainsworth's work on attachment and includes research into privation and whether negative effects can be reversed, as well as research into deprivation, including how negative effects can be reduced. Cross-cultural research into attachment types is included, as is research into day care, including its advantages and disadvantages for the child. Features, explanations and therapies for autism are included in the content too. The methods covered are questionnaire and interview, observation and cross-cultural research, including the use of meta-analysis. Ethics also feature, including the UNCRC (1989) and the focus on the child's right to participation and to protection. As in clinical psychology, there is a review of Year One material around the analysis of both qualitative and quantitative data. Also as in clinical psychology, grounded theory is required alongside thematic analysis with regard to analysis of qualitative data. There is one classic study and one contemporary study from a choice of three, one key question to examine, and one practical investigation to carry out. Studies, key question and practical are all linked to the content.

Health psychology in your course covers issues around drug taking, such as withdrawal and tolerance, and explanations of drug addiction, including one biological and one learning explanation. Treatments for drug addiction are also required as well as one anti-drug campaign and the psychological strategies behind it. The methods covered are the use of animals in laboratory experiments to study drugs as well as the ethics involved, and the use of humans to study drugs, again including ethical issues. The cross-cultural research method used to study drug misuse is also included. As in clinical psychology, there is a review of Year One material around the analysis of both qualitative and quantitative data. Also as in clinical psychology, grounded theory is required alongside thematic analysis with regard to analysis of qualitative data.

There is one classic study and one contemporary study from a choice of three, one key question to examine, and one practical investigation to carry out. Studies, key question and practical are all linked to the content.

Structure of each topic area/application

Each application follows the same structure, to help your learning, and this was the same structure for the topic areas in Year One:

- some content to focus on, involving theories, ideas and studies in the area of focus
- methodology, to see how psychology works
- studies – a classic and a contemporary one in the area of focus, although in clinical psychology there are three studies in this section
- a key question in the area of focus
- a practical investigation for you to carry out in the area of focus
- issues and debates.

Issues and debates

Issues and debates are important as they allow discussion of different aspects of psychology, from its emphasis on researching in a scientific way to how its findings can be used as a form of social control. You are asked in Paper Three, at the end of your course, to consider such issues and debates. In order to highlight such issues and debates throughout the course, so that you can build your understanding of them, they feature as part of the structure of each topic area, both the four topic areas in Year One (social, cognitive and biological psychology, and learning theories) and the applications in Year Two (clinical psychology and a choice of one from criminological, child and health psychology). As an A level student you can choose to look at them throughout your course or you can choose to study them at the end of your course. In Book One, issues and debates were briefly summarised towards the end of the book. Here in Book Two, issues and debates are found towards the end of the book as part of 'Psychological skills'. However, they can be examined in any of the three A level papers so you need to consider them in relation to the applications in Book Two (and in relation to the four Year One topic areas) as well as looking at them as a synoptic part of Paper Three.

Year Two of the A level course – a brief summary of psychological skills (Paper Three)

Year Two covers two applications examined in Paper Two and also the 'Psychological skills' section, examined in Paper Three.

There are three sections to the psychological skills element of the A level course. The first is a review of research methods, which covers all the methodology in the A level course, both in Year One and in Year Two. The second section is a review of studies, focusing on the classic studies in your course as well as on being able to discuss issues using unseen studies. The third section is the issues and debates section.

Review of research methods covers the many research methods in the A level course, including experiment, observation, interview, questionnaire, case study, twin and adoption studies, animal experiments and content analysis.

Designs include longitudinal, cross-sectional, cross-cultural, meta-analysis and correlation research. Methodological issues range from hypotheses and controls to sampling and types of data. There is also emphasis on ethics, when using both human and animal participants. Also analysis of both qualitative and quantitative data is reviewed. You will have covered all this material over the A level course so this is a revision section. However, there is the inclusion of the convention of published psychological research, including the role of peer reviewing, which you must cover and has less focus throughout the course than the other material in this section.

Review of studies covers the requirement to draw on and compare all the classic studies you covered in the Year One topic area and Year Two application, as well as the requirement to review the classic studies synoptically in terms of issues and debates. You also need to be able to use principles of understanding, evaluation and synopticity on unseen material.

Issues and debates covers 11 issues. These are briefly listed here. You need to know about (a) 'ethical issues in animal and human research' and (b) 'practical issues in the design and implementation of research', issues you will have covered throughout the course. You will have covered (c) 'reductionism in the explanation of behaviour' and (d) 'psychology as a science' in learning theories in Year One. You also need to know about (e) 'cultural and gender issues in psychological research', and your learning about obedience and prejudice in social psychology will help with this issue and debate. For (f) 'role of nature and nurture', your coverage of cross-cultural research methods and twin and adoption studies will help you. You need to be able to (g) 'compare ways of explaining behaviour using different themes', which you will have done throughout your course, such as different learning explanations, and you need to show (h) an 'understanding of how psychological understanding has developed over time', which you will have seen, such as if you looked at Milgram's and Burger's work on obedience. You need to know about (i) 'the use of psychological knowledge in society', which you looked at when studying key questions for society in the topic areas. Finally, you need to cover (j) 'the use of psychology in social control' and (k) 'issues related to socially sensitive research', again issues you will have covered in the course.

The exam papers

A level

Paper One has 90 marks, lasts two hours and covers the four foundation topic areas in your course – social, cognitive and biological psychology, and learning theories (these are covered in Book One). It is worth 35 per cent of your A level.

Paper Two has 90 marks, lasts two hours and covers two applications in your course – clinical psychology and a choice of one from criminological, child and health psychology (these are covered in this book, Book Two). Paper Two is part of Year Two and is worth 35 per cent of the A level.

Paper Three has 80 marks and lasts two hours. It covers what are called 'Psychological skills'. The paper covers all the methodology in your course as Section A, a review of your classic studies and what you know about studies as Section B, and an 'issues and debates' section, Section C (these are covered in this book, Book Two). It is worth 30 per cent of the A level.

Types of questions

All exams will have some short-answer questions and some open-response extended writing. The short-answer questions can range from 1 mark for naming a mental health disorder to 4 or 6 marks, for example, for describing a theory, study, part of a study, or for giving an explanation of something, such as explaining one treatment for a mental health disorder. Open-response extended writing questions are currently 8, 12, 16 or 20 marks. There are no multiple-choice sections in the exam papers.

Taxonomy/injunctions

In your specification, near the end, you will find a taxonomy (pp. 77–78). This is a list of injunctions, which are words that tell you what to do in an answer. For example, 'describe' or 'assess'. Be sure to read through the taxonomy so that you know what each 'command word' requires you to do.

For example:
- 'calculate' requires you to show working
- 'analyse' means examine parts of something to uncover the meaning or essential features
- 'assess' requires you to come to a conclusion after weighing up evidence
- 'compare' means look at similarities and differences but not needing a conclusion or judgement
- 'describe' means you don't need a justification for your points
- 'explain' requires points with justifications
- 'discuss' needs an exploration of different views but without needing a judgement or conclusion
- 'evaluate', importantly, requires you to 'come to a supported judgement of a subject's qualities and relation to its context' (p. 78)
- 'to what extent' means look at information, give a balanced and reasoned argument and then a judgement or conclusion.

Remember, 'assess', 'evaluate' and 'to what extent' all require you to come to a judgement or a conclusion and 'explain' requires a justification.

There are other injunctions but they are more obvious. These are 'complete', 'define', 'determine', 'draw', 'give', 'identify', 'interpret', 'justify', 'name', 'plot', 'predict', 'state' and 'suggest'. See what is required for each injunction by referring to the specification.

Writing an answer

Your writing needs to be as concise as possible and to be clear and effective. Points have to be made clearly, showing knowledge and also understanding of that knowledge. It is useful to make a point and then think of an elaboration on that point – when you have given your answer, consider writing something else as well.

Essays (open-response extended writing) should be written logically, with a conclusion if required (depending on the injunction). For example, if you are asked to consider something about psychology in relation to two theories, you could deal with one theory at a time, which might be logical (depending on the exact question).

Always answer the question in full and tailor your answer for that question. A good way to do that is to refer to the question in your answer to show the reader you are focusing on it.

Assessment objectives

You will be assessed on assessment objectives, which you can find in full in your specification (p. 4):

- Assessment Objective One (AO1) – demonstrate knowledge and understanding of scientific ideas, processes, techniques and procedures.
- Assessment Objective Two (AO2) – apply knowledge and understanding of scientific ideas, processes, techniques and procedures (in various contexts).
- Assessment Objective Three (AO3) – analyse, interpret and evaluate scientific information, ideas and evidence, including in relation to issues, to make judgements and reach conclusions and to develop and refine practical design and procedures.

In summary, you will be assessed on what you know and understand, how you can apply that knowledge and understanding to new contexts and how you can evaluate, interpret and analyse what you have learned.

Know ⟶ Apply ⟶ Evaluate

About this book

Website

 There is a website to go with this book, which you can access here: www.hoddereducation.co.uk/edexcelpsychology2

Where material is on the website, a note will be made and the website icon will appear. The 'Psychological skills – methods' part of your course can be found on the website as it revises material. Answers to progress checks are also on the website. You need to know one key question for clinical psychology and your other application; one key question is given in the book and an additional key question can be found on the website for your interest. Practical investigations for the four applications are also worked through on the website.

What the chapters cover

- Chapters One and Two cover clinical psychology. Chapter One focuses on the content, studies and key question, and Chapter Two covers the method material, including the practical investigation.
- Chapters Three to Five follow the specification and cover one of the 'option' applications in the order in the specification. Each of these three chapters is divided into the relevant areas, following the specification. You will need to cover just one of the three chapters, depending on which option you choose.
- Chapter Six covers review of studies for your course, covering Section Two of 'Psychological skills'.
- Chapter Seven covers issues and debates, Section Three of 'Psychological skills'.
- The Glossary follows.

On the website, you can find the review of methods for your course, covering Section One of 'Psychological skills', as well as suggested progress checks answers.

Advice and guidance

Throughout the chapters, there is advice to guide you. Use the following features carefully as they will be very useful:

- *Explanation/definition* boxes provide details on emboldened key terms in the text and can be used to build a glossary to help understanding. They are found the first time a term is used.
- *Explore* boxes will enhance your learning.
- *Progress checks* test your understanding, and the suggested answers can be found on the website to help your understanding and learning.
- *Study hints* are there to help you to learn about exam techniques and processes, as well as giving tips for learning.
- *Study of interest* sections bring in additional aspects for your interest and can be used in discussion.
- *Test yourself* questions are for you to check what you have learned and practise writing exam-style answers.
- *Individual differences and developmental psychology* icons can be used to track such issues through your course.
- *You need to know about* tables are given at the start of each chapter – you can use them to check your learning after you have read the material.
- *Year One links* are there to help you to use your Year One material to improve your understanding and revision.
- *Practical links* help you to link to a relevant practical investigation.
- *Maths links* help you to link to the maths requirement in clinical psychology.

Individual differences and developmental links

In your course, while you are covering the required content, you are also asked to consider any parts of the content that can link to the study of differences between individuals and to the study of how we develop.

Individual differences

Individual differences are an important part of your course. In all the topic areas there is focus on individual differences, including the four Year One topic areas and the Year Two applications. In psychology, a lot of focus is on how people are the same, such as the way the brain works (covered in biological and clinical psychology) and aspects of memory (covered in cognitive and criminological psychology), as well as learning explanations (such as for drug addiction in health psychology). Alongside these similarities, however, there are differences in individuals, such as intelligence (IQ) and personality. Gender can also give people 'individual differences', as can other characteristics, such as temperament. Even identical twins, who share 100 per cent of their genes, exhibit individual differences. In your course, you need to be aware of individual differences in people, alongside all the similarities that are discussed. In this textbook, there is an 'individual differences' icon (shown at the start of this section) to alert you when to take notes about this area of interest in psychology.

Developmental psychology

Developmental psychology is an important area in psychology. Developmental psychology follows someone's development from conception to adulthood and into older age. Areas within developmental psychology include learning theories – from our learning come our gender behaviour and cultural norms and beliefs as well as behaviour, such as our relationships coming from early attachment experiences (child psychology). When the nature–nurture debate is discussed, you can think about developmental psychology, not only the nurture element, though how we are brought up affects our development (as attachment theory in child psychology, social explanations of anti-social behaviour in criminological psychology and learning theories of drug addiction in health psychology show), but also our nature, as issues about our biology can also affect our development. For example, maturation processes (which are inbuilt processes that change us as we grow, such as puberty and ageing) affect our development. You need to be ready to discuss developmental issues and such issues are mentioned in the content of each of the topic areas in your course (social psychology, cognitive psychology, biological psychology and learning theories in Year One and clinical psychology and the other three applications in Year Two). This textbook uses a 'developmental psychology' icon (shown at the start of this section) to alert you to links.

How to use this book

You should work through Paper Two first, reading Chapters One and Two to cover clinical psychology. Then study one from Chapters Three to Five, to cover your chosen 'other' application. You should then look at Chapters Six and Seven and the 'Psychological skills – methods' section online, to cover the three sections of 'Psychological skills', for Paper Three. Chapters Six and Seven and the online 'Psychological skills – methods' will help with revision, before you start revising in more detail.

Chapter Seven, covering issues and debates, relates to all the topic areas in your course, including the four Year One topic areas (social, cognitive and biological psychology and learning theories) and the two applications (clinical psychology and one from criminological, child and health psychology). You could read Chapter Seven after Chapters One and Two, so you relate issues and debates and clinical psychology, and then read Chapter Seven again after Chapter Three, Four or Five, so you relate issues and debates and your other chosen application. When revising, you need to relate issues and debates to the Year One foundation topic areas too.

Active learning is best

You are advised to read through each chapter without taking notes. Then go back through each section and make your own notes. Focus on terminology; making your own definitions for each term can be particularly useful. Use lots of headings in your notes and make your notes as clear as possible. For example, each study, theory or concept could have its own heading and summary. When carrying out your practical, keep a separate folder for your notes. Your teacher might be able to give you a pro forma for keeping notes about practical investigations.

How psychology works

Throughout Year One and in Year Two as well there is strong emphasis on how psychology works, referring to the 'study' of mind and behaviour. 'Psychological skills – methods' (online) reviews the method material you covered in your course and will give you a good picture of how psychology works. Some of the issues and debates in Chapter Seven also relate to how psychology works, such as whether psychology is 'doing science' and issues of ethics and reductionism, as well as practical issues when doing psychological research.

Studies in psychology

Chapter One has a classic study, a compulsory contemporary study, and another contemporary study for you to cover, and Chapter Two has a case study and a study using interviewing. You will also cover a classic and a contemporary study focusing on your chosen 'other' application. As part of your studying, you might like to read through all the studies in those sections, to get a good picture of how studies are written up, what they entail and how similar research methods are, with similar evaluation points about them.

About key questions for society

For clinical psychology and your chosen 'other' application, you will study a key question for society based on the material you have covered, as you did for the four foundation topic areas in Year One. The key question relates to the issue and debate 'the use of psychological knowledge within society'. You need to focus on a question society needs answering where the answer can draw on psychological understanding. This will help you to relate what you study to the 'real world' and should help to make psychology interesting.

About practical investigations

For each of the two applications you cover, you will carry out a practical investigation to practise the skills you have learnt in the methodology and content sections, as you did in the Year One topic areas. For clinical psychology, you have to carry out a content analysis looking at attitudes to mental health. For your chosen 'other' application, you can choose the research method from a specified list of three methods. With regard to the specific practical investigation you undertake there is choice, though your practical investigation must relate to the material you have covered in the application.

Psychology is a science and science involves:
- putting forward a theory
- developing a hypothesis of what might be expected from the theory (a hypothesis is a statement of what is expected)
- testing the hypothesis.

Each practical investigation that you carry out should come from a theory and be planned to test that theory. Check that you understand the theory that your practical is testing. This will make for a more interesting and better investigation and will also mean that you will have a better understanding of the issues.

 Worked-through practical investigations for clinical psychology and your other chosen application can be found on the website.

 Edexcel Psychology for A level Book 2

Choices in Year Two of your A level course

It is important to note that there are some choices in your course:

- In clinical psychology, you have a choice of your 'other' mental disorder, though schizophrenia is compulsory. There are two contemporary studies listed for each of the three 'other' disorders you can choose from and you need to cover one of those two studies. In this book, all three 'other' disorders are covered for your interest.

- In clinical psychology, in the method section, you have to cover a study using the case study method and one using the interview method and you can choose the two studies. There is one example of a case study and one of a study using interviewing offered in your specification – those two examples are the ones given in this book.

- There are three 'other' applications and all three are given in this book. You can choose one after reading all the chapters, though it is likely that you will have chosen one of them before using this textbook, which means you do not need to study the other two chapters, just the chapter relating to your chosen 'other' application.

- In the three 'other' applications (you choose one of them), there are three contemporary studies listed and you choose one from three. In this book, for all three applications, all three of these studies are explained for your interest. You may have chosen just one of these or you can choose one after reading them all.

- In criminological psychology, you can choose the two treatments for offenders within set limits (e.g. one treatment has to be cognitive-behavioural) and you can choose which characteristics of the defendant you study.

- In health psychology, you can choose the explanations and treatments for drug addiction, within set limits, such as needing one learning and one biological explanation.

- You have a choice of a key question in each topic area. One key question is given in the book for clinical psychology and the other applications. Another key question for each application is provided on the website for your interest. However, you may have chosen a different one already. If that is the case, you might like to read the ones offered here and on the website, to help your learning of the concepts and ideas in the topic area.

- You have a choice about the focus of your practical investigations, though some of what you have to do in your practical investigations is given in the specification. In this book, what is required for each practical investigation for each of the applications is explained, and for each application there is a worked-through practical on the website. However, you will have carried out your own practical investigations, so you need to use those in the exams. You might like to read through the examples, however, to help your learning.

Year One of your A level course, which includes the AS

Book Two covers Year Two of your course, as has been explained. Year One covers four foundation topic areas, which are social, cognitive and biological psychology and learning theories. These four foundation topics make up the AS course. The AS does not require any of the Year Two material. Book One covers the Year One/AS material.

Year One also covers a lot of basic methodology, which is drawn on in Year Two, such as interviewing as a research method, which is covered in clinical psychology, and sampling being reviewed if you choose to study criminological psychology.

Year Two builds on the foundations that you will cover in Year One. For example, your learning about synaptic transmission and how messages are sent in the brain, in biological psychology, is used again when you consider, perhaps, drug therapy for schizophrenia or depression, or if you cover health psychology and issues around drug addiction and withdrawal.

Your Year One learning will underpin a lot of Year Two requirements, both the content and the methods.

The Edexcel website

- Edexcel has its own website (www.edexcel.com), with a section for psychology. Use it to find out more about your course, including the specification. The specification outlines everything you need to know for your course, and this textbook follows every aspect of Year Two.
- Use the specimen assessment materials (SAMs), which include specimen exam papers and mark schemes. The mark schemes will help you to see how to answer the questions and score the marks.

Take charge of your own learning and you will do very well.

Maintaining your interest in psychology

You will have clear reasons for studying A level or AS psychology. Remember those reasons and make sure you get what you want out of your studying. Use websites and other sources, such as books and magazines, to maintain your interest. Treat your studies separately from your interest and then from time to time try to bring the two together. This takes time and practice, but it is worth being patient. If you joined the course because you want to know what makes people do certain things or what makes us like we are, then you *will* find the answers by studying psychology, even though some of what you learn first may not seem relevant – it *is* relevant and its relevance will become more obvious as you move through the course.

Acknowledgements

Thank you, Francesca, Susan, Julie, Caterina, Kate and Rebecca, and all at Hodder for their hard work on this book. Thank you to my grown-up family, such an important part of my life: Alex, Jenny, Doug and Sarah; remembering Kevin, Paul and Lee; including Matt, Leanne, Chris and Amy; and, not least, Alastair, for his patience, good humour, love and support.

For Jonathan: live long, prosper and enjoy.

Photo and artwork credits

The Publishers would like to thank the following for permission to reproduce copyright material.

Page 3: © Cory Docken/iStock/Thinkstock; *page 6*: © Jupiterimages/Creatas/Thinkstock; *page 8*: © Suprijono Suharjoto/Fotolia; *page 13*: © University of Pittsburgh; *page 15*: © MAXFX/Fotolia; *page 18*: © Digital Vision/ Photodisc/Thinkstock; *page 21*: © Black Star/Alamy; *page 56*: © Chris Rout/Alamy; *page 88*: © AntonioGuillem/iStock/ Thinkstock; *page 93*: © Dmitri Kotchetov/iStock/Thinkstock; *page 101*: © Library of Congress Prints and Photographic Division; *page 124*: © Ssilver/Fotolia; *page 139*: © Newscast Online; *page 140*: © Muhammad_Karim/iStock/Thinkstock; *page 142*: © Darrin Klimek/Photodisc/Thinkstock; *page 144*: © Poplasen/iStock/Thinkstock; *page 146*: © Ahlapot/ iStock/Thinkstock; *page 150*: © Ingram Publishing/Thinkstock; *page 170 (left)*: © Shironosov/iStock/Thinkstock; *page 170 (centre)*: © Yaron Yarden/iStock/Thinkstock; *page 170 (right)*: © MAHESH PURANIK/iStock/Thinkstock; *page 173*: © Anatoliy Samara/iStock/Thinkstock; *page 175*: © Jupiterimages/Thinkstock; *page 185*: © moodboard/Thinkstock; *page 190*: © Monkey Business Images/Stockbroker/Thinkstock; *page 225*: © Mark Bowden/istock/Thinkstock; *page 233*: © KatarzynaBialasiewicz/iStock/Thinkstock; *page 234*: © REX Shutterstock; *page 246*: © John Powell Photographer / Alamy; *page 253*: © Juan CARLOS/AFP/Getty Images; *page 262*: © Images of Birmingham Premium / Alamy; *page 272*: © fkienas/iStock/Thinkstock; *page 277*: © Stockbyte/Thinkstock; *page 286*: © Greg Blomberg / Alamy; *page 290*: © Stockdisc / Corbis; *page 300*: © Jupiterimages/Photos.com/Thinkstock; *page 305*: Meinzahn/Thinkstock; *page 315*: © Pete Maclaine / Alamy; *page 329*: © lekcej/iStock/Thinkstock; *page 330*: © Elizabeth Loftus; *page 342*: © Justin Kase zfivez / Alamy; *page 347*: © Steve Parsons / PA Archive/PA Images; *page 356*: © Nikreates / Alamy; *page 358*: © Maria Teijeiro/Photodisc/Thinkstock; *page 362*: © Picture Partners/Alamy; *page 363*: © Ewastudio/iStock/Thinkstock; *page 369*: © Photo Researchers, Inc./Science Photo Library; *page 370*: © The Image Works / TopFoto; *page 375*: © Thomas, aged 2 years 4 months, in *Foster Care for Ten Days. Young Children in Brief Separation* (1971) James and Joyce; *Separation and the Very Young* (1989) Robertson J and Robertson J; *page 378*: © Copyright The Open University 2015; *page 395*: © Comstock/Thinkstock; *page 402*: © Lionel Bonaventure/Getty Images; *page 404*: © Brian Harris; *page 409*: © Romrodinka/iStock/Thinkstock; *page 414*: © Kim Gunkel/Getty Images; *page 424*: © ElizabethHoffmann/iStock/ Thinkstock; *page 440*: © Paul Springett 07/Alamy; *page 446*: © Kai Chiang/istock/Thinkstock; *page 450*: © Alexsokolov/ iStock/Thinkstock; *page 467*: © Comstock/Stockbyte/Thinkstock; *page 480*: © The Image Works / TopFoto; *page 482*: © NHS; *page 485*: © Andy Crump/Science Photo Library; *page 501*: © Jonathan Welch/Alamy; *page 512*: © Jeff Dunn/ Photolibrary/Getty Images; *page 514*: © Philip Allan/Jennifer Reynolds; *page 521*: © Chagin/iStock/Thinkstock; *page 540*: © Dejan Krsmanovic/iStock/Thinkstock; *page 542*: © Lucianne Pashley/ age fotostock/Alamy; *page 553*: © Fuse/ iStock/Thinkstock; *page 558*: © Iyoshi Takahase Segundo/iStock/Thinkstock; *page 571*: © Marmaduke St. John / Alamy; *page 575*: © Yaacov Dagan / Alamy; *page 584*: © Mimi Forsyth/AGE Fotostock/Superstock; *page 602*: © Phodo/iStock/ Thinkstock; *page 603*: © Piksel/iStock/ThinkStock; *page 607*: © Pawel Bienkowski / Alamy; *page 611*: © Emily Riddell/ Lonely Planet Images/ Getty Images; *page 613*: © Monkeybusinessimages/iStock/Thinkstock; *page 635*: © Jyliana/ iStock/ThinkStock; *page 640*: © Tatiana Gladskikh/iStock/Thinkstock; *page 642*: © Diego Cervo /123RF; *page 644*: © Stockdevil/iStock/Thinkstock; *page 648*: © AMilkin/iStock/Thinkstock; *page 650*: © Albert Bandura; *page 662*: © Michael Price/iStock/Thinkstock; *page 666*: © Murad RM / Alamy; *page 667*: © BananaStock/Thinkstock; *page 675*: © RGB Ventures / SuperStock / Alamy; *page 680*: © Anna Omelchenko/iStock/Thinkstock.

Page 167 (Table 2.2): reprinted, with permission, from Vallentine, V. *et al.* (2010) 'Psycho-educational group for detained offender patients: understanding mental illness', *The Journal of Forensic Psychiatry & Psychology*, 21(3), 393–406; *pages 331 and 332* (Tables 3.29, 3.30 and 3.31): reprinted, with permission, from Loftus, E.F. and Palmer, J.C. (1974)

'Reconstruction of automobile destruction: An example of the interaction between language and memory', *Journal of Verbal Learning and Verbal Behavior*, 13(5), 585–589; *page 594* (Tables 5.18 and 5.19): adapted, with permission, from Dixit, S. *et al.* (2012) 'Biosocial determinants of alcohol risk behaviour: An epidemiological study in urban and rural communities of Aligarh, Uttar Pradesh', *National Journal of Community Medicine*, 3(3), 447–451.

Chapter One: Clinical psychology – content, studies and key question

General overview

This chapter is about clinical psychology, an **application** in psychology, which means that theories and studies are applied to issues of concern to society and the individual. Clinical psychology covers many areas and focuses on describing, explaining and treating mental disorders. In your course you will touch on just some of these issues. You will look at some general issues around diagnosing mental illnesses and then focus on two disorders. As with your Year One studies, in the Year Two applications you are required to know studies in detail. For clinical psychology you need to know *three* studies as well as one key question in the area you are studying. You will also carry out a practical investigation based on the content you cover.

Definition

Application refers to theories and studies in a specific area of psychology that are used to look at particular issues for an individual or society.

Explore

You will find it helpful to explore more about mental health issues as you prepare to work through this chapter. 'Mind' is one of a number of organisations that focus on mental health and mental ill health: www.mind.org.uk

Study of interest

Oei *et al.* (2013) carried out a study to see whether a standard measure used to test for depression, anxiety and stress is reliable in other cultures. Hispanic, British, American and Australian cultures use the DASS-21 (Depression and Anxiety Stress Scale with 21 items) reliably and validly. The researchers pointed out that DASS-21 had not been tested for validity in Asia, where people often express different emotional reactions to particular situations. If a scale is not valid it will not give an accurate measure. For example, if stress is defined as not having the resources to cope with a situation, but those 'resources'

are seen differently in Asia, then stress will be experienced differently. Oei *et al.* (2013) used statistical analysis on data from six nations and found that using 18 of the items (DASS-18) made the measure more valid. The DASS is used a lot in counselling and similar situations because it is relatively easy to administer and gives a quantitative result. A score at the start of treatment can be recorded and the DASS used at any time during the treatment and at the end so that progress can be measured by a reducing DASS score. It is important that studies such as this one are carried out as it is important that measures of depression, anxiety and stress are accurate.

Explore

You can find versions of the DASS measure on the internet – there is one with 42 items and one with 21 items. Try: **www.iwsml.org.au/images/mental_health/Frequently_Used/Outcome_Tools/Dass21.pdf.**

Look at the scales to get an idea of what clinical psychology can involve. Remember that scoring must always be carried out by a professional, so avoid using the scale on someone you know, or drawing conclusions about your own score from the scale.

STUDY HINT

(w) Progress check answers can be found on the website accompanying this book.

Summary of learning objectives

Content

You need to learn about issues around defining abnormality (in mental functioning), including the four 'Ds': deviance, dysfunction, distress and danger. In the area of diagnosis you need to look at two different classification systems, the Diagnostic and Statistical Manual of mental disorders (DSM) and the International Classification of Diseases (ICD). With regard to DSM you will be looking at the DSM-IV-TR or the DSM-5, as well as the DSM more generally (see page 10). **Reliability** and **validity** of diagnosis are important issues, as indicated in the Oei *et al.* (2013) study described above. You also need to learn about schizophrenia and one other mental health disorder from a choice of anorexia nervosa, obsessive compulsive disorder (OCD) or unipolar depression. When looking at schizophrenia and your other chosen disorder you need to cover symptoms and features of both, explanations for both, and treatments for both.

Definitions

Reliability – when something done again gets the same results, including when a diagnosis is repeated.

Validity – measuring what is being said to be measured, including in a diagnosis.

STUDY HINT

Emboldened terms in the text are defined in a glossary of terms. If you already know a term from Year One, test yourself or look at the meaning in the glossary to help build your knowledge of psychology and make links to your Year One studies. If a term is new to you, look at what it means and begin making a glossary of your own for Year Two.

STUDY HINT

Often in clinical psychology (and in other topic areas) there are a lot of studies to learn because these give you evidence to use in your exam answers. One way of recording such information is to use index cards with the name(s) and date on one side and a brief summary of what the evidence is on the other side. Then you can practise learning names and dates from evidence or evidence from names and dates. Another approach is to draw up a table of studies with name(s) and the date in one column and evidence in the other. Try to find a way to revise that suits you and to write notes ready for revision from the beginning of your course.

Year One link: Year One Method sections have covered reliability and validity issues so you should be familiar with both terms and their meanings.

Individual differences and developmental psychology

All topic areas in this course require you to consider two issues in psychology and these are individual differences and developmental psychology. In each topic area you will find reference to where these issues are within the content or the key question. You need to be able to make links between these two issues and areas that reflect them. Each issue has

its own symbol in this textbook to alert you to these links (see below). Individual differences refers to how people might be inherently different, such as in their personality or intelligence. Gender, as well as other genetic or biological differences, can result in individual differences, too. Developmental psychology is an area of study that focuses on how humans develop from before birth through to adolescence as well as beyond and into old age.

Year One link: Year One topic areas consider both individual differences and developmental issues in the content sections. Year Two applications do the same.

 Individual differences

In clinical psychology the links that must be learned about are:
- how cultural effects can lead to individual differences in mental health disorders
- how culture can affect diagnoses of mental disorders, affecting validity and reliability; culture can make individuals different.

 Developmental psychology

In clinical psychology the link that must be learned about is:
- issues around genes and mental health, such as a genetic or biochemical explanation for schizophrenia, which can affect development.

Method

Methodology refers to how psychology is 'done'; it is the study of **research methods**. Method in clinical psychology is covered in Chapter Two. The main methods used in clinical psychology are **case studies** (page 156) and **interviews** (page 161) and you will study one case study and one interview to help you learn these research methods. Other methodological issues you need to know about are **longitudinal**, **cross-sectional** and **cross-cultural** designs in a study (page 143), as well as **meta-analysis** (page 152) and the use of **primary data** and **secondary data** (page 154). You will need to be able to analyse the data gathered using these methods, including using both descriptive and inferential statistics for quantitative data gathered (page 177) and thematic analysis and **grounded theory** for qualitative data gathered (page 169). With the exception of grounded theory, you have already covered these analysis methods together with interviewing in Year One. You will have looked at case studies of brain damaged patients, but perhaps not at case studies in general. One further issue covered in the method section for clinical psychology is the **Health and Care Professions Council** (HCPC) guidelines for clinical practitioners (page 142), which is about ethics in clinical practice.

Definitions

Research methods refers to the main ways data are collected in a study, such as using an experiment, a case study, a questionnaire or an interview.

Methodology considers how a study is carried out and issues around doing psychology.

Health and Care Professions Council (HCPC) became the governing body of psychologists in 2008. The HCPC keeps a register of psychologists and social work professionals who meet their standards and they regulate these professions too.

Case study is a research method where one person or a small group is involved in a detailed study which produces a lot of data.

Interview is a research method where an interviewer asks questions of an interviewee. There are different types of interview, including structured, semi-structured and unstructured interview.

Grounded theory means gathering qualitative data without a research question driving the gathering of those data and then using coding to uncover themes and ideas in the data. From those categories theory can be generated. The theory comes from the data rather than the theory driving the gathering of the data, as happens in a positivist tradition.

Longitudinal design is a psychological study that involves studying the same participant or participants over a period of time to make comparisons in the data gathered over that time period. There are also **cross-sectional designs**, where at one moment in time data are gathered from participants and comparisons are made at that one moment in time. Some studies use a **cross-cultural design**, which means they gather data in different cultures and compare the data from the different cultures.

Meta-analysis refers to a study that uses data gathered from a number of other studies which have sufficiently similar research questions that their findings can be compared and conclusions drawn using results from all the studies. Such studies gather **secondary data**, which means the data that are used in the study were already gathered for a different study. **Primary data** are when data are gathered first-hand for the study in question.

A case study can be carried out to look at the support a self-help group can offer and how effective a group might be in supporting those with a mental disorder. Lavarenne *et al.* (2013) is an example of such a study.

Explore
You can find out more about the HCPC at:
www.hcpc-uk.co.uk/aboutregistration/professions/index.asp?id=14

Method link: For clinical psychology, the method, maths and practical investigation are in Chapter Two.

Studies

The classic study you need in clinical psychology is Rosenhan (1973) 'On being sane in insane places'.

The required contemporary study focuses on schizophrenia: Carlsson *et al.* (1999/2000) 'Network interactions in schizophrenia – therapeutic implications'. This is a **review** of work in the area rather than a **study**.

Definitions

Review in psychology: this is similar to a study but it is more of a theoretical examination of a research question using what is already known.

Study in psychology: this is where researchers take a research question and then gather data to consider that research question, drawing conclusions accordingly.

You will also choose one contemporary study from a choice of two (see below) for your chosen mental disorder (anorexia nervosa, obsessive compulsive disorder (OCD) or unipolar depression).

● Anorexia nervosa – choose from:
   ● Scott-Van Zeeland *et al.* (2013/2014) Evidence for the role of EPHX2 gene variants in anorexia nervosa, *or*

- Guardia *et al.* (2012) Imagining one's own and someone else's body actions: dissociation in anorexia nervosa.
- Obsessive compulsive disorder (OCD) – choose from:
  - Masellis *et al.* (2003) Quality of life in OCD: Differential impact of obsessions, compulsions and depressions co-morbidity, *or*
  - POTS team including March *et al.* (2004) Cognitive-behavioural therapy, Sertraline and their combination for children and adolescents with OCD.
- Unipolar depression – choose from:
  - Kroenke *et al.* (2008) The PHQ-8 as a measure of current depression in the general population, *or*
  - Williams *et al.* (2013) Combining imagination and reason in the treatment of depression: a randomised control trial of internet-based cognitive bias modification and internet-CBT for depression.

Key question

You have a choice of key question to study. The course suggests that, focusing on how clinical psychology can help to explain or deal with such an issue, you choose from how different societies define mental health disorders or what the issues are surrounding mental health in the workplace. You can, however, choose any issue.

Practical investigation in clinical psychology

You have to carry out one practical research exercise within clinical psychology using **content analysis** and you must look at attitudes to mental health. You will choose your own practical research exercise within your learning, so it is not possible to state in this book what that might be. Chapter Two discusses the practical investigation in clinical psychology using a **summative content analysis** to help you with this section (page 181).

A worked example can be found on the accompanying website. You may have looked at how attitudes to mental health have changed over time or how different sources report mental health. Your key question could be how different societies define mental health, showing their attitudes to mental health, and you could collect data from different sources to examine that question.

You need to gather data relevant to topics you have studied in clinical psychology and your practical investigation must be ethical throughout. You must use at least two sources when collecting your data.

Definitions

Content analysis refers to a method of gathering and analysing data. It means looking in detail at some content – which can be newspaper articles, studies, children's books, drawings, stories, a film and so on – and analysing that content using particular categories.

Summative content analysis refers to looking at some content and counting specific key terms in that content (the key terms are decided beforehand). There are other types of content analysis.

Year One link: You will have looked at content analysis in your study of learning theories.

Practical link: Chapter Two discusses the requirements of a practical investigation in clinical psychology (page 181) with the actual practical found on the website.

Maths link: Chapter Two looks at the maths you need for clinical psychology (page 177) so that you can analyse your practical investigation. You will be familiar with this from your Year One studies.

Issues and debates

The 11 issues and debates chosen for your course are: ethics; practical issues in research design; reductionism; comparing explanations; psychology as a science; culture and gender; nature-nurture; how psychology has developed over time; issues of social control; using psychology in society; and issues around socially sensitive research.

Chapter Seven looks at issues and debates in detail.

> **STUDY HINT**
> These issues and debates appear in each topic area for Year One and Year Two, in the same order, in the specification. For each topic area there are examples against each of the issues and debates in the specification to show how material from that topic area can illustrate the issue or debate. You can use the specification for ideas relevant to each of the issues and debates.

> **STUDY HINT**
> Make the summary of learning objectives into a checklist. Table 1.1 gives a suggested list. However, you could add detail, which would help your learning.

Table 1.1 What you need to know for clinical psychology

You need to know about:	
The four Ds relating to diagnosis of mental disorders	The use of case studies, including one example (looking at mental health)
The DSM (DSM IV-R or DSM V) and ICD classification systems and reliability and validity of such classification systems	The use of interviews, including one example (in clinical psychology)
Symptoms and features of schizophrenia, including thought insertion, hallucinations, delusions, disordered thinking	Analysis of quantitative data focusing on the methods listed for clinical psychology, including descriptive and inferential statistics (the four tests from Year One)
Three explanations for schizophrenia, including the functioning of neurotransmitters, one other biological explanation and one non-biological explanation	Analysis of qualitative data using thematic analysis and grounded theory
Symptoms and features of one disorder from anorexia nervosa, obsessive compulsive disorder (OCD) and unipolar depression	A classic study: Rosenhan (1973)
Two explanations for one disorder from anorexia nervosa, obsessive compulsive disorder (OCD) and unipolar depression, one biological and one non-biological theory/explanation	A contemporary study looking at schizophrenia: Carlsson *et al.* (1999/2000)
One biological and one psychological treatment (use different topic areas) for schizophrenia	One contemporary study from a choice of two per mental disorder from anorexia nervosa, obsessive compulsive disorder (OCD) and unipolar depression for one of these disorders
One biological and one psychological treatment (use different topic areas) for one disorder from anorexia nervosa, obsessive compulsive disorder (OCD) and unipolar depression	One key question that can be explained using concepts, theories and/or research from clinical psychology in your course, and the concepts, theories and research in question
An awareness of HCPC (Health and Care Professions Council) guidelines for clinical practitioners	One practical investigation focusing on attitudes to mental health and relating to your studies in clinical psychology in your course. This must be a summative content analysis
The use of longitudinal, cross-sectional, cross-cultural designs; meta-analysis; and primary and secondary data when researching mental health	Individual differences and developmental psychology linking to clinical psychology
Issues and debates (see Chapter Seven for more detail)	

An introduction to clinical psychology

Clinical psychology is about diagnosing, explaining and treating mental illness. Your course focuses on schizophrenia and one other disorder, chosen from anorexia nervosa, obsessive compulsive disorder (OCD) and unipolar depression. Unipolar depression is generally referred to in this chapter simply as 'depression'; bipolar depression is a different disorder, sometimes called manic depression. This textbook covers schizophrenia and all three of the optional disorders.

- Diagnosis involves a clinician listening to a patient to see whether any of their symptoms match those in a checklist of the features and symptoms of a mental disorder.

- Explanations of mental disorders concern what might cause the disorder and what the course of the illness/disorder might be.
- Treatment of mental disorders concerns what might help a person with that disorder; treatments can be biological (e.g. drug therapy) or they might have a non-biological focus, such as examining someone's thought patterns (e.g. cognitive-behavioural therapy – CBT) or focusing on issues like social support.

Psychology makes basic **assumptions** about human nature and human behaviour. For example, in clinical psychology, one idea is to think of mental disorders as illnesses to be diagnosed and treated, perhaps with drugs (the so-called 'medical model'), while another is to group types of treatments within a particular approach to psychology, such as biological or non-biological.

Definition

Assumptions refers to an area of psychology where the underpinning beliefs and ideas support this being a particular area, such as clinical psychology, which focuses on the mental health or mental disorder aspect of humans.

Year One link: You have already looked at basic assumptions for each of the Year One topic areas (social, cognitive, biological psychology and learning theories).

Defining mental disorder: what is meant by abnormality?

You will look more at how abnormality is defined when reading about the required content in clinical psychology in your course. This section provides a short introduction to what clinical psychology is all about. There are a number of definitions of 'abnormality'; for example, that with regard to mental health it means being outside the majority, which is a statistical definition. The fact that there are many definitions shows that it is not an easy term to define. It depends, for example, on what is 'normal'. It could be said that anything not normal is abnormal. However, it is not easy to define normal either, as it is a concept that depends on culture – what is normal in one culture might be abnormal in another. Many issues in society, such as health and mental disorders, are said to be **socially constructed**. This means they differ from society to society and are not 'externally real'; they are best understood within their social context. For example, some cultures see the 'hearing voices' part of schizophrenia as a negative experience, while some see it as a positive experience (Luhrmann *et al.*, 2015, see page 29). This would suggest that the way schizophrenia is constructed is down to culture as well as (or instead of) it being an 'illness' in itself. One of the key questions in clinical psychology is about how different societies define mental health disorders (see online Appendix, page 1).

Definition

Social constructionism is the idea of features and issues in a society being constructed by that society rather than having some external existence. Evidence for social constructionism is found when looking at how features of society can change over time, and mental disorders fit into that category.

Someone wearing a chicken suit would not be defined as abnormal except in certain circumstances – the situation affects whether or not a behaviour conforms with social norms.

Explore

Walker (2006) has written about social constructionism in the context of mental health. To find out more, go to: **www.recoverydevon.co.uk/download/The_Social_Construction_of_Mental_Illness.pdf**

STUDY HINT

Use the content, studies in detail and key issue sections of this chapter to extend your idea of what clinical psychology is, so that you can define what is meant by 'clinical psychology'.

Study of interest

Bulanda *et al.* (2014) looked at the SPEAK Programme (Share, Peace, Equality, Awareness and Knowledge) where school students ran information workshops for younger students at risk from mental health issues. The at-risk younger students' understanding about mental health was measured before and after the programme. Measures about social distance were also taken (social distance means how much someone would avoid people with mental health issues). After the programme, measures of understanding and of social distance had both changed, suggesting that even a short intervention with young people around mental health awareness can have an effect and that knowledge can help to overcome stigma. This study is useful in aiming to reduce stigma as it suggests that even a quite simple education programme run by young people for young people can have an effect on views of mental disorders.

Diagnosing mental disorder

This section provides a brief introduction to diagnosis, while the content section of this chapter looks in more detail at the reliability and validity of diagnosing mental disorder. Mental disorders are difficult to diagnose. Often the patient shows no physical symptoms, so diagnosis relies on the presence of a list of symptoms and features. For example, to diagnose a phobia the patient must experience an intense and irrational fear, not just a fear, as you will have seen when studying learning theories in Year One. A fear becomes a phobia when it interferes with the way a person wishes to live their life. People suffering from a phobia can usually point to an exact thing they fear – this distinguishes a phobia from generalised anxiety. Someone who does not quite fall within the list of 'requirements' for the disorder is not diagnosed with it, although they continue to live with the symptoms. Features of mental disorders may also be subjective, such as how long a person feels they have been suffering.

Explaining mental disorder

Explanations for mental disorders are not fixed or definite and there is often more than one explanation for a particular disorder. It could be argued that if there is more than one explanation, then this indicates more than one disorder. Perhaps there is a label attached to certain symptoms that are then thought of as one disorder, when in fact similar symptoms have different causes and relate to different disorders. For example, schizophrenia can be caused by a single bad experience, known as reactive schizophrenia, but it may be genetic, so there is not one single experience that triggers it, as indicated by the fact that there may be many cases of schizophrenia in one family. Another explanation for schizophrenia is expressed in the dopamine hypothesis, which suggests that it is caused by the presence of excessive dopamine (a neurotransmitter). Some people have claimed that dysfunctional families can cause mental disorder. Sociologists have suggested, for example, that low socioeconomic status might be a cause for schizophrenia. Others have said that schizophrenia is just a state that some people are in, and not a 'disorder' or 'medical problem' at all (e.g. Szasz, 1960). These are the sorts of issues that surround explanations for mental disorder, and some of them are covered in detail in this chapter.

Treating mental disorder

Mental disorders are treated in a variety of ways. For example, anti-schizophrenic drugs may be used to treat schizophrenia, while other medical treatments include ECT (electroconvulsive therapy). Non-medical therapies such as psychotherapy may be used, particularly in the treatment of depression, where cognitive-behavioural therapy (CBT)

is currently a popular treatment. Specific treatments are used for specific mental disorders, as you will have seen when studying learning theories in Year One. For example, systematic desensitisation may be used in the treatment of phobias. The content section of this chapter covers some treatments and related issues in more detail.

Explore
Looking at what a clinical psychologist does will help you to understand what clinical psychology is. A starting point for your research is the NHS website:
www.nhscareers.nhs.uk/explore-by-career/psychological-therapies/careers-in-psychological-therapies/psychologist/clinical-psychologist/

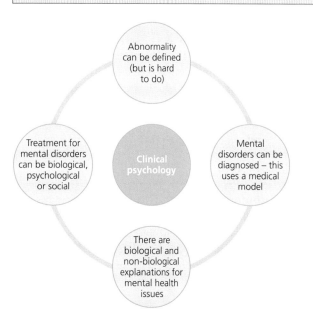

Clinical psychology is about the study of mental health and mental disorders.

Progress check 1.1

Define what is meant by the term 'clinical psychology'.

STUDY HINT
Answers to progress checks can be found on the accompanying website to this book.

STUDY HINT
Your course requires a general overview of what 'clinical psychology' involves, so make some notes on this aspect.

Test yourself

Explain what is meant by clinical psychology, drawing on two of its main assumptions. **(6 marks)**

Content in clinical psychology

In this section you will focus on two mental disorders: schizophrenia and your chosen disorder from a choice of anorexia nervosa, obsessive compulsive disorder (OCD) and unipolar depression. Schizophrenia and all three of the other disorders are covered in this section. You are required to know the symptoms and features of the two disorders (schizophrenia and your other chosen disorder), explanations for them and treatments of them.

First, though, you need to consider issues around diagnosis and issues about defining abnormality and mental disorders. You must consider the four Ds of diagnosis and the two classification systems used to diagnose mental disorders – the **Diagnostic and Statistical Manual of Mental Disorders** (DSM) and the International Statistical Classification of Diseases and Related Health Problems (ICD). You need to look at issues of validity and reliability with regard to diagnosis of mental disorders.

Diagnosis of mental disorders: the four Ds

Psychopathology looks at the symptoms and features of mental disorders, explanations that can offer ideas about causes for mental disorders and treatments for mental disorders. Psychopathology also looks at how abnormal behaviour is defined, including what makes something a 'mental disorder'.

Definitions

The Diagnostic and Statistical Manual of Mental Disorders (DSM) is a list of mental health disorders, with their symptoms and features intended to aid diagnosis.

Psychopathology is a term which refers to either the study of mental illness or mental distress or those behaviours and experiences that may indicate mental illness or some form of psychological impairment.

Four Ds are used to define abnormality. They are: deviance – there must be behaviour or emotions that go against social norms and are not approved of; the experience of distress; some form of dysfunction and problems with living; and some danger to others or to the individual themselves.

When defining abnormality, the **four Ds** are: deviance, distress, dysfunction and danger.

1 **Deviance** refers to behaviour and emotions that are not the norm in a society. Not only do the behaviours and emotions have to deviate from social or cultural norms, they must also be seen as unacceptable by the society. For example, it may not be the norm in a society to be exceptionally clever, but it is accepted by society and is even seen as a positive, so it is not classed as deviance.

2 **Distress** refers to when someone with a disorder experiences negative feelings. It is thought that abnormality in a mental health sense is accompanied by feelings of distress.

3 **Dysfunction** refers to a person's behaviour not being successful in relation to carrying out everyday tasks and living their life in general. However, dysfunctional behaviour can be deliberate and does not on its own signal a disorder.

4 **Danger** refers to danger to others or to the individual. Violent behaviour directed towards others signals danger, while behaviour that is a danger to the individual themselves would include suicidal thoughts.

The four Ds are useful in summarising how mental health professionals might define abnormality, but there is no clear scale between normal and abnormal, only issues of judgement. It is important to remember that sometimes there are explanations for the presence of the four Ds where mental disorder might not be diagnosed. For example, a person might experience some distress, act a little oddly (deviance), seem to be a danger to themselves and frequently take time off work (dysfunction), all of which might signal they are having a difficult time. However, they may have been recently bereaved rather than suffering from a mental disorder.

Mental illness can be dysfunctional (one of the four Ds) and can stop someone from being productive at work or even from going to work.

Davis (2009) suggests that using the four Ds can help practitioners to see when a condition might need a DSM diagnosis. One of the difficulties of diagnosis of mental illness is deciding when a characteristic or trait is problematic enough to become a clinical diagnosis. The four Ds can assist in making a decision, as matching the four Ds to the DSM-IV-TR (Diagnostic and Statistical Manual fourth text revised edition) can help to show their usefulness even though there are issues to consider when using them in diagnosis.

- Deviance can be difficult to use in diagnosis because different mental disorders can show similar deviance. However, some diagnoses are clearly illustrated by deviance, such as paedophilia, where the symptoms shown in the DSM clearly indicate deviance. Distress must also be present as well as dysfunction and there are other issues in the diagnosis of paedophilia too, such as the individual must be over the age of 16 years and 5 years older than the 'subject of the desire' (Davis, 2009).
- Dysfunction is also difficult to use in diagnosis, because many life events and issues can be dysfunctional. One example of a mental disorder that illustrates the importance of dysfunction in mental disorders is Major Depressive Disorder, Recurrent, without Psychotic Features. Davis (2009) points out that to receive this diagnosis the episodes of depression must affect normal everyday functioning with regard to a person's work or social life. In fact the dysfunction must occur in more than one part of the person's life for the diagnosis to be given. Examples of lack of functioning include insomnia, being unable to work, relationships being affected and a decrease in pleasure in many areas of the person's life.
- Distress is quite hard to measure as a person may be unable to function but does not experience feelings of distress, while someone else can feel a great deal of distress and yet still be able to function. Hypochondriasis is a diagnosis that is about fear of having a serious disease, based on misinterpreting bodily symptoms, and the main feature of this disorder is distress. Treatment is therefore based on reducing this distress by getting the person to focus on things that are right, to stop focusing on their bodily symptoms and to decrease the time they focus on their distress.
- Danger can be understood as one of the four Ds by looking at the example of nicotine dependence, a diagnosis that is about danger to the person from smoking-related illnesses and also danger to others because of inhalation of second-hand smoke. Davis (2009) cites figures showing that 10 per cent of all current and former smokers in the USA have a smoking-related chronic disease, which illustrates the 'danger' from smoking-related diseases. Mental illness itself has dangers. Davis (2009) also cites figures that individuals suffering from mental illness have a 25 per cent higher chance of dying from unnatural causes.
- Davis (2009) discusses a fifth 'D', which is **duration**. Duration refers to the length of time the individual has had the symptoms. For example, different types of schizophrenia may be diagnosed depending on how long the patient has experienced symptoms. Schizophrenia Undifferentiated requires symptoms to have lasted for more than a few hours, whereas Schizophreniform Disorder is a possible diagnosis if

symptoms have lasted one month but not longer than six months. It is clear that duration of symptoms is important in diagnosing mental disorders.

Definition

Duration in relation to the four Ds of diagnosis: this is a fifth D which refers to the length of time a symptom has lasted; this is important in diagnosing a mental disorder.

Evaluation of the four Ds of diagnosis

Strengths

- Davis (2009) has shown how the four Ds can be used with the DSM-IV-TR, and adds a fifth – duration. The four Ds have a practical application because they are useful for professionals when considering when a patient's symptoms or issues become a clinical diagnosis.
- The four Ds support the validity of the DSM as a diagnostic classification system in that various diagnoses are shown to focus on specific Ds, showing each has value. Davis (2009) offers evidence for this claim.

Weaknesses

- There is likely to be subjectivity in the application of the four Ds – what a professional views as dysfunctional, such as not going to work, for example, might not be considered dysfunctional by the individual themselves. It might be dysfunctional more for society, for example.
- Questions about a lack of objectivity of the four Ds raises issues about their reliability. If the four Ds are used by two different professionals, they may not reach the same conclusion about mental disorder.
- It could be claimed that, as Davis (2009) suggested adding a fifth D (duration), the four Ds are insufficient in themselves as a tool, which is a criticism.

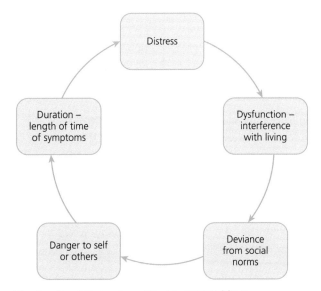

The four Ds of diagnosis and Davis's (2009) fifth D

Progress check 1.2

Explain the four Ds of diagnosis with reference to mental disorders by providing one example of a diagnosis to illustrate each 'D'.

STUDY HINT

When answering questions about the DSM classification system and diagnoses, you can make links to the four Ds and vice versa.

Year One link: Notice that evaluation of the four Ds uses terms such as validity, reliability, objectivity and subjectivity. Your course asks you to know about these issues, which you will have frequently covered in your Year One studies.

Test yourself

Using the idea of the 4Ds, discuss difficulties in defining abnormality. **(6 marks)**

Reliability and validity of the four Ds

Reliability and validity are two important issues that will be discussed in detail later in this chapter, but we need to consider them here in relation to the four Ds and the diagnosis of mental disorders.

You have come across these terms before, when looking at research in psychology in Year One, and they have the same meaning when applied to diagnosis.

Year One link: Recall your learning about validity and reliability when carrying out research in psychology. Reliability means that you will get the same result if you repeat a study, while validity refers to findings that can be applied to real life.

A study can be said to have 'validity' if what is measured is what is claimed to be measured. For example, if a researcher studying anxiety draws conclusions about it from a study, but it turns out that the people involved in the study were actually suffering from depression rather than anxiety, then the researcher's conclusions would not be valid.

Findings can be said to have 'reliability' if the same findings are found when a study is repeated. For example, a researcher conducts a study and the findings suggest there is a link between depression and loss in early childhood (such as loss of a parent). However, when the study is repeated with different participants (or even the same participants), this time no such link is found, so the results of the first study can be said to lack reliability.

Validity and reliability are important issues in clinical psychology, particularly with regard to diagnosing a mental disorder. If one doctor diagnoses depression and another diagnoses anxiety – and perhaps a third doctor diagnoses schizophrenia – then that patient would not think they had been reliably diagnosed. Reliability of diagnosis is important for the individual, as treatment depends on diagnosis. If a person is not being treated for the right disorder then they are unlikely to improve.

Classification systems for mental health

You need to know the two main classification systems for mental health, the DSM and the ICD. For the DSM you need to know the DSM-IV-TR (sometimes seen as DSM IVR) or the DSM-V and both are covered here. The DSM-IV-TR was mentioned earlier when the four Ds were discussed. 'IV' means 4th edition and 'TR' means 'text revised'. 'V' means 5th edition, and this is referred to as the DSM-5 in this book from now on. You also need to know about the ICD system, currently the ICD-10, which means the 10th version is currently being used. This section will also consider issues of reliability and validity in diagnosis when using such classification systems.

Progress check 1.3

What do 'ICD' and 'DSM' stand for respectively?

We begin by looking at the *Diagnostic and Statistical Manual of Mental Disorders* (DSM). The DSM is published by the American Psychiatric Association (APA) and provides criteria from which a mental disorder can be diagnosed. It is used around the world. The DSM was first published in 1952 and since then there have been six revisions, from the DSM-I to the current DSM-5. The DSM-IV was published in 1994 and the text revision was published in 2000. The DSM-5 was published in May 2013.

The DSM system was developed in response to the need for a census of mental health disorders; the US army had developed a system to diagnose mental disorders using mainly descriptions and classifications, such as **neuroses** and **psychoses**. From such classifications and descriptions, lists of symptoms gradually developed and were refined, and the DSM evolved.

Definitions

Neuroses are mental health issues that fall just outside normal functioning, but the individual is still in touch with reality and knows they are ill.

Psychoses are mental health issues where the individual has lost touch with reality and is not on a continuum with normal mental health.

Study of interest

Brown *et al.* (2014) carried out a study looking at the DSM-5 criteria for anorexia nervosa. They pointed out that the new criteria (in the DSM-5) included changes that relied on clinical judgement more and their focus was on possible problems with validity of diagnoses if clinical judgement was involved. They found that when they looked at diagnosis of anorexia nervosa (AN) using the DSM-5 there was a higher frequency of AN than would be found using the DSM-IV and higher numbers using the broadest definition in the DSM-5. The researchers found that 'low-weight' should be defined using BMI less than 18.5 kg and there should be a way of measuring weight phobia rather than inferring it. This is an interesting study that claims that judging issues such as low weight and weight phobia can lead to over-diagnosis of those with AN, as measured by the rise in numbers diagnosed from DSM-IV to DSM-5. This questions validity of diagnosis of AN using DSM-5.

The DSM-IV-TR: a multi-axial system

The DSM – up to and including the DSM-IV-TR – is a multi-axial system, consisting of five axes: each diagnosis of a disorder is split into five levels called axes that relate to different aspects of a disorder. A patient is assigned a category according to their symptoms; the nearest prototype for a mental disorder suggested by these symptoms provides the diagnosis.

- Axis I considers clinical disorders, major mental disorders, developmental disorders and learning disorders. Some common disorders include schizophrenia, depression and phobias. Axis I also looks at other conditions that may be focused upon and these tend to be problems that need immediate attention from a clinician.
- Axis II looks at underlying personality conditions, including mental retardation. The axis has a rating scale to measure mental retardation. Some common personality conditions include paranoid personality disorder and anti-social personality disorder as well as obsessive compulsive personality disorder. Problems in this area may not need immediate attention but should be taken into account as they can affect treatment.
- Axis III is about medical and physical conditions. Some common physical conditions include brain injuries and existing diseases. Axis III is about general medical conditions and these are important because even if the problem seems to be a mental one, psychological disorders can arise from physical illnesses, such as diabetes or heart problems.
- Axis IV focuses on psychosocial and environmental factors that affect the disorder. Factors include poverty and dysfunctional families. Any other factors in the person's environment that might affect their functioning are considered.
- Axis V is an assessment of global functioning. The question asked is how is the patient functioning? There is an overall rating of someone's ability to cope with normal life. The rating scale goes from low scores, which indicate a persistent danger for the client to severely hurt themselves, to 100, which refers to a superior level of functioning with reference to a range of abilities.

Progress check 1.4

Explain the five axes of the DSM, up to and including the DSM-IV-TR.

STUDY HINT

If you are asked to 'explain' something, you must be able to describe it and then justify your description by adding more detail such as a study as evidence. For example, if you have to explain the DSM multi-axial system you need to do more than list the five axes; you need to add a bit more in each case, such as an example of the type of condition covered by each particular axis.

Explore

Find out more about the DSM multi-axial system at: www.psyweb.com/DSM_IV/jsp/dsm_iv.jsp

Changes in the DSM

There have been a number of revisions to the DSM, partly in response to criticisms such as that arising from Rosenhan's study (1973) of what it was like to be sane in insane places. This study is explained in detail later in this chapter (page 101). Rosenhan found that eight 'normal' people (in the sense that they had no psychiatric symptoms and showed no abnormal behaviour) were accepted as mentally ill by mental health institutions, highlighting the lack of validity in diagnosis of mental illness at that time. As a result, the DSM was revised to take such criticisms into account.

We can also see how the DSM has changed in terms of its attitude towards homosexuality and how it responds to new research and changing cultural attitudes. During its revision, the DSM is studied by many groups of people, who consult research data as well as other types of data relating to diagnoses. Sometimes social groups lobby to get a category changed. For example, in 1974 the DSM-II no longer listed homosexuality as a category of disorder, both in response to research such as that by Kinsey and to protests from gay activists. The category 'homosexuality' was replaced with 'sexual orientation disturbance'. In 1980 the DSM-III replaced the category 'sexual orientation disturbance' with 'ego-dystonic homosexuality', but that was removed in 1987. The DSM-IV-TR has the category 'sexual disorder not otherwise specified', which is characterised as 'persistent and marked distress about one's sexual orientation', which emphasises that it is not sexual orientation that is the problem but any persistent and marked distress about it.

The DSM-5

One of the goals of the DSM-5 is to harmonise with the ICD system, which was not the case for previous DSMs. The DSM-5 has not continued with the multi-axial system – Axis I, Axis II and Axis III. Instead, the DSM-5 lists all disorders in its Section II. Axis IV has become psychosocial issues and the context of a presenting issue and Axis V, global assessment of functioning, has been dropped. The DSM-5 has three sections: Section I, Section II and Section III.

- Section I simply explains the way the DSM-5 is organised and introduces some of the changes, such as moving away from a multi-axial system and bringing in Section III.
- Section II gives diagnostic criteria and codes. Chapters in Section II cover neurodevelopmental disorders; schizophrenia spectrum and other psychotic disorders; bipolar and related disorders; depressive disorders; anxiety disorders; obsessive compulsive and related disorders; trauma and stressor related disorders; dissociative disorders; somatic (bodily) symptom disorders; feeding and eating disorders; and others. The chapters in Section II are relevant to the topics of schizophrenia, obsessive compulsive disorder, anorexia nervosa and unipolar depression, which are the four mental disorders covered in this chapter. Neurodevelopment disorders covered include autism spectrum disorder, which is part of child psychology and is an option in your course (see Chapter Four). The schizophrenia spectrum includes schizophreniform disorder, which was mentioned earlier when the four Ds were discussed. Others mentioned when we looked at the four Ds include depressive disorders, including major depressive episode, as well as paedophilia and substance-related and addiction disorders – these disorders each have their own chapter within Section II.
- Section III is about emerging measures and models. This section is about the future of diagnoses. In Section III there are diagnostic categories that need more research before they are included in Section II and there are tools for diagnosis as well. For example, some patient-rated and clinician-rated measures relate to symptoms that go across all DSM diagnoses, as well as measures of disability and information about cultural context and its influence on how a mental disorder might be presented by a client. David Kupfer, the chair of the DSM-5 Task Force, suggests that the DSM-5 is a 'living document' (Moran, 2014). Section III enables self-assessment by the patient to give the patient a voice, and also means cultural issues can be taken into account. New diagnoses are found in Section III as well. These are diagnoses that need more work before they can go into Section II. Also if a diagnosis is in Section II it will be 'medicalised'. Some symptoms and features do not occur often and do not always move into a Section II diagnosis, so they were fitted into Section III. One example of a disorder in Section III that helps to illustrate the purpose of this section is internet gaming disorder, which is separate from internet gambling disorder. Internet gaming disorder is characterised by someone experiencing five of the following nine symptoms during the past year:
  - a preoccupation with games
  - psychological withdrawal symptoms such as irritability
  - tolerance (a need to spend an increasing amount of time playing games)
  - lack of success in controlling their game participation
  - loss of interest in previous hobbies
  - carrying on in spite of knowing the problems

- deceiving family or therapist
- using gaming to escape a bad mood
- jeopardising job or relationship.

This disorder is in Section III because it is not yet fully accepted as a clinical disorder.

Explore
Find out more about the DSM-5 and issues of diagnosis by watching this YouTube video, which considers the DSM-5 in some detail, including cultural issues and issues around diagnosis, as well as talking about the recovery model: www.youtube.com/watch?v=BjnPfFS4-yo

Dr David Kupfer, clinical psychologist and chair of the DSM-5 Task Force

Progress check 1.5

Explain the three sections of DSM-5.

Evaluation of the DSM including the DSM-5

Strengths

- The DSM allows a common diagnosis to be reached by clinicians. Through its many revisions, the DSM has stood the test of time. Even with the problems outlined above, it is perhaps the best attempt at diagnosis in existence, given the limited understanding of mental disorders. When more than two doctors use the DSM, they should come close to the same diagnosis.
- Goldstein's (1988) study tested the reliability of diagnosis between the DSM-II and the DSM-III and

is briefly explained later in this chapter (page 168). She found there was evidence of reliability within the DSM-III (but less so between the DSM-II and the DSM-III).

- The DSM-5 underwent field trials before publication, which included test-retest reliability where different clinicians independently evaluated the same patient.

Weaknesses

- The DSM is seen as a confirmation of the medical state of mental disorder, as sufferers are 'patients' and 'treatment' is suggested. Mental health issues are 'disorders' and 'illnesses' and so 'cures' are looked for. However, it might be said that some mental disorders are simply ways of living, and who is to say whether they are 'illnesses' or not. RD Laing (1927–89) suggested that schizophrenia is another way of living, where a person is trying to get back to their true self, and it is not therefore a medical illness. The recovery model (page 27) is moving away from a medical focus on mental health issues.
- There was criticism that those reviewing the DSM-5 had to sign an agreement that they would not talk about the process of reviewing this version of the DSM, which meant there was no transparency. It was argued that this meant the DSM-5 lacked credibility, in that the results of any testing could not be challenged. It was later claimed that the development of the DSM-5 was very careful and transparent, more so than other versions, because the public were able to comment on it but there is still dispute over its development.
- Among the criticisms of the DSM-5 was the fact that it does not link mental disorders to any biological underpinnings. Criticism of individual diagnoses has also been made, such as using the name 'borderline personality disorder', which is said to reinforce stigma and to have no useful information in its title.
- The British Psychological Society has expressed concern about the DSM-5 because the DSM-5 brought in social norms to be considered when making a diagnosis and this requires the clinician to make judgements about such norms or to use their own social norms. Deviance and dysfunction (two of the four Ds) relate to culture and social norms as they might be different in different cultures.

Progress check 1.6

Evaluate the DSM-5 in terms of one strength and one weakness.

Explore

Find out more about RD Laing's ideas; you may find it useful to read his book *The Divided Self* (1960). Laing did not deny that those needing help needed treatment as such, just that the medical model failed to recognise other ideas about their functioning in society. The recovery model is now a model used by mental health professionals and looks at someone *recovering* their mental health rather than managing their symptoms, though this might be a little idealistic.

The following link is to an article about Laing's ideas regarding mental health:
www.theguardian.com/books/2012/sep/02/rd-laing-mental-health-sanity

Test yourself

Explain criticisms of the DSM-IV-TR or the DSM-5.
(6 marks)

Reliability and validity of the DSM classification system

This section considers the reliability and validity of diagnoses using the DSM classification system, including cultural issues, which, as we saw earlier when trying to define what is meant by 'normal' (page 13), can affect validity. This section also focuses on studies that investigate and produce evidence of issues of culture and validity. Whether a diagnosis stands the test of time (reliability) and is correct because the treatment works (validity) is extremely important, as is whether someone is unfairly treated as a result of a doctor's misdiagnosis, arising from the doctor's failure to take their culture and beliefs into account.

Reliability of diagnoses using the DSM

The DSM's reliability rests on the question of whether one person's set of symptoms would lead to a common diagnosis by different physicians. If different doctors give different diagnoses for the same set of symptoms (i.e. for the same person), then the diagnoses are not reliable and treatment may not work. A diagnosis is valid if it leads to treatment that works and predicts the course of a mental disorder, because then it is measuring what it claims to measure. If a diagnosis is not reliable, because there is no consistency in the diagnosis of an individual's disorder, then it will not be valid, because the individual's symptoms will be given different diagnoses by different doctors, who will suggest varying treatment options and different predictions.

The following studies looked at the reliability of the DSM (before the DSM-5).

Goldstein (1988)

Goldstein tested the DSM-III and found that there was reliability. She looked at the effect of gender on the experience of schizophrenia and also re-diagnosed 199 patients using DSM-III when they had originally been diagnosed using DSM-II. There were some differences but, as DSM-III was a revised version of DSM-II, this was to be expected. What was of interest, however, is that Goldstein asked other experts to carry out the re-diagnosis separately, using a **single-blind technique**.

Goldstein realised that she herself was aware of the hypothesis and so she asked two experts to re-diagnose a random sample of eight patients. The experts were given copies of case histories with any reference to the original diagnosis removed. She found a high level of agreement and inter-rater reliability (see Study hint). This suggests that DSM-III is a reliable tool. As later versions of the DSM have focused on improving validity and reliability, it is likely that the DSM-IV-TR is also reliable. The DSM-5 was said to have reliability for the same reasons (page 17).

Definition
Single-blind technique is a technique that does not allow the hypothesis of a piece of research to be known to people other than the researchers, so that it cannot be a cause of bias in judgement/data.

STUDY HINT
Some terms mentioned in this section, such as 'inter-rater reliability', are referred to as 'method' terms. These terms are discussed in detail in Chapter Two, which looks at method, maths and the practical investigation for clinical psychology.

Brown *et al.* (2001)

Brown *et al.* (2001) set out to test the reliability of the DSM-IV. They studied anxiety and mood disorders in 362 out-patients in Boston, USA. The patients underwent two independent interviews using the anxiety disorders interview schedule for the DSM-IV, known as the lifetime version (ADIS-IV-L). For most of the DSM-IV categories there was good-to-excellent reliability, with inter-rater reliability. If there was disagreement it tended to focus not on what the symptoms were but whether there were enough of them, whether they were severe enough or whether they had lasted long enough. The study also showed boundary problems for some disorders such as generalised anxiety disorder and major depressive disorder, meaning that sometimes it was hard to diagnose disorders at the boundaries of these types of disorder. The study highlighted some problems with the DSM, but overall it emerged as reliable.

Stinchfield (2003)

Stinchfield's (2003) study tested both reliability and validity. It looked at the diagnosis of **pathological** gambling (a gambling habit that is severe enough to cause someone to have problems in living and functioning). The study looked at 803 men and women from the general population of Minnesota and 259 men and women who were on a gambling treatment programme. A questionnaire using 19 items was used to measure the DSM-IV diagnostic criteria for pathological gambling. There were other validity measures as well. It was found that the DSM-IV diagnostic criteria were reliable and valid. The DSM criteria were used to sort out those who were linked with pathological gambling and those who were not.

Gambling can be a diagnosed disorder.

Definition
Pathological is behaviour diagnosed as abnormal due to its extreme or excessive nature.

Kirk and Kutchins (1992)

The above three studies have shown that, in general, from the DSM-III to the DSM-IV, reliability is thought to have improved to the point where it is no longer an issue. Kirk and Kutchins, in their review paper (1992), argued that there are methodological problems with the studies used to test the reliability of the DSM up until 1992, and that these limit the **generalisability** of the findings. The three studies outlined above used interviews and questionnaires to gather data. Kirk and Kutchins argued that training and supervision of interviewers in general was insufficient and that they lacked the commitment and skills to be accurate. They also pointed out that the studies they looked at tended to take place in specialised research settings, which means their findings might not relate to clinicians in normal clinical settings. As an unreliable diagnostic tool also lacks validity, Kirk and Kutchins suggested that the DSM could lack validity.

Definition
Generalisability means findings can be said to be true of the target population not just the sample used.

Assessment of Kirk and Kutchins' points:
- Some of the points about interviewing – such as that different interviewers may affect the situation and lead to different data – might be important when considering generalising findings from studies. However, Goldstein (1988) did not use interviewing to test reliability – she used re-diagnosis using secondary data, and also found reliability.

- The patients in the studies described above were not all from research settings. The 'gamblers' in Stinchfield's study were on a gambling treatment programme, not in a research institution. The patients in the study by Brown *et al.* were out-patients at a hospital.
- Kirk and Kutchins' study took place before Brown *et al.* and Stinchfield's studies showed that the DSM-IV and DSM-IV-TR could be regarded as reliable. It might be concluded that further work has been done since the DSM-II and reliability has improved.
- Goldstein (1988), Brown *et al.* (2001) and Stinchfield (2003) all provide evidence that diagnosis is reliable.

STUDY HINT

In your exam you will be asked to consider psychological research in relation to a particular question and you will be expected to refer to research studies in your answer. It is a good idea to have evidence for claims you make in your answer and to use studies to back up your answer.

Reliability of diagnoses using the DSM-5

Stetka and Ghaemi (2014, cited in Cooper, 2014) suggest that just under half of clinicians had moved over to the DSM-5 a year after it had been released, with some clinicians commenting that they were concerned about its reliability (Cooper, 2014). Cooper discusses the idea of a diagnosis having reliability and says that if a figure of 0.6 is reliable enough, that might mean that a patient judged as having schizophrenia by one clinician has a 60 per cent chance of being diagnosed as having schizophrenia by another clinician, which is unlikely to be considered acceptable by most people. In 1974, Spitzer and Fleis said that 0.7 as a reliability estimate was 'only satisfactory' (in Cooper, 2014), concluding that the reliability of the early DSMs was not good. It is against this background that the DSM-5 was written, with a strong focus on reliability.

However, according to Cooper (2014), in the development of the DSM-5 it was thought that attaining a reliability figure of between 0.6 and 0.8 would be very good, and even between 0.2 and 0.4 would be acceptable (Kraemer *et al.*, 2012a, in Cooper, 2014), so it looked as if expectations regarding reliability had changed from the earlier DSMs. For example, schizophrenia had a reliability estimate of 0.81 in the DSM-III trial and just 0.46 in the DSM-5 trial, according to Cooper (2014), and she gives other examples too of such differences. The question was whether, with this sort of evidence, the DSM-5 could be said to have reliability. The DSM-5 Task Force (the group who worked on the development of the DSM-5) thought they had achieved reliability (Regier *et al.*, 2013, cited in Cooper, 2014).

Explore

Look at Rachel Cooper's (2014) article on the reliability of DSM-5 to find out more:

www.madinamerica.com/2014/09/how-reliable-is-the-dsm-5/

It seems that there might be reliability in the DSM-5 for some mental disorders, but not for others, as shown by the field trials undertaken in preparation for DSM-5. For example, autism spectrum and ADHD in children and PTSD (post-traumatic stress disorder) and binge-eating disorder in adults had good or very good reliability according to the trials, whereas major depressive disorder and generalised anxiety disorder both had rather low reliability scores. Dr David Kupfer, the Task Force chair, suggested that some disorders have symptoms that vary a lot over weeks and so it is harder to find reliability for those diagnoses.

Explore

You can find out more about the DSM-5 field trials at:

www.dsm5.org/research/pages/dsm-5fieldtrials.aspx

Before concluding that the DSM-5 has reduced reliability compared with the DSM-III, DSM-IV and DSM-IV-TR, it is worth noting that the DSM-5 is not easily compared, because the DSM-5 has new diagnoses that are more fine-tuned than in previous versions. For example, 'eating disorder' has become 'binge eating', which is more specific. Also in the DSM-5 trials there was more careful methodology used, such as clinicians interviewing patients independently rather than jointly as they did in the DSM-III trials. Cooper (2014) argues that though reliability in the form of a statistic might be lower in the DSM-5, this may not matter that much for the following reasons:

- If a diagnosis leads to drug therapy, for instance, and the consequences of getting a diagnosis wrong are important, then reliability would be important.
- However, if a diagnosis is a *guide* to what treatment might suit an individual and there are a number of treatments that could be useful, reliability is less of an issue.
- If the focus is on *recovery* of mental health for each individual, then the actual diagnosis might not be as important as what treatment or therapy is offered. (The recovery model is considered later in this chapter, page 27).

Progress check 1.7

How does asking more than one clinician to diagnose the same patient (as was done in the DSM-5) lead us to be able to draw conclusions about reliability?

Validity of diagnoses using the DSM

If the DSM were not reliable it would not be valid either. If a diagnosis was repeated and this time the DSM provided a different diagnosis, then it would not be a valid diagnosis (it would not be measuring what it claimed to measure). Reliability and validity go together. A diagnosis is valid if it predicts the course of a disorder 'in real life' and the treatment suggested by the diagnosis is useful 'in real life'.

> **STUDY HINT**
> It is wise to keep validity and reliability separate in an exam answer, although you can make the point that if diagnosis is unreliable then it cannot be valid.

Construct validity

If the DSM is to define mental disorders, then mental disorders need to be **operationalised**. Lists of symptoms and behaviour are the result of making a mental disorder measurable. It has been argued, however, that in operationalising a concept such as depression, something is lost from the understanding of the nature of the whole experience of depression, which means that the DSM is not a valid tool. There is a lack of **construct validity**, in that the constructs drawn up, for example, to represent depression, might not be representative enough.

Definitions

Operationalising variables means making them fully measurable so that what is done in a study is precise, replicable and clear.

Construct validity refers to how far the constructs that are being measured (for example, in the case of depression, the number of days the patient has lacked the motivation to go to work) represent that mental disorder.

Year One link: You will know about the idea of operationalisation of variables, such as making an independent and dependent variable measurable, from your Year One studies.

Another problem with validity is that although revised versions of the DSM (up to but not including the DSM-5) have taken into account personal and social factors (Axis IV), as well as how the person is functioning (Axis V), this is taking these factors into account in relation to a mental disorder. Such factors might in fact be separate from the mental disorder. For example, if someone with depression is not functioning well in society, it might not be because of depression but for some other reason (such as unemployment, solitude or financial problems). So a diagnosis of depression would not be valid in that case.

Some people argue that a number of categories, such as those related to sexual issues (for example, female hypoactive sexual desire disorder – having a low sexual drive), should not be in a list of mental disorders. Both epilepsy and circadian rhythm sleep disorder used to be listed as a mental disorder but now are not. These changes to what is considered a mental disorder suggest low validity.

Concurrent validity

Concurrent validity is when the result of a study or test matches a result from another study or set of data done at the same time. So if a diagnosis using the DSM comes up with the same mental disorder that another diagnosis has given at the same time, then the new diagnosis is likely to have concurrent validity. For results to have concurrent validity the second diagnosis has to match a first diagnosis or result that has been shown to be valid.

Predictive validity

Predictive validity is the same as concurrent validity, except that the result being compared was obtained at different times, so instead of two results being compared with one another at the same time to see if one result backs up the other result, two results are compared in different time periods. To find predictive validity, a test would be carried out and a result collected. Then another or different measure would be done some time later that would test the same feature. If the test results matched the earlier measure then this shows predictive validity. For example, the DSM could be used to diagnose a mental disorder, then another later measure for that mental disorder – perhaps a doctor's view, family comments, the person's own self-rating or observations by mental health personnel – could be taken to see if the diagnosis and the other measure agreed. If they do agree, then the diagnosis (and, therefore, the DSM) would be said to have predictive validity.

Convergent validity

Convergent validity is when a test result converges on (gets close to) another test result that measures the same thing. A correlation test would be carried out. If two scales measure the same construct, for example, then a person's score on one should converge with (correlate with) their score on the other. The difference between convergent validity and predictive/concurrent validity is that in convergent validity the two measures should measure exactly the same thing, whereas in the other two types of validity (concurrent and predictive) there can be a different way of measuring in each case. Convergent validity does not mean that one test predicts the result of the other test. Carroll (1989, cited in Pies, 2013) explains that clinicians use convergent validation. They look at signs, symptoms, the course of an illness, how someone responds to treatment, family history and other data and from those measures come up with a diagnosis that is valid.

Definitions

Concurrent validity refers to when the results of two tests, done at the same time and which focus on the same issue, come up with the same results or match. This would seem to suggest that they measure what they claim to measure. One of the tests can then be used to predict the outcome of the other one.

Predictive validity is when one measure that occurs is intended to measure something later, and when that later measure is done, the two results can be compared to make sure they agree, indicating that there is indeed predictive validity. As with concurrent validity, one of the tests can then be used to predict the other.

Convergent validity is when two measures of the same construct agree with one another, thus strengthening the validity of the measures.

Year One link: In cognitive psychology you looked at internal, ecological and predictive validity. You can now add construct and convergent validity to the types of validity you know about.

Explore
To find out more about issues of validity and diagnosis (and reliability too), try doing an internet search. The following link can start you on your search:
http://datause.cse.ucla.edu/da_validity.php

Progress check 1.8
Compare predictive and concurrent validity.

Progress check 1.9
Compare construct and convergent validity.

The following studies have looked at the validity of the DSM.

Kim-Cohen *et al.* (2005)

Kim-Cohen *et al.* studied the validity of the DSM-IV with regard to conduct disorder in five-year-old children. This was a longitudinal study. The study was to test the concurrent, convergent and predictive validity of the DSM-IV with regard to conduct disorder. A longitudinal study that was already underway was following 2,232 children and these children were used as the focus of this study. Researchers interviewed the mothers of the children and asked teachers to complete postal questionnaires, in both cases asking about conduct disorder symptoms over the last six months.

Children with three or more symptoms were diagnosed as having a conduct disorder and if a child had five or more symptoms, they were diagnosed as having moderate to severe conduct disorder. The study found that 6.6 per cent of children were diagnosed with conduct disorder and 2.5 per cent with moderate to severe conduct disorder. The study also found that the children who were diagnosed with conduct disorders were significantly more likely than comparison children to say that they had anti-social behaviours (self-report). They were also more likely to behave disruptively during observational assessment and to have risk factors relating to conduct disorder. Five year olds diagnosed with conduct disorders were significantly more likely than comparison participants to have behavioural and educational difficulties at the age of seven.

The different measures in this study – mother's responses to an interview, teachers' responses to a questionnaire, comparisons with other children with regard to anti-social behaviours using self-report data, observational data and data about behavioural and educational difficulties at the age of seven – all led to a diagnosis of conduct disorder, so it was concluded that the diagnosis was valid. This is an example of using different data sources to check for validity.

If a mother, teacher and a child separately make the same points about the child's behaviour, then there is likely to be validity in the data, which is confirmed by use of the three different sources.

Hoffmann (2002)

Hoffmann looked at the different diagnoses of alcohol abuse, alcohol dependence and cocaine dependence to see if such differences showed up using a structured interview that was computer-prompted, and to see if they corresponded to the DSM-IV-TR criteria. The study looked at prison inmates. It was found that the DSM diagnosis was valid and the interview data supported the idea that dependence was a more severe syndrome than abuse (both alcohol and cocaine abuse). The symptoms from the automated interview matched the DSM diagnosis.

Lee (2006)

The purpose of this study was to see if the DSM-IV-TR diagnosis of ADHD (attention deficit hyperactivity disorder) would be suitable for Korean children. The study also focused on gender differences in the features of ADHD recognised in the DSM, such as inattention and hyperactivity/compulsivity. The DSM-IV-TR contains 18 ADHD criteria with regard to children's behaviour.

Lee's study used a questionnaire with 48 primary school teachers and asked them to rate the behaviour of the children they taught. In total 1,663 children were rated – 904 boys and 759 girls. The idea was to compare the DSM-IV-TR criteria for diagnosing ADHD with criteria arising from the questionnaire data. If the two agreed, then the DSM-IV-TR could be said to be valid (concurrent validity). Another measure used the ADHDT (attention deficit hyperactivity disorder test) to find out what behavioural and psychological characteristics are related to ADHD and to see if those characteristics match those used in the DSM-IV-TR diagnosis.

Previous studies showed that children with ADHD often had oppositional defiant disorder (ODD) as well, and had problems with their peers and with discipline. If this study found those features too, this would be evidence for the validity of the DSM-IV-TR (construct validity). The findings of Lee's study meant that correlations could check for validity, as different measures were used. Teachers' opinions were associated with the ADHD diagnosis using the DSM-IV-TR, so it was concluded that the DSM has validity. The other measures also gave findings that fitted the DSM criteria (such as inattention, hyperactivity and impulsivity). The study's findings suggest that for girls the fit with the DSM criteria was not as complete as for boys.

Evaluation of validity of diagnosis and the DSM

Strengths

- The studies described above (Kim-Cohen *et al.*, Hoffmann and Lee) show that the DSM, particularly the later versions before the DSM-5, was valid in its diagnoses. Different mental health issues were chosen in the different studies cited here, which

reinforces this conclusion. It is likely that symptoms for disorders such as alcohol abuse, dependence, cocaine abuse, pathological gambling and ADHD are well established, given that the DSM has had many revisions to date. Different research methods such as interviews and questionnaires yield data that, for those with mental health disorders, match the DSM criteria.
- The claim that the DSM is valid is supported by the claim that it is reliable, as reliability and validity go together. If the DSM is not reliable it will not be valid.
- Great efforts have been made to make the DSM-IV-TR more valid, such as adding culture-bound syndromes (see later in this chapter).

Weaknesses

- It has been said that **co-morbidity** is hard to diagnose using the DSM, a system which relies on the health professional choosing the closest match from lists of symptoms and features.
- It could be claimed that splitting a mental disorder into symptoms and features is **reductionist** and that a holistic approach might be more valid. For example, in a counselling situation symptoms are treated as aspects of the whole person and mental health is the focus, not mental disorder. In counselling a diagnosis is not as important as treating the individual.
- It is possible that questionnaires and interviews produce the findings they are searching for. For instance, if it is well known that 'children with ADHD are impulsive and hyperactive', and teachers know which children have that label, they will then say that those children are impulsive and hyperactive – the diagnosis is self-fulfilling.

Definitions

Co-morbidity is the state of having more than one mental disorder or, more generally, more than one illness or disease.

Reductionist/reductionism is the idea of breaking down a complex phenomenon into simpler components.

Progress check 1.10

Explain two weaknesses in regard to validity of diagnosis using the DSM.

Issues and debates

Reductionism is one of the issues and debates for your course. Using a classification system can be said to reduce mental disorders, which affect the whole person, into a list of features and symptoms. This can lead to treatment that is thought to fit the symptoms, such as drug therapy, but it can mean a less holistic view of the individual is taken.

Validity of diagnoses using the DSM-5

In an article in Medscape, Pies (2013) discusses the validity of the DSM-5 by considering the idea of the DSM being the 'bible' for diagnosis. He regards the DSM-5 as a 'useful but incomplete' text, an 'informative but fallible guide'. It is suggested in the article that the DSM-5 should include more neuroscience and more psychodynamic explanations of disorders, showing that the DSM-5 does not offer diagnoses for every mental disorder and take into account every explanation; there is more that can be done. This suggests that validity of the DSM-5 can be questioned; that it is more of a guide giving current thinking than an absolute list of all diagnoses that are possible. Pies feels that what the DSM (including the DSM-5) does not offer is a 'comprehensive understanding of the patient', which is what clinicians want.

These comments suggest that having a 'shopping list' of symptoms and features that suit different mental disorders and ticking the symptoms and features off against that list does not suit the complexity of individual patients. This means that such a classification system will lack validity with regard to diagnosis of individuals. Having said that, clinicians obtain information from many different sources – the patient's family history, their signs and symptoms, the course of their mental disorder and how treatments affect them – and then aim for convergent validity. Diagnosis is not simply a case of reading from a manual and making a diagnosis that is then fixed; this means that the diagnosis for each *individual* can be valid.

Kupfer (2013) claims that the DSM-5 has made good progress and is the 'strongest system currently available for classifying disorders'. There is a revised chapter to show how disorders can relate to one another, how disorders are linked to age, gender and cultural expectations, and how key disorders are now combined into a single continuum where possible (such as autism spectrum disorder). Self-assessment tools are included so patients can be involved in their diagnosis and there is guidance to help clinicians, such as cultural guidance, that was missing from previous versions of the DSM.

Explore

Cultural issues in the DSM-5 are discussed on a YouTube video that you may find helpful:
www.youtube.com/watch?v=e9C_K37i2R4

Cultural issues, validity, diagnosis and the DSM

With regard to its list of symptoms and features, studies have suggested that the DSM-IV-TR is both reliable and valid. However, one area where there has been a great deal of criticism of previous versions of the DSM is its usefulness across different cultures. If the classification system is not useful in different cultures, then its validity must be in question. Section III of the DSM-5 discusses the need to be aware of and careful about cultural bias in diagnosis. One of the key questions suggested in your course is provided on the website accompanying this book and focuses on how different societies define mental health disorder. The material in this section can be used for the key question.

Culture does not affect diagnosis – mental disorders are 'scientific'

The DSM was developed in the USA and is used widely in many other cultures. This is a valid use if mental disorders are clearly defined with specific features and symptoms; for instance, schizophrenia or depression present as the same illness all over the world, with particular symptoms and features. In other words, mental disorders are scientifically defined illnesses that are explained in a scientific way. It is interesting that one study cited above (Lee, 2006) was conducted in Korea deliberately to see if the DSM-IV-TR was valid in a non-Western culture and it was found that it was valid (for ADHD).

Culture does affect diagnosis – a spiritual model

Some studies have shown that culture *can* affect diagnosis. For example, symptoms that are seen in Western countries as characterising schizophrenia (such as hearing voices) can be interpreted in other countries as showing possession by spirits, which renders someone special in a positive rather than negative 'disorder' way.

Evrard (2014) writes about how hearing voices can be because of a mental disorder but it can also be an individual difference and interpreted as an exceptional experience. Depending on cultural interpretations of what is being measured, the DSM is not always valid. A clinician from one culture must be aware that a patient from another culture is guided by their own frame of reference.

In some cultures possession by spirits would not be seen as a mental disorder. Cultural factors are important when diagnosing mental disorders – clinicians must take into account the fact that what people say is within their cultural context and must be 'heard' as such.

Cultural differences in schizophrenia

The following studies illustrate the role of cultural differences in diagnosis, using the example of schizophrenia.

Differences in how hallucinations are interpreted/understood

Luhrmann et al. (2015) found that in the USA hearing voices was seen as a negative experience, whereas in India and Ghana hearing voices was seen as more positive (page 29). This suggests the experience of a mental disorder might be different across cultures. If a patient is from a different culture to their clinician, cultural differences in what they say about their disorder might affect the clinician's diagnosis, thus challenging the validity of the diagnosis.

Differences in how treatment affects people

Myers (2010) found from a case study that by using the recovery model (page 27), efforts to help people to become more empowered citizens tended to generate more stress for those diagnosed with schizophrenia if their lives were already stressful. This suggests that cultural differences (e.g. around work patterns) can lead to different reactions to treatment. Myers cautions against using the same model of treatment in all cultures and says that sociocultural conditions affect outcomes for those with schizophrenia. Outcomes are already better in the developing world than in the USA and techniques to get better outcomes need to be 'locally relevant' (Myers, 2010).

Outcomes for schizophrenia are better in the developing world

Kulhara et al. (2009) reviewed various studies and confirmed that in developing countries there is a larger proportion of people having a good outcome for schizophrenia (with fewer having a poor outcome) than in developed countries. This is called the 'favourable outcome hypothesis in developing countries'. However,

Kulhara et al. suggest that it is not culture that should be used to explain variance in outcomes but other factors should be explored in research. They suggest that with cultural differences come other factors that might cause the differences in outcomes.

Increased catatonia in other cultures – or different treatment regimes?

It does seem that there are actual cultural differences in mental disorders like schizophrenia. It has been reported that catatonic schizophrenia is on the decline and this could be because of health measures that prevent the development of this type of schizophrenia. A person with catatonic schizophrenia may be very still, while another person may be very excited – it is associated with extremes of behaviour. Chandrasena (1986) reported more incidences of catatonia in Sri Lanka (21 per cent compared with 5 per cent among British white people). However, it was found that in Sri Lanka it was less likely that patients had received early interventions with drug treatment; this was not therefore a cultural difference in the attitude to the mental disorder, but a difference in treatment availability.

Increased auditory hallucinations in Mexican-born people than white Americans

More auditory hallucinations were reported to doctors by patients who were Mexican-born Americans than those who were non-Mexican-born Americans. The study by Burnham et al. (1987) looked at this using self-reports and interviewing. When they checked the evidence they found that there was a difference; no other explanation could be found, so it was determined that culture had led to the difference.

Increased grandiosity in white Americans

White Americans were reported (using patients' records) as showing more 'grandiosity' as a symptom compared with Americans of Mexican origin, again showing cultural differences. It is important to look at individual symptoms when looking for cultural differences in symptoms of mental disorders because the DSM looks at a *set* of symptoms; without specific studies, such cultural differences might not be found.

> **STUDY HINT**
> Note that there is evidence of sub-cultural differences in the research discussed in this chapter. Goldstein (1988) (page 168) suggested that females have a less severe course through schizophrenia than males. You can use such evidence to evaluate the claim that schizophrenia across cultures has mainly similarities but some differences.

Schizophrenia in all countries has more similarities than differences

Lin (1996) summarised schizophrenia in other cultures and noted that it is found in all cultures that have been studied and the prevalence seems similar across all cultures. With regard to symptoms, similarities outweigh the differences. Good outcomes appear more likely in developed countries, as has been mentioned earlier.

Evaluation of cultural differences in schizophrenia

It is important to note that just because the symptoms under the heading 'schizophrenia' appear similar and occur in all cultures as far as is known, it does not mean that schizophrenia in all cultures is in fact the same illness, with the same cause and the same course through the illness – an assumption made by the DSM.

STUDY HINT

There are many studies that illustrate issues of reliability and validity and the use of the DSM in diagnosing mental health issues. To help your revision, you might like to draw up a table with details of the name of each study, brief details of what the study involved, the study's findings and the conclusion that can be drawn about the issue being illustrated.

Progress check 1.11

Using research explain some cultural issues that can affect validity of diagnosis of a mental disorder.

Overcoming cultural bias in diagnosis

Section III of the DSM-5 focuses on issues to be taken into account when using Section II, which contains the list of mental disorders. Section III includes the need to be aware of cultural differences in people presenting for diagnosis, to make sure that any diagnosis is valid and unaffected by cultural issues. It is important for the DSM classification system to note which features might be affected by culture so that a different emphasis can be placed on them – one that takes into account the patient's cultural differences. In order to give greater reliability and validity, less emphasis must be placed on symptoms that show cultural differences and more emphasis on symptoms and features that seem to be universal. For example, something bizarre in one culture might not be bizarre in another culture (such as hearing voices), so 'bizarreness' might be a symptom that has less emphasis placed on it when making a diagnosis using the DSM.

The review of the DSM-IV to create the DSM-IV-TR looked at removing 'bizarre' from the list of symptoms,

but it was so central that it was not felt this could be done. Instead, a warning of the need to be mindful of cultural differences that the judgement 'bizarre' can entail was added. The DSM-5 has continued with that warning.

A move away from emphasis on first-rank symptoms and interpretation

One problem with schizophrenia is that **first-rank symptoms** tend to be weighted as more important when making a diagnosis. First-rank symptoms include hearing voices, delusions and other features of distortions in thinking. However, first-rank symptoms are also more open to interpretation, which means that there might be cultural issues with regard to interpretation. Flaum *et al.* (1991) found a lack of reliability when using the DSM with regard to first-rank symptoms and that was with a similar sample from one culture. Therefore, it is likely that such unreliability would be magnified if using first-rank symptoms across different cultures. Minimising first-rank symptoms and taking care with 'bizarre' features would mean less unreliability with regard to diagnosis across cultures.

Explanation
In schizophrenia, **first-rank symptoms**, according to Schneider (1959), include auditory (heard) hallucinations, thought insertion and delusions. These are positive symptoms. (Negative symptoms include withdrawing from usual activities and lacking emotion.)

Focus more on negative symptoms as they are more 'objectively' measured

With regard to diagnosis of schizophrenia, there should be a greater emphasis on symptoms that are objectively measured. Flaum *et al.* (1991) suggest that negative symptoms (for example, poverty of speech) are more objectively assessed and measured than positive symptoms like hallucinations.

STUDY HINT

Note that studies and research findings are given in the sections of this chapter about reliability, validity and diagnosis. This is because research findings are likely to form part of an examination question. Make sure you can give evidence as well as make general claims.

Culture-bound syndromes

Culture-bound syndromes are mental health problems (or other illnesses) with a set of symptoms found and recognised as an illness only in one culture. Many psychiatrists reject the idea of culture-bound syndromes. However, the most commonly recognised ones are listed in the DSM-IV.

Penis panics

In some cultures males may think that their penis will retract into their bodies – and women may think the same about their breasts. This is known as genital retraction syndrome (GRS). Such panics have been found around the world but mainly in Africa and Asia. The origin of the idea may be related to witchcraft.

Kuru

Kuru is an incurable brain disease found in Papua New Guinea. The symptoms are headaches, shaking and aching limbs; death can occur, in the worst cases, within about 18 months. It is related to Creutzfeldt-Jakob disease and is only found in one area in Papua New Guinea and nearby tribes, where there is intermarriage. It might be related to the funeral practice of eating the brain. Kuru is not a mental disorder, but its symptoms are similar to mental disorder.

Evaluation of cultural issues, validity, diagnosis and the DSM

Strengths

- The DSM-IV-TR takes account of cultural issues in acknowledging culture-bound syndromes, for example. Taking account of culture should improve validity of diagnosis.
- There has been an attempt to remove focus from bizarre symptoms in schizophrenia, as it was acknowledged that such symptoms are open to interpretation and that there are cultural issues in such interpretations.

Weaknesses

- Other features of symptoms of schizophrenia that are listed in the DSM could lead to cultural bias. First-rank symptoms (like 'bizarreness') should perhaps receive less emphasis, and a strength is that this has been suggested. The weakness is that a clinician may not follow this suggestion.
- Negative symptoms of schizophrenia are more objectively measured and so should be given greater attention, whereas in practice, the focus is on positive symptoms (including bizarreness, because this includes hallucinations).
- There might be some cultural differences in the symptoms of schizophrenia (such as grandiosity and auditory hallucinations) so these should be considered separately rather than as elements of a range of symptoms.

Test yourself

With reference to the DSM classification system (the DSM-IV-TR or the DSM-5), and using psychological research, evaluate diagnosis in terms of validity and reliability. **(16 marks)**

The ICD

A popular diagnostic system, different from the DSM, is the International Statistical Classification of Diseases and Related Health Problems (ICD), which is used more frequently than the DSM in some parts of the world. The ICD includes a look at the general health of a population and is used to monitor **incidence** (when a health problem occurs) and **prevalence** (how frequently a health problem occurs). It is the ICD that provides **mortality** (numbers of deaths) and **morbidity** (numbers of diseases) for the World Health Organization (WHO). All WHO member states use the ICD for such figures. The WHO was established in 1948 and its goal is to achieve the highest level of health, including mental health, for all people. ICD-10 was accepted in May 1990 and is the current version, though it is currently under revision and ICD-11 will be released in 2018. The ICD addresses all diseases, not just those involved in mental disorders, unlike the DSM.

Explore

ICD-10 is free and has public access so you can investigate more for yourself at:

www.who.int/classifications/icd/icdonlineversions/en/

Definitions

Mortality figures are about deaths while **morbidity** figures are about numbers of diseases. The **incidence** of a disease refers to when it occurs and the **prevalence** is how widespread it is or how frequently it occurs.

Categories of the ICD-10 (2015)

ICD-10 (2015) starts with the following categories (and goes up to XXII):

I Certain infectious and parasitic diseases
II Neoplasms
III Diseases of the blood and blood-forming organs and certain disorders involving the immune system
IV Endocrine, nutritional and metabolic diseases
V Mental and behavioural disorders
VI Diseases of the nervous system

Table 1.2 shows the results of a study by Reed *et al.* (2011), which asked 4,887 psychiatrists around the world whether they used the ICD. The figures show that the ICD is used worldwide, with 70 per cent of the study's participants saying they used ICD-10 most for mental disorders in their day-to-day clinical work compared with around 23 per cent using DSM-IV (the version being used at the time of the study). Evana *et al.* (2013) carried out a similar study using 2,155 psychologists – the results are shown in Table 1.3. In this study, however, 51 per cent of participants used ICD-10 and 44 per cent used DSM-IV, so the split is different. The US used ICD-9 until October 2014.

Table 1.2 Worldwide usage of ICD-10 (Reed *et al.*, 2011)

Area	No. of psychiatrists using the ICD-10
Americas	540
Europe	2,774
Africa	83
South East Asia	463
Eastern Mediterranean	315
Western Pacific	712

Table 1.3 Worldwide usage of ICD-10 (Evana *et al.*, 2013)

Area	No. of psychologists using the ICD-10
USA	108
Latin America	165
Africa	121
Eastern Mediterranean	224
Asia	139

Comparing the ICD with the DSM

Reed (2013) suggests a number of reasons for changing to the ICD from the DSM. These reasons can be used to show comparisons between the two classification systems.

- The ICD is produced by the WHO, an agency of the United Nations, whereas the DSM is produced by the American Psychiatric Association (APA), which is a single nation professional body.
- The ICD is a free and open resource whereas the DSM is a revenue source for the APA.
- The ICD is available to countries and service providers whereas the DSM is available to psychiatrists only.
- The ICD is multilingual and multidisciplinary whereas the DSM is US-dominated and in the English language only.
- The ICD covers all health conditions while the DSM covers only mental disorders.

Jakobsen *et al.* (2005) claim that there is significant agreement between the ICD and the DSM, which suggests reliability in diagnosis (page 25). Although Andreasen (2000) suggests that emphasis in the diagnostic criteria in both classification systems is on psychosis, which improves reliability, as the symptoms are easier to assess than cognitive impairments. This means that reliability is gained at the expense of validity.

Reliability of ICD-10 with regard to schizophrenia

In general it seems that ICD-10, like the newer DSM versions, gives reliability when it comes to diagnosis of schizophrenia. As Lee (2005) has said, 'there are more similarities than differences in diagnoses of schizophrenia'.

The following studies focus on the reliability of ICD-10 and schizophrenia.

Jakobsen *et al.* (2005)

Jakobsen *et al.* (2005) used a random sample of Danish in-patients diagnosed with schizophrenia and a sample of out-patients with a history of psychosis to look at the reliability of the ICD-10 with regard to schizophrenia. An ICD-10 diagnosis showed 93 per cent sensitivity and 87 per cent predictive value when it came to a diagnosis of schizophrenia and showed good agreement between the ICD-10 and diagnosis using another measure. Jakobsen *et al.* (2005) concluded that the ICD-10 gave a reliable diagnosis of schizophrenia.

Hiller *et al.* (1992)

Hiller *et al.* (1992) compared the ICD-10 with the DSM-III-R to look at their validity and reliability. The researchers used both classification systems on the same set of patients who were suffering from affective (about feelings and emotions) and psychotic (not in touch with reality) disorders. The ICD-10 gave higher reliability for all the disorders looked at except for bipolar disorder. Reliability was tested using more than one

rater. Reliability was reasonably high overall, with 0.53 agreement when diagnosing using the DSM-III-R and 0.59 agreement when using ICD-10. Affective disorders gave good agreement; there was moderate agreement for schizophrenia, though for schizoaffective disorder there was not enough reliability. It was thought that schizoaffective disorder was not sufficiently separate from schizophrenia and bipolar disorder. In order to be diagnosed, schizophrenia must have had symptoms lasting for six months in the DSM-III-R and lasting for one month in the ICD-10, which affected frequency rates. Therefore, there seems to be reliability when using both classification systems but there are also some issues around which diagnosis is made.

Cheniaux *et al.* (2009)

Cheniaux *et al.* (2009) looked at various diagnoses, including schizophrenia, bipolar depression and unipolar depression. They used inter-rater reliability, as is usual in such studies, and their aim was to look at reliability of diagnosis using the DSM-IV and the ICD-10. Two trained psychiatrists used interviewing to assess the diagnosis of 100 in-patients. They found that schizophrenia was more frequent using the ICD-10 than if using the DSM-IV. Only for schizoaffective disorder, which was also looked at, did the reliability between the two classification systems drop below 0.50. Bipolar disorder was the one most reliably diagnosed.

Evaluation of the reliability of ICD-10 in diagnosing schizophrenia

Strengths

- Studies tend to show that the ICD-10 is a reliable measure of schizophrenia and it also compares well in terms of reliability with the DSM-III-R (Hiller *et al.*, 1992, and Jakobsen *et al.*, 2005).
- Studies use inter-rater reliability, which means more than one person uses the classification system or systems with the same patients and when they come up with the same diagnosis, reliability can be claimed. There are careful controls to ensure that the raters work independently to avoid bias.

Weaknesses

- Schizophrenia was diagnosed more frequently when the ICD-10 was used than when the DSM-IV was used (Cheniaux *et al.*, 2009), which suggests some lack of reliability between the two systems (this could be due to differences in duration – six months for the DSM and one month for the ICD).

- Similarly, schizoaffective disorder was not reliably diagnosed according to Cheniaux *et al.* (2009) and Hiller *et al.* (1992), so reliability is in doubt for some disorders related to schizophrenia.
- The reliability figures were around 0.50 agreement, which leaves a lack of agreement also to be accounted for.

> **STUDY HINT**
> We have used the example of schizophrenia to explain the need to focus on reliability and validity. The information covered here on schizophrenia will also be useful when you are learning about schizophrenia as part of your studies of content in clinical psychology.

Validity of ICD-10 for schizophrenia

Pihlajamaa *et al.* (2008)

Pihlajamaa *et al.* (2008) looked at the validity of schizophrenia diagnosis using the DSM-III-R, the DSM-IV and the ICD-10 in order to compare them. Their study looked at 877 people born in Helsinki in Finland between 1951 and 1960 who had had at least one diagnosis of schizophrenia, schizophreniform disorder or schizoaffective disorder (**core schizophrenia spectrum** diagnoses). Case notes were available for 807 of the people identified and so they were the sample used.

The researchers used the case notes in the Finnish Hospital Discharge Register to look at diagnoses according to the Register as well as the three classification systems (the DSM-III-R, the DSM-IV and the ICD-10) and compared the diagnoses to look at their validity. Validity was said to exist when individuals received the same diagnosis from the different diagnostic systems as stated in the Register.

This study was about having more than one measure (the diagnosis in the Register and the ones done separately using the diagnostic classifications) to see if the diagnoses matched. If they matched, that would mean they were valid. Using the DSM-III-R diagnosis and the Register diagnosis, individuals had the same diagnosis 75 per cent of the time and using the ICD-10 diagnosis and the Register diagnosis, they had the same diagnosis 78 per cent of the time. This study looked at the core schizophrenia spectrum diagnoses. Other validity figures, such as comparing people with schizophrenia alone, or using the DSM-IV and the Register, were also around 70 to 80 per cent. The researchers concluded that generally, when taking information from case studies in the Register, the Register diagnosis and comparing them using the ICD-10 and the DSM, it could be seen that diagnoses were valid. However, they did find some issues if people had a diagnosis of both a core schizophrenia spectrum disorder and bipolar I disorder.

Explanation

Core schizophrenia spectrum disorders come under the spectrum of psychotic disorders, which includes schizophrenia, schizoaffective disorder, delusional disorder, schizotypal personality disorder, schizophreniform disorder, brief psychotic disorder and some other psychoses linked to substance misuse or medical conditions.

Jansson *et al.* (2002)

Jansson *et al.* (2002) wanted to look at the ICD-10 criteria for schizophrenia compared with other diagnostic systems. They looked at concurrent validity of the ICD-9 and the ICD-10, which means they wanted to see if the two would yield the same diagnosis for the same individual at the same moment in time. The researchers looked at 155 patients in Copenhagen from 1998 to 2000. The sample included psychotic patients and those that were non-psychotic but seemed to be within the schizophrenia spectrum.

A large amount of data were gathered by interview, including many different assessments, notes, interviews from second informants, diagnostic criteria and family history. The diagnoses were then compared to check the validity of the different classification systems. The ICD-10 and the DSM-IV gave the best diagnostic agreement (0.823). However, the researchers reported differences in diagnoses for individuals and some differences between diagnostic systems, including between the ICD-9 and the ICD-10. They thought that the boundaries for schizophrenia needed redrawing as it was not clear exactly where the boundaries were, given the amount of data they analysed and the differences in diagnosis that were found.

The ICD-10 seems to be less valid than the ICD-9 in some situations, which seems to be because the ICD-9 focuses on features such as autism and self-dissolution whereas the ICD-10 focuses more on noticeable psychotic phenomena and negative symptoms. This study has a lot of complexity, which is not reported here, but the basic point is that there is validity in the diagnostic classification in general, but when looking more at the detail there are differences.

Evaluation of the validity of the ICD-10 and diagnosis of schizophrenia

Strengths

- In general when the ICD-10 is used to diagnose schizophrenia the diagnosis matches a diagnosis using a different system, which suggests that the ICD-10 is valid (e.g. Pihlajamaa *et al.*, 2008).
- According to Jansson *et al.* (2002) the ICD-10 and the DSM-IV gave in excess of an 80 per cent agreement in diagnosis, which is high, though it must be said that the study also reported differences.

Weaknesses

- Jansson *et al.* (2002) found that different classification systems focused on different features and symptoms in schizophrenia (such as the ICD-10 and the ICD-9), which threatens the validity of the two systems. There is a general suggestion that there is a different focus and so validity of diagnosis is less likely.
- Studies of validity of diagnosis of schizophrenia are hard to carry out given differences in the disorders, such as whether the core schizophrenia spectrum disorder is considered or specific diagnoses like schizoaffective disorder. In general it seems that the complexity of the disorders is an issue when it comes to claiming validity of diagnosis. The complexity is further seen in that other disorders, such as bipolar disorder, have some features of schizophrenia. Ellason and Ross (1995) suggest that people diagnosed with dissociative identity disorder have more features and symptoms of schizophrenia than those with schizophrenia. These were positive symptoms (page 29).

STUDY HINT

Draw up strengths and weaknesses tables to suit the material you must learn, as that will help your learning and your revision.

Progress check 1.13

What is the difference between reliability of a diagnosis and validity of a diagnosis?

Test yourself

With reference to the ICD-10 classification system, and using psychological research, discuss issues of validity and reliability. **(16 marks)**

Diagnosis: the medical model

So far, in looking at the issue of 'diagnosis', there has been evidence that what is being used is a medical model of mental 'ill health'. For example, illnesses are diagnosed using lists of symptoms and features and classification systems produce such lists for a clinician to use in making a diagnosis. The diagnosis then informs the treatment offered and a 'cure' is sought or some way of helping the individual 'to get better'. Often that help is in the form of medication to rebalance biological factors that might be producing or prolonging the mental disorder. There is clear evidence here that mental disorders within society are regarded as the responsibility of the medical profession.

The recovery model: against the medical model

Recent focus in clinical psychology is on *recovery* of mental health, which means focusing on helping people to overcome mental disorders. The Care Quality Commission, cited in Speed and Harper (2015), report that 84 per cent of mental health service users received medication in the previous year and 87 per cent of those had been prescribed medication for over a year, showing the prevalence of drug therapy. In contrast just 47 per cent had received intervention apart from medication.

Arenella (2015) suggests that the recovery model is a good thing, coming after the 1990s' focus on the brain and the 2000s' focus on behaviour. The recovery model moves away from mending broken brains and giving relief of symptoms and focuses on the whole client and how personal relationships can help with healing. The focus is on recovering good mental health; there is less emphasis on diagnosis and more on what can be done to support the individual in regaining their mental health. Schizophrenia, for example, has been (and is) treated with medication and not considered open to counselling intervention, but the recovery model has highlighted that support can help. Lavarenne *et al.* (2013) used the case study method and you can use this in your study of clinical psychology (page 158). They showed how a group could act as the 'ego boundary' for individuals with mental disorders including schizophrenia, which is in line with recovery model thinking. Arenella (2015) also suggests that the recovery model is gaining ground over medication and the medical model when it comes to mental health issues because drugs are expensive and there is a backlash against the costs involved in supporting those with mental disorders. Instead, the focus on recovery can involve comparatively cheaper professionals, from psychiatrists to social workers.

However, a problem with the recovery model is that focusing on the individual's recovery of mental health can lead to a lack of emphasis on social issues such as unemployment, poverty and welfare issues and more emphasis on the individual getting back to their 'normal' life. The idea of focusing on an individual's recovery can mean missing wider factors and focusing just on empowering an individual, whereas that may have the opposite effect if the social factors impacting on and disempowering individuals are not also considered. The recovery of our mental health presupposes that mental health existed in the first place, whereas political and social issues suggest this is not the case for many. Such issues include inadequate education, homophobia, violence, neglect and racism, so to recover good mental health these issues must also be addressed.

Beresford (2015) has written an article called 'From recovery to reclaiming madness', which emphasises the issue mentioned above – that recovering mental health presupposes there was mental health in the first place. 'Recovery' sounds like 'getting better' and seems to have its basis in the medical model, though when it is looked at as 'recovering mental health' there is less emphasis on the medical model. Beresford (2015) focuses more on surviving a mental disorder and recovering mental health, at least to some extent, rather than 'recovery' meaning getting over what is 'wrong' with the patient.

Explore

One recovery programme that you can investigate is called Wellness Recovery Action Plan© or WRAP©, which will help you to see recovery ideas in action. Take a look at the following link to investigate this programme further: www.mentalhealthrecovery.com/wrap/

There are also a number of YouTube videos focusing on the recovery model. Try the following: www.youtube.com/watch?v=_2SDbSuX3kQ

You may also like to investigate the SAMHSA (Substance Abuse and Mental Health Services Administration) website, which has a lot of information about mental health, including ideas about recovery: www.samhsa.gov

STUDY HINT

The recovery model is about how people with mental issues *could be treated* rather than about actual diagnosis. However, it is included within the section looking at diagnosis as it helps to emphasise that one criticism of diagnosis is that it assumes mental health issues are 'illnesses'. The recovery model is outlined here to show alternatives to that assumption. When studying your notes, try to learn how the material covered fits into your studies.

Progress check 1.14

How does the recovery model go against diagnosing a mental disorder?

Schizophrenia

This section focuses on schizophrenia, looking at **symptoms** and **features**, followed by a look at three explanations for the illness, one of which is neurotransmitter functioning, which you must cover in your studies. This is followed by another biological explanation, again which you must cover, and this book

has chosen to look at genes. The third explanation must be non-biological and this book covers the social causation hypothesis. Lastly, you need to cover two treatments for schizophrenia. Three are given for your interest. One treatment must be biological and here drug therapy is chosen; one must be a non-biological treatment and here CBT and a treatment focusing on social issues called assertive community treatment (ACT) are chosen, the latter to help with social explanations and the former because of its wide usage for schizophrenia. (You also need to know about one other disorder from a choice of three; later in this chapter we will cover three disorders and you will need to study one of these using the same approach used in this section on schizophrenia.)

You will already know quite a bit about schizophrenia from your study of abnormality and diagnosis earlier in this chapter, so you can draw on that understanding here. The information on schizophrenia in this section will help to illustrate some of the earlier points in this chapter with regard to diagnosis of mental disorders.

Explanation

Features of a mental health disorder usually involve statistics about the disorder, or aspects of it, such as how the illness develops or how other factors such as gender and age link.

Symptoms are things that characterise a disorder with regard to how the person thinks, feels or behaves.

STUDY HINT

Make sure you can separate features from symptoms in case you get an exam question that asks you about only one of them.

Study of interest

Sjöblom *et al.* (2013) carried out and wrote up a single case study of a woman whose brother became mentally ill, focusing on her experiences of psychiatric care. The researchers comment that for people with mental health issues, siblings can become very important, particularly as parents grow older and perhaps can no longer help the person with mental disorder. Also, the person with mental illness may not have children and so any nephews and nieces may be especially precious.

Sjöblom *et al.* wanted to gather detailed, in-depth data about one woman's experiences. They used in-depth semi-structured interviewing which they repeated over a two-year period and which they analysed using content analysis. Main areas of focus were her brother's time in psychiatric care, her feelings and emotions and her view of her contact with psychiatric care. The findings showed that siblings in such situations need time to talk about their experiences of psychiatric care. The study was one of the first opportunities the woman had had to talk about it and her need for attention and support was clear.

This study shows the importance of social support and social isolation for those with schizophrenia and also underlines how schizophrenia impacts on siblings, an area not well researched. The study also shows how the research method followed the research question – a study focusing on feelings and emotions needed a method that gathered in-depth and detailed qualitative data.

Symptoms of schizophrenia

Schizophrenia is a mental illness that can affect the way someone thinks, speaks or feels to such a degree that they lose their grip on reality. There are a number of ways of characterising schizophrenia, including giving first- and second-rank symptoms or positive and negative symptoms. First-rank symptoms include hearing voices and ideas about being guided by others. Second-rank symptoms include flattened emotions. Positive and negative symptoms are explained below. With regard to symptoms you need to know in particular about disordered thinking and thought insertions, including hallucinations and delusions, but it is useful to know other symptoms too.

STUDY HINT
When describing symptoms and features of schizophrenia, you could use the information about markers in the blood and detection of certain eye movements, but they are not currently listed in a diagnostic classification. It is therefore better to focus on 'listed' symptoms and features, and then use additional information in discussion.

According to the DSM-IV-TR a diagnosis of schizophrenia requires one to six months of **positive** and **negative symptoms**. For example, in the DSM-IV-TR two or more of a list of symptoms over a one-month period can mean a diagnosis of schizophrenia (see below).

Explanation
In schizophrenia **positive symptoms** are where there are additions to behaviour and symptoms that can be seen and noted (i.e. the presence of something). **Negative symptoms** are the absence of something, usually the absence of normal functioning.

Positive symptoms of schizophrenia

Positive symptoms are additions to behaviour and actual symptoms that can be noted, such as delusions and hallucinations. Positive symptoms include first-rank symptoms such as delusions and hallucinations; they are about changes in thinking in the person. In your course you are required to learn about thought insertion, hallucinations, delusions and disordered thinking and these are covered in the description of positive symptoms described below.

- **Hallucinations** refer to seeing or hearing things that are not there, but may also involve smells or feelings of being touched by someone or something. Hearing voices in some cultures is not seen as a sign of mental disorder, but of a personal spiritual capability. In these cases the voices are often kind and positive, whereas in others diagnosed with schizophrenia, the voices are often harsh and critical. Critical voices provide a running commentary on what the person is doing. Controlling voices tell the person what to do – usually uncharacteristic acts. Sometimes the voices talk to one another. They may tell someone to do something or warn the person of danger.

STUDY HINT
Luhrmann *et al.* (2015) carried out a study of hallucinations and found that in some cultures the voices heard were interpreted as harsh and critical but in other cultures they were seen as kind, so there are cultural differences in how schizophrenia is characterised. You could refer to this when discussing features and symptoms of schizophrenia in relation to issues of culture (page 28).

- **Delusions** (false beliefs) refer to a person thinking their movements are being controlled by someone else. A common form of delusion is the paranoid delusion, where the sufferer believes that someone is trying to mislead, manipulate or even kill them. Someone suffering from delusions of grandeur will think they are in a prominent position of power, such as a king, or that they possess special powers, such as to cure cancer. Delusions can also take the form of a person thinking that unrelated things are in fact intended to relate to them; they may feel that a newspaper headline carries a secret message for them. Delusions can lead to strange behaviour, such as covering windows to shut out the sound of the voice of God. Delusions are beliefs that remain even when shown not to be true or beliefs that are not logical. Delusions of persecution are when someone thinks others are trying to harm them, spying or plotting against them.

- Thought disorders make someone's speech hard to follow. Someone with schizophrenia might lose concentration at work or complain of having muddled thinking; they may become disorganised. Further developments of thought disorders are '**thought insertion**' (a person thinks their own thoughts are put there by someone else) or 'thought broadcasting' (thinking others can hear their thoughts).
- **Disordered thinking** is when someone finds it hard to put their thoughts into logical sense. Thought blocking is when someone stops in mid-sentence in the middle of a thought and they may say the thought has been taken out of their head. Someone might make up words that have no meaning, called 'neologisms'.
- Movement disorders tend to mean agitated movement, such as repeating movements over and over. However, someone can become catatonic, which means not moving or responding to others.

Definitions

Thought insertion is when someone thinks someone else is putting thoughts into their head. It is a positive symptom of schizophrenia.

Disordered thinking is when someone finds it hard to put their thoughts into a logical order to make them make sense. This is a positive symptom of schizophrenia.

Hallucinations are a positive symptom of schizophrenia and focus on seeing (or smelling or hearing) something that is not there.

Delusions are beliefs that are not borne out by reality, such as believing you are being persecuted or you are famous. Delusions are also positive symptoms of schizophrenia.

Evaluation of positive symptoms

Positive symptoms tend to have greater weight when diagnosing schizophrenia but, as explained earlier in this chapter (page 29), they can be affected by cultural differences so perhaps should not be weighted as strongly as negative symptoms, which might be more objectively measured.

Negative symptoms

Negative symptoms are where normal functioning is not present, such as a loss of emotion, speech or motivation. Such symptoms often start before positive ones, sometimes years before schizophrenia is diagnosed. This is known as the **prodromal** period. Some negative symptoms are described below.
- Lack of energy and apathy, for example, no motivation to do daily chores.

- Social withdrawal, for example, avoiding family and friends and not going out.
- Flatness of emotions, where a person's face becomes emotionless and the voice dull with no rise and fall of intonation.
- Not looking after appearance and self and generally not adhering to expectations with regard to preserving a sense of self.
- Lack of pleasure in everyday things and everyday life.
- Speaking little even when required to interact.

People with negative symptoms need help because they tend to neglect everyday tasks such as preparing food or personal hygiene tasks. They can seem lazy and not willing to help themselves, but this is due to their schizophrenia.

> **STUDY HINT**
> When asked about symptoms of schizophrenia, try to choose a wide category for a symptom, such as hallucinations, delusions or thought disorders, rather than a narrower category such as 'thought broadcasting', so that you will have plenty to say about the symptom. Make sure you are able to answer a question about one of the four symptoms specifically covered in your course – hallucinations, delusions, thought insertion and disordered thinking.

Definition

Prodromal period is the early period in schizophrenia, before the onset of psychotic symptoms. In this period patients still have insight and have not yet experienced a psychotic break with reality.

Evaluation of negative symptoms

Negative symptoms seem less affected by cultural factors and it has been suggested that they can be more objectively measured. Hearing voices, for example, is difficult if not impossible to measure. Lack of energy, flatness of emotions or social withdrawal might be more easily monitored. However, prodromal features have been found to be present in many adolescents and cannot be taken to indicate the onset of schizophrenia on their own.

> **STUDY HINT**
> Separating symptoms into positive and negative ones can be useful, but note that 'positive' and 'negative' are not themselves symptoms. Therefore, when answering a question that asks for the symptoms of schizophrenia, give an explanation of the symptoms themselves (e.g. social withdrawal and delusions).

Cognitive symptoms of schizophrenia

Cognitive symptoms in schizophrenia include difficulty in concentrating and paying attention, problems with working memory and difficulty with executive functioning (understanding information and making decisions).

Year One link: Cognitive symptoms in schizophrenia link in part to working memory and you can use what you know about working memory from your study of cognitive psychology to understand such symptoms.

> **Positive symptoms:** hallucinations, delusions, thought disorders (including disordered thinking and thought insertion) and movement disorders (agitated or catatonic)

> **Negative symptoms:** flatness of emotions (flat affect), social withdrawal, apathy, not looking after self, lack of pleasure in life, not speaking much

> **Cognitive symptoms:** poor working memory, poor executive functioning (understanding and decision-making), difficulties in concentration, difficulties in paying attention

Symptoms of schizophrenia

Explore

YouTube has lots of videos about schizophrenia for you to explore. However, choose carefully, as this sort of material can be upsetting. You may like to try the following:
www.youtube.com/watch?v=bWaFqw8XnpA

Progress check 1.15

Explain two symptoms of schizophrenia.

Features of schizophrenia

It is hard to separate features from symptoms. Symptoms are what the person presents with to the doctor. Features are wider – for instance, that there are different types of schizophrenia or that schizophrenia is found in all countries where research has been carried out. According to Jablensky (2000), schizophrenia is found in any nation at a rate of about 1.4–4.6 per 1,000 people. These are features of schizophrenia because they are not symptoms but 'facts' about the disorder. About a quarter of people who have had a schizophrenic episode recover and do not get another one. About a quarter of those who have schizophrenia have it continually without any breaks. That leaves 50 per cent who have periods of recovery and periods of symptoms. The positive symptoms, such as hallucinations

and delusions, can be overcome but the negative symptoms tend to remain.

- A feature of schizophrenia is that there is psychosis, which refers to a separation from reality, unlike neurosis, where there are mental health issues but no separation from reality.
- Another feature is that schizophrenia is a serious mental health condition with about 1 per cent of the population experiencing schizophrenia. Others suggest this figure is lower at around 0.7 per cent, but whichever figure is correct, it indicates that in a population as a whole, the number of those affected by schizophrenia is quite high.
- The average life expectancy for someone with schizophrenia is around ten or more years less than average. This might be because of the physical health problems associated with schizophrenia or the higher suicide rate.
- Duerr (2013) suggests that adolescents with psychotic symptoms are nearly 70 times more likely to attempt suicide.
- Schizophrenia tends to be diagnosed during adolescence and up to the age of about 30.
- People who are experiencing social problems, such as poverty and unemployment as well as possibly homelessness, are more likely to develop schizophrenia than other sections of the population.

Explore

A common misconception is that people with schizophrenia have a multiple or split personality. However, split personality, if it exists, is not the same at all. Learn more about dissociative identity disorder (multiple personality disorder) by taking a look at the following:
www.psychologytoday.com/conditions/dissociative-identity-disorder-multiple-personality-disorder

---

Explore

There is lots of information on the web about schizophrenia. You may like to start by looking at the following:
www.nimh.nih.gov/health/topics/schizophrenia/index.shtml

Types of schizophrenia

A feature of schizophrenia is that there are many different types.

- Paranoid schizophrenia is characterised by someone being suspicious of others and having delusions of grandeur. There are often hallucinations as well.
- Disorganised schizophrenia is characterised by speech being disorganised and hard to follow, as well as the person having inappropriate moods for a given situation. There are no hallucinations.

- Catatonic schizophrenia is when someone is very withdrawn and isolated and has little physical movement. They may assume unusual body positions.
- Residual schizophrenia is where there are low level positive symptoms but psychotic symptoms are present.
- Schizoaffective disorder is when someone has symptoms of schizophrenia and of a mood disorder such as depression. This is not exactly a type of schizophrenia and is diagnosed separately, but it is included here to show such combinations of mental disorders can occur. The 'schizo' part is the psychosis and the 'affective' part refers to the 'mood'. Mood symptoms can be depression or manic, as well as mixed.
- Undifferentiated schizophrenia is when the person does not fit the other types described above.

STUDY HINT
What you have learned about the *nature* of schizophrenia can be referred to as a *feature* of the disorder. For example, Goldstein (1988) (page 168) found that women aged 45 and under have a less severe course through the illness. Gender difference in the course of schizophrenia is therefore a feature of schizophrenia.

Progress check 1.16

Using two examples, compare features with symptoms of schizophrenia.

Diagnosing schizophrenia

Having looked at the symptoms and features of schizophrenia, it is interesting to consider whether in future it might be diagnosed using a blood test or eye tracking – both of which can offer **biomarkers** for schizophrenia. As yet there is no physical way of diagnosing schizophrenia, although research is looking at the possibility of using both these tests in future.

Definition
Biomarker is a biological marker that can signal a disease or problem. It is a biological state that can be measured.

Blood testing to diagnose schizophrenia

A recent article in *Schizophrenia Bulletin* (a journal focusing on schizophrenia) suggests that a blood test may become possible as a way of diagnosing the disorder. Perkins and others (reported in 2014) analysed blood samples of 32 patients with symptoms that seemed to show psychosis and from 35 control patients. The researchers were looking for biomarkers of inflammation, oxidative stress, metabolism and hormones (previously it had been suggested that these markers are at abnormal levels in those with schizophrenia). Perkins and her team (in the US) found that they could, using 15 markers in the blood, predict which of the 32 patients went on to develop psychosis (meaning some developed schizophrenia, some an unspecified psychosis, two had major depression with psychotic features, one had bipolar disorder, one had schizoaffective disorder and one had delusional disorder). This information suggests that a blood test might be able to diagnose such psychoses in the near future.

Eye tracking to diagnose schizophrenia

Sweeney *et al.* (1994) carried out a study using psychotic patients and matched controls and found that those with schizophrenia were slow and different in their eye movements. If there are specific issues with eye movements in those with schizophrenia, such movements might be used to diagnose schizophrenia. Benson and his team (2012) also worked to see if simple eye tests could identify schizophrenia. They had some success (using patients with schizophrenia and controls) in identifying those with schizophrenia using eye-movement abnormalities.

Explore
In 2013 Assistant Professor Miriam Spering of the University of British Columbia made a video that discusses eye tracking and schizophrenia. Take a look at the link below if you'd like to explore more on this issue.
www.youtube.com/watch?v=Q9DIW_z6i_E

STUDY HINT
Note that suggesting that a blood test and/or tracking eye movements might help in the diagnosis of psychosis, in particular schizophrenia, means that the use of a diagnostic classification system to establish diagnosis will become less important. You can use information like this when evaluating the use of the DSM or the ICD. Be ready to use any relevant material from the sections when looking at an issue.

At present, only a psychiatrist can make a diagnosis of schizophrenia using symptoms and features found in a classification system such as the DSM or the ICD, as described earlier in this chapter, until perhaps a blood test, eye test or some other test becomes available.

Three explanations for schizophrenia

You are required to learn about three explanations for schizophrenia. One of these explanations is the function of neurotransmitters together with one further biological explanation and one non-biological explanation.

We begin this section by looking first at the functioning of neurotransmitters as an explanation for schizophrenia. This is followed by another biological explanation, the role of genetic factors in schizophrenia. The non-biological theory or explanation that is covered in this section is the role of life experiences in schizophrenia, including how they can increase the chance of a person developing schizophrenia.

Neurotransmitter functioning such as involving dopamine and/or glutamate

Environmental influences focusing on social factors

Genetic variation with evidence from twin studies, family studies and DNA sampling from those with schizophrenia and controls

Three explanations for schizophrenia

Neurotransmitter functioning and schizophrenia

For some time the main focus when considering the role of neurotransmitters on schizophrenia has been the neurotransmitter dopamine. However, newer research is now looking more closely at the idea that schizophrenia comes from excess dopamine and other hypotheses are now being put forward, including the glutamate hypothesis. The main study in your course focusing on schizophrenia is Carlsson *et al.* (1999/2000) (page 105), which explains in great detail both the dopamine hypothesis and the role of glutamate in schizophrenia and how they interact. Carlsson *et al.* explain how neurotransmitter functioning relates to schizophrenia and you should refer to that study throughout this section. Note that at present there is no actual 'answer' to the question of how neurotransmitter functioning might cause schizophrenia, but quite a lot is known about this issue and more continues to be discovered.

The dopamine hypothesis

Research suggests that the presence of an excess number of dopamine receptors at the synapses in the brain contributes to schizophrenia. It is possible that an increase

in dopamine in one site in the brain (the mesolimbic pathway) contributes to positive symptoms and in another site (the mesocortical pathway) contributes to negative symptoms of schizophrenia. The illustration below shows the dopamine pathways in the brain.

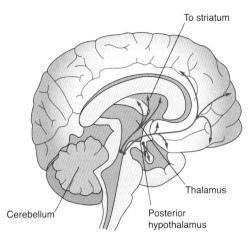

Dopamine pathways in the brain

There are many ways in which such sensitivity to dopamine can arise, from genetic inheritance to brain **lesioning**, so the conclusion seems to be that there are many ways to develop schizophrenia, or at least many ways in which such 'supersensitivity' to dopamine can occur. Much of the research looking at how excess dopamine receptors arise has been done on animals. Other research has been carried out on humans using PET scanning and other scanning methods.

Definition

Lesioning involves damaging a part of the brain to see the effect on behaviour. This tends to be done using animals but can be carried out with humans, though as part of a surgical procedure to help someone rather than as an experiment.

Year One link: Review your learning about synaptic transmission and the role of neurotransmitters in sending messages around the brain (Edexcel for A Level Book 1 Psychology, page 139).

Explaining the dopamine differences

Dopamine receptors can be present in the brain in different numbers and it has been suggested that development of the receptors in one area might inhibit their development in another. For example, lack of activity in the prefrontal cortex and limbic system might lead to lack of inhibition of their production in the striatum; this area of research is currently being studied. There is some evidence that people with schizophrenia have enlarged ventricles and smaller frontal lobes and that they also have a higher incidence of head injury in childhood. Any of these features link with prefrontal cortex damage. The prefrontal cortex finishes developing in adolescence, which links with the (common) onset of schizophrenia at this age.

Evaluation of the dopamine hypothesis

Evidence for the dopamine hypothesis (strengths of the explanation)

1 Amphetamines produce symptoms similar to those of excess dopamine.

Some evidence comes from the effects of drugs such as amphetamines, which can cause an excess of dopamine, resulting in symptoms of psychosis. This psychosis is called 'amphetamine psychosis' and the symptoms are similar to the positive symptoms of schizophrenia. However, excess dopamine also has a stimulant effect, such as overconfidence and high alertness, which are more symptoms of mania than schizophrenia, so the explanation does not fit exactly using this evidence.

2 Phenothiazines block dopamine receptors and reduce schizophrenic symptoms.

Phenothiazines (a group of drugs including chlorpromazine, given to people with schizophrenia) alleviate the symptoms of schizophrenia and work by blocking dopamine receptors. If the receptors are blocked, then less dopamine will be taken up so that the effects of excess dopamine are avoided. This supports the conclusion that excess dopamine is a cause of schizophrenia.

3 People with schizophrenia are more sensitive to dopamine uptake.

Scanning shows that if those with schizophrenia are given amphetamines there is greater release of dopamine than if people without schizophrenia are given amphetamines. This suggests that those with schizophrenia are more sensitive to excess dopamine than other people (Carlsson *et al.*, 1999/2000) – again, evidence that dopamine is involved in the disorder.

4 Drugs to increase dopamine production in sufferers of Parkinson's disease give psychotic symptoms.

People given Levodopa (which increases dopamine production) for Parkinson's disease can experience symptoms similar to schizophrenia. This is another piece of evidence that dopamine relates to schizophrenic symptoms.

5 Some genes link with dopamine production and are found with greater frequency in those with schizophrenia.

Genes that are likely to increase sensitivity to dopamine are found in those who develop symptoms of schizophrenia, so it is likely that there is a genetic

explanation for schizophrenia as well. More about a genetic explanation is given later in this section.

6 Brain differences might link with dopamine sensitivity.

Those with schizophrenia seem to have differences in their brain, such as grey matter differences in the front and temporal lobes. Such brain changes, at an early age, link with sensitivity to dopamine.

Progress check 1.17

Give two pieces of evidence that link dopamine excess at the synapse with schizophrenia.

Evidence against the dopamine hypothesis (weaknesses of the explanation)

1 PET scans show that blocking dopamine receptors does not always remove symptoms.

PET scans have suggested that drugs that block dopamine do not reduce the symptoms of schizophrenia in patients who have had schizophrenia for ten years or more, even if the block is 90 per cent effective. However, if antipsychotic drugs are administered early on in the disorder, then more than 90 per cent of patients respond.

2 Blocking dopamine receptors takes a few days to work.

It is also interesting that anti-schizophrenic drugs block the dopamine receptors almost immediately but any calming effect is not noticed for several days. This suggests that something other than excess dopamine is causing the psychotic symptoms. (This is the same criticism as is made against the neurotransmitter malfunctioning explanation for depression, explained later in this chapter on page 58.)

3 Amphetamines produce only positive symptoms.

Amphetamines only produce symptoms that are like the positive symptoms of schizophrenia, which suggests that the dopamine hypothesis is not a sufficient explanation. There are symptoms of mania where amphetamines are used; these are not involved in schizophrenia.

4 Different types of dopamine receptor in different brain areas give different results.

Research suggests that the striatum, limbic system and cortex are the three areas of the brain where there are excess dopamine receptors in everyone. When the striatum was examined in schizophrenic patients it was not found that there were more dopamine receptors than in non-schizophrenic patients. Also, there were fewer dopamine receptors in the prefrontal lobes of schizophrenic patients. Research has suggested that the decreased level of dopamine receptors in the prefrontal lobes links with negative symptoms of schizophrenia. Although this still focuses on dopamine and psychotic symptoms, it is not just that there are excess dopamine receptors. Different types of dopamine receptors (D1, D2, D3 and so on) give different results from excess or reduced receptors.

5 Glutamate might also be implicated.

Another neurotransmitter, glutamate, is also thought to cause psychotic symptoms if its production is blocked. Again, this shows up in those who take recreational drugs, such as PCP (also known as 'angel dust'). So perhaps dopamine is not the only neurotransmitter involved in the development of schizophrenia. However, animal studies (such as Schwabe *et al.*, 2004) have shown that if an animal is sensitised to PCP it is also sensitised to dopamine

and there is an increase in the number of dopamine receptors in the brain. This suggests a relationship between PCP and dopamine, which might explain the psychotic symptoms, rather than glutamate alone. More about the role of glutamate is found in Carlsson *et al.* (1999/2000), the required study for schizophrenia in clinical psychology (page 105).

6 Social and environmental factors are involved.

Social and environmental factors seem to trigger schizophrenia, so a biological explanation is not sufficient. Perhaps stressful events in life can trigger production of excess dopamine. The link between social class and schizophrenia is described below, as the third explanation for schizophrenia.

Table 1.4 Strengths and weaknesses of the methodology used to study the dopamine hypothesis

Strengths	Weaknesses
Many different sources of evidence point to dopamine receptors being involved in some way in schizophrenia, from animal studies to PET scanning. Evidence also comes from unrelated events, such as how medication affects those with Parkinson's disease or how using recreational drugs leads to psychotic symptoms.	Animals are used to investigate dopamine pathways and the effects of drugs on them. Lesioning is also used with animals to explore the effects of dopamine on their functioning. It is possible that findings from animal studies cannot legitimately be generalised to humans, because there are obvious differences in animal brains and the functioning of their nervous systems.
Dopamine receptors are implicated in many different studies, which tends to give the hypothesis reliability.	PET scanning is a reliable and objective measure. However, it is not a very sophisticated technique because detail is hard to study, even though functioning of the brain can be looked at.
'Biological' research methods such as scanning and animal studies can have good controls and tend not to involve subjective interpretation of data, so such methods are scientific, which means the findings are credible.	Another aspect of schizophrenia may have caused the differences in dopamine receptors, rather than dopamine receptor differences causing schizophrenia.

The glutamate hypothesis

Carlsson *et al.* (1999/2000) present a review of how neurotransmitter functioning links to psychosis and a fairly detailed account of their study can be found later in this chapter (page 105). Carlsson *et al.* support the dopamine hypothesis, which they found evidence for in a study in 1994 (Hietala *et al.*, 1994, cited in Carlsson *et al.*, 1999/2000). They accept that schizophrenia-like symptoms link to excess dopamine in the brain and in their 1999 review they investigate whether this is due 'just' to excess dopamine or whether there is more to it. The various studies cited by Carlsson *et al.* (1999/2000) show that there is indeed more to it – for example, animal studies have shown that where animals were treated with an NMDA **antagonist**, this led to a lack of glutamate but did not always lead to an increase in dopamine. If NMDA antagonists are psychostimulants and lead to psychosis-like symptoms and they inhibit dopamine release (Waters *et al.*, 1996, cited in Carlsson *et al.*, 1999/2000) then this does not support the idea that excess dopamine causes schizophrenia. It seems that there is more to schizophrenia and psychotic behaviour than excess dopamine – glutamate seems also to have a role.

Definitions

An **antagonist** blocks the receptor at the site of the receptor and deactivates it. An **agonist** activates the receptor at the site of the receptor so a message is passed on.

Progress check 1.18

Explain why there is debate about whether it is useful to experiment on animals to find out about human neurotransmitter functioning.

STUDY HINT

When learning new terms, you could 'translate' them every time you read them to help you learn their meaning. For example, for 'antagonist' you could think of a cartoon of someone aggressively pushing away a neurotransmitter trying to link to a receptor and, for 'agonist', think of a cartoon where the receptor happily receives the neurotransmitter.

More evidence that glutamate has a role in the development of schizophrenia and it is not just excess dopamine that gives psychostimulation is that PCP (angel dust) is an NMDA receptor antagonist (blocks glutamate receptors). PCP leads to lower levels of glutamate, increased dopamine and psychostimulation. However, glutamate receptor antagonists can cancel the psychostimulant behaviour of PCP even though there is still an excess of dopamine. Findings like this suggest that 'simple' excess dopamine cannot be the cause of psychotic behaviour. Dopamine seems to have a role, but there are other neurotransmitters implicated in the process as well.

STUDY HINT

In a topic area such as clinical psychology, the studies you need to cover can help to illustrate points about the content, just as Carlsson *et al.* (1999) can explain neurotransmitter functioning as an explanation for schizophrenia. Use material from across a topic area to answer questions, as well as material from your Year One studies (such as in biological psychology, where you learned about neurotransmitter functioning). Make notes about such links whenever you can, to help your learning and revision.

Evaluation of the glutamate hypothesis

Strengths

- The glutamate hypothesis works with the dopamine hypothesis and expands on it rather than replacing it. This is a strength as it means evidence for the dopamine hypothesis, which is strong evidence, can be incorporated into the glutamate hypothesis. The idea that glutamate has a role as well as dopamine adds to the original hypothesis, enabling a body of knowledge to be built and adding to its scientific credibility.
- Though the evidence is complex (because the idea of neurotransmitter functioning at the synapses in the different brain regions is very complex), there is quite a lot of evidence from neuroimaging and animal studies to show that blocking glutamate relates to psychotic symptoms (such as negative affect in schizophrenia). The findings of the studies tend to support one another, which suggests they are reliable.

Weaknesses

- Whenever animal studies are used to explain human behaviour, questions are asked about generalisability of the findings. Perhaps especially when looking at areas of human functioning like psychoses, which has mental roots even if manifested in behaviours, using findings from animal studies might lack validity. What seems like erratic behaviour and is seen as a psychostimulant

in animals might not relate to psychotic behaviour in humans as clearly as is claimed.
- Another weakness might be using PET scanning to obtain evidence about neurotransmitter functioning, even if scanning humans. Carlsson *et al.* (1999) mention how when undergoing scanning humans might feel under pressure and are likely to respond differently from normal. This means that any findings, especially those focused on brain activity linked to psychotic functioning, might not have validity.

Progress check 1.19

Give evidence that shows that limited glutamate might link to psychotic-like symptoms.

Conclusion of the neurotransmitter functioning explanation for schizophrenia

Dopamine and glutamate are neurotransmitters and both seem to have a role in schizophrenia. Excess dopamine at the synapse seems to be an explanation for psychostimulation in animals and psychotic behaviour in humans. Alongside that, however, glutamate seems to have a role – one that may even be more important than dopamine. Excess dopamine might be present but may not itself be the cause.

You can use the dopamine and glutamate hypotheses to discuss the role of neurotransmitter functioning in schizophrenia in answer to an exam question.

Evaluation of the neurotransmitter functioning explanation for schizophrenia

As research progresses in this area, using both animals and neuroimaging to uncover more information about the complexity in neurotransmitter functioning in the brain, there are fairly consistent findings that excess dopamine is present when there are psychotic symptoms. Even when glutamate is found to have a role, the excess dopamine is still found. Evidence for glutamate having a role is quite strong, including from animal studies, and findings reinforce one another so there is reliability. Neurotransmitter functioning does therefore seem to explain schizophrenia, at least on some level.

However, the criticisms of animal studies and using their findings to explain human neurotransmitter functioning are clear. Humans are animals but their brain functioning is different. Regions of the brain are similar to those in animals but not the same. Prefrontal cortex functioning and decision-making appear to differ in humans, for example. Animal brains 'work' using neurotransmitters and synaptic transmission so studying animals has some validity as human brains also use synaptic transmission using neurotransmitters. However, psychostimulation in animals can be said not to match psychotogenic behaviour in humans.

There is enough evidence to show that neurotransmitter functioning has a role in schizophrenia to accept it as an explanation. However, there are weaknesses in the arguments as well. Perhaps, too, neurotransmitter functioning takes place because of other issues in humans, such as genetic make-up or stimulation from the environment. Genes as an explanation for schizophrenia are looked at next, followed by an environmental explanation.

Genetic explanations for schizophrenia

There is evidence from twin and family studies for a genetic factor in schizophrenia. If identical twins are more likely to both have schizophrenia than non-identical twins, this suggests a genetic explanation, at least in part, for schizophrenia. If a family has more members with schizophrenia than might be expected in the general population, this too can be evidence for a genetic explanation for schizophrenia.

Twin studies used to gather evidence for a genetic explanation for schizophrenia

Twin studies involve comparing **MZ (monozygotic)** and **DZ (dizygotic)** twins to see what differences there are in the incidence of a certain characteristic. MZ twins are identical in genetic make-up (sharing 100 per cent of their genes), as they have developed from one egg. DZ twins share 50 per cent of their genes like any other brother/sister pair, as they have developed from two eggs.

The idea in studying twins is that if a characteristic is completely genetically given (**nature**), MZ twins would both show the characteristic. If a characteristic is not genetically given but comes from environmental influences and factors (**nurture**), then MZ twins will not share that characteristic any more than DZ twins. In practice, it is not expected that a characteristic is totally shared between MZ twins, so a higher sharing of that characteristic for MZ twins than for DZ twins is thought to indicate a genetic component for that characteristic.

Definitions

Nature refers to what comes from our biology and what we are born with, while **nurture** refers to what comes from our experiences and interactions with our environment.

Monozygotic (MZ) twins are identical and share 100 per cent of their genes. **Dizygotic (DZ) twins** are not identical and share 50 per cent of their genes.

With regard to schizophrenia, if one twin has schizophrenia and the condition is inherited, it would be expected that for MZ twins the other twin would be more likely to have schizophrenia too, but with DZ twins this would be less likely. Gottesman and Shields (1966) set out to study this (page 37).

Year One link: Twin studies as a research method were covered in biological psychology in Year One.

Issues and debates

The issue of how much a characteristic results from nature and how much from nurture is one of the issues and debates in your course. It is discussed in Chapter Seven of this book. Twin studies are useful when discussing the nature-nurture debate in psychology.

Evaluation of the 'twin studies' research method

Table 1.5 Strengths and weaknesses of twin studies

Strengths	Weaknesses
There is no other way to study genetic influences so clearly, because no other humans share 100 per cent of their DNA.	MZ twins share their DNA but even in the womb they may experience different environments, which may lead them to develop differently.
Although the amount of shared DNA differs, both MZ and DZ twins usually share the same environment, providing a natural control over environmental effects.	MZ twins may be treated more alike than DZ twins because their appearance and gender are identical, so their environment may not be as controlled as might be thought.

Study of schizophrenia using twin studies: Gottesman and Shields (1966)

Aims

Gottesman and Shields (1966) wanted to look at how far schizophrenia was genetic and also to try to replicate other studies that had found a genetic link with schizophrenia.

Procedure

The researchers gathered secondary data from one hospital, about twins who had been diagnosed with schizophrenia. Starting in 1948, they accessed 16 consecutive years of records to obtain information. Out of 392 patients that seemed to fit their criteria, they found that 68 patients were one of twins and had some sort of diagnosis of schizophrenia or related psychosis.

Three patients were discounted because they were from overseas and a further three discounted because it was not easy to tell if they were MZ or DZ twins, leaving 62 patients. Of these, five cases showed that both MZ twins had been diagnosed with schizophrenia, leaving 57 pairs where at least one had been diagnosed as having schizophrenia. Gottesman and Shields then tracked down the other twin in each case.

There were 31 males and 31 females in the group of patients (patients were the 'diagnosed' half of the pairs), born between 1893 and 1945 and with ages from 19 to 64. The average age was 37. They used blood and visual tests to check whether the twins were MZ or DZ. Data were collected in multiple ways: using hospital notes, case histories for the twins, tape recordings of 30-minute samples of verbal behaviour gathered by semi-structured interviews (these gathered primary data), personality testing and a test to look at thought disorders.

The question was whether, when one twin had developed schizophrenia, the other was also diagnosed with schizophrenia, and whether they were MZ or DZ twins. In practice, the researchers also recorded disorders close to schizophrenia but not indicating a full diagnosis.

Gottesman and Shields looked at the **concordance** rate within MZ twins to see in what percentage of cases when one twin was diagnosed with schizophrenia, the other one was too. They did the same with DZ twins and found a relatively high concordance rate for MZ twins and schizophrenia or a related disorder. They found a much lower concordance rate for DZ twins.

Definition

Concordance means agreement, for example, when one twin is found to have the same characteristic as the other twin.

Results

The results were reported in terms of concordance looking at the following features:

- Pairs where both twins were diagnosed as having schizophrenia.
- Pairs where one diagnosis is a psychiatric one but not schizophrenia, and the other twin has schizophrenia.
- Pairs where there appears to be psychiatric abnormality from some of the researchers' own measures.
- Pairs within normal limits.

Table 1.6 Number and percentages of twins in particular categories in the study by Gottesman and Shields (1966)

Category of twins	MZ		DZ	
	Number	%	Number	%
1 – both diagnosed with schizophrenia	10	42	3	9
1+2 – both diagnosed with schizophrenia or close	13	54	6	18
1+2+3 – both somehow rated abnormal	19	79	15	45
Normal	5	21	18	55
Total	24	100	33	100
(Note: numbers are cumulative in the first three rows.)				

Progress check 1.20

What is the percentage of MZ twins and the percentage of DZ twins that are rated abnormal in some way in Gottesman and Shields (1966)?

Gottesman and Shields's study showed that in MZ twins there was a concordance rate for schizophrenia of between 35 per cent and 58 per cent and in DZ twins a concordance rate of between 9 per cent and 26 per cent. This means that, for MZ twins, around 42 per cent of the time when one twin has schizophrenia the other has it too. For DZ twins the average figure is around 17 per cent. If the most severe cases of schizophrenia were looked at, the concordance rate for MZ twins was between 75 per cent and 91 per cent. The study therefore strongly suggests that there is at least some genetic basis for schizophrenia.

Conclusions

The researchers thought that the **diathesis–stress model** was the one that best explained the results. This model suggests that behaviour comes in part from genetic predisposition and in part from environmental triggers. Gottesman and Shields thought that particular genes predispose someone to schizophrenia by lowering the threshold for coping with stress. Even if it is suggested that there is a single gene for schizophrenia (Gottesman and Shields believe there is a set of genes responsible), their explanation still stands – that there is a genetic tendency to schizophrenia, which environmental factors can trigger.

Gottesman and Shields concluded that the 11 other studies they looked at did agree with one another, and although there were methodological criticisms, such as the sampling, they felt that the results of the studies were compatible and that their study supported previous findings. They therefore felt that their findings – that there is a genetic element in schizophrenia – were reliable.

Overall, Gottesman and Shields (1966) concluded that, in Western societies at least, the identical twin of someone with schizophrenia is at least 42 times as likely to have schizophrenia as someone from the general population, and a fraternal (non-identical) twin of the same sex is at least nine times as likely. Therefore, genetic factors seem to be responsible for the specific nature of most schizophrenias. Certain genes are necessary for schizophrenia to occur but environmental triggers may also be required. If there is not a 100 per cent concordance rate between identical twins then the characteristic must have some environmental explanations, and studies do not find a 100 per cent concordance rate.

Explanation

The **diathesis-stress model** takes into account both genetic explanations and environmental factors to explain a characteristic. It is about being predisposed towards a characteristic genetically and there perhaps being stress in the environment or some environmental cause to trigger the characteristic.

Strengths of Gottesman and Shields (1966)

- The study replicates other studies and the results are backed up by them, which means they are likely to be reliable. For example, Inouye (1961) in Japan found a 74 per cent concordance rate for people with progressive chronic schizophrenia and 39 per cent where twins had mild transient schizophrenia. These figures are similar to those of Gottesman and Shields.
- It addresses criticisms of previous studies by detailing the sampling carefully so that it was understood which twins were included and why. There is great detail about the different diagnoses, for example, whether the diagnosis was schizophrenia, some other psychosis or some abnormality. There is care when measuring both the 'twin' situation and the diagnosis.

Weaknesses of Gottesman and Shields (1966)

- The researchers felt that a concordance rate simply notes whether if one twin has some abnormality, the other has it too. It would have been useful to have information about the degree of the abnormality, such as a scale showing 'schizophrenia' through 'other psychiatric diagnoses' to 'some abnormality' to 'normal'.
- The researchers suggest there might be different forms of schizophrenia. They also suggest that some of the disorders diagnosed might come from life experiences (such as being a prisoner of war) rather than genes, and the study did not easily distinguish between reasons for schizophrenia.

Other suggestions for a genetic basis for schizophrenia

Tiwari et al. (2010) consider the evidence for genetics in schizophrenia, looking at which genes might be implicated. They suggest there is evidence for common genes and rare copy number variations when looking at genetic causes for schizophrenia. Tiwari et al. also suggest that genes that make someone susceptible to schizophrenia overlap with genes that make someone susceptible to bipolar disorder, which is an interesting link given the difficulty in separating the two when diagnosing mental disorders. Tiwari et al.'s (2010) review supports the idea that family, twin and adoption studies suggest a strong genetic component in schizophrenia. They cite a meta-analysis of twin studies (Sullivan et al., 2003) that arrives at a figure of 81 per cent heritability, which is higher than Gottesman and Shields found, but similar to other more recent findings. For example, Lichtenstein et al. (2009, cited in Tiwari et al., 2010) thought that the heritability figure was about 64 per cent. These high figures suggest that genes are the largest explanation for schizophrenia, though Tiwari et al. also point to there being environmental factors, as the percentages would predict (studies do not show that there is a 100 per cent genetic underpinning for schizophrenia).

Family history

Uncovering the genes that underpin schizophrenia is not easy, as Tiwari et al. (2010) point out. Fewer than one third of people with schizophrenia have a family history of schizophrenia, which suggests that there is complexity in the genes in question. More direct genetic influence could be found if schizophrenia came through the family line, but for many, that is not the case.

Looking for chromosomal problems in families with schizophrenia does uncover some genetic evidence. Patients with a section of 22q11 missing (known as '22q11 deletion') do show psychotic symptoms similar to the symptoms of schizophrenia and the frequency of these symptoms for those with 22q11 deletion is 18 per cent, greater than the 1 per cent for schizophrenia in the general population.

Another study reported in Tiwari *et al.*'s review is where a large Scottish family with a high incidence of psychiatric disorders (including schizophrenia) had the DISC1 gene disrupted. The DISC1 gene was also implicated in another family with a history of psychiatric disorders. Other gene differences were found in other families. However, there was no clear chromosomal abnormality that related to schizophrenia, even though some of the genes found seemed to predispose someone to psychiatric disorders.

Common variants

From the many studies looking for genes that link to schizophrenia, it seems that there are common variants that interact and the **alleles** involved will be shared by unrelated individuals. This could be why family studies and twin studies show some evidence for genetic underpinning in schizophrenia but do not uncover the genes responsible. It is the *grouping* of genes and variants that should be studied. This means the genotypes of individuals must be studied as well as using samples from people that share DNA.

Definition

An **allele** is an alternative form of a gene; it is a variant of a gene. One gene can have more than one variant (or allele).

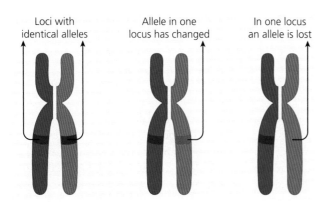

| Loci with identical alleles | Allele in one locus has changed | In one locus an allele is lost |

There can be variation in alleles, which can be a genetic base for schizophrenia.

DNA pooling

DNA pooling takes place by using DNA from those with schizophrenia and DNA from controls (people without schizophrenia) to look for differences in allele frequency between the two groups. (DNA pooling is used in studying other disorders as well.) The differences in allele frequency becomes the estimate of the association between the genes and, in this case, schizophrenia. Mah *et al.* (2006) found a significant marker in the Plexin A2 gene (PLXNA2) though replication of this finding has produced mixed results. Tiwari *et al.* (2010) cite other studies where different genes and variants are found to link with schizophrenia but they conclude that using DNA pooling does not lead to solid conclusions.

Copy number variation and schizophrenia

Tiwari *et al.* (2010) explain in their review of genes and schizophrenia that given that two thirds of schizophrenia cases are where schizophrenia occurs sporadically, it is not unexpected that any genetic cause comes from rare variations in genes. Rare variations can include mutations, deletions and duplications and it is hard to study such variations. Copy number variations are **submicroscopic**, underlining the difficulty in studying them.

Definition

Submicroscopic means unable to be detected with a microscope.

The most well-known deletion is on 22q11, as mentioned above. Another copy number variant is in the Xq23 region, found in 52 per cent of cases of schizophrenia. Kirov *et al.* (2008, cited in Tiwari *et al.*, 2010) found 13 copy number variants in 93 patients with schizophrenia. These copy number variants were not found in 372 controls.

Tiwari *et al.* (2010) mention many more copy number variants and it is clear that a conclusion about what variants of genes align with schizophrenia has not yet been arrived at.

Progress check 1.21

When discussing examining gene variants that might link to schizophrenia, which two features/actions might be at work with regard to the genes themselves to cause variation?

Other factors related to a genetic explanation

Tiwari *et al.* (2010) mention other factors in schizophrenia that come from the environment. These include maternal infection affecting the foetus, taking cannabis and epigenetic modification, where genes not only act on the organism at the start of its development but continue to affect the organism's development. Environmental factors can affect body mechanisms that are driven by genes, such as stress (cortisol) and hormones. To understand genetic factors there is a need to study such environmental factors as possible triggers as well.

Progress check 1.22

Which two features of a person's environment (including during their time in the womb) might be explanations for schizophrenia?

Evaluation of a genetic argument for schizophrenia

Strengths

- There have been a lot of studies done with large samples, including studies in more than one country. For example Shifman *et al.* (2008, cited in Tiwari *et al.*, 2010) found a female-specific association in the reelin gene (RELN), which was confirmed in UK patients of European ancestry. The finding was not confirmed when looked for in Irish, American and Chinese people. However, these three populations, when studied, did show similar trends. It can be seen from the large studies carried out that even though the findings do not always support one another, there are common findings between some of the studies. A weakness here is that the evidence about reelin protein is not confirmed by all studies, but a strength is that large-scale studies do support one another. Given the complexity of what is being studied, and that such large studies may have differences but also common findings, this suggests that there is a genetic basis to schizophrenia, but exactly what that is is not yet known.
- Another strength is in the different ways genes and variations are studied, not all of which are explained in this section. Family studies can help to identify gene issues, such as deletion in a section of 22q11, which shows symptoms of psychosis. Twin studies suggest a high likelihood that genes explain schizophrenia. DNA pooling is used to compare the DNA of those with schizophrenia against controls to look for gene variants and differences. Having many methods can help if the same findings are uncovered as this helps with

reliability. A weakness is that what is being studied is so complex, such as the fact that copy number variants are submicroscopic. However, there are some similar findings that are found using different methods, so there is some reliability in claiming that genes can help to explain schizophrenia.

Explore

You may like to read more about gene variants and schizophrenia and what is known about them. Although this area is complex, you can skim read to grasp some of the ideas. Here is a link to a study by Shifman *et al.* (2008), which you can access online and which continues some of the points made in this section.
http://journals.plos.org/plosgenetics/article?id=10.1371/journal.pgen.0040028#pgen-0040028-g003

Weaknesses

- Weaknesses are hinted at in the strengths above, such as the fact that this area of study is so complex, including complexity in the variants and because variations exist within individuals rather than being easy to find in patterns in families. It seems as if there might be genetic underpinning to schizophrenia, but with more than one gene implicated and complexity in the variants, considering deletions and duplications, for example.
- The focus on genes and variants in genes means that there is less focus on any interaction with environmental factors. In MZ twins, for example, there is not a 100 per cent concordance rate with regard to schizophrenia and if genes were wholly responsible then that would be found. There is room for environmental factors either to 'cause' schizophrenia or to lead to epigenetic modification. It is likely that both environmental stressors and genetic features are what lead to schizophrenia and the review of genetic features of schizophrenia by Tiwari *et al.* (2010) confirms that environmental factors should also be examined. A criticism of studying genes in relation to schizophrenia is that it is reductionist, focusing on parts rather than on the 'whole' characteristic in question.

Issues and debates

Looking at explanations for schizophrenia involves both genetic and environmental explanations and this is a useful area to refer to when discussing the nature-nurture debate. Looking at gene variants to find causes for schizophrenia is reductionist, so this is also a useful example of reductionism for that issue and debate.

Year One link: In the learning theories area of your course you learned about psychology as a science and about reductionism. You could draw on that learning when evaluating the genetic explanation for schizophrenia.

Progress check 1.23

Briefly state two weaknesses of the genetic explanation for schizophrenia.

Non-biological explanations for schizophrenia: the social causation hypothesis

In their review, Tiwari *et al.* (2010) list some environmental factors that relate to schizophrenia. Environmental factors include growing up in an urban environment, cannabis usage, male gender and stress and malnutrition, all of which seem to point to an increased risk of developing schizophrenia (Tandon *et al.*, 2008, cited in Tiwari *et al.*, 2010). Tiwari *et al.* (2010) say that maternal infection, such as influenza during pregnancy, and drug misuse need to be taken into account when looking for explanations for schizophrenia and they cite van Os *et al.* (2008) for evidence of this claim. Cannabis usage is a risk factor for psychosis and seems to lead to faster development of prodromal symptoms as well as the psychosis itself.

Environmental factors that increase the risk of developing schizophrenia are wide and numerous and just one has been chosen here as the non-biological explanation of schizophrenia. Since the 1950s, it has been recognised that there is a higher rate of schizophrenia in the lower social classes. This has led to the social causation hypothesis, because it seems that something in someone's social position in life must be at least in part an explanation for schizophrenia.

Social class

There is evidence that people in the lowest social classes and groups such as immigrants have a higher incidence of schizophrenia than others in the UK. It appears therefore that social class might either be a cause of schizophrenia or at least be involved in its development. In the UK an incidence of about 4 people per 1,000 has been found, both in the lowest social class in the white population and in black immigrant groups. This is a lot higher than the 1 per cent that is generally accepted as the rate of schizophrenia in the general population. Studies regularly show that schizophrenia is found more in the lower social classes, among the unemployed and those living in deprived city

areas. Those in lower social classes also experience a different course for the illness and receive different medical care.

Official statistics and census figures confirm such differences. Lower social class patients are more likely to be brought to get medical help by the police or social services, to become compulsorily admitted and to become long-term cases. In the 1960s it was thought that being lower class was a causal factor in schizophrenia. This was known as the social causation hypothesis, also known as the environmental 'breeder' hypothesis. The idea now is to suggest that social class shows someone's position in society, including stress levels related to their position, and that is likely to be the explanation for schizophrenia not social class itself.

Cooper (2005) suggests that for single men the rate of schizophrenia in social class 5 (unskilled labourers) was 4.1 times as high as in social class 1 (higher managerial), which is evidence that social class is at least a feature in schizophrenia. Lower social class is a risk factor for schizophrenia, as it involves social adversity. (Today often seven categories of social class are given, but at the time of Cooper's study there were five.)

Social adversity

Schizophrenia is more associated with living in cities than rural communities, so it might be that something in city life leads to schizophrenia (Eaton *et al.*, 2000). A study that took place in Sweden (Hjem *et al.*, 2004) showed that 'social adversity' in childhood relates to the development of schizophrenia later in life. Pressures in childhood and adolescence (social adversity) link to being in a lower social class and also link to schizophrenia.

Features in the environment that might affect the development of schizophrenia:
- adversity in adult life
- unemployment and poverty
- social isolation
- living in inner-city areas with poor housing and overcrowding, and high levels of crime and drug use
- separation from parents as a child.

Progress check 1.24

The social drift hypothesis is that people with schizophrenia are found in lower social classes and experience more poverty and unemployment because of their disorder, which can be characterised as not finding it easy to take care of oneself. The social causation hypothesis says that social factors such as poverty and unemployment as well as the area someone lives in can be an explanation for schizophrenia. With regard to schizophrenia explain the difference between social drift and social causation.

Immigrant populations

In the UK, census data have consistently shown a higher incidence of schizophrenia in the Afro-Caribbean and black immigrant population (e.g. the 1991 and 2001 censuses), again pointing to social situation as a possible causal factor. It is estimated that there are four times as many incidences of schizophrenia in these populations as in the white indigenous population, and some studies suggest a higher figure than that (for example, Fearon *et al.*, 2004).

It is not thought that there is a genetic reason for higher levels of schizophrenia in black immigrants. The evidence for this is as follows:

- The risk of schizophrenia is greater not only for Afro-Caribbean immigrants but also for African-born black immigrants and, to an extent, for Asian immigrants.
- In Caribbean countries the incidence of schizophrenia is similar to that for the indigenous UK population – lower than for immigrants in the UK.
- The rate for second generation Afro-Caribbean immigrants is higher than for first generation immigrants.
- It is not thought that those who came into the UK as immigrants in the 1950s and 1960s had weaker mental health; it is thought that immigrants would have been 'upwardly striving' individuals.
- Afro-Caribbean people with schizophrenia are likely to be unemployed, living in poor inner-city areas and in a worse situation than other Afro-Caribbean people. They are likely to be living alone and to have been separated from their parents when younger.
- The immigrant population tends to be disadvantaged with regard to educational attainment, social class, standard of housing and discrimination. They also tend to live in over-crowded conditions.

Living in an 'alien' neighbourhood

Brown (2010) wrote a review focusing on the environment and susceptibility to schizophrenia. The review covered many aspects of the environment, including the environment before birth and issues such as drug-taking. He also wrote about urban living and the effects of living in different neighbourhoods relating to immigrant status. These are issues covered in the social causation hypothesis. Brown (2010) reported that Veling *et al.* (2008) carried out a study in The Hague and found that when immigrants were in neighbourhoods in which their own ethnic group did not predominate there was a higher rate of psychotic disorders compared to neighbourhoods where it did. This suggests that social factors can affect the *development* of

schizophrenia, not that they *cause* schizophrenia. Social factors may act, perhaps with other factors particular to the individual (such as their early experiences or genes), in such a way that triggers or does not prevent schizophrenia. Veling *et al.* (2007, cited in Brown, 2010) claim that experiencing discrimination accompanies an increased risk of schizophrenia (they also include other psychoses).

Year One link: You need to know three explanations for schizophrenia, one being neurotransmitter functioning, one other biological explanation and one explanation that is not biological. The two biological explanations draw on material you learned in biological psychology. The social causation hypothesis focuses on social issues, such as discrimination, and sits within social psychology. Note how the applications in Year Two fit with the fundamentals of psychology you learned in Year One.

Evaluation of social class as a risk factor for schizophrenia

There are problems in claiming that social adversity, including poverty, unemployment, social isolation and living in inner-city areas, is responsible for someone developing schizophrenia.

- White people in the lowest socioeconomic groups do not show the increased risk of having mental disorders that black immigrants to the UK do. This suggests that there is more to this than simply social adversity and lower class status.
- A tendency to schizophrenia seems to come from what happens to someone in childhood and the early stages of their lives, rather than developing because of lower socioeconomic status and related issues (Cooper, 2005). Therefore, the link between schizophrenia and low socioeconomic status might come from children living in these circumstances as much as from the social status of an adult.

Evaluation of the social causation hypothesis

Strengths

- The idea that social adversity contributes to developing schizophrenia helps to explain the fact that, although there are more people with schizophrenia in the lower classes, they are concentrated in inner-city areas, and that black immigrants are more likely to be diagnosed with schizophrenia than white lower-class groups.

The diathesis-stress model considers that stressors in the environment work with an individual's biological features such as genes when considering issues like schizophrenia. A strength of the social causation hypothesis is that it helps to explain the environmental part of the interaction between biology and environment in the cause of schizophrenia.

- There are many studies that have shown that social factors relate to the incidence of schizophrenia. Brown (2010) reviewed findings looking at environment and schizophrenia and uses evidence from many studies. These include Mortensen *et al.* (1999, cited in Brown, 2010) in Denmark, who found a two-fold increase of risk of developing schizophrenia for those born in the capital compared with those born in a rural region. Veling *et al.* (2008, cited in Brown 2010) showed in The Hague that there was more schizophrenia in people living in a place where their ethnic group was not predominant compared with places where their ethnic group did predominate. Kirkbride *et al.* (2007, cited in Brown, 2010) found that those who experienced less social capital (which refers to connectedness and support) were more likely to develop psychosis. These newer findings support the earlier findings of Eaton *et al.* (2000), who also found that there was more schizophrenia in urban settings than in rural settings. These findings support one another and suggest reliability in the claim that social factors at least affect whether schizophrenia is developed, even if they are not the actual cause of it.

Weaknesses

- Those in lower socioeconomic groups, living alone, unemployed and living in poverty might be more likely to be diagnosed with schizophrenia, suggesting a diagnosis problem, not an environmental problem.
- It is hard to separate environmental factors to see if they cause schizophrenia, as they could be the result of schizophrenia, as suggested by the social drift hypothesis. The social drift hypothesis suggests that those with schizophrenia drift into the lower social classes and into adversity because of the disorder, such as not being able to work, and also through symptoms of the disorder, such as difficulty with personal care.
- In urban regions crowded living conditions can lead to toxins in the environment, for example (such as leaded fuel), and there are other risk factors too, such as not having social support and instability among communities, leading to social isolation and difficulties in communication. In general it might be claimed that there are social factors that can help to explain schizophrenia but it is hard to know which social factors are involved, as social factors interact and are hard to isolate for study.

March *et al.* (2008, cited in Brown, 2010) point to key social pathways which might unravel this complexity. This might be by focusing on studying 'place', which will encompass the different social factors that can then be understood by such an approach.

Progress check 1.25
Why is it said that if an area for study is complex, it is considered a weakness and a difficulty for research?

Test yourself
1 Compare two explanations for schizophrenia, one biological and one non-biological (for the biological explanation do not use the neurotransmitter explanation). **(8 marks)**
2 Evaluate the neurotransmitter explanation for schizophrenia. **(12 marks)**

Treatments for schizophrenia

One of the two treatments for schizophrenia that you cover in your course must be from biological psychology – this book covers drug treatment. The other treatment must come from a different topic area in your course. The topic areas are social, cognitive, biological and learning. Although you need to know two treatments, three are covered in this section for your interest and they relate to biological, cognitive and social psychology. The biological and social treatments are likely to be new to you but you may have covered cognitive-behavioural therapy as a treatment for phobias when you studied learning theory in Year One.

Year One link: When looking at treatments for schizophrenia, draw on your understanding of neurotransmitter functioning and how drugs work (which you covered in biological psychology). If you looked at CBT as a therapy for phobias when you covered learning theories, draw on that understanding too.

Antipsychotic drug treatments for schizophrenia

Drug therapy was hailed as an important step forward in the 1950s, as up to then treatment for psychotic patients was rudimentary and did not allow patients to function normally. Drug treatment in many cases will allow some form of normal functioning.

The neurotransmitters dopamine and glutamate were suggested as possible explanations for schizophrenia (page 33). It follows that if neurotransmitter functioning causes schizophrenia symptoms, drug treatments that affect such functioning can help to treat those symptoms. Drugs such as phenothiazines are used for this purpose, for example, chlorpromazine (first used in 1952), which acts by blocking dopamine receptors so that there is no excess dopamine.

The drugs used in the treatment of schizophrenia are called 'antipsychotic' drugs and they work to suppress hallucinations and delusions. Usually the first psychotic episode results in drug prescription. Antipsychotic drugs are known as 'typical' and 'atypical'. **Typical antipsychotic drugs** are well-established while **atypical antipsychotic drugs** are newer ones. Atypical drugs tend to have fewer side-effects and act in different ways to typical antipsychotic drugs. Drug treatment can be referred to as **chemotherapy**, which is an overall term for therapy using chemicals.

Explanations

Typical antipsychotic drugs are established drugs that were introduced back in the 1950s when such drug treatments were first used in the treatment of schizophrenia. They include Haldol (haloperidol), prolixin and thorazine. These drugs are neuroleptics because they act at the neuron and though they can be effective, they cause side-effects.

Atypical antipsychotic drugs used for the treatment of schizophrenia include clozapine and newer antipsychotics that cause fewer side-effects.

Chemotherapy is an overall term for drug therapy and drug treatment.

Glutamatergic means 'relating to glutamate'.

Each patient is only put on one antipsychotic drug at a time, although antidepressants can be used at the same time and anticonvulsants might also be prescribed. Some clinicians prefer certain drugs and some people respond differently to different drugs, so there is no single drug for each particular mental disorder.

> ## Explore
> The Royal College of Psychiatrists has a leaflet about antipsychotics - the link is below. You may like to explore more about drug therapy and schizophrenia using the internet.
> www.rcpsych.ac.uk/healthadvice/treatmentswellbeing/antipsychoticmedication.aspx

Antipsychotic medication can reduce the positive symptoms (page 29) of schizophrenia in about two weeks, though the initial typical antipsychotics seem not to work on the negative symptoms or cognitive symptoms. Atypical antipsychotic drugs seem to be better for negative symptoms

and for improving cognitive functioning. Clozapine (an atypical antipsychotic) can improve delusions and hallucinations and seems to be helpful for those that do not respond well to other drugs, but its side-effects can be serious, such as lowered white blood cell count. Most antipsychotic drugs work on the dopamine system. Atypical antipsychotic drugs increase the release of dopamine and acetylcholine and have effects on the **glutamatergic** system that typical antipsychotic drugs do not have. Atypical antipsychotic drugs may also be called second generation antipsychotics (SGAs). Carlsson *et al.* (1999/2000) explain more about problems with this focus on the dopamine system (page 105).

> ## Progress check 1.26
> Briefly evaluate clozapine with regard to its effectiveness - an atypical antipsychotic drug for schizophrenia.

Side-effects of antipsychotic drugs

Chlorpromazine, thioridazine, haloperidol and trifluoperazine are examples of typical antipsychotic drugs. Side-effects of these drugs can include:

- sleepiness and tiredness
- shaking and muscle spasms
- low blood pressure
- problems with sex drive
- weight gain.

Risperidone, olanzapine and quetiapine are three atypical drugs. Common side-effects of atypical antipsychotic drugs are similar to those listed above for typical antipsychotic drugs.

> ## Explore
> Look up these typical and atypical antipsychotic drugs to read about and compare their effects and side-effects. NHS Choices is a good place to start and here is the link to risperidone:
> www.nhs.uk/Medicine-Guides/Pages/
> MedicineOverview.aspx?condition=Schizophrenia and Psychosis&medicine=Risperidone&preparation=Risperidone 1mg orodispersible tablets sugar free

> ### STUDY HINT
> When you learn about Rosenhan's study later in this chapter (page 101), it is worth noting that pseudo-patients diagnosed as having schizophrenia in remission were prescribed different drugs for the same diagnosis. There are different preferences for treatment by different drugs; one is not necessarily 'better' than another at controlling symptoms.

Atypical antipsychotic drugs are different from antipsychotic drugs as they produce fewer 'extrapyramidal' symptoms and have a lower risk of tardive dyskinesia. Dyskinesia refers to repetitive, purposeless involuntary body movements and is a neurological disorder. Tardive dyskinesia refers to a form of dyskinesia that is hard to treat and does not come to light for some time. Extrapyramidal side-effects (EPSE) are also movement disorders and they include Parkinson-like symptoms such as tremor or rigidity, as well as spasms. It can be seen that if atypical antipsychotic drugs cause fewer of these side-effects they will be preferred, though as tardive dyskinesia can take some time to show itself, it is not certain that atypical antipsychotic drugs are better in this respect.

Progress check 1.27

Explain tardive dyskinesia and extrapyramidal side-effects in relation to antipsychotic drug use.

Effectiveness of drug treatment

Meltzer *et al.* (2004)

Meltzer *et al.* (2004) carried out studies to look at the effectiveness of drug treatment in schizophrenia. They chose 481 patients with schizophrenia and randomly assigned them into groups. The groups were given a placebo, an investigational drug (there were four of them) or haloperidol (an established antipsychotic drug) for six weeks. The investigational drugs were four new antipsychotic drugs (new in 2004).

The study gathered information about positive and negative symptoms, severity of the illness and a score from a psychiatric rating scale. The study found that haloperidol gave significant improvements in all aspects of functioning tested compared with the placebo group, so the study appeared to have validity. Two of the new drugs also showed improvements in several of the measures (such as positive and negative symptoms) compared with the placebo. There were two groups of new drugs that did not show improvements, however. This study shows that haloperidol (an older antipsychotic) improves symptoms for the patient, and that some new drugs at least also show improvements over a placebo. This is evidence that drug treatment works, at least to an extent.

Guo *et al.* (2011)

The researchers state the reason for carrying out the study was that the effectiveness of atypical and typical antipsychotic drugs for those with early-stage schizophrenia had not been confirmed. The research was done in

China and its aim was to look at seven antipsychotic drugs used in the early stages of schizophrenia to establish their effectiveness and safety. The study involved 1,133 people with schizophrenia or schizophreniform disorder within five years of the disorder starting. The seven drugs were chlorpromazine, sulpiride, clozapine, risperidone, olanzapine, quetiapine and aripiprazole. Individuals were each only taking one of the drugs. The researchers measured the rate of discontinuing the treatment (Table 1.7) and clinical outcomes as well as tolerability.

Table 1.7 Rate of treatment discontinuity within 12 months of starting

Drug	Percentage of patients stopping the treatment
Chlorpromazine	41.4%
Sulpiride	39.5%
Clozapine	36.7%
Risperidone	40.2%
Olanzapine	39.6%
Quetiapine	46.9%
Aripiprazole	40.2%

Table 1.7 shows that there was a very similar percentage in those stopping taking the drug for all seven drugs, with quetiapine having the largest percentage stopping and clozapine having the smallest. The researchers confirm that there was no significant difference in the stopping rates ($p=.0717$). Guo *et al.* (2011) confirm that there were no significant differences in people being intolerant to the different drugs or patient decisions about the drugs, as well as no significant differences with regard to discontinuation. Chlorpromazine and sulpiride showed more extrapyramidal symptoms (page 46), while weight gain was more common with clozapine and olanzapine. The researchers concluded that for early stage schizophrenia, the seven drugs were very similar in the measures they used. It was clear that there was a high drop-out rate. It is hard to say whether the drugs were effective or not from this study, but it can be said that no drug was more effective than another.

Hartling *et al.* (2012)

Hartling *et al.* (2012) carried out a review and meta-analysis to look at the effectiveness of first-generation and second-generation medications for schizophrenia. They looked at studies using randomised trials which lasted at least two years, and included 114 studies. They found that for core illness symptoms there were few differences. It was difficult for the researchers to reach strong conclusions but they did find what they called 'moderate-strength' evidence, showing that haloperidol had benefits over olanzapine for improving positive symptoms, though they found some evidence that olanzapine was better than haloperidol for improving negative symptoms. There was some evidence of a higher risk of tardive dyskinesia for chlorpromazine as against clozapine with the risk differences being 5 per cent as opposed to 9 per cent. They say that their conclusions cannot be that firm because all studies had some risk of bias and the follow-up was often too brief to measure adverse effects over time. They also said that the studies tended to use selective populations so generalisability was limited. Hartling *et al.* could not conclude with regard to first- and second-generation antipsychotic drugs that one was better than the other.

STUDY HINT

Hartling *et al.* (2012) mention not being able to generalise from the studies in their meta-analysis because samples were selective or biased. This is useful evidence to use when discussing generalisability of research. Hartling *et al.* (2012) carried out a meta-analysis, which is one of the research methods you have to cover for clinical psychology in your course. You can therefore use their study as an example of that type of research method.

Summary of the findings

The list below provides a summary of the findings of the three studies – Meltzer *et al.* (2004), Guo *et al.* (2011) and Hartling *et al.* (2012) – with regard to effectiveness.

- Meltzer *et al.* (2004) found that halperidol gave significant improvements in all areas of functioning compared with a placebo, which is a starting point for saying that antipsychotics work.
- Meltzer *et al.* (2004) found that two of the newer atypical antipsychotic drugs showed improvements over a placebo in both positive and negative symptoms, and two did not. This means there are differences in their performance but that there are atypical antipsychotic drugs that are successful.
- Guo *et al.* (2011) found few differences when they compared seven antipsychotic drugs, in particular when they measured discontinuation over a year.
- Guo *et al.* (2011) found some differences, even though mostly they found very little difference. They found that chlorpromazine and sulpiride showed more extrapyramidal symptoms and weight gain was more common with clozapine and olanzapine.
- Hartling *et al.* (2012) looked at many studies and found that for core symptoms there were generally few differences.

- Hartling *et al.* (2012) found haloperidol had benefits over olanzapine for improving positive symptoms.
- Hartling *et al.* (2012) found there was some evidence of a higher risk of tardive dyskinesia for chlorpromazine as against clozapine. This reflects the finding of Guo *et al.* (2011) that chlorpromazine (and sulpiride) showed more extrapyramidal symptoms.

Progress check 1.28

Give two pieces of evidence that show effectiveness of drug therapy for schizophrenia and two pieces of evidence that show they are not that effective.

Evaluation of drug therapy for schizophrenia

Strengths

- Drugs are thought to be better than former (pre-1950s) treatments for schizophrenia as they are seen as more ethical and more effective. For example, before drug therapy for schizophrenia, treatment included insulin shock therapy, while in 1910 Winston Churchill called for sterilisation of people with severe mental illness. Drug therapy was welcomed as being much more humane.
- Drug treatment rests on strong biological evidence about the causes of schizophrenia so is underpinned by theory, which helps in considering its effectiveness. Refer back to the information in this chapter on the dopamine hypothesis and the glutamate hypothesis (page 33) to add to this strength. For example, antipsychotic drugs target dopamine at the synapse. Carlsson *et al.* (1999/2000) – the study you have to cover when looking at schizophrenia – discusses newer drugs (including clozapine) and how they work, so you can use this study.
- Use the information here about the effectiveness of drug therapy to explain its strengths. For example, you can explain their effectiveness in the treatment of positive and negative symptoms. Clozapine, for example, is said to be effective even though it can have serious side-effects that need to be monitored.

Explore

Go to the link below to read an article by Rachel Whitehead, published in *The Guardian* on 29 October 2011. The article explores how those with schizophrenia were treated in the past and will give you some background on this issue.
www.theguardian.com/commentisfree/2011/oct/29/100-years-schizophrenia-treatment

---

Weaknesses

- Patients with schizophrenia often do not continue to take the drugs that are prescribed for them. It is estimated that this is the case in about 50 per cent of patients and Guo et al.'s (2011) study backs up that finding. The percentages showing the number of patients discontinuing medication for each of the drugs looked at in Guo et al.'s study is not quite 50 per cent, but it is over 30 per cent and up to 46.9 per cent. It might be that problems with functioning mean that someone who has schizophrenia is unable to remember to take their medication regularly or they may find the side-effects too uncomfortable.
- From an ethical point of view, drugs have been described as a 'chemical strait-jacket' and some people think that such control by society is unacceptable.
- Drugs have side-effects that are unpleasant and can themselves require medication. This is the case, for example, with clozapine, which means people have to be closely monitored using blood tests every one–two weeks, to check their white blood cells. Antipsychotic drugs are not a 'cure-all' treatment, as they seem to help most with positive symptoms of schizophrenia rather than negative ones.
- Drugs do not take into account a patient's environmental or social problems, which might contribute to re-hospitalisation and relapses. Social treatments, such as assertive community programmes, can address such issues. Assertive community programmes are briefly explained later in this section, for your interest and to show that there are social therapies as well as biological and cognitive ones.

> **STUDY HINT**
> Rosenhan 1973 (page 101) found that patients in the institutions in his study preferred to hide their drugs rather than take them. This is evidence that people with schizophrenia do not take their medication. Use evidence from different parts of clinical psychology when discussing the different areas you are studying.

Cognitive-behavioural therapy

Cognitive-behavioural therapy (CBT) is set within both cognitive psychology and learning theories because it has both a cognitive element and a behavioural element. The behavioural element links to operant conditioning principles, focusing on rewarding oneself and also links to social learning theory as there can be modelling of behaviour. This link to the behavioural element is more apparent when discussing CBT for OCD or anorexia nervosa. When thinking about both schizophrenia and depression the focus is more on cognition and thinking.

Drug therapies can be helpful for hallucinations and delusions in schizophrenia, which are positive symptoms. They tend not to be so helpful for negative symptoms, although clozapine can be helpful. Cognitive symptoms are also important and there is a cognitive element to schizophrenia. Cognitive-behavioural therapy addresses the thinking and behaviour involved in schizophrenia. The case study that is given in Chapter Two, focusing on schizophrenia and methods for researching schizophrenia, is Lavarenne et al. (2013) (page 158). Lavarenne et al. (2013) claim that a support group that is run for people with schizophrenia acts as a boundary for them, helping what the researchers call their fragile ego boundaries. This suggests that people with schizophrenia can be helped in their everyday living and CBT can help. Lavarenne et al.'s (2013) study also suggests that social support can help someone with schizophrenia, and this idea is briefly considered later in this chapter (page 48).

Explanation

Cognitive-behavioural therapy focuses on thought (the cognitive part) and behaviour and how they link (as well as how emotions fit in). The focus is on thinking and how emotions follow our thoughts, which then means we behave in certain ways, and the consequences lead back to our thinking. Changing the thinking or the behaviour can break the cycle (if it is unhelpful).

Year One link: You may have already studied cognitive-behavioural therapy if you chose it as a treatment for phobias when looking at learning theories in your Year One course.

Cognitive symptoms in schizophrenia include difficulties in concentrating and paying attention, problems with working memory and difficulty with executive functioning, which is about understanding information and making decisions. CBT can help people to focus on their thinking, though this is more about learning to cope with the disorder and helping cognitive symptoms than about 'curing' them. The social deprivation hypothesis suggests there are also issues with lack of social support and feelings of social isolation and CBT can help in those areas as well.

Cognitive-behavioural therapy in general

Cognitive-behavioural therapy tends to take the view that disorders and distress are down to cognitive factors. Beck in 1970 and Ellis in 1962 focused on maladaptive cognitions – thinking that is not helpful in a situation and is not suitable – i.e. it does not help someone to adapt to a situation or to function. Maladaptive thinking, according to CBT, maintains emotional distress and behavioural problems. Beck claimed that the maladaptive thinking comes from schemas and general beliefs about the world and about oneself – and about the future. CBT acts to focus on these thoughts and schemas, to change them so that the emotions and behaviours that arise from the maladaptive thoughts also change.

> **STUDY HINT**
> CBT is also offered for depression and other disorders and later in this chapter you will explore more about CBT when considering treatment for unipolar depression and OCD. The discussion of these disorders will each include a specific focus on how CBT can be used. General points about CBT apply to schizophrenia and these disorders, so it can be useful to know how the treatment works in general as well as more specifically.

CBT for schizophrenia

Dickerson (2000) reviewed studies looking at CBT for schizophrenia and her review gives useful information about the use of CBT for schizophrenia. She talks about a set of CBT interventions for schizophrenia which have been used in the early stages and in the later stages. Dickerson (2000) cites Bustillo *et al.* (1999), saying that many of those with schizophrenia have symptoms and social disability throughout their lives, while Shepherd *et al.* (1989, also cited in Dickerson, 2000) suggest that fewer than 60 per cent of sufferers achieve full remission. This suggests that if a treatment alleviates at least some of the issues, then it is useful. Full effectiveness is not expected.

CBT has been used to focus on cognitive approaches and specialised cognitive behaviour therapies have been developed for schizophrenia (e.g. Alford and Correia, 1994, cited in Dickerson, 2000). One of the main reasons for using CBT is that drug therapies do not address all the symptoms of schizophrenia. Many people are distressed by their symptoms and use various coping mechanisms to deal with them (e.g. Strauss, 1989, cited in Dickerson, 2000). Also researchers like Alford (1986, cited in Dickerson, 2000) claim that psychotic symptoms can be helped by cognitive interventions.

Different forms of CBT intervention are used in the UK, but the different forms do have common underlying assumptions. Biological factors are seen as being important in schizophrenia but it is assumed that how someone experiences and expresses their psychotic symptoms will be about psychological factors and so can be modified by psychological interventions. Psychological interventions aim to reduce the stress involved. CBT interventions are less likely to target psychological issues such as hallucinations and delusions; they focus mainly on the distress experienced and on coping mechanisms.

> **Progress check 1.29**
> Outline some assumptions underpinning CBT as a therapy for schizophrenia.

CBT for schizophrenia, consistent with CBT in general, focuses on the way someone structures their world cognitively and challenges the difference between psychosis and normality. It is assumed that normal cognitive processing is involved in the maintenance of some psychotic symptoms. Also normal cognitive mechanisms are thought to be helpful for someone coping with symptoms of schizophrenia. Kates and Rockland (1994, cited in Dickerson, 2000) explain that CBT is an individual therapy to strengthen coping, and focusing on the person's life at the time. CBT also targets psychotic symptoms.

Process of CBT for schizophrenia

CBT for schizophrenia focuses on the individual, with one-to-one sessions weekly over a number of weeks or longer. The therapeutic relationship is important, as it is in all such therapies, and focuses on the therapist being non-threatening and supportive. There is collaboration where the patient and the therapist work together to discuss specific symptoms (Alford and Beck, 1994, cited in Dickerson, 2000). There is focus on the subjective experience of the symptoms and then specific symptoms and problem areas are targeted to work on them. The patient's symptoms are focused on rationally, accepting them and the patient's experience of them.

CBT approaches include belief modification, focusing and reattribution, normalising and cognitive therapy following an acute phase, and there are other approaches as well. These are outlined here to give an idea of how CBT for schizophrenia works.

- Belief modification is where delusional thinking is challenged directly and there is testing against reality. Evidence for the delusional belief is challenged and exploration of the delusional belief being only one version of events is carried out.

- Focusing and reattribution looks at auditory hallucinations to reduce the frequency of the voices and to reduce the distress they bring. The therapist focuses on physical attributes of the voices first (number, loudness, tone, gender and other characteristics of the voices, according to Dickerson, 2000). Then the content of the voices is looked at and the patient records what the voices say for homework. The focus in the third stage is on what the patient's beliefs and thoughts are about the voices. The therapist aims to show that the voices are self-generated (and presumably not to be feared, but to be accepted).

- Normalising involves de-stigmatising the psychotic experience and looking at this experience rationally. Cognitive distortions from the illness are discussed and stressful events before the illness are also discussed, in order to see the illness as more 'normal'. Standard CBT techniques such as examining the evidence, looking for alternative explanations and challenging faulty thinking are used. Relaxation techniques and activity planning may also be used. The psychotic symptoms are looked at as more normal and less of a catastrophe, to reduce the fear and distress related to them.

- Cognitive therapy following an acute phase involves four different procedures (which run together, not one after the other):
  - Cognitive therapy to challenge and test key beliefs, with a supportive and non-threatening relationship between the patient and the therapist.
  - Group therapy, where members of the group are encouraged to see the irrationalities and inconsistencies of the other group members. Coping strategies are encouraged in the group.
  - A third approach involves sessions with families so that patients do not become absorbed in their psychotic symptoms.
  - The fourth part involves structured activities.

Progress check 1.30

List four CBT approaches focusing on schizophrenia.

NICE guideline 178, modified February 2014

The National Institute for Health and Care Excellence (NICE) produces guidelines under the heading 'preventing psychosis' and the first recommendation is that individual CBT is offered, with or without family intervention. The second recommendation is to offer interventions for depression and anxiety disorders and/or related disorders.

For the first episode, medication is recommended and it is for subsequent acute episodes that CBT is mentioned again, as well as family intervention this time.

The guideline also contains recommendations about cultural and ethnic differences, which will be of relevance when you are considering cultural issues in schizophrenia. The guideline indicates that CBT is recommended as a treatment for schizophrenia, as is medication.

Explore

NICE guideline 178 covers the treatment and management of psychosis and schizophrenia in adults. Use the following link to view the guideline:
www.nice.org.uk/guidance/cg178/resources/guidance-psychosis-and-schizophrenia-in-adults-treatment-and-management-pdf

Effectiveness of cognitive-behavioural therapy (CBT)

Hoffmann et al. (2012) carried out a review of meta-analyses to summarise the effectiveness of CBT. They looked at 269 meta-analyses and from those chose 106 that looked at CBT for disorders including schizophrenia, substance misuse disorder and other psychotic disorders, as well as depression, aggression and other issues. They found that the strongest support for CBT was its use for anxiety disorders, anger control problems and general stress, as well as other issues, but not listing schizophrenia or psychotic disorders. Eleven of the meta-analyses compared response rates to CBT with those from other treatments or controls. In seven of these reviews CBT showed a higher response rate than the comparison condition (another treatment or a control group), which in general suggests that CBT is very effective, even though for these studies the focus was not directly on schizophrenia.

Other studies considering effectiveness of CBT

The following studies are all cited in Dickerson (2000).

- Chadwick and Lowe (1994) considered an intervention using CBT principles that was about belief modification. They found that 10 out of 12 deluded patients showed a decrease in their conviction about their beliefs and 5 out of 12 rejected their delusion, which shows some success for this therapy. Such studies tend to have a small number of patients and to use self-report data at the end of therapy, so the results might not be reliable and might not be valid, as well as possibly not being generalisable.

- Bentall et al. (1994a) considered reattribution of auditory hallucinations as a strategy for helping with schizophrenia and found that three out of six patients did then reattribute the voices to themselves and a further three (not the same three) reported fewer hallucinations as well as a reduction in the stress involved. However, there was a small number of participants and no control group or follow-up, so the findings must be understood with those limitations.
- Kingdon and Turkington in 1991 found that 35 out of 65 patients with schizophrenia (54 per cent) in a five-year follow-up were free of symptoms when normalising and standard CBT techniques were used. Of the 65 patients, 62 were living in the community. However, there was no control or comparison group as with other studies cited here, so no baseline measure, for example.
- Drury et al. (1996a and 1996b) looked at CBT in an acute phase and found that CBT patients showed fewer psychotic symptoms at week 7 of a 12-week intervention than those in a comparison group. The CBT group average (median) stay in hospital was 49 days compared with 108 days for the comparison group. The comparison group had another therapy, activities and informal support. There were some criticisms of the study, such as how the two groups were initially matched and also there was no control in the comparison group over the amount of therapist attention.

> **STUDY HINT**
> For each of the studies showing the effectiveness of CBT for people with schizophrenia there are limitations of the studies. When making notes, aim for an equal amount of content and evaluation as you will need to be able to evaluate any evidence you offer.

Progress check 1.31
Some evaluation points are offered at the end of each of the list of studies cited in Dickerson (2000), focusing on the effectiveness of CBT for schizophrenia. List the evaluation points given there.

Evaluation of CBT as a treatment for schizophrenia

Strengths

- Studies have shown that CBT is effective, including meta-analyses that have found CBT is effective for positive symptoms of hallucinations and delusions (e.g. Gould et al., 2001, cited in Hoffmann et al., 2012). Zimmerman et al. (2005, cited in Hoffmann et al., 2012)

show that CBT can be useful alongside drug therapy for people in an acute phase of schizophrenia. The studies listed above give evidence for its effectiveness. A strength of CBT is that studies have found it to be effective, so much so that it is recommended by NICE guidelines.
- A strength of CBT for schizophrenia is that it need not only focus on schizophrenia but also on any stress, distress, depression and anxiety that the patient is experiencing alongside schizophrenia (e.g. Turkington and McKenna, 2003). The therapy is used for many different disorders and as someone with schizophrenia is likely to be experiencing at least distress, it is useful to use one therapy for more than one of their symptoms.
- A strength of CBT is that the therapist and patient work collaboratively on issues of concern to the individual and the relationship between them is non-threatening and supportive. This gives some power to the patient, perhaps more than when drug therapy is involved. This is a strength for ethical reasons, giving the individual power over what happens to them, and also a strength because if the person is involved in their own therapy directly, it could be argued that it will be more tailored to their needs and, therefore, more likely to be successful.

Issues and debates
You will look at social control as an issue in psychology, as one of the issues and debates in your course. You can use ideas about CBT and drug therapy in schizophrenia to discuss issues of social control in psychological therapies.

Weaknesses

- CBT can be distressing for the individual as they have to focus on distressing symptoms such as hallucinations and delusions. They must also question their own beliefs, which includes questioning their own sanity, and this too can be stressful. While thinking about ethics as a weakness, it is worth considering how far someone is able to give informed consent to treatment given their psychosis (although this is not to say they cannot; it simply depends on the severity of their psychosis at the time). Because CBT enables the individual to be involved in their own therapy, this suggests they are able to give consent to the treatment.
- When testing CBT for effectiveness in schizophrenia, mostly this is not done using controls or competing therapies, as mentioned when we considered its effectiveness earlier (page 69). Without randomised controlled trials it is hard to claim effectiveness. Evidence tends to come from self-report data after therapy, and such data might be neither reliable nor valid. When there has been a control treatment there was no significant difference in using CBT (Sensky et al., 2000, Lewis et al., 2002, cited in Turkington and McKenna, 2003).

However, there have been studies that have used randomised controlled trials and these have found CBT to be effective for schizophrenia. Barrowclough *et al.* (2006) found no significant differences between CBT and their usual treatment (which was the control); however, when they looked at group CBT they did find reductions in feelings of hopelessness and low self-esteem. Perhaps the weakness here is that some of the studies claiming effectiveness did not use controls or comparison groups and findings about effectiveness are perhaps not as strong as findings about drug therapy.

Explore

You can find a debate focusing on the question 'Is cognitive-behavioural therapy a worthwhile treatment for psychosis?' at the link below. It gives arguments both 'for' and 'against' this claim and you can use the material when evaluating or discussing CBT as a treatment for schizophrenia.

http://bjp.rcpsych.org/content/182/6/477

Treatments other than drug therapy or CBT

Dickerson (2000) reviews treatments other than CBT. She suggests that psychodynamic individual therapy was not found to be better than more structured therapies so is not often found. Personal therapy has been found to be effective for some patients, according to Hogarty *et al.* (1997) cited in Dickerson (2000). Token economy, based on reinforcement principles of operant conditioning, was found to help in institutions (Allyon and Azrin, 1968) and can help with specific behaviour, such as what someone with psychosis might say (see diagram below). However, token economy does not seem to generalise well outside the institutional setting (e.g. Himadi *et al.,* 1991, cited in Dickerson, 2000).

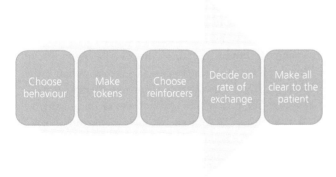

How token economy would work for someone with schizophrenia in an institution

A psychosocial treatment – assertive community treatment (ACT)

Though two treatments for schizophrenia have been explained in this section, here is just a brief look at how social psychology principles can be used in therapy. This links with CBT as it has been said that group CBT can be effective and one approach to CBT – when the psychotic episode is acute – involves group therapy as well as individual therapy. Lavarenne *et al.* (2013) in their case study showed how the group acted as a boundary for individuals (page 158). We have also seen there is a social explanation for schizophrenia associated with a lack of social support and social isolation. All these issues suggest that there is a social element to schizophrenia, and so a social treatment is of importance.

One psychosocial treatment is assertive community treatment (ACT), which is used to help patients with schizophrenia who have frequent relapses and bouts of hospitalisation. This therapy is used by community mental health services with clients who have difficulties meeting personal goals, getting on with people, making and keeping friends and living independently. Leonard Stein and Mary Ann Test were two of the US developers of ACT, which was originally called the Madison Project because it was developed in Madison, Wisconsin.

ACT links with the idea of deinstitutionalisation and care in the community. In the 1970s large numbers of patients were discharged from hospitals and strong community support for these people was required.

Characteristics of assertive community treatment

- A focus on those who need the most help from the community health service.
- Helping with independence, rehabilitation and recovery, and to avoid homelessness and re-hospitalisation.
- Treatment of the patient in real-life settings – visiting them and helping, rather than offering therapies, with enough staff to offer this support and related treatment.
- Working with other professionals, such as psychiatrists, nurses, social workers and people with whom the treatment has worked, so that a whole team can focus on the individual in question.
- A commitment to spend as much time with the person as necessary in order to rehabilitate and support them, offering a holistic treatment that looks at all of their needs in a multidisciplinary approach.

Outcome study focusing on patients in the Netherlands, van Vugt *et al.* (2011)

Van Vugt *et al.* (2011) carried out a study looking at ACT in the Netherlands. They wanted to look at the outcomes for individuals using an ACT programme and how faithful the programme had to be to the original to have successful outcomes. They studied 20 different out-patient treatment teams and 530 patients with severe mental illness took part in the study. The researchers assessed outcomes for the patients three times during the study and counted the number of hospital days and the number of homelessness days they experienced over a two-year follow-up study. Van Vugt *et al.* (2011) found that team structure was most related to better outcomes and concluded that it was important to stick to the original model for ACT, which depends strongly on the structure of the team.

Outcome study focusing on patients in Japan, Nishio *et al.* (2012)

Nishio *et al.* (2012) focused on seeing if ACT was helpful for patients making the transition from institution to the community. The researchers looked at 41 people hospitalised for severe mental illness who met the conditions for having ACT. Conditions included age, diagnosis, residence, use of mental health services, social adjustment and ability to function in daily life. The number of days and frequency of hospitalisations were measured as well as frequency of emergency visits over a one-year period before and a one-year period after hospital discharge. The measures showed a significant decrease in the number of days and in the frequency of hospitalisations. One year after discharge there was no change in life satisfaction, although their Global Assessment of Functioning score increased significantly and their antipsychotic medication dose significantly decreased. These results were taken to show that ACT does enable people to live for longer in the community without symptoms becoming worse and without deterioration in their quality of life.

Outcome study focusing on staff in Australia, Harvey *et al.* (2012)

Harvey *et al.* (2012) explain that how well ACT works for patients depends on how the treatment is implemented, which agrees with the findings of van Vugt *et al.* (2011) explained above. Harvey *et al.* (2012) studied four ACT teams using a validated questionnaire. Their study focused on outcomes for the staff of running the programme, which is a different focus from looking at outcomes for patients and is an interesting way of evaluating a treatment programme. The study found that the outcomes for staff were not good, with one team showing high levels of emotional exhaustion. It was found that burnout was associated with the stress of working in a team. There were differences between the four teams studied, which suggests that it is important to focus on effective team working and leadership as well as sticking to the ACT model.

Effectiveness of ACT for schizophrenia

- There is some problem with replicating the programme in less populated areas and where people needing such support are widely spread.
- ACT tends to be used with other interventions as well, such as social skills training and family therapy.
- There have been many outcome studies that have shown the success of a programme of assertive community training (PACT). This programme began with people with schizophrenia and has been extended to those with other mental illnesses.
- Nishio *et al.* (2012), in Japan, found some measures of success in their study and concluded that ACT could be successful, although their study focused on serious mental illness, not just schizophrenia.
- Van Vugt *et al.* (2011) found (in the Netherlands) that provided the model was adhered to, ACT could be effective, and that it was the team structure that was important.
- Harvey *et al.* (2012) raised questions about the difficulties for staff of running the programme, which should be considered when considering the effectiveness of providing such a treatment.

Evaluating ACT

Dixon (2000) points out that since the 1980s ACT has been seen as the model for mental health practice. Bond *et al.* (2001) summarised 25 controlled studies that looked at the effectiveness of ACT – called an evidence-based treatment, because there is evidence for its effectiveness. They concluded that, compared with standard community care, ACT was highly effective because it engaged clients, prevented re-hospitalisations, increased housing stability and improved the clients' quality of life.

ACT is used in severe mental health cases, not only schizophrenia. The more carefully implemented an ACT programme is, the more effective it is. Surveys tend to suggest clients appreciate ACT (e.g. Mueser *et al.*, 1998) and studies looking at its effectiveness report no negative aspects of the programme. ACT seems to work with all age groups, both genders, and across different cultures.

However, there are critics. Gomory (2001), for example, suggests that ACT is paternalistic and coercive, in that the client does not have the choice of whether or not to undergo such treatment. This is about social control and the client not having control. It is suggested that about 11 per cent of clients feel forced into the treatment. It seems that case managers are more active in setting limits for clients who have more symptoms, more arrests, many hospitalisations and more recent substance abuse, so there may be some coercion in such severe cases. Bond (2002), however, points out that by preventing hospitalisation the treatment increases a client's choice, and by helping them to live in the community, the treatment increases their freedom.

Strengths

- It is thought to be good for those who have many relapses, because it might be problems with living outside the hospital that lead to such episodes. Social skills training and family therapy can help someone to improve their interactions with others. Treatments based on improving the individual to function in society have been shown to help and can be incorporated into an ACT programme. The strength here is that it has been shown to work when focusing on social interactions for someone with schizophrenia and it shows the importance of such social interactions.
- In a review of evidence, Bond (2002) found that ACT was extremely effective in most mental health disorders, across gender, age and culture, and suggests that it allows client choice. Only about 11 per cent of clients in surveys say they find it restricting. The strength here is that it has been shown to be effective by studies.

Weaknesses

- Although therapies such as ACT help to prevent relapses they do not seem to have an effect on actual functioning, and reducing positive and negative symptoms of schizophrenia or helping with employment prospects. Supportive employment programmes would have to be provided, as well as ways to reduce the effect of symptoms of schizophrenia.
- ACT works best in heavily populated areas where there is a high incidence of people with schizophrenia needing care in the community. This is because of the effort and intensive focus that is required as part of the treatment. Adequate staffing is required to undertake this hands-on therapy. This links back to social deprivation as an explanation for schizophrenia. If urban heavily populated areas seem to have more people with schizophrenia than rural areas, perhaps ACT works best in urban areas because

there can be that focus – teams can be brought in because there are enough cases to warrant it. The weakness here is that it might not be provided where there are not many cases of schizophrenia, because of cost implications.
- Gomory (2001) pointed out that the client is offered little choice and surrenders all responsibility for making decisions and taking care of themselves. This is an ethical consideration about a person having control over decisions about them.

Progress check 1.33

Explain two weaknesses of ACT as a therapy for schizophrenia.

Unipolar depression

For your course, alongside schizophrenia, you need to know about one other disorder from a choice of **unipolar depression**, obsessive compulsive disorder (OCD) and anorexia nervosa. All three are given in this book, but you only need to learn about one of them. There is useful information about each, including diagnosis, explanations and treatment of mental disorders, so you might want to read about all three even if you only learn in detail about one.

We begin by looking at unipolar depression and this section will look in turn at symptoms and features, explanations and treatments of unipolar depression. Unipolar depression is also known as major depression, clinical depression, recurrent depression or unipolar disorder. It is usually abbreviated to 'depression' and this short form is often used in the discussion that follows. Depression in the sense of a low mood is not a disorder, so the word unipolar is used to indicate a disorder with one aspect. Bipolar depression indicates depression with two aspects – mania and depression.

Depression is sometimes called the 'common cold' of mental illnesses. It is a mood disorder that features sadness, disappointment, self-doubt, loneliness and hopelessness. The feelings can be intense and last a long time. The individual might cope with daily activities but such activities are difficult.

Explanation

Unipolar depression is characterised by lethargy, feelings of despair and hopelessness and loss of interest in usual activities. Unipolar depression is also known as clinical or recurrent depression and is diagnosed as major depressive disorder (MDD).

Study of interest

Amey (2010) explains her own case of unipolar depression and, importantly, her experiences of psychotic mania, which were apparently brought on by being given tricyclic antidepressant treatment (dosulepin). Amey had a 16-year history of depression and had been receiving sertraline, then alongside the sertraline she was given dosulepin. Within days she had symptoms of mania and the dosulepin was stopped but the sertraline continued. Two months after that she was sectioned (i.e. detained under Section II of the Mental Health Act) and admitted to hospital with psychotic manic symptoms. Amey (2010) says that there should be more understanding of how antidepressants can bring on an episode of mania. This study is interesting because it is a personal story and it helps to show the difficulties of living with depression, not least the difficulties with medication that is prescribed.

Symptoms of unipolar depression

The symptoms of unipolar depression include extreme lethargy, disturbed sleep (which can mean early waking, waking up tired or difficulty in getting to sleep), permanent anxiety and irritability, feelings of despair and hopelessness, lack of concentration, loss of interest or pleasure in usual activities, lack of sex drive and irrational fears and suicidal thoughts. Headaches and digestive problems are also reported. There are other disorders with similar symptoms, such as sleep and anxiety disorders and obsessional behaviour.

There is no test for depression; diagnosis relies on self-report data or information from family and friends. There are different levels of depression giving different diagnoses. Someone can have mild depression, which has some impact on someone's life, moderate depression, which has significant impact, or severe depression, which means

it is hard to get through daily life. Unipolar disorder is severe depression. Bipolar disorder is a form of depression, but here 'depression' does not include that disorder, or postnatal depression, which is a special form of depression too. Another special form of depression is seasonal affective disorder (SAD), which tends to be found in the winter. These special forms are not included in this section because your course asks you to focus on unipolar depression.

Table 1.8 Psychological, physical and social symptoms of depression

Symptoms of depression	
Psychological	Continuous low mood and sadness; feeling hopeless and helpless; low self-esteem; irritable and intolerant; no enjoyment in life; anxiety; suicidal thoughts; thoughts of self-harm; feelings of guilt; feeling tearful.
Physical	Slow movements and speech; aches and pains such as headaches and cramps; disturbed sleep.
Social	Having problems at work; avoiding social activities; avoiding friends; family life difficulties.

Explore

There are many websites about depression. One example is on YouTube, which you can access using this link: **www.youtube.com/watch?v=IgSVR54LZzY**

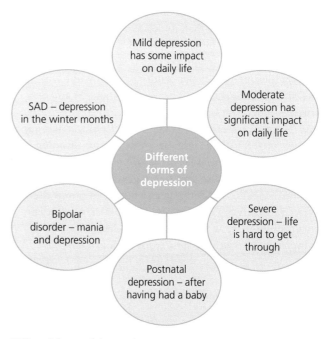

Different forms of depression

There can also be cognitive symptoms in depression, such as difficulty with memory and difficulty with concentration. Ideas of guilt and low self-esteem are cognitive issues and thinking about suicide also is about thinking.

Anxiety is a different disorder but can go with depression, with one making the other worse. Anxiety leads to repetitive thinking and a busy mind, which makes concentration difficult as well as leading to negative thoughts.

For there to be a diagnosis of major depression patients must have suffered at least one episode, which means depression that has lasted two weeks or longer and with five or more of the main symptoms given above.

Depression is characterised by lethargy, feelings of despair and hopelessness and loss of interest in usual activities.

Explore

Depression can be a factor in other illnesses, such as Parkinson's. A study reported in the medical journal *Neurology* went further and suggested that depression could signal the start of Parkinson's. Here is the link to some information (from May 2015) about this study (Gustafsson *et al.*, 2015):
www.theatlantic.com/health/archive/2015/05/is-depression-a-symptom-of-parkinsons-disease/393800/

Features of unipolar depression

Depression is twice as common in women as in men, although men are more likely to commit suicide and in the US around 3.4 per cent of those with major depression do commit suicide, which underlines its severity. The rate of suicide for unipolar depression is lower than for bipolar depression (where the rate is about 80 per cent). Over a lifetime, 10–25 per cent of women will have major depression and 5–12 per cent of men. At any one time, 5–9 per cent of women will be clinically depressed and 2–3 per cent of men. Young *et al.* (1990) carried out a study of 498 patients with major depressive disorder, both males and females. With regard to increased appetite and weight there were significant gender differences, but in impairment of functioning and other symptoms there were no significant differences. Young *et al.* concluded that though more women suffer with depression, the symptoms are relatively similar for both genders.

Depression is most common from the ages of 25 to 44, with the average age for developing depression being mid-20s. Some cases of depression only occur once, whereas other people suffer permanently, though with more or less severity, over the years. Depressed individuals tend to live a shorter life than non-depressed people, possibly because depression relates to heart disease and other illnesses. Depression tends to affect work and family life as well as functioning, such as sleeping and eating. According to the Anxiety and Depression Association of America, around 14.8 million adults (6.7 per cent of the adult population) suffer from major depressive disorder in the US, which affects their everyday lives. In the US anxiety is the most common mental illness, with 40 million adults affected. According to the NHS, in the year 2010–2011 depression affected over 4.7 million people in the UK and figures for 2012 indicated an increase of a further 500,000, so numbers are rising. Mind, the mental health charity, carries out a survey every seven years to measure the number of people in England who have different types of mental health problems each year. The latest set of figures available is for 2009 (Table 1.9). Table 1.9 shows that mixed depression anxiety is the most prevalent condition with depression next. Haase and Brown (2015) cite Moussavi *et al.* (2007), suggesting that 15 per cent of the population in industrialised nations suffer from depression, with it being the leading cause of disease globally by 2030.

Table 1.9 Most common mental illnesses

Condition	Cases in the adult population in England (%)
Depression	2.6
Anxiety	4.7
Mixed depression and anxiety	9.7
Eating disorders	1.6
Obsessive compulsive disorder	1.3

Source: www.mind.org.uk

When someone has had an initial episode of depression there may be years before they experience another one, if they have one at all. However, as episodes become more frequent, the shorter the time seems to be between each one. If someone has had one episode of depression, there is a 50–60 per cent chance they will have another; where someone has had two episodes, there is a 70 per cent chance they will experience a third, and then a 90 per cent chance of a fourth if they have had a third. About one third of people who have had major depression recover completely and about one third partly recover.

Co-morbidity as a feature of depression

Major depression often appears with other disorders, including with schizophrenia (Kessler *et al.,* 1996). Anxiety often goes along with depression as can drug misuse. Co-morbidity means that more than one illness or disorder co-exists in someone. This can have implications for treatment and therapy so is worth mentioning as a feature of depression. Goes *et al.* (2007) used semi-structured interviewing and 4,724 participants with recurrent major depressive disorder or bipolar disorder to look at psychotic features that link to severe depression. They found that compared with major depressive disorder, a diagnosis of bipolar disorder did accompany psychotic symptoms, whereas unipolar disorder did not. You should therefore check which form of depression is being discussed when considering links to psychosis. Rothschild *et al.* (2015) discuss unipolar major depression with psychotic features (hallucinations and delusions), however, and see this as a subtype major depressive disorder, so psychosis can go with unipolar depression as well as bipolar disorder.

Explore
To find out more about major depressive disorder, try the following link:
www.healthline.com/health/clinical-depression#1

Brain structures and depression

Unipolar depression shows emotional reactivity and this has been linked to amygdala activity. It is thought there are disruptions in executive control that link to the prefrontal cortex (Siegle *et al.,* 2005). Siegle *et al.* (2005) looked at 27 patients with unipolar depression (diagnosed using the DSM-IV) and 25 healthy controls. The participants completed tasks requiring executive control and processing of emotions. At the same time the participants underwent fMRI scanning. Siegle *et al.* (2005) found that depressed participants showed more amygdala activity than controls when doing the emotional tasks and lower activity in the dorsolateral prefrontal cortex than controls when doing the executive control tasks. This is evidence that depression is associated with (raised) limbic system activity when processing emotionally and (lowered) prefrontal activity when doing cognitive tasks.

Year One link: In biological psychology you will have read that the prefrontal cortex is linked to decision-making and the amygdala (in the limbic system) to emotions (including aggression). You can use this material when understanding biological issues in unipolar depression. In biological psychology you will have looked at fMRI scanning and you can use Siegle *et al.* (2005) as an example of such scanning.

Explore
A number of areas of the brain have been found to be implicated in major depressive disorder.

Do some research on the internet to find a diagram of the brain and identify the location of the following structures:
- Prefrontal cortex
- Anterior cingulate cortex
- Nucleus accumbens
- Amygdala
- Hippocampus
- Insular cortex

Two explanations for unipolar depression

When looking at explanations for unipolar depression you need to cover one biological explanation and one non-biological explanation. Depression can be triggered by a significant life event, hormone or neurotransmitter deficiency, or other areas of a person's life, such as drug dependency and alcoholism.

In this section a biological explanation is considered – the monoamine hypothesis – along with a psychological explanation – aspects of faulty thinking.

Biological explanation: the monoamine hypothesis

The monoamine hypothesis is like the dopamine and the glutamate hypotheses you looked at when learning about neurotransmitter functioning as an explanation for schizophrenia. An explanation for depression is a decrease in monoamine neurotransmitters such as serotonin and noradrenaline in the central nervous system (Krishnan and Nestler, 2008, cited in Haase and Brown, 2015). For unipolar depression it is serotonin, noradrenaline and dopamine that are considered. In the case of depression, there is not enough dopamine whereas for schizophrenia one explanation for the condition is that it is caused by an excess of dopamine. Although there are differences between the two conditions, therefore, the similarity between the two is in the mechanisms indicated, involving synaptic transmission and the role of neurotransmitters.

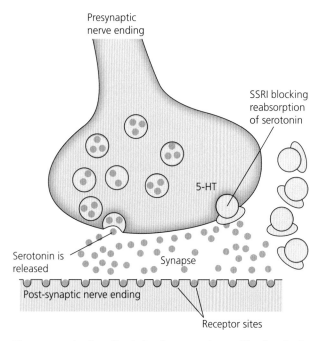

The monoamine hypothesis involves neurotransmitter functioning in depression including the idea of too little serotonin. Selective serotonin reuptake inhibitors (SSRIs) block the reuptake of serotonin into the presynaptic neuron so there is more in the synaptic gap, preventing its depletion.

Monoamines are a group of neurotransmitters that contain amino acid. Monoamine transporters include serotonin, norepinephrine (noradrenaline) and dopamine transporters. As with other neurotransmitter functioning, monoamine transporter action stops when there is reuptake

into the presynaptic neuron. Monoamines are thought to be important for emotions and cognition, and drugs that improve the effects of monoamine neurotransmitters help with not only depression but also anxiety and schizophrenia.

Definition

Monoamines are neurotransmitters that contain an amino group; they come from amino acids such as tryptophan and the thyroid hormones. Neurotransmitters include serotonin, noradrenaline and dopamine.

Year One link: Recall your learning in biological psychology when you looked at neurotransmitter functioning at the synapse, including the role of reuptake into the presynaptic neuron.

One role of serotonin (also known as 5-HT) is to regulate other neurotransmitters; without regulation, erratic brain functioning and thinking patterns occur. Low levels of serotonin can produce low levels of another neurotransmitter, norepinephrine (which is required for someone to show alertness, energy, anxiety and attention to life). Some antidepressants can be used to increase levels of norepinephrine (called serotonin noradrenaline reuptake inhibitors). Others are used to increase levels of another monoamine neurotransmitter, dopamine (dopamine is related to the ability to show attention and motivation, to feel pleasure and reward).

Progress check 1.34

Which three neurotransmitters are discussed in the monoamine hypothesis for depression and what is their role in human functioning (in relation to depression)?

Many antidepressants work by increasing the patient's levels of serotonin. Selective serotonin reuptake inhibitors (SSRIs) are widely used drugs for depression (page 68), underlining the idea that serotonergic transmission has a role in depression. It could be concluded then that lack of serotonin is a biological cause of unipolar depression – an explanation known as the monoamine hypothesis. Preventing serotonin from being taken back up into the presynaptic neuron, as SSRIs do, does help with depression and also helps to increase serotonin at the synapse. A conclusion that low levels of serotonin 'cause' depression follows from this (Haase and Brown, 2015). Delgado (2000) discussed the role of monoamine deficiency in depression and underlined the link not only to deficiency of serotonin in the central nervous system, but also to depleted levels of norepinephrine and/or dopamine. As drugs that raise levels of these neurotransmitters in the brain help with symptoms of depression, this suggests, according to Delgado, that depression comes from deficiency in these neurotransmitters. Lack of serotonin appears to be related to anxiety and compulsions. Symptoms of depression such as disruption of sleep patterns also seem to relate to deficiencies in monoamine neurotransmitters.

Serotonin receptors are found in different central nervous system cells and serotonin from the raphe nuclei is important in regulating behaviour, including moods, sleep and appetite. Serotonin is released from the presynaptic neuron into the synapse where receptors in the postsynaptic neuron pick the serotonin up, which 'sends a message' to the postsynaptic neuron. Serotonin can travel quite a way from its release site (the presynaptic neuron) before binding to receptors in the postsynaptic neuron. A serotonin transporter is involved in 'carrying' the serotonin. Evidence for this explanation of serotonin functioning is that Karg *et al.* (2011, cited in Haase and Brown, 2015) suggest that changes in the gene encoding the serotonin transporter are linked to depression that is triggered by stress. Interfering with serotonin transporter functioning, such as by SSRIs, means more serotonin and more signalling through postsynaptic serotonin receptors, which can help with depression.

Year One link: You should recall from biological psychology that the central nervous system consists of the brain and the spinal cord and that neurons are cells. You also need to recall the structure of neurons.

> **STUDY HINT**
> One of the treatments for depression discussed later in this section is the use of antidepressants. Relating antidepressants to the ideas discussed here about neurotransmitter functioning at the synapse will help you to understand how antidepressants work.

Alternative/additional explanations

The monoamine hypothesis is still considered the main explanation for unipolar depression, but other explanations are also now considered alongside this hypothesis, although these explanations still hold to the idea that serotonin has a role in our moods and monoamines are important in depression. Alternative explanations can link to issues around serotonin, with the explanations not 'against' the hypothesis so much as expanding on how unipolar depression is explained by biological factors.

Genetic or environmental factors

The diathesis–stress model shows that a biological explanation may link to a stress trigger. It suggests that people with a pre-existing genetic or environmental vulnerability to depression (the diathesis) will have it triggered by stressful life events or one single event. Heritability is about 40 per cent for depression in women and 30 per cent for men, according to a Swedish study, which is evidence for a genetic link. A further study found that the serotonin transporter gene had a moderating effect on depression following a stressful life event. It seems possible, therefore, that biological make-up can predispose one person to develop depression where another person in the same situation will not. Haase and Brown (2015) discuss the immune system as a possible explanation for depression and how the immune system affects serotonin transporter regulation. Stress can impact on the immune system. These ideas suggest that serotonin has a role in depression (along with other monoamine transporters like dopamine) and neurotransmitter functioning can link to other issues in the individual such as stress and the immune system, cortisol and/or genetic factors.

> ## Progress check 1.35
> Explain one point about genes and how they can link to depression.

Synaptic plasticity and neurogenesis

Lee and Kim (2010) suggest that **synaptic plasticity** has a role in unipolar depression. **Neurogenesis** is important too. Synaptic plasticity refers to how synapses can become stronger or weaker, affected by activity at the synapse and the number of neurotransmitter receptors at the synapse also changes over time. An interesting feature of antidepressants is that their effects are delayed in that it takes time for them to begin working when a patient first begins to take them. An explanation for this seems to be that increasing monoamine transmitter levels leads to the release of **neurotrophic factors** (factors that affect the growth and survival of neurons) and this leads to synaptic plasticity, which has an effect on the hippocampus (Krishnan and Nestler, 2008, cited in Haase and Brown, 2015). Changes in hippocampal cells and in the hippocampal structure link to depression. The hippocampus continues to produce new neurons by neurogenesis (most parts of the brain do not do this). It has been found in people with depression that they have a 10–15 per cent decrease in the size of the hippocampus (e.g. Campbell *et al.*, 2004, cited in Haase and Brown, 2015).

Eisch and Petric (2012) suggest that neurogenesis has a role in depression. SSRIs increase neurogenesis and clinical studies show there is more brain-derived neurotrophic factor in depressed people, which is evidence for such neurogenesis (Autry and Monteggia, 2012, cited in Haase and Brown, 2015). Studies using mice and also other studies show a strong link between brain-derived neurotrophic factor (BDNF), depression and transmission of serotonin. These ideas suggest that the monoamine hypothesis stands but that there is more happening, such as the production of neurons in the hippocampus and issues around synaptic plasticity. SSRIs affect such processes and it can take time for changes to take place because it takes time for the effects of antidepressants to be felt.

Definitions

Neurogenesis refers to the making of neurons from cells.

Synaptic plasticity refers to how synapses can become weaker or stronger over time depending on activity of neurotransmitters at the synapse.

Neurotrophic factors are responsible for the growth of neurons and maintenance of neurons.

Progress check 1.36

How do synaptic plasticity and neurogenesis relate to depression?

STUDY HINT

One way of learning new terms is to 'translate' them every time you read about them until you have fully learned their meaning. You could have a 'shorthand' phrase to remember them by. For example, 'synaptic plasticity' can be seen as 'flexible changing synapses' perhaps.

Evaluation of the monoamine hypothesis

Strengths

- If the explanation is that there are monoamine deficiencies, and drugs that replace those deficiencies work, then this is evidence for the hypothesis. Haase and Brown (2015) make this claim, as did Delgado (2000).
- The different monoamines link to the symptoms differently and treatment reflects those differences, again supporting the hypothesis. For example, anxiety, compulsions and lack of interest, energy or concentration can all be explained by deficiency in monoamines. Tricyclic antidepressants and benzodiazepines link to anxiety symptoms and SSRIs work to improve mood, for example. SSRIs are used for generalised anxiety disorder.

- There is a lot of evidence linking monoamine functioning to depression, including animal studies and the use of different research methods. Krishnan and Nestler (2008), in their review of the neurobiology of depression, discussed the research methods involved. They report on the scanning of depressed patients after their death (which found changes in grey-matter volume, including in the hippocampus), fMRI and PET scanning (amygdala activity correlates with dysphoria, which is, roughly, unhappiness and irritability as an emotional state) and animal models of depression (such as Monteggia et al., 2007). When many different research methods point in a similar direction that gives strength to a hypothesis. However, Krishnan and Nestler (2008) conclude by saying that there are 'enormous gaps in the knowledge of depression and its treatment' (p. 901) and say it is 'imperative' to look beyond monoamine mechanisms. The strength here, therefore, is that there is a lot of evidence for monoamine activity in depression, with the caveat that much more needs to be known.

Weaknesses

- There are drugs that affect depression but whose action is not related to monoamine neurotransmitters, putting the monoamine hypothesis in doubt. Chaki et al. (2006) mention drugs focusing outside the monoamine system, including focusing on receptors within the glutamate and neuropeptide systems. Palucha and Pilc (2005) also mention glutamate receptors, such as studies showing activity that acts as an antidepressant when considering glutamate receptors.
- SSRIs do not help everyone with depression, according to Haase and Brown (2015), which suggests that lack of serotonin is not a complete explanation. Trivedi et al. (2006, cited in Haase and Brown, 2015) found only one third of people using the SSRI citalopram were in complete remission.
- Experiments where monoamines are depleted do not cause symptoms of depression.
- Delgado (2000) said that evidence for there being deficiency in a specific monoamine system in depression has not been found. A problem is the difficulty in measuring monoamines in humans. Monoamine depletion does not make depression worse and neither does it lead to symptoms of depression in healthy non-depressed volunteers. Antidepressants do work in monoamine systems, but it is hard to be sure that monoamine deficiency causes depression.

- MRI scans have shown some physical differences in the brain in people with depression as compared to those without, so these might be related to the cause of depression rather than faulty monoamine neurotransmitter functioning. One such brain difference is a smaller hippocampus. It may be that drugs increasing serotonin levels affect depression because those heightened levels act to increase the hippocampal area. This increase in the mass of the hippocampus might lift mood and improve memory. So serotonin level is still a factor in the explanation, but its action affects brain mass not monoamine deficiency. Issues around hippocampus volume in depression have been discussed earlier (page 59).
- A different biological explanation implicates the parts of the nervous system related to stress and includes an increase in levels of cortisol. This also goes against the monoamine hypothesis.
- Goldberg *et al.* (2014) revisit the monoamine hypothesis of depression and suggest that there is a role for GABA, shown using scanning and laboratory findings. This is not to say that monoamines do not have a role, but that GABA also is important and increasing GABA might be a way forward for therapy.

Progress check 1.37

Briefly explain two pieces of evidence for the monoamine hypothesis for depression and two pieces of evidence against.

Social factors in depression

For your course you only need to know one biological and one non-biological explanation for unipolar depression. However, in line with this book's approach to looking at schizophrenia, this brief section focuses on a particular study and looks at the importance of social interactions when it comes to mental disorder like depression. Brown *et al.* (1986) carried out a well-known study that shows the importance of social support in depression, which can link to what was said earlier about social isolation and schizophrenia (page 44). This is additional material that might be useful in a discussion about unipolar depression.

Brown *et al.* (1986)

Brown *et al.* (1986) looked at factors involved in depression and considered only women. They used interviewing to find out how self-esteem and support factors affected the development of depression.

Background

Depression is usually measured using a life-event score rather than looking at a specific life event, and data are usually gathered from the respondent using a standard questionnaire. However, data from semi-structured interviews with a researcher suggest that specific life events are significant in the development of depression. In particular, it is claimed that life events with a severe long-term threat or entailing major difficulties that last two or more years can bring about depression. However, only a minority develop depression in such circumstances, suggesting the need to consider vulnerability factors: what causes one person and not another to develop depression in response to the same life event?

Previous research has suggested that vulnerability factors include low self-esteem, lack of close relationships and a woman's relationship with her husband. However, some studies (e.g. Lewinsohn *et al.*, 1981) suggest that self-esteem is not low before depression – it becomes low after the onset of depression, in which case low self-esteem cannot be a cause of depression. When studies look at social support they do not often distinguish core support from general social support, although they show that, in general, social support can protect against depression.

Brown *et al.* considered such issues and chose to use detailed questioning and investigator-based judgements rather than questionnaires, so that they could find some depth and detail in the data. They chose to look at self-esteem and support factors before the onset of depression in order to investigate causation and they chose to separate social support into two areas: wider social networks and core support/core relationships.

One feature of studies into depression is that they tend to be cross-sectional and to look at depression once it has arisen. When someone is asked after the onset of depression what life events they encountered before they became depressed, the data they give might be affected by the depression. Longitudinal studies that follow a person and gather data about their lives *before* they develop depression are necessary, so that possible causes of developing depression can be identified.

> **STUDY HINT**
> In clinical psychology you learn about the longitudinal approach when carrying out research. You could use Brown *et al.* (1986) as an example of this research approach.

Brown *et al.* (1986) used a prospective design so that depressive episodes would not affect the data. They decided on two periods for data collection: 'Time 1' (before any depression) and 'crisis support' (at the time of the depression and afterwards). They took measures at both these times, which were one year apart.

Hypotheses

There were a number of hypotheses:

- The existence of crisis support protects against the onset of depression, even if there is low self-esteem and lack of general support.
- Lack of support and low self-esteem are vulnerability factors and they increase the risk of depression given a later provoking agent.
- Support from a husband, partner or other close relationship (at Time 1 or at the time of crisis) will relate to a reduced risk of depression.

> **STUDY HINT**
> Consider issues around social adversity and schizophrenia, as issues such as poverty, unemployment and lack of social support can also lead to depression. Depression can go along with schizophrenia and they are not separate. Consider, too, ACT as a treatment for schizophrenia, to help to see the importance of social support for mental health.

Procedure

The study took place in Islington, North London. Women whose husbands were in a manual occupation, who had at least one child under 18 living at home, and who were aged between 18 and 50 were sent a letter by their GP asking if they would be willing to take part in the study. Women who fitted the criteria and all single mothers (who were included because they feature highly in women developing depression) were put into a sample. From this sample a number were randomly chosen for the study. In total, 435 women were found; 91 per cent of them (395) were involved in the first part of the study.

The first part had two phases:

- At first contact (Time 1) measures of self-esteem and personal ties were measured. Psychiatric history was also collected at this point.
- The second phase (12 months later) collected data about any onset of psychiatric disorder in the 12 months following the first contact. Measures of life-event stress and social support were also taken.
- The measures were carried out carefully and by experienced interviewers. There were tests for reliability, with 60 women being interviewed intensively and 21 used in a reliability study. Of these 21, 11 were seen by two interviewers and 10 were rated by a second person using tapes of the original interviews. Satisfactory inter-rater reliability was found.

Year One link: Recall issues around reliability that you covered in your Year One studies, including the role of inter-rater reliability and how it is achieved.

Results

In all, 353 women agreed to a follow-up interview at the end of the year (89 per cent of the original sample). Forty-two of the remaining participants were not followed up and of these, three had moved abroad and two refused because of illness. There were 50 cases of depression at first contact out of the 353 women who agreed to a follow-up interview, so they were excluded. Therefore, 303 women were interviewed and their data analysed to see if there was onset of depression over the 12 months after first contact. About half of them (150) had had a severe event or major difficulty in the 12-month follow-up period after the first contact and 32 of the women had the onset of depression.

Life events and onset of depression: Of those who had developed depression in the 12-month follow-up period, 91 per cent (29 out of 32) had experienced a severe event in the 6 months before the onset of depression (involving a loss, failure or disappointment). This compared with 23 per cent of the women with no onset of depression who had experienced a severe event in the 6 months before the interview.

Self-esteem and the onset of depression: Of those who had a provoking agent (life event), 33 per cent of those who developed depression had negative evaluation of self and 13 per cent did not. Table 1.10 (Brown *et al.*'s findings) shows the relationship of those with negative evaluation of self and those without it set against those with a provoking agent (major life event) and those without one.

Table 1.10 Vulnerability and onset of depression looking at negative evaluation of self and provoking agent

	Provoking agent	
Negative evaluation of self	**Yes (% of those with onset)**	**No (% of those with onset)**
Yes	33% (18 out of 54)	4% (1 out of 27)
No	13% (12 out of 96)	1% (1 out of 126)

Table 1.10 shows that many more of those participants with a provoking agent developed depression than those without one. It also shows that people with negative evaluation of self were more likely to develop depression following a provoking agent. Those without negative evaluation of self were less likely to develop depression, even in the presence of a provoking agent. Just one person developed depression

without a provoking agent and without negative evaluation of self.

Social support: The majority of women with core crisis support (92 per cent, or 85 out of 92) saw it as helpful and there was no difference in their perception of support being helpful and whether they developed depression or not. It is interesting that where a woman said she had confided in a close tie (core support) at first contact, but not at crisis support and so felt let down, 42 per cent (14 out of 33) developed depression. Of those who had had no support either at first contact or at crisis, 44 per cent (4 out of 9) developed depression.

Conclusions

In general those who were married or had a close tie had a lower chance of the onset of depression, although if they had confided in their husband and were then let down at crisis by not having such support, then the risk of the onset of depression increased. This sort of result clearly shows the complexity of social support situations, where support is given and expectations are aroused but not fulfilled, and someone feels let down. Of course, this is not just about support from a husband, because he might be involved in the situation. An example is a miscarriage or an unplanned pregnancy, where the husband would be involved but is unable to give support. It is possible that self-esteem is an internalisation of social support and that lack of support lowers self-esteem, which is why negative evaluation of self also relates to the onset of depression. A provoking agent seems to be necessary for the onset of depression in most cases.

Strengths of Brown *et al.* (1986)

- The interviews, both at Time 1 and at crisis support (12 months later), gave the in-depth and detailed data that were required for the analysis of such complex inter-related concepts as self-esteem, core social support and major life events.
- There was inter-rater reliability, which strengthens the results arising from the data.
- The data were likely to be valid, as they were gathered carefully by trained interviewers using a semi-structured interview, allowing detailed information to be explored.
- Sampling was carefully carried out by contacting all eligible women and then carrying out random sampling. This meant that all the women had an equal chance of being chosen, which removes a source of bias.

Weaknesses of Brown *et al.* (1986)

- It was hard to separate out the concepts that were scored as numbers and then percentages, because qualitative data were in some cases 'reduced' to quantitative data. For example, the presence or lack of support from a husband at crisis point seemed easy to assess, but then it was shown that such lack of support meant, at least in some cases, that the husband was part of the situation rather than a bystander.
- This was a study of working-class women with at least one child still at home; generalising the findings to all women might not be possible.

Non-biological explanation: the cognitive model of depression

Various biological explanations for depression have been identified above, together with the social elements associated with diathesis–stress. A further explanation is psychological: having accepted that environmental stressors and biological factors can cause unipolar depression, it has been found that an individual's method of coping can affect the course of the disorder and that thinking processes might, in fact, cause the disorder. It does appear that making changes to thinking patterns can help a patient cope with depression. This suggests that distorted thinking is, at least in part, a cause of depression.

> **STUDY HINT**
> For both the monoamine hypothesis as an explanation for depression and the idea of distorted thinking as an explanation, the argument has been that if a treatment works, this points to the fact that what the treatment is focusing on is the cause of the problem. You can use arguments like this when evaluating treatments and therapies; however, this is not really proof. Just because a treatment works does not mean its basis is what has caused the problem. Remember to consider such issues when presenting an argument about explanations.

In the 1960s, Beck developed the cognitive model of depression, which considers three aspects of thinking. He looked at cognitive errors that people make about themselves (a negative view of themselves), at faulty patterns of thought and schemata and at distorted processing of information. Beck's ideas were discussed earlier when cognitive-behavioural therapy (CBT) was considered as a treatment for schizophrenia (page 49).

Year One link: Although cognitive explanations of depression do not relate directly to models of memory, which you covered in cognitive psychology, you can use the basic ideas from cognitive psychology to understand what is being said about schemas and faulty patterns of thought. Bartlett's ideas about how we reconstruct memories (and thoughts) using our schemas gained from experiences can link to Beck's ideas.

Seligman put forward a similar theory when he suggested that depression is a form of **learned helplessness**; this is when people learn to give up trying to put things right because they have experienced only failure. CBT, an example of cognitive therapy and a treatment for depression, arises from such theories and is explained in detail later in this section. Cognitive therapy focuses on looking at unhelpful thinking to re-evaluate it, looking at evidence, perhaps, and uncovering core beliefs that guide such thoughts and the schemas that go with that thinking.

Study of interest

Forsyth *et al.* (2010) carried out a review of 427 in-patients who had undergone CBT for depression. This was an Advanced Practice Nurse-led CBT group and the study looked at the patients' negative and positive thinking before and after the therapy. The thinking was measured using the Automatic Thoughts Questionnaire at the start of the therapy and again at the end. They found a significant change in both thinking, leading to more positive thinking from the start of the therapy to the end of the therapy (p=.001). This is evidence that CBT has a good effect on negative and positive thinking – though there is always the possibility that being part of research caused the difference in thinking that was measured, or being part of a group in therapy might have helped rather than the therapy itself.

Explanation

Learned helplessness has been studied using animals. Animals that receive a shock when they move to a certain spot learn to avoid that place even when the shock no longer occurs. They have learned that they were helpless to avoid the shock and that learning remains. The theory says that people show helplessness following learning even after the unpleasant response to their behaviour has stopped. Also there can be generalisation from one learning experience to other situations.

Explore

You can learn more about learned helplessness at the following links:

http://study.com/academy/lesson/how-seligmans-learned-helplessness-theory-applies-to-human-depression-and-stress.html

www.youtube.com/watch?v=gFmFOmprTt0

Year One link: Learned helplessness links to classical conditioning where an association is made between a stimulus and a response. Usually there would be extinction if the pairing no longer happens; perhaps learned helplessness is when that extinction has not taken place. You looked at classical conditioning in learning theories.

There are three aspects of Beck's cognitive model of depression:

- the **cognitive triad** – a negative view of self, the world and the future
- cognitive errors – faulty thinking, along with negative and unrealistic ideas
- schemata – patterns of maladaptive thoughts and beliefs.

Definition
Cognitive triad refers to a negative view of three issues – of the self, the world and the future.

Progress check 1.38
Explain the importance of the cognitive triad in explaining depression.

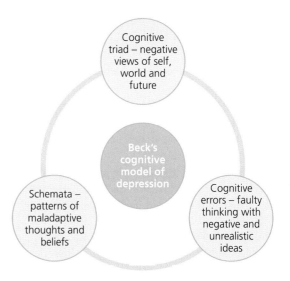

Beck's cognitive model of depression

In people with depression, it was found that the cognitive triad involves the person having negative thoughts about themselves (feeling inadequate and unworthy), about the world (feeling defeated or deprived) and about the future (believing that the suffering will continue).

The main issue concerns how an individual assigns meaning to an event. Genetic factors and early experiences affect thinking and schemata are built up from interactions and experiences. Through such experiences beliefs are built up and these beliefs set up assumptions about the world. A person will adhere to their core beliefs and operate according to the principle that *if* they do this *then* that will happen. This sort of thinking can involve **negative automatic thoughts**.

Explanation
Negative automatic thoughts are automatic because they come from core beliefs from experiences; they are distorted because they do not fit the facts; they are unhelpful because they are hard to change and lead to unwanted feelings; and they are plausible and accepted as facts.

Explore
To find out more about CBT, look at the Beck Institute for Cognitive Behaviour Therapy at the following link:
www.beckinstitute.org/history-of-cbt/

Schemata are built up through experiences of the world and involve developing positive and negative beliefs and attitudes to interpret the world. A generalised negative belief pattern will make someone vulnerable to depression. Clark and Beck (1999) explained that the negative belief pattern involves schemata about thinking, emotions, motivations and behaviour. The way to overcome depression, according to the cognitive model, is to change maladaptive interpretations by considering alternative thoughts and interpretations of events. If evidence is presented that there are other interpretations, an individual can change their cognitions.

Definition
Schemata (or schemas) are ways of seeing and understanding the world that come from experiences of the world. Schemata are organised patterns of not only information but of relationships as well. They involve a structure of ideas and a framework for representing the world.

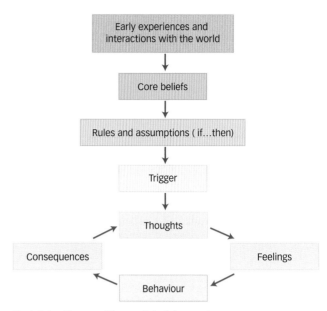

Explaining the cognitive model of depression

The likely schemata of a depressed person include:
- cognitive schemata that lead to seeing actual or threatened loss
- affective (emotions) schemata leading to sadness
- physiological (biological) schemata that make someone feel tired and unable to do things
- motivational schemata that lead to helplessness and lack of direction
- behavioural schemata that lead to withdrawal and inactivity.

Progress check 1.39
Explain what 'schemata' are (with regard to information processing) and relate them to how cognitive ideas can explain depression.

Evidence for the cognitive model for depression and for CBT

The cognitive model for depression led to focusing on cognition in therapy and to CBT. Evaluating CBT as a therapy therefore can help when evaluating the cognitive model. If someone is helped by focusing on cognition in therapy and on issues around schemata and negative automatic thoughts, then it is tempting to say that those negative thoughts 'cause' the depression.

STUDY HINT
One of the treatments for depression covered in this section is CBT. You can use the material in this section about the cognitive model for depression to help your understanding of CBT. You can also use what is said later in this section about CBT to help you understand and evaluate the cognitive model for depression.

- Hollon *et al.* (2002) reported on many attempts to evaluate CBT and found that it performed well in controlled trials. It appears that CBT helps for at least as long as drug treatment.
- Bothwell and Scott (1997) found that faulty thinking and errors in cognitive processing – especially with regard to needing approval and having low self-esteem – linked with the symptoms of depression continuing after hospital care.
- Watkins and Baracaia (2002) found that knowing more about mental processes helped to reduce relapse in those with depression and helped to stop them going over thinking in their heads and constantly problem solving (ruminating).
- Teichman *et al.* (2002) looked at relationships between self-concept, hostility between self and partner, a partner's level of depression, involvement in house activities and how severe depression was. They found that self-concept was the most marked link with the severity of the depression. As self-concept involves how people see themselves and what they think about themselves in relation to the outside world, this is evidence for the cognitive model of depression.
- Strunk and Adler (2009) focused on cognitive therapy for depression and on the negative thoughts of someone with depression. Their study focused on predictions of those with depression about their future life events, how they would be rated by someone who knew them and how they would do on a vocabulary test. They used 85 participants, who made the predictions in the three chosen areas (about the future, their self-esteem and their cognitive ability). The participants had a wide range of levels of depression. Strunk and Adler (2009) found that in all three judgements how optimistic or pessimistic someone was depended on their symptoms of depression. The participants who had the highest levels of symptoms of depression were more pessimistic on all three tasks. It was not that the judgements were more or less accurate, but they showed pessimism whether that pessimism was justified or not. These findings support the cognitive model of depression.

Brain functioning related to the cognitive model of depression

The cognitive model of depression is separate from the monoamine hypothesis and ideas about how depression and biology link. That is because in the cognitive model thinking is focused on and addressed. You will have seen in your study of cognitive psychology that thinking is not separate from brain functioning. Studies of patients with brain damage show how brain damage relates to memory, for example, which is about information processing in the brain. Negative automatic thoughts are about information processing in the brain. Research has looked at how brain functioning might underpin the cognitive model, to help in evaluating the model. A model has perhaps more strength if it can be explained by reference to biological processing.

Disner *et al.* (2011) is a review of neural mechanisms in the cognitive model of depression, focusing on Beck's ideas about bias in processing, thoughts, schemata and attention being important in depression. The researchers are Disner, Beevers, Haigh and Aaron Beck – note that Beck continues to work in the area of depression, as this study shows. Disner *et al.* (2011) conclude that there is different brain functioning in different brain structures for the different processes considered, such as memory, attention and so on. However, they conclude that emotion processing regions in the brain combined with cognitive control mechanisms underlie the model.

Disner *et al.* suggest that the emotion areas of the brain are where depression starts, with the cortical areas maintaining the depression because of thoughts and the way cognitive control takes place. They say that people with mood disturbance (issues at the subcortical emotional level) attend to sad stimuli, which is not the case for others. They mention the prefrontal cortex is where decision-making and attention to stimuli takes place. Areas like the ventrolateral prefrontal cortex and the dorsolateral prefrontal cortex are where top-down processing takes place (decision-making about what to focus on and what stimuli to select).

Year One link: Use what you learned about brain structure and function in biological psychology to help you understand the role of the prefrontal cortex in depression (or more precisely, differences in the brain and functioning between someone with and without depression).

The diagram opposite shows the importance of schemas, as Beck's cognitive model emphasised, and also a role for environmental triggers and vulnerability factors. There is also emphasis on emotional stimuli as well as processing in the brain, including attention and memory features of processing.

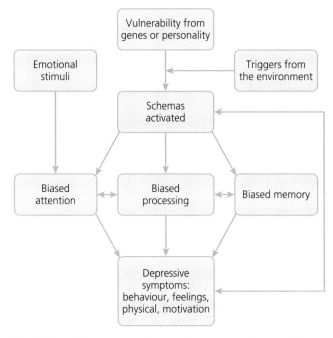

How information processing features in the cognitive model of depression. Source: Disner *et al.* (2011)

The role of emotions, areas of the brain and depression

In those with depression who are processing negative stimuli there is about 70 per cent more intense activity in the amygdala, which lasts about three times longer than in healthy controls (e.g. Siegle *et al.*, 2002, cited in Disner *et al.*, 2011). This increased amygdala activity seems to be automatic. Antidepressant medication seems to decrease the amount of amygdala activity in response to negative stimuli (e.g. Anand *et al.*, 2007, cited in Disner *et al.*, 2011). If stimuli trigger this sort of reaction, this is said to be **bottom–up processing**, because the processing comes from sense data from the environment, not from thought processes in the brain. The idea is that such bottom-up processing signals cause bias in **top-down processing**, which is about thoughts generated internally. Other issues might involve, for example, connection problems between the thalamus and the dorsal anterior cingulate cortex – messages might be re-routed via the emotional part of the cingulate cortex. There is much more to such functioning and what is known about it; these ideas are just examples of the sorts of processing issues that might underpin the claims of the cognitive model of depression. There are other examples in the review by Disner *et al.* (2011), such as how, in healthy people, processing of happy faces takes place in the right fusiform gyrus but as depressive symptoms increase this activity reduces. Depression is perhaps not about negative thinking so much as about reduction in positive thinking.

Explanation

In psychology, '**bottom-up**' refers to behaviour or individual components that generate or explain a theory or idea, and which leads to more complex cognitive processing. '**Top-down**' refers to moving from complex processing or a theory or idea, to explain behaviour and the individual components.

Explore

You can find out more about Disner *et al.*'s (2011) review of neural mechanisms of the cognitive model of depression (briefly described above) using the link below.
www-psych.nmsu.edu/~jkroger/lab/
COURSES/375/2011%20%20Disner%20-%20Neural%20
mechanisms%20of%20the%20cognitive%20model%20
of%20depression.pdf

Evaluation of the cognitive model of depression

Strengths

- Cognitive vulnerability models, such as Beck's, that look at maladaptive schemas with ideas about helplessness have been supported by the evidence. Jacobs *et al.* (2008) summarise research about there being a cognitive role in depression in young people and show many studies supporting this idea. For example, they cite Kistner *et al.* (2006), who studied 667 children/young people and found that inaccurate self-perceptions led to increased symptoms for depression and also that more symptoms led to more inaccuracy in self-perceptions. Jacobs *et al.* (2008) also cited Gibb *et al.* (2006), who looked at 448 children aged 9 to 11 and found that depression predicted a change in score on the CASQ (Children's Attributional Style Questionnaire). Jacobs *et al.* (2008) say that of the 14 studies they looked at, 8 showed that negative self-perception links to depression symptoms.
- Alloy and Abramson (1999) undertook a longitudinal study of those with depression to evaluate Beck's schema theory and the idea of hopelessness. Some college students were identified as having negative self-schemata. The researchers found that students with negative thought patterns were more at risk from depression, so this study was taken as evidence for the cognitive model – that modes of thinking can cause depression.
- The cognitive model takes into account genes, early experiences and learning and suggests that developmental issues can lead to certain thinking patterns and core beliefs that predispose someone to depression. There is also biological evidence backing up the claims of the cognitive model (see Disner *et al.*, 2011), again adding evidence for the model.

Weaknesses

- It is hard to find evidence for the cognitive model's claim that negative thinking actually causes depression, rather than simply being present in those with depression. Negative thinking seems to disappear when the depression stops, which might suggest that faulty thinking comes with depression rather than being a cause of it.
- It is difficult to distinguish between thinking which *causes* depression and thinking *caused by* depression. The same issue arises with a neurochemical explanation, because depressed thoughts are likely to alter brain chemistry – or brain chemistry could cause depressed thoughts. It is hard, if not impossible, to test which came first.

Two treatments for unipolar depression

Treatment for depression tends to be carried out in the community, though patients can be hospitalised if they are a risk to themselves or pose a risk to others. The use of psychotherapy and antidepressant drugs is common. You need to study two treatments – one must be have a biological basis and the other must be 'non-biological'. In this section biological (drug) treatment and psychotherapy using CBT are the two treatments considered. 'Psychotherapy' refers to therapies and treatments that are psychological in nature as opposed to 'medical' treatments. Psychotherapy covers more than CBT – it also covers person-centred approaches and any therapy where someone talks with another person is covered under the wide term 'psychotherapy'.

Drug treatment

Antidepressants are used to treat depression. They work on the principle that since low levels of serotonin can cause depression, increasing serotonin levels will help. Drugs such as Prozac work in this way. However, the fact that Prozac seems to improve depression does not prove that low levels of serotonin are the cause (see weaknesses of the monoamine hypothesis, page 60). It has also been found that while serotonin levels are quickly raised by drug treatment, improvement in the symptoms of depression may not follow for weeks, which suggests it might be more than low serotonin levels that explain depression.

There are four types of drugs used in treating depression.

- **Selective serotonin reuptake inhibitors (SSRIs).** Examples include fluoxetine (Prozac), sertraline (Zoloft), paroxetine (Paxil) and citalopram (Celexa) – brand names are shown in brackets. SSRIs seem to have less severe side-effects than tricylic or MAOIs.
- Tricyclic antidepressants (older type of drugs) inhibit reuptake of serotonin and norepinephrine and to an extent dopamine. They tend to cause more side-effects, so SSRIs and atypical drugs tend to be prescribed first. Examples of tricyclic antidepressants include amitriptyline (Elavil), clomipramine (Anafranil) and imipramine (Tofranil).
- **Atypical antidepressants** are new drugs which also target other neurotransmitters like norepinephrine and dopamine as well as serotonin. Atypical antidepressants include bupropion (Wellbutrin) and trazodone (Desyrel). Trazadone, cymbalta and remeron affect norepinephrine and serotonin and may be called serotonin norepinephrine reuptake inhibitors (SNRIs).
- **Monoamine oxidase inhibitors (MAOIs)** are a fourth type of antidepressant drug and the oldest. All these drugs have side-effects because neurotransmitters play many roles. Serotonin, for example, is involved in many aspects of physiological function. MAOIs must not be combined with SSRIs as this can lead to serotonin syndrome. Combining MAOIs with certain food and drink can also be a problem. Restricted foods include

cheese and chocolate. Examples of MAOIs include phenelzine (Nardil) and tranylcypromine (Parnate).

Definition

Selective serotonin reuptake inhibitors (SSRIs) are drugs to help with depression that prevent the reuptake of serotonin in the presynaptic neuron. It may be the reuptake that means not enough serotonin is in the synapse to be picked up by the postsynaptic receptor so preventing the reuptake is a way of improving mood.

STUDY HINT

For revision learn the names and action of some antidepressants, including their side-effects, so that you can add depth to any answer.

Progress check 1.41

List the four types of drugs used for depression.

Definitions

Monoamine oxidase inhibitors (MAOIs) are drugs that help to prevent depression and can also treat Parkinson's disease. They inhibit activity of monoamine oxidase enzymes.

Atypical antidepressants are newer drugs which target serotonin as well as other neurotransmitters such as norepinephrine and dopamine.

Side-effects of antidepressants

- SSRIs: nausea, insomnia, anxiety, dizziness, weight change, headaches and fatigue. They can also increase suicidal thoughts and suicidal behaviour and can increase hostility. In older people they can increase the risk of falling and getting fractures and they cause serious side-effects if someone suddenly stops taking them.
- Atypical antidepressants – nausea, fatigue, weight gain, nervousness, blurred vision and dry mouth. Bupropion (Wellbutrin) causes fewer side-effects and can give more energy than other antidepressants.
- Tricyclic antidepressants and MAOIs have more severe side-effects so are only used as a last resort if the others do not work. Side-effects include weight gain, dry mouth, blurred vision, increased heart rate and disorientation.
- MAOIs have side-effects including insomnia, weight gain, headaches and dizziness.

Withdrawal of antidepressants

Treatment with antidepressants has to be withdrawn gradually to avoid **withdrawal symptoms**, including anxiety, dizziness, insomnia, stomach upsets, flu-like symptoms and vivid dreaming. These withdrawal symptoms are called antidepressant discontinuation syndrome and are not the same as withdrawing from a drug that is addictive. The withdrawal symptoms arise from the changes in neurotransmitter functioning that occur when the drug is no longer taken.

Explanation

Withdrawal: the symptoms that occur when someone stops taking a drug they have been using.

Withdrawal symptoms occur when someone stops taking an antidepressant. For example, if serotonin levels suddenly slow, the body is likely to respond with symptoms caused by the drop in levels. There are likely to be both physical and emotional symptoms.

Explore

The Royal College of Psychiatrists has produced a leaflet about withdrawal from antidepressants which gives useful information. Take a look using the following link:
www.rcpsych.ac.uk/healthadvice/treatmentswellbeing/antidepressants/comingoffantidepressants.aspx

---

Evidence for drug treatment as the 'best' treatment for depression

- In 2005 the World Health Organization (WHO) published a report on the most effective way of diagnosing and treating depression, which stated drugs are 'well-documented treatments' for depression (as is psychotherapy) and seeming to back the use of medication at least to an extent. The report points to a 'large number of studies' that show that antidepressants are effective for severe depression in adults although it adds that the goal should be complete remission (from depression) and to achieve that, other interventions are needed. The report claims that no matter what therapy is chosen first, about one third of patients will not respond to it or will not tolerate it, so this is evidence that even if medication can be useful, it should not be the only treatment.
- The WHO report (2005) gives conclusions about specific drugs and considers amitriptyline as less well tolerated than other tricyclics and SSRIs, even though it is effective. This evidence came from a meta-analysis, Barbui *et al.* (2003), which showed that SSRIs seemed to be better than tricyclics even though tricyclic antidepressants are still prescribed a lot in the US and in Europe.

- Geddes *et al.* (2003), cited in the WHO report (2005), carried out a review and found that using drug treatment for depression showed a relapse rate of 18 per cent compared with 41 per cent for a placebo group. Also the treatment seemed to last up to three years. This seems to support the claim that drug therapy is effective.

Evidence against drug therapy as the 'best' treatment for depression

- An article in *Psychology Today* discusses the effectiveness of drug therapy for depression (Muller, 2013). The article says that such medication is worth $300 million to the industry. Muller is critical of the way drugs for depression are prescribed without sufficient attention to the individual's past history, which might show clear reasons for depression and anxiety, with the implication that those reasons could be treated using psychotherapy. It is suggested that the idea of depression coming from a chemical imbalance might not be the only theory. If the explanation for depression is chemical imbalance, it makes sense that correcting the imbalance is the first treatment to be considered, but this does not mean it is the best or only treatment.
- Muller cites a study done in the Netherlands where 222 patients had their symptoms examined over ten years. It was found that 76 per cent of those who had not received medication recovered and, importantly, did not relapse, compared with 50 per cent who recovered without relapse having taken medication.
- The WHO report (2005) says that 5–10 per cent of the population in Western Europe is affected by major depression. The report suggests that effective strategies for managing depression include clinical education as well as nurse care management and integration between primary and specialist health care. These ideas are similar to those that led to the idea of ACT for schizophrenia (page 52). Vallentine *et al.* (2010) found that psycho-education helped offender patients in understanding their disorder, in a study related to schizophrenia, but still showing the value of education.
- Caporino and Karver (2012) carried out a study to see what treatments for depression were acceptable to adolescent girls. They asked the girls to rate four individual treatments (CBT, interpersonal therapy, family therapy and drug therapy) and three treatment combinations. They found that psychotherapy (non-drug treatment) was more acceptable to the girls than combining psychotherapy and pharmacotherapy (drug treatment), with drug treatment on its own not being seen as acceptable. This suggests that even if drug therapy is seen as effective, it might not be seen as acceptable. However, only adolescent girls featured in the study so perhaps the findings cannot be generalised to the rest of the population.

Explore
The World Health Organization (2005) report on the most effective way of diagnosing and treating depression can be accessed at the link below if you would like to read more about this.
www.euro.who.int/__data/assets/pdf_file/0003/74676/E86602.pdf

Progress check 1.42
Give one piece of evidence that shows the effectiveness of drug therapy and one piece of evidence that suggests drugs are not always effective.

Comparison of drug treatment and group-based CBT as a treatment for depression

A 2008 study (Kuyken *et al.*) reported that a group-based form of CBT (mindfulness-based cognitive therapy – MBCT) is at least as successful in treating depression as medication like Prozac, even in the long term. MBCT was found to be better at preventing relapse, offered a more effective change in quality of life and was more cost effective.

The aim of the study (which was carried out by British researchers from Exeter and London universities) was to compare the effectiveness of treatments for depression. It looked at 123 people who had had repeated episodes of clinical depression. The participants were randomly placed in one of two groups. One group carried on with their antidepressant treatment and the other group took part in the MBCT course. The MBCT group was given the choice of whether to stop their medication or not. As explained in the section on the cognitive model for depression earlier in this chapter (page 63), MBCT targets negative thinking.

There was an 8-week trial and groups of between 8 and 15 people from the MBCT group attended meetings with a therapist. Group exercises were based on Buddhist meditation techniques and members of the group were taught to focus on the present rather than the past, for example. Many reported greater control over their negative thinking following the group meetings. Over the 15 months after the trial ended, about 47 per cent of the MBCT group had a relapse. However, those who continued the antidepressant treatment without the MBCT had a 60 per cent relapse rate. The MBCT group reported a much better quality of life.

The researchers thought that MBCT had given the participants skills for life, whereas medication did not. This is evidence against the use of drug therapy. Note, however, that some of the MBCT group may have continued with their drug treatment at the same time.

Evaluation of drug treatment for depression

Strengths

- Antidepressants can be prescribed to boost mood so that other therapies like CBT can be used. Although it takes a few weeks for antidepressants to work, this may be necessary where mood is too depressed for an individual to focus on making a change in their thinking.
- Researchers continue to seek more effective antidepressants with fewer side-effects. Atypical antidepressants, for example, have fewer side-effects than the 'old' tricyclic antidepressants.
- There is theoretical evidence to back the use of antidepressants, in particular the newer ones that address not only low serotonin levels but also levels of norepinephrine (noradrenaline) and dopamine.

Weaknesses

- A government study (2006) showed that fewer than 50 per cent of those with depression who take antidepressants become symptom free. Many relapse into depression again even if they keep taking the medication.
- Antidepressants ease symptoms but are not seen as a cure for depression. It is suggested that therapy works just as well and is more likely to prevent relapse. CBT involves the client learning their triggers for depressive episodes and in acquiring the tools to combat such episodes, so it is likely to be better at preventing relapse.

> **STUDY HINT**
> This section looks at drug therapy and CBT as treatments for depression. You can often use evidence for the effectiveness of one as evidence against the use of the other.

Non-biological treatment: cognitive-behavioural therapy (CBT)

> **Explore**
> Use the link below to read a report about use of CBT in depression and related areas. Table 1 on p.376 of the report shows NICE recommendations for the psychological treatment of depression and anxiety disorders. It also shows how CBT is recognised as a treatment in these areas.
> www.iapt.nhs.uk/silo/files/clark-2011-implementing-nice-guidelines-the-iapt-experience.pdf

Cognitive-behavioural therapy (CBT) comes under the umbrella term of '**psychotherapy**'. CBT is an evidence-based therapy. In the UK CBT is funded by the government because studies have shown its effectiveness.

You have already looked at the use of CBT as a therapy for schizophrenia (page 48) and you can use the basic ideas mentioned in that section when considering it as a therapy for depression here.

Definition

Psychotherapy is a broad term for counselling, psychodynamic therapy and other similar forms of therapy.

CBT developed from Beck's cognitive model of depression (page 49). Faulty thinking patterns, including negative automatic thoughts, are regarded as arising from schemata that are built through early experiences. Depression can be treated by helping the individual to focus on their negative automatic thoughts and then to consider new ways of thinking. From a list of possible faulty ways of thinking, the client is encouraged to consider which, if any, apply to them. The CBT practitioner then offers a number of different tools to help cope with negative automatic thoughts, including identifying the triggers for these thoughts so that the cycle can be broken.

The cognitive model suggests some thinking patterns that are found in those who are depressed:

- all-or-nothing thinking – something that goes wrong is taken to indicate that everything will always be wrong
- catastrophising – a single negative event is blown up into the precursor of disaster
- crystal ball thinking – guessing negatively what someone else will do or say or what will happen
- over-generalisation – for example, loneliness means that you are disliked
- negative mental filter – the negative aspects of a situation are focused upon, while positive ones are 'filtered out'
- disqualifying the positive – when someone gives a compliment and it is brushed to one side
- jumping to conclusions – when something unwanted happens the individual concludes they are worthless or have something wrong with them, rather than seeking another explanation
- magnification and minimisation – exaggeration of the importance of minor problems
- emotional reasoning – a job like cleaning up the house seems overwhelming and hopeless
- 'should' statements – thinking other people should do things and getting worked up about it
- labelling and mislabelling – such as breaking a diet once and thereafter labelling oneself a failure or 'fat pig'
- personalisation – blaming oneself for things that are beyond our control.

Explore
You will find lots of information about CBT on the internet. Here is a link that includes more about the downward arrow technique:

https://understandingcbt.wordpress.com/tag/downward-arrow-technique/

How CBT works in practice

A CBT therapist usually enters into a contract to see a client for about six sessions, with each session lasting around 50 minutes. A review would then take place. The first session involves contracting and setting the scene about what is expected. For example, ethical issues such as confidentiality and privacy will be discussed, as well as other issues such as the client having to do homework to help themselves to overcome any thinking they feel is faulty.

In each session, an agenda is set with the client so that they decide what issues they would like to raise. Those issues are then focused on. At first the client talks about themselves so that their **frame of reference** can be understood by the therapist. It is important to focus on the client's own words and meanings, as the aim is to help them to uncover their own core beliefs and thinking patterns. The therapist summarises what the client has said to check full understanding and also works with the client using CBT tools. For example, if a client repeatedly mentions their 'stupidity' in some situations, the therapist can ask what 'stupidity' means to them. David Burns (a therapist central to the development of CBT) developed what he called the **downward arrow technique**, a process by which a negative automatic thought can be investigated. The investigation might start from the thought 'I should have visited my mother at the weekend'. The therapist and client would explore this thought by asking 'if that were true, what would that mean?' The client might say 'I should care about my mother more' and then, on being asked what that would mean, might say 'I am a bad person'. By using such techniques the client and therapist can together uncover core beliefs. Once these are revealed, evidence can be found that the beliefs are not altogether true. For example, the therapist can ask the client if he/she is really a 'bad person' and find evidence that that is not the case.

Definitions

A person's **frame of reference** is their way of looking at things, including understanding their own words and how they use them. The **downward arrow technique**, developed by Burns, involves the use of taking something important for the client and examining 'what it means' to the client, drilling down until they cannot answer any more about what it means. At that stage they will have reached a core belief.

The therapist can use other tools as well, such as the list of thinking patterns given above. For example, when a client says they are a bad person for not visiting their mother they might be catastrophising (thinking that if they do not visit their mother something really bad will happen to her). Another tool is to look at self-concept. Clients are asked to talk to family and friends about their views of the client to discover elements of themselves they have not known about before, potentially improving their self-esteem.

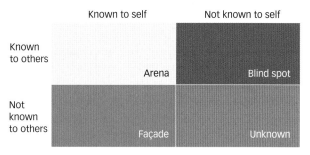

The Johari window can help people to see how to use feedback from others to know themselves better, potentially improving their self-esteem, particularly in their blindspot.

CBT for depression

The approach used for CBT suits depression (and anxiety) very well, since it focuses on negative automatic thinking, which is also a feature of depression. Information about how CBT works in general also applies when explaining how it works for depression. However, CBT for schizophrenia can be specific and different, because the characteristics for schizophrenia are often more specialised.

A study looking at CBT effectiveness: Stiles *et al.* (2006)

Stiles *et al.* (2006) carried out a study that looked at the effectiveness of CBT as compared to person-centred and psychodynamic therapies, over a three-year period in 58 NHS settings in the UK. In all, 1,309 patients who had received CBT, person-centred therapy or psychodynamic therapy were studied. The researchers used the clinical outcomes in routine evaluation – outcome measure (CORE-OM) at the beginning and end of their treatment. The therapists wrote down which therapy was used on an 'end of therapy' form. Clients were divided into six groups. Three groups were each treated with one of the three therapies (CBT, person-centred, psychodynamic) and three groups received one of these therapies and an additional treatment (such as integrative or art therapy). They found that all six groups showed marked improvement and no one group stood out as being more improved. It was concluded that theoretically different approaches tended to have equivalent outcomes, as previous studies have shown.

> **STUDY HINT**
>
> If you use Vallentine et al. (2010) as an example of interviewing in clinical psychology, you will learn more about using the CORE-OM. Stiles et al. (2006) use the same measure, which underlines the value of using standardised questionnaires in studies, so that findings can be compared.

Evaluation of Stiles et al. (2006)

There was no control group, some data were missing, the clients were not randomly allocated to the groups (the treatment was selected for them) and there was no supervision of the actual treatment. This means there are some limitations with the study.

Studies looking at CBT effectiveness for depression

Farrer et al. (2011)

Farrer et al. (2011) considered the reduction of depression in people with chronic mental health problems using internet-based CBT. This was a six-week intervention and the CBT involved weekly telephone tracking for one group but not for a control group. The participants were people calling in to a helpline service. All of the 155 callers had moderate to high distress and there was then randomisation, with some having internet CBT with phone follow-up every week, others having internet CBT only, some having the phone follow-up only and others having treatment as usual. Farrer et al. found that depression was lower for those having internet CBT (iCBT), both with and without phone follow-up, compared with treatment as usual. This finding was the case right after the treatment/intervention and also six months afterwards, when there was a follow-up collection of data. The phone support did not add any advantage to the iCBT. Farrer et al. (2011) suggest that CBT (internet based in this study) is effective for those with depression.

Williams et al. (2013)

If you choose depression as a main disorder for your course (remember, you can choose from depression, anorexia nervosa and OCD), then you must choose one of two studies that focus on depression. One of these two studies is Williams et al. (2013) (page 115), which looks at the use of internet CBT combined with an imagery-based treatment. Williams et al. found that CBT alone and when combined with an imagery-based treatment was successful. This does not show that drug therapy is unsuccessful but it does show that psychotherapy is successful.

> **STUDY HINT**
>
> One of the studies for depression in your course, Williams et al. (2013), looked at iCBT and found it to be effective. Use the material in the studies to inform your understanding of the content
>
> Farrer et al. (2011) discuss the use of randomisation into groups. You can use this study as an example of using experiments in clinical psychology as well as the features of using experiments, such as randomisation.

Hoffmann et al. (2012)

Hoffmann et al. (2012) carried out a review of meta-analyses looking at studies using CBT to summarise issues about its use. Hoffmann et al. used 269 meta-analyses of studies and used 106 of them to come to conclusions about the use of CBT. They show a long list of disorders CBT is used for, suggesting that CBT is applicable to many disorders. They found that CBT is the most effective when using with anxiety disorders, anger control and general stress, not specifically depression, though it has been found to be effective for depression. Andersson and Cuijpers (2010) found that CBT for depression was more effective than control conditions (cited in Hoffmann et al., 2012). Eleven studies looked at response rates for CBT and other treatments (or controls) and found CBT had a higher response rate than other conditions in seven of the studies, with only one of them showing CBT had a lower response rate. Hoffman et al. conclude that evidence that CBT is effective is strong, though they comment that studies had not focused on subgroups like ethnic minorities and those of low income, so that was an idea for further research.

The Beck Institute

The Beck Institute claims that in 'hundreds of clinical trials' CBT has been shown to be effective for depression as well as many other disorders.

Whitfield and Williams (2003)

Whitfield and Williams (2003) suggest that the evidence for CBT for depression has the 'strongest research base for effectiveness'.

Studies showing CBT might not be that effective

- Hoffmann et al. (2012) found some evidence that CBT was equally effective as other psychological treatments but not more effective, such as Beltman et al. (2010).
- Hoffmann et al. (2012) found that drug therapy and CBT had similar effects on depression (e.g. Corry and Andrews, 2004).
- Chan et al. (2006, cited in Hoffmann et al., 2012) found that drug therapy could be useful as an addition to CBT and a combination was more effective than just using CBT.
- Whitfield and Williams (2003) mention that specifics about how CBT should be administered in order to be successful need more focus. They say that weekly meetings are not necessarily shown to add to its effectiveness and instead self-help rather than weekly meetings might add to its effectiveness; for instance, iCBT (internet-based CBT) has been recognised as being effective (e.g. Farrer et al., 2011).

Evaluation of CBT

Strengths

- This therapy is evidence-based. Kuyken et al. (2008) suggested that a form of CBT was more effective in preventing relapse and in improving quality of life than the use of antidepressants.
- CBT is backed by government funding in the UK and is a large part of the initiative to improve access to psychological therapies (IAPT). This might be because it is fairly quick to show results and is relatively cheap to provide.

Weaknesses

- CBT depends for its efficacy on the idea that depression comes from faulty thinking, such as negative automatic thoughts. However, these might be a result of the depression, not a cause of it. Some studies have found that when depression is removed so are negative thoughts. This does not mean, however, that there is not a causal relationship between cognitive processing and depression – just that it is hard to demonstrate.
- Many of the data about the effectiveness of CBT come from self-report and such data are often said to be unreliable. The client might want to please the therapist and say that the therapy is working, for example, which would make the data invalid. Or it might depend

on how they were feeling when they completed a questionnaire, which would also make the data unreliable.
- Stiles et al. (2006) found that, in general, all psychotherapies have the same success rates in spite of their different theories and techniques. It is hard to differentiate between the end results of different therapies. Person-centred therapy focuses on the client's own frame of reference and offers them unconditional positive regard. Psychodynamic therapy allows the client to examine their early experiences and reveal what could be called core beliefs, to help them understand their thinking about themselves and to achieve a more positive self-regard.

Progress check 1.44

Explain one piece of evidence that shows CBT's effectiveness as a therapy for depression and one piece of evidence that queries its effectiveness.

Test yourself

1. Compare two treatments for depression, one biological and one non-biological. (8 marks)
2. Evaluate the neurotransmitter explanation for depression. (12 marks)

Obsessive compulsive disorder (OCD)

For your course, in addition to schizophrenia, you need to know about one other disorder from a choice of unipolar depression, obsessive compulsive disorder (OCD) and anorexia nervosa. There is useful information about diagnosis, explanations and treatment of each of these mental disorders, so you might want to read about all three before you decide which one to focus on.

For each disorder you study for your course, you need to know about symptoms and features, two explanations and two treatments. For OCD, the two explanations offered in this book are about brain areas and brain functioning (biological) and the cognitive model (non-biological). There are other explanations for OCD, such as focusing on learning theory, but the two chosen in this book match those chosen for explanations of schizophrenia and depression too. For example, brain structure as well as cognitive explanations are discussed in relation to OCD, as they were for schizophrenia and depression, which means learning about one disorder can help your learning about another. Finally, two treatments are covered. These are medication and CBT, again chosen because they match the treatments used for schizophrenia and depression.

Study of interest

Boeding et al. (2013) carried out a study looking at how a person's partner was involved in their OCD. The researchers looked at 20 couples and focused on OCD symptoms and how the couple functioned, including in their relationship and engaging in 'accommodation' of the OCD (taking the OCD symptoms into account, helping and so on). The idea came from noting how carers and family of those with OCD might help out with the rituals. The measures were taken before CBT and after 16 sessions of CBT. It was found that before treatment there was accommodation from the partner and this accommodation affected the partner's self-reported rating of their own satisfaction, with using accommodation meaning there was less satisfaction. Also a partner who helped (i.e. who showed accommodation) meant there was not such a good response to treatment either. It was possible that continuing the support and help meant less response to treatment, so fewer treatment gains or those who struggle with OCD even after treatment need partner help more. Boeding et al. (2013) suggest from their findings that involving a partner in the treatment can be beneficial.

Symptoms and features of OCD

Features of a disorder are facts and figures about it and general ideas about it. Symptoms are what people experience from the disorder. Features of OCD are considered first, then symptoms.

Features of OCD

OCD is an anxiety disorder which focuses on worry about things (**obsessions**), and reducing the anxiety related to the worry (**compulsions**). Compulsions are the tasks that people carry out to relieve their obsessive thoughts – they reduce their anxiety by using rituals and different behaviours. Obsessions are the persistent thoughts which the individual cannot get rid of even though they want to; obsessions are the focus of their anxiety, worry and fears.

People with OCD recognise the difficulties and that their behaviour is irrational. OCD is not a psychosis, more a neurosis. According to the ICD-10 (World Health Organization, 2007) key features of OCD are distressing and recurrent thoughts that are intrusive (obsessions) and compulsive behaviours.

Definitions

Obsessions in OCD are the thoughts that are persistent, irrational and unwanted.

Compulsions in OCD are the tasks that people do to relieve the obsessions, such as having an obsessional fear about contamination which leads to the compulsion of continual washing of hands.

OCD includes repeated checking, ideas about contamination, hoarding and ruminations (intrusive thinking). There are also other obsessions and compulsions – any unwanted obsessions and compulsions that have an impact on someone's quality of life come under the disorder 'OCD'.

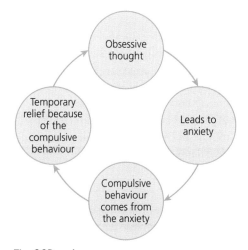

The OCD cycle

Progress check 1.45

Look at the list below and for each statement decide whether it is an obsession or a compulsion.

Statement about someone with OCD	Obsession or compulsion?
Repeatedly checking that a door is locked	
Being afraid that there will be a fire	
Collecting things even though there is no space for them	
Worrying that something is dirty and will contaminate	

OCD is thought to be the fourth most common mental illness in Western countries and affects males, females, adults and children. OCD-UK estimates that OCD affects about 1.2 per cent of the population, which suggests that over 700,000 people are living with OCD in the UK at any one time. The National Institute of Health (NIH) suggests that in the US about 1 per cent of the population over 12 months will have OCD and 50.6 per cent of the cases are severe. These figures are from Hanna et al. (2007) citing Kessler et al. (2005a, 2005b) and two studies looking at prevalence. Grohol (2005) gives some different figures, suggesting about 2.3 per cent of the US population has OCD in one year. So there are some variations in figures but OCD is clearly a prevalent disorder. Sasson et al. (1994) estimate that worldwide about 2 per cent of people have OCD. Grohol (2005) says OCD tends to start in childhood or adolescence and affects males and females equally.

STUDY HINT
For any disorder you study, be ready to discuss features as well as symptoms separately as you can be asked about them separately.

Symptoms of OCD

A diagnosis will be given when there are a lot of obsessions and compulsions that take up much of someone's time during the day, causing them distress and interfering with their daily living.

Symptoms of OCD are described below.

- Checking – this is a compulsion and tends to come from a fear that some damage or something bad will occur like a fire or some harm. Checking can include checking stoves, door locks, house lights, appliances or water taps, to avoid the feelings of fear that otherwise can predominate. Checking is often carried out over and over for hours, such as going back to see if a door is locked a great many times. This can lead someone to be late for work or affect their life in other important ways.

- Contamination – avoiding this is also a compulsion. The fear is that things are contaminated and might cause illness, either to the individual or to a family member. Contamination can be about shaking hands, touching door knobs, using public phones, eating in a restaurant or with clothes. As with checking, washing or cleaning to avoid contamination can be done over and over again, until something feels clean. To avoid contamination there can be rituals, such as repetitive hand washing. There can also be mental contamination, coming from someone else, who might make the individual feel 'like dirt' and the response is the same as for other contamination – washing or showering to 'wash the dirt away'.

- Hoarding – this is a compulsion. It is when someone finds it impossible to throw things away, even if they are broken or useless. A person can have difficulty in throwing things away, they might buy or collect things even when they have no more space left because of not throwing things away, and they might find it hard to organise things as well. Hoarding can be to prevent the harm which a person perceives might occur if they throw something away, such as hurting themselves on the object. Hoarding can be about feeling they might need the object at some stage, which can come from them being deprived at some stage in their life. There can be emotional hoarding as well, which is holding on to things that have special significance, such as when objects tend to be trusted more than people so someone develops relationships with objects (such as a teddy bear).

- Ruminations – this refers to thinking for a long time in a way that is not productive, such as dwelling on life after death or mortality. People with OCD can go over and over thoughts in their minds for a long time, weighing evidence and so on. Intrusive thoughts are when obsessional thoughts are disturbing and extremely upsetting. Such thoughts can be about religion, fear of violent thoughts or relationships.

Two explanations for OCD

You need to cover one biological and one non-biological explanation for OCD. Brain functioning and the cognitive model for OCD are covered. Cognitive explanations and brain functioning are commonly seen as causes for disorders and they underpin common treatments too.

Cognitive functioning as an explanation for OCD

OCD is characterised by obsessions, which are thoughts of fear and worry, and so a cognitive explanation is indicated. Compulsions are behaviours that help to calm the fear and worry, which suggests a learning explanation for the behaviours; however, in this section it is the cognitive rather than learning explanation that is considered. We look at the cognitive explanation first, followed by brain functioning as an explanation for OCD. This is because the cognitive explanation is supported by findings about brain functioning, so it makes sense for the cognitive explanation to be presented first in this book.

Cognitive characteristics that link to OCD are described below.

- Self-doubt (Salkovskis and Forrester, 2002, cited in Greisberg and McKay, 2003) – self-doubt might lead to repetitive actions, so can help to explain rituals found in OCD.
- Need for perfection – in a person with OCD this often means a rigid definition of success which they are constantly striving for. For example, they may not feel they have washed their hands correctly and so keep washing them. They repeat actions until they feel 'right' to them.
- Responsibility – is when someone feels they have to do more, no matter what they have done (e.g. Ladouceur et al., 2000, cited in Greisberg and McKay, 2003). They overestimate the importance of their own thoughts and actions in respect of a specific outcome; this idea of responsibility is important when using CBT for OCD (Salkovskis, 1999).

The role of external criticism in OCD

Pace et al. (2011) discuss the role of external criticism in OCD within the cognitive model. They suggest that criticism might lead to vulnerability that contributes to the development of OCD and also it might be a factor in maintaining OCD. Pace et al. (2011) carried out a review looking at external criticism and OCD. Criticism is about making a judgement and generally means an unpleasant judgement where someone is inconsiderate. Criticism is seen as a negative concept, focusing on issues such as failure. Smith and Peterson (2008, cited in Pace et al., 2011) say that criticism is a stressor and has been linked to physical and psychological problems. Criticism can be a 'critique', which might not be negative, however, generally it is perceived by the OCD sufferer as negative. This is about cognition and how others' responses are interpreted, rather than 'reality'. It is about how someone perceives judgements from others and how they might be seen as negative, or indeed as judgements when they might be just comments.

The cognitive model of OCD focuses on the role of appraisals (Salkovskis, 1985, cited in Pace et al., 2011). Distress comes from appraisals (judgements) that focus on responsibility, where someone has beliefs about being responsible for doing harm to others or to oneself. It is the personal responsibility that comes with the obsessions that brings the distress, intrusive thoughts and wish to 'neutralise' (Salkovskis et al., 1998, cited in Pace et al., 2011).

It has been shown that most people in the population have intrusive thoughts at some stage in their lives; however, the difference between intrusive thoughts and obsessions are about how often they occur, how intense they are, how distressing they are and whether they lead to misinterpretations (Salkovskis and Harrison, 1984).

Six cognitive variables in OCD

Pace et al. (2011) outline six cognitive variables in OCD:

1. Beliefs related to a high focus on responsibility
2. Over-importance of thoughts
3. Excessive focus on the importance of controlling one's thoughts
4. Overestimating threats
5. Difficulty in tolerating uncertainty
6. Requiring perfection.

The variables that link to criticism are responsibility and perfectionism. There is focus on upbringing and early experiences, because they can underpin someone's response to criticism. Self-worth and social acceptability are also of interest when it comes to criticism and its role in OCD. Also important are the compulsions, such as checking and cleaning, which are there to allay the fears and obsessions that characterise OCD. Some research has indicated that there are people with OCD who do not show the beliefs in the six domains (Taylor et al., 2006), which suggests that there are other beliefs too, not just those listed above.

Cognitive biases in OCD

Rachman (1998) suggests there are two important biases that lead to misinterpretations of thoughts which in turn lead to OCD. One bias is that thinking about something unpleasant increases the chances that it will happen and the other bias is believing that having an immoral thought is the same as behaving in an immoral way. These two biases are what make intrusive thoughts so distressing for someone with OCD; they seem to be revealing something about the self that is threatening. The two biases lead to what is called 'thought-action fusion' (TAF), which means merging the thought and the action as if they are the same and overestimating the significance of the thoughts.

Progress check 1.47

Explain thought-action fusion in relation to OCD.

Inflated sense of responsibility

Salkovskis (1999) suggested that OCD arises from having an inflated idea of one's own responsibility and that is what makes intrusions more frequent and distressing. The responsibility in question is the sufferer's idea that they are responsible for preventing harm coming to oneself and to others. This inflated sense of responsibility leads to compulsions, which are behaviours intended to put things right and to make up for the 'harm'; the compulsions reduce the distress. Salkovskis explains that the compulsions are self-fulfilling in that they reduce the distress and anxiety, but they reinforce the idea that the thoughts are doing harm and so the compulsions are repeated more often, which focuses even more attention on the thoughts.

Evidence for the cognitive model of OCD

- Tolin et al. (2006) suggest as part of the cognitive model of OCD that dysfunctional beliefs are related to OCD, including the symptoms matching the thoughts and the idea that the OCD sufferer has more obsessive compulsive cognitions than someone in the general population. OCD sufferers tend to also have anxiety and depression, which have cognitive features, but when studying OCD it is important to separate OCD from anxiety and depression as they are different disorders. However, even after controlling for anxiety and depression, it has been found that behaviour (compulsions) and cognition (obsessions) correlate in people with OCD (Stekett et al., 1998, cited in Novara et al., 2011). Stekett et al. (1998) also found that people with OCD scored higher on cognitive measures than people with anxiety disorders. Overall it was found that there was a correlation between how severe the OCD

symptoms were and the level of dysfunctional thinking a sufferer experienced. This is evidence for the cognitive model of OCD (Novara et al., 2011).

- Libby et al. (2004) looked at cognitive appraisals in 28 young people aged 11–18 years with OCD, 28 young people with anxiety disorders and 62 people without disorders. Libby et al. used the Responsibility Attitude Scale to look for raised responsibility thinking, the Thought-Action Fusion Scale to look at how thought and action linked and the Multidimensional Perfectionism Scale to look at perfectionism. They found that those with OCD had higher scores than the other two groups regarding raised responsibility as well as thought-action linking. They also had higher scores on concern over mistakes, which is an aspect of perfectionism. Libby et al. also found that inflated responsibility predicted severity of OCD symptoms (higher feelings of responsibility gave more severe symptoms).
- Frost and Steketee (2002) say that there is a lot of evidence for cognitive-behavioural models of OCD and a strength is that the cognitive-behavioural model has led to effective treatments.

Evidence against the cognitive model for OCD

- Abramowitz et al. (2005) suggests that for 'the average' OCD patient cognitive therapy does not help any more than **exposure and response prevention** (**ERP**), which is not a cognitive therapy as such. Masellis et al. (2003) discuss ERP and therapy effectiveness for OCD (page 129). ERP is based on flooding, which means someone faces their anxiety and intrusive thoughts and sticks with them, which can help to alleviate the worry without using the compulsions. This is evidence against the cognitive explanation for OCD because if cognitive therapy is not the most effective that might suggest that the cognitive explanation is not the only explanation or not a useful explanation for OCD.
- Foa et al. (2005, cited in Abramowitz et al., 2005) found that ERP is more effective than a pill placebo and is at least as good as or better than drug therapies (such as clomipramine) for OCD. Abramowitz et al., however, take time in their review to explain that ERP overlaps with cognitive treatments and should not be seen as purely behavioural. Not only does CBT involve behavioural ideas such as exposure (for example, not locking the door more than three times and being made to experience the anxiety), but ERP involves cognitive ideas too, such as discussion about dysfunctional beliefs. It can perhaps be said, therefore, that a cognitive explanation for OCD is insufficient rather than wrong.

- Mowrer (1960) suggested that obsessions and compulsions develop through association with something. For example, if someone does something they are punished for (such as playing with mud outside), they may associate the fear of punishment with being dirty so they would feel better (and have their behaviour reinforced) if they stay clean. Rituals can help to avoid the learned fear (such as ritualistic washing). Rachman (1985) developed ERP (page 86), which involves training a person to experience a different response to their obsession. ERP works for people with OCD, so this is evidence for a learning theory model of OCD and evidence against the cognitive explanation (because although thoughts are still involved, they are not the *explanation* for the OCD symptoms).

Explanation

Exposure and response prevention (ERP) is a therapy for anxiety that is used for OCD, where the patient faces their fears (such as not washing their hands after touching what they think is contaminated) and experiences the fear until it subsides. The patient is encouraged to avoid carrying out the response that is a ritual for them.

Year One link: Flooding is based on learning principles. If someone is immersed in something they fear, in the end their body will not be able to maintain the alarm reaction and the person will feel as if they are calming down. They can, therefore, learn a calm response to what they fear and this can work with fearful thoughts too. You may have learned about flooding as a treatment for phobias when you covered learning theories.

Progress check 1.48

Give two pieces of evidence for the cognitive model of OCD and two pieces of evidence against it.

Biological evidence for the cognitive model of OCD

- Greisberg and McKay (2003) reviewed what is known about OCD and neurophysiology. They suggest a difficulty in executive functioning and decision-making, including memory deficits, in those with OCD. Memory problems are most noticeable in tests when organisation is needed. Specific brain areas that have been suggested include the frontal lobes linked to executive functioning and decision-making (Lezak, 1995, cited in Greisberg and McKay, 2003). One idea is that because those with OCD recognise that there is no rational reason for the compulsions, it might relate to a problem with cognitive control. Doubting (another symptom of OCD) may not only be about decision-making difficulties but also due to encoding difficulties, perhaps around not identifying which information needs to be stored (Christensen *et al.*, 1992, cited in Greisberg and McKay, 2003).

- Greisberg and McKay report, however, that studies do not consistently find problems in frontal lobe functioning or memory. Christensen *et al.* (1992, cited in Greisberg and McKay, 2003) assessed 18 patients with OCD (without depression) and matched controls for different types of memory and for executive functioning. They found that there was some difference for non-verbal memory and those with OCD did not do so well when speed was required for the processing task. Importantly those with OCD had less confidence in their answers. There were some differences but not in all types of memory.

- Martinot *et al.* (1990, cited in Greisberg and McKay, 2003) looked at 16 patients with OCD and 8 controls. They used PET scanning and found that those with OCD took significantly longer to do tasks such as counting backwards or giving the days of the week in reverse order and made more errors. Martinot *et al.* (1990) found more functioning in the left cortex in the OCD patients when they were doing a Stroop test. The Stroop test is a mental task where someone has to read out the colour ink a word is written in when the word is a 'colour' word, such as the word 'blue' written in red ink. Those with OCD found the Stroop test more difficult and they also showed more frontal cortex activity so it seems that performance difficulties in that area are linked to the problems with functioning that were found.

Explore

You could try carrying out a Stroop test yourself, perhaps using just yourself and friends as participants - remember to adhere to good ethics.

1 Write out a list of 'colour' words, perhaps five words repeated four times randomly, so a list of 20 words. Write them out in the same colour ink as the meaning of the word ('red' in red ink and so on).

2 Using exactly the same list write the words out in the 'wrong' colour ink (use random colours).

3 Read the colour ink of the 20 words out loud and time how long it takes. Counterbalance who does the condition where the colour words are in the 'right' colour ink and the other condition. It should take quite a bit longer (in seconds) to read out the 'wrong' colour ink. Explore more to find out why that is.

The Stroop test is often used when looking at disorders and you could explore more about that too. Henik and Salo (2004) wrote about the Stroop test and schizophrenia - use the following link to find out more:

http://ucdirc.ucdavis.edu/people/papers/henik_salo_BCNR2004.pdf

The information above provides some evidence to show that a biological explanation for OCD and a cognitive explanation for OCD may not be separate, although they have a different focus, with one looking at how the brain functions and the other explanation looking at thinking patterns related to how a person functions. The evidence presented here should show that brain functioning underpins cognitive functioning and that the cognitive model of OCD can be supported by biological evidence. An example is that the cognitive model involves executive functioning and cognitive control, which occurs in the prefrontal lobe.

Evaluation of the cognitive model of OCD

Strengths

- The biological evidence seems to point to issues with decision-making, executive functioning and memory and shows differences for those with OCD compared with controls. This biological evidence can be used as evidence for the claims of the cognitive model for OCD, such as how compulsions are seen as senseless by the person with OCD and yet they still carry them out. The cause of compulsions does seem to be a problem with control over cognitions and with decision-making. Biological evidence supports the cognitive model.
- If a therapy based on an explanation is successful that can provide support for the explanation. CBT is successful as a therapy for OCD (van Oppen et al. 1995, cited in Abramowitz et al., 2005, found ERP and CBT to be equally effective) and works on the idea that thoughts guide feelings, which lead to behaviour, which reinforces the thoughts, as Salkovskis suggests when discussing the role of responsibility in OCD.
- It could be argued that the cognitive model for OCD gives power to the patient when working to overcome their OCD. The individual can work to change their intrusive thoughts, for example, by changing their behaviour and this is in their power. Someone can stick with their anxiety and stop themselves from locking the door more than, say, three times, and gradually they may move away from the intrusive thoughts that harm might happen. When a successful therapy comes from an explanation that is a strength for that explanation.

Issues and debates

You can use the idea of giving power to a patient as being a strength of a therapy when discussing the issue and debate about social control.

Weaknesses

- If symptoms of OCD are cognitive in nature, such as anxious and self-doubting thoughts and ideas about perfection, then using a cognitive model to explain OCD is in a way just repeating these symptoms. Explaining the symptoms using features of the brain seems a better explanation; perhaps the cognitive model is more of a description and so less useful.
- ERP, which is a therapy largely based on learning principles, is found to be just as effective as cognitive therapy (CT) or CBT according to Abramowitz et al. (2005), which goes against cognitive explanations for OCD. McLean et al. (2001) and Vogel et al. (2004), according to Abramowitz et al. (2005), found ERP seemed to be more effective than CBT.
- There is conflicting evidence about whether ERP, CT or CBT is the most effective therapy for certain symptoms in OCD. For example, though some studies show ERP to be more effective than CBT, van Oppen et al. (1995, cited in Abramowitz et al., 2005) found ERP and CBT to be equally effective. Looking at specific symptoms there are differences in treatments and their effectiveness, though no definite finding that cognitive treatment is better for cognitive symptoms. For example, the strength of dysfunctional beliefs does not predict that CBT is better than ERP as an effective treatment. Sometimes CBT helps patients who have difficulty accepting their ideas make no sense (overvalued ideation) and sometimes it does not (e.g. Taylor et al., 2003). However, compulsive hoarding might be better treated by CBT and ERP according to Steketee and Frost (2003, cited in Abramowitz et al., 2005).
- If the cognitive model for OCD is useful, then treatments based on it would perhaps be the most useful, and sometimes they are, but there is evidence that this is not always the case. This suggests the cognitive model is not sufficient as an explanation of OCD. Another important point is that ERP focuses on changing behaviour and CBT and CT focus on changing dysfunctional beliefs, but in OCD of course the behaviour and the beliefs are linked, suggesting that the cognitive model is helpful as an explanation but must draw in behavioural explanations too.

Progress check 1.49

It is argued that a strength of an explanation is that a successful therapy arises from the explanation and a weakness of an explanation is that the therapy arising from it is not the most successful. Explain this argument in relation to the cognitive explanation for OCD.

Brain functioning as an explanation for OCD

Brain structure and functioning that supports the cognitive model for OCD has been briefly mentioned above in terms of memory deficits, for example. However, evidence is contradictory and while some OCD sufferers show abnormal brain structures, others do not (e.g. Riffkin *et al.,* 2005). It is possible that problems with brain functioning might come from OCD, rather than be a cause of OCD. These are the issues discussed here when looking at a biological explanation for OCD. It has been found that neurotransmitter levels are different in OCD, with OCD linking to lower levels of serotonin. However, in the biological explanation given here, we will look at brain activity and brain structure as an explanation for OCD.

Changes in brain activity

Brain scans have shown that people with OCD seem to show more activity in three brain areas: the basal ganglia, the prefrontal orbital cortex and the cingulate gyrus.

- Specific cells in the basal ganglia, the caudate nucleus, seem to show different levels of activity in those with OCD and this area filters thoughts from other areas. The area is important in managing repetitive behaviours, so drug therapy for OCD decreases activity in this area. This provides evidence that activity in this area is important for OCD.
- The prefrontal orbital cortex is implicated in OCD. Decisions about appropriate social behaviour occur in this brain area in the front of the brain and less activity in this area (or damage) leads to feelings of being uninhibited, having lack of guilt and making bad judgements. If there is more activity in the prefrontal cortex this leads to worry and concerns, such as about being neat and clean and fears about acting inappropriately.
- The cingulate gyrus is the third area to show differences in brain activity in those with OCD. This area is associated with emotional responses and is where compulsions (activities to relieve the worry) arise.

The cingulate gyrus, basal ganglia and prefrontal cortex are strongly linked in the brain and have many cells affected by serotonin, which is interesting given the link to low levels of serotonin and OCD.

Other brain areas that might be involved in OCD are the striatum, thalamus and anterior cingulate cortex. The circuit between the areas shown in the following illustration (the striatum, thalamus and anterior cingulate cortex and the prefrontal orbital cortex, basal ganglia and cingulate gyrus) is thought to relate to primitive behaviour. It triggers behaviour like hand washing, because of links to aggression, sexuality and bodily excretions. It is thought that the brain in those with OCD might not easily ignore urges from the circuit.

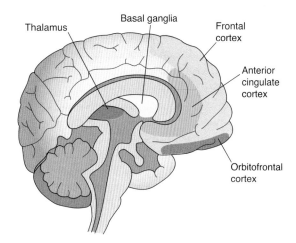

The circuit linking the frontal, orbitofrontal and anterior cingulate cortices, the basal ganglia and thalamus is thought to relate to OCD.

Explore
To find out more about OCD, go to the link below, which discusses various explanations (including the brain activity explanation):
http://ocd.about.com/od/causes/a/Causes_OCD.htm

Progress check 1.50
List four brain areas where activity is said to differ in those with OCD compared to controls.

Evidence for brain activity explaining OCD

- In patients with OCD the cingulate gyrus, basal ganglia and prefrontal orbital cortex are active when at rest (compared with controls without OCD) and they become more active as OCD symptoms are stimulated. They are no longer overactive following drug therapy or CBT (Whiteside *et al.* 2004). These three points are taken as evidence for these areas being implicated in OCD.
- Hou *et al.* (2012) carried out a study focusing on the orbito-striatal circuits in OCD patients. The researchers used fMRI scanning when patients were at resting state to look for dysfunctional brain regions in OCD patients. They used 28 patients with OCD and 23 controls. Hou *et al.* (2012) found that those with OCD had increased activity (amplitude of low-frequency fluctuation – ALFF) in the bilateral orbitofrontal cortex, the anterior cingulate cortex and the cerebellum and parietal cortex (p<.01). In addition, scores on the Y-BOCS (Yale-Brown Obsessive Compulsive Scale) correlated with activity in the bilateral

orbitofrontal cortex. This is evidence for brain activity being implicated in OCD, though perhaps not necessarily causing it.

- Menzies *et al.* (2008) and Robbins *et al.* (2011), both cited in Hou *et al.* (2012), also show that it is the orbitofronto-striatal circuits where activity is found to differ in people with OCD and so it seems that these circuits are important in the disorder.
- Hou *et al.* (2012) cite many studies supporting the idea of the brain areas listed in this section being important in OCD. For example, Almaca *et al.* (2007, cited in Hou *et al.*, 2012) found abnormalities in the orbitofronto-cortex in those with OCD. Hou *et al.* explain that studies using different forms of scanning, including a PET study, which measures blood flow, found abnormal activity in the same areas. Hou *et al.* (2012) measured ALFF, which is different from blood flow; however, they still found the same in relation to how brain activity differs in those with and without OCD.

Year One link: You learned about fMRI scanning in biological psychology. You can use Huo *et al.* (2012) as an example of its use and you can use strengths and weaknesses of fMRI scanning to evaluate Huo *et al.* (2012).

Evidence against brain activity explaining OCD

- More recent studies using scanning have found differences in other brain areas, such as the parietal cortex and cerebellum (e.g. Sanematsu *et al.*, 2010, cited in Hou *et al.*, 2012), which suggests the actual brain areas active in OCD are not completely known. Brain activity is of course complex and difficult to study.
- Kireev *et al.* (2012) looked at activity of the anterior cingulate cortex in OCD patients and found that the function of that brain region in such patients takes place in other brain areas instead. This suggests that simply saying there is different activity in the anterior cingulate cortex in those with OCD is insufficient. Brain region activity in one area (or lack of it) can be compensated for in another area. This shows the complexity of brain activity and the difficulties of finding specific brain regions that relate to a specific disorder like OCD.
- Kireev *et al.* (2013) looked at people with OCD where drug therapy had not worked. They also considered how surgery focusing on the anterior cingulate cortex had not worked for those with OCD. They concluded this was because decision-making and cognitive control, which is found in the anterior cingulate cortex, can be redistributed to other brain regions, so operating

on that area may well not work. Kireev *et al.* think that OCD might come from a functional deficit in the anterior cingulate cortex but that other brain areas can take over those functions. Though this does not give evidence against the brain activity explanation for OCD, it does suggest a complexity that is hard to unravel.

- Evidence for the cognitive explanation for OCD can be used to argue against the brain activity explanation, though it can be argued that the two support one another.

Evaluation of the biological explanation about brain functioning and OCD

Strengths

- Studies looking at brain activity in those with OCD compared to those without OCD use different measures. Hou *et al.* (2012) used measures of amplitude of low-frequency fluctuation (ALFF) when carrying out fMRI scanning and others used PET scanning and measured blood flow, with all finding differences in the same brain areas. The use of different scanning techniques with similar findings gives evidence for brain activity being implicated in OCD and adds to reliability of the findings.
- fMRI is comparatively low cost compared to other types of scanning, is more available and is non-invasive, so it is a useful method to use (Liu *et al.*, 2009). Resting-state fMRI is particularly helpful as there can be comparisons between those with OCD and those without, with the fears and anxiety not being part of the differences if both are in a resting state. The research methods, therefore, are strong and seemingly reliable and ethical, which is a strength when looking at findings. As many studies of brain activity (see Huo *et al.* 2012) come up with similar findings, the use of robust research methods adds to the reliability of the findings. This means evidence for brain activity as an explanation for OCD is strong.
- The areas thought to be involved in OCD (because activity in those areas differs for those with OCD) do relate to symptoms of OCD, such as contamination (relating to hand washing) and areas relating to cognitive control. Cognitive factors in OCD support the brain activity explanation and vice versa.
- If the circuit under discussion in the brain activity explanation relates to serotonin functioning (which is suggested) and selective serotonin reuptake inhibitors (SSRIs) help with OCD, the fact that the treatment helps does give support for the explanation.

Weaknesses

- If problems with brain processing are found in those with OCD compared with controls, this might be because of the symptoms of OCD, such as thoughts about perfection or worry, rather than the cause of such symptoms. For example, OCD symptoms may be caused by problems with memory tasks that come from low self-esteem and worry rather than problems with processing (e.g. Otto, 1992). This is one reason for scanning people in a resting state if possible, though it could be argued that worry, a symptom of OCD, will still be present in a resting state.

- It is hard to say whether brain activity issues explain OCD or whether brain activity issues accompany symptoms and so are not the cause of the symptoms but part of them. Brain activity and thoughts are related of course and it is not easy to say whether thoughts change brain activity or vice versa as they cannot really be separated. Even in a resting state there will be thoughts and emotions that affect brain activity.

Progress check 1.51

Give one piece of evidence to support the brain activity explanation for OCD and one piece of evidence against.

Two treatments for OCD

When looking at schizophrenia and unipolar depression the two treatments described for each of these were drug therapy and CBT. The same treatments have been chosen for OCD, as these are the two most common forms of treatment for OCD. You can use what you learned about drug therapy and CBT in schizophrenia to remind yourself of the basics for each therapy.

Explore

To explore more about treatments for OCD, try the link below.
www.nhs.uk/Conditions/Obsessive compulsive-disorder/Pages/Treatment.aspx

Drug therapy

The basics of drug therapy, focusing on neurotransmitter functioning at the synapse and issues such as reuptake and drug take up at receptors, are covered earlier in this chapter in the sections on the use of drug therapy for schizophrenia (page 44) and for depression (page 68). They are not repeated here as the same processes apply. The focus in this section is on which drugs are used for OCD and specifically how they work for OCD.

STUDY HINT
The POTS team study looking at the success of combining sertraline and CBT when treating OCD will be useful when looking both at drug therapy and CBT. The POTS team study can be found on page 133 of this chapter.

Drug therapy for OCD

Drug therapy works by altering the balance of chemicals in the brain. For OCD, as with many brain disorders, the drugs prescribed are SSRIs. This is because it is serotonin that is involved in the brain circuit thought to relate to OCD. SSRIs that are prescribed for OCD include citalopram (Cipramil), fluoxetine (Prozac) and sertraline (Lustral and Zoloft). SSRIs do not work for quite a few weeks and tend to be taken for about a year before reviewed. Side-effects of SSRIs can include dizziness, fatigue and dry mouth.

A tricyclic antidepressant, such as clomipramine, can be used if SSRIs do not work for an individual. NICE guidelines say clomipramine (a non-selective serotonin reuptake inhibitor) should only be used if at least one SSRI has been tried and has not worked.

SSRIs and non-selective serotonin reuptake inhibitors work by blocking the reuptake of serotonin by the presynaptic neuron, leaving more serotonin available for the postsynaptic neuron. There is evidence that it is a lack of serotonin that links to OCD symptoms, which supports the idea of increasing the serotonin levels in the synapse ready to be taken up by the postsynaptic neuron.

Progress check 1.52

Fill in the table below by completing the 'explanation' column.

Term	Explanation
Postsynaptic neuron	
Presynaptic neuron	
Synapse	
Reuptake	

STUDY HINT
Evidence for explanations of OCD, both when discussing brain activity and the cognitive explanation, touched upon the effectiveness of therapies derived from the explanations. When considering the effectiveness of therapies you can draw on evidence for the explanations.

Effectiveness of drug therapy for OCD

- Stanford School of Medicine suggest that about 40–60 per cent of OCD patients respond to SSRIs or clomipramine, though it is not possible to know which patient will respond to which drug. They report that in studies fluvoxamine, paroxetine and sertraline are equal in effectiveness to clomipramine. What tends to happen is that the drug is prescribed and then increased to the highest dose that can be tolerated, then over a period of 10 to 12 weeks symptoms decrease by about 40 per cent in approximately 60 per cent of patients. Symptoms will return if the drugs are stopped and in around 20 per cent of patients a drug will not work again if it is stopped and then re-started.
- Dougherty et al. (2011) discuss progress in treating OCD. They suggest that serotonergic reuptake inhibitors are successful with some other drugs (such as clonazepam) being effective but having more limited evidence about their effectiveness. Dougherty et al. (2011) claim that first line treatment is ERP and serotonergic reuptake inhibitors (SRIs). Cognitive therapy is a second line treatment as are other drugs. Evidence for the effectiveness of SRIs comes from randomised controlled trials and placebo controlled studies. SSRIs have been shown to be effective and SRIs are more effective than non-SRI tricyclics. Dougherty et al. (2011) use a table to show the many studies and their findings, including Denys et al. (2003) showing that paroxetine and venlafaxine are equally effective and Stein et al. (2007) showing that escitalopram and paroxetine are significantly better than a placebo. Dougherty et al. (2011) agree with the account from Stanford School of Medicine that there is an improvement of around 40 per cent and up to 60 per cent of patients respond to SSRIs.
- Abramowitz (1997) carried out a review looking at the effectiveness of both psychological and drug treatments for OCD. Abramowitz found that ERP was effective in reducing OCD symptoms, as was cognitive therapy, and in fact the two had overlapping procedures. He suggests that medication focusing on serotonin levels was effective too, including clomipramine, though this was not significantly better than other such medication.
- The POTS team looked at therapy for OCD and their study used four conditions – one placebo group, one group receiving just CBT, one receiving just sertraline and one receiving CBT and sertraline combined (page 134). They found all three types of therapy were effective compared with the placebo. The combined therapy was better than the single therapies, even though all three showed significant effectiveness. This is evidence for drug therapy and CBT and, interestingly, evidence that the two combined work best.

> **STUDY HINT**
> If you choose OCD as a disorder to focus on (alongside schizophrenia), then the POTS team's study of OCD is one of the two studies provided for you to choose from. It is explained later in this chapter on page 133 and can be used to show the effectiveness of sertraline, the effectiveness of CBT and as an evaluation point about the effectiveness of either drug therapy or CBT because it claims that a combination of both is best.

Evidence against the effectiveness of drug therapy for OCD

- There are few studies that follow drug therapy over time (Dougherty et al., 2011) and studies show high rates of OCD symptoms returning despite drug therapy and recurring if drug therapy is stopped. Romano et al. (2001, cited in Dougherty et al., 2011) found that patients using fluoxetine who either continued their treatment or were in a placebo group had one-year relapse rates of 17.5 per cent if continuing with the fluoxetine and 38 per cent if in the placebo group. This is evidence that drug therapy, though found to be effective in many studies, might have high relapse rates.
- Koran et al. (2002) carried out a study on OCD patients taking sertraline. Some of the patients continued on the sertraline while others were given a placebo. Koran et al. found a relapse rate to OCD symptoms of 21 per cent in those remaining on sertraline and a 59 per cent relapse rate for those who stopped sertraline and went onto a placebo. This finding supports Romano et al. (2001, cited in Dougherty et al., 2011), which suggests some reliability in the claim that medication can work, but there is a fairly high rate of relapse and more so if medication is stopped.

> **STUDY HINT**
> When discussing a therapy it is useful to know some studies that give findings about its effectiveness so make some notes when you can, ready to answer a question about effectiveness in the exam.

Evaluation of drug therapy for OCD

Strengths

- As reported by Dougherty et al. (2011) there are many studies that show the effectiveness of SSRIs and SRIs over placebo or control groups, which suggests reliability in the findings. Denys et al. (2003) showed that paroxetine and venlafaxine are equally effective and Stein et al. (2007) showed that escitalopram and paroxetine are significantly better than a placebo (both cited in Dougherty *et al.*, 2011). There are many studies giving similar findings, which contributes to reliability.

- Studies use randomised controlled trials so there is careful use of a control group to measure against. Placebo controlled trials are used, again giving a careful baseline measure, which is useful as there is control over the participant's thoughts about taking medication, since they will not know whether they are in a placebo group or not. The use of careful control groups adds objectivity and credibility to the claims that drug therapy is effective.

Weaknesses

- Studies showing the effectiveness of drug therapy sometimes use participants who have not tried SRIs and sometimes participants for whom at least one of the drugs has not worked. This means that groups are not always comparable, which should be taken into account (according to Dougherty *et al.*, 2011).
- The studies show the effectiveness of drug therapy but also point out that how individuals react to the different drugs cannot (yet) be predicted, not all individuals respond well to drugs at all, and many individuals do not respond to at least one of the drugs. This is relevant to your understanding of individual differences and means that, although drug therapy might be considered applicable to everyone, in fact it must be adapted to each individual. This suggests that the explanation that OCD relates to lowered levels of serotonin is perhaps not as simple as it seems, because otherwise we would expect everyone to respond in the same way to SSRIs.
- There are quite high relapse rates not only if a drug is stopped but also over time. Koran *et al.* (2002) and Romano *et al.* (2001) both cited in Dougherty *et al.* (2011) showed 17.5 per cent and 21 per cent relapse rates respectively when a drug was continued, and 38 per cent and 59 per cent respectively in their placebo groups. Though continuing with a drug meant lower relapse rates regarding OCD symptoms, there was still quite a high relapse rate and stopping taking the drug led to an even higher relapse rate.

Progress check 1.53

Explain two limitations of drug therapy as a treatment for OCD.

Cognitive-behavioural therapy (CBT)

Whittal and McLean (1999) discuss CBT for OCD. They say that although exposure and response prevention (ERP) is a first line treatment, there can be a high drop-out rate

and also some individuals do not benefit from ERP; such individuals may instead benefit from CBT. CBT for OCD involves challenging beliefs and appraisals, looking for evidence for them and, by not finding strong evidence, reducing their intensity.

CBT for OCD patients

The basic idea of CBT is to focus on thoughts, not so much in themselves, but for the emotions they bring and the behaviour that follows. The same thought in different people leads to different responses – both emotional responses and actions. In CBT the individual focuses on an example of obsessive thoughts and examines what was happening at the time to help them understand the obsessions and compulsions that come from their obsessions. First, the therapist explores the thoughts, emotions and behaviours that result and which help to maintain those thoughts. The therapist will then help the patient to begin to look at alternative ways of understanding their thoughts.

The diagram below shows how using compulsions to allay fear from obsessive thoughts does not allow for the obsessive thought about the house catching fire and the responsibility that goes with it being stopped or even reduced. The more someone checks the gas the more they think about the house catching fire and the more real the idea becomes. CBT involves the patient focusing on the likelihood of the house catching fire and on the gas being turned off, then experiencing the anxiety caused by not checking the gas before leaving the house.

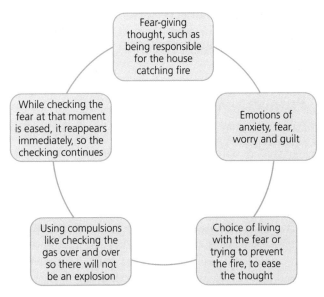

The cycle of obsessive thoughts and beliefs that are maintained by rituals and compulsions

A main focus of CBT can be to show that although compulsions are behaviours that are adopted to allay fears and worries, in reality they help to keep such fears alive. Compulsions may give temporary relief from anxiety but the rituals confirm the belief, maintaining the OCD cycle.

Examples of compulsions and how CBT might deal with them

Checking: this is a compulsion and the patient with OCD will be encouraged to think about what would happen if they did not check. ERP can be included here, which means exposing the patient to the fearful thought, preventing them checking and enduring the anxiety. CBT examines the thinking behind compulsions more deeply than ERP because the person thinks through what would happen if they did not check, challenging the belief itself. The role of CBT is not to say there is no risk (e.g. of harm) if the checking does not take place, but instead the patient is encouraged to assess how great a risk there is and the reality of that risk.

Avoiding: this is also a compulsion; by avoiding a feared situation the person with OCD does not find out what would happen (or not happen) if they faced the situation, so their fear is perpetuated by the avoidance. The therapist uses behavioural experiments to help to show what would happen, such as themselves touching what the patient is avoiding, to demonstrate no harm comes to the therapist and therefore no harm will come to the patient.

> **STUDY HINT**
> Refer back to discussions on how CBT works covered elsewhere in this chapter when putting together an explanation of how it works. Remember, though, that when discussing a therapy in relation to a specific disorder you must focus your discussion on that particular disorder.

Progress check 1.54

Explain, using one example, how CBT can be effective for obsessions and compulsions in OCD.

CBT and ERP

CBT for OCD involves focusing on thoughts, feelings and behaviour and also can involve ERP. ERP involves someone facing their anxieties and worry by not using their compulsions that neutralise those fears. It is not easy to do this but gradually the anxiety can greatly reduce and even disappear when compulsions are prevented. Different exposure tasks are involved, to focus on the obsessions and related compulsions one by one.

CBT involves an element of 'facing fears', such as experiencing anxiety up to a point. For example, experiencing the anxiety and measuring it using a clock face – the person sticks with it until about 7 o'clock on the clock face as a measure and then they stop. This helps them to face their fears. They visualise a clock face, choose a level they think they can cope with, and picture it as a time on the clock. Usually, this would go past 6 o'clock, to get past a half way point, but 9 o'clock would be thought of as too much. It is a visual way of using a measure. This is not the same as ERP but has a similar focus, so there is an element of ERP in CBT and that makes it hard to separate them when looking at the effectiveness of psychotherapy for OCD. ERP is a recommended therapy for OCD.

Evaluating the effectiveness of CBT as a treatment for OCD

Strengths

- Abramowitz (1997) suggests that ERP shows the most consistent findings when looking at disorders and van Balkom et al. (1994) suggests ERP is more effective than other treatments.
- Both ERP and cognitive therapy can be successful with no differences being found to suggest they work on different mechanisms. Steketee (1993) indicates that ERP suggests cognitive restructuring, again demonstrating that the effectiveness of ERP and cognitive therapy are not easily separated.
- Whittal et al. (2010) carried out a study where CBT was compared to **wait list controls** and stress management training (SMT). Whittal et al. found that there were lower scores on the Yale-Brown Obsessive Compulsive Scale (Y-BOCS) for both the treatments compared with the wait list controls. They also found lower OCD-related cognitions and less depression for the two treatment groups (CBT and SMT) compared with the wait list controls. CBT and SMT showed similar effectiveness with regard to some symptoms with few differences in the follow-up period. However, CBT showed larger changes than SMT on most OCD-related cognitions. The researchers concluded that psychotherapy was successful (both SMT and CBT) and that there were lasting improvements in OCD symptoms.
- Foa (2010) evaluates CBT for OCD. She talks about cognitive therapy (CT), which focuses on negative automatic thinking and on helping patients to uncover and change how they interpret such thoughts. CBT involves focusing on negative automatic thinking like CT but involves focus on behaviour too. What is said about CT can be applied to CBT. Foa (2010) outlines a study by van Oppen et al. (1995) where they compared cognitive therapy with ERP. A group of 71 OCD patients were

randomly assigned either to a cognitive therapy group or to exposure to their fear using ERP. The cognitive therapy focused on overestimating danger and inflating personal responsibility and behavioural experiments were added too. Van Oppen *et al.* (1995) found both therapies were effective and there were no differences. Note that the van Oppen *et al.* study was cited in Whittal *et al.* (2010) as well, where similar points about CBT and ERP were made. Eddy *et al.* (2004, cited in Foa, 2010) in a meta-analysis of 15 clinical trials looked at ERP, CT and control conditions too. They found that about two thirds of those who finished the treatment improved though only about one third of them met criteria that could say they had recovered. ERP was more effective than CT and individual therapy was more effective than group therapy.

Weaknesses

- The POTS team found that CBT was effective for OCD; however, they also found sertraline effective, which means CBT is not the only effective treatment. Also they found that CBT and sertraline together was the most effective treatment, which is evidence perhaps that CBT can be effective but more can be done in terms of combining it with another therapy like drug therapy.
- Cordioli (2008) claims that CBT is effective for about 70 per cent of patients with OCD who try CBT. However, it is also said that many patients do not respond to CBT and so again more needs to be done to increase its effectiveness.
- Van Oppen *et al.* (1995, cited in Abramowitz, 1997) used a cognitive outcome measure but did not find that ERP was better for the behaviours and cognitive therapy was better for the obsessions.

Definition
Wait list controls are the control group in a study that are on a waiting list for the treatment so they can be compared well with the treatment group.

Progress check 1.55
Give one piece of evidence that shows CBT is effective for OCD and one piece of evidence that suggests it is not effective.

Evaluation of CBT as a treatment for OCD
Strengths

- CBT is thought to be better than medication in terms of lower rates of relapse in CBT when discontinued; there are no side-effects with CBT as there are when taking medication.

- Many researchers claim CBT is effective, including Greist *et al.* (2003) and Abramowitz (2006) as well as the National Institute for Health and Clinical Excellence (NICE) (2006). It seems unlikely that so many researchers could be wrong; CBT is called an 'evidence-based' therapy because there is so much evidence.

Weaknesses

- Although the POTS team found that CBT is an effective therapy for OCD compared with a placebo group, they also found sertraline was effective and most effective was a combination of CBT and sertraline. This suggests that CBT is effective, but perhaps other treatments and combinations of treatments are more effective.
- Although CBT and ERP are fairly consistently found to be effective, perhaps with ERP having the edge, it should be noted that CBT is similar to ERP in that both involve behavioural experiments and challenging irrational thoughts. Singling out what it is about CBT in particular that is effective (compared to ERP and also cognitive therapy) is difficult.

Test yourself

1 Compare two explanations for obsessive compulsive disorder (OCD), one biological and one non-biological. **(8 marks)**
2 Evaluate one non-biological treatment for OCD. **(12 marks)**

Anorexia nervosa

For your course, in addition to schizophrenia, you need to know about one other disorder from a choice of unipolar depression, obsessive compulsive disorder (OCD) and anorexia nervosa. There is useful information about diagnosis, explanations and treatment of each of these mental disorders, so you might want to read about all three before you decide which one to focus on.

For each disorder you study for your course, you need to know about symptoms and features, two explanations and two treatments. In this section the symptoms and features of anorexia nervosa are explained, before looking at two explanations – one biological and one non-biological. Two treatments are covered, again one biological and one non-biological. For the treatments the two explanations must be from a different topic area (from social psychology, cognitive psychology, biological psychology and learning theories).

STUDY HINT

Two studies focusing on anorexia nervosa are given later in this chapter on page 120. Use the information in them when discussing anorexia nervosa.

Study of interest

Crisafulli *et al.* (2008) looked at attitudes to anorexia nervosa. They wanted to see if people would think differently about someone with anorexia nervosa depending on whether they read a biological/genetic explanation for anorexia nervosa or a sociocultural explanation. Crisafulli *et al.* (2008) used undergraduate student nurses who were allocated randomly to two conditions. The conditions were reading information that emphasised biological/genetic or sociocultural explanations for anorexia nervosa. Then the participants completed questionnaires to find out their attitudes towards people with anorexia nervosa. It was found that those who read the biological/genetic explanations for anorexia nervosa tended to blame those with the illness less than if they read about sociocultural explanations, although the results were not that strong. The researchers wanted to replicate the findings in larger scale studies, but in the meantime they felt that in order to reduce the blame and stigma attached to having anorexia nervosa more information about biological and genetic underpinnings should be available.

STUDY HINT

If you use Vallentine *et al.* (2010) as an example of the use of interviewing in clinical psychology, you will read about the success involved in giving offenders information about their disorder – what the researchers called 'psycho-education'. You can use this idea of the value of information about a disorder when evaluating Crisafulli *et al.* (2008) and their conclusions about anorexia nervosa.

Symptoms and features of anorexia nervosa

Features of anorexia include prevalence, how much it can cost to treat it, age of onset and gender figures, while symptoms are focused on what characterises anorexia nervosa.

Features

Anorexia nervosa (AN) is an eating disorder and is different from bulimia nervosa, another eating disorder. AN is a serious illness with one in 20 patients treated being likely to die from the illness. AN is around ten times more common in females than in males (Lindberg and Hjern 2003, cited in Silverstone, 2005) and mostly starts in adolescence. It occurs in 1–4 per cent of women and 0.2–0.3 per cent of males in their life time (Smink *et al.*, 2012), though these figures are approximate and relate to Western countries. Woodside *et al.* (2001) suggest that in a Canadian community full anorexia nervosa was found in 0.66 per cent of females of all ages. Silverstone (2005) suggests that the lifetime prevalence in females is around 0.5 per cent, which suggests that one women in every 200 develops anorexia at some time in her lifetime. If the illness is treated early on and if there is a good parent–child relationship, then the outcome is likely to be better.

Symptoms

The main symptoms of anorexia nervosa are not eating, deliberately losing weight and food being an important focus in life, to the point where it may even dominate. Those with anorexia nervosa tend never to reach the stage of feeling full after eating and limit what they eat and drink. They are underweight and can become dangerously underweight. Another symptom is feeling fat when the opposite is the case.

There are two types of anorexia nervosa, the restricting type (weight loss by restricting food intake) and the purging type (weight loss by self-induced vomiting). In the latter type, some sufferers also take diuretics or laxatives, making the effects of malnutrition worse. Some of the main symptoms of anorexia nervosa are described below.

A symptom of anorexia nervosa is a strong focus on weight and body image.

Deliberate weight loss

Losing weight deliberately is one of the main symptoms and is usually done by avoiding food and drink in order to control the body's appearance. A sufferer might also take laxatives, exercise excessively or use appetite suppressants to help with weight loss. Measuring to see if a person is under- or over-weight is usually done by calculating their body mass index (BMI), which is weight in kilograms divided by the square of height in metres (for people over 18 years old; those younger are measured differently). People with anorexia nervosa tend to be about 15 per cent below the weight that would be expected for their size. Normal BMI for an adult is between 20 kg/m^2 and 25 kg/m^2. Adults with anorexia nervosa typically have a BMI of below 17.5 kg/m^2 and a BMI of less than 15 kg/m^2 indicates an extreme case of anorexia nervosa. The DSM-IV requires that the individual weighs less than 85 per cent of their 'normal' weight though the DSM allows room for judgement by the clinician, such as taking into account body build and weight history. ICD-10 says the individual must have a BMI of equal to or less than 17.5 kg/m^2. A diagnosis of AN also requires other features/symptoms.

Unrealistic body image in relation to body size

Anorexia nervosa leads people to think they are fat when they are thin. An individual with anorexia nervosa has an extreme fear of gaining weight. An important point is that those with anorexia nervosa do not see themselves in a mirror as others see them; instead they see themselves as larger than they are. Self-esteem seems to be dependent on their body weight and shape.

> **STUDY HINT**
> Guardia et al. (2012) did a study to see whether girls with anorexia nervosa only judged their own body size as larger than it was, or whether they judged the body size of someone else in that way too. They found that it was just their own body they did not see 'correctly'. This study (see page 125) is one of the two in your course for anorexia nervosa.

Physical symptoms

Physical symptoms are caused by poor diet and low weight and include exhaustion, sleeping difficulties, difficulties with concentration, dizziness and feeling cold.

Other symptoms

People with anorexia nervosa may wear baggy clothes to hide their thinness and put heavy weights in their pockets when being weighed. They tend to lie about how much they eat. Sufferers do feel hungry and they can like food, but they find the consequences of eating frightening. Appetite is not different; for example, patients experience reduced hunger and feel more full after a test meal the same as other (non-anorexic) participants (Halmi and Sunday, 1991).

Depression, often accompanied by social withdrawal and insomnia, is common. These symptoms can be so severe that major depressive disorder can be diagnosed.

OCD symptoms such as obsession with eating and compulsions such as checking calorie values of all food items can also be found in someone with anorexia nervosa. With regard to links to OCD it should be noted that perfectionism is a feature of anorexia nervosa. Perfectionism is often found in children who later develop anorexia nervosa. Halmi et al. (2003, cited in Silverstone, 2005) interviewed 324 people with anorexia nervosa and found obsessional thoughts and/or compulsive behaviour in around 70 per cent of them.

Health risks

There are a number of health risks experienced by those suffering from anorexia nervosa.

Chemical imbalance in the body and osteoporosis (thinning of the bones)

Osteoporosis arises from a lack of calcium and vitamin D as well as a lack of oestrogen. Chemical imbalance such as low potassium levels resulting from over-use of laxatives causes tiredness and may cause kidney damage.

Irregular menstruation and bowel difficulties

Levels of hormones such as oestrogen can be affected by a poor diet, which can in turn affect menstruation. Frequent use of laxatives can cause bowel problems, such as permanent constipation. Apart from the amenorrhoea (loss of menstruation), males and females experience the same symptoms (Woodside et al., 2001, cited in Silverstone, 2005).

Teeth, hair and skin problems

Fluid disturbances in the body can cause swelling of hands and feet and stomach acid can affect the condition of teeth (due to vomiting). Thinning hair may occur and those with anorexia nervosa can develop 'lanugo', a covering of fine downy hair on their body.

Infections and anaemia

Anaemia results because the body is low in iron and leads to dizziness and fainting. Infections occur because the body's defence system is not working well.

Heart problems

Heart problems arise from a poor diet and issues with weight, including low blood pressure.

Two explanations for anorexia nervosa

Biological explanation

Collier and Treasure (2004, cited in Silverstone, 2005) suggest that little is known about the biology underpinning anorexia nervosa. There is some evidence for each of the following:

- genetic differences in anorexia nervosa
- brain processing, such as when focusing on emotional stimuli
- brain structures and activity
- serotonin activity.

There is no firm single biological explanation though the evidence for genetic underpinning seems quite strong. Therefore, the genetic explanation is given first before the other biological ideas are briefly explained so that you can use them when evaluating the genetic explanation.

Genes and anorexia nervosa

According to Kipman *et al.* (1999) if genes are an explanation for anorexia nervosa then the frequency of anorexia nervosa in relatives of someone with it should be higher than in the general population. Also identical twins should be more concordant for anorexia nervosa than non-identical twins, meaning that if someone is an identical twin of someone with anorexia nervosa there is a higher likelihood of them having the same (or a similar) disorder than if they have a non-identical twin with the disorder. Using family and twin studies means a **heritability estimate** can be made, which involves estimating the percentage of any difference between family members or twins that is due to genes (leaving the rest to environmental factors as causes). If genes can explain anorexia nervosa it might be something about the anorexia nervosa itself that is similar or the same between relatives, rather than other features, such as depression.

Definition

Heritability estimate is the percentage of a characteristic that is due to genes, worked out using family and twin studies to look for similarities between them in relation to that characteristic.

Family studies

Family studies tend to show a higher risk for anorexia nervosa in female relatives of someone with the disorder than in female relatives of controls (Kipman *et al.*, 1999), which seems to be evidence of genetic factors underpinning the disorder. However, in a family there might be similar ideas that build, thus leading to anorexia nervosa in relatives, and also there might be something in the family interactions that leads to the disorder, such as over-protectiveness of parents. Kipman *et al.* (1999), however, argue that these features of families are not likely to explain why those relatives not sharing the same home environment (e.g. cousins and aunts) still show a higher tendency to anorexia nervosa when someone has the disorder in that family than do relatives of control participants (e.g. Herpetz-Dahlmann, 1988, cited in Kipman *et al.*, 1999). Kipman *et al.* (1999) report that the closer the relative, the higher the risk. It is restrictive type anorexia nervosa that increases the risk of the disorder in families, rather than the purging type (Gershon *et al.*, 1984, cited in Kipman *et al.*, 1999).

Twin studies

Monozygotic twins (MZ) share 100 per cent of their genes and dizygotic twins (DZ) share 50 per cent of their genes, so if MZ twins show a higher concordance rate for anorexia disorder than DZ twins this suggests that at least some part of anorexia nervosa is due to genes. An exact concordance rate is not possible as studies vary and there are issues such as being sure that the zygoticity is properly decided (it is not always known whether twins are identical or not when doing a study). However, when more than one study finds similar results, such as a higher concordance rate for anorexia nervosa, then this is evidence for genes being involved. Kipman *et al.* (1999) looked at a great many twin studies involving anorexia nervosa and came up with a heritability estimate of 71 per cent, given that 46.2 per cent of the 106 MZ twins involved were concordant for the disorder and 7.1 per cent of the 56 DZ twins were concordant.

Evidence for a genetic explanation of anorexia nervosa

- There is some evidence that monoamine functioning relates to anorexia nervosa and there might be a genetic variability that increases the likelihood of developing the disorder. Collier *et al.* (1997, cited in Kipman *et al.*, 1999) suggest the $5HT_{2A}$ gene is implicated, for example (5HT is serotonin).

- Connan *et al.* (2003) suggest that people have a genetic predisposition to the illness and then early life experiences can lead to changes in the hypothalamic-pituitary-adrenal (HPA) axis. The changes in the HPA axis lead to higher rates of corticophin releasing hormone (CRH) and this is what changes appetite regulation.

- Woodside *et al.* (1998) show that first degree relatives are more likely to share having anorexia nervosa compared with the general population, though this connection is found less in third degree relatives. This is evidence for a genetic basis for the disorder.

- Identical twins show a higher concordance rate for anorexia nervosa than non-identical twins, which suggests a genetic basis. Holland *et al.* (1988, cited in Silverstone, 2005) looked at 25 identical twins (MZ twins) and 20 non-identical twins (DZ twins), all female, where one of the twins in each pair had anorexia nervosa. They found 56 per cent (14) of the 25 MZ twins were concordant (both had anorexia nervosa) compared with 5 per cent (1) of the 20 DZ twins.

- Kipman *et al.* (1999) give the concordance rate for MZ twins as about 44 per cent and for DZ twins about 12.5 per cent, which underlines the idea of a genetic factor in anorexia nervosa.

- Gu *et al.* (2002) looked at families where at least two relatives had anorexia nervosa (the restricting form) and found linkage on chromosome 1p.

- Scott-Van Zeeland *et al.* (2013/2014) found evidence for gene variants linking to anorexia nervosa. Their study focused on EPHX2 gene variants.

> **STUDY HINT**
> Scott-Van Zeeland *et al.* (2013/2014) give evidence for EPHX2 gene variants having a role in anorexia nervosa, which suggests there is a genetic basis for the disorder. You can use this study (see page 120) when discussing genes as an explanation for anorexia nervosa. Always try to use material from different sections in a topic area if you can, to gain an overall understanding of an issue.

> ## Explore
> The following link provides some information about genes and anorexia nervosa:
> www.apa.org/monitor/mar02/genetic.aspx

> ## Progress check 1.57
> Explain how twin studies support a genetic explanation for anorexia nervosa.

Other biological explanations of anorexia nervosa

Biological explanations of anorexia nervosa point to genes to an extent, but there are other biological issues associated with the disorder and it is worth considering them as a contrast to the genetic explanation. There is some evidence that other biological explanations are underpinned by genetic variance, such as when considering the role of monoamines, including serotonin. You can use other biological explanations to evaluate the genetic explanation and also as evidence against it.

Evidence for brain processing differences in those with anorexia nervosa

Hatch *et al.* (2010) looked at alterations in the 'emotional brain' for those with anorexia nervosa. They wanted to find biological markers for anorexia nervosa to help with research in the area, so that new treatments could be developed. This suggests that not enough is known about brain functioning in anorexia nervosa to develop suitable drug therapy to help. The study tested 28 adolescent females with anorexia and some matched healthy controls. Those with anorexia nervosa were tested when admitted to hospital and then again after weight gain. The healthy controls were tested at the same times. The study looked at emotion processing when underweight and when not (and at the same times for the controls too) and found significantly reduced emotion-focused activity in the temporo-occipital regions in those with AN who were underweight and also when they had gained weight. This suggests that there are differences in judging relevant emotional signals in those with anorexia nervosa. The judgements of those with anorexia nervosa were different from the controls, both when underweight and after weight gain, so the differences did not depend on weight or nutritional status of the body. Drug treatments focusing on the emotion-focused processing areas in the brain might be useful for anorexia nervosa.

Brain structure abnormality

Early on in the course of the disorder, abnormalities in the brain are found in sufferers. For example, Swayze *et al.* (2003, cited in Silverstone, 2005) used brain scanning to show that ventricles were enlarged with a reduction in white matter. In the temporal lobe and in the parietal and orbitofrontal lobes blood flow can also be reduced (Chowdhury *et al.*, 2003, cited in Silverstone, 2005).

Serotonergic pathways

Steiger *et al.* (2001, cited in Silverstone, 2005) suggest that there is altered serotonin activity and reduced 5-HT binding in those with anorexia, which persists even after weight gain. Perhaps the (low) serotonin levels contribute to the obsessions and compulsions that come with anorexia. 'Reduced 5-HT binding' means less serotonin uptake in the postsynaptic neuron so there is less serotonin activity (5-HT is another term for serotonin). Kipman *et al.* (1999) mention monoamines as having a role in anorexia nervosa, but it may be genes relating to monoamines that explain the illness, rather than the idea that neurotransmitter functioning and genes are separate.

Evaluation of a genetic explanation for anorexia nervosa

Strengths

- There is a lot of evidence for a genetic explanation for anorexia nervosa, suggesting that there might be genes that predispose someone to the disorder. For example, twin studies show a higher concordance rate in monozygotic twins compared with dizygotic twins (e.g. Kipman *et al.*, 1999). Family studies too show that closer relatives are more likely to show a link to anorexia nervosa than more distant relatives or the general population, which is also evidence for a genetic explanation.
- Twin studies and family studies are usually well carried out and controls are carefully considered, such as whether a similar environment in the home might be causing the higher levels of anorexia nervosa in relatives (and identical twins) of someone with the disorder than in the general population. Evidence that it is not just similar environment causing the familial link is that relatives of someone with anorexia nervosa that do not share the home, such as cousins and aunts, also have a higher likelihood of having the disorder. There are issues around whether the twins are correctly allocated with regard to zygoticity, but the concordance rate is different enough for the findings to be accepted.
- It has been suggested that if anorexia nervosa is seen as having a biological cause (such as a genetic one), then there will be less stigma attached and less blame. Crisafulli *et al.* (2008) carried out an experiment to see if there would be less stigma attached if someone was told that anorexia nervosa was down to biological/genetic explanations than if they were told it was due to sociocultural factors. They found those who received the biological/

genetic explanation were less likely to blame individuals with the disorder. If this is helpful to those suffering from anorexia nervosa, then this is perhaps a strength.

Weaknesses

- Twin studies suggest that for anorexia nervosa there is around 50 per cent concordance for monozygotic twins. This leaves the other 50 per cent to be explained. Heritability estimates are about 70 per cent, again leaving around 30 per cent to be explained. Genes are said to be involved in the disorder, but they are likely to predispose someone towards developing anorexia nervosa rather than being its sole cause. This is a weakness in that it shows that this is a complex disorder with possibly multiple causes. This does not necessarily help with treatment.
- There is not enough known about genetic factors and anorexia nervosa. Studies are being done, such as Scott-Van Zeeland *et al.* (2013/2014), and gene variants linked to anorexia nervosa are being isolated and studied, but more needs to be learned. Biological explanations include brain activity and processing (including neurotransmitter functioning) but it is not known how far such activity relates to underpinning genes or to environmental influences.

Progress check 1.58

Explain two weaknesses in the genetic explanation of anorexia nervosa.

Cultural factors

Eating disorders tend to be found more in industrialised countries where the idea of being thin is more emphasised. Garner and Garfinkel (1980) looked at sociocultural factors in the development of anorexia nervosa. They carried out a study looking at dance and modelling students, choosing those because the career choice would mean a focus on body shape. They gathered height and weight information from all the participants (183 dance students and 56 modelling students) and used the Eating Attitudes Test (EAT). They also used 59 non-dance female university students, 68 people with anorexia nervosa and 35 music students. They found that in the dance and modelling groups there was more anorexia nervosa and there were more concerns over dieting. All but one of the dance students developed anorexia nervosa while studying dance. These findings suggest that sociocultural factors affect anorexia nervosa, such as pressure to be thin, and cultural expectations.

Garner and Garfinkel (1980) found more anorexia and focus on diet in dance (and modelling) students than in non-dance or music students.

> **STUDY HINT**
>
> If you studied Becker *et al.* (2002) in learning theories in Year One of your course, you will have seen that they too used the EAT questionnaire. When discussing studies, make reference to studies that use a similar method (in this case a standardised questionnaire) in order to make comparisons between different study findings.

Chadda *et al.* (1987) suggest family interaction patterns and parental attitudes to weight, as well as the desirability of being thin, are all factors in explaining the disorder. Chadda *et al.* (1987) report on the case of a 13-year-old female, giving depth and detail of a case study approach, showing the importance of sociocultural factors in the illness. For example, they say she was praised for her dieting and 'this resulted in a fall in her weight, which won her recommendations from the family' (p. 108).

Engl (1998) claims that anorexia nervosa is found mainly in white women in Western cultures (where there is often a focus on being thin and pressure to look thin) (Garner, 1993, cited in Engl, 1998). Anorexia nervosa is thought to be rare outside Western countries and rare in black women in industrialised countries. In North America and Western Europe anorexia nervosa is less common among women in ethnic minorities (Streigel-Moore *et al.*, 2003, cited in Silverstone, 2005). However, Simpson (2002) found rising numbers of anorexia nervosa in non-Western societies. This seems to suggest that there are cultural differences in anorexia nervosa but that changes might be occurring. Chadda *et al.* (1987) support the idea that prevalence of anorexia nervosa has increased over the last 20 years or so, which ties in with Becker *et al.*'s (2002) findings.

Explore

Chadda *et al.*'s (1987) case study of a 13-year-old girl with anorexia nervosa can be accessed at the following link: www.ncbi.nlm.nih.gov/pmc/articles/PMC3172455/pdf/IJPsy-29-107.pdf

Summary of cultural issues that might explain anorexia nervosa

- Living in an industrialised country.
- Being within Western norms (Engl, 1998).
- Following a career path that has expectations of 'thinness', such as dance or modelling (Garner and Garfinkel, 1980).
- Having family interaction patterns that support being thin (Chadda *et al.*, 1987).
- Being white and female rather than black (Garner, 1993, cited in Engl, 1998).
- Exposure to images of thinness which become aspirational (Willemsen and Hoek, 2006).

Evidence for cultural factors explaining anorexia nervosa

- Streigel-Moore *et al.* (2003, cited in Silverstone, 2005) found no Afro-American women with anorexia nervosa in a US sample of 2,000 women compared to 1.5 per cent of white women. This suggests a cultural basis for the disorder.
- Becker *et al.* (2002) found that in Fiji, before television was introduced, girls were unlikely to be concerned with diet and slimming, but after television was introduced there was evidence that they were more conscious of their body image and diet. Their scores on a questionnaire about eating and dieting were much higher after television had been introduced. For example, 0 per cent said they used self-induced vomiting to control weight in 1995 compared with 11.3 per cent in 1998. This suggests that culture is a factor in anorexia nervosa, though the study looked at eating behaviours rather than at anorexia nervosa directly.
- Garner and Garfinkel (1980) looked at sociocultural factors in the development of anorexia nervosa. They carried out a study looking at dance and modelling students (chosen because they were likely to be focused on body shape). They found that in the dance and modelling groups, compared with other participants (music students, non-dance/modelling students and people with anorexia nervosa) there was more anorexia nervosa and there were more concerns over dieting.

Year One link: Becker *et al.* (2002) is one of the contemporary studies in learning theories in your course that you may have studied.

Evidence against cultural explanations for anorexia nervosa

Engl (1998) thought that in the Caribbean there would be few cases of anorexia nervosa, given that it is more prevalent in Western industrialised countries. Being overweight in Curaçao, the Caribbean Island chosen for the study, was socially acceptable and still appears to be so today. Engl (1998) reports looking at medical records on the Island and looking for symptoms and signs of anorexia nervosa (i.e. not diagnosed as such, but fitting the DSM criteria). They found six cases of anorexia nervosa, all women, five being Creole (mixed ethnicity) and one being Portuguese. The women had an average BMI of 14.6 and all had amenorrhoea. On the island there were 2.6 cases of anorexia nervosa in 100,000 women in each year. Engl (1998) point out that this range matches that in Western countries. The point of this study is that within the Caribbean culture studied there was no pressure to be thin or images of thinness for women to copy (although this might be less true today). Families were not likely to pressure girls to be thin in the way that Chadda *et al.* (1987) reported. Engl's (1998) study goes against the claim that cultural factors explain anorexia nervosa.

Further evidence for cultural issues affecting the development of anorexia nervosa

It is important to note that the women in Engl's (1998) study were white or mixed ethnicity, not black, so the claim that anorexia nervosa is not found in black women might still apply and perhaps their ethnicity protects them. Willemsen and Hoek (2006) report a case of a black woman from Curaçao with anorexia nervosa who attended a centre for eating disorders in The Netherlands. This study was important to follow up to determine whether a black woman with anorexia nervosa had been found. They found the woman had grown up in the black community in Curaçao and never thought of losing weight when she was young; indeed she wanted to be more voluptuous, according to Willemsen and Hoek. They found that the woman's ethnicity did not prevent her from developing anorexia nervosa when she moved to The Netherlands, where being thin was valued, and this changed her way of seeing her body. Willemsen and Hoek say that watching television seems to have affected her perception of what was desirable regarding her body weight and shape. When the woman lived in Curaçao she had gained weight to become more attractive and then, because of relationship problems, she lost weight in order to be less attractive.

When she moved to a country where thinness was more valued she wanted to be thin because it was thought of as more attractive. This suggests that it is culture rather than ethnicity that protects someone from developing anorexia nervosa.

Year One link: In learning theories you covered social learning, which suggests that we learn by imitating what we observe, provided we are motivated and rewarded for doing so. You can use social learning theory to explain cultural factors in relation to anorexia nervosa.

Progress check 1.59

Complete the table by putting a tick against the issues that link to a cultural explanation for anorexia nervosa and a cross for those that do not.

Feature	✓ or ✗	Feature	✓ or ✗
$5HT_{2A}$		Family support for being thin	
Being in a Western culture		Having television	
MZ twins – higher concordance		Serotonin functioning	

Evaluation of the cultural explanation for anorexia nervosa

Strengths

- Many studies have claimed that anorexia nervosa arises from the pressure to be thin in a culture that values thinness as part of being attractive. For example, Garner and Garfinkel (1980) found that dance and modelling students were more likely to develop anorexia nervosa and to diet than music students or non-dance/modelling students. Willemsen and Hoek (2006) found that a black woman who developed anorexia nervosa had grown up in a culture that valued voluptuousness as being attractive. She developed anorexia nervosa after moving to a culture that valued thinness.

- Social learning theory (developed by Bandura and with experiments to support it) suggests that people copy what they observe in certain circumstances. For example, females are likely to imitate other females and to imitate role models. If role models are thin and female, girls are likely to imitate them, resulting in a strong desire to be thin. Wanting to be thin can lead to anorexia nervosa, which is characterised by a very strong urge to lose weight, for example. This means experimental evidence backs the idea that cultural factors explain anorexia nervosa, which is a strength of the explanation.

Weaknesses

- The cognitive features of anorexia nervosa include dissatisfaction with one's body image, low self-esteem and cognitive distortions about weight. This is an alternative explanation for anorexia nervosa, as are genetic (biological) explanations. Other explanations suggest that even if culture has some influence, it is unlikely to be the only factor.
- There is some evidence to show that anorexia nervosa exists in other cultures, including those where being voluptuous rather than thin is considered more attractive. Engl (1998) reported finding anorexia nervosa in Curaçao, with a 'Western' prevalence rate, for example, which goes against the 'culture' explanation. However, it was said that Engl (1998) did not find anorexia nervosa in Curaçao in black women, so there are some doubts about Engl's claims. Engl (1998), nonetheless, went through medical records carefully and took care to identify anorexia nervosa. Because the culture was 'against' thinness in women, the findings are interesting and counter the claim that culture is involved in anorexia nervosa.

Progress check 1.60
Explain two strengths of the cultural explanation for anorexia nervosa.

Two treatments for anorexia nervosa

There seems to be no single treatment for anorexia nervosa that works. Lock and Fitzpatrick (2009) suggest that early intervention is the most effective. Force feeding someone, for example, by gastric tube when they are in hospital, is a treatment that is used so that the person gains weight, which is a priority. Goals of treatment for anorexia nervosa include weight gain followed by prevention of weight loss, a change in eating behaviour, reduction in preoccupations with body image, focus on depression and OCD and any medical conditions related to the anorexia nervosa arising from the symptoms (Aigner et al., 2011).

Drug therapy and family-based therapy (FBT) are the two treatments considered here.

Drug therapy is chosen because it is a biological therapy (as required by your course). Drug therapy is used to treat the depression and anxiety that accompanies anorexia nervosa, and atypical antipsychotic drugs have shown some success.

CBT is an evidenced-based treatment and is considered to be useful in addressing the behaviours and thoughts that might have led to the disorder. However, FBT is viewed as more successful than individual therapy (Espie and Eisler, 2015) so is the treatment chosen here. Some of the other reasons for choosing FBT in this section are as follows:

- CBT has already been explained in relation to the other disorders described earlier (schizophrenia, unipolar depression and OCD) and FBT is different to CBT.
- Those with anorexia nervosa are often adolescents and it can be beneficial to focus on the whole family rather than just the patient. This is because family interactions have been shown to unconsciously contribute to anorexia, such as praise when someone diets (though not of course intending for the focus on losing weight to lead to anorexia nervosa).

Family-based therapy (FBT)

Family therapy helps to focus on what, for the patient, can be a dysfunctional role within the family. Family-based therapy (FBT) is used for anorexia nervosa as family support can be helpful and because dysfunctional family roles may be part of the disorder. The patient's eating behaviours can maintain that role too.

For the most part FBT will take place with the family and the patient present. There can also be sessions without the patient present, because that can help the family see the roles they play in respect of the patient's eating issues. Family-based therapy can last a year; for example, Lock et al. (2010) gave 24 one-hour sessions over the course of a year. Their family-based treatment had three phases:

1. Therapy began by focusing on complimenting parents on their parenting so that they did not feel personal responsibility for the disorder. Families were encouraged to think about how to help the child to return to their normal weight.
2. Parents were helped to give control of eating and weight to the young person in accordance with the age of the individual.
3. The focus then moved to making sure the child–family relationship was a healthy one.

Maudsley family-based therapy

The Maudsley is a well-known hospital in London, providing both in-patient and community mental healthcare. The Institute of Psychiatry is based at the Maudsley Hospital and it conducts a lot of research there, including research in clinical neuroscience. The 'Maudsley method' is a specific type of family therapy where parents feed the person who has anorexia nervosa to help them to gain weight and to achieve better eating habits. This tends to work best near the start of the illness.

Le Grange and Lock (2005) discuss family-based treatment of adolescent anorexia nervosa as carried out at the Maudsley. They explain that weight gain is the most important focus but that using in-patient and day hospitals is very disruptive for the family and for the young person with anorexia nervosa. In addition, weight gain is not enough for the person to recover from anorexia nervosa. In view of this, the Maudsley offers an out-patient family-based treatment. The aim is to prevent hospitalisation by drawing parents in and helping them to help the young person so that the young person's normal development can continue. Eisler *et al.* (1997) studied the Maudsley approach and found that between 75 and 90 per cent of young people had reached their normal weight at a five-year follow up. There had also been improvement in other areas, such as psychological functioning. Le Grange and Lock (2005) in the US discussed the use of FBT, similar to the Maudsley approach, and reported similar positive results with about 20 treatments over 6–12 months, leading to around 80 per cent of patients with anorexia nervosa having full weight restoration at the end of the treatment.

In the Maudsley approach parents work to restore the young person's weight to normal levels, give control over eating back to the young person and use discussion to encourage normal development for the individual. The Maudsley approach does not see parents as responsible for the young person's disorder but as a resource to help in recovery.

STUDY HINT
You have probably noticed that in some areas of your course, some names appear often, such as Le Grange when looking at FBT, and also Lock. This can help you to remember the most important researchers in the area you are studying and to find out more by doing an internet search related to the names.

The Maudsley approach has three phases:

1 The weight restoration phase is first, where the dangers of malnutrition are focused on and the family's reactions to eating habits is looked at. Parents are helped to feed the young person and the therapist helps in a joint attempt to get the weight back to normal for that individual.

2 The young person needs then to take control over their eating. This phase begins once the patient has accepted the parents' demands that they eat and once their weight is improving. After focusing on weight gain, there is a focus away from thinking always about eating and tension over eating is reduced as far as possible. Alongside that, concerns can be looked at with regard to family relationships. Normal development is encouraged, such as the young person going out for a meal with their friends.

3 When the young person is maintaining their weight, the focus moves to them establishing a healthy identity, and includes supporting them to make their own decisions and to establish appropriate relationships with parents and siblings.

Progress check 1.61

Explain the three phases of the Maudsley family-based therapy.

Evidence for the effectiveness of family-based therapy

- In a five-year follow up study looking at the Maudsley family therapy, Le Grange and Eisler (2009) found that up to 90 per cent of those involved fully recovered, which is strong evidence for the effectiveness of FBT. A general figure given by Silverstone (2005) is that only 50 per cent of those attending specialist referral centres will fully recover. This suggests FBT is a useful therapy.

- Nauert, in an online account, suggests that more than 50 per cent of those receiving FBT using the Maudsley approach in Chicago (Le Grange led the programme there) were in full remission after 12 months, compared with 23 per cent of those using adolescent-focused individual therapy (AFT). These are different figures from those found by Le Grange and Eisler (2009,) but they still show effectiveness of the therapy. Nauert does say that after a year just 10 per cent of patients relapsed, which matches the 90 per cent claim of Le Grange and Eisler (2009), again showing effectiveness of the therapy. With regard to AFT, 40 per cent relapsed according to Nauert.

- Lock *et al.* (2010) carried out a study using a randomised clinical trial comparing FBT with AFT for young people with anorexia nervosa. A total of 121 participants aged 12 to 18 years with anorexia nervosa were assessed before the treatment (a baseline measure), at the end of the treatment and also at follow up at 6 and 12 months. There were no differences between the two treatments at the end of the therapy – both had the same success rate. However, after 6 months and at 12 months the family-based therapy was found to be better with regard to full remission. FBT was also better at the end of the treatment when it came to partial remission. Lock *et al.* (2010) concluded that AFT and FBT were both successful treatments but it was FBT that was better long term in maintaining full remission.

Evidence against the effectiveness of FBT

- Dimitropoulos *et al.* (2015) investigated family-based treatment with young people with anorexia nervosa. James Lock and Daniel Le Grange, as well as others, were involved in this study. The study involved content analysis, 7 interviews and 6 focus groups involving 34 clinicians. The study found that individual clinicians did vary the family-based therapy to increase its appropriateness with regard to the development of the young people – who were the age of transition into adulthood and so into adult care rather than paediatric care. The clinicians tended to work with the patient in a more collaborative way, spending more time with the individual before engaging with the family and giving the individual more time to focus on their own eating habits without support of parents. Clinicians said that it was the age of the individual with the eating disorder, their level of independence and the idea of transferring to adult support (given their age) that was the main focus in making changes to the usual family-support therapy approach. This suggests that FBT is successful with young people but when the young person is about to transfer away from paediatric support clinicians take a different approach.

- Dare *et al.* (2001, cited in Fairburn, 2005) carried out a study of 84 adult patients (mean age 26.3 years) who were given one of four treatments. These were focus psychoanalytic psychotherapy, CAT (cognitive analytic therapy), FBT and out-patient sessions with a trainee psychiatrist. All three of the psychotherapies were better than the out-patient sessions. Across all three psychotherapies there was a good outcome for 13.8 per cent of the sample and a substantial improvement for 18.5 per cent of the sample. When using an adolescent sample in the same study there was a good outcome for 37.5 per cent and 25 per cent improved substantially, suggesting that though therapies including FBT can

work with adults, they work better with adolescents. This might indicate, as has been said, that anorexia nervosa improves more if treated earlier. Fairburn (2005) concludes his review by stating that treatment outcome for adolescents is good but for adults it is in general poor. Fairburn (2005) concludes that treatments are really not that good for anorexia nervosa (the percentages improving are low even for the adolescents).

Evaluation of family-based therapy for anorexia nervosa

Strengths

- There is a lot of evidence to show that FBT works for young people with anorexia nervosa. Lock *et al.* (2010) found that FBT was successful after a 6-month and 12-month follow-up (though they found that adolescent-focused individual therapy was as successful as FBT at the end of the therapy, though not so successful at follow-up). Le Grange and Eisler (2009) found that 90 per cent of young people on the Maudsley Hospital family-based therapy programme reached full recovery, which is a very encouraging figure.
- Studies that are carried out (for example, Lock *et al.*, 2010) tend to have reasonably large sample sizes and there are strong controls to ensure that the treatment is the same for all participants. This means that conclusions are more reliable and more credible.

Weaknesses

- Family-based therapy is focused on children and adolescents, with studies often focusing on adolescents. It is found to be successful for that age group, where family interactions are likely to be different from when a young adult is living away from home, for example. This suggests that family-based therapy is suitable for specific age groups and not others, which could be seen as a limitation.
- FBT can be adapted each time it is used, as Dimitropoulos *et al.* (2015) discovered. They found that clinicians varied the treatment according to the individual, including their level of independence (for example, they saw the individual before a family meeting). If FBT is varied then it is harder to study and draw conclusions about. This is because different studies might be looking at different therapies in effect; they are not comparing the same treatment.

- The figures showing the success rate for FBT for young people are good if you are one of the people it worked for. However, there are those who it does not work for and that is a limitation. Also studies are likely to look at cases were FBT has already been chosen as a suitable treatment, so perhaps the participants are those likely to do well on the programme. This might mean there is bias in conclusions drawn about effectiveness from such studies.
- NICE Guidelines (2004) suggest that there is limited evidence in respect of specific treatments for anorexia nervosa, including family therapy, such as Geist (2000), who found insufficient evidence that family group education was better than family therapy, or Russell (1987), who found family therapy was not better than individual supportive psychotherapy. There are studies that suggest family therapy is not that good, though such studies tend to report 'limited evidence', which perhaps means there is some support for FBT.

Explore

You can find out more about the strengths and weaknesses of FBT using this link:

www.scienceofeds.org/2013/04/22/family-based-treatmen-for-adolescents-with-anorexia-nervosa-hype-or-hope/

Medication and anorexia nervosa

Drug therapy has not been shown to be very effective for anorexia nervosa, although antipsychotics and antidepressants are used.

Antipsychotics

- Chlorpromazine has been used and did lead to weight gain but a serious side-effect was that some patients suffered seizures (Dally and Sargant, 1966).
- Antipsychotics that blocked dopamine also enabled patients to achieve some weight gain (a main purpose in treating anorexia nervosa), but they did not affect any of the other symptoms (Vandereycken, 1984, cited in Silverstone, 2005).
- Atypical antipsychotic drugs might be more successful. Powers et al. (2002, cited in Silverstone, 2005) found that in a study of the use of olanzapine with 18 patients, 10 gained weight, but 4 did not complete the study and 4 lost weight, so these findings are mixed in terms of success. In another study, also looking at olanzapine, patients said they had lower levels of anxiety and less difficulty with eating (Malina et al., 2003, cited in Silverstone, 2005). Atypical antipsychotic drugs focus mainly on dopamine

functioning and Kaye (2008, cited in Aigner et al., 2011) suggests that altered dopamine functioning in the striatum might contribute to anorexia nervosa symptoms. This suggests that antipsychotic drugs can be useful in anorexia nervosa.

Summary of antipsychotic use for anorexia nervosa

- Chlorpromazine and antipsychotics that block dopamine enable weight gain but are not otherwise useful.
- Olanzapine (an atypical antipsychotic) enables weight gain and can help to reduce anxiety and eating difficulties.

Antidepressants

- Tricyclic antidepressants have side-effects, including those that affect the heart, so they tend not to be used.
- Selective serotonin reuptake inhibitors (SSRIs) such as fluoxetine have been used and studied, but studies tend not to demonstrate effectiveness of their use for treatment of anorexia nervosa. However, Kaye et al., (2001, cited in Silverstone, 2005 and Aigner et al., 2011) suggest that at higher doses fluoxetine can help to prevent relapse when someone has finished therapy and is receiving 'maintenance' therapy. SSRIs can help with the anxiety and depression that accompany anorexia nervosa. Serotonin function can be disturbed by anorexia nervosa and this disturbance can continue after recovery, so focusing on serotonin levels using medication can be helpful (Kaye, 2008, cited in Aigner et al., 2011).
- Citalopram did not help with weight gain (Fassino et al., 2002, cited in Silverstone, 2005) but did help with depression and with obsessions and compulsions.
- Venlafaxine, an antidepressant that stops the reuptake of serotonin and noradrenaline, was as good as fluoxetine in respect of weight gain if there is CBT as well (Ricca et al., 1999, cited in Silverstone, 2005).

Summary of antidepressant use for anorexia nervosa

- Fluoxetine can help with maintaining weight and recovery.
- SSRIs can help because they focus on serotonin levels, which can help to reduce anxiety and depression as well as, possibly, other symptoms of anorexia that may be caused by low levels of serotonin.
- Citalopram helps with depression, obsessions and compulsions that can accompany anorexia nervosa.
- Venlafaxine can be as good as fluoxetine with regard to weight gain if there is CBT alongside its use.

Year One link: In biological psychology you will have looked at different brain structures and might have considered the hypothalamus and its role in governing issues such as food intake, metabolism and appetite.

Progress check 1.63

Name two drugs that provide some level of help in treating anorexia nervosa and briefly outline the way in which they help.

Guidelines for drug therapy for eating disorders

Aigner *et al.* (2011) write about guidelines for drug treatment of eating disorders. Although they include bulimia nervosa as well as anorexia nervosa, they are useful because they also help to describe a therapy. Aigner *et al.* (2011) state that for anorexia nervosa the UK NICE Guidelines (2004) do not suggest drug therapy as the first choice as such medication is disappointing in respect of core symptoms, promoting weight gain and affecting depression. The New Zealand Guidelines (2004) recommend using family therapy, CBT and dietary advice, but not drug therapy (Aigner *et al.*, 2011). However, the New Zealand Guidelines do say that antidepressants can help with co-morbid symptoms (like anxiety and depression) and olanzapine might help more directly too. In the Cochrane review carried out by Claudino *et al.* (2006, cited in Aigner *et al.*, 2011) there was not enough evidence found to recommend antidepressants for anorexia nervosa.

Effectiveness of drug therapy

It would appear from the studies that drug therapy for anorexia nervosa has limited use and is not recommended as a first-line treatment.

- Zhu and Walsh (2002) and Casper (2003), cited in Silverstone (2005), suggest that drugs have limited value for anorexia nervosa, possibly because patients do not take the medication and instead try to hide it.
- Mitchell *et al.* (2013) found that antidepressants could be effective in bulimia nervosa but less so with anorexia nervosa. Atypical antipsychotics were found not to be that useful for anorexia nervosa.
- Halmi *et al.* (1986) carried out a double blind placebo controlled trial with amitriptyline and cyproheptadine (a tricyclic antidepressant) in 72 females with anorexia nervosa. They found a significant weight gain for cyproheptadine only.

> **STUDY HINT**
> Use what you have learned about research to recall what is meant by:
> - 'double blind' — both participants and those running the trial are unaware of who is in a placebo group and who is in the experimental group
> - 'controlled' — all else is the same except one group has the drug and the other has the placebo pill
> - 'placebo' — a pill where the medication being tested is not present; it is given so that all patients receive a 'pill' without knowing which contains the medication, as a control.
> The more you use these terms and the more familiar you become with their meaning, the more easily you will understand and remember them.

Progress check 1.64

Name two drugs and their associated studies that suggest they do not appear to offer help with anorexia nervosa.

- Crisp *et al.* (1987, cited in Aigner *et al.*, 2011) found that clomipramine (a tricyclic antidepressant) did not give significant weight gain for 16 patients with anorexia nervosa, compared with a placebo.

Effectiveness of drug therapy – atypical antipsychotics showing some effectiveness

Despite the studies above which showed that drug therapy is less helpful in the treatment of anorexia nervosa, some atypical antipsychotic drugs showed some success.

- Olanzapine shows weight gain and some other improvements in those with anorexia nervosa (e.g. Babarich *et al.*, 2004, cited in Aigner *et al.*, 2011).
- Court *et al.* (2010, cited in Aigner *et al.*, 2011) found that using low-dose quetiapine (an atypical antipsychotic drug) showed psychological and physical improvements with few side-effects, using 33 patients with anorexia nervosa.
- Bosanac *et al.* (2007, cited in Aigner *et al.*, 2011) also found improvements in respect of weight gain and other measures using quetiapine.
- Trunke *et al.* (2010, cited in Aigner *et al.*, 2011) used aripiprazole with five patients with anorexia nervosa and there were what Aigner *et al.* (2011) described as 'promising results' when the drug was used for more than four months.

Evaluation of drug therapy for anorexia nervosa

Strengths

- Drug therapy can help with weight gain, which is a strength, as weight gain is a main goal of therapy for anorexia nervosa (e.g. Babarich et al., 2004, cited in Aigner et al., 2011). Drug therapy can also help with the anxiety and depression that may accompany anorexia nervosa; again, this is a strength.
- Studies that show the usefulness of drug therapy, such as for weight gain, tend to be controlled trials (e.g. Crisp et al., 1987, cited in Aigner et al. 2011), which means credible and reliable findings.

Weaknesses

- There is quite a lot of evidence to show that drug therapy is not directly useful for anorexia nervosa even though it can help with symptoms of anxiety, depression, obsessions and compulsions. This means drug therapy is not the treatment of choice and indeed NICE Guidelines do not recommend it as a first choice.
- A treatment is carried out within a setting and NICE Guidelines (2004) suggest that the success of a treatment can depend on it being carried out in an appropriate setting. For example, being treated as an out-patient allows more normal development for the individual, which family-based therapy takes into account, compared to being an in-patient. Being an in-patient, however, enables there to be a focus on the weight gain needed, for example. NICE Guidelines (2004) say some family-based therapy is 'essential', which suggests that drug therapy alone will not be enough. The Guidelines say that drug therapy is used to support psychological treatments and for management of co-morbid conditions (such as depression). This shows that drug therapy for anorexia nervosa has limitations.
- Drug therapy does not seem tolerated as much as psychotherapy for those with anorexia nervosa (Treasure, 1998, cited in NICE Guidelines, 2004). Also studies often do not consider how problems with nutrition in those with anorexia nervosa might affect drug action (e.g. Halbreich and Kahj, 2000, cited in Nice Guidelines, 2004, showed that antidepressants might not work as well if oestrogen levels are low).

Test yourself

1 Compare two explanations for anorexia nervosa, one biological and one non-biological. **(8 marks)**
2 Evaluate one biological treatment for anorexia nervosa. **(12 marks)**

Summary

In the content section you need to know about the following:

- The diagnosis of mental disorders including the 4Ds — deviance, dysfunction, distress and danger.
- The DSM and ICD-10 classification systems for mental health, including validity and reliability. For the DSM you need to cover either DSM-IV-TR or DSM-5.
- Schizophrenia, including features and symptoms, three explanations (neurotransmitter functioning, one other biological explanation and one non-biological explanation).
- One other disorder from unipolar depression, obsessive compulsive disorder and anorexia nervosa. For your chosen disorder you need to cover features and symptoms and two explanations (one biological and one non-biological).
- Two treatments for schizophrenia (one biological and one non-biological). These must be from different topic areas.
- Two treatments for your chosen disorder from unipolar depression, obsessive compulsive disorder and anorexia nervosa (one biological and one non-biological). These must be from different topic areas.

Studies in clinical psychology

For this section you need to look at three studies in detail, the first of which is the classic study for clinical psychology in your course, Rosenhan's study of 'being sane in insane places', which looks at the issue of diagnosis and disorder. The second study, Carlsson et al. (1999/2000), focuses on schizophrenia. The third study will relate to the mental disorder you chose to study, from a choice of unipolar depression, anorexia nervosa and obsessive compulsive disorder. For each of these three disorders your course asks you to cover one study from a choice of two named studies.

In this chapter all three option disorders are covered together with both studies for each of the three option disorders. Table 1.11 shows the studies covered in this chapter. In total you will cover three studies, but you may like to read for interest about what is being done in the area of the other two disorders you are not choosing to study.

Table 1.11 Studies

Disorder	Study
Diagnosis and disorder	Rosenhan (1973) 'On being sane in insane places'
Schizophrenia	Carlsson et al. (1999/2000) 'Network interactions in schizophrenia – therapeutic implications (a review)'
Unipolar depression	Kroenke et al. (2008) 'The PHQ-8 as a measure of current depression in the general population' OR Williams et al. (2013) 'Combining imagination and reason in the treatment of depression: a randomised controlled trial of internet based cognitive bias modification and internet-CBT for depression'
Anorexia nervosa	Scott-Van Zeeland et al. (2013/2014) 'Evidence for the role of EPHX2 gene variants in anorexia nervosa' OR Guardia et al. (2012) 'Imagining one's own and someone else's body actions: dissociation in anorexia nervosa'
Obsessive compulsive disorder (OCD)	Masellis et al. (2003) 'Quality of life in OCD: Differential impacts of obsessions, compulsions and depressions co-morbidity' OR POTS team including March et al. (2004) 'Cognitive-behavioural therapy, sertraline and their combination for children and adolescents with OCD'

Diagnosis and disorder: Rosenhan (1973)

David Rosenhan 'sent' people into mental hospitals posing as mentally ill patients to see if their sanity would be identified. It was not. The study relates to issues surrounding the use of the DSM and its validity and reliability (page 14), as well as issues around defining abnormality (page 6).

Background

Rosenhan (1973) was interested in the difficulty of defining abnormality, including problems with defining 'sane' and 'insane', as well as defining mental disorders such as schizophrenia. If it is difficult to define such terms, then questions have to be asked about the accuracy of diagnosis. For example, the question of whether 'mental illness' lies in the person, the observer or the person doing the diagnosis needs to be addressed. The DSM (*Diagnostic and Statistical Manual of Mental Disorders*) offers lists of symptoms which can be matched to those presented by a patient, in order to diagnose a specific illness, thus distinguishing the 'sane' from the 'insane'.

St Elizabeth's Hospital in Washington DC is believed to be one of the 12 psychiatric hospitals used by Rosenhan in his study 'On being sane in insane places'. It is now closed and boarded up.

Rosenhan's study placed 'normal' people (who did not have, and had never had, symptoms of a psychiatric disorder) in an institution to see if they could be distinguished from 'the insane context in which they are found' (Rosenhan, 1973, p. 238). The study assumed that the hospital staff were competent, that the individual behaved as they normally did, and that there was no suggestion that they had had any previous mental health problems. Given these factors the study questioned whether the setting alone would be sufficient to lead to the person being accepted as mentally ill.

Aims

The main aim was to see if eight sane people who gained admission into 12 different hospitals would be 'found out' as sane. A further aim was to find out what the experience of being in such an institution was like, and what it feels like to be viewed as 'insane'.

Procedures: study 1

Sample

The sample involved eight **pseudo-patients** (three women and five men) taking part in the study. One was a 20-year-old graduate and the other seven were older and were made up of three psychologists, a paediatrician, a psychiatrist, a painter and a housewife.

They all used pseudonyms to avoid any diagnosis giving later embarrassment. Those employed in mental health provided a different occupation to avoid being treated differently. Rosenhan was one of the pseudo-patients; the hospital administrator and chief psychologist where he carried out the research knew about him, but nobody else did. The other seven were unknown.

Definition

Pseudo-patients is the term Rosenhan used for the people in his study who had no mental disorder and yet when placed in an institution they were not 'found out'. They were called 'pseudo-patients' because they were not real patients, but from the point of view of the staff at the relevant hospitals they *were* patients.

STUDY HINT

This study helps to illustrate the wide-ranging features of research methods and the difficulty of allocating a specific research method to every study. In some ways Rosenhan's study is similar to an experimental case study because there are controls and some manipulation with regard to what the participants said to doctors and so on; however, there are no conditions as such. The study is in the field, but not in the natural setting of the participants, so it is not quite a field study, while it also has the features of a case study because of the gathering of in-depth data, both quantitative and (predominantly) qualitative.

Settings

The settings were varied so that the findings could be generalised. The 12 hospitals, for example, were located in five different states in the USA and were varied in character (e.g. old/new, good ratio of staff to patients or not, private or not).

Hospital admission

The pseudo-patients called the hospital for an appointment. Then they arrived at the admissions office saying that they had been hearing voices. The pseudo-patients said the voices were unclear but seemed to be saying 'empty', 'hollow' or 'thud'. These words were chosen because they seemed to place an emphasis on the person's life (for example, life being hollow). Other than this and changing their name and some of their personal history, each pseudo-patient gave details of their own life. None of their current behaviours or history was pathological.

On being admitted the pseudo-patients stopped simulating symptoms of abnormality in any way. Some were a little nervous, not having believed they would be admitted so easily, but otherwise all behaved as they would 'normally'. They were given medication, which they did not swallow, responded to instructions from staff and chatted to other patients. Each pseudo-patient was told they would have to get out by convincing staff they were sane. All but one wanted to be discharged almost immediately, as hospitalisation was extremely stressful. Therefore, they behaved 'sanely' and were 'paragons of cooperation'.

Results: study 1

The pseudo-patients were never detected. All except one were admitted with a diagnosis of schizophrenia in remission. No records or behaviour by hospital staff showed that there were any doubts about the authenticity of the patients. 'Rather, evidence was strong that, once labelled schizophrenic, the pseudo-patient was stuck with that label' (Rosenhan, 1973, p. 241). 'In remission' meant 'able to be discharged' rather than anything else. Between 7 and 52 days were spent in hospital by the 'patients', with an average of 19 days.

Factors to note

- The hospitals were considered good or excellent and not to blame for the failure to recognise sanity.
- The pseudo-patients were not carefully observed, so it was not observation of behaviour that led to the label 'schizophrenia'.
- It was not that the false diagnosis was applied because the pseudo-patients did not behave sanely. Visitors, and indeed other patients, felt they were 'sane'; during the first three hospitalisations 35 out of 118 patients on the admissions ward voiced their suspicions, such as 'you're not crazy. You're a journalist or a professor' (this was because of the note-taking). In the study, Rosenhan states 'The fact that the patients often recognised normality when staff did not raises important questions' (p. 241).

Rosenhan suggests that, in general, doctors are more likely to err on the side of caution – that is, to call a healthy person sick rather than a sick person healthy. This partly explains the findings. However, psychiatric diagnoses carry stigma, making the implications of misguided psychiatric diagnoses in some ways more serious than medical ones.

STUDY HINT

Rosenhan discusses how doctors are more likely to say that a healthy person is unwell, which is a Type II error, than to say a sick person is healthy, which is a Type I (optimistic) error. You can use this information to remind yourself of Type I and Type II errors in statistical testing (see 'Psychological skills – methods' section online for a review of these). Doctors have a strong bias towards a Type II error (Scheff, 1966, cited in Rosenhan, 1973).

Procedures: study 2

Rosenhan wondered whether the diagnosis of 'insane' for 'sane' people could be reversed. Staff at a teaching hospital doubted the findings of the first study, so Rosenhan told them that sometime in the next three months one or more pseudo-patients would attempt to be admitted. Each staff member was asked to rate patients presenting themselves on a scale of 1 to 10 to reflect the likelihood of them being the pseudo-patient.

Results: study 2

Judgements were given on 193 patients admitted for psychiatric treatment, of which 41 were judged with high confidence by at least one staff member to be pseudo-patients, 23 were considered suspect by at least one psychiatrist and 19 were thought to be pseudo-patients by one psychiatrist and one other staff member. There were, in fact, no genuine pseudo-patients (as far as Rosenhan knew).

'Any diagnostic process that lends itself so readily to massive errors of this sort cannot be very reliable', stated Rosenhan (p. 242). 'Once labelled schizophrenic there is nothing the pseudo-patient can do to overcome the tag', which 'profoundly colours others' perceptions of him and his behaviour' (p. 243). One explanation for the failure to detect sanity is that 'insanity' is a powerful central trait, and therefore all behaviours and characteristics are coloured by the label 'insane' and normal behaviours are thus overlooked.

> **STUDY HINT**
> If you decide to study criminological psychology, consider Rosenhan's comments about labelling — that once labelled 'schizophrenic' it is a difficult label to remove. You may like to consider how labelling might be an explanation for crime, when considered with the idea of a self-fulfilling prophecy.

Rosenhan found that 'normal' family background was interpreted as 'abnormal' in diagnosis. For example, acknowledged changing patterns of closeness between a pseudo-patient and his mother and father over the years was interpreted as 'manifests a long history of considerable ambivalence in close relationships' (p. 244). The records for this pseudo-patient mentioned 'angry outbursts' and 'spankings' of the children (untrue). The facts were unintentionally distorted to 'fit' with a 'popular theory of the dynamics of schizophrenic reaction' (p. 244). Rosenhan also questioned why the extensive note-taking undertaken by the pseudo-patients did not elicit questions from the hospital staff. Three pseudo-patients had their writing diagnosed as an aspect of their pathological behaviour: 'Patient engages in writing behaviour' was recorded.

It is unlikely that someone is insane all the time, just as usually we are not angry or depressed all the time. However, it seems that once a person is labelled 'insane' all their behaviour is understood through that label. Rosenhan suggested that it is perhaps because the state of insanity is not understood that the label is so strong. For instance, schizophrenia cannot be easily understood and so is interpreted as threatening to others, whereas a broken leg is easily understood and is not interpreted as threatening to others. Moreover, mental illness is treated differently from physical illness as it allegedly lasts forever.

Hospital environment

Rosenhan was interested in the hospital environment. The staff and patients were separated, and professional staff had glassed quarters in the corner of a ward, which the pseudo-patients called 'the cage'. Staff emerged from the cage, did their tasks, and then returned. When 'time out of the cage' was measured it was found (in four hospitals) that the average was 11.3 per cent of the whole time. There was little mingling time with the patients. On an average day the nurses came out of the cage 11.5 times per shift. Doctors (especially psychiatrists) were even less available and were rarely seen on the wards. Those with most power had least to do with the patients. Rosenhan wondered if staff learned from their superiors.

It is interesting that Rosenhan talks about the attitudes of the staff to the patients, because in the practical investigation work for clinical psychology (on the website) studies are briefly mentioned that focused on the attitudes of mental health staff to patients and they did show negative attitudes, as Rosenhan suggests. However, a summative content analysis carried out for the practical investigation found six articles in three newspapers where there was positivity towards those with mental disorders and stigma and negative stereotyping were not found.

Further experiments

The pseudo-patients asked a member of staff a question periodically (such as 'when will I be discharged?'), and always asked politely. In general, staff avoided continuing such contacts. In contrast, a student at Stanford University was attended to and answered when she asked staff there for help, such as how to find an area of the campus. She was helped without exception, even when her questions were trivial. However, if she went to the university medical school and asked to see a psychiatrist she was helped less than if she asked to see a doctor. It was concluded therefore that a mental health issue was something that would be avoided by members of the public.

Table 1.12 Responses by psychiatrists and nurses/attendants to self-initiated contact by pseudo-patients and responses to a student on campus (non-medical)

Responses	Psychiatrists in the hospitals	Nurses/attendants in the hospitals	Faculty members on a university campus (non-medical)
Moves on, head averted	71%	88%	0%
Makes eye contact	23%	10%	0%
Pauses and chats	2%	2%	0%
Stops and talks	4%	0.5%	100%

Progress check 1.65

Use the percentages in Table 1.12 to show why it was concluded that staff did not interact much with patients as much as might happen in the 'outside world'.

Powerlessness and depersonalisation

Eye contact and verbal contact make a person feel they are 'seen' as an individual, while a lack of such contact is depersonalising. The pseudo-patients observed a lot of avoiding and depersonalisation of patients in the hospital. The patient is powerless, deprived of legal rights if committed to the psychiatric hospital. There is no privacy. Pseudo-patients at times felt invisible and 'unworthy of account' (p. 251). The medication given to the pseudo-patients was not swallowed (nearly 2,100 pills were given out, with just two being swallowed). However, such behaviour went unnoticed and the pseudo-patients found the medication of other patients hidden away, which reinforces the idea that patients were invisible and staff did not notice them or their behaviour. The pseudo-patients showed behaviour that was a way of becoming a 'person' – such as engaging in psychotherapy with other patients – to counter the feelings of depersonalisation that they were experiencing.

Origins of the depersonalisation

Rosenhan (1973) suggests that one reason for the depersonalisation of the patients involves attitudes to those who are mentally ill – on the one hand fear and distrust and on the other hand a wish to help. Such ambivalence might lead to avoidance. A further reason, according to Rosenhan, is the hierarchical structure of the hospital: those in senior positions have very little contact with the patients and all staff follow their lead. A third reason for the depersonalisation might be financial, though Rosenhan adds that he felt that more staffing would not change the depersonalising of patients, so financial factors were not a main cause. Finally, there is the suggestion that the use of medication means patients are being treated so contact is not necessary.

Conclusions

Rosenhan (1973) concluded that the sane cannot be distinguished from the insane in psychiatric hospitals. In the hospital environment special meanings are given to behaviour and patients in such an environment experience powerlessness, depersonalisation and segregation.

Rosenhan looked for suggestions to offer help to those who are mentally ill, deriving ideas from his study. First, Rosenhan felt this was an argument against using labels and diagnosis. He felt it would be more helpful to keep the patient in a better environment, and mentions community mental health facilities. He felt that perceptions of someone with a mental disorder were distorted in a psychiatric hospital, and those distorted perceptions were not helpful for the individual as increased sensitivity to their needs was necessary. Second, Rosenhan thought if staff read his study and similar materials then they might be helped to understand how patients experienced such hospitals. He adds that the pseudo-patients felt the staff really cared and were committed to the patients, and it is important to note that he felt there was no malice or stupidity in their actions. Third, he felt more data from actual rather than pseudo-patients would be valuable.

STUDY HINT

Rosenhan (1973) is the classic study in clinical psychology for your course, so be sure to know it well. Note that its main focus is on diagnosis and defining abnormality, rather than on schizophrenia. It is not a study of schizophrenia as such.

Progress check 1.66

Give some evidence from Rosenhan (1973) to suggest whether care in the community or care outside an institution would be better for those with mental health issues.

Evaluation of Rosenhan (1973)

Strengths

- The kinds of hospitals used were varied, so that findings could be generalised. Twelve hospitals were involved, strengthening the findings and allowing them to be generalised. If just one hospital had been involved it might have been that hospital alone that 'labelled' mental illness.
- The design was simple. The pseudo-patients just had to be themselves, so it is unlikely that any treatment of them was due to their behaviour being similar to someone with a mental illness. The fact that some of the bona fide patients realised that the pseudo-patients were not mentally ill backs this observation up and suggests that their behaviour was validly 'normal'.
- By using 8 people in 12 hospitals the study was able to be replicated and the same results were found. The study is therefore regarded as reliable.
- The findings are strong because the idea of people being perceived through the use of labels was clear and is likely to still be the case, although the study was carried out over 40 years ago.

Weaknesses

- The pseudo-patients said that they heard voices, a standard symptom of schizophrenia, so it is perhaps not surprising that they were considered to have schizophrenia. (This does not, however, explain why the patients were not subsequently realised to be sane, unless each hospital was being cautious.) It is perhaps equally unsurprising that pseudo-patients were wrongly identified in Study 2 as staff were (wrongly) informed that some would be presenting themselves for treatment in a three-month period. These 'lies' are likely to have guided the results and this means the studies were not natural and, to that extent, not valid.
- In the 40 years since the study was carried out, institutions have changed their working practices considerably and there is a great deal more emphasis on care in the community, so it might be wrong to conclude that mental illness is still hard to diagnose.

> ### Progress check 1.67
> Give two strengths of Rosenhan's (1973) study.

Contemporary study relating to schizophrenia: Carlsson *et al.* (1999/2000)

Carlsson *et al.* (1999/2000) is the study you have to cover relating to schizophrenia, although it is more of a review of findings in the area of schizophrenia rather than a study. The focus is on the dopamine hypothesis and how investigations into the way neurotransmitters function in the brain suggests that there is more to psychotic functioning than excess dopamine at the synapse. It seems other neurotransmitters are implicated and the interactions between neurotransmitters are important as much as the amount of dopamine present.

> **STUDY HINT**
> When considering explanations for schizophrenia you need to learn about neurotransmitter functioning as one of your explanations. You can use Carlsson *et al.*'s (1999/2000) findings in your discussion.

Carlsson *et al.* (1999/2000) is a study about neurotransmitter interaction in schizophrenia and implications for therapy. It is a **review** of what is known in the area of study, rather than a study that gathers actual **empirical data**. The review claims that as more knowledge is uncovered about how different neurotransmitters work together, drug therapy can be informed and hopefully improved. Animal studies have suggested that instead of drugs being used to paralyse neurotransmitters and neural circuits, these circuits might be able to be stabilised, which can help in avoiding side-effects from drug therapy. Some findings show that drugs affecting glutamate function may help to control negative symptoms of schizophrenia.

Carlsson *et al.*'s (1999/2000) article uses some evidence from their own past work and some evidence from the work of others, including evidence using mice, to look at the role of neurotransmitters in schizophrenia. Their review is set out in the way the article is set out, using separate sections. Though you can think of the introduction as the background, the middle parts as the results of their review and there is also a conclusion at the end. The discussion is found throughout.

They start by explaining how scanning supports the dopamine explanation for schizophrenia. Though new evidence has shown how dopamine interacts with other neurotransmitters and has shown the complexity of neural networks. Issues with dopamine and glutamate are two models of schizophrenia being tested. Being able to stabilise neural networks is a treatment now supported. Drugs that act on dopamine, serotonin and glutamate receptors are put forward as treatments for schizophrenia.

Definitions

A **review** is published in a journal just like a study, but does not gather **empirical data** in the way a study does. A review considers what is known in an area of research and is useful for seeing what needs to be studied and what conclusions can be drawn about that area of research.

Empirical data are data gathered directly, using touch, sound, smell, taste or sight.

Year One link: Look back at what you learned about neurotransmitter functioning in biological psychology in your Year One course.

Background

Research shows how there is a **dopaminergic dysfunction** in schizophrenia (the dopamine hypothesis) (Carlsson *et al.*, 1995, cited in Carlsson *et al.*, 1999).

Evidence for the dopamine hypothesis comes from scanning. For example, PET scanning shows an increase in dopamine in patients with schizophrenia (those not in remission) than in controls (e.g. Hietala *et al.*, 1994, cited in Carlsson *et al.*, 1999/2000). There is greater amphetamine-induced release of dopamine in the basal ganglia brain area in those with schizophrenia as shown by SPECT and PET scanning. This rise in dopamine release correlates with positive psychotic symptoms (e.g. Laruelle *et al.*, 1996, cited in Carlsson *et al.*, 1999/2000, p. 343).

> **STUDY HINT**
> Carlsson *et al.* (1999/2000) discuss PET scanning as a method, so you can use the study as an example of scanning when discussing scanning as a research method in Paper 1. Controls are mentioned and the validity of scans is questioned in the study, both of which provide useful material when discussing methodological issues.

Definitions

The suffix 'inergic' means 'relating to', for example, **dopaminergic** means 'relating to dopamine'. **Dysfunction** means problems in functioning.

There are weaknesses with this dopamine explanation for schizophrenia:

- These correlations are not 'perfect' – some people with schizophrenia are in the 'normal' range regarding dopamine release. There is the suggestion that only a 'subpopulation' of those with schizophrenia have the dopamine dysfunction.
- Another weakness of the dopamine hypothesis is that some patients showing stress or reaction to amphetamine showed the dopamine dysfunction, so it may have come from a stress experience and not from schizophrenia.
- Also the evidence was gained from those experiencing acute schizophrenia and may not be found in those with chronic schizophrenia. An **acute** phase of schizophrenia is when someone suddenly shows strong psychotic symptoms, though schizophrenia is usually seen as a chronic disorder because it lasts a long time.
- According to Carlsson *et al.*, Laruelle *et al.* found that dopamine release from amphetamine was normal for those with schizophrenia in **remission**. This fits with patients in remission being more affected by side-effects of antipsychotic drugs than when undergoing an episode of schizophrenia. An issue is that anti-psychotic drugs focus on lowering levels of dopamine and if dopamine levels are normal, as they may be in those with schizophrenia in remission, this would mean the levels with the drugs would be lower than normal. Such dopamine levels may mean a 'failure of the reward system' as dopamine affects the reward system. This lack of rewards would affect people negatively. Anti-psychotic drugs focusing on lowering levels of dopamine may not suit everyone with schizophrenia.

Definitions

When a disorder or illness is **acute** it means it is sudden in onset and is severe (the opposite of this is 'chronic', which means long term and underlying). **Remission** means not being experienced at a particular time. In schizophrenia acute would refer to the illness being 'active' rather than in remission.

Aims

- Carlsson *et al.*'s (1999/2000) main aim in their review was to show neurotransmitter functioning between neurons in specific brain areas. They used evidence from others (such as Moghaddam and Adams, 1998, and their findings about the effects of the recreational drug PCP ['Angel Dust']).
- They also wanted to use what is known about neurotransmitter functioning and psychosis to provide more of an explanation for schizophrenia than simply the dopamine hypothesis.

- Another aim was to use their understanding of psychosis and links to neurotransmitter functioning to produce new antipsychotic drugs that could be more effective with fewer side-effects.

Method

A review does not have a procedure as such, nor are there participants in the sense that data are not gathered directly. However, Carlsson et al. (1999/2000) do mention findings of various studies. For example, they discuss studies using rodents to test neurotransmitter functioning and related brain structure functioning; studies with those with acute schizophrenia and schizophrenia in remission; and evidence from studies looking at mice.

Their method, however, was to review the methods and findings of studies in the area they were looking at, and to use the other studies and the data-gathering studies to build a body of knowledge about the area of dopamine and schizophrenia.

Results of the review

Carlsson et al. (1999/2000) mention that it is unlikely that dopamine is the only dysfunctional neurotransmitter in schizophrenia. Also dopamine change may come from some other change in people with schizophrenia. The explanation of raised levels of dopamine causing schizophrenia is likely to be too simplistic. They list noradrenaline, serotonin, acetylcholine, glutamate and GABA as likely neurotransmitters to relate to schizophrenia. Dopamine is easier to study in the live brain that these other neurotransmitters. Serotonin too is measurable and serotonin turnover relates to dopamine (Ågren et al., 1991, cited in Carlsson et al., 1999/2000).

> **STUDY HINT**
> Carlsson et al. (1999/2000) show how what is studied in a research area can depend on the methods available for studying that area. As further methods are tried and new ones become available, there might be new findings. Understanding of particular areas may be affected by the methods available to study those areas. This is a useful evaluation point when evaluating research.

Glutamate has a role in schizophrenia

One piece of evidence suggesting glutamate has a role in schizophrenia is that the recreational drug, PCP (phencyclidine – Angel Dust), which can lead to psychosis (with schizophrenia-like symptoms), links

to the NMDA receptor, a glutamate receptor subtype. PCP blocks the receptor and is an NMDA receptor antagonist, which means it limits glutamate. Such NMDA antagonists are psychostimulants (in rodents) and **psychotogenic** in humans (Lodge, 1989, cited in Carlsson et al., 1999/2000). In their review, Carlsson et al. (1999/2000) discussed both psychostimulants and psychosis and both are taken in this summary to mean 'psychotic behaviour'. PCP leads to psychosis and blocks glutamate receptors so perhaps glutamate deficiency has a role in psychosis.

Definition
Psychotogenic refers to a drug or other agent that produces symptoms similar to psychosis, such as hallucinations.

Glutamate and dopamine release

Having seen that excess dopamine has been shown to link to at least acute schizophrenia and blocking of glutamate functioning has also been shown to relate to psychotic behaviour as occurs in schizophrenia, this next part of the discussion is about how glutamate and dopamine relate to one another.

Dopamine neurons seem to be affected by glutamatergic neurons acting as 'accelerators' or 'brakes' and if the brake or the accelerator dominates then there will be either an increase or a decrease in the functioning of dopamine. This shows that dopamine and glutamate interact. In normal functioning, it appears that the brake is the most dominant response but not by much; there is a balance between the brake and the accelerator. If there was reduced glutamate functioning this can raise dopamine release. However, if amphetamine or something else raises dopamine suddenly there is a reaction that means strongly weighting the reaction to the brake. In animals if an NMDA antagonist is put with amphetamine there is a sudden rise in dopamine. This explanation of how glutamate and dopamine affect one another can explain the dopamine enhancement that comes from amphetamine in those with schizophrenia. However, there might be a glutamate deficiency and this might be the explanation rather than excess dopamine.

Treating animals with NMDA antagonists can give a slight increase in the release of dopamine (Miller and Abercrombie, 1996, cited in Carlsson et al., 1999/2000), which is some evidence of a connection between the two. However, some NMDA antagonists seem to stop dopamine release and so decrease it (Waters et al., 1996, cited in Carlsson et al., 1999/2000). It seems that it is not just increased dopamine that accounts for the psychotogenic reaction to NMDA antagonists.

NMDA antagonists seem to stimulate the turnover of serotonin more 'consistently' according to Carlsson *et al.* (1999/2000) and serotonin seems implicated in schizophrenia as well as dopamine. PCP (an NMDA antagonist) causes release of more dopamine but it seems that the psychostimulation that PCP brings can be cancelled by a glutamate receptor agonist, even though this leaves the excess dopamine. So it seems that the psychostimulation brought about by PCP does not come from the excess dopamine but is more complex.

Carlsson and Carlsson (1989, cited in Carlsson *et al.*, 1999/2000) found that MK-801, which is a NMDA antagonist, can bring about movement in mice which have no dopamine or noradrenaline circulating. NMDA-receptor antagonists could also bring about movements when there was no dopamine present (in mice). Abnormal movements that were seen in mice included moving forward seemingly without intention and not being able to move between behaviours. It is thought that failure of glutamate functioning (in the cerebral cortex) linked to being able to choose different behaviours (hard to choose if functioning is not normal). Carlsson *et al.* (1999/2000) suggest that if it is glutamate deficiency that explains schizophrenia and this is in the cerebral cortex, this can explain problems with cognition and flexibility – negative symptoms in schizophrenia. They also suggested that glutamate problems in the basal ganglia could relate to positive symptoms of schizophrenia. They found that various monoamine agonists (dopamine, serotonin and noradrenaline are monoamines) and various NMDA antagonists worked together. Agonists they looked at included clonidine and a serotonin-related agonist. Carlsson *et al.* (1999/2000) used all their evidence, which is to an extent explained here, to propose an explanation for schizophrenia based on interaction between more than one neurotransmitter to form a network of pathways that link to schizophrenia.

The thalamic filter

There is a theory that it is the interaction between dopamine and glutamate pathways running to the striatum from the lower brainstem and cortex that relates to psychotic behaviours. The two neurotransmitters are antagonists in that one is inhibitory and the other stimulating. The two neurotransmitters function in the pathways that relate to the filtering off of sensory information to the thalamus to protect from sensory overload. If dopamine receptors are over-active or the glutamate pathway is under-active then confusion or psychosis can ensue. The idea of action to limit sensory overload in the thalamus is called the 'thalamic filter'. A problem lies in studying brain functioning such

as the role of glutamate. Carlsson *et al.* (1999/2000) say glutamate has a role in cell metabolism as well as a role as a neurotransmitter, and it is hard to measure glutamate release.

Two experimental models of schizophrenia – implications for therapy

Carlsson *et al.* (1999/2000) say it is hard to choose between the two neurotransmitter explanation of schizophrenia. One is hyperdopaminergia – '**hyper**' means active and hyperdopaminergia refers to the 'excess dopamine' hypothesis. The other explanation is hypoglutamatergia – '**hypo**' means underactive and hypoglutamatergia refers to the 'inhibited glutamate' explanation of schizophrenia. Carlsson *et al.* (1999/2000) discuss the implications for drug therapy. Some people might get on better with one type of drug than another, given that drugs focus on certain neurotransmitter functioning rather than a combination of such activity. Clozapine and other atypical antipsychotics (page 45) involve both antidopaminergic and antiserotonergic activity but because atypical antipsychotics work in different ways at different places in the brain it is hard to predict their effects. Carlsson *et al.* (1999/2000) say drugs that can work with the glutamatergic system in different ways would be useful.

So are drugs that act on dopamine no longer considered valuable?

A way of knowing how useful drugs relating to dopamine availability are is to find more out about how dopamine works. Carlsson *et al.* (1999/2000) explain that they have developed drugs/compounds that can stabilise the dopaminergic system without lowering levels of dopamine too far, which is the concern.

STUDY HINT

Note that evidence for neurotransmitter functioning in different parts of the brain highlighted by Carlsson *et al.* is from rodents. You can use your understanding of the use of animals in experiments to evaluate the claims of Carlsson *et al.* (1999/2000).

Year One link: Recall your learning about the practical and ethical aspects of using animals in experiments and then use the findings to help to explain human behaviour and functioning.

Progress check 1.68

Explain how NMDA receptor antagonists relate to glutamate deficiency.

Definitions

Hypo in a medical sense means 'insufficient'.

Hyper in a medical sense means 'too much'.

Conclusion and discussion

Carlsson et al. (1999/2000) end their review by drawing together their interpretations.

- They suggest that there might be subpopulations of those with schizophrenia and there might be different causes for schizophrenia within these subpopulations.
- Glutamate deficiency seems to need studying to help to explain schizophrenia.
- It might be a glutamate deficiency that leads to more responsiveness to dopamine, giving excess dopamine.
- There is more serotonin activity too. It is thought that both dopamine and serotonin contribute to both positive and negative symptoms of schizophrenia (page 29).
- More needs to be known about the glutamate function in order to understand issues about schizophrenia, such as that psychotic episodes seem to mean lasting deterioration in the patient.
- More focus on other neurotransmitters, such as acetylcholine, GABA and neuropeptides, is needed.

Year One link: Recall the 'presynapse' and the 'postsynapse' from what you study of biological psychology. Presynaptic activity occurs in the neuron that is releasing the neurotransmitter into the synapse; postsynaptic activity occurs in the neuron that is receiving the neurotransmitter.

Evaluation of Carlsson et al.'s (1999/2000) review

Strengths

- Sendt et al. (2012) have written a review of studies called 'Beyond dopamine: Glutamate as a target for today's antipsychotics'. You can see from the title that they back Carlsson et al.'s ideas, including putting forward what they call the 'glutamate hypothesis'. Their review confirms Carlsson et al.'s ideas about glutamate deficiency being important in schizophrenia and about the dopamine hypothesis not being sufficient as an explanation for schizophrenia. Sendt et al. agree with Carlsson et al. that drugs focusing on dopamine do not work for many people with schizophrenia and that drugs should focus on the glutamate deficiency. They also agree that negative and cognitive symptoms in those with schizophrenia seem to come from a dysfunction of glutamate. These ideas confirm Carlsson et al.'s claims.
- Carlsson et al. (1999/2000) used evidence from studies using rodents, people with Parkinson's, people with Huntington's and people with schizophrenia, both acute and in remission. They also mentioned studies using primates and had done previous studies (e.g. Carlsson and Carlsson, 1989). This is a wide range of evidence that points to the issue of glutamate deficiency being important in explaining psychotic symptoms and in questioning the dopamine hypothesis. Though using animal studies to draw conclusions about humans can be questioned, Carlsson et al. drew on evidence using humans as well, which strengthened their claims. They also showed how findings from one study support findings from other studies (such as the role of NMDA antagonists), which suggests their review conclusions were reliable.

Weaknesses

- Though Carlsson et al. (1999/2000) used studies using humans as well as animals, nonetheless, it is important to question the validity of drawing conclusions from animals and relating them to humans. Carlsson et al. themselves (1999) suggested that animal studies show ambiguous results when making claims about excess dopamine and psychostimulation, which undermines the use of animal studies when discussing schizophrenia in humans and relevant drug therapy for humans.
- When discussing the dopamine hypothesis, Carlsson et al. (1999) suggested that scanning used to look at neurotransmitter functioning in people might not have valid findings because being scanned is stressful and can affect 'normal' functioning. Findings about neurotransmitter functioning using scanning and humans

might, therefore, not be valid, and not just when studying dopamine functioning.

Progress check 1.69

How can glutamate deficiency explain the negative symptoms of schizophrenia?

Contemporary study relating to unipolar depression: Kroenke et al. (2008)

Kroenke *et al.* (2008) is a study about how depression is measured and looks at how far a patient health questionnaire (PHQ) depression scale is valid when measuring unipolar depression. The study focuses on validity of measurement using self-report data and links to issues of diagnosis and problems if a diagnosis is not valid. To test for validity the researchers measured depression using the PHQ-8 (the patient health questionnaire with eight items) using a score of equal to or greater than 10 on the questionnaire, and then compared that measure of severity of depression with the DSM-IV algorithm for depression, which the PHQ-8 items are based on. The DSM-IV method of measuring depression involves a structured psychiatric interview using the PHQ-8, whereas the PHQ-8 is easier to administer if taking the score of less than 10 or equal to and more than 10 as the cut off for depression. If taking this measure from the PHQ-8 is as good as when diagnosing depression using the interview, then the PHQ-8 will be useful as a standard questionnaire for measuring depression. Diagnosing using the PHQ-8 items by interviewing is more time-consuming and perhaps, therefore, less useful than a score of equal to or more than 10 on the PHQ-8.

> **STUDY HINT**
> In clinical psychology you must look at issues around diagnosis, including reliability of diagnosis. If someone is diagnosed twice will they get the same diagnosis? If so, it is a reliable one. You also consider validity of diagnosis. Is someone's diagnosis suitable for the treatment they are offered and does their diagnosis suit all of their symptoms? Kroenke *et al.* (2008) look at the validity of diagnosis, so you can use their study when discussing such issues.

Kroenke *et al.* (2008) found that both methods of measuring depression (the PHQ-8 score and the algorithm method using the PHQ-8 in a structured interview) identified depression in people similarly. A score of equal to or more than 10 on the PHQ-8 did uncover depression, so was seen as a valid measure.

Aims

Kroenke *et al.* (2008) wanted to see if they could use the PHQ-9 (patient health questionnaire with nine items), which is a well-used measure for finding out about depression, to obtain a score which would be a valid way of diagnosing depression. Earlier research suggested to them that a score of equal to or more than 10 would be a valid cut off point and that is what they wanted to test. They used PHQ-8, in fact, because the ninth item on the questionnaire, which was about self-harm, was not suitable to be asked in a telephone interview. Kroenke *et al.* (2008) wanted to see if a score of equal to or more than 10 on the PHQ-8 would diagnose depression as well as using the PHQ-8 questions as a diagnostic algorithm rather than to give a score. They felt that having a score would be quicker and easier when trying to look at depression over a whole population (in this case the US population) than using a diagnostic algorithm, so there was a practical application element to their aims.

Background

Kroenke *et al.* (2008) begin their report by explaining that unipolar depression (referred to throughout the report simply as 'depression') is the most common mental disorder and a major public health problem, which affects productivity in the workplace. They explain that psychiatric interviewing is successful in uncovering depression, but when a survey of a large population is required to look at the prevalence of depression, interviewing is perhaps not suitable and having a measure that is easier to administer on a large scale is useful. In the US the PHQ-9 is the patient health questionnaire that is used for diagnosing depression and it has nine items, so is not too burdensome on respondents who are asked about their health. The nine items are from the DSM-IV criteria for depression. The PHQ-9 has been used as a valid measure and is good for uncovering the severity of depression. It is useful when self-administered as well as when telephone administered. Kroenke *et al.* (2008) cite Huang *et al.* (2006a and 2006b) as showing that the PHQ-9 is useful for uncovering depression in different racial groups; they cite Klapow *et al.* (2002) as saying it is useful for older people too and they also give evidence that the PHQ-9 can uncover depression in other medical conditions as well.

The focus of Kroenke *et al.* (2008) is to use a version of the PHQ that contains eight items, to look at scores of equal to or more than 10 on the questionnaire and to test its validity against a diagnosis using the DSM-IV criteria in the PHQ-8 rather than the score itself. The idea is that the PHQ-8 score of 'less than 10 or equal to and more than 10' is easier to use than the DSM-IV criteria to judge depression – and that a score of equal to or more than 10 can show clinical depression in people.

A PHQ-9 score (Table 1.13) can indicate whether someone has depression, including its severity, and treatment can be indicated by the score too.

Table 1.13 PHQ-9 scores

PHQ-9 score	Provisional diagnosis	Treatment recommendation (patient preferences should be considered)
5–9	Minimal symptoms	Support, educate to call if worse, return in one month
10–14	Minor depression	Support, watchful waiting
	Dysthymia (mild but persistent depression)	Antidepressant or psychotherapy
	Major depression, mild	Antidepressant or psychotherapy
15–19	Major depression, moderately severe	Antidepressant or psychotherapy
>20	Major depression, severe	Antidepressant and psychotherapy (especially if not improved on monotherapy)

Explore

Find out more about Kroenke et al. (2008) and the PHQ-8 depression scale at:

http://patienteducation.stanford.edu/research/phq.pdf

Questions in the PHQ-8 and PHQ-9 are shown below. The main question is 'How often over the last two weeks have you been bothered by the following problems?':

1 Little interest or pleasure in doing things
2 Feeling down, depressed or hopeless
3 Trouble falling/staying asleep, sleeping too much
4 Feeling tired or having little energy
5 Poor appetite or overeating
6 Feeling bad about yourself or that you are a failure or have let yourself or your family down
7 Trouble concentrating on things such as reading the newspaper or watching television
8 Moving or speaking so slowly other people may have noticed, or the opposite – being so fidgety or restless that you have been moving around a lot more than usual
9 Thoughts that you would be better off dead or of hurting yourself in some way (PHQ-9 only).

STUDY HINT

Link the items in the PHQ-8 and PHQ-9 with what you have learned about the symptoms of depression earlier in this chapter (page 55). Kroenke et al. (2008) can be used as evidence when discussing such features and symptoms.

Methods

Different methods were used to collect data to compare the findings about diagnosing depression.

Behavioural Risk Factor Surveillance Survey (BRFSS)

The study used the BRFSS, which is used by all US State Health departments. The aim of the BRFSS is to collect information about the health of people in different states. Trained interviewers telephone adults to ask them to complete the survey. The data from the different states are then pooled to obtain a national picture. This is an example of a method that uses interview, using a standardised questionnaire.

The BRFSS has three parts:
● Core questions that are asked in all states.
● Other modules that ask about specific illnesses and areas (including mental health).
● Questions added by individual states. Added questions in 2006 included many states asking about severity of depression and diagnoses of anxiety.

The BRFSS sample was used in Kroenke et al.'s (2008) study.

PHQ-8

The PHQ-8 uses eight of the nine DSM-IV criteria for depression and was used to find out about depression (its prevalence and severity) across the US general population. As stated above, only eight questions were asked, rather than nine, because the ninth is about suicidal thoughts and self-harm, which were considered unsuitable to be addressed in a telephone interview. Kroenke et al. (2008) cite Huang et al. (2006a) to indicate that removing this item would not greatly affect scoring because it is rare to find such thoughts in the general population. Kroenke and Spitzer (2002, cited in Kroenke et al., 2008) found identical scoring when looking at severity of depression in the PHQ-9 and the PHQ-8.

The PHQ-8 was standardised to match the BRFSS questions by focusing on the 'how many days in the past two weeks' question when asking whether the respondent had experienced depression. This response was then matched against the usual PHQ-8 question, which was broader and asked 'how often in the past two weeks ...' For example, '12 to 14 days' matched with 'nearly every day'. Points were then allocated, for example, 3 points for 'nearly every day'/'12 to 14 days' and 0 points for 'not at all'/'0–1 days'. The PHQ-8 overall gives a score of 0–24, with 0–4 points indicating no significant depression and 15–19 points being moderately severe depression and so on.

Health-related quality of life questions

There were three health-related quality of life (HRQoL) questions. These asked about a person's physical health and whether it was 'good' or 'not good'; about their mental health and whether that was 'good' or 'not good' and about whether their health prevented them from taking part in 'usual activities'. The HRQoL also asked people for personal data, such as details of their employment and any other diagnosis they had been given, such as anxiety disorder.

In total there were 198,678 respondents from 38 states in the study who completed all of the PHQ-8 questions. Nearly all of the respondents (99.95 per cent) also completed at least one of the first three HRQoL questions. As is likely from such a large sample there was a good range of people of different ages (adults) and a range of different ethnicities (with 78 per cent being non-Hispanic white).

Year One link: Kroenke *et al.* (2008) use self-report data and questionnaires, so you can use this study as an example of such use. The study can also be used to evaluate the use of self-report data and questionnaires (and interviewing).

Results

The two scores used were either a) equal to or more than 10 on the PHQ-8, or b) a diagnosis of major or other depression using the PHQ-8 DSM-IV algorithm for depression rather than the score.

All the personal data relating to employment status, race, age and gender were analysed to look for differences in having a score of under 10 or equal to and more than 10 or in having a diagnosis of major or other depression (or not).

Analysis of personal characteristics

Kroenke *et al.* (2008) found that depressed people were more likely to be female, non-white, unemployed or not able to work, younger than 55, unmarried and less educated.

Table 1.14 Differences in gender between the PHQ-8 score (either under 10 or equal to and more than 10) and the PHQ-8 DSM-IV diagnosis score (either no depression or major/other depression)

Gender	No depressive disorder (diagnosis) N = 180,625	PHQ-8 score less than 10 N = 181,638	Depressive disorder (diagnosis) N = 18,053	PHQ-8 score equal to or more than 10 N = 17,040
Female	61.0%	60.7%	67.4%	71.3%
Male	39.0%	39.3%	32.6%	28.7%

Table 1.14 shows that the differences in gender are similar in all the scores – both the PHQ-8 scores (either under 10 or equal to and more than 10) and the results from the PHQ-8 diagnostic algorithm. Where the percentage of women in all the categories is between 60 and 70 per cent, the percentage of men is between 30 and 40 per cent. This suggests that there are few gender differences in the different measures because the sample contained 61.6 per cent women and 38.4 per cent men, and the split is the same across the different measures, showing few gender differences. However, the two percentages that are about depression (the diagnosis and the PHQ-8 score of equal to or more than 10 – the final two columns in Table 1.14) are higher in the women but lower in the men, so it seems that women are more likely to show depression.

Analysis of PHQ-8 scores

Table 1.15 shows that the figures from the diagnostic algorithm are distributed as would be expected if the PHQ-8 is a valid score. This is because when the PHQ-8 score is equal to or more than 10 (the first row of scores), the numbers in two of the three columns are higher where there is some depression (major and any depression) measured using the PHQ-8 algorithm than they are in the 'no depression' column. For example, there are 0 scores of major depression if the PHQ-8 score is less than 10 and 8,476 scores of major depression when the PHQ-8 score is equal to or more than 10. Also for 'any depression' there are 12,556 scores if the PHQ-8 is equal to or more than 10 but less than half that (5,497 scores) if the PHQ-8 is less than 10. Also the number of those with no depression is a lot higher if the PHQ-8 score is less than 10 than if it is equal to or more than 10, which would be expected. This does show that the PHQ-8 score of equal to or more than 10 does identify those with depression and is a cut-off point, which was what Kroenke *et al.* (2008) wanted to find out.

Table 1.15 Distribution of the PHQ-8 scores (either under 10 or equal to and more than 10) against the scores from the PHQ-8 DSM-IV diagnosis in the BRFSS sample

BRFSS sample:	Scores from the PHQ-8 diagnostic algorithm				Totals
PHQ-8 score around 10	Major depression	Other depression	Any depression	No depression	N = 198,678
≥10	8,476	4,080	12,556	4,484	17,040
<10	0	5,497	5,497	176,141	181,638

Kroenke *et al.* (2008) calculated percentages to study the differences between the two measures they were interested in – the PHQ-8 score of under 10 or equal to or more than 10 and the PHQ-8 diagnosis using the algorithm. They found that a PHQ-8 score of 10–14 is 15 times more likely to occur in someone with depression than in someone without, for example.

The following results were found for the 17,040 respondents who scored equal to or more than 10 on the PHQ-8:
- 8,476 (49.7 per cent) had major depressive disorder diagnosed
- 4,080 (23.9 per cent) had other depressive disorder diagnosed
- 3,887 (22.8 per cent) had depressed mood diagnosed only
- 597 (3.5 per cent) had neither of the two criteria that diagnose depression.

Clearly those with a high PHQ-8 score (equal to or more than 10) were more likely to be diagnosed with depression using the PHQ-8 diagnosis algorithm than those with a PHQ-8 score of lower than 10.

STUDY HINT

It is useful to use percentages to show differences in scores and to make them comparable. You can use Kroenke *et al.*'s (2008) findings to show how percentages can be used when displaying data.

Health-related quality of life impairment and depression

Table 1.16 Mean number of impaired days in the past 30 days in health-related quality of life domains, focusing on those with a PHQ-8 diagnosis of depression and those with a PHQ-8 score of equal to or more than 10

HRQoL (health-related quality of life)	Mean number of days self-rated as impaired	
	Depressive disorder from the PHQ-8 using the algorithm	PHQ-8 score of equal to or more than 10
Physical health not good	10.09	10.76
Mental health not good	14.37	15.34
Activity limited days	9.49	10.23

Table 1.16 shows that when the DSM-IV criteria of the PHQ-8 diagnose depression, the mean number of days that someone says there is impairment for them is very similar to when the PHQ-8 score of equal to or more than 10 is used as a measure of depression. This suggests that the PHQ-8 is as good a measure of depression as the algorithm, which is what Kroenke *et al.* (2008) predicted.

Progress check 1.72

What do the 'scores' in Table 1.16 relate to?

Table 1.17 Mean number of impaired days in the past 30 days in health-related quality of life domains, focusing on those with a diagnosis of depression or without, and those with a PHQ-8 score of equal to or more than 10 or a score of under 10

HRQoL (health-related quality of life)	Mean number of days self-rated as impaired			
	No depressive disorder from the diagnosis using DSM-IV categories	PHQ-8 score of less than 10	Depressive disorder from the DSM-IV categories diagnosis	PHQ-8 score of equal to or more than 10
Depressive symptoms	1.44	1.43	13.70	15.57
Anxiety symptoms	3.24	3.21	15.15	17.25
Fatigue	9.33	9.30	20.98	23.13
Sleep problems	6.98	6.93	17.04	19.17
Pain-limited days	2.14	2.14	9.16	10.19

Table 1.17 shows how low the mean number of impaired days is when the PHQ-8 score is less than 10 and when the DSM-IV-derived categories on the PHQ-8 give no diagnosis of depression. It also shows how much higher the mean number of impaired days is when the PHQ-8 gives a score of equal to or more than 10 and the diagnosis shows depression. Table 1.17 shows how similar the scores are between the PHQ-8 and the diagnosis of depression. The PHQ-8 score of less than 10 matches closely the diagnosis of 'no depression' and the PHQ-8 score of equal to or more than 10 matches closely the diagnosis of depression.

Conclusions and discussion

Kroenke *et al.* (2008) were pleased to have been able to use the BRFSS (Behavioural Risk Factor Surveillance Survey) sample for their study because it had such a large sample and seemed to represent the target population (population of the USA). They claimed that their study was the first to test the PHQ-8 in such a large survey.

The main finding was that the prevalence of depression (i.e. the number of people with depression) was similar when the PHQ-8 score of equal to or more than 10 was used as a cut off for depression (8.6 per cent) to when the PHQ-8 diagnostic algorithm was used (9.1 per cent). The researchers also found that the two ways of measuring depression gave similar findings when looking at the personal data characteristics of those with or without depression (sociodemographic characteristics). In addition the results of looking at health-related quality of life were similar when using the two measures of depression. Of those with a PHQ-8 score of equal to or more than 10, 96.5 per cent either had depression or some core depressive symptoms. These findings support the prediction of the study: that using a score of equal to or more than 10 on the PHQ-8 was a valid way of diagnosing depression and compared well with using the PHQ-8 as a diagnosis tool rather than using the score and the cut-off point suggested.

Kroenke *et al.* (2008) reported in their findings that around 9 per cent of the population have depression, which agrees with other studies, such as Kessler *et al.* (2003, cited in Kroenke *et al.*, 2008), who found that over a 12-month period the prevalence of having major depression in the US population ranged from 6.6 to 10.3 per cent. Kroenke *et al.* (2008) look at other studies too, such as in Germany, where Martin *et al.* (2006, cited in Kroenke *et al.*, 2008) found that 7.2 per cent of respondents had a PHQ-9 score of equal to or more than 10. Kroenke *et al.* (2008) concluded that the percentages they found (9.1 per cent using the diagnostic algorithm and 8.6 per cent using the cut-off point of a score of 10) might be a bit conservative and may have slightly overestimated the prevalence in the US population.

The usefulness of the findings of the study are that the PHQ-8, using the cut-off score of 10, would be useful in population-based studies or in postal or web-based surveys. Kroenke *et al.* (2008) discussed the PHQ-8 as missing the ninth item about suicide and self-harm and suggest that it can be useful to exclude that item, but in some cases it would be useful to include it by using the PHQ-9. For example, a study of GPs' decision-making showed that knowing about suicidal or self-harming thoughts was useful for GPs when making a diagnosis, so in those circumstances the PHQ-9 might be better than the PHQ-8 (Smith and Gilhooly, 2006, cited in Kroenke *et al.*, 2008).

Kroenke *et al.* (2008) discussed how the findings might lead to the DSM-5 and perhaps the ICD-11 recommending the idea of diagnosis using both the criteria and the scoring together. Their study goes on to explain other research that has looked at validity and reliability of the PHQ-9; for example, research has shown the PHQ-9 to be reliable when compared with the Hospital Anxiety and Depression scale (HADS) when looking at 32 GP practices in Scotland (Cameron *et al.*, 2008, cited in Kroenke *et al.*, 2008). Gilbody *et al.* (2007a, cited in Kroenke *et al.*, 2008) found in a study in the UK that PHQ-9 was valid compared with clinicians' methods of diagnosing depression in primary care. This suggests that PHQ-9 is both valid and reliable across different countries.

The researchers also explained some limitations of their study:

- They point out that the BRFSS does not include those who cannot respond to a phone survey or institutions, such as those without a phone or those with more severe mental health issues. These groups have higher depression rates so that means the scores in this study using the BRFSS sample might underestimate depression scores in the population. This points to a lack of generalisability.
- There was no testing of the switch to asking the BRFSS question about 'number of days' rather than the usual PHQ-8 question of 'how often over the last two weeks' (rather than days). The study findings would be strengthened if the validity of this change were to be tested.
- Although the two measures did seem to identify depression to the same extent, there was some 'non-overlap' which needs to be accounted for in the groups that were identified by the two measures.
- The researchers also thought that although the score on the PHQ-8 seemed to be a valid measure of depression, for individuals, a more clinical and in-depth approach would be better when making judgements about their care.

Evaluation

Strengths

- A strength is the size of the sample. Nearly 200,000 respondents made up the sample, and the analysis of personal data suggests that this was a representative sample of the US population. This means there can be generalisability of the findings to the target population. Kroenke *et al.* (2008) mention a problem with generalisability in that the sample did not include those without a phone or those in an institution, so there is some limitation in its generalisability, but the large sample with representativeness in terms of sociodemographic data is a strength.

- Another strength is the quantity of evidence from other studies that Kroenke *et al.* (2008) draw upon to support their findings about the validity of the PHQ-8 scoring as a measure of depression. The researchers are able to show that other studies have come up with similar findings, such as Martin *et al.* (2006, cited in Kroenke *et al.*, 2008), who found that in Germany 7.2 per cent of respondents had a PHQ-9 score of equal to or more than 10, which is not so different from Kroenke *et al.*'s scores (8.6 per cent and 9.1 per cent for the two measures used). This gives reliability to their findings.

Weaknesses

- Kroenke *et al.* (2008) point to some weaknesses in their study. One is the problem of not being able to include those without a phone or those in institutions, especially as these are likely to be in the 'depression' category and so would affect the findings. They explain that such groups have higher rates of depression.
- Another weakness is that they did not test the validity of changing the main question in the PHQ-8 from a focus on 'how often in the last two weeks?' with answers such as 'very likely' to a focus on 'number of days over the last two weeks'. They moved from a more qualitative estimate to a quantitative measure, which may have changed responses sufficiently to be a different measure from the PHQ-9 and the PHQ-8 used in other studies.

Progress check 1.73

Give two reasons for questioning the results of Kroenke *et al.* (2008).

Contemporary study relating to unipolar depression: Williams *et al.* (2013)

Williams *et al.* (2013) focused on depression by looking at internet-based treatment, including cognitive-bias modification and cognitive-behavioural therapy and how they would work for depression if combined. Williams *et al.* (2013) used a randomised controlled trial to look at cognitive-bias modification alone and cognitive-bias modification followed by cognitive-behavioural therapy. Both treatments were conducted online and focused on major depression (unipolar depression). Some patients had an 11-week internet-based therapy plan, with one week focusing on cognitive-bias modification and ten weeks on cognitive-behavioural therapy; other patients were in a waiting-list group (this means they were going to have the therapy but for the purposes of the study they were in

the control group, with no therapy, as a baseline measure). It was found that 27 per cent of the patients showed clinical change in their depression after the cognitive-bias modification part of the therapy and that rose to 65 per cent after the intervention included cognitive-behavioural therapy. It seems that combining therapy and using an internet-based treatment can be effective.

Aims

Williams *et al.* (2013) looked at the effectiveness of treatment for major depression – unipolar depression, but referred to throughout this section as 'depression'. They wanted to know if a combined treatment of a seven-day cognitive-bias modification training programme with internet-based cognitive-behavioural therapy directly afterwards for ten weeks would be effective in reducing symptoms and issues around depression. They wanted to implement the intervention with one group of patients and measure the improvement in depression using self-report data by comparing the intervention group with a control group using baseline measures.

Background

Kroenke *et al.* (2008) began their report by highlighting depression as a common disorder and Williams *et al.* (2013) begin in the same way, showing the importance for society and for individuals of focusing on depression. Williams *et al.* (2013) point out that cognitive explanations for depression focus on bias in information processing, such as focusing on negative interpretations of things that can be seen differently. Williams *et al.* (2009) cite NICE Guidelines (2009) as recommending cognitive-behavioural therapy (CBT) as a main treatment for depression and point out that CBT does focus on cognitive bias. They also underline difficulties in providing CBT for those needing it as there are long waiting lists, for example (Lovell and Richards, 2000, cited in Williams *et al.*, 2013). Simon and Ludman (2009, cited in Williams *et al.*, 2013) suggest that what is needed is an accessible treatment that is cost-effective and this is what Williams *et al.* (2013) focus on.

Andrews *et al.* (2010, cited in Williams *et al.*, 2013) show that internet-based CBT (iCBT) has been shown to be effective and a way of increasing access to CBT.

Year One link: If you used CBT as a treatment for phobias in the learning theories part of your course, you may find it helpful in understanding Williams *et al.* (2013), who use a combination of iCBT and another therapy to see how effective the combination is for depression.

CBT looks at cognitive biases by examining someone's thought processes and linking them to feelings and subsequent behaviour patterns. It has been suggested though that a simpler version of this, using computerised training, can affect cognitive-bias more directly. This simpler version is called cognitive-bias modification (CBM). CBM uses mental imagery and is shown to be effective, for example, by Blackwell and Holmes (2010, cited in Williams *et al.*, 2013). CBM works by presenting people with scenarios that can be interpreted in different ways but are resolved in a positive way. It trains people to interpret ambiguous information in their daily lives in a positive way. Imagery-based CBM is called CBM-I. Williams *et al.* (2013) call CBM-I a bottom-up therapy as it goes directly to the issue of negatively interpreting information and starts with the behaviour that comes from the negative thoughts. The lower levels, which are the individual elements of the negative thoughts, are considered first. Williams *et al.* (2013) call CBT a top-down therapy as it begins by looking at the higher cognitive processes and more complex ideas to explain and change behaviour and its individual components.

Progress check 1.74

Explain why Williams *et al.* (2013) called CBM-I a bottom-up approach and CBT a top-down one.

Williams *et al.* (2013) suggest that combining CBM-I with iCBT would combine the bottom-up approach with a top-down one and might be successful. The combination could be put together and offered via the internet, with the advantage of providing an accessible treatment more quickly than waiting for face-to-face CBT, which is the treatment recommended by NICE Guidelines.

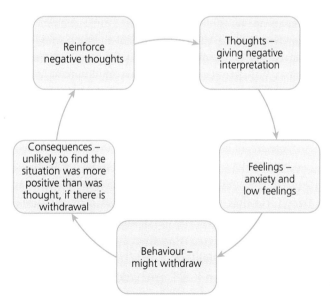

How a typical vicious circle might work to maintain depression

Williams *et al.* (2013) is a report on a randomised controlled trial (RCT) which gave seven days of CBM-I that was internet-delivered and then ten weeks of iCBT. This was the intervention group. The therapy was delivered remotely and measured change in depression by measuring severity, distress, anxiety, disability and repeated negative thinking. The researchers had a waiting list control (WLC) with which to compare any change from the treatment. They also looked at the success of the CBM-I part of the combined therapy and at how acceptable patients found the two parts of the treatment and their integration. Williams *et al.* (2013) predicted that the intervention group would show that the treatment had an effect compared with the waiting list control.

Method

The researchers found that a sample size of 21 or more in each group would suffice but they recruited more in case some dropped out. The participants were recruited in Australia after being screened using questionnaires. The participants were then phoned and a diagnostic interview took place. A total of 69 people were recruited and gave informed consent and were then put into either the intervention group or the waiting list control group randomly. There were 38 patients in the intervention group (having the treatment) and 31 were in the waiting list group. The waiting list group control underwent iCBT after the study was completed. Two Human Research Ethics Committees (HRECs) in Sydney approved the trial.

Year One link: Williams *et al.* (2013) obtained informed consent and the trial was approved by two HRECs. The researchers also mention recruiting more participants than they might need to find acceptable results, because some might drop out, suggesting they would give participants the right to withdraw. You can link these ethical points to your learning about ethics in the social psychology topic area of Year One.

Issues and debates

Williams *et al.* (2013) explain ethical considerations when setting up their study so this study is useful when discussing ethics in research — one of the issues and debates in your course.

Progress check 1.75

Explain how Williams *et al.* (2013) used a randomised controlled trial (RCT) design.

Measures used

Primary measures were used which looked at severity and distress with regard to depression.

- To measure depression Williams *et al.* (2013) used the Beck Depression Inventory 2nd edition (BDI-II) and the PHQ-9 (nine-item patient health questionnaire) developed by Kroenke *et al.* (2001, cited in Williams *et al.*, 2008). (The PHQ-9 is explained on page 111.)
- To measure distress the ten-item Kessler Psychological Distress Scale was used (K10).
- Interpretation bias was measured using the Ambiguous Scenarios Test – Depression (AST-D), using two versions of the test, counterbalanced (i.e. alternating which test was used) and a further measure as well, the Scrambled Sentences Test (SST).

> **STUDY HINT**
> If you have chosen unipolar depression as your disorder, then you will need to focus on the study by either Kroenke *et al.* (2008) or Williams *et al.* (2013). However, as both studies use the PHQ-9 measure of depression, this suggests that even if you don't look at both studies in depth, you should read both, as they can add to your learning.

Year One link: Williams *et al.* (2013) used online imagery to train someone to use positive interpretation, using two versions of a test showing ambiguous scenarios. They used counterbalancing when presenting the scenarios, which means they alternated which test was used. Remind yourself what counterbalancing means if you need to – you covered it in cognitive psychology in Year One.

There were also secondary measures in the form of measures of disability, anxiety and repetitive thinking, using other standardised scales. Other measures looked at how the patients managed the treatments. For example, a treatment expectancy and outcomes questionnaire was used to find out what patients thought of the treatment they had received. They asked three questions:

1 'How logical does the programme offered to you seem?'
2 'At this point, how useful do you think this treatment would be in reducing your depression symptoms?'
3 'Overall how satisfied are you with your treatment?'

The researchers measured using scales of either 0–4 (questions 1 and 2) or 1–5 (question 3). The higher score was the answer that was the most satisfied for all three questions.

> **Progress check 1.76**
> Williams *et al.* (2013) used standardised measures in their study. What is meant by 'standardised' in this context?

There were seven 20-minute sessions of CBM-I carried out, daily, over one week.

The iCBT was the Sadness Program, which features six cartoon-like situations showing a person with depression focusing on specific issues. Each situation includes homework, and email contact is offered to the patient to provide support. There is no face-to-face contact. Andrews (2013) claims that the Sadness Program is effective as a prescription for depression.

> **Explore**
> You can see Professor Gavin Andrews explaining the Sadness Program on a YouTube video at:
> **www.youtube.com/watch?v=x2SZCQRQAAM**

> **Explore**
> If you would like to read more about iCBT treatments, Williams and Andrews (2013) have written about another similar study which you may like to explore:
> **http://journals.plos.org/plosone/article?id=10.1371/journal.pone.0057447**

Procedure

- Before treatment began, all patients completed both primary and secondary measures (the Beck Depression Inventory, the Kessler Scale and so on).
- Then the patients in the intervention group did the seven-day CBM-I programme and the others were in the waiting list group.
- All patients after the seven-day period completed the primary measures again.
- Then the patients either did the iCBT programme or were in the waiting list group. This part lasted ten weeks.
- After the ten weeks all patients completed all the questionnaires again except for the AST-D and SST, which related to the CBM-I programme.
- At that stage the waiting list group started the iCBT programme.

Analysis

A Chi squared test was used to test for differences in demographic data and in pre-treatment scores to make sure that the intervention group and the waiting list group were not different. The data were nominal data.

Change in depression was also measured and was scored as a BDI-II score of less than 14 and a total score reduction as well.

Year One link: Williams *et al.* (2013) obtained nominal data when they gathered demographic data such as age, gender, employment status and so on. They compared the data between the two groups (the intervention group and the waiting list control group). This means they used an independent groups design and nominal data, looking for difference, so a Chi squared was appropriate. Use your Year One understanding to help here, and perhaps also use this study to illustrate the use of such statistical testing.

Results

Table 1.18 shows that there were some differences between the two groups, such as a higher percentage who were on antidepressants in the intervention group, although there were similarities too, such as in the gender split. Williams *et al.* (2013) reported that there were no significant differences in the two samples.

Table 1.18 Some of the demographic characteristics of the two samples in Williams *et al.* (2013)

Characteristic/ variable	Intervention group (N=35)	Waiting list control group (N = 28)
Gender		
Male	27 (77%)	21 (75%)
Female	8 (23%)	7 (25%)
Co-morbidity		
Generalised anxiety disorder	21 (60%)	14 (50%)
Social phobia	12 (34%)	7 (25%)
Medication		
No	18 (51%)	18 (64%)
Yes (antidepressants)	17 (49%)	10 (36%)

Table 1.19 shows the mean scores for some of the measures at baseline, after the CBM-I programme and after the iCBT (which was after both programmes). Note that the intervention group for each measure is given before the waiting list control group. The table shows that the

baseline measures tended to be similar between the intervention and the waiting list group, when looking at mean scores for each measure. For example, on the BDI-II measure the intervention group mean was 27.97 at baseline (before the treatments) and the waiting list control's mean was 28.00.

Table 1.19 Mean scores for some of the measures at baseline, after the CBM-I programme and after the iCBT (Williams *et al.*, 2013)

Measure	Group	Baseline	After the CBM-I programme	After the iCBT programme
BDI-II	Intervention	27.97	18.96	10.40
	Waiting list	28.00	24.82	20.54
PHQ-9	Intervention	12.38	9.88	5.15
	Waiting list	13.81	13.03	10.59
K10	Intervention	29.26	24.11	17.40
	Waiting list	28.62	28.33	24.45
AST-D	Intervention	4.18	4.67	N/A
	Waiting list	4.60	4.32	N/A

Explanation

A **baseline measure** is the measure taken at the start, before treatment or intervention takes place. It acts as a comparison so that improvement (or not) can be measured.

Progress check 1.77

In Williams *et al.* (2013), what is the intervention group and what is the waiting list control group?

Table 1.19 also shows a steady reduction in the primary measures (BDI-II, PHQ-9 and K10) for all the groups on all three measures. For example, the intervention group on the PHQ-9 had a mean score of 12.38 at baseline, then 9.88 after the cognitive-bias modification training and then 5.15 after the iCBT and the combined therapy. Also, the waiting list control group on the PHQ-9 had a mean score of 13.81 at baseline, then 13.03 after the cognitive-bias modification training and 10.59 after the iCBT and the combined therapy.

Table 1.19 also highlights the way the reduction in mean score in the primary measures was a greater reduction for the intervention group than for the waiting list control group. For example, on the BDI-II the intervention group fell from 27.97 at baseline to 10.40 after the combined treatment whereas the waiting list control group fell from 28.00 at baseline to 20.54 at the same time as the intervention group finished their combined treatment. The fall was much greater for the intervention group and that applies to the other primary measures too.

The AST-D measure, which focuses on depression measured by how ambiguous scenarios are interpreted, had similar scores for both the intervention and waiting list groups both at baseline and after the CBM-I intervention. Of course this measure related to the CBM-I treatment and not the iCBT treatment so data were only gathered on this measure at baseline and after the cognitive-bias modification treatment. There was a small increase in the mean score on the AST-D for the intervention group and an increase meant more positive interpretation, so there was some effect from the cognitive-bias modification treatment. On this measure the waiting list control group's scores were lower after the seven-day period, which suggests their negative interpretation of issues increased compared to the increase in positive interpretation in the group that had the CBM-I training.

Other findings

- An important result is that there were no significant differences between the two groups (the intervention and the control group) with regard to their characteristics or their baseline measures. Baseline measures of depression were not significant (p>.05), nor were age or gender (both p>.05).
- There were no differences either in the expectations patients had of the treatment (p>.05) and the amount of contact with the research team did not differ between the groups (though there was some difference in email contact because the intervention group needed more technical assistance).
- After CBM-I there were significant reductions in scores on the BDI-II, PHQ-9 and K10 in the intervention group. These were the primary measures.
- There were also significant reductions in the waiting list control but they were not as large as reductions in the intervention group.
- Clinically significant change was found in 27 per cent of the intervention group (seven patients) compared with 0.07 per cent of the waiting list group (two patients).

With regard to the secondary measures about anxiety and other such issues, the intervention group showed improvement in their depression compared to the waiting list group on all measures. Again, there was reduction in depression-linked features like anxiety for both groups, but the reduction for the intervention group was higher than the reduction for the waiting list control group.

Conclusions and discussion

The results suggest that CBM-I (cognitive-bias modification using imagery) for depression, delivered via the internet, can lead to a reduction in depression symptoms in just one week using just seven 20-minute sessions and no homework. It seems that repeated practice in using positive mental imagery can help in depression. Linden et al. (2012, cited in Williams et al. 2013) suggest that such improvement might link to brain areas involved in the generation of positive emotions and Blackwell et al. (2013, cited in Williams et al., 2013) suggest the improvement might come from increasing optimism.

The results also show that using the combined treatment of CBM and iCBT can be effective. Williams et al. claimed that the combined intervention effectively reduced depression symptoms, anxiety and disability in people with major depression.

> **STUDY HINT**
> In your study of mental health disorders you will need to be able to discuss treatments and how effective they are. You can use Williams et al. (2013) to show the effectiveness of combined treatments.

Williams et al. (2013) were also encouraged by the finding that patients felt the CBM-I intervention to be logical and understandable. They point out that to be effective a patient must see internet-based therapy as accessible and acceptable because the patient has to complete the programme.

Limitations of the study

- Williams et al. (2013) offer ideas about the limitations of their study. They suggest that the waiting list is a control group but it is not an active control group, because they are simply waiting. The researchers suggest that an active comparison would be better, where two groups have different interventions rather than one simply waiting.
- Another limitation they suggest is that there was no interview at the end of the intervention to measure the change in depression symptoms. Self-report data were relied upon and an interview to check for validity of the self-report data might be useful.
- It was not possible to show that using the CBM-I programme caused any change in the depression symptoms as there was no control over other things that happened to the patients over the time period.
- Also the measure that showed more positive interpretation was a measure that was similar to the scenarios in the CBM-I programme, which limits the conclusions about its effectiveness over other situations.
- It was also not known how far one programme impacted on the other. Perhaps using CBM-I first helped the iCBT programme (by improving the patients' motivation, for example) and that is something to look at in further research.
- A follow-up data collection would be useful so that the findings could be checked to see how long-lasting any effects were.

Progress check 1.78

What is meant by a 'follow-up' as mentioned in the conclusions of Williams *et al.* (2013)?

Evaluation

Strengths

- Williams *et al.* (2013) used a randomised controlled trial design with random allocation of patients to a waiting list control or an intervention for treatment of their depression. They tested to make sure the two groups did not differ in important ways, so when they found greater improvements in those who had the intervention they were able to conclude that the differences came from the intervention. Randomised controlled trials have credibility.

- They used a lot of different measures to look at depression before and after the intervention rather than just one measure. This means they were able to show reliable results as in the different measures there were similar findings – both the intervention and the waiting list control group showed reduction in depression 'scores' but the intervention group had a greater reduction.

Weaknesses

- Williams *et al.* (2013) gave some limitations themselves. They suggested they needed to use clinical interviewing as well as self-report data to measure the depression after the intervention(s). Interviewing would add qualitative data and depth to the scores from the questionnaires, which means validity can be shown.

- Another limitation was that they were unable to unpick the first intervention (CBM-I) from the second one (iCBT) and it would have been useful to see, for example, whether the CBM-I impacted on the iCBT effectiveness.

Contemporary study relating to anorexia nervosa: Scott-Van Zeeland *et al.* (2014, published online 2013)

Scott-Van Zeeland *et al.* (2013/2014) carried out a study focusing on anorexia nervosa and related gene variants. The researchers state that anorexia nervosa is complex and likely to have genetic and environmental causes.

Issues and debates

Scott-Van Zeeland *et al.* (2013/2014) mention both genes and environment when considering causes of anorexia nervosa, so this can be a useful study when discussing nature–nurture in human development, which is a debate in your course. They focus on gene variants underpinning anorexia nervosa, which relates to the 'nature' part of the issue.

Scott-Van Zeeland *et al.* (2013/2014) looked at different coding regions and gene sequencing, using different groups of people. They used 1,205 people with anorexia nervosa and 1,948 controls. They also used 261 people who developed severe anorexia nervosa and 73 controls and there they identified variants in the Estrogen Receptor-β (*ESR-2*) gene (note: estrogen = oestrogen; β= beta) and in the Epoxide Hydrolase 2 (*EPHX2*) gene.

Scott-Van Zeeland *et al.* (2013/2014) drew on other studies looking at similar areas, as well as the Bogalusa Heart Study sample, which had 58 people with 'eating disturbances' that they could study (as well as controls). Other evidence they used was body mass index (BMI) because *EPHX2* influences the metabolism of cholesterol so BMI might be a useful measure. The study found an association of gene variants within *EPHX2* giving susceptibility to anorexia nervosa. This is not about a single gene, but about specific combinations, which is not easy to study.

> **STUDY HINT**
> Scott-Van Zeeland *et al.* (2013/2014) is a study looking at causes of anorexia nervosa. You can use it to show a biological explanation for anorexia nervosa, which is part of your course.

Aims

Put simply, Scott-Van Zeeland *et al.* (2013/2014) wanted to look for genes as causes of anorexia nervosa. However, the reality was more complex than that because they knew that it was not one single gene that was involved, but combinations of genes and variations in genes. They wanted to use large sample sizes and careful examination of the DNA-sequencing in those with anorexia nervosa (and controls) in order to draw generalisable conclusions. Their overall aim was to 'identify genetic variants that contribute to anorexia nervosa'.

Background

Scott-Van Zeeland *et al.* (2013/2014) begin by saying that many 'environmental, behavioural and genetic' factors are associated with anorexia nervosa and a predisposition to anorexia nervosa (e.g. Kaye *et al.*, 2009, cited in Scott-Van Zeeland *et al.*, 2013/2014). Anorexia nervosa has a high risk of occurring in children in the same family, which suggests there is an 'inheritability' factor. However, neither a single gene nor a combination has been clearly picked out as a cause of anorexia nervosa. What is now helpful is the ability to study gene sequencing – what the researchers call 'genetic technologies', of which 'high-throughput genotyping' is an example.

The researchers discuss neuropsychiatric diseases such as autism and schizophrenia and put anorexia nervosa (AN) in this category. Associations in rare copy number variants (CNVs) have been linked to autism and to schizophrenia. The purpose of this study was to look for such features in AN. An issue they discuss is that neuropsychiatric diseases like anorexia nervosa will have complex causes and they suggest collections of rare single nucleotide variants (SNVs) might influence anorexia nervosa as well as the effects of other variants.

> **STUDY HINT**
> To make material more readable, shortened forms of some common terms are acceptable in your writing, such as AN for anorexia nervosa, CNVs for copy number variants and SNVs for single nucleotide variants. If you decide to write in this way be sure to say clearly first what each shortened form means. When you are reading it can help to occasionally use the full term and that is done in this book to help your understanding.

In order to study such gene variants there must be large sample sizes and sequencing looking at generations, as well as careful data analysis techniques. One problem is that when studying such complex issues, some are due to individual differences, including 'unique genetic profiles', which will not help towards the aim of uncovering genetic variants that link to AN.

> ## Progress check 1.79
> Why is it possible that individual differences affect findings that try to link gene variants to anorexia nervosa?

Scott-Van Zeeland et al. (2013/2014) underline the importance of having large sample sizes, patients with clear characteristics when it comes to anorexia nervosa and careful DNA-sequencing strategies and this was their aim when trying to find genetic features of anorexia nervosa.

Scott-Van Zeeland et al. (2013/2014) used a strategy that looked at 152 genes that seemed to be involved in feeding behaviours as well as looking at neurotransmitter functioning (specifically dopamine, GABA and serotonin).

They also looked at genes and regions that had been previously linked with anorexia nervosa including the *EPHX2* gene. Their aim was to 'identify genetic variants' contributing to anorexia nervosa. Their starting point was to use 261 people with anorexia nervosa and 73 controls (after exclusions of specific individuals). They also used a group of 500 people with anorexia nervosa and 500 controls. This starting point was to find links between single nucleotide variants (including rare SNVs) and anorexia nervosa.

The researchers wanted to go beyond what was already known about common SNVs that explain some of the heritability in AN – they wanted to know more. They also replicated previous findings and used 444 people with AN and 1,146 controls for this replication in order to look for a subset of variants. Then they looked at the impact of these variants on BMI using participants in the Bogalusa Heart Study. This detail is given here to indicate their focus on large sample sizes and careful measuring.

> **STUDY HINT**
> Scott-Van Zeeland et al. (2013/2014) used different groups, with controls each time, from which to draw conclusions, so there is an element of replicability in their study and they can claim reliability. You can use this study as an example of this sort of methodology.

Method

Participants

1) The initial phase

To do the initial sequencing the researchers used DNA samples from 262 people with AN and 80 controls (there was some further exclusion after this, to reach the final figures). They also had a lot of other information about the individuals, including 'phenotyping', which is explained later in this section.

Scott-Van Zeeland et al. (2013/2014) began with 300 women with features that showed they had anorexia nervosa. To be used in the study the individual had to have features including a lifetime BMI of 15 or lower and a history of being diagnosed with AN. Those with bingeing disorders were not included. There was a matched control group with BMI of between 18 and 29, matched by age and ethnicity. The participants had been what the researchers called '**phenotyped**'. Phenotyping was done using the Beck Depression Inventory (BDI) and the State-Trait Anxiety Inventory, as well as other questionnaires, such as the Yale-Brown-Cornell Eating Disorders Scale. This was done to obtain measures of the participants' functioning. This information had already been gathered before the study began. From the initial sample of 300, 262 women, and 80 controls, had DNA samples in the Price Foundation Sample Repository, so those were the numbers used.

Definition
Phenotype refers to our genetic make-up as well as our environmental influences.

Year One link: In biological psychology you learned something about genes when looking at the idea of survival of the fittest. Try to recall what genotype and phenotype refer to as that will help your understanding of this study.

2) The pooling-based replication phase
DNA samples from 500 people with AN were also used, with 500 controls – also from the Price Foundation sample. This group was separate from the 262 women and their 80 controls that were in the initial sample.

3) Replication studies
The researchers found more people by using replication studies, so they had an even larger sample. There is more about this later in the section describing the procedure and the results of the study.

Overall there were 1,205 people with anorexia nervosa in the samples and 1,948 controls in the study. A test was used to make sure only those of European descent were included, to help as a check on gene variants. The researchers did this by using 1,115 people with known ancestry to help them to identify those with European ancestry and others. At this stage a few of the participants were excluded from taking part because of their unclear ancestry.

Procedure

1) The initial phase
The study involved using the DNA of the 262 women and 80 controls and the researchers sequenced all of these individuals. The researchers give careful detail about how they did this sequencing. Part of the care in the study involved excluding those with missing information in the sequencing. Care is also shown in the way the researchers repeated what they did and also compared their genotype assigning to what was done in a previous sequencing study. It was found that their sequencing matched what was previously done, which shows reliability in their findings.

2) The pooling-based replication phase
In order to carry out replication, the researchers created 50 pools of data with DNA from 20 people. This involved 25 pools of DNA from 20 people with anorexia nervosa and 25 pools of DNA from 20 of the controls. They also included a pool from those sequenced previously in the initial phase. The aim of this phase was to compare allele frequencies in the pools with allele frequencies from the initial sequencing. (Allele means one of a pair of genes.) The researchers looked at 2,087 variants in this pool. Some variants were excluded, such as 15 of them being from one individual and 57 variants being missed when compared with previous genotype information. After some gene variants were excluded, the rest showed a very strong correlation with the initial allele frequencies from the initial phase. After some had been excluded there were 4,798 variants left for analysis from the pools.

Analysis
In the initial sequencing study there was analysis of the variants (the 4,798 not excluded) to look for an association with AN and also to look for a difference between those with anorexia nervosa and controls.

There was also statistical analysis in the pooled DNA replication study. The focus was on the frequency of variants in the DNA from those with anorexia nervosa compared with the frequency of variants in the DNA from the controls.

Two other groups were used – those with anorexia nervosa and those with eating disorders. These people had already been genotyped. Scott-Van Zeeland *et al.* (2013/2014) compared genotypes from these two groups with two control groups (with comparable ancestry backgrounds). They had 128 samples they could compare with their initial sequencing. They found a concordance rate of 97.7 per cent for SNPs (single nucleotide polymorphisms – common types of genetic variation) within *EPHX2*.

The researchers had other data about the participants, including BMI measures and also the phenotyped information from the questionnaires. They could then look at the sequencing they had uncovered and see the impact on the phenotype (the individual). They also had cholesterol measures so they could look at weight gain using change in the BMI over time. This meant they could look at the sequencing (gene variants) related to weight gain, for example. Scott-Van Zeeland *et al.* (2013/2014) considered total cholesterol level as the dependent variable in this part of the study. They used age, degree of European ancestry, BMI, genotype and a calculation of BMI multiplied by genotype, as the independent variables. Gender was also examined as an independent variable.

Scott-Van Zeeland *et al.* (2013/2014) also looked at brain regions that seemed to be relevant with regard to the sequencing they uncovered.

Results

Phenotype differences

It was found, using the phenotype data, that the people with AN (both in the replication parts of the study and in the initial phase) were significantly different from the controls in terms of BMI scores, anxiety levels and other health measures.

Ancestry

It was found that the sample in the initial stage did match those with European ancestry (though one was excluded because of not matching enough), so it seems that genetic background differences in ancestry in the sample were not likely to affect the results.

Results of the initial sequencing

There was no single genome that had significance, which was what the researchers expected from previous research in the area. They found the two variants that seemed to be most statistically significant were in the Estrogen Receptor-β gene (*ESR2*). The top two sets of variants (after analysis) were 35 variants in the *ITPR3* gene and 14 variants in the *EPHX2* gene (Epoxide Hydrolase 2 gene). The *ITPR3* gene encodes the Inositol 1,4,5-trisphosphate receptor, a type 3 protein.

Results of the pooling-based replication

The analysis of the pooling-based replication results was to look for frequency differences in allele between the anorexia nervosa sample and the controls. Just one set of variants in the *EPHX2* gene showed significance in this difference, which suggests that the results of the initial sequencing were reliable, as that gene also showed a link in the initial sequencing. Eight of the fourteen variants that were identified in the initial phase (in the *EPHX2* gene) were identified in this replication phase.

Table 1.20 Two genes that seem to feature in anorexia nervosa and the allele frequencies for both those with anorexia nervosa and controls (the initial phase sample and the pools samples)

Gene (just one example variant each)	Those with anorexia nervosa		Controls	
	Initial discovery phase	Pooling-based replication	Initial discovery phase	Pooling-based replication
EPHX2	0.0785	0.0859	0.1319	0.1061
ESR2	0.0383	0.0294	0.1096	0.0412

Table 1.20 does not provide enough information to show the differences between those with AN and the controls because not all of the data are given. However, it gives an idea of the differences in the findings between the controls and those with AN. It also shows to some extent that the pooling-based replication backed the findings of the initial discovery phase. One exception is the pooling-based replication of the initial phase in the control groups.

A further replication

In another replication, using the other cohorts, there was evidence for *ESR2* gene variants, which also supports the findings of the initial phase. This suggests a role for oestrogen in AN.

Variants in the *ESR2* and *EPHX2* genes with other measures

To look more at the specific variants in the *ESR2* and *EPHX2* genes, Scott-Van Zeeland *et al.* (2013/2014) focused on those in some of the samples they used and found some links. They also looked at those variants and depression and anxiety scores that had been collected (for this they used 261 cases of those with AN from the samples they had been using). The researchers did find that these gene variants (in the *ESR2* and *EPHX2* genes) related to the psychometric measure of anxiety and depression. There was also a significant interaction between variants in *EPHX2* and BMI and depression scores. Women with anorexia nervosa who carry the identified *EPHX2* variants showed higher BDI (Beck's Depression Inventory) scores and decreasing BMI scores.

Progress check 1.81

Which two gene variants related to measures such as anxiety and depression?

Longitudinal measures

Scott-Van Zeeland *et al.* (2013/2014) found that one *EPHX2* variant affected the relationship between weight gain (increasing BMI over time) and cholesterol measures. This was found in the females in the samples, but males too in one of the samples.

Consideration of brain areas

The researchers looked at where *EPHX2* linked to brain activity and found the gene is expressed in 'neural tissues of relevance to feeding behaviours, anxiety and other anorexia nervosa associated phenomena' (p. 729). One area is the paraventricular nucleus of the thalamus. Studies link the paraventricular nucleus to food and water intake (Leibowitz, 1978, cited in Scott-Van Zeeland *et al.*, 2013/2014), weight gain in rats (Bhatnagar and Dallman, 1999, cited in Scott-Van Zeeland *et al.*, 2013/2014) and stress response (Miller *et al.*, 2009, cited in Scott-Van Zeeland *et al.*, 2013/2014). The study does mention abnormal activity in the corpus callosum and hippocampus and this suggests a sex-specific effect of the *EPHX2* gene in anorexia nervosa. Another brain area mentioned is the subcallosal gyrus, which links to depression and is connected to the thalamus and the limbic system.

Year One link: Recall the different parts of the brain you looked at in biological psychology in Year One when reading about how the *EPHX2* gene links to certain brain areas which in turn relate to issues that link to anorexia nervosa.

Scott-Van Zeeland *et al.* (2013/2014) suggest that anorexia nervosa has a genetic link.

Discussion and conclusions

- Scott-Van Zeeland *et al.* (2013/2014) found some evidence that the *ESR2* gene variants are implicated in AN and they felt this was important given that the condition is observed more in females than males and that it tends to start in adolescents. The *ESR2* gene is oestrogen-related and oestrogen might have a role in anorexia nervosa.
- They had looked at the *EPHX2* gene because links had been found between it and anorexia nervosa in earlier studies.
- The *EPHX2* gene was known to influence cholesterol functioning as well (also a link to their study). They found the *EPHX2* gene variants were associated with cholesterol levels in one of their samples and also were related to other symptoms in their samples, such as anxiety and depression.
- Scott-Van Zeeland *et al.* (2013/2014) used their evidence and evidence from animal studies to show links between the *EPHX2* gene and a gene product that has a role in fat regulation in response to diet.
- A further discussion point was that low levels of cholesterol might decrease serotonin activity, leading to depression, which links back to lower cholesterol levels. Lower cholesterol levels are also linked to self-harming behaviour and suicidal thoughts in those with anorexia, so there are useful ideas here that relate to the findings of Scott-Van Zeeland *et al.* (2013/2014).
- *EPHX2* gene enrichment in the brain is found in areas associated with feeding behaviours, depression and stress, which also underlines the link between brain functioning, genes and emotions such as depression.

Evaluation

Strengths

- One strength of Scott-Van Zeeland *et al.*'s (2013/2014) study is the number of participants, both those with AN and controls. They say that this was necessary when studying genetic functioning as large numbers were needed to show significant differences in gene variants between those with AN and the controls. Overall they looked at 1,205 people with AN and 1,948 people without AN, as controls.
- A similar strength is that they used data from other studies and samples from other studies when drawing their conclusions. The researchers had an initial phase and then aimed to replicate the findings in various ways. Not only did they use samples from other studies to look at the gene variants, but they also used other data, such as scores on depression and anxiety scales, to look at how those scores fit with gene variants that were highlighted as being important. There is reliability because they replicate their findings.

Weaknesses

- One weakness is possibly in the complexity of what they are studying and how they went about obtaining findings. They did take into account, for example, ancestry, to try to control for any gene variation being due to something other than anorexia nervosa. However, claiming a cause and effect conclusion between the gene variants (e.g. the *EPHX2* gene variants they discuss) and having or not having AN is not suitable because there may have been other differences between the groups (other than simply one having anorexia nervosa and the control group not having the disorder).

- A weakness the researchers highlight, which seems to go against a strength offered by the study, is that there needed to be even larger numbers for replication of the results to be carried out. The idea of very large numbers is to counter the criticism that there might be other differences between the two groups, other than one group only having AN. They say at the start that their study must have large sample sizes, patients where there are a lot of data available, including about their phenotype and their illness and so on, and good DNA-sequencing strategies. These are the three areas where there might be weakness in their study, and not having large enough numbers seems to be seen by the researchers as a weakness despite the apparently large numbers they used.

Progress check 1.82

Explain how having a large sample is both a strength in this study and a weakness.

Contemporary study relating to anorexia nervosa: Guardia *et al.* (2012)

Guardia *et al.* (2012) focus on how someone with anorexia nervosa views themselves in terms of their body image. Not only are the researchers interested in body image itself, but also how those with anorexia nervosa see their body in action. An example the researchers give is judging whether your body could pass through a door-like opening. Even when the opening is large enough, someone with anorexia nervosa might not think they can pass through the opening. Guardia *et al.* (2012) wanted to see if someone with AN has problems with judging their own body actions but whether their perceptions (such as of the body actions of others) are wrong in a more general sense. They found that someone with AN had problems judging their own body actions but not with judging the body actions of someone else in the room. As the overestimation of their size seemed to relate to their size before the AN developed, it was thought that perhaps the central nervous system had not 'updated' to the new body size, so there was an incorrect representation of the body's size when the person had AN.

Aims

Guardia *et al.* (2012) wanted to see whether problems in judging body actions (such as deciding whether a body fits through a space) occurred only when judging one's own body or whether it was a problem in judgement overall. The question was whether people with AN would be different from a control group in judging whether a gap was large enough for their body to pass through. Another condition was to ask whether the gap was large enough for another person in the room to pass through. The aim was to see differences in judgement according to whether the person was judging their own body or someone else's body and also to look at differences between those with AN and controls.

Background

Anorexia nervosa affects between 0.5 and 1 per cent of women but a small percentage of men (Hudson *et al.*, 2007, cited in Guardia *et al.*, 2012). Studies have found that those with anorexia see themselves as larger than their actual size (e.g. Schneider *et al.*, 2009, cited in Guardia *et al.*, 2012). Altered body image is a symptom of AN and also can help to maintain non-eating behaviour as there can be increased body dissatisfaction. Previous studies looking at AN and body image tend to ask people with the condition to point to body images to show which they think matches their own body size. The body mass index (BMI) of the individual is then compared to the BMI of the person in the picture they choose and the difference between the two shows the under- or overestimation.

People with anorexia nervosa often see themselves as much larger than they really are.

Guardia et al. (2012) point out (citing De Vignemont, 2010) that this way of measuring body image does not separate the emotions around body image, which is top-down processing because it comes from thoughts and ideas of the body during actions – what the researchers call 'body schema'. It has been suggested that the parietal cortex and the right superior parietal lobe in particular might give these dysfunctions in body schema (e.g. Nico et al., 2010, cited in Guardia et al., 2012). This is about disturbances in recording information about the body, such as visual information and tactile information.

Guardia et al. (2010) also used controls in the same way as the 2012 study reported here and looked at whether those with anorexia thought an opening was wide enough for them to pass through. Guardia et al. (2010) found that those with AN did not think they could pass through an opening that was clearly wide enough, showing that those with the disorder overestimated their body size and may have a changed perception of space. This finding led the researchers to do another study, the one reported here, which looked at not only whether those with AN overestimate their body size but whether they also overestimate someone else's body size.

Guardia et al. (2010) describe how Vartanian and Germeroth (2011) showed participants ten photographs of women ranging from underweight to obese and asked them to estimate their body weight. The researchers also asked the participants to rate their own dietary restraint, which was about how far they limited their own eating. Those with high dietary restraint underestimated their own weight more than those with low dietary restraint, even though when judging the weight of others in the photographs there was no difference between those with high or low dietary restraint. This suggests that people might under- or overestimate their own body size, but they do not tend to under- or overestimate the body size of others.

It was interesting that those with high dietary restraint underestimated their own weight whereas people with AN overestimated their own weight, which shows that anorexia nervosa is more than simply being 'on a diet'.

Smeets et al. (1999, cited in Guardia et al., 2012) found that it was not direct perception of body size that led those with AN to overestimate their body size. They found no differences between people with AN and normal and thin control groups when measuring perceptual signals and asking participants to judge differences between their own and someone else's body. This suggests that those with anorexia nervosa do not have an incorrect perception when they look at their body, so it is not that they see themselves as different from what they are. If the reason for

overestimating body size does not come from what they see, then it must come from top-down processing focusing on their visual body image – from how they represent what they see. Patients with AN were more accurate then controls when seeing someone else's body form and just as accurate with someone else's body actions (Urgesi et al., 2010, cited in Guardia et al., 2012).

After looking at these findings the issue is the problem of distinguishing between the overestimation of body size being due to problems in how the body itself is represented and how emotions and attitudes about the body lead to problems (top-down processing). In general it is thought that the same 'internal representations' are used to judge whether a body can pass through a space as those used for actually passing through the space. For example, Kohl and Roenker (1980, cited in Guardia et al., 2012) found that mental rehearsal can improve performance, which suggests the two areas of processing are linked. Roth et al. (1996) found that brain areas that are active when imagining a movement are active when that movement takes place as well. These results (and those of other studies) show that having a task that involves imagery about movement is suitable for measuring body movement 'for real' and for assessing body schema.

The hypothesis was that someone with AN will make errors in judging their own body actions (in so far as they say their body would fit through an opening) more than a control group would.

Method

Guardia et al. (2012) start their method section by explaining the ethics of their study. The study was approved by an independent ethics committee. Each participant was given an information sheet so that they could give informed consent when taking part; parental consent was given for anyone under 18 years old.

Year One link: Recall from social psychology and your other Year One studies the British Psychological Society's Code of Ethics and Conduct (2009). There are four ethical principles – competence, integrity, respect and responsibility. Obtaining informed consent fits into these principles. When ethical issues are mentioned in studies, remind yourself of the four principles and what they are, to help in your evaluation of studies.

Participants

A total of 50 young female participants took part, 25 with AN from an eating disorder clinic and 25 healthy controls. They were all students and the two groups were matched for age and education. A check took place to make sure there were no perceptual problems and the AN patients fulfilled DSM-IV-R criteria for a diagnosis. A psychiatrist carried out an interview to check there were no co-morbidities. Controls had a BMI of between 18.5 and 25.

Table 1.21 shows that the two groups are similar in many ways, though their current BMI is of course different (given that one group has AN) and their shoulder width is different (smaller for the anorexia nervosa group). Another large difference was in the scores for the body shape questionnaire, again perhaps not unexpected.

Table 1.21 Some demographic and clinical data for the participants in Guardia et al. (2012) (scores are mean averages)

	Anorexia nervosa group (N = 25)	Control group (N = 25)
Age (years)	23.84	24.48
Educational level	13.16	13.8
Height (m)	1.645	1.649
Current BMI (kb/cm²)	15.645	22.06
Shoulder width (cm)	37.66	41.542
Body Shape Questionnaire score	123.96	66.708

Progress check 1.83

Although there are no statistics in Table 1.21 to show significant differences, explain the three areas that show differences between the controls and those with anorexia nervosa.

Procedure

Collecting demographic and clinical data

Assessment of height, shoulder width and weight were standardised. The researchers measured changes over time in nutritional status by looking at weight before the disorder, six months before the study, one month before the study and weight at the time of the study. The researchers gathered data about body dissatisfaction and concern about weight using questionnaires, including the Body Shape Questionnaire and the Eating Disorder Inventory-2 (which showed the drive for thinness and the body dissatisfaction scores).

The experimental procedure was that 51 different openings from 30 cm to 80 cm were projected onto a wall in random order. Each opening/aperture was presented four times. The opening reached the floor so it looked like a door. This was to maintain ecological validity. An experimenter was used in the study as well as the participant. The experimenter was 28 years old, 1.60 m in height, weighed 52 kilograms and her shoulder width was 38 cm. She stood 5.9 metres from the wall onto which the opening was being projected.

There were two conditions: The first was when the person judged their own body and whether it would fit through the opening. This was the first person perspective and was referred to as '1PP'. Each person had to imagine themselves walking through the opening and to say whether they could walk through at normal speed without turning sideways. The second condition was that the participant had to imagine the experimenter (who was standing next to the participant) going through the opening. This was the third person perspective and was called '3PP'. The participants could move to get a better view of the experimenter and had to say whether the experimenter could walk through the opening without turning sideways.

An opening was said to be a perceived critical aperture when it had a 'yes' response 50 per cent of the time. A ratio was obtained by dividing the perceived critical aperture (size) by the shoulder width of the participant. When the perceived critical aperture was 1, that is when it was equal to the shoulder width and there was a chance of not passing through. A ratio of higher than 1 meant there was a safety margin. Less than 1 meant the body could not pass through the opening, although actual calculations to achieve the scores were worked out a little differently.

Progress check 1.84

In Guardia et al.'s study (2012) explain what is meant by 1PP and 3PP.

Results

There were no significant differences in age, educational level or height. Both the mean BMI and mean shoulder width differed between the two groups, as Table 1.21 shows. The anorexia nervosa group had a significantly higher score on the Eating Disorder Inventory-2 and the Body Shape Questionnaire scores were also significantly higher in the anorexia nervosa group.

- In the 1PP condition (where the person judged whether their own body would pass through the opening) the mean perceptual ratios were higher for the anorexia nervosa group than for the controls.
- The mean ratio for the AN group was 1.321 and for the controls it was 1.106 (p=.001). In the 3PP condition (where the person judged whether the experimenter's body would go through the opening) the mean

perceptual ratios were the same. In the 3PP condition, although the average ratio for the AN group was higher (1.227) than for the control group (1.137), the difference was not statistically significant.

- There was also a statistically significant difference between the mean ratios for those with AN in the 1PP and the 3PP conditions. Where the patients with AN rated their own body for going through the opening the mean ratio was 1.321 and where those with AN rated the experimenter's body for going through the opening the mean ratio was 1.227. With the controls there was no significant difference between the 1PP and the 3PP conditions.

Table 1.22 suggests that those with anorexia nervosa rated their own body (in so far as it would pass through the opening) differently from how they rated the experimenter's body. They also rated their own body differently from how the controls rated theirs.

Table 1.22 Different ratios in the two conditions for both the anorexia nervosa group and the control group (Guardia et al., 2012)

	Anorexia nervosa group (N = 25)	Control group (N = 25)
1PP (rated own body)	1.321[ac]	1.106[a]
3PP (rated experimenter's body)	1.227[bc]	1.137[b]

a means the difference between these two scores was statistically significant
b means the difference between the two scores was not statistically significant
c means the difference between these two scores was statistically significant

Discussion and conclusion

The aim of the study was to find out whether the ability to make judgements about one's own body size and that of someone else is affected by AN. Those with AN significantly overestimated their own 'passability' (i.e. their decision about whether their body could pass through an opening) in relation to a control group. The patients also said they felt larger than they were, which goes with this finding. Another important result was that, although those with AN made errors when judging their own passability, they did not make such errors when judging the passability of the experimenter. The control group's judgements were the same when judging their own passability or the experimenter's passability – they did not make the error when considering their own body size that the AN patients did.

Guardia et al. (2012) explored explanations for their findings. They rejected eye height as an explanation of the different judgements as the participants in the two groups did not differ with regard to mean height. The researchers thought that the overestimation of the ratio between the size of the opening and the shoulder width arose, in those with AN, from an overestimation of their own body schema. This was not so much a perceptual error on its own as those with AN were better at judging the body size of the experimenter. The researchers suggest that the reason for the overestimation regarding their own body schema, in those with AN, might be problems in integrating information from the various senses. A size-weight illusion is when two objects of the same weight but different sizes are judged and the smaller is judged as the heavier (though they are the same weight) (Charpentier, 1891, cited in Guardia et al., 2012). It was thought that the size-weight illusion comes from the integration of conflicting sensory input from vision and touch. Case et al. (2012, cited in Guardia et al. 2012) found that those with AN are not as sensitive to the size-weight illusion, which suggests there is a problem with their integration of sensory input compared with those who do not have AN. The overestimation of body size in those with AN might come from problems with integrating sensory input. This might explain why those with AN feel bigger and heavier than they are.

Another illusion that can help to explain Guardia et al.'s (2012) findings is the rubber hand illusion. This is an illusion that comes from a set up situation. The participants see a dummy hand being stroked with a paint brush. At the same time their own hand is being stroked with a paint brush but out of their sight. If the dummy hand is similar to the participant's hand and if the visual and tactile information arrives at the same time, some people might feel that the dummy hand is part of their own body and is feeling the stroking. It is found that AN patients have a stronger rubber hand illusion than controls (Eshkavari et al., 2012, cited in Guardia et al., 2012). It is thought that perhaps those with AN rely mostly on visual information, which contradicts the claim that those with AN are less affected by the size-weight illusion.

It was interesting that the participants' perceptions of their body size were related to their weight before they developed AN. Also the greater the weight loss the larger the perceived passability ratio. Guardia et al. (2012) suggest that perhaps the body schema had not been updated by the central nervous system.

Guardia *et al.* (2012) considered limitations of their study.

- They cite Morgado *et al.* (2011) as showing that people don't like being near someone they do not feel close to, and this suggests that ideas about our bodies are affected by emotional and psychosocial factors, not just perception. Morgado *et al.* (2011, cited in Guardia *et al.*, 2012) asked people to imagine passing through an opening with life size pictures of two of their classmates either side of it. The closer the participants felt to the classmates the more they felt able to pass through the opening. However, Guardia *et al.* (2012) did not include the emotional element in their study so such top-down processing should not have occurred to affect the judgements of whether the participant was able to get through the opening.
- Another limitation was the sample itself, which was quite small, and not all of the patients reported a history of weight change. There should be replication of the study to see if the findings were reliable.
- Guardia *et al.* (2012) also point out that the controls in their study were closer in body size and weight to the experimenter than were those with AN. It would have been better to have an experimenter the same weight and size as those with AN when they were doing the condition involving a judgement of someone else's body. This was ethically not possible as it would have involved a patient making a judgement about another patient and might have meant confidentiality was compromised.
- The study does not ask people to go through an opening and then watch to see when they felt they needed to turn sideways. Perhaps using imagery means there is a lack of validity.

Evaluation

Strengths

- Having a matched control group is a strength of Guardia *et al.* (2012). If all else is kept the same and the difference between the two groups is that one group consists of AN patients and the other does not, then cause and effect conclusions are more easily drawn. Without a control group there is no data to compare the AN group to. As the controls did not misjudge their size when deciding whether their body could fit through an opening as much as the AN group misjudged their size, this was taken to show that the AN linked with that misjudgement.
- A strength with Guardia *et al.* (2012) is that there was a lot of other research showing similar findings, including Guardia *et al.* (2010). Guardia *et al.* (2010) had already found that those with AN did not think they could pass through an opening that was

clearly wide enough. This showed a problem in perception of their own body (in those with AN) and led Guardia *et al.* (2012) to then look at whether those with AN would also have a misperception of someone else's body size. Their findings in the 2012 study replicated those in the 2010 study in that those with AN did misjudge their body size when it came to judging whether they could pass through an opening without turning sideways. Schneider *et al.* (2009) were also said to have found that people with anorexia nervosa misjudge their own body size. All this evidence (and there was more) suggests reliability in the idea that those with anorexia nervosa overestimate their body size.

Weaknesses

- One limitation that the researchers put forward is that the control group and the anorexia nervosa group in fact did have differences – in their shoulder width and their BMI. The weight and size of the experimenter's body matched that of the control group much more than it matched that of the AN group. To have sufficient control over variables, those with anorexia nervosa, when judging whether the experimenter's body could pass through the opening, should have had an experimenter with a body size and weight similar to their own too. Ethically, this was not possible, but it is an issue with the study that might have affected the findings.
- The researchers felt that their sample was not that good because it was rather small, given requirements for size of sample. They also suggested that their study needed to be replicated to check for reliability in the findings. Also with regard to the sample not all of those with AN reported a history of weight change.

Contemporary study relating to OCD: Masellis *et al.* (2003)

Masellis *et al.* (2003) is one of the contemporary studies in your course that focuses on obsessive compulsive disorder (OCD). If you have selected OCD as your chosen disorder, you have a choice of two studies that focus on OCD and both are given in this chapter.

> **STUDY HINT**
> Though you only have to learn about one contemporary study in detail for your chosen disorder, you will probably find it interesting and useful to read through the other study in order to gain a fuller picture of the disorder.

Summary

Masellis *et al.* (2003) asked people with obsessive compulsive disorder (OCD) about their quality of life, in particular how far their illness intruded on their lives. They asked about their obsessions, compulsions and depression, to see the effects of these three features of the illness on their quality of life. The researchers found that the depression had the greater intrusion, the obsessions also were intrusive, but the compulsions were less intrusive. The researchers thought that the compulsions existed to reduce the anxiety caused by the obsessions, so it made sense that the compulsions were seen as less intrusive. It made sense that the depression was seen as intrusive too. The researchers also commented that treatment for OCD tends to focus on the compulsions, which from the findings did not seem as helpful as treatment that focused on the obsessions and depression.

> **STUDY HINT**
> Masellis *et al.* (2003) refer to OCD as an 'illness'. This shows a focus on a medical model. As the researchers refer to 'illness' this is the term used here as well. You can use this study to show how the medical model features in research into mental health.

Background

OCD affects one adult in 40, which is around 2.5 per cent of the population, at one time in their lives (Masellis *et al.*, 2003). The researchers say it is the fourth most common disorder. As obsessions and compulsions take up so much of someone's life if they have OCD it is a very disabling disorder. OCD is a disorder that comes and goes and is hard to treat, with anxiety affecting people in personal, social and financial ways. Little research has been done on the impact of OCD on sufferers' lives. Hollander *et al.* (1966, cited in Masellis *et al.*, 2003) found that 73 per cent of people with OCD were affected with regard to their family relationships and 62 per cent had impaired friendships. Koran *et al.* (1966, cited in Masellis *et al.*, 2003) found people with OCD were affected in their roles in life as well as in social functioning, being more impaired than people with medical conditions like diabetes or people in general.

> **STUDY HINT**
> Masellis *et al.* (2003) cite evidence for various features of obsessive compulsive disorder. You can use this evidence when describing or discussing the disorder as well as when talking about the study itself.

In OCD impairments include difficulties with reading and carrying out tasks that require concentration. According to Masellis *et al.* (2003) studies have not looked at whether obsessions in OCD are more limiting than compulsions. Compulsions are time-consuming rituals, while obsessions relate to intrusive thoughts. Rituals require time and intrusive thoughts require concentration. One or the other may be more limiting for the individual. For example, getting stuck in ritual hand-washing means other tasks are not carried out and a social life can be hard to maintain, as well as being distressing for the individual.

Aims

Quality of life is affected by an anxiety disorder and Masellis *et al.* (2003) say this is perhaps particularly the case for those with OCD. One primary aim of the study was to assess how obsessions and compulsions affect the quality of life of the individual. Another aim was to assess the effect of depression on the quality of life of those with OCD as depression can accompany OCD as a primary diagnosis. Co-morbidity refers to someone experiencing more than one disorder (or illness) at the same time, and having depression as well as OCD is an example of co-morbidity. Rates of major depression in those with OCD can be between 28 and 38 per cent according to Karno *et al.* (1988, cited in Masellis *et al.*, 2003).

The aim, then, was to look at the quality of life of those with OCD and the impact of obsessions, compulsions and depression on individuals. It was thought that quality of life ratings would be affected by how severe the obsessions and compulsions were. The more severe the symptoms, the poorer the quality of life. Depression itself would mean poor quality of life too.

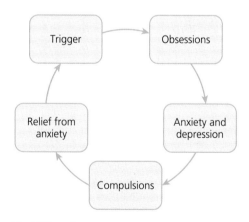

The OCD cycle

Methods

Participants

A group of 43 patients who met the DSM-IV criteria for OCD were involved, all from a university-based teaching hospital in Canada. They had to be between 18 and 65 years old to take part and had to have symptoms of OCD. Those with schizophrenia, bipolar disorder or substance use disorder were excluded. There were 18 males and 25 females in the sample, of whom 25 were single, 16 married or co-habiting and 2 separated, divorced or widowed. Their average age was 34.9 years.

Measures

The Yale–Brown Obsessive Compulsive Scale (Y-BOCS), the Illness Intrusive Rating Scale (IIRS) and the Beck Depression Inventory (BDI) were used with all participants.

- The Y-BOCS has ten items and is a standardised scale for assessing the severity of the obsessions and compulsions. It uses a five-point Likert scale from 0 (no symptoms) to 4 (severe symptoms). It has high validity and reliability.
- The IIRS measures how far symptoms interfere with quality of life using objective measures and perceived interference. There are 13 domains, including health, financial situation, relationships and community involvement. This measure uses a seven-point Likert scale from 1 (not very much) to 7 (very much). The total score is from 13 (minimum intrusion) to 91 (extreme intrusion).
- The BDI uses 21 items, using a four-point scale. It uses self-report data assessing severity of symptoms and it is a reliable and valid measure.

> **STUDY HINT**
> Masellis *et al.* (2003) used standardised measures to gather their data, gathering information about the obsessions and compulsions, quality of life and depression of their participants. They used self-report data and said that the scales used had validity and reliability. They mention the use of Likert scale questions too. These issues feature in your course, so you can use this study as an example of their use.

Statistical methods

- One test was to see if any variables predicted how intrusive the illness (OCD) was for people. Variables were clinical ones (about the illness) or demographic ones (relating to age, gender, etc.).
- Another analysis included correlating the BDI, Y-BOCS obsessions and Y-BOCS compulsion scores. The obsession and compulsion scores were expected to correlate highly.

Progress check 1.85
What are demographic variables in a psychology study?

Results

- Age, age of onset (of the OCD), marital status, gender and education were tested against the amount of intrusion affecting people's quality of life and were found not to predict the intrusion score of the illness.
- There was a significant positive correlation between compulsions score on the Y-BOCS and intrusiveness ($r = 0.53$, $p < .001$) and a significant positive correlation between obsessions scores on the Y-BOCS and intrusiveness ($r = 0.62$, $p < .01$). This means that the higher the obsessions and compulsions score on the Y-BOCS, the higher the intrusiveness score.

Year One link: You have learned about correlations when studying biological psychology in Year One. Remind yourself about positive and negative correlations and issues around significance and levels of significance. $p < .01$ is quite a strong level of significance so the relationship is quite significant, for example.

- The depression score and the obsessions and compulsions scores were analysed together. A higher depression score predicted intrusiveness of the illness on people's lives (significant at $p < .0001$). Higher obsession severity predicted intrusiveness of the illness too ($p < .05$) and the more severe the obsessions the more there was intrusion on quality of life for someone. The compulsions score did not associate with illness intrusiveness ($p = 0.91$), however. As obsessions and compulsions did correlate with intrusiveness of the illness, this suggests obsessions correlate highly with intrusiveness as compulsions did not.
- Depression seemed to account for 54 per cent of the score relating the illness to the intrusiveness. The obsession score on the Y-BOCS accounted for 39 per cent of the quality of life intrusion. This showed that depression accounted more for the intrusion score, with obsessions accounting for some of the score too. This analysis confirms that compulsions were not the main issue relating to the illness intruding on quality of life.
- Results suggested that depression affected the intrusiveness scores most, and obsessions were next important (from the measures taken in this study).

Progress check 1.86
What does $p < .0001$ and $p < .05$ mean when referring to results of a study?

Discussion

Previous studies show obsessions and compulsions affect quality of life (e.g. Koran *et al.*, 1996, cited in Masellis *et al.*, 2003). Masellis *et al.* (2003) found the severity of obsessions affected how much OCD intruded on someone's life. Compulsions were less intrusive. It seems obsession thoughts and impulses lead to anxiety whereas compulsions are strategies to reduce the anxiety.

Current treatments attend more to the compulsions than the obsessions (e.g. Kozak and Foa, 1997, cited in Masellis *et al.*, 2003), which may not be helpful given the findings of Masellis *et al.* (2003). Also, according to Freeston *et al.* (1997, cited in Masellis *et al.*, 2003) between 17 and 44 per cent of OCD patients do not present with compulsions, again suggesting a treatment focusing on compulsions may not be the most successful treatment. Cognitive therapy, focusing on obsessions, may be more useful for someone with OCD.

As depression related to OCD symptoms, the findings of the study suggest that treatment of the depression is also needed. Masellis *et al.* (2003), however, point out that use of selective serotonin reuptake inhibitors (SSRIs) is seen as no more effective than a main psychological treatment (ERP, exposure and response prevention – a type of exposure therapy) (Stanley and Turner, 1995, cited in Masellis *et al.*, 2003). The evidence for this claim comes from meta-analyses reviewing the effectiveness of SSRIs and ERP.

> **STUDY HINT**
> Masellis *et al.* (2003) give evidence from a meta-analysis (Stanley and Turner, 1995). You can use such examples when discussing meta-analysis, a research method you need to know about in clinical psychology.

> **Explore**
> ERP is a treatment for OCD, based on the idea of flooding. This link is to a story about OCD that might be a place to start your research:
> http://psychcentral.com/lib/erp-therapy-a-good-choice-for-treating-ocd/00010858

Year One link: In learning theories you may have covered flooding as a treatment for phobias. Make links from ERP to flooding and to what you learned about classical conditioning. ERP works on the principle of replacing a fear response to something with a relaxed response to it.

Masellis *et al.* (2003) point to a main strength of their study – the importance of using reliable and valid measures of quality of life. They also explain limitations of the study. One limitation is that it is cross-sectional rather than longitudinal so it is hard to draw conclusions about a causal connection between OCD symptoms of compulsions, obsessions and depression.

Quality of life may affect symptoms if things become difficult for a person so that they start to focus more on their obsessions and compulsions. This is the opposite of saying the symptoms affect quality of life. Another limitation is that the ratings done by each individual are likely to rely on how they felt at that moment. As the symptoms of the obsessions and depression come and go in OCD, one moment in time (a cross-sectional approach) can capture just the quality of life and self-report data at that time. This may not give a true long-term picture. Masellis *et al.* (2003) argue that a longitudinal design would be better for these reasons.

> **STUDY HINT**
> Masellis *et al.* (2003) mention the cross-sectional nature of their study as a limitation. The limitation is that they did not follow the participants and the course of their disorder over time and so were unable to record links between symptoms and quality of life. You can use this as a comment when discussing cross-sectional and/or longitudinal designs in clinical psychology.

The researchers also say the sample was not large enough to draw strong conclusions about how obsessive compulsive symptoms link to aspects of quality of life. The study, however, did find a direct association between obsessions, depression that goes with OCD, and quality of life.

> **STUDY HINT**
> As part of your course you need to know how to write up parts of a psychology report. Masellis *et al.* (2003) illustrate how to write a discussion:
> • Summarise the findings.
> • Refer to the background literature to see how the findings relate to what others have found.
> • Consider some real life practical applications of the findings.
> • Describe the strengths and limitations of the study before coming to a final conclusion.
> You can use this pattern when describing how a discussion should be presented.

Evaluation of Masellis *et al.* (2003)

Strengths

- Masellis *et al.* (2003) point to one of the strengths of their study, which is their use of standardised scales for measuring depression, obsessions and compulsions as well as measuring quality of life. The scales they use have been used before and tested for validity and reliability, so they can draw reliable and valid conclusions from their findings.
- Another strength of their study is the careful analysis using different statistical testing, including correlation analysis, as well as looking at how far each of the factors (depression, obsessions and compulsions) affected the quality of life scores (intrusiveness). They report strong levels of significance for some of the results and their analysis shows how compulsions seem to relate less to intrusiveness of OCD than obsessions. This finding is strong enough to be used when suggesting treatment for OCD. The statistical testing gives strength to the claims.

Weaknesses

- A weakness of the study, again reported by Masellis *et al.* (2003), is that they used a cross-sectional design and so only have self-report data from participants at one moment in time. OCD is an illness that can vary in effect over time, as can depression, so the results just show how someone feels about their illness and how it affects their quality of life at one point in their life. A longitudinal design would mean more data from each individual and tracking the course of the illness could perhaps show more successfully how quality of life (which is something that is affected over time) is affected by OCD.
- Another weakness that Masellis *et al.* (2003) point to is the size of the sample. A total of 43 patients were involved and there was a range of ages and a reasonable balance of males and females. The researchers suggest that this was not enough from which to draw strong conclusions, perhaps because they gathered self-report data and OCD affects people in different ways, so 43 people gave just their individual experiences. There is some depth and detail in their data, as they used three different scales to measure the different dimensions of OCD. However, the researchers felt that they did not get data from enough people to be sure their conclusions were strong enough to generalise to everyone with OCD.

Progress check 1.87

What were the reasons for Masellis *et al.* (2003) suggesting a longitudinal design would be better in their study?

Contemporary study relating to OCD: The Pediatric OCD Treatment Study (POTS) Team (2004)

The Pediatric OCD Treatment Study (POTS) reports on a randomised controlled trial looking at treatments for children and adolescents with obsessive compulsive disorder (OCD). It is thought from research that short-term OCD-specific cognitive-behavioural therapy (OCD-specific CBT) is effective with children and adolescents and that selective serotonin reuptake inhibitors (SSRIs) can also be effective. The POTS team (2004) looks at these two treatments, combined and separate, and their relative effectiveness. The study was done in the US with 112 patients who volunteered for the study. The participants/patients were aged from seven to seventeen years old.

The patients were randomly assigned to one of four conditions. One condition was using CBT alone, one was using sertraline alone, one condition was where both CBT and sertraline were used and a final condition was where there was a pill placebo. Of the 112 patients, 97 completed the 12 weeks of treatment and the findings showed there was a statistically significant advantage in having CBT alone, in having sertraline alone and in having the combined treatment. All were effective compared with the placebo. The combined treatment was better than the other two, even though all three showed significant effectiveness.

Progress check 1.88

What were the four conditions in the POTS team (2004) study?

Aims

The POTS team wanted to evaluate the effectiveness of CBT on its own, using an SSRI (sertraline) alone, as well as looking at CBT and sertraline together. They wanted to see how effective these three treatments were as initial treatment(s) for children and adolescents with OCD.

Background

The POTS team start by showing that around 1 in 200 young people has obsessive compulsive disorder (OCD) (Flament *et al.*, 1988, cited in POTS team, 2004). Around one third to one half of adults with OCD developed it during childhood or adolescence. This suggests that early intervention in childhood or adolescence can be very beneficial. Clomipramine, fluvoxamine, sertraline and fluoxetine are found to be effective drug therapies for OCD. In 30 to 40 per cent of adults drug therapy reduces OCD symptoms (Greist *et al.*, 1995, cited in the POTS team, 2004). This suggests that those on drug therapy alone would still have symptoms. Franklin *et al.* (2000, cited in the POTS team, 2004) suggest CBT is an effective treatment for OCD in adults, and March *et al.* (1994) as well as Franklin *et al.* (1998) suggest CBT is an effective treatment for OCD in children and adolescents.

STUDY HINT
When you are learning about OCD symptoms and features (as well as treatment and therapy) you can use the information from the POTS team study (2004). Masellis *et al.* (2003) also has information that can be used. This is perhaps a reason for looking at both studies in your chosen disorder as you can obtain general information from both.

The POTS team study (2004) was funded by the US National Institute of Mental Health to evaluate CBT alone, sertraline alone and a combination of the two as an effective way to treat OCD in children and adolescents.

Methods

The four conditions

Four 'treatments' were used and evaluated, all lasting over 12 weeks: CBT alone, sertraline alone (drug therapy), CBT and sertraline together and a control condition using a placebo pill. There was discussion about having CBT with a placebo pill as well, as this would control for expectations about taking medication in the treatment of CBT with sertraline, but this was thought too costly to do and also not ecologically valid.

This 12-week period using the four conditions was Stage 1 of the overall POTS team study, and is the part reported here this study. There was a Stage 2 part, which was a 16-week study about discontinuing treatment (following the 12-week treatment period). At the end of the 12 weeks all the placebo patients were offered CBT, medication or a combination.

Participants

The sample was a volunteer one. The sample was formed of 112 out-patients from an initial 154, who were aged from seven years old to seventeen years old. They all had a primary diagnosis of OCD using DSM-IV. The patients who were excluded were 31 that were deemed not to be eligible, 10 not interested and 1 excluded at the baseline measure because of not having OCD symptoms.

The sample of 112 were randomised to the four conditions, with 28 receiving CBT, 28 receiving sertraline, 28 receiving CBT and sertraline combined and 28 given a placebo pill. In the sample 46 per cent of the patients were children aged 11 years or younger and 54 per cent were adolescents aged 12 years and above. The ethnic origin of the sample was 92 per cent white.

STUDY HINT
The POTS team study uses a volunteer sample, which you can refer to when discussing sampling methods in your course. The POTS team also use participants diagnosed with OCD using the DSM-IV so you can also use this study as an example of using the DSM-IV.

The study was done in the USA at three different sites – Duke University, The University of Pennsylvania (Penn) and Brown University. Patients were recruited by advertisement in print and on the radio and also by referral from mental health clinicians. All the patients (and at least one of their parents) gave written informed consent to take part and each of the three sites approved the study through a review board.

The POTS team tried not to exclude certain patients or keep others because they wanted a representative sample. To include a patient in the study they had to be the right age (seven to seventeen years) and have a DSM-IV diagnosis of OCD, which came from the Children's Yale-Brown Obsessive Compulsive Scale (CY-BOCS) and the Anxiety Disorders Interview Schedule for Children (ADIS-C). Their CY-BOCS score had to be over 16. They also had to have an IQ of over 80 and not to be on anti-obsessional medication at the start of the study. Participants were excluded if they had major depression or bipolar, Tourette's syndrome or any developmental disorder. There were some other conditions as well around their state of health (such as intolerance to sertraline or a failed trial of CBT for OCD). The POTS team wanted their results to be generalisable so they included patients who had ADHD (attention-deficit hyperactivity disorder) who were stable on medication.

Progress check 1.89

Why were some of the patients excluded from the POTS study?

STUDY HINT

Look at the answer to Progress check 1.89 online. You will see that the answer focuses on why some patients were excluded in this particular study, rather than reasons for exclusion in general. When you are asked this type of question about methodology of a study, be sure to focus your answer on the particular study rather than offering a general answer.

Procedure

Participants were screened using telephone screening and then various consent and inclusion/exclusion procedures were gone through. The participants were then given a baseline assessment and randomised to the four conditions. The researchers found that the groups were not different when looking at their baseline scores and there did not seem to be any bias in selecting the four groups. The researchers did know that those in the CBT group were not having medication and those in the combined group were on active medication; however, they did not know which were in the placebo group and which were in the sertraline-only group.

Interventions

- The patients in two conditions, the one with sertraline only and the one with the placebo, had psychiatrists available to monitor them and also to encourage them to resist OCD. There was a weekly review and readjustment of the medication, which was given in increasing doses in the first six weeks. After the six weeks they were seen every other week.
- The CBT treatment consisted of 14 visits over the 12 weeks involving psychoeducation, cognitive training, mapping OCD target symptoms and exposure and response prevention. Visits were mostly weekly and lasted about an hour.
- Those in the combined CBT and sertraline group had the CBT treatment of the CBT-only group and were given sertraline at the same time. The visits for CBT and for readjustment of medication were timed so the patient only had to visit once.

Measuring the outcomes

All patients were assessed at baseline and at week four, week eight and week twelve by the same independent evaluator, who did not know which condition a patient was in. The CY-BOCS was used to measure distress and degree of resistance and similar issues around OCD. A score of equal to or less than 10 matched remission.

Analysis

Analysis focused on the impact of treatment on the outcome at the 12-week point. The researchers set the level of significance at p.05 with a two-tailed hypothesis (the treatment could either help or hinder the OCD symptoms) and they mentioned this might yield a Type I error.

Year One link: The POTS team (2004) study mentions a two-tailed focus, with a p.05 level of significance and the possibility of a Type I error. You can refer back to your Year One studies to check on the meaning of these features of a study in psychology. For example, a Type I error is made if the level of significance is wrongly set generously and p.05 is generous (it allows for 1 in 20 results to go against the prediction and still the hypothesis is accepted).

Results

The POTS team first looked at the demographic data to be sure that the four groups were similar with regard to age and gender. Table 1.23 shows some of the demographics and baseline measures by group.

Table 1.23 Baseline demographics and clinical characteristics by group (POTS team study, 2004)

Characteristics	CBT alone N = 28	Sertraline alone N = 28	Combined CBT and sertraline N = 28	Placebo alone N = 28
Gender				
Male – number	14 (50%)	17 (60.7%)	11 (39.3%)	14 (50%)
Female – number	14 (50%)	11 (39.3%)	17 (60.7%)	14 (50%)
Mean age in years (SD in brackets)	11.4 (2.8)	11.7 (2.4)	11.7 (2.8)	12.3 (3.0)
CY-BOCS mean score – total of obsessions and compulsions mean scores	26	22.5	23.8	25.2

Table 1.23 gives information about gender, mean age in years and scores on the CY-BOCS at baseline for the 112 patients. You can see the figures are very similar across the four conditions although the gender split is different for the two conditions where sertraline is used, with more males in the sertraline-alone group and more females in the CBT + sertraline group. Other than that it can be seen that the randomisation to the four conditions worked to give what looks like an unbiased sample in each.

Although there were 28 in each group at the start, in practice some did not complete the treatment. Those failing to complete the treatment were:

- CBT only – three participants
- sertraline only – two participants
- combined treatment group – three participants
- placebo treatment – seven participants.

All 112 were included in the analysis, however.

The baseline CY-BOCS scores were very similar, showing a similar level of obsessions and compulsions at the start of the study. There were no statistically significant differences between the four groups at the start of the study, which is the important point. Table 1.24 shows the mean score on the Children's Yale-Brown Obsessive Compulsive Scale (CY-BOCS), for each treatment group from baseline to the twelfth week.

Table 1.24 Mean score on the CY-BOCS, for each treatment group from baseline to the twelfth week (POTS team study, 2004)

Week	CY-BOCS mean score (adjusted for other variables) with standard deviation in brackets			
	CBT alone	Sertraline alone	Combined CBT and Sertraline	Placebo group
Baseline/start	26 (4.6)	23.5 (4.7)	23.8 (3.0)	25.2 (3.3)
4	20.6 (6.5)	18.5 (7.5)	18.1 (6.8)	22.4 (5.4)
8	18.1 (7.9)	16.9 (8.2)	14.4 (8.1)	22.5 (4.4)
12	14.0 (9.5)	16.5 (9.1)	11.2 (8.6)	21.5 (5.4)

Progress check 1.90

Draw a graph to show the results in Table 1.24 (the mean CY-BOCS scores) and briefly explain the pattern.

Table 1.24 gives mean scores that show a trend over time (p<.001) and by treatment (p<.001).

Summary of some of the results shown in Table 1.24

- In all of the four conditions the CY-BOCS scores (means) fall over time, showing the treatment is successful over time, though that includes the placebo 'treatment'. At four weeks and eight weeks the placebo condition's scores do not really fall, but remain very similar, but at 12 weeks there is a fall, so overall in all conditions the trend is for the scores to fall over time.
- As the scores fall, towards the 12-week measure, there is a tendency for the standard deviation to rise. This suggests that the spread of scores at baseline is the smallest with a large spread as the scores fall. This means that there is more variation in the scores as the treatment progresses, which might point to a variation in the success of the treatments that the overall mean does not show clearly.

Progress check 1.91

In Table 1.24 the standard deviation is given. In general what does the standard deviation of a set of scores show? Use two examples from the table to illustrate your answer.

- Although the baseline measures start as very similar, at the end of the 12-week period there are differences in the scores across the conditions. The placebo score (21.5) is very similar to the four baseline scores, but the other three conditions show quite a large reduction in score at the end of 12 weeks. The CBT-alone condition has a score of 14.0 at the 12-week period, the sertraline-only condition has a score of 16.5 at that point and the combined treatment has the lowest score of 11.2.

The POTS team analysed the results of the study and found that combined treatment was better than CBT (p=.008), which is better than sertraline alone (p=.006), which is better than the placebo (p=.001). They found that CBT alone was statistically significantly better than the placebo at p.003 and sertraline alone was significantly better than the placebo at p.007. However, CBT alone or sertraline alone did not differ in their effectiveness.

Year One link: In the results for the POTS team study levels of significance are given to show the significance of certain results. For example, combined treatment is better than just CBT and the level of significance is 8 in 1,000 being due to chance, which is a strong claim. When reading about such results, recall your learning of levels of significance to help your understanding.

Overall the results showed that the placebo had the least effect, as would be expected, CBT alone and sertraline alone were both similarly effective and the combined treatment was the most effective.

There were some statistically significant differences between the sites, with, for example, CBT alone at Penn (the University of Pennsylvania) being better than CBT alone at Duke University ($p=.05$). Sertraline alone at Duke was better than sertraline alone at Penn ($p.02$). The combined treatment and placebo were similar between these two sites and Brown was not included in this analysis as the numbers were too small. This suggests that the combined treatment was less affected by the different sites, which is a point to note as it might mean that combined treatment is less affected by individuals administering it. The diagram below shows the overall findings of the POTS team study looking at effectiveness of CBT-alone, sertraline-alone, combined CBT and sertraline or a placebo.

Conclusions and discussion

The aim of the POTS team study (2004) was to look at the benefit of the combined CBT and sertraline treatment compared to each being used separately, as well as the merits of the treatments compared with a placebo. The conclusions were that the combined treatment or CBT alone was the best treatment. One site's results suggested that the combined treatment was better than CBT alone, but the other site did not confirm this trend. Medication, in the form of sertraline in this study, was better than the placebo. The team concluded that children and young people with OCD should start with CBT alone as a treatment or with CBT and an SSRI.

The team then considered limitations of their study. They felt that the results sufficiently supported their earlier work for them to be confident about claiming effectiveness of the SSRI for OCD and the effect sizes of the results were what led to this confidence. They felt that the findings could be generalised to children and adolescents with OCD and so treatments could be used accordingly.

The researchers were interested in the site differences, which they did not expect, as they felt the administration of the treatments would be the same across sites. CBT alone showed more impact at Penn than at Duke though there was no site effect for the combined treatment. They thought perhaps there was a therapist effect that accounted for the differences between the sites, even though they had taken care to match the therapies (e.g. using supervision, case conferences and training meetings). The researchers wondered if patient characteristics varied between the two sites rather than there being therapist difference, although they did not find differences between the patients on the different sites when they analysed the data. They felt that the site differences affected the generalisability of the findings.

The POTS team pointed out that it is useful for clinicians to know that combined CBT and medication is a successful treatment for children and adolescents with OCD but that it would be helpful to know which treatment would suit which individual best, which this study did not show. For example, SSRIs can lead to suicidal thoughts or mania in children with certain clinical characteristics, so it is important to consider individual characteristics when suggesting treatment.

The team felt that their findings would both give information about medication as a treatment for children and adolescents with OCD and also show the value of psychosocial treatments (in this case, CBT). The team say that CBT was not being used [in 2004] for most young people with OCD, either with medication or alone, and their findings suggested that CBT either with or without medication could be effective.

| The placebo had least effect (mean CY-BOCS score of 25.2 at baseline to 21.5 at 12 weeks) | The sertraline alone condition was next best (mean CY-BOCS score of 23.5 at baseline to 16.5 at 12 weeks) | The CBT-alone condition was next best (mean CY-BOCS score of 26 at baseline to 14.0 at 12 weeks) | The combined CBT and sertraline was best (mean CY-BOCS score of 23.8 at baseline to 11.2 at 12 weeks) |

Overall findings of the POTS team study (2004)

Evaluation

Strengths

- The POTS team study used randomisation to groups, which should mean a lack of bias in the conclusions that would come from there being differences in the patients in the four different groups. This sort of control, using randomised controlled trials, means that cause and effect conclusions can be drawn. The researchers tested to see if there was bias in characteristics between the four groups and found that there was no bias, which strengthens their claims about the effectiveness of the therapies.

- By using three sites and finding that the combined treatment was the most effective (with CBT alone a close second) across the sites, this helps the generalisability of the findings. It was the case that there were some site differences, but overall the findings that the combined therapy and CBT alone were the best choices were the case across all three sites. If just one site had been used, such as the University of Pennsylvania, where CBT alone was more effective than at Duke University, such subtleties in findings would not have been known about.

Weaknesses

- The team wondered about the generalisability of their findings. They felt that there was no bias in characteristics between the four groups, but they found site differences in the findings, which suggests perhaps that there were individual differences in the samples for those two sites

that led to differences in the findings. CBT alone was more effective on one site (Penn) than CBT alone at Duke University. The POTS team did suggest that the difference could be down to therapist differences, but they wondered if it was because of differences in the sample, which does threaten generalisability somewhat.

- As the team point out, randomised controlled trials find cause and effect conclusions for groups of people and they felt it was useful to discover that CBT and an SSRI together was a successful treatment for the age group considered, and that CBT alone was successful. Sertraline was also successful. All treatments were better than a placebo. However, this did not help clinicians with prescribing for individuals who might react differently, for example, to SSRIs depending on the individual characteristics of their OCD. Individual differences are important and research was needed to find out more, for example, about which conditions in young people might lead medication to produce either mania or suicidal thoughts, or similar issues.

Progress check 1.92

Why is generalisability important in the POTS team's (2004) research?

Test yourself

Focusing on the disorder you have chosen (from a choice of unipolar depression, anorexia nervosa or OCD), and one of the two studies for that disorder, answer the following questions:

1 Explain the procedure of one of the studies named in your course focusing on your chosen disorder other than schizophrenia. **(4 marks)**

2 To what extent can the findings of the study you wrote about in question 1 be considered suitable for generalising to the target population? **(8 marks)**

3 Evaluate one of the studies named in your course focusing on your chosen disorder other than schizophrenia. **(16 marks)**

Summary

In the studies section you need to know about:
- Rosenhan's (1973) study about 'being sane in insane places'.
- Carlsson *et al.*'s (1999/2000) study looking at biological aspects of schizophrenia.
- If choosing unipolar depression as your other disorder, either Kroenke *et al.* (2008) about measuring depression or Williams *et al.* (2013) focusing on internet CBT for depression.

- If choosing anorexia nervosa as your other disorder, either Scott-Van Zeeland *et al.* (2013/2014) focusing on related gene variants or Guardia *et al.* (2012) on how someone with anorexia nervosa views themselves in terms of their body image.
- If choosing OCD as your other disorder, Masellis *et al.* (2003) looking at obsessions, compulsions and quality of life, or the POTS team study (2004) looking at CBT and drug therapy for OCD.

Key question in clinical psychology

In this section you need to be able to describe one key question in clinical psychology using the areas covered in this chapter. Suggested key questions include asking how different societies define mental disorders and what are the issues surrounding mental health in the workplace. This chapter considers one of these key questions for society.

 The other key question can be found on the accompanying website.

Year One link: As in topic areas in Year One, each of which had a key question that was studied, you need to be able to describe your key question and say why it is 'key' for society. Then you need to be able to apply concepts, research and theories to help to explain the key question, including answers.

> **STUDY HINT**
>
> The practical investigation for clinical psychology, which is introduced in Chapter Two and worked through on the accompanying website, looks at attitudes to mental health in the media, particularly newspapers. You may like to use some of the review of the literature given there, when discussing how different societies define mental health disorders (the key question given online).

> **STUDY HINT**
>
> The key question 'How do different societies define mental health disorders?' can be found on the website accompanying this book.

Social isolation occurs more in some cultures than others and can affect the course and outcome of a mental health disorder. How different societies define mental health disorders is important and can be affected by cultural traditions.

Progress check 1.93

Explain two findings that show that different societies define mental health disorders differently.

What are the issues surrounding mental health in the workplace?

Mind, a charity focusing on mental health, reported one in five people take a day off work because of stress, one in four people have thought about resigning because of stress and one in ten do resign a job due to stress. However, for many people their workplace provides more than a job – it gives them their 'identity' and is the place where most of their friends can be found. In November 2014 the BBC reported that more than 11 million working days are lost each year because of stress and depression. A research briefing from the Parliamentary Office of Science and Technology in October 2012 claimed that poor mental health in the workplace has a cost to the UK of around £26 billion a year. It is claimed that changing the environment at work and giving training to managers can reduce absenteeism and improve productivity. The briefing claimed that in 2000 44.6 per cent of all sickness absence from work was due to poor mental health.

> **Explore**
>
> *The Guardian* published an article in September 2014 about mental health in the workplace, which you may like to read:
> /www.theguardian.com/society/2014/sep/10/mental-health-workplace-employers
>
> Do some internet research to find further articles related to this key question.
>
> Here is a link to the 2012 Parliamentary paper 'Mental Health and the Workplace', mentioned above:
> http://researchbriefings.files.parliament.uk/documents/POST-PN-422/POST-PN-422.pdf

In a paper published by the Mental Health Foundation, Gray (1999) explains the issues surrounding mental health in the workplace. She points out that a workforce that is psychologically healthy benefits employers and the individuals themselves. A CBI (Confederation of British Industry) survey (1997) found that 98 per cent of companies thought that mental health of employees was of concern to the company, so it is clear that this is a recognised issue. The issue of mental health in the workplace does not seem to relate to companies not recognising its importance; it seems to be more about what is done in the area of mental health in the workplace.

Gray (1999) found that fewer than one in ten of the companies surveyed had an official mental health policy. Gray (1999) suggests that it is excessive stress in the workplace that is the issue, leading to 'fatigue, impaired judgement and decision-making and exhaustion' (p. 2). Psychological effects include problems with sleep, poor concentration and aggression, and issues like this can lead to accidents at work, as well as problems for the individual. As evidence for there being stress at work, Gray (1999) says that out of 270 company managers 88 per cent said there was a moderate or high level of stress in their company, with 39 per cent saying it had got worse over the past year.

Mind has some ideas for taking care of yourself at work, such as talking to people instead of sending emails, asking about someone's weekend and listening to their answer, finding out how someone really is and giving a colleague a lift to or from work. This is about improving social relationships to promote well-being. Issues in the workplace relating to mental health include isolation as well as stress.

Physical activity is another issue related to mental health at work. Mind suggests that regular physical activity relates to lower levels of depression. In the workplace people are often physically inactive, so walking or moving around at work can help. The unvaried routine of going to work, doing the work and going home again can affect someone's mental health as it is possible that a person stops noticing what is happening during the day, and this can link with depression. Mind advises that taking note of our surroundings can help to counter this.

The unvaried routine of the daily commute to work can lead to depression in some people.

Progress check 1.94

Give two pieces of information that show that mental health in the workplace is an issue for society.

Issues around mental health in the workplace are issues for society, as the Parliamentary Office of Science and Technology figures about productivity and absenteeism suggest. Underlying the key question 'what are the issues surrounding mental health in the workplace?' is what should be done by society with regard to such issues.

Using concepts, theories and research to explain the key question

When discussing mental health in the workplace the focus tends to be on stress at work. Stress affects both a person's physical and mental health and symptoms include anxiety, depression, fatigue, sleep problems, difficulty with concentrating and possibly aggression.

Depression commonly affects people in the range 25–44, with the average age for developing depression being mid-20s, which fits in with working patterns. This suggests that work might lead to depression or that people at work can develop depression. Whichever way it is interpreted, it is clear that there needs to be an emphasis on such mental health issues within the workplace.

Depression tends to affect work and family life as well as functioning, such as sleeping and eating. According to the Anxiety and Depression Association of America, around 6.7 per cent of the adult population suffer from depression, and this affects their everyday lives. In the US anxiety is the most common mental illness with 40 million adults affected. Depression affected over 4.7 million people in the UK in 2010–11 according to the NHS.

Brown (1986) carried out a study looking at depression in women and found that of those who had had no support, either at first contact or at crisis, 44 per cent (4 out of 9) developed depression. This suggests that social support at work is very important, not only because social support seems to prevent depression from developing but also because it is an important factor in helping someone with depression.

Social support is also thought to be important in the quality of life of someone with schizophrenia while social isolation is seen as a factor in starting or maintaining mental health issues. This again underlines why social support at work is important for mental health in the workplace. The diathesis-stress model, when related to schizophrenia, considers that stressors in the environment work with biological features of an individual such as genes, which underlines the importance of environment, including the workplace.

If neurotransmitter functioning or the way the brain is activated are explanations for mental disorders, as has been suggested for schizophrenia, depression and OCD, for example, then perhaps the workplace is not responsible for the development of mental health disorders in workers. However, cognitive factors can link to neurotransmitter functioning, as seen in OCD, and intrusive thoughts leading to fear and worry (which are symptoms of OCD), which can worsen in a workplace where there is insufficient support. Many people spend much of their time at work, so it is important that a workplace offers the required support to avoid workers with mental health disorders experiencing social isolation.

CBT has been shown to be an effective therapy for mental health disorders, including depression and OCD, for example. CBT works by challenging negative automatic thoughts, for example, to reduce the negative emphasis (such as the thought 'nobody likes me' being changed to 'not everyone will like me'). CBT requires the individual to do homework on inappropriate thinking and this is something that could be offered in the workplace, as it is not particularly time-consuming (perhaps 50 minutes each week). Such an approach can be effective for mental disorders such as depression and if a workplace was able to offer support, it is likely people would increase their productivity. For example, a 2008 study (Kuyken *et al.*)

reported that a group-based form of CBT (mindfulness-based cognitive therapy – MBCT) is at least as successful in treating depression as medication like Prozac, even in the long term. It was better at preventing relapse, offered a more effective change in quality of life, and was more cost-effective.

Test yourself

Focusing on one key question you have studied relating to clinical psychology, evaluate the key question for society, using concepts, theories and/or research that you have covered in your course. **(16 marks)**

Summary

In the key question section you need to know about:

- One key question of relevance to today's society discussed as a contemporary issue and a question for society.
- Concepts, theories and/or research that you have studied within clinical psychology that can be used to give answers about the key question you have chosen.

Chapter Two: Clinical psychology – method, maths and practical investigation

General overview

In clinical psychology you need to study various methodology issues, including an awareness of the Health and Care Professions Council (HCPC) and their guidelines for clinical practitioners. This chapter looks at researching mental health and the use of longitudinal, cross-sectional and cross-cultural methods, meta-analysis and primary and secondary data. You need to know about the use of case studies, including an example of a case study, and the use of interviews together with an example of an interview. As well as these specific methodological issues you need to revise your understanding of analysis of quantitative data using both descriptive and inferential statistics from your Year One studies. You also need to recall thematic analysis and look at how grounded theory is used to analyse qualitative data.

Health and care professionals, including clinical practitioners, must register with the Health and Care Professions Council (HCPC) and follow their guidelines.

STUDY HINT

Progress check answers can be found on the website accompanying this book.

Health and Care Professions Council

You need to have an awareness of the Health and Care Professions Council (HCPC) guidelines for clinical practitioners. The HCPC has standards that those registered with the Council must abide by to remain on the Register.

- In July 2009 it was announced that statutory (legal) regulation for psychologists would no longer be done by the British Psychological Society (BPS) but would instead come under the HCPC.
- Statutory regulation exists to protect the public and to ensure good practice. Sanctions can be applied for failure to comply with the requirements of the HCPC, such as removing someone from the Register.
- Clinical psychologists, health psychologists, counselling psychologists, educational psychologists, occupational psychologists, sport and exercise psychologists and forensic psychologists must all register with the HCPC. These are all examples of health and care professional titles that are protected by law. This means that anyone using the title must be registered with the HCPC, or they may be subjected to prosecution and possibly a fine
- The BPS continues to oversee the content of psychology training courses as the HCPC does not state what must be covered by a professional training course. The HCPC does, however, visit training course providers to make sure the required standards of education and training are being met.

HCPC Standards in relation to practising psychologists

The HCPC publishes standards relating to the character, health, proficiency, conduct, ethics and training of health and care professionals.

- Character: criminal convictions or cautions must be revealed and a character reference is required, signed by someone of 'professional standing in the community', such as a doctor, solicitor, bank manager, justice of the peace or religious official.
- Health: a person registered with the HCPC must stop work if their health affects their judgement. A long-term health condition or disability is not a barrier to registration, but if a person's health affects their work or might affect their work it must be declared.
- Standards of conduct, performance and ethics: in essence, this includes acting in the best interest of service users, respecting confidentiality of service users, maintaining high standards of personal conduct, providing important information about conduct and competence, acting within the limits of personal skills and experience and referring to others when necessary.

It is important to communicate well, supervise tasks you have set others, obtain informed consent when providing care and services, keep accurate records, deal carefully with infection and stop practising if health affects judgement. Someone must behave with honesty and integrity to avoid damaging public confidence in their profession.

Explore

You can learn more about the HCPC using their website. This is a link to the HCPC requirements concerning conduct, performance and ethics: www.hcpc-uk.org/assets/documents/10003B6EStandardsofconduct,performanceandethics.pdf

Year One link: Note that the ethics of the HCPC fits closely with the ethics of the British Psychological Society that you studied in social psychology in Year One.

Progress check 2.1

Give three ways in which the HCPC guidance on ethics and professional conduct matches BPS guidance about ethics and professional conduct.

Standards of proficiency for practitioner psychologists were developed in 2007 and then reviewed in 2009–10 to ensure they still met their purpose.

- The practitioner psychologist must understand the need to act in the best interests of service users and be familiar with the requirements of the HCPC.
- The psychologist must understand the need to respect every service user and this includes their role in the diagnostic and therapeutic process and in maintaining health and well-being.
- Clinical psychologists, educational psychologists, health psychologists and forensic psychologists are asked to understand how to manage the power imbalance between them and their clients. Counselling psychologists are asked to recognise boundaries that are appropriate and they too must understand the power situation that exists between themselves and their clients.
- The practising psychologist must work in a non-discriminatory way and maintain confidentiality as well as obtain informed consent from their clients.
- They must exercise a duty of care, manage themselves successfully and work autonomously as well as be able to work as part of a multi-disciplinary team.

- Standards of education and training are set out, focusing on training in the profession, such as training in psychology as a profession.
- Those who are registered must have a continuous up-to-date record of continuing professional development (CPD). CPD activities must be a mixture of learning and practice. All CPD undertaken must benefit the service user.

Registering with the HCPC

Registering with the HCPC involves two stages:

- Stage 1: The HCPC checks that a trainee has passed all elements of a programme that they have undertaken, such as a doctorate in clinical psychology, where the academic, clinical and research elements must all be passed.
- Stage 2: The trainee (now qualified) can apply for registration. The HCPC will require a character reference, health reference and information about the applicant.

Test yourself

Explain the standards that the Health and Care Professions Council (HCPC) require registered practising psychologists to adhere to. **(8 marks)**

Researching mental health

Your course includes some specific issues about researching mental health, such as the use of longitudinal, cross-sectional and cross-cultural methods as well as meta-analysis. The use of primary and secondary data must also be understood.

Longitudinal designs

In this section longitudinal research is called 'longitudinal designs'. That is because using a longitudinal approach is not a research method as such; it is a way of carrying out a study. Although these studies may be called 'longitudinal studies', this chapter will mainly refer to 'designs' in order to distinguish what is said from discussions about specific longitudinal studies. 'Longitudinal' means taking place over a period of time rather than at one moment in time.

- An observation can be repeated using the same variables over a period of time, such as repeating the observation every month for a period of six months. This design would be a longitudinal one.
- A questionnaire can be used longitudinally, for example, when a questionnaire is given at the start of an intervention and then administered at the end too. This is a 'before and after' study and can be seen

as a longitudinal design. The data are collected over a period of time, which is longitudinal, and the same participants are involved, which also fits a longitudinal design. The intention is to study how the intervention (in this example) affects the participants over time, which again fits the definition of longitudinal. Vallentine *et al.* (2010) – which is the study described later in this chapter (page 162) – used before and after measures using two questionnaires (and other measures, including a semi-structured interview at the end of the intervention). They returned to the participants over time, taking details of any violent incidents at three and six months before and after an intervention that involved psycho-education training for the participants.

Longitudinal designs are used to study developmental trends over time and are often used in child psychology, for example, looking at how a baby develops language, perhaps up to the age of three years old. Longitudinal designs/studies follow the same participants or a single participant over a period of time, using the same individual(s). Many longitudinal designs are observations and do not involve manipulating variables. This is because one of the aims is to see how a characteristic or behaviour develops, so the researchers don't wish to interfere with the behaviour observed to make it unnatural, as the study would then lack validity.

Cohort studies are longitudinal in design because they involve following one cohort of people, such as a school year group (a cohort is a group that has similar experiences; often the similarity is the year they were born in) over a period of time (perhaps through primary school, for example). It is difficult to say how long a study has to last to be called 'longitudinal'. Someone might follow a patient through a treatment that lasts a few weeks, which would be a longitudinal design, while another might follow a patient from their diagnosis through a long course of their life, which could be years. That too would be a longitudinal design. It is not just the length of time that makes a study longitudinal, it is following the same individual(s) over time in some way, gathering data from them more than once and comparing any changes over time.

Example of a longitudinal study in clinical psychology

Hankin *et al.* (1998) carried out a ten-year longitudinal study looking at gender differences in how depression emerges in young people from pre-adolescence to young adulthood. Hankin *et al.* (1998) used a birth cohort, which means they used everyone born in that year. They used structured interviews which they administered five times over ten years. They started to see more females emerging with depression than males as the cohort reached the ages

of between 13 and 15. However, they report that the largest gender difference was between 15 and 18 years old. They compared those that went to university with those that did not and found no differences in depression rates between those two samples and no differences in gender and depression between those two samples either. There was no gender difference in how severe the depression was or how often it recurred. The increase was in overall rates of depression and in the severity of the symptoms and that increase took place between 15 and 18 years of age. The conclusion was that between 15 and 18 years old is an important time when studying how vulnerable someone is to depression because there are higher depression rates then and a large increase in gender differences in depression at that time.

The focus here is on the longitudinal element of the study, which is the way participants were selected, and the procedures of the study. The sample was a complete birth cohort from the Dunedin Multidisciplinary Health and Development Study. This is a study of people in New Zealand born between 1st April 1972 and 31st March 1973, in Dunedin. The sample contained 1,037 children (of whom 52 per cent were male). A diagnosis of depression was taken at 11, 13, 15, 18 and 21. The fact that data were gathered on five occasions is what makes this a longitudinal study. Other data were taken from this group at ages 3, 5, 7 and 9, and also at ages 11, 13, 15, 18 and 21, so the cohort was studied more than the use of the interviews explained here indicates. The study explains that the DSM-III was used as well as other means of diagnosis and the interview used was 'very structured'.

Hankin *et al.* (1998) suggest that between the ages of 15 and 18 is a time to watch for the development of depression and that girls are more likely to suffer from depression at that age than boys. This was a longitudinal study gathering data from aged 11 to aged 21.

Evaluation of longitudinal designs in clinical psychology

Strengths

- Longitudinal designs are good because they follow the same people or person over a period of time so there are no individual differences that might affect the results. The participants each time are the same and are often from the same cohort, so they are likely to have had very similar experiences, at least in some ways. If research focuses on someone with a mental disorder which is specific to them, then it makes sense to follow the course of their illness to take into account individual differences.

- Another strength is that it is a good way of finding out how we develop – in fact if someone is going to study how someone or something develops over time, they will by definition be using a longitudinal design. Development is hard to study any other way. A cross-sectional design (page 145) can be used, but it will mean different people are studied, which raises issues about individual differences, which might affect the findings. If a researcher wants to see how a mental disorder affects someone's functioning over time, then they will use a longitudinal design because it enables the study of development.

Weaknesses

- A difficulty is keeping the participants in the study for long enough to draw conclusions about their development or about the issue being studies. Participants are likely to drop out of the study as they might move away or they may decide they no longer want to take part. Vallentine et al. (2010) found that the patients who started in the group focusing on psycho-education could be moved to another institution before finishing the group. There were also patients who refused to have their data used, as was their

right. However, if there is something particular about those that do not finish a study that makes them different from those that do finish (perhaps in motivation) then that can add bias to the results.

- There are also potential ethical difficulties. For example, following someone or a group of participants over time can be more intrusive than studying them just once. A longitudinal study tends to be about someone's development so the data gathered might also be intrusive. Respecting someone's privacy can be more difficult than in a cross-sectional design (page 162) where intrusion might be quick and less personal. If someone has already consented to be part of a study they might find it hard to refuse later. This can be especially the case for those with a mental disorder, who may be classed as more vulnerable because of their disorder, which is likely to affect their functioning.

Progress check 2.2

Explain two problems of using a longitudinal design in clinical psychology.

Cross-sectional designs

A cross-sectional design is one where data are collected at one moment in time, over a short period – it provides a 'snapshot' of something. Like longitudinal designs, cross-sectional designs tend to be used to look at development in some way, but instead of following the same person or people over time, they focus on getting different people at the same moment in time. The difference in the people is what will be of interest. For example, language in children can be studied longitudinally by following a baby (or some babies) through their development of language perhaps until the age of three years old. Alternatively, three groups of children can be used. One small group of babies, one small group of 18-month-old children and one small group of three year olds. Then comparisons can be made about what each group can do in the way of using language – this is an example of a cross-sectional design.

Progress check 2.3

What is meant in psychology by a cross-sectional design?

Example of a cross-sectional design in clinical psychology

Studies suggest that smoking cigarettes is more common in those with schizophrenia than in the general population and it is thought that biological, social and psychological (**biopsychosocial**) factors influence this behaviour. For example, it is thought that nicotine might be used as self-medication for schizophrenia symptoms – Addington *et al.* (1998, cited in Wijesundera *et al.*, 2014). However, those with schizophrenia who smoke have more hospitalisations, which perhaps suggests smoking does not help their symptoms (Goff *et al.*, 1992, cited in Wijesundera *et al.*, 2014). Nicotine might help by improving cognitive functioning, while increasing dopamine activity (which nicotine does) might reduce negative symptoms in schizophrenia (Wijesundera *et al.*, 2014).

> **STUDY HINT**
> Wijesundera *et al.* (2014) is offered as an example of a cross-sectional study in clinical psychology, but it also has a focus on drug therapy in schizophrenia as well as on explanations for schizophrenia (such as neurotransmitter activity). You can use the material in this study wherever it fits in your course.

Wijesundera *et al.* (2014) carried out a study to look at tobacco use and antipsychotic medication in out-patients with schizophrenia in one hospital in Sri Lanka. They used systematic sampling (every third patient diagnosed with schizophrenia using the ICD-10 was chosen). The researchers thought that smoking in schizophrenia might depend on the drugs the individual was taking – for example, typical antipsychotics are linked to an increased risk of smoking. Some studies suggest that clozapine reduces smoking in those with schizophrenia (e.g. Drake *et al.*, 2000, cited in Wijesundera *et al.*, 2014). Wijesundera *et al.* (2014) report that when 12 patients treated with halperidol changed to clozapine cigarette smoking was reduced (McEvoy *et al.*, 1995, cited in Wijesundera *et al.*, 2014). In fact, clozapine also seems to reduce alcohol intake in those with schizophrenia (Drake *et al.*, 2000, cited in Wijesundera *et al.*, 2014).

Progress check 2.4

What possible bias is there in using a selective sample, as Wijesundera *et al.* (2014) did?

> **STUDY HINT**
> Wijesundera *et al.* (2014) used the ICD-10 classification system, so you can use this study as an example of the use of this classification system.

Year One link: In Year One, in social psychology, you looked at four types of sampling – volunteer/self-selected, random, opportunity and stratified. Selective is another way of selecting a sample, as was the case in Wijesundera *et al.* (2014), who took every third patient with the required diagnosis. Review what you know about sampling when you are looking at Year Two studies.

Explanation

Biopsychosocial factors are often looked at when studying a mental disorder. Causes of a mental disorder may be biological, social or psychological, but it is common to look at all three under the title 'biopsychosocial'.

Wijesundera *et al.* (2014) wanted to look at how prevalent smoking was in those with schizophrenia in a country where smoking rates were low overall. They also wanted to see how smoking linked to antipsychotic treatment. Sri Lanka in general has a low prevalence of smoking and smoking in females is rare. Smoking was measured by using self-report data, severity of illness was measured using a standardised scale (Brief Psychiatric Rating Scale – BPRS), and nicotine dependence was measured using the Fagerstrom Test (a standardised test). There were 148 males (48.5 per cent), the average length of the illness was 12.63 years (SD 8.38) and the mean age of the 306 participants was 38.93 years (SD 10.98).

It is suggested that smoking tobacco affects symptoms of psychosis and schizophrenia and some medication (such as clozapine) reduces the risk of smoking cigarettes (Wijesundera *et al.*, 2014).

Year One link: Studies in psychology provide mean averages when giving information about the age of participants or length of time of an illness (as shown in the summary of Wijesundera et al. (2014) given in this section). The standard deviation is very often given when a mean average is offered. This is so that the reader can see the spread of scores around the mean average. Remind yourself about the function of the standard deviation of a set of scores, how to calculate it and what it means. You need to understand this information when it is given in studies in psychology (even if the information is not always reported in the summaries of studies provided in this book).

Explore
You may like to do some internet research to find out more about a standardised test or scale. For example, the Brief Psychiatric Rating Scale (BRPS) is explained more at this link:
www.public-health.uiowa.edu/icmha/outreach/documents/bprs_expanded.pdf

Progress check 2.5

Studies tend to use standardised scales and tests, such as those used by Wijesundera et al. (2014). What does 'standardised' mean in relation to a scale or test and why is this important?

In Wijesundera et al. (2014) medication being used by the participants (who were diagnosed as having schizophrenia) was:

- oral atypical antipsychotic medication – 103 participants
- clozapine – 136 participants
- oral typicals – 29 participants
- depot typicals (older typical antipsychotic drugs) – 38 participants.

None of the females in the sample smoked cigarettes although smokeless tobacco was used by some. Of the males in the sample, 20.27 per cent smoked (the measure was smoking in the last 30 days). Tobacco use for the males was 30.41 per cent. Smokeless tobacco was used by 10.14 per cent of males and 1.90 per cent of the females. The researchers found that when patients who were being treated with clozapine were not in the analysis, that increased the prevalence of tobacco use to 41.6 per cent of males and 3.2 per cent of females, with 29.9 per cent smoking.

As only males smoked, females were not included in the overall analysis when looking at tobacco use and antipsychotic drugs. Tobacco use was lowest in those treated with clozapine (19.41 per cent) and highest in those treated with depot antipsychotics (47.83 per cent). Risk of tobacco use in males with schizophrenia was lower in those on clozapine, which was what the researchers expected from other studies.

Wijesundera et al. (2014) is an example of a cross-sectional study. The researchers did not follow the same patients over a period of time to see how their smoking and tobacco use developed depending on the type of antipsychotic drug they were on, as this would be a longitudinal design. Instead they took a cross-section of males and females with a diagnosis of schizophrenia at one moment in time in one hospital in Sri Lanka and gathered data about both their tobacco use and the antipsychotic drugs they were taking, to look for a relationship between the two.

Explore
To find out more about the difference between cross-sectional and longitudinal designs, try the following link:
www.youtube.com/watch?v=LL2CESAd8KA

Evaluation of cross-sectional designs related to clinical psychology

Strengths

- It provides a useful way of studying something that might take a long time to study naturally and can be done in a short space of time, which can be more efficient in practical terms. If a longitudinal design is not possible, perhaps for ethical reasons or because results are needed quickly in order to affect policy and practice, then a cross-sectional design is a practical alternative.
- A cross-sectional design can be cheaper than a longitudinal design. A cross-sectional design also requires less commitment in terms of time from a researcher or a team of researchers than a longitudinal design. The researcher sets up the study, gathers the data and then writes the study up before moving on. Requiring less time commitment is a strength in itself, as is the possibility of reduced costs of researchers.

Weaknesses

- There might be a cohort effect because the study looks at different people at the same moment in time and those people will belong to a different cohort. For example, a study in Norway which looked at the use of GP services by patients with schizophrenia showed that

17 per cent had no GP consultation, 26.2 per cent had one or two, 25.3 per cent had three to five and 16.1 per cent had more than five consultations (Hetlevik et al., 2015). There is no mention of a cohort effect, but perhaps older people were less likely to consult a GP because of cultural differences they experienced through their life. Perhaps the culture when they were younger was not to 'bother' a GP, whereas younger people at the time of the study felt more able to visit the GP when they needed to. This is an invented example of what is meant by a cohort difference, but it demonstrates how there might be a cohort effect that affects the results of a study.

- Cross-sectional designs are not good at finding out the causes of something like a mental disorder because they are descriptive research. Because they are a snapshot at one moment in time they are unlikely to include any historical information about a patient or participant, and they do not gather any information about the future either. They are not useful for seeing the course of a mental disorder, or how it began, what might have caused it, or how treatment might work for an individual.

Progress check 2.6

What does it mean to say a study shows a cohort effect?

Test yourself

Compare longitudinal and cross-sectional designs in terms of their strengths and weaknesses when researching in clinical psychology. **(6 marks)**

Cross-cultural designs

Cross-cultural designs are carried out by researchers who want to compare some behaviour or attitude in different **cultures**. Cross-cultural psychology refers to studying people's behaviour and thoughts across different cultures to see what is common across cultures and what is culturally specific.

Year One link: In Year One, when studying social psychology, you will have looked at the influence of culture on prejudice. One study, Guimond et al. (2013) considered how countries using a multicultural policy (meaning different cultures live alongside each other) were different from countries using an assimilation policy (where minority cultures adhere to a majority cultural way of living). There was more pro-diversity in countries that were multicultural. This was a cross-cultural study that gathered data from the UK, Germany, Canada and the USA. You can use studies like this up to a point but in clinical psychology try to use examples from clinical psychology as your understanding of method in clinical psychology should always use examples that are relevant to the particular topic.

If behaviour or way of thinking is found to be the same across cultures it might be argued that it comes from human nature and not from upbringing (nurture). However, if behaviour/way of thinking is different in different cultures it might be thought that it came about because of environmental influences in the different cultures. This is an argument about what is **universal** in humans and what is not.

Explanation

A **cross-cultural design** is used when researchers want to look at a particular behaviour or pattern of thinking between different cultures. In order to do this, they compare data from the cultures they are interested in. The researchers may not always gather data themselves from the different cultures; they may use data already gathered about one culture and compare it with data from another culture that looks at the same thing.

Definitions

Culture can be defined as the way a group of people share their decisions and behaviour, such as sharing norms in a society.

When something is said to be **universal** it means it is found in all cultures, which suggests it is in our nature and comes from our biology. All cultures have babies babbling and then using language, for example.

Year One link: If you studied Sebastián and Hernández-Gil (2012) as your chosen contemporary study when you looked at memory in cognitive psychology, you will have read about cross-cultural comparisons. Sebastián and Hernández-Gil (2012) gathered data from Spanish speakers about their digit span and then compared it with data from another study that used English speakers to study digit span. When the researchers compared the Spanish-speakers' digit span with that of the English speakers they were making cross-cultural comparisons.

Cross-cultural research does not only look for universals in human behaviour and thinking. In fact it is difficult to demonstrate such universals because each culture might develop their own way of thinking or behaving, even though they are similar to or even the same as other cultures. For example, there might be similar patterns in child development across cultures, but that might be equally due to the fact that cultures develop in a similar way or because that characteristic is a universal part of human behaviour or thinking.

Progress check 2.7

How does using cross-cultural designs help in discussing the nature–nurture debate?

There is, however, a problem in studying possible universals. If the same study is done in many different cultures a criticism could be that the method used is not received in the same way in different cultures. The same method needs to be used if comparisons are to be made, but the same method might not be testing the same thing in different cultures. This criticism is difficult to overcome.

Emic and etic – studying within a culture or studying across cultures

Current interest is in using cross-cultural studies to look at the variance or differences in cultures, which are of interest as much as the similarities or universals. There is interest in how individual cultures operate and make choices. The **emic** approach looks at behaviour within a culture and focuses on one culture to understand it. The **etic** approach looks at cultures from the outside and draws on data from many cultures. When researchers are looking for universal laws of behaviour and comparing cultures, this is the etic approach. However, because the researchers in these cases often take a Western approach, it is claimed that looking at one other culture, which is the emic approach, is really an etic approach because the Western-related ideas of the researchers are present in the study, guiding the methods used and so on. This means the culture is not really being studied within a culture.

Definitions

Emic is an approach to studying cultures that looks at a culture from within it, to find out about its norms and ideas.
Etic is an approach to studying cultures that looks at norms and ideas between cultures.

STUDY HINT
If you study child or health psychology as part of your Year Two studies you will come across cross-cultural designs and studies again. You can use your understanding here to help with understanding the issues in those topics (and vice versa).

Issues and debates

Issues of nature and nurture in humans is a debate in your course. More about this particular debate is found in Chapter Seven. Make sure you are able to discuss these issues as relevant to clinical psychology in your course. You can use discussion about cross-cultural designs in psychology studies. Using a cross-cultural design is one way of finding out what aspects of our behaviour or thinking are universal.

Example of a cross-cultural study in clinical psychology: Tsuang *et al.* (2013)

Tsuang *et al.* (2013), in a study called 'The cross-cultural nature of the relationship between schizotypy and mixed-handedness', explored the relationship between **schizotypy** and handedness and looked at how this relationship stands up between different cultures. The background of the study is that positive schizotypy is associated with being **non-right-handed**. Non-right-handed means being either left-handed or mixed handed. Positive schizotypy is a term that covers paranoia (beliefs about conspiracy or fear of something, such as 'everyone is out to get me'); magic ideation (the idea that things that we do not usually link causally might do just that, such as 'the radio broadcaster knew I was listening to him'); and perceptual aberrations (having mental images but not having control over them and seeing them as 'real'). Most studies link schizotypy with non-right-handedness (e.g. Annett and Moran, 2006, cited in Tsuang *et al.*, 2013). Schizotypy refers to how personality can range from states of being dissociative to more extreme psychosis, rather than someone being 'psychotic' or 'not psychotic', while schizotypal can be seen as meaning 'schizophrenia-prone'. Sommer *et al.* (2001, cited in Tsuang *et al.*, 2013) found that the frequency of non-right-handedness in people with schizophrenia compared with controls is almost twice as high. This focus on handedness is also found in autism and in non-psychiatric neurological disorders, according to Tsuang *et al.* (2013).

Definitions

Non-right-handedness refers to someone who prefers their left hand for writing, sport and so on, or to someone who can use both hands and so has no preference (mixed-handed).

Schizotypy means prone to schizophrenia but not necessarily having that diagnosis. Positive schizotypy symptoms include paranoid ideas (ideas of persecution), perceptual aberrations (such as hallucinations) and magic ideation (thinking cause and effect thoughts that are not rational).

Most studies that linked non-right-handedness with schizotypy were done in Western populations, according to Tsuang *et al.* (2013). Gregory *et al.* (2003), an early study in this area, used Asian adults and did not find the association between non-right-handedness and schizotypy. In Japan, Asai and Tanno (2009) showed that mixed-handed Japanese participants had the strongest positive schizotypal traits (this study corrected for social pressure against left-handedness). Tsuang *et al.* (2013) concluded that in Asia there was social pressure against non-right-handedness and this might have affected earlier findings (e.g. Gregory *et al.*, 2003). Tsuang *et al.* (2013) wanted to find out whether both left-handedness and mixed-handedness were associated with higher schizotypy and also whether social pressure against left-handedness affected associations between handedness and schizotypy.

Tsuang *et al.,* from 2009 to 2010, measured handedness using a questionnaire given to 1,315 undergraduates; they measured schizotypy using different questionnaire items. The questionnaire about handedness focused on writing, throwing a ball, striking a match and similar actions. There was also a question about whether they had had to change their writing hand from left to right. This question was to check social pressure against left-handedness. The schizotypy questionnaire took 12 questions from the Chinese Health Questionnaire (CHQ), 35 questions from the Perceptual Aberration Scale (PAS) and 74 questions from the Schizotypal Personality Questionnaire (SPQ). The SPQ questions assessed the DSM-III-R aspects listed for schizotypal personality disorder. The PAS and the SPQ have been tested for reliability using test-retest (retest after one week) with 0.80 agreement for the PAS and 0.86 agreement for the SPQ. The SPQ has also been shown to have convergent, discriminant and criterion validity (Raine, 1991, cited in Tsuang *et al.,* 2013).

Studies have found that people with a high score for positive features of schizotypy tend to be non-right-handed. This seems to be the case across different cultures when the findings take into account any social pressure with regard to handedness.

Progress check 2.8

Why is it important for studies about handedness and schizotypy to control for social pressure on handedness (social pressure meaning issues like pressure not to use the left hand for writing)?

STUDY HINT

Note that Tsuang *et al.* (2013) mention test-retest and reliability, as well as different types of validity. You can use this study when discussing such issues.

Tsuang *et al.* (2013) found that those that were shown to be fully left-handed from their answers to the questionnaire had the highest score for positive schizotypy. They found that this focus on left-handedness and schizotypy remained despite correcting for social pressure on being left-handed, which meant the findings did not seem to come from cultural pressure on handedness. The findings were, therefore, thought to apply cross-culturally. This was because such findings have been found in many Western world studies as well as in Japan, and Tsuang *et al.*'s study was in Taiwan. The researchers felt they could claim to have found that the idea of left- or mixed-handedness accompanying positive schizotypy was true across cultures. That is what made them call their study 'cross-cultural'.

Confirmation that Tsuang *et al.*'s (2013) study was cross-cultural

One of the aims of Tsuang *et al.* (2013) was to see whether findings from studies in the West (that schizotypy related to non-right-handedness) would be the case in different cultures. They mention that a study in Asia had shown that this was not the case. However, they also mention that in Asia social pressure on not using the left hand for writing might mean people had swapped from being left-handed. If that were the case, and such people called themselves 'right-handed', that might account for the lack of a link showing up between schizotypy and non-right-handedness. They saw that a Japanese study had come up with the link after controlling for social pressure to change away from left-handedness. They did their own study in Taiwan, taking into account that they needed to control for such social pressure, and after asking about social pressure to change away from left-handed writing, they concluded that there was a link between positive schizotypy symptoms and non-right-handedness in Taiwan. Their conclusion that this link was found in studies done in the West, in Japan and in Taiwan, and that this was a study that drew the cultures together, make it a cross-cultural study.

Example of a cross-cultural study in clinical psychology: Mandy *et al.* (2014)

Mandy *et al.* (2014) chose to test the DSM-5 diagnosis of autism spectrum disorder. They suggested that the USA and UK testing had supported the new diagnosis of autism spectrum disorder and they wanted to see if the diagnosis would generalise to other cultures/countries. Mandy *et al.* used 130 young people with autism spectrum disorder and 110 with autism phenotype (which is a broader diagnosis) in Finland. They then compared their Finnish sample with UK participants (where the sample involved 488 with autism spectrum disorder and 220 with autism phenotype). They found that the DSM-5 model fitted well in Finnish autism spectrum disorder. The autism phenotype diagnosis did not fit so well in Finland but fitted in the UK. They concluded that there might be cross-cultural variability in the milder autism diagnosis, though not perhaps for the autism spectrum disorder diagnosis. Mandy *et al.* (2014) asked other researchers to do more cross-cultural work like theirs and they mention that this is particularly useful because of the ICD-10 being revised to become the ICD-11, meaning such studies would be useful in informing the revision of the ICD.

Confirmation that Mandy *et al.*'s (2014) study was cross-cultural

Mandy *et al.* (2014) already knew that the USA and UK were thought to accept the use of the diagnosis of autistic spectrum disorder in the DSM-5. It was known that samples from the USA and from the UK supported the diagnostic criteria and found validity. Mandy *et al.* wondered if the diagnosis would be valid in other cultures. They gathered data in Finland and compared the data with the UK samples, finding that for autistic spectrum disorder the diagnosis was suitable in the UK and in Finland, but for the broader category of autism phenotype the Finnish sample did not fit the diagnosis. As the study used data from the UK and from Finland to see if in both cases the diagnosis was valid, this was a study conducted 'cross-culturally'. In addition, because their conclusion was about the diagnosis in two different cultures, that also makes the study 'cross-cultural'.

Evaluation of cross-cultural designs

Strengths

- Cross-cultural designs allow generalisations between cultures to build a body of knowledge. For example, if schizophrenia is diagnosed using the ICD-10, which is used in many different cultures and countries, then knowing that 'schizophrenia' is found universally is important. Studies like Tsuang *et al.* (2013) that suggest that schizotypy goes with non-right-handedness universally can help to show that schizophrenia is a universal disorder and so classification systems like the ICD-10 or the DSM can be used cross-culturally.

- Cross-cultural designs can use scientific methodology to look for general laws of human behaviour. The same study using the same tools (instruments for measuring the variables, such as a questionnaire) can be used in different cultures, and provided controls remain in place, similarities in findings can be attributed to similarities between the cultures.

Weaknesses

- In order to compare data, studies have to use the same method and procedures. An issue in using the same method cross-culturally is that what is understood in one culture might be different in another. For example, questionnaire items in one culture might not suit norms and ideas in another culture. If the method affects the findings, then that affects any conclusions about cross-cultural similarities and differences.
- If features of a culture tend to be socially constructed (meaning they develop within a culture to suit that culture), then behaviour, thoughts, attitudes and emotions, for example, are not comparable between cultures as what is being measured might be different. Validity of measurement would only be found within the culture the issues are set in.

> ### Explore
> You can read more about the purpose of cross-cultural research. Here is a link to get you started: **http://miguelescotet.com/?s=cross-cultural+research**
> You may also like to watch this short YouTube video about cross-cultural research. The video features an American interviewer asking American women in Italy what they think of Italian men and then asks Italian men what they think of American women. What is likely to be the influence of the interviewer? This video helps to demonstrate the difficulties of cross-cultural research. The link is: **www.youtube.com/watch?v=oeSALGpaxRM**

Test yourself

Discuss the strengths and weaknesses of using cross-cultural designs in psychology. **(8 marks)**

Meta-analysis

Meta-analysis means analysis of analyses and is a way of using results from different studies, about the same issue, and studying them as a whole to look for an overall picture about that area of study. It is more a technique of analysis than a research method, because it uses studies that have already been carried out with the research methods chosen and separate analyses already done. If a number of studies separately find the same answer, and then those studies are analysed together (a meta-analysis) then that answer becomes stronger as the studies support one another. A meta-analysis can also help to adjudicate where studies find different answers. For example, if one study finds that being overweight means less likelihood of developing dementia and other studies have found the opposite, that might be something worthy of a meta-analysis.

> ### STUDY HINT
> When discussing designs and ways of doing research in psychology it can be useful to use examples of the design, both as evidence for how it is used (and perhaps for strengths and weaknesses in its use) and also to help explain the design.

> ### Explore
> A recent news item in *The Guardian* suggested that people who are overweight have a lower chance of developing dementia when older. You can read about this at: **www.theguardian.com/society/2015/apr/10/underweight-people-face-significantly-higher-risk-of-dementia-study-suggests**

In clinical psychology one use of a meta-analysis is in looking at the effectiveness of a treatment. If a treatment is evaluated by different studies, drawing their findings together to look at the effectiveness of that treatment can be beneficial.

Example of a meta-analysis in clinical psychology: Stafford *et al.* (2015)

Stafford *et al.* (2015) carried out a meta-analysis to look at treatments of psychosis and schizophrenia in children, adolescents and young adults. The group included mainly those under 18 years old, but some older participants were included, so that the average age of participants was 25 years old. Stafford *et al.* (2015) were interested in how effective and safe treatments were for that age group. The researchers looked at many randomised controlled trials (RCTs). RCTs use a group that has an intervention (e.g. a treatment) and a control group that does not get the intervention (they are usually either in a waiting group or they receive a placebo, depending on the study) so that the two groups can be compared to see the effects and effectiveness of treatment. Stafford *et al.* used any study that compared any drug, psychological or combined treatment for psychosis or schizophrenia that looked at children, adolescents or young adults. Stafford *et al.* (2015) assessed the studies they included to look for bias and they graded the studies for the quality of their results. They used 27 trials, which had 3,067 participants in total. They compared the trials looking at symptoms, relapse, state of global functioning, psychosocial functioning, depression, weight and 'drop out' from the treatment.

Stafford et al. (2015) found that in children, adolescents and young people, antipsychotic drugs give a small improvement regarding psychotic symptoms, lead to weight gain and lead to drop out due to side-effects. The researchers did not find trials that looked at psychological treatments for under-18 year olds. There was some (low) evidence that family psychological treatments and CBT for individuals affected (positively) the number of days to relapse. The researchers concluded that more evidence was needed to see the benefits of psychological treatments focusing on this age group, both treatments on their own and combined with drug therapy. They also concluded that antipsychotics seemed not to have the improvement in terms of benefit for children, adolescents and young adults (when balanced with risk) that was there for adults.

Use of a meta-analysis technique in Stafford et al. (2015)

Stafford et al. (2015) used 27 studies selected from a number of journals. The studies had to focus on children, adolescents or young people and to compare types of treatment. They had to focus on psychosis or schizophrenia and to have used randomised controlled trials. The researchers did not include:

- studies of that age group that looked at bipolar disorder only
- studies of those who were resistant to medication
- studies that gave the treatment but without the control condition.

They also excluded studies that involved fewer than ten participants per group and studies not available in English.

After selecting studies carefully, the researchers then assessed them for bias and gave them a grade according to the quality of the study. Having prepared the studies for analysis in this way, the researchers then 'meta-analysed' all the data to see what overall conclusions they could draw about both drug therapy and psychological treatments used for psychosis/schizophrenia in the particular population (children, adolescents and young people).

This study illustrates how a meta-analysis can be done. A meta-analysis is about using secondary data (i.e. data gathered in another study with a specific hypothesis, meaning it was primary data at that time, but secondary data when used again in a meta-analysis).

Progress check 2.9
What makes Stafford et al.'s (2015) study a meta-analysis?

STUDY HINT
For the method section of clinical psychology in your course you need to know about secondary and primary data, so you can use Stafford et al. (2015) as an example of the use of such data.

Explore
Stafford and others have been involved in other meta-analyses too, including one that looked at early interventions to prevent psychosis. Here is a link to that meta-analysis: www.bmj.com/content/346/bmj.f185

The Stafford et al. (2015) study used in this section can be found at this link if you are interested in finding out more: www.ncbi.nlm.nih.gov/pmc/articles/PMC4324833/

Evaluation of meta-analysis as a technique

Strengths

- An advantage of meta-analysis is that it is a way of finding out trends about an issue and any relationships that might exist. A meta-analysis involves statistical analysis and because it uses more data than single studies (the meta-analysis combines the results of studies) then the power of the statistical result is larger than the result of the single studies.
- Smaller samples in studies become a large sample in a meta-analysis, so there can be better generalisability of findings. Also studies may be in different cultures, which might enable the meta-analysis to draw conclusions and to generalise about the universality of an issue (if the results from the different cultures relate to one another).
- A meta-analysis can help to uncover patterns that can then be the subject of further research. This can help in building a body of knowledge.

Weaknesses

- A difficulty is that the studies that the meta-analysis draws on are unlikely to be identical in their research method, procedure, sampling and decision-making. Putting the results of different studies together needs careful decision-making to make sure that the data that are compared are fairly comparable. Stafford et al. (2015) had to discard results in order to choose just the data that could be compared, for example.

- Badly designed studies that are used in a meta-analysis lead to a poor meta-analysis, which is why Stafford *et al.* (2015) chose to grade the quality of the studies they used. It can be argued that if there is doubt about the quality of a study, such as there being bias, then that study, if used, is going to give bias to the results of the meta-analysis.
- A meta-analysis will draw on studies that have been published in an area of study, and this means unpublished studies of course will not be used. This might show **publication bias** and distort the findings of the meta-analysis. Studies that show negative or non-significant results are less likely to be published. Ferguson and Brannick (2012) have published a paper about publication bias in psychological science and include implications for the use of meta-analysis.

Explore
You can read Ferguson and Brannick's (2012) paper on publication bias and implications for meta-analysis using this link: **http://psych.colorado.edu/~willcutt/pdfs/Ferguson_2012.pdf**

Definition
Publication bias in psychology refers to the tendency of journals and publications not to publish results that have negative or non-significant results. This might not be deliberate, it might be that such dissertations are not put forward for publication, for example, or it may be that another study is then carried out to look for more significant results by the researchers.

Test yourself

1 Explain the usefulness of a meta-analysis in psychology. **(4 marks)**
2 To what extent is the design of a study – focusing on cross-sectional, longitudinal, cross-cultural and meta-analysis – important when evaluating the study? **(12 marks)**

STUDY HINT
When looking at one of the designs you need to cover in this section (longitudinal, cross-sectional, cross-cultural and meta-analysis), first the design is explained, then an example is offered, followed by an explanation of how that example illustrates the design in question and then strengths and weaknesses are suggested. You could draw up a table to show these four pieces of information summarised for each of the four designs to aid your revision.

Primary and secondary data

Year One link: You will know about qualitative and quantitative data from your study of social psychology and your Year One learning. You may also have cone across primary and secondary data in Year One, even if not in such a focused way.

Data can be qualitative or quantitative, primary or secondary. Primary data are gathered first hand from source, directly by the researcher(s). For example, you will recall from your Year One studies that Milgram (1963) collected primary data when he studied obedience in a laboratory and Bandura *et al.* (1961) collected primary data when they looked at children copying role models. In clinical psychology in your course, you have covered Rosenhan's (1973) study, which gathered primary data from first-hand observations. Lavarenne *et al.* (2013), offered as a case study in clinical psychology in your course, gathered data from a small support group for patients with schizophrenia and related mental disorders and found the group seemed to give the individuals boundaries that they did not have as individuals. Lavarenne *et al.* (2013) (page 158) used data from one of the group sessions, which were primary data. Psychological studies usually gather primary data. Questionnaires, observations, content analyses and experiments are all ways to gather primary data and there are others.

Secondary data have already been gathered by researchers and are used by others for further research. For example, government statistics from a census can inform researchers about the number of females living alone. A meta-analysis (page 152) in which researchers pool data on a particular topic uses secondary data because the data studied are not gathered first hand. Twin studies tend to use secondary data because otherwise twins would find themselves the subject of many studies. Instead, a twin study tends to gather a lot of data that other researchers can then draw upon. Brendgen *et al.* (2005) is a twin study you may have covered in biological psychology where the researchers used twins recruited to the Quebec Newborn Twin Study in the Montreal area of Canada, recruited from birth from November 1995 to 1998. In clinical psychology, Gottesman and Shields (1966) in their classic study used data from twins too, which were secondary data (they gathered primary data as well) (page 37). Stafford *et al* (2015) in their meta-analysis outlined earlier in this section (page 153) used secondary data because they used data from other studies.

Year One link: You looked at twin studies when covering biological psychology and will have considered the use of secondary data then.

STUDY HINT
Make sure you can write a definition for the terms given in this chapter, such as primary and secondary data, with an example for each from clinical psychology.

Progress check 2.10

What is meant by 'primary data' and 'secondary data' in research?

Evaluating the use of primary and secondary data in research

Primary and secondary data can be compared in terms of cost (one is relatively more expensive than the other), validity (one is more valid, perhaps) and strength of conclusions (one is more trustworthy and credible). Primary data may be more recently gathered than secondary data.

Relative cost

Primary data are expensive to obtain because each researcher or research team has to start from the beginning of a study and follow the whole study through, finding participants, organising materials and running the study. Secondary data are cheaper because they already exist. A lot of psychological research is carried out using other people's research and government statistics, which provide secondary data from which to draw conclusions.

Validity

Primary data are gathered first hand, following careful operationalisation of variables and using carefully chosen procedures. Consideration is given to what is being gathered in terms of data so that it relates to 'real life'.

Operationalising the independent variable (the variable being manipulated) is done so that it represents what is to be measured. In general, therefore, primary data should be valid because the study is designed and carried out for the main purpose of the research.

Secondary data, on the other hand, are likely to have been gathered for some other purpose or for an unclear purpose. Often secondary data have already been analysed, which can bring in an element of subjectivity. If secondary data gathered for one purpose are used for another they may not be valid for that second purpose.

Year One link: Methodological issues like operationalisation of variables and use of an independent and dependent variable in a study were covered in Year One, such as when experiments were discussed in cognitive psychology.

Credibility

Primary data might be considered to be more trustworthy, in that they have greater validity than secondary data. If data are collected objectively, with careful planning and sampling, controls in place and other features of methodology adhered to, then they are likely to be scientifically gathered for the stated aim of the study. This means they are more credible. If, however, data gathered for one purpose are used for a different purpose or aim, then this use of secondary data might lack credibility.

Time period

Primary data are likely to be gathered at the time of the study and conclusions will be drawn at that time. Secondary data, however, might have been gathered some time ago. Conclusions drawn from this data might not be valid, as cultures, for example, change over time, as do people.

Table 2.1 provides an evaluation of the strengths and weaknesses of primary and secondary data.

Table 2.1 Strengths and weaknesses of primary and secondary data

	Primary data	**Secondary data**
Strengths	Operationalisation is done with the research aim in mind, so there is likely to be validity with regard to the aim.	Relatively cheap compared with primary data, as they are already collected.
	More credible than secondary data, because they are gathered for the purpose with chosen research method, design etc.	Can be large quantities of data, so there might be detail. Can be from different sources, so there is a possibility of comparing data to check for reliability and validity.
Weaknesses	Expensive compared with secondary data because data gathered from the start.	Likely to be gathered to suit some other aim, so may not be valid for the purpose of the study.
	Limited to the time, place and number of participants etc., whereas secondary data can come from different sources to give more range and detail.	When analysed to be presented as results, there may have been subjectivity. May have been gathered some time before, so not in the relevant time period.

Example of a study using both primary and secondary data

Gottesman and Shields (1966) is outlined in Chapter One (page 37) and is a study which gathered both primary and secondary data. Another study that used both primary and secondary data is Hach *et al.* (2004), which compared interview data with medical records to see if diagnosis of mental health disorder was valid.

Hach *et al.* (2004)

Hach *et al.* (2004) looked at the prevalence (frequency) of mental disorders and the prescription of drugs for mental disorders in young women in Germany. A total of 1,555 18–25 year olds were involved in the study. The aim was to consider the patterns of drug use in young women in Germany in relation to how common mental disorders were.

A standardised interview was used to diagnose mental disorders using Axis I of the Diagnostic and Statistical Manual of Mental Disorders (DSM-IV) (explained in Chapter One – page 11). The interview also asked the women what medication they were being prescribed. The researchers gathered information about each woman's diagnosis from her doctor using medical records, including the medicines prescribed. The interviews provided primary data and the doctors' diagnoses and prescriptions were secondary data from records.

For each person, the researchers compared the DSM diagnosis from the interview with the doctor's diagnosis. They also compared the medication the women said they were on with the medication that was being used according to the records. They found that mental disorders were frequent among the young women. There was not much agreement between the diagnosis from the interviews and the doctor's diagnosis. However, there was general agreement between what the women said they had been prescribed and what their medical records said about their prescriptions. The conclusion of the study was that the prescription of drugs by doctors for mental health issues should be checked, as the validity of the mental health diagnoses might be questioned. This study shows that using both primary and secondary data can help to show the usefulness of one or the other. In this case, it might have led to questioning about the doctor's (or the interviewer's) diagnosis.

> **STUDY HINT**
> You can use Hach *et al.* (2004) as evidence for questioning the DSM's reliability and validity. When repeated (in this case through interviewing), a diagnosis did not yield the same result, which is about reliability. Also if the diagnosis does not predict what seems to be the issue uncovered by interview, that questions the DSM's validity.

> **STUDY HINT**
> Use your Year One glossary if you wrote one, or start one for Year Two. Alternatively, use the glossary in this book. Make sure you know the meaning of terms such as credibility and subjectivity as they are used a lot when evaluating psychology.

Test yourself

Using psychological research, explain for both primary and secondary data why they are useful and what they are used for. **(8 marks)**

Use of case studies in clinical psychology

In your course you need to know about the use of case studies in clinical psychology. Case studies look at one individual or a small group in depth to gather detailed data, usually from a number of sources. You need to know about the case study research method, including one study in clinical psychology that uses the case study method. Lavarenne *et al.* (2013) is the case study suggested in your course and is the one used here as an example.

> **STUDY HINT**
> Some subjects look at case studies and use the term 'case study' to mean any study. Note how in psychology 'case study' is itself a research method and has a particular meaning. Just as you need to refer to 'experiments' only when the research uses an experimental method, so you need to refer to case studies only when the research uses that method.

Features of case studies

Case studies are interested in individuals and in detail about them. They can be said to have an **idiographic** approach, which means focusing in detail on a topic and on individuals. The opposite would be a **nomothetic** approach, which means looking for general rules about behaviour by drawing on data gathered, focusing on large numbers and finding cause and effect results in order to generalise to laws of behaviour.

Case studies are used to find out detail about something rather than for building cause and effect understanding. They describe someone or a small group as much as they explain them. Case studies are called a 'research method' here, though they are not quite the same as other research methods, like experiments. This is because case studies use other research methods like interview observation or questionnaire to gather data about the case they are interested in. However, they are an overall research method.

They gather mainly qualitative data, because such data give the richness and detail that a case study is looking for. A case study will often use more than one way of collecting data, such as questionnaires for people who know the individual being focused on, or experiments on brain damaged patients, for instance, as well as observations and interviewing to find out more. This means that a lot of the data are qualitative but there can be quantitative data too.

Definitions
Nomothetic means a tendency to generalise from instances to more general claims, such as is done in science. Empirical data are collected ('empirical' means gathered directly using sense data, sight, sound and so on) and from those data, general laws are derived.

 Idiographic means looking at specific, subjective and more personal features of people (in psychology). The focus is on the individual. Idiographic can link to individual differences, where laws are not the focus of interest, but individuals are.

Triangulation
A strength of a case study is that **triangulation** can be used to look for reliability and validity. Triangulation in the context of psychology research means taking data from different sources (at least two) and checking whether the data agree. If the same data are gathered using different means, then the data are reliable (which means if you do a test again, you will get the same result). The data are also likely to be valid, because if data match and some data at least come directly from an individual, then the data are likely to be measuring what they claim to measure, which gives the data validity. Triangulation, being likely to confirm reliability and validity, adds **credibility** to the results of a study. Case studies tend to use more than one means of collecting data, so they are usually credible findings.

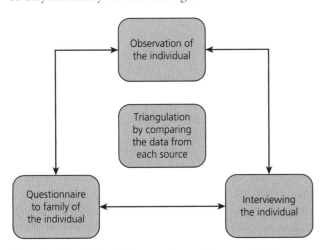

Example of how triangulation can be used in case studies

Year One link: You will have studied the idea of psychology as a science when you looked at learning theories in your Year One studies. Link the ideas here about a nomothetic view to what you know about psychology as a science.

Definitions
Triangulation is used in the context of psychological research. This refers to using two or more ways of collecting data so that the data can be compared to look for validity and reliability, giving credibility.

Credibility, in the context of psychology, refers to how believable the data are, considering issues such as objectivity and subjectivity, competence and trustworthiness of researchers. Case study data can include some subjectivity perhaps, given researchers are likely to build a relationship with the individual; however, if triangulation shows matching data using different sources then it is likely that data are objective.

Year One link: Recall from your Year One learning issues used to evaluate research methods. You may have learnt about triangulation, for example, and you will have covered validity, reliability, credibility, objectivity and subjectivity, all of which are drawn upon in the material regarding case studies. Case studies can describe rare events, such as the case study of Henry Molaison (HM) that you looked at in cognitive psychology in your Year One studies. This was a rare event of specific damage to the brain and it helped researchers to understand how memory 'works' in the brain. This is an example of a case study of an individual where there is an attempt to generalise to laws about how memory works. However, the main focus is to describe the case. The generalising takes place when other similar cases are examined. If you studied Schmolck *et al.* (2002) as a contemporary study in cognitive psychology, you will have seen how individual cases can be put together to help draw conclusions (in this case about brain damage and how the brain functions).

Evaluation of case studies as a research method in psychology

Strengths

- Case studies are good at finding out detail and depth about an individual or small group and such detail means rich data to draw conclusions from. The advantage here is that the case study allows depth, which is hard to find using other research methods. Experiments, for example, gather focused data, looking at a specific hypothesis rather than wider and richer data focused on the whole individual or group. Case studies allow that richness, variety and detail, where other methods often do not.

- Case studies can look at rare situations and individuals where samples of such individuals are by definition going to be difficult to find. If a wide sample of a certain type of person is not easily available, meaning data cannot be collected in a more general way, a case study is a way of gathering a lot of information about a rare occurrence. For example, if someone has specific brain damage, as Henry Molaison did, then knowing a lot about that case can be very beneficial for building knowledge.

- As case studies tend to use more than one way of collecting data, triangulation can be used to test for both reliability and validity and also to show credibility in the findings.

Weaknesses

- A main difficulty is that the focus on one individual or small group means that generalising the findings to others is not really possible. The sample is so limited it is not going to represent a wider population and so results are limited in their usefulness.

- Another limitation is that a case study is often carried out by one researcher or a small team, and the researcher(s) will get to know the individual who is the focus of the case study very well. This might not

cause bias in what is recorded as data, but it is possible that there is subjectivity in the data gathered and the findings might be affected by the researcher's input.

Progress check 2.11

Give one strength of using the case study method in psychology and one weakness of using this method.

A study using the case study method

You need to know one study in clinical psychology using a case study method and the one given here is Lavarenne et al. (2013).

Lavarenne et al. (2013)

Abstract/summary

Lavarenne et al. (2013) explained one meeting of a small group that met to support one another. They were psychotic patients with what Lavarenne et al. called 'fragile ego boundaries'. By 'psychotic' patients they meant those with schizophrenia or schizoaffective illness. Such disorders were covered in Chapter One. The researchers discussed how the group provided boundaries for the patients and was a solid place for people with a poor sense of self. The focus was on group therapy, provided in the group, and how the social support provided helped the individuals to develop a sense of themselves.

Background/introduction

Lavarenne et al. (2013) take time in the introduction to explain the group that was the subject of the study. The group was for out-patients (not those in a hospital, but those that came for treatment from outside) that had 'severe disturbances' (p. 293), mainly schizophrenia or schizoaffective disorder. This was the 'Thursday' group that met once a week for 45 minutes. There were leaders and they discussed how the group would work and what would be focused on; they developed a theme for the meeting and planned codes for each patient. The idea of codes is explained later in the method section (page 169). The group had run since 1985 and in that time had served both out-patients and in-patients.

The purpose of the study was to look at the group, considering how it might provide a firm boundary so that people could take part in such groups if they did not have a strong sense of self. Lavarenne et al. (2013) cite McWilliams (2011) as suggesting that psychosis is about having weak ego boundaries, which backs the claims here that the group itself could provide the boundaries. McWilliams (2011, cited in Lavarenne *et al.,* 2013) gives examples of fragile boundaries, such as a person fearing they will break apart or be annihilated, together with wishing to be a part of someone else. It is thought that the person finds both their internal and external realities too tough to deal with so they retreat into fantasy. Taking these ideas into account, Lavarenne *et al.* (2013) wanted to see if a group like the Thursday group could provide boundaries that each individual in themselves appeared to lack.

To explain the idea of fragile ego boundaries further you can recall Freud's ideas about the unconscious being a large part of our mind even though it is inaccessible. Freud talked about the id being the unconscious part of the mind that represents what is wanted by an individual – their needs and desires. He talked also about the superego, which is our conscience, coming from society and our parents – what we ought to do and what we ought to be like. The third element of our personality according to Freud is the ego. The ego is the rational part of our personality and works to satisfy the demands of both the id and the superego. You can see that having problems with ego boundaries – such as where the self sits in all the demands from the mind – is something that might fit with psychosis and this is the sort of explanation Lavarenne *et al.* (2013) considered.

It is possible to think of the idea of ego boundaries without Freud's explanations, by thinking of the ego as the 'I' that is in our heads. If someone does not have a clear sense of 'I' inside themselves and they find it hard to separate themselves from the outside world, then that would be a case of having a fragile ego boundary; you can see the link to psychosis here.

Explore
An article in *Psychology Today*, called 'Before the Madness', can help to show what is meant by our ego boundary. Go to the following link if you would like to explore more:
www.psychologytoday.com/blog/out-the-darkness/201207/the-madness

Lavarenne *et al.* (2013) discuss Ormont (1994), explaining that having ego boundaries is our emotional insulation and with weak emotional insulation we might feel vulnerable and might defend ourselves against feeling this way. The group members seemed to suggest in different ways that they were struggling with such boundaries and it seemed that reality and fantasy were blurred in individuals with weak emotional insulation. The group perhaps served the purpose of strengthening that insulation as it provided the boundaries for the members. This was what the researchers wanted to investigate.

Year One link: In your Year One studies you looked at Freud's ideas about personality and about the unconscious, when looking at his explanation for aggression.

Aims

The aim of the study was to use the group to provide a firm boundary so that members of the group could interact and participate even if they themselves had fragile ego boundaries. The study wanted to look for evidence of the group providing such boundaries.

Method

Being a case study, there was no procedure as such, and the study wrote about one session of the group, to give evidence for what took place in the group. That evidence was the 'results' of the study. The basic idea of the group and the ideas behind it were given in the background section. In this section more about the group is explained and the results section gives the observations of the particular session that was chosen to be the focus of the study.

Participants

The Thursday group had ten members and not all attended regularly as three had difficulty in attending. Only six attended the session of interest and one person was missing. Members were able to continue to attend the group for years, while some came just for a few weeks – the group was open-ended. Some attended for a few meetings, while others kept on attending. The group's purpose was to be a container for the depression, anxiety and psychosis that the members experienced. All members were on drug therapy. The aim of the group was to develop a 'sense of connectedness' (p. 294) in its members and the leader role was to be there and to bear the illnesses of the group with them, so they did not feel alone. This idea of a group being a container and holding the group for a while is perhaps hard to grasp and it is this purpose of the group that was being investigated in this study.

About the group

The group was such that each member could participate as much or as little as they wanted to. If they shared experiences, then they knew someone else would know about those experiences. Lavarenne *et al.* (2013) cited one group member as saying 'it kind of holds you and accepts you' (p. 295) when talking about the group, which helps to explain its purpose. There was coding that leaders applied to what happened in the group. Therapists used coding to record issues like members showing manic or depressed thoughts or behaviours and they noted talk of loneliness, dreams, relationships or illness. They also coded whether someone made insightful comments and/or participated in the group. The recording was done immediately after the session. With a lot of data being gathered, the leaders began to note improvements in members, such as them developing insight or supporting others.

Results during the session – what was discussed

One session was used to record the data. There was a lot of data, as would be expected in a case study, so only some of the data are given here. It is hoped that what is chosen to be included here is a good snapshot of the session. Each bullet point below represents some data about one of the six members in the group. The session in question was the last one before the Christmas break, which meant perhaps there was more fragility in the group as support would not be available for a short while.

- One member of the group with schizophrenia gave out a calendar and a card to the others in the group; he also liked to give tapes (with recordings on them) out so that the members passed them round between them. Lavarenne et al. (2013) suggested that sharing the tapes connected the members physically as they were passed round and this might have reinforced the group boundary – this may have helped the person with schizophrenia's own ego boundary as well.
- Another group member, also with schizophrenia, could not accept the calendar he was offered and said that accepting a gift meant selling oneself. This group member had grandiose ideas (characteristic of schizophrenia) about a multinational engineering project he worked on, the OPEC pipeline, naming countries involved 'as if he were sewing together pieces of fabric to make a quilt' (Lavarenne et al., 2013, p. 297). The one giving the gift was confused when the calendar was rejected, and the leaders had to reassure him that it was not a rejection of him as a person. The grandiose ideas showed blurring of boundaries.
- Another patient also spoke of what can be interpreted as fragile boundaries. She talked about nightmares that she could not recall, related to her work (she worked as a volunteer). She explained to the group that it was suggested she was tested for sleep apnoea, but she preferred to do her own therapy, such as thinking good thoughts before going to sleep. This seemed to show blurring between waking and sleeping and between fantasy and reality. This member was sad because another group member, 'her friend', had said he would no longer attend the group, suggesting perhaps that her 'self' was to an extent in the group.

- On hearing about the nightmares, a fourth group member talked about having an out-of-body experience, when he could not get his spirit back into his body. Lavarenne et al. (2013) said 'he felt his boundary to be extremely fragile in that experience' (p. 297). This person's girlfriend was asking for clearer boundaries between them (she used to be his fiancée). He liked to be in charge of the space between them or he got angry. This seemed to be about his boundaries.
- A fifth member of the group talked about having a lot of people in the house over Christmas and how he would not like it. He was planning to go out to shovel snow or take a walk, to get out of the house. This was about how much closeness and distance he could tolerate and showed good sense of his own boundaries, which seemed reasonably strong at that point, compared with the member of the group who could not accept the calendar as this would invade his weak (Lavarenne et al., 2013, called this 'porous') boundaries.
- The sixth member of the group to be mentioned here also contributed. She talked about limiting her food intake, mothering her daughter, looking after other young relatives and helping with their homework and swimming every day. This was interpreted as dealing with her own fragile boundaries through restricting behaviours and self-sacrificing behaviours.

Results after the session

- After the session one of the leaders talked about the member who had the OPEC pipeline fantasy and suggested that this fantasy was holding his fragmented self together, symbolising the boundary between his self (the inside) and the outside world for him. Running the pipeline around the world and refusing the gift of the calendar seemed to be a way of containing his self. The leaders also thought that the work with OPEC was a fantasy; they felt it was a delusion related to finding his identity and merging his identity with his father (his father was an engineer and had been employed by OPEC). Interestingly this group member was discharged and still chose to spend all his free time in the dayroom of the ward he was a patient in, though he changed chairs after a while. He spoke and seemed to enjoy the group at that time. He still confused reality, fantasy, memory and identity of self and others, which showed his fragile ego boundaries.

Conclusions

It seemed that each of the six members of the group talked about issues that related to efforts to hold themselves together. Guntrip (1962, cited in Lavarenne et al., 2013) suggested that the 'psychotic' lives just in an inner world because of being so cut off from others and cutting themselves off from others. However, people just cannot live as 'isolated units' (p. 300). Therefore, the emotional fantasy world inhabited is a replacement for objects lost from the real world. This explains perhaps the member's fantasy about the multinational pipeline, a constructed world that replaced the 'real' world of people and gave him a boundary. Lavarenne *et al.* (2013), from their studies of the group, felt that this person would come to see the group as an object that could support him and the group may have existed as an object for all members in the same way. The group provided a boundary between self and others, which meant a relationship between self and others could take place.

Progress check 2.12

What are the researchers looking for in the Lavarenne *et al.* (2013) case study and what do they find? Explain one issue that might be an issue of bias in this study.

Evaluation of Lavarenne *et al.* (2013)

Strengths

- Lavarenne *et al.* (2013), as a case study, gathered rich and detailed data in a way that a different type of study would not achieve. The leaders made notes about what happened during the group session and after the session and the data came from the group itself. A questionnaire might have shown how the group members see the group, which would have value, and interviewing also might have obtained rich data from individuals, but only observational data of the group interacting was able to show the relationships between the members, giving enough detail that could be interpreted as being about boundaries.
- Another strength is that the data were valid because they were not interpreted by researchers. What happened was written up as a case study and so the data must have measured what they claimed to measure. The individuals acted and spoke in the group and those words and actions are the data.

Weaknesses

- This particular group of six people in one 45-minute session in one group showed issues around boundaries and setting boundaries between themselves and others, in order to have an improved boundary of their 'self'. It is hard to generalise from these individuals to say that other similar groups are helpful because they act as a boundary for the members. These were six individuals in one group and case studies are difficult to generalise from. Nevertheless there were six people in the group, all with schizophrenia or

related psychosis, and there were similarities in their experiences (such as around fantasies). This does perhaps enable some generalisability, though it would be limited to a similar group with a similar purpose, led in a similar way and so on.

- Case studies often involve more than one data-gathering method, but Lavarenne *et al.* (2013) employed observation and review after the session rather than using questionnaire, interview, analysis of stories or other methods that might have gathered data and enabled triangulation. There were comments from another study, showing what the members got from the group (not in the same session), which helped to verify the data. However, this was a short case study of one group lasting 45 minutes, using one means of data gathering, so triangulation was not possible. A weakness is that the data might be subjectively remembered and recorded. It was not possible to use triangulation to check for objectivity.

Progress check 2.13

Give two features of Lavarenne *et al.* (2013) that make it a case study, excluding that the researchers call it a 'single-session group case study' in the title of the study.

Test yourself

Assess the use of the case study as a research method in clinical psychology. **(12 marks)**

> **STUDY HINT**
>
> When looking at the use of case studies in clinical psychology in this book you have looked at one study, Lavarenne *et al.* (2013). This study gives information about schizophrenia and you can use it when discussing schizophrenia in an exam question.

Use of interviews in clinical psychology

Interviewing can take the form of questionnaires, in which case this is a **structured interview**. The questionnaire will remain the same for all respondents, so each person is asked the same questions in the same format. Another form of interviewing is the **semi-structured interview**, where there are set questions (as in a questionnaire) but there is also some freedom for the interviewer to explore issues in order to extend answers. When an interviewer is free to explore areas without any set questions, this is known as an **unstructured interview**. In spite of its unstructured format it will still have a schedule and general areas for the interviewer to cover.

Definitions

A **structured interview** has set questions asked in the same order in the same way by the interviewer with no room to vary questions. A **semi-structured interview** has an interview schedule and topics to cover but the order topics are covered in and the exact wording of questions can vary. An **unstructured interview** enables the interviewee to guide the course of the interview and gives more data in terms of quantity; also valid data are more likely.

The interviewer will find out about the **personal data** required for the study, such as gender, age, marital status, employment status and other details of relevance. The interviewer will use some **standardised instructions** at the start of the interview so that the respondent is aware of ethical issues such as confidentiality and the right to withdraw. The respondent will also be told something about the interview and what the purpose is.

Definitions

Personal data refer to information about the participant, such as their age, gender and educational experiences. Used in questionnaires and interviews to enable analysis relating to such features of the participants.

Standardised instructions in a psychology study are where each participant is given the same instructions so they are not affected differently. This acts as a control. Standardised instructions are an opportunity to set out ethics in a study, such as enabling informed consent if enough information is given, and clearly setting out the right to withdraw.

Year One link: You learnt about interviews and questionnaires from the work you covered in social psychology, including the different types of interviewing. Ethics were also covered there.

Evaluation of the use of interviews

Strengths

- Unstructured interviews are useful for obtaining qualitative data because issues can be explored and the respondent is able to use their own words and ideas. The qualitative data offered by interviews give more depth and detail than quantitative data.
- Data tend to be more valid in interviews than questionnaires because the interviewee responds using their own words.

Weaknesses

- The interviewer may affect the findings because of the way questions are asked, the way he or she is dressed or other characteristics. This is known as **interviewer bias**.
- There might be **subjectivity** involved in analysing interviews. When categories and themes have to be identified from in-depth and detailed data, usually involving a transcript, the researcher may allow personal judgements and experiences to affect their analysis. **Objectivity** is required to build a body of knowledge, so subjectivity must be avoided where possible in research.

Definitions

Interviewer bias is a type of researcher bias, where something about the researcher affects the results of a study. This can be their dress or way of speaking.

Subjectivity means a researcher can affect the data by what they choose to record or how they generate themes from qualitative data, which will affect results too.

Objectivity is always required in science; it means not affected by personal feelings or opinions (of the researcher in the case of interviews), which is why controls are put in place to avoid subjectivity.

Studies using interviewing

You need to know one study that used interviewing as a research method. The study suggested in your course is explained here (Vallentine *et al.*, 2010), together with another study (Goldstein, 1988) that used interviewing and is also useful for your study of schizophrenia.

Study 1: Vallentine *et al.* (2010)

Abstract/summary

Vallentine *et al.*'s (2010) study was about educating people about their psychological disorder with a focus on offender patients. The aim was to look at the usefulness of group work that used cognitive-behavioural therapy (CBT) for patients in a high security hospital. The study looked at 31 patients with a mental illness that attended a group called 'understanding mental illness' to learn about their illness and to look at coping strategies. Before the group work, questionnaires were used, and they were used again afterwards to measure changes. The measures used were relapse and change in behaviour. Also semi-structured interviews were used and these found that patients reported benefits from the group. The quantitative questionnaires, however, failed to find benefits.

Background/introduction

Psycho-education is about giving information to patients regarding their mental health issues. Not only are explanations and symptoms considered, but also coping strategies. Such training is seen as helpful in treating mental health issues (e.g. Drake *et al.*, 2001, cited in Vallentine *et al.*, 2010). Also such information helps when seeking informed consent for treatment. Evidence has shown that such psycho-education can lead to patients being more compliant with medications and with treatment for their mental disorder, which is another advantage. Psycho-education has also been linked with reduction in relapse and readmission (Bauml *et al.*, 2006, cited in Vallentine *et al.*, 2010). This is all evidence that psycho-education is a worthwhile undertaking.

However, Vallentine *et al.* (2010) reported some disadvantages in using psycho-education. They suggested learning about their mental ill-health could lead to lower self-esteem for individuals and bring feelings of hopelessness (e.g. Hasson-Ohayon *et al.*, 2006, cited in Vallentine *et al.*, 2010). On a more positive note it was suggested that such training could be useful as a treatment programme. Psycho-education training is reasonably cheap and quick and even just increasing compliance regarding other treatment was seen as worthwhile as that can prevent relapse and readmissions.

Vallentine *et al.* (2010) explained that studies looking at the value of psycho-education in high-security settings needed to be done as evidence was from low-security or community settings, thus raising questions about generalisability to high-security settings. Patients in high-security settings may have more severe illnesses, and may be less complaint regarding treatment so validity in generalising from findings from less secure settings might be questioned.

> **STUDY HINT**
> Vallentine *et al.* (2010) first looked at how psycho-education is useful for those with mental disorders and then suggested that studies finding out about this effectiveness did not look at patients in high-security settings. The point here is about lack of generalisability to high-security settings from findings from lower security settings. You can use this study as an example when discussing issues of generalisability in studies. There is an issue about validity too, as it is suggested here that studies must be done in the 'right' setting for there to be valid findings. To see how psycho-education helps those in high-security settings, the study must be done in such a setting.

In the high-security group, learning information about the mental disorder and retaining such information might have been more difficult due to the severity of the disorder. The idea was that if someone was in a high-security setting it might be thought that their disorder was more severe and they may have less insight into their disorder. Those in a high-security setting would not have their family or relatives to work with them, which might be done more easily in a community setting. Staff in the high-security hospital might be those that offer support rather than family and relatives. These differences suggested that previous studies looking at outcomes of psycho-education for mental disorder, because they focused on community and low-security institutions, could not be so easily generalised to patients in high-security settings.

Aim(s)

Vallentine *et al.* (2010) aimed to study the usefulness of psycho-education within group work for offender patients in a high-security forensic hospital setting. Problems compared with a study in a community setting included that many patients stayed for up to eight years and 'readmission' was not a measurable **outcome**.

Definition

Outcome in relation to a therapy is about its effectiveness. Outcome measures look at how far a treatment has been effective (or not).

Outcome measures: quantitative

The variables measured in this study were:
- relapse, measured by medication change
- level of care, measured by whether a patient was on a high- or a low-dependency ward
- engagement in therapy
- number of violent incidents.

> **STUDY HINT**
> Note here that the variables needed to be operationalised to make them measurable. For example, relapse was not easily measured so a quantitative measure was used — medication changes. When discussing the importance of operationalisation of variables you could use Vallentine *et al.* (2010) as an example. You could also use these examples when discussing validity of findings of a study because often operationalising can mean loss of validity. For example, relapse may be more than just a change in medication.

Outcome measures: qualitative

The patients' view of the group work after it was carried out was gathered using semi-structured interviews. Questions included asking about the patients' experience of relating to and with group facilitators, because such interpersonal relationships had been found by other studies to be important.

Research questions/hypotheses

The researchers predicted that patients would report improvements in their well-being and mental health after the group work. It was also thought that they would say they not only understood their mental health issue(s) more afterwards but would also be open to other suggested treatments after the programme – more than they would have been without it.

Method/procedure

Participants

A total of 42 male patients assessed as being likely to be helped by knowing more about their illness were referred to the 'understanding mental illness' psycho-education group. Most had the ICD-10 diagnosis of schizophrenia, schizotypal and delusional disorders (80 per cent) and in that group 64 per cent had the diagnosis of paranoid schizophrenia.

There was a biased sample in Vallentine et al.'s (2010) study because the group were all men assessed as likely to benefit from the group work and the unit that the group work took place in needed commitment from patients to attend. Note such biases as they may be necessary for ethical or practical reasons; however, they can be useful in any discussion critiquing the findings.

Measures

- CORE-OM (clinical outcomes in routine evaluation – outcome measure) was one of the questionnaires used. This is widely used to measure the effectiveness

of therapy. It consists of a questionnaire covering four domains: subjective well-being; problems/symptoms; social life/functioning; risk to self/others (Evans et al., 2002, cited in Vallentine et al., 2010, p. 396). A low score in CORE-OM means fewer problems (in each of the four domains).

- SCQ (self-concept questionnaire) was the other questionnaire used. This is a 30-item questionnaire giving self-report data on self-esteem. SCQ has high **internal consistency** and **test–retest** reliability as well as good concurrent validity (Ghaderi, 2005, cited in Vallentine et al., 2010) and clinical validity (Robson, 1989, cited in Vallentine et al., 2010).

Year One link: In social psychology in Year One you learned about items in a questionnaire (questions), self-report data (what people say about themselves) and questionnaires (using a rating scale, having standardised instructions and using both open and closed questions). You can use your Year One understanding when learning about Vallentine et al.'s (2010) work.

Definitions

Internal consistency is where questionnaire items that measure the same construct give the same score. If a questionnaire has one question asking about someone's rating of their own well-being and then another question also asking for their opinion about their well-being, the same score should arise from both questions.

Test-retest relates to reliability. If a questionnaire is carried out twice, on different occasions (a test and then a re-test) using the same participants, the same results will be expected if the questionnaire is reliable.

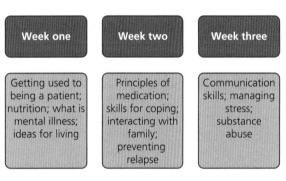

Explore

You can find out about test-retest by looking at an example using the following link:

www.scielo.br/pdf/rbepid/v11n3/en_05.pdf

- The number of incidents of violence were noted, ranging from minor verbal comments to interpersonal violence, which staff recorded as standard, so that measure was available.
- Changes in medication, changes in staff and engagement in other therapies were also recorded. These measures were there to look for a change after the group work in terms of engagement and compliance regarding accepting other treatments and therapies.
- A semi-structured interview was used to evaluate the participants' experience of the group, looking at positive and negative comments in terms of suggestions for improvement and what benefits they felt they had experienced.

Year One link: Vallentine et al. (2010) used semi-structured interviews. You can recall from Year One the different types of interview (semi-structured, structured, and unstructured).

Procedure

Groups ran for 20 sessions and over a three-year period; four groups were run. Each session was an **intervention** using psycho-education to focus on schizophrenia, depression and anxiety. The emphasis was on preventing **relapse**.

Definitions

Relapse refers to re-occurrence of something (usually a disorder). For example, in the case of depression, a returning episode of depression after a 'cure' or an improvement.

Intervention in the context of mental disorder refers to a treatment or therapy that is designed to affect the outcome for patients. An intervention sets out to affect the situation, to lead to an improvement in outcome.

- The psycho-education programme considered symptoms, treatment options and ways of coping. Group work included presentations, discussions and small group work.
- The CORE-OM was given to all participants but the SCQ was just used in groups 3 and 4. Both measures were used before and after the programme was administered.
- Information about medication was gathered three, six and twelve months after the group ended and came from a centralised pharmacy database. Importantly, the information included which prescriptions were above BNF (British National Formulary) limits (which would indicate high doses).

- Each group consisted of up to nine patients at the start, with various facilitators such as a nurse therapist and assistant psychologist. Senior clinical psychologists provided supervision each week. It was the lead researcher who carried out the semi-structured interviews at the end of the group and data were transcribed before being stored electronically.

STUDY HINT

Vallentine et al.'s (2010) study is an example of using interviews in clinical psychology, which mentions gathering qualitative data about participant experiences and transcribing the data. Use the study to show use of such features in research.

Week one	Week two	Week three
Getting used to being a patient; nutrition; what is mental illness; ideas for living	Principles of medication; skills for coping; interacting with family; preventing relapse	Communication skills; managing stress; substance abuse

Possible programme for a psycho-education group

Explore

You can find out more about psycho-education by doing some research online. Here is one link that takes you to a study looking at schizophrenia. You could just read the abstract as that gives a good idea of what is being claimed in the study by Bauml et al. (2006).

www.ncbi.nlm.nih.gov/pmc/articles/PMC2683741/

Progress check 2.14

Give some possible features of a psycho-education programme focusing on mental disorder.

Data analysis

Participants were either 'completers' of the programme or 'non-completers' depending on whether they stayed in the programme to the end or not. Data were compared between completers and non-completers to look for group differences. An individual's data were examined to look for 'clinically significant change', defined as 'whether post intervention an individual's reported level of functioning has moved closer to an average reported score for the normal population' (p. 397). To do this comparison, means and standard deviations from the study participants were used as well as those for a non-clinical (normal) population.

The semi-structured interview data were analysed using content analysis to find themes. Coding units were drawn from the data and descriptive categories were generated. A second person also coded the data to check reliability of the scores, giving a 60 per cent agreement across the themes.

> **STUDY HINT**
> Vallentine *et al.*'s (2010) study uses content analysis of qualitative data to generate themes from the data and to draw up coding categories. There was also inter-rater reliability. These are all features you need to know about in your course, so this study is useful as an example of these methodological issues.

Results: quantitative data from the questionnaires and other sources

In the group, 7 participants dropped out, 3 refused to let their data be used and out of 41 only 31 participants took part. A total of 21 completers took part in the interview because 3 more refused and 7 had left the hospital since taking part in the group. There were no significant differences with regard to age, diagnosis or length of admission between the completers and the non-completers, so they were comparable.

- Analysis of the CORE-OM and the SCQ did not show significant differences between the completers and non-completers, which was *not* what was expected.
- The CORE-OM showed clinically significant change for five people in terms of well-being, five people in terms of problems/symptoms and six people in their social/life functioning, as well as for three people with regard to risk. It was just that there was not a significant difference overall. With regard to the CORE-OM just one participant had a *reliable* change and that was on the subjective well-being scale (see Table 2.2).
- The SCQ showed nearly half of the completers showing a reliable change (see Table 2.2). Social/life functioning and subjective well-being showed more than half of participants having a positive shift in scores, though some participants showed no change from pre-test to post-test and two showed a reliable negative shift.
- For both the CORE-OM and the SCQ more than half of the participants showed an improvement in self-esteem (though again some reported reduced self-esteem and some reported no change in self-esteem).
- Overall the use of the education programme did not show significant change.

- Medication changed little over the time of the study.
- There were no significant differences in number of incidents pre- and post the session. For the completers the number of incidents was lower than for the whole group at the start, but this was not a significant difference.
- With regard to moving to a lower security setting, there were some differences. In both groups some participants made such a move. Completers seemed to stay on their wards, which suggests it might have been a time of security for them.
- Those who completed the group did engage more in ward-based treatments later compared with non-completers. There were not enough data to find out if these differences were statistically significant.

> **STUDY HINT**
> The figures in Table 2.2 in brackets are percentages and are useful, because no matter what the scores/measures are, a percentage gives a comparison figure.

Results: qualitative data from the structured interviews

Of the 31 completers, 21 completers were interviewed because 7 patients had been transferred out of the high-security setting and 3 refused to be interviewed. All of those interviewed said they thought the group was valuable and gave useful information. They all said they had experienced misunderstanding when diagnosed, either because they did not understand the explanation given or because they were not given an explanation. All said they would have liked such material and were entitled to it and all said they found a visit from the pharmacist useful in explaining medication. They all said they would recommend the group to others.

Themes identified were:
- What participants had valued and why
- What was helpful about the group
- Clinical implications identified by patients
- What was hard or not helpful

Results: qualitative data from the semi-structured interviews

The study reports some of the comments, focusing on what the participants valued, how the information helped, what clinical implications there were and what was unhelpful.

Data included:
- What participants valued (statements from Vallentine *et al.*, 2010, p. 401):
  - 'Knowing the basic stuff gives you piece of mind that you can get out, it gives you hope.'

Table 2.2 Clinical and reliable changes for the CORE-OM and SCQ in Vallentine *et al.* (2010, p. 400)

Scale	Positive direction (%)	No change (%)	Negative direction (%)	Clinical change (%)	Reliable change (%)
CORE-OM (N=26):					
Well-being	15 (57.7)	5 (19.2)	6 (23.1)	5 (19.2)	1 (3.8)
Problems/symptoms	12 (46.2)	4 (15.4)	10 (38.5)	5 (19.2)	0
Social/life functioning	14 (53.8)	2 (7.7)	10 (38.5)	6 (23.1)	0
Risk	7 (26.9)	15 (57.7)	4 (15.4)	3 (11.5)	0
SCQ (N=11)	6 (54.5)	2 (18.2)	3 (27.3)	2 (18.2)	5 (45.5)

- 'Hearing other people's experiences made me feel better about my own.'
- 'Knowing about my illness is important for recovery.'
- How the information helped:
  - 'It helped me to understand the symptoms I've got and how different treatments help.'
  - 'If you don't know your diagnosis then you've got no chance of improving yourself.'
- Clinical implications identified by patients:
  - 'It gives you piece of mind.'
  - 'Not knowing your diagnosis can be confusing, it is helpful for people to know so that they can help themselves.'
- What was unhelpful:
  - 'It made me feel guilty about my past.'
  - 'It was difficult talking in front of the group.'
  - 'Getting up early in the morning is difficult, I feel very lethargic in the morning.'

> **STUDY HINT**
> The statements made by participants in Vallentine *et al.* (2010) help to show how themes were developed from the content analysis and should help you to see how qualitative data are analysed.

Discussion and conclusion

The results showed that there were positive and negative changes in the various measures taken after the psycho-education group took place. Hasson-Ohayon *et al.* (2006, cited in Vallentine *et al.*, 2010) found similar findings. Clinically significant changes were identified even though the group changes were not significant. There were not really any reliable significant changes in the CORE-OM data (except for one), which suggests there might have been measurement errors. For both the CORE-OM data and the SCQ data more than 50 per cent of participants showed general improvement in well-being and social functioning, so there were changes demonstrated. It might be that overall there were no significant changes because

the participants, being offenders in a high-security setting, showed complex needs and functioning and so it takes longer for changes to appear.

It is possible that a psycho-education group lowers someone's self-esteem (some showed a change in a negative direction), as it might highlight to them their 'loss of potential' in their life (p. 403). Also there might be individual differences in that someone with less insight into their illness might show different changes following the group than someone who already has a good insight.

With regard to medication no significant changes were seen up to six months after the group. This might, however, be because of those doing the prescribing and also as there was no control group it cannot be claimed that attending the group meant medication levels stayed the same. A cause and effect relationship cannot be shown.

The semi-structured interviews gave qualitative data that showed how participants valued knowledge about their illness and how this knowledge gave them power. The interviews also underlined the lack of previous information received by the participants. This shows the semi-structured interviews were useful and their data could be used to inform future practice (such as building in explanations of someone's diagnosis).

> **STUDY HINT**
> In Vallentine *et al.*'s (2010) study the semi-structured interviews gave qualitative data that were useful in planning for the future. The participants gave the data directly and there was validity. You can use these findings to show the value of using interviewing as a research method.

Evaluation of Vallentine *et al.* (2010)

Strengths

- The two questionnaires were standardised and statistical testing was used to look at differences between their pre-test scores and their post-test scores. The same questions were asked before and after, which helps reliability.

- The questionnaire scores and other measures gave quantitative data and the semi-structured interviews gave qualitative data after the group work. This means one type of data could be used to verify another type of data. For example, there were no significant changes in the two questionnaire scores after the group, but there were changes in individuals. The qualitative data from the interviewing showed how all the participants said they valued the group and would recommend it. This does suggest that although findings were 'not significant', changes had nonetheless taken place and the psycho-education programme was both welcomed and useful. The questionnaires on their own would not have supported such strong conclusions.

Weaknesses

- The researchers suggested that there might be bias in the measures used, such as the measuring of medication changes. They felt that such issues might have been controlled by the pharmacists rather than the participants, so saying that there was no medication change might not measure a change in the participant's behaviour after the group.
- Using one group session (albeit of 20 weeks' duration) might not be enough to show change for offenders who are in high-security institutions as they are likely to have severe problems and complex needs. The researchers themselves offered this as a possible weakness in their findings (the fact that no significant changes were found as a whole). They said change may 'appear as a more gradual process' so perhaps they needed to use different measures or use a more longitudinal approach.

Progress check 2.15

How did the qualitative data gathered by Vallentine et al. (2010) using semi-structured interviews add to the quantitative measured used?

Study 2: Goldstein (1988)

Goldstein's study (1988) looked at differences in how males and females experience schizophrenia, and used both secondary and primary data from interviews. Secondary data were used when looking at case histories of patients diagnosed with schizophrenia to see if the diagnosis was reliable. Goldstein used trained interviewers to gather data about the symptoms of the patients and questionnaires administered by an interviewer to gather information about their past histories, family structure and previous experiences. Her study is summarised here.

> **STUDY HINT**
> You need to know about both primary and secondary data and you can use Goldstein (1988) to illustrate the use of such data.

Aims

Goldstein's aim was to see if females with schizophrenia experience a less severe course of the illness than males. She also wanted to see if a diagnosis using the DSM-III was different from a previous diagnosis that used the DSM-II (see Chapter One). Her aim was to look at other factors affecting the course of schizophrenia, including subtypes of the illness, premorbid history (past experiences and environments before the illness) and social functioning.

Procedures

Goldstein and others re-diagnosed 90 patients from a New York psychiatric hospital, to see if the schizophrenia diagnosis (and subtypes) remained the same. In general, she found some differences in diagnosis between the two DSM systems but it was interesting that she found reliability in diagnosis between herself and the others carrying out the diagnoses with her, even though the others were blind to her hypothesis. She used trained interviewers to go through symptoms to check them to aid the diagnosis, as well as the hospital's case histories.

Goldstein also wanted to know about past experiences and other data such as age, class, ethnicity, whether married or not, level of education, level of social functioning and gender, and she used questionnaires to obtain this data. Secondary data and records were used to find out two important features of the course of the illness for each patient: the number of re-hospitalisations and the lengths of each stay in hospital.

> **STUDY HINT**
> Goldstein (1988) is an example of using interviewing to check symptoms and diagnosis made. You can use her study as an example of interviewing.

Results and analysis

The main part of the study was to look at gender differences. Goldstein looked at gender and the number of re-hospitalisations, gender and lengths of stay in hospital each time, and then at gender against these two features of the course of the illness (re-hospitalisation and lengths of stay) and other factors, such as premorbid factors and social functioning. She carried out complex analyses to separate these different features and to study their effects on one another.

Goldstein found that women with schizophrenia did have a less severe course for the illness than did men. Women had fewer re-hospitalisations and shorter lengths of stay. Premorbid factors affected the re-hospitalisations more than they affected the length of a stay. Social functioning affected lengths of stay more than the number of re-hospitalisations.

> **STUDY HINT**
> You can use Goldstein's (1988) findings about gender and schizophrenia as well as social functioning and schizophrenia in your study of schizophrenia and issues around diagnosing mental disorders and to discuss various method issues.

Conclusions

Goldstein concluded that her study reinforced the findings of many other studies – that women had a less severe experience of schizophrenia than men. She also concluded that the DSM-III was a reliable tool for diagnosis, though between the DSM-II and DSM-III there were some differences. She found that premorbid functioning and social functioning were both important features of the illness.

Evaluation of Goldstein (1988)

Strengths

- Goldstein used secondary data which were already available and factual (the number of re-hospitalisations and lengths of stay), so the data were objective and needed no interpretation.
- She asked two experts to check her own diagnoses using the DSM-III and was, therefore, able to show that her diagnoses were reliable.
- She used interviewing to gather information about symptoms, so she was able to explore issues. This is necessary when studying patients with a mental health disorder, where issues such as symptoms may not be easy to describe or record.

Weaknesses

- Goldstein did not include patients over 45 and it has been shown that 9 per cent of women who are diagnosed with schizophrenia are over 45, whereas this is not the case for men. Women over 45 have a more severe form of the illness.
- Her sample was relatively small and mainly white middle class American patients in a particular region (New York), all of which may have meant that the findings were hard to generalise.

- The interviewers may have affected the data by the way they asked questions about, for example, symptoms.

> **Progress check 2.16**
> Explain how Goldstein (1988) used secondary data in her study.

Test yourself

1 To what extent is interviewing a valid way of gathering data relating to clinical issues in psychology? **(12 marks)**
2 Choose two research methods used to study schizophrenia and evaluate two studies (each study should use one of the research methods). **(12 marks)**

> **STUDY HINT**
> When looking at the use of interviews in clinical psychology in this book you have looked at two studies, Vallentine et al. (2010) and Goldstein (1988). Both give a lot of information about schizophrenia that you can use when discussing that mental disorder in questions.

Analysis of qualitative data: thematic analysis and grounded theory

The final part of this chapter on 'method' in clinical psychology looks at how to analyse both qualitative and quantitative data. Analysis of quantitative data fits with the maths element of your course and is reviewed under the heading of 'maths' (page 177). Analysis of qualitative data is covered first and these type of data can be analysed using **thematic analysis** and grounded theory (page 172). You covered thematic analysis in Year One, when you studied social psychology. Grounded theory may be new to you. Both are explained in this section.

Thematic analysis

Thematic analysis involves looking at qualitative data and picking out themes and patterns in the data. Boyatzis (1998) says that thematic analysis is a way of 'encoding qualitative information'. Themes are the patterns and they help to describe the overall data, often in relation to a specific research question. Themes/patterns are identified from coding, they then become categories and the data can be examined carefully, allocating the data to the different categories.

Thematic analysis takes place by:

- familiarising oneself with the data
- generating codes
- looking for themes in the codes
- reviewing the themes
- defining and naming the themes
- producing the report.

The researcher must be very familiar with the data in order to generate the codes and also then to identify themes in the codes that suit the particular research question.

Year One link: When studying social psychology in Year One you will have studied how qualitative data can be analysed using thematic analysis. Recall your material from Year One to help with your Year Two studies here. What you learn here in Year Two will also help your understanding of your Year One material.

Definition

Thematic analysis is a way of analysing qualitative data by generating categories. Researchers transcribe (write out) the data and then sort it into patterns and themes.

Thematic analysis involves generating codes, which can come from theory, from how the researcher understands their data or from previous research. Thematic analysis is a main tool for analysing qualitative data and can be used in other ways to analyse qualitative data, including grounded theory. Braun and Clarke (2006) argue that it should be a method of analysis in its own right.

Explore

You can find out more about thematic analysis, including how to do thematic analysis, at the following link: http://eprints.uwe.ac.uk/11735/2/thematic_analysis_revised

These pictures show people jumping with their arms outstretched. They all seem to show happy people. A difference though is that two pictures show water and one shows holding hands. This is a way that themes can be generated from data, though in psychology usually (but not always) written data would be focused on.

Issues of thematic analysis

Issues of thematic analysis include how 'long' a pattern or theme should be, so that it is put into a category and coded. A pattern would tend to suggest there are quite a few instances of that point or theme, and that it would be quite a large theme, so that a lot of the data would fit into it. That would be efficient in terms of reducing the size of the qualitative data. However, it is not about counting the instances a pattern arises or how much of the data would fit into that pattern. It is not about bringing quantity into the data. A pattern that did not appear often but was judged to be a theme would be accepted by a researcher. The researcher would judge whether an idea is a theme according to the research question and importance of that pattern. A researcher would look for data that captured something in relation to the research question, rather than for ideas that appeared 'most often', for example. This would be thematic analysis driven by theory.

A researcher might want to capture all the data that has been collected, in which case themes are more likely to be ideas or features of the data that appear often. This would be thematic analysis driven by the data (and more like grounded theory). There are no rules about how large a theme must be to be a 'theme'.

Content analysis (page 181) involves categorising qualitative data and counting instances of categories. Content analysis is very similar to thematic analysis but is more likely to involve quantity (such as frequency of an idea or feature in the data).

STUDY HINT

Note that thematic analysis is not just used in psychology, it appears in studies of literature as well, so if you are using YouTube videos or material to help your learning, make sure the focus is on psychology.

Thematic analysis can be viewed as the same as content analysis and the same as grounded theory. Explain these similarities.

Using thematic analysis in clinical psychology: Lim *et al.* (2014)

Lim *et al.* (2014) used thematic analysis of the evidence found in other studies looking at placement (work) and support as an intervention for those with schizophrenia or schizoaffective disorder. Their focus was on implementing an IPS (individualised placement and support) programme and its effectiveness for individuals on the programme. Lim *et al.* (2014) wanted to look at neurocognitive enhancement therapy (used in this area) and how it might help to improve the outcomes for individuals on IPS programme. They wanted to look at IPS programmes and their effects depending on age of the recipients (comparing younger and older clients). The themes that came from the thematic analysis involved dealing with change that is required from workers (those implementing the programme) when using IPS programmes for those with such disorders. Themes that arose from the analysis included:

- only a vague rationale was given for the idea of return for investment when using the IPS programme
- stress was placed on the structures put into place to provide such a programme for individuals
- differences in outcome measures
- a lack of focus on how the programme was run for individuals (differences in how it was run)
- differences in how any control group was treated (defined as 'treatment as usual', but this was not well defined).

The researchers concluded that there was a need for a lot of discussion around these themes and a focus on best practice, to clarify these issues for the workers working with schizophrenia in this way.

STUDY HINT
In their study, Lim *et al.* (2014) mention Braun and Clarke's (2006) account of how thematic analysis should be done, which is a useful link to the explanation of thematic analysis offered in this book. When you are reading studies, make a note of any such links, as that will help your learning.

Choosing the sample studies

Lim *et al.* (2014) describe their procedure. They say they used a literature search using the internet and found 358 **articles**. An article is usually a study, but can also be a review article (a written account of what has been found in an area). The researchers then used the titles and abstracts (summaries) of all those articles to find working age people with schizophrenia who were working in some way. The search found 22 studies. The researchers then looked for a diagnosis of schizophrenia and research designs that involved randomised controlled trials (RCTs) (page 152), cross-sectional designs (page 145) or cohort studies (page 144). This left eight studies that could be used in the thematic analysis.

STUDY HINT
Recall what you learned about randomised controlled trials, cross-sectional designs and cohort studies earlier in this chapter to help in your understanding of Lim *et al.* (2014). You can use this study as an example of these methodological issues.

Definition

In psychology **article** refers to a paper published in a journal, often a study that has gathered data. It can be a meta-analysis (which is still a study) or it can be a review of what has been done in a particular area of study.

Carrying out the thematic analysis

Lim *et al.* (2014) followed steps suggested by Braun and Clarke (2006). The steps were familiarisation with the data, generating initial codes and then building and reviewing themes. To do the coding they coded each study 'line by line, from the introduction to the conclusion' (p. 98). They used 627 excerpts from the data and had 417 codes initially. Then using thematic analysis of the codes and grouping excerpts, checking the data and going back to the themes, they put the 417 codes into 40 categories. The first author did the initial coding, then the second author did the initial coding (separately) and the third author reviewed so that there was consensus. Themes and patterns came from the codes. There is a lot of information in the results section of this study, but the results are not explained in detail here as the focus is on the use of thematic analysis.

STUDY HINT
As with the other methods and methodology described in this chapter, remember to focus on the use of such methods and methodological issues in clinical psychology and to use examples from clinical psychology, as that is the topic area of interest.

What makes Lim *et al.* (2014) a thematic analysis?

The researchers follow the steps put forward for doing thematic analysis, such as starting with familiarisation with the data and then coding carefully before building themes. The separate authors act as coders so that reliability can be shown. Themes and patterns come from the coding, which is how thematic analysis works.

Evaluation of thematic analysis

Strengths

- Thematic analysis is a flexible way of analysing qualitative data. It can be done using categories and themes that come from theory, or it can be used to generate categories and themes from data directly. Thematic analysis does not need a theory to drive the analysis and, unlike grounded theory, it does not need to derive a theory from the data; it can do either.
- Another strength is that it is a way of maintaining a richness in data and yet summarising a large amount of qualitative data in a manageable way.
- Thematic analysis allows insights that are not anticipated by the researcher and presents correct and detailed data in a way that does not lose its richness. Participants can be collaborators, for example, and can verify the data once they are analysed, which maintains richness. Participants do not have to be trained to understand the data after the analysis; the data are accessible to everyone as they are written in a clear format, again maintaining the richness and detail.

Weaknesses

- It is hard to explain how thematic analysis is done in a way that captures the active part of the process. There is a tendency to think of themes emerging from the data, which in a way they do, but if a researcher sees that their data show repetition about a certain phrase or feature when many interviews are considered, then that phrase or feature seems to 'emerge', but it's because the researcher has noticed the feature or phrase. A weakness is that it is hard to say how the analysis is done in general terms. Ely *et al.* (1997, cited in Braun and Clarke, 2006) say it is thinking about the data and creating links that gives the themes; they do not 'reside in the data'.
- If data come from a questionnaire or an interview, they come from questions put to the participants, and that is often the case. It can be hard to find themes in the data that are not driven by the questions in the questionnaire or interview, as that has already guided the data offered. It is important to derive themes from the data

over and above the researcher's choice of questions to the participants (though the questions might uncover themes too). It can be hard to separate the participants' responses to questions when giving data from themes that arise from the data.

- Thematic analysis can be said to have some subjectivity. Those analysing the data are likely to make judgements, for example, about what makes data form into a 'theme'. Without guidance as to how much data about an idea there must be for it to be a theme or how many times an idea has to be found to make it a theme, there must be judgement and where there is judgement there can be subjectivity. Science is about objectivity so that there is no bias in data. However, using more than one researcher to analyse the data may give reliability and remove subjectivity.

Progress check 2.18

Explain two strengths and two weaknesses of using thematic analysis when analysing qualitative data.

Grounded theory

Grounded theory is a way of analysing qualitative data and means not using existing theory but finding theory from the data – the theory is grounded in the data. The goal of analysis is to generate a useful theory from the data – a theory that explains that data (McLeod, 2001, cited in Braun and Clarke, 2006). Grounded theory is a research method as much as a method of analysing data, because it focuses away from the **positivist** tradition of 'doing science'. Science is about taking a theory, deriving a hypothesis from the theory, testing the data empirically (from the senses) and then accepting, adapting or rejecting the theory because of what was found.

Grounded theory focuses in the opposite direction and avoids the adoption of a theory before looking at the data; it involves looking at the data first before arriving at a theory. The researcher using grounded theory looks at the data, sees themes and ideas that are repeated, uses them as categories and groups the data accordingly. After that a theory is put forward. Note that when grouping the data and using coding, grounded theory is no different from thematic analysis. It is just that grounded theory is a method that does not analyse data with a theory already in mind. Thematic analysis is more a term for the technique used.

Glaser and Strauss (1967) originally put forward the idea of grounded theory. The aim of the theory is to retain the richness of the ideas and interactions between people contained in qualitative data and to produce coding that enables those meanings captured to be presented fairly and in a manageable form. The aim is not just to make the data manageable, but most importantly to show new ways of understanding behaviour, including shared meanings between people. Shared meanings between people include language so coding qualitative data using language has value when trying to understand the reality of participants.

From observing or videoing children playing a game, you can code data and then build a model of how the game is being played. This is different from having a theory about how the game is played and then observing to verify the theory. Grounded theory means going from the observations to the model/theory rather than vice versa.

Definitions

Positivism refers to the methods of the natural sciences. A theory is looked at, a hypothesis comes from the theory and data are gathered accordingly. Then the theory is amended, accepted or rejected depending on the findings of the examination of the hypothesis. This is 'doing science' because the theory comes first.

How grounded theory takes place

The stages of analysis when doing grounded theory are given below. Grounded theory is no different from thematic analysis at this stage.

- First, coding is done. Coding involves taking text in small pieces and putting the text into a heading that suits it. This is about identifying the idea in each bit of text.
- Second, codes are collected into concepts, which groups the data together. The idea is to see how the coded data might fit together and in that way generate concepts that are 'wider'. This process will not be static once the concepts are chosen; it will be an active process, with concepts changing as the analysis proceeds.

- The third process takes the concepts and groups them into similarities (and differences); this is where a theory can start to develop. The researcher will take notes about this process so that their notes can be read alongside the analysis, and their thought processes can then be followed. This can be called 'memoing'.
- The theory comes from collecting the categories together; it is about forming a model that can explain the data. The process is more circular than it seems here as the model might mean looking back over categories and revising the theory accordingly.

Explore
YouTube has some clips on coding data. Here is a link to one about how to code and it links to thematic analysis as well. www.youtube.com/watch?v=GZKZKUycqFU

Progress check 2.19
What is memoing (in grounded theory)?

Inductive and deductive thinking

Grounded theory uses both **inductive** and **deductive thinking**:

- Deductive thinking refers to going from a theory to 'deduce' what will arise from that theory. An example is 'if all men are mortal, and Henry is a man, then, by deduction, Henry is mortal'. It is assumed that the claims (in this example, that Henry is a man and that all men are mortal) are true. If the claims are true, by definition (in this example) Henry is mortal. It would be the job of the researcher to check the claims, and if the claims are true then the conclusion must be true.
- Inductive thinking refers to the ideas arising from empirical evidence. The idea is that specific observations using sense data (so empirical observations) are carried out and then from the specifics, a general theory is derived.
- In reality, in science there is both deductive reasoning (developing the hypothesis from the theory) and also inductive reasoning (gathering empirical data, testing a hypothesis and also generating new ideas when data do not fit a hypothesis).
- Grounded theory focuses on inductive reasoning but there is deductive reasoning too. In grounded theory the data drive the concepts and from the concepts come the theory, which uses induction. However, checking back from a possible theory to the concepts and back again in order to build the theory can involve deduction.

- If a researcher only wants to describe data then grounded theory is not a suitable method. Thematic analysis can describe data and present the analysis of data into categories that show themes. Grounded theory is about developing a theory from the data – it involves explaining the data, not simply describing it.

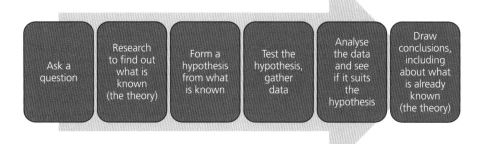

Scientific method

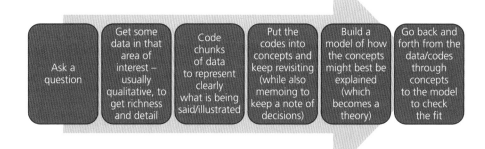

Grounded theory

Definitions

Deductive thinking means going from a theory to predict what might happen, according to the theory, and then testing the idea against reality to see if it is the case.

Inductive thinking means observing something empirically (using data from the senses) and then developing a model of how things might 'be' from the data gathered.

Progress check 2.20

Decide whether these statements represent inductive reasoning or deductive reasoning.

1 Watching how people with schizophrenia behave in a group and noting how they talk in the group.

2 Coding the notes and observations and then developing a theory about the interactions of the participants in the group from those notes and observations.

3 Using previous research to see that having social support can help those with schizophrenia and then noting down examples of where those with schizophrenia get social support (such as observing in a support group). Then checking whether or not that social support is helpful and making a statement about this.

Issues and debates

The terms used here, such as positivism and deductive and inductive thinking, are useful when considering psychology as a science. One of the issues and debates in your course focuses on psychology as science so these issues are useful in such a discussion.

Example of grounded theory used in clinical psychology: Coldwell *et al.* (2011)

Coldwell *et al.* (2011) published a paper called 'How people with psychosis positively contribute to their family: a grounded theory analysis' and that study is briefly looked at here as an example of the use of grounded theory in clinical psychology. Coldwell *et al.* (2011) point out that usually when writing about psychosis or schizophrenia the diagnosis takes the view that the individual is not contributing to society or to their family but is a burden on the family. The researchers say that no study has looked at how people with the diagnosis of psychosis or schizophrenia might contribute to their family, and that is the focus of this study.

The researchers were interested in what factors might help or hinder contributions by someone with this diagnosis to the family. They interviewed six people diagnosed with schizophrenia and six who had a relative with schizophrenia, and then analysed their data using grounded theory. Coldwell *et al.* (2011) in their abstract (summary) said that the 'emergent theory' (p. 353) suggests that those with psychosis do 'contribute positively to their family' (p. 353). The researchers point to individual, family and social factors in this contribution and also to the availability of the opportunity to contribute. As there seemed to be psychological rewards from contributing to the family, the researcher suggested that the process of contributing should be encouraged.

Choosing the sample

Six people with schizophrenia and six people with relatives with schizophrenia were interviewed to gather the data.

Doing the grounded theory analysis

The interviews were face-to-face and semi-structured. A literature review raised some key topics for the interviews to focus on. The interviews lasted 90 minutes and full detail was captured by taping the interviews.

Coldwell *et al.* (2011) used one-to-one, face-to-face, semi-structured interviewing of six people with schizophrenia and six relatives of someone with schizophrenia to find out about how people with psychosis can contribute to the family. Using grounded theory, they found that contributions can and do happen.

The interview data were analysed using grounded theory. The researchers kept a reflexive journal and memos and analytic auditing was done, so that the reliability of the analysis could be checked. As themes began to emerge they were explored using follow-up interviewing so that there was more understanding of the categories that were emerging from the data.

Themes showing contributions to the family included giving practical support (e.g. picking a nephew up from school) and providing emotional support (e.g. a sister saying she could phone her brother and talk about their mother). Another theme was personal enhancement (e.g. a relative saying 'she has taught me a lot of my mental skills' and 'the positive side of that is that I am today who I am').

Results of the study are not explained here as the focus is on using the study as an example of grounded theory in clinical psychology.

What makes Coldwell *et al.* (2011) an example of grounded theory?

The researchers kept a reflexive journal to chart their decision-making during the analysis and used memoing to check reliability as well as auditing of the analysis. This is done in grounded theory. Also they derived themes from the coding and then went back to the participants to carry out more interviewing to test the themes, which is the process of deriving theory that is grounded in data.

However, the researchers did find the themes that they wanted to focus on in the initial interviews from a literature review, so there was some theory guiding the data gathering perhaps. However, because they found that studies did not tend to focus on how someone with schizophrenia could contribute to a family, there were few ideas to rely on, so the data did drive any theory or framework that the study might put forward to explain their data. Having said that, in the conclusion, Coldwell *et al.* (2011) suggest that their theory added to ideas coming from the USA and Israel showing that people with psychosis do contribute to the family in a positive way. Though this is grounded theory, there is mention of previous ideas guiding the questions asked, so perhaps that means it is not entirely a new area of study developed from the data.

Progress check 2.21

What makes Coldwell *et al.* (2011) an example of grounded theory?

Evaluation of grounded theory as a way of analysing qualitative data

Strengths

- There is validity in that the coding is done carefully using meaning from the data in chunks, and then codes are developed into wider concepts, going backwards and forwards from the codes to the concepts in order to build the concepts. This means that the participants' own thoughts and feelings are used to drive the analysis, which means the concepts should measure what they claim to measure, which gives validity.
- Grounded theory uses specific terms to explain how it is done and is explicit in its guidance, which, when it comes to deriving theory from qualitative data, is not done in any other way. Thematic analysis can analyse qualitative data and content analysis also can analyse qualitative data and give categories, but it is grounded theory that then goes on to develop a theory to explain the data. Grounded theory allows the creativity that is needed to move from data about people to draw up ideas about how to explain that data.

- Another strength is that using grounded theory allows the richness and detail of the qualitative data to survive the analysis. The concepts that come from the coding bring the richness of the data to the analysis, rather than losing the detail.

Weaknesses

- It is perhaps impossible to code and categorise data into concepts without some theory in mind. Thomas and James (cited in Charmaz, 2009) suggest that we cannot put out of mind theories when analysing qualitative data.
- Another similar criticism is that the search is for the shared meanings of individuals that have given the data and yet the way grounded theory is carried out has a formula and is prescribed. This means it would appear to go against the idea of encapsulating rich meaningful data in the meanings of the participants (rather than those of the researcher(s)).
- It could be argued that it is not appropriate to ignore previous research to aim to generate a completely new model or theory from empirical data. The original question is likely to have come from previous research and previous findings, probably including previous theory.
- **Engaged theory** is another idea. It focuses on generating concepts from data, as does grounded theory, but engaged theory uses existing theory to help in the analysis.
- It is not possible perhaps to generalise from the findings of a study using grounded theory to say that any theory that comes from that data can explain all examples of what is being understood. The data will come from a specific culture in a specific time-frame, using specific participants. Generalising is, therefore, limited.

Explore
Hussein *et al.* (2014) wrote a paper called 'Qualitative Report' which you can use to understand more about grounded theory, including its advantages and disadvantages: www.nova.edu/ssss/QR/QR19/el-hussein13.pdf

Explanation
Engaged theory involves giving a framework that can move from analysis of empirical data (data from sight, sound and so on) to a theory for understanding the data (about people and social interactions). It is about theories that can offer a framework for understanding the world and engaging with it, sometimes with a view to changing it. Engaged theory does not accept the idea of grounded theory that data can be collected without a theory in mind.

Test yourself

Compare thematic analysis with grounded theory as a way of analysing qualitative data. **(6 marks)**

Analysis of quantitative data using descriptive and inferential statistics

Maths

In your course in clinical psychology the 'maths' element is not separated from the 'method' section. It is useful in this chapter to focus on maths separately, but note that there is nothing new to learn for clinical psychology – you simply need to use the maths that you learned in Year One and apply it to your understanding of clinical psychology. You are not asked to apply your maths understanding to the practical investigation in clinical psychology, but it can be useful to do so, to enhance your learning (see material on the accompanying website).

Year One link: In Year One you covered:

- descriptive statistics, including the mean, median and mode, which are measures of central tendency
- range and standard deviation, which are measures of dispersion

- use of percentages
- ways of presenting data using graphs, including bar chart, histogram, scatter diagram and frequency graph
- presenting data in tables.

Draw on your understanding of descriptive statistics from Year One, when studying your Year Two material.

Analysis of quantitative data: descriptive statistics

Measures of central tendency

The mean average: add up the scores in a set of data and divide by the number of scores in the set.

The median: find the middle score in a set of data and if there is no exact middle, work out what score would be in the middle.

The mode: find the most common score in a set of data, the score that appears the most.

Measures of dispersion

The range: take the lowest score from the highest score to find the range.

Standard deviation: work out the difference of each score from the mean average and do the required calculation.

Percentages: these provide a useful way of displaying data because they are always a number out of 100 and that means two statistics can be compared. For example, we can say that a study has 18 males and 25 females, but it may be clearer to the reader to say that 42 per cent of the participants were male and 58 per cent were female.

Graphs

Bar charts: represent data in groups, where the length of the bars represents the score in each data set. A vertical bar chart can be called a column bar chart. Bar charts can have vertical or horizontal bars. A simple example would be two bars, separated from one another, and vertical. One bar shows that females have a mean score on a depression scale of 40 and another bar shows males have a mean score on the same scale of 20. The 'male' bar would be half the height of the female 'bar'.

Histogram/frequency graph: a histogram, like a bar chart, uses bars. However, the bars represent the frequency of scores and a histogram can show whether the distribution of scores is normal or skewed. A histogram shows the frequency of scores and so is a frequency graph in a way. There is such a thing as a cumulative frequency graph, which you might want to investigate, but a histogram should generally suit your purpose. For example, a cumulative frequency means that if we measure the reaction time of someone pressing a button when they recognise a word, those participants that are really slow will be at the start. The next category of scores can then take into account those first slow participants and the graph can give the 'very slow and quite slow' score. The next category would be the next fastest so you have 'very slow, quite slow and not too slow' and so on.

Scatter diagram: shows the relationship between two scores and relates to a correlation. Each plot on the scatter diagram is put on the line where the two scores meet. For example, if a person aged 16 years scored 5 digits in a digit span test and another person aged 18 years scored 7 digits, the plots would be placed accordingly.

Tables

Frequency tables: A frequency table displays the scores and also the frequency of each score, ready to do a histogram or frequency chart.

> **STUDY HINT**
> Make sure you know the meaning of all the terms within descriptive statistics in your course and that you can carry out any necessary calculations and draw any necessary graphs or tables. You may be asked about descriptive statistics and/or you may be asked to calculate or display data using the required format — for example, calculating a standard deviation or mean average, or drawing up a frequency table. For terms you are unsure of, check the glossary at the back of this book.

Analysis of quantitative data: inferential statistics

Year One link: In Year One you covered the material regarding inferential statistics that you need in Year Two. Remind yourself of the issues involved in carrying inferential testing as well as the four inferential tests: Mann Whitney U, Wilcoxon, Spearman's and Chi squared. Issues you need to know include:

- levels of measurement
- levels of significance
- Type I and Type II errors

- issues around choosing a statistical test, such as the design of the study – independent groups, repeated measures and matched pairs – whether the study is looking for a difference or a relationship and whether the hypothesis is directional (one-tailed) or non-directional (two-tailed)
- normal and skewed distribution.

When a test result is known, you need to know about critical and observed/calculated values and sense checking data.

Levels of measurement

Levels of measurement are nominal, ordinal and interval/ratio. Whether a day is 'hot' or 'cold' involves putting the temperature into categories and are nominal data. Whether you rate a day as '10' for 'very hot' or '2' for 'really cold' or somewhere in between, you are putting the temperature into an order, which is ordinal. If you give the temperature in degrees Celsius, that is giving a 'real' number, which is interval/ratio data. Interval and ratio data are in fact different, but can be treated as the same for your course.

> **STUDY HINT**
> The headings in this maths section (such as 'levels of measurement' or in the section on descriptive statistics 'measures of central tendency') are terms for which you need to know about their meaning and their usage in psychology studies.

Probability and levels of significance ($p \leq .10$, $p \leq .05$ and $p \leq .01$)

When reading results we need to know what probability there is that the results are due to chance or some variable other than the one under investigation. A researcher will choose this level of probability according to what is known in the area already. In psychology a level of 10 per cent due to chance ($p \leq .10$) means not significant. A level of 5 per cent ($p \leq .05$) is taken as significant and a level of 1 per cent ($p \leq .01$) is especially significant.

One per cent due to chance means 99 per cent of the findings are said to be due to the manipulation that took place in the study. That is quite high: 99 people go with the hypothesis, only 1 goes against it, so $p \leq .01$ is a high level of significance.

When using critical values tables you need to know what level of significance a researcher chose, so that you can say whether the result of a test is significant or not. The symbol ≤ means 'equal to or less than', > is the symbol for 'greater than' and 'p' stands for 'probability that the results are due to chance'. Make sure you know these symbols.

Progress check 2.22

Is a probability of 10 per cent that results are due to chance acceptable in psychology?

Experimental design

The research or experimental design is the way participants are distributed in a study. If one participant only does one condition in a study then this is going to be a between subject or independent groups design. The term 'unrelated' is sometimes used but in your course the term used is 'independent groups'.

If one participant does all the conditions then that is a within subject or repeated measures design. This can be called 'related' but in your course the term used is 'repeated measures'. The only other possibility is if you use different people in all of the conditions but those people are matched in important ways so that they are 'as if the same person'. This is called 'matched pairs'.

Difference or relationship

In psychology, studies often look for a difference between two (or more) variables. Experiments tend to have two parts to the independent variable and a difference between the two is what is being looked for. For example, if we say children have a lower digit span than older people, we are looking for a difference in digit span between the two age groups.

However, some studies look for a relationship. They look to see if two variables are related to one another. If we say that the older someone gets the longer their reaction time when driving to avoid cones on a test track, then we are saying there is a relationship between age and reaction time.

One- or two-tailed

One-tailed hypotheses predict the direction, such as saying older people have a *longer* digit span than younger people.

Two-tailed hypotheses do not predict the direction of the result, such as saying that age affects self-esteem. We do not know whether self-esteem improves with age or gets worse, so the hypothesis is two-tailed.

Progress check 2.23

A researcher gives the hypothesis 'females have a higher score on a depression scale than males'. Is this hypothesis one- or two-tailed?

Normal and skewed distribution

Data are normally distributed if the mean, median and mode are very similar. A histogram can show whether data are normally distributed. There would be a normal rise and fall in the data, with the highest part of the graph in the middle – a bell-shaped curve would arise if the points of the histogram were joined by one line.

Data are skewed if measures of central tendency do not match one another. For example, if the mode is very different from the mean, then data will be skewed. Also if there is more than one mode.

Choosing a statistical test

To choose a test you need to know the design of a study, the level of measurement of the data and whether a test is a test of difference or looking for a relationship.

A Mann Whitney U test suits an independent groups design, a test of difference and more than nominal data.

A Wilcoxon test suits a repeated measures or matched pairs design, but is otherwise similar to the Mann Whitney U – it needs to be for a test of difference and more than nominal data.

A Spearman's test is for correlations when the data are ordinal or interval/ratio.

A Chi squared test is for tests of difference, independent groups design and nominal data.

Year One link: In your Year One studies you are likely to have learned a table showing when each of the four tests is used. Look back at this table so that you can learn which test to choose.

Progress check 2.24

If a researcher uses a matched pairs design in a study looking for a difference between two variables, and the data are ordinal or interval, what test should be chosen?

Observed and critical values and using critical values tables

When you carry out a statistical test (there are four in your course) you will be looking for the observed or calculated value. This is the result of your test, for example, $\chi^2 = 5.01$ (a result for the Chi squared test).

You need to choose or know the level of significance that is suitable, $p \leq .05$ being the 'highest' that is acceptable in psychology.

The critical value is the value you are comparing your result with for a particular test. There are critical values tables (these are in your specification and also at the front of your exam papers, so you don't have to learn them). You can use the critical values tables to find the critical value in your case.

You need to know N, which is the number of participants, or df, which is the degrees of freedom. For the Chi squared you need to know that a 2 by 2 table has 1 df and a 2 by 3 table has 2 df. For Spearman's you need to know the number of participants. For the Mann Whitney U you will have two sets of data (independent groups) and you need to know N (number of participants) in each group. For the Wilcoxon test you need to know the number of participants, minus participants that have 0 difference between their two scores. (This is clearer when you use the tables to look for significance.)

You need to know whether the hypothesis was one- or two-tailed. Then use the tables to find the critical value and compare it with the observed/calculated value. The critical values tables in your specification/exam papers will tell you whether your value has to be more than, equal to or less than the critical value. You can then say whether your result was significant or not and at what level of significance.

Progress check 2.25

Why do you need to know what the experimental hypothesis is (in an experiment) in order to use a critical values table to see if your result is significant or not?

Sense checking data

You can check your result by using sense check data. This means looking at a set of scores to see whether they look different enough to be significantly different or whether they look related enough to show a significant relationship.

Type I and Type II errors

After you have chosen to accept your experimental or alternate hypothesis (because your observed/calculated value from the test was significant when you checked against the correct critical values table), you may not know that you have made either a Type I or a Type II error. This means you may have either optimistically (but wrongly) accepted your experimental or alternate hypothesis (which is a Type I error) or you rather pessimistically accepted your null hypothesis and said the findings were not significant when they were (this is a Type II error). You would only find out about this error if someone repeated your study and found different results.

STUDY HINT
Hopefully this brief run through the use of inferential statistics to analyse quantitative data has reminded you about the meanings of all the ideas and terms offered here. You could make a list of all the terms in this section and then prepare cards with the term on one side and an explanation on the other to use for revision.

Progress check 2.26

If I accept an experimental hypothesis but someone else replicating my study finds that the results were not significant, does this mean I might have made a Type I or a Type II error?

Test yourself

Explain how to use critical values tables for a Spearman's test. **(4 marks)**

Practical investigation in clinical psychology

In each topic area in your course that gives the foundations of psychology (social, cognitive and biological psychology, and learning theories) and applications of psychology (clinical plus criminological, child or health psychology) you will carry out a practical investigation. Only Psychological Skills does not include a practical investigation (Topic 9 in your course).

In clinical psychology, where mental disorders are the focus, it is not ethical to carry out experiments or even observations or interviews at the level at which you are studying. You might be very capable of interviewing someone with a mental disorder or someone working in the field of mental disorders. However, there are many A level Psychology students at any one moment in time so a lot of such interviews would be taking place and the ethics would be hard to track and control. Therefore, for clinical psychology, the practical investigation is a little different. You are asked to carry out a content analysis on some data that relate to mental disorder.

 An idea for a practical investigation in clinical psychology can be found on the website.

However, you will be carrying out your own investigation and it is your practical that you will answer questions about in your examination. What is given in this book will hopefully help your understanding.

Requirements of the clinical psychology practical investigation

Your practical investigation must be ethical, so check with your teacher about the ethics of your content analysis. Although you are being asked to carry out a content analysis because of the issue of ethics, the intention of the practical must also be ethical.

You must explore attitudes to mental health using a summative content analysis and at least two sources to look at attitudes to mental health. Options offered in your course are: a) looking at how attitudes to mental health have changed over time; or b) looking at how different sources report mental health.

You do not have to carry out an analysis of the data as a summative content analysis itself gives the analysis, though you might want to see if the data fit into categories enough to carry out a Chi squared test, perhaps. Content analysis will gather nominal data (categories) and will be not be comparing data from the same person, so a Chi squared would be the right test.

However, you might prefer to keep your categories broader to represent the richness of the qualitative data, in which case you may decide not to use a statistical test.

Types of content analysis

Year One link: You will have looked at content analysis when studying learning theories in Year One. You now have to carry out a summative content analysis, so draw on your previous learning for this purpose.

The data that you will analyse will be qualitative data from at least two sources, such as newspapers or magazine articles. Content analysis is an overview term and within it there are three ways of analysing qualitative data. Hseih and Shannon (2005) say that content analysis has three different approaches, which are: conventional, directed and summative. You are asked to carry out a summative content analysis. (Hseih and Shannon used examples relating to end-of-life care and so relate to clinical psychology, which is useful for your course.)

Content analysis is used to interpret the meanings in qualitative data and as such has a lot in common with grounded theory and thematic analysis. Content analysis, however, is more about describing the data by generating categories. Grounded theory attempts to develop concepts and categories, but aims to explain data and formulate some framework or theory to explain them.

Conventional content analysis involves coding categories arising straight from the text. Directed content analysis starts with a theory or the findings of research to give the researcher a guide as to what categories to use. A summative content analysis is about counting keywords or content and then interpreting the content accordingly.

Explore
You can read Hseih and Shannon's (2005) article using this link, or find a different link to look at content analysis of qualitative data: www.iisgcp.org/pdf/glssn/Supplemental_Reading_on_Coding_2.pdf

The use of content analysis has grown according to Hseih and Shannon, from 97 studies reporting the use of content analysis in 1991 to 332 in 1997 and 601 in 2002 (p. 1277). Content analysis, like thematic analysis, is flexible, because the analysis of the content can be creative and intuitive or systematic.

Conventional content analysis

If the aim of a study is to describe an area of interest, it is likely that conventional content analysis will be used. Conventional content analysis is useful where data from other studies are limited, and it is useful for generating ideas for further study. In this type of content analysis preconceived categories are avoided and categories, as well as the names of categories, come from the qualitative data. This is about the researcher allowing new insights to come from the data and is inductive (data first, theory afterwards).

A conventional content analysis will use open-ended questions, with the interviewer asking for clarity from participants. Questions are prepared to obtain rich, detailed data unaffected by a researcher's ideas about possible theory and categories. The analysis involves becoming very familiar with the data before starting any analysis. Codes come from small parts of text, even words, to find concepts that emerge. Words seem to capture a concept, the researcher makes notes about their thinking and labels are then generated that cover more than one key idea. Categories come from linking the codes so that 'meaningful clusters' are generated. Morse and Field (1995, cited in Hseih and Shannon, 2005, p. 1279) suggest that 10–15 clusters are manageable and meaningful. Theory from other research might be brought into the discussion of a study that uses conventional content analysis, but the analysis comes from the data inductively.

Conventional content analysis does not lead to a theory as much as grounded theory does and might also be more limited in the amount of data, because it can focus on a small event or area of interest.

Directed content analysis

If a researcher has found out quite a bit about their area of interest from previous research and there is some existing theory, but the researcher wants to find out more, they might choose to use directed content analysis. A directed content analysis is where the idea comes from previous theory. The aim is to either find something out that adds to current understanding about an area or confirms current understanding.

To carry out directed content analysis a researcher can set up key concepts or variables from existing theory or studies. The researcher can have strict definitions for the categories they are looking for and then can analyse the qualitative data, looking for the specific categories.

Although open-ended questions are likely, such as in interviewing, there can then be more targeted questions focusing on the categories that are already known, which makes directed content analysis different from conventional content analysis.

Summative content analysis

This section focuses on summative content analysis as that is the type of content analysis you are being asked to carry out. A summative content analysis begins with words and content in the test. These words and/or content are identified in the text and then counted. This type of content analysis turns qualitative data into quantitative data by counting the instances of the chosen word(s) and/or content. According to Hseih and Shannon (2005), Potter and Levine-Donnerstein (1999) call this type of counting of words and content 'manifest content analysis' (p. 1283). Then summative content analysis also involves 'latent content analysis', which means interpreting the content after the words/content have been counted. Although at the stage of counting the words the data are quantitative, offering an interpretation goes back to qualitative data. This is about underlying meanings in the content.

A summative content analysis can start with counting the pages that refer to the area of interest (in your practical investigation that is attitudes to mental health), and then there can be interpretation of the content, which can involve evaluation of the quality of that content (Hseih and Shannon, 2005, p. 1285). Not only can the pages be counted but specific words are counted as well, giving word frequency counts. Then interpretation might include noting who speaks those words and in what context, so that goes back to qualitative data and adds richness. The word being counted might have different meaning in different contexts and that can be part of the interpretation. To verify any interpretation, researchers using summative content analysis can go back to their

participants to check their interpretation, if they are analysing interview data, for example. There must be credibility in the analysis. Another person can count the instances of the words (or specific content), for example, to check for reliability.

Progress check 2.27

Allocate these three statements to the relevant type of content analysis:

A A researcher is interested in a specific point that other research and theory explains to an extent but not completely.

B A researcher is interested in how something is talked about in a context or a situation, and they want to know how many times a word is used and then interpret the usage of that word.

C A researcher wants to immerse themselves in data about a certain topic that is not known about and from which general ideas about patterns and key concepts are required.

Steps in doing a content analysis (no matter which type):

1 Give the research question, once chosen.
2 Select the sample.
3 Define the categories.
4 Give the procedure for coding.
5 Do the coding.
6 Consider how trustworthy the analysis is.
7 Analyse the results of the coding.

Comparing the three types of content analysis:

- In conventional content analysis the study begins with observation, codes come from the data and codes are defined during the analysis.
- In directed content analysis the study begins with the theory, codes come from the theory or previous research and they are defined before analysis (though can be developed through the analysis).
- In summative content analysis, the study begins with keywords, which come from a literature review or the researcher's area of interest and are identified before the analysis (though can be developed during analysis).

Evaluation of content analysis

Strengths

- Content analysis aims to get large quantities of qualitative data into manageable units. Categories are patterns and themes. The strength here is that content analysis is a way of analysing a large amount of data and can present interpretations of the data. This does not go as far as grounded theory, which aims for theory as interpretation, and it does not stop at description if it is a summative content analysis. Content analysis is therefore useful because it does not require generation of a theory and the analysis can, therefore, be a fairly straightforward way of making data manageable.

- Content analysis might come from observation or interview data, but if other sources are used, such as media sources, it does not require involvement with people and so, in that sense, can be seen as more ethical.
- Content analysis can be part of data-gathering methods and if combined with other data (such as from observation) then triangulation (page 157) can take place, which can show validity and reliability in data.
- Replication is possible as the data can be given to someone else to analyse, for example, another coder, so there is inter-coder reliability (if the coding agrees of course, but if not, there can be discussion).
- A content analysis goes directly to the data and so aspects of social interaction can be studied directly. This limits bias when gathering the data, even though there might be bias in the analysis.

Weaknesses

- Although content analysis is flexible because it can range from a creative intuitive approach to generating categories to a very systematic approach of counting occurrences of particular words, this can be seen as a weakness because content analysis is, therefore, hard to define (Tesch, 1990, in Hseih and Shannon, 2005).
- In conventional content analysis it can be hard to get the overall understanding of the data that gives the key categories. The findings might not represent the data and might lack validity. Credibility, meaning trustworthiness, is required and peer debriefing, using triangulation or persistent observation, can help to give the data credibility. However, it must be acknowledged that starting with a deep understanding of the data is hard.
- Content analysis can be said to be reductionist in that it reduces data into parts from the whole. If data are complex and it is hard to derive from the data a small enough number of categories to represent the data validly, then reducing the richness of the data can reduce the validity.

STUDY HINT

A worked-through example of a summative content analysis focusing on how different sources represent mental health can be found on the website accompanying this book.

Test yourself

Explain seven stages in carrying out a summative content analysis. **(6 marks)**

Summary

- You need to have an awareness of the Health and Care Professions Council guidelines for clinical practitioners.
- Longitudinal and cross-sectional designs are involved when researching mental health as well as cross-cultural methods.
- Secondary and primary data are both used in research in mental health, as are meta-analyses.
- Lavarenne et al. (2013) used the case study method to look at psychotic patients with fragile boundaries and there are other studies that use the case study. You need to know one such study and how case studies are used in clinical psychology.
- Vallentine et al. (2010) used interviewing to look at how far psycho-education worked for detained offender patients; there are of course many other examples of the use of interviewing in clinical psychology. You need to know one such study and how interviews are used in the area of mental disorder.
- Analysis of data from studies uses descriptive and inferential statistics if they are quantitative data.
- Qualitative data are analysed using thematic analysis and grounded theory.
- Summative content analysis is another way of analysing qualitative data in clinical psychology. You must carry out a practical investigation using summative content analysis as a method.

Chapter Three: Criminological psychology

General overview

Criminological psychology is an application in psychology. This means that theories and studies are applied to issues of concern to society and the individual. Criminological psychology is about the definition of crime and the causes of crime and anti-social behaviour. It is about the identification and treatment of offenders undertaken by forensic investigators.

Study of interest

Arsuffi (2010) carried out a case study of a homicide by an older adult offender and focused on **assessment, case formulation** and treatment. Case studies of people who commit crimes can be useful in showing how assessment uncovers information about the person; formulation focuses on what treatment might suit the individual and then treatment is administered. Her case is called Mr A, and he gave consent for the study to take place and for it to be reported upon, though it is reported carefully and briefly here. Mr A had a bout of depression when younger and at retirement. He had medication for his depression at retirement though he attempted suicide soon afterwards, being hospitalised but making a good recovery. Mr A's wife had been losing her eyesight and he was concerned about her. He was 78 years old and she was 76 years old. One night she was late back and he worried as usual. The next morning he woke with a 'muzzy head', went to the shed because he thought he had left the door open all night, picked up shears from the shed and went back upstairs. He then just recalls the scene afterwards and he phoned the police. In prison it was clear that Mr A had symptoms of depression and possible suicide. He was convicted of manslaughter of his wife on the grounds of diminished responsibility and given a hospital order. Assessments looked at level of functioning, risk of re-offending and personality factors. An assessment helps to develop a formulation, which is an explanation of what happened, and to decide on interventions that would help the client and reduce the risk of re-offending. It also helps to see if the client would be responsive to treatment. Assessments used included the Young Schema Questionnaire (YSQ), which looked at schemas Mr A used, and showed he had unrelenting standards, approval seeking and self-

sacrifice, as well as punitiveness. Cognitive interviewing did not uncover any details about the murder or Mr A's motivation, though such interviewing was hampered by his mental illness symptoms and the nature of the offence. Cognitive-behavioural therapy (CBT) was used to help him to manage the stress, anxiety and depression and included assertiveness training. CBT was chosen because it was forward-looking and prevented focus on the event. Formulation showed Mr A used negative thinking and **catastrophising**, and attachment theory helped to explain his depression as he might have seen himself as unlovable with insecure working models of relationships.

> **STUDY HINT**
> The content of criminological psychology in your course has a section on understanding the offender, offence analysis and case formulation, for which Arsuffi's (2010) case study is useful. Also, it is a case study, which is one of the methods you need to know about.

Definitions

Assessment in criminological psychology refers to assessing the risks and needs of an offender. **Case formulation** in criminological psychology refers to forming a model taking account of an offender's problems, possibly underlying causes and links to theory and research. **Catastrophising** is one of a list of unhelpful ways of thinking used in CBT and refers to where a single negative event is blown up into the precursor of disaster.

In criminological psychology, you will focus on explanations of crime and anti-social behaviour focusing on gender differences and including biological and social explanations. This is about people who might commit crime or behave in an anti-social way, and why. You will look at understanding the offender, how offences are analysed and case formulation, which is like diagnosis, putting together the story of the offender. You will look at two treatments for offenders and one study for each treatment to focus on their effectiveness. One treatment must be cognitive-behavioural and one must be biological. You will also look at factors affecting eyewitness testimony and that influence jury decision-making, as these are two areas where psychology has made a large contribution when considering the fairness of the justice system. Criminological psychology draws on your understanding of foundations of psychology – social, cognitive and biological psychology and learning theories.

In the method section, you will also draw on your learning of foundations of psychology. You will look at field and laboratory experiments, which are covered in cognitive psychology, and issues including sampling, evaluation and analysis of qualitative and quantitative data, which are all foundations of psychology. However, you need to relate it to the study of criminological psychology, which means applying your understanding. You need to know two studies in detail as well as one key question, and you will carry out a practical investigation.

What a defendant looks like or talks like can affect the decision of a jury.

STUDY HINT
Progress check answers can be found on the website accompanying this book.

Roles of the forensic psychologist

A forensic psychologist is involved in the justice system and is there as an expert in psychology. They might assess competence to stand trial or consider mitigating factors when sentencing is considered. A psychologist can be involved with inmates and offenders to evaluate and formulate a plan for treatment. They may also provide the

treatment or intervention in prisons or other institutions, and they might be involved in civil proceedings, such as divorce and custody cases. Some of the different roles and how they relate to what you will cover in your course are explained in this chapter, such as case formulation. Criminological psychology is a large area of study, and you will cover a small part of it. In this chapter, criminal psychologist and forensic psychologist mean the same thing. To become a forensic psychologist, you need a degree, British Psychological Society (BPS) membership, and to have undergone forensic psychologist training that is approved by the Health and Care Professions Council (HCPC). Training can be a Doctorate in Forensic Psychology or a Master's and a BPS qualification.

Forensic psychologists as clinical psychologists

There are ways in which psychologists working in the area of crime (not literally!) can be involved in criminal proceedings. They can be involved in a clinical capacity, as a clinical psychologist would, such as assessing someone to give a clinical judgement. In your course, you will look at the use of psychological formulation to understand how the offending behaviour helps the individual to function. You look at two treatments for criminal behaviour, relating to the 'clinical' role of a criminal or forensic psychologist.

Forensic psychologists as researchers

Psychologists working with offenders can do research – not just academic research, but research to help with a case. They might do experiments to give evidence to help courts in a specific case, such as with eyewitness testimony issues. Experiments have also been carried out on jury decision-making, though these tend to be by academic researchers.

Forensic psychologists as advisors

Psychologists also advise the police, such as the best way to interview an offender or about their behaviour. There is cognitive interviewing and there are ethical interview techniques to consider.

Main duties of a forensic psychologist
- Specialist risk assessment for offenders
- Training and mentoring trainee psychologists
- Contributing to writing strategies
- Writing formal reports on offenders
- Giving expert advice, e.g. regarding parole
- Developing treatment programmes and rehabilitation programmes for offenders

Study of interest

Nagi and Davies (2015) were interested in low-secure mental health units in the UK and supporting the families of people in such units. These units provide health care and treatment for people with mental health problems (in this study, schizophrenia was the focus) who require a secure setting (Mental Health Act, 1983) and who may be in such units for months or even years. It is recommended (e.g. British Psychological Society, 2010; NICE, 2014) that support be provided to families of those with schizophrenia and it is this support that Nagi and Davies studied. Although family support is recommended, Finlay et al. (2013, cited in Nagi and Davies, 2015) suggest that families do not feel heard and do not get much information from professionals. Family psycho-education is an intervention that Nagi and Davies (2015) suggest; their paper is called 'Bridging the Gap', which illustrates that the intervention is about supporting families using understanding and knowledge. This intervention involves three one-hour (or 1.5 hour) sessions focusing on developing knowledge, building understanding and managing risk and relapse. A goal is also to help families engage with professional services, with sharing of information between the family and the professional services. There are different purposes within the programme. NICE guidelines suggest a programme needs to offer education about the issue, support (such as for carers) and a treatment function, such as prevention of relapse. Also a programme can help with forensic formulation in giving information and background material about the individual and with risk management. The individuals themselves are encouraged to attend the family sessions.

Nagi and Davies (2015) included six people in their study, all with a diagnosis of schizophrenia and a history of drug misuse, in their psycho-education programme. Three families had three sessions and three received two sessions, though the overall time was the same – three or four hours of intervention. Families said that they found the intervention useful and the materials accessible and user-friendly. They found the new information about the individual useful – in particular, information around the

mental health disorder and their offending behaviours. Staff also found the interventions useful and said they had helped to fill in some gaps, such as about warning signs that might lead to offending behaviour. This study reports on a fairly simple intervention that can help an individual, staff and families.

STUDY HINT

Nagi and Davies (2015) talk about family psycho-education. If in clinical psychology you used the recommended example study as an interview, then you looked at a psycho-educational group for offender patients (page 162). The study was Vallentine et al. (2010). You can link what you found there in relation to the success of giving offenders information about their condition to what Nagi and Davies recommend about giving families information.

Progress check 3.1

State three roles of a forensic psychologist.

Summary of learning objectives
Content

You need to know about biological and social explanations of crime and, within the explanations, give consideration to gender issues. For the biological explanations, you need to look at brain injury, the amygdala and aggression, XYY syndrome and personality. You have looked at the role of regions of the brain, including the amygdala related to aggression, in biological psychology, so you know something about these explanations. Also Raine et al. (1997) was the classic study in biological psychology, relating brain region differences to crime in those pleading not guilty to murder by reason of insanity. For the social explanations, you need to look at labelling and the self-fulfilling prophecy, which are explanations that say we become what people expect us to become, including in relation to criminal behaviour. Social learning theory can also help to explain criminal behaviour – although you do not need to learn about this directly, it is touched upon in this chapter.

You also need to know about understanding the offender, offence analysis and case formulation. You will look at the cognitive interview and at ethical interview techniques. Also you need to cover the use of psychological formulation to understand how the offending behaviour works for the offender in helping them to function. Formulation means gathering information to put together a hypothesis that can help to give a framework for treating or dealing with an offender.

The next section is about treating offender behaviour. You need to cover two treatments, including their strengths and weaknesses, and also one study for each of the two treatments. One treatment must be a cognitive-behavioural treatment, such as CBT, social skills training, anger management or assertiveness training. The other treatment must be a biological one, such as improving diet or hormone treatment.

You also need to look at factors affecting eyewitness testimony, including reliability, focusing on how information after the event (post-event information) can affect testimony, as well as the weapons effect. The weapons effect is uncovered by psychology experiments and refers to how, if a weapon is present when a crime is committed, a witness will focus on the weapon so may miss other features of the event. You need to look at studies in this area.

The final section considers factors relating to jury decision-making, including characteristics of the defendant and how pre-trial publicity can affect the jury's decision. You need to look at studies in this area.

Individual differences and developmental psychology

All topic areas in your course require you to consider two special issues in psychology – individual differences and developmental psychology. In each topic area, you will find reference to where these issues are within the content or the key question. You need to make links between these two issues and areas that reflect them. Each issue has a symbol in this textbook to alert you to these links. Individual differences refers to how people might be inherently different, such as in their personality or intelligence. Gender too can give individual differences, and you need to consider gender when looking at explanations of crime. Other genetic or biological differences can also give individual differences.

Developmental psychology is an area of study focusing on how we develop from before birth to adolescence, and also beyond into old age.

Year One link: Year One topic areas consider both individual differences and developmental issues in the content sections. Year Two applications do the same.

Individual differences

In criminological psychology, the links that must be learned about are:
- personality as a factor in criminal and anti-social behaviour
- individual differences in whether a self-fulfilling prophecy occurs in relation to developing criminal behaviour.

Developmental psychology

In criminological psychology, the links that must be learned about are:
- the self-fulfilling prophecy and labelling as explanations of criminal and anti-social behaviour because the behaviour then develops through interactions with others
- social learning theory as a theory about how we develop and can explain criminality and anti-social behaviour
- other explanations of criminal or anti-social behaviour, such as biological explanations, which can also explain development.

Method

You will be used to learning about method in each topic area. The main methods for criminological psychology are field and laboratory experiments, in particular how they are used to assess eyewitness testimony, and case studies. You need to know about the same four sampling techniques that were covered in social psychology. You also need to know about issues of reliability, validity, objectivity, credibility and ethics in research, and you will be used to evaluating using these features of research. You also need to know about ethical guidelines when doing research in psychology, including the BPS Code of Ethics and Conduct (2009) and risk management, and also principles of the Health and Care Professions Council (HCPC) for undertaking psychological formulation and intervention.

Year One link: Sampling is covered in social psychology. You covered field and laboratory experiments too, as well as the BPS Code of Ethics and Conduct (2009) and risk management in social psychology. You will be able to draw on your Year One learning.

As with other topic areas, you need to know how data are analysed in psychology. You need to know about analysis of quantitative data using measures of central tendency, frequency tables and measures of dispersion (range and standard deviation), as well as analysis of quantitative data using inferential statistics. Correlations are required, which you covered in biological psychology, as well as meta-analysis, found in clinical psychology. You also need to know about issues relating to inferential statistics, including the four tests in your course (Chi squared, Mann Whitney U, Wilcoxon and Spearman's), as well as issues of statistical significance, levels of measurement and critical and observed/calculated values. Analysis of qualitative data is required, including thematic analysis and grounded theory. All except grounded theory and meta-analysis has been covered in Year One, and reviewed in clinical psychology too. Grounded theory and meta-analysis were both covered in clinical psychology (pages 172 and 152).

Year One link: Analysis of quantitative data using descriptive and inferential statistics and analysis of qualitative data using thematic analysis has all been covered in Year One, so be sure to revise the material for Year Two studies.

Studies

The classic study in criminological psychology is Loftus and Palmer (1974), a well-known study that asks students to watch films of a car accident and then asks about their estimate of the speed of the cars using words like 'hit' and 'smashed', to find whether those words changed estimate of speed, which they did. This study relates to eyewitness testimony and is a lab experiment, so you will be able to use it in your study of methods as well as in the study of content, when you look at factors affecting eyewitness testimony.

You will choose one contemporary study from three, all of which are covered in this chapter:
- Bradbury and Williams (2013), who look at the effects of race on juror decision-making

- Valentine and Mesout (2009), who study **eyewitness identification** under stress in the London Dungeon
- Howells *et al.* (2005), who consider outcomes and predictors of change related to brief anger management programmes with offenders.

All four studies are given in this chapter so you can choose one to focus on and also because they are useful for your studies in criminological psychology.

Definition
Eyewitness identification refers to whether someone can identify someone they have seen as a witness or not.

Key question

You have a choice of key question to study. The course specification suggests that you choose from whether eyewitness testimony is too unreliable to trust or whether jury bias should lead to the abolishment of juries (one of which is in this chapter and the other, about jury decision-making, is on the accompanying website). However, you can choose any issue.

Practical investigation in criminological psychology

You have to carry out one practical research exercise within criminological psychology and there is a choice about using a questionnaire, interview or experiment. You will do that within your learning, so it is hard to foresee in this book what you will have done. There is one practical investigation in criminological psychology using an experiment to look at the effect of defendant attractiveness on length of sentence in a drug-related crime, which is worked through on the accompanying website.

You need to gather data relevant to topics you have studied in criminological psychology and your practical investigation must be ethical throughout. You will also write up some of what is needed in a psychology report – the research question and hypothesis, sampling and data collection tools as part of the method, data analysis, results and discussion. The data have to be quantitative for analysis, though there can be qualitative data as well, and you need to use an inferential test when analysing your data. You also have to consider strengths and weaknesses of your practice investigation and possible improvements.

Year One link: You will have looked at questionnaire and interview as research methods in social psychology and at experiment in your

Year One study of cognitive psychology. Your practical will focus on issues you have studied in criminological psychology but the research methods are the same.

Issues and debates

The 11 issues and debates chosen for your course are: ethics; practical issues in research design; reductionism; comparing explanations; psychology as a science; culture and gender; nature–nurture; how psychology has developed over time; issues of social control; using psychology in society; and issues around socially sensitive research. Chapter Seven looks at issues and debates in detail.

STUDY HINT

The issues and debates appear for your course in each topic area for Year One and Year Two, in the same order, in the specification. For each topic area, there are examples against each of the issues and debates to show how material from that topic area can illustrate the issue or debate. You can use the specification for ideas relevant to each of the issues and debates.

STUDY HINT

Make the summary of learning objectives into a checklist. Table 3.1 gives a suggested list. However, you could add detail, which would help your learning.

Table 3.1 What you need to know for criminological psychology

You need to know about:	
How crime and anti-social behaviour can be explained, including focusing on gender differences; biological explanations including brain injury, amygdala and aggression, XYY syndrome and personality	The use of field and laboratory experiments to study eyewitness effectiveness (you can bring in other methods too)
How crime and anti-social behaviour can be explained using social explanations, including labelling and self-fulfilling prophecy, again considering gender differences	Case studies as well as sampling techniques in research in psychology: random; stratified; volunteer; opportunity
Understanding the offender and offence analysis and case formulation focusing on cognitive interviewing and ethical interviewing techniques and the use of psychological formulation to understand how the offending behaviour functions for the individual	Issues of reliability, validity, objectivity, credibility and ethics in research in criminological psychology
Two treatments for offenders (and strengths and weaknesses), including one cognitive-behavioural treatment and one biological treatment (and one study for each looking at their effectiveness)	Ethics to include BPS Code of Ethics and Conduct (2009), risk management and HCPC principles for undertaking psychological formulation and intervention
Factors influencing eyewitness testimony, including reliability as affected by post-event information and weapon focus (and studies in the area)	Analysis of quantitative data, including descriptive and inferential statistics (the four tests from Year One) and related issues
Factors influencing jury decision-making, including defendant characteristics and pre-trial publicity (and studies in the area)	Analysis of qualitative data using thematic analysis and grounded theory
Individual differences relating to content you have covered in criminological psychology, including personality and self-fulfilling prophecy and how they relate to individual differences in crime and anti-social behaviour	The classic study in criminological psychology, Loftus and Palmer (1974), and their study of how changing a word can affect judgement of speed and eyewitness testimony
Developmental psychology linked to criminological psychology, including self-fulfilling prophecy explanations, social learning explanations and biological explanations, which can all explain how people develop in relation to crime and anti-social behaviour	One contemporary study from a choice of three: Bradbury and Williams (2013); Valentine and Mesout (2009); Howells *et al.* (2005)
One practical investigation focusing on an area of criminological psychology in your course and using an observation, a questionnaire or an experiment as the research method	One key question that can be explained using concepts, theories and/or research from criminological psychology in your course, and the concepts, theories and research in question
Issues and debates (see Chapter Seven for more detail)	

STUDY HINT

You can see there is a lot to cover in criminological psychology, but you have covered a lot of the foundations for this application, such as sampling techniques, lab and field experiments, ethical issues, analysis of qualitative and quantitative data, and biological and social ideas to draw upon, including social learning, from learning theories. Be ready to draw on your previous learning.

An introduction to criminological psychology

Criminological psychology is about all aspects of crime and anti-social behaviour, from looking at causes of crime, to considering issues around the offender to understand them, to treating them.

Defining crime

Crime is an act (or omission of an act) that is against the law. Crime also implies a punishment – or at least some treatment to prevent **recidivism**. Criminological psychology is about applying psychological principles to all aspects of crime. Recidivism is when someone repeats a crime or a behaviour for which they have either been punished or received treatment. It means returning to and repeating behaviour that should have been extinguished. There are rates of recidivism but only criminals who are caught again, or who reveal their renewed criminal activity, are counted, so reported rates are probably lower than reality. **Anti-social behaviour** may not be about an unlawful action as such but is considered part of criminological psychology, because it involves actions that citizens dislike and which could become crime at some stage. Anti-social behaviour is any behaviour that affects other people negatively and, in psychology, is often used to mean aggressive behaviour. In the UK, anti-social behaviour orders (ASBOs) were created for behaviour that might cause harassment, distress or alarm to others, illustrating how close anti-social behaviour is to criminal activity. Behaving anti-socially includes being drunk or using threatening behaviour and playing loud music at night. The Crime and Disorder Act 1998 defines anti-social behaviour as 'acting in a manner that caused or was likely to cause harassment, alarm or distress'. Getting an ASBO means not being allowed into particular places, such as a town centre, or not spending time with 'known' trouble-makers, or drinking in the street.

Explore

You can find out more about anti-social behaviour orders (ASBOs) using the following link, and you can find further information on the internet: **www.gov.uk/asbo**

Definitions

Crime is a behaviour or an action that is an offence and punishable by law. **Anti-social behaviour** refers to any behaviour that is seen negatively by others in the sense of harassing them or causing alarm or distress. **Recidivism** refers to someone relapsing into criminal behaviour after having had some treatment and/or been released into the community.

STUDY HINT

In this chapter, 'crime' or 'anti-social behaviour' can be used as one term to refer to both crime and anti-social behaviour. However, in an exam question, expect there to be clarity, and watch for questions about anti-social behaviour as well as about crime.

Photo posed by models

Anti-social behaviour may not be criminal but it is behaviour that has a negative effect on a person or people in society, and it is therefore studied within criminological psychology.

Explore

Look up the government website **www.nidirect.gov.uk/anti-social-behaviour** to find out what is thought about anti-social behaviour and what is being done about it in the UK.

Progress check 3.3

What is anti-social behaviour?

Crime as a social construct

Society and legal processes decide what is and is not a crime in a particular society. Some actions may be a crime in all countries but crime is often seen as socially constructed, which means that different countries and cultures understand the concept differently and, if what is a crime differs between countries and cultures, then crime is a construct. Therefore, it is hard to argue that an action is a crime without considering the context and the situation. Psychology considers such aspects when studying what crime is, including whether someone is 'of sound mind' or whether there was intention in their action(s). In this chapter, you will look at the idea of the self-fulfilling prophecy, which suggests that people are 'constructed' by how others respond to them. Crime is constructed by each society according to what that society thinks should be against the law and how some behaviour should be punished.

Issues and debates

Compare the idea of social constructs in a society with scientific understanding. If something is scientifically 'proved' then it should be true of all people in all cultures and is likely to come from nature. It is a universal law of behaviour. If something is a construct, in that it differs between cultures, then it is likely to be about nurture. So the concepts of social constructionism, universal laws and science are useful when you discuss the nature–nurture debate later in your course.

Causes of crime

Causes of crime are often split into nature and nurture aspects of behaviour. For example, personality, genes and brain structure have all been said to be causes of criminal behaviour. These are biological aspects of crime, and crime then comes from someone's nature. However, an accident or head injury can affect someone's biology and their behaviour, so crime might not be 'born' but can be 'made' and is still biologically caused. You will cover biological explanations including brain injury, brain structure (the amygdala), genes (XYY syndrome) and personality.

Others say that crime is caused by environment and nurture. Theories include labelling and the self-fulfilling prophecy, which is about stereotyping – predicting behaviour and then, by expecting such behaviour, producing criminal or anti-social behaviour. Most theories about nurture and crime are about the (bad) influence of families. Criminal behaviour might be copied, for example, or encouraged, or expected. In your course, you cover labelling and the self-fulfilling prophecy as explanations of crime, and social learning is considered too.

Progress check 3.4

Relate the idea of how crime or anti-social behaviour might be copied or encouraged to learning theories in your course.

Issues and debates

Your study of criminological psychology can be used when discussing the nature–nurture issue. You could use biological explanations of crime, such as it being about personality, to discuss a nature explanation, and you could discuss social explanations of crime, such as that it comes from what others expect of us, to discuss a nurture explanation.

Identifying criminals, making judgements and treating offenders

In the following content and method sections, you will learn more about problems with eyewitness testimony and you can choose this as a key question or as your practical investigation. You will also look at two ways (of many) of treating offenders, which will add to your understanding. Another area of criminological psychology is how a jury is affected by the defendant. For example, would you be more likely to think someone dressed in a suit and without a strong regional accent is innocent than someone dressed in jeans and speaking in a strong local accent? It appears that juries are affected by issues such as race and attractiveness, and these are issues studied in your course. Eyewitness testimony and interviewing are areas focusing on identifying offenders; formulation and jury decision-making can be about making judgements about offenders.

Forensic psychologists cover many areas that relate psychology to crime and are interested in **rehabilitation**, which is about preparing someone to become a productive and settled member of a community. Forensic psychologists also carry out research, so they work within criminological psychology. A degree in criminology, however, would also cover sociological aspects of crime, including recidivism rates, and how gender, race or class might affect criminal activity.

Definition

Rehabilitation is about preparing someone to become a productive and settled member of a community.

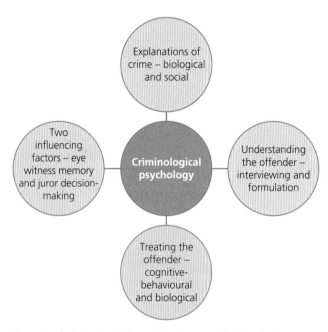

Aspects of criminological psychology covered in this chapter

Progress check 3.5

Explain, using two examples, what criminological psychology is.

Test yourself

Explain the role of a forensic psychologist to show what criminological psychology focuses on.
(6 marks)

Content in criminological psychology

In your course, the content part of criminological psychology is split into four sections. First, explanations for criminal and anti-social behaviour are covered. Biological explanations are followed by social explanations. Then issues around understanding the offender are considered, including types of interviewing and issues around formulation. A third section gives two treatments, one cognitive-behavioural treatment and one biological treatment. The final section has two parts: one looking at factors affecting **eyewitness memory** and the other looking at factors affecting juror decision-making.

Definition

Eyewitness memory can be recall or recognition of what has been seen.

You need to cover biological and social explanations for crime and anti-social behaviour. There are quite a few biological explanations for you to study, but for social explanations you just have to study labelling and the self-fulfilling prophecy, although social learning can help to link to learning theories and is an alternative explanation.

Defining terms

Crime has already been defined earlier, as has anti-social behaviour. It is worth defining aggression and violence too as some studies have found that there are brain issues involved in aggression but not in violence as such. For example, damage to the frontal lobes can give aggression, which can be about violence, but might not be. The Definitions box below defines **anger**, **aggression**, **instrumental aggression**, **reactive aggression** and **violence**.

Definitions

Anger is an emotion and anger management is about controlling that emotion. Anger is not good or bad, it is how someone feels. **Aggression** is focused on how someone behaves, such as using threatening behaviour or physical assault, but this might not cause harm and might not be against social norms, so is not violence. Aggression is seen as bad in our society because it is not controlled, planned behaviour, which is what society praises. **Instrumental aggression** is when someone uses aggression to achieve a goal, such as using threatening behaviour; harm could result but it is not the aim. **Reactive aggression** is when someone is hostile and wants to hit out at someone perhaps because of a perceived injustice. **Violence** is when aggression moves to behaviour that does physical harm and goes against social norms. Violence can be planned behaviour. Violence is thought of as 'bad' and goes against social norms in a much stronger way than aggression. Aggression can lead to violence of course and anger can be an emotion involved in both aggression and violence.

Gender and crime/anti-social behaviour

You have to look at biological and social explanations of crime and anti-social behaviour and you also have to consider gender differences relating to such explanations. The explanations are given separately in this section. Within each explanation, there is a section that considers gender differences in the explanation. First, however, some general evidence about gender differences in explanations of crime and anti-social behaviour is given.

In general, more males than females show anti-social behaviour

In general, crime and anti-social behaviour relates to males more than females, so you will expect to see a lot of studies using men as participants and referring to males. For example, Elbogen *et al.*'s (2012) study, which you will come across later when looking at biological explanations of crime and anti-social behaviour, found in war veterans that being young related to showing aggressive behaviour, as did being male. Steffensmeier and Allan (1996) agree that the 'gender gap is universal' and that men are more likely than women to commit criminal acts.

The government in the UK publish statistics showing offender characteristics, including gender. It is interesting to focus on anti-social behaviour and aggression to see if they relate more to male offenders than female offenders.

Among the many statistics, the custody rates of males and females (2014 figures) are given in relation to aggravating factors (focusing on aggression) in sentencing for theft, dishonesty and fraud and in relation to 'higher culpability' and 'greater harm' in assault and public order offences. Some examples are included from these particular figures to show gender differences. Tables 3.2 and 3.3 show that males have higher custody rates, although the female figures are not that low.

Table 3.2 Custody rates by gender relating to theft, dishonesty and fraud giving aggravating factors

Aggravating factors (focus on aggression)	Custody rates (%)	
	Females	Males
Intimidation or force used	67%	78%
Member of group or gang	50%	70%

Table 3.3 Custody rates by gender relating to assault and public order giving 'higher culpability' and 'greater harm' factors

'Higher culpability' and 'greater harm' factors (focus on aggression)	Custody rates (%)	
	Females	Males
Threatened/actual use of weapon/equivalent	37%	66%
Intention to cause more serious harm	67%	83%
Deliberately causes more harm than necessary	55%	81%
Sustained or repeated assault on the same person	44%	72%

Explore

Statistics published in November 2014 focusing on women and the criminal justice system, from which the figures above were taken, can be accessed using this link: www.gov.uk/government/statistics/women-and-the-criminal-justice-system-2013

The Dunedin Longitudinal Study and gender differences in anti-social behaviour

Moffitt *et al.* (2003) say that the 'most robust' finding about anti-social behaviour is that it is found more in males than in females. The Dunedin Longitudinal Study reported in Moffitt *et al.* (2003) followed 1,000 males and females in New Zealand from birth to the age of 20 and did not find an overall difference between the genders in the causes of anti-social behaviour. However, there was some difference in gender when looking at a more serious pattern of anti-social behaviour, and a pattern that shows persistent anti-social behaviour is found more in males. Moffitt *et al.* (2003) report that, for every ten males that show this pattern of persistence in anti-social behaviour, there is just one female. It is said that neurocognitive problems, a temperament showing lack of control, and hyperactivity are factors found more in males and also in people who persistently show anti-social behaviour. Moffitt *et al.* (2003) suggest that female anti-social behaviour rises at the time of female puberty and the gap between the genders is then at its closest; males and females also show similar patterns in their drug use and abuse; and in relationships male and female violence is about equal. However, in general, anti-social behaviour and violence is found more in males.

Bowen *et al.* (2008): The Avon Longitudinal Study of Parents and Children

The Avon Longitudinal Study of Parents and Children focuses on anti-social and problem behaviours among young children, including gender differences in anti-social behaviour. The study reports that more males than females reported being involved in anti-social behaviour and males reported being involved in more anti-social and problem behaviours than females. Those at high risk of involvement in anti-social behaviours showed resilience (88 per cent), which means they were at high risk but did not engage in the anti-social and problem behaviours. It was found that girls were more likely to show resilience than boys. When boys did show resilience, this linked to school enjoyment, high levels of pro-social behaviour and having mothers with good parenting skills. The findings back up the general claim that crime and anti-social behaviour are found in males more than females.

> ### Explore
> The NHS news website contains a March 2013 article that considers guidelines on child anti-social behaviour. The article is about conduct disorder, a mental health condition that causes defiance as well as aggression and anti-social behaviour. In the article, it is said that conduct disorders are more common in boys than girls: 7 per cent of boys and 3 per cent of girls aged 5–10 years are said to have conduct disorders. You can access the article here:
> www.nhs.uk/news/2013/03march/pages/new-guidelines-on-child-antisocial-behaviour.aspx

> ### Progress check 3.6
> Give three pieces of evidence showing that males feature more than females when looking at crime and anti-social behaviour.

Biological explanations of crime and anti-social behaviour

Biological explanations that you need to cover include brain injury, the amygdala and aggression, XYY syndrome and personality.

Brain injury as an explanation for anti-social and criminal behaviour

Brain injury can lead to aggressive behaviour. In 1966, Charles Whitman killed around 16 people. An autopsy showed he had a large brain tumour which affected the amygdala, a brain area known to be linked with aggression. Although it was not shown that the brain tumour caused the shootings, it may have been a factor. Other studies, such as the case study of Phineas Gage, have suggested left and right prefrontal lobe damage leads to aggression. For Phineas Gage, his personality changed after his accident, although it was suggested that the change was temporary and he was more 'himself' again later in life. These real-life incidents provide evidence that is used when looking at brain injury as an explanation for criminal and anti-social behaviour. Various studies with evidence for and against the brain injury explanation for criminal and anti-social behaviour are explored in this section.

> ### Explore
> You can look up the case of Charles Whitman here:
> **www.biography.com/people/charles-whitman-11495598**
> or here:
> **www.dailymail.co.uk/news/article-2872736/Victims-1966-Texas-tower-shooting-angered-museum-s-recent-decision-display-sniper-s-rifle-bearing-handwritten-notes.html**

> ### Explore
> Damasio *et al.* (1994) wrote an article about Phineas Gage. You can access it here: **www.antoniocasella.eu/dnlaw/Damasio_1994.pdf**. However, be warned that the article describes the brain damage quite graphically.

Brower and Price (2001): frontal lobe problems and criminal behaviour

Brower and Price (2001) reviewed how frontal lobe problems link to criminal behaviour – reviews are helpful as they summarise findings from research. They found that anti-social and criminal behaviour related to brain injury in the frontal lobes, which is evidence that such brain injury can be an explanation for criminal and anti-social behaviour. The prefrontal lobe is associated with problem-solving and decision-making so it makes sense to say that damage to that area will lead to more aggression and possibly violence. Brower and Price conclude that focal orbitofrontal injury is associated with increased aggression, specifically impulsive aggression. However, they did not find studies that showed that frontal network dysfunction can predict violent crime. There was a link with impulsive aggression but not with violent crime.

Brower and Price helpfully define what they mean by 'aggression' and 'violence', and it is worth looking at the difference. By 'aggression', they meant 'threatening behaviour or physical assault directed at someone else or at the environment'. By 'violence', they meant 'actions that inflict physical harm in violation of social norms' (p. 720).

Year One link: In biological psychology, you looked at brain regions and their association with aggression. You will have seen that the prefrontal cortex relates to aggression and you will have looked at evidence, such as the case of Phineas Gage. Recall that material as it will be relevant in this section.

Progress check 3.7
Explain the difference between aggression and violence.

Case study evidence for frontal lobe injury relating to aggression

Blumer et al. (1975, cited in Brower and Price, 2001) say that case studies have shown how anti-social personality can arise after frontal lobe injury and there is evidence for this link that goes back to 1835. The damage tends to be to the orbitofrontal cortex and as behaviour when that brain region is damaged tends to be poor control over impulses, outbursts and lack of interpersonal sensitivity, the area is said to be for decision-making and impulse control (Duffy and Campbell, 1994, cited in Brower and Price, 2001). Brower and Price (2001) cite Tranel (1994), Meyers et al. (1992) and Blair and Cipolotti (2000) as case studies of sociopathy and anti-social personality disorder where there is frontal lobe damage and make the link between the brain injury and the 'sociopathy', which relates to criminal and anti-social behaviour. However, Brower and Price (2001) mention one report (Labbatte et al., 1997) about two cases that show improvement in impulsive and anti-social behaviour after frontal brain injury as adults.

There is evidence that links such damage to aggression and anti-social behaviour but it is interesting to find studies that show the opposite. This can help to underline the difficulties of researching in these areas. What case studies tend to do is look at damage, look at changed behaviour, and then relate the two together, which might not be strong evidence of a cause-and-effect finding. Studies of people injured in war show that damage to the frontal lobes tends to mean aggression and violent behaviours compared with controls without head injury. In one study (Vietnam Head Injury Study, Grafman et al., 1996, cited in Brower and Price, 2001) around 14 per cent of the brain injury patients were in fights compared with around 4 per cent of those without the damage to the frontal lobes. Brower and Price (2001) state that the problem is that there is no evidence about the aggression of the individuals before the injury and also evidence is retrospective, meaning the study goes back to the time of the head injury and there may have been forgetting.

> **STUDY HINT**
> Brower and Price (2001) use evidence from case studies when drawing conclusions about the role of brain injury in criminal and anti-social behaviour. You can use such evidence when discussing the case study research method, which is required in your study of criminological psychology.

> **Explore**
> You can access Brower and Price's (2001) review here if you would like to know more:
> www.ncbi.nlm.nih.gov/pmc/articles/PMC1737651/pdf/v071p00720.pdf

Progress check 3.8
Explain one strength and one weakness of case study evidence in psychology.

Diaz (1995): traumatic brain injury (TBI) and association with crime

Diaz (1995) was interested in the insanity defence, which is pleading not guilty by reason of insanity. This plea can relate to structural and functional brain issues, including brain injury. Diaz confirms that the most common areas of brain damage from trauma are the frontal lobes, the temporal lobes and the brain stem, and a lot of studies relate frontal lobe damage to anti-social and possibly criminal behaviour. Volkow and Tancredi (1987, cited in Diaz, 1995) found that two out of four violent psychiatric patients showed frontal lobe damage as shown using PET scanning.

Diaz also commented that there are individual differences in brain damage which can affect resulting behaviour.

Year One link: Raine *et al.* (1997), the classic study in biological psychology, used PET scanning to look for brain differences in people pleading not guilty by reason of insanity compared with controls. Review this study as it can be used as evidence in this section.

Huw Williams (October 2012): links between brain injury and offending in young people

TBI is a type of acquired brain injury (ABI) and an ABI is damage that was not there at birth. ABI can come from an accident but also from stroke and infection. TBI is caused by a 'trauma' rather than stroke or infection and is likely to happen because of a fall, fight or road accident. An open injury is the least common and is an actual injury to the brain from penetration through the skull. A closed TBI is when an external force damages the brain from a jolt or a blow to the head. Young people are the most at risk of a TBI and it affects about 8.5 per cent of the population, with males more at risk than females (www.nhs.uk, accessed July 2015).

In 2012, the *Daily Mail* claimed that young people who have ABI can behave in a criminal way, with 60 per cent of young adult male prisoners in custody having some kind of TBI, according to an Exeter University report produced by Huw Williams and reported on the NHS website. The study was also reported by BBC News (October 2012). The thought is that it is the inability to prevent impulsivity that is behind the problems, and this links to the evidence that prefrontal lobes are 'for' executive function and control. One issue with young people having a brain injury is that their brain is not fully developed until around the age of 25, and impulse control and planning are among the last areas to develop.

> ### Explore
> You can read about Williams' study using this link:
> **www.bbc.co.uk/news/uk-19998710**

The consequences of head injury include reduced awareness of emotions, loss of memory and concentration, poor control over impulses and poor social judgement. There can be increased aggression and attention problems. You can see how this relates to aggressive behaviour, and possibly to criminal behaviour as well, such as might come from poor impulse control. The report on brain injury in young people reports that head injury in offenders is likely to be found in 50 to 80 per cent of offenders, compared

with less than 10 per cent in the general population. This is evidence for TBI being an explanation for criminal behaviour. A study in Sweden showed that 8.8 per cent of patients with brain injury committed violent crime, compared with 3 per cent in the general population.

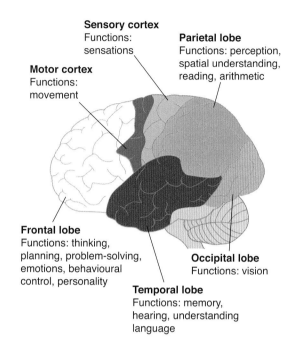

The frontal lobe is often the focus of brain injury and its functions include behavioural control.

Findings from various studies

- Yeudall *et al.* (1982), cited in Brickman *et al.* (1984), suggest a lot of frontal and temporal lobe abnormalities or brain damage have been found in juvenile delinquents.
- Pincus (2001) suggests there is physical and sexual abuse found among offenders and also acquired brain injury and/or brain dysfunction.
- Pincus (2001) found a correlation between drug abuse, brain damage and aggression – in particular, alcohol impacts on the effects of frontal lobe damage.
- Barnfield and Leathem (1998) in New Zealand found 'disproportionately high rates' of TBI in prison populations.

(Source: www.braininjuryaustralia.org.au, accessed July 2015)

Elbogen *et al.* (2012): war veterans, PTSD and traumatic brain injury

Elbogen *et al.* (2012) looked at the idea that people who have increased anger and irritability after experiencing traumatic events are more likely to exhibit anti-social behaviour. They thought that war veterans with post-traumatic stress disorder (PTSD) or TBI who say they have emotions of anger and irritability would show higher arrest rates for criminal behaviour. They studied 1,388 Iraq or Afghanistan war veterans and found that 9 per cent reported being arrested since their return from military service. Those with PTSD or TBI reporting anger or irritability were indeed more likely to be arrested than other veterans. They found, though, that being younger, male, a witness of family violence, misusing drugs or having a criminal history and having anger or irritability with PTSD did all relate significantly to arrests. However, arrests were not related to exposure to combat or to TBI. They found that veterans with PTSD and negative feelings might be more at risk of criminal arrest and also drug abuse, and a criminal history made them more at risk of arrest, so there were non-PTSD factors as well. However, TBI did not relate to the greater likelihood of being arrested for criminal behaviour. This is evidence against the claim that TBI causes criminal or anti-social behaviour. However, Grafman *et al.* (1996, cited in Brower and Price, 2001) noted findings from the Vietnam Head Injury Study (VHIS) that 14 per cent of brain-injured patients were in fights compared with 4 per cent of those without frontal lobe damage.

Table 3.4 Summary of evidence for brain injury as an explanation for criminal and anti-social behaviour

Study	Summary of findings relating to brain injury and criminal/anti-social behaviour	For or against the argument that brain injury relates to criminal/anti-social behaviour
Brower and Price (2001)	Anti-social and criminal behaviour relate to frontal lobe brain injury.	For
Blumer *et al.* (1975, cited in Brower and Price, 2001)	Frontal lobe injury links to anti-social personality.	For
Labbatte *et al.* (1997, cited in Brower and Price, 2001)	Frontal brain injury in two cases improved impulsivity and anti-social behaviour.	Against in a way. Shows relationship but not in the expected direction
Grafman *et al.* (1996, cited in Brower and Price, 2001)	14% of brain injury patients were in fights compared with 4% of patients without frontal lobe damage.	For
NHS website (accessed July 2015)	60% of young male adult prisoners in custody have some kind of TBI.	For
Swedish study on the NHS website (accessed July 2015)	8.8% of patients with brain injury committed violent crime compared with 3% in the general population.	For
Barnfield and Leathem (1998)	In New Zealand, disproportionately high rates of TBI are found in prison populations.	For
Elbogen *et al.* (2012)	Factors in war veterans relating to criminal behaviour include PTSD with anger and irritability, being young and male, witnessing family violence, misusing drugs or having a criminal history. However, factors did not include having TBI.	Against
Diaz (1995)	Diaz suggests that 'no scientifically proven information is currently available on the potential association of TBI, drug use and violent crime'.	Possibly against
Lewis *et al.* (1986, cited in Diaz, 1995)	All 15 people studied who were sentenced to death with no further appeal had a history of severe brain injury, though Diaz points out that it is not clear that the damage caused the criminal behaviour as it could have been unrelated to it.	For

STUDY HINT
To help with your exam preparation, you could reproduce Table 3.4 and add another column to give some evaluation points for some or all of the studies.

Progress check 3.9

Explain two pieces of evidence that go against the claim that brain injury explains criminal and anti-social behaviour.

Gender and brain injury as an explanation for criminal and anti-social behaviour

Both Charles Whitman and Phineas Gage, the two real-life studies given at the start of this section, were male, though of course this is not proof that brain injury affects males more than females. The NHS website reporting on brain injury does suggest that young people are most at risk of a TBI and it affects about 8.5 per cent of the population, with males more at risk than females (www.nhs.uk, accessed July 2015). Amongst other factors, Elbogen et al. (2012) found that being male was a risk factor for showing violence and anti-social behaviour, looking at war veterans. There was some evidence offered here that males show more violence and anti-social behaviour than females. However, evidence mostly looks at brain biology and issues such as prefrontal lobe damage, and the results are not thought to be different according to gender. It might be that more males have a TBI, perhaps because they are more likely to be war veterans, are more likely to be involved in fights and perhaps also more likely to have a car accident, rather than that there is a direct gender–biology link. Social factors might put males in the position of having brain injury more than females.

Bruns and Hauser (2003): review of TBI

Table 3.5 Severity of incidence in people hospitalised with TBI according to Bruns and Hauser (2003), citing figures in Minnesota 1965 to 1974

Severity of TBI	Male	Female
Mild	149	71
Moderate	69	29
Severe	17	6
Fatal	35	10

Bruns and Hauser (2003) have a section on gender differences and state that males are 'uniformly at higher risk of TBI than are females' (p. 7). They give evidence for this claim, such as in Olmsted County (US) in the adolescent and young adult age groups, the ratio of males to females is more than two to one. Although in the geriatric age group, focusing on older people, females have more TBI incidences than males. Bruns and Hauser suggest that in young adults a high ratio of males to females in terms of TBI might be because of interpersonal violence and motor vehicle collisions. In South Africa, the ratio of TBI was more than four males to one female and the greatest difference in gender was in young adults. They put this down to the amount of interpersonal violence. These figures seem to be evidence for males showing differences in behaviour that cause them to have more traumatic brain injury rather than males responding in a more violent way after TBI.

Summary of gender differences in brain injury affecting crime and anti-social behaviour

It seems that there are gender differences in having TBI more than gender differences in aggressive responses from having TBI. It seems that the biological explanation of brain injury as a cause of crime and anti-social behaviour does not show gender differences in the biology but does show gender differences in people experiencing traumatic brain injury.

Evaluation of brain injury as an explanation for criminal and anti-social behaviour

Strengths

- There is a lot of evidence to suggest that brain injury relates to anti-social behaviour and aggression. It is more that brain injury in the frontal lobes prevents executive functioning and control over impulsivity and so aggression and anti-social behaviour, perhaps including criminal behaviour, are more likely. Evidence comes from Grafman et al. (1996, cited in Brower and Price, 2001) and others. There seem to be reasonably consistent findings that frontal lobe brain injury relates to problem behaviour.

- Evidence for brain injury explaining criminal and anti-social behaviour comes from case studies and from studies using brain scanning, as well as from the use of tests of executive functioning. Methods also include simply looking at violent prisoners and non-violent prisoners and comparing whether they report brain injury or not. Therefore, many different methods are used to come to similar conclusions about frontal lobe damage and aggression. This gives findings reliability and credibility.

Weaknesses

- Studies tend to show an association between frontal lobe brain damage and aggression in behaviour, which can relate to criminal or anti-social behaviour. However, as Diaz (1995) points out, scientific evidence is hard to find. There are other factors relating to criminal behaviour, such as being young and male, witnessing violence in the family, having previous convictions or possibly having PTSD with anger and impulsivity as well as drug and alcohol misuse. It is hard to pinpoint brain injury alone as a cause for criminal behaviour, even though some studies show a relationship. Finding cause-and-effect conclusions is hard given the evidence that must be used (such as case studies and scanning) and the complexity of the behaviour.

- There are individual differences in brain injury and differences between individuals in behaviour that is affected (e.g. Diaz, 1995). This means it is hard to draw strong conclusions that a certain brain injury will lead to certain behaviour. Notwithstanding the amount of evidence that does relate brain injury, in particular in the frontal lobes, to aggression. When there are individual differences in people studied, issues about generalisability are raised.

The amygdala as an explanation for aggressive behaviour

As mentioned earlier, Charles Whitman, who was responsible for killing around 16 people, was subsequently, after his death, found to have a brain tumour affecting the amygdala. It was not shown that the tumour accounted for his behaviour, but it could have done. The amygdala is involved in fear and aggression, as well as social interactions, and it is thought to be involved in crime. The role of the amygdala in criminal and anti-social behaviour is covered in this section.

Year One link: You have looked at brain regions and their functioning, including links to aggression, when you studied biological psychology. Draw on that understanding in this section.

Yang et al. (2009): link between smaller volume of the amygdala and anti-social behaviour

Yang et al. (2009) looked at 27 psychopathic people and 32 controls and used structural MRI to measure amygdala differences. One of the researchers working with Yang in this study is Adrian Raine, who with others carried out the classic study in biological psychology in your course, and you can probably see that the two studies relate somewhat in their aims and findings.

Year One link: Raine et al. (1997) is the classic study in biological psychology, where PET scanning is used to look at regions in the brain – in particular, those connected with aggression and crime. Recall the study so you can relate the findings to what is given here about the role of the amygdala.

The aim of Yang et al. (2009) was to look for regions in the amygdala that are problematic in psychopaths. The volume of the amygdala of each person was measured. Yang et al. (2009) found that people with **psychopathy** had volume

reductions on both amygdalae (bilateral) compared with the controls. They had 17.1 per cent less volume in the left amygdala and 18.9 per cent less volume in the right amygdala. There were also deformations in the surface of the amygdalae. There were significant correlations between the reduced volumes and the psychopathy scores and the strongest correlations related to emotions and interpersonal abilities and the amygdala volume. Yang et al. (2009) point out that psychopathy relates to manipulative personality and anti-social behaviour, such as poor behavioural control, so their findings support the idea that the amygdala is involved in criminal or anti-social behaviour or in the control of such behaviour, as a smaller volume in the amygdala seemed to mean more anti-social behaviour and less control.

Definition
Psychopathy is defined as 'a personality disorder characterised by a severe affective deficit, lack of respect for the rights of others and the norms of society' (Woodworth and Porter, 2007, cited in Mossière and Dalby, 2008).

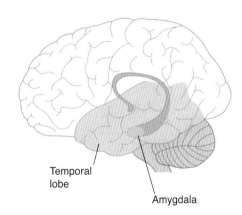

Temporal lobe

Amygdala

The amygdala is for moral reasoning, conditioning regarding fear and controlling behaviour.

An important issue discussed by Yang et al. is the link between the amygdala and conditioning, including conditioning related to fear. If there is an impairment in the amygdala this might affect conditioning related to fear and as psychopathy can link to lack of fear Yang et al.'s findings make sense. The amygdala also relates to rewards and moral reasoning so again if there is amygdala impairment that links to psychopathic behaviour.

Progress check 3.10
Yang et al. used controls in their study. What does it mean to say controls were used in the context the term is used in this study and why is it good to use controls?

Pardini et al. (2013): lower amygdala volume and links to violence and aggression

Pardini et al. (2013) carried out a study using scanning. Adrian Raine was a member of the team. They found that men with lower volumes of the amygdala were a lot more likely to show aggressive and violent behaviour, as well as psychopathic traits showing up three years later, than a control group of men with normal sized amygdala. This finding supports the finding of Yang et al. (2009). This was a longitudinal study and 56 men with histories of violence were recruited. They looked at violence and psychopathic traits in the three-year follow-up and also looked at the association between level of aggression and psychopathic tendencies of the participants in childhood and adolescence. As the researchers predicted more aggression and psychopathic traits after three years, this suggested to them that the volume of the amygdala might be a biomarker for 'severe and persistent aggression'.

> **STUDY HINT**
>
> Pardini et al. (2013) use a longitudinal design because they follow their participants and take data again after three years to look at their behaviour in terms of violence and aggression. You can use the study as an example of a longitudinal design. Yang et al. (2009) used a cross-sectional design. Such examples are useful when a criminological psychology example is appropriate.

Glenn et al. (2009): less amygdala activity in psychopaths

Glenn et al. (2009), again including Adrian Raine in the team, found it was not just the size of the amygdala but its functioning that is reduced in people with psychopathic tendencies. Glenn et al. focused on moral reasoning and the neural circuitry underlying it, so not just brain structures but also brain functioning involving neurotransmitters. The researchers were interested in circuit functions that relate to immoral individuals who show psychopathic traits. They used fMRI scanning and found that more 'psychopathic' individuals had reduced amygdala activity during moral decision-making, which they take as evidence that psychopaths show deficits in brain regions that are for moral reasoning. This finding means that psychopathic individuals would worry less about causing harm to others – this is the link to criminal and anti-social behaviour.

> **STUDY HINT**
>
> In biological psychology, you looked at three scanning techniques, one of which was fMRI scanning. You can use Glenn et al. (2009) as an example of fMRI scanning if a study within criminological psychology is relevant.

> **Explore**
>
> You can access the abstract of Pardini et al. (2013) using this link: www.ncbi.nlm.nih.gov/pubmed/23647988. You can access Glenn et al. (2009) using this link: http://repository.upenn.edu/cgi/viewcontent. cgi?article=1058&context=neuroethics_pubs.

Progress check 3.11

Pardini et al. (2013) and Glenn et al. (2009) had related but different findings. Explain the findings and how they are related but different.

Bufkin and Luttrell (2005): review of studies using scanning

Bufkin and Luttrell (2005), in their review of studies using scanning to look at aggressive and violent behaviour, give a table of studies, some of which are given here, showing that they focus a lot on brain regions like the prefrontal lobes rather than, or as well as, the amygdala, so it looks as if there are parts of the brain other than the amygdala implicated in aggression and violent behaviour. The amygdala is in the temporal lobe, so even when it is not mentioned, it is referred to in some of the studies.

Table 3.6 Some of the studies listed in Bufkin and Luttrell which used scanning to look at brain regions and aggression/violence

Study	Participants	Methods	Results
Elst *et al.* (2000)	48 patients – 24 with temporal lobe epilepsy and 24 matched health controls	MRI (magnetic resonance imaging)	44% of patients who were aggressive showed problems with the amygdala.
Amen *et al.* (1996)	40 psychiatric patients showing aggression and 40 matched controls who were not aggressive	SPECT (single-photon emission computed tomography)	Less activity in the prefrontal cortex in aggressive patients as well as more activity in left basal ganglia, left temporal lobe and anteromedial frontal cortex.
Volkow and Tancredi (1987)	Four psychiatric violent patients and four normal matched controls	PET (positron emission tomography)	50% of the violent patients had reduced functioning in the frontal lobes and there were left temporal lobe problems in all the violent patients.
Raine *et al.* (1997)	41 murderers pleading NGRI (not guilty by reason of insanity) and 41 matched controls	PET	Less activity in the lateral prefrontal cortex of the murderers as well as the medial prefrontal cortex and the posterior parietal cortex. Murderers also showed less activity in the corpus callosum and reductions in the left amygdala, thalamus and medial temporal lobes.
Tonkonogy (1991)	14 violent and 9 non-violent patients with organic mental disorders	MRI	Just 1 of the 14 patients showed orbitofrontal lesions. Violent patients were more likely to have less tissue in the temporal lobe, particularly in the amygdalo-hippocampal region or nearby areas.

STUDY HINT
Raine *et al.'s* (1997) study was in Bufkin and Luttrell's review and you can use it when discussing the amygdala and brain regions relating to aggression.

Explore
You can access Bufkin and Luttrell (2005) using this link if you want to find out more or to read about the other studies reviewed: www.acdlaonline.com/zoomdocs/presentations/neuroimagingaggession(1).pdf

STUDY HINT
If you are trying to learn a list of names, you could try working them into a sentence. Elst, Volkow and Tancredi, Amen, Tonkonogy, and Raine are five studies that use scanning to relate aggression to brain regions including the amygdala. Use the initials V & T, E, A, T and R to help you to remember. You could try a sentence such as 'Rory EATs Vegetables and Treats'. When creating a mnemonic, make it relevant to you. Also, be sure to learn which study 'belongs' to which name. In an exam, if you remember the point of a study but not the name, use the study anyway, but it is good to recall the name(s) of the researcher(s).

Evaluation points relating to the amygdala explaining anti-social behaviour

Though Bufkin and Luttrell (2005) list studies that include the amygdala or the temporal lobe as a region affected in people that show violence and aggression, their list also shows studies that mention frontal lobe functioning, which relates to brain injury as an explanation of criminal and anti-social behaviour. It seems that there is evidence for the amygdala being involved in psychopathy, and related to that behaviour can be anti-social or criminal behaviour. However, other areas of the brain can be damaged or dysfunctional and can lead to aggression, violence or anti-social behaviour. Possibly there is not one single explanation for criminal and anti-social behaviour. The observed behaviour might be explained in different people in different ways.

STUDY HINT
When discussing these studies, you can use evaluation points about the use of neuroimaging/brain scanning as a research method, since a number of these studies adopt that method.

Gender and the amygdala as an explanation for criminal and anti-social behaviour

It is not generally emphasised that male and female brains differ with regard to the functions of brain regions like the amygdala. Blakemore and Choudhury (2006) looked at white and grey matter differences between children aged 11 years and found some differences. However, they suggested that differences in male and female brains with regard to the frontal cortex needed to be studied further, and they did not mention specific regions such as the amygdala. Studies looking at the role of the amygdala in anti-social and aggressive behaviour seem not to highlight gender differences. However, it might just be that gender has not featured as a variable of study.

Shirtcliff *et al.* (2009): gender differences in neurobiology relating to amygdala functioning

Shirtcliff *et al.* (2009) reviewed the neurobiology of empathy and callousness and considered implications regarding gender for anti-social behaviour. Although their review does not emphasise gender differences, they do include a passage on gender differences towards the end of the paper. They say that there are differences between the genders, citing Zahn-Waxler *et al.* (2005). They state that girls show more empathy than boys (Zahn-Waxler, 2000, cited in Shirtcliff *et al.*, 2009) and there are more instances in conduct disorder and anti-social behaviour in boys than in girls (e.g. Moffitt, 1993a, cited in Shirtcliff *et al.*, 2009). Cale and Lilenfeld (2002, cited in Shirtcliff *et al.*, 2009) show that gender differences carry on into adulthood and relate to psychopathy. Importantly, with regard to biological explanations of crime and anti-social behaviour, they point out that the neurobiology involved in empathy and callousness is different in males and females, with more empathy-related neurocircuitry being active in females (e.g. Hein and Singer, 2008, cited in Shirtcliff *et al.*, 2009). They also show that stress response is different according to gender (e.g. Wang *et al.*, 2007, cited in Shirtcliff *et al.*, 2009). They conclude that 'the neurobiology of anti-social behaviour may be fundamentally different in males and females'. They do not mention the amygdala specifically; however, they do earlier state that the amygdala is critical for emotion responses and might be the most important limbic area with reference to emotion, so there may indeed be gender differences in the amygdala which can help to explain crime and anti-social behaviour.

Explore
You can access Shirtcliff *et al.*'s (2009) review using the following link, which gives a great deal of information about neurobiology relating to empathy, callousness and anti-social behaviour: www.ncbi.nlm.nih.gov/pmc/articles/PMC2729461/. The gender passage is towards the end of the paper.

Hyde *et al.* (2014): the amygdala, emotions, anti-social personality and psychopathy

Hyde *et al.* (2014) used both men and women in their study looking at anti-social personality disorder and psychopathy, relating these to negative emotionality and amygdala reactivity to perceived threat and to distress. They found higher scores for psychopathy to be associated with lower negative emotionality and lower amygdala activity. They found higher anti-social personality scores associated with higher negative emotionality and higher amygdala activity. This suggests that the amygdala has a role in anti-social behaviour, at least in some way. What is interesting is that, although men and women were used in the sample, gender was not used as a variable in the findings. This suggests that it might not be that there are *no* gender differences in amygdala functioning and negative emotionality, but that gender is not a variable of interest for some researchers.

Summary of gender differences in the amygdala affecting crime and anti-social behaviour

In general, it seems that there are no gender differences in amygdala functioning and neurobiology related to anti-social behaviour. Blakemore and Choudhury (2006) suggest that there are not many differences but more research is needed. Hyde *et al.* (2014) did not report gender differences in their study, but this does not mean that there weren't any, just that they did not look at them. Shirtcliff *et al.* (2009) give gender differences such as in empathy (more in girls) and conduct disorders (more in boys). They confirm that the amygdala is important in emotions and so it can be assumed that differences in emotionality between the genders might come from differences in the amygdala. Shirtcliff *et al.* (2009) give some evidence for biological differences in brain functioning between males and females when they point out that the neurobiology involved in relation to empathy and callousness is different in males and females, with more empathy-related neurocircuitry active in females (e.g. Hein and Singer, 2008, cited in Shirtcliff *et al.*, 2009).

Evaluation for the amygdala explanation for criminal behaviour and/or anti-social behaviour

Strengths

- Just some of the evidence is presented here. However, it is clear that there is a lot of evidence relating to amygdala size and possibly functioning to suggest that lower volume or less activity relates to problems with moral reasoning and control over behaviour, as well as problems in learning fear responses to stimuli. Though the focus tends to be on psychopathy, psychopathy relates to aggression and anti-social behaviour so the evidence for the amygdala as an explanation for criminal and/or anti-social behaviour is strong.

- Studies tend to use neuroimaging, which is a research method that can show reliable findings because more than one person can analyse the scan pictures. There is validity in what is being measured too, if the amygdala is highlighted and then measured using the scan pictures.

Weaknesses

- Scanning is seen as scientific, objective, reliable and, to an extent valid, which are strengths. However, when relating what is found in the scans to behaviour, it is harder to achieve those qualities. For example, psychopathic tendencies are hard to relate to crime and violence directly and there are many factors that relate to crime and violence, including age, gender and early life experiences. A scan might show reduced amygdala volume, but relating this to aggression and criminal behaviour does not have the same objectivity and reliability.

- As some studies show, it is not just the amygdala that is implicated in aggression. Studies have shown links between aggression and prefrontal lobe functioning, for example. Also some studies use the size of the amygdala and others the level of activity, so it is not certain what it is about the amygdala or how its relationship to other brain areas relates to criminal and anti-social behaviour.

Progress check 3.12

Briefly explain two weaknesses of the amygdala explanation of crime and anti-social behaviour.

Issues and debates

Biological explanations can be seen as reductionist, which can mean they are not strong as explanations. Looking at part of what might explain crime and anti-social behaviour might be useful to show a relationship and to suggest a treatment. However, if there are other factors explaining the behaviour, any treatment would not be that successful. 'Behaviour' is likely to come from both biology and environment. Reductionism is one of the issues and debates in your course.

XYY syndrome as an explanation of crime and anti-social behaviour

XYY syndrome relates to chromosomal abnormality. Males have an X and a Y chromosome and females have two X chromosomes. XYY syndrome means there is an extra chromosome at birth, with an additional Y chromosome in males. XYY is also called 47,XYY because the individual has 47 chromosomes instead of the usual 46 (23 pairs), with an extra Y chromosome. There is also 47,XXY, which is when someone has an additional X chromosome.

People with 47,XYY syndrome will be taller than normal and, in some cases, have severe acne. In 47,XYY, testosterone levels are normal, with normal sexual development and normal fertility. 47,XYY syndrome people may have reduced intelligence and there can be learning difficulties, as well as developmental delays in speech and language. There can also be difficulties in development of physical skills such as walking, as well as behavioural and emotional difficulties.

The features and symptoms of XYY syndrome vary between individuals. About one in 1,000 boys will have XYY syndrome.

Explanation

XYY syndrome refers to a male who has an additional Y chromosome so instead of being XY, there is an additional Y. This is sometimes called 47,XYY as there are 47 chromosomes rather than the usual 46.

Progress check 3.13

Explain what 47,XYY means.

XYY syndrome and crime

From here, the syndrome is called 'XYY' only. There is no obvious connection with crime and anti-social behaviour in what has been said about XYY syndrome regarding symptoms and characteristics. The link comes only from observations of XYY syndrome people in criminal populations. For example, Jacobs *et al.* (1965) suggested that men with XYY syndrome were more aggressive than XY men and they found that there was an over-representation of XYY men in the prison population, with 15 XYY men for every 1,000 prisoners. These sorts of observations led to an apparent link between XYY and crime and anti-social behaviour. XYY syndrome is also called Jacobs' syndrome because of Patrick Jacobs' work. Around 75 per cent of cases are not diagnosed or detected; finding out someone has an XYY chromosome pattern can be accidental or may never happen. Some incidences of XYY syndrome are uncovered before birth.

Public misconception of a link between XYY and violent crime

There is a general feeling among the public that XYY goes with violent crime. Alien 3 is set in a penal colony for XYY males, unable to be rehabilitated because violent crime is 'in' their genetic make-up. Films like this perpetuate the idea that XYY goes with being a violent criminal, though research certainly does not find evidence for that claim. Another media representation of XYY was when Richard Speck in 1966 claimed he had XYY syndrome and that this explained his rape and murder of eight women. It turned out he was XY in any case, and the violence had nothing to do with XYY syndrome, but such links can persist. These links can lead to a self-fulfilling prophecy (see page 224) in that someone can be labelled and then fulfils their incorrect label. These are the reasons XYY is included in your course, not because XYY is a genetic formation that 'means' violence.

Witkin et al. (1976): no direct link between crime and XYY syndrome

Witkin et al. (1976) carried out a study in Denmark looking at 4,591 men in the top height distribution (a total group of 28,884 men) and found only 12 cases of XYY. They found for the XYY men that 41.7 per cent of them compared with 9.3 per cent of those with an XY chromosomal pattern were more likely to be involved in crime, but this was not violent crime and not a large difference. In fact, the difference between XYY/XXY and XY was not significantly different when background variables were controlled for. Those with XXY syndrome showed a higher crime rate too but less than XYY, and there was not a significant difference. Just one of the people with XXY syndrome was convicted of an aggressive act, so there did not seem to be any link

with aggression and the syndrome. They did find lower intelligence in both the XXY and XYY syndromes when compared with XY males. Witkin et al. felt that XYY and XXY males tended to have low intelligence and to be taller than average, which might be what led to their over-representation in the prison population, because of the social reaction such characteristics might produce. The study suggested it was not the biological differences in having an extra chromosome that led people to be over-represented in prison populations.

Stochholm et al. (2012): some link but not when social variables taken into account

In a study in Denmark, Stochholm et al. (2012) looked at men aged 15–70 years diagnosed with XXY or XYY syndrome. XYY, according to Stochholm et al. (2012), does not lead to observable physical differences, except regarding height. The researchers compared number of convictions in men with Klinefelter's syndrome (XXY) and men with XYY syndrome, comparing these with incidences of crime in the general population (controls). They considered eight types of crime, including homicide, burglary, violence and traffic crime. There were 934 men diagnosed with Klinefelter's syndrome (KS) and 161 with XYY syndrome. They found that there were significantly more convictions in those with KS compared with controls (p<.001). The crimes that showed increases included sexual abuse, burglary, arson and 'others'. There was a decreased risk of traffic-related and drug-related crimes in those with KS. In those with XYY, there was a significant increase in number of convictions compared with controls (p<.005) in all crimes except drug- and traffic-related crimes. When variables were controlled for, such as education, fatherhood, retirement and cohabitation, the differences between those with XYY or XXY syndrome and controls were very low for some crimes, but some still showed an increase, such as sexual abuse, arson and others.

Stochholm et al. (2012) concluded that, when social variables were controlled for, the risk of conviction was similar to controls. However, there was an increased risk of convictions for sexual abuse, burglary, arson and 'others'. The researchers concluded that the raised risk of conviction was down to socioeconomic conditions that related to having the syndromes.

Re and Birkhoff (2015): review of the evidence about 47,XYY syndrome and deviance

Re and Birkhoff (2015) provide a review of evidence over the last 50 years relating to XYY syndrome and crime. Their conclusion is that there is no link between XYY syndrome and crime. Re and Birkhoff focus on the question 'Are we born guilty?' Re and Birkhoff raise the idea that XYY syndrome can be associated with problems with impulse control, low tolerance of frustration, aggressiveness and a tendency towards anti-social behaviour (e.g. Ross et al., 2009). However, these features might also link with environmental factors, such as dysfunctional families (e.g. Witkin et al., 1976). Re and Birkhoff refer to Linden and Bender (2002), which suggests that XYY needs to be found early so that there can be intervention in families and in the child's education to reduce the effects of the disorder. The main focus here, when considering Re and Birkhoff's (2015) review, is to look at findings relating the aggressiveness, deviance and criminal behaviour. Studies tend to show no relationship between XYY syndrome and criminal or aggressive behaviour. For example, Welch et al., cited in Re and Birkhoff (2015), in their study on inmates with aggressive, mental retardation and tallness, concluded that since only one of these inmates had XYY syndrome it could not be claimed that XYY related with aggression, deviance or a low IQ. Those doing studies in prisons did find men there with XYY syndrome. However, as Witkin et al. (1976) point out (page 224), when there are differences between XYY and XY males, these can be explained by social factors. Witkin et al. (1977, cited in Re and Birkhoff, 2015) found that crimes committed by prisoners with XYY syndrome tended to be minor and without violence, and they did not find more crime in those with XYY syndrome. Theilgaard (1983, cited in Re and Birkhoff, 2015) found no evidence that XYY males are more aggressive or violent than XY males and no more likely to commit crime.

The review of Re and Birkhoff did find some evidence linking XYY to crime. Gosavi et al. (2009, cited in Re and Birkhoff, 2015) looked at 94 criminals convicted of murder in India and said there was an association between the criminal behaviour and XYY syndrome. Briken et al. (2006, cited in Re and Birkhoff, 2015) suggested a link between XYY chromosome abnormality and sexual offences when they looked at 166 offenders with characteristics of XYY and analysed 13 of them, finding three of them with XYY syndrome. However, other studies tend to suggest that, even when there is a link, it tends to come from unfavourable living conditions and not from genes (e.g. Stochholm et al., 2012). Re and Birkhoff (2015) conclude that XYY syndrome is not shown conclusively to relate to crime or anti-social behaviour. There is evidence that people with XYY syndrome have deficits in IQ, language and speech delays, learning disabilities, poor writing ability and social and emotional problems. It has been suggested that some disorders such as attention deficit hyperactivity disorder (ADHD), pervasive development disorder, autism spectrum disorder, some issues with control over impulsivity, aggressiveness and some other disorders and features might connect together and be found in someone with XYY syndrome. Within these characteristics, there might be a link between XYY and criminality, but not directly, as has been shown. Re and Birkhoff (2015), importantly, end by emphasising a possible link between features of XYY syndrome and social and environmental factors – a link that might help to explain a correlation between XYY syndrome and prison populations, and a link that something can be done about. Re and Birkhoff (2015) point out that the analysis of studies in their review 'shows that there is no statistical evidence that a 47,XYY man is predisposed, just because of genotype, to aggressive and deviant behaviour'.

Table 3.7 Five studies used in Re and Birkhoff's (2015) review and their conclusions

Study	Population	Number of participants	Number of 47,XYY males	Conclusion
Fryns et al. (1995)	1963–1992 patients in the Lueven Centre for Human Genetics	98,725	50	XYY males with mild to borderline 'mental retardation' have more behavioural abnormalities.
Götz et al. (1999)	1967–1979 infants at birth	34,380	19	Found low IQ and slightly more anti-social behaviour when looking at 16 XYY males and 45 controls.
Gosavi et al. (2009)	Convicted murderers in India	94	2	XYY and criminal behaviour show an association. Needs more research.
Briken et al. (2006)	Sexual offenders	13	3	High frequency of XYY males in sexual homicide.
Stochholm et al. (2012)	XYY male criminals aged 15–70	161	161	A moderately increased risk of conviction in XYY men but the increase goes when socioeconomic variables are controlled for.

List ten variables/characteristics other than chromosomal difference that have been suggested might explain any findings that those with XYY syndrome are or were over-represented in the prison population.

Gender and XYY as an explanation for criminal and anti-social behaviour

In other explanations for criminal and anti-social behaviour, it has been possible to discuss gender differences. However, XYY relates to males only, and therefore XYY is an explanation for criminal and anti-social behaviour that can focus only on males.

XYY syndrome used to be thought of as, and sometimes called, 'super-male' disease because males with an XYY chromosomal pattern tended to be tall and have a large build, and they were thought to be aggressive and non-empathic. However, this is no longer what is thought about XYY. Nonetheless the syndrome does affect just males and they can be labelled in some way and can fulfil any expectations that a culture has about masculinity when judging their masculinity differently from the 'norm' with regard to height and build. Gender is an issue in XYY because of how such boys/men are seen in a society, rather than it being an issue between boys and girls.

Summary of gender differences in XYY affecting crime and anti-social behaviour

XYY syndrome is a chromosomal issue in males only, so differences between males and females cannot be discussed with regard to this explanation. The 'male' aspect of XYY, however, can affect the individual because environmental factors, such as labels, can affect an individual, possibly through a self-fulfilling prophecy (page 224), and it is likely to be labels relating to masculinity that apply.

Evaluation of XYY syndrome as an explanation of crime and anti-social behaviour

Strengths

- If XYY syndrome is found early, and around 25 per cent seem likely to be found before birth, then issues around physical development, and behavioural and emotional issues can be addressed early (e.g. Re and Birkhoff, 2015). Studies seem to suggest that it is not that an XYY chromosome pattern leads to criminality, but there might be labelling and a self-fulfilling prophecy that can lead those with XYY syndrome into crime. A strength of examining XYY syndrome is that from results of studies action can be taken to prevent a link with criminality. This is not so much a strength of the explanation of crime and anti-social behaviour because there appears not to be a link between XYY and crime; it is a strength of researching into such a link, to help to prevent it.

- There is a lot of research into XYY syndrome and deviant behaviour so reviews such as Re and Birkhoff (2015) can show rather conclusively that a link is not shown. Having a lot of evidence can help to support an argument, although in this case there is little support for the explanation (that XYY syndrome leads to crime and anti-social behaviour) from the evidence.

Weaknesses

- A problem with studies looking at XXY and XYY syndrome is the classifying of the men into XXY, XYY or XY patterns, as this has been incorrect in some studies. XYY syndrome tends to lead to men being extra tall and having acne and scars, and possibly these were the characteristics that were used to classify the men, which is not enough to be sure they were XYY.

- Even in studies that find XYY does relate to crime, even if not to a great extent, such as Gosavi et al. (2009, cited in Re and Birkhoff, 2015), there could be labelling and a self-fulfilling prophecy as the cause of the link. This point relates to the issue about nature–nurture. Genetically, someone might have XYY syndrome but any effect from the genetic difference can be down to environmental influences. A problem is in splitting nature and nurture when looking for a cause.

Issues and debates

When it is thought that genes, such as XYY syndrome, can affect how someone is seen in a society and how they are treated because of it, that is a useful example of how nature–nurture interact and are not separate. Stochholm et al. (2012), for example, can be used as evidence for this idea. You can use this argument when discussing the nature–nurture debate, which is one of the issues and debates in your course.

Personality as an explanation of crime and anti-social behaviour

Certain personalities have been related to criminal and anti-social behaviour. It is suggested that looking for a specific personality to explain crime and anti-social behaviour would mean such behaviour can be attributed to just some people and not everyone (Barlow, 1990, cited in Reid, 2011). If we can 'blame' someone's personality, that could mean nobody else is to blame. However, 'personality' is hard to pin down. The section above, which looks at XYY syndrome and finds few links between XYY syndrome and criminal behaviour, except for possible links associated to how people with XYY syndrome are treated in society, shows that popular opinion is not always supported by **empirical** evidence. With 'personality ' too it can be claimed that, although it is a way of categorising people, personality might not be something that 'exists' outside its label. There are researchers who say that personality is not a useful concept when explaining crime (e.g. Brown, 2006, cited in Reid, 2011). However, there is research that does relate personality to crime, as discussed in this section.

Year One link: You will have looked at personality in social psychology when studying obedience and prejudice as in both cases personality has been said to have a role. You can draw on your understanding of personality from social psychology when looking at personality as a biological explanation of crime and anti-social behaviour.

Temperament

It is generally accepted that people are born with a **temperament**. Temperament is also discussed in Chapter Four, which focuses on child psychology. Temperament means the aspects of personality that are deemed to be innate, and these include extraversion and introversion, which are discussed later when considering Eysenck's biological theory of personality. Some models of personality that relate personality to crime draw on temperament, such as Cloninger's model, which is a **biosocial model**, so temperament is part of theory relating personality to crime. When looking at personality as a biological explanation of crime and anti-social behaviour, it is temperament that is important, although 'personality' tends to be the term used.

Definitions

Empirical data are data gathered directly through touch, smell, taste, sound or sight.

Temperament refers to the innate part of personality, the part that is in our biology. A **biosocial model** of crime draws on genes, neuropsychology, environment and evolution to explain criminal behaviour and brings in temperament as an innate factor.

Models of personality used in criminological research

Akers and Sellers (2009, cited in Reid, 2011) discuss ways in which personality has been linked to crime and anti-social behaviour. One way has been to develop models of personality to see which traits in a person relate to anti-social behaviour.

Four personality models based on traits have been used in criminological research:

- The five-factor model (FFM) (McCrae and Costa, 1990): the five traits are often called the 'Big Five': agreeableness, conscientiousness, openness, neuroticism and extraversion. McCrae and Costa thought that these five traits are universal and can be used to describe personality in different countries and cultures. The Big Five are also thought to have biological underpinnings, as discussed later in this section.
- The psychoticism-extraversion-neuroticism (PEN) scale (Eysenck, 1977): in this model anti-social behaviour is said to come from high levels of psychoticism, neuroticism and extraversion. Eysenck's model is considered later in this section.
- Tellegen's three-factor model (1985, cited in Reid, 2011): Tellegen's three factors can be related to Eysenck's three dimensions. Tellegen has positive affect/feelings as one of his factors, and that can go with extraversion. Tellegen has negative affect/feelings as another factor than can go with neuroticism. The third factor is constraint avoidance, which can go with psychoticism.
- The temperament and character model (Cloninger et al., 1993): Cloninger et al. suggested anti-social behaviour is

linked to low avoidance of harm, high novelty-seeking and low dependence on reward. Cloninger *et al.*'s ideas too can be related to Eysenck's three dimensions. There is behavioural activation and novelty seeking, which goes with extraversion, and behavioural inhibition and harm avoidance, which goes with neuroticism. A third dimension for Cloninger *et al.* is behavioural maintenance and dependence on reward, which can go with psychoticism.

Explore
Biological dimensions of personality are considered in the following article: www.personalityresearch.org/pen.html

Another way of looking at personality according to Akers and Sellers (2009, cited in Reid, 2011) is to see some people as deviant and abnormal with a 'criminal personality'. This is about psychopaths and characteristics, such as being harming and manipulative as well as callous and self-centred. This is a disorder, now considered 'anti-social personality' rather than psychopath or sociopath, and is in the DSM-IV-TR.

In your course, you have to look at personality as a biological explanation of crime and anti-social behaviour so both the 'personality trait' explanation and the 'anti-social personality disorder' explanation are considered here.

The Big Five personality traits

The Big Five refer to agreeableness, conscientiousness, openness, neuroticism and extraversion. These are frequently referred to when personality is discussed.

Year One link: You may have come across the Big Five in social psychology when looking at personality relating to obedience and prejudice so you can review your learning there.

In your course, you focus on personality as a biological explanation of crime and anti-social behaviour so it is important to link personality to biology. Jang *et al.* (1996) used a twin study to look at the Big Five personality traits and linked them to genetic underpinnings. They used 123 pairs of identical twins and 127 pairs of non-identical twins and found genetic influence in all of the Big Five dimensions of personality. They found between 40 and 60 per cent to be down to genes. Neuroticism came out at 41 per cent, extraversion at 53 per cent, openness at 61 per cent, agreeableness at 41 per cent and conscientiousness at 44 per cent, all quite high figures. However, there is

clearly a role for environment too in such personality dimensions as the figures are not 100 per cent. This means that identical twins were more similar in these dimensions than non-identical twins; however, they were not wholly identical. Jang *et al.* (1996) found that non-shared environment accounted for the rest with regard to each dimension, so clearly people's environment does affect their personality as well as their biology. This relates to the nature–nurture debate, giving evidence for a result that is frequently found when looking at biology versus environment, which is that about half of our characteristics, including personality, are down to our biology and our nature, and the other half are down to our nurture.

Year One link: You may have chosen to look at Brendgen *et al.* (2005), which was a twin study listed as one of the contemporary studies in biological psychology. They looked at non-shared and biological aspects of social and physical aggression, which has a similar focus to Jang *et al.*'s study. Brendgen *et al.* found evidence for biological causes for physical aggression and evidence for non-shared environmental effects for social aggression. Brendgen *et al.*, like Jang *et al.* and other twin studies, showed that there are both genetic and environmental factors for many characteristics, such as aggression and personality factors.

Eysenck's theory of personality includes neuroticism and extraversion. However, psychoticism makes up 'disagreeableness' and 'non-conscientiousness' so although similar to the Big Five, his theory has differences. As has been shown by Jang *et al.* (1996), neuroticism and extraversion have been shown to have genetic underpinning and Eysenck also thought that personality, focusing on extraversion, neuroticism and psychoticism, had a biological basis. There is evidence that the Big Five have biological underpinnings.

Eysenck's personality theory of crime

Eysenck has a well-known theory of personality which relates to crime. Eysenck suggested that personality is divided into dimensions, including an extravert–introvert scale and neurotic–stable scale, and he later added a psychoticism scale. He thought that extraverts need excitement so are more likely to seek out crime, and also they do not condition easily. By this, he meant that classical conditioning, associating stimuli with responses, and operant conditioning, which suggests that we repeat what we are rewarded for doing, do not have the same effects on extraverts. This would suggest extraverts would be more involved in criminal or anti-social behaviour. Also people high in psychoticism, according to Eysenck (1982), are egocentric, impulsive, cold, lacking in empathy for others and aggressive. Eysenck (1977) thought that extraversion, instability (neuroticism) and psychoticism would characterise criminals according to his theory of personality.

Progress check 3.16

You have looked at various biological explanations for crime and anti-social behaviour up to now and one of them mentioned a difficulty with 'being conditioned'. Which explanation was that?

Three dimensions of personality according to Eysenck

The three dimensions of personality have not been fully explained up to now and neither have they been linked clearly to crime and anti-social behaviour. In this section, the dimensions will be explained and then examined with regard to how they link to biology. Finally, they are linked to criminal and anti-social behaviour.

With regard to the dimensions, here is a brief outline of what characterises each personality (Eysenck and Eysenck, 1985, cited in Jang, 1998):

- Someone high in extraversion is sociable, optimistic, popular and might be unreliable.
- Someone low in extraversion is quiet, reserved, reliable and introspective.
- Someone high in neuroticism is moody, unstable, worried and anxious.
- Someone low in neuroticism is even-tempered, calm, emotionally stable and carefree.
- Someone with high psychoticism is hostile, socially withdrawn, uncooperative and troublesome.
- Someone with low psychoticism is sociable, empathic, conventional and altruistic.

What is interesting is that Eysenck and Eysenck (1985) suggest that the three dimensions – extraversion, neuroticism and psychoticism – are universal, which means they are found in all cultures.

Issues and debates

Eysenck found that his three personality dimensions were universal as they are found in different cultures. The Eysenck Personality Inventory was used in different countries and the

three dimensions were found consistently. You can use this as an example of cross-cultural research and as an example of nature in the nature–nurture debate.

Explore

The paper by Jang (1998) on Eysenck's personalities can be found here: www.personalityresearch.org/papers/jang.html

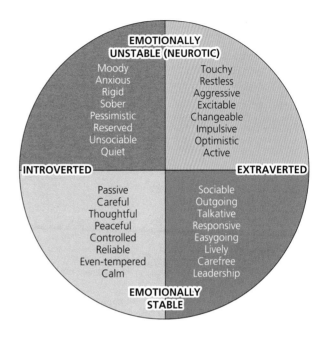

Eysenck's idea about introversion and extraversion and neuroticism and stability. The psychoticism dimension was added later.

Extraversion, introversion and arousal

Eysenck (1977) linked arousal levels to extraversion. Arousal is a biological reaction that can be measured by skin conductance, sweating or brain activity. Arousal involves activation of the reticular activating system, which is in the brain stem, and there is also activation of the autonomic nervous system and the endocrine system.

STUDY HINT

This is a small detail, but note that extraversion is 'extra' and introversion is 'intro' as it is easy to muddle up the terms.

Arousal and the autonomic nervous system

The autonomic nervous system (ANS) is involved in the fight-or-flight response, which is arousal. It involves the body getting ready for action and this is done by the sympathetic part of the autonomic nervous system. Heart rate speeds up, digestion is affected, as is breathing rate, and pupils dilate, all to help the body to act quickly. The parasympathetic part of the autonomic nervous system plays the part of getting the body state back to resting. If the body is in a more or less permanent state of arousal, the immune system is affected as well as the body's workings. The body is always ready for action so energy is being used up. This really is what stress is – the body ready for action and not having the chance to go back into a resting state. Deep breathing, relaxation and drinking water can be good strategies to help the body to 'stand down' from the arousal state. Stress is defined as not thinking you have the resources to cope. You can see that this might lead to being permanently in a state of arousal.

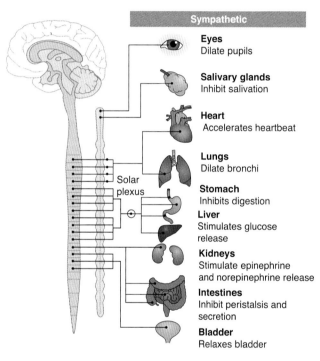

The role of the sympathetic part of the autonomic nervous system, preparing for fight or flight

Arousal in the cortex

There is also cortical arousal, which means the brain is ready for action. Neurotransmitters are involved, including acetylcholine, norepinephrine, dopamine and serotonin. Stimulation of the neurons in the arousal system gives brain activity. The limbic system and posterior cortex are two areas in the brain's arousal system and, for example, activation of the locus coeruleus releases norepinephrine to give wakefulness. There is activation in the dopaminergic

system as well. Brain regions that are involved include the nucleus accumbens, the striatum forebrain, the prefrontal cortex and the limbic system – you will have come across these areas in your course before, e.g. when looking at the reward pathways in the brain. You don't have to know about the brain's arousal system in much detail but it is worth knowing something about it as it relates to Eysenck's ideas about biological elements of personality affecting behaviour.

Year One link: You looked at how neurotransmitters work at the synapse in biological psychology so recall that material to help in understanding how personality can relate to biology.

Arousal in the reticular activating system

The reticular activating system (RAS) is important in Eysenck's theory – in particular, the ascending reticular activating system (ARAS), which refers to messages 'ascending' through the brain stem and into the brain. The reticular activating system is responsible for wakefulness and moving between sleep and waking states. The RAS connects the brain stem to the cortex and includes connections with the thalamus and hypothalamus as well as other areas. Its purpose relates to wakefulness and sleep, with faster brain waves showing wakefulness and REM sleep and slow waves showing non-REM sleep. When someone is awake the ARAS receives sensory information and relays it to the cortex. The reticular activating system also controls the fight-or-flight response. The RAS has excitatory and inhibitory functions which affect neurotransmitter transmission to achieve states of wakefulness or sleep.

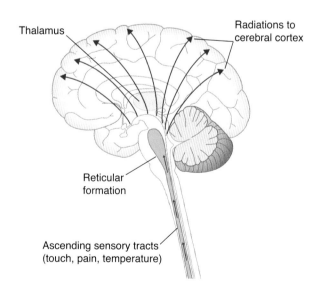

The brain stem reticular formation

Explore
You can find out more about the reticular activating system using this link:
www.just.edu.jo/~mafika/226_NS/RAS_EEG_226.htm

Eysenck linked extraversion to a state of arousal in the brain, which is one of the ways that his theory of personality is biological. Extraverts are under-aroused and need external stimulation. Eysenck talks about nervous systems as being strong or weak. He points out that a strong or weak nervous system relates to his extraversion and introversion dimension, with 'weak' linking to introvert and 'strong' linking to extravert (Eysenck, 1967). Gray (1964, cited in Eysenck and Levey, 1972) showed that the 'strong' and 'weak' nervous system being referred to relates to arousal of the reticular activating formation, and Eysenck (1967) agrees. Low thresholds of the reticular activating system relating to sending signals to the brain (referring to activation happening quickly, meaning a low threshold before there is activity) would relate to a 'weak' nervous system and introversion. High thresholds (referring to activity happening more slowly as there is a higher threshold to reach) would relate to extraversion and a 'strong' nervous system. The inhibitory influence of the RAS on brain activity has a different effect, with low thresholds of this influence (inhibition of action happens more quickly) relating to the strong nervous system and extraversion. According to Eysenck and Levey, there is some evidence for this. A 'weak' nervous system can mean low thresholds before there is activity, which means activity happens sooner. Therefore, for an introvert, activity happens sooner. High thresholds for activity means activity is triggered later so for an extravert it takes longer for there to be activity, which characterises a 'strong' nervous system. As evidence for this idea, introverts (with a weak nervous system) would have lower pain thresholds as activation would happen sooner, and this is found (Smith, 1968, cited in Eysenck and Levey, 1972).

Geen (1984) also showed that introverts had higher arousal levels as they chose a lower level of noise than did extraverts so for introverts the optimal level of stimulation given by the noise was not as loud as for extraverts – the arousal for introverts happened more quickly. Geen took this to show that introverts were at a higher level of arousal than extraverts. Eysenck argues that introversion relates to greater brain arousal (excitation) as activity happens more quickly, and relates to greater likelihood of conditioning occurring, given that activation happens more quickly. Eysenck found that there were particular conditions with regard to introversion relating to more conditioning taking place. He found that introverts react

better to partial reinforcement because reinforcement acted more quickly for introverts and so partial reinforcement would give an association quickly. He also found that weak unconditioned stimuli worked better for introverts; strong unconditioned stimuli did not. For example, a weak puff of air could cause the eye blink and a conditioned stimulus to be related to the eye blink in an introvert – there was no need for a strong puff of air. Also for introverts conditioning worked better if there was a small gap between the conditioned and unconditioned stimulus being presented together. A small gap between the two led to an association being quickly formed.

Year One link: Recall features of classical conditioning and Pavlov's work from your study of learning theories.

STUDY HINT
You need to be able to relate Eysenck's personality theory to biological functioning, so you should take some of the evidence here to show how introversion and extraversion relate to someone's biological make-up. The personality explanation of crime and anti-social behaviour is biological, so be sure to learn the underpinning biology.

Progress check 3.17
Explain one piece of evidence that shows that introversion means a low threshold for activity, so activity happens more quickly, and extraversion means a high threshold, so activity happens more slowly.

Neuroticism and arousal

Neuroticism links to activation thresholds in the sympathetic nervous system so, like extraversion, has biological underpinning. Neuroticism in someone with a low activation threshold regarding the fight-or-flight response, which is activated by the sympathetic part of the autonomic nervous system, would mean being jumpy and experiencing a fight-or-flight reaction to what others would see as minor stressors. The other end of the neuroticism scale is stability and stable people, with a high activation threshold, would have a slower-to-respond fight-or-flight reaction and would be calmer in the face of stressors.

Psychoticism and testosterone or size of brain regions

Psychoticism seems to relate to hormones, in particular testosterone, and to aggression. There are links to the sex hormones, and psychoticism might relate to how much testosterone is released into the body by the endocrine system. If psychoticism relates to testosterone, then you would expect people high on the psychoticism dimension to be male, which is what Eysenck found. However, women do have testosterone in their bodies, which can account for the women high in psychoticism. Psychoticism is perhaps also related to high levels of cortisol in the central nervous system (Eysenck, 1998) and those high in psychoticism might have low levels of cortical arousal, as do extraverts.

Another feature of arousal, which is a different explanation from Eysenck's but of interest, is Gur *et al.*'s (2002) idea that it is the size of the amygdala, hippocampus and other limbic regions that goes with emotional arousal in relation to the size of the frontal cortex, which controls behaviour. Gur *et al.* found that women have a larger frontal brain area in relation to the limbic regions than do men and this might show why women have more control over impulses so are less often found at the high end of the psychoticism dimension. Psychoticism means low in impulse control so this explanation might show why there are fewer women at the higher end of the psychoticism scale.

Year One link: You have looked at the role of hormones, including testosterone, in aggression so you can relate that learning to Eysenck's ideas about personality and, in particular, psychoticism.

Eysenck's personality theory as an explanation of crime and anti-social behaviour

Having looked at Eysenck's biological theory of personality, it is important to relate it to crime and anti-social behaviour. You can see that there is evidence for Eysenck's theory relating to biology as he links aspects of someone's biology to their behaviour. For him, behaviour is determined by biology. **Determinism** means every action and situation is given and predetermined rather than changed by events around it. The conditions around a situation are such that the situation could not be any other way. This means people have no way of changing what 'is'. Eysenck's personality theory, being rooted in biology, means that their behaviour is determined by their biology. For example, introverts are more easily conditioned and need less stimulation as well as being more quickly stimulated, such as having a lower pain threshold. Extraverts seek out arousal and condition less easily and these factors are *determined* by biology not changed or changeable by the environment.

Explanation
Determinism is the idea that an action or situation has to occur as it has occurred because of preceding factors and universal laws. Something that is determined, such as our biology, cannot be changed by definition.

Clearly when relating Eysenck's theory to crime and anti-social behaviour, it is a biological theory of personality and it is someone's personality that leads them into crime and anti-social behaviour.

Eysenck thought that anti-social behaviour and crime would come from someone high in extraversion in that their arousal levels would be low and so they would seek stimulation. It would also relate to neuroticism because the fight-or-flight reaction would be quicker to trigger in someone high in neuroticism so there might be more aggression found than in someone more stable. There would be more anti-social behaviour in someone high in psychoticism too, which relates to aggression.

Eysenck *et al.* (1977)

Eysenck *et al.* (1977) wanted to use personality variables to classify criminal behaviour, focusing on extraversion, neuroticism and psychoticism. They used 156 prisoners with an age range of 18–38. They classified the prisoners into those who had carried out 'violent' crimes, 'property' crimes and 'fraud' crimes. There were two other categories, called 'inadequates', who were those with a lot of convictions over a short time but not violent crimes or robbery, and 'residual', into which they put all the prisoners who did not fit into the four other categories. They used the Eysenck Personality Questionnaire (EPQ) as well as physical measures, such as EEG (electroencephalograph, which measures heart rate), eye blink and skin conductance. They found that conmen had low psychoticism scores and those in the 'violent' and 'property' categories had low scores in neuroticism compared with the high scores for those in the 'residual' and 'inadequate' category. Extraversion did the opposite to neuroticism, with those in 'residual' and 'inadequate' categories having low scores and 'violent' and 'property' criminals having high extraversion scores, though there was not a statistically significant difference. The conclusion was that criminal behaviour could be predicted by personality type, at least to an extent. The EPQ is the questionnaire used and the Eysenck Personality Inventory (EPI) is the result of the questionnaire.

Explore
You can see the questions asked using the Eysenck Personality Inventory using this link, and there is a study to read about too, looking at the reliability of the EPI: http://medind.nic.in/icg/t09/i1/icgt09i1p27.pdf

Table 3.8 The findings of Eysenck *et al.* (1977)

Personality characteristic	Category of crime	Low or high incidence
Psychoticism	Conmen (fraud)	Low
Neuroticism	Violent crime or property crime	Low
Neuroticism	Residual or inadequate	High
Extraversion	Violent crime or property crime	High
Extraversion	Residual or inadequate	Low

Progress check 3.18

How does Table 3.8 give support for Eysenck's claim that extraversion and neuroticism are different types of personality?

Explore

You can read Reid's (2011) article about crime and personality here if you would like to know more:
www.studentpulse.com/articles/377/crime-and-personality-personality-theory-and-criminality-examined

Eysenck *et al.* showed some evidence linking extraversion to violent crime, though perhaps little evidence that neuroticism and psychoticism relate to aggression and anti-social behaviour.

Other evidence for Eysenck's biological theory

McGurk and McDougal (1981) compared 100 delinquent with 100 non-delinquent college students and found the delinquent group higher in psychoticism, extraversion and neuroticism, as Eysenck's theory would predict. The non-delinquent students were low in extraversion and neuroticism. This supports Eysenck's PEN theory relating to crime and anti-social behaviour. Steiner *et al.* (1999) showed a link between being high in psychoticism and showing a pattern of recidivism, which means re-offending frequently. This too supports Eysenck's theory.

Explore

You can explore biological aspects of criminal behaviour, including Eysenck's personality theory, using this link:
www.integratedsociopsychology.net/crime-biological_factors4.html

Progress check 3.19

McGurk and McDougal (1981) compared two groups when drawing their conclusions. Explain what they did and the advantage of doing this when considering the strength of the conclusions.

STUDY HINT

When reading about the findings of studies, it is useful to consider the method(s) used so you are ready to evaluate the study.

Progress check 3.20

What was a possible limitation of McGurk and McDougal's (1981) method?

Evaluation of Eysenck's personality theory as an explanation of crime and anti-social behaviour

Strengths

- The data Eysenck and others gather as evidence for his personality theory tend to come from the Eysenck Personality Inventory (EPI). This has been found to have reliability. Tiwari *et al.* (2012) used a short form of the EPI, a Hindi edition (EPQRS-H), to test it for reliability. They used 78 men and 124 women in India and administered the questionnaire, which consists of 48 items that assess neuroticism, psychoticism, extraversion and lying. They found that the items did measure neuroticism, lying and extraversion and so showed reliability. However, it was not so good at identifying psychoticism. Reliability can be tested because the items used are such that the same thing is asked in a different way and those items that are the 'same' can be checked to see if they are answered consistently. Tiwari *et al.* felt that the scale had internal consistency, even though they queried the reliability of its measuring of psychoticism.

- The EPI can be used for practical purposes and if it gives predictions that are useful in practical situations it has validity. Eysenck's theory can help to explain crime and anti-social behaviour. It also helps in other fields. Bartram (1995) looked at the EPI to see how useful it was in selecting people to become pilots (he used the 16PF too, another personality test, but here the EPI is focused on). He found that people who apply for training to become pilots tend to be emotionally stable and more extraverted than the general population. The EPI helped to pick out personality factors that matched other selection criteria when it came to selecting applicants for pilot training, which suggests it has validity.

- Eysenck's model has been supported using experiments, which gives it strength, as they are scientific and can yield cause-and-effect conclusions. Experiments have been done, for example, related to classical conditioning.

Weaknesses

- There are issues with using the EPI to measure personality, including the query that Tiwari *et al.* raised about its reliability in respect of the psychoticism dimension. Tiwari *et al.* cite Katz and Francis (2000), Ivkovic *et al.* (2007) and others as also finding low internal consistency regarding psychoticism.
- Jang looks at the difficulty in Eysenck's model whereby impulsivity was originally in the extraversion part of his model but was then moved to psychoticism, where he felt it fitted better. This is not really explained and, if traits can be moved between dimensions, this seems rather arbitrary and does not support the model. Gray (1981) too felt that impulsivity should not have been moved. Gray felt that impulsivity and anxiety are important dimensions of personality. Clearly the traits that fit into the main factors are open to discussion, which suggests the model might be more about labelling than about 'fact'.

> **STUDY HINT**
> You have looked at the amygdala, XYY syndrome and brain injury as biological explanations of crime and anti-social behaviour so you can use those other explanations to evaluate Eysenck's personality theory of crime and anti-social behaviour. One way to evaluate a theory is to make one point about there being strong evidence for an alternative.

Progress check 3.21

Make a bullet list of strengths and weaknesses of Eysenck's biological personality explanation of crime and anti-social behaviour.

> **STUDY HINT**
> When evaluation points are written in detail, it can be useful to summarise them in a list or a table to help your learning.

Personality trait model and personality disorder

There is a difference between personality traits as an explanation for crime and anti-social behaviour and personality disorder as an explanation. Personality

disorders include paranoid, schizotypal, anti-social and borderline disorders. These are mental disorders diagnosed using a system like the DSM. Personality disorders are not accepted by all clinicians as evidence for them is scarce. Personality traits are found in everyone and are not disorders. Anti-social personality disorder is of interest when considering explanations of crime and anti-social behaviour, as are personality trait theories.

Anti-social personality disorder statistics

In North America, anti-social personality disorder is found in 4.5 per cent of men and 0.8 per cent of women, according to Robins *et al.* (1991), and 6.8 per cent in men and 0.8 per cent in women, according to Swanson *et al.* (1994). This shows that it is predominantly found in males. Torgensen *et al.* (2001) found 1.3 per cent in men and 0 per cent in women in a study in Europe, and another European study (Coid *et al.*, 2006) found 1 per cent in men and 0.2 per cent in women. Still the gender difference is found, even though there is a lower figure in Europe. However, Yang and Coid (2007) suggest that the condition is more severe in women, despite it being found less often. Fazel and Danesh (2002) found from looking worldwide at prison populations that the figures for anti-social personality disorder were 47 per cent of the population for men and 21 per cent for women, and in the UK 63 per cent of male remand prisoners, 49 per cent of male sentenced prisoners and 31 per cent of female prisoners are diagnosed with anti-social personality disorder (Singleton *et al.*, 1998). These figures come from the National Institute of Health (NIH) site in the US. Of course the diagnosis is what features highly in prison populations, especially in men. However, it is important to note that the diagnosis includes 'breaking the law repeatedly' and 'not showing remorse' as two of the features of the diagnosis, so it might be that anti-social personality disorder is a label for people whose behaviour and characteristics are such that they are likely to find themselves in prison (e.g. for showing anti-social or criminal behaviour).

Anti-social personality disorder as a biological explanation for crime and anti-social behaviour

Not only are there theories about personality and crime related to personality traits, like Eysenck's, but there is also interest in personality disorders and how these relate to crime and anti-social behaviour.

A diagnosis of anti-social personality disorder

Anti-social personality disorder features impulsive behaviour that is irresponsible and can be criminal. Characteristics of such a disorder include someone being manipulative, reckless and not caring about other people's feelings. Psychopathy is a severe form of anti-social personality disorder. The disorder affects men more than women and can come from a home where there is alcohol addiction or harsh parenting. This suggests there are environmental factors associated with anti-social personality disorder. However, Eysenck's theory of crime and anti-social behaviour includes the dimension of psychoticism, which seems to match the personality of someone with anti-social personality disorder and might relate to someone's biology.

The diagnosis of anti-social personality disorder is given if someone is aged 18 or over and exhibits three of the following, though importantly not when the behaviours come from another mental disorder:
- breaking the law repeatedly
- repeatedly being deceitful
- showing impulsivity and not planning ahead
- being irritable and aggressive
- showing a disregard for their own safety or the safety of others
- showing irresponsible behaviour consistently
- not showing remorse.

(Source: NHS website)

Psychoticism related to anti-social personality disorder

- Psychoticism was characterised earlier as hostile, socially withdrawn, uncooperative and troublesome.
- Anti-social personality disorder is characterised by being irritable and aggressive (hostile), showing irresponsible behaviour consistently (uncooperative) and breaking the law repeatedly (troublesome).
- You can see that the two 'labels' correspond to an extent.

Progress check 3.22

Explain how anti-social personality disorder is diagnosed.

Explore

Explore the Mind website to find out more about different personality disorders: www.mind.org.uk/information-support/types-of-mental-health-problems/personality-disorders/types-of-personality-disorder/#.VcOaLWBREok

STUDY HINT

When you look at social explanations of crime and anti-social behaviour, you will read about labelling and the self-fulfilling prophecy. You can use the idea of labelling to explain how someone might come to show the features of anti-social personality disorder from their experiences and perhaps not because of their biology.

Davison and Janca (2012): anti-social personality relates to factors other than just personality

Davison and Janca (2012) show that there is a well-established connection between anti-social personality disorder and criminal behaviour. Davison and Janca (2012) review the literature that relates personality disorder to offending. They say that personality disorder is found in serious offenders but personality disorder might feature more in some offences than others. Disorders that seem to relate to personality disorder include stalkers perhaps and men who kill their children. Davison and Janca (2012) conclude from their review that there are a lot of variables that go with personality traits and it is not just 'personality' when it comes to understanding crime and anti-social behaviour. Variables they list include substance misuse, mood disorders, ADHD, maladaptive cognitions, anger and situational factors. It is important to note that personality alone does not explain crime and anti-social behaviour – this is a useful evaluation point.

Explore

You can read Davison and Janca's (2012) paper using this link: www.medscape.com/viewarticle/754975_2

Moss et al. (1990): anti-social personality disorder can be affected by serotonin functioning

Moss et al. (1990) look at anti-social personality disorder and substance abuse to see if this is related to changes in response to serotonin, which is about biological explanations. Moss et al. (1990) used 15 men with anti-social personality disorder and 12 controls. They measured prolactin and cortisol responses in the men who were given m-CPP, which is a serotonin agonist. They found that those with anti-social personality disorder had a significantly lower prolactin response to the m-CPP than the controls and they had a significantly larger serotonin response than the controls. There was more aggression, negative feelings and needs in those with the lower prolactin response but no significant relationship between cortisol measures and other factors that were measured, such as aggression. Impulsivity did not relate to either cortisol or prolactin measures. The conclusion was that altering serotonin functioning was associated with aggression in those with anti-social personality disorder, which gives some evidence for biological issues being involved in anti-social personality disorder. However, Moss et al. in their introduction suggest that anti-social personality comes through genes *and* environment (Crowe, 1974, cited in Moss et al., 1990), suggesting it is not all about biology.

Perez (2012): psychopathy relates to impairment in the frontal cortex but also environmental issues

Perez (2012) looked at psychopathy and in particular brain dysfunction, such as showing impairment in the orbital frontal cortex, an area for executive functioning, so problems there can relate to problems with impulse control. Perez also found a strong correlation between attachment disorder and anti-social personality disorder, which agrees with the findings of Fonagy *et al.* (1997) and also suggests anti-social personality disorder, while perhaps being about brain region functioning, is not all down to someone's biology.

Fonagy *et al.* (1997): borderline personality disorder caused by disordered attachments

Fonagy *et al.* (1997) discuss the importance of early experiences, including attachment patterns between infants and their caregivers, as an explanation for crime and anti-social behaviour. Their explanation focuses on the development of an internal working model for relationships that comes from early experiences and they suggest that problems with an internal working model can explain later anti-social behaviour. Delinquent adolescents may have attachment disorder. One issue that might arise from having poor early attachments is that someone might not develop abilities in understanding the feelings and states of other people. This explanation of borderline personality disorder is not a biological one but shows that there are alternative explanations.

There are elements of biology in Fonagy *et al.*'s explanation, however, in that infants' formation of an attachment with a caregiver is thought to be an evolved state as an attachment aids survival.

Year One link: The idea of early attachment patterns being used to form an internal working model for later relationships comes from the psychodynamic approach to psychology and from Freud's ideas about the importance of early childhood and the development of the id, ego and superego. This is Freud's explanation of personality. You can draw on what you learned about Freud's theory in biological psychology to help in understanding Fonagy *et al.*'s 1997 points about crime and anti-social behaviour.

Progress check 3.23

Complete the table by putting the names of the studies against the summary of their findings.

Name of the study	Findings
	Specific disorders seem to relate to personality disorder, such as stalkers and men who kill their children. There are a lot of variables that go with personality traits to explain anti-social behaviour.
	In psychopathy, there is brain dysfunction, such as impairment in the orbital frontal cortex, which is an area for executive functioning so problems there can relate to problems with impulse control.
	Altering serotonin functioning was associated with aggression in those with anti-social personality disorder.

Evaluation of biological aspects of anti-social personality disorder

Strengths

- Moss *et al.* (1990) found differences in responses to a serotonin agonist in those with anti-social personality disorder using a control group so there was some objectivity in the findings. Perez (2012) found impairment in the orbital frontal cortex of people with anti-social personality disorder. Both these studies focus on impulsivity, which seems to be in someone's biology, and indeed Eysenck's personality theory shows how high levels of psychoticism, which also features impulsivity, go with anti-social behaviour. So there is evidence for biological aspects of anti-social personality disorder.

- Attachment is said by Bowlby to be a survival trait, suggesting that infants that form an attachment with a caregiver have a survival advantage. This argument is given in Chapter Four. Fonagy *et al.* (1997) suggest that poor attachment formation can lead to anti-social behaviour and problems later, which backs the idea that secure early attachment helps in building a successful internal working model for later relationships. A strength of the argument that anti-social behaviour comes from poor early attachment is that it has support from other theories, such as Bowlby, whose ideas were built on Freud's psychodynamic approach to personality. In this argument, there are biological aspects, such as relating to survival – when theories support one another, that can be a strength for all the theories.

Weaknesses

- There is evidence that anti-social personality disorder links to environmental factors as well as biological factors. For example, Fonagy *et al.* (1997) found that poor formation of attachments and other early experiences seemed to account for anti-social behaviour, and Perez's (2012) findings back up this idea that attachment disorder can go with anti-social behaviour. Therefore, even though there might be biological underpinnings for crime and anti-social behaviour as explained by anti-social personality disorder, there are also environmental aspects, such as regarding someone's upbringing, that are part of the explanation.
- A weakness of anti-social personality disorder as an explanation for crime and anti-social behaviour is that it can be seen as a label that describes someone showing anti-social and criminal behaviour as those behaviours feature in the diagnosis (and, therefore, definition) of anti-social personality disorder. This means showing the high percentage of males in prison that have anti-social personality disorder is not that useful, for example, as it is perhaps describing their behaviour and characteristics rather than explaining it.
- Some studies, like Perez (2012), show correlational evidence that relates anti-social personality disorder to impairment in certain brain regions. However, a cause-and-effect conclusion cannot be drawn from correlational data. The relationship might be caused by some other factor.

Gender and personality as an explanation for criminal and anti-social behaviour

Eysenck suggested that crime and anti-social behaviour comes from high extraversion tendencies, high neuroticism and high psychoticism. These factors have biological explanations, including functioning of the reticular activating system, functioning of the sympathetic part of the autonomic nervous system and hormone functioning including testosterone. Testosterone is said to explain psychoticism and indeed most people high in psychoticism are men, which backs up the testosterone explanation.

Psychoticism relates to anti-social personality disorder as they have features in common, such as impulsivity,

hostility, social withdrawal, uncooperativeness and a troublesome nature. More people with anti-social personality disorder are male than female and studies tend to involve males, such as Moss *et al.* (1990), as reported earlier in this section.

As was outlined when looking at anti-social personality disorder, there are gender differences in its prevalence. For example, in the UK 63 per cent of male remand prisoners, 49 per cent of male sentenced prisoners and 31 per cent of female prisoners are diagnosed with anti-social personality disorder (Singleton *et al.*, 1998, cited by the NIH).

Van de Shoot *et al.* (2010): anti-social behaviour relates to males more than females in adolescence

Van de Shoot *et al.* (2010), in the Netherlands, consider, among other issues, gender and anti-social behaviour. They found that most research looking at adolescents and anti-social behaviour studied male behaviour (such as Rodkin *et al.*, 2006, cited in van de Shoot *et al.*, 2010). Some studies look at more subtle anti-social acts and study females (such as Rose *et al.*, 2004, cited in van de Shoot *et al.*, 2010). Van de Shoot *et al.* state that, in general, boys are more anti-social than girls (e.g. Vaillancourt, 2005). This suggests that anti-social personality will be diagnosed more in males than females as it does entail overt anti-social behaviour rather than behaviour of a more subtle kind.

Lynn and Martin (1997): biological factors relate to psychoticism and neuroticism with strong gender differences

Lynn and Martin (1997) looked at gender differences in psychoticism, neuroticism and extraversion in 37 countries. They found that women had higher neuroticism in all the countries included in the study and men had higher psychoticism in 34 countries. Men had higher extraversion in 30 countries. Eysenck (1975) had found in Britain that women were higher than men on neuroticism, men were higher than women on psychoticism and there were no consistent gender differences with regard to extraversion. Lynn and Martin's (1997) findings confirmed Eysenck's in 1975 regarding neuroticism and psychoticism, though they did find gender differences in extraversion whereas Eysenck did not. The finding that there were no consistent gender differences in extraversion goes with Hesslebrock's (1991) findings that when it comes to anti-social personality disorder, its effects do not show gender differences in those diagnosed (though more men are diagnosed with anti-social personality disorder than women).

Issues and debates

Lynn and Martin (1997) found using mean scores from 37 countries that women had higher scores in neuroticism and men had higher scores in psychoticism. Eysenck (1975) in Britain had the same findings as Lynn and Martin, except he did not find gender differences in extraversion. This suggests that psychological understanding shows similarities over time. How psychological understanding changes over time is one of the issues and debates in your course.

Table 3.9 Some of Lynn and Martin's findings about gender and Eysenck's three personality dimensions, with mean scores (just 7 countries out of 37 are shown)

Country	Number	Extraversion		Neuroticism		Psychoticism	
		Men	Women	Men	Women	Men	Women
Australia	654	18.8	19.8	14.9	16.1	8.4	5.5
Brazil	1,396	18.1	17.1	13.8	15.8	4.5	3.5
Hong Kong	732	17.4	16.1	14.2	15.0	8.4	5.7
India	981	23.1	22.4	14.7	17.8	8.4	7.9
Mexico	988	20.4	20.9	13.3	15.0	5.2	3.8
UK	1,198	18.0	18.1	12.8	17.2	4.8	2.9
US	879	21.2	22.3	13.8	16.3	3.8	2.8

Table 3.9 shows how women are consistently higher on the mean for neuroticism and men are higher on the mean for psychoticism in a wide range of countries, including all those in this table. With regard to extraversion, gender differences are not found so often in Lynn and Martin's study and were not found in Eysenck's data. Lynn and Martin found men had higher extraversion in 30 of the 37 countries so it must just be the countries shown in Table 3.9 that suggest little difference in extraversion between genders.

Lynn and Martin conclude that as there are similarities in neuroticism and psychoticism with regard to gender, there is a biological explanation for these personality factors, because there are such strong cross-cultural similarities.

Issues and debates

Lynn and Martin (1997) suggest that neuroticism and psychoticism are two personality dimensions that come from our biology and our nature rather than our nurture. Other evidence given in this section suggests that personality is down to our upbringing. This is a useful area to use when discussing the nature–nurture debate.

Summary of gender differences in personality affecting crime and anti-social behaviour

Eysenck (1975) and Lynn and Martin (1997) found that females scored higher on neuroticism and males higher on psychoticism. Lynn and Martin's study was across 37 countries so this seems to be a universal finding. This shows strong gender differences in personality factors. The finding that there are gender differences also suggests a biological explanation for such factors as the factors were stable and similarly different by gender across so many countries. Also as psychoticism features more in males that supports the idea that anti-social personality disorder, also found more in males, has some biological underpinnings. However, Hesslebrock (1991), when looking at anti-social personality disorder, and various factors such as family background in alcoholism and childhood behavioural problems, found no gender differences. It was not that there weren't more males with an anti-social personality disorder diagnosis but when females and males with the disorder were included in the study, then there were few gender differences. Van de Shoot et al. (2010) found differences in the type of anti-social behaviour in males and females, with females exhibiting more subtle anti-social behaviour, which might account for gender differences as anti-social behaviour, being more overt in males, might be diagnosed more in males.

Issues and debates

When you read about a behaviour or characteristic being 'universal', which means found in all countries where it has been studied, you can use the behaviour or characteristic when discussing the nature–nurture debate.

Test yourself

To what extent is gender a variable when it comes to biological explanations of crime and anti-social behaviour? **(16 marks)**

Social explanations of crime and anti-social behaviour

You need to cover **labelling** and the self-fulfilling prophecy to explain crime and anti-social behaviour. Social learning theory is briefly included as well to help with discussion.

Labelling and the self-fulfilling prophecy go together as an explanation of crime and anti-social behaviour – the process of the prophecy is that someone is first labelled and then 'becomes' the label.

Year One link: Review your learning about social psychology and how it is defined. For example, social psychology considers interactions between individuals as well as the effects of groups. Labelling and the self-fulfilling prophecy fall within the social approach.

Labelling

Labelling involves a majority group considering a minority group as inferior, and using inferior terms when talking about them. There is a negative connotation to being 'labelled', though in theory someone can be labelled positively – for example, as 'bright'. When applied to crime or anti-social behaviour, labelling means referring to someone, for example, as 'a thief' or, when applied to education, referring to someone's ability, for example, as 'not good at maths'. Labelling links to stereotyping and usually someone stereotypes someone else and the label comes from the stereotype. A label can start from something one person says, rather than from stereotyping.

Explanation
Labelling is describing someone using one or more particular terms and often is used to refer to criminal behaviour. A label can be applied by someone to another person, and does not necessarily reflect the nature of the individual being referred to. That is where the idea of labelling as unfair comes from.

Labelling is putting a person into a category and the category often has connotations. Labelling can have the purpose of showing a lot about someone by giving them just one label.

Labelling theory
Labelling theory (Becker, 1963) refers to how someone's view of themselves comes from the terms used to describe them and how **self-identity** is shaped by how someone is classified in society. Labelling theory explains that deviance is not a 'thing' but a label given to minorities by majorities to pigeon hole them and show that their behaviour is outside cultural norms. This is where the negativity of labelling comes from. A **stigma** is defined as a negative powerful label that affects someone's **self-concept**. Giving someone a 'negative' label in terms of criminal or anti-social behaviour is likely to mean there is social stigma attached as it means the extreme disapproval of members of society. You can see that this idea reflects the idea of social constructionism, in suggesting that deviance is constructed by the majority to refer to cultural norms that are different from theirs. Labelling theory is a sociological theory. Becker (1963) came up with the idea of labelling, explaining deviance from social norms, and Goffman (1963) talked about stigma being a behaviour or reputation that discredits someone. Labels are about expectations people have of others. The majority in a social group label the minority as deviant and this puts pressure on someone being given the label to behave in the expected way.

Explore
You can access 'Outsiders' by Howard S. Becker using this link: www.personal.psu.edu/users/e/x/exs44/406/becker_outsiders_from_weitzer.pdf

Definitions
Stigma refers to a reproach or a 'mark of disgrace', and it refers to someone's reputation and their 'label', which affects their self-concept. **Self-concept** is someone's belief about themselves which is formed by responses of others, which can include labels given by society. **Self-identity** refers to the characteristics and qualities that people use to define themselves.

The issue with stigma is that it is hard to change the label, even if it is shown not to be true. There is **retrospective labelling**, which is going back to someone's past and reinterpreting it in the light of how someone has been labelled. Perhaps someone is labelled a criminal when they reach early adulthood. People who knew the person when they were younger might say things like 'he was always bad'. This would re-label earlier actions and is retrospective labelling. There is also **projective labelling** of someone who has been stigmatised. Projective labelling is using a label to say what will happen to that person in the future. People might say something like 'one of these days he is going to do something really bad'.

Definitions

Retrospective labelling means going back into the past and using a current label or stigma to explain 'retrospectively' someone's past behaviour, such as saying they were always bad (even though that was not said then). **Projective labelling** is using a current label or stigma to predict behaviour in the future and say they will do something bad.

Progress check 3.24

Fill in the gaps in the passage to explain the labelling explanation of crime and anti-social behaviour. Use the following terms: stigma; projective labelling; self-esteem; retrospective labelling; confident; others.

_____ is a negative label that affects someone's _____. This can mean someone is less sociable and less _____, which can confirm the label, such as someone being labelled as anti-social. There can be _____ to re-interpret past behaviour, such as saying they were always anti-social and uncaring about how their behaviour affected _____. There can be _____, which is about predicting future behaviour from a current label, such as saying they will 'turn out badly'.

STUDY HINT

To help you to understand the idea of labelling as a social explanation for crime and anti-social behaviour, you could make a list of the terms about labelling and write definitions alongside them. Or you could use index cards with a term on one side and the definition on the other.

Besemer *et al.* (2013)

Besemer *et al.* (2013) looked at the extent to which children of convicted parents had a higher risk of conviction themselves because of the focus on certain criminal families. The way criminal justice systems like the police focus on certain families is called **official bias**. You can see that labelling a child of such a family as 'criminal' is likely to happen and could influence their development and future. Besemer *et al.* (2013) looked at bias in terms of a convicted parent, low family income, low family socioeconomic status, poor housing and a poor job record for the father. These are factors that are used to label a family and factors that relate to a 'criminal' family, including predicting an increased conviction risk. This is not to say, of course, that all such families are criminal families, just that those factors are used to make such judgements.

Explanation

Official bias refers to the way the criminal justice system looks more at criminal families, which means people from those families are more likely to get caught and prosecuted, not because there is more criminal behaviour in those families but because they are focused on more.

Besemer *et al.* point out that the findings, which showed that children of criminal families are more likely to be convicted, do not show that such families transmit criminal behaviour to their children. The findings mean that such families are paid more attention to and so such children are more likely to be caught and prosecuted, and found guilty, than children from other families. The researchers used data from the Cambridge Study in Delinquent Development (CSDD), which is a longitudinal study following male children born in 1953–1954. The children were studied from the age of 8 to the age of 50. Police records of the parents of the 411 male participants were consulted. They found that a convicted parent was the strongest predictor of the child being convicted. Low family income and poor housing predicted the conviction of a child whether or not the parent had been convicted of crime. It seemed that the greatest risk for showing criminal behaviour was a convicted parent and after that it was social circumstances. There are practical factors involved in 'social circumstances', such as where someone lives and how likely there is to be a police patrol in that area.

It can be concluded from Besemer *et al.* (2013) that there is at least some effect of having a parent convicted and where someone lives on whether they are convicted of a crime. This can be about official bias in that the police focus on the families of convicted people. However, there seems to be a link unconnected to family, which is social circumstances. With regard to labelling, it is suggested that these factors in someone's environment can lead to labelling, such as in the environment or at school.

Explore

You can access the article by Besemer *et al.* (2013) using the following link: www.researchgate.net/profile/Sytske_Besemer/publication/259344063_Official_bias_in_intergenerational_transmission_of_criminal_behaviour/links/0a85e53ab72c39da8e000000.pdf

Livingstone et al. (2011)

Livingstone et al. (2011) looked at 'forensic' labelling (referring to crime and being a criminal) and the effect on self-stigma (how someone sees themselves negatively) for those with severe mental illness. The researchers looked at people in the criminal justice system with mental disorder and considered their mental health needs which had to be catered for outside an institution. They looked at people in Canada who had compulsory treatment in the community and at their level of self-stigma. They found from their quantitative data that labelling was not associated more with self-stigma, though self-stigma was associated with how severe their mental disorder was, their history of being in prison and their history of being homeless. However, Livingstone et al. (2011) found from their qualitative data that having the support of forensic mental health services seemed to come at the risk of stigma for the individual. Livingstone et al. (2011) wanted to look at forensic mental health services which were being provided as a separate service to see if this service would bring increased stigma and what its strengths and weaknesses would be.

> **STUDY HINT**
> Livingstone et al. (2011) used thematic analysis to find recurring patterns in their qualitative data. After becoming very familiar with the data, there was line-by-line coding and, by going backwards and forwards between the text and the codes, the codes were sorted and categorised and developed into four themes. It is useful to have an example of thematic analysis in criminological psychology (and in your course) as you need to know about such analysis of data.

Livingstone et al. (2011) used four main themes when analysing their qualitative data using thematic analysis:

- The first theme was 'group of criminals', which is the participants' view of how society sees them, and they gave data such as 'people are afraid of you'. One comment was, 'My family would label me "mental"' and another said, 'Forensic patients have a double stigma'. These data show that the participants felt perceived as having the 'negative attributes that characterise the forensic social group to which they belong'.
- The second theme was 'system designed for criminals', which showed how forensic patients (offenders with mental health issues) felt the forensic mental health system was 'a correctional system'. They said things like 'not really a hospital, more like a jail'.
- A third theme was 'rejected', which means they felt discriminated against and excluded.

- A fourth theme was 'Cadillac service', which means the way some forensic participants felt the forensic mental health services were better than those offered outside the forensic system. It was felt that the system was good and helpful. A Cadillac is seen as a prestige car in the USA. However, someone said 'being in forensics was good and helpful but it has a stigma'.

> **STUDY HINT**
> Livingstone et al. (2011) show the value of qualitative data when they offer quotes and evidence for claims that having a separate forensic mental health service seemed to be good, but it did seem to carry stigma. You can use this study when discussing the value of qualitative data.

The findings of Livingstone et al. were that, from the quantitative data, it appeared that the forensic mental health services did not bring stigma. However, qualitative data showed that the participants did feel that there was stigma.

Conclusions about labelling and stigma from labels

Besemer et al. (2013) found that there was a link between someone being convicted of a criminal offence and their parent having a criminal record. They also felt that other influences were social circumstances which affected whether someone got a criminal record, unrelated to whether a parent had one. It seems that people can be labelled according to things such as parental behaviour and social circumstances. Though the study was more about official bias, it is useful to show what is likely to be used to label someone a 'criminal'. Livingstone et al. (2011) looked at stigma that someone might feel when attending compulsory special forensic mental health services. They found people did feel that there was stigma and that they were being judged. If someone is being judged and there is stigma, then that suggests labelling is going on.

> **STUDY HINT**
> When answering a question about labelling, be sure to bring each point you make to focus explicitly on the question. For example, talking about stigma can link to labelling but you need to make that link in your answer.

Gender and labelling as an explanation for criminal and anti-social behaviour

Labelling seems a general theory that claims that a label can affect someone's behaviour, and it seems likely that both genders will be affected by labelling given the evidence presented here. There is some new evidence offered here, however, that suggests that labelling may affect the genders differently.

The Cambridge Study in Delinquent Development

The researchers used data from the Cambridge Study in Delinquent Development (CSDD), which is a longitudinal study following male children born in 1953–1954. It was interesting that they chose to look at males as this in itself suggests that males are seen as showing delinquent behaviour more than females. Figures have been given in this section backing the idea that aggression related to crime features more in males than in females.

Sutherland (1949): how boys and girls are socialised differently

Boys and girls experience different socialisation according to Sutherland (1949) and this can lead to more delinquency in boys. Girls are more supervised and more controlled and boys are encouraged to take more risks and to be aggressive, according to Sutherland. However, the study was done in 1949, so there might be differences in the 2000s.

Parsons (1995): how we learn specific gender roles

Parsons (1995) outlines different gender roles in nuclear families, which are 'traditional' families with a mother, father and children. The father has leader and provider roles and the mother has the role of providing emotional support. Though these ideas relate well to social learning theory, they can also be related to labelling theory. If boys are seen as taking more risks then 'risky' labels such as anti-social behaviour and delinquency might well be attached more to boys than girls. But this is speculation. Some evidence for labelling theory related to violent crime and for there being gender differences in how labelling theory affects individuals is given below.

Carlen (1990): women's crime is rational and thought out

Carlen (1990) gives some evidence for boys and girls being given different labels after interviewing 39 women convicted of offences. Carlen suggests that crime for women is about control and they turn to crime when it makes sense to do so, rather than to go against social norms. Heidensohn (1985) suggests that women conform to social norms more than men, which again suggests that males will show more criminal and anti-social behaviour and again this social understanding of gender might affect which labels are given to which gender.

Ramoutar and Farrington (2006): labelling is an important variable in violent crime, particularly for females

Ramoutar and Farrington (2006) look at gender differences in participation in violent crime and the frequency of violent crime. They look at labelling, social learning and personality theories and use 24 constructs that can explain participation and frequency of offending. They used 118 male prisoners and 93 female prisoners in Trinidad and carried out interviewing to ask about their participation in property and violent crime and the frequency of this participation.

They found that the constructs they considered – in particular, labelling – were more related to participation than to frequency and that they were related to both property and violent crime. There was similarity in gender between the constructs with regard to explaining frequency of crime but there was not so much similarity when looking at male and female participation in crime. They found that impulsivity was related to both participation and frequency and that was the case for both males and females. Gender differences seemed to be found with regard to participation in violent and property crime. However, this was not about impulsivity, which was found in both males and females.

Constructs that were considered included various types of reinforcement, such as vicarious reinforcement, from social learning theory. They also included parental approval of violence and parental discipline. They looked at victimisation in the neighbourhood and violence in the home. Importantly for the information required here, they considered both informal and formal labelling as constructs. Informal labelling was measured by asking how far a prisoner thought parents and neighbours had labelled them as deviant, including 'getting into trouble', 'unlikely to succeed' and 'doing illegal things'. Formal labelling was measured by what happened when they were first caught by police – 'labelled' would mean they were arrested; 'not labelled' would mean they were given a warning. Personality factors were also measured, such as impulsivity and low self-control, which relates to Eysenck's ideas about personality and crime (page 209). Table 3.10 shows the labelling variables/constructs and male- and female-related odds ratios for violent crimes.

Table 3.10 Odds ratios for participation taken from Ramoutar and Farrington (2006) relating to labelling, crime and gender differences

Labelling as an explanatory variable	Males (violent crimes)	Females (violent crimes)
Parental labelling	2.9*	19.2*
Neighbour labelling	2.2*	2.3*
Self-labelling	2.7*	3.4*
Formal labelling	1.8	2.9*

*p<.05 (one-tailed)

You can see that labelling has affected males and females more or less equally with the notable exception of parental labelling, which has affected females a lot more than males. Also there is some difference in the effect of formal labelling. Informal labelling seemed to be more important regarding male participation than formal labelling. Male prisoners who felt they were negatively labelled by parents and neighbours and those with a negative self-image were twice as likely to participate in violent crimes. This might not be a cause-and-effect conclusion showing that labelling causes crime. However, it is a relationship that suggests there is a link between labelling and violent crime. In females, the labelling variables, particularly parental labelling, showed a very strong relationship to participation in violent crimes. The more female prisoners felt that their parents labelled them negatively, the more likely they were to be involved in violent crimes. This relationship was not as strong for males. Negative self-labelling and official labelling also showed a relationship for females when looking at participation in violent crime. The researchers found relationships with the other variables too. Interestingly the researchers did not find a link between labelling and the frequency of committing violent crimes, just with participation in violent crimes.

> **STUDY HINT**
> You can use the evidence of Ramoutar and Farrington (2006) as evidence for the labelling explanation of crime and anti-social behaviour as well as for ideas about gender differences in the labelling explanation.

> **STUDY HINT**
> Just as Raine is an important name when looking at brain functioning and aggression, Farrington is an important name when considering social factors and aggression. It is useful to note such main figures in a field of study as it can help with searching for relevant information.

Summary of gender differences in labelling affecting crime and anti-social behaviour

Ramoutar and Farrington (2006) seem to give strong evidence for gender differences in participation in violent crime and not all their evidence is covered here by any means. What they do show are gender differences in how labelling affected violent crime. Females are much more affected by parental negative labelling than males and are also affected more by formal labelling, though males are affected by informal labelling as well. Carlen (1990) gives some evidence for boys and girls being given different labels, which suggests they might be differently affected. Sutherland (1949) suggested males and females

are socialised differently and Parsons (1995) highlighted different gender roles. Both socialisation and roles are likely to affect labels given to individuals and labels are likely, therefore, to be 'gendered'.

Evaluation of labelling as a theory of criminal and anti-social behaviour

Strengths

- Labelling theory has support from studies such as Besemer *et al.* (2013) and Livingstone *et al.* (2011), even though they do not look directly at labelling. The idea that certain factors like a convicted parent or coming from a 'criminal' family link to becoming a criminal is one that people tend to accept and it is from such acceptance that labelling arises. There is some evidence that being in a certain social position links with criminal behaviour and that being in a certain social position brings stigma, and labelling theory is backed by such evidence.
- Labelling theory has some support from evidence for the self-fulfilling prophecy (see next section), which tends to start with, and is therefore linked to, labelling.

Weaknesses

- It is hard to say that all criminal and anti-social behaviour comes from labelling. You have looked at different explanations for crime, including biological explanations, which have supportive evidence, which suggests there is not one explanation.
- It is hard to study labelling and its effect on criminal behaviour because an experiment could not be set up to label some participants and see what they then become. Some experiments have been carried out focusing on the self-fulfilling prophecy but in general it is hard to uncover one aspect of someone's development, like being labelled, and show that it is an explanation for criminal behaviour. For example, the longitudinal study mentioned that gave data for the Besemer *et al.* (2013) study found many factors implicated in explaining criminal behaviour, not just labelling. Isolating factors for study is not easy to do in methodological terms.

Stereotyping

Stereotyping means thinking of a whole group as having certain characteristics, usually using evidence from one member of the group and assuming that this evidence is true of all members. Sometimes there is no direct evidence and people stereotype from what they hear about a group. A label derived from the stereotype would involve one or more of those characteristics. The self-fulfilling prophecy (described below) develops from a label, which can be positive (such as 'clever') or negative (such as 'violent').

Self-fulfilling prophecy

The **self-fulfilling prophecy** (SFP) can be applied to criminal and other behaviours. The term came mainly from studies in schools that looked at how educational processes work. It has since been applied to other areas, such as crime, and it tends to focus on how children develop. The theory is that, when individuals are labelled in some way, they begin to see themselves in the way the label portrays them and, as they are expected to act according to the label, they do so. The self-fulfilling prophecy claims that people fulfil the expectations of others and become what others think and say they will become. This is good if someone is labelled 'clever' but unhelpful and destructive if someone is labelled 'bad'.

This concept of a SFP is also known as the **Pygmalion effect**. George Bernard Shaw wrote the play *Pygmalion*, which was later adapted into the film *My Fair Lady*. The story is about a London flower seller, Eliza, who has a strong Cockney accent. She is taken in by a professor of phonetics, who says he can turn her into a lady, which he does by training her. The idea is that, if someone is known as a lady and treated as a lady, she becomes a lady, which Eliza did. The Pygmalion effect refers to a positive self-fulfilling prophecy, which means someone is expected to succeed and to do well, which is what they do. There is another effect that the self-fulfilling prophecy explains, and that is when someone is expected not to do well or to display criminal behaviour, and that is what they do.

> **STUDY HINT**
>
> When writing, it is tempting to use abbreviations like 'SFP' for self-fulfilling prophecy, and you might like to do that in exam answers. Avoid doing this too often or where the abbreviation is not common practice. However, using abbreviations can save time. Spell out the term first and put the initials in brackets, and from then on you could use the initials. Never use initials without spelling them out first.

Explanations

The **Pygmalion effect** refers to the self-fulfilling prophecy, where higher expectations can lead to better performance. The **self-fulfilling prophecy** holds that someone is given an untrue label, which then affects their self-esteem or affects them in some other way. It is because of the label and expectations that arise from the label that someone behaves in a certain way and is then given positive feedback. The positive feedback leads to the prediction being fulfilled and someone becomes the label they are given – the false prediction comes true because of the prophecy.

The self-fulfilling prophecy involves various stages. First, there is labelling, then there is treatment of the person based on the label. This is followed by the individual reacting to expectations by behaving according to the label. The individual's behaviour, therefore, fulfils the expectations, which confirms the label, and so the behaviour continues.

The self-fulfilling prophecy predicts that something becomes true just because it has been predicted and not for other reasons. It is because of the expectation that the prophecy comes true. The prophecy fulfils itself because of the feedback after behaviour, which affects someone's self-belief. Merton (1948) came up with the term 'self-fulfilling prophecy' and explains it. He says that, first, there has to be a false label for a situation and this false label leads to new behaviour which makes the false label into a true one. You can see how the idea of a self-fulfilling prophecy highlights the importance of labelling to explain criminal behaviour.

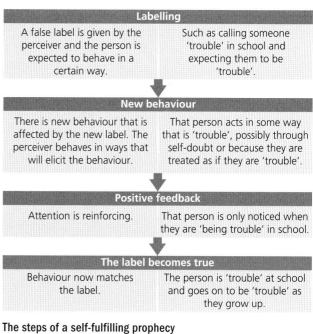

The steps of a self-fulfilling prophecy

The self-defeating prophecy

The self-defeating prophecy is the opposite of a self-fulfilling prophecy. If someone is given a negative or a positive label and they fulfil the expectation of the label, this is a self-fulfilling prophecy. If they are given a negative or a positive label and they get negative feedback, perhaps, then they may well not fulfil the label and instead do the opposite of what is predicted. This is a self-defeating prophecy because the person defeats and overcomes the expectation and the prediction.

Progress check 3.25

Decide whether the following three statements are examples of a self-fulfilling prophecy.

Statement	An example of a SFP?
You expect the brother of someone who has an ASBO to show anti-social behaviour, so you avoid him and tell others you think he will be aggressive, though unknown to you he is much quieter than his brother. He is aggressive because of feeling left out.	
Tom has a bad experience when he goes to a football match because some fans by the side of him support the other team so he does not go again.	
A teacher does not expect the class to do well at a test because she thinks they have not been revising, though they have. She does not encourage them and work with them to prepare for the test and they do badly.	

Rosenthal and Jacobson (1968)

Probably the best-known study of the self-fulfilling prophecy is not about crime but about education. Rosenthal and Jacobson (1968) carried out a study in which, at the start of a school year, they told teachers that certain pupils were 'about to bloom' and do well at school, though in fact they chose the pupils at random. The prophecy was not true for all the pupils. They had given all the pupils an IQ test, so the teachers thought the predictions had come from the test, though this was not true. At the end of that teaching year, the researchers tested the pupils again. Those who had been labelled as 'about to bloom' had improved in IQ score more (in the case of younger pupils) than the other pupils, and the researchers concluded that they had evidence for a SFP. The teachers must have treated the pupils differently from the rest and, as a result of that additional attention, the pupils did better – or perhaps they gained more confidence because the teachers perceived them to be brighter.

If a teacher has a false expectation of a child, according to the self-fulfilling prophecy, they are likely to fulfil that expectation because of it.

Evaluation of Rosenthal and Jacobson (1968)

Strengths

- This is a well-controlled study in which the teachers did not know the IQ test results and the children said to be 'about to bloom' were randomly chosen; this deceit meant that nothing could have affected the children, except for teacher attention, because they were not all 'about to bloom'.
- The study is replicable because it was carefully planned, so it can be tested for reliability. Other studies have found similar results when studying teacher–child interactions, such as Madon *et al.* (2004), who found that when both parents have false unfavourable beliefs about their child's likelihood of drinking alcohol, those parents have the strongest self-fulfilling effect. This is evidence that false beliefs can come true through a self-fulfilling prophecy.

Weaknesses

- The study is artificial and the teachers were given a false belief, which they then acted upon – perhaps they thought they were supposed to act on the information in some way, whereas in another situation, they may not have acted as they did; this is a validity problem.
- Perhaps it is not ethical to 'choose' some children, expecting that they will get special attention and 'bloom', when other children might not have been given special attention because of the study.

The SFP and crime

The link between crime and being lower class is clear in statistics, and it is possible that a reason for this is a self-fulfilling prophecy. If a young person is known to come from a poor family, for example, he or she might – through stereotyping – be labelled as 'bad'. Or the person may come from a family with criminal members, and again could be labelled as 'bad'. According to the prophecy, such individuals would be treated according to their label, would act as they were treated and eventually fulfil the prophecy. Other family members or others from that area might then also be labelled 'bad', and this could account for more criminals being found in the lower classes and poor areas.

Explore

If you would like to read more about the self-fulfilling prophecy, here is a link to start with:
https://public.psych.iastate.edu/madon/PAPERS%20 ON%20HOMEPAGE/EnclopediaSocialSciences.pdf

In Rosenthal and Jacobson (1968), with regard to the self-fulfilling prophecy as an explanation of criminal and anti-social behaviour, what is the significance of the finding that children thought by the teacher to be 'about to bloom' do better after a year in school even though the expectation is false?

Madon *et al.* (2003): the self-fulfilling influence of maternal expectations on children's underage drinking

Self-fulfilling prophecies occur when beliefs or expectations about behaviour for which there is no evidence come true when the beliefs are fulfilled. It is suggested that a mother's false expectations about her child's future drinking of alcohol may result in her expectations coming true. Parents can either overestimate or underestimate their children's future alcohol drinking behaviour.

Results of previous studies

Rosenthal and Jacobson (1968) showed that teacher expectations could lead to a self-fulfilling prophecy of a child's academic ability, but this was an unnatural study because the independent variable (whether a child was about to bloom) was set up. In naturalistic studies, expectations develop naturally and these are important, because they can affect achievement and occupational opportunities as well as personal development.

In general, although it is found that incorrect teacher expectations do lead to self-fulfilling prophecies, the effect is small. This is mainly because teacher expectations are found to be largely accurate, as they are based on valid information (unlike in Rosenthal and Jacobson's study).

Outside educational settings, however, it might be that the self-fulfilling prophecy occurs and has more of an effect. Child self-esteem, family social class and parental expectations are seen as factors that might affect whether a self-fulfilling prophecy occurs. For example, it could be said that children with low self-esteem are more likely to be affected by persuasive messages, and so are more affected by false expectations, or that children with high self-esteem have had more support and approval from their parents, so they might be more influenced by parental judgements and expectations. These are the sorts of issues that are considered in this study.

Aims

Madon *et al.* set out to look at the self-fulfilling prophecy in a natural situation outside the educational setting and with naturally occurring false expectations. Questions included whether mothers' expectations about their children's future alcohol use would predict their children's

future alcohol use. The researchers also looked at whether the accuracy of a mother's expectations limited the self-fulfilling prophecy. Another issue that was investigated was whether some children are more susceptible to a self-fulfilling prophecy than others – perhaps because of their self-esteem or social class.

Procedure

Participants

The study looked at 505 mother–child pairs. Only one child from the family was included, even if there were more. The pairs were found from families of seventh graders in 36 rural schools from 22 counties in a US state. There were 233 girls and 272 boys in the study.

Data

The data were gathered from a longitudinal survey using both questionnaires and interviews, and were correlation data. Researchers contacted the families to arrange an initial in-home visit, and then revisited the families who agreed to take part. There was an interview to gather general information and a written questionnaire. Family members completed the questionnaire individually and separately, and confidentiality was guaranteed. Questionnaires were carried out at the baseline (the start) and 18 months later. Family members were paid a small amount for taking part.

> **STUDY HINT**
> Note that this study is longitudinal, naturalistic, uses interviews and questionnaires, and produces correlation data. Therefore, it can be used as an example for all these features of methodology.

Assumptions

The study relies on the belief that valid background variables influence children's future alcohol use and mothers' expectations about their children's future alcohol use. To this extent, a mother's expectations are accurate (if based on valid background variables). Background variables in this study include the child's behaviour, attitudes, intentions, norms, the family demographics and environments (peer, social and family). Such variables have been shown to affect early alcohol use.

A mother's expectations can also affect a child's future alcohol use through a self-fulfilling prophecy. Only inaccurate expectations can be self-fulfilling (by definition). A mother's expectations are inaccurate if not based on valid background variables about her child's future alcohol use. There are moderator variables, such as self-esteem, social class and valence (the value in the sense of positive or negative) of the mother's expectations, and these can moderate the influence of a mother's expectations on her child's future alcohol use.

These beliefs come from the reflection–construction model (Jussim, 1991).

Measures

The questionnaires assessed variables related to family, peers and substance abuse. Baseline measures included a mother's expectation of her child's future alcohol use, as well as family income, the gender of the child and his/her perception of friends' alcohol use. The 18-month follow-up included a measure of the child's alcohol use up to that time.

Examples of questions for the children included: 'How many of your friends do you think get drunk at least once a week?' and 'If you had the money and wanted to get beer, wine or liquor, do you think you could get some?' Mothers were asked: 'On a scale of 1 to 10, rate how likely you think it is that your child in the study will drink alcohol regularly as a teenager'.

A reliability check was carried out by asking the children who answered 'yes' to a question about having drunk alcohol for more information, and getting a new score from them. The researchers could check this new score against the questionnaire score to look for a correlation in respect of past and future alcohol use. This was in case children said they drank alcohol because of **demand characteristics** or peer desirability. At baseline, 89 per cent said they had not drunk alcohol, so it was not thought that claiming to drink alcohol when they did not was a large problem.

Explanation

Demand characteristics cause bias if they are present in a study. This is when there are characteristics of a study that lead the participant to guess what is required — it is as if a certain response is demanded.

> **STUDY HINT**
> Recall what demand characteristics and social desirability mean when applied to data in psychology. You can see that using such terms when assessing a study is useful. Madon et al. (2003) took steps to avoid such biases. You can use their study when discussing such issues.

Results

It was important to know how much a mother's expectation was wrong, because only an incorrect expectation can cause a self-fulfilling prophecy. Predictor variables were studied (such as school, type of parenting, past alcohol use and self-esteem of the child) to find out what proportion of expectations about future alcohol use is

predicted from background variables and what proportion is incorrect. The accuracy of expectation can be shown by how far the expectation differs from the prediction according to the variables.

- If prediction of alcohol use is the same as predicted by background variables, there is no effect from the prediction.
- If prediction of alcohol use is greater than predicted by background variables, there is a positive difference and a negative effect (predicts more alcohol use), so a self-fulfilling prophecy would have a negative effect.
- If prediction of alcohol use is less than predicted by background variables, there is a negative difference and a positive effect (predicts less alcohol use), so a self-fulfilling prophecy would have a positive effect.

Overall, Madon et al. (2003) concluded that 52 per cent of the relationship between a mother's expectations and her child's future alcohol use is down to accurate maternal expectations and 48 per cent is down to self-fulfilling effects. There was a stronger relationship between a mother's expectations and the child's future alcohol use among high self-esteem children than low self-esteem children. Positive expectations that underestimated children's future alcohol use had a stronger self-fulfilling effect on children's future alcohol use than did negative expectations that overestimated future alcohol use.

Conclusions

Children with high self-esteem were more susceptible to self-fulfilling prophecies than those with low self-esteem, and self-fulfilling prophecies tended to be helpful rather than harmful. A mother's expectations were about half accurate and half self-fulfilling. There is no evidence of an effect from social class or family income.

> **Progress check 3.27**
> In Madon et al. (2003), with regard to the self-fulfilling prophecy as an explanation of criminal and anti-social behaviour, what is the significance of the finding that only certain children seemed to change their behaviour in light of their mother's (false) expectations?

Evaluation of the study

Strengths

- The mother's expectations are naturally occurring to an extent and this is a naturalistic study, so it has more validity than previous laboratory or field experiments.
- The reliability of the child's self-report data about his or her alcohol use was checked, so the study has reliability to that extent.

- A large amount of data were gathered so that many different factors could be considered, and the researchers looked at many explanations in addition to a self-fulfilling prophecy, so they accounted for the complexity of issues.

Weaknesses

- In general, mothers had low expectations with regard to their children's alcohol use – they did not think they would drink much. The children reported little alcohol use even at the end of the study, so the effect of expectations should be generalised taking this into account.
- There were some differences in the questionnaires that the mothers and children completed. Children were asked if they *ever* drank but their mothers were asked if the children would *regularly* drink. These are two different levels of drinking, so comparing the replies might not have been fair.

Jahoda (1954): study of names related to behaviour

An interesting study that is useful when considering whether behaviour can arise from a label gives strong evidence of the power of labelling. Gustav Jahoda (1954) studied the Ashanti (a Ghanaian ethnic group) and he noted that boys were named according to the day on which they were born. For example, Monday children were labelled according to the soul for that day (the *kra*), which would mean the child was quiet and peaceful. The *kra* for Wednesday, however, would lead to aggressive and quick-tempered characteristics in the child. If there was a SFP at work, then children born on Monday would be quiet and peaceful and children born on Wednesday would be more aggressive. Jahoda discovered from court records that children born on a Wednesday were more likely to be convicted for crimes against the person. There were noticeably fewer Monday children on record as having been convicted.

Evaluation of Jahoda's study

Strengths

- Data were valid and came from court records, so this was a naturalistic study where variables were not manipulated.
- The difference in name is clear and it is hard to see what other factors could have led to the findings, although other details about the tribe and their practices are not clear; on the face of it, the findings are powerful.

Weaknesses

- The study has not been replicated and so it is not certain that data are reliable.

- Factors other than the Wednesday name might have led to the convictions (though it is hard to see what they would be, other than the child being treated differently according to expectations).

Gender and self-fulfilling prophecy as an explanation for criminal and anti-social behaviour

Jahoda (1954) looked at boys when considering how names related to anti-social behaviour, which was interesting as it would be useful to know if the same applied to girls. Some studies looking at the self-fulfilling prophecy do look at gender and have found there to be gender differences both in responding to expectations and in being the person forming the expectations.

Dvir *et al.* (1995): self-fulfilling prophecy and gender

Dvir *et al.* (1995) claim that all studies that have confirmed the Pygmalion hypothesis have been done using men; there have been a few studies focusing on females but those had methodological issues. Dvir *et al.* point out that when women make up most of the participants, the Pygmalion effect is not found. Dvir *et al.* (1995) carried out two studies to test the Pygmalion hypothesis on women. The Pygmalion hypothesis is about the self-fulfilling prophecy, which means that when an untrue 'fact' about someone is planted, it will be fulfilled just because of the label being given. Higher expectations lead to better performance. They used Israel Defence Forces and led leaders to believe that the trainees in the experimental condition, which was the Pygmalion hypothesis condition, had 'higher than usual potential'. Experiment One focused on female officer cadets led by women and Experiment Two focused on men and women taking the same course but in separate groups. In Experiment One, where women were led by women, they found that there was an effect from giving the information about high potential. However, there was no evidence of the participants doing better because of expectations. In Experiment Two, there was a self-fulfilling prophecy in men led by a man and in women led by a man, but not in women led by a woman. It seemed that the Pygmalion effect could be found in women but perhaps not when the expectations come from a woman. They needed to look at women leading men, and that was a suggestion for further study.

This study using two experiments suggests that there are gender differences in whether a self-fulfilling prophecy occurs and that the gender of the person 'expecting' a certain behaviour is important, perhaps more than the gender of the person 'fulfilling' the expectation. This study was not about crime or aggression; it was about how expecting more tends to get more, even when such expectations rest on false assumptions or understanding.

However, it does give evidence for a self-fulfilling prophecy going in the 'right' direction. Crime and anti-social behaviour are not 'going in the right direction', however, and that might be a criticism of this study, as it might be of Rosenthal and Jacobson (1968) too (page 225). Dvir *et al.*'s study was valid in the sense that it took place in a natural environment – an officer-training course.

Summary of gender differences in self-fulfilling prophecy affecting crime and anti-social behaviour

Jahoda (1954) found that boys expected to have aggressive and violent characters, and named according to that character (which was not going to be a 'true' character as it was unlikely that all boys born on Wednesdays would have that character), seemed to be more responsible for violent crime. Girls were not studied. There is a tendency to focus on males when looking at crime and anti-social behaviour. Dvir *et al.* (1995) found a self-fulfilling prophecy when men were led by a man and when women were led by a man, but not when women were led by a woman. There seems to be a gender effect when considering the person having the expectations.

Evaluation of the SFP explanation leading to crime

Strengths

- Madon suggests that people with high self-esteem are more likely to be affected by their parents' predictions and she suggests that social class is not a factor in whether a parent–child relationship leads to a SFP. This shows that there are conditions when a self-fulfilling prophecy might be found; it is not that it works for all labels and all people. Madon *et al.* (2003) give findings with more detail and depth about the self-fulfilling prophecy. Rosenthal and Jacobson found that a positive false expectation was fulfilled, as did Madon, which strengthens her findings.
- This would further suggest that expectations about former criminals, such as labels applied to them in the local community, will lead to a SFP, in some cases at least, depending on the relationship between those giving the label and the person being labelled. This is useful as it gives the idea a practical application.
- Jahoda's study gives strong evidence for the effect of labelling.

Weaknesses

- Much of the research into the SFP has been in education, the teacher–child relationship being a special one where expectations might be fulfilled. However, other relationships might not have this effect.
- The problem with studying the effects of labelling at an individual level is finding a false belief, as Madon has explained. This is probably why there are few psychological studies of labelling and the SFP.

Progress check 3.28

Studies given as evidence for the self-fulfilling prophecy include Rosenthal and Jacobson (1968), Madon *et al.* (2003) and Jahoda (1954). They used different contexts in their studies. Explain the three contexts and provide one strength and one weakness of the contexts when using their studies as evidence for a self-fulfilling prophecy as an explanation for criminal and anti-social behaviour.

The social learning explanation of crime/anti-social behaviour

The social learning explanation is briefly looked at here as it is helpful as an alternative theory and, since you have covered the theory before, it is worth seeing how it relates to crime. However, for your course, you only need to study labelling and the self-fulfilling prophecy.

Role models, social learning theory and crime

Social learning theory suggests that behaviour, to an extent at least, comes from observing role models and imitating their behaviour. This is known as observational learning. Role models are those with whom people identify in some way – often someone they look up to. Thus people tend to imitate those of the same gender, possibly of a similar age, or people they see as powerful or having something to be achieved, such as celebrities. Bandura, Ross and Ross (1961), for example, showed that children imitated an adult model who was aggressive. They found that boys imitated physical aggression more than girls, who showed more verbal aggression than physical aggression. They also discovered that both girls and boys were more likely to imitate the adult male model than the female model. This suggests that there is also an element of expectation involved, such as that males are imitated more if they are aggressive, because it is expected that aggression is found more in males. There are some complex issues involved, but the basic idea is that behaviour can come from imitation of role models.

Year One link: Review social learning theory, which you covered in learning theories. Remind yourself about the modelling process and which role models are more likely to be imitated. Recall your study of Bandura, Ross and Ross's work (1961), which showed how young children copy aggressive behaviour, and of Bandura's other studies.

The role of reinforcement in social learning theory and crime

Social learning theory suggests that people commit crimes because of an association with others. Not only is it possible to be exposed to criminal models, it is also possible to be 'reinforced' for crime. Crime becomes not only acceptable but also desirable.

Reinforcement of criminal behaviour can be positive or negative. **Positive reinforcement** might come from financial or material gain from the crime, or approval from one's peers. **Negative reinforcement** might come from the removal of something unpleasant by committing the crime, such as removing disapproval from peers or removing financial hardship. Social learning theory would predict that, if someone commits a second crime, it is likely to be the same as, or similar to, the first crime, since that would match the patterns of reinforcement. Punishment is likely to deter criminal behaviour. These are the principles of operant conditioning, and social learning theory adopts these principles as well as the idea of observational learning.

Explanation

Positive reinforcement encourages behaviour because something pleasant happens in response to the behaviour.

Negative reinforcement encourages behaviour because something unpleasant is avoided in response to the behaviour.

Year One link: Review operant conditioning from the learning approach in your course.

Progress check 3.29

Using what you learned in learning theories, fit relevant terms into the table to describe the process of modelling according to social learning theory. Give the order of the process by numbering. The first answer is completed as an example.

Term referring to the modelling process	Explanation of the term	Order of the process
There must be a good reason to imitate the behaviour.	Motivation	4
The modelled behaviour has to be remembered.		
The modelled behaviour has to be noticed.		
The behaviour has to be able to be copied.		

Gender and social learning as an explanation for criminal and anti-social behaviour

Social learning theory is backed by evidence from Bandura's studies in the 1960s. One study (Bandura, Ross and Ross, 1961) found that gender was an important variable when children observe aggression acted out by adults. Boys seemed to show more physical aggression than girls but girls did show similar verbal aggression to boys. Girls showed more physical aggression if the model was male and more verbal aggression if the model was female. The gender of the model showing the aggression was also important, with the male model being imitated more, for example, and boys tended to imitate the model of their own gender, though this was less pronounced in girls. You can see just from this one study that gender has an impact on what is imitated. The study reported here focused on aggression, so is relevant when looking at crime and anti-social behaviour, though this was modelled aggression in an unnatural situation so there might have been a lack of validity in the results, which should be borne in mind.

Year One link: Recall your learning about Bandura, Ross and Ross (1961) in learning theories in your course, focusing on gender in their findings.

Explore

You can find a summary of Bandura, Ross and Ross (1961) using this link: www.simplypsychology.org/bobo-doll.html

Evaluation of social learning theory as an explanation of criminal behaviour

Strengths

- There is a lot of experimental evidence to show that behaviour is imitated, including aggressive behaviour;

some of this evidence is explained later in this section when looking at the role of the media.

- The theory has a practical application and can help to rehabilitate offenders, as appropriate role models can be used to help learn appropriate behaviour, alongside appropriate reinforcements.

Weaknesses

- The theory does not look at individual differences, only at how an individual is influenced by social factors; therefore, biological aspects are not considered.
- The theory does not account for criminal behaviour that is opportunistic and has not been observed first – it tends to account more for stealing, aggression and other crimes that are reasonably easily observed in society, rather than murders. Therefore, the theory does not account for all crime.

Progress check 3.30

What makes labelling and the self-fulfilling prophecy *social* explanations of criminal and anti-social behaviour?

Gender differences in biological and social explanations of crime and anti-social behaviour

You have looked at four biological explanations and two social explanations of crime and anti-social behaviour (plus social learning). In each of these explanations, there has been consideration of gender differences in anti-social behaviour and crime. Table 3.11 summarises these gender differences in biological and social explanations of crime and anti-social behaviour.

Table 3.11 Biological and social explanations for crime and anti-social behaviour and gender differences

Explanation	Summary of gender differences found regarding anti-social behaviour and crime in relation to the explanation
Brain injury	The biological explanation of brain injury as a cause of crime and anti-social behaviour does not show gender differences in the biology but does show gender differences in people experiencing traumatic brain injury.
Amygdala	In general, it seems that there are no gender differences in amygdala functioning and neurobiology related to anti-social behaviour. For example, Hyde *et al.* (2014) did not report gender differences in their study. Shirtcliff *et al.* (2009) gave gender differences such as in empathy (more in girls) and conduct disorders (more in boys). They confirm that the amygdala is important in emotions. Shirtcliff *et al.* (2009) point out that the neurobiology involved in relation to empathy and callousness is different in males and females with more empathy-related neurocircuitry being active in females (e.g. Hein and Singer, 2008, cited in Shirtcliff *et al.*, 2009).
XYY syndrome	It is clear from how XYY syndrome appears that it is a chromosomal issue in males only. The 'male' aspect of XYY can affect the individual because of environmental factors such as labels. The effect of labelling might bring about a self-fulfilling prophecy and it is likely to be labels relating to masculinity that apply.
Personality	Eysenck (1975) and Lynn and Martin (1997) found that females scored higher on neuroticism and males higher on psychoticism and this was in Lynn and Martin's study across 37 countries so this seems to be a universal finding. Psychoticism also features more in males, so that supports the idea that anti-social personality disorder, also found more in males, has some biological underpinnings. However, Hesslebrock (1991), when looking at anti-social personality disorder and various factors such as family background in alcoholism and childhood behavioural problems, found no gender differences. Van de Shoot *et al.* (2010) found differences in the type of anti-social behaviour in males and females, with females exhibiting more subtle anti-social behaviour, which might account for gender differences as anti-social behaviour, being more overt in males, might be diagnosed more in males.
Labelling	Ramoutar and Farrington (2006) show gender differences in how labelling affects violent crime. Females are much more affected by parental negative labelling than males and are also affected more by formal labelling, though males are affected by informal labelling as well. Sutherland (1949) suggests males and females are socialised differently and Parsons (1995) highlights different gender roles. Both socialisation and roles are likely to affect labels given to individuals and labels are likely, therefore, to be 'gendered'.
Self-fulfilling prophecy	Jahoda (1954) found that boys expected to have aggressive and violent characters, and named according to that character, seemed to be more responsible for violent crime. Girls were not studied. Dvir *et al.* (1995) found a self-fulfilling prophecy when men were led by a man and when women were led by a man, but not when women were led by a woman. There seems to be a gender effect when considering the person having the expectations. It seems there are gender differences to uncover.

Test yourself

1 Evaluate social explanations of crime and anti-social behaviour. **(12 marks)**
2 Compare research into biological and social explanations of crime and anti-social behaviour. **(12 marks)**
3 To what extent is gender a variable when it comes to social explanations of crime and anti-social behaviour? **(16 marks)**

Understanding the offender, offence analysis and case formulation

The first part in this section considers effective interviewing in criminological psychology, which can involve using the 'cognitive interview' and ethical interviewing. The second part covers an important aspect of the job of a forensic psychologist, which is to use formulation to understand the offence and how offending behaviour might be functional for an offender.

This section is all about getting information relating to an offender. This includes information before an offender is caught, which includes how interviewing of witnesses is carried out, and that is where focus on cognitive interviewing and ethical interview techniques comes in. There is getting information after an offender becomes an 'offender', which is after sentencing, and that is where using case formulation comes in. Interviewing the offender after sentencing to consider possible treatment can also involve a cognitive interview and must involve ethical interviewing techniques.

Focus on the offender but not forgetting victims of crimes

When focusing on understanding the offender, it is the offender and not the victims that are the focus in a textbook. This does not mean victims are not important. Forensic psychologists using interviewing to find out about offences from an offender or carrying out a case formulation, which is about summarising the case and putting forward a treatment plan, focus on the offender. However, a lot of focus is on reducing the risk of re-offending and potential victims are focused on in that

sense. It may seem as if the focus is on the offender and treating the offender; however, it is important to note that is the purpose of an interview or a case formulation. This is not to say that a crime is not heinous and to be remembered as such with due regard for any victims involved, even if that does not always come across.

Offender profiling

Offender profiling is only briefly outlined here. The idea that someone can draw clues from a criminal's patterns when a crime is committed is an interesting one, and something that appeals to the imagination. Offender profiling is not directly in your course so this material is just for your interest, though it may help your understanding of other areas of criminological psychology.

Offender profiling is the creation of a description of a criminal drawn from clues available from a crime scene or from past crimes. It is usually used in multiple crimes, such as murder or rape, because (sadly) more than one crime is often needed for a pattern to be noted. The profiler considers the geography, where the crime(s) took place, including road and rail links, barriers to travel, such as rivers, and so on. He or she will consider if the criminal needed to be strong, or able to drive – the scene can give such information or allow a best guess. There is consideration of the type of crime, such as if it is a sex crime, and whether there is something about the crime that is odd, as a criminal will often leave signals. If a crime scene is left tidy, for example, it would indicate a fussy person. There are studies looking at the effectiveness of offender profiling and how far it works to find a criminal. David Canter is a well-known 'name' in offender profiling and wrote an article (2000) about offender profiling and criminal differentiation. He points out that the issues relate to classes of crime, different offences and differences in offenders. He discusses salience, which is the importance of the frequency of criminal actions, and models of differentiation, which is how criminals can be distinguished from one other. There is also a look at patterns offenders might use. In your course, offence analysis is about understanding the offender after they have been sentenced in order to formulate an understanding of them and the aim is to put together a relevant and effective treatment plan. Offence analysis is not about offender profiling in order to catch a criminal, so there is a different focus.

Cognitive interviewing

The **cognitive interview** is a way of interviewing victims and witnesses relating to a crime to get as much retrieval as possible and reliable testimony. The aim is to avoid problems when interviewing about offences, such as issues around eyewitness unreliability (page 271). Its use has spread to interviewing in other contexts, including to look at warmth in the patient–provider relationship (Neumann *et al.*, 2011), to look at long-term recall of physical activities (Fisher *et al.*, 2000), to investigate aging (e.g. Dodson *et al.*, 2015), to look at sexual attitudes and lifestyles (Aicken *et al.*, 2013), and to focus on nutrition and nutrition messages for low-income populations (Carbone *et al.* (2002). However, most research using and looking at cognitive interviewing is about eyewitness testimony and enhancing memory recall for witnessed events. It has been used in interviewing by forensic psychologists when carrying out assessment and formulation regarding offenders too (see section on case formulation, page 248).

Explanation

The **cognitive interview** is a questioning technique used by police and forensic psychologists. The aim is to improve testimony so that it is reliable and not affected by how an interview is done, such as by leading questions.

How cognitive interviewing came about

Cognitive interviewing was developed by Geiselman *et al.* (1984) with the intention of improving police interviewing techniques. Geiselman *et al.* focused on improving the accuracy of eyewitness testimony. It was found that some training in retrieval techniques helped participants to recall more correct information about an event. The ideas behind the cognitive interview include the idea that memory is reconstructive and unlike a tape-recorder, as Bartlett (1932) illustrated, and the idea that there could, therefore, be confabulation (adding to what happened so it makes sense for the individual). There was other theory behind cognitive interviewing too, such as how a physical memory trace in the brain might decay and so memories are lost. Fisher and Geiselman (1992) wrote a training manual about using cognitive interviewing, which is now widely used.

Year One link: Recall your learning about the reconstructive model of memory and Bartlett's work, including his War of the Ghosts study and conclusions from it about the unreliability of memory.

The cognitive interview links what is known from psychology about how memory works with practical ideas about police interviews, aiming to develop more effective interviewing techniques with regard to witness testimony and offender accounts.

A typical British police interview (before cognitive interviewing)

Geiselman and Fisher (in a chapter written for a 2014 book) explain George and Clifford's (1992) work on summarising what a typical British police interview entailed. What they outlined matched the American police interview closely, according to Geiselman and Fisher (2014). The 'typical' police interview entails:

- a short attempt to establish rapport
- a direct question, such as 'Tell me what happened'
- an 'outburst' of crime-related facts from the witness
- an interruption where the interviewer asks short direct questions, such as 'How tall was he?' – these questions are generally facts that related to the crime and are asked in a standard order if there was more than one witness
- leading questions, such as 'He was wearing a red shirt, wasn't he?'
- the interviewer dominating the interview, with replies being rather brief, so the witness stays passive, waiting to answer questions.

20/11/2014
23:03:58

CAM 3

Police interviewing is not likely to include the 80 per cent talking from the witness that a cognitive interview proposes.

STUDY HINT
In the caption to the photo above, it would be tempting to write that such interviewing 'does not include 80% of the witness talking'. However, writing 'is not likely to include' is safer. In psychology, when writing answers, avoid being too definite because when discussing human behaviour, there are always (well, almost always!) exceptions.

Geiselman and Fisher (2014) reported that more recent interviews showed similar techniques being used and they cite, for example, Snook and Keating (2010) in Canada as evidence for their claim. The reason they criticise the 'typical' police interview is that the witness is encouraged in a way to withhold information, not to provide additional information, to give short answers and not to give any answers they are unsure of. This is not really a way of finding out what happened in a crime situation. An issue mentioned is that it has been known for some time that cognitive interviewing is more successful in getting recall from witnesses, so it is surprising to find that typical interviewing is still being used.

How cognitive interviewing is done

The cognitive interview is linked to the use of **mnemonics**, which are ways of remembering. Also the idea of remembering an event using schemas is used, and breaking up someone's schemas, such as using a novel viewpoint, is one of the techniques.

There are different retrieval rules involved:

- Mentally reinstating the environment and people in a situation: by mentally revisiting the event and forming a mental picture of the environment, someone recreates the cues in the environment and that can trigger memories. They are also asked to recreate their mental state and there too there can be cues that help recall.
- Giving an in-depth account: the interviewer asks about every detail no matter how insignificant it seems, to uncover information rather than getting only what a witness thinks is important. Also different pieces of information can trigger other memories.
- Describing the event in different orders, starting from different points: the person tells the story of the event first. Then they are asked to start from different points in their story, which might lead to more information being triggered and recalled.
- Reporting the event from a different viewpoint: by asking a witness to tell the story from another viewpoint, perhaps someone else's viewpoint, different information can be uncovered, such as asking what the bar tender saw.
- Other techniques: these include giving ideas to help memory, such as whether the car reminded them of the car of someone they know, or whether slang words were used.

In a bank robbery, there are likely to be quite a few witnesses and one technique is to ask one witness what the others are likely to have seen.

Definition

Mnemonics refers to special ways of remembering information. An example is 'Richard Of York Gives Battle In Vain' for the colours of the rainbow.

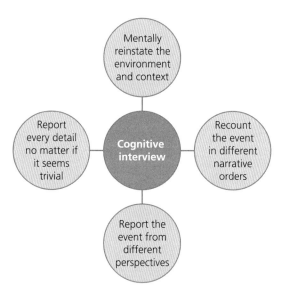

Different parts of a cognitive interview to improve memory and get more information about an event

Geiselman and Fisher (2014) point out advantages of the cognitive interview. They say that more information is gathered and less incorrect recall is found. They say that important elements in cognitive interviewing include forming a rapport with the witness, asking mainly open questions, asking neutral questions and avoiding leading questions, and using a funnel in the interview that starts with broader questions and narrows to more specific ones.

It is acknowledged that each witness will be different, so though there is a series of steps in cognitive interviewing, there is some room for tailoring the process to suit the individual.

Progress check 3.31

List the four main parts of the cognitive interview.

Relating aspects of cognitive interviewing to psychology theory

Reinstating the context

With regard to reinstating the context, the witness is asked to form an image of the environment and they can be asked not only about objects in the room and what was happening but also to reinstate their emotions at the time and any sounds and smells there were, and so on. The **encoding specificity principle** (Tulving and Thomson, 1973, cited in Memon and Higham, 1999) refers to the idea that a cue in an environment can be encoded with information and so can help recall. Reinstating the environment and context relating to what is to be remembered helps recall because it brings the retrieval cue to mind. Malpass (1996, cited in Memon and Higham, 1999) has reviewed this idea. Cues in the environment include the cognitive environment, which means bringing to mind thoughts and feelings at the time as well as the setting. Memon and Higham, although they say there is some evidence that context reinstatement can help recall of events (e.g. Milne, 1997, cited in Memon and Higham, 1999), say too that context reinstatement tends not to last long for recall to happen (e.g. Eich, 1995).

Explanation

The **encoding specificity principle** refers to the idea that a cue in an environment, which can be a cognitive environment, will be encoded with the memory and so if the cue is reinstated it will assist recall.

Reporting everything

According to Fisher and Geiselman (1992, cited in Memon and Higham, 1999), reporting everything might help with recalling detail because there is then no screening out of anything, even if there is only partial recall.

Using different perspectives

Using a different perspective means asking the witness to put themselves in the position of one of the other people present, which is about looking from a different perspective and so changing what is focused on, thus using different retrieval cues. This means using different pathways to the material. However, it is suggested that using this approach could lead a witness to make up what they think another person might have seen (e.g. Memon *et al.*, 1996a, cited in Memon and Higham, 1999). Memon and Higham say that the police tend not to use this part of the cognitive interview fearing that witnesses may be misled by being asked to take someone else's viewpoint (e.g. Kebbel and Wagstaff, 1996, cited in Memon and Higham, 1999). However, Milne (1997, cited in Memon and Higham, 1999) found that, though taking another's viewpoint does not seem to get *more* information than the other techniques, it can get as much correct information as using the other techniques.

> **STUDY HINT**
> Sometimes a reference for a piece of evidence will have a date with a letter after it, such as Memon *et al.*, 1996a. The 'a' means that in 1996 there was another article published by the author(s) so one is 1996a and one is 1996b.

Starting at different points in the story

A witness will tend to start at the beginning, or where they see the beginning is. However, starting from different points seems to give more focused and more detailed recall. An example would be starting from what was most memorable, or starting from the end or the middle. Geiselman and Callot (1990, cited in Memon and Higham, 1999) found recalling in forward order once and then going back in reverse order was more effective than going from the start twice. Though Memon and Higham (1990) report that there is no evidence (up to 1999) that going from the start and then recalling back from the end gives more information than just going through the story again, Milne (1997, cited in Memon and Higham, 1999) suggests that, with some specific prompts, the technique of forward and then backwards recall can help.

Important elements in cognitive interviewing

- Using open questions to encourage free response and detail.
- Asking neutral questions.
- Avoiding leading questions.
- Starting with broader questions.
- Narrowing to focus on specifics, like using a funnel approach.

Progress check 3.32

Make three comparisons between cognitive interviewing and police standard interviewing.

The protocol for cognitive interviewing

There are five sections to the protocol:

- An introduction establishes a relationship between the interviewer and the witness. This establishes a witness-focused approach.
- There is then the opportunity for the witness to tell the story of what happened without any interruption. This transfers control to the witness and the interviewer can acknowledge that, such as saying 'I was not there, you tell me what happened'. Snook and Keating (2010, cited in Geiselman and Fisher, 2014) say that there is an 80–20 rule, which means 20 per cent of the talking should be done by the interviewer with 80 per cent by the interviewee.
- Then the interviewer uses techniques such as imagery and scenes to help their recall. This is where the features of a cognitive interview come in, such as taking the view of another person at the scene or starting at a different point in the narrative.
- The interviewer reviews the information generated over the whole interview.
- The interview is closed in a way that means it could be continued if more information is required.

Explore
Memon *et al.*'s (1997) study about eyewithness performance in standard and cognitive interviews can be accessed using this link if you would like to know more: **cogprints. org/646/1/memon.memory.html**

The enhanced cognitive interview

The same four retrieval rules are found in the enhanced cognitive interview. These are changing the order for recall, mentally recreating the situation, starting the story at different places in the event and taking different viewpoints. The enhanced cognitive interview also includes ways of improving communication between the interviewer and interviewee, including preventing distractions as much as possible and giving time for a gap between a response and the next question. Using language that suits the witness also helps.

For the enhanced cognitive interview, using the protocol given earlier in this section, techniques would include:

- changing the order for recall
- mentally recreating the situation
- starting the story from different points in the event
- taking different viewpoints
- allowing a gap between a response and the next question
- using language that suits the witness
- avoiding any distractions.

Memon and Higham (1999) discuss features of the enhanced cognitive interview. They discuss how transfer of control from the interviewer to the witness might take place, giving several ways of it occurring during the rapport-building phase. They suggest the need for open questions, which means the witness has to elaborate on their replies and so there will be more witness talk than interviewer talk. They suggest not interrupting the witness by timing questions to suit the witness's patterns of retrieval rather than the interviewer asking questions to suit their own schedule. An example Memon and Higham give is if the witness is talking about a suspect's face, ask about eye colour and not shoe colour. Memon and Higham point out that an enhanced cognitive interview has aspects of the interview working together – for example, by not interrupting a witness's recall patter, the interviewer can, when the witness has finished, go about the context reinstatement element of the interview.

The effectiveness of the enhanced cognitive interview

In their meta-analysis, Köhnken *et al.* (1999) found there were more errors using the enhanced cognitive interview, which is interesting as it is meant to improve communication and so improve recall.

Memon and Higham (1999) consider the enhanced cognitive interview and mention that it is hard to separate different parts to study to check for effectiveness.

The effectiveness of the cognitive interview

When considering the four parts of the cognitive interview technique earlier, some evaluation points were included and these are briefly drawn together here.

Reinstating the context

Memon and Higham, though they say that there is some evidence that context reinstatement can help recall of events (e.g. Milne, 1997, cited in Memon and Higham, 1999), suggest there is evidence to say that context reinstatement tends not to last long for recall to happen (e.g. Eich, 1995).

Recording everything

Fisher and Geiselman (1992, cited in Memon and Higham, 1999) say recording everything might help because there is then no screening out of anything, even if there is only partial recall.

Using different perspectives

It is suggested that using this approach could lead a witness to make up what they think another person might have seen (e.g. Memon et al., 1996a, cited in Memon and Higham, 1999). Memon and Higham say that the police tend not to use this part of the cognitive interview fearing that witnesses may be misled by being asked to take someone else's viewpoint (e.g. Kebbel and Wagstaff, 1996, cited in Memon and Higham, 1999). Milne (1997, cited in Memon and Higham, 1999) found that, although taking another's viewpoint does not seem to get *more* information than the other techniques, it can get as much correct information as using the other techniques.

Starting from a different perspective

Geiselman and Callot (1990, cited in Memon and Higham, 1999) found recalling in forward order once and then going back in reverse order was more effective than going from the start twice. Memon and Higham (1990) report that there is no evidence (up to 1999) that going from the start and then recalling back from the end gives more information than just going through the story again. Milne (1997, cited in Memon and Higham, 1999) suggests that, with some specific prompts, the technique of forward and then backwards recall can help.

Other evidence about the effectiveness of the cognitive interview

- According to Memon and Higham, there have not been many studies (up to 1999) that separate out the different ideas in the cognitive interview so that they are researched separately and evidence gathered.
- Memon et al. (1996a) used an experiment where college students were interviewed about a staged event with three different conditions being used. They use context reinstatement, changed perspective, changed order and also a control group asked to 'try harder'. It was thought that all these conditions would have the same amount of recall, and that was what was found. The witnesses were aged 5–8 years old. They did note that the younger children had more problems with using the cognitive techniques, which was interesting.
- Milne (1997, reported in Memon et al., 1999) replicated Memon et al. (1996a) to an extent but also looked at the cognitive interview as a whole and found that the full cognitive interview condition achieved more recall than the other single technique conditions, except for context reinstatement. Context reinstatement is thought to be the most effective technique in the cognitive interview.
- McCauley and Fisher (1995, cited in Memon and Higham, 1999) suggest that the effectiveness of the cognitive interview is the improved communication and access to information using context reinstatement and so on, and that the factors work together to be effective.
- Johnson et al. (1993, cited in Memon and Higham, 1999) suggest using imaging when reinstating the

context might be a problem regarding accurate recall. For example, Johnson et al., (1979) found that people who repeatedly imagined a picture they had seen did have false recall. Suengas and Johnson (1988, cited in Memon and Higham, 1999) found that when people thought about characteristics of an imagined event, such as what it made them feel like, they began to think they had experienced the event. Focusing on an imagined event made the imagined event seem real.

- Roberts (1996, cited in Memon and Higham, 1999) thought that if witnesses focus on imagining a real event they might confuse the original event with what they imagined. There is a risk of creating false memories.
- Memon and Higham (1999) conclude their review of effectiveness of cognitive interviewing by suggesting that context reinstatement with imagery, used cautiously and if it is not suggestive and confusions are monitored, is the only effective cognitive technique used in the cognitive interview.

> ### Explore
> You can access Memon and Higham's review using this link:
> http://cogprints.org/640/1/memon.ci_review.html

Studies focusing on the cognitive interview technique

Arsuffi (2010)

At the start of this chapter a 'study of interest' was briefly outlined by Arsuffi (2010), who used the cognitive interview technique with Mr A, the participant in the reported case study. The cognitive interview was said not to help in getting information for an assessment and formulation about Mr A, who had been convicted of the manslaughter of his wife. It was said that mental health issues had probably prevented a cognitive interview being useful. This case study shows that cognitive interview techniques can be used outside the police role of building a case for court and can be used later in the process. Cognitive interviewing is used in many different areas, such as nursing, as well as with offenders. It is interesting though that Arsuffi (2010) reported the cognitive interview as giving little additional information. Perhaps, however, Mr A was already cooperative and giving what information he could and possibly, as Arsuffi suggested, his mental health issues prevented a cognitive interview from being successful. This might be a limitation of such interviewing.

Geiselman et al. (1985)

Geiselman et al. (1985) aimed to look at the effectiveness of the cognitive interview. They asked participants to watch a film of a violent crime and then 48 hours after watching the film the participants were interviewed (individually) by a policeman. Three methods were used. These were the standard interview, the cognitive interview and an interview using hypnosis. The number of facts that were correct and number of errors were recorded. For the cognitive interview, the average number of correctly recalled facts was 41.2 as opposed to 38.0 for the hypnosis and 29.4 for the standard police interview. With regard to the errors, there were no significant differences. The conclusion was that the cognitive interview led to better recall and more relevant information was recalled.

Köhnken et al. (1999)

Köhnken et al. (1999) carried out a meta-analysis of 42 studies that looked at cognitive interviewing. The study looked at the effects of cognitive interviewing on correct and incorrect recall. The studies covered around 2,500 interviewees and there was a strong effect size found for the cognitive interview increasing the number of correctly recalled details compared with a control interview. A 'control' interview would be a standard interview. There was also a small significant effect showing that there were more incorrect details from the cognitive interview, which is interesting. The accuracy of recall, calculated by working out the proportion of correct details relative to the total number of details, was not different between the two interviews, with figures of 85 per cent for the cognitive interview and 82 per cent for the standard interview. Staged events gave a larger effect size regarding correct detail than video films in the studies and there was a larger effect size regarding correct detail if the interviewee had participated in the event than if they had not. The enhanced version of the cognitive interview gave more errors than the original version of the cognitive interview. There were some interesting findings from this meta-analysis. One was that perhaps witnesses involved in the event in question would recall more than those who were bystanders, which might be useful to know. Another conclusion was that as staged events gave better correct recall than video, the more realistic a situation in an experiment, the more recall is affected, which suggests a lack of validity in some experiments. It was also found that correct details were not found more in a cognitive interview relative to what was recalled – perhaps more was recalled in a cognitive interview, which means more correct details, though, which is positive evidence for choosing to use cognitive interviewing, even though there was a lot more recalled overall, a lot of which might have been incorrect. A final conclusion is that the enhanced cognitive interview might not be better.

Holliday et al. (2012)

Holliday et al. (2012) looked at the effect of using a cognitive interview on young and older adults to look at their recall of a short film of a staged crime with some misinformation reported to them after they had watched the event. After the watching of the film and after the misinformation had subsequently been introduced, an interview was carried out. In one condition, this was a modified cognitive interview and in the other condition they used a control interview together with a recognition memory test. The modified cognitive interview found more correct details and better overall accuracy than the control interview, and this was the case in both age groups. The young adults recalled three times more correct information in the modified cognitive interview than the older adults did. The cognitive interview achieved more person details and more action details than the control interview. Also, importantly, older adults interviewed with the modified cognitive interview were not affected by **misinformation effects**.

Definition

The **misinformation effect** is when incorrect information after an event is somehow incorporated into the memory of the event and affects recall negatively.

Progress check 3.33

With regard to Holliday et al. (2012), give two independent variables in their experiment.

Progress check 3.34

Give one piece of evidence that shows that, although more accurate details are recalled using the cognitive interview, it is not that errors in recall are reduced. Also discuss one other piece of evidence looking at errors recalled depending on interview type.

Sooniste et al. (2015)

Sooniste et al. (2015) used the cognitive interview to look at differences in answering planned and unanticipated questions, using either a cognitive interview or a standard interview technique. Half the participants planned a non-criminal event and half planned a mock crime. Half were interviewed using cognitive interview elements and half using a standard interview. All participants had two sets of questions; one set was about their stated intentions in what they had planned and one set was about the planning phase itself. The ones who had planned a non-criminal act were told to tell the truth during the interview, whereas those who had planned a mock criminal act were told to hide their criminal intentions and to lie – they prepared a cover story that was structured similarly to the non-criminal intentions given by the participants telling the truth.

The hypothesis was that the truth-telling participants and the liars would anticipate the questions focusing on their intentions more than they would anticipate the questions about the planning phase. Liars would give less detailed answers to the unanticipated questions and, importantly, this detail would be affected by the type of interview. The researchers predicted that there would be a larger difference regarding richness and detail between liars' and truth-tellers' answers to the questions about the planning phase when a cognitive interview was used compared with a standard interview. This was an important hypothesis. They used 125 participants, and not just students. The study was done in Sweden and participants were recruited by advertisement, including on the website, and also **snowball sampling**. They were all told they could leave at any time and would be compensated for any discomfort. The design was independent groups. There were the two conditions of truth teller and liar and the two conditions of cognitive or standard interview. Participants were randomly allocated to the conditions as follows:

- A 'veracity' condition had truth tellers where the non-criminal activity was planned. There were 64 participants in this condition. This was a true intention condition.
- Another condition had liars where the mock criminal activity was planned. There were 61 participants. This was a false intention condition.
- Half of those in the truth-telling condition (31 participants) had a cognitive interview.
- Half in the liars condition (30 participants) had a cognitive interview.
- Half of the liars (31 participants) had a standard interview.
- Half of the truth tellers (33 participants) had a standard interview.

Definition

Snowball sampling refers to finding one participant who then introduces the researcher(s) to others and the size of the sample grows like a snowball.

Results

The liars rated their lying much higher than the truth tellers rated their own lying (p<.001), suggesting that the two groups did follow instructions to either lie or tell the truth. Table 3.12 shows the perceptions of the truth tellers and liars with regard to the planning phase.

Table 3.12 The perceptions of the truth tellers and liars regarding their view of the planning phase of the study. The mean average rating out of 7 is given.

Variable	Truth tellers' mean score	Liars' mean score
Truth degree	1.64	5.06
Motivation	5.99	5.78
Difficult to plan	3.25	4.24
Planning satisfaction	5.16	4.38
Time satisfaction	5.57	4.90
Question anticipated	3.17	3.78

The two groups were similarly motivated and liars were less satisfied with the planning phase than truth tellers. They were also less satisfied with the time allowed. Truth tellers said they found it easier to plan for future events.

Truth tellers' answers were seen as significantly more detailed than the answers of the liars when asked about the planning phase (p<.001). The cognitive interview was seen as giving more detailed answers to the main question on the planning phase than the standard interview (p<.001). The relationship between veracity (whether participants were truth tellers or not) and interview type (cognitive or standard interview) was found to be significant (p=0.02). The truth tellers' answers were significantly more detailed in both types of interview compared with the liars' answers – the significance level for the difference in detail using the cognitive interview was p<.001 and using the standard interview was p<.01. The difference between truth tellers and liars was more pronounced when using the cognitive interview.

Progress check 3.35

Sooniste et al. (2015) say that the relationship between whether the participants were telling the truth or not and whether they had a standard or cognitive interview was significant at p=.02. Explain this significance level.

Conclusions

There were other findings too, but those summarised here relate to the cognitive interviewing as that is the focus of this section. The researchers found that using a cognitive interview magnified differences in detail coming from truth tellers and liars, as it was thought. There were also other findings, including that liars gave less detail when questions were not anticipated, which could be a useful finding. Participants interviewed with a cognitive interview gave more detailed answers than those interviewed with a standard interview, which is in line with what other studies looking at the cognitive interview would predict and is what the cognitive interview was developed for. Unanticipated questions are worth asking in an interview as truth tellers gave more detailed answers about their planning than liars in both types of interviewing but it was in the cognitive interview that the difference was seen most. When they lie, people answer unexpected questions with less detail than expected questions and even less detail in a cognitive interview. So one way of finding out if someone is lying is by asking unexpected questions and seeing whether the answer is very detailed. If it is just as detailed as with expected questions, it might be the truth, but if less detailed, then the person might be lying.

This was a lab experiment, with all the caveats about lacking ecological validity. In this study, the participants planned what they were told to plan, which limited the validity. Also many of the participants were university students, which can limit generalisability. These are limitations that are often made against laboratory experiments (page 314).

Evaluation of the cognitive interview technique

Strengths

- The cognitive interview aims to get as much detail as possible from the witness using strategies such as starting from a different place in the 'story'. This is a strength as police may not know the value of different details at the time of the interview so being thorough is important. Also finding some detail can trigger other detail, so it is a useful technique for aiding recall. Holliday *et al.* (2012) found more correct details from both older and young adults using a modified version of the cognitive interview compared with a control interview. Memon and Higham say that there is some evidence that context reinstatement can help recall of events (e.g. Milne, 1997, cited in Memon and Higham, 1999). So there is evidence that the cognitive interview techniques can help with regard to correct details recalled.
- By not using leading questions, as shown by Loftus and colleagues (e.g. Loftus and Palmer, 1974; see page 330), there won't be the effects on testimony that such

questions give. For example, if someone asks about cars that 'smashed' into one another, it is shown that using the verb 'smashed' affects how fast someone thinks the cars were going. Recall is less affected if open and non-leading questions are used, including 'tell me about it', which is very broad. Studies looking at eyewitness testimony and finding it to be unreliable show how leading questions affect recall. This is evidence in favour of the open questioning techniques used in cognitive interviewing.

Weaknesses

- What is planned in theory might not be easy to do in practice. For example, the police might be in the middle of a large investigation and want to interview witnesses quickly, which may not give the best circumstances in which to concentrate on a cognitive interview. There needs to be the training and time taken. Building a rapport, giving control to the interviewee and letting them lead the interview is perhaps not easy to achieve in practice as, for example, the police might find it hard not to focus on what they want to know first.
- Even with training, it is difficult to avoid asking leading questions if the interviewer knows things about the event. It would take concentration not to lead a witness. The interviewing would need to be done by someone not only trained in such interviewing but who also practises it regularly so that open questioning becomes almost automatic for them. Asking only open questions takes practice.

> **STUDY HINT**
> When giving a strength or a weakness of something like the cognitive interview technique (or another process or theory), be careful not to say what the technique or theory is and offer that as a strength. For example, saying the cognitive interview asks for as much recall as possible and that is a strength – this is not that helpful as part of what the cognitive interview does is to ask for as much recall as possible.

Progress check 3.36

Explain why this answer is not enough as a strength of cognitive interviewing:

'The cognitive interview aims to get as much detail as possible from the witness using strategies such as starting from a different place in the "story". Also finding some detail can trigger other detail, so it is a useful technique for aiding recall.'

Ethical interviewing techniques

Interviewing an offender or someone charged with a crime, before being sentenced, has to be done ethically, as do all interviews. This can be challenging as the crime in question might be shocking and an interviewer is not going to be immune to such issues. It is the interviewer in charge of the interview who is responsible for working ethically. Conducting an ethical interview is more likely to get valid information than if the interviewer brings their own views and judgements into the interviewing process. There has to be 'due process', which means the criminal justice system tends to have the power in a situation, such as where someone is being interviewed before possibly being charged, and yet the individual has rights which must be adhered to.

Some ethical standards for interviewing relating to crime

- Every human being has worth and is to be treated with dignity. This relates to self-determination, part of the principles in the BPS Code of Ethics and Conduct (2009).
- An interview must be carried out in a non-judgemental way, with openness, and treat interviewees in a fair way.
- Interviewers must not affect the interview or the data gathered.
- In this regard, interviews must not involve coercion and material gained from an interview must not be suppressed.
- Interviewers should use different ways of getting information so that reliability and validity can be checked as far as possible.
- There should be no shortcuts in an interview; the truth must be the focus and not a confession.
- Anyone with special needs of any sort must be treated with additional care when interviewing, taking account of their needs.
- Interviewers should not bring in false information or use deception to get a confession as this is deceiving someone and is not ethical.

Savage and Milne (2007, cited in Roberts, 2011) put forward issues that should be covered in ethical interview. Issues include:

1 **P**lanning and preparation

   The planning phase is about the importance of planning an interview before carrying it out, such as noting aims and objectives as well as required outcomes. Topics of interest are noted and questions designed. The place and time of the interview are also planned as well as how it will be recorded.

2 **E**ngage and explain

   There is a need to build rapport with a suspect, which means explaining how the interview will take place and to answer questions to allay concerns. Witnesses are told what to expect.

3 **A**ccount

   The account is the invitation to a suspect to provide an account of their behaviour depending on what is being investigated. The way the account will be asked for and how it would be elicited from a witness is decided upon. The ethical interview includes ideas about different ways of doing this.

4 **C**losure

   Closure is about bringing an interview to a good conclusion and maintaining rapport. The aim is to avoid anger or anxiety as the interview ends.

5 **E**valuate

   Interviews should be evaluated against the required aims to look at the material obtained.

PEACE is a helpful way of remembering ethical interviewing. PEACE is a structure that is meant to build trust and the idea of 'Engage and explain' is that the person feels their needs are being listened to and taken into account in the interview planning.

Progress check 3.37

What does the acronym PEACE stand for (in relation to ethical interviewing)?

Some history, leading to PEACE

Roberts (2012) says that from the 1960s police behaviour regarding the arrest and interviewing of suspects was of concern and because of that there was a review carried out in the UK (Baldwin, 1992, 1993, cited in Roberts, 2012). Baldwin looked at 400 videos and 200 audio recordings of interviews carried out by the police and concluded that interviewing standards were low. Problems found were no rapport being developed with a suspect, looking for a confession and trying to get the suspect to accept the interviewer's version of events. Interviewers tended not to listen to the suspect and tended to interrupt. Baldwin (1993) suggested that some interviewers were aggressive and provocative and the worst took a macho approach.

Roberts (2012) reported that many of these issues were also found when witnesses to a crime were interviewed. Roberts (2012) reported a lot of studies showing the same thing about interviewing being accusatory (Stephenson and Moston, 1993, 1994) and persuasive (Inbau *et al.*, 2004). What was also found was that when interviewers were seen as weak and used an information-gathering approach, they tended to increase the chance of a suspect giving an account of the event.

Roberts (2012) reported reasons for a suspect not wanting to engage with an interview. These were psychological factors such as anxiety, fear, depression and anxiety; mental health status; intelligence; and general attitude towards the police (Shepherd, 1993, cited in Roberts, 2012). Other factors that seemed to lead to non-engagement included inappropriate listening by the interviewer, disruptions from the interviewer, not pacing an interview properly and not allowing time for reflection. It was thought that these factors all pointed to the interviewer signalling a lack of interest and as such they were barriers to communication. Another issue was failure to explain the interview situation properly, such as what was going to happen in the interview. This affects suspects as they do not know how to behave or what the police want, or what will happen to them (Shepherd, 1991, cited in Roberts, 2012).

It was Shepherd (1992, cited in Roberts, 2012) who used the term 'ethical interviewing' to explain interviewing that avoided the issues that made them unsuccessful. Interviewers should treat suspects with respect, as equals and with the same rights to dignity, self-determination and choice. Baldwin (1993, cited in Roberts, 2012) put forward the idea of rapport-based interviewing using a non-accusational approach. PEACE was the UK's effort at ethical interviewing.

Table 3.13 Summary of studies in Roberts (2012) to help with understanding issues of ethical interviewing

Name of researcher(s) (in Roberts, 2012)	Point relating to ethical interviewing
Baldwin (1992, 1993)	Carried out a review of police interviewing because of concerns about the process, including ethics
Stephenson and Moston (1993, 1994)	Suggested standard interviewing had a strong accusatory element
Inbau *et al.* (2004)	Suggested standard interviewing had a strong persuasive element
Shepherd (1993)	Suggested that there were psychological factors such as anxiety, fear, depression and anxiety; mental health status; intelligence; and general attitude towards the police that led suspects and maybe witnesses not to agree to being interviewed
Shepherd (1991)	Found there was a failure to explain to suspects (and witnesses) what would happen in the interview, so that suspects did not know how to behave, what the police wanted or what would happen to them
Shepherd (1992)	The 'ethical interview' was coined to explain interviewing that could avoid the issues that made them unsuccessful. Interviewers should treat suspects with respect, as equals and with the same rights to dignity, self-determination and choice
Baldwin (1993)	Put forward the idea of rapport-based interviewing using a non-accusational approach

Ethical v. cognitive interviewing

The focus on rapport is important because rapport leads to trust, which reduces anxiety and distress in a witness or suspect, meaning more information is likely to be disclosed in an interview. It also means more reliable information. This evidence is from Fisher and Geiselman (1992), who talked about using a cognitive interview. Using ethical interviewing and cognitive interviewing are similar in many aspects, including a drive to uncover as much correct information as possible. However, the ethical interview emphasises using rapport to reduce stress and anxiety for moral and ethical reasons as much as for producing correct information. Fisher and Geiselman (1992) also emphasise ethics when they suggest that rapport means showing empathy and active listening – paying attention to the needs of the witness or suspect not only improves the interview with regard to information yielded but adheres to ethical guidelines, such as allowing self-determination.

Year One link: Self-determination is part of the ethical principle of respect, which is explained in the BPS Code of Ethics and Conduct that you studied in social psychology.

In the PEACE model, closure is about getting any final information, if considering the efficiency of the interview. However, it is also about making sure the witness or suspect is not left feeling distressed or anxious by the interview (or no more than they will be anyway in the circumstances).

Approaches that can be used in ethical interviewing

The 'account' part of the PEACE model is where the suspect or witness tells the story the interviewer wants to uncover. There are different strategies that can be used within conversation management.

- Conversation management focuses on what is known from memory research. There are three phases: the suspect agenda, the police agenda and the challenge. These ideas are from Shepherd (1991, cited in Roberts, 2012).
- The suspect agenda starts with open questions about the offence and the suspect can say anything about it. The interviewer lets the suspect speak in their own words without interruption. The interview focuses on the suspect's agenda.
- The police agenda is to clarify the account though not to challenge it. Issues the suspect did not cover but are of police interest can be explored, and this is about getting fine detail. Roberts (2012) gives the example of a suspect saying they were driving a yellow car (the suspect agenda) and then the interviewer asking for more detail, such as its registration (the police agenda).
- The challenge phase is where an interviewer would explore any inconsistencies or inaccuracies that had come up in the other stages. The reason for leaving challenge to the end is to avoid confusion because of the questions or confabulation.

Year One link: Recall what you learned about the reconstructive model of memory and about confabulation, meaning a tendency to fill in gaps to make a story make sense.

- Challenge should be done calmly and in a controlled way without anger or threats, as Ord et al. (2008, cited in Roberts, 2012) say these raise the risk of suggestibility.

STUDY HINT

When you see phases of a process, or a list of ways of doing something, you could draw up a diagram to illustrate these points. Looking at material in a different way, a bit like taking a different perspective in a cognitive interview, can help your learning and subsequent recall.

Explore

Roberts wrote an article about police interviewing of suspects and concluded that interviewing techniques have changed over the years. You can read his article using the following link (a section on ethical interviewing starts on page 6): **www.internetjournalofcriminology.com/roberts_police_interview_criminal_suspects_ijc_dec_2012.pdf**

More issues around ethical interviewing

Mack *et al.* (2009) focused on nursing research looking at the experiences of adolescents, showing that interviews for adolescents in the area of health are 'particularly challenging'. Though the focus is on people with illness, the issues can relate to interviewing suspects and offenders. Issues include working at the developmental level of adolescence and adjusting interviews so the participants have the best possible experience when being interviewed. An issue is about establishing rapport with young patients. Current focus on doing research with young people is that they are a good source of data about their own experiences (e.g. Petersen, 2006, cited in Mack *et al.*, 2009). Interviewing is thought to need a direct, practical and naturalistic approach. This is connected to the United Nations Convention on the Rights of the Child (1989), which gives children and young people the right to participate in research about them and the right also to be protected.

Issues when wanting to interview adolescents is that an illness can affect their self-esteem (Suris, 2003, cited in Mack *et al.*, 2009) and also the diagnosis itself is likely to be stressful (e.g. Schmidt and White, 2006, cited in Mack *et al.*, 2009). Adolescents with illness may not want to consent to being involved in research because of other issues they are facing.

Mack *et al.* (2009) focus on ethical issues in interviewing adolescents with a diagnosis of illness, as follows.

Capacity

Capacity is about appreciating the benefits and risks of taking part in research (or in treatment). There is the capacity to give informed consent without parental permission, which is one issue. A child or young person has the right to participate, so should give their own consent if they wish to, and they have the right to be protected, which suggests parents should also give consent. It is not clear when a child can give assent (Ford *et al.*, 2007, cited in Mack *et al.*, 2009), which means they agree. However, mostly they should be able to assent to research and taking part in it. For a young person who has not reached the age of 18 years (in the UK), parents must give informed consent to a researcher approaching them to get their assent. These issues can apply to police interviewing of young people.

Protection of the child or young person

A researcher has to weigh up costs and benefits to each child of carrying out interviewing. This is about the well-being of vulnerable participants. Rapport should be developed and the interview should progress in a non-judgemental way, treating the adolescent with respect. There should be active listening.

Sharing power

There is also the issue of sharing power and the interviewer should give up some of the control in the situation. An adolescent could choose the interview date and time, for example. There can also be a reminder that the adolescent has the freedom to refuse to answer questions and that their opinion has value.

Although Mack *et al.* (2009) were looking at interviews of adolescents diagnosed with an illness, which is not the same as focusing on understanding offenders, the points about ethical interviewing with regard to this vulnerable group apply. The young person has the right to be heard and to participate in research about them and they have the right to be protected. Even if parents give informed consent for the young person to be interviewed, the young person must give assent. There should be rapport-building and the young interviewee should be respected and listened to carefully. They need to be reminded too that their data have value for the interviewer and that they can refuse to answer certain questions and withdraw at any time (depending on the situation, if it is about a criminal act). There should be active listening and some power given to the interviewee, such as when the interview takes place. These 'rules' for ethical interviewing could be applied in an offender situation for the same reasons as in a nursing situation, to do with respect, low self-esteem issues and the right to both participate and be protected.

Progress check 3.39

List three features you would expect in ethical interviewing.

Studies looking at ethical interviewing

Kebbell *et al.* (2010)

Kebbell *et al.* (2010) looked at the perceptions of sex offenders regarding police interviewing. The researchers wanted to see whether there was a relationship between how sex offenders viewed police interviewing and whether they confessed or not. The participants were 43 convicted sex offenders and they were interviewed using a questionnaire about different interviewing strategies. Twenty violent offenders were included so that comparisons could be drawn between their answers and answers of the sex offenders. The interviewing types were: evidence presenting strategies; ethical interviewing; displays of humanity; displays of dominance; use of minimisation and maximisation techniques; and showing an understanding of the cognitive distortions of sex offenders. It was found that evidence presenting strategies, ethical interviewing and displays of humanity were seen as more likely to get a confession. Interviewer dominance was seen to link to the reduction of the likelihood of a confession. This is evidence not only that interviews must be ethical, on moral grounds, but that ethical interviewing is also more effective.

Roberts (2011)

Roberts (2011) looked at police interviews with terrorist suspects focusing on risks, ethical interviewing and justice. The focus was on the social context within which interviews with terrorist suspects would take place and how the context might affect how the interview would be carried out by police officers. The idea was that there might be 'robust, even aggressive tactics'. Risks include getting unreliable information as well as the risk of such interviewing impacting on the community and affecting police–community cooperation. A way of improving such interviewing is to improve the cultural awareness of police officers and another way is to improve how interviewing is done. The use of ethical interviews is suggested, including focusing on the planning and preparation, engaging and explaining, the account, closure, evaluation of the interview and managing conversation. Roberts suggests that using ethical interviewing may improve reliability of interviewee information as well as affect how communities view police. This study gives information in favour of ethical interviewing.

Walsh and Milne (2010)

Walsh and Milne (2010) looked at the interviewing ability of investigators of benefit fraud in particular. They focused on the effects of training using the PEACE model, which is preferred by the British police. Walsh and Milne analysed 99 audiotapes of interviews of benefit fraud suspects. They then compared the performance of trained and untrained investigators to see if training using PEACE gave better interviewing. They measured 56 behaviours and procedures in order to categorise the interviews. They found that the trained investigators were better with regard to the effective use of open questioning, which it was said earlier in this section might be difficult and would need training. Using open questions led to more detail from suspects and, importantly, a 'comprehensive fulfilment of the necessary legal requirements'. This means the trained interviewer got more detail and adhered to the law successfully with regard to the interviewing. Unethical practices were rarely found in the interviewing. However, Walsh and Milne (2010) did not find much evidence of planning, which is the first part of the PEACE model. The

lack of planning was thought to have affected the structure and flexibility of the interviews.

The results of Walsh and Milne highlighted concerns with not enough rapport building, not enough focus on points that needed proof, not enough exploration of the suspects' motives and not enough summarising during an interview. They concluded that there was better interviewing after interview training but not enough to say there was increased professionalism. Walsh and Milne say that more training is needed in the PEACE model and in other appropriate interviewing skills.

> **STUDY HINT**
> You have probably noticed that when a particular area is being explored some names crop up quite a lot, such as Milne when looking at interviewing. When you notice this, you could use the name to research in the field further if you want to. It is common in academic circles for a few people to work in a specialist area, such as Fisher and Geiselman in the cognitive interview field.

Progress check 3.40

What are three benefits of using tapes of actual interviews when analysing how interviews are carried out?

Evaluation of ethical interviewing of offenders (and witnesses)

Strengths

- There is evidence that ethical interviewing is more effective than standard interviewing. Kebbell *et al.* (2010) found some interviewing techniques were better than others and included ethical interviewing in the 'effective' category. Roberts (2011) suggests that using ethical interviewing may improve reliability of interviewee information as well as affect how communities view police. Ethical interviewing is good regarding moral concerns, such as building rapport and acknowledging that harm should not be done and there should be self-determination. It is also good with regard to getting reliable, detailed information.
- Although it can be hard to separate effectiveness of ethical interviewing, using the PEACE model, from moral and ethical success in using such interviewing, a strength is that there is little need to separate the two aspects of interviewing as ethical interviewing seems to get more detail and more reliable recall in any case, as well as adhering to ethical principles. Fisher and Geiselman (1992) emphasise this point. They suggest

that rapport means showing empathy and active listening, including paying attention to the needs of the witness or suspect, which not only improves the interview with regard to information yielded but adheres to ethical guidelines, such as allowing self-determination.

Weaknesses

- A weakness with ethical interviewing is, even though it is said to be chosen by British police, it seems not to be used in all situations. Walsh and Milne (2010) showed that even interviewers trained in ethical interviewing were not that good at building the rapport required and it seemed that in the 99 audiotapes of interviews of benefit fraud suspects, even though ethical interviewing using the PEACE model is the required standard, it might not be used fully, which is likely to limit its effectiveness with regard to what is uncovered, but also with regard to ethics in the interview situation.
- In studies looking at ethical interviewing, there is often focus on what is recalled, including the detail and whether it is correct. This is similar to the cognitive interview in that, for example, building a rapport is said to help to relax witnesses and to aid recall. However, studies looking at the ethical implications alone of ethical interviewing seem to be harder to track down.

Test yourself

Explain similarities and differences between ethical and cognitive interviewing. **(12 marks)**

Psychological formulation relating to offenders

Formulation is what happens after conviction. It is about understanding the offender, analysing the offence and considering what function the offence might have for the individual.

Offence analysis and assessment of risk

Offence analysis comes from the assessment part of understanding the offender. Then there is case formulation before treatment is put into place. A difficulty for forensic psychologists is that they cannot observe the behaviour in order to analyse it or to assess risk. The answer is to find a similar offence and draw conclusions from that about a different offender or to look for behaviour and issues that go along with the offence – called contingencies – and, from what is observed, draw conclusions. The idea is to look at the **criminogenic** state and attitudes, though this is not reconstructing the situation at the time of the offence so some detail is going to be missed.

A problem with offence analysis and assessment is validity as data are often gathered using self-report methods which are retrospective and also will be interpreting the events. Hanson and Wallace-Capretta (2000, cited in Jones, 2010, in Daffern et al., 2010, eds) found that 'batterers' in their study did change their attitudes when treated. However, positive treatment scores did not predict a fall in recidivism. Self-reported improvements were associated with increased recidivism, which strongly suggests that self-report data are not valid. A related issue is that likelihood of reconviction might not be the best measure of risk. This is because offenders can report what attitudes and thoughts they want to, and these may be down to wanting to evade detection with regard to their risk of re-offending. It might be that reconviction measures just capture those who are not using good detection evasion skills. Jones (2004, cited in Jones 2010) claims that most offending goes undetected. There are issues in using behaviour once convicted to predict behaviour once released. Aggression once convicted might not match any aggression shown in the offence. It might be that the aggression before conviction was not detected, or it might be that being in prison leads to the aggression which would not occur once released. Assessing risk has these difficulties.

Definitions

Offence analysis refers to the analysis of a crime, including assessment of the offender. It is from the assessment that a formulation can be done. **Criminogenic** means anything that is likely to cause criminal behaviour, so refers to underlying reasons for a crime.

Photo posed by models

Street fighting has contingencies such as being with friends or possibly drinking alcohol. There can be criminogenic factors too such as money worries or low self-esteem because of job issues.

Progress check 3.41

In the account about using self-report data to assess risk of re-offending, what is the point made about validity?

Year One link: You looked at self-report data and questionnaires and interviews as ways of gathering self-report data in social psychology.

Offence cycles

The assumption is that whatever contingencies were around at the time of the offence, if repeated, are likely to lead to the offence happening again. Another assumption is that once an offender has committed an offence they can do it again in the same way. Therefore, treatment will focus on strategies to avoid the contingencies, such as avoiding high-risk situations. Also Ward *et al.* (2007, cited in Jones, 2010) suggest the focus should be on 'approach goals', which means setting up a lifestyle where there is no need to offend because needs are met. These are ways of breaking offence cycles. Either the situation that might lead to the offence being repeated should be avoided or a lifestyle set up where needs are met, or both.

Addiction to crime

Hodge (1997, cited in Jones, 2010) suggests that crime can be understood by thinking about addiction. There is a pattern of repetitive offending for some offenders and that might include tolerance, which is the need to do more to get the same effect; withdrawal, which is distress after some time not offending; craving, which is the distress from the desire to offend again; salience, which is the importance of the offending lifestyle for the person; conflict, which is an increasing awareness of the bad consequences of offending; and then relapse, which is offending again after a period of resistance.

Year One link: You could draw on issues around addiction to recreational drugs, which you learned about in biological psychology, to understand how, for some people, offending might be like an addiction.

Psychological similarity

There is a lot to offence analysis and assessment, and your course just mentions offence analysis briefly, with the focus on psychological formulation. Therefore, not much on offence analysis is given in this section, just enough for you to see some of the issues with assessment, and also because case formulation can include offence analysis.

One means of assessment is to look at patterns in reasons for offending. Behaviours can be said to be the same because they have the same function or come from the same psychological processes as behaviours at the time of an offence. Perhaps at the time of the offence an offender was humiliated over a relationship and so raped a stranger, which relieved the humiliation and gave a sense of power (Jones, 2010). In custody, the person may experience humiliation and in his room may fantasise about raping a woman, which reduces feelings of humiliation and gives a feeling of power. The point is that the function of the rape or rape fantasy was the same and knowing the function can help an assessment. There is a case for looking for functional similarity in offences and things to focus on include relationships and status, as well as psychological and cognitive states. Jones (2004, cited in Jones, 2010) suggests that where behaviour in a crime and how the crime was committed are similar to another crime, the function is likely to be similar.

Progress check 3.42

What does it mean to say that, in two different offences, there may be functional similarity?

Schema therapy

When you looked at the idea of memory being reconstructed, you looked at schemas and how people see the world through their schemas, which are built from experiences with the world. Young *et al.* (2003, cited in Jones, 2010) used schemas to understand people's experiences and their moods. Schema theory can be used in offence analysis as well. Young *et al.* (2003, cited in Jones, 2010) discuss patterns of behaviour that are repeated and they relate such behaviour to certain schemas or core beliefs. They call patterns of repeating episodes 'repisodes'. These are episodes in someone's life that repeat themselves, such as maladaptive responses to relationships or to difficult life events. There are core ways of thinking that shape someone's behaviour and such constructs can guide offending behaviour.

Explore

If you would like to read more about Young's ideas about schemas being used in therapy, here is a link:
www.contemporarypsychotherapy.org/vol-2-no-2/schema-theray/

Year One link: You learned about the influence of schemas on memory when you covered cognitive psychology.

Case formulation

Case formulation includes offence analysis because it goes from the assessment, which gives the information, to the analysis, and linking to theory, which can then hopefully suggest a useful and effective treatment plan.

Case formulation takes the key features of an offender – a 'case' – in order to choose suitable treatment. It can also help an offender to understand their own issues and can improve the therapeutic relationship between the offender and the therapist (Eells, 2007a, cited in Sturmey, 2010, in Daffern *et al.*, 2010, eds). Case formulation is done by clinical and counselling psychologists in clinical settings and relating to mental health issues, so it is not just done by forensic psychologists. In your course, you are asked to look at psychological formulation to understand the function of the behaviour for the individual. The example of someone experiencing humiliation in relationships and so turning to rape to get rid of such feelings and to capture a feeling of power is an illustration on how offending behaviour can be **functional** for the individual.

Definition

When behaviour is said to be **functional**, it means it serves a purpose, and looking at what function a behaviour fulfils for a person is about seeing what purpose the behaviour has for that individual.

In a forensic context, case formulation has the purpose of summarising the development of offending and related behaviour (Gresswell and Hollin, 1992, cited in Sturmey, 2010) and of predicting treatment that will be the most effective, as well as suggesting a rehabilitation programme for the individual client (Haynes and O'Brien, 2000, cited in Sturmey, 2010). In a forensic context, case formulation can also have a slightly different meaning, focusing on treatability, risk assessment and likelihood of re-offending, and can be something prepared for a judge, for example.

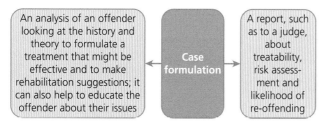

What case formulation means when applied to an offender

Case formulation tends to cover a range of offender mental health problems, some of which are long-standing and dangerous and so more common in forensic settings, such as arson, sexual offending, self-harm and aggression. Forensic mental health professionals also formulate more common conditions, such as depression and anxiety. Forensic psychologist courses include case formulation; it is an important part of the role. Case formulation helps in 'understanding offender histories, current offending behaviour and mental health problems' (Sturmey, 2010, p. 25).

Progress check 3.43

How might forensic mental health professionals formulate depression?

Defining case formulation

Formulation leading to diagnosis

Describing problems and predicting the best treatment can be called 'diagnosis', and you looked at diagnosis and related issues in clinical psychology. Risk assessment also describes problems and predicts treatment. It could be said that case formulation gathers together information that can then be used to make a diagnosis, such as in the case of depression, using information to pick out features and symptoms of depression and thus prescribing medication, such as SSRIs (selective serotonin reuptake inhibitors). Also there are manuals and protocols for certain treatments, which clinicians can turn to once the formulation shows the features and symptoms that suit such treatments. An example would be anorexia or OCD (obsessive compulsive disorder), which you may have covered in clinical psychology and which are discussed in Chapter One. The British National Institute for Health and Clinical Excellence (NICE) publish guidelines around diagnosis such that, after a diagnosis has taken place, a clinician can look up the preferred treatment and what it entails.

Formulation versus diagnosis

However, case formulation can be done in place of diagnosis, as is the case in counselling. There are limitations to diagnosis when it comes to predicting the most effective treatment. Diagnosis can be unreliable and lack validity. People with the same diagnosis might not react in the same way to the same treatment and evidence about the effectiveness of diagnosis often comes from randomised controlled trials, as you will have seen when studying clinical psychology, and these can lack external validity. There are also a large number of clients with multiple diagnoses who might need more than one treatment and some who have already undergone the recommended treatment without success. There are diagnoses where evidence-based treatments are not available and unique clients who do not fit diagnostic categories. You can see in the list of issues in Table 3.14 that there are problems with diagnosis.

> **STUDY HINT**
> The problems about diagnosis listed here are useful when considering diagnosis issues that were covered in clinical psychology, in Chapter One. You could look at your notes about diagnosis in clinical psychology and link the ideas in with those offered here to add depth to any discussion. However, in criminological psychology be sure to focus on offenders and in clinical psychology on those with mental health issues, though of course the two overlap.

Case formulation tends to be seen as 'beyond diagnosis' (Bruch and Bond, 1998, cited in Sturmey, 2010).

Table 3.14 Issues with diagnosis, suggesting that formulation goes 'beyond diagnosis' (adapted from Sturmey, 2010)

Issue with diagnosis	Explanation
Unreliability	You could go to two clinicians and get a different diagnosis as features and symptoms between different diagnoses could be similar and might require interpretation.
Lack of validity	A diagnosis might not predict all the features and symptoms displayed.
Individual response to treatment	One treatment plan might lead to different responses in different individuals.
Using randomised controlled trials	A problem with external validity – meaning problems with generalising from the results of artificial trials.
Multiple diagnoses	A problem with knowing which treatment plan to follow if there are multiple diagnoses in one person.
Failure to respond to treatment	A problem with clients who have already had the recommended treatment without success.
Diagnosis without treatment	There are a large number of diagnoses without fully laid-out treatment plans.
Uniqueness of individuals	A large number of clients have features and symptoms that do not fit into existing diagnoses.

Useful contexts for forensic case formulation

Drake and Ward (2003, cited in Sturmey, 2010) suggest four contexts where case formulation would be useful in a forensic situation:

- when an offender presents with complex problems and treatment is unclear – for example, presenting with substance abuse but also other problematic behaviour
- when not a lot is known about a problem, such as internet pornography
- when standard treatments have not changed behaviour in a significant way – for example, group treatment may not have worked with a sexual offender who had not found relationships with adult partners, perhaps because of unusual sexual experiences when young; he avoided adult sexual relationships and turned to sexual behaviour with his partner's children (the offending behaviour); it was only when a clinician identified the function of his behaviour for him, and addressed his problems with adult relationships, that the deviant sexual behaviour with children decreased
- when offenders do not progress and disrupt group functioning so cannot benefit from group treatment, or because they are not motivated to change for some reason.

These situations show that diagnosis is not enough in some forensic situations.

> **Progress check 3.44**
> Give three situations when formulation is more useful than diagnosis.

What is case formulation?

Eells (2007a, cited in Sturmey, 2010) says that a psychological case formulation is a hypothesis about someone's psychological, interpersonal and behavioural problems considering their causes, what has led to them and how they are maintained. Theories that can be used in a formulation include behavioural, cognitive and psychodynamic ones.

- Case formulations tend to be brief, not like the story of an offender's problems or a list of their presenting issues. There are specific features in case formulations. For example, a cognitive formulation might include ideas about underlying schemas.
- Case formulations try to integrate a lot of information from an offence analysis and assessment into some key

features. For example, a behavioural formulation might look at different behaviours and how they appear to serve the same function.

- Case formulations try to account for how the problems developed and also how they are being maintained. For example, a psychodynamic formulation might suggest that early experiences of relationships set the pattern for later relationships and might be seen in those later relationships.
- Most formulations are seen as tentative and ready to be revised in the light of new information. For example, if an offender does not respond to treatment suggested by an initial formulation and, because of that, new information comes to light, such as about their family situation, there can be a new formulation and a new treatment plan.

Year One link: When defining what a case formulation is, different areas in psychology have been mentioned. There can be cognitive formulation looking at thinking processes, and behaviour and psychodynamic formulation looking at the importance of early experiences. You covered cognitive psychology as well as the behavioural and psychodynamic approaches so you can draw on your learning about them to understand the different focuses with regard to formulation.

Another definition is that it is about preparing an evidence-based explanation of someone's difficulties, including what the difficulties are, where they have come from, how they developed and how they are maintained over time (e.g. Tarrier, 2006, cited in Hart *et al.*, 2011).

Formulations from different perspectives

'**Perspectives**' refers to different ways of looking at human behaviour and functioning. The ones covered are cognitive, behavioural and psychodynamic, all of which you have come across in your course, although they have not been referred to as perspectives.

Explanation
Perspectives in psychology are different approaches to answering questions about why we behave as we do and think the way we do. Perspectives each have a main assumption about such questions and what methods should be used to study such questions. Perspectives included are psychodynamic, behavioural and cognitive.

An example of a specific approach to formulation: the behavioural approach

The behavioural approach to formulation comes from Skinner's work on behaviourism, including the role of learning in offender behaviour and also behavioural treatment models. For example, someone might learn through fear to act in a certain way or they may not have been able to show behaviour for which they would be rewarded so they do not display good (rewardable) behaviour. Alternatively, they might not be able to behave in the way they used to behave to get rewarded. Loss is an important factor. Someone who has suffered loss might no longer be rewarded in the same way and might stop behaving in the way they used to. Loss can involve bereavement, divorce or retirement. Skinner (1971, cited in Sturmey, 2010) suggested that if someone's partner has died they can no longer be rewarded by that person and if there are many stresses because of the loss, the person might then be at risk of offending behaviour. The answer according to Skinner was to acquire skills in self-control and use of rewarding consequences for such self-control. People could slap their own hand for some behaviour they want to stop and can reward themselves for wanted behaviour.

Studies and articles looking at case formulation

In this section, studies/articles are detailed to give examples and evidence about case formulation. At the start of this chapter, there was a summary of a 'study of interest', which was a case study by Arsuffi (2010) – this also gives ideas about case formulation.

STUDY HINT
Articles are found in journals and when they are about a study they are written up in a particular format chosen by the journal. You need to know about the format for a psychology report: abstract, title, introduction, method, results, discussion, references. Articles are only accepted by a journal if they are **peer reviewed**. An editorial is a summary at the start of a journal issue.

Explanation
Peer reviewed refers to how a study or a review article is sent to a journal for publication and before being published is reviewed by people in the field to check that it is appropriate for publication.

Hart et al. (2011)

Hart *et al.* (2011) looked at case formulation. Their definition of formulation includes the process of gathering a lot of information, though they focus mainly on the product of this information gathering, which is an account of problems affecting the mental health of an individual in order to guide treatment for that individual. Hart *et al.* (2011) wanted to look at how forensic case formulation is done and also at its evaluation, which is useful as you need to be able to evaluate case formulation.

> **STUDY HINT**
> You might be interested to know that in the team of researchers summarised as Hart *et al.* (2011) is Peter Sturmey, whose ideas on case formulation have been included in this section. This emphasises how certain individuals become very involved in specific areas of study.

According to Hart *et al.* (2011), formulation includes the process of preparing the formulation and the product of the process, which is the formulation. Someone is formulating and then producing a formulation. There can be inference as the formulation can go beyond 'facts' and description to suggest explanations for the offending behaviour. Formulation has action as its aim in that it is about developing an understanding of an offender's problems and putting forward a treatment plan. Hart *et al.* (2011) cite Logan and Johnstone (2010) as saying that formulation is particularly useful for complex cases so that there can be joint working by different authorities in the justice system with an agreement come to about how to proceed.

> **Explore**
> You can access Hart *et al.* (2011) using this link:
> www.researchgate.net/profile/Mary_McMurran2/
> publication/233479011_Forensic_Case_Formulation/
> links/00b7d53625d6e2961a000000.pdf

Case formulations are driven by theory and theory guides treatment. Formulations are **individualised**, which means they are driven by the individual's history and data. The question is 'What will work for this person?', not 'What works for people with this problem?'. They are **narrative**, which means natural language is used and the approach is qualitative, taking into account the complexities of the individual and of human action. They are **diachronic**, which means they span from the past, through the present to the future – they span time. They are also **testable**, which means the formulation is explanatory and rests on theory and facts. Testability is necessary to make sure if it is not working for the individual it is changed. A formulation is also **ampliative**, which means a formulation does not simply summarise all the information on the offender but adds new information too. A summary can itself add new information if it means adding theory and explanation to data.

Definitions

Individualised when applied to a formulation means it focuses on an individual offender rather than a 'type'. **Narrative** means a formulation has qualitative elements and is written in clear, accessible language. **Diachronic** means a formulation is not just focusing on the past, present or future but spans all those time periods. **Testable** means a formulation is measurable, so it can be shown to be wrong and be amended. **Ampliative** means a formulation should not just repeat information already known but, by summarising and bringing in theory, should add new understanding of the case.

What formulation must be, according to Hart *et al.* (2011)

Hart *et al.* (2011), importantly for this section, focus on evaluating formulations. A formulation is usually evaluated in terms of its product, which is a treatment plan or a decision about risk of re-offending. However, the product relies on the process so the process of formulating can also be evaluated. An error in formulating can be important. A formulation error in not predicting an effective treatment for social anxiety might not be too serious. However, a formulation error that results in the wrong treatment for a high-risk offender might be more serious (Hart *et al.*, 2011). Evaluative criteria for formulations are presented in Table 3.15.

Table 3.15 Ideas for evaluating formulations according to Hart *et al.* (2011)

Term	Explanation – ideas to help with evaluating a formulation
External coherence	A formulation must be consistent with a theory that is generally accepted and familiar.
Factual foundation	A formulation must be based on information about the case that has quality and quantity.
Internal coherence	A formulation must rest on compatible theories and explanations.
Diachronicity	A formulation is coherent in how it ties past, present and future information together.
Simplicity	A formulation is not cluttered by unnecessary detail; it is short and focused.
Reliability	Different professionals should develop similar formulations for similar cases or the same case.
Generativity	A formulation gives predictions that are testable, including predictions about what to do about a case and any risk of violence.
Accuracy	Predictions from a formulation are accurate, giving predictive validity.
Acceptability	Offenders and others within a situation accept the formulation, which means it is likely to be collaborated with.

Theories in forensic case formulations

The risk-needs-responsivity model (**RNR model**) is a 'dominant rehabilitation model' according to Hart *et al.* (2011). There are three core principles: the **risk principle**, which is when the level of service delivered to an offender matches the risk to re-offending; the **needs principle**, which is focusing on criminogenic need, which means looking at reasons for the behaviour; and the **responsivity principle**, which means treatment should be the most effective, such as focusing on the acquisition of skills and matching the offender's learning style and motivations.

The RNR model fits into the General Personality and Cognitive Social Learning theory, which covers a range of more specific theories relating to personality, cognitive, behavioural and social factors. Eells and Lombart (2004, cited in Hart *et al.*, 2011) suggest that using different theories in a formulation is informative. Some formulations offer ideas from biological, psychodynamic, psychiatric, cognitive and behavioural approaches and then integrate these into one formulation.

Definitions
The **RNR model** is the risk-needs-responsivity model. The **risk principle** is that focus on treatment must be at a level that matches the risk the offender poses regarding re-offending. The **needs principle** means focus on the causes of offending behaviour, which means focusing on criminogenic factors. The **responsivity principle** is that the treatment must match the offender in terms of, for example, their learning style and motivation to change.

Progress check 3.45
Describe the RNR model of re-offending.

Effectiveness of formulation in improving treatment outcomes

Ghaderi (2006, cited in Hart *et al.*, 2011) suggested that there was mixed evidence with regard to whether formulation improves outcomes for offenders. McKnight *et al.* (1984, cited in Hart *et al.*, 2011) found that case formulation did predict effective treatments and also which treatments would not be effective. Ghaderi (2006) found formulation helped with suggesting a treatment plan for bulimia and the treatment was better than standard CBT (cognitive-behavioural therapy), which itself worked. Although Schulte *et al.* (1992, cited in Hart *et al.*, 2011) found formulation-based therapy was less effective than flooding, this might have been due to inexperienced therapists. Some therapies for some issues are so effective that case formulation might add nothing.

Explore
You can access a paper focusing on the formulation of violence risk, by Hart and Logan (2011), using this link:
www.sfu.ca/psyc/faculty/hart/Hart,_SFU_Website/Publications_files/Hart%20%26%20Logan,%202011,%20Sturmey%20%26%20McMurran,%20Formulation%20of%20violence%20risk.pdf

Whitehead *et al.* (2007)

Whitehead *et al.* (2007) focus on the Good Lives Model and rehabilitation and they use a case study research method. Theirs is a case study of a high-risk offender and takes the reader through the assessment, formulation, treatment planning and monitoring of this offender.

STUDY HINT
You can use Whitehead *et al.* (2007) when you are discussing the use of the case study research method in criminological psychology.

This section focuses most on the formulation process. Whitehead *et al.* (2007) suggest that with regard to treatment for adult violent offenders and the impact of treatment on reconvictions, programmes targeting criminogenic needs using cognitive-behavioural methods seemed to have the best effects (Dowden and Andrews, 2000, cited in Whitehead *et al.*, 2007). Dowden and Andrews (2000, cited in Whitehead *et al.*, 2007) concluded the RNR model of offender rehabilitation was the most suitable to use for these offenders. The suggestion is that criminogenic needs (which are the causes for the offending) must be targeted with intensity to match the intensity of the risk, and cognitive-behavioural interventions are best, including some treatment focusing on the individual, such as a lack of motivation or specific features of the individual.

The **Good Lives Model (GLM)** of offender rehabilitation can be contrasted with the RNR model. The GLM focuses on promoting the personal goals of the individual and at the same time reducing their risk of re-offending. This is similar to the idea of promoting a lifestyle that would mean moving away from criminogenic factors like peers or place lived in, and changing to a life that would not include crime. The focus is on personal identity and goals, with individuals as active agents with meaningful lives and good motivation.

Explanation

The **Good Lives Model (GLM)** of offender rehabilitation refers to taking the offender's personal values and preferences seriously and providing offenders with the skills and opportunities to develop their primary goals. A treatment plan would reflect these aims.

Progress check 3.46

Describe the GLM model of re-offending.

The case study

Mr C is the client in the case study reported by Whitehead *et al.* (2007). He gave written informed consent for his case to be discussed. Whitehead *et al.* made sure his identity was not revealed in their report. Mr C is a Maori from New Zealand, aged 28 years, and he was a prisoner out on parole. He was a member of a criminal gang, heavily tattooed and many of the tattoos proclaimed his allegiance to the gang. He showed an apparent preparedness to die for the gang. He had 20 convictions since aged 18 years for many different crimes, including burglary and violence. Most of his adult life was spent in prison and he showed a lot of violence while in prison. His last two convictions

were for aggravated robbery where he presented firearms to many victims, once including a child. He disclosed other violence apart from what he had been convicted for, including rape, though there was no evidence of deviant sexual interest in children.

Gang tattoos help someone to belong to a gang, which has functions for an individual. Violence and offending can, in this way, be functional.

In an interview, Mr C talked about his family background and early development. He was the middle child with a brother and a sister, and in the family he was exposed to violence and sexual abuse. He chose to live with his grandfather to 'avoid severe physical punishment from his parents' (p. 583). Mr C left school aged 15 without qualifications and had been involved in school truancy, assaults on other pupils and some drug misuse. This was when he started mixing with a criminal gang. Some of the gang members were relatives. Being with the gang reinforced his criminal and violent lifestyle. As an adolescent, he lived with two female prostitutes 'who took sexual advantage of him' (p. 584) and he began to use weapons and engage in 'nonconsensual' (p. 584) sex with females.

Whitehead *et al.* discuss how Mr C had been exposed to early modelled forced sex and also experiences of it himself, as well as peer approval of it and situations of dominance. Therefore, he had not had models for loving, intimate and equal relationships. For example, his belief was that rape only happened if a woman verbally said 'no'. This part of the case study illustrates formulation, where theory such as social learning is incorporated into the story.

There is a lot more in the case background but this gives ideas about information available for the formulation. Mr C was assessed as high-risk and violent. He underwent different therapies and when it came to treatment regarding rehabilitation, the GLM model was used. When being assessed, some correspondence was available written by Mr C and, while on the GLM programme, some more writing from him is presented in the case study. Here are extracts from the two pieces of writing to demonstrate the change during the course of his treatment programme. The study gives a lot more interesting detail and longer extracts, but space is short here. The first extract was from prison, after completion of a 100hr-long cognitive-behavioural programme focusing on criminogenic needs (underlying reasons) of violent offenders:

'I'm in now bro, been here for about a week, first day here smashed someone over...'

(p. 584)

The second extract was after a Good Lives plan, which considered the function of his offending behaviour. His criminogenic needs were linked to feelings of control, arousal from risk-taking and notoriety. He could not have a 'good life' because friendship was associated with his allegiance to the gang and 'offence-associated sexual arousal' (p. 591). Once an analysis of these needs had taken place, work was done to put into place skills so that Mr C could carry out his own goals and have a 'good life'. A Maori counsellor was used to 'provide culturally matched mentoring and support' (p. 592). The second extract included the following from Mr C:

'To change my life I need to change the way I think and live... To help just one person makes a difference even within myself to be educated is a big statement in my life... I'm given a chance to start a new life and way of living.'

(p. 593)

You can see the difference in the person making these two statements, which is evidence in itself for the effectiveness of the GLM of rehabilitation.

Mr C admitted to two violent incidents after his release. One was in retaliation for being pushed to the ground at a party, and he felt guilty as well as angry for not controlling himself better. The second time he 'smashed' someone in response to his partner being insulted and he reacted by wanting to join his gang again. However, he 'activated his safety plan' and got in touch with his support people. He was very distressed but he was rational enough that he could be reminded about his past goals and what he had said about not wanting to go back to prison. It is not that someone can completely withdraw from old habits; Whitehead *et al.* (2007) cite Prochaska and DiClemente (1982) and say 'one can go around the wheel of change many times before actually exiting the wheel. Mr C is no different'. The case study ends by saying that Mr C had had only a minor driving charge, but no other convictions, for 14 months after leaving prison.

Conclusions

The conclusion is that the GLM can work with risk management, by giving a more positive and motivating framework. The GLM works and 'working toward goals that are valued by the offender facilitates a collaborative approach to therapy and change' (p. 594).

Summary relating to case formulation

Whitehead *et al.*'s case study gives some insight into case formulation, such as how criminogenic needs were explained using Mr C's past experiences and behavioural theories, such as social learning and the idea of reinforcements guiding behaviour. The therapies and models, such as cognitive-behavioural therapies, the idea of risk management and the GLM are available for forensic psychologists putting together the formulation, which links the case detail, including the history and the criminogenic needs, with the available models and therapies, linking to theories underpinning them.

Progress check 3.47

What are some theories that are included in the case study presented here, which the formulation could draw on? Include how the theories can help to show the function of his offending for Mr C.

Strengths of Whitehead *et al.* (2007)

- As a case study, Whitehead *et al.* (2007) gives a lot of depth and rich detail about Mr C's offending and also his early experiences and background. The qualitative data give a full picture from which to draw up a formulation, which is individualised and has external cohesion and factual foundation. Case studies are a useful research method to use for offenders, whose cases are always going to have individual elements, and a case formulation must be focused completely on the one individual.
- The information in the case study is used not only to drive the formulation and treatment, but also to keep Mr C on track with his goals after he displays his violence and desire to be part of the gang after his release. Having support people who know all about his life and experiences helped to understand his need to go back to what he was used to and helped to communicate with him through a sound relationship underpinned by 'knowing' him. A case study can be very strong evidence for the effectiveness of a programme or model, like the GLM, which was the aim of this case study, and with regard to offenders can also be a strong way of working with an individual. It has both a theoretical and a practical element, which is a strength.

Weaknesses of Whitehead *et al.* (2007)

- A weakness of Whitehead *et al.*'s (2007) case study is that it is not easily generalisable to other offenders and it is not easy to say that the GLM will be as successful with other offenders just by drawing on one case study. The individual nature of the case study, which is its strength, is also a weakness.

- Another weakness is that reliability cannot be assured. It seemed as if the GLM was what led to the change in Mr C that was so clearly exemplified by the two statements from him, and indeed for 14 months he had managed not to re-offend. However, he had had two violent incidents, so it was questionable whether there would be recidivism. A problem with a case study is that it cannot be repeated to test for reliability, though follow-up procedures can help.

Progress check 3.48

Why is the case study a useful research method to use when looking at the risk of re-offending and how to deal with rehabilitation?

McMurran and Taylor (2013)

McMurran and Taylor (2013) wrote the editorial for a journal issue that was all about case formulation. You can see the importance of case formulation from the fact that there was a whole issue on the subject. The issue came about because of a new 'phase' relating to offenders with severe personality disorder, which was a co-ordinated approach to developing a new pathway for offender personality disorder (page 214). A 'pathway' is a treatment plan and a way of dealing with particular offenders. McMurran and Taylor point out that case formulation came from the idea that clinical psychologists use scientific methods to understand people's problems and to 'generate hypotheses about what might bring about change in such problems' (p. 227). The new pathway would cross service boundaries, which means it would not be just forensic psychologists involved but people in all the other services coming into contact with an offender with personality disorder, including probation services and other support networks. The issue would be in giving all the people the skills in formulation so they could 'reach a mutually acceptable, structured narrative about the offender's problems, which leads logically to effective planning of supervision, care and treatment throughout their pathway' (p. 227).

As McMurran and Taylor explain, it is hard to define case formulation, and different professional groups define it in different ways. The British Psychological Society define it as developing a hypothesis about someone's difficulties, which links with theory and practice and gives an intervention plan, and the Royal College of Psychiatrists says it includes reporting appropriate individual diagnoses. Adding to the base definition of case formulation are ideas around maintaining improvement from a treatment plan and motivating the offender to be involved with their 'pathway', as well as giving the offender an explanation that will help them to be involved in a good working relationship with others involved in the treatment plan.

Connell (2014)

Connell (2014) says that a difficulty when considering an offender and a suitable treatment plan is in organising a lot of detailed and complex information, which is often contradictory, into a clear and structured simple formulation which intervention can be based on and risk of recidivism reduced (Gresswell and Dawson, 2010, cited in Connell, 2014). A problem for occupational therapists is that how an offender feels can affect how they act, and they may have dysfunctional cognitive schemas – their ways of seeing the world. Occupational performance is where the individual and the environment meet. However, a difficulty is that the environment which an offender offends in is different from the prison environment and the offender will return to their own environment, so it is hard to work on occupational performance in a valid way. The focus in this study is on addressing 'risk-related lifestyle factors' in the offender. This report details an intervention that aims to show, using a case study, the advantages of identifying an offender's strengths and difficulties, predicting the risk of re-offending, finding offence paralleling behaviour (which means behaviour that relates to the offence behaviour) and looking at the effectiveness of intervention. The focus of occupational therapy is occupational adaptation, which helps people to meet their needs and to survive (Wilcock, 1993, cited in Connell, 2014). Connell's point is that offending behaviour is itself an occupation which is carried out to meet the offender's needs and to survive. It will be early experiences and issues – ones that often link to anti-social personality disorder – that stop someone being involved in **pro-social** occupation and lead them into anti-social occupation.

Definition

Pro-social: in a way that benefits society, being the opposite of anti-social, which means that society does not benefit from the behaviour.

Connell (2014) discusses using **functional analysis**, which is case formulation using behaviour theory and looking at human behaviour in terms of its consequences. Behaviour brings about consequences and, if consequences are rewarding or punishing, that can affect whether the behaviour is repeated or not. Functional analyses use the **ABC model**. 'A' is the antecedent, which is what happens before a behaviour, 'B' is the behaviour itself, which produces 'C', the consequences.

Year One link: You covered operant conditioning and its principles in learning theories so recall what you learned there about antecedent, behaviour and consequences and about the role of rewards and punishments in behaviour.

Explanation

Functional analysis refers to analysing behaviour in terms of its function, which means what it is for and what it achieves for the person. Functional analysis involves looking at what goes before the behaviour, the behaviour itself and the consequences that come from the behaviour. The **ABC model** refers to a way of looking at behaviour to see its purpose or function for the individual. 'A' is the antecedent (what leads to the behaviour), 'B' is the behaviour and 'C' refers to the consequences of the behaviour, whether they are rewarding or not.

Connell (2014) argues that occupational performance is behaviour and can be assessed using functional analysis. In your course, you are asked to look at psychological formulation to understand the function of behaviour for the individual so it is important not only to focus on case formulation but on how it focuses on the function of their offending behaviour for them. Functional analysis helps

to explain this important point, and the case study of Mr C also focused on how his offending behaviour was functional for him (Whitehead *et al.*, 2007).

Issues and debates

Reductionism is an issue and debate in your course. In a way, the ABC model reduces behaviour to antecedent, behaviour and consequence, which is an example of reductionism. In other ways formulation is individualised and takes a holistic view, taking the whole person into account, which is not a reductionist way of uncovering information. You can use such examples in a discussion about reductionism.

Connell (2014) uses a case study, that of Connor, who gave verbal and written consent for his material to be used – the name is a pseudonym to maintain anonymity. Just some parts of the case study are summarised here. Connor spent ten years in prisons in various cities. He was using heroin and alcohol and carrying out serious and violent offences. Connor hoped to get work when he was released and so assessment and formulation focused on understanding his problems in keeping a job.

It is the formulation part of the case study that is focused on here. Connell says that a detailed assessment informed the formulation, including the use of interviewing, psychometric testing and using clinical documentation. There were five events in Connor's life where functional analysis was used separately, with learning points that Connor may have taken from these events highlighted. The five events were his first experience of looking for a job, his adoptive parents moving house, his work experience in prison, the sequence of his offences, and offence paralleling behaviour. Examples of functional analysis are shown in Table 3.16.

Table 3.16 Examples of functional analysis relating to the behaviour of Connor (Connell, 2014)

Antecedent	Behaviour	Consequence
Unsuccessful at finding a job – sees the employment market as rejecting and unfair	Internal experience of shame, humiliation and failure	Foster parents cannot give alternative messages to support or help him to get a job
Foster parents were abusive and critical when he did not find work and said he could only live with them if he had a job	To avoid his foster parents criticising him, he stayed away for days and weeks	Marijuana reduced his motivation to look for work and his ability to find work – he gave up looking
Key learning points:		
He learned that work is valued highly and is about being socially acceptable so his beliefs about himself as a failure with others rejecting and criticising him are maintained. He learned to run away and avoid criticism and others, and he learned criminal activity as a survival strategy as well as learning to rely on drugs to cope with emotions.		

Connell (2014) suggests using this approach, using functional analysis, in case formulation when focusing on occupational therapy for someone wanting to find work outside prison. Connell admits that the approach

needs interpretation. However, a clinician can practise reflexively, which means noting any bias, and also can discuss issues with the offender, friends and family to help show the validity of any interpretation.

Ethical principles for understanding psychological formulation and intervention – HCPC

As part of the research methods section in criminological psychology, you need to cover the Health and Care Professions Council (HCPC) principles for understanding psychological formulation and intervention. This issue is covered here because it relates to case formulation and it is also briefly summarised in the research methods part of this chapter (page 328).

In this section on understanding the offender, you have read about two case studies looking at formulation: the case of Mr C (Whitehead et al., 2007) and the case of Connor (Connell, 2014). Also there was the case of Mr A briefly outlined at the start of this chapter (Arsuffi, 2010). In those cases, it was mentioned that the individual had given permission for their data to be used as a case study and also that privacy had been maintained. You can see from the 'names' given to the individuals that care has been taken not to make them identifiable. These are ethical issues.

The HCPC has Standards of Proficiency for practitioner psychologists. The Standards of Proficiency are 15 statements that apply to all professionals regulated by the HCPC, including forensic, clinical and counselling psychologists who all use formulation. There are also standards that are specific to the separate professions and they also are in the Standards of Proficiency document. The standards focus on safe and effective practice, which is different from doing research, but very similar in many ways to the BPS Code of Ethics and Conduct (2009) principles that you are familiar with through doing this course. The HCPC regulates all psychologists. Before someone can be registered with the HCPC, they must meet the standards in the document, including those for the specific profession they work within.

HCPC Standards of Proficiency

- Being able to practise safely and effectively, which relates to the BPS principle of competence.
- Being able to practise within the legal and ethical boundaries of the profession, which relates to adhering to BPS guidelines and to the principles of respect and dignity of clients or participants, including self-determination. There must also be maintenance of health and well-being, which relates to the BPS principle of responsibility and doing no harm. The principle of informed consent fits into this standard and the duty of care agenda, as well as issues of power.
- Being able to maintain fitness to practice, which is about competence and integrity.
- Being able to practise in an autonomous way and to use professional judgement, which is about responsibility.

- Being aware of the impact of culture, equality and diversity on practice. An example might be how Whitehead et al. (2007) used a Maori counsellor for Mr A, so that cultural issues could be addressed.
- Being able to practise in a non-discriminatory manner.
- Understanding the importance of confidentiality, which is included in the BPS Code of Ethics and Conduct and which the case studies used in this section specifically mention.
- Being able to communicate effectively, which can affect formulation because there is a need to explain a formulation to an offender and suitable language must be used in order to communicate clearly.
- Being able to work appropriately with others, and this standard includes understanding the need to engage service users and carers in planning and evaluating assessments, treatments and interventions to meet their needs and goals, so is directly focusing on issues like formulation. A particular focus is on working with the offender to communicate about any formulation and treatment plan.
- Being able to maintain records appropriately.
- Being able to reflect on and review practice.
- Being able to assure the quality of their practice. This includes revising a formulation in the light of any new evidence.
- Understanding the key concepts of the profession's knowledge base, which includes understanding issues around formulation and current models such as the Good Lives Model for rehabilitation, for example. This standard also includes knowing about scientific enquiry and would cover avoidance of bias in a formulation. In this standard, there are specific standards listed for clinical psychologists, counselling psychologists, educational psychologists, health psychologists, and others, including forensic psychologists. Those standards for forensic psychologists include understanding: how psychology is applied to the legal system, a range of theories, including psychological, social and biological perspectives, psychological models, including mild to severe problems in offenders, problems with biology or neuropsychological aspects, and problems involving psychosocial factors, such as life events and health conditions. There is also a requirement to understand the development of criminal and anti-social behaviour and psychological interventions for offenders as well as for victims and others involved in the legal system.

Issues and debates

Psychology as science is one of the issues and debates in your course and you can see that being able to work scientifically is in the HCPC standards. Clearly psychology as science is important in practising psychology.

Drawing on knowledge and skills to inform practice. For forensic psychologists, this includes being able to plan training, including assessing training, and to research using psychological methods, concepts, models and theories in forensic psychology. There is also the requirement to be able to work within a lifespan approach and to look at someone's developmental level and social situation.

- Finally, understanding the need to establish and maintain safe practice.

> **Explore**
> You can access the HCPC document focusing on Standards of Proficiency for practitioner psychologists using this link: www.hpc-uk.org/assets/documents/10002963sop_practitioner_psychologists.pdf. These standards applied from 1 July 2015.

From the standards listed here you should be able to recognise the British Psychological Society's Code of Ethics and Conduct (2009), which is a code required in your course, and some links are made for you. For most standards, there is more detail than is given here, and you can see that practising ethically is very important, as you would expect.

Year One link: Remind yourself about the ethical principles in the BPS Code of Ethics and Conduct (2009), which you studied in social psychology.

You will cover more about the HCPC when you learn about clinical psychology. Draw on what you learned there when discussing HCPC principles for understanding psychological formulation and intervention.

British Psychological Society Generic Professional Practice Guidelines (2008)

You need to know the HCPC principles. However, a brief look at the BPS guidelines is included here to underline some of the important issues. The BPS guidelines look at setting up a contract with a client, getting valid consent, focusing on confidentiality, looking at records and record keeping, supervision and working in multi-disciplinary teams (where different professions are represented, such as social workers, probation officers, care workers, forensic psychologists and occupational therapist perhaps).

> **Explore**
> You can access the BPS Generic Professional Practice Guidelines using this link: www.bps.org.uk/sites/default/files/documents/generic_professional_practice_guidelines.pdf

The guidelines have the objectives of defining good psychological practice for all psychologists, strengthening their identity, working for the benefit of the public and members and providing guidance on legal matters.

There are four key ethical values, which are respect, competence, responsibility and integrity, and five core competencies, which are assessment, formulation, intervention or implementation, evaluation and research, and communication. Formulation is pulling together knowledge from the assessment and draws on psychological theory and research to give a framework to describe a client's problems or needs. It is specifically mentioned in the BPS document, which shows its importance with regard to ethical practice. You can see that these competencies match those of the HCPC standards, which is to be expected as they are focusing on the same professions. The HCPC 'took over' regulation of psychologists from the BPS.

Issues and debates

Ethics in psychology is an issue and debate in your course so make notes about the HCPC standards so you can use them in a discussion as appropriate.

HCPC sanctions

The HCPC, which covers professional psychologists, use sanctions to maintain their standards. You can access the HCPC website (www.hcpc-uk.org) to look at media releases which will show you some of the cases they deal with and sanctions used. For example, a psychologist can be suspended from the HCPC register for a set period for delaying medico-legal reports that are required. A specific case (reported in August 2015) involved reports being delayed, which meant treatment was delayed (for two children). Another case featured a practitioner psychologist who crossed professional boundaries and breached client trust by having a relationship with a client (reported in June 2014). There are not that many cases featuring professional psychologists but looking through them helps to show the ethics required of them.

Evaluation of psychological formulation

Strengths

- A case formulation is a way of summarising a great deal of information about one individual, interpreting it according to a theory or theories, and from that putting together a treatment plan that should be effective with regard to rehabilitation. As such, it is a name for a process and a product that is needed. Going from a lot of unconnected information to formulate and justify a treatment plan would not be possible without a simple, diachronous (going from the past through the present to the future), externally coherent and internally coherent formulation (Hart *et al.*, 2011). This means that a good formulation that is well put together is a strength for the offender with regard to understanding their behaviour and putting together a plan for changing it. It is the formulation itself that can have strengths and weaknesses rather than using case formulation in general, which is necessary for its purpose.

A strength is that a case formulation goes beyond diagnosis. Diagnosis focuses on mental health disorders and issues in general, such that depression, for example, is treated in a general way, perhaps by either medication or psychotherapy. Formulation is more personal and, even though it may include diagnosis, as indeed an offender may be depressed or anxious and their symptoms might 'fit' into a diagnostic category, it is more than a diagnosis; it is a personal plan tailored to suit the needs of the individual. A formulation takes into account all aspects of someone's life, from their early experiences, through their temperament and personality, to a study of their relationships and social interactions. It is from the whole of someone's life experiences that the formulation is derived, which is a strength. It is individualised, one of Hart *et al.*'s (2011) categories for evaluating a formulation.

Weaknesses

- As Connell (2014) says, there is interpretation in doing a case formulation. The person doing the formulation takes a lot of information from an assessment and then puts together a simple and concise summary that must be valid and needs to inform a treatment plan for an individual offender. Interpretation means some information will be chosen to be left out and other information will be left in. Also interpreting from examples of behaviour and incidents in someone's life to involve theory in an explanation can bring bias according to a clinician's preferences regarding theory, for example. Checking back with the offender and those who know them, as well as using a reflexive journal to chart the formulation, can help with validity. However, a case formulation may well be different depending on who carries it out, which does suggest it might lack reliability as well as validity.
- A problem is that a case formulation takes place at one moment in time with the information available then. Other things may happen to change the formulation and also if a formulation is done when the offender is in prison, being in a different environment can affect risk of re-offending. A formulation needs to be flexible. However, that does raise questions about its reliability and validity and also about is usefulness if it is subject to change.

Test yourself
Evaluate two ways of understanding the offender.
(16 marks)

Treatments for offenders

You need to cover two treatments for offenders, including strengths and weaknesses. For both treatments, you also need to cover one study that looks at the effectiveness of the treatment.

You need to look at one cognitive-behavioural treatment, which can be CBT, social skills training, anger management or assertiveness training, or a different treatment that draws on cognitive-behavioural principles. In this chapter, anger management is covered as a cognitive-behavioural treatment. This is because one of the contemporary studies in criminological psychology in your course is Howells *et al.* (2005), which looks at the effectiveness of brief anger management programmes with offenders and so can be used as the study looking at effectiveness of the therapy.

You also have to look at one biological treatment, such as improved diet or hormone treatment. Hormone treatment for sexual offences is considered in this section. Biological treatments tend to be used for specific crimes rather than for all offenders.

Cognitive-behavioural treatments

One treatment is considered in this section – anger management programmes. You need to know about the treatment, consider strengths and weaknesses and cover one study looking at effectiveness.

Anger management programmes

Offenders can be treated using anger management programmes, which focus on people with aggressive behaviour that needs to be controlled.

Explore
You can look at the British Association of Anger Management website using the following link: **www.angermanage.co.uk/**

Anger management in general uses strategies such as identifying what triggers anger and learning to control those triggers. Proper eating regimes are suggested, as well as relaxation techniques. Learning to cope with different opinions from others is also important in the programme. Cognitive-behavioural therapy (CBT) can be useful to help someone to control angry outbursts. Anger management programmes can be one-to-one but more often involve group work. In this section, focus is on anger management of offenders, although anger management programmes are used for other people too, such as school pupils.

Anger is considered a normal, healthy response, but if it develops into rage that takes a person over, it is not healthy and puts strain on the body. It can be said that anger can trigger aggressive 'outbursts', which may lead to criminal behaviour, such as harming someone else. Some offenders are put on anger management programmes as part of their treatment because of the nature of the offence or because of personal characteristics.

This theory of anger as an outburst links to Freud's ideas of 'negative' emotions being locked away in the unconscious, only to burst out. Freud believed sport and other energetic activities could release such emotions.

Year One link: You have covered Freud's explanation of aggression in biological psychology when you looked at catharsis and the importance of releasing aggression as a contrast to biological explanations of aggression.

Currently, however, there is more focus on what triggers the outburst of anger or aggression and how that trigger (which is often centred on learned thought patterns) can be changed. Such anger is thought of more as inappropriate thinking patterns and reactions than as 'outbursts'. Anger management is a cognitive-behavioural treatment and there is focus on thinking patterns, which is the 'cognitive' part, and behaviour, which is the aggressive reaction.

When someone seems to show 'uncontrollable' anger at name-calling, for example, this is not in fact uncontrollable but is perceived by that person as a necessary response, because, perhaps, name-calling is a huge insult in their culture. In order to help individuals to manage their anger, it is necessary to understand their frame of reference – to know what is triggering the anger. Instead of being seen as 'uncontrollable', it is viewed rather as an understandable response to someone's provocative behaviour. This focuses on individuals' thinking patterns and reactions.

An example of what happens in an anger management programme

A programme could take the form of a twice-weekly group meeting. A trained practitioner is likely to run the group, which in a prison might be a forensic or prison psychologist. There are also programmes set up to train prison officers in running anger management sessions. First, there is focus on helping the group to work together, concentrating on social skills, to make sure that everyone is listened to and that there are ground rules for letting each person contribute.

Explore
The government 'Justice' site gives a list of offender behaviour programmes in prisons, including anger management programmes, and briefly outlines them, if you would like to know more: www.justice.gov.uk/offenders/before-after-release/obp

Group skills are used, such as having a **check-in** for each session, where each person briefly explains how they are feeling, describes their day or talks about their progress in the group. During the sessions, different techniques are used to help the members talk about their feelings. Relaxation techniques are also used.

Definition
Check-in refers to everyone saying how things are going for them as an individual before the 'work' starts. This helps to bridge entering a session and the session itself and can help with joining a group together with a common purpose.

Gradually, group work can turn to discussions of what makes each person angry, and such sessions would end with positive thoughts about group members' progress, what they enjoy, or being positive about someone they dislike. Members may be asked to think about the last time they were angry and what their thoughts were at the time, or to reflect on the last time they were kind.

The sessions progress in this way, by introducing the idea of changing the thoughts that relate to an angry response and ending with something positive. It is suggested that the course of group sessions ends by lengthening the time between the sessions, so that the support framework is not removed immediately.

What a ten-week course might cover

Issues that might be covered in a short anger management course include:
- what anger is not
- how to stop anger affecting you
- knowing the difference between rage and anger
- how to stop taking things personally
- why stress can lead to anger
- what negative cycles are and how to stop them
- child, parent and adult anger
- how to manage and resolve conflict
- how to express anger clearly
- coping strategies.

Controlling Anger and Learning to Manage It (CALM™)

One such programme is CALM™ (Controlling Anger and Learning to Manage It). CALM™ teaches participants, focusing on men, to monitor and understand their emotions in order to prevent problematic behaviour. Participants learn the skills necessary to reduce the frequency, intensity and duration of anger to lessen the likelihood of aggression.

The CALM™ sessions are practical, highly structured, sequential and designed for delivery to groups of adolescent and adult males at risk of inappropriate, violent behaviour, and in many cases, criminal recidivism. Personal assignments, modelling, role-play, teamwork and self- and peer-evaluation are used to teach and promote lasting change of inappropriate and unproductive thought and behaviour patterns. This emphasises how anger management programmes are cognitive and behavioural in focus.

There are 24 group sessions and the programme has a complete script so can be delivered after only a short training programme. Participants have a workbook to work through and it is written at a fairly low reading level to take into account males with poor reading skills.

General points about anger management for offenders

Jerry Deffenbacher is a psychologist who focuses on anger management. You may have seen Deffenbacher's work mentioned in Howells *et al.* (2005), one of the contemporary studies for criminological psychology in your course.

Deffenbacher suggests that individuals differ in their anger, such as how quickly they get angry and how intense their anger can become. He suggests that individual differences in anger can come from genes or the environment. Some children might be born with a touchy temperament, whereas others might have a calmer temperament.

People tend to be taught not to display anger, which means we tend not to learn how to handle it. Anger management programmes include focusing on how to handle anger.

Studies looking at the effectiveness of anger management for offenders

Blacker et al. (2008)

Blacker *et al.* (2008) explore a drama-based programme called 'Insult to Injury', set up to explore anger, aggression and violence. The programme was to help offenders look at situations that might trigger anger and consider strategies and skills for dealing with such situations to avoid anger. The drama-based approach was used so that strategies could be practised and evaluated. Howells *et al.* (2005) cited Watt and Howells (2003), who suggested that one reason anger management programmes might not be effective is that there is no time allowed for practising skills, and this drama-based programme responds to that criticism. The drama-based approach provides a safe and secure environment. Issues such as masculinity, power and control, victim awareness, and pride and shame were explored using the active drama-based approach and CBT. There was just one group and testing anger levels before and after the group session gave data to see if the session was effective. Sixty-two adult male offenders from six UK prisons took part in the nine-day course. Significant anger reductions were found. The researchers concluded that using a drama-based approach could be used with anger management programmes to help with effectiveness.

The Midlands Art Centre was involved in showing how a drama-based approach can enhance an anger management programme.

Howells *et al.* (2005)

Howells *et al.* (2005) look at an anger management programme that was run with various groups of offenders to see whether anger issues are improved by attending the programme. They also consider whether the individual's motivation to complete an anger management course – their 'readiness' – affects how successful the programme is. In Howells *et al.* (2005), there is information about other studies that have looked at the effectiveness of anger management programmes. Howells *et al.* (2005) is explained in detail later in this chapter (page 346) because it is one of the contemporary studies in criminological psychology in your course. You should use it as a study that looks at the effectiveness of anger management programmes even if you do not use it as your contemporary study. Howells *et al.* (2005) found that the anger management programme was not all that successful, though it did lead to the treatment group having more knowledge about anger than the control group. They found that more readiness before the programme correlated with better outcomes in the anger variables they measured. They thought that, as the control group completed the measures, which meant focusing on their anger, there was some learning for the control group too, which helped to prevent differences between the treatment and control groups. If you choose to study anger management, you should look more at Howells *et al.* (2005) later in this chapter.

Frank (2006)

Frank (2006) wrote a dissertation focusing on evaluation of an anger management programme in a detention facility. Like Howells *et al.* (2005), Frank (2006) points out that outcome studies looking at anger management treatments with offenders are scarce and she cites Dowden *et al.* (1999), as did Howells *et al.* (2005). Frank's paper evaluates a psycho-educational anger management group that also focuses on substance abuse. The group is in a privately owned detention centre in the US. She wanted to explore the experiences of the group and also to look at the effectiveness of the programme. Seventy-four offender volunteers attended seven-week long groups focusing on psycho-education and facilitated by clinical psychology graduate students. Thirty-one of the detainees completed pre- and post- group measures. The measures assessed readiness to change anger and substance use, and collected self-report data about anger levels and satisfaction with the programme. This was a similar design to that used by Howells *et al.* (2005).

Analysis of results showed that attending the group increased motivation to change how anger was dealt with, which shows some effectiveness in itself. The findings were similar to Howells *et al.* (2005). Frank (2006) found no significant differences between the pre- and post-treatment measures when considering people who completed both measures. Howells *et al.* (2005) found some differences between their treatment and control groups, such as in knowledge of anger, but Howells *et al.* (2005) in general did not find that the anger management programme was effective in making changes, which was similar to Frank's findings. Frank found that participants knew what had been covered, again showing similarity to Howells *et al.*, who also found anger knowledge had been improved by the programme. Frank also found the group was seen as a positive experience by participants. Frank had some findings showing differences between Spanish and English speaking detainees and the outcomes of the anger management/substance abuse group. She suggested that looking more at English and Spanish speaking needs would be worthwhile as they seem different. Also Frank emphasised that studying the impact of readiness to change and how it affects treatment outcomes would be worthwhile.

Watt and Howells (2010)

Watt and Howells (2010) evaluated an anger management programme for violent offenders in Australia. The programme was the Skills Training for Aggression Control (STAC) programme. Two studies looked at the effectiveness of the STAC programme with adult male inmates. In one study, there were 39 participants and in the other study there were 50 participants. The studies used a pre- and post-test design. Violent offenders were compared with a wait list control and the dependent variables were anger knowledge, trait anger, anger expression, observed aggressive behaviour and prison misconduct. The second study focused on the idea that offenders with high levels of trait anger would gain more from the treatment. As with other studies given here, Watt and Howells (2010) did not find treatment gains from the STAC programme when comparing the treatment and the control groups. Also there were no more gains in those with more trait anger. Although the STAC programme has had support, Watt and Howells, given their findings, suggest it might not be that useful for violent offenders.

> **Explore**
> Watt has done a lot of work in the area of anger management, including evaluation of programmes, as has Howells. Take note of 'names' that do a lot of work in an area of study and explore more by researching using those names.

Watt et al. (1999)

Watt et al. (1999) in Western Australia evaluated cognitive-behavioural anger management programmes for violent offenders. Violent male adult offenders on an anger management programme were compared with offenders on a waiting list, who acted as a control. The two groups were measured in terms of anger knowledge, anger expression, observed aggressive behaviour and misconduct in prison. The study found no special gain for the offenders on the treatment programme when compared with the control group, so it was suggested that anger management programmes with violent offenders may not have value.

Towl and Dexter (1994)

Towl and Dexter (1994) evaluated nine anger management programmes in England and Wales and used a self-report questionnaire, which they administered at the start of each programme and then again between 7 and 14 days after the end of the programme. Fifty prisoners completed the questionnaires and reported a drop in feelings of anger at the end of the programme. However, when considering the data in depth, it was clear that six prisoners had experienced an extreme drop in anger, whereas the others tended to remain unchanged. The data from those six had been enough to

produce a significant change overall. However, the prisoners did report a drop in their internal anger and some decrease in their anger turned towards others (external anger). Overall, the results were fairly encouraging.

Law (1997)

Law (1997) carried out a similar study to that of Towl and Dexter, looking at four anger management programmes. They found that prisoners were trying to control their anger to a greater extent after the programme.

The Ministry of Justice Report (2012/2013)

The Ministry of Justice reports on their accredited treatment programmes for offenders. The 2012/2013 report states that the NOMS Violence programmes, focusing on sexual offending, have moved on from moderate cognitive skills and anger management programmes to include more high-intensity work that is specialised for high-risk offenders, some with personality disorder. The new programmes include the newer research findings, theories and methods. There is focus on risk factors that contribute to violence, including weapons, gang influence and identity issues. This shows the influence of research into anger management and violence, and how programmes are changed in the light of findings about their effectiveness. The report considers programmes for general offending too, which consist of life skills training and cognitive-behavioural theory looking at problem-solving, social skills, positive relationships and self-control, and not just focusing on anger management. Domestic violence programmes are likely to involve anger management focus, according to the report. In 2012/2013, the report states that general offending programmes were the highest proportion of programmes started in probation, at 41 per cent, and the highest in prisons, at 49 per cent. Violence programmes were the lowest number started in probation, at 6 per cent, and the lowest in prisons, at 2 per cent. The report helps to place anger management in a range of accredited programmes for offenders and suggests that it is part of a suite of programmes. When evaluating anger management, it would be useful to consider individuals, to take note of which other programmes they might have been on or are on.

> **Progress check 3.50**
> A lot of studies looking at the effectiveness of anger management programmes for offenders find some success but, in general, offer a pessimistic view that such programmes do not have strong positive outcomes for offenders. Give evidence for this statement using two studies in your answer.

The success of anger management programmes for offenders

As you have seen, some studies show good outcomes from anger management programmes with offenders, such as Blacker et al. (2008), who found a drama-based group helped as part of an anger management programme, and Law (1997), who found that prisoners were trying to control their anger to a greater extent after an anger management programme.

However, in the main, the studies do not show that anger management programmes for offenders are successful. There are some successes, such as Howells et al. (2005), showing that knowledge of anger was better after the programme. Also readiness before a programme should be considered as it can predict whether a programme is successful. However, for violent and high-risk offenders, as well as less 'risky' offenders in some studies, anger management programmes are not found to be effective.

A criticism has been made that anger management programmes do not focus on the victim and the harm caused, nor do they deal with issues of morality. Offenders can gain from victims a better understanding of why violence is unacceptable. This element could be added to anger management programmes. Perhaps focusing on the harm anger can do might make the programmes more effective.

It has also been suggested that men convicted of domestic violence become less physically violent after attending an anger management programme but may be more verbally and emotionally abusive. The programmes perhaps show people other ways of hurting people, and this is backed up by evaluations of specific programmes. This is a worrying conclusion about their 'effectiveness'. Dobash et al. (1996) found domestic violence projects do succeed in that, 12 months after an intervention, offenders reduced their violence and controlling behaviour and their women partners reported better relationships with their men and better quality of life. This suggests domestic violence programmes, which can include anger management, are successful. Kelly and Westmarland (2015) report that experimental designs have found limited effects of the programmes (e.g. Gondolf, 2007) so interviewing with men was included as well as an ethnographic approach, which means researchers immerse themselves in a situation or programme to get in-depth data. The conclusion includes the idea that most men can take steps towards improvement with a programme that considers their anger (the Domestic Violence Perpetrator Programme) and it is not thought that it is a way of signposting a different way of being violent.

Explore
If you want to read more about Domestic Violence Perpetrator Programmes, here is the link to the full report: www.dur.ac.uk/resources/criva/ProjectMirabalfinalreport.pdf

Prisoners evaluate the success of programmes for them, but they might be positive because of the change of routine, or they might feel they should say they value the sessions to show they are improving. Some prisoners are asked to keep anger diaries, which can be a useful measure of the success of a programme. It is hard to be sure about effectiveness as prisoners are in a situation where they may give answers they think they 'should' give.

Evaluation of anger management programmes

Strengths

- Studies show the success of anger management programmes from self-report data, which are likely to be valid as they come from the prisoners themselves. However, there is the question about how well prisoners understand their anger issues and also that prisoners are a 'captive audience' and might have a reason for keeping emotions and issues to themselves. In general, self-report data are considered to be valid, however. Also if the same person is giving their data before and after the programme, any issues in the data should be found in both pre- and post-treatment measures, so any changes can perhaps validly be said to come from the treatment.

- Although Howells et al. (2005) found that their control group changed in line with their treatment group, which seems to be evidence for the treatment not being successful, the measures that the control group completed might have informed them about anger such that they improved too. This suggests that anger management programmes might be successful because of the information they give rather than the skills that are practised. This is perhaps a positive outcome for the programmes. The anticipation of dealing with their anger might have helped the control participants and, if the assessments helped with that, and they reflect the programmes, that supports the programmes, at least to an extent.

Weaknesses

- The programmes do not include a discussion of morality or understanding from a victim's point of view, which has been said to limit their success. Perhaps it is not that anger management is not successful with offenders, as the studies suggest, but that the programmes do not contain the right elements and looking at the harm anger does, as well as specific harm an offender has done, might be helpful.

It has been claimed that men convicted of domestic violence turn physical aggression into other ways of expressing aggression, such as verbal or emotional abuse. However, this is now *not* thought to be the case, and Kelly and Westmarland (2015), in a report on Domestic Violence Perpetrator Programmes, suggest that many men can benefit from them. However, when considering individual differences in how anger management programmes are received by individuals, a weakness is that there might be some unwanted effects.

Progress check 3.51

How is using self-report data both a strength and a weakness when evaluating anger management for offenders?

Test yourself

Using psychological research, evaluate one cognitive-behavioural treatment for offenders. **(20 marks)**

Biological treatments for offenders

Hormone treatment is considered in this section as a biological treatment for offenders. You need to know about the treatment, consider strengths and weaknesses and cover one study looking at effectiveness.

Hormone treatment for offenders

Hormone treatment tends to be focused on sex offenders and that is how it is considered in this section. Bradbury and Kaye (1999) report on the treatment of sexual deviation. Generally it is thought that psychological treatment and drug treatment together are most effective. This section focuses on drug treatment – in particular, treatment using hormones. Bradbury and Kaye (1999) say that use of drugs for sexual deviancy assumes that such behaviour comes from biological drives and suppressing sexual drive would reduce those drives. The goal is to maintain 'normal' sexual drives but to suppress deviant behaviour.

Some focus is on **paedophilia**, defined as 'the deviant erotic urge' focused on children. **Paraphilia** refers to abnormal sexual drives that tend to involve dangerous activities. Before looking at drug therapy, it is worth noting that surgical castration and neurosurgery have been used with very low recidivism rates reported – about 5 per cent after a long time. Surgical castration has importance because it was from this that drug therapy for deviant sexual urges was developed, following understanding that came from such procedures. Androgen suppression using anti-androgens and hormonal agents (Bradbury and Kaye, 1999) has the same effect on sexual behaviour as surgical castration.

Explanation

Paedophilia is when someone experiences an abnormal or unnatural attraction towards children. **Paraphilia** refers to abnormal sexual drives that tend to involve dangerous activities and intense sexual arousal to atypical situations or individuals.

SSRIs, not hormone treatment, for sexual offenders

If paraphilias are considered to be part of OCD disorders then specific serotonin reuptake inhibitors (SSRIs) have been suggested as treatment, such as sertraline, which has been used for paedophilia. Studies support the use of SSRIs for paraphilias, such as Greenberg and Bradbury (1997, cited in Bradbury and Kaye, 1999). Also SSRIs might work not because paraphilias relate to OCD disorders but because 5HT (serotonin) has a role in the 'neurobiology of sexual behaviour' (Bradbury and Kaye, 1999). An advantage of using SSRIs is that their side-effects are not as potentially serious as anti-androgen and hormonal treatment. However, in this section, hormone treatment is the focus, not SSRIs as drug therapy.

Hormone therapy for sexual offenders

Bradbury and Kaye say that using anti-androgens and hormonal agents is successful when treating paraphilias, including sex offenders, and recidivism rates are reduced, by reducing sexual fantasies, sexual arousal and drive, and sexual behaviour.

Anti-androgens

Cyproterone acetate (CPA) has anti-androgenic, antigonadotropic and progestational effects. It quickly reduces sexual drive and deviant fantasies, though it is not available in the USA, just in Canada, according to Bradbury and Kaye (1999). There are side-effects, such as liver dysfunction and adrenal suppression. It is as effective as castration in reducing recidivism related to offenders.

Hormonal agents that are not anti-androgens

Medroxyprogesterone acetate (MPA/Depo-Provera) is a hormonal agent and is the one used most in the USA. Side-effects included weight gain, decreased sperm production, and gall bladder and gastrointestinal dysfunctions. MPA brings reduction in sexual drive and deviant sexual fantasy, and possibly aggression.

LHRH (luteinizing hormone-releasing hormone) analogues are used to treat paraphilias and act as a pharmacological castration because they exhaust the hypothalamic pituitary axis (HPA). Bradbury and Kaye (1999) suggest that these hormones are likely to be important in treating severe deviation.

Progress check 3.52

Name two main hormone types used for treating sexual offenders and, for each, give one hormone used and two side-effects.

> **STUDY HINT**
> To help your learning, you could draw up a table of each treatment, what it does and its side-effects.

Review of sexual offender treatment programmes

Perkins *et al.* (1998) reviewed treatment programmes for sexual offenders, working in the UK. A review is useful as it can show what treatments are being used, though this one is from 1998 so there are likely to have been changes since then. The hormone treatments are what are focused on in this summary of the review. Perkins *et al.* (1998) comment that more clinical trials are needed using a randomised controlled trials design.

> **STUDY HINT**
> Randomised controlled trials are used a lot in studies looking at effectiveness of drug therapy in mental disorders, for example, so you will come across them in your coverage of clinical psychology. Use what you have learned to understand why they are thought to be needed when looking at treatment for sexual offenders.

For the highest risk sex offenders with the most disturbed backgrounds and psychopathic personality characteristics, Perkins *et al.* (1998) recommend using a combination of group-based cognitive-behavioural interventions looking at underpinning needs (criminogenic) and personality factors together with anti-libidinal medication. It is interesting that Perkins *et al.* suggest analyses based on individual experiences when looking at treatment 'impact and outcome' (p. 3). Perkins *et al.* (1998) review pharmacological treatments, including anti-androgens (Bradbury, 1990, cited in Perkins *et al.*, 1998) and serotonergic drugs (Pearson, 1990, cited in Perkins *et al.*, 1998). Emory *et al.* (1992) evaluated Depo-Provera (MPA) and concluded that such treatment lowered the sexual interest of the patients and

was useful in allowing engagement with psychotherapies. Federoff *et al.* (1992, cited in Perkins *et al.*, 1998) looked at MPA and found that 15 per cent of those using MPA re-offended, compared with 68 per cent of non-users. Perkins *et al.* (1998) concluded that hormone medication helps as long as there is informed consent given to have the treatment and the ability to withdraw from the medication.

Progress check 3.53

Give two pieces of evidence from Perkins *et al.*'s (1998) review that show that hormone treatment is effective in that it reduces sexual drive in offenders.

> **Explore**
> You can access the review of sex offender treatment programmes by Perkins *et al.* (1998) using this link, if you would like to know more about all treatments, not just hormone treatment: www.ramas.co.uk/report4.pdf

Studies on the effectiveness of hormone treatment for offenders

Thibaut *et al.* (1998)

Thibaut *et al.* (1998) looked at hormone treatment for sex offences. They point out that **androgens**, which are hormones, in humans are said to regulate sexuality, aggression, cognition, emotion and personality, which suggests that there is a role for hormones in the treatment of offenders. Thibaut *et al.* mention what they call 'organic' treatments reducing the plasma testosterone levels or lowering androgen effects on cells. Such treatments might reduce the likelihood of re-offending when it comes to sexually aggressive men. Thibaut *et al.* found GnRH analogue (triptoreline) was helpful when used with 11 sex offenders, if used with psychotherapy and with offenders ready for treatment.

> **Definition**
> **Androgen** is a male sex hormone; testosterone is an androgen. Other androgens are dihydrotestosterone (DHT) and androstenedione, less well-known but also important in male development.

Meyer *et al.* (1992)

Meyer *et al.* (1992, cited in Bradbury and Kaye, 1999) looked at 40 men treated with MPA, most of them paedophiles. They were treated for between six months and 12 years. There was a control group (21 participants) who refused the treatment and just had psychotherapy. Of those on MPA, 18 per cent re-offended and 35 per cent re-offended after the treatment stopped. These figures were compared with 55 per cent of the control group who re-offended. This study shows the effectiveness of MPA as a treatment for sex offenders.

Turner *et al.* (2013)

Turner *et al.* (2013) consider the use of testosterone-lowering medication (TLM) in sex offender treatment in addition to psychotherapy. They used observation to look at the frequency of prescribing TLM and other medications in forensic psychiatric hospitals in Germany (those for offenders) for sex offender treatment. They asked the prescribers about the effects and side-effects of TLM. They asked the heads of the 69 German forensic psychiatric hospitals and out-patient clinics to complete a questionnaire asking about offender characteristics and treatment methods used. They counted the number of patients on TLM and other drugs for reducing sexual drive and they found out about effects and side-effects.

Thirty-two of the institutions took part, reporting on 3,963 patients, of which 611 were sex offenders. The sex offenders had mainly been convicted of child sexual abuse or sexual assault/rape. Almost all of them were undergoing psychotherapy and 39.8 per cent were also on drug treatment: 15.7 per cent of the sex offenders were treated with TLM; 10.6 per cent were treated with a gonadotropin-releasing hormone agonist; 5.1 per cent were treated with cyprotersone acetate. Of the sex offenders treated with these hormone treatments, between 26 and 75.4 per cent of these showed improvements measured by reduced sexual thoughts. In addition, 21.3 per cent of the sex offenders were treated either with SSRIs (11.5 per cent) or antipsychotic medication (9.8 per cent). It was concluded that there was some evidence of hormone therapy being effective, though controlled clinical trials were needed to show the efficacy of TLM. Also, the main side-effects meant it should be prescribed carefully and after a full assessment of benefits and risks, given the ethical implications.

Maletzky (1991)

Maletzky (1991) found that offenders treated with hormonal agents did not show different rates of sexual recidivism than similar offenders not treated with hormonal agents.

Table 3.17 Evidence from studies relating to hormone treatment for sexual offenders

Study	Findings
Thibaut *et al.* (1998)	GnRH analogue (triptoreline) was helpful when used with 11 sex offenders, if used with psychotherapy and with offenders ready for treatment.
Meyer *et al.* (1992)	Of those on MPA, 18 per cent re-offended and 35 per cent re-offended after the treatment stopped, compared with 55 per cent of the control group who re-offended.
Turner *et al.* (2013)	Of the sex offenders on hormone treatments, between 26 and 75.4 per cent showed improvements measured by reduced sexual thoughts.
Maletzky (1991)	Offenders treated with hormonal agents did not show different rates of sexual recidivism than similar offenders not treated with hormonal agents.

Main study looking at the effectiveness of hormone treatment for offenders

Maletzky *et al.* (2006) found anti-androgens compared to no treatment led to lower rates of sexual recidivism and decreased sexual arousal in response to stimuli that might before have led to arousal. This finding was confirmed by self-report data. This is the study chosen to be explained in more detail in this section, which requires you to know one biological treatment for offenders and one study focusing on the treatment's effectiveness.

Maletzky *et al.* explain that a 1999 House Bill in Oregon required certain offenders to be assessed before release to see if treatment using MPA would help to reduce their risk. Under this programme, 275 men were evaluated from 2000 to 2004, and Maletzky *et al.* (2006) reviewed these men. MPA goes under the trade name Depo-Provera. The men were split into three groups: men who needed MPA and went on to get it; men who were recommended MPA but did not get it; men who were not thought to need MPA. The researchers collected data on recidivism, including re-offending, violation of parole and reincarcerations, and they also noted whether the recidivism was sexual. They found that men receiving Depo-Provera committed no new sexual offences and committed fewer other offences compared with the other groups. The men judged to need it but did not get it committed a new offence, with around 60 per cent of these new offences being sexual. They felt that anti-androgens were valuable, though in addition to cognitive-behavioural treatment programmes.

Background

In general, it is claimed (Maletzky *et al.*, 2006) that sexual offenders are not an immediate risk for re-offending. Even with more serious offenders, perhaps 80 per cent will not be an immediate risk once released. However, there might be risk in the future (e.g. Hanson, 2000, cited in Maletzky et al., 2006) if there is no community-based treatment. Having said this, Maletzky et al. (2006) suggest that there are still those who might pose an immediate risk and these might benefit from medical treatment to reduce sexual drive quickly. This thinking is what led Oregon to pass a Bill saying that medication might be suitable for those deemed a risk. The Bill means that, while in prison, offenders must be assessed to see if medication would be suitable. What is important here is that if an offender was thought to be a risk, the medication could be ordered as a requirement of supervision after prison. A problem was in how to determine whether an individual offender needed medication. Criteria included whether the person had a current or past conviction of a sexual crime, whether they were within six months of release, whether their incarceration was for a second crime, whether they lacked intellectual capacity and whether they had shown excessive sexual drive. Difficulties were in finding people to make such assessments and finding doctors to do the prescribing.

At the time of the Bill, MPA was the most widely used medication to reduce sexual drive in offenders, though since then depo-leuprolide (Lupron) has had a lot of attention, as well as fluoxetine or sertraline. Maletzky et al. (2006) suggest the side-effects of MPA are not as bad as those with leuprolide, which requires X-rays because of loss of bone density, so MPA is still seen as a useful alternative. It has also been suggested that SSRIs do not reduce sexual drive as much as hormonal agents (Maletzky and Steinhauser, 2002, cited in Maletzky et al., 2006).

The evaluations of the MPA programme began in January 2000. There were 275 inmates selected to be evaluated: for 141 of them (51.3 per cent), MPA was considered not to be appropriate; 134 (48.7 per cent) were thought to be a sufficient risk that MPA should be prescribed.

Aims

The aims of the study were to evaluate the offenders who had been assessed for appropriateness of MPA on or before release. The study followed up the people who had been judged appropriate and the ones who had not, including those who did not take up the programme even if it was judged appropriate. The aim was to see the outcomes of being on MPA compared to not being on the treatment.

Methods

This was a retrospective review because it looked back over the history of the 275 inmates after their release to look at the recidivism rate and to compare those on the MPA programme with those not on the treatment. It was clinical judgement that was the main factor in deciding which offenders would be suitable for MPA.

The 134 deemed suitable for MPA were released and their parole officers contacted to see if they were being given the MPA. Some would not receive it despite the recommendation because the community they returned to might not have the resources to provide it or a treating therapist or parole officer might not think it was necessary. The dose of MPA was given by injection every two weeks. Of the 134, 79 (59 per cent) received medication and 55 (41 per cent) did not. The average doses and timing of the injections was not known. However, most of the men were released to the Portland area, where Maletzky was prescribing the medication, so there was some knowledge about the dose and it was in general between 200 and 400mg every other week.

Questionnaires were used to collect the outcome data. These were whether a new offence had been committed since release, whether there had been a violation of parole conditions, whether the offender had been re-arrested, whether any re-arrest was down to sexual problems and whether the offender was employed. The supervising officer also said whether they thought the offender was 'doing well' or not.

Results

Out of the 275 original offenders, 134 (48.7 per cent) were recommended to receive MPA and 141 (51.3 per cent) were not. The crime itself was looked at against whether MPA was recommended and it was found that a lot of the recommendations were for offenders who had committed the most shocking crimes. It was also noted that, with regard to those recommended to receive MPA, supervisors 'made certain' (p. 308) that almost 70 per cent of homosexual paedophiles received MPA as opposed to just 46 per cent of men with heterosexual paedophilia and just 33 per cent of men with mixed offences. This was a significant difference when analysis was carried out.

> **STUDY HINT**
> While reading a study, you could look out for method points so you are ready to evaluate. For example, notice that Maletzky et al. (2006) use the expression 'made certain' when describing the differences between those who received the medication and those recommended to receive it. This suggests that the supervisors focused more on homosexual paedophiles than heterosexual paedophiles, which is information over and above giving the figures.

Table 3.18 Outcomes for all those recommended to receive Depo-Provera (MPA)

Event	Received MPA (N = 79)		Did not receive MPA (N = 55)		Not recommended to receive MPA (N = 141)	
	N	%	N	%	N	%
New offence	4	5.1	17	30.9	38	26.9
Sexual in nature	0	0	10	58.8	21	55.3
Violation	11	13.9	19	34.5	59	41.8
Sexual in nature	1	1.3	12	63.2	22	37.3
Back in prison	0	0	11	20.0	19	13.5
Sexual in nature	0	0	9	81.8	6	31.6
Employed	59	74.6	41	74.5	97	68.8
Doing well	70	88.6	24	43.6	89	63.1
Not doing well	9	11.4	31	56.4	52	36.9

Progress check 3.54

Describe the outcomes of Maletzky *et al.* (2006) in terms of recidivism.

Table 3.18 shows that those who received the medication committed fewer new offences and no new sexual offences compared with the other two groups. They also committed fewer parole violations, did not return to prison and were seen to be 'doing well' more often than men recommended to receive the MPA but not receiving it, although there were more men not recommended to receive it said to be doing better. Employment figures showed no significant differences.

Chi squared tests were carried out on the outcomes showing significant differences in those receiving the medication:

- There were fewer new offences in those receiving MPA (p<.0001) and none of the offences was sexual in nature.
- There were fewer parole violations in those receiving the medication (p=.009).
- Those receiving medication were less likely to have returned to prison (p<.0001).
- Those receiving medication were more likely to be said to be 'doing well' (p<.0001).

Conclusions

The conclusion was that those recommended to receive and receiving MPA were less likely to re-offend than those recommended it but not receiving it. The 'not taking MPA' group had similar findings whether it was recommended for them or not. About 31 per cent of those recommended but not receiving the treatment committed a new offence and about 60 per cent of these new offences were sexual ones. This compares to around 27 per cent of those not recommended the treatment committing a new offence and about 55 per cent of the new offences being sexual. These are very similar figures. This seems to suggest that deciding who 'needed' the medication and who did not was not a valid measure.

Maletzky *et al.* (2006) noted the differences in supervisor attention regarding giving the medication: over 50 per cent of heterosexual paedophiles recommended for the medication did not receive it, whereas just 30 per cent of homosexual paedophiles and 41 per cent of those who had raped did not receive the medication after being recommended it. However, supervisors had to think about the cost of the medication and of providing it, so the figures about the different focus on the different offences may not be useful.

It seemed as if the MPA did reduce sexual drive because, even when there were re-offences by those receiving the medication, they tended not to be sexual in nature. The researchers point out that most of the men in the study had been out of custody for two years so the findings had some significance. One difficulty was that the questionnaire did not give information about how long the MPA had been given or whether it had been discontinued. However, sexual re-offending tends to occur within the first six months after release and the medication is intended to be there at the start before other therapies start working, so that situation should have been reached by most of those in the study. Also, the finding that more of those on the medication were 'doing well' than those recommended it (but not receiving it) perhaps showed that the medication was successful in reducing sexual drive. However, supervisors had to make a subjective judgement about 'doing well', so it is hard to draw firm conclusions about that.

Strengths of Maletzky *et al.* (2006)

- There are a lot of studies showing that hormone treatment is successful in reducing sexual drive. For example, Turner *et al.* (2013) found TLM to be successful in reducing sexual drive (though they did suggest controlled trials and further research were needed). Thibaut *et al.* (1998) found GnRH analogue (triptoreline) effective in reducing sexual drive too. Maletzky *et al.* (2006) had support for their findings from other studies, including Emory *et al.* (1992), who evaluated Depo-Provera and concluded that such treatment lowered the sexual interest of the patients. When findings are supported by other studies, it strengthens them.

- The idea of getting the supervisors to give a quality judgement about 'doing well' did add to the data, which measured a variety of different outcomes and not just recidivism. The outcomes seemed to come to the same conclusions about whether MPA was an effective treatment for sexual offences, with new offence, violation of parole or being back in prison all being lower for the 'received medication' group. This suggests findings are reliable and using many outcomes helps to validate the findings.

Weaknesses of Maletzky et al. (2006)

- Maletzky et al. (2006) suggest a limitation for their study is that data were collected retrospectively, which means looking back on a situation, and that can depend on memory, which is unreliable. The reason for someone being back in prison relied on the supervisor's memory, though the researchers did check records to confirm reports.
- Also some data were qualitative, such as the judgement about 'doing well', rather than quantitative, which again affects reliability. It is hard to draw conclusions from a subjective judgement about whether an offender is 'doing well' or not. 'Doing well' could have been decided based on any re-offending.

Progress check 3.55

What would you say about the generalisability and validity of the results of Maletzky et al. (2006)?

Evaluation of hormone treatment as a treatment for offenders

Strengths

- A strength with hormone treatment is that studies have shown its effectiveness and the findings support one another. There are a lot of studies showing that hormone treatment is successful in reducing sexual drive. For example, Turner et al. (2013) found TLM to be successful in reducing sexual drive, Thibaut et al. (1998) found GnRH analogue (triptoreline) effective in reducing sexual drive, Maletzky et al. (2006) found MPA reduced sexual drive and re-offending, and Emory et al. (1992) evaluated Depo-Provera and concluded that such treatment lowered the sexual interest of the patients. These findings support the effectiveness of hormone treatment.
- Notwithstanding ethical issues, and there are many (see weaknesses below), hormone treatment has shown success. The principle is fairly simple in that sexual drive comes from hormones and so altering hormones should affect the sexual drive, and that does seem to be supported by the evidence. Though this treatment suits only sexual

offenders, it seems to be effective. It is hard not to think of the side-effects and issues about control; however, it is possible that the treatment is welcomed by the offender even though it is aimed at helping possible victims. It would be useful to have more qualitative data about how the participants, such as in Maletzky et al. (2006), felt about the treatment and the possible effect on their behaviour.

Weaknesses

- Studies tend to look at sexual offenders having anti-androgen therapy but also psychotherapy. A weakness of hormone therapy is that it does not stand alone so it is hard to evaluate on its own. Psychotherapy includes cognitive-behavioural treatments and supervised probation or parole, as well as community-based interventions. When there is more than one therapy, it is hard to say which therapy is effective.
- Hormone treatment can be expensive and hard to administer and supervise. Maletzky et al. (2006) found that 41 per cent of sexual offenders recommended to receive MPA did not receive it for various reasons, including cost and availability. They went on to re-offend more than those receiving MPA, which is a consideration when weighing up costs and benefits of a treatment.
- There are ethical issues with hormone treatment. In Oregon, hormone treatment had to be received by those it was recommended for as a condition of them being released. This is about the rights of the offenders. In Maletzky et al. (2006), 41 per cent of those recommended to receive MPA did not, which might also be about their rights. Use of Depo-Provera can be called 'chemical castration', which makes the point about ethical issues. In America, there are protests about making people take drugs, including anti-androgens for sex offenders, and it is argued that this goes against the Eighth Amendment (which prohibits federal government from imposing excessive bail, excessive fines, or cruel and unusual punishments). In 2008, treatment was used in Portugal for sex offenders in prisons, though it was emphasised that taking part was voluntary. In 2010, in the UK hormones were used to treat a man as part of his sentence. There are clearly a lot of ethical issues involved in 'hormone treatment' or 'chemical castration', and there are differences in countries about how it is used.

STUDY HINT

When discussing strengths and weaknesses of a treatment, it is useful to explore each in detail because a strength so often brings with it a weakness (such as the strength of hormone treatment being its effectiveness and the weaknesses being ethical issues and side-effects) and discussion of either a strength or a weakness can help to show full understanding.

Issues and debates

One of the issues and debates in your course is about social control and how psychological understanding can be used in social control. Hormone treatment is clearly about social control and you can use it when discussing issues.

Test yourself

1 Explain two ways of treating offender behaviour.
  (6 marks)
2 Assess the effectiveness of one biological and one cognitive-behavioural treatment for offenders.
  (16 marks)

Factors influencing eyewitness testimony

In this section, you will look at factors influencing eyewitness testimony and the unreliability of eyewitness memory. Two factors that you must cover in relation to the unreliability of eyewitness memory are post-event information and weapon focus.

You come across eyewitness testimony again when you look at research methods used to study it, including lab and field experiments. You also look at eyewitness testimony when you cover the classic study and, if you chose it, one of the contemporary studies. The unreliability of eyewitness memory is the main key question in this chapter. You can use material from the different sections to cover a variety of issues in criminological psychology.

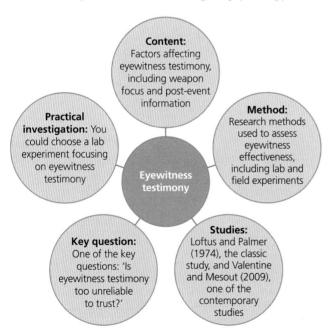

Where eyewitness testimony fits into criminological psychology in your course

In the section on studies, you will cover Loftus and Palmer's (1974) study (page 330) as the classic study in criminological psychology. They looked at how the wording of a question could lead to unreliable eyewitness testimony. You can also choose to study Valentine and Mesout (2009) (page 337) as one of the contemporary studies in criminological psychology, which looks at the influence of stress on eyewitness identification. Therefore, you will be learning more about the influence of wording in a question and the influence of stress on eyewitness testimony, making it unreliable in certain circumstances. Loftus and Palmer (1974) is a laboratory experiment and Valentine and Mesout (2009) is a field experiment. These are two useful examples of the research methods used to look at eyewitness testimony so you can also apply these to the methods part of this chapter.

Loftus and Palmer (1974): the effect of wording on estimate of speed

Loftus and Palmer (1974) was a laboratory experiment. They showed students films of car accidents. The independent variable was the word used in a question asking for estimate of speed of the car and the word was, for example, 'hit' or 'smashed'. The dependent variable was the estimate of speed. The hypotheses were that 'smashed' suggests a higher speed than 'hit' and that 'smashed' suggests broken glass where 'hit' does not.

Valentine and Mesout (2009): the effect of stress on eyewitness identification

Valentine and Mesout (2009) carried out a field study where they manipulated what happened to see the effect, so it was an experimental study. The study involved all participants in a scary place being faced with a 'scary person' and then, as an eyewitness, trying to identify that person. Valentine and Mesout (2009) used three independent variables, which were gender, state anxiety and trait anxiety, to see the effect on various dependent variables, including number of descriptors of the 'scary person' and whether or not the 'scary person' was picked out from a photo line-up.

> **STUDY HINT**
> These two studies are only summarised here as they are given in good detail later in this chapter. One looks at how wording in a question affects judgement like estimate of speed and the other looks at the influence of stress on eyewitness testimony. You can use both these factors as ones that impact on the reliability of eyewitness testimony. However, the two factors listed in your course are weapon focus and post-event information so be sure to focus on them too.

Progress check 3.56

Loftus and Palmer (1974) did a lab experiment and Valentine and Mesout (2009) carried out a field experiment. What is the main difference between these two research methods?

Yarmey (2004): eyewitness recall and photo identification

There are concerns about generalising from laboratory study findings and their associated lack of realism and validity. These are criticisms of Loftus and Palmer's (1974) lab experiment, as you will see (page 330). Field experiments help to raise both the generalisability and the ecological validity of studies. Such concerns are of particular importance in the field of eyewitness memory because of the need to apply findings about eyewitness testimony to actual court procedures. Valentine and Mesout (2009) carried out their study in a natural setting/situation, so their study has the advantage of more ecological validity than a laboratory experiment, which can lack external validity too. Yarmey (2004) is explained here as another example of a field experiment and of how eyewitness testimony is studied and what factors are involved when considering the unreliability of eyewitness testimony. Yarmey's study will be useful for you as an example of a field experiment looking at eyewitness testimony if you choose not to cover Valentine and Mesout (2009) as the contemporary study.

Year One link: You will have looked at predictive, ecological and internal validity in cognitive psychology as well as generalisability. Field and laboratory experiments were covered in cognitive psychology so you will already know a lot of the issues with those research methods, which you can recall here.

Yarmey said that, in general, research has found that objects and people more relevant and central to situations are better remembered by witnesses, and that witnesses tend to remember what fits best with their expectations. Haber and Haber (2001) analysed 48 studies on eyewitness identification in a line-up, where the person to be identified (the target) was present. They found that in 51 per cent of cases the target was correctly identified by the witness. In 27 per cent of cases a target was wrongly identified. In other studies, where the target was not included in the line-up, there was a 57 per cent chance of incorrect identification. These figures show the unreliability of eyewitness testimony.

Research has found that eyes are a main feature used in identification, so it was thought that covering the eyes would affect identification. Masking a hairline by use of a hat also reduces identification, according to previous studies.

It is thought that people identify others using eyes and hairline, so cap and dark glasses can hinder identification.

The cognitive interview technique (page 233) suggests that going over the event before recall and being asked open questions helps witness recall. This is called giving enhanced retrieval instructions.

Aims

Daniel Yarmey's aim was to look at the effects on both males and females of being part of a field experiment related to **eyewitness recall** and photo identification. Another aim was to see how far a disguise (sunglasses and a baseball cap) affected retrieval. One issue was whether instructions given just before recall, to review an incident, would affect the identification. The study also used a four-hour time gap and investigated the effect of this gap on eyewitness recall. Yarmey went on to compare what students believed about the success rate of photo identification before the study with the actual findings of the study.

Definition

Eyewitness recall is information given by an eyewitness without a prompt.

Procedure

There were 215 male and 375 female participants, ranging in age from 18 to 70. Only white participants were used to avoid any race bias. Participants were randomly assigned to one of a number of conditions, as follows:

- being prepared (told that they were going to be an eyewitness) or not
- a disguise present (sunglasses and baseball cap) or not
- retrieval instructions enhanced or not
- tested immediately or delayed by four hours

- the gender of witness (male or female)
- whether the target was present or not in a line-up.

Two white women were the targets (person to be identified).

Progress check 3.57

Why was it important that the target (the person to be identified) was always female and always white? What might be the consequence of using two different women?

Participants were approached by a target in a public place and asked to help look for lost jewellery or asked for directions. After two minutes, a female researcher went up to the participant and asked him or her to take part in the study. The researcher either asked then and there about the identification of the target or four hours later. Witnesses were given a questionnaire with 16 items, eight about the physical characteristics of the target and eight about her clothing. They rated their confidence about their answers on a seven-point scale. After completing the questionnaire, witnesses were given a set of six photos. In half the cases, the target was present in the photos, and in half the target was absent. Participants were asked to identify the target female (they were told she might not be in the photos, and they were shown each photo only once). At the end of the study, there was a debriefing.

Another part of the study was to give the whole scenario in written form to students. The students were asked to comment on what they thought would happen and what would affect eyewitness recall.

Results

As there were so many conditions, the results and analyses were complex. In many cases, significant differences were found between the various conditions. When the target was present in the photo line-up, about 49 per cent of participants correctly identified the target, and 62 per cent correctly said that the target was not there in the 'target absent' condition.

It is interesting to compare the findings about correct identification in the photo line-up with the student predictions. For example, it was found that where 62 per cent of the participants correctly said the target was not in the photos in the 'target absent' condition, students thought this would happen for only 47 per cent of the participants. Whereas 49 per cent of the participants correctly identified the target when her photo was included in the photo line-up, 63 per cent of the students thought that, in that condition, the target would be correctly identified. This is a significant overestimate.

Another finding was that the participants who were prepared for the test were better at recall but were not better at photo identification. With regard to physical characteristics, this study found that age estimates were reasonably accurate – more so than height or weight estimates.

Conclusions

This study found that about 50 per cent of the time a witness makes a correct identification in a line-up when the target is present, which corresponds closely with the findings of Haber and Haber's meta-analysis (2001). Yarmey's study also has practical applications, as it casts doubt on the assumption that jurors should accept eyewitness accounts as accurate just because the eyewitness was there. Students judging what would happen were not accurate, and jurors are likely to have similar assumptions to the students.

Evaluation

Strengths

- The photo line-up findings support Haber and Haber's findings (2001), which suggests that there is some reliability in this study. Both studies found that witnesses tend to be about 50 per cent accurate in line-up identification when the target is present.
- The study was carried out in a natural environment for the participants and so has ecological validity. The target female simply approached the first person available when she was ready and the participants were going about their normal business.

Weaknesses

- While this study found that age was better identified than other physical characteristics, such as height and weight, Yuille and Cutshall's study (see below) found more or less the opposite, so not all findings of studies into eyewitness recall support one another.
- The photo line-up is not the same as a real life line-up – a photo of a face is not the same as the actual person being there. There would have to be more focus on facial characteristics, such as hair and eyes, rather than build, stance and other forms of body language, which would also have been present. This means that the task lacks validity, even though the study has ecological validity.

Progress check 3.58

The strengths of Yarmey (2004) suggest that the study is both valid and reliable. Explain what each of these terms means.

STUDY HINT
Yarmey (2004) can be used as an example of a field experiment when discussing research methods used to study eyewitness testimony.

Yuille and Cutshall (1986)

Yuille and Cutshall carried out a study interviewing real witnesses of a real crime, so their study is different from the laboratory studies of Loftus and others. It is a field study because it looks at what happened in a natural setting, and it is more of a case study than an interview because, although data were gathered by interview, the study looks in detail at a particular crime. If you study Valentine and Mesout (2009) as your chosen contemporary study, you will see that they talk about Yuille and Cutshall's (1986) study, which is another reason for using this study here.

STUDY HINT
Yuille and Cutshall (1986) carried out a field study. However, it was not a field *experiment* because the experimental method was not used. They studied a situation that had actually occurred and did not set the situation up or manipulate an independent variable. A field experiment is a study in the field so can be called a 'field study' but not every 'field study' is a field experiment. It is worth sorting out the difference so that you don't make a mistake when discussing field experiments as a research method used to study eyewitness testimony.

The researchers began their study by pointing out that research on eyewitness testimony has focused on situations in the criminal justice system, and studies (e.g. Woocher, 1970) suggest that judges and juries do not focus on errors in eyewitness testimony, accepting it as truth. Malpass and Devine (1981) suggested that there was a need to know that laboratory findings could be generalised to more realistic situations. One problem, for example, is that slide sequences and filmed events are not relevant to real-world events. Even staged live events do not represent the seriousness or consequences of actual events. If observers are deceived into thinking that events are real, this has ethical consequences. Another concern is that the participants in laboratory studies are not representative – of 41 research articles about eyewitness testimony from 1974 to 1982, for example, 92 per cent (38 articles) tested only students. There are problems with generalising from this group to the general public. Therefore, field observations are required to help to generalise laboratory study findings.

STUDY HINT
In the description of the background to Yuille and Cutshall (1986) are issues that you can use when discussing methodology in general – for example, the point about using only student participants, and the validity problems of laboratory experiments. This is why you are asked to do so much evaluation in your study of psychology.

Yuille and Cutshall (1986) used witnesses who had observed a gun-shooting incident that occurred on a spring afternoon in Vancouver, Canada. A thief entered a gun shop, tied up the owner and stole some money and guns. The owner freed himself and picked up a revolver. He went outside to take the car registration number but the thief had not got into the car and he fired two shots at the store owner from a distance of about six feet. The owner, after a short pause, fired all six shots from his revolver. The thief was killed but the store owner recovered from serious injury. Witnesses viewed the scene from different locations – from passing cars, buildings or in the street.

The researchers chose this case because:
- there were enough witnesses to compare their accounts
- the thief was killed and the weapons and money recovered, so there was a lot of forensic evidence to verify the witness accounts
- the death of the thief closed the file, so research would not interfere with a police case
- there were many visible elements to the scene (car, gun boxes, a blanket) so the eyewitness statements could be checked and compared
- witnesses could be asked about elements the police would not have focused on, so previous police questioning would not interfere with or affect the study results.

Aims
- To record and evaluate witness accounts.
- To examine issues raised by laboratory research.
- To look at witness verbatim (word-for-word) accounts – their accuracy and the kind of errors made.

Research shows that loss and distortion of memory takes place over time. The idea of the study was to look at eyewitness interviews immediately after the event, which were conducted by a police officer, and to compare these with interviews carried out by research staff longer after the event. Misleading questions were incorporated into the research interviews to see how an eyewitness might be affected by distortion. This is about post-event information, one of the factors affecting reliability of eyewitness testimony that you have to cover.

Procedure

Twenty-one witnesses to the gun shooting were interviewed by police after the incident. Twenty out of the 21 were contacted by the research team and 13 agreed to the research interview – two had moved from the area and five did not wish to take part. The other witness was the store owner, who did not want to relive the trauma.

The police had interviewed the witnesses and recorded the interviews by hand. Each witness was asked to describe the event in their own terms and then the officer asked a series of questions to amplify what had been said. The reports were verbatim.

About four or five months later, 13 of the witnesses were interviewed by the researchers and the interviews were recorded on audiotape and transcribed. The same procedure was followed – their own account followed by questions.

- There were also two misleading questions: one involved a headlight in the thief's car. Half of the witnesses were asked if they had seen *a* busted headlight and the other half were asked if they had seen *the* busted headlight, using Loftus's procedure, which you will read about in Loftus and Palmer (1974) (page 330). There was no broken headlight.
- The second misleading question was about the colour of a quarter panel of the car. Half were asked about *the* yellow quarter panel and the other half about *a* yellow quarter panel. The colour of the quarter panel was in fact blue.

> **STUDY HINT**
> The two misleading questions are set out clearly in this account as they are examples of post-event information, which you need to cover as a factor that affects eyewitness testimony. This is misinformation too, another interesting factor in eyewitness testimony. You can use this study when discussing such factors.

The interview also asked about the degree of stress each witness experienced at the time of the accident. This used a seven-point scale, with 1 being perfectly calm and 7 being extremely anxious. They were asked about their emotional state before the incident and any problems afterwards, like sleeplessness.

A careful scoring procedure was used, because details from the research interviews had to be compared with details from the police interviews, as well as needing the actual details of the incident. The researchers divided the incident up into 'action' details and 'description' details, and the 'description' details were further divided into 'object' and 'people' descriptions. Various reconstructions were set up and evidence was carefully researched so that the actual details were revealed.

> **STUDY HINT**
> In Yuille and Cutshall, there is an example of sorting out qualitative interview data into categories to help with analysing the data. You can use this when discussing types of data and the value of them.

An example of how details were divided up is shown using the statement 'He turned around and shot the guy in the shoulder', which was divided up into three action details. There were some difficulties with the scoring — for example, 'He looked like he was in his early 20s' was scored as incorrect, even though he did look as if he was in his early 20s, because he was in fact 35.

Results

Table 3.19 Total reported classifiable details from 13 witnesses

	Police interview	Research interview
Action details	392 (60.35%)	551.5 (52.20%)
Person descriptions	180 (27.72%)	267 (25.27%)
Object descriptions	77.5 (11.93%)	238 (22.53%)
Total	649.5	1056.5
The percentage figures are the proportions of the details or descriptions that the researchers laid down.		

It can be seen that the researchers obtained more detail than the police. This was because they asked questions of no interest to the police, such as what the blanket was like that covered the thief's body. The police achieved more action details than object or person details and the researchers had half action and half description details.

There was variability in what the witnesses reported but this was because they had seen different amounts of the incident. Of the 13 participants, 7 were central witnesses and 6 peripheral witnesses. However, both groups were equally accurate. In the police interviews, 84.56 per cent of the central witnesses were accurate, compared with 79.31 per cent of the peripheral group. The accuracy remained similar and high for most of the witnesses even after four or five months had passed, and errors were relatively rare. There were different details recalled through the interviews of the researchers, which were not recalled for the police.

The misleading information had little effect on answers – ten said there was no broken headlight or no yellow quarter panel, or said they had not noticed the detail.

Conclusions

The researchers point out that this was the first investigation of eyewitness testimony that involved a real incident and real witnesses. As there were only 13 witnesses and this was a unique event, it is not easy to generalise from the findings. They conclude, however, that their findings show that eyewitnesses are not incorrect in their accounts, as was suggested by laboratory studies. Most of the witnesses were extremely accurate and remained so up to five months after the incident. It is possible that this was because the incident was memorable and unusual.

The researchers suggest they may have been investigating **flashbulb memory**, which is when a specific and relevant event is recorded in memory in great detail. It was found that those directly involved in the event remembered more, so the researchers suggest that laboratory studies would not capture this involvement, which could explain why these findings are different from laboratory study findings.

Definition

Flashbulb memory: the name given to a memory of a specific and relevant event that is recalled in a lot of detail as if the detail is lit up and in focus.

It is interesting that the effort to mislead the witnesses did not succeed, which goes against some laboratory study findings.

There was some investigation of the effects of arousal on memory, although that detail is not given here in the results section, and in general it was found that stress did not affect memory negatively. The researchers found that witnesses at the time felt more adrenaline than stress and that stress came later, so these areas need more research. Judges sometimes reject a witness account because of some incorrect detail, but Yuille and Cutshall here show that, although some detail may be wrong (such as the colour of the blanket), that does not make other details wrong, and that the witness testimony should not then be rejected.

Evaluation

Strengths

- This is a field study that looks at a real incident with real witnesses. It has validity that laboratory experiments do not have and it was carried out because of that validity.

- Great care was taken when counting details from the real incident to make sure that witness testimonies did not alter what 'really' happened. Such care enables the findings to be seen to be reliable.

Weaknesses

- There are problems in generalising from this specific and unique incident. The researchers themselves suggest that this could be a case of flashbulb memory, which is a specific type of memory different from what is studied in the laboratory, so generalising the findings to use them to criticise laboratory studies may be unfair.
- The scoring of the interviews was done conservatively, with some inaccuracies noted even when the response in fact made sense. However, as the accounts were found to be largely accurate, emphasising inaccuracies would not have affected the findings in this case. Scoring turns qualitative data into quantitative data and there is always the chance of interpretation and bias when doing this.

Summary of factors affecting eyewitness testimony considered so far

So far eyewitness testimony has been shown to be unreliable because of stress in the situation, the wording used when questions are asked and issues such as a hat covering a hairline or eyes not being visible. Other factors that have been mentioned in this section so far include how objects and people that are more relevant and central to situations are better remembered by witnesses, and that witnesses tend to remember what fits best with their expectations. Also going over the event before recall and being asked questions is said to help witness recall. This is called giving enhanced retrieval instructions, though Yarmey, who brought this up, did not find that going over the event before starting the recall of it helped.

Yuille and Cutshall (1986) throw doubt on the claims that eyewitness testimony is unreliable, however, because they found even four or five months after a real shooting, recall was good and accurate. Though they did wonder whether they were testing flashbulb memory rather than the more normal eyewitness memory and also the event would be very relevant and central to the witnesses to the shooting, so that might account for the findings. Valentine and Mesout (2009) showed stress affected eyewitness testimony negatively, though Yuille and Cutshall's participants would have been in a stressed state and still had good recall.

Factors that seem to make eyewitness testimony unreliable include:
- stress
- words used in questions

- eyes and hairline regarding faces
- focus on what is expected in a situation
- relevant and central features in an event
- going over an event before recall (enhanced retrieval instructions).

Progress check 3.59

Complete the following table to match the study to the factor affecting eyewitness testimony to show evidence for each factor.

Study giving evidence for the factor	Factor affecting eyewitness testimony
	Stress
	Words used
	Eyes and hairline
	Going over an event before recall

Central information in this scene might be the tram in the centre with some people directly in front, including a pushchair. Peripheral information might be the white car parked by the tram or the man in a brown coat.

Focusing on post-event information and weapon focus as affecting eyewitness reliability

The two factors affecting reliability of eyewitness testimony that you have to focus on are post-event information and weapon focus.

Post-event information

You looked at the effect of misleading information, which if given after the event is **post-event information**, when reading about Yuille and Cutshall's (1986) study, where they planted incorrect misleading information to see if participants would pick up on it. However, participants were not misled by being asked about the 'yellow' quarter panel, which was blue, for example.

Loftus and Palmer (1974), in their question, wrote that the cars 'hit', 'collided', 'bumped', 'smashed' or 'contacted', which was intended to mislead (and was post-event as the question was asked after the films were watched) as the word was intended to convey a different meaning about the accident watched. The post-event question affected the estimate of speed. In the second part of their experiment, they asked about 'broken glass', when there had in fact been no broken glass, and found that 'smashed' suggested broken glass more than 'hit'. This was post-event misleading information. In their study, unlike Yuille and Cutshall, they found participants were 'led' by the questions and, importantly for eyewitness reliability, they were 'misled'. The question came after the event, which was watched on film, so this was post-event information.

Post-event information is information given after the event and can be misleading information, as in Loftus and Palmer's and Yuille and Cutshall's studies. The idea is that information given after the event can be incorporated into the memory and thus lead to an incorrect memory, making eyewitness testimony unreliable, although Yuille and Cutshall's results did not back this finding. Also post-event information can be leading and correct, misleading and incorrect, or neutral, as you will see when reading about Sutherland and Hayne's (2001) study (page 278).

Definition

Post-event information when referring to eyewitness unreliability is information encountered after an event has occurred; the implications are that it interferes with memory of the event.

Gieselman et al. (1986) pointed out that eyewitness accounts can be a leading cause for the miscarriage of justice (Sutherland and Hayne, 2001). An issue is that, in the time between the event and a trial, a witness is going to come across more information, such as from other witnesses, lawyers, the media or the police, and this post-event information may well affect their testimony (Sutherland and Hayne, 2001). This is why studying the effects of post-event information is so important.

The misinformation effect

Loftus used laboratory studies to look at the effect of giving the wrong information to a 'witness'. The aim was to see if the witnesses involved would incorporate the wrong information into their 'witness statement', or if they would even notice. The idea is that memory is reconstructive and not like a tape recording. Witnesses will use past experiences and information, not only from the event but from those around and from any questioner, when they are telling their story (post-event information).

Year One link: Recall your learning about the reconstruction theory of memory, which includes Bartlett's (1932) *War of the Ghosts* study and the idea of schemas guiding what we recall. We use confabulation, reconstruction and rationalisation to make something make more sense.

Explore

You can read about reconstructive memory, including about the misinformation effect, using this link: http://psych.wustl.edu/memory/Roddy%20article%20PDF's/Roediger%20&%20DeSoto%20(2015).pdf

---

When questions included misinformation, Loftus discovered a misinformation effect. This is the effect of using leading questions when the question includes inaccurate information (after the event). In laboratory experiments, this wrong information affected what participants said they saw. The misinformation effect is where incorrect information that someone receives after an event can be incorporated into their memory for that event and of course this would make eyewitness memory unreliable.

One example is when participants witnessed a car accident at a junction where there was a stop sign (Loftus *et al.*, 1978). After the participants had seen the film of the accident, half were given information that the stop sign was a 'yield' (give way) sign. Those who had seen the 'yield' sign information were much more likely to recall a 'yield' sign, whereas the other half of the participants were more likely to be accurate and remember a stop sign. Loftus *et al.* (1978) found that information that was consistent with the original information (accurate information) improved recognition, whereas conflicting information reduced recognition – this is the misinformation effect. In another study, participants recalled a 'barn' that they were asked about but which was not there (Loftus, 1975).

Loftus also found that, if there was a time lapse between the viewing of the film and being asked questions about what they had seen, participants were even more open to the (post-event) misinformation effect and more likely to change their memories to include the misinformation.

Progress check 3.60

Using the four studies outlined briefly above, answer the following questions. The four studies are the 'stop/yield sign' study, the 'barn' study, the 'broken glass' part of Loftus and Palmer (1974), and the 'time taken before recall' study.

1 For two of the studies, what is the hypothesis?
2 For two of the studies, what is the IV and what is the DV?
3 For the 'stop/yield sign' study, what is the experimental design?

Consideration of central versus peripheral information and neutral, leading or misleading post-event information

Sutherland and Hayne (2001) carried out an experiment to test the effect of post-event information. They wanted to look at recognition questions, such as 'Did the perpetrator have a gun or a knife?', which are about **recognition** because a choice is offered about what was in the scene. They also wanted to look at recall of the event, asking such questions as 'What did the perpetrator look like?', which is about **recall** as there is no information offered. Sutherland and Hayne point out that the usual procedure for eyewitness research is to look at 'recognition' by using closed questions rather than at 'recall', which requires open questions.

Another aim was to look at both misleading post-event information and leading post-event information as some of what a witness encounters between the event and their testimony is going to be accurate post-event information. For example, the media may print correct details of the event that the witness did not know about. A final aim was to look at central versus peripheral aspects of the event to see if these affect testimony. Studies tend to mislead participants with regard to peripheral information, such as a 'stop' sign versus a 'yield' sign on the road (Loftus *et al.*, 1978, cited in Sutherland and Hayne, 2001). Pirolli and Mitterer (1984, cited in Sutherland and Hayne, 2001) found that adults were more accurate regarding recognition for central items than for peripheral items. Sutherland and Hayne thought that adults' account of central information would be less affected by post-event information than their account of less important details. Sutherland and Hayne were interested in whether police interviewing might affect an account of an event, given that police questioning might be giving post-event information. So they asked participants specific questions giving post-event information to replicate that interview situation. The questions could be answered by recognition as two answers were given for participants to choose from, or it could be answered using free recall (not giving a choice of answer).

Definitions

Recognition refers to an awareness that something being looked at (or heard, and so on) has been perceived before. Specifically regarding post-event information, recognition refers to someone being asked a question and given a choice for their answer, which includes the right answer. **Recall** is to remember and bring something back to awareness — to 're-call' it. Specifically regarding post-event information, recall refers to someone being asked a question without answers to choose from, so memory is relied upon differently in recall than in recognition.

To recap, Sutherland and Hayne's aims were:
- to look at recognition questions, such as 'Did the perpetrator have a gun or a knife?', which are about recognition because a choice is offered about what was in the scene
- to look at recall of the event, asking such questions as 'What did the perpetrator look like?', which is about recall as there is no information offered
- to look at both misleading (incorrect) post-event information and leading (correct) post-event information
- to look at central versus peripheral aspects of the event to see if these affect testimony
- to see whether police interviewing after an event might affect an account of an event.

Sutherland and Hayne (2001) used 24 undergraduates from an introductory psychology course aged from 18 to 32 years. They were put into a direct recall or a recognition group as they were recruited.

Session one

All students watched a short video clip where a two-and-a-half-year-old child is separated from her caregiver while out shopping. In the video, a policeman finds the girl and asks her for her name, address, phone number and where her caregiver is. The policeman then takes her to the police station and tries to phone her home. Then the caregiver comes to collect her. The participants then rate the video for its suitability as a public service announcement, which is a distracter task to prevent rehearsal. They had been told that the research was about rating the video for its suitability.

Session two

Then, 24 hours later, participants were asked six questions about the video:
- Two of these post-event information questions were leading ones, consistent (correct) with the video information. For example, 'In the video, Mary was given a white bear. Who gave her the bear?'

- Two of the questions were misleading, with material inconsistent (incorrect) with the video content. For example, 'In the video, Mary was given a green bear. Who gave her the bear?'
- Two of the questions were neutral, with no additional information given. For example, 'In the video, Mary was given a bear. Who gave her the bear?'

As well as the two consistent leading questions, two inconsistent misleading questions and two neutral questions, the researchers included three questions that related to central features of the video and three questions relating to peripheral features (i.e. not in central vision). In order to choose central and peripheral features of the video, the researchers asked ten different participants to free recall about the video 24 hours after having seen it; the central questions were chosen from the features remembered most, and the peripheral questions came from the features remembered least. The central features were a three-legged dog, the child's caregiver and a teddy bear given to the child, and the peripheral features were the colour of the shop assistant's shirt, the name of the suburb the child lived in and distinctive earrings worn by the caregiver's friend (Sutherland and Hayne, 2001, p. 253).

> **STUDY HINT**
> You can see that Sutherland and Hayne set up their experiment very carefully, including how they chose central and peripheral features in a scene. You could practice devising a few experiments yourself from their study, to help in learning about method issues. Also Sutherland and Hayne's (2001) study will be useful as a laboratory experiment when discussing the method part of criminological psychology in your course.

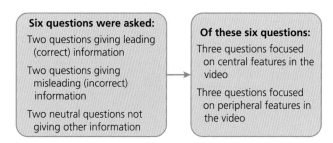

Six questions were asked:
Two questions giving leading (correct) information
Two questions giving misleading (incorrect) information
Two neutral questions not giving other information

Of these six questions:
Three questions focused on central features in the video
Three questions focused on peripheral features in the video

The questions Sutherland and Hayne (2001) asked

> ## Progress check 3.61
> Give one independent variable and the dependent variable that goes with it, from Sutherland and Hayne (2001).

Each participant was asked one neutral, one leading and one misleading question from central information in the video and one neutral, one leading and one misleading question from peripheral information in the video, so each was asked six questions. Questions were asked in the order the information was found in the video.

Session three

Then, 24 hours after the post-event information session, participants were interviewed individually. They were told at this stage that the experiment was to test their memory regarding the video and the reason for the deception was to prevent rehearsal.

All the participants were asked to describe the video in as much detail as possible. Then, participants were asked a series of six specific questions, some in the free recall condition and some in the recognition condition. In the recognition condition, participants had to select their response from two possible answers, called the recognition test procedure, as they had to recognise the answer to the question. One of the answers was correct and one was the misleading item that had been presented in session two. Participants in the recall condition had to answer the same questions but giving their own answers, which was recall, so this was the recall test procedure. Afterwards, participants were fully debriefed.

Results

- Participants answered more questions correctly when given the two-choice recognition task (mean = 4.83) than when giving their own answers (mean = 3.33)
- Participants answered more questions correctly if they had leading post-event information (mean = 1.71) than if they had neutral post-event information (mean = 1.25) or misleading post-event information (mean = 1.13).
- Participants answered more questions correctly when the questions referred to central aspects of the video (mean = 2.58) than when they focused on peripheral information (mean = 1.50).
- When asked about central information, the recognition and recall conditions showed few differences. However, when asked about peripheral information, recognition gave more correct responses than recall (p<.001).
- For central details, leading information did not affect correct responses. However, when asked about peripheral details, leading information increased correct responses but misleading post-event information had no effect on the number of correct responses.

The test condition (recall or recognition) affected the testimony (p<.001), the category of information (central or peripheral) affected the testimony (p<.001) and the post-event type of information (neutral, leading or misleading) affected the testimony (p<.001).

Conclusions

Sutherland and Hayne confirmed Loftus's findings about post-event misleading information and found that participants were more likely to choose the misleading option as an answer when they had been previously exposed to misleading information than if they were exposed to neutral or leading post-event information. However, when they generated their own responses, they were less likely to give misinformation. This suggests it is the questioning procedure that affects the 'testimony', which is what has been claimed in other eyewitness testimony research. The practical application here is with regard to interviewing witnesses as giving post-event information when questioning witnesses is likely to affect their account of an event. It was also found that adults' reports about central aspects of the video were less affected by post-event information than their accounts of peripheral aspects. With regard to peripheral aspects, misleading information increased errors and leading information increased correct responses so it was the peripheral information that was more affected by post-event information than central aspects of the event. Using recognition showed more effect from misinformation, which is of concern because eyewitnesses might receive a lot of misinformation. Using open-ended questioning was more successful in avoiding the misinformation effect and this has implications for interviewing eyewitnesses to help with reliability. Cognitive interviewing involves asking open questions and this study supports that approach.

As a limitation, Sutherland and Hayne suggest that their study lacks ecological validity to an extent because their participants did not witness a stressful crime first-hand. However, they think that some of their procedure had ecological validity because witnesses might well be asked about details that, to them, were peripheral at the time and also relevance of their eyewitness information might only come clear once they hear about the crime. Therefore, the researchers claim there is some validity in their study.

> **STUDY HINT**
> In an exam question on eyewitness testimony, aim to be very accurate in terms used. Such as referring to eyewitness testimony (e.g. Loftus and Palmer, 1974), eyewitness memory (e.g. Valentine and Mesout, 2009), eyewitness identification (e.g. Valentine and Mesout, 2009), **eyewitness recognition** (e.g. Valentine and Mesout, 2009) or eyewitness recall (e.g. Yuille and Cutshall, 1986). These terms are summarised in Table 3.20.

Definition

Eyewitness recognition occurs when given a choice.

Table 3.20 Terms used in eyewitness research

Term	Explanation
Eyewitness recall	This is when a witness recalls information without a choice of statements to help recall. Open questions are used to get the witnesses' own version of events from their memory.
Eyewitness recognition	This is when a witness is given a choice somehow, such as a choice of statements or a photo line-up.
Eyewitness testimony	This is the general term for a witness giving evidence in court. In this chapter, it is used as a general term for eyewitness input, including when being interviewed.
Eyewitness identification	This is about identification specifically. It means pointing to someone or a picture of them and saying it was them the witness saw.
Eyewitness memory	This can cover recall and recognition and involves accessing what is stored about an event or situation.

Creating false childhood memories

Loftus has also carried out research into planting false early memories to see if people accept those memories as accurate (Loftus and Pickrell, 1995). It seems they do. Again, she used laboratory experiments. To be sure that any planted memory would not be too traumatic for participants – ethical considerations being important – she came up with the idea of having been lost in a shopping mall as a child. The participants were asked to try to remember incidents from their childhood; a relative helped with three real incidents and also the fake one about being lost (the researchers having first checked that each participant had not been lost in this way).

The scenario is that the child became lost in a shopping mall and started crying. The child was then comforted by an elderly woman, and was finally reunited with a family member. The participant read all four stories and had to say what they remembered about each event. They could write that they did not remember the event if they could not recall it. The question was, would they 'remember' the 'being lost' story, which was false?

Explore
There is a YouTube video of Elizabeth Loftus and the 'lost in a shopping mall' study, which you can access here: **https://www.youtube.com/watch?v=PQr_IJvYzbA**

The results were that 29 per cent (7 of the 24 participants) 'recalled' being lost. Then, after being interviewed again about the story at a later date, 25 per cent (6 of them) still claimed they remembered. Of the events that actually took place, 68 per cent were remembered. Loftus concluded that memories are reconstructed from present and past experiences, but also that some 'memories' might be completely false, such as being 'given' after the event, which affects how we view eyewitness testimony. Loftus was actually interested in this issue because of the false memories that therapists can instil in their clients, but this work on false memories also has implications for witness testimony. The false memory was post-event information and was incorporated into memories already there. This backs up the misinformation effect – that incorrect information can be incorporated into memories and that makes them 'false'.

Explore
You can hear Elizabeth Loftus talking about 'the fiction of memory' using this link: **www.youtube.com/watch?v=PB2Oegl6wvI&spfreload=10**

Progress check 3.62
Give four features of post-event information that might affect the reliability of eyewitness testimony.

Implications of post-event information for eyewitness testimony

The misinformation effect underlines how memory is reconstructed and not like a tape-recorder and yet it might be seen to be reliable and like a tape-recorder in a court of law. This can affect the reliability of eyewitness testimony. In Yarmey (2004), students overestimated how well a target would be identified in a photo line-up. This helps to show that generally eyewitness reliability might be overestimated, which is not good news for a defendant where eyewitness testimony is central evidence in the case. Not only is the court situation of interest, but also getting the testimony in the first place in as reliable a way as possible is important. As Sutherland and Hayne pointed out, interviewing after an event would get more correct testimony if open questioning were used (see page 233 on cognitive interviewing) and eyewitness testimony is more reliable if there is no misleading post-event information encountered. As information about things that are central to the witness are better remembered and information police might be interested in might well not be central for the witness, that too is likely to affect eyewitness reliability, and post-event information can affect a witness differently depending on whether it is about what was central for them in an event and what was peripheral. Overall, it is clear that eyewitness testimony can be unreliable in different ways, for different reasons.

Individual differences in eyewitness testimony – gender

Areh (2010) looked at gender-related differences in eyewitness testimony. They looked at the accuracy of recall for details of an event and the number of details recalled. They used 280 participants (57.5 per cent female, 42.5 per cent male), with an average age of 19 years.

Progress check 3.63

Work out the number of females and the number of males in Areh's sample. Areh gives the percentage figure. What is the usefulness of having a percentage figure?

Participants watched a recording of a violent robbery, which was said to have been caught on surveillance camera, and they were told their help was needed with the criminal investigation. This gave the procedure some ecological validity.

The females were more reliable eyewitnesses than the males. Females were more accurate when describing people, in particular when describing victims. Males were more accurate in describing the event and were more confident about describing the place the incident took place in. The males were more confident but they were less often correct – females were highly accurate when describing places. There were no gender differences in how much detail was recalled, which might have been because a checklist was used with details listed and perhaps what was on the checklist were the most notable details.

It is generally thought that there are small gender differences and they relate to specific cognitive abilities between the two sexes (e.g. Lippa, 2005, cited in Areh, 2010). Shapiro and Penrod (1986, cited in Areh, 2010) found women were better at face recognition, for example, though they made more errors than men; Rehnman and Herlitz (2007, cited in Areh, 2010) agreed that women are better at face recognition. Areh (2010) cited other information about gender and eyewitness testimony, saying females are also better than males in recall of everyday tasks (e.g. Lindholm and Christianson, 1998), of stories (Zelinski et al., 1993) and of names (Herlitz et al., 1997). Women also have better episodic memory. With regard to eyewitness memory, Linholn and Christianson (1998, cited in Areh, 2010) suggest women have more elaborate categories for person information, which is why there is a female advantage.

Year One link: Recall what you learned about episodic memory in cognitive psychology.

Results of Areh (2010)

- Gender differences were most apparent for victim description, with females recalling significantly more correct details than males.
- Females reported fewer false details than males.
- Females were better than males at place description.
- Males had more confidence in their accuracy than females, as can be seen in Table 3.21, with males consistently perceiving themselves in a better way than females perceive themselves.

Table 3.21 shows the results of Areh (2010), giving gender differences in their own view of their accuracy. Scores are mean average of self-perceived accuracy, with 1 meaning they thought they would recall no details and 7 meaning they thought they would recall a lot of details. When measuring confidence, 1 meant no confidence and 7 meant full of confidence.

Table 3.21 Mean average of self-perceived accuracy (Areh, 2010)

Variable	Male	Female
Memory of the incident	3.38	3.25
Memory of the women	3.55	3.61
Memory of the man	3.78	3.78
Memory of the place of the incident	4.64	4.25
Confidence in one's memory	4.32	4.05

The idea that gender affects the reliability of eyewitness testimony is useful and is another variable to consider when judging the unreliability of eyewitness testimony. We now turn to another variable of interest: the 'weapon focus'.

Weapon focus

Weapon focus can be called the weapons effect and is a factor affecting eyewitness testimony. When a weapon is in a scene, a witness tends to focus attention onto the weapon and so other information is not well recalled.

Explanation

Weapon focus refers to the way a weapon a perpetrator is holding is focused on, taking attention away from other aspects of a situation or event so they are less well recalled and described.

Taylor (1982) claimed that, when a witness concentrates on a weapon in a scene, that leaves no attention available for seeing other things in the scene. Or a scene where there is a weapon might allow recall of some other things in the scene, but there is a 'reduced ability' (Loftus, 1979, cited in Loftus *et al.*, 1987). Yarmey and Jones (1983) asked psychology researchers who had published articles on eyewitness testimony about weapon focus and nearly 90 per cent of such experts agreed that in a crime a victim is going to focus on a gun, which will mean they don't focus on the criminal's face (cited in Loftus *et al.*, 1987). What is important here is that lay people think victims 'get a good look' (p. 56) at the gun *and* the face (e.g. Deffenbacher and Loftus, 1982, cited in Loftus *et al.*, 1987).

Laboratory study looking at weapon focus and implications for eyewitness reliability

An early study raising the issue of weapon focus is given here to explain the idea and to give some evidence for it. The study was carried out by Loftus *et al.* (1987).

Background

Loftus *et al.* (1987) use Johnson and Scott (1976) as a study providing some evidence for the weapon effect. Johnson and Scott (1976) had participants sit outside a laboratory waiting to take part in an experiment. A receptionist was there but then left. Participants in the 'no weapon' condition overheard a conversation about equipment failure and saw someone enter the room with a grease pen. The other condition was the 'weapon' condition, where participants heard a hostile conversation and heard crashing of objects. These participants saw someone enter the room holding a letter opener covered with blood. Later, participants were tested on their memory for the event. Nearly all those in the weapon condition described a weapon of some sort, whereas in the other condition participants did not describe the grease pen. In the 'weapon' condition, there was 33 per cent identification of the person coming into the room from 50 photos. In the 'grease pen' condition, there was 49 per cent correct identification. It seemed as if there was a weapon effect, and Loftus *et al.* (1987) wanted to test weapon focus for themselves.

Procedure – Experiment 1

Loftus *et al.* (1987) carried out a study looking at weapon focus. They showed 36 student participants slides of a customer in a restaurant. In one version of the slides, the customer was pointing a gun at the cashier and the cashier gave them some money and in the other version the customer hands the cashier a cheque and the cashier hands some money over. Those participants who saw the gun tended to focus on it and were less able to identify the 'customer' in a line-up than those who were in the condition where the cheque was presented. In one part of this experiment, eye movements of participants were recorded while they viewed the slides. Participants fixed their eyes more on the weapon than on the cheque, and fixations on the weapon lasted longer than fixations on the cheque. In another part of the study, when they asked for details of the scene, the participants in the condition where the gun was seen had worse memory for the event than those in the condition where the cheque was handed over to the cashier.

> **Explore**
> You can read about this study by Loftus *et al.* (1987) here: https://webfiles.uci.edu/eloftus/ LoftusLoftusMessoWeaponFocusLPagesHB87.pdf

Results – Experiment 1

Questionnaire data: Regarding a questionnaire using 20 items asking about the event, those in the 'weapon' condition were correct on 45.8 per cent of the items and those in the control (cheque) condition were correct on 50.3 per cent of the items, which was not a significant difference (p>.05). When asked about the person with the gun/cheque (the target), again those in the 'weapon' condition did less well, but only just. Those in the 'weapon' condition were correct on 45.5 per cent of the items and control participants were correct on 51.5 per cent of the items (p>.10). Regarding the questionnaire items, there did not seem to be much of a weapon effect as recall was similar in the two conditions, though all the participants could describe the object in the target's hand.

> **Progress check 3.64**
> Loftus *et al.* (1987) found no significant difference in recall between the 'weapon' and the control condition. They state that the significance level was p>.05 and p>.10. What does p>.05 and p>.10 mean?

Line-up data: Seven of the participants in the control condition chose the right person (38.9 per cent) and only two of the participants in the 'weapon' condition did so (11.1 per cent). This difference was significant at p<.05. This is evidence for a weapon effect, which takes attention away from features of the criminal.

Eye movement data: Participants made more fixations on the gun than on the cheque. Average fixations were 3.72 on the gun and 2.44 on the cheque, and this difference was significant at p<.01. The length of the eye fixations on the weapon was 242.0 milliseconds whereas with the cheque it was 200.3 milliseconds. A millisecond is a thousandth of a second. The difference in length of fixations between the two conditions was significant at p<.025. This shows the weapon was focused on more than a similar object in a scene that was identical except for the weapon.

Procedure – Experiment 2

In Experiment 2, Loftus *et al.* (1987) used the same slides as in Experiment 1. This time there were 80 students as participants, with 40 in each of the two conditions. Eye movements were not measured this time, but questions about the target person and the 12-person line-up were used again.

Results – Experiment 2

With regard to questions about the person with the weapon or cheque, participants in the weapon condition were correct on 56 per cent of the items and control participants were right on 67 per cent of the items, which was a significant difference at p<.05.

With regard to the line-up, those in the weapon condition were less accurate than controls. Those in the weapon condition were correct 15 per cent of the time and control participants were correct 35 per cent of the time (p<.05).

General conclusions

Loftus *et al.* (1987) put the two experiments together and claim they have the first real support for the idea of weapon focus. In Experiment 1, those seeing the weapon spent longer looking at it than the control participants looked at the cheque. There were more eye fixations on the weapon in that condition than there were on the cheque in the other condition. A consequence of focusing on the weapon was that, in the line-up, there was less identification of the target person. There was more identification in the 'cheque' condition. In Experiment 2, participants were less likely to identify the person in the weapon condition and also they were less accurate when answering questions about the person coming into the room.

Loftus *et al.* (1987) thought that the way the weapon had an effect on recall depended on the slide. It did not affect all slides; whether the weapon was in view seemed to be important. This, they thought, was something that could be investigated.

The researchers thought that the weapon might be related to higher stress levels. Valentine and Mesout (2009) found that higher anxiety related to fewer correct details of an event being recalled and Loftus *et al.* (1987), much earlier, thought that this was the case too.

Loftus *et al.* (1987) also thought that it might be that a weapon is unusual, whereas a cheque in a restaurant is not. They wondered whether a banana instead of a gun would

also have been focused on because it, like a gun, is unusual. Again they suggested this idea as needing further research.

Progress check 3.65

What new research into weapon focus did Loftus *et al.* (1987) suggest?

Issues and debates

One issue and debate in your course is practical issues in the design and implementation of research. Loftus *et al.* (1987) worked very hard to design a carefully controlled experiment and yet still came up with a possible confounding variable (the unusual nature of the gun). You can use this as an example of practical issues in the design and implementation of research in psychology.

Strengths of Loftus *et al.* (1987)

- A strength is that this is a laboratory experiment with a lot of controls, so the results are objective and cause-and-effect conclusions can be drawn about the weapon effect and the unreliability of eyewitness memory.
- Another strength is there is reliability, as Loftus *et al.* did the study twice using different participants and, with regard to identification issues and details of the person, they had similar findings each time.

Weaknesses of Loftus *et al.* (1987)

- As with many laboratory experiments, there is some doubt about ecological validity. The scene was something reasonably familiar in that people in a restaurant give cheques to a cashier and it is thought that holding up a restaurant by pointing a gun at a cashier might be something that is done in real life. Nevertheless, the participant is not experiencing the gun or the fear as a real eyewitness is likely to, so there is a lack of validity.
- As the researchers say, it might be that it is not the weapon that is the issue but the fact that it is unusual in the situation. Possibly anything unusual in a scene will be focused on to the detriment of other details being attended to. More work needed to be done to rule out this confounding variable.

A meta-analysis review of the weapon focus effect

Steblay (1992) carried out a meta-analysis of 19 studies looking at weapon focus and its effect on eyewitness memory. The hypothesis looked at is 'that the presence of a weapon during commission of a crime will negatively affect an eyewitness's ability to later identify the perpetrator' (p. 1). Steblay found a significant difference overall between the weapon-present and weapon-absent conditions, with weapon-presence meaning lower identification accuracy. When looking at actual identification in a line-up, the effect was small and it was moderate for accuracy with regard to describing features. There were factors found that affected the weapon focus effect.

Explore
You can access the meta-analysis carried out by Steblay (1992) using this link: **http://web.augsburg.edu/~steblay/weaponfocusmetaanalysis.pdf**

Table 3.22 Summary of some of the studies reviewed in Steblay (1992) ('arousal' means the stress in the situation)

Study	Number of participants	Arousal	Mode	Weapon	Interval before testing
Bothwell (1991)	27	Low	Video	Gun	Same day
	28	Low	Video	Knife	Same day
Cutler and Penrod (1988)	175	Moderate	Video	Gun	Same day
Johnson and Scott (1976)	48	High	Staged	Opener	–
Kramer (1990)	62	Low	Slides	Cleaver	Same day
Loftus et al. (1987)	36	Moderate	Slides	Gun	Same day
	80	Moderate	Slides	Gun	Same day
Maass and Köhnken (1989)	86	High	Staged	Syringe	Same day

The conclusion drawn by Steblay is that the presence of a weapon does significantly affect eyewitness performance. The overall effect size is not that high but it suggests weapon focus is a variable that affects line-up identification accuracy as well as accuracy in describing someone's features. Although quite a few of the studies use college participants, some studies have used other participants, which adds to the generalisability of the results. Steblay concludes that the weapon effect is found in different scenarios, including real-life enactments, video and slide presentations. Also the effect was found when there was high or moderate arousal and when the line-up had the offender present or when the offender was not in the line-up. The weapon effect was also shown with different time intervals between seeing the event and doing the recall and identification. The meta-analysis supported the idea of a weapon focus interfering with identification of an offender and also recall of details, such as about their appearance. This suggests that in real life an eyewitness account is likely to be affected by a weapon and that any line-up identification should be used with care, as well as other information about the scene.

Strengths of Steblay (1992)

● This was a meta-analysis that drew on a number of studies using similar procedures to look at weapon focus. As the studies used similar procedures, such as using slides of an event and then using a line-up and questions to find out if focus on the weapon affected identification of the 'criminal' and/or information about

them, they could be compared. This gives additional participants and more data, so if the findings from the studies agree this strengthens them. They did agree and so the claim that weapon focus can affect eyewitness identification of a criminal and their description of the criminal is stronger than if based on just one study.

● The studies use the experimental method – a situation was set up where only the 'weapon' varied. Having strong controls means cause-and-effect conclusions can be drawn and there is objectivity and reliability in the findings.

Weaknesses of Steblay (1992)

● Even though the studies were similar in many ways in their procedure, there were differences – for example, in the weapon used and in how the scene was experienced by the participants. Such differences may have meant the data were not comparable.

● A lot of the studies were experiments and this means they may lack ecological validity. There is some attempt at validity, such as when the scenario is something people might experience, like the restaurant scene with a gun and a cheque relating to a cashier in Loftus et al. (1987). However, watching an event on screen is not the same as experiencing it. Valentine and Mesout (2009) (page 337) showed that high anxiety affected number of descriptors correctly recalled in a field situation, so laboratory experiments might not be valid, and so applying their findings to real eyewitnesses may not be appropriate.

A study in the field looking at weapon focus and eyewitness memory

Maass and Köhnken (1989) conducted a study looking at witness effectiveness. In their study, 86 non-psychology university students were approached by a woman holding a pen or a syringe. She either said or did not say that she would give them an injection. The participants were then asked to identify the woman in a line-up, and those exposed to the syringe rather than the pen performed worse in their identification. Participants remembered less facial detail the greater their fear of injections. This study supports other research that claims that, when a weapon is present in a situation, people will focus on the weapon rather than the person or what is happening. In Maass and Köhnken's study, participants seemed to focus on the syringe more than the pen.

Experimental features of Maass and Köhnken (1989)

- Experimental hypothesis: participants will remember more details about a woman who approaches them holding a pen than if she approaches holding a syringe.
- Directional or non-directional: directional (they will remember more in the 'pen' condition).
- Independent variable: whether the woman holds a pen or a syringe.
- Dependent variable: how much they remember about the woman – measured by whether they pick her out in a line-up.
- Experimental design: independent groups (half had the 'pen' condition and half had the 'syringe' condition). In fact, half also had the 'administering an injection' statement.

In Maass and Köhnken's study, a woman walked towards the participant holding either a pen or a syringe.

The conclusion from Maass and Köhnken (1989) is that there is a weapon effect, as other studies have shown.

Strengths of Maass and Köhnken (1989)

- This was a study done in a fairly natural setting, in the university and with students. The set up about an injection might not have been completely natural; however, there was some 'real-life' in the situation, such as having a syringe and a reason for it, or a pen.
- There were good controls, which meant that the independent variable, which was whether there was a syringe (a sort of weapon) or a pen, was all that varied between the two conditions, so that gave objectivity and reliability to the study findings.

Weaknesses of Maass and Köhnken (1989)

- This was a staged incident so, although a syringe might well give stress, it would perhaps not be the same as witnessing a real event where a syringe was used as a weapon or where a more obvious weapon like a gun was used.
- Students were the participants so perhaps it is hard to generalise the findings. The students might have been used to taking part in experiments so might not react as a real eyewitness would react. This is about validity but also about generalising the findings as the sample did not represent the required population (which would be all eyewitnesses).

Threat, novelty and timing effects on weapon focus effect on identification in line-ups

Erickson *et al.* (2014) looked at weapon focus effect. The effect is accepted – the focus of this study was more about how weapon focus arises. Erickson *et al.* (2014) raise the point that weapon focus might work because attentional cues are narrowed to the weapon perhaps because arousal (page 210) increases. Alternatively, weapon focus might work because weapons are novel objects, which take more attention than appropriate objects. Erickson *et al.* (2014) used a crime set-up where there was a normal, novel or threatening object. Also the object was either visible before the culprit's face was visible, during the face being visible or after the face was visible. Also, both **target-present** and **target-absent** line-ups were used, which means in one line-up situation the culprit is in the line-up (target-present), but not in another line-up situation (target-absent). There were also questions about the scenario to test recall, as well as identification in a line-up. The results were that both the novel object and the threatening object (the weapon) led to more misidentification in the line-up where the culprit was not in the line-up (target-absent).

Definitions

Target-present means the person to be identified in an experiment looking at eyewitness testimony is in the line-up, whether a live one or a photo line-up. **Target-absent** means the person to be identified in an experiment looking at eyewitness testimony is not in the line-up, whether a live one or a photo line-up.

Year One link: When studying cognitive psychology, you looked at how schemas are used to reconstruct memories. There are studies looking at the role of schemas in memory and experiments often include expected and unexpected objects in a scene to see whether a schema for the scene 'puts in' objects that were not there or whether unexpected objects are better recalled as they are outside the schema. This sort of explanation fits with the ideas about weapon focus, so recall your learning of reconstructive memory and the role of schemas. Steyvers and Hemmer (2012), one of the contemporary studies in cognitive psychology, is useful for this information.

Issues and debates

In your course, one issue and debate is understanding how psychological understanding has changed over time. You could trace research into weapon focus from Loftus *et al.* (1987), who more or less started it off, and then consider Erickson *et al.* (2014), who accepted that there was a weapon focus effect and wanted to look at variables more closely. This is an example of how psychology research builds a body of knowledge.

Erickson *et al.* (2014) follow Loftus *et al.*'s (1987) suggestions for an experiment to see whether it was the gun that led to the identification problems or whether it was because it was a novel object in the situation. Loftus *et al.* (1987) wondered whether any novel object would have the same effect. Erickson *et al.* pointed out that the presence of the weapon might raise state anxiety so narrowing attention and not leaving attentional resources for other things in a scene. Another explanation is that the weapon is unexpected in the scene and so attention

is focused on what is unexpected. The weapon focus effect itself is accepted and, according to Erickson *et al.* (2014), 87 per cent of researchers looking into eyewitness testimony agree that a weapon in the scene impairs eyewitness ability to identify the culprit's face. Erickson *et al.* also point out that almost all studies looking at weapon focus effect have used target-present line-ups, though, notably, Maass and Köhnken (1989) used the target-absent procedure. Erickson *et al.* argue that target-present and target-absent look at two types of memory – one is recognition of the perpetrator in the line-up; the other is about rejecting the people in the line-up. This is why Erickson *et al.* (2014) used both target-present and target-absent conditions.

The other issue of interest is timing. The researchers wonder whether the face being visible first, at the same time as the weapon, or afterwards would affect testimony. Kramer *et al.* (1990, cited in Erickson *et al.*, 2014) found that the weapon focus effect, decreasing accuracy of memory, was found not to differ depending on whether the face was seen first or the face and weapon were seen together, though Kramer *et al.* did not look at the situation where the face was seen after the weapon. Threat, novelty and timing were the three conditions of interest in Erickson *et al.* and they also wanted to look at target-present as opposed to target-absent line-ups.

Participants and design

Erickson *et al.* (2014) used 1,263 undergraduates in the USA. The conditions were:
- object: neutral, novel and weapon
- timing: face seen before, during or after the weapon
- line-up: target-present or target-absent.

Materials

The set-up was a row of people photographed as if at a bar, although they were in a lab. The photo was taken from a bartender's point of view, from behind the bar. Seven volunteers could be seen from the waist up facing the camera and gesturing as though ordering drinks and two other volunteers sat at a table in the background.

One of the people held an object out to the camera: the normal object was an empty glass; the novel object was a rubber chicken; and the weapon was a realistic 'airsoft' gun. Photos were added to a set of slides for participants to see.
- With regard to the timing condition: 'before' showed the object only and then the face; 'during' showed the face and object together at the same time; 'after' showed the face only and then the object only.
- Photo line-ups were used. The target photo was in a different place in different line-up photos in the target-present condition.

- Follow-up questions asked about the participants' perceptions of threat and surprise and how much attention they paid to the object.

Aims

- Erickson *et al.* (2014) wanted to test the weapon focus effect, which is that there is less identification of the target person in a line-up if a weapon is present than when a novel or neutral object is present.
- They also wanted to see if the poorer memory for the target person was found in a target-present line-up differently from a target-absent line-up.
- They wanted to see if the timing of the object and face in the scene affected the weapon focus effect.

- They wanted to see whether a novelty object and a threat object had a different effect on the identification of the perpetrator.

Results

Not all of the results are reported here but there are enough to give you the main findings. In the target-present condition, 69.50 per cent correctly identified the person, 16.20 per cent said the person was not there and 14.30 per cent incorrectly identified someone else. In the target-absent condition, 52.30 per cent correctly rejected the line-up and 47.70 per cent incorrectly identified someone else. Table 3.23 summarises the results of Erickson *et al.* (2014).

Table 3.23 Proportions of target selections and line-up rejections depending on whether the condition was target-present or target-absent and looking at the three different objects

Target-absent (TA) or target-present (TP) in line-up	Object (glass is neutral; chicken is novel; gun is weapon)	Timings		
		Face before object (before)	Face and object together (during)	Face after object (after)
TP target so is right	Glass	.73	.71	.75
	Chicken	.68	.63	.70
	Gun	.79	.53	.72
TP reject so is wrong	Glass	.10	.22	.17
	Chicken	.16	.15	.09
	Gun	.12	.34	.12
TA reject so is right	Glass	.55	.55	.74
	Chicken	.54	.46	.51
	Gun	.48	.43	.46

Progress check 3.68

In the 'gun' results in two of the line-up options, you can see that when the face and object are presented together there is quite a dip in accuracy compared with when the face and object were presented separately. Give the figures that lead to this claim.

STUDY HINT
Be ready to answer questions in the examination using figures in tables. Practise studying figures in tables to prepare.

Some main results:
- The gun produced significantly fewer identifications of the suspect compared with the glass (p=.030) but the chicken did not make a significant difference (p=.297).

- The face before the object and the face after the object were both significantly different from the face and object being presented together, so timing seems to make a difference. There was lower identification of the face if it appeared during the presentation of the object than if it was before or after the object was presented. Though there was no difference in timing coming from which object was used.
- The glass led to more line-up rejections in the target-absent condition than the gun or the chicken, which goes with the weapon focus hypothesis. Rejecting a line-up was correct in the target-absent condition so there was more identification when the glass was the object than when there was threat (the gun was the object) or novelty (the chicken was the object).

Some results from the responses to the questions, which are given in Table 3.24:

- Looking at attention, the glass had significantly less attention than the chicken or gun (p<.001). The chicken and gun did not differ significantly (p>.30). The 'after' condition meant less attention than the 'before' or 'during' conditions.
- Looking at surprise, the glass was seen as significantly less surprising than the chicken (p<.001) or gun (p<.001). The chicken and gun were not significantly different from one another with regard to the surprise element and timing had no effect.
- Looking at reported threat showed that the gun was seen as more threatening than the chicken or glass (p<.001 in both cases). The chicken and glass did not differ from one another and there was no effect from the timing differences.

Progress check 3.69

Explain two results shown in Table 3.24.

Conclusions

The conclusion was that the weapon focus effect was replicated and there is impaired memory of perpetrators of crimes when a weapon is present. When the face and object were present in the same slide, there was a weapon focus effect, with the fewest identifications of the target in the gun condition, followed by the chicken, and most identifications in the glass condition, as would be expected. There was a drop of 18 per cent in identifications from the glass condition to the gun condition. However, the chicken condition was not that much different from the glass

Table 3.24 The mean responses to questions giving ratings of attention, surprise and perceived threat for all three objects (timings all put together)

Question	Object type		
	Glass (neutral)	Chicken (novel)	Gun (weapon)
Attention paid (1 = paid more attention to the face; 10 = paid more attention to the object)	4.96	6.38	6.59
How surprised were you? (1 = not at all; 10 = very)	3.56	7.86	8.01
How surprised would you be? (1 = not at all; 10 = very)	3.36	7.06	7.01
How frightened were you of the object? (1 = not at all; 10 = very)	1.76	2.00	5.53
How frightened would you be of the object? (1 = not at all; 10 = very)	2.27	2.04	8.11

condition, so the novelty effect did not seem to be at work. Erickson *et al.* found that the gun and glass were correctly identified by almost all participants. However, this was not the case with the chicken, which was correctly identified less often, so if participants could not tell it was a chicken that would account for the novelty effect not being found.

What was interesting was that in the target-present condition the weapon focus effect was not found. The timing did have an effect, with fewer target selections when the face and object were presented together than when they were presented separately. This suggests that when there is attention on any object, there is less attention on the face. It was in the target-absent condition that the weapon focus effect was found most. The gun and the chicken conditions produced more false identifications than the glass, and the differences were significant. This does suggest that, when a weapon or unusual object is present in a scene, there might be more mistakes made by an eyewitness, with obvious effects on someone innocent of the crime. Erickson *et al.* concluded that they had found a weapon focus effect and that it came from surprise and novelty of the object rather than from threat. The researchers suggest that members of the public need to know about such issues with eyewitness memory to help to prevent wrongful identification of perpetrators and hence possible wrongful convictions.

Strengths of Erickson *et al.* (2014)

- Erickson *et al.*, as with many studies looking at the weapon focus effect, used a lab study that was carefully set up with controls and so cause-and-effect conclusions could be drawn.

- The study goes beyond looking at just one hypothesis, such as testing the 'threat' explanation against the 'novelty' explanation. It looks at timing of face and object being presented, which adds more evidence to what is already known, for example, and also shows that a target-present line-up gives different findings to a target-absent line-up. The study uses complex analysis and many variables, which helps to add detail to the findings.

Weaknesses of Erickson *et al.* (2014)

- There might be a lack of ecological validity because, although the staged situation was realistic to an extent and might have been people in a bar, which had some validity, the chicken was not identified as much as the glass and gun, which might suggest there was a lack of realism in the situation.
- Students were used in the study, as they are in a lot of psychology studies. It is generally offered as a criticism when students are the participants, because generalising from just students to say the findings can be applied to everyone might not be appropriate.

STUDY HINT

If you go through the evaluation points of the lab experiments used when discussing the unreliability of eyewitness testimony, you will see that there are similarities, because it is often the research method that is being evaluated. For example, for weaknesses, you can consider generalisability and validity and, for strengths, you can use reliability, objectivity, cause-and-effect and credibility in terms of science. It is useful to think of these issues, as well as ethics, when evaluating studies.

Test yourself

To what extent is eyewitness testimony unreliable?
(20 marks)

Juror decision-making

There are factors that affect juror decision-making, as you might expect. As you will have seen in cognitive psychology, memory is not like a tape-recorder. Schemas are used through which the world is seen. Such schemas, influencing the way people are judged, will be involved in juror decision-making. Earlier in this chapter, we looked at the effect of labelling on becoming a criminal or behaving in an anti-social way (page 219), and labelling can be done by jurors, using stereotyping. These are the issues looked at in this section. 'Jury' decision-making

is where a whole jury can be affected by issues about a defendant and 'juror' decision-making is more about how an individual juror is affected – the terms tend to be used interchangeably in this section.

In your course, you are asked to look at factors affecting jury decision-making, including characteristics of the defendant and the effects of pre-trial publicity. You need to look at studies in these areas. You do not need to look at group processes that are involved that affect the decision a jury comes to, just focus on the two areas of defendant characteristics and pre-trial publicity. The concepts you will look at are social and cognitive ones. For example, labelling is about social interactions and how others affect someone's behaviour, and the use of schemas is about cognitions.

Year One link: Recall what cognitive psychology is about in general, such as the way the brain processes information, and what social psychology is about in general, such as looking at how people are influenced by others around them.

Jury decision-making is an area of interest in criminological psychology and it has practical implications because it is part of the judicial system and a jury has power over a defendant. Saying someone is guilty of a crime is a responsibility and, if juries are biased in their decision-making, there is a key question for society of whether juries should no longer be used in a position of power. This is one of the key questions in your course (and is explored on the website accompanying this book). In an area like this, psychological research has implications for legal policy (Bornstein and Greene, 2011).

In this section, first, characteristics of the defendant are looked at, using studies as evidence for points made. Second, the effects of pre-trial publicity are considered, again using studies as evidence.

Trial by jury should mean people representing the general public give their opinion based on all the evidence. However, jurors are individuals and can be affected by characteristics of a defendant or what is said about a trial before it begins.

Defendant characteristics and jury decision-making

First, some general information about defendant characteristics is considered. Then some specific characteristics are chosen and looked at in more detail. Two characteristics are focused on in this section. Race is chosen because it features in one of the contemporary studies in your course, Bradbury and Williams (2013). Attractiveness is also discussed. A section on gender of the defendant is provided on the website accompanying this book. However, there are other characteristics you can look at, such as accent.

General information

Devine *et al.* (2000) carried out a review of research focusing on jury decision-making between 1955 and 1999. They considered studies looking at actual juries and those using mock juries. Mock jury trials are where a jury is set up and a fictitious trial carried out or reported where there can be manipulation of variables. You are looking at characteristics of the defendant and issues about the case focusing on any publicity before the trial.

Studies looking at jury decision-making tend to be experimental, looking at an independent variable, such as the race of a defendant, and the dependent variable, such as how many years a mock jury would think would be appropriate for the defendant, or whether they would say the defendant in the mock situation was guilty or not. You can use evaluation of the experimental method when evaluating the factors affecting jury decision-making. Some evaluation points about mock jury studies are given later in this section (page 303).

Devine *et al.* (2000) discuss research looking at defendant characteristics. They discuss how human judgement is affected by schemas and scripts and how characteristics of a defendant can affect a juror's decision. Characteristics include race, gender, social class, attitudes and physical attractiveness.

Explore

You can access Devine *et al.*'s (2000) review using this link: http://static1.squarespace.com/static/5046753fe4b032e1c6aa75b9/t/51844f1ae4b0b930f1c93d59/1367625498585/DL.pdf

Simple effects tend not to be found with regard to race as a defendant characteristic (e.g. Shaw and Skolnick, 1995, cited in Devine *et al.*, 2000). It is not that all studies show a racial bias. However, defendant race and juror race have been shown to link and some studies have shown that the race of the defendant can affect jury decision-making. One of the contemporary studies in your course is Bradbury and Williams (2013), who looked at the effects of race on juror decision-making (page 333). The study gives evidence that, with regard to a black defendant, it makes a difference if the majority of the jury is white and it also makes a small difference if the majority of the jury is Hispanic. Not much has been done on gender as a defendant characteristic, according to Devine *et al.* (2000). However, there are studies on the impact of socioeconomic status of the defendant on jury decision-making. Judson *et al.* (1969, cited in Devine *et al.*, 2000) found that those of low socioeconomic status tended to receive the death sentence more often, though Gleason and Harris (1976, cited in Devine *et al.*, 2000) found no effect for socioeconomic status of the defendant in a laboratory experiment. Physical attractiveness has also been studied and shows some evidence of bias against defendants seen as unattractive. Izzett and Leginski (1974, cited in Devine *et al.*, 2000) found that juries seem to be more lenient towards an attractive defendant.

STUDY HINT

 The practical investigation on the website accompanying this book focuses on attractiveness of a defendant and decisions about sentencing. Attractiveness is one of the characteristics considered in this section, alongside race and (on the website) gender.

Progress check 3.70

There are three characteristics of the defendant that have been mentioned in this general introduction as not being fully confirmed by studies as affecting jury decision-making. List the three characteristics.

The race of the defendant

Mitchell *et al.* (2005) carried out a meta-analysis looking at race and jury decision-making, and some of the findings are given here. Bradbury and Williams (2013) (page 333) looked at majority white and majority Hispanic juries and how race of the majority of the jury might influence judgement of a black defendant. Another study referred to here is Carter and Mazzula (2013), which looks at in-group and out-group bias in jury decision-making, finding racial bias. A final study is Glaser *et al.* (2015), which looks at the possibility of the death sentence and the effect on verdicts for black and white defendants. Glaser *et al.*'s (2015) study is considered in more depth so, with Bradbury and Williams (2013), there are two studies looked at in depth concerning the influence of the race of the defendant.

Mitchell *et al.*'s (2005) meta-analysis

Mitchell *et al.* (2005) report on a meta-analysis of mock jury trials looking at the effects of **racial bias** on juror decision-making. As Devine *et al.* (2000) said in their review, evidence from studies is mixed, some showing such racial bias and others not.

Definition

Racial bias means not treating minority group defendants equally; when applied to juror decision-making, it means black defendants being treated 'more harshly' by jurors and juries than white defendants (Mitchell *et al.*, 2005).

Explore
You can access Mitchell *et al.*'s (2005) review of studies looking at mock juror decision-making and racial bias here: **http://digitalcommons.utep.edu/cgi/viewcontent. cgi?article=1016&context=christian_meissner**

Mitchell *et al.* (2005) defined racial bias as different treatment of racial out-groups and found that there is a small but significant effect of racial bias in decision-making but the effect is more pronounced in certain situations.

STUDY HINT
Later in this section, Table 3.25 gives some of the findings concerning effects of race of the defendant on jury decision-making. It is useful when making notes to summarise the main findings in different ways, such as tables and bullet points, so that you have an overview of the studies.

STUDY HINT
Meta-analysis as a research method was covered in clinical psychology and is detailed in Chapter Two, with a review in the 'Psychological skills – methods' section on the website. You can use evaluation points about meta-analysis as a method when evaluating a study using meta-analysis.

Mitchell *et al.* (2005) start their meta-analysis by showing that there is racial bias in the American justice system, such as Human Rights Watch (2000), reporting that black male drug users are 13 times more likely to be sentenced to jail than white male drug users. This was the case even though drug use between the two groups is equivalent.

STUDY HINT
You need to carry out a practical in criminological psychology, and juror decision-making is a suitable area within which to design an experiment. While reading the material, look out for a suitable hypothesis that you could test in a jury-like situation. A possibility is to write a story about a male drug user, with some detail, and then ask participants to give a 'sentence' for this person. You could have two versions of the case, with exactly the same detail and the same question for each participant, except that for half the participants the story says the drug user is white and for the other half the drug user is black. The practical used in this chapter and found on the website accompanying this book uses a similar idea but with attractiveness as the variable, and controlling for race, age and education level.

Year One link: You studied in-group and out-group behaviour, including in-group hostility to the out-group, when you looked at social identity theory in social psychology. Social identity theory is an explanation for prejudice and the idea of racial bias in juror decision-making relates to the effects of prejudice.

Mitchell *et al.* (2005) cite studies such as Austin and Allen (2000), showing that minority defendants, in particular black defendants, are given longer sentences and sentenced to death more often. Austin and Allen looked at actual defendants and looked at whether there being more minority defendants than whites in the Pennsylvanian prison system (1990–1994) was because of differences in committing of crimes or because of racial discrimination in the justice system. They found that only 43 per cent of the commitment rate targeting minority defendants was due to the arrest rate; race explained the rest. Baldus *et al.* (2002, cited in Mitchell *et al.*, 2005) found that black defendants are given much longer sentences than white defendants when there is a white victim. However, there are studies that have not found race of the defendant to be a main factor, such as Williams and Holcomb (2001, cited in Mitchell *et al.*, 2005), who found that defendant race did not predict death sentence in Ohio. Some studies find that black defendants are treated more harshly than white defendants, especially in murder and rape cases. However, Poulson (1990, cited in Mitchell *et al.*, 2005) found that white defendants were treated more harshly than black defendants, using mock jury decision-making.

Progress check 3.71
What is an advantage of using actual crime figures and statistics about prisoners when looking at race of the defendant and conviction rate compared with using mock jury studies?

Mitchell *et al.* (2005) discuss two meta-analyses looking at race of defendant and juror decision-making which drew different conclusions. Sweeny and Haney (1992, cited in Mitchell *et al.*, 2005) included 14 studies and found a small significant effect of racial bias, showing that white participants were more likely to give black defendants longer sentences than white defendants. They found differences in findings depending on the year of the study, the region it was carried out in, the type of crime, the sample and how the race was shown to the participants/jurors. Also there were differences in whether the study specifically mentioned race and whether the victim's race was specified. Studies that mention the race of the defendant and those specifying the race of the victim showed more racial bias.

Factors affecting whether race affects a sentence (Sweeney and Haney, 1992, cited in Mitchell *et al.*, 2005) include:

- the year the study was published
- the region the study was carried out in (South v. not South, in the US)
- the type of crime (rape v. not rape)
- the sample (student v. community)
- the method of showing defendant race (pictures v. words)
- specific mention of race or not
- mention of victim's race or not.

> **STUDY HINT**
> There are a lot of different variables that have been found to affect the effect of defendant race on sentencing. In the practical for this chapter (on the website accompanying this book), some are controlled for (age, gender, specific mention of race and education level) but others are not (e.g. region the study was done in and to an extent the sample used, though there was an attempt to control variables in the sample). If you carry out a similar practical, getting ideas about important variables from studies is important.

Mitchell *et al.* (2005) also report a meta-analysis carried out by Mazzella and Feingold (1994), which looked at race of the defendant and also physical attractiveness, socioeconomic status and gender of both the defendant and the victim. This meta-analysis looked at 29 studies. Mazzella and Feingold (1994, cited in Mitchell *et al.* 2005) did not find racial bias when they looked at judgements of guilt or sentencing decisions focusing on race alone. They felt that there were other variables that affected racial bias in sentencing or judgement of guilt. The crime itself was an important factor. Black defendants were given longer sentences for certain homicide crimes and white defendants were given longer sentences for fraud.

Progress check 3.72

List some variables that seem to affect whether there is racial bias found in jury decision-making.

Results of Mitchell *et al.*'s (2005) meta-analysis focusing on in-group and out-group

It was thought that mock jurors would show in-group favouritism and would be more lenient to defendants of their own racial group.

- Mitchell *et al.* (2005) looked at 34 studies and found that participants were more likely to give a guilty verdict for defendants of a race different from their own than for defendants of their own race. The meta-analysis found that variables affecting the decision included race of the participant (the juror), sample type, how the dependent variable was measured, whether or not there were jury instructions and the date of the study. They found that race of the participant, dependent variable measure, presence or absence of instructions and the date of the study significantly affected whether there was racial bias in decision-making or not.

- Sixteen studies were looked at to consider racial bias in sentencing and it was found that longer sentences were given out to defendants of a different racial group from the participant/juror, though this result was not strongly significant. This suggests in-group favouritism and out-group hostility/bias.

Progress check 3.73

To show that there are mixed results when considering the impact of the race of the defendant on juror decision-making, give one study's finding that shows there is an effect of the race of the defendant and one study's findings that shows there is not.

Carter and Mazzula (2013)

Carter and Mazzula (2013) carried out a study using 210 mock jurors representing different racial groups. The study showed the mock jurors an employment case and asked about whether the person had been discriminated against. They found both in-group and out-group bias, which backs up Mitchell *et al.*'s (2005) findings. Carter and Mazzula focused on **extralegal factors**, which refer to feelings and ideas about the defendant and any factor outside the evidence which affects the jury's decisions. Extralegal factors are what are being discussed when considering factors that might affect juror decision-making.

Definition

Extralegal factors are those factors that might affect jury decision-making that are not connected to the courtroom, such as biases towards a defendant. **Racial identity** refers to someone's investment in their own race and culture and also focuses on power differences with regard to race.

Race is an extralegal factor that has been found to affect mock and actual juror decisions, as Mitchell et al. (2005) have shown, though Carter and Mazzula underline the finding that studies have shown different results about the influence of race in jury decision-making and the evidence is still inconclusive. Carter and Mazzula wanted to look at a juror's **racial identity** rather than the defendant's race, so their study is not detailed here. However, there are aspects of their study that relate to juror decision-making and the race of the defendant. They agree that it is usually accepted that the defendant's race affects jury decision-making (e.g. Sweeney and Haney, 1992, cited in Carter and Mazzula, 2013). As well as race of the defendant, focus has been on the race of jurors and how that affects their decision-making, with them showing in-group favouritism. Bradbury and Williams (2013), one of the contemporary studies in this chapter, does not look at black juries and black defendants as they accept that this is not likely to lead to racial bias against black defendants. They focus instead on majority white and majority Hispanic jurors and how they make judgements relating to black defendants. This is evidence for it being out-group hostility that leads to racial bias in jury decision-making, which is what Carter and Mazzula (2013) look at. Carter and Mazzula, in their introduction, repeat the point that some studies have not found racial bias in juror decision-making and, like Mitchell et al. (2005), they cite Williams and Holcomb (2001) as not finding racial bias.

Table 3.25 Findings about race of the defendant and racial bias in jury decision-making (Mitchell et al., 2005)

Study/name	What was found	Race of defendant affects decision-making
Devine et al. (2000) meta-analysis	Evidence from studies is mixed, some showing such racial bias and others not showing racial bias.	Mixed
Mitchell et al. (2005) meta-analysis	There is a small but significant effect of racial bias in decision-making and the effect is more pronounced in certain situations.	Yes
Austin and Allen (2000)	Only 43 per cent of the commitment rate (more minority defendants than whites in the Pennsylvanian prison system) targeting minority defendants was due to the arrest rate; race explained the rest.	Yes
Baldus et al. (2002)	Black defendants are given much longer sentences than white defendants when there is a white victim.	Yes
Williams and Holcomb (2001)	Defendant race did not predict death sentence in Ohio.	No
Mitchell et al. (2005) meta-analysis	Some studies find that black defendants are treated more harshly than white defendants, especially in murder and rape cases.	Yes
Poulson (1990)	White defendants were treated more harshly than black defendants, using mock jury decision-making.	No
Sweeny and Haney (1992) meta-analysis	There is a small significant effect of racial bias showing that white participants are more likely to give black defendants longer sentences than white defendants.	Yes
Mazzella and Feingold (1994) meta-analysis	Did not find racial bias when they looked at judgements of guilt or sentencing decisions.	No
	Black defendants were given longer sentences for certain homicide crimes and white defendants were given longer sentences for fraud.	Yes

Carter and Mazzula (2013) are interested in racial identity. According to them, racial identity focuses on someone's 'psychological investment' in their race and culture and also looks at 'power differentials' regarding race. The meaning people apply to race is what affects how they see their world and how they make sense of themselves as racial 'beings'.

Carter and Mazzula point out that racial identity models have been developed for different racial groups, such as non-Hispanic whites having abandoned racism and having developed a non-racist identity. A racial identity model for racial minorities, however, shows they have abandoned a reliance on white culture and looking for acceptance, and have looked instead towards developing a positive racial identity as a member of a minority group (Helms, 1995, cited in Carter and Mazzula, 2013). Carter and Mazzula summarise a theory for whites, which they describe as being about contact, reintegration, immersion and autonomy. They summarise a theory for 'people of colour', which they describe as being about dissonance, resistance and internalisation of a minority group racial identity. Their point is that views about racial identity will affect juror decision-making and these are views about a juror's own racial identity and about the racial identity of other people. The race of the defendant will affect juror decision-making in this way.

Glaser *et al.* (2015)

Glaser *et al.* (2015) focus on whether a case has the possibility of the death sentence. This would not apply in all countries. However, the study is chosen here as it shows the influence of race of the defendant on jury decision-making, which is the important focus. Glaser *et al.* (2015) carried out an experiment that gathered data using a survey and they used a representative sample to look at the effect of defendant race on sentence severity. Their study gave participants a summary of a triple murder trial that gave the possibility of death sentence or life without parole and also manipulated defendant race. Those who were told that life without parole was the maximum sentence were not significantly more likely to convict a black defendant (67.7 per cent) than a white defendant (66.7 per cent). Those who had a death sentence as the maximum sentence showed a higher likelihood of convicting a black defendant (80.0 per cent) than a white defendant (55.1 per cent). These results suggest it is the death sentence that gives the difference in juror decision-making regarding racial bias, which has civil rights implications. It would be expected that a higher penalty would mean a juror would need more evidence before voting guilty (Ellsworth and Ross, 1983, cited in Glaser *et al.*, 2015). However, there is evidence to suggest that black defendants are treated more harshly when it comes to sentencing (e.g. Goff *et al.*, 2008, cited in Glaser *et al.*, 2015). Eberhardt

et al. (2006, cited in Glaser *et al.*, 2015) found there was more severe punishment given to black defendants. This suggests that there would be higher conviction rates for black defendants (Sommers and Ellsworth, 2000, cited in Glaser *et al.*, 2015) and harsher sentences for black defendants (Mitchell, 2005, cited in Glaser *et al.*, 2015).

Glaser *et al.* (2015) go on to look at findings about juror decision-making and defendant race and repeat what has been said in other studies, such as Mitchell *et al.* (2005), mainly suggesting that there are different variables affecting whether the race of the defendant affects the jury decision-making and that overall it is hard to show that race of the defendant directly affects decision-making (Mazella and Feingold, 1994, cited in Glaser *et al.*, 2015). Mitchell *et al.* (2005) in their meta-analysis suggest a small but significant effect of racial bias in decisions about guilt.

> **STUDY HINT**
> The practical for this chapter (found on the website accompanying this book) is an experiment using the method of Glaser *et al.* (2015), though focusing on the effect of physical attractiveness on decision-making. It is worth coming back to Glaser *et al.* (2015) when reading about the practical investigation, to learn more about method when studying jury decision-making.

Hypothesis

Glaser *et al.* (2015) thought that the possibility of a death penalty would reduce the conviction rate because jurors tend to want more evidence because of the seriousness of the penalty. They thought that jurors would be more concerned about the effects of their decision on a white defendant than they would be about their decision's effect on a black defendant.

Glaser *et al.* (2015) used a case summary that was written to convey guilt to a juror though not so convincingly that there would not be some variation. The independent variables were the sentence, which could be either death sentence or life imprisonment, and the race of the defendant. The way they manipulated race was to use stereotypical black or white names.

Participants

Participants were 276 American adults randomly selected from a high-quality national survey database that had come from careful sampling techniques. An internet survey was used to collect the data. The median age of the sample was 46 years, half of the sample were women, 84.8 per cent were white, 6.2 per cent Hispanic and 4.7 per cent black.

Design

They used an independent groups design and the dependent variable was whether to convict or acquit. Two conditions were death sentence or life imprisonment without parole. Two conditions were the race of the defendant – Black or White.

Materials

Glaser et al. (2015) put together a realistic scenario of a triple murder, taken from various real-life trials, and the goal was to get a high conviction rate. The trial summary was four pages long and written like a court document. The four conditions (the maximum possible penalty and the race of the defendant) were embedded into the summary. The maximum sentence was repeated three times during the summary. The defendant's race was signalled by using names. 'Black' names were Darnel, Lamar, and Terrell, and 'white' names were Andrew, Frank and Peter. Surnames were neutral (Hill, Rogers and Wilson). Pilot testing was done on the names and also on the conviction rate, which came out at 70 per cent, and the summary was said to be realistic.

Procedure

The summary was read and then a decision to acquit or convict was given straight afterwards with some instructions, such as to imagine themselves as a juror and voting to convict if this was 'beyond reasonable doubt'.

Results

- Glaser et al. (2015) found a main effect of the race of the defendant. There was a greater tendency to convict black defendants (73.9 per cent) than white defendants (60.9 per cent). This was a significant difference at p=.021.
- There was no main effect of maximum sentence on the verdict (p=.934).
- There was a significant interaction of maximum sentence and defendant race (p=.034). Sentence severity was affected by the race of the defendant, with 25 per cent more black than white defendants 'convicted' when the condition was the death sentence as the maximum sentence than when the maximum sentence was life without parole (p=.002).

Conclusions

Glaser et al. (2015) concluded that the race of the defendant affects jury decision-making, including how a jury is swayed and that black defendants are negatively affected. The possibility of a death sentence affects black defendants differently (and more negatively) than white defendants. This raises questions about how a juror sees a black defendant. Are they seen as more guilty or is capital punishment seen as more appropriate than for white defendants? Another idea is that violence in the mind of a juror is consistent with a black stereotype.

There were not that many non-whites in the sample so it was not possible to look at the effects of race of the juror on the decision-making. There were some limitations to the study, mostly focusing on its lack of ecological validity. One limitation is that the juror made a decision alone, whereas juries discuss their decision. Another limitation is that instructions to the jury about sentencing were not given as they would be in a real trial.

Strengths of Glaser et al. (2015)

- The study was experimental and so had careful controls. For example, the story of the trial was the same for all participants and the survey was carried out over the internet so all the instructions were the same for everyone. The stories were identical except for the name of the defendant and the maximum possible sentence.
- Sampling was randomly done and was said to be nationally representative. There were 50 per cent male and 50 per cent female and a variety of ages, as well as a reasonable split with regard to race. Generalising from such a sample should be possible, although having a large percentage of white participants it was not possible to look at the effect of race of the participant on their verdict.

Weaknesses of Glaser et al. (2015)

- One main limitation was regarding lack of ecological validity. The trial was realistic; however, it was not real and the verdict was not real. The participants were not jurors, so there was a lack of validity in the study.
- Also on ecological validity, this was a decision made by a single participant/juror rather than a discussion between 12 jurors. This point is raised by the researchers, who suggest building on their study and including discussion to represent jury decision-making more appropriately.

Progress check 3.74

Glaser et al. (2015) found that, in the condition where the death penalty was the maximum sentence, there were more guilty verdicts for black defendants than white defendants. Suggest two reasons for this finding.

Thomas (2010)

Thomas (2010) produced a report for the Ministry of Justice about whether juries are fair. Some studies are given in the report, including focusing on race of the defendant. Thomas discusses a key question: 'Do all-white juries discriminate against black and minority ethnic (BME) defendants?' The study used 41 all-white juries and gave them an identical case where only the race of defendants and victims was varied. Unlike many studies looking at race of the defendant and juror decision-making, this study was done in England using Winchester and Nottingham juries. The finding was that all-white juries did not discriminate against BME defendants and all-white juries were not more likely to convict a black or Asian defendant more than a white one. When race of the juror was looked at, it was found that white jurors had lower conviction rates overall when they were on racially mixed juries. White jurors in a racially diverse area like Nottingham were more likely to convict the white defendant when he was accused of assaulting a BME victim than when assaulting a white victim. This result was not found in Winchester. This suggests that the area the crime was carried out in is important. Thomas (2010) reports that gender of the juror affected jury decision-making, with female jurors more open to persuasion. Male jurors rarely changed their minds.

Thomas (2010) reviewed jury decision-making in Crown Court trials and found that BME defendants were three and a half times more likely to face a jury verdict in the Crown Court than would be expected given their representation in the general population. Then again, Thomas (2010) did not always find that race of the defendant affected jury decision-making. She found that white and Asian defendants both had 63 per cent jury conviction rate and for black defendants it was a 67 per cent jury conviction rate, so very similar.

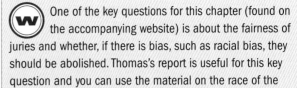
The gender of the defendant

Gender is a characteristic of the defendant that can affect jury decision-making and it is explained as a section on the website accompanying this book. Progress checks are left here for you to monitor your progress if you choose to study gender as one of the characteristics.

The physical attractiveness of the defendant

Another characteristic of the defendant looked at here is physical attractiveness. There have been a lot of studies looking at the idea that a more attractive defendant will be treated more leniently than an unattractive one. Efran (1974) is one such study; Sigall and Ostrove (1975) is another. A lot of studies were done in the 1960s and 1970s showing the effects of defendant attractiveness on jury decisions. Studies are still being done, which shows the enduring interest of this area of study.

Weiten and Diamond (1979)

Weiten and Diamond (1979) summarise studies that look at defendant attractiveness. They list a lot of studies showing that a more attractive defendant tends to be treated more leniently, including Sigall and Ostrove (1975) and Stephan and Tully (1977), as well as Izzett and Leginski (1974). They go on to say that gender and race are not found to be as important as attractiveness, which is interesting. As has been seen in the section on race, there were studies showing that the link between race of the defendant and jury decision-making was not as clear as might be thought and the section on gender (found on the accompanying website) shows that studies have not focused in great numbers on the effect of gender of the defendant alone on jury decision-making. With regard to attractiveness, the findings seem to be more secure. Weiten and Diamond carried out their review in 1979, so a lot of studies have been carried out since then.

Explore

You can find Weiten and Diamond's (1979) review using this link: www.law.northwestern.edu/faculty/fulltime/diamond/papers/ACriticalReviewJurySimulation.pdf. It is useful for the basics of this area of study, as a lot of classic studies were carried out about that time looking at bias in jury decision-making.

Issues and debates

One issue and debate in your course is about how psychological understanding has changed over time. Studies looking at the characteristics of the defendant and the bias they suggest in jury decision-making started in the 1970s and have continued ever since, so you can use this area of study to show changes over time. Use the dates of studies presented here to help you.

Sigall and Ostrove (1975)

Sigall and Ostrove (1975) carried out a study on offender attractiveness and jury judgement. They looked at the physical attractiveness of the defendant and the nature of the crime and how attractiveness-related the crime was. Participants read an account of a crime and then 'sentenced' the defendant to a number of years in prison. Sigall and Ostrove thought that when a crime is not related to attractiveness, like a burglary, an attractive defendant would get a more lenient sentence than a non-attractive defendant. When the crime was related to attractiveness, such as swindling someone, the attractive defendant would get a harsher sentence. They found what they predicted, which suggests the physical attractiveness of the defendant affects judgements made about them, though this depends on the crime itself.

Explore

You can find Sigall and Ostrove's study using this link: www.communicationcache.com/uploads/1/0/8/8/10887248/beautiful_but_dangerous-_effects_of_offender_attractiveness_and_nature_of_the_crime_on_juridic_judgment.pdf

Progress check 3.79

What is the variable, other than attractiveness of the defendant, that Sigall and Ostrove (1975) thought affected whether defendant attractiveness leads to more leniency from a jury?

Efran (1974)

Efran (1974) used both a survey and an experiment. He gave a survey to college students and found that 79 per cent of them thought that a jury decision about guilt or innocence should be based on character and previous history, and 93 per cent of them said physical appearance should not bias a jury's decision. This established that the students did not think physical attractiveness should have a place in jury decision-making. The experiment was done to see if attractive defendants would be valued more positively than unattractive ones. Efran found that physically attractive defendants were rated as guilty with less certainty ($p<.05$) and with the recommendation of less severe punishment ($p<.005$) than unattractive defendants. This showed the importance of feelings and thoughts about attraction on judgements.

Taylor and Butcher (2007)

Taylor and Butcher (2007) carried out a mock juror study to look at reactions to defendant attractiveness. The study was done in the UK and used 96 participants: 48 white and 48 black. Participants were given a fictitious write-up of a mugging, with a photograph of the defendant attached. The photos varied, though the story of the crime was the same for all participants. Some of the photos showed an attractive defendant and in some the defendant was not attractive; some photos showed a black defendant and others showed a white defendant. The researchers found that the participants (jurors) were more likely to find the less attractive defendants guilty than the attractive ones. However, race had no effect on the verdict. Unattractive black defendants were, however, given harsher sentences if found guilty than white defendants, regardless of the race of the participant (juror). It seems that jury decision-making tends to be affected by two (or more) extralegal defendant factors.

Schvey et al. (2013)

Schvey et al.'s (2013) study was given when discussing the effect of a defendant's gender on jury decision-making (on the accompanying website) and the study also involved the effect of their body weight. It was found that obese females were judged more harshly by males and it can be said that this is about attractiveness, though it was weight that was the variable being tested. You could use the study, however, and suggest that body weight is part of how attractiveness is judged, so the findings might be relevant to a discussion on how attractiveness affects jury decisions. There is the assumption here that body weight relates to attractiveness – you would need to make the link.

Patry (2008)

Patry (2008) looked at the effect of attractiveness on jury discussion. A few studies given in this section on defendant characteristics have mentioned how they were testing just individual participants as jurors, which means there is a lack of ecological validity because jurors make decisions based on discussion. Patry thought that mock jurors who did not discuss would be more likely to find a 'plain-looking' defendant guilty than if there were discussion. Participants were randomly assigned to four conditions: attractive and deliberation; attractive and no deliberation; plain-looking and deliberation; plain-looking and no deliberation. Patry found that deliberation meant jurors were more likely to find the attractive defendant guilty.

Abwender and Hough (2001)

Abwender and Hough (2001) look at interactions between defendant attractiveness and gender of the juror and also between defendant race and juror race, when considering making judgements and sentencing. The 'story' the participants read was about a murder where the defendant's attractiveness and race were varied. The participants rated guilt and recommended sentencing. Women participants were less lenient with regard to the unattractive female defendant than the attractive female defendant and the men showed the opposite. Black participants showed more leniency to a black defendant than to a white defendant, and the Hispanic participants showed the opposite. White participants showed no race bias. It was thought that there was in-group favouritism among black participants. The study was carried out in the US and was a mock jury study.

Background

Abwender and Hough (2001) suggest that it is the defendant's physical attractiveness that is one of the most widely studied extralegal variables and the general finding is that an unattractive defendant is at a disadvantage both regarding being found guilty and having a more severe sentence. Dion et al. (1972, cited in Abwender and Hough, 2001) suggested that it is the belief that 'what is beautiful is good' that leads to lenience being shown to attractive defendants. Mazzella and Feingold (1994), in their meta-analysis, suggest, according to Abwender and Hough (2001), that juries see attractive defendants as more likeable and treat them more leniently.

However, Mazzella and Feingold (1994, cited in Abwender and Hough, 2001) suggest that the advantage of being attractive only works for some crimes, such as rape and robbery. For some crimes, as Sigall and Ostrove (1975) suggested, like swindle, it might be that juries see someone using their attractiveness to their advantage. Mazzella and Feingold (1994, cited in Abwender and Hough, 2001) suggested jurors might judge attractive defendants more harshly as they do not live up to 'expectations'.

Mainly though it is the attractiveness-leniency effect (ALE) that is most frequently shown (Abwender and Hough, 2001). What Abwender and Hough are interested in is defendant attractiveness and interaction with juror characteristics. Darby and Jeffers (1988, cited in Abwender and Hough, 2001) found that participants (jurors) who rated themselves as attractive behaved differently from those who rated themselves unattractive. Those who rated themselves as attractive were biased in favour of attractive defendants, whereas those rating themselves as unattractive showed leniency towards both highly attractive and highly unattractive defendants. This showed that there were mitigating factors according to juror characteristics, which is what Abwender and Hough wanted to look at. It seems that similarity between the juror and the defendant might lead to more leniency.

Another juror feature that seems to affect the idea that jurors are more lenient to attractive defendants is gender. Abwender and Hough's (2001) ideas about gender of the defendant and gender of the juror, and how both seem to affect whether attractiveness of a defendant leads to more leniency, are discussed in the section on gender of the defendant (on the accompanying website). Abwender and Hough (2001) show how there is a tendency for attractive defendants to be treated more leniently. There is a related factor of the crime being committed, which can affect the effect of defendant attractiveness. The gender of the juror affects the ALE, as does the gender of the defendant. Another extralegal variable is defendant race, which was discussed earlier. Regarding race, Abwender and Hough (2001) use Mazella and Feingold's (1994) meta-analysis findings and confirm that black defendants are not routinely treated more harshly than white defendants. However, in the case of negligent homicide, white defendants are favoured. There is also the general finding of in-group favouritism, where the race of the juror and the race of the defendant affect judgement, and similarity of race means more lenience.

Hypotheses

1. The attractiveness of a female defendant accused of negligent homicide interacts with participant gender. Male participants show a stronger reverse ALE than female participants. A 'reverse' ALE refers to the opposite of the finding that attractiveness of the defendant leads to more leniency – it means that attractive defendants are treated more harshly.

2. Defendant race interacts with 'juror' race and black jurors show stronger in-group favouritism (leniency when juror and defendant are both black) than white jurors.

> **STUDY HINT**
>
> The term 'hypothesis' should be clarified here as there is the alternative and the null hypothesis. Generally, the null hypothesis is specified and 'hypothesis' in a study will be the alternative one if unspecified. In an experiment, the alternative hypothesis is the experimental hypothesis. In an exam question, check which hypothesis is being used and if there is no specification, take it to be the alternative or the experimental hypothesis and not the null hypothesis.

The researchers note that they did not expect so many participants to identify themselves as Hispanic so they did not have a hypothesis about that but did analyse their data separately.

Method

There were 207 participants used, after some were excluded for various reasons. There were 89 black (62 females and 27 males), 55 Hispanic (33 females and 22 males) and 63 white (34 women and 29 men). They were aged from 19 years to 51 years.

The 'story' used in this study was a case of a negligent homicide where a 25-year-old woman was stopped by the police for reckless driving. She was intoxicated but the officer did not arrest her, calling a taxi for her instead. The woman got out of the taxi, returned to her car and went home again. It was on the way home that she hit and killed a pedestrian.

In Abwender and Hough's 'story', when a police officer stopped a female car driver and did not arrest her but called a taxi for her, she returned for her car and subsequently knocked down and killed a pedestrian. Would a juror make a judgement about her guilt based on her attractiveness?

There were four versions of the story, with details changed of the defendant's race (black or white) and their attractiveness (attractive or unattractive).

Progress check 3.80

What were the independent variables in this study and which characteristics of the defendant are controlled for?

The participants were asked to complete a questionnaire with two dependent variables. What was measured was the impression of the person's guilt rated on a seven-point Likert-type scale (1 was guilty and 7 was not guilty). They also measured the recommended jail sentence (0 to 99 years) for the defendant. Participants were also asked to rate the defendant's attractiveness, likeability, degree of intoxication and level of responsibility for the incident.

Questionnaire packets were posted out to those willing to participate and there was a postage-paid envelope enclosed for the data to be returned to the researchers.

Results

Defendant attractiveness:

- Both male and female participants with the story using an attractive defendant rated her as significantly more attractive than those with an unattractive defendant. Defendant race, participant race and participant gender did not affect these ratings of attractiveness.

Juror gender and defendant attractiveness:

- Male participants recommended longer sentences for the attractive defendant than for the unattractive defendant.
- Female participants recommended longer sentences for the unattractive defendant.
- Defendant likeability correlated with ratings of defendant attractiveness, as might be expected.
- The researchers found defendant gender differences in the recommended sentence for attractive defendants and for unattractive defendants. Female participants recommended shorter sentences than male participants for the attractive defendant. For the unattractive defendant, male participants recommended shorter sentences than female participants.
- Male participants who rated the defendant unattractive also rated her less responsible for the incident, though there was no such relationship when participants were female.

Defendant and juror race:

- Black participants (jurors) gave higher ratings of guilt to the white defendant than to the black defendant. This was a significant finding.

- Hispanic participants gave higher ratings of guilt to the black defendant than to the white defendant. This was close to being a significant finding.
- White participants gave reasonably similar ratings of guilt to the black and the white defendant. This was not a significant finding.

Conclusions

The researchers felt they had found that female participants showed the attractiveness-leniency effect and they punished the unattractive defendant more. However, males recommended longer sentences for the attractive female than for the unattractive one. Male participants also rated the unattractive female as less responsible for the incident.

It was found regarding race that white jurors did not show differences regarding guilt and sentencing depending on race of the defendant. However, black participants showed more leniency to black defendants and Hispanic participants showed more leniency to white defendants. The finding here supports Bradbury and Williams's (2013) claim that black jurors do not show racial bias towards black defendants.

The findings back up Mazzella and Feingold's (1994) claims that people judge attractive defendants as needing to come up to higher standards and so when they do not live up to those standards (such as in the case of negligent homicide) they are punished more. Though the male participants were more likely to be influenced by the female defendant's attractiveness and less likely to see them as 'should have known better', which seemed to be more the view of female participants. Abwender and Hough (2001) felt that 'what is beautiful is good' was too simplistic to explain their findings. They found that defendant attractiveness was affected by juror gender. They also found that race of the defendant did not lead to racial bias, though their findings about Black jurors and Black defendants, as well as Hispanic jurors and Black defendants, meant that 'justice is not colour blind' (Johnson et al., 1995, cited in Abwender and Hough, 2001, p. 611). Hispanic jurors seemed to show bias against black defendants in favour of white defendants. Black jurors showed solidarity with black defendants, which supports the idea of in-group favouritism, and black jurors behaved more harshly to white defendants. White jurors did not show racial bias.

Strengths of Abwender and Hough (2001)

- There is the usual strength of mock jury studies that there is careful manipulation of the independent variable(s), careful measuring of the dependent variable(s) and careful control over other extraneous variables so that they do not become confounding ones. For example, Abwender and Hough (2001) measure likeability as well as attractiveness and found there was an effect from likeability. They also measured estimate of responsibility as well as guilt, which was rated on a seven-point scale. They gathered careful data about important variables and, using an experimental design, were able to draw strong conclusions. The element of science in the design gives strength to the conclusions.

- To an extent, the researchers could look at reliability because they gathered a lot of data using different variables. For example, ratings of defendant attractiveness correlated with ratings of defendant likeability, and there was a correlation found. This would be expected and, when results are as expected from other sources, this suggests results are reliable.

Weaknesses of Abwender and Hough (2001)

- The researchers felt generalisability was difficult as their sample was seen as generally high academic achievers and almost all from the lower socioeconomic strata. They felt though there was some generalisability because their sample was racially diverse and geographically diverse. The sample was all from the USA though, so generalising to other societies might not be appropriate.
- Ecological validity is also in doubt as the study involved a pack of questionnaires being sent out to participants for them to complete individually and return. This is not a naturalistic task and findings would lack validity.

Progress check 3.81

In mock jury studies, which have an element of experiment in their design, why is there generally the strength of good controls and the limitation of lacking ecological validity?

Issues and debates

Mock jury studies tend to isolate variables for study, such as the race and attractiveness of the defendant, as in Abwender and Hough (2001). This is a reductionist approach. Looking at the whole juror-defendant interaction in a courtroom is hard to replicate using a mock jury study approach (probably impossible). You can use this example when discussing reductionism as an issue and debate in your course.

Gunnell and Ceci (2010)

Gunnell and Ceci (2010) were interested in how different people process information differently. This study is chosen because it brings cognitive elements into the study of defendant attractiveness and jury decision-making and discusses information processing.

Also it can relate to individual differences in jurors leading to them making different judgements. In cognitive psychology, you will have looked at information

processing and the impact of individual differences, so it should be interesting to look at another way of studying the effects of defendant attractiveness on juror decision-making.

Year One link: Gunnell and Ceci focus on juror information processing and you can recall looking at information processing in cognitive psychology.

Gunnell and Ceci (2010) focus on cognitive experiential self-theory (CEST), which is a theory putting forward the idea that information processing goes through a rational and an experiential pathway. The rational pathway focuses on analysis, fact and logic, and the experiential pathway is about emotions and personal experiences. Gunnell and Ceci look at whether extralegal biases, like defendant attractiveness, affect people influenced by the experiential system (E-processors) more than by those influenced by the rational system (R-processors). The study involved participants looking at a trial transcript and the profile of a defendant and choosing a verdict and sentencing. They found that E-processors and R-processors did not differ in rate of convicting attractive defendants. However, they found E-processors were more likely to convict less attractive defendants than R-processors. R-processors were not affected by attractiveness when deciding about sentences. E-processors gave more lenient sentences to attractive defendants and harsher sentences to less attractive defendants. E-processors, more than R-processors, said that extralegal factors would affect their verdicts. The score of emotionality 'trumping' rationality in a person correlated with harsher sentencing and extralegal influence. The study showed an 'unattractive harshness' effect when considering guilt, an attractiveness leniency regarding sentencing and more susceptibility to extralegal factors in E-processors. This was a different way of looking at the effect of extralegal factors like defendant attractiveness and showed that not only might variables in the juror like gender and race affect their decision-making but something about their preferred way of processing might also affect their decisions.

Gunnell and Ceci (2010) summarise their main findings:

- E-processors convicted less attractive defendants 22 per cent more than R-processors.
- E-processors sentenced less attractive defendants to 22 months more in prison on average than they sentenced attractive defendants.
- R-processors did not differ in their sentencing according to defendant attractiveness.
- The more someone was scored as 'more experiential' than rational, the more likely they were to sentence the less attractive defendant to a harsher sentence.
- E-processors were more likely to say that extralegal factors would have changed their verdicts (such as when they were told later about charity work of the defendant).

- The more someone was scored as 'more experiential' than rational, the more likely they were to say extralegal factors would affect their verdict.
- There was a trend in that E-processors tended to rate less attractive defendants as being the type of person to commit crime.
- E-processors were more 'conviction prone' than R-processors, giving more convictions regardless of attractiveness.

Importantly, there was no overall attractiveness-leniency bias. This finding is consistent with Erian *et al.* (1998, cited in Gunnell and Ceci, 2010), who found attractiveness did not predict the allocation of guilt but did predict sentencing. What was important was that less attractive defendants did get more guilty judgements from E-processors. It was more that an unattractive harshness bias was found in E-processors than that an attractiveness-leniency bias was shown. Gunnell and Ceci (2010) concluded that different processing preferences did affect juror decision-making. They thought that for an E-processor, if the criminal looks like what a criminal is expected to look like, then it is less stressful for the E-processor to give a guilty verdict.

Strengths of Gunnell and Ceci (2010)

- They used four different 'attractive' defendants and four different 'less attractive' criminals, which helped to avoid one 'face' being judged for different reasons relating to attractiveness or being less attractive.

The point is that one face might be seen as different in a specific way, such as 'baby faced', which is seen as good, and that would be a particular type of attractiveness rather than 'attractive' in general. The same argument applies for one 'less attractive' face. The researchers felt this was a strength of their study.

- The use of actual case materials and actual jury instructions was also seen as a strength of the study. This helps with validity.

Weaknesses of Gunnell and Ceci (2010)

- The researchers used a sample of undergraduates with a limited age range rather than a community sample, so generalising is not possible. The researchers themselves thought that they may have had more 'R-processors' because their sample consisted of university students.
- As with other mock jury studies, there is no discussion in this study and no idea how the different processing preferences might affect jury discussion and the resulting outcome.

Summary of studies looking at attractiveness of the defendant

There has been a lot of material relating to the attractiveness of a defendant and the influence of this characteristic on jury decision-making. A brief summary of the studies is given in Table 3.26.

Table 3.26 Summary of some of the studies looking at the effect of defendant attractiveness on jury decision-making

Study	Explanation of the study regarding defendant attractiveness and jury decision-making
Weiten and Diamond (1979)	List a lot of studies showing that a more attractive defendant tends to be treated more leniently, including Sigall and Ostrove (1975) and Stephan and Tully (1977), as well as Izzett and Leginski (1974).
Sigall and Ostrove (1975)	Found attractive defendants were given more lenience than unattractive ones; however, it did depend on the crime. For example, swindle meant less lenience for an attractive defendant over an unattractive one.
Efran (1974)	Found that physically attractive defendants were rated as guilty with less certainty ($p<.05$) and with the recommendation of less severe punishment ($p<.005$) than unattractive defendants.

Mock jury studies

A lot of studies looking at characteristics of the defendant and effects on juror decision-making use mock jurors, as has been seen. You can use evaluation points about mock jury studies when discussing their findings. Some ideas are given here.

> **STUDY HINT**
> Use tables, such as Table 3.27 on the next page, to list some of the studies using mock juries that you have read about in this section. Look at what you need to learn and organise information to help that learning, such as focusing on the method of mock juries.

Strengths of mock jury studies

- They allow variables that might affect juror decision-making to be tested using a lot of control over extraneous variables that the more naturalistic situation of a real court case and jury would not allow.
- They enable the actual decision-making to be studied, whereas jury decision-making takes place out of the public eye so is not directly accessible.

Weaknesses of mock jury studies

- They are not real trials and would not involve the stress and responsibility of an actual trial where someone may be convicted, and that has implications for them and often for others. There is a lack of validity.

- Mock jury trials are not generalisable to real jury trials because of the lack of external validity mentioned and because they tend to involve small samples and confounding variables.

Evaluation of the effects of the characteristics of the defendant on juror decision-making

Strengths

- Many studies use the mock jury idea and the strengths of doing that apply to this area of research (as do the weaknesses). Mock juror studies enable the relatively ethical study of jury decision-making when actual juries are not available. Also they enable specific extralegal variables to be manipulated for study, with controls over other variables and consequential cause-and-effect conclusions drawn. They give a strong body of evidence (Monahan and Loftus, 1982, cited in Gunnell and Ceci, 2010).
- Another strength of the research looking at characteristics of the defendant and the effect on juror decision-making is its usefulness for society. There is clearly a need to know if jurors are affected by extralegal factors and discussion about such factors should be thought about if there can be something like 'unattractive harshness bias' or 'attractiveness leniency'. A jury decision should be a fair one and research into

characteristics of the defendant affecting such a decision strongly suggests it is not. A strength of research is when it has a clear practical application.

Weaknesses

- A problem with looking at the effects of characteristics of the defendant on juror decision-making is that it does not seem that in real life one characteristic at a time affects the juror. Variables are combined, such that gender, race, physical attractiveness and other features of a defendant when combined can affect a juror's decision in a way that separately they may not. Studies have to bring in more than one variable, just as Gunnell and Ceci (2010) looked at different ways of processing and the attractiveness of the defendant. This shows how juror characteristics are important too. Using reductionist methods like experiments can mean the whole picture is not studied. There is a lack of ecological validity.
- Another limitation of studies seems to be generalisability. Frequently research uses students – for example, Gunnell and Ceci (2010). A community sample is needed as jurors represent the community from which they are drawn.

Test yourself

Evaluate how characteristics of the defendant can influence jury decision-making. **(12 marks)**

Table 3.27 Studies on jury decision-making that use mock jury trials

Study using mock juries	More information
Poulson (1990)	Found that white defendants were treated more harshly than black defendants.
Carter and Mazzula (2013)	Carried out a study using 210 mock jurors representing different racial groups. The study showed the mock jurors an employment case and asked about whether the person had been discriminated against. They found both in-group and out-group bias.
Thomas (2010)	One study used 41 all-white juries and gave them an identical case where only the race of defendants and victims was varied. Unlike many studies looking at race of the defendant and juror decision-making, this study was done in England using Winchester and Nottingham juries. The finding was that all-white juries did not discriminate against BME defendants and all-white juries were not more likely to convict a black or Asian defendant more than a white one.
McCoy and Gray (2007)	Found males are more likely to be found guilty than females in a mock jury study in cases of alleged sexual abuse relating to children.
Ahola et al. (2009)	Found mock jurors issue shorter sentences to a female defendant than to a male defendant in certain crimes, including homicide
Mossière and Dalby (2008)	Found juror age affected sentencing but did not find an effect from gender. Younger jurors recommended a guilty verdict more often and recommended probation more often than older jurors. Older participants recommended not guilty more often but when there was a guilty verdict they recommended incarceration more.
Abwender and Hough (2001)	Male participants recommended longer sentences for the attractive defendant than for the unattractive defendant. Female participants recommended longer sentences for the unattractive defendant. Gender of the juror seemed to affect the attractiveness-leniency idea.

The effects of pre-trial publicity

As well as characteristics affecting jury-decision-making, jurors can be influenced by **pre-trial publicity**. Pre-trial publicity means information in the media about a case and a defendant can argue that what a jury has read and heard about their case might prejudice the case when it comes to trial. As with characteristics of the defendant, pre-trial publicity can also prevent a fair trial. If publicity is widespread enough, it can be hard to get 12 people who don't know about the case to be on the jury.

Definition

Pre-trial publicity means media and other coverage of a case before the trial takes place. It is assumed that jury members will have read or heard about a case that has had a lot of publicity (or indeed any case with any publicity can be a problem) and the question is raised about how, in such cases, there can be a fair trial as the jury will be swayed by what they have heard and read.

Courts may impose 'gagging' orders on the media in high-profile cases in order to avoid problems with pre-trial publicity affecting not only juror decision-making but also choosing a jury in the first place. A problem is that a defendant has the right to be tried fairly and by jury in certain circumstances, and so 'gagging' is put into place. However, the idea of free speech also must be considered. 'Trial by newspaper' is to be avoided.

When you looked at eyewitness memory, the misinformation effect was shown to be important – how information after an event has been witnessed can be incorporated into memory. False memory is an example of this and earlier in this chapter, the study about a shopping mall incident was explained to show how a false memory can be incorporated into memory to become 'real' (page 281). Pre-trial publicity could have the effect of giving misinformation to a juror and that information might be incorporated with the trial evidence and might then affect the juror's decision-making.

Negative publicity of a case before the trial takes place can affect jury decision-making, leading to bias against a defendant.

Thomas (2010)

Thomas (2010), in her report about the fairness of juries, discusses a study conducted in Nottingham, Winchester and London focusing on media reporting of trials. The study looked at long high-profile cases and shorter ones too, and drew conclusions about the effects of media reporting. It was found that jurors on high-profile cases were 70 per cent more likely to recall media coverage than those on standard cases (11 per cent). Most of the jurors saw reports during the trial rather than beforehand, which is not pre-trial publicity. However, a third of jurors (35 per cent) heard pre-trial publicity. Jurors in trials with a lot of publicity remembered TV reports and reports in national newspapers, whereas those in standard cases remembered reports in local newspapers. When jurors recalled the emphasis of reports – and 66 per cent did not recall detail – they tended to remember publicity suggesting defendant guilt. In high-profile cases, 20 per cent of the jurors who did remember media reports about the case found it hard to put reports out of their mind while serving as a juror on the case. Jurors also looked at their cases on the internet during the trial, which they are not supposed to do. This information suggests that pre-trial publicity can negatively affect the defendant.

Explore

You can read about pre-trial publicity and problems with defendants receiving a fair trial using this link: **http://blog. justis.com/can-pre-trial-publicity-prejudice-a-fair-trial**

Steblay et al. (1999)

Steblay et al. (1999) carried out a meta-analysis to review the effects of pre-trial publicity on juror verdicts. Forty-four tests were looked at and findings were often in support of the idea that participants exposed to negative pre-trial publicity are more likely to find a defendant guilty than if there is less or no negative pre-trial publicity.

Background

Steblay et al. (1999) mention how often a case is publicised in the media and the last name of a criminal brings back memories about their trial. In America, as in other countries, there is the press right of freedom and the right of people to a fair trial, and these two rights clash. Courts try to see if pre-trial publicity has violated a defendant's rights and try to rebalance any such problems, such as moving the trial to a place that might be less prejudicial because of lower community awareness.

Steblay et al. (1999) point out that studies of real jurors and cases have not linked pre-trial publicity directly with juror verdicts (e.g. Linz and Penrod, 1992) and studies tend to be carried out in the lab so lack ecological validity. A problem too in carrying out a meta-analysis is that studies can use video of a trial or a written scenario. Different ways of running an experiment make the findings from experiments hard to compare.

> **STUDY HINT**
> You can use Steblay et al.'s (1999) account of difficulties of a meta-analysis in the area of pre-trial publicity when you discuss meta-analysis as a research method.

Steblay et al. (1999) suggest that from 44 studies of pre-trial publicity, with the hypothesis that negative pre-trial publicity leads to more guilty verdicts than jurors who have more neutral pre-trial publicity, 23 support the hypothesis and 20 found no significant difference at $p<.05$. One study found the opposite – that negative pre-trial publicity significantly led to fewer guilty verdicts. This overall finding suggests that there is no 'pre-trial publicity' effect (e.g. Fulero, 1987, cited in Steblay et al., 1999).

What is good about a meta-analysis is that studies are put together so the sample is larger and also underlying patterns can be sought, which lessens effects of extraneous variables on the results of single studies. Also a meta-analysis can uncover variables that affect the main effect.

Aims

The aims of Steblay et al. (1999) were to see the effect of negative pre-trial publicity on juror's judgements of defendant guilt and to identify conditions where the pre-trial publicity effect is most likely to occur, when it did occur. Also the aim was to look at the impact of different studies using different methodology and to identify areas for future research.

> **Progress check 3.82**
> Steblay et al. (1999), and the researchers carrying out the studies they used, considered the effects of negative pre-trial publicity on a guilty verdict. Why do you think they focused on negative pre-trial publicity? What do you think would be the point of focusing on positive pre-trial publicity?

Method

In their meta-analysis, Steblay et al. (1999) included surveys and mock jury experiments where participants were given negative information about a defendant and a crime before a trial. The dependent variable was 'guilty or not' in some studies and in others was measured on a Likert scale. Three studies had a 'not

sure' option, but those answers were not included in the meta-analysis. Twenty-three studies were found, with 44 tests of the hypothesis. Dates of the studies were from 1966 to 1997. Sample sizes were from 37 to 535 participants. Three of the researchers separately coded the studies and then compared their coding, with 100 per cent agreement after discussion. Information coded included the origin of the pre-trial publicity (real or made up), the origin of the trial (real or made up), the sample size and type of study (experimental or survey) and information about a control group. Also coded were other variables, including the pre-trial publicity medium (e.g. newspaper or video), how long before the pre-trial publicity and juror decision, and type of crime.

Results

The overall finding supported the hypothesis that participants (jurors) exposed to negative pre-trial publicity were more likely to judge a defendant guilty than those who had no pre-trial publicity or no negative pre-trial publicity. The percentage of guilty verdicts in the negative pre-trial publicity condition was 59 per cent and, in the control conditions, the mean percentage of guilty verdicts was 45 per cent.

Steblay et al. (1999) provide information about a lot of variables that related to the claim that negative pre-trial publicity affects juror decision-making leading to more guilty verdicts. Some of these are given here.

Survey versus experiment/simulation design

The largest effect size in the studies looked at came from two teams of researchers who used surveys. They contacted participants, found their knowledge about a case, and then compared those with high knowledge of the case with those with low information. They found that case knowledge went with the participant being likely to give a guilty verdict. The higher the case knowledge, the more there was a guilty verdict. The experiments, which used a controlled amount of pre-trial publicity, also showed negative pre-trial publicity went with a guilty verdict but the effect size was lower.

Also the longer delay between pre-trial publicity and the decision about guilt, using community residents as participants, asking for the verdict before the trial, and real pre-trial publicity all related to a larger effect of pre-trial publicity on guilty verdict in the surveys.

Participants

When the participants were from a pool of potential jurors and so were from the community, there was a larger effect size (a higher relationship between having negative pre-trial publicity and reaching a guilty verdict) than when students were used.

Time sequence

One important point is when the verdict was asked for. Asking for a verdict after the pre-trial publicity but before trial information seemed to be the most effective, though there were significant results even if the verdict was asked for after the trial information, just at a lower effect size. The longer delay between negative pre-trial publicity and the juror judgement gave the larger effect.

Pre-trial publicity content

More than one type of information about the crime and the defendant gives the greatest effect on a guilty verdict. 'Different types of information' included arrest information, a confession, prior record, any incriminating evidence, and other information about the crime. Also how specific the negative pre-trial publicity was affected the verdict. If pre-trial publicity was general, there was less of an effect (though the effect was still significant) than if it was specific.

Medium

Using a combination of video and printed materials gave the largest effect, and using video or print alone gave less of an effect than using them together.

Type of crime

One of the survey tests had the greatest effect, and it was a drug case. Murder or sexual abuse tended to have the largest effect sizes apart from that one drug case.

Summary of the results

The results showed that pre-trial publicity has a significant effect on participants judging whether a defendant is guilty or not and this finding comes from surveys and experiments. The surveys gave the highest link between pre-trial publicity and guilty verdict. There was a larger effect between exposure to negative pre-trial publicity and giving a verdict of 'guilty' in the following conditions: when the verdict was given before the trial, when potential jurors were used as participants, when a lot of negative

information was in the pre-trial publicity, when pre-trial publicity was real, when the crime was murder, sexual abuse or drug related, and when there was longer between the pre-trial publicity exposure and the verdict. Other variables that reduced the effect included using students as participants and using general rather than specific pre-trial information.

Conclusions

The overall conclusion was that negative pre-trial publicity affects jurors' decisions about guilt of the defendant. Jurors exposed to negative pre-trial publicity are more likely to give a guilty verdict than those not exposed to it or exposed to limited pre-trial publicity. Steblay et al. (1999) felt that, because they had larger sample sizes overall, they were able to find significance even when studies found limited significance, so using meta-analysis was useful.

The researchers felt they had found a lot of different factors involved in the link between negative pre-trial publicity and a guilty verdict and more research was needed looking at those variables. For example, they found that the largest effect of the negative pre-trial publicity was before the trial, which is important for the jury decision-making process and contradicts the idea that a defendant is innocent until proven guilty. Their findings also back the idea that, in a community where a crime is known about and reported, there is likely to be bias in any decision about the defendant and moving the trial to another area might be a fairer decision than having the trial in the relevant community.

Steblay et al. (1999) point out that surveys seemed to show the stronger link between pre-trial publicity and a guilty verdict. However, they gave correlation data, which means lack of control over confounding variables.

Year One link: In this section, extraneous and confounding variables have been referred to. Look back at what you learned in cognitive psychology where variables were discussed, alongside looking at the experimental method to remind yourself what these terms mean.

Progress check 3.83

Why is using the survey method and correlation data going to mean lack of control over confounding variables, as Steblay et al. (1999) claim?

Steblay et al. (1999) mention the importance of pre-trial publicity for giving jurors schemas and they discuss the idea that such schemas are likely to be hard to combat in the justice system, which will mean bias in the system. They suggest there is a need to use some strategies to combat pre-trial publicity-induced schemas in jurors.

Explore
You can access Steblay et al. (1999) using this link if you would like to read more: http://web.augsburg.edu/~steblay/PretrialPublicity.pdf

Strengths of Steblay et al. (1999)

- The researchers themselves point to a main strength of using meta-analysis, which is having large sample sizes when carrying out statistical analysis. Where individual studies might not find a significant result, using a meta-analysis, which means pooling the data from different studies, can show significance in the findings, which is what Steblay et al. were able to do.
- Another strength is that they could look at many variables related to the finding about negative pre-trial publicity and a guilty verdict, because they could look carefully at all the studies they were able to include and compare them in respect of particular variables. For example, they could use quite a bit of data related to whether the verdict was given before the trial or not, which seemed to affect the verdict. They found that a juror was biased against the defendant because of negative pre-trial publicity even before the trial began, which is an important finding. Drawing together a lot of studies meant getting more data about variables involved, affecting the overall conclusion.

Weaknesses of Steblay et al. (1999)

- A problem with meta-analyses is that the different researchers will use different definitions of some of the variables of interest, such as using a video to show pre-trial publicity in an experiment versus using a real trial and real pre-trial publicity in a survey. Putting together findings that come from different means of gathering data and different ways of measuring variables means the findings may lack validity.
- Another weakness is that, although coding was done carefully, it would mean interpreting the data, which tends to mean a lack of validity. The researchers did code separately and made sure their coding agreed; however, they had the same aims in mind, which is likely to have led to the same decisions, which means the data may lack validity.

STUDY HINT
When you are making notes about strengths and weaknesses of a study, check that each point relates directly to the study and is not a general point. In an exam answer, check what you write and make sure that the study is identifiable from each point. This will help you to write enough and to show understanding of the point you are making.

Progress check 3.84

In the table below, identify which of the evaluation points are general and which are specific.

Evaluation comment about Steblay et al. (1999)	General	Specific
There might be interpretation of data when putting the data into categories.		
The three coders might have interpreted the data in the same way because they were all researchers in the study.		
Inter-rater reliability is found when more than one person rates the data.		

Ruva and McEvoy (2008)

Ruva and McEvoy (2008) carried out an experiment looking at the effects of being exposed to pre-trial publicity. They were interested in effects on juror memory and decision-making. Mock jurors read news articles with negative pre-trial publicity, positive pre-trial publicity or unrelated articles. Five days later, participants watched a videotaped murder trial and made decisions about guilt. Half of the jurors gave the verdict and had a memory test straight after watching the video; the other half did the same but two days after watching the video. Neither the verdicts nor the guilty ratings differed between those giving them immediately and those giving them after two days ($p=0.87$ and $p=0.78$ respectively). They found that being exposed to pre-trial publicity affected the verdict and also perception of credibility of the defendant. What was also interesting was the finding that the pre-trial publicity was seen as part of the trial evidence, which memory studies looking at false memory and the effect of misinformation would predict. It was both negative and positive pre-trial publicity that affected juror decision-making.

Ruva and Guenther (2015)

Ruva and Guenther (2015) looked at pre-trial publicity and its effects on mock jurors' decisions, their impressions and their memory. They looked at negative pre-trial publicity and its effect on the jury as well as what might cause bias in decision-making. The study was in two parts. The first part of the study looked at pre-trial publicity and effects on the verdict, and on impressions of the defendant and the lawyers in the trial. The 320 university students had negative pre-trial publicity about a criminal trial they were going to see or they read crime stories not related to 'their' trial. An additional condition was that some 'jurors' deliberated about the verdict and some gave the verdict individually. It was found that negative pre-trial publicity led jurors to vote guilty more often, to make memory errors and to rate the defendant lower in credibility. Deliberation had an effect on jury decision-making as well. Those who had negative pre-trial publicity and deliberated had lower memory accuracy. Those who deliberated and did not have the pre-trial publicity showed reduced guilty verdicts, which meant there was a leniency bias. The effect of pre-trial publicity on guilty ratings was affected by juror memory and also by their ratings of the defendant and the prosecuting attorney.

The second part of the study used content analysis on 30 mock jury deliberations to see how pre-trial publicity affected those deliberations and jury decisions. They found that juries who had read negative pre-trial publicity discussed evidence that was ambiguous as if it were from the prosecution and were less likely to discuss lack of evidence compared with juries that had not had negative pre-trial publicity. The ones having negative pre-trial publicity were also less likely to attend to jury instructions. The researchers concluded that jury deliberations and instructions were not enough to reduce the bias from pre-trial publicity. Bias came from memory errors, biased impressions and distortions before decisions were made.

Honess et al. (2003)

Honess et al. (2003) looked at factual recall and affective (emotional) recall of pre-trial publicity and their influence on jury reasoning and verdict. They used a simulated fraud trial. This was an interesting study because it was real-life pre-trial publicity in a high-profile fraud case and what was looked at was the reasoning about the trial evidence and verdicts. Fifty mock jurors were shown a video simulation of the trial material and the reasoning of the mock jurors as well as their verdicts were recorded. The researchers looked at the effects of recalling the facts in the pre-trial publicity compared with recall of the feelings and thoughts from the pre-trial publicity. Honess et al. (2003) found that it was the recall of the feelings and evaluation thoughts about the trial that affected reasoning against the defendant and confidence in guilt rather than recall of the facts, although the effect from the feelings and evaluation

was itself affected by reasoning done throughout the presentation of the evidence itself. Although this study is not looking at emotional reasoning as opposed to rational reasoning, as in Gunnell and Ceci (2010) when they considered characteristics of the defendant, Honess et al.'s (2003) focus is similar in that it looks at facts from pre-trial publicity versus emotions and evaluation thoughts about the defendant and the case. Just as emotional reasoning seemed to affect sentencing in Gunnell and Ceci's (2010) study, so it was the emotions and evaluations from pre-trial publicity that seemed to affect jury decision-making.

> **STUDY HINT**
> As you need to be able to use studies when discussing the effects of pre-trial publicity on juror decision-making, two studies (including one meta-analysis) are given in some detail to help. Other studies are explained briefly to add detail.

Progress check 3.85

In the table below, tick which is affective/evaluative information and which is factual information. The information is from a real case.

Information	Affective/evaluative	Factual
This was a brutal, despicable assault.		
The victim was murdered and dismembered.		
The man was a serial killer in the making.		

Background

Honess et al. (2003) use the Maxwell fraud trial in the UK, which involved much pre-trial publicity. Kramer et al. (1990, cited in Honess et al., 2003) suggest that factually biased pre-trial publicity, such as giving information about previous convictions, is different from emotionally biased pre-trial publicity, such as that which arouses negative emotions – for example, talking about injuries. Brown and Kulik (1977, cited in Honess et al., 2003) suggest that highly emotional material is more likely to be remembered so there is an argument for not just looking at being exposed to pre-trial publicity but looking at what the content of the pre-trial publicity is. When recalling pre-trial publicity, people can remember facts, such as the charge itself, or they can remember feelings or evaluation, such as the consequences for the victim. An emotional response to pre-trial publicity might not be the same as an evaluative response, but they are close enough and both might impact on how trial evidence is processed. Otto *et al.* (1994, cited in Honess *et al.*, 2003) suggest that evaluations or impressions from pre-trial publicity are hard to ignore and affect juror judgement. Honess *et al.* (2003) are interested in how evidence presented at the trial might moderate what has been read or heard in the way of pre-trial publicity. They looked at jury reasoning through the trial to track how trial evidence affected pre-trial publicity effects.

Aim

The aim of the study was to focus on free recall of naturally occurring pre-trial publicity and to measure juror reasoning throughout a simulation of the trial the publicity related to, to see the impact of pre-trial publicity on reasoning.

Hypotheses

1 Affective/evaluative recall of pre-trial publicity will have a stronger relationship with anti-defendant reasoning and confidence in the defendant's guilt than factual recall.
2 Impact of affective/evaluative recall of pre-trial publicity on the verdict will be, to an extent (or wholly), mediated by the reasoning that was developed during the presentation of the evidence.
3 Accurate case knowledge will be related to anti-defendant reasoning and confidence in the defendant's guilt.

Method

The Maxwell case

The Maxwell fraud case had four defendants accused of defrauding people by misusing pension funds. There was a lot of pre-trial publicity because the family are so high profile. A video simulation of the case was used, which included the charges, the judge's introduction and the opening statements of both prosecution and defence counsel.

> ### Explore
> You can read about the Maxwell case using this link or explore more using the internet: http://australian-guardians.org/?page_id=808

The judge in the Maxwell case mentioned pre-trial publicity, saying 'in deciding whether a defendant is proved guilty, the jury considers evidence placed before them in court, not allegations or abuse that they may have read in the newspapers or heard broadcast…' (Honess *et al.*, 2003, p. 1407).

> ### Explore
> An article in *The Telegraph* (March 2001) shows what pre-trial publicity there was in the Maxwell case. Of course the participants were expected to have read about it 'naturally' in Honess *et al.* (2003), but you might find it interesting to look the case up. Here is a link to the article: www.telegraph.co.uk/news/uknews/1328574/Inexcusable-role-by-Kevin-Maxwell-in-pension-raid.html

Participants

Public notices recruited participants, so this was a volunteer sample. There were 50 participants, 23 male and 27 female, with an age range of 18–52 years.

Procedure

Participants were interviewed to find out about their recall of pre-trial publicity about the Maxwell case and also about their knowledge of the case. Then participants were asked to act as mock jurors, to consider the arguments and the evidence presented in the opening statements and to reach a verdict with regard to the main defendant.

The simulation was in four equal time periods, with the first three periods focusing on the prosecution opening statement and the last one on the defence opening statement. The participants were interviewed after each of these time periods to find out about their reasoning of the evidence and what their verdict would be at that time. The interviewers were graduate assistants who did not know the aims of the study and were not involved in the analysis.

> ### STUDY HINT
> This case was a real one and the defendants were real too. There is a need to consider the ethics of using defendants whose names are known. The names are not given here, for example, and the case itself is not really what this study is about. The point is about pre-trial publicity and how it can bias jury decision-making rather than being about the charge and trial of individuals. Using a real case has advantages because the pre-trial publicity and the participants' memory of it are real. However, there are disadvantages when it comes to ethics. If you choose to write about this study, avoid discussing the Maxwell case as such, though you can refer to it if it is helpful regarding a point you are making. Your answers in exams must always have due regard to ethical principles.

Recall of pre-trial publicity

Participants were asked to recall all they had seen or heard in the media about the case and what they knew about the verdict (if they had such knowledge). The data were collected during the trial for 32 of the participants and soon afterwards for 18 participants. There was content analysis carried out of the transcripts of the participant's recall.

Year One link: You studied the use of content analysis in learning theories so you can recall what you learned there. Also content analysis was part of clinical psychology (see Chapter Two).

Content analysis looked at units of text that were factual and those that were affective/evaluative. Affective refers to emotions. Two coders did the categorising to check for inter-rater reliability. The coding by the two coders agreed, so there was reliability.

Case knowledge

After the free recall, participants answered questions to give information about their knowledge of the case. They answered about the number of defendants, the identity of the defendants, the charges and about any victims. Their responses were scored for accuracy and level of detail and a score was given to each participant – a 'case knowledge' score.

Reasoning about the evidence

Interview data were collected at each time period, focusing on the participants' reasoning about the evidence. Interviewers were trained to ensure consistency. Interviewers had to avoid making judgements about participant answers and not discuss answers. The interviews had to be non-directive and relaxed. Along with each interview, participants were asked whether they thought the main defendant was guilty or not guilty and they gave themselves a confidence rating for their verdict (10 was 'extremely confident). If their verdict had changed, they were asked to explain the change.

Progress check 3.86

There are some interesting methodological points in Honess *et al.* (2003). They used two coders in the content analysis. They used trained interviewers when collecting data about the participants' reasoning and they used the same questions when asking for case knowledge. Explain why each of these methodological decisions was taken.

Content analysis of reasoning about trial evidence

Interviews were transcribed and content analysis was carried out by two independent graduate assistants. Categories were derived from the content analysis.

- Categories for reasoning about the prosecution case:
  - Pro-prosecution reasoning (e.g. 'you can see lies building up…')
  - Doubt concerning guilt (e.g. 'maybe it was bad management not fraud…').

- Categories for reasoning about the defence case:
  - Approval of defence counsel reasoning (e.g. 'the defence is right, he had not been told…')
  - Rejection of defence counsel reasoning (e.g. 'no, he must have known what was going on…').

Results

Hypothesis 1

Affective/evaluative recall of pre-trial publicity will have a stronger relationship with anti-defendant reasoning and confidence in the defendant's guilt than factual recall.

- Accurate knowledge about the case positively associated with both affective/evaluative and factual recall, as would be expected.
- Pro-prosecution reasoning and confidence in guilt were closely related.
- Approval of the defence argument meant less confidence in guilt.
- Affective/evaluative recall of pre-trial publicity related more strongly with anti-defendant views than did factual recall. Affective/evaluative reasoning related significantly to pro-prosecution reasoning, less approval for the defence argument and to confidence in guilt. This supports Hypothesis 1.

Hypothesis 2

Impact of affective/evaluative recall of pre-trial publicity on the verdict will be, to an extent (or wholly), mediated by the reasoning that was developed during the presentation of the evidence. This is saying that, as the trial progresses, there will be less effect from affective/evaluative pre-trial publicity recall. Confidence in guilt would be lower at the end of the prosecution evidence as the impact of affective/evaluative pre-trial publicity lessens.

- Affective/evaluative recall was related to pro-prosecution reasoning.
- Affective/evaluative recall was related to confidence in guilt at the end of the prosecution opening statement.
- There was some mediation from the trial information on the affective/evaluative recall's influence on final confidence in guilt. This means that there was less confidence in guilt at the end of the four periods than would have been expected if confidence was based just on the affective/evaluative recall of pre-trial publicity.

Hypothesis 3

Accurate case knowledge will be related to anti-defendant reasoning and confidence in the defendant's guilt.

- Confidence in reasoning and guilt did not relate clearly to pre-trial knowledge. Any effect of pre-trial knowledge disappeared as more information was given to jurors.

Conclusions

It was found that recall of the emotional and evaluative parts of pre-trial publicity was what impacted on a juror, with them being more anti-defendant and having more confidence in the defendant's guilt than if they recalled factual pre-trial publicity. Pre-trial publicity has an effect on jury decision-making but it is the emotional content and the publicity that gives evaluative judgements that gives more bias against the defendant and towards the defendant's guilt. Honess *et al.* (2003) thought that affective/evaluative recall of pre-trial publicity may have led participants to have an explanation from that, which guided the way they viewed and heard the evidence. Prior case knowledge did not affect reasoning or verdict; it was the evaluative and emotional part of the pre-trial publicity that affected reasoning and verdict. This supports the idea that it is not the facts that affect juror decision-making but other parts of the publicity before the trial.

Strengths of Honess *et al.* (2003)

- A strength is that real pre-trial publicity and case knowledge were involved. Participants were not given articles to read about a fictitious case, but a real one, so there was validity in that part of the study. The trial itself was a simulation, however. It did use materials from the actual trial, including the opening statements of the prosecution and the defence, so again there was validity, which is often lacking in mock jury studies.
- A strength was in the study design. For the content analysis, two coders were used who were not aware of the aims of the study and whose analysis agreed, so there was reliability. Similarly, the interviewers were trained so that the interviewing of the participants was consistent, again showing reliability.

Weaknesses of Honess *et al.* (2003)

- Even though the case was real, the participants were mock jurors so the responsibility of the case and of the verdict was not present and, to that extent, there was a lack of ecological validity.
- Some participants took part after the verdict and some took part before the verdict, which was said not to have impacted on the results but it might have done. Perhaps doing the whole study at the time of the trial but before the verdict would have been preferable.

> **STUDY HINT**
> Honess *et al.* (2003) used a mock jury design, to an extent, and so evaluation of mock jury studies can be used to evaluate Honess *et al.* (2003).

Daftary-Kapur *et al.* (2014)

Daftary-Kapur *et al.* (2014) looked at the influence of pre-trial publicity on mock juror decision-making, in particular looking at the focus of the pre-trial publicity, such as whether it was slanted towards the prosecution or the defence. They used a shadow jury using a real trial, to try to improve ecological validity of mock juror studies. For the study, 115 mock jurors, who were community members eligible for jury service, were exposed to pre-trial publicity naturally in the place where the case happened, and 156 mock jurors were exposed to the pre-trial publicity experimentally. It was found that the jurors were influenced by both the slant of the pre-trial publicity and the quantity of it. Jurors exposed to pro-prosecution pre-trial publicity gave a verdict in that direction and jurors exposed to pro-defence pre-trial publicity gave a verdict 'for' the defence. Jurors exposed to more pre-trial publicity tended to be more biased. There was no significant difference between those naturally exposed and those experimentally exposed, which suggests that laboratory studies looking at pre-trial publicity do have external validity. The researchers concluded that studies claiming the biasing effects of pre-trial publicity were supported by their study.

Table 3.28 Summary of some of the studies and findings about pre-trial publicity and jury decision-making

Study	Findings about pre-trial publicity and juror decision-making
Thomas (2010)	Found that when jurors recalled the emphasis of media reports — and 66 per cent did not recall detail — they tended to remember publicity suggesting defendant guilt. In high-profile cases, 20 per cent of the jurors who did remember media reports about the case they were on found it hard to put reports out of their mind while a juror on the case.
Steblay *et al.* (1999)	Found that jurors exposed to negative pre-trial publicity were more likely to give a guilty verdict than those not exposed to it or exposed to limited pre-trial publicity.
Ruva and McEvoy (2008)	Found that being exposed to pre-trial publicity affected the verdict and also perception of credibility of the defendant. There was a finding that pre-trial publicity was seen as part of the trial evidence, which memory studies looking at false memory and the effect of misinformation would predict. Both negative and positive pre-trial publicity affected juror decision-making.
Brown and Kulik (1977, cited in Honess *et al.*, 2003)	Suggest that highly emotional material is more likely to be remembered, so there is an argument for not just looking at being exposed to pre-trial publicity but looking at what the content of the pre-trial publicity is.

Evaluation of research into pre-trial publicity affecting jury decision-making

Strengths

- Studies that use an experimental method and a simulation involve careful controls and often a control group, so cause-and-effect conclusions can be claimed. By isolating independent variables, measuring dependent variables and controlling extraneous variables, scientific procedures are carried out, which gives credibility to the findings. However, credibility regarding validity can be questioned.
- Enough studies have been done looking at the effects of pre-trial publicity (particularly negative pre-trial publicity) that meta-analyses have been carried out. This is a strength because samples can be merged, meaning larger numbers are available for statistical analysis, which strengthens results, as Steblay *et al.* (1999) claim.

Weaknesses

- Mock juror studies using the experimental method tend to lack ecological validity, though there are studies that use real pre-trial publicity and recreate a trial that uses real information, such as Honess *et al.* (2003), so there is some validity in these cases. Nonetheless, unless real jurors are used in real-life situations, there will be limitations with regard to validity. Studebaker *et al.* (2002) suggest that the internet can be used to look at the effects of pre-trial publicity in an actual trial taking place, which might help with problems regarding lack of ecological validity.
- Although there have been studies with community samples, many studies use students and it is thought that this limits their generalisability.

Evaluation of research into jury decision-making in general

Strengths

- Methods include going through records of real jury trials, which will have valid data, and also using mock trials, which can show reliability because of their controls. When data from both agree, as can happen regarding race of the defendant and jury bias, that strengthens the findings about bias in jury decision-making.
- A problem is that variables work together in real-life situations, such as obesity and gender of a defendant, and gender of a juror, all affecting decision-making together (Schvey *et al.*, 2013). Mock jury trials can and do manipulate more than one variable so that they can capture such complexity. This does mean that studies might not be taking into account all influencing variables, which is a weakness, but studies have tended to look at more than one variable, and that is a strength.

Weaknesses

- Quite a lot of studies used students rather than members of the community and this is thought to bring bias in the decision-making, which means a lack of generalisability if the sample does not represent the target population.
- The dependent variable is often not measured in a valid way – for example, asking a participant to give a sentence in years, which is not something a real jury would do. This shows a lack of ecological validity

Test yourself

Using two studies, assess how pre-trial publicity negatively influences jury decision-making. **(16 marks)**

Summary

- There has been a lot of very interesting material in this content section for criminological psychology, including biological explanations of crime and anti-social behaviour. Explanations given were brain injury, the role of the amygdala in aggression, XYY syndrome and personality.
- You also looked at social explanations of crime and anti-social behaviour, including labelling, the self-fulfilling prophecy and social learning.
- Then there was a focus on understanding the offender, including looking at cognitive interviewing and ethical interviewing.
- More on understanding the offender included offence analysis and case formulation, including formulation with regard to looking at the function of behaviour for the individual.
- Then treatment for offending was discussed. One cognitive-behavioural treatment is required, and anger management was covered.
- One biological treatment is also required, and hormone treatment was covered.
- What followed then were two sections looking at the criminal justice system and crime. First, you looked at eyewitness memory and factors affecting it, including weapon focus and post-event information. The focus was on its unreliability.
- Second, jury decision-making was focused on to look at bias. Factors influencing jury decision-making include characteristics of the defendant, and race and physical attractiveness were looked at, with a section on gender provided on the accompanying website.
- Another issue that can cause bias in jury decision-making is pre-trial publicity, which marked the end of the content section for criminological psychology.

Methods in criminological psychology

With regard to methods in criminological psychology in your course, there is not much that is new to you, so you will be able to draw on what you have already learned to a great extent. Even what is new has often been covered in the content section of this book, and you can draw on that material as well.

You need to cover research methods used to assess eyewitness effectiveness, including laboratory and field experiments. You also need to cover case studies as a research method. You have to know about issues of reliability, validity, objectivity, credibility and ethics in research in criminological psychology, which have been used when evaluating studies in the content and studies sections of this chapter. You need to recall the four sampling techniques that you learned in social psychology, analysis of both quantitative and qualitative data and use of both descriptive and inferential statistics. You need to review your knowledge of ethics, including the BPS Code of Ethics and Conduct (2009) and risk management. There is some new material about how the Health and Care Professions Council (HCPC) regulate undertaking psychological formulation and intervention, which is covered in the content section of this chapter (page 257). This method section works through what you need to cover, referring you to different parts of your course or this chapter as necessary.

Research methods

The laboratory experiment as a research method to assess eyewitness effectiveness

Laboratory experiments used to examine witness effectiveness look for cause-and-effect relationships by controlling as much as possible about the situation, the setting and participants, while changing one variable (the independent variable – IV) to see the effect(s) of that change on another variable (the dependent variable – DV). They test a hypothesis that is generated from a theory and then the theory is amended or confirmed according to the results of the experiment.

Year One link: Review your learning about laboratory experiments, including checking your understanding of the terms 'hypothesis', 'independent variable' and 'dependent variable'. You covered laboratory experiments in cognitive psychology.

Loftus's laboratory experiments

One laboratory experiment that is well known in the study of eyewitness effectiveness is that of Loftus and Palmer (1974). This is the classic study in criminological psychology that you must know in detail, and it is explained thoroughly in the studies section (page 330). You can use your knowledge of the detail of their study in questions about laboratory experiments looking at eyewitness testimony.

Elizabeth Loftus carried out many laboratory experiments in the field of eyewitness testimony and often used students as participants. Eyewitness testimony is an account people give of an incident they have witnessed. 'Witnessing' in this case means they have seen the incident – it is a legal term. You cover the unreliability of eyewitness testimony in the content part of criminological psychology, so you can read more about it there (page 271).

Loftus's basic method was to show students a film or give them a scenario and then ask them questions about what they had seen. The questions were sometimes 'leading', by using particular words, and sometimes 'misleading', by including incorrect information. The idea was to find out what it was about questioning that might lead a witness to give 'false' information, albeit not deliberately.

Loftus is a forensic psychologist and she acts as an expert witness in the area of eyewitness testimony. She has drawn attention to factors such as how a jury will place trust in witness testimony, especially if the witness is confident. If a witness is wrongly confident then this can have serious consequences for a defendant. If a witness reports in a biased way what he or she saw, then this too has serious consequences. The unreliability of eyewitness testimony is the key question in this chapter so you can read more there (page 354).

Ear-witness testimony

Although your course focuses on eyewitness testimony, it is worth noting that research has also been carried out on 'ear-witness' testimony – when witnesses report on what they have *heard* rather than on what they have *seen*. For example, Cook and Wilding (1996) carried out a study to see if people remember more when they hear something from a well-known voice or a voice they have heard only once. They found little difference. There is no need for you to know any details about ear-witness testimony, but it is useful to be aware that research has taken place in this area.

How useful are laboratory experiments in studying witness effectiveness?

Laboratory experiments, especially since the 1970s, have been the main way of investigating witness effectiveness. This is because everything can be controlled except the

IV, so that researchers can claim that the IV causes the change in the DV. If all participants who watch the same film, for example, are in the same situation and have many other similarities (such as being students), and then half of them are given information about a yield sign and half are not (after viewing a stop sign), then if more participants remember a yield sign in that group, it could be claimed that the misinformation caused the 'memory'. Loftus's study focusing on a stop and yield sign is explained in the section on eyewitness testimony (page 278). A case study, observation or questionnaire asking about memory would not have given this information about a cause and effect. Laboratory experiments are scientific, and a body of knowledge can be built using such firm foundations.

> **STUDY HINT**
> Field experiments used to look at witness effectiveness are examined later in this section. When you have studied these, discuss the relative advantages and disadvantages of laboratory experiments compared to field experiments. When learning material, preparing comparison points is a good way to check your understanding.

> **STUDY HINT**
> In this method section, you need to look at issues of reliability, validity, objectivity, credibility and ethics in relation to research in criminological psychology. Use those issues when considering the use of laboratory experiments in criminological psychology.

The lack of ecological validity in laboratory experiments is important in that any attempt to apply the findings of these studies to real eyewitnesses in real cases may not be appropriate because laboratory experiments are not like real life.

Witnessing a car accident might be more stressful than watching one on film that you are not involved in.

Evaluating laboratory experiments in terms of reliability and validity

Research methods can be evaluated in terms of their reliability and validity. Reliable data are data that have been found more than once by repeating a study. If data are found only once and then not again when a study is repeated, you would not want to base real-life policy and practice on them. Valid data are data about real-life situations and behaviour.

Year One link: Review or recall your study of validity and reliability. These were two evaluation areas you will have come across often when learning about psychology. The reliability and validity of laboratory experiments was discussed when you looked at cognitive psychology, including three types of validity.

Reliability

Laboratory experiments are replicable because of the strong controls. They are replicable because they are clearly detailed and someone else can repeat them exactly. They are usually repeated by the researchers to test the findings for reliability, and they may also be repeated by others. Researchers such as Loftus and her students have carried out so many studies that have come up with similar findings that their work appears to be reliable. If the results are scientifically gathered and reliable, they have greater weight. This is even more important if the results are going to be used in real situations, as Loftus's results have been. In Loftus *et al.* (1987), when they looked at weapon focus, they did two experiments in the same study, which showed reliability.

Validity

Laboratory experiments are, however, not usually valid with regard to the setting, because of the strong controls in place. This means they lack ecological validity. The very controlled situation – watching a film, being asked questions, the film possibly having no relevance to the participant, and using students as participants – means that ecological validity is likely to be low. The whole set-up is not like a 'real' car accident or a 'real' situation that is witnessed. Valentine and Mesout (2009), one of the contemporary studies in this chapter (page 337), found that someone high in anxiety would not be such a reliable witness as someone low in anxiety, so stress, like being involved in or watching a car accident, can affect memory.

Year One link: Review evaluation of laboratory experiments from your learning of cognitive psychology.

The external validity of artificial lab settings

Anderson and Bushman (1997) wrote a paper on artificial 'trivial' laboratory settings and looked at the **external validity** of lab experiments. **Internal validity** is when the controls in an experiment are strong enough for the researchers to believe that the IV caused any changes in the DV. Laboratory experiments can have high internal validity. There cannot be external validity without internal validity because a study that is not controlled enough to show that the IV caused changes in the DV will not give results that can be generalised 'outside' that situation.

Definitions

External validity means how far findings can be generalised to other situations, which relies on the study being enough about real-life behaviour that findings can be generalised.
Internal validity means measuring what is claimed to be measured with regard to isolating the variable to be studied and controlling for all other variables so that findings can claim cause and effect because there are no confounding variables.

Anderson and Bushman (1997) discuss aggression in their paper and not eyewitness testimony but many of their points apply. Aggression is part of criminological psychology in your course but this section about laboratory experiments is a discussion about research in eyewitness testimony. If you are using Anderson and Bushman's argument in this section, be sure to relate it to eyewitness lab experiments by referring to them in your answer.

Anderson and Bushman carried out a meta-analysis looking at five situational variables and three individual variables. The situational variables were provocation, violent media, alcohol, anonymity and trait aggressiveness. The individual variables were sex, personality type and trait aggressiveness. Anderson and Bushman argue that laboratory experiments can involve variables that relate to the real world. They use examples relating to aggression. To use examples from eyewitness studies it might be said that watching slides of someone pointing a gun at a cashier is more stressful than watching someone hand a cheque to a cashier (Loftus *et al.*, 1987; see page 283).

STUDY HINT
In the data analysis section of methods in criminological psychology, you need to look at meta-analysis so prepare some studies in criminological psychology that use meta-analysis, such as Anderson and Bushman (1997), as examples.

Explore
You can read Anderson and Bushman's (1997) account of how laboratory experiments can have external validity using this link: www.researchgate.net/profile/Brad_Bushman/ publication/51993041_External_validity_of_trivial_ experiments_The_case_of_laboratory_aggression/ links/02bfe513125f773727000000.pdf

STUDY HINT
You could add some notes here as evidence for the idea that lab experiments can represent real-life variables, such as fear and stress.

Evaluation of the laboratory experiment research method

Strengths

- Laboratory experiments are replicable because of strong controls, so they are testable for reliability. Loftus's experiments had strong controls.
- Laboratory experiments use scientific methodology, such as forming a hypothesis from a theory and controlling all aspects except the IV. Erickson *et al.* (2014), looking at weapon focus, had a lot of different independent and dependent variables, and extraneous variables were carefully controlled.

Weaknesses

- Laboratory experiments are not ecologically valid, because they do not take place in the participant's natural setting, such as a gun in an experiment not being the same as a real weapon in real life.
- Laboratory experiments might not be valid with regard to the task – for example, watching a car accident on film is not the same as watching it in real life. This is about internal validity.

STUDY HINT
Some strengths and weaknesses of the lab experiment as a research method for looking at eyewitness testimony have been covered here. You will find more detailed evaluations relating to individual laboratory experiments used in eyewitness testimony. Use the evaluations offered there when discussing the lab experiment as a research method. When offering a strength or a weakness in this area, be sure to make each point relate to eyewitness research.

Progress check 3.87

What do you think is the most important part of what makes a study an experiment?

The field experiment as a research method to assess eyewitness effectiveness

Field experiments have a lot of the features of laboratory experiments but are carried out in the participants' natural setting.

Field studies and field experiments focusing on eyewitness testimony

Another way in which witness effectiveness is tested is to use field experiments, because these are based in real situations – they avoid the accusation that laboratory experiments are not ecologically valid and lack external validity. Field experiments and field studies are not the same – a field experiment has all the features of an experiment, whereas there are field studies that tend not to have control over the IV and DV. In this section, it is important to focus on field experiments testing witness effectiveness rather than field experiments in general, though the features of field experiments in general, as well as strengths and weaknesses, apply.

Year One link: Review your learning about field experiments, which you studied when learning about the cognitive approach.

Field studies

Field studies tend to use methods that gather descriptive (qualitative) data rather than numerical (quantitative) data. **Qualitative data** are where attitudes, opinions and stories are gathered. **Quantitative data** are based on numbers, such as percentages or the number of 'yes' or 'no' answers given. Field studies can use research methods such as **ethnography**, case studies or tests carried out in real-life settings.

In ethnography, a researcher gets involved in the whole setting being studied, using many different research methods. This is similar to carrying out an in-depth case study. Field studies are not field experiments if there is no manipulation of an independent variable to see the effect on a dependent variable, and if there are no controls. However, field experiments can be called field studies because they are studies carried out in the field.

Explanation

Qualitative data are rich, detailed, in-depth and like a story.
Quantitative data feature numbers, such as miles or age.

Definition

Ethnography is a research method for getting involved in a culture or situation, where the researcher obtains data directly from participants and the researcher immerses themselves in the culture sufficiently for data to be valid.

STUDY HINT

In this method section, you are asked about field experiments. Make sure you do not get this confused with field studies. In practice, if you call a field experiment a field study you will not be wrong, but it might be incorrect to call a field study a field experiment (if there are no controls and no manipulation of the IV).

One field study that has been covered in this chapter is Yuille and Cutshall (1986) (page 274), who looked at eyewitness memory for a real shooting four of five months after the event, so refer to this when you are discussing eyewitness effectiveness. However, do not use it if you are discussing field experiments – even though it is a study 'in the field', it is *not* an experiment.

Progress check 3.88

What is it about Yuille and Cutshall's (1986) study that means it is *not* an experiment?

Field experiment v. field study

Yuille and Cutshall (1986) manipulate a few questions, such as asking about a yellow quarter panel on a car when it was in fact blue. However, in the main there is no manipulation and so it has few elements of a field experiment; mainly the results are gathered by interview and questions.

Valentine and Mesout (2009) is one of the contemporary studies for criminological psychology in your course (page 337). They did not manage to give two parts to the IV; they just let all the participants meet up with the 'scary person'; there was not a 'not scared' condition. However, they did manipulate IVs to look at the results, such as those with high versus those with low anxiety and the number of descriptors of the 'scary person' they managed. There might be some doubt here but there are a lot of features of a field experiment and, though Valentine and Mesout do not name their research method, you can justify it as a field experiment.

Hopefully these two examples will help you to see the difference between field studies and field experiments.

Field experiments

Field experiments are just like laboratory experiments in terms of their aim to find cause-and-effect conclusions by controlling what can be controlled, and varying the IV to see what the effect is on the DV. The difference is that laboratory experiments take place in a controlled and artificial environment and field experiments take place in the field, which is the participants' natural environment.

Yarmey (2004)

Yarmey (2004) carried out an experiment in a public place, which makes it a field experiment. A young woman approached people individually and they spoke to her for about 15 seconds. Then, either two minutes later or four hours later, they were questioned about the woman and asked to identify her in a photo. When the woman was seen, she either had dark glasses and a baseball cap or she did not, and some witnesses were warned they would be tested and others were not. Therefore, there were a number of different conditions. This study is explained in more detail in the content section (page 272).

Explore

Although focusing on different areas in criminology, not eyewitness memory, the Cambridge Centre of Experimental Criminology website provides some interesting examples of research: **www.crim.cam.ac.uk/research/experiments/**. Criminology is the study of criminal behaviour and does not just focus on psychology, but this area of research might interest you. Remember to focus on eyewitness research, though, when discussing lab and field experiments in this part of your course.

How useful are field experiments of witness effectiveness?

After a period of about 30 years of using laboratory experiments to study witness memory, more recently there has been a tendency to use field experiments instead, such as Yarmey's work. This is mainly to produce more ecologically valid results – for example, much research now focuses on police line-ups and identification of people by witnesses. Field experiments can reassure practitioners in police forces that findings about eyewitness memory are important, and that the guidance the police are asked to implement is sound. Features that are required in order for field experiments to be seen as valid are **double-blind techniques** and **random assignment** to groups, as these help to rule out **confounding variables.**

Definitions

Double-blind techniques mean that neither the experimenter or person administering the task(s) nor the participant knows which condition is being used at any one time. This technique avoids bias. **Random assignment** means a participant is put into one of the groups randomly, avoiding bias. **Confounding variables** are those that affect the results of a study as they were not controlled for.

STUDY HINT

In this chapter, double-blind procedures and random assignment to groups have been discussed when looking at studies into the effectiveness of treatment of offenders. When you come across terms in this book, be sure to look them up in the Glossary if you are unsure about their meaning.

Progress check 3.89

What is the main difference between field and laboratory experiments as research methods?

Controls and procedures of field experiments must be thorough. Well-controlled and carefully planned field experiments are valuable because they have the reliability and scientific status of laboratory experiments, while also having validity because of their real-life settings and real-life situations.

Evaluating field experiments in terms of reliability and validity

Reliability

Field experiments are reliable if the procedures are carefully controlled and planned. If they are repeated, they tend to get the same results and are as reliable as laboratory experiments. However, because they take place in the field, in some ways this is an uncontrolled environment, which could mean there are confounding variables, making the findings unreliable.

Validity

Field experiments are valid with regard to the setting, which means they have ecological validity, because they occur in the participants' natural setting or a setting that could be natural for the task (or both). However, the task is still manipulated to see the effect of different conditions on the DV, so the task itself might not be valid. Usually, researchers try to use a task that is realistic even if set up. Therefore, field experiments have more validity than laboratory experiments. Having said that, laboratory experiments looking at eyewitness testimony try to use realistic scenarios, such as Erickson et al. (2014) having people sitting at a bar and Loftus et al. (1987) having a gun or a cheque pointed at a cashier in a restaurant. These scenarios were on slides; however, they were realistic scenarios.

Year One link: Review the evaluation of field experiments from your coverage of cognitive psychology.

Strengths of field experiments

- Field experiments are replicable to an extent because of strong controls, so they are testable for reliability. Yarmey (2004) used a lot of different IVs, such as the time before someone was asked about the target person (the person they had met), and he controlled all variables as much as possible. For example, the two people who separately approached the participants were both white and a similar age.
- Field experiments are ecologically valid, because they take place in the participant's natural setting. In Yarmey (2004), the woman walked normally and looked for, for example, jewellery, as someone might. Valentine and Mesout (2009) used participants who were going on the London Dungeon tour anyway and the manipulation happened during the tour.

Weaknesses of field experiments

- Field experiments might not allow enough control over variables to be reliable, because the setting is not as controlled as it is in a laboratory experiment. Valentine and Mesout could not control what other people were doing in the labyrinth when the 'scary person' appeared and Yarmey (2004) could not control what others were doing in the vicinity when the target woman approached the participant.
- Field experiments might not be valid with regard to the task either – for example, a line-up that has been set up is not the same as identifying a real-life criminal. Valentine and Mesout (2009) and Yarmey (2004) both used photo line-ups, which are perhaps not real life, though police do sometimes use photos. Also in the studies the participants were not real witnesses, so there was less responsibility and stress.

Ethical issues in the lab and field experiment research methods to study eyewitness testimony

Both laboratory and field experiments involve manipulating an IV to see the effect of that manipulation on a DV, and there are a lot of controls. When people are controlled (as participants in experiments tend to be), there are various ethical issues involved.

Year One link: Review the ethical issues you studied in social psychology. These include obtaining informed consent, debriefing, not using unnecessary deceit, providing the right to withdraw, being competent, and ensuring privacy and confidentiality. These ethical issues come under the four principles of the BPS (2009), which are respect, responsibility, integrity and competence.

The BPS sets out a code of ethics. These guidelines must be followed by students of psychology, no matter which research method is used. Laboratory and field experiments are not in themselves ethical or unethical – it all depends on the procedure and the decisions made by the researcher(s). For more about ethics, see later in this method section (pages 327 and 328).

Informed consent and deceit

The participant should be told as much as possible so that he or she can give informed consent. Any deceit must be kept to a minimum. However, there will almost certainly be some deceit involved, because the manipulated variable will have to be kept secret so that participants do not deliberately change their behaviour. Any change in behaviour needs to be shown to be because of the IV rather than an awareness of the investigation. Both laboratory and field experiments are likely to require some level of deceit, so there is unlikely to be fully informed consent. Loftus and Palmer (1974) did not tell participants that there was a verb difference in the questions they were asked. Yarmey (2004) did not tell participants that the woman asking for help was part of a psychology study. Valentine and Mesout (2009) did not tell the participants that the 'scary person' was staged just for them. There are more examples of deceit in what you have covered in the study of eyewitness testimony because the situation someone is to witness tends to have to be secret. Valentine and Mesout (2009) obtained informed consent from the participants meeting the 'scary person' only after the tour, for example. This is about respect.

Distress

Participants are not supposed to be unduly distressed or have harm caused to them. They should leave a study in the same emotional state as that in which they started. This is about respect and responsibility.

Progress check 3.90

Review the following studies, which have been presented when reliability of eyewitness testimony was examined, and in each case, note down where there is a need for deceit and one other ethical issue in the study.

1 Loftus's barn study (page 278)
2 Maass and Köhnken's study about the pen/syringe (page 286)
3 Yarmey's study asking participants to identify someone who had approached them (page 272)

Debriefing

As there is usually some deceit involved in a study, and consent is not totally informed, there must be a thorough debrief to make sure that participants are happy with and understand what was done, and that they are happy to have their results used in the study. Valentine and Mesout (2009) mention explaining their study to the participants.

Right to withdraw, privacy and confidentiality

Participants must be told they can withdraw at any time and they should be reminded of this at times throughout the study. They should be asked if they want to withdraw their involvement at the end, too, and this can be done as part of the debrief. The participants' identity must be kept secret, to preserve their privacy and to maintain confidentiality. Valentine and Mesout (2009) mention saying to participants that they had the right to withdraw and did not have to give a reason. As for confidentiality, it is rare that personal details such as names would be taken or that an individual could be identified.

Competence

The researcher must be competent to carry out the study and, if in any doubt, must consult with a colleague or someone else who is competent. For example, Loftus is seen as competent in the field, as are others.

Comparing field and laboratory experiments in terms of ethics

One main difference that makes field experiments less ethical than laboratory experiments is that participants in some field experiments cannot be asked for consent at all, let alone informed consent. This is because participants are found in the field and in public places, so they are often not prepared beforehand to let them know they are in a study. This was the case with Yarmey's (2004) study. Participants are asked for their consent afterwards, but this could be seen as less ethical than laboratory experiments, where participants usually know they are taking part in a study beforehand.

Test yourself

1 With reference to two studies, explain how the experimental research method is used to study eyewitness effectiveness. **(12 marks)**
2 Assess the field experiment and the laboratory experiment as ways of studying eyewitness effectiveness. In your answer, refer to validity, reliability and ethical issues. **(16 marks)**

Case studies

As well as laboratory and field experiments, you also have to cover the use of the case study research method in criminological psychology. You will have looked at case studies as a research method in clinical psychology and at case studies of brain-damaged patients in cognitive psychology, so you can draw on that understanding when looking at case studies used in criminological psychology. You do not have to focus just on researching eyewitness effectiveness this time, just on aspects of criminological psychology.

The aim of using a case study

- Case studies can help to shed light on a situation because they go into depth and detail.
- They can help as examples to highlight something specific, such as the result of specific brain damage.
- They can help to describe a technique, such as the process of assessing, doing a formulation and treating an offender.
- They can be used to show gaps in knowledge and to give in-depth understanding in a particular area from which hypotheses can then be generated to test them using other research methods, such as the experiment.

> **STUDY HINT**
> Information about the case study research method is found in Chapter Two, where case studies are explained relating to clinical psychology. Also the 'Psychological skills — methods' section on the accompanying website reviews the method in your course, including case studies. You could draw the material together so that you have a good understanding of the case study research method.

Some case studies used in this chapter

At the start of this chapter, a case study was included as a study of interest. Arsuffi (2010) (page 184) looked in detail at one person to track his assessment, formulation and treatment. Phineas Gage (page 194) is the subject of a case study and, though not a criminal of course, had brain damage that helped to explain aggression, which can link to crime. Yuille and Cutshall's (1986) study (page 274) has elements of an experiment because they use misinformation to see if it affects witness testimony; however, their study involves a specific incident, a murder, and the 21 witnesses who were interviewed by police about the murder (though not all of the witnesses took part in Yuille and Cutshall's study), so there are elements of a case study too. You can use these examples to explore the differences between case studies and experiments when doing research in criminological psychology.

Progress check 3.91

Give two examples of how case studies are used in criminological psychology.

Differences between case studies and experiments

Differences between experiments and case studies include the type of data gathered, differences in the sample and in generalising, differences in how a study is written up, ecological validity, reliability and reductionism.

Qualitative v. quantitative data

Case studies gather qualitative data. They may involve some quantitative data, such as using tests (e.g. in case studies of people with brain damage) or questionnaires, but a main focus is on depth and detail, which requires qualitative data. Experiments gather quantitative data so that there can be careful measurement and analysis in the quest for cause-and-effect conclusions.

Small sample, unique v. large sample, generalisable

Case studies are limited to just one person or a small group. Arsuffi focused on Mr A and what happened to him and those around him. Experiments tend to use large numbers if possible, to get a representative sample so that there can be generalisation. Case studies are hard to generalise as they look in depth at a unique situation, which is not as useful as experiments for finding universal laws about humans.

Written up as a story v. inferential statistics

Case studies tend to be written up as a story, with thematic analysis or the use of grounded theory, for example, if themes are required. Themes can be counted and there might be some analysis, such as using a Chi squared test, to see if differences between categories are significant. However, inferential testing is unlikely. It is often the story that is required, giving the depth and detail of the situation and examples from it as evidence.

Ecological validity

Case studies gather rich, detailed information about one person or a small group and often involve gathering a lot of data examining different aspects of the person's or group's life. They can involve different research methods as well, such as observing, interviewing and examining documents. If the same data are arrived at using different methods, there can be triangulation, which means using different sources to verify what has been found, and

this would mean data are likely to be ecologically valid. Experiments can have validity, as Anderson and Bushman pointed out. When discussing the validity of experiments in eyewitness testimony, there is validity in the variables that are tested as people can be made to feel anxious if watching slides of someone using a gun. However, for the most part, experiments keep people apart from real situations and so can lack ecological validity.

Reliability

Case studies tend not to be repeated and indeed it would be hard, if not impossible, to repeat them as situations rarely arise again. Even going back to Mr A, who Arsuffi (2010) studied, might mean gathering some different data. There might be a similar case study done at some stage, so there can be comparisons, but that is unlikely. In general, it is hard to show reliability with regard to case studies. If different research methods are used and there are similar findings, that does show some reliability. Experiments, however, are set up to be replicated and reliability is one of the features they aim for in the quest for scientific research that can be used to build a body of knowledge. Case studies of people with brain damage can show reliability because they use testing, such as of recall, and there can be replication. Although case studies of people with brain damage mostly do not come directly into criminological psychology, they do discuss aggression and evidence from them can be used to explain crime and anti-social behaviour. For example, they can show how the prefrontal lobe is for decision-making and control and having damage to that brain region might explain someone's lack of control.

Reductionism

Case studies embrace as much data as possible so that a rich and detailed picture can emerge. Data are qualitative and wide-ranging. Experiments have the intention of narrowing what is being measured to independent and dependent variables and controlling any **extraneous variables**. Experiments reduce what is being studied to small parts so that there can be objectivity and cause-and-effect conclusions. Experiments are reductionist and this is so there can be reliability, objectivity and credibility. For example, Erickson *et al.* (2014) used three different 'object' conditions in their study of eyewitness identification. They used a glass, chicken and a gun to represent a neutral, novel and threatening object. This was reducing witness situations to something measurable and some realism would be lost in the process. There are pros and cons about using a reductionist approach, as the case study and experimental methods illustrate.

Issues and debates

When considering the case study as a research method in criminological psychology, and also considering the experiment as a research method, you can see that quite a few of the issues and debates for your course are covered. These include psychology as science and reductionism, and also practical issues in the design and implementation of research. You can use examples from this section when discussing such issues and debates.

Definition

Extraneous variables are those that should be controlled for and can affect results in a study. These include situational and participant variables.

Exploratory, descriptive or explanatory

Case studies can be used to *explore* a particular aspect of people or a situation because of the focus on depth in the data and the use of different methods to uncover good detail. They can *describe* a situation or someone's life experiences. Experiments tend to look for *explanations* and cause-and-effect conclusions. Experiments are more likely to look for reasons for something, such as eyewitness unreliability, and so are explanatory. However, case studies can also look for *explanations*, such as case studies of brain-damaged patients, which are looking for an explanation of behaviour. It can be useful to look at studies and research methods to see whether their aim is exploring, describing or explaining some person, group or situation.

Case studies in criminological psychology

The *Journal of Forensic Psychology* has a section that reports only on case studies. Kirsch (2010) has written an introduction to this separate section and her introduction helps to explain the value of case studies in criminological psychology.

Explore

You can access Kirsch's introduction to the case study section in the *Journal of Forensic Psychology* here: **www.forensicpsychologyunbound.ws/OAJFP/Case_Studies_files/Kirsch%202010.pdf**

Kirsch mentions Phineas Gage and HM, as well as Freud's case studies, which have been covered in your course. Kirsch gives the example of Murphy (2010), who discussed an individual with an autistic spectrum disorder to look into his violent behaviour. Kirsch explains how Mart and Connelly (2010) carried out a case study to look at how seizures can relate to criminal behaviour and lack of control over violence, and how Barnao *et al.* (2010) present an in-depth discussion about a treatment model relating to

three patients. They used case examples to discuss a model they put forward for treatment of patient offenders. Kirsch (2010) uses these examples to show the value of the case study research method in criminological psychology.

Explore

You can access Mart and Connelly's (2010) case study using this link if you would like to use it as a case study example in criminological psychology: **www.forensicpsychologyunbound.ws/OAJFP/Case_Studies.html**

The uses of case studies

- Case studies provide examples giving details as evidence for treatment success (or otherwise).
- They can explore a new area of study to give information from which hypotheses can be drawn.
- They can examine particular incidents for evidence to back up findings using other research methods.
- They can provide an assessment of an individual to help treatment planning.
- They can help as examples to highlight something specific, such as the result of specific brain damage.
- They can help to examine a process, such as the process of assessing, doing a formulation and treating an offender.

(Adapted from Kirsch, 2010)

Blagden et al. (2012)

Blagden *et al.* (2012) carried out a case study to look at the practical usefulness of using **repertory grids** with sexual offenders who are in denial about their offending. Repertory grids are ways of uncovering personal constructs, which are ways people see and understand the world, and they are used in various treatment situations.

Blagden *et al.* (2012) used a 'single case study design' by using a repertory grid with an individual to uncover their **personal constructs**, which are their ways of understanding others.

Explanation

Repertory grids are used in interviews to look at someone's personality and what variables they use to understand people. The theory is that people have personal constructs about others. A repertory grid enables the comparison of people someone knows, and involves thinking about three such people at a time, thinking of a way in which two are the same and one is different, thus finding out how someone thinks about people. **Personal constructs** are our way of understanding other people, such as seeing them as mean or generous. One person might look at people as happy or sad, another might see them as rich or poor — we have different ways of understanding the people around us, and these are our personal constructs.

Pole 1	Me	John	Hana	James	Sophie	David	Ella	Niamh	Harry	Ali	Pole 2
Passionate		\							X	\	Rational
Impetuous			\		\	X					Careful
Controlling	X			\	\						Easy-going
Self-absorbed				\	\			X			Supportive
Controlled		\	X			\					Demonstrative

An example of a repertory grid

They found that what was uncovered about the individual was useful in setting out an idea about a formulation and seemed to be a starting point for intervention. Blagden *et al.* (2010) point out that there are problems in generalising from this single case study and research on a larger scale might be worth doing following their exploratory case study. Their main contribution is to understanding 'total deniers', who are sex offenders not recognising themselves as such. Blagden *et al.* (2012) say that these offenders are seen as untreatable but that using repertory grids can help an initial formulation. They claim that a main strength of their study is in providing information about offenders where there is usually so little information to go on and suggesting a start with regard to treating these 'deniers'.

Background

'Deniers' are sexual offenders who do not accept that they have committed an offence and the problem is that treatment programmes for sexual offenders focus on the offender accepting responsibility and overcoming any denial. Blagden *et al.* (2012) cite McGrath *et al.* (2009) as finding that 91 per cent of treatment programmes in the USA have the responsibility of the offender for their actions as a main target. Denial does not seem to add risk for recidivism (e.g. Mann *et al.*, cited in Blagden *et al.*, 2012) so perhaps is not a need that has to be addressed. However, if denial means no treatment, that is clearly something that needs to be focused on. 'Denial' here is total denial.

Method

The case study focused on Bryan, who was 54 years old and was convicted on two counts of rape. He denied the accusations and saw the criminal justice system as unfair, having a sceptical approach to treatment and to psychologists because of previous experiences. He was willing to do a programme but not if he had to discuss his offence. Blagden *et al.* (2012) report that a semi-structured interview was carried out and then a repertory grid was administered. Bryan was asked to comment on three

people, giving a way in which two were the same and one was different, and in this way his personal constructs were built up. After the constructs were noted, Bryan rated them on a seven-point scale. The grid could then be analysed.

Results

Constructs that were important for Bryan when defining himself were 'unsettled', 'sad', and 'negative outlook on life'. These features were thought to be anxiety, including anxiety about the future. When looking at how Bryan saw 'me now', the constructs were around low self-esteem, negative outlook on life, unsettled and lonely. There was also the finding that Bryan found his 'ideal self' unreachable.

Year One link: Ideal self is part of the superego according to Freud and refers to what someone thinks they should be like, with evidence coming from the idea of society and others. Review your learning of Freud's ideas about the personality (id, ego and superego), which you learned about in biological psychology as a contrast to the biological view of aggression and the person.

The findings about Bryan's view of himself might relate to him being in denial about his offences and also explain why he was socially isolated and unwilling to engage in treatment, as well as being defensive. The grid also showed that 'victim' meant to him someone uncaring, jealous and devious, which suggests he blamed his victim and there was little empathy. His victim was also seen as different and isolated from others so he saw himself and his victim similarly, which was interesting. There is only some information given here, but hopefully it illustrates the value of using a case study when researching in a novel area using a technique that was novel in that specific situation.

Conclusions

The grid technique seemed to uncover some useful and relevant factors that could help case formulation. You looked at case formulation in the content section of this chapter (page 248). Such a formulation is required for there to be a successful treatment plan. The findings suggest that a therapist could keep in mind the isolation Bryan felt and reasons for his cynicism about treatment. Blagden *et al.* (2012) suggest that Bryan had cognitive barriers that were preventing treatment and 'deniers' need room to construct their identity differently. Finally, Blagden *et al.* (2012) mention that someone in denial might actually be denying the offence because they are innocent. Sexual offences like the one Bryan was convicted of often rest on witness testimony and memory, which can be unreliable, though of course this cannot be known in the case of Bryan.

Summary of case studies in criminological psychology

Just a few case studies have been used in this section to discuss the use of the method in criminological psychology. Others were used when discussing psychological formulation, such as Whitehead *et al.* (2007) (page 252). In general, you can see that they are used when depth and detail is required and often for issues surrounding treatment, when individual approaches are often necessary. Case studies take an idiographic approach rather than a nomothetic approach. An idiographic approach refers to something individual and private and means looking at what makes people unique. A nomothetic approach means looking for laws of human behaviour that show what is common in people, focusing on universal laws. Case studies are chosen by those taking an idiographic approach and a repertory grid shows an idiographic approach to understanding each person's personality through their own personal constructs. Experiments are used by researchers focusing on finding laws about people (a nomothetic approach) and behaviour that can apply to everyone, such as the weapon focus effect showing that people in general attend to a weapon in a situation when it is present.

Issues and debates

You can use the idiographic versus nomothetic approach when discussing psychology as science. Science is about building a body of knowledge, which is about uncovering universal laws about behaviour – that is a nomothetic approach to understanding people. Generally, an idiographic approach to understanding people is not seen as 'science'.

Evaluation of case studies as a research method in criminological psychology

Strengths

- Case studies are useful for getting in-depth and detailed data regarding the uniqueness of one person or a small group, or one situation. By getting such detailed information, they can help with planning a treatment, for example, and can aid case formulation to help to ensure that a treatment plan will be effective for an offender. They have a practical application, which is a strength.
- When there is a novel situation or something hard to study, such as working out how to help a sexual offender 'in denial', a case study of such a person can help to unpack causes for the denial and is a way of getting data in a novel situation where there can be no theory from which to derive a hypothesis because not enough is known.

Weaknesses

- As in other areas, the case study research method has difficulty with generalising from the study of a unique individual (or small group), and it takes an idiographic approach, which means it is not about generating general laws of behaviour. It is not easy to generalise from studying a unique person or situation. Blagden *et al.* (2012) mention this limitation in their case study. They can only use their material with Bryan, though they do suggest that the idea of using a repertory grid with sex offenders 'in denial' might be generalised.
- There might be subjectivity in the way a case study is carried out, which can affect the data gathered, and there might be subjectivity in the analysis of the study, such as choosing which data to include in a report of the results. Subjectivity might mean that there is bias in the data and any interpretation needs to be logged in a reflexive journal and reported with the findings so a judgement can be made about possible bias. Bias is a weakness in a study, such as one looking at reasons for offending because it means validity can be questioned.

> **STUDY HINT**
> When reading a question about 'case studies', look carefully at whether the question is about case studies as a research method or case studies in particular, such as Blagden *et al.* (2012). You could write out a few questions yourself to see how they may seem ambiguous as this will help you with understanding a question in an exam.

> **STUDY HINT**
> When evaluating a research method in a specific application in psychology, as you will do with case studies and field and lab experiments in criminological psychology, be sure to suit your answer to the application. Note how in the evaluation points made regarding the use of the case study research method, each point is related to the application explicitly. Your answers need to do the same.

Progress check 3.92

Complete the table using what you know about case studies. For each statement, put a cross in the box to indicate whether it is true or false.

Statement about the case study research method	True	False
Case studies are replicable and can be shown to be reliable.		
Case studies use more than one research method, which helps with triangulation, thus helping to show validity.		
Case studies take a nomothetic approach to understanding people.		
Case studies tend to use qualitative data most because they aim to gather rich, in-depth data.		
Case studies are useful for reducing real-life behaviour into small parts to explain it.		

Test yourself

Evaluate the strengths of case studies as a research method used in criminological psychology. **(12 marks)**

Sample selection and techniques

You need to cover random, stratified, volunteer and opportunity sampling.

Ⓦ All four sampling techniques are explained in the 'Psychological skills – methods' section online, where methods are reviewed. Remember to review evaluation points for each of the sampling techniques as well, both strengths and weaknesses.

Year One link: Review your learning about the four sampling techniques (random, stratified, volunteer and opportunity) in social psychology.

- Random sampling is when each person in the sampling frame, which is the people you are drawing the sample from, have an equal chance of being in the sample. You can do that by having all names in a 'hat' and drawing the sample out one-by-one or by using random number tables.
- Stratified sampling is when you need representatives of specific groups in the sample, such as certain age groups and both males and females in each age group. You choose a certain number from each 'strata'.

- Volunteer sampling is when the study is advertised and people are asked to turn up or respond to an advertisement. Alternatively, you could get a large group of people together and ask for volunteers.
- Opportunity sampling is also called 'convenience' sampling and means taking who you can get and who is available at the time.

Progress check 3.93

Explain which of the four sampling techniques in your course is considered the most representative.

Issues of reliability, validity, objectivity, credibility and ethics

Reliability

Reliable data are data that are found again when a study is repeated and they refer to consistent results. If someone only gets a finding once, it is not very reliable. You saw when studying weapon focus effect that many of the studies found there was an effect in that memory was impaired when a weapon was in a scene. There was reliability because other studies came up with the same finding. Similarly, studies looking at the effectiveness of anger management seemed to suggest it was not that effective for offenders. These findings are reliable because they occur in more than one study and they are consistent. Eyewitness studies tend to be reliable because experiments are used, as seen earlier in this method section. Other research in criminological psychology, such as focus on case studies, might be less reliable. Studies looking at the effectiveness of treatments for offenders tend to be reliable because they try to use randomised controlled trials. Case studies are less reliable, not because there is something wrong with the data as such, but because they are not so replicable and so reliability is hard to show. It is not that criminological psychology is reliable or not, or valid or not; it is the research method in question that you need to evaluate.

> **STUDY HINT**
> When discussing reliability, validity, objectivity, credibility and ethics of research in criminological psychology, be sure to give examples from criminological psychology.

Validity

Valid data are data that apply to real life and can be used in policy and practice. If findings have no validity, they are not that useful. The weapon focus effect was found consistently but Loftus *et al.* (1987) suggested it might be that the gun in their scenario was novel in the situation rather than because it was a gun that showed unreliability in eyewitness testimony. This suggests the 'weapon focus' should be 'novel object focus', which questions the validity of the explanation. Erickson *et al.* (2014) suggested it was because it was novel as they found some unreliability in eyewitness testimony when the focus was on a rubber chicken, which was novel in their scenario, as well as when it was on a gun. If it is concluded that a weapon means lack of attention on other details in a scene and leads to unreliable testimony, that would not be a valid conclusion from Loftus *et al.* (1987) as it does seem that it might be the novelty of a gun that gave the findings. So anything novel might cause the same attention problems and also lead to unreliability in eyewitness testimony. Eyewitness studies have problems with ecological validity as a rule because they tend to be experiments, as is discussed earlier in this section. However, Anderson and Bushman (1997) suggested that variables can represent real-life situations and so laboratory experiments can have external validity.

Year One link: In cognitive psychology, you learned about ecological validity, predictive validity and internal validity so recall the differences and use those different types of validity here.

Progress check 3.94

Explain the idea that when a research method is good for reliability, that makes it less good regarding validity.

Objectivity

Research in criminological psychology, as has been shown, often uses laboratory or field experiments or randomised controlled trials. When biological explanations of crime and anti-social behaviour are considered, 'biological' methods are used, such as scanning or animal laboratory experiments. These methods involve objectivity and are examples of psychology as science, so they also involve credibility. When scientific methods are used and cause-and-effect conclusions are looked for, there should be objectivity, reliability, credibility and cause-and-effect findings. Objectivity means the results are not affected by experimenter effects or bias and this is attained by using careful and thorough controls. Loftus's work involves thorough and careful controls so is useful as an example. Experiments as research methods are discussed earlier in this section so look back there for examples of objectivity in criminological psychology research.

It can be argued that case studies lack objectivity, as subjectivity can be found. Perhaps a researcher working with one person using a case-study approach gets close to them, which can help in getting rich, valid, in-depth data, which are the strengths of case studies. An example of a case study, given earlier in this section, is Blagden *et al.* (2012) (page 322). Data can be interpreted either when a choice is made about whether to include them or when analysis is carried out, such as thematic analysis.

Credibility

Credibility in psychology refers to whether a study has had sufficient controls or been carried out in an objective way so there is no bias in the results and they can be accepted as 'credible' enough to be used to build a body of knowledge. If there is subjectivity in a study, that can negatively affect its credibility. Credibility is about trustworthiness and expertise and it is about objectivity and subjectivity. Trustworthiness can be a subjective opinion but it is also about results having no bias, and having objective measures and reliability. Expertise can relate to competence, which is about someone carrying out a well-controlled, ethical and objective study. Case studies can be done competently of course, and objectively; it is not just about experimental methods. However, usually, credibility comes from scientific methods.

Scientific credibility can be about how far scientific findings are accepted. It could be said that they lack credibility if they lack validity, for example. These are the issues to discuss when claiming credibility when applied to research findings. Loftus is well-known in the area of eyewitness testimony and carries out experiments, so an experiment she is involved in should have credibility, in general: the study itself would need to be looked at specifically as well. When research into the effectiveness of a treatment for offenders is carried out, it has credibility if it uses a randomised controlled trial method. Researchers that do not randomly allocate people to a treatment or control group would need to explain why not and would need good reason if their results are going to have credibility. One of the studies in the studies section in this chapter, Howells *et al.* (2005) (page 346), cannot use randomisation but has a treatment and a waiting list control group, which has some credibility. Howells *et al.* make sure they explain the situation and why they did not use randomisation.

Ethics

You need to cover ethics in this method section, both the BPS Code of Ethics and Conduct (2009) and risk management, which were both required in social psychology in your course, as well as specific ethics in criminological psychology. The specific ethics involve the Health and Care Professions Council (HCPC) principles for undertaking psychological formulation and intervention. These are considered in the ethics section (page 328).

Research in criminological psychology, as with all research, must be ethical. All the general ethical principles apply, covered by respect, responsibility, integrity and competence, which are the four principles in the 2009 BPS Code of Ethics and Conduct. There are some issues with experiments looking at eyewitness testimony that you could consider when discussing ethics in criminological psychology research.

Using students

One issue is the use of undergraduates, who often take part in studies as part of their psychology course, which could be said to be putting pressure on them. Erickson *et al.* (2014) used students in this way, though as it is widely accepted and the researchers would have competence, there is some argument that it is fine to do so. Loftus and Palmer (1974) used students in the same way. Putting pressure on someone relates to the principle of responsibility. Also the principle of respect asks for people to be given self-determination so even if students give an overall agreement to taking part in studies as part of their course, they must be given the right to withdraw.

Getting consent that is 'informed'

Another ethical issue is informed consent. Valentine and Mesout (2009), one of the contemporary studies in criminological psychology, could not explain to their participants that the 'scary person' they met in the labyrinth was part of a study, but they did explain as soon as they could. Informed consent was obtained once the participant had finished the tour. Valentine and Mesout (2009) also got informed consent from participants doing another part of the study where their heart rate was monitored. Eyewitness studies, in particular, rely on the participant not knowing about the various conditions so there tends not to be informed consent, which is where debriefing comes in. Informed consent is part of the principle of respect.

The need for deceit

Another ethical issue is deceit, which comes under respect, though the principle does say deception might be necessary 'in exceptional circumstances to preserve the integrity of research' (Code of Ethics and Conduct, 2009, p. 14). If there has been deceit, it must be kept to a minimum, as in Valentine and Mesout's (2009) study.

Depriving a control group

Another issue when considering studies looking at the effectiveness of treatment is using a control group which is then deprived of the treatment. This is about responsibility and it is why waiting list controls are often used. They at least will get the treatment, even if later. Howells *et al.* (2005), one of the contemporary studies in criminological psychology, used a treatment group and a control group. It was interesting that, probably because the waiting list control group did all the questionnaires and assessments both before and after the treatment, the control group reduced their anger as did the treatment group, so the treatment seemed not to be effective when measured against the control group. It seemed that being part of the study had perhaps motivated the controls to focus on their anger. These are the sorts of ethical issues that need to be considered, though in this case the control group gained from the study.

> **STUDY HINT**
> Issues like reliability, validity, objectivity, credibility and ethics have been mentioned often throughout your course. Just some ideas are given here relating to how to discuss these issues in relation to research in criminological psychology. You could have a section in your notes for these issues and bring in studies where you notice the issues arise, so that you have examples to draw on.

Progress check 3.96

Using examples, explain why deceit is a particular issue when the experimental method is used.

Data analysis

Data analysis includes analysis of quantitative data using descriptive statistics and inferential statistics, and all the issues involved therein. You also need to know about analysis of qualitative data, using both thematic analysis and grounded theory.

Year One link: All the issues around data analysis that you need to know about were covered in Year One, so review them for this application. There is just one exception, which is the use of grounded theory for qualitative data.

You covered all the issues around data analysis that you need here in clinical psychology too, including grounded theory for qualitative data, so you can review all that you need by referring to Chapter Two. The 'Psychological skills – methods' section online also reviews data analysis. Remember, however, that you do need to know and understand such issues in criminological psychology and could be asked about them in the criminological psychology section of your examination.

In criminological psychology, you need to recall information about:

- measures of central tendency: mean, median and mode
- measures of dispersion: range, standard deviation and frequency tables
- correlations and meta-analyses as used to analyse quantitative data
- inferential statistics, including the four tests used in your course: Wilcoxon, Mann Whitney U, Spearman's and Chi squared
- levels of measurement, issues of statistical significance and observed/calculated and critical values, including using tables
- analysis of qualitative data using thematic analysis
- grounded theory and qualitative data analysis.

Progress check 3.97

Name the four inferential tests you need to know about, two ways of analysing qualitative data and three levels of measurement.

Test yourself

Explain why inferential testing is useful when analysing results in psychology. **(4 marks)**

Ethical guidelines

You need to know about the BPS Code of Ethics and Conduct (2009) and risk management issues. You also need to know about the Health and Care Professions Council (HCPC) principles for undertaking psychological formulation and intervention.

BPS Code of Ethics and Conduct and risk management

The BPS Code has four main principles: respect, responsibility, integrity and competence. Some of these have been discussed when considering ethical issues in research in criminological psychology (page 327).

Risk management is about making sure participants are safe as well as researchers and other people involved in the study. For example, Valentine and Mesout (2009) carried out their research in the London Dungeon so could rely on the London Dungeon risk management procedures when participants did the tour, though the researchers needed to be careful with the intervention they introduced, which was a 'scary person' stepping out and blocking the participant's path in the labyrinth, as that was in addition to the usual tour.

Year One link: You covered the BPS Code of Ethics and Conduct (2009) as well as risk management in social psychology and it is reviewed in the 'Psychological skills – methods' section online, so you can recall what you need to know and be ready to relate the ideas to research in criminological psychology.

The BPS Code of Ethics and Conduct has been covered elsewhere in your course and some of the issues have been covered in this method section. Be sure you can discuss issues around respect, responsibility, integrity and competence using examples from criminological psychology. For example, consider case studies such as Blagden *et al.* (2012), where they study Bryan's responses to a repertory grid task, and where there are issues of privacy and confidentiality when publishing the case study, perhaps especially because at the end of their report they raise the issue of whether he was 'in denial' or in fact not guilty.

HCPC principles for undertaking psychological formulation and intervention

The HCPC principles were considered in the section on psychological formulation earlier in this chapter (page 257), so presented here is just a review of that material. The main source of information is the HCPC Standards of Proficiency document, which lists 15 standards, and within those gives some guidance that is specifically for forensic psychologists. You can access the Standards of Proficiency document to find out more. The standards are summarised here (see page 257 for more detail).

HCPC Standards of Proficiency

- Being able to practise safely and effectively.
- Being able to practise within the legal and ethical boundaries of the profession.
- Being able to maintain fitness to practice.
- Being able to practise in an autonomous way and to use professional judgement.
- Being aware of the impact of culture, equality and diversity on practice.
- Being able to practise in a non-discriminatory manner.
- Understanding the importance of confidentiality.
- Being able to communicate effectively.
- Being able to work appropriately with others.
- Being able to maintain records appropriately.
- Being able to reflect on and review practice.
- Being able to assure the quality of their practice.
- Understanding the key concepts of the profession's knowledge base.
- Drawing on knowledge and skills to inform practice.
- Understanding the need to establish and maintain safe practice.

Forensic psychologists need to be able to use a lifespan approach taking into account someone's developmental path and social situation, for example.

Explore

You can access the HCPC document focusing on Standards of Proficiency for practitioner psychologists using this link: **www.hpc-uk.org/assets/documents/10002963sop_practitioner_psychologists.pdf**

Year One link: Remind yourself about the ethical principles in the BPS Code of Ethics and Conduct (2009), which you studied in social psychology.

Summary

- Laboratory experiments are used a lot in the study of eyewitness testimony and have the strength of following a scientific approach, focusing on objectivity, reliability and credibility, so claiming cause-and-effect conclusions.
- Lab experiments in this chapter that focus on eyewitness testimony include Loftus and Palmer (1974), other Loftus studies and Erickson et al. (2014).
- Field experiments have the strengths of laboratory experiments, but, being in the field, in a naturalistic environment, there are necessarily fewer controls and so the findings might be less reliable. They may be more ecologically valid as there is a realism that is not present in lab experiments.
- Field experiments in this chapter that focus on eyewitness testimony include Yarmey (2004) and Valentine and Mesout (2009), who have a lot of experimental elements in their study.
- Case studies in criminological psychology are often found when looking at treatments for offenders, including when carrying out a case formulation.
- Studies in this chapter using the case study research method include Blagden et al. (2012), Yuille and Cutshall (1986), whose study has case study elements, and Arsuffi (2010), who looked at assessment, formulation and treatment of one offender.
- Sampling techniques are important in psychology, including random, stratified, volunteer and opportunity sampling, all of which were covered in social psychology too.
- Issues of reliability, validity, objectivity, credibility and ethics in research in criminological psychology are important, as they are in all psychology research.
- Data analysis of quantitative data includes descriptive statistics (mean, median, mode, range, standard deviation, graphs and tables), correlations and meta-analysis, and inferential statistics, including four non-parametric tests: Mann Whitney U, Wilcoxon, Chi squared and Spearman's. Issues of statistical significance, levels of measurement and observed/calculated and critical values are also important.
- Data analysis of qualitative data includes thematic analysis and grounded theory.
- Ethical issues in research are always important, including the BPS Code of Ethics and Conduct (2009) and risk management.
- In particular in criminological psychology, the Health and Care Professions Council principles for undertaking psychological formulation and intervention are important.

Studies in criminological psychology

For this section, you need to cover two studies in detail. Loftus and Palmer (1974) fits in well both with the methodology section of this chapter and with the content section. It is the classic study for criminological psychology in your course. It is described and evaluated in detail here.

The other study must be one from a choice of three contemporary studies. All three are given in this section to help your learning. They are:

- Bradbury and Williams (2013), who looked at the effects of race on juror decision-making
- Valentine and Mesout (2009), who looked at eyewitness identification under stressful conditions
- Howells *et al.* (2005), who looked at brief anger management programmes with offenders to consider the outcomes of such programmes and what might predict change in the offender.

Howells *et al.*'s (2005) study fits in with cognitive-behavioural treatments for offenders in this chapter. Bradbury and Williams's (2013) study is useful because juror decision-making is part of the content in this chapter, and Valentine and Mesout (2009) looks at eyewitness testimony, also part of the content in this chapter.

Loftus and Palmer (1974)

Loftus and Palmer carried out two experiments within this study and both are explained here.

Elizabeth Loftus has carried out a lot of research into eyewitness memory and her study with Palmer is just one of those studies. They got students to watch films of car accidents and then to answer questions relating to what they had seen. Loftus and Palmer (1974) kept things the same in their study for the most part but changed a verb to see what the effect of that change in one of the questions would be. They wanted to see whether the word 'smashed' led to someone thinking a car was going at a faster speed and whether it would lead people to 'remember' smashed glass at the scene, even though there was none.

Elizabeth Loftus

Background

According to researchers such as Bird (1927), people are inaccurate at reporting numbers relating to time, speed and distance. This is particularly true of speed, and one study of air force personnel who knew they would be asked about speed found estimates varying between 10 and 50mph, even though the car they were watching was only going at 12mph (Marshall, 1969). There are likely to be variables that could influence estimates of speed, which is what Loftus and Palmer's study is about.

Aims

The aim was to see if the phrasing of a question would affect estimates of speed, applying these findings to the idea of leading questions in court. A leading question is one that suggests to the witness what answer is desired or leads him or her to the desired answer. Bransford and McCarrell (cited in Loftus and Palmer, 1974) found that the verb 'hit' and the verb 'smashed' suggested different rates of movement and Loftus and Palmer also thought that such verbs might suggest different consequences of events they are referring to. Their aim was to see if the verb 'hit' indicated a more gentle event than the verb 'smashed'.

Experiment 1

Procedure

Forty-five students were put into groups. Seven films were shown, each involving a traffic accident, with each film lasting between 5 and 30 seconds. After every film, the participants had a questionnaire to fill in. First they were required to give an account of the accident, and then to answer specific questions. The critical question was the one asking about the speed of the vehicles. Nine participants were asked: 'About how fast were the cars going when they hit each other?' Equal numbers of the rest were asked the same question, but with the word 'hit' being replaced by 'smashed', 'collided', 'bumped' or 'contacted'. The same procedure was followed for each film. The different participants saw the films in a different order.

Progress check 3.99

How does Loftus and Palmer's (1974) study procedure represent leading questions in court?

Results

Four of the seven films used staged crashes which were intended to show what can happen to people when cars 'crash' at a certain speed, so the speed of the cars was known. One was travelling at 20mph, one was at 30mph and two were at 40mph. Table 3.29 shows the average speeds estimated, according to the words used in the question. For the cars where the accident was staged and the speed known, for the car travelling at 20mph, the mean estimate was 37.7mph. For the car travelling at 30mph, the mean estimate was 36.2mph and for the cars travelling at 40mph, the mean estimates were 39.7 and 36.1mph. This shows that people are not very good at estimating speed and the estimate of around 40mph was a common one.

Table 3.29 Estimated speeds, according to which word was used in the question (Loftus and Palmer, 1974)

Word used	Mean speed estimated in miles per hour (mph)
Smashed	40.8
Collided	39.3
Bumped	38.1
Hit	34.0
Contacted	31.8

It can be seen from Table 3.29 that 'smashed' gave the highest mean estimate of speed (40.8mph) and 'contacted' the lowest mean estimate (31.8mph). 'Collided', 'bumped' and 'hit' had speed estimates that were fairly well spaced and decreased according to the perceived severity of the verb.

> **STUDY HINT**
> When there are not too many results, such as in Loftus and Palmer's Experiment 1, you can learn the exact numbers, so here you could learn the mean speed estimates in response to the different verbs used in Experiment 1.

> **STUDY HINT**
> As part of the content in criminological psychology in your course you have to learn about factors that influence eyewitness testimony, so Loftus and Palmer's (1974) study will be useful for you when you are covering that material.

Conclusions

It was concluded that the form of a question can affect a witness's answer. Perhaps the participant is uncertain in judging speeds between 30 and 40mph, so he or she uses the word in the question to help. Or it is possible that the question changes the memory of the accident so the participant sees the accident as more severe if the word 'smashed' is used. If it is about changing memory, then other aspects of memory may be affected. Loftus and Palmer's second experiment was run to test that idea.

Experiment 2

Procedure

There were 150 students involved in this experiment, put into various groups. A film with a multiple car accident was shown, followed by a questionnaire. The film lasted less than one minute, with the accident taking four seconds. The questionnaire at the end of the film asked participants to describe the accident in their own words and then to answer more questions. Fifty participants were asked about the speed using the word 'smashed' as part of the question ('About how fast were the cars going when they smashed into one another?'). Fifty participants were asked the same question with the word 'hit' replacing 'smashed', and 50 participants were not asked about speed. One week later, the participants came back but were not shown the film again. They were asked more questions, including 'Did you see any broken glass?' There was no broken glass in the film, but it was thought that the word 'smashed' used in the question the week before would lead to more broken glass being 'remembered' by those participants.

Results

Table 3.30 'Yes'/'no' replies to the question 'Did you see broken glass?', according to the question asked the previous week (Loftus and Palmer, 1974)

Response	'Smashed'	'Hit'	Control (not asked about speed)	Total
Yes	16	7	6	29
No	34	43	44	121

Progress check 3.100

Reproduce Table 3.30 using percentages instead of numbers for the 'yes' and 'no' replies. Use one significant figure. Explain the advantage of using percentages instead of actual figures.

The mean estimate of speed for the question including the word 'smashed' was 10.46mph and for 'hit' it was 8mph. These mean averages were statistically different at $p<0.05$. A Chi squared test was carried out and the result was 7.76, which was significant at $p<0.025$. The probability of saying yes in response to 'smashed' was 0.32 and in response to 'hit' was 0.14. 'Smashed' gave more 'yes' answers to a question about whether there was broken glass (Table 3.30) and a higher estimate of speed.

There is an issue here about whether a higher speed estimate, notwithstanding the verb used, might lead to a greater likelihood of saying 'yes' to broken glass. It might be the speed that is thought to give the broken glass and not the verb ('smashed' giving 'yes' to broken glass more than 'hit'). To test this, Loftus and Palmer worked out the probability of saying 'yes' to there being broken glass according to the estimate of speed and also according to whether the verb used was 'hit' or 'smashed' (Table 3.31).

Table 3.31 The probability of participants saying 'yes' to the question about seeing broken glass related to estimate of the speed of the car

Verb condition	Speed estimate (mph)			
	1–5	6–10	11–15	16–20
Smashed	.09	.27	.41	.62
Hit	.06	.09	.25	.50

Table 3.31 shows that as the estimate of speed rises so does the likelihood of 'seeing' broken glass, but the probability of saying 'yes' to 'seeing' broken glass is consistently lower when the verb used is 'hit' compared to 'smashed', so it is the verb (perhaps as well as the estimate of speed) that guides the 'recall' of broken glass and not just the estimate of speed.

Conclusions

The way the question is asked can affect the answer given, and the word change in the question had consequences a week later. Memory is fed by the event and by external information provided afterwards. Over time these are integrated into one memory. The film provides the internal memory, and the 'smashed' or 'hit' question adds external information (post-event information). Integrate the two and the memory is of a crash that is more severe than it was (broken glass was seen to represent 'severe'). The findings link with studies on verbal labels, which have been shown to affect recall. Verbal labels cause a shift in memory to 'fit' the label better. For example, Carmichael *et al.* (1932, cited in Loftus and Palmer, 1974) found that people reproduce drawings according to the label a drawing is given and not just from the drawing itself. This suggests that the label is incorporated into the memory of the seen object. In Loftus and Palmer's (1974) experiments, for example, a car crash for some was labelled a 'smash'.

Evaluation of Loftus and Palmer (1974)

Strengths

- Loftus and Palmer (1974) carried out a laboratory experiment in Experiment 1 with clear controls, such as all participants watching the same film and being asked identical questions, except for one word change. The controls and careful documenting of the procedure mean that the study is replicable – in fact, the researchers replicated it themselves when doing Experiment 2 and found again that the use of the word 'smashed' gave a higher estimate of speed. Therefore, the findings are reliable.
- By using estimates of speed, the researchers gathered quantitative data and so they did not have to interpret the data at all, which makes their study more objective. They were able to use inferential statistical testing to see how far their results might be due to chance.

Weaknesses

- The students who were participants might not have been under the same emotional strain as if they had been witness to a real car accident, so the findings might not have validity.
- When an experiment is carried out using students as participants, it is said that the findings might not be generalisable to the whole population. This is

not because students are not allowed their opinions but because, being students, they may have different motivation when carrying out the study.

- There might have been demand characteristics in the study, in that the students were able to work out what was required so they answered accordingly. There were questions in addition to the key one, and it would not have been clear that other participants had a different word in the key question, but participants may have picked up that this was about the car accident and that the word 'smashed' was meant to be leading, for example.

Explore

You can access Loftus and Palmer's (1974) study using this link if you would like to read the full study: **https://webfiles. uci.edu/eloftus/LoftusPalmer74.pdf** (note there is an error in the file: the mean estimated speed for 'smashed' was 40.8 and this file gives 40.5).

There is also a YouTube video on the study here: **www.youtube. com/watch?v=16yIMHtLUTg**

You can read more about the study using this link: **www.simplypsychology.org/loftus-palmer.html**. Here you will find some questions about the study that you could answer to test your understanding, as well as further information, such as the use of independent measures/independent groups.

Progress check 3.101

Evaluate Loftus and Palmer (1974) in terms of validity, generalisability and reliability.

Bradbury and Williams (2013)

Bradbury and Williams (2013) look at the issue of black defendants being less likely to be convicted by juries with more black jurors and more likely to be convicted by juries with more white and Hispanic jurors. This issue relates to **diversity** in public participation in issues such as court proceedings involving jurors and is about **equality**. Bradbury and Williams focus on the diversity of jurors and how that affects their decision-making. In particular they focus on the effect of race on juror decision-making. They recommend that when juries are selected there should be 'careful consideration of which members of the public are and are not participating' (p. 564), saying that this might affect the decisions that are made.

Explore

You can access Bradbury and Williams (2013) directly using this link: **http://libres.uncg.edu/ir/asu/f/Williams_Marian_Bradbury_2013_Diversity_Citizen.pdf**

Definitions

Diversity, in the sense used when discussing people in a society, means aiming to value people's differences and to recognise and respect them, so it would involve having a representative group taking in different beliefs and groups. **Equality** means making sure people are treated fairly with no group being favoured over another group; equality includes race, gender, disability, religion, belief, sexual orientation and age.

STUDY HINT

The key question on the website accompanying this book relating to criminological psychology is about bias in juror decision-making and whether juries should be abolished. You can use Bradbury and Williams (2013) when discussing this key question.

Background

Bradbury and Williams (2013) spend a lot of time at the start of their paper looking at public participation and juror participation. Their hypotheses are that black defendants are more likely to be convicted by a jury made up of a higher number of white jurors and that black defendants are more likely to be convicted by a jury made up of a higher number of Hispanic jurors.

Citizen participation in decision-making and citizen juries

Bradbury and Williams start their paper by mentioning the aim of increasing citizen involvement in decision-making in government, citing, for example, Stewart (2007). They say that one definition of citizen participation is that it is where members of society share power with public officials around making important decisions (Roberts, 2008, cited in Bradbury and Williams, 2013). It is about citizens being 'personally involved and actively engaged' (Roberts, 2008, p. 7, cited in Bradbury and Williams, 2013). Research generally shows that there should be a lot of citizen participation and it needs to be 'better explained and understood' (Stewart, 2007, p. 1069, cited in Bradbury and Williams, 2013).

An important consideration when involving citizens in decision-making is that administrators must trust those citizens and administrators and the citizens must work together. Another consideration is that participation must be more than **tokenism**. Tokenism refers to a gesture being made in policy and practice to include someone or some people from members of minority groups. The issue is that it is a gesture and not 'true' inclusion. This is Arnstein's (1969, cited in Bradbury and Williams, 2013) view and she says that actual participation in decision-making is rare. Mostly citizen participation would involve citizens being consulted and then not being involved in policy decisions after the consultation. Delegating power to citizens is rare.

Definition

Tokenism refers to a gesture being made in policy and practice to include someone or some people from members of minority groups, which could refer to citizens when considering public administration. The issue is that it is a gesture and not 'true' inclusion.

One area where citizens are delegated power is in juror decision-making. Smith and Wales (2000, cited in Bradbury and Williams, 2013) say that a jury is a group of citizens who are randomly chosen to make decisions on a particular issue, which can be setting a policy agenda or choosing between different policy choices. A jury goes through witness statements, guided by a trained 'moderator' and reports on their findings and recommendations. The jury is there to represent the general public. This is about the citizen jury; however, juries in the legal system have similar powers.

A main issue is with representativeness of a citizen jury. One issue about getting representativeness is that diversity of the public being represented might not be considered. John (2009, cited in Bradbury and Williams, 2013) found that participants in a citizen jury did not differ much in their characteristics when compared with non-participants. However, John did agree that there might be a link between inequality in participation and the output and outcomes of the jury. Bradbury and Williams conclude that a jury must be randomly selected and must have direct power over public decisions.

Juries in the legal system

Bradbury and Williams take the ideas about what makes good citizen jury decision-making and apply the ideas to juries in the legal system. They say that juries in the legal system are not studied enough when it comes to them being a participation mechanism, in particular when considering that power is delegated to them. They look at how power is delegated to them and they look at whether a jury's racial make-up affects its decision-making.

Bradbury and Williams are examining the right of people to be tried by an impartial jury. Twelve jurors have to reach a unanimous decision if the decision is to be successful. Juries should represent the community and protect the accused from the state's resources and power,

as well as being impartial. Each member of the jury has an equal voice in the decision-making.

Once the randomly selected pool of jurors has been chosen, the pool is 'whittled down' to just 12 people. Neubauer (2008, pp. 295–296, cited in Bradbury and Williams, 2013) says 'many lawyers believe that trials are won or lost on the basis of which jurors are selected' and this emphasises the importance of the selection process. The lawyers in the trial, both prosecution and defence, can protest about members of the pool on the grounds that they do not represent the community. Also there are two challenges that can be made where, in each case, a potential juror can be excluded during the **voir dire** process. Challenges have to be on the basis that a particular juror would not be impartial.

According to Bradbury and Williams (2013), working in the US, there is also the peremptory challenge which can be used to form a jury into one that is not open-minded and objective. A limited number of peremptory challenges are used with the aim of rejecting potential jurors who may be favourable for the opposition. However, in England, the Criminal Justice Act 1988 removed the right of peremptory challenge because it was seen as leading to unfairness. In Ireland, challenge without cause shown is permitted and each side has seven challenges. In New Zealand, there are six such challenges. As you can see, there are differences regarding peremptory challenge in different judicial systems.

Definition

Voir dire means 'tell the truth' and the truth must be accurate and given honestly. It is about the competence of a jury (as well as other competencies, such as that of a witness). 'Voir dire' means lawyers for the prosecution and defence questioning jurors about their backgrounds and biases, and jurors can be accepted or rejected on that basis.

Juror bias

The idea of challenging jurors because of various characteristics shows the belief that such characteristics can affect decision-making. Barkan and Bryjak (2004, cited in Bradbury and Williams, 2013) suggest that life experiences affect a juror's assessment of witness evidence and so on, and that such experiences concern issues of race, age, gender and social class, and other similar variables. Studies have been done to look at how such factors might affect juror decision-making. Ford (1986, cited in Bradbury and Williams, 2013) carried out a review of the evidence and found it was unclear whether demographic factors influence juror decisions.

In-group/out-group bias

One way in which jurors might be biased in their decision-making is that in-group bias may occur if a juror shares demographic characteristics with the defendant and that juror may see the defendant in a more favourable way. This suggests that jurors serve the community best if they represent the demographics of the community and not sharing characteristics with a defendant.

Year One link: Recall what you learned about social identity theory (SIT) in social psychology and how out-group hostility can occur just because an in-group and an out-group are formed. This is the theory behind the idea that jurors can show in-group favouritism and out-group hostility.

When researching juries, mock juries are often used as it is hard to study real jury decision-making. One reason is that there is plea-bargaining, which means the jury does not often make the decision about guilt. The majority of cases where a jury might be used are resolved using plea-bargaining according to Neubauer (2008, cited in Bradbury and Williams, 2013). Real trials are preferable as valid data would be gathered and mock jury studies can be accused of lacking validity because of the difference in stress and emotions between a mock trial and a real one, for example.

Bowers et al. (2004, cited in Bradbury and Williams, 2013) looked at 353 trials where the defendant was black and the victim was white. They found that mixed-race juries showed more conflict during their deliberations, discussed possible mitigating circumstances more, and talked more about race affecting judgements. Wishman (1986, cited in Bradbury and Williams, 2013) found that black jurors were less likely to convict black defendants because of 'feeling of brotherhood' (p. 116). Juries with a high percentage of white jurors are more likely to convict black defendants, suggesting out-group bias.

> **STUDY HINT**
> Quite a lot of detail is given here about study findings regarding race and juror decision-making because you need to know about race and juror decision-making for the content part of your course. Therefore, what is discussed in Bradbury and Williams (2013) can be useful elsewhere in your studies.

Aims

Bradbury and Williams (2013) look at how power is delegated to juries and whether a jury's racial make-up affects its decision-making. Bradbury and Williams are examining the right of people to be tried by an impartial jury. They want to look in particular at the race of a juror with regard to the race of the defendant and to look for out-group bias, in that a jury that is all or predominantly white is more likely to convict a black defendant. They want to see whether jurors of the same race as a defendant would be more likely to want to acquit the defendant and jurors of a different race would be more likely to want to convict.

Hypotheses

Bradbury and Williams set out two clear hypotheses:

1 'Black defendants will be more likely to be convicted by juries composed of a higher number of white jurors' (p. 571).
2 'Black defendants will be more likely to be convicted by juries composed of a higher number of Hispanic jurors' (p. 571).

Hypothesis 2 focuses on whether members of minority groups support one another. Also it is interesting to study Hispanics as, according to Bradbury and Williams, they have been excluded from doing jury service because of language and citizenship issues (Enriquez and Clark, 2007). This has led to mock jury studies when looking at Hispanics, with their validity and generalisability issues. One study found that Hispanic jurors tended to be more lenient to white defendants than to black defendants (Abwender and Hough, 2001, cited in Bradbury and Williams, 2013). This study is the basis for Hypothesis 2, which states that Hispanic jurors will be more likely to convict a black defendant.

> **Progress check 3.102**
> Explain why mock jury studies are said to lack validity and generalisability.

Method

One way of getting data about juries and their decisions is to use data from trials and to compare juries where there was deadlock in the decision with juries that convicted defendants. Deadlock means the jury cannot come to a unanimous decision and the jury is then a 'hung' jury. Deadlock can become a non-unanimous verdict. It is only reached after there has been extended deliberation.

Data that were gathered included the charge, the sentence, the jury decision, demographic characteristics of the defendant and of the victims, jury selection, trial evidence and jury deliberations. A strength of this way of gathering data is that the data come from real trials and not mock trials with mock juries.

Bradbury and Williams felt that the data they collected might not be representative of all trials and all jury decision-making so there were difficulties with generalisability. However, they did feel they could draw conclusions about the racial make-up of juries and how that make-up could affect decisions. Thus the data suited their aims.

They chose to look at only black defendants, which included 60 per cent of all defendants in the jurisdictions they were using. Whites made up 10 per cent of the defendants and Hispanics made up 24 per cent of the defendants.

Bradbury and Williams could just have looked at race of jurors to consider whether this affected their decisions. However, they wanted to see if other variables were more important than the race of the juror (the defendant's race was set as black). They looked at the quantity of the evidence, the length of jury deliberations and any written instructions for the jury.

The dependent variable

The dependent variable was whether there was a conviction or not. A conviction (yes) was coded 1 and no conviction (no) was coded 0. A conviction for any charge, even if there was more than one charge and others did not result in a conviction, was coded 1. Acquittals and hung juries were coded 0.

The independent variable

The independent variable was the racial make-up of the jury. Races of interest were white, Hispanic and black, and the focus was on the effect of race of jurors on conviction or otherwise of a black defendant.

Progress check 3.103
How would you define the terms 'dependent variable' and 'independent variable'?

Control variables

Five variables that needed to be controlled and could become confounding variables included:
- the strength of the prosecutor's case – this was measured by 'above one' representing when jurors felt the prosecutor's case was stronger than the defence's case and 'below one' when the jurors felt the prosecutor's case was weaker than the defence's case
- the quantity of the prosecutor's evidence – this was measured by the number of exhibits and witnesses presented by the prosecutor

- length of the trial
- length of deliberations – Bradbury and Williams thought that the longer the jury's deliberations took place the more a possible in-group bias for black jurors would be counteracted
- written instructions – written instructions from the judge to remind the jury of their role and responsibilities would affect how much shared demographics with the defendant would affect black jurors in particular.

Bradbury and Williams also felt that the type of crime was important when it came to juror decision-making. They coded violent crime as 1 for 'yes' and 0 for 'no'. They coded property crime as 1 for 'yes' and 0 for 'no'. Drug crimes were assessed against violent and property crimes to see what effect drug crimes have on conviction to cope with another possible confounding variable. Drug crime was given 1 for 'yes' and 0 for 'no'. They also felt that attorney type was important as some defence attorneys might not do as well as others. A private attorney should be negatively correlated with conviction rate as private attorneys are thought to be better.

Progress check 3.104
What does the term 'confounding variable' mean?

Results

- The results were that a higher percentage of white jurors on a jury meant the jury was more likely to convict black defendants than juries with a higher percentage of black jurors. The odds ratio was 1.022, $p < .01$. The juries with a higher percentage of black jurors were the baseline measure for the findings.
- Also a higher percentage of Hispanic jurors on a jury meant the jury was more likely to convict black defendants than juries with a higher percentage of black jurors. The odds ratio was 1.019, $p < .10$. However, the finding about having Hispanic jurors on a jury was only significant at $p < .10$ so there is not much support for Hypothesis 2, which was that juries with a higher proportion of Hispanic jurors are more likely to convict black defendants than juries with a higher percentage of black jurors.
- Juries were less likely to convict black defendants of violent crimes compared with drug crimes. The odds ratio was 0.395.
- Juries were less likely to convict black defendants of property crimes compared with drug crimes. The odds ratio was 0.339, though this finding was again at $p < .10$ so marginally significant.

- The strongest finding was that juries with a higher percentage of white jurors were more likely to convict black defendants, with a weaker finding that juries made up of a higher percentage of Hispanics were also more likely to convict black defendants.
- Although the significance for the finding about Hispanics on a jury affecting conviction of a black defendant was low, Bradbury and Williams saw this hypothesis as exploratory given the lack of previous findings in this area, which is why they wanted to report the finding that a higher percentage of Hispanics on a jury affected conviction of a black defendant.

Conclusions

The finding that black defendants are more likely to be convicted of drug crime than of violent crime, notwithstanding the racial characteristics of the jury, is a useful finding for the criminal justice system to note. It might be important for the defence team to look for a trial by jury for violent crimes. Lawyers for black defendants might also prefer, from these findings, to have black jurors. Bradbury and Williams acknowledge that the idea of black jurors for black defendants is already known but they say their evidence adds to this knowledge.

Bradbury and Williams make the point that it is not that any jury will represent the public; it is important that the focus is on who from the public is making the decisions on behalf of the public as the composition of a jury, for example, appears to affect the decisions made.

Evaluation of Bradbury and Williams (2013)

Strengths

- Bradbury and Williams emphasise that a strength of their study is that they collect data from real trials that have taken place and real juries. This gives their data validity, which mock jury studies lack.
- They use social identity theory to underpin their hypotheses, suggesting that juries with a higher percentage of black jurors would favour a black defendant because of in-group favouritism and so that could act as a baseline against which to measure juror decision-making when the jury had a higher percentage of whites and when the jury had a higher percentage of Hispanics. Using a well-researched and evidenced theory adds weight to their hypothesis. Science involves a theory from which hypotheses are generated and then testing empirically before accepting the hypotheses (or not) and amending the theory. Bradbury and Williams, by using a theory to underpin their hypotheses, were

'doing science', which is a strength. Also their collecting of the data could be objective as it was a case of analysing reports of trials, not collecting data directly.

Weaknesses

- Although Bradbury and Williams use real trial data, which is a strength, they point out that the trials might not be representative of all trials by jury. For example, they only chose trials where the defendant was black. They suggest that a more representative sample of offences and trials are studied using their methods as that would help the generalisability of the findings.
- They accept their experimental hypothesis 2 that 'black defendants will be more likely to be convicted by juries composed of a higher number of Hispanic jurors', even though the findings were just $p < .10$, so the finding is weak. They want to accept the experimental hypothesis because they felt that not much had been done in the way of research in the area of Hispanics on juries so for a pilot study $p < .10$ was acceptable. However, it could be argued that the finding was limited.
- They classified any conviction in the trial as a 'conviction', whereas in practice a defendant might have been convicted of one charge and acquitted of many others. This might affect the findings and perhaps a different way of scoring 'conviction' might have helped to show a fuller picture.

Valentine and Mesout (2009)

Valentine and Mesout (2009) focused on eyewitness identification under stress. Both Loftus and Palmer (1974), the classic study in your course, and Valentine and Mesout (2009) will be useful for you when covering eyewitness testimony.

> **STUDY HINT**
> The key question in this chapter relating to criminological psychology is about the unreliability of eyewitness testimony — you can use both Loftus and Palmer (1974) and Valentine and Mesout (2009) when discussing that key question.

> **STUDY HINT**
> In clinical psychology, you may have chosen to use Vallentine et al. (2010) as an example of an interview (see Chapter Two). Just be careful with the spellings in Vallentine et al. (2010) and Valentine and Mesout (2009) as they are different. Making a list of studies for your course and giving a very brief outline of what they are about can help to avoid any confusion.

Valentine and Mesout (2009) carried their study out in London. They see as important the lack of validity in eyewitness experiments with regard to replicating the stress of the eyewitness in a situation where they might be called upon to give evidence. One weakness of Loftus and Palmer's (1974) study was said to be its lack of ecological validity because the films of the accidents were unlikely to replicate the stress involved in watching a 'real' accident. This is Valentine and Mesout's point about the use of experiments to study eyewitness identification.

> **STUDY HINT**
> In the methods part of criminological psychology in your course, you need to look at laboratory experiments for studying eyewitness memory. You can use Valentine and Mesout's study and their criticism of lab experiments as not having validity when commenting on the use of lab experiments as a research method.

Valentine and Mesout chose to study the ability of visitors to describe and identify someone they met in the Horror Labyrinth in the London Dungeon. They wanted to look at the ability to identify someone taking into account state anxiety, which was measured using a heart rate monitor. High heart rate was taken as showing high state anxiety. Afterwards visitors were asked questions to measure their state and their trait anxiety. They found that high state anxiety meant giving fewer correct descriptors of the person, giving more incorrect details and making fewer correct identifications from a line-up. They found that trait anxiety did not affect eyewitness memory. Trait and state anxiety are defined later (page 340).

> ## Explore
> You can access Valentine and Mesout's (2009) report using this link: www.valentinemoore.co.uk/trv/londondungeon.pdf

Background

Valentine and Mesout (2009) start by showing the practical focus of their study because it was about fairness in the criminal justice system. They cite Scheck *et al.* (2000) as saying that 'wrongful' convictions happen in both the UK and the USA. They said that 215 people were shown to have been wrongfully convicted when DNA analysis became possible. In 75 per cent of such cases, it was mistaken eyewitness identification that led to the wrong conviction (these figures were correct at the time of their study, in 2009).

> ## Explore
> Valentine and Mesout (2009) use the Innocence Project to get figures about wrongful conviction due to eyewitness identification. You can access the website of the Innocence Project and find out more using this link: www.innocenceproject.org/causes-wrongful-conviction/eyewitness-misidentification

Valentine and Mesout explain how, without looking at stress in an 'eyewitness' situation, the processes that might affect eyewitness testimony cannot adequately be studied. They appreciate that putting participants into a stressful situation such as would be experienced by a victim of crime is not ethical. However, they emphasise that it is important to look at the effects of stress on eyewitness identification.

Arousal was discussed when Eysenck's personality theory was looked at as a biological explanation of crime and anti-social behaviour (page 210). Valentine and Mesout also consider arousal because they want to look at the effects of stress on memory. Arousal affects performance and arousal refers to the alarm reaction that is the sympathetic nervous system preparing the body for action. Preparation affects the body, such as giving a dry mouth and a raised breathing and heart rate. There is a theory of arousal that says that performance is improved by being in a state of arousal, because of this preparation of the body. However, as arousal continues, the body runs out of energy in a way and heightened arousal cannot be continued, with the result that performance then drops off. This means some arousal improves performance but performance gets worse again as arousal of the body continues. Valentine and Mesout (2009) suggest that arousal improves memory performance just as it improves other types of performance but that, as arousal continues, memory performance reaches an optimum level and then starts to fall again. This is the U-shaped curve and is explained by the Yerkes-Dodson law.

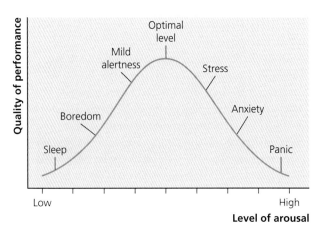

The Yerkes-Dodson law (1908) suggests that some arousal can help performance. However, too much means performance levels fall off.

However, Valentine and Mesout (2009) cite Christianson (1992) as suggesting that memory for 'central details' is improved by arousal – it is peripheral detail that is impaired by stress. Whether you use the Yerkes-Dodson explanation for how stress affects arousal or Christianson's explanation, you can see that stress affects performance and is likely to affect memory, which includes eyewitness memory.

Yuille and Cutshall (1986) carried out a field study where they looked at a real-life crime and went back to witnesses some time after the event to study their eyewitness memory. They found that people who experienced stress in the situation recalled more of the event, which supports the idea that arousal can help memory. However, Yuille *et al.* (1994) found that how much someone was involved in an incident affected their eyewitness recall, which shows a confounding variable. Valentine and Mesout list studies that have looked at involvement in an incident and recall (see Table 3.32).

Table 3.32 Studies in Valentine and Mesout (2009) that relate to involvement in an incident and eyewitness recall

Study	What was found
Yuille *et al.* (1994)	Police trainees who took part in a stressful stop-and-search scenario had better eyewitness recall than trainees who took part in a less stressful scenario. Stress affected recall.
Hulse and Memon (2006)	Police firearms officers in a 'shoot' scenario where they fired a weapon did not show differences in recall compared with those in a 'no shoot' condition. Opening fire or not opening fire did not affect recall. This was the only study cited where the more stressful condition did not seem to affect recall.
Stanny and Johnson (2000)	In a repeated measures design, witnesses who showed arousal (physiological) during a 'shoot' scenario showed less recall than when they were in a 'no shoot' scenario. Both police and civilians were used as participants, both showing less recall in the more stressful situation. Stress affected recall.
Ihlebaek *et al.* (2003)	Witnesses seeing a realistic live but staged bank robbery recalled fewer details than witnesses who watched the same simulation on video. Stress affected recall.
Peters (1988)	Participants received an injection. Their eyewitness identification of the nurse giving the injection was not as good as their identification of a researcher, even though they interacted with the researcher for a similar length of time after the injection as they interacted with the nurse. The more they showed physiological arousal while awaiting the injection the stronger the effect with regard to identifying the nurse. Stress affected recall.
Morgan *et al.* (2004)	Soldiers were kept in a mock prisoner of war camp for 12 hours. They then either had a high-stress interrogation that included physical confrontation followed by a low-stress interrogation with no physical confrontation, or vice versa. The design was counterbalanced. Soldiers did not identify their interrogator in the high-stress condition as well as they did in the low-stress condition. Stress affected recall.

Progress check 3.105

Using three studies, explain evidence that stress affects eyewitness recall.

In this chapter, arousal refers to the sympathetic nervous system's preparation of the body for action, such as increasing heart and breathing rate. However, with regard to neural control systems controlling our responses to what is happening in the environment it is said that we have two such control systems. There is the **arousal mode** of attention control and the **activation mode** of attention regulation. The arousal model directs attention to what is most interesting and informative in the situation and, in physiological terms, this means lowering blood pressure and heart rate. This is done in order to remain wakeful and responsive. This is a different use of the term 'arousal' from the one used to describe the fight/ flight response. Then there is the activation mode, which is the stress response to a situation. When a situation increases **cognitive anxiety** (worry) and **somatic anxiety** (physical) then the fight-or-flight mode is activated and, in this explanation, this mode is called the 'activation mode'. Valentine and Mesout use Deffenbacher *et al.*'s (2004) distinction between the activation way of controlling attention, which is the increased heart rate, blood pressure and muscle tone referred to as arousal earlier in the chapter, and the arousal way of controlling attention, which decreases the heart rate, blood pressure and muscle tone; attention control is about paying attention only, not preparing the body for fight or flight. The activation mode versus the arousal mode way of explaining control over our attention to environmental situations is an explanation for eyewitness attention. In the activation mode, memory is enhanced in general, whereas in the arousal mode memory for central aspects of the situation is enhanced. It is as if the arousal mode is increasing our attention in a helpful and purposeful way with regard to decision-making and the activation mode moves more into panic. A main point is that there is a **catastrophic** drop in attention when the situation is very stressful.

Explanations

Activation mode is the stress response to things in the environment when there is cognitive and somatic anxiety and the activation mode brings increased blood pressure and heart rate. **Arousal mode** is the vigilance response where there is wakefulness and alertness but, without a threat in the environment, there is lowered blood pressure, heart rate and muscle tone.

Cognitive anxiety is worry about a situation. **Somatic anxiety** is the physiological response, such as sweating and increased breathing rate. **Somatic** refers to physiology and physical explanations – think of 'soma' as 'body'.

The **catastrophe model** of stress goes against the Yerkes-Dodson law, which states that performance rises with some arousal/stress but falls as arousal is maintained. The catastrophe model suggests that performance rises with arousal coming from cognitive anxiety without too much somatic anxiety, but with rising cognitive and somatic anxiety, performance starts to fall. Importantly, if there is a rise then in somatic anxiety, with cognitive anxiety remaining high, that brings a sudden (**catastrophic**) drop in performance. Then if arousal drops, performance can lift again, but not back to its original level.

STUDY HINT
You need to separate ideas about arousal that we looked at when considering Eysenck's personality explanation of crime and anti-social behaviour and those that refer to the body's preparedness for fight or flight from the arousal and activation mode of attention control that are used to explain eyewitness unreliability. It is as if the activation mode is the 'arousal' response in the usual use of the term, so be sure to make a note to avoid any possible confusion.

Valentine and Mesout refer to **trait anxiety** and **state anxiety**. Trait anxiety comes from someone's character and varies from individual to individual. It refers to what will cause anxiety in one particular person, perhaps because of their coping strategies, and is about their 'traits' that link, for them, to anxiety. State anxiety comes from emotional responses to threatening situations and refers to the 'state' someone is in because of anxiety.

Explanation

Trait anxiety refers to someone's traits or characteristics that lead to anxiety or the management of anxiety. This is about individual differences. **State anxiety** refers to the emotional response to stressors and is the physical arousal from stress; it can affect mental processing as well as physical responses.

Moving away from Valentine and Mesout

Previous studies show greater stress affects eyewitness recall

Although this is not all in Valentine and Mesout (2009)'s introduction, it might help here to give some evidence for this catastrophic drop in attention when there is a highly stressful situation – this evidence fits with the **catastrophe model** of stress. Table 3.33 gives some studies and their findings. Valentine and Mesout in fact use these studies in their discussion section to show how their own results support the findings of these studies.

Table 3.33 Evidence that attention drops sharply when a situation is very stressful

Study	Evidence that eyewitness success drops sharply in response to high-stress situations
Bothwell *et al.* (1987)	There was 68 per cent correct identification compared with 32 per cent in the high-stress condition.
Peters (1988)	There was 66 per cent correct identification compared with 41 per cent in the high-stress condition.
Morgan *et al.* (2004)	There was a fall from 62 per cent hit rate to 27 per cent hit rate.
Valentine and Mesout (2009)	Low anxiety people had a 75 per cent hit rate using a photo line-up compared with 18 per cent hit rate for a highly anxious person.

Deffenbacher *et al.*'s (2004) meta-analysis of the impact of stress on memory found low differences between high- and low-stress conditions when looking at both correct identifications and accuracy of recall of details. Differences were found more in a condition when the target person was in the line-up than when they were not, and differences were found more for eyewitness recognition than for face recognition. Also there was a larger effect size when a staged crime was used to induce stress compared with another way of 'stressing' someone. The negative effects of stress were more apparent in people with higher anxiety, neuroticism and greater vulnerability to stress, for example.

The effect of the time interval before recall

Deffenbacher *et al.* (2008) is another meta-analysis, this time looking at the effect of a time gap between an incident and recall. Previous studies had found that the longer the time the memory was retained before recall the more the negative effect on memory. For example, Deffenbacher (1986), also a meta-analysis, found that as retention interval increased, forgetting also increased. Shapiro and Penrod (1986), a meta-analysis, also found the retention interval length affected eyewitness recall. Deffenbacher *et al.* (2008) found that longer retention intervals mean worse memory for a once-seen face ($p < .005$).

> **STUDY HINT**
>
> In this account of Valentine and Mesout's (2009) study, some additional information has been given. This is partly to help with understanding Valentine and Mesout's study and partly because in the content part of criminological psychology in your course you need to know about factors affecting the reliability of eyewitness memory, so this information will be useful there, as well as when considering the key question about the unreliability of eyewitness testimony.

Aims

The main aim of Valentine and Mesout (2009) was to look at the idea taken from the catastrophe model, which is that performance rises with some arousal but then, if both cognitive and somatic anxiety remain high, there can be a 'catastrophic' drop in performance. Valentine and Mesout (2009) set up a situation that gave physical threat but was an everyday life occurrence, with the aim of looking at cognitive anxiety from the situation and effects on eyewitness identification. This was so they could see the effects of a threatening situation on eyewitness identification.

As part of their study, they wanted to validate the State Anxiety Inventory (SAI) as a measure of state anxiety so they used some participants to go through the conditions of the eyewitness part of the study, including meeting the

'scary person' and at the same time having their heart rate monitored. Then, after the whole experience, the researchers correlated the heart rate with the self-report state anxiety measure to make sure the self-reported state anxiety was a valid measure. This part of the study is called the 'validation of the SAI' part of the study and the main procedure is called the 'eyewitness' part of the study. This part of the study can also show that the situation in the Dungeon is scary, so it validates the claim that the scenario is stressful.

Method

Measures

- State and trait anxiety were measured using self-report data and also heart rate was measured to validate the self-report data regarding state anxiety. The self-report measure of anxiety used the Spielberger (1983) State-Trait Anxiety Inventory. The State Anxiety Inventory (SAI) had 20 items, such as 'I was tense' and 'I felt frightened'. The Trait Anxiety Inventory (TAI) had 20 statements such as 'I feel inadequate'. Both the SAI and the TAI used a four-point scale for each item. The TAI was only used in the 'eyewitness' part of the study. The SAI and the heart rate measure were used in the 'validation of the SAI' part of the study.
- A questionnaire was used to measure free recall and cued recall of the 'scary person', who is described later in this section.
- The line-up consisted of a photographic line-up using nine people, including the actor in the study. The others in the photo line-up were similar in appearance, age and ethnic origin, and in gender, to the 'scary person' and wore the same make-up etc.
- The dependent variable was the recall of the appearance of an actor and also the identification of the actor from a 'culprit-present' line-up. They used the 'culprit-present' description to say that the actor would be in the line-up as some studies test eyewitness identification using a line-up without the 'culprit' present.
- Recall of the appearance was measured using self-report data. There was also a questionnaire
- They used a correlation design as they did not have a non-stressful condition as a control.

Year One link: Recall what you learned about correlation design in biological psychology.

Participants

- For the 'validation of the SAI' part of the study, 20 participants, all employees of a London department store, were used. Two people had a different baseline heart rate from the sample so their data were not included. There were ten women and eight men in the sample, with an average age of 26.1 years, and age range of 18–48 years.

- For the 'eyewitness' part of the study, 56 people volunteered to complete questionnaires after their visit to the London Dungeon in return for a reduced admission price. There were 29 women and 27 men, with a mean age of 31.0 years, and an age range of 18–54 years.

Materials

In the tour of the London Dungeon, the Horror Labyrinth is the first exhibit and it consists of floor to ceiling mirrored walls giving a maze within Gothic vaults. Visitors go around the maze in groups of 30 people and the aim is to disorientate people. It is dark and crowded and there is the sound of a heart beat 'playing', as well as screams and scary noises. There are some separate 'scares' too. A screaming skeleton can be triggered when someone trips an infra-red beam and an old woman sitting in a rocking chair is seen behind a mirror.

For the study, an actor dressed in a dark robe with theatrical make-up giving a pale face and scars is the 'scary person'. The actor stepped out in front of a participant and blocked their path.

The London Dungeon, the setting of Valentine and Mesout's (2009) study

The actor varied on each day and there were 50 actors used, most of them playing the 'scary person' on different occasions.

Design

Validation of the SAI part of the study

Heart rate was measured when participants walked slowly to get an average baseline heart rate for each person. Then their average heart rate was recorded while they were in the labyrinth, also walking slowly, and they encountered the 'scary person'. After the labyrinth visit, how the participant felt was recorded using the SAI and self-report data. The researchers correlated the two average heart rates with the SAI scores to measure change in heart rate after the visit to the labyrinth and to validate the SAI as a measure of state anxiety. These were the 18 participants in the 'validation of the SAI' condition. The purpose of this part of the study was to validate the use of the SAI as a measure of state anxiety. If heart rate change correlated with self-reported state anxiety, that validated the scale.

'Eyewitness' part of the study

The dependent variables measured were the number of correct descriptors of the 'scary person' recalled, the number of incorrectly reported descriptors and the identification of the person in the photo line-up (or not). The independent variables were gender, state anxiety score in the labyrinth and trait anxiety score. The median SAI score was used to split people up into 'high anxiety' and 'low anxiety' groups so that there could be analysis between high and low anxiety and identification from the photo line-up or not.

Progress check 3.106

When analysing high and low anxiety in relation to identification of the person in the photo line-up or no identification, explain which inferential test would be suitable.

STUDY HINT

Recall what a median of a set of scores is and what role it can play. The median is the middle in a set of scores. It seems that Valentine and Mesout took scores below the median to be low anxiety and scores above the median to be high anxiety. You could consider the evaluation point that scores close to the median perhaps should not have been included in the groups as they represent 'middle anxiety'. This sort of analysis of a study can help with understanding it.

Progress check 3.107

Give two dependent variables in Valentine and Mesout's (2009) study and two independent variables.

Procedure

'Validation of SAI' part of the study

The 'validation of the SAI' part of the study involved getting informed consent from participants and then a wireless heart monitor was used to record first the baseline heart rate at slow walking pace (walking for seven minutes) and then heart rate in the labyrinth again at slow walking pace (again walking for seven minutes). The heart rate in the labyrinth involved meeting the 'scary person'. The participant then completed the tour and around 45 minutes after leaving the labyrinth the participants completed the SAI. They circled their response to the question: 'How did you feel when you were in the labyrinth?'.

'Eyewitness' part of the study

The 'eyewitness' part of the study involved participants agreeing to complete some questionnaires at the end of the study in return for the reduced admission charge but informed consent was not obtained. The procedure for the 'eyewitness' participants was the same as for the 'validation of the SAI' participants and it was at around 45 minutes after the meeting in the labyrinth that informed consent was obtained and the purpose of the experiment was explained to the participants. Each participant was also told at this point that they could withdraw from the study at any time and did not need to give a reason for doing so. Then these participants completed the SAI, as with the participants in the other condition, being asked to circle their response to the question: 'How did you feel when you were in the labyrinth?'. Then these participants completed the Trait Anxiety Inventory (TAI) being asked to circle their response to: 'How do you feel generally?'. After that they did the questionnaire about their memory of the 'scary person' and they then responded to cues to get recall, such as the person's gender, age, height and hair colour. Participants were asked not to make guesses about what they recalled. Finally, these participants looked at the photo line-up showing nine people with the 'scary person's' photo being placed randomly amongst the other pictures each time. The participants said 'yes' or 'no' to the person being in the line-up and then rated their response from 1 to 100 per cent for confidence.

Results

'Validation of SAI' part of the study

In the 'validation of the SAI' part of the study, the mean baseline heart rate of the 18 participants was 74.7 beats per minute (bpm) and their mean heart rate in the labyrinth was 86.9bpm, which was significantly higher when in the labyrinth (p<.001). Their mean state anxiety score (on the SAI) was 43.2. A correlation test was carried out and the baseline mean heart rate showed a significant association with the SAI score (p<.001). This suggests that the SAI was a valid measure of stress response.

'Eyewitness' part of the study

State and trait anxiety scores

In the 'eyewitness' part of the study, the mean state anxiety score was 49.0.

It was found that:
- females (52.8 mean score) had a higher state anxiety score than males (45.3 mean score) (p<.01)
- there was no gender difference in trait anxiety, however, and the mean trait anxiety score was 36.8.

Free recall and cued recall descriptors of the 'scary person'

With regard to free and cued recall of the 'scary person', the two scores were divided into noun and adjective phrases and put into one score. The descriptors were judged as correct or not correct by two judges by comparing what was recalled about the scary person and what they were actually wearing and what they looked like. The judges had each actor's age, height, weight, hair colour and eye colour as well as a photograph to help in judgement of facial features. There was some leeway given, such as height was taken to be correct if within two inches and age within two years. If a statement used 'might' it was not accepted as correct. The decisions of the two judges who worked independently matched for 94 per cent of the items, which was taken to show inter-judge reliability.

It was found that:
- participants rating themselves as having lower state anxiety recalled significantly more descriptors than other participants (p<.001). The lower the state anxiety, the higher the number of descriptors recalled, as shown in Table 3.34. There was higher state anxiety reported by females than by males (p<.005).

Table 3.34 Correlation scores between the number of correct descriptors and other variables – gender, state anxiety and trait anxiety

Variables	Number of correct descriptors	Gender	State anxiety score	Trait anxiety score
Number of correct descriptors	1.00	−.08	−.41**	−.11
Gender		1.00	.36*	.08
State anxiety score			1.00	.09
Trait anxiety score				1.00
Means	6.25	1.48	49.0	36.8
Standard deviations	3.01	0.50	10.5	6.54

*p<.005 **p<.001

Valentine and Mesout also compared the number of incorrect descriptors with the variables gender, state and trait anxiety and found similar findings to when recall was scored and analysed using the same variables.

It was found that:

- people who reported higher state anxiety reported more incorrect details (p<.001).

Identification from the photo line-up

With regard to identification from the photos, the accuracy or inaccuracy of this identification was tested against gender, state anxiety and trait anxiety.

It was found that:

- state anxiety did affect the identification of the 'scary person' in the array of photos (p<.005)
- there was nearly an effect of gender on the identification of the 'scary person' but it was not quite significant (p<.059).

Progress check 3.108

Explain what Valentine and Mesout (2009) meant when they said that there was *nearly* a gender difference in whether the 'scary person' was identified in the photo array or not but the difference was not quite significant.

Year One link: Recall what you have learned about levels of significance in cognitive psychology as well as in other topic areas, so that you understand what is meant by p<.01, and so on, in Valentine and Mesout (2009).

High state anxiety category and low state anxiety category and identification in the line-up

In order to analyse state anxiety more, each person was allocated a label of high or low state anxiety using the median state anxiety score to split the participants into the two groups. The other category to be tested was whether there was correct or incorrect identification, but the 'incorrect' category had very few people in it so in order to carry out the analysis the 'incorrect' category became an 'inaccurate' category and included people picking out the wrong person from the photos as well as just those saying the person was not in the line-up.

It was found that:

- participants who reported high state anxiety were less likely to be correct in identifying the 'scary person' in the photo 'line-up' (χ2 = 12.95, p<.001)

- males made more correct identifications than females (χ2 = 8.81, p<.005).

Table 3.35 Two-by-two table for low and high state anxiety and accurate or inaccurate identification. Inaccurate identification is split into identifying a wrong photo or not identifying a photo at all.

Categories	Low state anxiety	High state anxiety	Total
Identification of the 'scary person'	21	5	26
Identification of one of the other photos	6	15	21
No identification made	1	8	9
Total	28	28	56

Progress check 3.109

Carry out a Chi squared test using the information in Table 3.35. To do the test, put together the incorrect answers as one score ('identification of one of the other photos' and 'no identification made' should be put into one score). Show the working.

You can see by looking at Table 3.35 that the scores seem significantly different.

> **STUDY HINT**
> It is good practice to use sense checking when you read results tables so that you can see whether results are likely to be statistically significant or not. You can be asked to use sense checking in an exam question.

Rating of confidence about identification attempt

It was found that:

- accuracy of identification from the line-up was associated with confidence rated before the identification took place (p<.001)
- accuracy of identification from the line-up was associated with confidence rated after the identification took place as well (p<.001).

Conclusions

- The labyrinth at the London Dungeon was a scary experience and did raise heart rate in the validation group as well as raising state anxiety scores in that group.

- Women reported higher state anxiety in the labyrinth than men so there is a gender difference.
- There was a negative relationship in that the higher someone's anxiety, the less they reported appearance accurately when a situation was stressful.
- The higher the state anxiety, the more incorrect descriptors were included. Alternatively, higher state anxiety led to more 'might have' answers, which were judged to be incorrect.
- High state anxiety strongly affected eyewitness identification: 17 per cent of those above the median on state anxiety correctly identified the 'scary person' in the photos compared with 75 per cent of those scoring in the lower part of the state anxiety scale. This finding agrees with other studies showing impaired eyewitness identification under stressful conditions (see Table 3.32).
- Confidence about ability to identify the 'scary person' was associated with that ability, both confidence before the identification and confidence afterwards, suggesting people know what they know.
- Eyewitness identification under stressful conditions is less accurate in females than in males, which can have implications when using eyewitness identification in the criminal justice system.
- Someone's judgement of their state anxiety is good and correlates with their heart rate measure.
- There might be a problem in results from laboratory experiments if the element of stress is not involved in the study and it is likely that the potential for error in eyewitness identification is much more than lab studies suggest.

Evaluation of Valentine and Mesout (2009)

Strengths

- Their study was naturalistic and had ecological validity. They used people who were going to visit the London Dungeon in any case and were going to go to the labyrinth. Mostly the people simply did the tour as they would have done, with just the change that a cloaked and scarily made up 'scary person' stepped out in front of them and stood in their way. Valentine and Mesout (2009) deliberately planned a study that was not a laboratory experiment because they wanted to test the effect of state anxiety on people's eyewitness identification. Their study was more natural and, therefore, had more valid findings than laboratory studies.
- The study used 56 participants from the general public with quite a large age range and using both males and females, so there should be reasonable generalisability. The participants selected themselves by being amongst

the visitors to the London Dungeon at the specific time and by agreeing to complete questionnaires after their visit. Therefore, there might be differences between them and 'general' eyewitnesses. However, that is not thought to be likely. If anything, by choosing to go somewhere scary participants would be less likely to show anxiety and they had the confidence to agree to do the questionnaires, so if they are seen to have high state anxiety, that suggests the sample could be generalised from.
- Two judges rated the descriptors as accurate or not and did the rating separately. There was a very high level of agreement between them. This suggests that the number of accurate and inaccurate descriptors recorded for each individual were likely to be reliable.
- The findings have a practical application. Not only is it useful to know that people in a high state of anxiety are likely to have their recall affected and their ability to identify a 'culprit', but also it is useful to know that this applies in particular to female eyewitnesses.

Weaknesses

- Possibly there were some issues with the ethics of the study because, although one set of participants gave informed consent, the others did not. They consented to complete the questionnaires at the end of their tour and they agreed to be in the study. However, the researchers could not inform them fully about what was to take place as the 'scary person' encounter had to be a surprise. Valentine and Mesout got informed consent from the participants as soon as they could and explained their right to withdraw, so the study does adhere to ethical guidelines; however, there could be said to be some ethical issues. Another ethical point is that the participants were put into a situation which was, for some, highly stressful.

> **STUDY HINT**
> You have to cover ethical issues in the method part of criminological psychology in your course and you can use Valentine and Mesout's study to explain some of the ethical principles, such as giving the right to withdraw and getting informed consent from participants.

- There are some aspects of the scoring that might have affected the results. For example, as Valentine and Mesout (2009) explain, by counting as 'incorrect' any descriptor statement that made a suggestion rather than a definite claim (such as 'might have had dark hair') the results would perhaps come out as more 'incorrect' than if the tentative descriptor, if reasonably accurate, had been taken as 'correct'.

Related to the weakness just explained, it is important to note that Valentine and Mesout collected some qualitative data in the form of descriptions of the 'scary person' and then changed them into quantitative data by using categories. This can help with analysis of the data so can be a strength. However, it can mean that detail and depth are missed from the data, which reduces them somewhat.

Progress check 3.110

Explain reliability and validity issues in Valentine and Mesout (2009).

Howells *et al.* (2005)

Howells *et al.* (2005) carried out a study looking at treating offenders. The other three studies in this section have covered either eyewitness memory or juror decision-making so they are all looking at factors that affect conviction of offenders. Howells *et al.* (2005) focus on treatment of offenders and the study fits into the content part of your course where two treatments must be covered. One of the two treatments must be a cognitive-behavioural treatment and one must be a biological treatment. Importantly, for each treatment you need to cover a study of its effectiveness. Anger management programmes draw on cognitive-behavioural principles and so can be used as the cognitive-behavioural treatment, and Howells *et al.* (2005) look at the effectiveness of brief anger management programmes so you can use this study both as the contemporary study in criminological psychology and as the study looking at the effectiveness of a cognitive-behavioural treatment.

Howells *et al.* (2005) look at brief anger management programmes with offenders. They say such programmes are a common form of rehabilitation, especially for violent offenders. They say there is a need for information about the effectiveness of anger management for serious offenders. They carried out an intervention study using offenders and then compared them with controls on a waiting list for the programme. They found no statistically significant differences between the experimental and control conditions and any changes found were small.

Background

Howells *et al.* (2005) emphasise how cognitive-behavioural treatments are 'the method of choice' when aiming to reduce offenders' recidivism and reconviction using psychological interventions (e.g. McGuire, 2002, cited in Howells *et al.*, 2005). The focus is on what it is about a programme that is likely to lead to success and which characteristics of a programme are likely to mean no effect. Howells and Day (2002, cited in Howells *et al.*, 2005) point to violent offenders being an important group for rehabilitation programmes.

Howells *et al.* (2005) say that aggression and violent crime in fact need not include anger – for example, psychopaths may not act because of anger. Also anger does not lead to violence all the time, in fact not that often, so anger is seen as contributing to violent crime rather than being the cause of it. Spielberger (1991, cited in Howells *et al.*, 2005) found, however, that on average prisoners do have higher anger scores than would be found in the community. Also violent offenders have higher anger scores than non-violent offenders. So anger relates to offending and relates to violence, though not always, and there are other variables too. Anger seems to be a common emotion in institutions, such as shown by the results of Cornell *et al.* (1999, cited in Howells *et al.*, 2005), who looked at adolescent offenders and found that anger predicted aggression. Zamble and Porporino (1990, cited in Howells *et al.*, 2005) found the frequency of anger increased the longer someone was in prison as well. All this evidence suggests that treatment focusing on anger can be useful for offenders.

According to Howells *et al.* (2005), anger management seems to be one of the most usual rehabilitation programmes for offenders. This means there needs to be evidence that anger management reduces anger and related behaviours. Studies seem to show the effectiveness of anger management, such as Deffenbacher *et al.* (2002, cited in Howells *et al.*, 2005). There are meta-analyses that suggest anger management is effective, such as Sukhodolsky *et al.* (2004, cited in Howells *et al.*, 2005). Howells *et al.* (2005) cite a meta-analysis by DiGiuseppe and Tafrate (2003), which looked at 57 studies and focused on two different types of effectiveness. DiGuiseppe and Tafrate (2003) found that **absolute efficacy** is about whether anger management is better than doing nothing and that **relative efficacy** is about whether anger management is better than other possible treatments or programmes. Howells *et al.* (2005) add **component efficacy**, which refers to which part of anger management intervention is the most effective.

Explanations

Absolute efficacy, when it comes to assessing the effectiveness of a treatment, looks at whether the treatment is better than nothing. **Relative efficacy,** when it comes to assessing the effectiveness of a treatment, looks at whether it is better than other possible treatments. **Component efficacy,** when it comes to assessing the effectiveness of a treatment, looks at which part of a treatment is the most effective.

DiGiuseppe and Tafrate's (2003) meta-analysis, according to Howells *et al.* (2005), does provide evidence that anger management shows absolute efficacy and is better than nothing. However, showing that anger management has relative efficacy, meaning it is better than other possible treatments, is harder. They showed there was some component efficacy, in that the relaxation training, the cognitive therapy and the desensitisation parts of an anger management programme were effective.

Progress check 3.111

What is meant by 'meta-analysis'?

An issue in looking at the effectiveness of anger management is that violent offenders only form part of the people having treatment. To look at the effectiveness of anger management for violent offenders would mean having them as the group being studied. Andrews and Bonta (2003, cited in Howells et al., 2005) suggest that programmes should target offenders who seem to have a high likelihood of re-offending and a high need for intervention, and only few anger management programmes that have been evaluated have been targeted at high-risk offenders. Howells et al. (2005) do report on some such studies. For example, Dowden et al. (1999) in Canada found that an anger management programme for high-risk offenders reduced recidivism in that group compared with untreated controls. The programme Dowden et al. (1999) evaluated involved an intensive 50 hours of treatment with a lot of what are seen as beneficial features in anger management programmes. On the other hand, Watt and Howells (1999) (page 263), reported in Howells et al. (2005), did not find an anger management programme to be effective when used with prisoners in Australia.

Howells et al. (2005) cite Howells and Day (1999), saying that a problem with anger management programmes is poor engagement with them and think that this might be down to not having been ready for the treatment. By 'ready' they mean that offenders tend to have characteristics that make them 'unready' for treatment and which are likely to stop them engaging in a treatment and also to prevent change. Howells et al. (2005) end their background account by saying that there are not many studies looking at the effectiveness of anger management programmes with high-risk offenders, even though there is convincing evidence that anger management is effective in other populations. Howells et al.'s (2005) study concerns the evaluation of the absolute efficacy (which means asking 'is it better than nothing?') of brief anger management programmes for offenders.

> **STUDY HINT**
> It was said about anger management as a treatment when looked at in the content section that it was not that effective, so compare the studies there (page 261) with Howells et al. (2005) here.

> **Explore**
> You can access Howells et al. (2005) using this link:
> www.researchgate.net/publication/228367068_Brief_anger_management_programs_with_offenders_Outcomes_and_predictors_of_change

Feltham Prison in Middlesex, which opened as a remand centre in March 1988, is the sort of institution where anger management treatment can be used. Howells et al. (2005), however, is a study carried out in Australia.

Aim(s)

The aims of Howells et al. (2005) were:
- to see whether anger management is more effective in producing change than no treatment
- to see if pre-treatment offender characteristics can predict any improvement in treatment – in particular, this means looking at what level of need and readiness there is in offenders with regard to treatment.

Method

Participants

All the 418 participants were male, with a mean age of 28.8 years, who had been referred to anger management programmes in South and Western Australia. Of the participants, 86 per cent came from prison-based anger management programmes with others being community correction-based. They were all offenders, with sentences ranging from one month to 26 years and four months. Sixty-five per cent said they were from Australia or New Zealand, 19 per cent said they were Aboriginal or Torres Straight Islanders and 16 per cent said they were European, Asian or other. Over half called themselves single, and 73 per cent had not completed an anger management course before, 20 per cent had completed an anger management course, 4 per cent had completed more than one and 3 per cent had tried one but had not completed it.

With regard to violence, 14 per cent had committed a non-violent offence, 42 per cent had committed violence but without bodily harm, 30 per cent had committed violence with bodily harm, 8 per cent had committed grievous bodily harm and 6 per cent had committed injuries causing death. This meant that most of the referrals involved violent offenders and they were at high risk of re-offending as assessed using risk assessment measures.

The post-intervention assessment was completed by 285 of the 418 participants – this was the measure taken after the treatment; 78 of them completed the two-month follow-up and 21 completed the six-month follow-up. The small numbers at the follow-up sessions were kept small rather than the low numbers showing dropout from the study.

Progress check 3.112

Why did Howells *et al.* (2005) make the comment that they chose to use small numbers of participants in the follow-up parts of the study?

STUDY HINT

Longitudinal designs are covered in clinical psychology in your course, in Chapter Two, and are reviewed in the 'Psychological skills – methods' section online. They are studies done over a period of time. Studies looking at the effectiveness of therapies often use follow-up sessions to see if any effectiveness has been long-lasting, as you will have seen when covering clinical psychology. It is worth noting that follow-ups rarely continue after a year, which can be seen as a weakness in the design, because effectiveness is intended to be there for longer than a year.

Research design

Howells *et al.* (2005) were able to take control participants from those waiting for the intervention so there was no random allocation to the two groups. The intervention group, which had the treatment, completed measures before the treatment began, when it ended and then again two months and six months later, as follow-up measures. Control participants completed the measures at the same times and were offered the programme some weeks later.

The anger management programmes

The programme was based on a 'cognitive approach to behaviour change' (p. 300) and ran for ten two-hour sessions with trained facilitators carrying out the programmes with groups of offenders. The treatment was based on Novaco (1997) and the content of the programme included structured exercises looking at the

skills of identifying provoking situations, relaxation, assertion, prevention of relapse and restructuring.

Procedure

Self-report data were collected from both control and treatment group participants at the same time, which was before the treatment, after it, then two months afterwards and then six months afterwards. The data were collected with the participants in a group but giving their data individually, though when there were reading problems there was verbal administration of the measures. There was also a checklist of the programme that one facilitator and one randomly selected participant completed to check the content of each session of the programme. It was found that the content of the sessions matched the manual being followed. There were also data about the aggression of each participant, completed by two correctional officers for the prison participants and one staff member for participants on a community programme. The aggression data were collected using the Staff Rating Scale for Aggression (SOAS). Participants reported on their own behaviour too and databases were used to get data about incidents and charges for six months after the programme, recording their number and severity. These last data about incidents and charges showed these events were so infrequent that the data were not used in the analysis.

Measures

The self-report measures used were the Spielberger State-Trait Anger Expression Inventory (STAXI), which was used to measure state and trait anger, anger expression and anger control, and the Novaco Anger Scale (NAS-PI), which was used to measure anger intensity as well as how someone would react in certain situations. Spielberger (1991, cited in Howells *et al.*, 2005) has shown the reliability and validity of the STAXI and Novaco (1994, cited in Howells *et al.*, 2005) has shown the NAS to have test-retest reliability. Mills *et al.* (1998, cited in Howells *et al.*, 2005) found concurrent validity of the NAS as used in an adult prison.

Other measures were also used. The Modified Watt Anger Knowledge Scale (WAKS) measures understanding of how to deal with anger effectively and a 19-item version of the WAKS was used in this study before and after treatment for all participants and at the follow-up times for the treatment group. Another scale was used to measure verbal aggression, aggression against property, auto-aggression and physical aggression, which was the Modified Overt Aggression Scale (MOAS).

Howells *et al.* (2005) also wanted to measure treatment readiness. They used the Anger Stages of Change Questionnaire (SCQ), which measures motivation to change, including precontemplation (thinking about thinking of change), contemplation (thinking of change) and action. The other scale they used to measure treatment readiness was the Serin Treatment Readiness Scale (STRS), which uses 11 items, with participants choosing the most applicable response on a five-point scale. An interview is used with the STRS and it was administered before and after treatment with both groups.

Table 3.36 The six scales used to gather self-report data by Howells *et al.* (2005)

Scale	What it measured in the study	The purpose of the measure
The Spielberger State-Trait Anger Expression Inventory (STAXI)	Anger itself: Used to measure state and trait anger, anger expression and anger control	Measured type of and issues around anger before and after the treatment to look for effectiveness
The Novaco Anger Scale (NAS-PI)	Anger itself: Used to measure anger intensity as well as how someone would react in certain situations	Measured the strength of and triggers of anger before and after to look for effectiveness
The Modified Watt Anger Knowledge Scale (WAKS)	Knowing how to deal with anger: Used to measure understanding of how to deal with anger effectively	Measured change from the intervention with regards to understanding how to deal with anger
The Modified Overt Aggression Scale (MOAS)	Knowing how to deal with anger: Used to measure verbal aggression, aggression against property, auto-aggression and physical aggression	Measured change from the intervention regarding types of aggression
The Anger Stages of Change Questionnaire (SCQ)	Readiness for anger management: Used to measure motivation to change, including precontemplation (thinking about thinking of change), contemplation (thinking of change) and action	Measured how ready someone was for the treatment
The Serin Treatment Readiness Scale (STRS)	Readiness for anger management: Used to measure treatment readiness	Measured how ready someone was for the treatment

STUDY HINT

There are six scales used in Howells *et al.* (2005), all with initials to help to identify them. When you are remembering which scales are used in a study, it is useful to draw up a table, as in Table 3.36. You could also have a column for the independent and dependent variable being tested to help you remember the study itself.

Year One link: Howells *et al.* (2005) used scales in their study to measure variables such as anger and readiness for a programme before and after the treatment, in order to test its effectiveness. You learned about Likert-type scales in social psychology as well as the use of questionnaires and interviews.

Progress check 3.113

As well as the six scales used to gather self-report data, Howells *et al.* (2005) used the Staff Rating Scale for Aggression (SOAS). Explain the purpose of this scale in their study.

Results

Analysis involved looking at pre-treatment scores and post-treatment scores to look for differences between the treatment group and the control group. Some of the results are given in Table 3.37.

Table 3.37 Some of the means for the control and treatment groups and pre- and post-treatment, focusing on anger measures

Dependent variable (scale used)	Treatment (T) or control (C)	Pre-treatment mean	Post-treatment mean	Mean change
State anger (STAXI)	C	11.2	11.9	+0.7
	T	12.4	12.1	−0.3
Anger control (STAXI)	C	22.5	23.0	+0.5
	T	20.7	22.2	+1.5
Anger expression (STAXI)	C	26.3	23.4	−2.9
	T	28.6	24.2	−4.4
Cognitions (Novaco)	C	29.3	28.4	−0.9
	T	30.9	29.0	−1.9
Arousal (Novaco)	C	27.9	26.7	−1.1
	T	29.2	27.9	−1.4
Knowing about anger (WAKS)	C	9.08	10.03	+0.95
	T	8.55	10.35	+1.80
Action (SCQ)	C	2.31	3.12	+0.81
	T	2.80	4.32	+1.52
MOAS weekly score (knowing about anger)	C	1.12	1.09	−0.03
	T	0.95	0.52	−0.41

Howells *et al.* (2005) suggest that the data collected show a trend for improvements over time, with the treatment group showing 'slightly better improvement' (p. 302) on most outcomes. Analysis controlled for **social desirability** in the case of the Novaco scales, as is recommended.

Definition

Social desirability is a form of bias in results. It refers to how people might respond in a study according to what they think is socially desirable, which will affect the responses.

Analysis found that the improvements were not statistically significant, as Table 3.37 suggests when sense checking the data. The conclusion from these data had to be that the anger management programme had not been effective. It was interesting that changes in the treatment group were reflected in the waiting list group (the control group), such as 'knowing about anger' improving in both groups: the prisoners who undertook the anger management programme did improve their knowledge more than the control group prisoners (p<.05), but the control group prisoners did also improve their knowledge about anger.

Progress check 3.114

Suggest reasons for the prisoners in the control group improving their knowledge about anger (although not as much as those in the treatment group).

Changes in the two follow-ups

Howells *et al.* (2005) used the follow-up data to look for changes over time. In one analysis, they looked at pre-treatment, post-treatment and two-month follow-up scores and compared them. In another analysis, they looked at pre-treatment, post-treatment, two-month and six-month follow-up scores and compared them. They reported linear trends, which meant a score increased or decreased over the time period. They also reported trends that showed change overall even if a score dipped or peaked in the middle, such as a trend that showed an initial improvement and then a flattening of the improvement or the improvement being lost over time.

At the two-month follow-up, a linear trend was found for anger control, angry cognitions (thoughts), anger arousal, anger behaviour and total anger score (using the Novaco scale). This suggests that on these variables there were initial improvements and more improvement over time. These improvements did not continue at the six-month follow-up but by then just small numbers were involved, so any improvement might not have shown up. Trait anger was reduced over time from the pre-treatment score to the two-month follow-up score and then there was just a slight increase, which was seen as a flattening effect. In general, it was thought that any effect from the anger management programme continued up to the two-month follow-up but not really after that, though at six-months the gains seem to have at least been maintained. There is some suggestion that the six-month figures were not reliable due to the sampling and small numbers at that stage. Overall, at six months, there seemed to be a decreasing trend in any gains. There seems to be a consistent long-term improvement in anger knowledge; however, that improvement does fall over time.

Treatment readiness variables

It has been shown in this study that the anger management programme was not that effective. However, Howells *et al.* (2005) had thought that there might be individual differences that masked effectiveness of such programmes. They thought that this might be to do with how ready an individual was to undertake the programme.

Howells *et al.* (2005) noted that the pre-treatment and post-treatment scores did show differences. However, the change from one score to the other was found in both the control and the treatment participants. They felt that they should look at changes, not between the two groups, but in the group as a whole. They thought that those with the more negative symptoms at the 'pre-treatment' stage might show the most improvement over time regardless of whether they were on the programme or not. Results showed that anger arousal, anger knowledge, action (being ready for treatment) and the self-rated weekly MOAS score (knowing how to deal with anger) were the four variables where there were better gains for those who had poorer scores.

With regard to relating treatment readiness to change on the measures of anger after the treatment, there were significant negative correlations for the treatment group, showing the more readiness, the lower the measures after treatment. Anger control increased with increase in readiness score but not significantly. With regard to the control group, the more there was readiness the less the improvement in anger outcomes. Table 3.38 shows the significant correlations in the treatment group measuring readiness score against anger outcome variables. There were no significant changes in the control group. However, where there are significant changes in the treatment group, the control group scores are shown too for comparison.

Table 3.38 Correlations between the score on the Serin Readiness Scale and changes pre- and post-treatment in the anger measures

Change in outcome variable from pre- to post-treatment	Serin Readiness Scale (STRS)	
	Control group	Treatment group
STAXI:		
Change in state anger	−.01	0.16*
Change in trait anger	+.05	−.26***
Change in anger expression	+.26	−.25**
NAS		
Change in total score	+.21	−.26**
Change in provocations score	+.12	−.27**

* p<.05; **p<.01; ***p<.001

Progress check 3.115

What does it mean to say in Table 3.38 that the correlation between readiness score and change in anger expression is −.25**?

Howells *et al.* (2005) conclude that being ready to undergo treatment is a variable that affects the outcome of the treatment and that treatment is more effective for those ready for it. The correlations between readiness score and outcome scores are different between the treatment and control groups, showing the readiness has affected the treatment effectiveness. Readiness score has predictive validity only for those who did the programme so it is a good predictor of whether a programme is going to be effective.

Year One link: You looked at predictive, internal and ecological validity in cognitive psychology so you can review what you learned about these types of validity. The 'Psychological skills – methods' section (online) reviews method issues as well, including the different types of validity.

Conclusions

General conclusions focusing on anger reduction

- Howells et al. (2005) claim that the samples were large enough, even after some scores were not used because of non-completion, for the data to give reliable conclusions.
- They found that the overall effectiveness of anger management programmes is small.
- The treatment group did improve, though not significantly.
- The control group also improved a little, suggesting that completing the assessments was beneficial.
- A positive finding was that the treatment group improved their knowledge about anger, as did the control group, although not as much.
- One explanation for the improvement in anger knowledge is that the assessments themselves (e.g. WAKS) are informative, giving similar information to the treatment programme and control group.
- A conclusion is that anger management programmes are educational and that is what was successful. They are educational in giving knowledge about what anger is, what effects it has and perhaps how to make changes.
- It was hard to check for maintenance of improvements over time given by the programme as there were not many improvements. The knowledge of anger improvements did seem to last the six months of the study. At the two-month follow-up, improvements on general anger measures and angry thinking had continued, which again is encouraging. Howells et al. (2005) felt that some improvement had come from the programme and that had, to an extent, been long-term.

Participant characteristics that related to effectiveness of the programme

- It was thought that individual differences are important when considering treatment for offenders and it is useful to know which treatment might work with which group, as this is both cost-effective and treatment-effective.
- Findings suggested that being ready for anger management did affect the effectiveness of treatment for participants in the treatment group.
- Offenders in the treatment group who were motivated to change and were ready to focus on their anger issues showed more improvement on many of the anger measures than those not so ready.
- Those less motivated to change showed less improvement.

Overall conclusions

As Howells et al. (2005) did not find the expected result that anger management programmes are effective, they considered why their results did not match previous ones showing effectiveness. If a programme is low in effectiveness, this can be because of low motivation of the participants, complexity in the programme, lack of integrity in the programme or not enough chance to practise the skills covered in the programme (Watt and Howells, 1999, cited in Howells et al., 2005).

Howells et al. had shown that the programme integrity was high, as explained earlier. There was a checklist of the programme that one facilitator and one randomly selected participant completed to check the content of each session of the programme and this showed programme integrity.

They agreed with Watt and Howells in saying that low participant motivation might affect the success of a treatment programme because they found motivation was a factor in treatment success. Howells et al. (2005) felt that programme complexity and not enough chance to practise the skills might have been a problem in the programme they implemented. They thought that the programme might be too short for what was needed. They also thought that using high-risk offenders as participants might be a factor in the lack of success of the treatment, as they have 'multiple problems' (p. 308). Problems might include anti-social personality disorder, substance abuse issues, problems with verbal skills and lack of family support. These problems are alongside any anger problems and might affect the success of treatment that is purely anger-focused.

Motivational problems might come from pessimism of those in high-security settings and offender resentment and distrust. There are issues specific to offender populations and these might affect the effectiveness of anger management for these individuals. They may also have concerns about revealing their emotions in a high-security setting. Novaco (1997, cited in Howells et al., 2005) highlights 'the long histories of failure, institutionalisation, and social rejection that characterise such clients and which entrench their anger and aggression' (p. 309).

In Howells et al. (2005), the anger management offered did not seem to be as successful as other studies predicted using different clients. Howells et al. (2005) felt it was reasonable to account for the difference in results by pointing to different motivational issues and the issue of there being multiple problems in individuals. They felt anger management programmes should be more intensive for offenders, perhaps by making them longer and by focusing less on educational factors and more on therapeutic ones.

Evaluation

Strengths

- Howells *et al.* (2005) said themselves that they had a large sample and felt that this helped the reliability of their findings. Having a large sample helps to rule out individual differences and to generalise the findings to other offender groups.
- They checked the integrity of the programmes by ensuring that all the programmes covered the same material and were delivered in the same way so it was 'as if' one programme was delivered to all those in the treatment group. If programmes were different, their effectiveness could not be compared.
- Ethically there was strength in that Howells *et al.* (2005) ensured that the control group participants were not deprived of the treatment as they were on a waiting list.
- Howells *et al.* (2005) used more than one scale for each of the main measures, which were measuring anger, knowledge about anger and readiness of the participants. By using a lot of measures, data could be compared to check for reliability and validity.
- They found that readiness did predict success on an anger management programme and it was good to find predictive validity so that readiness measures could be used to assess which offenders may benefit from an anger management programme. This is a cost-effective way of offering treatment to offenders and also is effective for the individual.

Weaknesses

- Howells *et al.* (2005) relied mainly on questionnaire self-report data. It is not that self-report data are not reliable, but there are issues with questionnaires gathering self-report data. Novaco's scale has to be scored taking social desirability into account, for example, which raises issues about how far offenders feel able to reveal their anger issues or to admit to lack of knowledge, given their situation. Data may not have been valid. There were some data from staff about the offenders' aggression, which went some way to confirming the data, but not in the detail that was gathered by self-report and used in the study.

- There were relatively small numbers at the two follow-ups, which the researchers admitted affected their ability to draw conclusions about any long-term improvements.
- The control group participants tended to improve on the measures without the treatment to a very similar extent to the treatment group. It was thought that doing the assessments gave them information about anger so they were 'educated' about it in the same way as those in the treatment group. This suggests that doing assessments about anger issues might be a treatment in itself. On the other hand, the control group participants were awaiting treatment so might already have been tuned in to issues about anger and they might already have made a start on their anger issues. It may not have been that the programme was not effective, but that it was not effective when compared with a waiting list group focusing on some of the issues involved and doing the assessments. This was an issue with the design of the study.

Progress check 3.116

A weakness of Howells *et al.* (2005) is that the control group showed changes in anger issues that were similar to changes in the treatment group (when there were changes). Suggest a way of improving the study to avoid the issue of the control group, without the treatment, also showing improvements.

STUDY HINT

You will be asked to suggest improvements to studies, such as those you have learned about or ones given in an exam that you won't have seen before. It is a good idea to practise doing this for your main studies (the classic and contemporary studies) so you are ready to suggest improvements for unseen studies too.

Test yourself

With regard to one contemporary study in criminological psychology, to what extent is the method that was used suitable for the aim(s)? **(16 marks)**

Summary

- Loftus and Palmer (1974) carried out a laboratory experiment to look at the effects of words used in a question on eyewitness testimony.
- They found that using 'smashed' to describe a car accident led to a higher estimate of speed than using 'hit' or 'collided', for example.
- They also found that if someone was asked about cars 'smashing' into one other, a week later they were more likely to 'recall' broken glass in a scene, even if there was no broken glass.
- Bradbury and Williams (2013) were interested in what might affect juror decision-making, including the effect of having a higher percentage of white jurors when 'judging' a black defendant and the effect of having a higher percentage of Hispanic jurors when the defendant is black.
- Bradbury and Williams (2013) found an effect of juror race on conviction when the defendant is black, in particular when there is a higher percentage of white jurors, and less so when there is a higher percentage of Hispanic jurors.
- Another study that looked at eyewitness testimony is Valentine and Mesout (2009), who found that stress affects identification of someone, including picking them out from a photo 'line-up'.
- Valentine and Mesout (2009) found that state anxiety affected number of descriptors correctly recalled about a 'scary person' who was encountered in a scary situation, with stress leading to less accurate recall.
- Valentine and Mesout (2009) also found a gender difference in how stress affects recall, with females' testimony/memory being affected more by stress than males.
- Howells *et al.* (2005) focused on the effectiveness of an anger management programme with regard to high-risk offenders. They used self-report measures to look at anger issues, including score for state anger and for knowledge about anger, and they compared the scores before and after the treatment.
- Howells *et al.* (2005) found that the control group of waiting list offenders and the treatment group changed in the same way, so the anger management treatment in general did not have different outcomes from not receiving treatment.
- An important finding in Howells *et al.* (2005) is that readiness for anger management can affect how successful an anger management programme is and can predict its success. In practical terms, readiness could be measured and could be a factor in deciding which offenders might benefit from anger management.

Key question in criminological psychology

As with other topic areas, in criminological psychology you need to cover one key question that is of relevance to today's society. You must be able to use what you have studied in criminological psychology to explain the key question, using concepts, theories and research.

The two key questions suggested in the specification are:

- Is eyewitness testimony too unreliable to trust?
- Should jury bias lead to the abolishment of juries?

One of these is considered in the content part of this chapter and is also described in this section. The other key question, on jury bias, can be found on the accompanying website. However, you may choose any key question. Note you need to learn just one key question, but considering others can help your learning.

Is eyewitness testimony too unreliable to trust?

You have studied eyewitness testimony in various parts of this chapter, including the content section (page 272), method section (page 314) and studies section (pages 330 and 337). There is a lot of information you can use to address the question of whether eyewitness testimony is too unreliable to trust.

Describing the key question as a question for society

First, the key question is described to show why it is of interest to society. The reliability of eyewitness testimony is in doubt and this has implications for defendants. If someone is convicted of a crime on the basis of faulty eyewitness memory, then a key question for society is how to avoid such miscarriages of justice.

Two factors that affect eyewitness memory are post-event information, including the 'misinformation effect' and weapon focus. Other factors include the stress of the situation and the time interval between the experience and the recall. The issue is that people are convicted on the basis of eyewitness testimony and if that testimony is not accurate they will have been wrongly convicted.

When a witness is in court giving an account of what they witnessed, they have power given to them by the court proceedings because they are being asked questions formally, as if they have something to offer. Weight is in this way given to their testimony. If research in psychology shows that such testimony can be unreliable for a number of reasons, this might be enough for a society to decide that eyewitness testimony is too unreliable to trust.

One example is that of Kirk Bloodsworth, who in 1984 was convicted of rape and murder, the conviction resting mainly on five eyewitness accounts. After nine years in prison, he was found to be innocent because of DNA testing. The Innocence Project uses DNA to uncover such wrongful convictions. Since the 1990s, of the 239 convictions that were overturned because of DNA evidence, 73 per cent were based on eyewitness testimony (Arkowitz and Lilienfeld, 2009). This is about fairness and justice and not convicting someone when they are not guilty. Also this might mean the real perpetrator is not charged or convicted, which also has implications for society. What is important as well is that if an eyewitness is shown to have been incorrect in their identification and testimony, then the eyewitness is likely to find that very upsetting, also something to be avoided. Ronald Cotton was wrongfully convicted of rape after eyewitness misidentification by one of the victims and was subsequently shown to be innocent. The witness was very much affected by the event but also their incorrect testimony, and clearly Ronald Cotton was also a victim.

Eyewitnesses are seen as credible by a jury and make a deep impression on a jury, according to Tversky and Fisher. Eyewitness testimony can be unreliable, not because of perjury, but because of misremembering. In a trial, it might be a case of who to believe and eyewitnesses tend to be believed as if what they are saying is an exact replica of what happened. The court relies on eyewitnesses and it is part of the common-law system. The jury rely on eyewitness accounts and people rely on a jury's judgement. Clearly a very important key question for society is: 'Is eyewitness testimony too unreliable to trust?'

Explaining the key question using concepts, theories and/or research

Gieselman et al. (1986) pointed out that eyewitness accounts can be a leading cause for the miscarriage of justice (Sutherland and Hayne, 2001). An issue is that, in the time between the event witnessed and a trial, a witness will come across more information, such as from other witnesses, lawyers, the media or police, and this post-event information may well affect their testimony (Sutherland and Hayne, 2001).

Sutherland and Hayne (2001) show that there are different factors involved in post-event information and how eyewitness accounts of an event can be affected by it. They found that information that was central for the witness was less open to distortion from misleading post-event information than information that was peripheral. The issue here is that often an eyewitness is asked to report on peripheral aspects of a situation, features that they were not focusing on. Therefore, misleading post-event information is likely to be unreliable. If a situation is such that the event was central for the individual, then post-event information might have less effect and testimony should be more reliable.

Sutherland and Hayne also showed that recognition of information is more likely to be incorrect than recall of information. Free recall seemed to lead to more correct recall. This means that, in a line-up, whether a real-life one or a photo one, where recognition is being tested, post-event misinformation can affect testimony. If someone free recalls what they remember about a person rather than having them in a line-up, that would be more reliable, but identification of someone by an eyewitness is often seen as very reliable because they were actually there. So not only is identification possibly unreliable, but it is trusted, which adds to the difficulty when using eyewitness testimony to convict someone.

Post-event information is not always a bad thing. If it is accurate, it possibly aids recall, according to Sutherland and Hayne (2001). If it is neutral, it does less harm too. It is when it is misleading post-event information (misinformation) that it can lead to wrongful conviction because the testimony is unreliable.

Loftus and Palmer (1974) showed that a word in a question can change what people recall or think about an event. They found that 'smashed' when describing a car accident led to a false memory of broken glass, whereas 'hit' did not. They also found that people estimated a higher speed for a car when they were asked about when cars 'smashed' into one another than when they were asked about them 'hitting' each other. This is about using leading questions and it is known to sway eyewitness testimony. This is misleading information as well as leading information as there is no right verb for cars 'smashing' into one another, but the verb chosen affects the testimony.

Valentine and Mesout (2009) showed how people with higher levels of anxiety recalled fewer correct descriptors of a 'scary person' than those with lower levels of anxiety. They showed that stress at the time of the incident can negatively affect testimony, which is important for the reliability of eyewitness testimony. Someone anxious at the time might not record as many features as someone less anxious. In a crime situation, it is likely that there is stress for eyewitnesses so their testimony should be relied on perhaps less than if an eyewitness is less anxious, perhaps because they are less involved. This perhaps goes against the idea of the weight of evidence from a 'key witness'.

Areh (2010) found that females are more reliable eyewitnesses than males. Females were more accurate when describing people, in particular when describing victims. Males were more accurate in describing the event and were more confident about describing places. Males were more confident but they were less right; females were highly accurate when describing places. There were no gender differences in the quantity of details recalled. This has implications for the unreliability of eyewitness testimony. Perhaps male eyewitnesses are less reliable.

Another issue that focuses on eyewitness unreliability is the weapon focus effect. Loftus et al. (1987) showed that there is less likelihood that a perpetrator will be identified if there is a weapon in a situation than if there is a neutral object (such as a cheque). Many studies, as explained in a meta-analysis by Steblay (1992), suggest that there is a weapon effect in that a weapon in the scene affects eyewitness testimony. A number of these studies used college participants, but there were also studies using other participants, so results seem to be generalisable. Erickson et al. (2014) confirmed the weapon focus effect, particularly in participants identifying the offender in a target-absent line-up, which is a concern when accepting eyewitness identification of an offender. Erickson et al. found that it was more the novelty of having a weapon in a scene than that it was threatening. However, it was still shown that having a novel object in a scene held someone's attention to the detriment of them focusing on the culprit's face.

STUDY HINT
Information is given here as evidence for the unreliability of eyewitness testimony. If you are asked to 'evaluate' or 'assess' the unreliability of eyewitness testimony as a key question for society, answer in a logical and organised way, such as giving evidence for unreliability, then evaluating the evidence and, importantly, each time relating the evidence to witness unreliability, and, finally, drawing points together to form a conclusion.

Progress check 3.117

Is eyewitness testimony too unreliable to trust? Answer this question giving four pieces of evidence.

STUDY HINT
Another key question looking at whether jury bias should lead to trial by jury being abolished is examined on the website accompanying this book.

It is mainly in the Crown Court that jury trials are found in England and Wales.

Progress check 3.118

One way of assessing evidence from studies is to evaluate the methodology involved in the study. Many studies looking at jury decision-making use mock jury studies. What are two problems regarding validity of mock jury studies?

STUDY HINT
When presenting an argument, such as giving an explanation of a key question for society, one way of evaluating is to consider the evidence itself and evaluate the methods used. Evidence is only as good as the way a study is carried out, and studies include an examination of their limitations by the authors, which can be useful in discussion.

With regard to criminological psychology, assess how psychological understanding can inform one key question for society. **(16 marks)**

Summary

- In criminological psychology, as in other topic areas, you need to describe one key question for society using material you have covered to inform your description.
- You also need to explain a key question for society using concepts, research and theories from your study of criminological psychology.
- One key question covered in your course is the unreliability of eyewitness testimony, which has important implications for society and for individual defendants if they are convicted unfairly on the grounds of unreliable witness testimony.
- Another key question covered in your course is bias in jury decision-making, which can lead to unfair convictions and sentencing. Such bias may include racial and gender bias, as well as bias resulting from physical attractiveness of a defendant.

Practical investigation in criminological psychology

As with other topic areas in your course, in criminological psychology you have to carry out a practical investigation. In this application, you have a choice of research methods. You can carry out an investigation into what you have covered in criminological psychology using a questionnaire, an interview or an experiment.

You will be doing your own practical and will need to know about it from start to finish. Such information cannot be covered here as the experiences from your course will help you to learn and to answer questions about your own practical.

What you need to do for the practical investigation

Your practical investigation must gather quantitative data, though it can gather qualitative data as well or convert qualitative data into quantitative data for analysis. In the experiment outlined on the accompanying website, quantitative data are gathered. You must use the relevant test for your practical. In the experiment outlined online, which focuses on juror decision-making, an independent

groups design is used and the inferential test required is a Mann Whitney U test. You need to include a research question/hypothesis, research method, sampling, ethical considerations, data collection tools, data analysis, results and discussion. Also look at strengths and weaknesses of the practical and possible improvements. These features of a practical investigation are given in the practical online, though not in detail.

> **STUDY HINT**
>
> When preparing for the examination, both when revising your practical investigations and when revising method in general, or studies, be ready to offer possible improvements. Your course assesses your understanding of 'possible improvements'.

> **STUDY HINT**
>
> An experiment focusing on issues with jury decision-making is worked through on the website accompanying this book.

You will have done a practical investigation in criminological psychology using a questionnaire, an interview or an experiment. Evaluate your practical investigation in criminological psychology in terms of reliability, validity and generalisability. **(16 marks)**

Summary

- You have to carry out a practical investigation using a questionnaire, an interview or an experiment.
- Your practical must cover some area you have studied in criminological psychology for your course.
- You can collect qualitative data. However, for analysis purposes, you need quantitative data, so either collect that as well or convert your qualitative data into quantitative data, perhaps using content analysis.
- You need to know about the hypothesis/research question, sampling, ethical considerations and data collection tools.
- You also need to focus on data analysis and the results of your practical investigation.
- As part of the results, you need to use the relevant inferential test from the four you have covered in your course, so be sure that your practical investigation will suit one of the tests.
- You need to be ready to discuss your practical investigation, including giving strengths and weaknesses and, importantly, considering possible improvements.

Chapter Four: Child psychology

General overview

This chapter is about child psychology, an application in psychology, which means that theories and studies are applied to issues of concern to society and the individual. Child psychology includes theories about problems in child development and about children's usual developmental progression. You will look at what happens when very young children are not cared for, as well as the effects of being separated from a main caregiver; the issue of day care is also explored. Developmental issues are important and in your course autism will be investigated with regard to how it affects a child's development. As you are accustomed from your Year One studies, in the Year Two applications you have to know one classic study and one contemporary study chosen from a list of three. As with Year One topic areas you need to cover one key question for society where you can draw on what you have covered in child psychology. You will also carry out a practical investigation based on the content you cover.

Attachment between parent and child is an important feature of a child's development.

Explore

You can use the internet to look at what a child psychologist's job involves. This will help you to understand what child psychology covers, though you will only be covering some of what it entails. http://psychology.about.com/od/psychologycareerprofiles/a/child-psychologist.htm

Study of interest

Bevington *et al.* (2015) used attachment theory to help develop a therapy for young people with difficulties. They talk about Adolescent Mentalisation-Based Integrative Treatment (AMBIT), which is a team-based therapy for working with hard to reach 'highly troubled' young people. The treatment is based on attachment theory. 'Mentalising' means understanding behaviour in terms of someone's (or one's own) mental state. The idea of mentalising fits in with attachment relationships, which form a basis for communication in a social situation. An infant, through attachments, experiences their own mental states through someone else understanding and communicating their mental states to them. This 'someone else' is someone trusted and it is their facial expressions and the words they use as well as tone that indicate to the infant that their mental state has been understood. Bevington *et al.* (2015) discuss how mentalising can go wrong in the face of emotions and if it breaks down (either the patient not understanding their mental state or the worker not understanding the patient's mental state) then the relationship tends to break down too. Bevington *et al.* (2015) suggest AMBIT as a model of practice. The focus is on attachment theory and aims to move the relationship between a patient and a worker to learning about things like the patient's mental state rather than using rigid command structures (such as where the worker is in charge).

STUDY HINT

Bevington *et al.*'s (2015) article shows that the way attachments are formed in young children shapes their later relationships. This emphasises individual differences in people, brought about by their individual attachment experiences, among other influences. You need to be able to discuss individual differences in people, so it is useful to make a note when you come across a link to individual differences.

Summary of learning objectives

Content

You need to know about Bowlby's work on **attachment**. In the area of attachments you also need to know about the work of Ainsworth, including the **strange situation procedure** and types of attachment. You need to cover research into **deprivation**, including long-term and short-term effects, and the reduction of negative effects of deprivation. Another important area linked to attachments is research into **privation**, including whether effects are reversible. You need to cover cross-cultural research into attachment types and nature–nurture issues that arise about development. Day care has been said to be a type of separation and you will look at research into day care, including advantages and disadvantages of day care for the child, and what makes good and poor quality day care. You also need to be able to describe the features of autism, together with one biological and one other explanation for the condition. With regard to autism you also need to know therapies for helping children with autism.

Definitions

Attachment is a warm, continuous loving relationship that connects someone with another person and which begins in infancy. Attachment is a two-way process that relates to how people react when they are hurt or separated from their attachment figures.

Deprivation refers to attachments being removed so that the child is deprived of love and care.

Privation refers to when there has been no attachment of the child in the first place so no attachment is taken away; the infant is privated.

Explanation

There are types or styles of **attachment** according to Mary Ainsworth and others. Some infants are securely attached, some show an ambivalent-insecure attachment and some have an avoidant-insecure attachment. A fourth type was later added called a disorganised-insecure attachment. These are covered in more detail in the content section of this chapter.

The **strange situation procedure** refers to Ainsworth's structured observation procedure where a mother and infant interact with a stranger and the focus of importance is the reunion between the mother and infant to see what type of attachment will be exhibited. The strange situation procedure is covered in more detail in the content section of this chapter.

Individual differences and developmental psychology

All topic areas in your course involve you considering two special issues in psychology and these are individual differences and developmental psychology. In each topic area you will find reference to where these issues are within the content or the key question. You need to be able to make links between these two issues and areas that reflect them. Each issue has its own symbol in this textbook to alert you to these links. Individual differences refers to how people might be inherently different, such as in their personality or intelligence. Gender too can give individual differences, as can other genetic or biological differences. Developmental psychology is an area of study focusing on how we develop from before birth to adolescence and also beyond and into old age.

Year One link: Year One topic areas consider both individual differences and developmental issues in the content sections. Year Two applications do the same.

Individual differences

In child psychology the links that must be learned about are:

- how attachment types can affect individuals differently, such as because of differences in chid temperament
- gender and temperament, which can mean that day care is experienced differently by different individuals, for example.

Developmental psychology

In child psychology the links that must be learned about are:

- how day care and attachment interactions (including deprivation, privation and separation) affect a child's development
- the effects of autism on development.

Method

The main methods for child psychology are observation, questionnaire and interview and how they are used in child psychology. Cross-cultural research is also covered as well as the use of meta-analysis in child psychology. Issues of cross-sectional and longitudinal designs are covered too.

Meta-analysis (page 152), cross-sectional (page 145) and longitudinal design (page 143) and cross-cultural research method (page 148) were all covered in Chapter Two so you can draw on what you learned there to help your learning in child psychology. Clinical psychology also focuses on the use of interviewing to gather data.

Year One link: Questionnaire and interview research methods were covered in social psychology in Year One and observation was covered in learning theories in Year One.

You need to know about the ethics of researching children, including children's rights and the United Nations Convention on the Rights of the Child (UNCRC) (1989) and participation and protection rights. These issues are probably new to you as they apply to research with children, which so far in your course you have not covered in much detail.

Data analysis is important in method in child psychology. You need to know about analysis of quantitative data using measures of central tendency, frequency tables, measures of dispersion (range and standard deviation) as well as analysis of quantitative data using inferential statistics. Issues relating to inferential statistics include the four tests in your course (Chi squared, Mann Whitney U, Wilcoxon and Spearman's) as well as issues of statistical significance, levels of measurement and critical and observed values. Analysis of qualitative data is required,

including thematic analysis and the use of grounded theory. All of this material (except grounded theory) was covered in Year One and reviewed in Chapter Two. Grounded theory was covered in Chapter Two (page 172).

Year One link: Analysis of quantitative data using descriptive and inferential statistics and analysis of qualitative data using thematic analysis has all been covered in Year One, so be sure to revise the material for your Year Two studies.

> ### Explore
> You can find out more about the UNCRC using this link: www.unicef.org/crc/files/Rights_overview.pdf

Studies

The classic study you need in clinical psychology is van IJzendoorn and Kroonenberg (1988), which is a meta-analysis looking at cross-cultural patterns in attachment.

You will choose one contemporary study from three, all of which are covered in this chapter:

- Cassibba *et al.* (2013), who looked at attachment in Italy
- Gagnon-Oosterwaal *et al.* (2012), who looked at issues for internationally adopted children
- Li *et al.* (2013), who considered issues in day care, focusing on high quality day care.

> ### STUDY HINT
> One of the contemporary studies in biological psychology was Li *et al.* (2013). Be sure not to confuse these two studies that have the same name and date. They focus on entirely different areas of research so there should be no confusion.

Key question

You have a choice of key question to study. Focusing on how child psychology can help to explain or deal with an issue, the course suggests that you choose from looking at what issues parents should take into account when deciding about day care for their child or whether international adoption is good or bad for the child. You can, however, choose any issue.

Practical investigation in child psychology

You have to carry out one practical research exercise within child psychology and there is a choice about using a questionnaire, interview or observation; you will choose your own practical research exercise within your learning, so it is not possible to state in this book what that might be.

The website accompanying this book discusses one practical investigation in child psychology using a questionnaire to help you with this section. A questionnaire is used that gathers both quantitative and qualitative data – whichever method you use you must gather quantitative data as this is required for analysis.

You need to gather data relevant to topics you have studied in child psychology and your practical investigation must be ethical throughout, with particular attention paid to the ethics of researching with children. You will also write up some of what is needed in a psychology report – the research question and hypothesis, sampling and data collection tools as part of the method, data analysis, results and discussion.

Year One link: You looked at questionnaires and interviews as research methods in social psychology and in observation in your Year One study of learning theories. Although your practical will focus on issues you have studied in child psychology, the research methods will be the same.

Issues and debates

The 11 issues and debates chosen for your course are: ethics; practical issues in research design; reductionism; comparing explanations; psychology as a science; culture and gender; nature-nurture; how psychology has developed over time; issues of social control; using psychology in society; and issues around socially sensitive research. Chapter Seven in this book looks at issues and debates in detail.

Table 4.1 What you need to know for child psychology

You need to know about:	
Bowlby's work on attachment	The use of cross-cultural research in child psychology, including the strange situation procedure and nature–nurture issues. Also cross-sectional and longitudinal designs
Ainsworth's work on attachment including types/styles of attachment and the strange situation procedure	Meta-analysis using cross-cultural, research to draw conclusions about universality
Research into deprivation, including short-term and long-term effects of deprivation and how negative effects of deprivation can be reduced	The ethics of researching with children, including the UNCRC (1989) and protection and participation rights
Research into privation and whether the negative effects of privation can be reversed	Analysis of quantitative data, including descriptive and inferential statistics (the four tests from Year One) and related issues
Research into day care, including advantages and disadvantages for the child and what makes good and poor quality day care	Analysis of qualitative data using thematic analysis and grounded theory
Autism – the features of autism; one biological explanation for autism; one other explanation for autism; therapies for helping children with autism	The classic study in child psychology is van IJzendoorn and Kroonenberg (1988) and their meta-analysis looking at cross-cultural attachment types
Individual differences relating to content you have covered in child psychology, including how attachment type and day care can affect children differently, such as because of temperament or gender	One contemporary study from a choice of three: Cassibba *et al.*, (2013), Gagnon-Oosterwaal *et al.* (2012) or Li *et al.* (2013)
Developmental psychology linked to child psychology. Child psychology focuses on development, including the effects of day care, attachment and autism on development	One key question that can be explained using concepts, theories and/or research from child psychology in your course, and the concepts, theories and research in question
Observation as used in child psychology, including gathering both qualitative and quantitative data, tallying, and types of observation (participant, non-participant, covert and overt)	One practical investigation focusing on an area of child psychology in your course using either an observation, a questionnaire or an interview as the research method
Questionnaire and interview as used in child psychology including gathering qualitative and quantitative data. Issues of semi-structured, structured and unstructured interviews, sampling, open and closed questions, social desirability and demand characteristics	Individual differences and developmental psychology linking to child psychology
Issues and debates (see Chapter Seven for more detail)	

An introduction to child psychology

Child psychology is part of developmental psychology, and focuses on infants and young children, though 'child' also refers to young people and adolescents. Child psychopathology is included as well – this looks at problems with child development.

A young child involved in a psychological test

Teachers, social workers, educational psychologists, clinical psychologists and other care workers are interested in child psychology. It could be said that one side of child psychology is research to gain understanding of children, and the other side is the application that helps with issues and problems faced by children. In general, there are academic researchers and practising psychologists and these two groups tend to be separate, although some practising psychologists also carry out research.

Child development from birth to adolescence

The main focus of child psychology is the development of a child from birth to adolescence. The United Nations Convention on the Rights of the Child (1989) defines childhood as being up to the age of 18. Cognitive developmental psychology focuses on how a child develops its thinking processes, but your course focuses more on emotional development and how having little or no care at a young age can affect the child. You will look at academic research in child psychology and at the work of practising psychologists who apply academic understanding, such as when considering how to help a child with autism.

How childhood affects later experiences

Another important feature of child psychology is the claim that what individuals experience in childhood (through early childhood, middle childhood and adolescence) affects their adult experiences. With this approach, child psychology is not just about children but also about adults. Your course touches on this area – for example, when showing how Bowlby thought that a difficult attachment pattern as a young child can lead an adult to have problems with relationships in adulthood.

> **STUDY HINT**
> For each of the topic areas in your course you need to know what the area is about. For child psychology too you need to know what child psychology is and what it covers, so be sure to take notes about child psychology in general.

Progress check 4.1

Explain two features of child psychology.

Test yourself

Explain what is meant by child psychology. **(4 marks)**

Content in child psychology

In this section you will focus on Bowlby's and Ainsworth's work on attachment, including types of attachment and the strange situation procedure. Cross-cultural issues concerning types of attachment are covered, including nature–nurture issues. Research into deprivation and privation is covered, as well as looking at autism as a developmental disorder. Day care is also studied.

Bowlby's theory of attachment and maternal deprivation

John Bowlby (1907–90) was a psychoanalyst who followed the ideas of Freud. He thought that an infant was strongly affected by the first few years of his or her life. Bowlby's family was upper-middle class and he saw little of his own mother during the day, when he was looked after by a nanny. He was sent to boarding school at the age of seven. These experiences may have affected his views on the importance of attachments in early life. By attachment, Bowlby meant that an infant should have a warm, continuous loving relationship with one person. Attachment is a two-way process, as the mother will also attach to the child.

Psychodynamic roots

Bowlby studied medicine and then psychoanalysis and he worked with maladjusted and delinquent children. His interest in such children led to the formation of his theories on the importance of early attachment for later development. Where psychodynamic theory suggests that relationship problems can arise from fantasies about relationships with parents, Bowlby thought that real relationships with parents could be the cause of later problems, which meant that he moved away from his psychodynamic roots. However, he used psychodynamic ideas: for example, he thought that the child's mother or main caregiver acted both as ego and superego, before these could develop in the child.

Year One link: You looked at the psychodynamic approach to explaining aggression when you covered biological psychology, so review what you learned there about the id, ego and superego, and about the role of the unconscious.

Bowlby's work with deprived and disturbed children led to the World Health Organization asking him to write a report on the effect of homelessness on the mental health of children in Europe following the Second World War. Bowlby considered the evidence at the time and published *Maternal Care and Mental Health* in 1951, in which he stated that a strong attachment with the mother (or permanent mother figure) was necessary for the positive mental health of the child. This led to changes in policy and practice in institutions. For example, there were alterations in visiting procedures in hospitals to allow parental visits (discussed later in this section).

However, Bowlby later stated that there was little evidence at the time and not much theory from which to draw conclusions, so from 1969 he worked again on his ideas about the importance of attachments and further developed his theory.

'Mother love in infancy and childhood is as important for mental health as are vitamins and proteins for physical health.'

John Bowlby, 1953

An evolutionary basis to attachment

Bowlby considered many other theories in addition to psychodynamic ideas, including the work of Konrad Lorenz (1952) and others, who were using **ethological** studies. Lorenz had noticed that animals such as ducks and geese, when hatched, followed the first moving object they saw, which was usually the mother. By following their mother (called **imprinting**), such animals would be more likely to survive.

Definitions

Ethology is the study of animals in their natural setting.
Imprinting is the term for certain animals, such as ducks, that follow the first moving object they see, usually the mother, though in experiments it can be a rubber glove (Guiton, 1966).

Imprinting is when newborn animals, such as ducks, follow the first moving object they see, which is usually the mother.

Bowlby thought that human infants might have a similar 'attachment' instinct that would ensure survival, so he put forward the idea of the evolutionary basis of attachment. **Evolution** theory holds that any behaviour or characteristic that aids survival will mean that an organism survives to reproduce its genes, so a behaviour or characteristic will be passed on through genes. Any behaviour that goes against survival means that an organism will not survive to reproduce its genes and that behaviour will die out. This is survival of the fittest.

Year One link: In biological psychology you looked at evolution and survival of the fittest, including looking at evolution as an explanation for aggression. You can draw on your understanding of evolution here.

Definition

Evolution refers to how what is inherited over time changes due to survival of the fittest, which means certain genes survive and others die out.

Bowlby's theory agreed with evolution theory because he thought that babies came into the world with an innate tendency to attach and bond to a main carer that would enable their survival. He maintained that infants are biologically programmed to form attachments. Separation, insecurity or fear would trigger the instinct to turn to the attachment figure. Crying and smiling are instincts to keep a baby close to its mother and the mother too has an instinct to form an attachment with the baby.

Bowlby's theory of maternal deprivation

Bowlby suggested that children deprived of their mother – their attachment figure – would have problems later in life. He acknowledged that the bond could be with a main attachment figure, not necessarily the natural mother. Bowlby referred to **monotropy**, which means a warm and loving relationship with one person. He thought that this first main attachment was different from any other attachment. Bowlby thought that social, emotional and intellectual development would be adversely affected if the mother–child bond was broken early in life – this is the **maternal deprivation hypothesis**. Bowlby believed such problems in adulthood are permanent and irreversible, meaning that once there are problems, nothing can be done about them. Problems included delinquency and **affectionless psychopathy** in young people according to Bowlby. Evidence for these ideas about maternal deprivation come from Bowlby's 44 juvenile thieves study, which is explained later in this section (page 365).

Definitions

Monotropy refers to Bowlby's idea that a child has an innate need to have one main attachment figure.

Maternal deprivation hypothesis refers to Bowlby's idea that if an infant does not have a continual attachment with one main attachment figure in their early life then as the child gets older problems will come from having been deprived of the attachment.

Affectionless psychopathy is Bowlby's term for what can develop if a child is deprived of attachment; it means showing little concern for others and being unable to form relationships.

Maternal deprivation means having an attachment broken through separation, and the first two years of life are very important. By 'deprivation', Bowlby seems to have intended both not having formed an attachment in the first place and having an attachment broken through separation. He was criticised for not separating deprivation (having an attachment broken) from privation (not having formed an attachment at all). Issues about privation are dealt with later in this chapter (page 386).

Attachment includes features such as providing a **safe haven** when the child is afraid. He or she can return to the attachment figure/caregiver for comfort. There is also

a **secure base** provided by the attachment figure so that the infant can explore. By keeping the infant close, the attachment protects the child. Another mechanism is that, when separated from the attachment figure, the child will seek them out for comfort and show distress and **separation anxiety**, which has the effect of drawing the attachment figure back to the infant – a useful survival mechanism.

Definitions

A **safe haven** refers to someone the young child can turn to when afraid and an attachment figure provides that safe haven. A **secure base** refers to when a young child explores the environment but keeps returning to be reassured and to check that all is well. They return to their attachment figure. **Separation anxiety** refers to the worry and fear a child might experience on being away from their attachment figure, which draws them back to safety.

STUDY HINT

By learning the meaning of the following terms, you will have explained Bowlby's theory of attachment: attachment, deprivation, privation, evolution, monotropy, maternal deprivation, safe haven, secure base and separation anxiety.

Main features of Bowlby's theory of attachment

- A child has an innate need to form an attachment with one person. This special attachment to one person is called monotropy.
- This strong relationship with one person should continue unbroken for the first two years of life if adverse effects are to be avoided.
- The maternal deprivation hypothesis holds that a broken attachment (or lack of an attachment) leads to relationship problems for the child on reaching adulthood.
- Broken attachment leads to delinquency and affectionless psychopathy.
- Attachment provides a safe haven for when the child is afraid and a secure base from which to explore the world.
- Separation distress/anxiety serves to draw the attachment figure back to the infant and is a survival mechanism.

Progress check 4.2

Explain how having a secure base and the mechanism of separation anxiety help a child with their development.

Bowlby's focus on loss

Deprivation and separation from a main attachment figure is all about loss. The idea of loss in early childhood connecting to later emotional ill health links back to the psychodynamic approach, within which Bowlby was working. **Object relations theory** developed within the psychodynamic approach and focuses on the way infants learn from their own relationships about how such relationships work, and from which they develop **internal working models**. Their later relationships are based on these models.

Definitions

Object relations theory refers to how an infant experiences their family and objects around them and how these affect their later social relationships and interactions.

The **internal working model** refers to a cognitive framework or schemas made up of mental representations of how the world and others are seen.

Year One link: Recall what you learned about schemas in Year One when you learned about the reconstructive theory of memory and Bartlett's War of the Ghosts study. Though the internal working model idea is different from the focus on cognition, because it also focuses on emotions, such as how someone interacts with others, it follows the same idea that our behaviour is guided by mental representations of the world.

Object relations theory, which is linked with theorists such as Melanie Klein, focuses on fantasy relationships as much as real relationships, but Bowlby talked specifically about real relationships. Bowlby believed that infants build internal working models for relationships from their experience of attachments. Their internal working model would be about loss if they experienced separation or a lack of the warm, loving relationship that characterises a strong attachment. People use their internal working models when interacting with others in life.

There is evidence for early experience of loss affecting later experiences. Brown and Harris (1978) found that girls who had lost their mothers before the age of about 12 years were more likely to be depressed as adults. Tracey (2011) studied the impact on daughters of their mother's death in childhood and gathered qualitative data to look at the 'lifelong impact of this loss'. The 26 women who were the participants in the study talked about yearning for a mother figure in adolescence and effects on their own parenting. Tracey (2011) used face-to-face interviews that were recorded. She reports that the absence of a mother 'was felt to have undermined

their self-esteem and sense of security' (p. 20). 'Loss' was something that the women talked about. Tracey's (2011) study is evidence for Bowlby's claims about loss.

Explore

You can find a brief news item about Tracey's study using this link if you would like to know more:
http://news.ulster.ac.uk/releases/2006/2830.html
You can look more at object relations theory and attachment theory using this link:
http://changingminds.org/disciplines/psychoanalysis/concepts/object_relations.htm

Defining deprivation and separation

Deprivation refers to an infant having the attachment with its main caregiver broken, either for a short or for a long time. Separation refers to when an infant is no longer with its main caregiver for some reason, again either short term or long term. Separation leads to deprivation. Divorce (where a parent loses contact with the child) or the death of one or both parents leads to long-term separation. There is also short-term separation, for example, when a parent goes into hospital or is away for some reason.

Explore

There are YouTube videos on attachments which you can explore. Here is a link showing Bowlby himself speaking, which you could start with, focusing on attachment and loss:
www.youtube.com/watch?v=VAAmSqv2GV8.
Another link, focusing on Bowlby's work on attachment is:
www.youtube.com/watch?v=js2XdP9FL5Q.

Evidence for the importance of attachments

Bowlby provided evidence for his theory by carrying out a study of 44 juvenile thieves. This study is explained here. Bowlby found that young people who had experienced separation from their mothers were more likely to have problems later in life. Bowlby also drew on evidence from others, including Harlow, the Robertsons, Spitz, Goldfarb and Lorenz. This evidence is also given in this section.

Bowlby's study of 44 juvenile thieves (1944)

In 1944 John Bowlby published a study of young people who were thieves to find out about their background and to see if he could understand the reason for them becoming thieves.

Background

In 1938 nine crimes out of ten were thefts and half of these were committed by someone under the age of 21. Over one-sixth of the thefts were carried out by children under 14. There was also recurrence of crimes – at the age of 16, one-third of those who appeared in court had been charged before. Bowlby realised that it would be useful to study youthful stealing and look at how early delinquency starts. 'Almost all recent work on the emotional and social development of children has laid emphasis upon the child's relation to his mother', Bowlby claimed. He had talked to mothers and found that love for their child might be only one aspect of the relationship: 'often an intense though perhaps un-admitted dislike and rejection of him (the child) also came to light'. A large proportion of juvenile delinquents had had long periods away from home, which might be a factor, as well as possible traumatic events in early childhood. These were the sorts of issues that Bowlby focused on in his study, working within the psychodynamic approach.

Procedure

The study was carried out at the London Child Guidance Clinic from 1936 to 1939. Bowlby gathered various kinds of data using interviews, case histories and psychological testing to try to look for patterns in the backgrounds of young people at his clinic, in an attempt to establish why some would become delinquents.

There were various ways in which a child was assessed when he or she first came into the clinic. A psychologist carried out mental tests to assess intelligence, as well as undertaking an assessment of the child's emotional attitudes towards the tests. A social worker then noted preliminary psychiatric history. This testing and case history lasted about an hour. The social worker and psychologist gave reports to the psychiatrist (Bowlby), who then interviewed first the child and then the mother – this took another hour. A case conference followed and a tentative diagnosis was formed. Often more interviews followed, along with psychotherapy and the mother talking further to the social worker, so more in-depth data were gathered.

Only a few cases were studied because of the depth required – such as finding out about the emotional influences within the home, which affect the development of the child's object relationships. Bowlby admitted that more such studies were needed to substantiate the findings of his study.

Progress check 4.3

List the different methods Bowlby used to collect data in his 44 juvenile thieves study.

Results

Bowlby gathered a lot of clinical material, which formed the results of his study:

- A total of 44 cases of children stealing were studied – 22 were referred to the clinic by a school, 2 by a school at the parents' request, 8 were referred by parents directly, 3 were referred at a court's request and 9 were referred by probation officers.
- There was also a control group – this consisted of 44 children who were not thieves but who also attended the London Child Guidance Clinic. Their age and intelligence were similar to the 44 thieves – this was to compare the thieves with other maladjusted children. Bowlby said he would have preferred some 'ordinary' schoolchildren as well, as another control group.
- In the group, 15 of the thieves were under nine years old and half were under eleven. Only one child under eleven had been charged.
- There were 31 boys and 13 girls in the main group and 34 boys and 10 girls in the control group. The clinic usually had 60 per cent boys and 40 per cent girls, so the groups were not representative of the usual intake.
- The average intelligence of both the thieves and the control group was quite high (using standardised tests). About one-third of each group was of above-average intelligence.
- In 22 cases there was chronic and serious stealing, mainly over a long period. In seven cases the stealing had lasted for more than three years. However, eight of the thieves had been involved in only a few thefts and four had only been involved in one.

Characters of the thieves

Bowlby wanted to define juvenile delinquency and thought there might be three different types: some children had been unstable for years, some had received a sudden shock (such as bereavement) and some had an exceptional moral lapse. Bowlby then looked through all the data and sorted the thieves into six groups:

A Normal
B Depressed
C Circular
D Hyperthermic
E Affectionless★
F Schizoid

*The main category for the study was 'affectionless', which Bowlby defined as having a lack of normal affection, shame or sense of responsibility.

Two of the 44 thieves were normal in character but 42 had abnormal characters. The diagnosis rested on careful examination, but the problem was that psychiatric examination was not useful because the children were on their best behaviour and hid things. For this reason, Bowlby drew his conclusions about character based on his discussions with the mother and the school. Group E, the affectionless character, is the one of interest in this study, so only two of the other groups are briefly outlined here to give an idea of other categories.

Group A: Normal

One child had been stealing since the age of 14, but only from his mother. However, his mother was taking a lot of his earnings. Another child was reasonably normal too – he was eight and was only stealing a few pennies.

Group B: Depressed

Five children suffered with mild depression, two of them having a very low IQ. Some children were severely depressed and often this arose from a specific event.

Group E: Affectionless

Fourteen of the children had what Bowlby called an affectionless character – a lack of affection or warmth of feeling for anyone. They had been undemonstrative and unresponsive from infancy. Two of the children sometimes showed affection but matched the personality type in other ways. They lied, stole and had no sense of loyalty, emotional ties or friendships. Bowlby thought that the affectionless character was depressive at an earlier stage in life and had suffered complete emotional loss of mother or foster mother during infancy and early childhood. He thought that misery lay below the mask.

Comparison with controls

There were no affectionless characters among the control group, but there were more depressed characters. Eight of the control group were of a type not found in the thieves (an over-conscientious child type referred to as 'priggish').

Table 4.2 shows that Group E, the affectionless characters, clearly stand out as being thieves and Bowlby focused on this differentiation between the thieves and the control group.

Table 4.2 Distribution of thieves and controls by character type

Character	Thieves	Controls
A: Normal	2	3
B: (i) Depressed	9	13
(ii) Priggish	0	8
C: Circular	2	1
D: Hyperthermic	13	10
E: Affectionless	14	0
F: Schizoid/schizophrenic	4	9
Total	44	44

Conclusion

Table 4.3 shows that 93 per cent of the affectionless thieves (13 out of 14 of them) were level IV with regard to stealing – the highest level, which is defined as stealing in a persistent and serious way. Out of the 23 persistent thieves (level IV), 13 were affectionless too (56 per cent). Bowlby linked the affectionless character with a lack of attachment and having some strong emotional loss in infancy.

Table 4.3 Distribution of thieves by character type and degree of stealing

Character	Degree of stealing (IV = highest)				
	I	II	III	IV	Total
Normal	0	2	0	0	2
Depressed	1	4	3	1	9
Circular	0	0	2	0	2
Hyperthermic	2	2	2	7	13
Affectionless	0	0	1	13	14
Schizoid/schizophrenic	0	0	2	2	4
Total	3	8	10	23	44

Progress check 4.4

Using Table 4.3 of Bowlby's results showing levels of stealing, answer the following:

1. What percentage of the thieves is in the category of the highest level of stealing (IV)?
2. What percentage of the thieves is characterised as affectionless?

Evaluation

Strengths

- There are a lot of in-depth and detailed data gathered from a number of different sources, including both qualitative and quantitative data and different research methods, so data are likely to be valid. This study has the strength of being a case study.

- There was a matched control group of similar children (in that they attended the same clinic) who were not thieves, so the findings about the thieves could be compared with these controls. This gave Bowlby the ability to show that fourteen of the thieves were affectionless characters whereas none of the controls was, so he could draw a conclusion that it looked as if the affectionless character would link with stealing. Without the control group he would not have been able to draw such a strong conclusion.

Weaknesses

- Bowlby himself said he would have liked to have had another control group, this time children from a 'normal' school and not the clinic, as the control group he used also had problems. He would have liked more in the sample too, so he could generalise.

- Bowlby covered many areas such as emotional state, IQ, age and experiences with the mother. However, in a child's development there are many other areas of interest as well, such as the relationship with the father and other relatives, and experiences at school. He focused on loss in early childhood, but there may have been other variables of importance that he did not focus on. Perhaps, for example, the lack of affection in infancy was genetic.

- What was learned about maternal deprivation used retrospective material relying on memory, which might mean the data are not valid.

Progress check 4.5

Explain two limitations to the study that Bowlby himself pointed out.

Harlow's study of monkeys and attachments

Harlow and his colleagues studied rhesus monkeys. In one well-known study (Harlow and Zimmerman, 1959), infant monkeys who had been removed from their mothers were the focus of study. One set of infants was allowed access to a towel-covered wire 'monkey' as well as a food-giving wire 'monkey'. Other monkeys could access only the food-giving wire monkey. Those monkeys who could get comfort from the towel-covered monkey did so, and at

the end of the study they were better adjusted physically and mentally. Harlow concluded that such comfort was important for the developing monkey and that it is not food alone that connects mother and infant. His research linked to the idea that attachment was part of the mother–infant relationship for monkeys. Bowlby used this as evidence that this was true for human children as well.

STUDY HINT

Harlow did experiments with animals when finding out about the need for contact comfort. You can use evaluation points relating to generalising from animals to humans when considering Harlow's findings, such as the usefulness of generalising from monkeys and also the disadvantages considering they are not human and the situation was unnatural for them.

Year One link: You looked at the use of experiments using animals when you studied learning theories, so you can use that material when considering how Bowlby used Harlow's findings.

Evaluation

Strengths

- Harlow filmed the studies and it is clear that the monkeys rushed to the towelling 'mother' when they were frightened or startled. There is validity to the findings, as there is 'real life' in the situations set up – it is clear that the monkeys really were frightened.

- Harlow used monkeys, which are close to humans in their genes (chimps share 98 per cent or more of their genes with humans), so there can be generalisation from infant monkeys to human babies, to some extent.

- Schaffer and Emerson (1964) found that young children formed multiple attachments rather than one single attachment. A baby tended to form an attachment to the mother, father, brothers, sisters, grandparents and others. This is evidence that attachment is not just about who feeds the child, as was thought by some theorists. Harlow also found that monkeys 'attached' to a 'mother' who did not feed them, so Schaffer and Emerson's findings support Harlow's findings.

Weaknesses

- Animals are not the same as humans, so generalising behaviour of monkeys to say it is true of human babies as well might not be legitimate.

- Ethically, Harlow's work has been questioned, as the monkeys were often frightened. Other studies have looked at whether monkeys without an early attachment figure make good mothers themselves, and they do not. Animals should be distressed as little as possible, whereas Harlow's work affected quite a few monkeys (those in the initial study and their offspring, who were deprived of good mothering).

Explore

You can find YouTube videos showing Harlow's work with monkeys. However, Harlow's work was widely criticised for its ethics and you might find looking at his work distressing, so you may prefer not to access this material. Here is a link if you would like to know more: www.youtube.com/watch?v=_O60TYAIgC4

Harlow found monkeys would cling to a cloth 'mother' in favour of one that fed them, showing their need for contact comfort.

Robertson's naturalistic observations

In 1948 Bowlby employed James Robertson to make careful observations of children in hospital or institutions. Robertson had worked with Anna Freud, Sigmund Freud's daughter, in her residential children's nursery. People working at this nursery were told to make detailed notes about the children's behaviour, so Robertson was well trained in observation. He was much affected by the distress of the children he observed in hospital over a period of three years and made a film called *A Two-Year-Old Goes to Hospital* (1953). The film showed Laura, aged two, who was in hospital for eight days for an operation. Bowlby and Robertson realised that this film was going to be important evidence that young children suffer enormously without their attachment figure near, so the sampling of the child was random and a clock showed the real time of the filming.

Robertson's film and detailed observations showed that children deprived of their attachment figure went through three stages. First, there was protest, and the child cried. At this stage a child also showed anger and fear, and Bowlby thought that this might be a survival instinct –

loud protest to attract the attention of the caregiver. Then there was despair, when crying became more intermittent and the child may appear to have 'settled in'. Finally there was detachment, where – on the face of it – the child adjusted, as he or she stopped protesting and gave up on crying and appeared to have become 'happy'. Table 4.4 shows London hospital visiting times when Robertson was carrying out his observations.

Table 4.4 London hospital visiting times in 1953

Hospital	Visiting times
Guy's Hospital	Sundays 2–4 p.m.
Westminster Hospital	Wednesdays and Sundays, 2–3 p.m.
Charing Cross Hospital	Sundays 3–4 p.m.
St Bartholomew's	Sundays 2–3.30 p.m.
St Thomas's	No visits for the first month, but parents could see children asleep between 7 and 8 p.m.

Explore

You can watch some of Robertson's film on YouTube if you would like to know more. Here is a link: www.youtube.com/watch?v=s14Q-_Bxc_U

Protest – distress, crying and searching for attachment figure

Despair – quiet, withdrawn, appears to have 'settled in'

Denial/detachment – interacts with others and shows more interest by repressing longing for mother, appears 'happy'

Three stages when a child's attachment breaks

This final stage links with Spitz's claim that the child was severely depressed, and this claim is explained below. (Bowlby noticed that widows and widowers showed the same three phases in the face of their loss – protest, despair and detachment – and he went on to write about this type of grieving.) There were controls when making the film, to give scientific value to this evidence. The film led to great changes in procedures in hospitals. Robertson's graphic visual evidence further convinced Bowlby and his team of the importance of early attachments. Mary Ainsworth was part of the team involved in this study, and they were joined later by Rudolf Schaffer. The work of Ainsworth and Schaffer is explained later in this section.

Short-term separation and deprivation can lead to distress (Robertson and Bowlby, 1952) and it is **long-term separation and deprivation** that moves the child into detachment, which should be avoided. Detachment leads to the caregiver being rejected on their return and children are likely to show anger.

Definitions

Short-term separation and deprivation is where the attachment figure returns after just a short break, such as if the mother is away in hospital for a week. **Long-term separation and deprivation** is where the attachment figure perhaps does not return, because they have died, or perhaps they do not return for some time and then not fully back into the child's life, such as in divorce.

This mother and baby are communicating with each other and an attachment is formed.

Evaluating Robertson's research

Strengths

- Naturalistic observations such as those of Robertson produce valid data, because they involve real situations, such as a real child who is separated from his or her attachment figure.
- Robertson later reported research observations of young separated children as the films 'Young Children in Brief Separation'. He found similar responses (protest, despair, detachment), so there was a form of replication and similar data were found.

Weakness

- Robertson used naturalistic observation, with its related problem of reliability: since the actual situation will not be repeated, the observation cannot be replicated.

> **STUDY HINT**
> You can use the studies explained in this section giving evidence for Bowlby's ideas about attachments when you are discussing methods used in child psychology. Bowlby used interviewing, Harlow used animal experiments and Robertson used naturalistic observation.

Spitz's study of children in institutions

When Bowlby worked on the World Health Organization report he researched studies at the time in the area of attachments, including the work of René Spitz, who had studied institutionalised children (1946). A hospital, prison, orphanage or residential home is an institution and, when children live in such a place, they are called '**institutionalised**'.

Spitz studied children in hospitals and he found that children deprived of their attachment figure became depressed. If an infant had formed an attachment with his or her mother for the first six months of life, development was good. However, if that attachment was broken (such as by a child going into hospital), then over a three-month period of being deprived of the attachment figure the child became increasingly depressed. At first the depression was partial but after a short time it became severe, which he called **hospitalism**. Partial depression meant the child would cry and cling to observers, but after about three months the child's condition would get worse and he or she would move into severe depression. Hospitalism refers to the wasting away of the infant and in some cases leading to death. **Anaclitic depression** refers to the problems with an infant's physical, emotional and social development arising from separation from the primary caregiver.

Definitions

Institutionalised means living in an institution like a hospital or a prison; **institutionalisation** means taking on the norms, social roles and beliefs of an institution.

Hospitalism relates to anaclitic depression and was used in the 1930s to refer to infants in hospital who faded away, probably because of lack of social contact, with some even dying.

Anaclitic depression refers to problems with an infant's physical, emotional and social development arising from separation from the primary caregiver.

Children still in the partially depressed stage when reunited with their mothers would readjust after about two or three months. Children still in hospital when they were severely depressed experienced weight loss, insomnia, illness and displayed a lack of emotion in their faces. These children would not make the attempt to move and refused to interact with their carers who were caring for their physical but not their emotional needs. As the years went by it was discovered that if these children remained in an institution then some died.

Spitz found that separation and being deprived of the main caregiver had extreme consequences for a child. He went further, however, by suggesting that the lack of stimulation in an institution, where children lay in cots with no stimulation around them, was also to blame for their decline. Bowlby drew on this evidence of depression for his maternal deprivation theory.

Evaluation of Spitz's studies

Strengths

- As with Robertson's work, Spitz studied real children in real institutions so the data were ecologically valid – the situation and setting were real.
- Spitz's work continued over a long period and he continued to find that deprived children had a lower IQ and problems with development. When he introduced more care for the children they had fewer problems, so the depth of his work adds to the validity of the findings.

Explore
You can see a film showing Spitz's work if you would like to know more. You can see the distress and depression, and in some cases there is a very sad ending, so you may prefer just to watch some of the film. Here is the link:
www.youtube.com/watch?v=0cOH-239mSU

Weaknesses

- Spitz did not carry out experiments with controls and careful sampling. He used observations, testing (e.g. **intelligence quotient (IQ)** and **development quotient (DQ)**) and interviewing, and his sampling and observations were possibly biased, as there were no controls. He may have noted situations where separation led to problems and low IQ, rather than all situations.
- Measurement of both DQ and IQ is difficult, as it means applying standardised measures that are criticised, for example, with regard to cultural differences. IQ in particular is based on Western ideas and cultural attitudes, so someone who was not aware of such ideas and attitudes might do less well on such tests.

Definitions
Development quotient (DQ) is a score that comes from observing physical and mental milestones in young children and is used before IQ can be measured.
Intelligence quotient (IQ) is a score that comes from written tests that children complete when they are old enough.

Explore
You can find information about the 44 thieves study, including information using Spitz's study and Harlow's work, on YouTube. Harlow's work on monkeys has been criticised for its ethics so you might find his work upsetting. Here is a link if you would like to do that:
www.youtube.com/watch?v=Polyrv5GPUc

Goldfarb's study of children in institutions

Goldfarb (1955) studied 15 children who had stayed in an institution up to the age of about three before being fostered. He compared them with a group of children who had been fostered from about six months of age. The aim was to see if later fostering would be successful. He found that those who were adopted or fostered later showed problems in adolescence more than those who were fostered early. Those who were fostered later were emotionally less secure, intellectually behind the other group and less mature. Goldfarb concluded that babies should not be put into institutions and he thought early deprivation would lead to later problems. Bowlby used this as evidence for his maternal deprivation hypothesis.

Evaluation of Goldfarb's study

Strengths

- His work has validity because it concerns real children who were in the institution and fostered at certain periods.
- He managed to find a control group of children who were fostered early to use as a baseline measure for developmental achievements, against which he could measure his 'late fostered' group of children.

Weaknesses

- It is possible that the early fostered group had something in common, such as personality or physical looks, which made them more likely to be chosen for fostering, so the sample of later fostered children might have been biased.
- There are so many different aspects of fostering, with many different experiences for a fostered child, so that it is hard to draw the conclusion that it was the early or late fostering that 'caused' any differences in development, particularly in a group of only 15 children.

Explore
You can look at ideas around the work of Spitz and Goldfarb using this link:
http://family.jrank.org/pages/1232/Orphans-Early-Literature-on-Institutionalization.html

Lorenz's findings about imprinting

Ethological studies, like that of Lorenz (1952), which showed how animals use imprinting as a survival mechanism, suggested to Bowlby that the attachment process in humans had the same purpose and is important for an infant's development. Lorenz used **precocial species**. Humans are **altricial species**, which means newly born or hatched young are not mobile in the way precocial species are.

Definitions

Precocial species are those where the young are fairly mobile and mature from the moment they are born or hatch. Examples are geese. Altricial species are those where the newly born or hatched young are not that mobile. Examples are humans.

Evaluation of Lorenz's findings

Strengths

- Lorenz used ethology and studied animals in their natural surroundings, so his findings are likely to have ecological validity. These were not experiments in an unnatural situation like a laboratory.
- There were experiments carried out later that replicated Lorenz's findings. In one study (Guiton, 1966) some male chicks were reared in isolation and fed only by an assistant in yellow gloves. The male chicks imprinted on the yellow rubber gloves and later attempted to mate with them, though they were then kept with normal females and developed normal sexual behaviour. This shows that imprinting is innate and does not discriminate species from other moving objects.

Weaknesses

- It is not easy to establish that findings from animals can be said to be true of humans, as there are differences between animals and humans, such as use of language and problem-solving abilities.
- Only certain animals show imprinting – precocial species that can move as soon as they are born – so the findings might be specific to those sorts of animal, not to humans or other animals.

Early maternal deprivation and brain functioning in young people: Olsavsky et al. (2013)

The studies used up to now were those that Bowlby used as evidence for the maternal deprivation hypothesis and were done in the 1940s and 1950s. It is interesting to see what research is currently being done in this area. A study is outlined here that shows the use of fMRI scanning to obtain evidence for the effects of early maternal deprivation on young people.

Olsavsky et al. (2013) suggested that in altricial species the amygdala is affected by maternal stimuli. When humans are seen to show indiscriminate friendliness to others, which fits with the detachment phase of maternal deprivation, there is altered amygdala development. Olsavsky et al. (2013) put forward the hypothesis that maternal deprivation would mean reduced amygdala discrimination between mothers and strangers and also increased reporting by parents of friendliness towards 'anyone'. The researchers used 33 young people who had previously been institutionalised and 34 in a control group, all aged from four to seventeen years old. All underwent fMRI scanning to look at amygdala response to mother or stranger. Then parents assessed their child for indiscriminate friendliness. It was thought that amygdala response in those who were institutionalised would not be different whether the focus was the mother or a stranger, though it would differ in the control group. Also the experimental group would be assessed as showing more indiscriminate friendliness.

It was found that the institutionalised children did show less difference in amygdala functioning between mothers and strangers compared with the control group, and also reduced amygdala discrimination was associated with more indiscriminate friendliness. These two findings meant the hypothesis was accepted. The effects were found to increase, depending on age at adoption. The conclusion was that the amygdala is related to maternal deprivation and that maternal deprivation is likely to lead to indiscriminate friendliness.

Year One link: In biological psychology you looked at brain structures and functioning and you also looked at the amygdala as a place for emotions and aggression.

STUDY HINT

Olsavsky et al. (2013) used a questionnaire to obtain parent data about indiscriminate friendliness, so you can use their study as an example of using a questionnaire in child psychology as a research method. You could use it as an example of using fMRI scanning when you discuss fMRI as a method in biological psychology, as you studied it in biological psychology in your course.

Evaluation of Olsavsky et al. (2013)

Strengths

- If fMRI scanning showing amygdala activity is related to the effects of maternal deprivation, it can be used to identify children and young people affected by such deprivation, which means in practical terms treatment can be offered. Therefore, the study findings have practical applications, as the researchers point out.
- Using information from fMRI scans, questionnaire data from parents and information about adoption age gave the researchers different data they could relate together, which suggests there might be validity in their findings. This validity is further supported by the much earlier work around Bowlby's time, where age at adoption and detachment, which can be measured by indiscriminate friendliness, were found to relate to maternal deprivation. Being able to triangulate findings helps to show validity.

Weaknesses

- Olsavsky et al. say that parental report gave the diagnosis of indiscriminate friendliness rather than them using a structured interview and so the diagnosis might not be accurate.
- There is the possibility that it is being institutionalised rather than actual maternal deprivation that has caused any issues in amygdala functioning and indiscriminate friendliness. Although knowing that age at adoption related to the amygdala and friendliness issues is evidence, what is giving the problems is showing that this is the maternal deprivation and not the institutionalisation.

> **Explore**
> You can find Olsavsky et al.'s (2013) study using this link if you would like to know more:
> http://labs.psychology.illinois.edu/DSNLab/resources/pubs/Olsavsky_etal2013BP.pdf

Neurodevelopmental effects of early deprivation in institutionalised children: Pollak et al. (2010)

Pollak et al. (2010) carried out a study to look at institutionalised children aged eight to nine years old who had been institutionalised either for a short period or for a longer period, to look for neurodevelopmental differences (differences in brain functioning). The researchers also had a group of children brought up in the birth family as a control. They used 132 children and three groups. Pollak et al. (2010) had a group who had been in an institution and then adopted at aged 12 months or older. These were called the post-institution group (PI). The children were adopted from Asia, Latin America, Russia and Eastern Europe and Africa. They had a second group who were adopted early, mainly from foster care, and they called these the early-adopted group (EA). These children had spent two months or less in institutional care. The children were from Asia and Latin America and this group meant there could be comparison with children who had lost their birth families and had been adopted into another culture. There was a third group of children born and raised in their birth families in the USA.

The study used testing to obtain data across different cognitive domains, including spatial working memory, memory for faces and a memory for narrative/stories. Learning processes were also tested, including visual memory and attentional ability. The aim was to see what differences in cognitive processes would be found in children who had experienced deprivation and neglect – the institutionalised group (PI). The PI group differed from the other groups in terms of visual memory and attention as well as in inhibitory control; however, other tests involving auditory processing showed no differences in the PI group. The PI group performed well on tasks about manipulation and planning too. Overall the PI group did not show many differences in neurodevelopmental functioning with the other two comparison groups. It was in general visual processing that showed more differences between the PI and the other groups rather than auditory processing and also differences in inhibitory control and attention. The conclusion was that perhaps some aspects of brain circuitry related to behaviour might be affected by deprivation and similar early experiences.

Limitations

The sample of children came from families who volunteered to participate and perhaps parents who thought their child would do well (or perhaps particularly badly) were the ones who volunteered, so there might be bias in the sample. For reasons of access their sample did not include in the early adopted group (EA) children from Eastern Europe (where adoption takes longer), which also suggests bias in the sample.

> **STUDY HINT**
> There is quite a lot of evidence here for the idea that maternal deprivation/separation has consequences for the child, with the longer the separation, the more severe the consequences. Table 4.5 summarises the studies used here as evidence for the maternal deprivation hypothesis. Make your own copy of Table 4.5 and add a further column for evaluation points, to help your learning.

Table 4.5 Summary of studies used as evidence for the maternal deprivation hypothesis

Study	Summary
Bowlby (1944)	A group of 44 juvenile thieves and 44 controls were tested in various ways and it was found that maternal deprivation linked to affectionless psychopathy. The conclusion was that early separation from the main attachment figure leads to later problems.
Harlow and Zimmerman (1959)	Monkeys preferred to cling to a cloth 'mother' than one that gave food. The conclusion was that within infants there is an instinct to form a bond and receive comfort.
Robertson (1953)	Filmed Laura in hospital without her attachment figure to show there was protest, despair and detachment. The conclusion was that separation and deprivation had very severe consequences if it was not kept to a minimum.
Spitz (1946)	Showed how children in an institution without social stimulation and support went into a depression and some even died. The conclusion was separation and deprivation had very severe consequences for young children.
Goldfarb (1955)	Showed that later adopted children had more problems. He concluded that separation after the age of about three years old would have negative consequences – those adopted earlier had fewer problems.
Lorenz (1952)	Showed how certain animals followed the first moving object they saw, which would usually be the mother, and this was a survival instinct. This showed that perhaps human infants have a similar survival instinct – to form an attachment.

Table 4.6 Recent evidence regarding maternal deprivation focusing on brain issues

Study	Summary
Olsavsky et al. (2013)	Showed that amygdala functioning did not give as much differentiation between mothers and strangers in institutionalised children and young people as much as it differentiated in controls. Also institutionalised children were more likely to be characterised as showing indiscriminate friendliness, which links to detachment. The older the age of adoption the more the lack of discrimination linked to amygdala functioning between mothers and strangers and the more likelihood of showing indiscriminate friendliness. The findings are said to support the maternal deprivation hypothesis.
Pollak et al. (2010)	Found some differences in cognitive processing in children who had long-term deprivation by being in an institution for 12 months or more before adoption (PI group) compared with children who had been adopted after short-term separation/deprivation and children who remained with their birth parents. They found visual processing showed more differences between the PI and the other groups than auditory processing and also there were differences in inhibitory control and attention. Perhaps some aspects of brain circuitry related to behaviour might be affected by deprivation and similar early experiences.

Progress check 4.6

Using two studies give evidence to show that maternal deprivation leads to difficulties in later functioning.

Test yourself

Evaluate Bowlby's maternal deprivation hypothesis as an explanation for problems in a child's functioning. **(20 marks)**

Reducing negative effects of deprivation and separation

From the evidence it is clear that the negative effects of deprivation can be reduced by avoiding separation from the main caregiver, though this is probably not a helpful suggestion because separation is not always a matter of choice. If avoiding separation is impossible then, according to both Spitz and Robertson, reducing the length of the separation can be useful. Again, this is not really a helpful solution in many cases. In cases of the death of the caregiver or unavoidable separation, it is not possible to pick the attachment back up again, so neither of these two actions would work. Short-term deprivation or separation can be helped in a different way from long-term deprivation or separation perhaps and these can be treated separately.

Ways to help include having a replacement attachment figure if the separation is short term, providing individual care and stimulation, perhaps especially if the separation/deprivation is longer term, and ideas for coping with divorce and separation, which tend to be long term.

Easing short-term separation with a replacement attachment figure

James Robertson and his wife Joyce, who also worked with Anna Freud, became involved with what Robertson had witnessed in hospitals. They fostered, observed and filmed four different children whose mothers were going into hospital for the birth of a new baby. Another child observed was John (aged 17 months old), who stayed in a residential nursery for nine days. He tried to get comfort from those working at the nursery, but did not succeed as staff changed frequently and they had little time to mother him. John became increasingly distressed and his visiting father could not comfort him. When his mother returned, John rejected her.

Jane was a child of the same age as John, but this time Joyce Robertson fostered the child while the mother was in hospital. The Robertsons met the mother and father with the child before the separation took place. Joyce Robertson became a fully available substitute mother keeping alive Jane's experience and expectation of mothering. When reunited with her mother, Jane happily accepted her.

Three other children, Thomas, Kate and Lucy, were also fostered by the Robertsons during the separation from their mother. They settled better than 'John', were less distressed and accepted the mother when reunited with her. The Robertsons concluded that replacing the attachment bond by providing a substitute mother could work. In fact, they observed that the younger children (Jane and Lucy) found it hard to part from the new attachment figure in their lives (*Separation and the Very Young*, 1989, Robertson J and Robertson J).

In their research observing children when they were separated from their mothers, the Robertsons found Thomas (2 years, 4 months) was well-prepared for the separation and fully supported by his substitute mother.

Providing more individual care and stimulation

Some studies in orphanages showed that improvements could be made if there was someone provided to support the children (Skodak and Skeels, 1945) or if there was more stimulation. Improvements in IQ were found if there was more stimulation or a lower child-to-carer ratio. This idea is returned to when the effects of day care are discussed later in this content section. It also seems from the evidence that the earlier the intervention, the better (e.g. Goldfarb). The effects of institutionalisation seem to be able to be overcome – they are **reversible** – but only if additional care and more stimulation are introduced. Success also depends on the age of the child and how long the deprivation lasts.

Definition

Reversible is an important word when discussing the effects of deprivation, separation or privation in child psychology. It means that problems caused can be put right.

Coping with divorce and separation

The above ideas are used when advising parents on how to cope with separation through divorce and other similar situations. A young child is likely to go through the stages of protest, distress and despair, unless steps are taken to ensure an attachment figure is there for them and that routines and familiar situations are maintained as far as possible.

Older children can understand more, so decisions can be discussed with and explained to them, to minimise anger and distress. When learning the method material in child psychology you will read about the rights of the child set out in the United Nations Convention on the Rights of the Child (1989), which explain that a child has the right to participate in decisions about them and the right to be protected.

Bowlby thought that the attachment process had an evolutionary basis and, in times of fear and threat, a young child would turn to his/her attachment figure. If fear and threat are reduced by offering explanations and comfort, problems from separation can be reduced, as the Robertsons found. The 'fight or flight' response is a survival trait that prepares someone for action when needed, and such a response can be triggered in young children when they are faced with a threat such as the departure of someone they rely on.

Explore

You could look up what advice is given about helping children to cope with separation and divorce and see how these ideas from psychology fit that advice. It is likely that the advice has come from these ideas, such as providing a routine in the way that the Robertsons did for the children they fostered, and providing care and reassurance. This is a link to start with if you would like to know more:

www.helpguide.org/articles/family-divorce/children-and-divorce.htm

Progress check 4.7

Explain two reactions a child might be expected to show when there is separation from their main caregiver and two ways such reactions could be reduced/helped.

Evidence to suggest maternal deprivation might not have such severe consequences

- Schaffer and Emerson (1964) found that babies could form multiple attachments and if a baby gets suitable responses he or she can attach to any caregiver. It seems likely, therefore, that even if there is separation and deprivation with regard to the mother or the main caregiver, someone else who the baby has formed an attachment with will be there to prevent deprivation and its effects.
- Skeels (1949) found that girls who stayed in an orphanage differed in their IQ compared with girls who at the age of three years old went to a school for what was then called 'the mentally retarded'. Of course this happened naturally without Skeels setting up the situation. Skeels found that the girls who were moved got attention and stimulation from older girls in the school whereas those in the orphanage did not get that stimulation. At the start, before the move, both groups had an average IQ of 64 points. When they were four years old the group that had remained in the orphanage went down to an average IQ of 60, whereas those who had moved to the school had an average IQ of 92. Stimulation seemed to have helped intellectual development and lack of stimulation seemed to have caused problems with intellectual development, not maternal deprivation itself.

- Rutter (1970) studied delinquent teenage boys and did not find a link between early maternal separation and the delinquency. He found that the type of relationship with parents before the separation was important and he thought it was stress in the home that was a factor (though not perhaps the cause) in later delinquency as much as the separation itself.

Test yourself

To what extent can negative effects of deprivation (both short-term and long-term) be reduced? **(16 marks)**

Evaluation of Bowlby's ideas

Strengths of Bowlby's theory of attachment

Bowlby drew on a great deal of evidence, which was a strength of his theory. He read up on studies by such psychologists as Spitz and Goldfarb, as has been shown. For his first report (the one for the World Health Organization), he admitted there was not that much evidence, but after that he continued to gather theory and evidence from a wide variety of studies.

He also drew on many different theoretical areas, such as ethology and evolution theory in his explanation of the maternal deprivation hypothesis. He explored the psychodynamic background and he brought in ideas from child development, such as conclusions about the effects of separation on DQ and IQ (through Spitz, Goldfarb and others).

Bowlby also commissioned and supervised the work of others, such as James Robertson's observations of children in hospital. A strength of his theory is the amount of evidence he amassed from many different sources, including his own, using naturalistic observation, ethology and interviews.

Bowlby's work led to changes in hospital visiting policies as well as in institutional practices. Hospitals opened up to parents and institutions recognised the need for a replacement attachment figure, such as a named worker for a child. The need for stimulation was recognised, as was the need to plan for a period of separation.

Weaknesses of Bowlby's theory of attachment

The observational studies in institutions lacked careful procedures. Neither Spitz nor Goldfarb gave great detail about their research methods when gathering evidence, so their procedures could have been biased. For example, the group in Goldfarb's study who were fostered early might have been chosen for a reason, such as seeming more settled or placid. The 15 who were fostered after the age of three might have had something in common (unattractiveness?), which means the sample was biased. Spitz's observations did not involve a controlled sample either.

Animal studies may not be generalisable to humans. Harlow and his colleagues studied monkeys and found they ran to towelling-covered 'mothers' when they were stressed. From this he drew the conclusion that monkeys needed comfort as well as food, and Bowlby surmised that this was true of human babies as well. However, drawing conclusions from monkeys and saying they are true of humans might not be possible, because animals and humans have differences in brain structures as well as in other abilities such as problem-solving and use of language.

Year One link: You looked at the issues of using data from animals and generalising to humans when you studied learning theories.

Bowlby's own study of 44 juvenile thieves can be criticised and evaluation points were offered when his study was looked at earlier. For example, he used a control group as well as the thieves, but he himself said that it was a pity that this control group also consisted of children in an institution, when children in a 'normal' school may have been a better control group. Table 4.7 gives a summary of the strengths and weaknesses of Bowlby's theory of attachment

Table 4.7 Strengths and weaknesses of Bowlby's theory of attachment

Strengths	Weaknesses
Bowlby drew on many studies and their findings.	He used evidence from animals, such as Harlow's and Lorenz's work, and it might not be legitimate to generalise from animals to humans.
He drew on many different theoretical perspectives.	Some of the studies whose findings he used did not use well-documented or well-controlled studies.
He used or drew on many different research methods.	His own study of 44 juvenile thieves, for example, lacked a 'normal' control group.
His theory had clear practical application and was acted upon.	

STUDY HINT
Evidence for Bowlby's maternal deprivation hypothesis was given from several studies in this chapter, including Harlow's work, the work of Spitz, Goldfarb (1955), Bowlby's own study (1944), the Robertsons, Lorenz and Olsavsky et al. (2013). For all these studies strengths and weaknesses were considered and you can use those points when evaluating Bowlby's work.

Test yourself

Using research evidence, evaluate Bowlby's maternal deprivation hypothesis as an explanation of 'juvenile delinquency' and problems in young people. **(16 marks)**

Ainsworth's work on attachments

Mary Ainsworth worked with John Bowlby, extending his ideas by looking at different types of attachment, also called attachment styles, as well as considering issues such as sensitive parenting. Ainsworth was Canadian but came to England with her husband. She had already been researching in the area of attachments before starting work with Bowlby.

Ugandan studies

Ainsworth left London in 1954 to live in Uganda where she studied mother–child interactions. She noticed that there was a relationship between the **responsiveness** of the mother and the reactions of the child. Some mother–child interactions were secure and comfortable but others were tense and full of conflict. She found that the type of interaction was related to how responsive the parent was to the child's needs. She also noted that infants used their mothers as a safe/secure base from which to explore.

Definition
Responsiveness as applied to parenting: this refers to when a parent responds to a child's needs and signals in a swift, warm and caring way.

The strange situation test

Following her observations in Uganda, Ainsworth developed her own research methodology to study types of attachment between mothers and their babies. She used a structured observation and set up a test using standard procedures, so that each mother and child had the same experiences and a child's responses could be carefully recorded for comparison. A one-way mirror was used so that the patterns of attachment could be observed and children used were between 12 and 18 months old. Her procedure was called the strange situation, because the significant period was after children were put into a situation that was strange for them, and when they were experiencing separation from their mother (or main caregiver). Observers carefully recorded the child's response to the mother when she returned.

As explained earlier in this section, Harlow found that a monkey put into a stressful and fearful situation would cling to a towelling 'monkey', seemingly to get comfort. Therefore, an attached child is expected, after the stressful and fearful situation of being alone with a stranger, to cling to the mother for comfort. These are the issues Ainsworth was researching.

One version of the strange situation had eight parts, as shown in Table 4.8. Each part of the procedure lasted about three minutes. The reunions were the important times and the focus was on how the young baby responded to its mother when she returned. Steps 5 and 8 were the times when the baby's reaction to the mother was carefully noted and, from its reaction, the baby was classified into one of three attachment types/styles. Each step ideally lasted for three minutes. However, the mother was in control and could shorten the step or stop the procedure at any time. The observers in the strange situation procedure looked at proximity and contact seeking, maintenance of contact, avoiding contact and proximity and resisting contact and comfort. They also looked at moving around the room and exploring, searching behaviours and emotional indicators such as crying. Time sampling was involved in the observation, noting behaviour a few times each minute.

Table 4.8 Version of the strange situation, involving eight steps

Step 1	The parent and baby enter the room, which is in a laboratory but set up with toys and chairs to be comfortable for the participants.
Step 2	The parent does not interact with the baby, who is left to explore.
Step 3	The stranger goes into the room, talks to the parent, then approaches the baby. At this stage the parent quietly leaves the room.
Step 4	This is the first separation. The stranger tries to interact with the baby.
Step 5	The parent comes in and comforts the baby, then leaves again. This is the first reunion followed by the second separation.
Step 6	The stranger leaves the infant alone.
Step 7	The stranger enters the room and begins to interact with the baby again. The mother is still out of the room. The second separation continues.
Step 8	The parent comes in, greets and picks up the baby, while the stranger quietly leaves. This is the second reunion.

In the strange situation procedure a mother, child and stranger interact to see the reactions of the child.

Attachment types

Ainsworth and her colleagues reported that three attachment types were found from the strange situation procedure (although later another one was added). The three original attachment types are:

- securely attached (Type B)
- anxious avoidant or insecure avoidant (Type A)
- anxious resistant or insecure ambivalent/resistant (Type C).

Securely attached

Ainsworth called **securely attached** the children who were distressed when their mother left and wanted comfort from her when she returned. Ainsworth thought that a securely attached child would use his or her mother as a safe base and would also show separation anxiety when the mother left. So she was expecting distress when the mother left and for the child to seek comfort on the mother's return. This type of attachment is linked to a responsive mother who attends to the child's needs. In Ainsworth's study in the USA in 1978 around 70 per cent of infants were securely attached.

Definition

Securely attached is one of Ainsworth's attachment types and means the child is distressed when their mother leaves and wants comfort from the mother when they return.

Characteristics of a 'securely attached' child

The child shows separation anxiety and is distressed when the mother leaves. Also the child shows stranger anxiety, avoiding the stranger when alone with them but friendly when the mother is there. The child is positive and happy when the mother returns and will use the mother as a safe base to explore the environment.

Anxious avoidant

Anxious avoidant was the label given to children who were not distressed when the mother left and tended to avoid her when she came back. The child plays normally throughout the strange situation procedure. Anxious avoidant can be called avoidant insecure. It could be that the mother is neglectful or abusive and that the child has learned not to depend on her, and so is equally happy with the stranger as with the mother. However, other studies have given different (less negative) interpretations, such as coming from different parental expectations. In Ainsworth's study in Baltimore (1978) around 15 per cent of the sample of 26 families had babies who were anxious avoidant.

Definition

Anxious avoidant is one of Ainsworth's attachment types and refers to the child not being distressed when the mother leaves and avoiding the mother on her return.

Characteristics of an 'anxious avoidant' child

The child does not show distress when the mother leaves and plays normally with or without the stranger. The child does not seek comfort when the mother returns and does not show interest. The stranger and the mother can comfort the child equally.

Anxious resistant

Children were called **anxious resistant** when they stayed close to their mother rather than exploring, and became extremely distressed when she left. They went for comfort when she came back but then rejected her comforting. Anxious resistant can also be called ambivalent insecure or insecure resistant. There were not many anxious resistant children found in the USA sample that Ainsworth tested – only around 15 per cent. It is not a common attachment type in the USA. It is suggested that the mother of a child showing this attachment type is someone the child cannot rely on all the time, and so is not sure about her. McCarthy and Taylor (1999) suggested that children with abusive experiences were more likely to show ambivalent attachments and those with anxious resistant attachment were more likely to have problems with maintaining adult relationships. There may be cultural or other reasons for differences in attachment type.

You will read more about culture and attachment type when you learn the classic study for child psychology in your course (page 452) later in this chapter.

Definition

Anxious resistant is one of Ainsworth's attachment types and means the child will stay close to the mother without exploring and will be very distressed when the mother leaves. The child will seek comfort when the mother returns but might resist comfort offered. There is an element of ambivalence.

Characteristics of an 'anxious resistant' child

An anxious resistant child is wary of strangers and does not explore much even with the mother present. The child can be very distressed when the mother leaves and tends to resist contact with her or push her away when she returns. The child might seek comfort and then reject it as well as showing anger towards the mother on her return. The infant explores less and cries more than in the other two attachment types.

Explore
Use the link below to read more about attachment types and the impact on relationships. You can relate what is being said about partner choice to attachment type, but be sure to read critically, remembering evaluation points about attachment types and the research that they were derived from.
www.psychologytoday.com/blog/compassion-matters/201307/how-your-attachment-style-impacts-your-relationship

STUDY HINT
It is worth making notes about what behaviour children with each attachment type are likely to show as you may be asked to apply your understanding of attachment types. For example, you could be given a description of a child and asked which attachment type the child's behaviour suggests.

Progress check 4.9
Consider a child who is very distressed when the mother leaves and does not explore their surroundings much. They seek comfort when the mother returns but then can reject any comfort offered. Which attachment type is the child displaying?

STUDY HINT
It is not difficult perhaps to picture the securely attached child, but the other two types are harder to remember. You could think of the avoidant child as being independent and *avoiding* contact and the resistant child as being clingy but *resisting* contact to help you remember the difference between anxious avoidant and anxious resistant.

Support for the maternal deprivation hypothesis

Ainsworth's work on attachment type backs Bowlby's attachment theory in that securely attached children have a positive working model of themselves perhaps and can explore because they are reassured at having a safe base. However, avoidance of the mother may mean the child feels rejected and so rejects the mother.

Evaluation of the strange situation procedure

Strengths

- There is good reliability in that the strange situation procedure has been used many times in different cultures and does show in the main the three types of attachment (though with different percentages than in the USA). Wartner *et al.* (1994) used the strange situation procedure and found in Germany that 78 per cent of children were classified in the same way at six years old as they were when they were one year old.
- The procedure is replicable and was carried out with many mother–child dyads (a dyad is a pair), which is what gives reliability and also credibility. An advantage of a structured observation is that the same interactions are being observed for each mother–child pair, such as the same stranger being used, so there are controls, which strengthens credibility.

Weaknesses

- The strange situation is an artificial situation and is a structured observation. It can be said to lack ecological validity because the child is in an artificial situation and environment and the comings and goings of the mother and stranger follow a script.
- Lamb (1977) suggested that there might be different attachment types with the father, and the strange situation only looks at mother–child interactions, which limits the usefulness of conclusions. Again this is about validity – the strange situation procedure looks at mother–child attachment types, not attachment types in general.
- There is the possibility that the child's responses at one time would not be the same another time, perhaps if the child is unwell or there has been a change in the child's circumstances.
- Ethically perhaps the strange situation is not appropriate as the child is made distressed by the study – though the mother can come in to the child at any time during the procedure.
- Also it could be said that a child is left by the mother in 'real life' occasionally so the situation is not that artificial.

- The strange situation has been used in different cultures and found different proportions of securely attached children. There is a suggestion that the situation is culture-bound and perhaps not suitable in other cultures where upbringing expectations are different.

> **STUDY HINT**
> When discussing structured observations as a research method used in child psychology you can consider the strengths and weaknesses of the strange situation procedure. For example, there is strength in the credibility, replicability and reliability, but weakness in validity.

A fourth type after Ainsworth: disorganised and disorientated

In 1990 Main and Solomon suggested that there is a fourth attachment type – disorganised and disorientated (Type D). This type of attachment is characterised by the child both approaching the mother on her return and avoiding her. This can arise from an abusive situation when a child wants to escape from the situation but the person they are frightened of is their safety net. Children can dissociate from what is going on and feel detached, which leads to a disorganised attachment with the mother/parents. It seems that loss in the parent's life can lead to a disorganised attachment between parent and child, and it is how well the parent has made sense of their own loss that affects the parent–child relationship. It might be that the parent has suffered abuse and becomes emotional when dealing with their own child. Main and Hesse (1993) found that mothers of children with disorganised attachment type had suffered loss or trauma close to the birth of the child and had become very depressed. For mothers whose parents had died before they finished their schooling, 56 per cent had children with disorganised attachments.

Characteristics of a 'disorganised' child

A child with a disorganised attachment has the difficulty of unpredictable parenting and no strategy for making themselves feel safe. A child with a disorganised attachment might approach the parent for comfort and then pull away from them or they might hit them or run away. This is what is meant about being 'disorganised'.

> **Explore**
> You can read more about how childhood attachments influence adult relationships, including the work of Bowlby and Ainsworth, using the internet. Here is a link to a YouTube video if you would like to know more: www.youtube.com/watch?v=2xOziE-Jlac

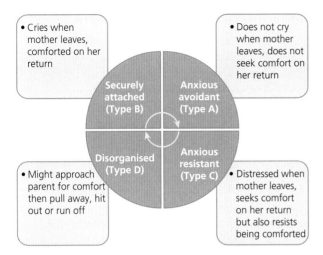

- Cries when mother leaves, comforted on her return

Securely attached (Type B)

- Does not cry when mother leaves, does not seek comfort on her return

Anxious avoidant (Type A)

Disorganised (Type D)

- Might approach parent for comfort then pull away, hit out or run off

Anxious resistant (Type C)

- Distressed when mother leaves, seeks comfort on her return but also resists being comforted

Ainsworth's three attachment types and the additional 'disorganised' type

Links between attachment types and mothering styles

Ainsworth, along with colleagues, such as Ainsworth and Bell (1969), looked at the type of mothering that might produce a certain attachment type in a child. They observed the children they used in the strange situation before that procedure was carried out. The observation was for three months and they were able to draw conclusions about the responsiveness of the mothering. For example, a mother who was insensitive to her infant's responses during feeding and to the infant's physical needs, who showed little face-to-face interaction and was less attentive when the child was distressed did not have an infant who was securely attached in the strange situation procedure – the child was likely to be insecurely attached. Mothers who had responded to their infant's needs in the first three months of their life, and who were sensitive to their child's demands, had securely attached children.

Insecure avoidant (anxious avoidant) children in Ainsworth's study were called Group A and securely attached children were known as Group B. Insecure ambivalent (anxious resistant) children were called Group C – they seemed both to welcome the mother back at first and then to push her away. Children who were insecure in their attachment had mothers who tended to push them away more and who were less sensitive to their needs.

STUDY HINT

Try to remember which attachment type is Type A, which is Type B, Type C and Type D, because in studies they may be referred to in that way. One way of remembering is that securely attached is Type B, perhaps counter-intuitively, because it was the one found most in Ainsworth's USA sample. Then Type D is [D]isorganised. Type A is [A]voidant and so Type C is left for resistant. Try to find ways of remembering like this as it will help you to learn the material.

Progress check 4.10

Explain what mothering style would be expected for a securely attached infant.

Reactive Attachment Disorder (RAD)

Reactive Attachment Disorder is found when normal attachments in early childhood are not formed and there may have been neglect and abuse or sudden separation from caregivers, change in caregivers or lack of responsiveness from caregivers from the age of six months to three years. RAD can present as withdrawal from social interaction or the opposite, which is being over-familiar with strangers. Both the ICD-10 and the DSM-IV-TR have RAD as a disorder. When there is over-familiarity, which is disinhibition, the disorder is called 'Disinhibited Attachment Disorder' (DAD). The DSM-5 splits RAD into Reactive Attachment Disorder and Social Engagement Disorder.

STUDY HINT

You covered both the ICD-10 and the DSM (either IV, IV-TR or 5) in clinical psychology. Recall what was said about such classification systems there.

It is thought that RAD comes from problems with internal working models of relationships, stemming from not forming healthy attachments themselves. You can see how this links with the work of Bowlby and Ainsworth on attachments.

Explore

If you would like to learn more about RAD and related disorders try the following link:

http://cogprints.org/3800/1/Richters_&_Volkmar.pdf

Another, perhaps less academic, link is:

www.mayoclinic.org/diseases-conditions/reactive-attachment-disorder/basics/definition/con-20032126

Using the strange situation in cross-cultural studies

Cross-cultural studies are those carried out in more than one culture in order to compare findings. Ainsworth, for example, used the strange situation in Uganda and another study used children from Baltimore in the USA; the findings were then compared.

Ainsworth's work in Uganda

In Uganda, around 1963, Ainsworth studied 26 families and observed their interactions, watching mother–child relationships. She also interviewed the mothers and gathered data about the mother's sensitivity. She found that mothers who knew a lot about their babies when interviewed were sensitive to their infant's needs. They tended to have children who were what Ainsworth called securely attached, in that they did not cry much and used their mother as a secure base from which to explore. In contrast, less sensitive mothers had children who cried more and did not explore as much.

Ainsworth's work on the Baltimore project

In Baltimore, also around 1963, 26 families were observed, following each family from birth of the child through the first year. Naturalistic observations were used, looking at such issues as face-to-face interaction, responsiveness to crying and physical needs, feeding and close bodily contact. The observations took place in the family home, but the final observation involved the mother and child going to a laboratory to take part in the strange situation procedure, which was devised for that purpose. The main focus of the study was the pattern of interactions in the home and conclusions about the sensitivity of the mother related to the attachment type of the child. Most of the focus, however, was on the results from the strange situation procedure, tending to overshadow the evidence about the mother's responsiveness.

Comparing Uganda and Baltimore

There were many similarities in the attachment types and types of mothering in the two cultures. The general conclusion was that securely attached infants used their mothers as a secure base from which to explore and had sensitive mothers, whereas insecurely attached infants cried more, explored less and had less sensitive mothers. If this was found in two different cultures, perhaps there was a biological basis for such attachment types when linked to parenting style and maybe this was true of all cultures. If there were differences in attachment types linked to parenting styles in different cultures, then the links may have come from nurture and the differences in environment.

Issues and debates

Cross-cultural studies are ways of looking at the nature–nurture debate. This is a strength of such studies, so you can use this comment in evaluation. They can help to show which human behaviours and characteristics come from learning by interacting with the environment and which are 'universal' laws of behaviour or characteristics.

Other cross-cultural studies of attachment types

In Germany, in a study by Grossman et al. in 1985 that used the strange situation, more avoidant attachment types were found than in the Baltimore study. In Japan and Israel (in the Kibbutzim) there were more ambivalent types. The Israeli study was carried out by Sagi et al. (1985) and the Japanese study by Miyake et al. (1985).

Cross-cultural study showing universality in attachment types: Jin et al. (2012)

A more recent cross-cultural study was carried out by Jin et al. in Korea and published in 2012. In this study 87 Korean mothers and their children aged 12 to 15 months were studied using the strange situation to look for cultural differences in attachment types. Jin et al. also observed children in a ten-minute free play session, after the strange situation procedure, to look at maternal sensitivity. The observations were video-taped. The aim of the study was to help to see whether attachment types were universal or culture-specific and the Korean results were compared with Ainsworth's finding from her Baltimore study. Her findings as generally reported were that about 70 per cent were securely attached and the remaining 30 per cent was split evenly between anxious avoidant and anxious resistant (these percentages come from interpretation of her data). In Jin et al. (2012) in Korea 78 per cent were securely attached and 22 per cent were insecure. In the Korean sample, as expected, there were a greater number of securely attached infants, which reinforces the idea that attachment types are found in similar proportions across cultures and countries. (This is generally reported to be the case, in spite of the differences found in Germany, Israel and Japan, as reported above.) However, there was just 1 per cent Korean babies classified as avoidant. The Korean study found the link between maternal sensitivity and infant security that was expected following Ainsworth's findings. When comparing Eastern and Western cultures, there were some differences in the behaviours of the securely attached children. For example, the Korean infants stayed less close to their mothers and explored more. When the Korean mothers returned to their infants, they were more likely to get down on the floor and play with their infants straightaway, and to stay there.

STUDY HINT
Use these studies as examples of cross-cultural research when answering questions about this research method.

Explore
You can look at the Korean study, which was available as a dissertation before publication, using this link: www.lib.utexas.edu/etd/d/2005/jinm06088/jinm06088.pdf

Jin *et al.* (2012) cite van IJzendoorn and Sagi-Schwartz (2008), arguing that there are four hypotheses when it comes to cross-cultural support for attachment theory. These hypotheses are that there is universality in that in nearly all cases all infants have an attachment with one or more caregiver and also that secure attachment is the norm. The other two hypotheses are that secure attachment comes from sensitive mothering, meaning swift and sensitive responses to the baby's signals, and that secure attachment means competence in later social and emotional interactions. From these four predictions, Jin *et al.* (2012) expected to find universality in that all the Korean children would show attachment behaviour and they expected to find the majority securely attached. They also thought that there would be low numbers of disorganised attachment, similar to the 15 per cent generally found in all countries tested. This figure came from van IJzendoorn and Kroonenberg (1988), which is the classic study in child psychology in your course (page 452). They also expected insecure infants to be in the resistant and not the avoidant category because of findings in Japan, which is similar to Korea in culture. Table 4.9 shows the Korean sample findings and the Baltimore, USA findings.

Table 4.9 Comparison of attachment types in two cultures

	Avoidant – Type A	Secure – Type B	Resistant – Type C
Korea sample	1 (1%)	66 (78%)	18 (21%)
Baltimore USA sample	22 (21%)	70 (67%)	13 (12%)

When 'disorganised' as a category was introduced the Korean sample percentages were 1 per cent avoidant, 72 per cent secure, 18 per cent resistant and 9 per cent disorganised.

Jin *et al.* (2012) concluded that having the norm of secure attachment is universal. However, they felt that mothering was different in different cultures, such as in the US and Western cultures mothers are more likely to encourage their infants to explore so the infants are the ones to seek proximity when they are distressed. However, in Korea and Japan mothers tend to encourage their children to remain close so the mothers are the ones who approach and stay near the infant after separation. That would make infants in Korea and Japan show less proximity-seeking behaviour.

Evaluation of Jin *et al.* (2012)

Jin *et al.* (2012) thought that perhaps the validity of the strange situation procedure was challenged because the mothers in Korea went straight to the infants, so the observers could not watch what the infant would do in the way of seeking out the mother. They felt, however, that their findings both reinforced and were reinforced by van IJzendoorn and Kroonenberg's (1988) meta-analysis. They suggested that home observations would be useful, which suggests that they felt the structured observational procedures of their study lacked the validity that naturalistic observations would have.

STUDY HINT
You can use these evaluation points when discussing observation as a research method, cross-cultural design as a research method and the classic study, van IJzendoorn and Kroonenberg (1988).

Progress check 4.11
Explain two limitations Jin *et al.* (2012) suggest in their study.

Evaluating cross-cultural studies and universality of attachment types

It was at first thought that there were more avoidant children in Germany because of a lack of responsiveness on the part of the parents. However, it was then suggested that it might be because parents valued independence more, making it more a matter of cultural features of parenting style.

In Japan and in Israel in the Kibbutzim it was suggested that there was less emphasis on getting on with strangers, so children were less used to other people and therefore more ambivalent when tested using the strange situation. What was thought to be a matter of difference in sensitivity of mothering was later thought to be because of a different cultural emphasis. The strange situation was perhaps more suitable for testing certain cultures – those that emphasised sensitive mothering in the same way as in the UK and the USA.

However, further examination of the findings of the studies suggest that, in fact, similar responses by the mothers led to similar attachment types, so it is now thought that the findings from the different cultures support each other more than was at first thought. The issue of whether the strange situation is suitable for use across different cultures is still being debated.

Evaluation of the cross-cultural studies using the strange situation task

Strengths

- The same procedure was used in the different cultures so, in theory, conclusions from each study can be compared with one another fairly. This gives the findings reliability in that the same procedures were used.
- There did seem to be consistency in the patterns observed – for example, the three types were identified in each of the studies.
- In general the main attachment type is securely attached and, when a different attachment type is found to predominate, this tends to be explicable by looking at cultural preferences regarding acceptable behaviour, rather than by 'bad' mothering.

Weaknesses

- By using a procedure developed in the USA in cultures as different as Germany, Japan and Israel, it might be that the task itself gives differences in findings as much as differences in sensitivity of the mothers. For example, Japanese children who are less used to strangers than American children might be more fearful and so respond differently, rather than have a different attachment type. Also as Jin *et al.* (2012) showed, different cultural norms can show different mothering styles, such as in Korea and Japan mothers seeking out their children first when reunited.
- Cultures have many differences, including family structure, parenting styles, what is expected and how

children are seen in a society. With so many different factors involved it is hard, if not impossible, to draw conclusions about which feature causes which effect. Where there are such complex issues, measuring them equally and fairly to allow comparisons is difficult, if not impossible.

> **STUDY HINT**
>
> The classic study van IJzendoorn and Kroonenberg (1988) can be used when discussing cross-cultural studies and the universality of attachment types as well as the validity of using the strange situation procedure.

Evaluation of Ainsworth's ideas about attachments

Strengths

- Like Bowlby, Ainsworth worked in the field of attachment and the effects of separation for many years, so she was able to draw on a wealth of data for her conclusions. She carried out many studies, and others used her strange situation procedure and drew similar conclusions.
- Ainsworth devised a well-controlled procedure for measuring attachment types, which was carried out in a laboratory and observed by many people. Therefore, inter-observer reliability could be found, and the procedure does seem to be reliable, because the same attachment types are found in different studies.
- Ainsworth could be criticised for using a procedure that was controlled and laboratory-based, but she also used naturalistic observation and interviews to make her findings valid and true to life.

Weaknesses

- A problem with the strange situation is that it is a laboratory procedure using an unnatural environment, so it could be the unnatural environment that causes the reactions of the infant to the mother, rather than (or as well as) being left alone with a stranger. This means there is a problem with validity.
- It could be argued that, if a fourth attachment type had to be added, then Ainsworth's conclusions were not complete, which is a weakness.
- If attachment depends on responsiveness and possibly also on the child's temperament, then it is hard to measure such complex issues. Scientific conclusions require measurable concepts.
- Attachment types were cleverly measured using the strange situation technique and sensitivity of mothering was measured by using observations. However, the

temperament of the child was not taken into account, which emphasises the complexity of the child's interactions.

Test yourself

Evaluate Ainsworth's research looking at attachment types and mothering styles. **(16 marks)**

Child temperament and attachment

Although Ainsworth did not look at child temperament and attachment, these issues have been considered and are important when considering the effects of individual differences on a child's development. Hong and Park (2012), researching in Korea, have written a review on the impact of attachment, temperament and parenting on human development. In their review they discuss temperament traits in children, which are biologically given. They describe temperament as a 'neurobiological element of the individual' and they suggest that individuals differ in terms of 'emotions, sociability and self-control'. Temperament comes from genes but is affected by development such as child-rearing practices, which makes it **epigenetic**.

Definition

Epigenetic means something that comes from genes but is also affected by the environment.

Year One link: You probably came across the term 'epigenetic' in biological psychology.

Thomas and Chess (1956) (cited in Hong and Park, 2012) used 133 individuals in 84 families using a longitudinal design and followed the individual from three months old into adulthood. They concluded from their study that there were nine dimensions to temperament and they classified temperament into three types. Thomas and Chess thought that 40 per cent of the children were 'easy', which meant

they were usually cheerful and adapted to new things quickly. It was found that 10 per cent were 'difficult' children, which meant they were easily frustrated and negative in social interactions, 15 per cent were 'fearful', which meant they had low activity and withdrew in the face of new stimuli, and 35 per cent were not easily classified into these three groups. Other studies suggest uninhibited and inhibited as two temperament types, with an intermediate type too (Kagan and Fox, 2006, cited in Hong and Park, 2012).

Parenting and temperament

Caregivers need to respond to the individual differences in a child that come from their temperament. However, if a mother is stressed because of things going on in her life it can be hard to deal with a child with a difficult temperament or problem behaviours. Goossens and van IJzendoorn (1990, cited in Hong and Park, 2012) showed that securely attached infants develop different attachments with their different caregivers, which suggests that parenting can affect a child's temperament. Chess (1977, cited in Hong and Park, 2012) suggests that it is about goodness of fit between the child's temperament and their family and others around them. Fonagy et al. (1991, cited in Hong and Park, 2012) suggest that reflective parenting can help and this means understanding self and others within issues like mental states and intentions, so mothers under pressure are more likely to have securely attached children if they reflect on the child's motivations rather than their actions.

Explore

You can read Hong and Park's (2012) review using this link if you would like to know more:
www.ncbi.nlm.nih.gov/pmc/articles/PMC3534157/

Guyer et al. (2015) discuss temperament and parenting styles. They talk about a temperament they call 'behavioural inhibition' (BI), which relates to social reticence and withdrawal from unfamiliar situations. They suggest that parenting style and temperament can together affect behaviour and they also suggest that there can be impact at the neural level, affecting 'cognitive and emotional responses to social challenges'. They used fMRI scanning to look at how different parenting styles affected neural responses when adolescents experienced peer rejection. They used two groups, one with BI and one without BI. They looked at authoritarian and authoritative parenting and three brain regions – the ventrolateral prefrontal cortex, the striatum and the amygdala. These three areas relate to social anxiety, which they felt linked to behavioural inhibition (BI). They found that the young people having BI in their childhood as a temperament showed lower response in the ventrolateral prefrontal cortex than those without BI in their childhood when parenting was authoritarian. However, all of the participants showed decreased response in the caudate when there were higher levels of authoritative parenting. This was in response to peer rejection. BI in early life seemed to show more neurobiological sensitivity to parenting styles, particularly authoritarian, or harsh, parenting.

Test yourself

Assess how individual differences might relate to attachment type and/or parenting style. **(8 marks)**

Research into privation

Privation is different from deprivation in that a child will not have formed any attachment and will lack almost all types of socialisation. With deprivation there would have been an attachment that a child would then be deprived of.

> **STUDY HINT**
> Be ready to compare the meaning of the terms privation and deprivation.

Study of 'Genie'

One of the best-known studies looking at the effects of privation is of a young girl called Genie, who was discovered after nearly 13 years of neglect, having been locked away in a room by her parents. One conclusion from the in-depth study of her development after she was found was that she did not develop normal language or motor movements (e.g. walking), so early privation was thought to lead to irreversible problems. However, nobody knows whether Genie would have developed normally without the privation. Perhaps her parents thought or knew that there were developmental problems in the first place, which is why they locked her away.

> **STUDY HINT**
> When looking at a question in an exam, make sure you read all the words carefully. You might be asked whether the effects of privation are reversible, which is a question with a different focus from being asked to evaluate the effects of privation.

In this section you will look at some studies of privated children to see what the effects of privation are and whether negative effects can be put right, i.e. if such problems are reversible.

Curtiss's study of Genie (1977)

Genie was discovered in California, USA at the age of about 13. She had been locked away by her parents and had very little socialisation. Curtiss was one of the researchers who studied and looked after Genie (not her real name) and who wrote up the case study.

Background

Genie's mother said that she had a stormy relationship with her husband, who threatened to beat her, and she lived in fear. Her husband did not want children and was violent towards Genie's mother. When their first daughter (not Genie) was born, she seemed healthy and normal but she cried a lot and her father, irritated by the crying, put her into the garage so he would not have to listen to her. This child died of pneumonia at the age of two. A boy was born three years later and the mother tried to keep him quiet and good. The boy had development problems, being late to walk and talk. The husband's mother took the boy and he thrived, later to return to his parents.

Genie was born three years after that. Her birth weight was normal and she had good head control when checked at four months. She had a hip dislocation that required a pillow splint. At five months she was said to be alert – this is important later, as it suggests that Genie was a 'normal' baby.

Genie's mother said that Genie was not very cuddly and resisted any solid food. It was also known that Genie's father disliked Genie and did not allow his wife to pay her much attention. At 14 months Genie had an illness and was feverish. She saw a paediatrician who said she showed signs of possible retardation, but it was hard to assess her development because of the fever. Genie's father used this diagnosis as an excuse for the later abuse Genie suffered.

Not long afterwards Genie's father's mother was killed by a truck. Genie's father became embittered, moving the family into his mother's home and cutting them off from the outside world. Genie's father soon isolated Genie completely, tying her to a 'potty chair' during the day and into a crib at night. The room Genie was in was isolated from the rest of the family and there was little for her to hear. She occasionally made a noise to attract attention but was then beaten, so she stopped. Genie's mother began to go blind and found it hard to go to speak to her, and her brother imitated his father and did not speak to her either.

Genie's father thought she would not live beyond the age of 12 so he promised that after that age, if Genie lived, her mother could get help for their daughter. However, he went back on his promise – but when Genie was 13 her mother had a violent argument with her husband and threatened to leave if he did not contact her own mother to get help. Genie's mother took Genie and left the home. When they went to get help from the welfare office a worker there saw Genie and realised that something was very wrong, and the police were called. Genie's parents were charged with child abuse, but on the day of the trial her father killed himself. Genie was admitted to hospital with severe malnutrition.

Genie at the start of the study

Susan Curtiss provides a great deal of evidence about Genie's progress (or lack of it) when taken in by psychologists to help her and study her. At first Genie could not chew food, stand upright or straighten her arms and legs. She made few sounds and was incontinent. She was, however, alert and curious.

The researchers were interested primarily in her language skills. They knew she did not speak but wanted to discover how much she understood, so they started by questioning the staff in the hospital she had been taken to. They said she seemed to understand a few words, focusing on single words rather than sentences, and that she could understand if pointing was used in addition to words. She had very little language use at all, but she did imitate some words that were spoken to her.

Aim

The aim of the study was primarily to help Genie, but also to see if a child of just over 13 could learn language.

Procedure

Much of the data were gathered by working with and observing Genie. There were also weekly interviews with Genie's mother, but it seemed that she would say what she thought social workers wanted to hear, so the detail was not reliable. Information about Genie's early life had to be gathered from Genie's own behaviour and the few comments she made. There were daily doctor's reports about Genie, and videotapes and tape recordings were made and catalogued, becoming a rich source of data. Psychological testing was used, with observations and language tests.

Case study evidence

Early progress

From January 1971 Genie was in the hospital and she started to become more social, as well as to develop cognitively and intellectually. When tested she could achieve some things an eight- or nine-year-old could do (such as cleaning up and bathing herself), but for other activities she only reached the level of a two year-old (such as chewing food). She displayed some awareness – in one incident in a classroom a teacher asked a child with two balloons how many balloons the child had. The child said 'three' and Genie, looking startled, gave the child another balloon. This suggests an understanding of numbers.

In time, language began to emerge and she started asking for the names of things around her. Curtiss's account gives many examples of how Genie learned language. She moved to a rehabilitation centre and began to develop, but her development was not normal. For example, she had delayed responses – she could be asked to do something but would respond up to ten minutes later. She also chose the path of least effort and seemed lazy. Her language, however, did develop and by 1972 she used language for the first time when thinking about a past event.

In 1974 Genie asked for a cracker. Curtiss asked 'how many do you want?' and Genie replied 'five'. Then Curtiss said 'how about fewer?' and Genie replied 'four'. When asked 'how about fewer than that?' she said 'three', and three crackers were given to her. It seemed that Genie was starting to understand and use English, with the help of sign language, although her understanding was incomplete.

Case study analysis

Genie's progress in language was analysed in relation to what was thought of as the **critical period** for language learning. A critical period means that something has to be learned by then or it is not learned at all. It was thought that the critical period for language development was from two years old to puberty. The critical age has to do with the brain's maturity – it is not mature enough before the age of two and is fully mature by puberty. Animal studies showed critical periods for development of processes such as attachment – although it is now thought that perhaps instead of critical periods, **sensitive periods** should be considered. A sensitive period is a time when it is best to learn a particular attribute or have a particular experience, but it can still occur outside that period.

> ## Definitions
>
> **Critical period** means something has to develop or be learned by a certain time or it will not develop or be learned at all. Language was said to have a critical period and Bowlby thought attachment might have a critical period.
>
> **Sensitive period** means something tends to develop or be learned within a certain time period, and tends to be better developed or learned then, but that the period can be extended.

At the time of Genie's study, critical periods were being investigated. A problem with studying humans and critical periods was that experiments could not be carried out – a human could not be deprived to see what the results of such deprivation would be. In Genie, though, and in other so-called **feral** children, there was a natural experiment. Genie had been deprived of stimulation until puberty.

If she could still learn language, then this was evidence against there being a critical period.

Definition
Feral is the term for a child that has had no attachment or socialisation from birth or from very close to their birth.

The difficulty with this study was that, although Genie did learn a lot of language and other skills, it could not be said that her development had caught up or that her behaviour and language use was 'normal', so it could not be concluded that there was no critical period for language development. Another difficulty was that there had been perhaps some language stimulation in Genie's development, but how much and what that was is not known. One feature of the study is that it was claimed that the language that Genie did develop was that associated with the right hemisphere of the brain, and tests were done that supported the idea that Genie was a 'right hemisphere thinker'. She used the right hemisphere for language and her language was abnormal. It was concluded that her case supported the idea of there being a critical period for 'normal' language development.

'Genie' today
After the study, when the arrangements for Genie's care were cut short because of a loss of funding, Genie went to stay in a residential home. Her case was not further studied, partly because it was recognised that the psychologists involved in the case had tried to help her to develop, but had also used her as the 'subject' of a study and there was thought to have been excessive testing, given her situation. In 2008 ABC News reported Genie was living in California in confinement and was not using language. There is of course an issue of privacy and confidentiality which protects 'Genie'.

Explore
Find out more about Genie. There are various films available that show Genie when she was being studied and looked after. Here is one link you could consider:
www.youtube.com/watch?v=hmdycJQi4QA
You could also look up the stories of other feral children and consider how far you think lack of socialisation leads to abnormal development.

Effects of the privation
It seems that Genie did not recover from the privation she experienced as a young child. She did not learn language normally, for example, and she had difficulty walking. However, she did learn some language and learned to recognise people. There might have been some reversibility. Quite rightly, not enough is known about Genie now, because of the issue of ethics, for it to be known if there was more reversibility than there seems, but it does seem unlikely. Also if she did have developmental issues as a young child then any problems might be down to those issues and not to the privation.

Evaluation

Strengths
- This case study had so much information gathered during its course that the data are rich, detailed and thorough. There are both qualitative and quantitative data gathered, using many different research methods, so the data are valid.
- The study gave Genie a pseudonym so that she could not be recognised and the family could not be traced. Her privacy was able to be protected so that after the study she could live anonymously and not be bothered by journalists. From an ethical point of view, this is a strength.

Weaknesses
- A major problem with the study is that it could not be shown that Genie would have developed normally with good socialisation, because there was the suggestion that she may have had developmental problems in infancy. It could be that after being discovered she did not develop normally because of inherent problems rather than because of her experiences.
- There are ethical difficulties about the study because Genie, although cared for during the study and living in the homes of psychologists, was the 'subject' of a study and was subjected to a great deal of testing and questioning. This could be seen as taking advantage of her situation and not treating her properly. For example, there was little mention of informed consent, a right to withdraw or debriefing. It might have been hard to cover these sorts of ethical issues given the unusual circumstances, but even so the testing would not be something that rehabilitation would normally entail.

STUDY HINT
Genie is an example of a privated child, so use this study when writing about privation and the importance of attachments.

Progress check 4.12
Explain one strength and one weakness of using the study of Genie to say that the effects of privation are not reversible.

The Czech twins: Koluchová (1972)

The psychologist Jarmila Koluchová looked at the story of identical twin boys who were born in Czechoslovakia in 1960. At first their development was reasonably normal, though they lost their mother not long after they were born and were brought up in an institution for a year, then cared for by an aunt for another six months. The twins seemed to have followed a pattern of normal development in their first 18 months. The twins' father had remarried and, when they were about 18 months old, they went to live with their father, stepmother and her four children.

However, their father was not often at home and their stepmother locked them away in a room and beat them. This carried on for over five years until they were found and rescued. When they were discovered, aged seven, the twins had rickets (a bone disease caused by lack of vitamin D), were small for their age, could not talk and could not recognise pictures, so an IQ test was not possible. They were frightened of the dark and of other people. Their stage of development was that of a three year old. It was predicted that they would not develop normally and would remain behind in intellectual development.

The boys were placed in a school for children with severe learning difficulties, which also helped with their physical development. Then they were adopted by a woman who took great interest in them and gave them exceptional attention. Over time they began to catch up with children of their own age and went to a normal school. By the time they were 11 their speech was normal. Eventually, by the age of 15, their IQ was normal for their age. They both continued through school and went on to train in electronics.

Koluchová reported on the twins again in 1991 and both were married with children and were said to be happy, stable and to have warm relationships with their families. One is a computer technician and the other a technical training instructor. The main point is that, after such severe privation, the boys gradually caught up and led normal, happy lives. Their story suggests that the effects of privation are reversible. Sometimes this study is reported as a study of deprivation but, as the twins hardly formed an attachment to an adult before they went back to live with their father, it is presented here as a study of privation.

Evaluation of the Koluchová study

Strengths

- It is known that the twins were normal in their development when they left the care of their aunt at the age of about 18 months. Therefore, when they were later found to be severely behind in their development, this could be said to be because of the privation they

experienced. There was a normal baseline against which to measure their lack of progress.
- This was a case study, and so a great deal of information was gathered using different methods, such as IQ testing, interviewing and observing. The depth and detail of the material suggests that the data are valid about the twins' real experiences.
- The study was longitudinal and so the development of the twins could be tracked over many years, which helps when drawing conclusions about whether privation is reversible. It is known, for example, that the twins married and had children, whereas a much shorter study would not have documented any later development.

Weaknesses

- The boys had each other and so could attach to each other, which may have been why they were able to catch up, develop normally and shake off the effects of their privation.
- They would have formed an attachment with their aunt and perhaps others in the social agency, so perhaps they were deprived rather than privated.
- It can never be completely known what life is like for the boys now they are adults, and they may not be happy and well adjusted. There is no reason to say they are not, but information about underlying anxieties and problems might not have been uncovered even now that they are adults.

> ## Progress check 4.13
>
> Explain why the study of twins carried out by Koluchová is said to be an example of privation.

> ## Explore
>
> You can read an article written in 1976 in the *British Medical Journal* about the twins, if you would like to know more, using the following link:
>
> www.bmj.com/content/2/6041/897

> **STUDY HINT**
> Use Koluchová as an example of a longitudinal study when answering questions about such research methods.

Children in Terezín: Freud and Dann (1951)

Anna Freud and Sophie Dann (1951) studied six children who were kept in the ghetto of Terezín, arriving there before the age of one. (Terezin was a garrison town in Czechoslovakia, and it became a

Jewish ghetto during the Second World War, from where people were sent to extermination camps such as Auschwitz.) The children were looked after by adults 'passing through' – before the adults were sent to gas chambers or a similar fate. These children did not have the chance to form an attachment and are considered to have suffered privation.

When the camps were liberated, the children were brought to Britain. Later they were fostered and followed up to see how well they recovered from their early privation. When they were found in Terezín, they could not speak much, but were strongly attached to one another, showing separation distress/anxiety when separated. The children developed normal intelligence, though one sought psychiatric help as an adult and another described feeling isolated and alone. It seems that the effects of privation can be reversed, though in some cases not without problems in adulthood.

Evaluation of the Freud and Dann study

Strengths

- This was a longitudinal study that followed the children through to adulthood, so information about the long-term effects of the privation could be found. This means that conclusions could be drawn to say that the effects of privation could be reversible. A longitudinal study is a good way of finding out such relevant information because the same people are followed through the whole situation, so conclusions can be drawn more firmly.

- This was a real study of real children who endured privation in a situation that, for ethical reasons, could not have been set up. This study offers valuable insights into such situations and is unique. This is the value of a case study – it is in-depth, detailed, valid and more ethical than setting a situation up for study.

Weaknesses

- Although the study is said to be about privation, it is suggested from the data that the children formed attachments with each other, so they may not have been as privated as is suggested. However, it is clear that they were privated of adult care that would provide a safe base, so to an extent this criticism is not well founded.

- The study is not replicable and there are so many complex factors to consider that it is hard to draw conclusions about the effects of early privation. For example, the children's temperaments may have affected their survival and subsequent recovery, or other factors about the specific situation.

A study of internationally adopted children: Eigsti et al. (2011)

Eigsti et al. (2011) looked at **internationally adopted children** to look at language and cognitive outcomes. They used 46 internationally adopted children to see if the length of institutionalisation in children adopted from orphanages abroad related to language skills and core cognitive processes. The children had come to the USA from the age of two to about seven years old and had been living in the USA for one to nine years. This study is explained here as a suggested study of privation though the history of each child is not known sufficiently to say if there was privation or deprivation. Privation seems more likely.

Definition

Internationally adopted children are children who are adopted from another country (and usually another culture). There is interest in them because not only have they been privated and institutionalised before being adopted but there are cultural effects too as they are adopted into a different culture. There are issues about children giving their consent to the adoption and issues about them 'being bought', too.

> **STUDY HINT**
> If using a study as evidence when discussing privation (or deprivation) be sure to make the link in your answer as is done here. Do not expect the examiner to make links that are not clear; be sure to use evidence in a way that explicitly addresses the issue in question. This advice applies to all areas of your work.

The researchers found that language skills were affected by the length of time spent in an institution compared with 24 controls who were not adopted. Eigsti et al. (2011) present evidence that there can be language issues in children who are adopted after the age of 12 months and they relate the issues to brain functioning. They offer a model of stress showing that stress from 'disrupted caregiving' can affect the brain. They say there is no effect on the striatum, such as the caudate nucleus, but that stress affects the limbic system, including the hippocampus, which is involved in memory and learning. They say also that stress affects 'prefrontal circuits' and there can be impaired cognitive control. These impairments lead to memory and cognitive control deficits and these impact on language acquisition and in particular vocabulary.

Issues and debates

One of the issues in your course focuses on psychology developing over time. You could use the way newer studies about deprivation and privation and their effects on the child tend to look at brain functioning, which is different from the methods and focus of older studies.

Eigsti et al. (2011) used 70 children (reasonably balanced regarding gender) aged from four to 13 years old. The group consisted of 46 international adoptees and 24 from a control group of non-adopted children recruited by word of mouth or by referral from the adopted participants. The study looked at four groups:

- those adopted aged 1 to 12 months
- those adopted aged 13 to 24 months
- those adopted at age 25+ months
- a control group.

Data were gathered by assessment in a Developmental Cognitive Neuroscience Lab at the University of Connecticut, with the child and a parent present. Parents filled in questionnaires and were interviewed. Children completed a lot of tests in one session, including language skills tests focusing on interpreting spoken directions, following directions, listening to and repeating sentences and understanding relationships between words. Explicit memory was tested, as was cognitive control and implicit learning. The study found that adoptees did not do as well as the controls on standardised language tests, which was what was expected – though the adoptees were within the normal range of scores. Vocabulary was lower in the adoptees. The study also found that institutionalisation related to explicit memory ability too, which suggests that language and memory abilities relate to one another. The adopted children did not control their attention as well, suggesting that early 'adversity' may have affected development of 'prefrontal cortical structures or connectivity'. There was some relationship between the length of time the children experienced institutionalisation and the difficulties in language and cognitive abilities, but the relationship was not a strong one and the researchers did not conclude that there was a link.

Evaluation of the Eigsti et al. (2011) study

Strength

- Eigsti et al. used adopted children and a control group so they had a baseline for the various measures, against which they could look for differences in the 'adopted' group.
- They had adopted children from a variety of countries, which could be a strength in terms of being able to generalise, even though it may have introduced confounding variables.

Weaknesses

- A limitation is the sample. Internationally adopted children vary considerably in respect of individual differences and it is hard to generalise the findings because they are not a heterogeneous group. Also the history of the adopted children was based on information from the parents, which was based on the institution's records, so might not be reliable. Some institutions had a higher staff–child ratio than others; some children experienced maltreatment while others did not. Though perhaps all this variability means the findings have even more generalisability, because the sample was more representative of all the differences, which is a strength.
- The cognitive abilities of the birth parents were not known but are likely to have had a strong influence on the abilities of the children. However, the adopted families will also have had a strong influence so that might override the problems of not knowing the abilities of the biological families.
- Another limitation is that there was the stress of being in the institution and that was the model that was being tested. Also in the institution the children might have been less exposed to language than the controls and that might be what caused the differences in language and cognitive ability that were found.
- What is difficult is knowing whether the institutionalisation was about privation or deprivation. If children are in an institution from birth or early in their lives, this is taken to be privation and this study is included as a study of early privation, though that is not known.

Explore

You can find Eigsti et al. (2011) using this link if you would like to know more:

http://eigsti.psy.uconn.edu/wp-content/uploads/sites/664/2014/05/Eigsti_IntAdop_2011.pdf

Issues and debates

Institutionalised children are assumed to have endured privation or deprivation and stress and that is assumed to cause the problems that they have, not unreasonably. However, often inherited characteristics are not known about, which is about the child's 'nature'. You can use this as evidence of difficulties in looking at causes for behaviour and characteristics if both nature and nurture cannot be known.

Progress check 4.14

Explain two limitations of Eigsti et al.'s (2011) study of internationally adopted children and their language, memory and cognitive control abilities.

Are the negative effects of privation reversible?

The conclusions from both the Koluchová and the Freud and Dann studies are that the effects of privation are reversible. The Czech twins grew up to get married, have children, achieve good jobs and maintain warm relationships. The six children studied by Freud and Dann did the same, though it seems that one or two had some problems. However, the study of Genie showed that she did not recover from her early privation. Genie developed some language use but it was far from normal and she did not relate normally to adults. Eigsti et al. (2011) found some differences in language and cognitive abilities between the adopted children and the controls, which suggests at least long-term issues following privation and institutionalisation.

Comparing three privation case studies: Genie, the Koluchová study and the Freud and Dann study

Differences between the case studies

It could be that, because Genie was found at the age of 13 – which is much older than the age at which the twins and the Terezín children were rescued – she may have passed the critical age for learning language and normal development.

A further consideration is that, in the cases of the twins and the Terezín children, they had each other for support.

Indeed, it was documented that the children had formed attachments with each other. Genie had nobody. Perhaps any individual, even another child, is better than nobody when it comes to socialisation.

Similarities between the studies

All three are case studies, so they use the same research methods, and all are longitudinal in that they follow the participant(s) through to adulthood. They have similar validity and a similar lack of reliability.

All three studies involved at least one person who, after the privation was revealed, took care to help the child or children:

- Genie was helped by some of the researchers.
- The twins were fostered by a committed and caring woman.
- The children from Terezín were eventually fostered and cared for.

It could be that the effects of privation are reversible only if this good quality care is given afterwards.

Reversibility of the effects of early privation: Eigsti et al. (2011), the newer study

Eigsti et al. (2011) also looked at adopted children where there was every sign that they had been well cared for since their adoption – for example, parents were happy for them to take part in the study and also put forward names of families that could act as controls, so were engaged in the study. The adopted children were found to have some language, memory and cognitive control differences compared with the controls; however, mostly their development was in normal limits. Perhaps their experiences after their privation had been enough to reverse the effects of privation. Again it is possibly that the negative effects of privation are reversible but only if good-quality, focused and continued care is in place for the child.

STUDY HINT

When discussing the issue of whether the effects of privation are reversible it is good if you can use evidence both for and against the argument of reversibility and then draw a conclusion in answer to any question.

Conclusion about the reversibility of the effects of privation

Genie is the example that shows the effects of privation are not reversible. However, her privation was extreme and prolonged. The twins that Koluchová studied had each other and were also found at a much younger age. The Terezín children also had each other and adults did try to care for them, again at a younger age than Genie was when she was found. Internationally adopted children are not the same as the case studies presented here because they are often adopted much earlier and also their early experiences cannot be assumed to be as bad. They seem to have some left-over issues from their privation, though this is not certain, although their development according to Eigsti *et al.* (2011) was in the normal range. The evidence presented here suggests that negative effects of privation are reversible if, at an early enough age, the child receives good-quality care.

Test yourself

To what extent are the negative effects of privation reversible? **(16 marks)**

Day care

Day care could be considered a form of short-term deprivation and the discussion about deprivation, attachments and separation distress/anxiety applies to an extent to this section on day care, though this is more about separation anxiety than about deprivation.

Generally, findings from studies suggest that, for some children, good-quality day care can be beneficial because it offers them stimulation and experiences they would often not get in the home. However, poor-quality day care is not a good thing and there is a suggestion that, for children under one year old, too long in day care (such as more than 20 hours per week) is detrimental. It is not only the quality of the care that is important but the length of time day care lasts. These are the sorts of findings considered in this section. You need to consider advantages and disadvantages of day care for children and also what makes good- and poor-quality day care.

> **STUDY HINT**
> Note that you can use the question of benefits and detriments of day care for a child as the key question that you cover in your study of child psychology, and for the related practical.

Defining day care

Day care is a term used for any situation where a child is cared for by someone other than its parents for some part of the day. Day care can take place for a short time, such as in a crèche, or every day of the week, such as in a full-time nursery; some day care is privately run and some is government run. Day care can be called child care, such as in the USA. In the UK all types of day care are now subject to government inspection as well as government curriculum rules. This has not always been the case, and research into day care took place before such rules were put into place. In fact, many of the rules now in place arose from the research findings. One study, Belsky and Rovine (1988), was influential in changing views of day care, and Jan Belsky is a prominent figure in the area of day care research.

Definition

Day care is the term for any situation where a child is cared for by someone other than a parent or legal guardian for some or all of a day and where the child tends to be cared for by someone other than immediate family.

> **Explore**
> Look up the Foundation Stage Curriculum and Every Child Matters to become familiar with the kinds of regulation to which day care providers have to adhere.
> **www.foundationyears.org.uk/eyfs-statutory-framework/**
> **www.education.gov.uk/consultations/downloadableDocs/EveryChildMatters.pdf**

Rules for day care provision

Rules for day care include what washing facilities are required, how many staff there must be and what other facilities are provided, including window space and floor space per child and how many children can be in a room depending on its size. There are health and safety rules too and other rules, such as how long children must play outside each day.

Issues such as staff-to-child ratios have been decided because research into day care has shown that, where there are sufficient staff, children benefit more. As well as these practical details, day care providers must also follow a curriculum and 'tick boxes' when a child achieves certain milestones. This is to ensure that all children in day care are receiving the same stimulation and experiences, with a view to making sure all children have equal opportunities. A formal curriculum can also help to make sure that day care is good quality, as research shows it must be to be successful for the child.

Research into day care

There are many day care studies, and only a few can be explained here. Belsky used data from the NICHD (National Institute of Child Health and Human Development) Study of Early Childcare and Youth

Development and from the EPPE (Effective Provision of Pre-school Education) project in the UK. Those are two pieces of research given here.

You need to look at the disadvantages and advantages of day care for the child and what makes poor- and-good quality provision. The NICHD study of Early Childcare and Youth Development is considered later when discussing Sosinsky *et al.* (2007), who used the NICHD study of Early Childcare and Youth Development, as an example of longitudinal design in research in child psychology (page 442). Siraj-Blatchford *et al.* (2008) reviewed the EPPE study data and showed that the 12 case studies were still useful in training staff about day care, and their study is also given as an example of longitudinal research in child psychology (page 443). The NICHD study data tend to be more against day care for a child and the EPPE data tend to support day care for a child, so these two studies are offered here so that you can use them in an argument about the advantages and disadvantages of day care for a child. Both studies raise issues about what make good-quality (and poor-quality) day care, too.

The NICHD study of Early Childcare and Youth Development (USA)

The NICHD study began as the Study of Early Child Care (SECC) and then became the Study of Early Child Care and Youth Development (SECCYD). The NICHD study was a longitudinal study following children from birth and its aim was to find out the effect of child care on children. In general this is a study that highlights the disadvantages of day care. The study was funded by the Institute of Child Care, which meant that the study was commissioned privately.

Aim

The aim was to look at the effect of child care on children and on young people as the study went on until the children were 15 years old.

Procedure

The study was longitudinal and involved gathering data by different means, including observation, interview and survey. The 1,200 children involved were followed from birth to when they started school. The study started in 1991 and worked with more than 1,300 children and their families. The study started looking at the effects of child care on the children but researchers did follow the children until they were 15 years old, hence the change of the name of the study. Table 4.10 shows the four phases of the NICHD SECCYD, the children's ages and the number of children/families taking part.

Table 4.10 NICHD study of Early Childcare and Youth Development (USA)

Year	Children's age	Number of children/ families taking part
1991 to 1994	Phase I, aged 0 to 3 years	1,364 enrolled
1995 to 1999	Phase II, up to 6 to 7 years	1,095 enrolled
2000 to 2004	Phase III, up to 11 to 12 years	1,073 enrolled
2005 to 2007	Phase IV, up to 14 to 15 years	1,056 enrolled

Results and conclusions

Length of time in day care

The NICHD SECCYD study concluded that children who spent early, continuous and intensive time in day care were likely to have more behavioural problems (such as aggressiveness or disobedience) later than children who did not. The problems were as rated by parents and teachers. This means that length of time in day care affects outcomes.

Type of day care

Another issue is the type of day care. It was found that nursery-type care (as opposed to care in someone's home) led to improvements in cognitive and language development but also increased behavioural problems such as aggression and disobedience.

Quality of day care

A third finding was that the quality of the day care was important. Low-quality day care was particularly bad for children with mothers who lacked sensitivity. Good-quality day care was a matter of the responsiveness of the staff, how attentive staff were and also how stimulating the environment was. High-quality care tended to mean higher cognitive and language functioning in the children. Children in higher quality child care had better language and cognitive development up to the age of four and a half and they were more cooperative than those who had lower quality care during the first three years. The higher the quality of care and the smaller the number of children an adult cared for, the more positive the care giving.

What is good-quality day care according to the SECCYD?

The study looked at adult-to-child ratio, group size and training of staff. These were the features of day care that it was felt could be subjected to rules. The study also looked at day-to-day experiences of children in day care and observations were used looking at social interactions between children and adults, activities with toys and other activities.

Features of day care that were or could be regulated

The SECCYD concluded the following made good-quality day care with regard to what could be regulated:

- the lower the number of children an adult is caring for the higher the quality day care and the better outcomes for a child
- smaller groups meant better observed quality of care
- there were better developmental outcomes for children and better quality of observed care if the staff had undergone higher education.

Day-to-day child care

Positive care giving is sensitive, encouraging and has frequent interactions between the caregiver and the child. Some examples of this are described below.

- Showing a positive attitude, encouraging and generally being cheerful.
- Hugging and holding the child's hand, having positive physical contact.
- Responding to vocalisations, commenting on what the child does and repeating the child's words, as well as answering the child's questions.
- Asking questions, encouraging the child to talk.
- Talking in a specific way, such as praising or encouraging, teaching and telling stories and singing.
- Encouraging development, such as encouraging walking in young children and helping to finish puzzles or do up zips in older children.
- Advancing behaviour, such as encouraging a child to smile, laugh and play with other children.
- Reading books and stories to the child, letting the child turn the page and touch the book or pointing to pictures in an older child.

Quality day care, according to the SECCYD, involves many activities including reading to a child, pointing to pictures and engaging the children.

The quality day care that the SECCYD found

Only a small percentage of the younger children in Phase I had positive care giving, with the percentage falling with age, going from 18 per cent to 6 per cent in the first three years, which is very low. However, the SECCYD found that only a very small percentage had poor-quality day care (around 4 per cent). About 30 per cent of children had a reasonable amount of positive care giving so day care centres were 'good but not outstanding' (p. 11). The source for the information given here is the 'NICHD Study of Early Child Care and Youth Development: Findings for children up to Age 4½ Years'. The document claims that 'fewer than 10% of arrangements were rated as providing very high quality child care' (p. 11). However, it also explains that fewer than 10 per cent of child care gave children very low-quality experiences.

Table 4.11 Estimates of positive care giving in day care centres

SECCYD estimates of positive care giving	
Child care settings where children get a lot of positive care giving	9%
Child care settings where children get a fair amount of positive care giving	30%
Child care settings where children get some positive care giving	53%
Child care settings where children get hardly any positive care giving	8%

Source: The NICHD Study of Early Child Care and Youth Development (ECCYD)

STUDY HINT
When using percentages take care to use them correctly. Table 4.11 does not say, for example, that 53 per cent of children get some positive care giving. It says that in 53 per cent of the *settings* children were getting some positive care giving. When making notes check that you write things down correctly because it is easy to make mistakes with figures.

Explore
You can find the NICHD document reporting the findings for children up to four and a half years old using this link if you would like to know more:
www.nichd.nih.gov/publications/pubs/documents/seccyd_06.pdf

Advantages for a child of having quality child care

The SECCYD study cited background research showing that children from disadvantaged households benefit from high-quality day care. However, the study found that child care quality and a child's development did link, but did not specifically depend on the economic or social status of the family. This goes against what was previously thought. There was a finding that if a child's development was slow at 18 months then quality day care was a benefit as it seemed to impact more on those children than on other children. There is a suggestion that the individual differences of a child predicted how beneficial good-quality day care was for the individual child.

Disadvantages of being in day care for children

At a young age children seemed to benefit from spending time in group child care; for example, they tended to be more cooperative with care givers at the age of two years old. However, by four and a half years old the children who had spent more time in child care centres tended to show more disobedient behaviour and more aggression than those with less experience of child care centres.

Overall conclusion from the SECCYD study

The overall conclusion, when the findings were reported for the children when they were up to four and a half years old, was that the quality of child care is linked somewhat to cognitive development in children up to pre-school. Quality of child care is also slightly linked to social development in the infant to toddler years. The children who did get higher quality care had 'slightly more positive outcomes' (p. 15) than those in lower quality care. You can see that the study did not give strong support that high-quality care makes a lot of difference for children, but it should be noted that in general the study did not find high-quality care. There was also the finding that being in day care centres is positive in terms of cognitive development up to the age of four and a half years and in terms of social behaviours up to the age of three years. 'Large-group settings' are associated with more problem behaviour at school-entry age, however.

> **STUDY HINT**
> The part of the SECCYD study reported here focuses on children in their pre-school years because the focus in your course is on day care for young children. Also the focus is on what makes good-or poor-quality care because that is the focus in your course. The other focus on day care in your course is advantages and disadvantages of day care for a child, so those issues are reported too.

A brief summary of findings of Phase IV when the children were 15

Vandell et al. (2010) published findings of the SECCYD study in Phase IV and their report is entitled 'Do Effects of Early Child Care Extend to Age 15 Years?'. Vandell et al. (2010) compared child care in children from birth to four and a half years old with their functioning at age 15. They found that quality and quantity of child care related to adolescent functioning, which helps to show the strength of early experiences with regard to later development. Their findings backed the findings at age four and a half years, such as higher quality care going with higher cognitive-academic achievement at age 15. There were more positive effects when quality of care was higher. Interestingly, more hours in day care (non-relative care) predicted more risk taking and impulsivity, which seems to go with the finding that children who were in day care longer when they were near pre-school age behaviour did seem to be more aggressive and to show more problem behaviour.

> **Explore**
> You can read Vandell et al.'s (2010) findings using this link if you would like to know more. The SECCYD is a large longitudinal study with a great many findings — too many to cover in this textbook.
> www.nieer.org/pdf/Effects_of_Early_Child_Care_Extend_to_Age_15.pdf

Evaluation of the NICHD SECCYD study

Strengths

- This was a longitudinal study, which followed a large number of children from birth to when they went to school and up to the age of 15, so the coverage was thorough and researchers were able to bring in many different aspects of the child's experiences from which to draw conclusions. Longitudinal studies are a better way of studying development than cross-sectional studies because the same children are involved and results are more secure.
- More than one research method was used, which means that data from different research methods can be compared to check for validity and reliability. Using a different method is a bit like repeating the study so that, if the same results are found, then reliability can be claimed. If different methods find the same results then this suggests that findings are valid too.

Weaknesses

- The area of child care involves so many variables and child development is so complex that it is hard to draw any meaningful conclusions. Researchers have to look for issues such as social background and the quality of the day care, but factors such as the temperament of the child, the quality of their attachments, and cultural issues can also be important. It is difficult to take account of all these factors. For example, the study did not include mothers under the age of 18, nor did it include very poor children. Also many of the children observed up to four and a half years old did not experience very high-quality care so it was hard to draw conclusions taking every variable into account.

- Any study of child care that takes place in one culture should perhaps have its findings generalised only to that culture. Cross-cultural studies, for example, have found differences in attachment types in different cultures. This suggests that the findings of a study of child care in the USA ought only to be generalised to the USA. In this section, this study is being compared to a UK study and generalised outside the USA.

Progress check 4.15

Explain what the SECCYD found with regard to the effects of good-quality day care on children.

The Effective Provision of Pre-School Education (EPPE) Project in the UK

A project in the UK similar to the NICHD study was the EPPE project (1997–2003). This study, which received government funding, followed children from the age of 3 up to 11, and there was a special project for pre-school children. The EPPE project was another longitudinal study following children in order to learn about their development. In general this is a study that highlights the advantages of day care.

Aims

The aims of the study were to look at the impact of pre-school provision on a child's intellectual and social/behavioural development, as well as to find out if social inequalities could be reduced by attendance in pre-school settings. The researchers (Sylva *et al.,* 2004) also wanted to see whether some types of setting were better than others.

Procedure

The study was of 3,000 children, consisting of observations, as well as interviews with parents and practitioners. The participants were from many different social backgrounds in an attempt to provide a range in the sample, to look at issues such as social background. There were two main groups: children in some types of day care centre and children who stayed at home. The 'home' children acted as a control group and 144 centres took part in the study.

Results and conclusions

A general finding was that high-quality care improved social, intellectual and behavioural development. The study found that the earlier a child started in a day care centre, the better the intellectual improvement. Children also had better sociability, independence and concentration the longer they had been in day care. It was found that full-time attendance led to no better gains than part-time attendance. An important finding was that disadvantaged children were better off in good-quality day care, particularly if they experienced a mixture of social backgrounds in the day care centre.

Explore

You can find the EPPE final report (Sylva *et al.,* 2004), using this link, if you would like to know more:
www.ioe.ac.uk/RB_Final_Report_3-7.pdf

Key findings of the EPPE study focusing on pre-school age

- Pre-school experience helps a child's all-round development.
- Starting before the age of three years gives better intellectual development.
- Full-time attendance is no better than part-time attendance.
- Disadvantaged children benefit from good-quality provision in particular, when children come from different backgrounds.
- High-quality provision gives better intellectual, social and behavioural development.
- Where staff have higher qualifications provision is of higher quality and children make more progress.
- Good-quality care means 'warm, interactive relationships' and a good proportion of trained staff.
- Nursery school provision and integrated centres (nursery schools with extended provision and family support services) have higher quality than playgroups, private day nurseries or local authority day centres.

Features of good-quality day care when working with three to five year olds

The 12 case studies carried out to show good practice suggested seven important areas:

1 The quality of adult–child verbal interactions and the existence of 'sustained shared thinking'. The recommended action was to encourage sustained shared thinking, which means the adult being aware of the child's interests and understanding and the child and adult working together to develop an idea.

2 Initiations of activities, meaning both the adult and the child initiated activities, where adults extended their thinking. The recommendation was to 'work towards a balance of adult and child initiated activity' (p. 7).

3 Knowledge and understanding of the curriculum (by the staff).

4 Knowledge about how young children learn, including focus on training of staff to achieve this knowledge. The recommendation was to provide training courses for staff.

5 Encouraging children to engage in challenging play and giving instruction (involving **sustained shared thinking**). The recommendation was to have trained teachers on the staff.

6 Encourage high levels of parental involvement, including sharing educational aims with parents so they can support the child at home.

7 Use discipline and behaviour policies where staff and children rationalise and talk through behaviour.

Definition

Sustained shared thinking means the adult being aware of the child's interests and understanding and the child and adult working together to develop an idea.

Report on the EPPE 3–11 (not focusing on day care directly): Sammons *et al.* (2006)

The EPPE 3–11 is the EPPE longitudinal study as it moved on from the 2004 findings, where the children were younger, and looked at them as they got older. This was Phase 2 of the Project and looked at the children aged 7 to 11. Phase 2 had three tiers:

- Melhuish *et al.* (2006) in Tier One focused on value added in the children using national tests as measures.
- Tier Two looked at 2,500 children in the original sample and measured their academic and social and behavioural progress.
- Tier Three used observations of teacher and child behaviour in the classroom, focusing on 125 classes drawn from the original sample.

Sammons *et al.* (2006) reports on the classroom observations. This study is mentioned because it is an example of use of naturalistic observations, so may be useful when you are discussing methods in child psychology. It is also mentioned to show that a longitudinal study carries on over time and it is likely that there are reports at intervals during that time. For the EPPE study focus has been on the pre-school findings and for the NICHD SECCYD the same sort of time scale is covered. However, both the EPPE and NICHD SECCYD continued.

Some findings of Tier Three of the EPPE project

- There was significant variation in teacher practice and pupil behaviour in the classroom, covering both good- and poor-quality care regarding educational experiences.
- In general students were engaged and classrooms were 'positive'.
- Some children attend poorer quality settings.
- Poor pupil behaviour and classroom disorganisation was found where schools were in areas of social disadvantage.

These findings were not directly related to individual children to see how their early day care experiences might affect their later experiences in school, so are not directly related to day care, but they do show briefly how the EPPE study continued.

Progress check 4.16

Explain three of the seven areas of good practice identified in the 12 EPPE case studies, for the purposes of showing effective provision.

Evaluation of the EPPE study

Strengths

- The procedure was carefully planned to include children from different social backgrounds, including a control group of 'home' children. This means that conclusions could be drawn more securely.
- The same advantages apply, both of the longitudinal design and the many research methods used, as explained when looking at strengths of the NICHD study.

Weaknesses

- A possible weakness is that the study had government funding and there is a question of how far the findings reflected government policy. However, this is true of much research and this weakness should not be exaggerated as the research team is well respected in the field and it is more likely that the funding did not affect the findings.
- The complexity of the issues and the related problem of drawing conclusions, as already discussed for the weaknesses of the NICHD study, also apply here.
- The research was based on English day care provision and so generalising the findings to any other country might not be appropriate.

Comparing the NICHD and EPPE findings

- The findings from the EPPE project were more positive with regard to use of day care than the NICHD study. The EPPE finding that children did not benefit more from being in day care for the full day compared with part-time attendance reinforces the NICHD conclusions. However, the NICHD researchers went further and suggested that too long in day care was a bad thing for the child (at an older age), which the EPPE team did not conclude.

- The EPPE idea that children benefit the earlier they start attending a day care centre goes against the general conclusion of other studies, including the NICHD research, that a very young child does not benefit from much day care. Conclusions from Jan Belsky's work were that too much time in day care before the age of one was bad for the child, for example, which the EPPE findings do not support.

- Both the EPPE and the SECCYD study suggested that good-quality day care meant well-qualified staff, a good child–adult ratio and warm relationships and caring between care givers and the child.

- The methods used to gather the data were similar in that both studies used observations to conclude about the quality of provision. Though the EPPE study included 12 case studies looking at centres who were effective (in the middle and upper range of effectiveness). The case studies were there to offer examples of best practice.

- The EPPE study suggested that by school age a child who had experienced day care would show more independence and less anxiety with regard to social behaviour, though the SECCYD study suggested that older children who spent quite a lot of time in group day care might show behavioural difficulties.

- The SECCYD has a list of good practice that differs from the EPPE list. However, there are similarities, such as in the SECCYD asking questions and encouraging the child to talk as well as reading with the child and pointing to pictures being similar to focusing on the quality of adult–child verbal interactions.

> **STUDY HINT**
> You need to be able to talk about good-quality and poor-quality day care as well as advantages and disadvantages of day care for the child. It would be useful to draw up a table for both of these issues, so that you have prepared material; make sure you can make comparisons between the studies too. Learning material is important, but being able to *use* the material is also very important.

Belsky's conclusions

Belsky considered the findings of the NICHD and EPPE projects and suggested that the UK government should put in place measures such as changing tax policies and encouraging parental leave, in order to ensure that children did not spend too long in day care. In 2006 Belsky concluded that good-quality child care, including child care in day care centres, can lead to better cognitive and language abilities. However, the more time spent in day care, especially more time in centre-based care, tended to lead to more problem behaviour. The important features of day care are quality, quantity and type of day care.

Evaluation of research into day care

Strengths

- Studies have taken into account as many factors that can affect a child's experience of day care as possible, such as the social background of the family, how long the child is in day care, how stimulating the environment is, and the quality of staff–child interactions. Studies have been carefully planned to try to draw strong conclusions.

- Studies have used large and carefully chosen samples, again in order to avoid bias.

- Other studies support the findings, such as Melhuish *et al.* (2000), finding that greater staff training and qualifications affect the quality of day care in Ireland (cited in Sylva *et al.*, 2004).

Weaknesses

- As explained when evaluating the EPPE and SECCYD studies given in this section, the issue of the effect of day care on a child is complex. It would be hard, if not impossible, to take all the relevant factors into account, such as a child's temperament or position in the family (two features not often mentioned).

- Studies are often carried out within one culture, or within one country. Cross-cultural studies in other areas suggest that differences in culture affect findings about child development, so it might not be legitimate to generalise findings from one culture to another.

Belsky and Pluess (2011)

Belsky was involved in many studies looking at day care. One of his studies is briefly given here to offer a comparison to the two large longitudinal studies already described. Belsky and Pluess (2011) began by commenting that poor-quality child care is associated with poorer child functioning and they focused this comment on cognitive and language performance. They cited the SECCYD as showing that when early negative temperament is taken into account early child care experiences predict later problems in the child, such as them being impulsive and taking risks as well as **externalising behaviour**, which is aggression and delinquency. Belsky and Pluess take a child's temperament and individual differences into account and suggest that 'negatively emotional infants' are more affected by child care quality than less difficult children. This is another variable to take into account when making judgements about good- and poor-quality child care and about advantages and disadvantages of child care for the individual child.

Definition

Externalising behaviour, with regard to children, means behaviour such as aggression, delinquency and hyperactivity.

Belsky and Pluess (2011) looked at children at the age of 15 to see whether the 'negatively emotional child' was more likely to show externalising behaviour (aggression and hyperactivity, for example). The idea was to look at a child before they were pre-school age and then again at 15 to look for connections between their early childhood experiences and later characteristics.

Belsky and Pluess, looking at the data, found that children with the 'difficult' temperament of 'negative emotionality' if they experienced low-quality day care were more likely to show externalising behaviour than those who experienced high-quality day care. This was comparing their externalising behaviour with children with less difficult temperaments. Though the 'difficult' children who had low-quality day care showed more externalising behaviours at 15, they did not show more risk taking or impulsivity.

Belsky and Pluess used the SECCYD data from which to draw their conclusions. Earlier it was said that the SECCYD did not look enough at issues like temperament. It is worth noting that data were gathered about temperament, as Belsky and Pluess show, however, the SECCYD in the early report of findings up to four and a half years did not emphasise the impact of temperament.

> **STUDY HINT**
> You could remind yourself what Chess said about 'easy' and 'difficult' temperament when individual differences were considered earlier in this chapter (page 385).

Belsky and Pluess (2011) found that low-quality day care particularly affected children with a 'difficult' temperament. They felt a diathesis-stress model explained results because there was the underlying temperament and then the environment acting on the temperament to give behaviour and characteristics.

Summary of good-and poor-quality day care

The EPPE Project and the NICHD SECCYD both discussed what makes good-quality day care:

- SECCYD: Good-quality day care needs good adult–child ratios, trained staff and a warm caring relationship between the care giver and the child. With regard to interactions, there must be focus on responding to the child, such as asking questions and encouraging development, as well as physical contact and a positive attitude. Reading books and stories to the child, letting the child turn the page and touch the book or pointing to pictures in an older child are also important.

- EPPE: Disadvantaged children were better off in good-quality day care, particularly if they experienced a mixture of social backgrounds in the day care centre. High-quality care improved social, intellectual and behavioural development. The earlier a child started in a day care centre, the better the intellectual improvement. Children also had better sociability, independence and concentration the longer they had been in day care. Where staff have higher qualifications provision is of higher quality and children make more progress and also where staff understood child development. High-quality child care means being aware of the child's interests and working together as well as having a balance of child–adult initiated activities. High-quality care means having trained staff, including a teacher, who are familiar with the curriculum. Encouraging the child to engage in challenging play and giving instructions were recommended, as well as high levels of parental involvement to support the child at home.

Poor-quality day care:

- According to Belsky and Pluess (2011) poor-quality child care is associated with poorer child functioning. Low-quality day care in 'difficult' children seemed to relate to aggressive and problem behaviour at the age of 15.

- Belsky found that too long in day care under the age of one year old is not good and up to around 20 hours a week is suggested up to that age. Using the strange situation Belsky found less secure attachments where children under the age of one year spent a long time in day care. He found that at the age of five years old children may be more aggressive if they had spent a long time in day care under the age of one.

- SECCYD: The emphasis on good-quality care suggests that poor-quality care is not effective for the child. An example of poor-quality care would be where there are a large number of children for each carer, poorly trained staff and fewer good-quality interactions between the child and the care giver. The SECCYD said what good-quality care was but also emphasised that they did not find much excellent quality care. They did not find much very poor-quality care either, but found a lot fitted into a middle category.

- EPPE: The 12 case studies showed excellent quality care and the study suggested that they be used in training. The emphasis was on promoting high-quality care rather than listing what was poor-quality care. The understanding is that the case studies show what 'should' be offered and anything less is poor quality.

- Melhuish carried out a literature review of the effects of day care on children, in particular those with disadvantaged backgrounds, and suggested that poor-quality care can produce 'deficits' with regard to language and cognitive development. However, for disadvantaged children high-quality care can be beneficial in terms of cognitive, language and social development.

> **Explore**
> You can read Melhuish's review of the impact of early years provision on young children (focusing on those with disadvantaged backgrounds) at the following link: www.nao.org.uk/wp-content/uploads/2004/02/268_literaturereview.pdf

Summary of advantages and disadvantages of day care for the child

Advantages

The EPPE Project and the NICHD SECCYD both discussed advantages for the child of day care, such as an 18 month old with developmental delay seeming to benefit from good-quality day care (SECCYD) and in general children benefitting from day care such as in terms of intellectual, social and behavioural development (EPPE).

- SECCYD: Nursery-type care led to improvements in cognitive and language development but also increased behavioural problems such as aggression and disobedience (in the older child). There was a finding that if a child's development was slow at 18 months old then quality day care was a benefit as it seemed to impact more on those children than on other children. There is a suggestion that the individual differences of a child predicted how beneficial good-quality day care was for the individual child, which Belsky and Pluess (2011) also looked at. The children who did get higher quality care had 'slightly more positive outcomes' (p. 15) than those in lower quality care. Being in day care centres is positive in terms of cognitive development up to the age of four and a half years and in terms of social behaviours up to the age of three years.
- EPPE: A child who started child care before the age of three years old had better intellectual development. Sociability, independence and concentration improved in a child in high-quality day care. Disadvantaged children did well in day care, especially if the setting

had a mix of children from different backgrounds. There was an effect of type of day care with nursery schools and integrated provision being better for the child. By school age a child who had experienced day care would show more independence and less anxiety with regard to social behaviour

Disadvantages

Disadvantages included the time spent in day care, with the SECCYD suggesting that longer time in group child care led to behavioural difficulties in the child just before they went to school. The EPPE project suggested that full-time day care was no better than part-time day care but did not suggest that full-time day care was a disadvantage so much as that it gave no additional advantage.

- SECCYD: The study found that there was no specific difference in benefits in day care depending on the economic or social status of the family. A child who spent quite a while in group child care, when nearing school age, was found to show some behavioural problems such as aggression and disobedience.
- Belsky and Pluess (2011): Low-quality child care experiences predict later problems in the child such as them being impulsive and taking risks as well as externalising behaviour, which is aggression and delinquency – but this is dependent on the temperament of the child. It could be an advantage to know about this sort of issue as intervention might be useful. A child with 'negative' temperament and a 'difficult' child shows this relationship between child-care experiences and later behaviour. This is not really about disadvantages of day care but about the importance of taking temperament into account when judging the effects of day care on a child.

> **Test yourself**
>
> Evaluate day care provision for children up to school age with regard to advantages and disadvantages for the child. **(16 marks)**

Autism

You are required to consider autism as a developmental issue that affects a child's development. You need to know about the features of autism, one biological explanation and one other explanation for autism (here the 'other' explanation is a cognitive one) and therapies for helping a child with autism.

Year One link: Your learning about cognitive and biological psychology will help in understanding the explanations for autism offered here.

Features of autism

Usually it is **autistic spectrum disorder** (ASD) that is discussed rather than autism as such, because it is recognised that a child can show behaviour and characteristics that fall at any point between mild autism and severe autism. Mild autism is diagnosed as having Asperger syndrome and the autism spectrum runs from mild Asperger to severe autism. In this section we focus on autism.

Definition

Autistic spectrum disorder (ASD) refers to a range of conditions that are neurodevelopmental disorders (DSM-5), including Asperger syndrome and autistic disorder.

Autism is a developmental issue or disorder that affects more boys than girls. For Asperger syndrome, which is at the mild end of the autism disorder spectrum, there is usually thought to be a ratio of 10 boys to 1 girl. For autism the ratio is nearer to 4 boys to 1 girl. There are about 6 people in every 1,000 with ASD, and about 2 people in every 1,000 with autism, which is 0.2 per cent of the population.

There is not a complete set of symptoms of autism but a variety of characteristics – groups of these characteristics lead to a diagnosis of autism. People with autism find it hard, if not impossible, to read other people's emotions and so they are poor at empathising. They usually have problems with communication too, either in talking or reading, or both. However, some children with autism talk clearly, though there may be no understanding of the words, and some read well too, but again with little comprehension.

One main characteristic of autism is that people affected find it hard to form relationships. They are, however, good at systems, and up to 10 per cent have high ability in one special area that is usually connected with systems, such as playing the piano, doing maths, or drawing what is in the environment in perfect detail. Autistic people with this special ability are called **autistic savants**. Affected children often repeat patterns over and over again, when other children would have grown tired of doing so.

Definition

Autistic savant refers to a special form of autism where there can be outstanding ability in music, art or numbers with no especial need to practise.

Autistic savants show outstanding abilities in certain areas, such as maths.

A child is usually only identified as having autism between the ages of two and three. It is likely to become apparent by then that the child is not using normal eye contact, for example, or not anticipating the needs or intentions of others. There are usually problems in social interactions. This, along with repetitive behaviour, signals autism.

In the first year a child with autism does show some signs, such as not responding to their name, not being as interested in others, as might be expected and having delayed babbling. Problems with toddlers include difficulty in playing games with others and not imitating the actions of others, as well as not displaying anger and affection in a typical manner (see Table 4.12).

Table 4.12 Signs of ASD/autism in pre-school children

Feature	Likely sign of ASD
Spoken language	Delayed speech, repetition of words and phrases, speech with little intonation, preferring to use single words
Responding to others	Not responding to name being called, rejecting cuddles initiated by others, reacting negatively when asked to do something
Interacting with others	Not being aware of someone's personal space, not liking someone invading own space, not interested in interacting with other children of the same age, not enjoying social situations like parties, preferring to play alone, rarely using pointing or facial expressions to communicate, avoiding eye contact
Behaviour	Repetitive movements such as rocking, playing in a repetitive and unimaginative way, preferring routine, strong likes or dislikes towards food, such as regard to colour not taste

It is not that children with autism are not attached to their parents but they express this attachment in different ways, and those ways may seem to lack affection. Difficulties include interpreting what others are thinking and feeling, such as a smile not conveying meaning. A person with autism has problems in understanding that other people have different thoughts from them.

Summary of features

Social issues

- Failure to respond to name towards the end of the first year and delay in babbling.
- Difficulty in playing social games, preferring to play alone, difficulties with interacting with others.
- Difficulty in interpreting what others are thinking and difficulty in understanding that other people have thoughts different from them.
- Difficulty in regulating emotions, including difficulty in not losing control.

Communication issues

- By the age of one year most children start babbling, pointing to objects and know their name. However, children with autism do not use gestures to speak and do not use babbling at the same age in the same way. There are individual differences in that some children with autism use language better than others. When they start to use language, children with autism may use single words or a lot of repeat phrases. Some display **echolalia**, which means repeating exactly what they hear. Some children use language a lot, some do not, but it is more the pattern in language use where someone speaks and then someone else speaks that is different.
- Body language might not be typical either, such as facial expressions not matching what is being said.

Repetitive behaviours

- Children with autism tend to show repetitive behaviour such as jumping around, arranging objects, rocking, repeating sounds or hand flapping.
- This means there can be a narrow range of activities, such as lining toys up and doing the same thing for a long time. This tends to be at the expense of pretend play and a child will be upset if someone disrupts the order that has been created.
- There can be obsessions, such as a great depth of knowledge in a particular area.

Definition
Echolalia is a stage in autism where a child repeats word for word exactly what they have heard.

Effect of autism on a child's development

There are many ways in which a child's development is affected by autism, including finding it hard to make friends (because of problems with empathising) and finding communication difficult (including talking, reading and writing, which are all basic skills for learning).

Difficulties in making friends

Someone who has difficulty in empathising and in understanding the thoughts and emotions of others will find it hard to make friends. Children with autism tend to live in their own world, and indeed this is part of the condition. Advice for parents states that friendships are important to children with autism, even if they seem to prefer to be by themselves, and so friendships should be encouraged early on. Friendships can help prevent bullying, which can be a problem for children with autism. Parents can help by inviting other children home to play, and teachers can encourage play with other children at school. Children with autism often develop friendships through shared interests such as computers.

Bauminger and Shulman (2003), researchers in Israel, have studied friendships of high-functioning children with autism and compared them with children without autism. Both groups tended to have friendships with children of the same gender and age, so there were few differences there. However, their friendship patterns differed with respect to the number of friends, how often they met, how long they were friends and the activities they did together.

Bauminger and Kasari (2000) reported that children with autism were lonelier than other children but also understood loneliness less. They studied high-functioning children with autism between the ages of eight and fourteen. All the children with autism said they had at least one friend but the quality of their friendships was not as good, providing less companionship and security.

These studies suggest that autism affects a child's development in terms of not making friendships in the same way as children without autism. However, children with autism are able to make friends and share interests.

Problems with communication

Children with autism have problems with communication, including learning language, and with reading and writing. They tend to have difficulty with the meaning of words and sentences. Some children with autism cannot speak, whereas others can talk fluently, so it is hard to generalise. However, in general, children with autism have communication and learning difficulties.

It is in using language that children with autism tend to have greatest problems. Even children who use language tend not to use it with meaning: for example, they might continuously count without reference to objects, or repeat sentences they have heard when it is inappropriate to do so. Children with autism may be able to speak in depth and knowledgeably about a topic that interests them but they are unlikely to be able to engage in a conversation about the topic. As children with autism do not use appropriate eye contact and have problems with nonverbal communication, such as using gestures to converse, problems with communication are linked to problems with friendships. So language and other communication problems restrict their learning as well as restricting their social interactions and friendships.

Two explanations for autism

Autism is thought of as a problem with the brain's development, which is why a biological explanation and a cognitive (non-biological) explanation are offered in this section – both being about how the brain works. There is no social explanation of autism, as it is not thought that it is caused by social interactions, although those with autism do have problems with interacting. The non-biological explanation chosen is that children with autism do not develop a **theory of mind**, which is a cognitive explanation. There is more than one biological explanation – for example, there seems to be a genetic link, and it could also come from problems during birth – but this section considers the suggestion that those with autism have an extreme male brain. Both explanations come from Simon Baron-Cohen, a leading researcher in the area of autism and the autistic spectrum.

Theory of mind and autism: a cognitive explanation

Baron-Cohen *et al.* (1985) carried out a study of children with autism. He used a task that other investigators had used, where a child watches a researcher manipulate two dolls (Anne and Sally) in a pretend situation. Sally has a basket and Anne has a box. Sally puts a marble in the basket and then 'leaves' the scene. Anne then moves the marble from the basket into the box. This all takes place with the child watching carefully. Sally then returns. The important question asked of the child is where Sally will look for the marble. Children 'pass' the theory of mind test if they say that Sally will look in the basket. They 'fail' if they say she will look in the box. The child knows the marble is in the box, but Sally would not know that and a child has a theory of mind if he or she understands that Sally does not know.

Baron-Cohen and Frith studied 21 children with autism, 11 Down's syndrome children and 27 children without developmental difficulties. Only the children with autism did not have a theory of mind. They were in the main not

able to understand that Sally did not know what the child knew. Children from the age of about three have a theory of mind, but much older children with autism did not. Down's syndrome children also have a theory of mind.

Cognitive psychology considers how information is processed in the brain as well as how thinking processes develop. Therefore, the explanation for autism that there is no theory of mind is a cognitive explanation. To explain further the idea that people with autism have no theory of mind, researchers have looked at **low empathising** people and **high systematising** people. 'Low empathising' means not being good at understanding the emotions and feelings of others. 'High systematising' means having the ability to use internal rules to organise internal events. Someone good at systematising will be able to sort things into groups, plan and build structures, work out patterns and work things out in their heads (internally). Someone poor at empathising will find it hard to work out external events, which means it will be difficult to discern what other people are thinking.

Definitions

Theory of mind refers to how children after the age of about three are able to understand that other people have different thoughts from the child, and that others have different 'minds'. A person with autism seems to lack this theory of mind.

Low empathising means not good at understanding the emotions and feelings of others.

High systematising means being able to use internal rules and planning.

People with autism are high systematisers and low empathisers. A child who finds it hard to work out external events would not have a theory of mind because he or she would find it difficult to look at things from the point of view of someone else. In the Sally/Anne scenario the child would not be able to work out what Sally knew or did not know.

Simon Baron-Cohen

Sensory processing problems

Related to difficulties in understanding that others have minds, someone with autism can have problems with processing information from the senses, such as sight and movement. They may be hypersensitive to touch, for example, which is called 'sensory defensiveness', though others are under-responsive. Being under-responsive might account for someone not responding when their name is called. These cognitive issues are different from the idea that people with autism do not have theory of mind, but they are related to the claim that there are cognitive explanations for autism.

Measuring the theory of mind: Hutchins *et al.* (2012)

Hutchins *et al.* (2012) carried out two studies to look at theory of mind in typically developing children and children with ASD. Their research was to look at the Theory of Mind Inventory (ToMI) to see if it is useful as a measure of autism.

A total of 135 care givers completed the inventory for children with ASD. The children involved were 27 females (20 per cent) and 108 males (80 per cent). A group of 124 mothers of typically developing children were also asked to complete the ToMI. In this sample, which is the second study, there were 62 females (50 per cent) and 62 males (50 per cent). Hutchins *et al.* (2012) found excellent test-retest reliability and internal consistency, which showed the test's reliability. Hutchins *et al.* (2012) then used the test with 124 typically developing children and again found good reliability.

The researchers looked at a way of measuring theory of mind because of difficulties with what was being used. The tasks like the Sally/Ann task just measured pass or fail, which did not give much information, for example. Also such tasks require language ability, which might be a confounding variable. This means that a child with autism might not understand the question about where Sally should look for the marble rather than they do not understand that Sally has not seen the marble moved.

The ToMI has 48 statements with a response continuum, which means the respondent can choose from answers such as 'definitly not' and 'undecided'. Here are some examples of statements that are included in the ToMI.

- Statement 6: My child understands that people can be wrong about what other people want.
- Statement 26: My child understands that people often have thoughts about other people's thoughts.
- Statement 34: My child can pretend that one object is a different object (for example, pretending a banana is a telephone).
- Statement 40: My child understands that when someone shares a secret you are not supposed to tell anyone.

Table 4.13 Mean ToMI scores for both the ASD sample and the 'typical' sample

Age (in years)	Mean ToMI score for ASD sample	Mean ToMI score for 'typical' sample
2–3	-	10.9
3–4	4.96	12.8
4–5	5.97	14.61
5–6	8.80	15.53
6–7	10.8	15.8
7–8	8.72	17.82
8–9	11.1	17.45

STUDY HINT

Table 4.13 shows the mean scores on the Theory of Mind Inventory for both the ASD children and the 'typical' sample. You will be expected to understand and be able to deal with figures like these in the exam. For example, you could be asked approximately how much higher the mean score was for typically developing children than children with ASD aged 6–7 years. The answer would be to compare 15.8 with 10.8, which you can estimate is roughly 50 per cent higher (roughly 16 compared with 11 so just a bit less than half as much again) for the typically developing children. Be ready to do a sense check on data in this sort of way. You may also have to do calculations, such as percentages. When working out how much higher as a percentage the difference between the means for children aged 6–7 is, you need to work out the difference between the two, which is 5 (15.8 − 10.8). Then work out 5 as a percentage of the lower figure (because the focus is on how much higher a percentage the difference is than the lower figure): 5 ÷ 10.8 x 100 = 46%.

You can see from Table 4.13 that the typical sample had a much higher mean score on the ToMI than children with ASD. In both cases as age rose the scores rose, showing a developmental pattern. However, the children with ASD showed a marked difference in the score (much lower), which suggests the measure has some validity. The study also used the Peabody Picture Vocabulary Test-4. As the ToMI scores related to the scores on the Peabody Picture

Vocabulary Test-4 so validity was claimed. Another test was children's scores on a theory of mind task, separate from the ToMI, and that too showed validity. A Spearman's rho was carried out to compare competence on the ToMI test and theory of mind tasks and the result was a significant positive correlation (r=.66, p<.05). The use of different methods helped to show validity.

> **STUDY HINT**
>
> Hutchins *et al.* (2012) used a Spearman's test and mention that the test gathered ordinal data, so you can use this study as an example of such a test. You can see that the results were significant at .05, which means 5 per cent (or fewer) of the results will be due to chance, which is acceptable in psychology. 0.66 is a high correlation too and the researchers say it is positive, so as the score on the ToMI test rises so does the ability to do theory of mind tasks. You can use this sort of information to help you learn statistics in psychology.

Progress check 4.17

Using the figures in Table 4.13 that show the mean scores for ASD children and typically developing children by age, what is the percentage difference between the means at age 8–9? What would you conclude overall from the table?

Conclusions

The study showed that theory of mind may increase over time (which fits with the findings of Peterson *et al.*, 2005, cited in Hutchins *et al.*, 2012). It looks as if in typically developing children theory of mind is still developing as well as in children with ASD. The study showed good reliability and there was validity as well as consistency over time. The main conclusion is that the ToMI is suitable for assessing theory of mind.

Evaluation of Hutchins *et al.* (2012)

- Generalisability: Those with ASD were included up to the age of 17 but the sample size for the older ages was small so larger samples are needed to check the data at these ages. Also a larger sample of those with ASD with language difficulties would be better for generalising as their study tended to have children with 'functional' language.
- Evidence from other studies: Lerner *et al.* (2011, cited in Hutchins *et al.*, 2012) found that ToMI scores correlated with social skills, ASD symptoms and social impairments in the 'expected directions'. Hutchins *et al.* suggested that looking at how far ToMI scores predicted social functioning as measured by observations would support the validity of the ToMI.

- A strength of the study – and of the ToMI – was that validity and reliability were found for both typically developing children and children with ASD.
- Hutchins *et al.* (2012) felt that having scores from the ToMI was better than the 'pass' or 'fail' used in other measures of theory of mind, another strength.
- Another strength was that the ToMI was easy and quick to administer and not affected by child motivation, language or cognition issues, which makes it a useful clinical tool.

> **Explore**
>
> You can access Hutchins *et al.* (2012) using this link if you want to know more. (It was published online in 2011 but the journal article used was 2012 so that is the date given here.) Here is the link:
>
> www.curriculumconnection4sped.com/uploads/1/2/6/4/12648571/hutchins-prelock-bonazinga-2011.pdf

> **STUDY HINT**
>
> Hutchins *et al.* (2012) is more about method and finding out about autism than about autism itself though it does give some information about autism. When discussing methods it is worth noting that many studies are actually about methods and finding data.

Rethinking theory of mind: Sheeren *et al.* (2013)

Sheeren *et al.* (2013) agreed that problems with understanding the mental states of others is a feature of autism; however, they thought that older high-functioning people with ASD are more complex and using theory of mind as an explanation for autism is not sufficient. Sheeren *et al.* (2013) did a study of 194 school-aged children and adolescents with high-functioning ASD and used 60 typically developing children and young people as a comparison group. The method was to use five social stories – these had within them issues relating to theory of mind, such as sarcasm and double bluff. They found that the participants with high-functioning ASD did as well on the tasks as the typically developing group. The adolescents did better than the children in both groups. Sheeren *et al.* (2013) concluded that school-aged children and adolescents with ASD could use mental state reasoning, which goes against the theory of mind explanation for autism. There was mention, however, that those with ASD might not apply the theoretical ideas about mental state reasoning to their everyday social interactions. Some of the stories were more difficult than others; however, the difficulty was felt by both groups more or less equally.

Evaluation of Sheeren *et al.* (2013)

- Generalisability: The sample involved those with relatively mild autism, which might explain why the findings showed children and young people with ASD did have theory of mind and did as well as the typically developing group. Though the researchers found that severity of autism did not relate to how well the tasks were done, so Sheeren *et al.* (2013) felt that the sample having a lot of children and young people with relatively mild autism did not change their findings.

- Sheeren *et al.* (2013) felt they had not managed to test actual social interactions as they used stories, so validity was in doubt.

Individual differences in those with autism: Pellicano (2010)

Pellicano suggested that when it comes to theory of mind there are individual differences in those with autism. Sheeren *et al.* (2013) suggested that high-functioning ASD does not go with theory of mind difficulties in school-aged children and young people, which is already questioning the theory of mind as an explanation for all autism. Pellicano suggests that individuals with autism show differences in theory of mind, executive functioning and central coherence. Pellicano used 37 children (33 boys and 4 girls) with good cognitive abilities with an autistic spectrum condition and involved them in false-belief tasks (similar to the 'Sally/Ann' task – page 404). They also measured planning ability, cognitive flexibility and inhibitory control, which focuses on executive functioning, and cognitive functioning. These measures all took place at the start of the study when the children were aged from four to seven years and were repeated three years later, making this a longitudinal study.

Pellicano found that both executive functioning and central coherence predicted how well a child did on the theory of mind testing and predicted how theory of mind developed. The conclusions were that such general skills as planning and cognitive flexibility shape how theory of mind develops in the individual. Perhaps it is not the absence of theory of mind that explains autism but underpinning cognitive abilities and skills that are risk factors.

Evaluation of theory of mind as an explanation of autism

Strengths

- Baron-Cohen *et al.* (1985) carried out their study using children with autism, typically developing controls and children with Down's syndrome. This means they had different groups to compare the children with autism to. They found that children with autism did not seem to have theory of mind, while the other two groups were able to understand the view of another. The controls in the study helped the credibility of the conclusions.

- Studies like Hutchins *et al.* (2012) found that the ToMI was a suitable measure of theory of mind and in doing so found that children with ASD did less well on ToMI tasks, which reinforces Baron-Cohen *et al.*'s (1985) conclusions.

Weaknesses

- Pellicano (2010) found that that both executive functioning and central coherence predicted how well a child did on the theory of mind testing and predicted how theory of mind developed. It was concluded that it might be underpinning cognitive abilities that led children to appear not to have theory of mind or to have difficulties with that sort of thinking and these underpinning abilities could have differences in individuals with autism. It does not seem that not having theory of mind is a full explanation for all those with autism.

- Sheeren *et al.* (2013) found that high-functioning school-aged children and young people with ASD did not have problems with five stories set up as tasks to test theory of mind. They did as well as typically developing children who were used as a comparison group. There is the possibility that this was because some of the sample had mild ASD; however, it was not found that those with 'stronger' autism did less well than the others, so that was rejected as an explanation by Sheeren et al. (2013). This suggests that it is not only the issue about not having theory of mind that explains autism; there is more to it.

Progress check 4.18

Explain two pieces of evidence that suggest it is not the lack of theory of mind alone that explains autism.

Autism and the extreme male brain: a biological explanation

The idea that autism is an extreme male brain condition follows from the evidence that autistic people tend to be low empathisers and high systematisers. Baron-Cohen links the two explanations, as he has been involved in them both. In 2002 he put forward the idea that autism is a feature of having an extreme male brain.

Explore

You can read Baron-Cohen's paper about the extreme male brain theory of autism using this link:

http://cogsci.bme.hu/~ivady/bscs/read/bc.pdf

Year One link: You looked at brain functioning and brain regions in biological psychology. Although you did not cover male and female brain differences, it might help to recall what you did learn about the brain.

Males are supposed to be better at visuo-spatial tasks such as map reading and jigsaws, whereas females are often better at language tasks and they use both halves of the brain more (males tend to use mainly the right-hand half of the brain). This tends to reinforce the idea that girls are better at empathising and boys are better at systems, which, as there are more boys with autism than girls, suggests that autism is linked to male sex characteristics. People with autism also seem to be low at empathising and high systematisers, so that too goes with having a 'male' brain.

As children, girls tend to be more verbal and boys more spatial in their play, again fitting the characteristics of autism, as people with autism often have difficulties with language but are good at spatial tasks. Girls tend to show verbal aggression and boys more physical aggression – and to show verbal aggression perhaps girls have to know more what their victim is feeling. So this too fits with the idea of low empathising being a male brain feature and a feature of autism.

Year One link: When you looked at Bandura et al. (1961) in learning theories you looked at how boys and girls imitated male and female models differently, including showing different types of aggression. Girls showed more verbal aggression. You could use this evidence and relate it to Baron-Cohen's idea about autism and extreme male brain.

There is other evidence, too: people with autism tend to show greater growth in the brain, and boys' brains tend to grow more quickly than girls' brains. Females tend to be better at working out body language than males, which suggests they might be better at understanding interpersonal communication, something autistic people find hard.

Baron-Cohen's (2002) evidence for the female brain being better at empathising

Baron-Cohen (2002) suggests evidence for females being better at empathising and says that statistically significant differences have been found in the following (these are just some of the points he makes):

- Sharing and turn-taking: Girls show more concern for fairness than boys.
- Rough and tumble play: Boys show more 'rough housing', which is mock fighting, than girls do.
- Responding empathically to the distress of others: From one year old, girls show greater concern for sad looks.
- Using theory of mind: By the age of three years girls can infer better than boys what people might be thinking.
- Sensitivity to facial expressions: Women can decode non-verbal communication better than men.
- Disorders of empathy: Men have more disorders that relate to lack of empathy than women do, such as conduct disorder.

Baron-Cohen's (2002) evidence for the male brain being better at systemising

Systemising refers to focusing on input-operation-output in order. Baron-Cohen (2002) suggests evidence for males being better at systemising and says that statistically significant differences have been found in the following (these are just some of the points he makes):

- Toy preferences: Boys are more interested than girls in boy vehicles, mechanical toys and building blocks – all of which can be 'systematised'.
- Adult job choices: There are some jobs that are considered 'male' ones and they tend to focus on constructing systems.

- Maths, physics and engineering: These relate to systems and are male-dominated.
- Good attention to relevant detail: Attention to detail is superior in males and is a general feature of systemising.
- Mental rotation test: Males are quicker and more accurate and the task involves systemising.
- Map reading: Looking at features that are 3D and represented in 2D is about systems and males are better at map reading than females.

Boys are systemisers and more likely to be interested in construction toys; children with autism are even more likely to be interested.

Progress check 4.19

Explain two pieces of evidence that females have an 'empathising' brain and males have a 'systemising' brain.

Baron-Cohen's (2002) evidence for autism being an extreme form of the male brain

Having shown that males and females have different abilities, females being more empathising and males more systemising, Baron-Cohen then looked at autism and the extreme male brain. He says that autism is about problems with social development and communication and involves obsessional interests. He says that about 1 in 200 children (in 2002) are on the autism spectrum, including Asperger syndrome (AS). He points out that ASD includes males more than females and those with high-functioning autism or AS are ten males to every female. Baron-Cohen (2002) cites Bailey et al. (1998) as showing that there is some evidence for genes underpinning autism and he also cites his own research in 2000 (Baron-Cohen et al.) looking at the amygdala theory of autism. For example, the amygdala was found to be abnormal in size in those with autism and also being a brain structure that does not respond to 'cues of emotional expression'. Asperger himself, according to Baron-Cohen (2002), in 1944 suggested autism as 'an extreme variant of male intelligence', which began the idea of autism linking to male brain.

Evidence relating to impaired empathising:
- Mindreading: Girls are better than boys on theory of mind tests. Children with autism are even worse that typically developing boys and autism can be called a condition of mind blindness (Baron-Cohen, 1995, cited in Baron-Cohen, 2002).
- Empathy Quotient: Females do better than males on the Empathy Quotient questionnaire and those with high-functioning autism and AS do even worse than males (Baron-Cohen and Wheelwright, cited in Baron-Cohen, 2002).
- The Complex Facial Expressions test: Females score better than males and those with AS score even lower than males (Baron-Cohen et al., 1997, cited in Baron-Cohen, 2002).
- Eye contact: Females make more eye contact than males do and people with AS or autism make less eye contact than males (Lutchmaya et al., in press, cited in Baron-Cohen, 2002).
- Friendships questionnaire: Women score higher than males and those with AS score lower than males (Baron-Cohen and Wheelwright, cited in Baron-Cohen, 2002).

Evidence relating to superior systemising:
- Islets of ability: Some people with autism have special abilities and they tend to be in 'highly systemisable domains' like maths and chess (Baron-Cohen and Bolton, 1993, cited in Baron-Cohen, 2002). Mostly they are domains where males have a 'greater natural interest'.
- Attention to detail: Males pay more attention to detail and are better on tasks involving focused perception, which is required for systemising (Joliffe and Baron-Cohen, 1997, cited in Baron-Cohen, 2002). People with autism or AS have faster, more accurate visual searching than females or males and males are better than females (O'Riordan et al., 2001, cited in Baron-Cohen, 2002).
- Toy preference: Boys like construction toys and vehicle toys more than girls do and those with autism or AS seem to have this very strong toy preference.
- Collecting: Boys do more collecting of and organising of items than girls do and organising is one of the features of autism.
- Systemising Quotient: Males score higher on the Systemising Quotient questionnaire and so do people with autism and AS – even higher than typical males (Baron-Cohen and Reichler, cited in Baron-Cohen, 2002).

Biological evidence for extreme male brain

Baron-Cohen (2002) also gives biological evidence for autism being extreme male brain. He talks about finger length, for example, and how males have a longer ring finger than their second finger and people with autism and AS have this feature in a 'magnified' form. These differences in finger length possibly relate to prenatal testosterone. There is a higher risk of autism in families with talent in maths, physics and engineering (Baron-Cohen *et al.*, 1998, cited in Baron-Cohen, 2002). This suggests that the cognitive style of autism might be inherited. Baron-Cohen suggests that the cause of autism is in being exposed to excess testosterone prenatally (before birth), which is characterised by the 'extreme male brain'.

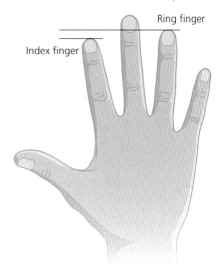

It is suggested that in males the ring finger is longer than the index finger and this feature occurs in autism too.

STUDY HINT
The idea of finger length is that it indicates prenatal testosterone levels, which may be a biological feature that helps to explain autism. Though this does not mean that the finger length difference is a cause of autism. If something helps to explain something, it does not mean it has caused it. Having no theory of mind can go with autism and can help to explain some of the features of autism but there can be another cause altogether. If your ring finger is longer than your index finger it probably does not say that much about you.

Conclusions

Baron-Cohen (2002) concludes that the male brain is systemising (Type S) and the female brain is empathising (Type E). The autism brain is extreme Type S and for males going from Type S to extreme Type S is not such a jump as for females going from Type E to extreme Type S.

STUDY HINT
Baron-Cohen is not talking about the brains of females and the brains of males, though it might seem that way; he is talking about the brain as having 'male' or 'female' traits, so females can have a 'male' brain.
You can see that Baron-Cohen has done (and is doing) a lot of work on explanations for autism. When writing about the explanations, you will probably cite Baron-Cohen's evidence a lot. Try to use the dates and full names of each study to differentiate them.

Progress check 4.20

Give two pieces of evidence for autism being extreme male brain according to Baron-Cohen (2002).

Testing the extreme male brain theory: Falter *et al.* (2007)

Baron-Cohen (2002) put forward a lot of evidence for the extreme male theory of autism; however, he did not offer evidence against the theory. Falter *et al.* (2007) tested visuo-spatial processing in autism. Visuo-spatial tasks are meant to be better in males and are thought, therefore, to be due to 'male brain'.

Falter *et al.* (2007) tested associations between three visuo-spatial tasks and finger-length comparing the ring finger and index finger. The study used 28 children with ASD and a matched group of 31 typically developing children. They found that the ASD group did better in mental rotation and figure disembedding tasks overall, which are two tasks that are reckoned to be 'male' tasks because males are better than females at them. However, these differences did not link to testosterone levels as measured by the index v. ring finger length differences. The three tasks included targeting, mental rotation and figure disembedding. Targeting meant moving a mouse cursor on a computer screen from a fixed cross in the centre of the screen to a target object. Mental rotation meant seeing if two objects on a screen were similar or not (rotated differently). Figure disembedding meant finding a smaller figure in a larger more complex picture.

The ASD children did do better on the mental rotation task, as has been said, but their improved performance was in the non-rotational aspects of the task. So the children with ASD did not do better in 'male' performance patterns. The finger lengths (index v. ring fingers) were not different for the children with ASD compared with the typically developing children. The issue about finger lengths is that it relates to prenatal testosterone which is the link to male brain. The children with ASD did worse on the targeting task than typically developing children, whereas if the extreme male brain theory is right they should do better. With regard to the figure disembedding task children with ASD did perform better than typically developing children and this does agree with the extreme male brain theory of autism.

Conclusions

Falter *et al.* (2007) used different ways of measuring 'male' brain and did not find evidence to support the extreme male brain theory of autism. The idea of high levels of testosterone fitting in with autism is not supported because the 'finger length' test showed no difference in those with ASD compared with typically developing controls. The mental rotation task and the targeting task did not support the extreme male brain theory. The mental rotation task was done better by those with ASD, however, what they did better on was not the 'male' part of the task. The targeting task was done less well by those with ASD.

Evaluation of Falter *et al.* (2007)

- Sample: All of the children, including those with ASD, had normal or better IQ, which might mean a bias in the sample. Other studies which showed differences in finger size in children with ASD did not match for IQ (Manning *et al.*, 2001, cited in Falter *et al.*, 2007).
- Falter *et al.* say that they cannot generalise to areas of cognitive performance seen in autism as their testing was specific and limited.
- They did not include a direct comparison of the sexes because they used tasks that have been said to be 'male' tasks.

Explore
You can access Falter *et al.* (2007) using this link if you would like to know more:
www.researchgate.net/profile/Greg_Davis7/publication/6165548_Visuo-spatial_processing_in_autism-testing_the_predictions_of_extreme_male_brain_theory/links/0deec51f6a63819449000000.pdf

Expanding on the extreme male brain theory of autism: Wen and Wen (2014)

Wen and Wen (2014) review the extreme male brain theory of autism. They focus on current risk factors for autism, which include parents being older, socioeconomic status and genetic predispositions in families of scientists and engineers. Factors relating to autism seem to link to testosterone. There is evidence that traits linked to males are also linked to those with ASD and to those with

anti-social personality disorder. For example, autism tends to mean lacking empathy in terms of cognitive problems such as theory of mind, whereas sociopathy means lacking in emotional empathy. Those with autism can lack empathy but without physical aggression.

STUDY HINT
Some of the arguments that Wen and Wen give can fit with the theory of mind explanation of autism, such as problems with empathy being cognitive.

Wen and Wen (2014) say it is clear that the traits of autism are 'male' traits, as Baron-Cohen (2002) has said, and because autism is four times as likely in males as in females. This adds to the idea that autism and the male brain seem to link, and a common link is testosterone. Wen and Wen say the important focus is on the 'social' brain, which is about social cognition – the idea that humans can make inferences about what goes on in the heads of other people.

Neuroimaging shows brain functioning related to social cognition, focusing on the amygdala, which is related to recognition of emotion and might differ in those with autism (Hughes, 2009, cited in Wen and Wen, 2014). The autism brain seems to be different in structure from the neurotypical brain. This is evidence for a biological explanation for autism that links to the 'extreme male brain' idea and also helps to explain the 'theory of mind' explanation of autism.

Wen and Wen (2014) suggest that prenatal factors can impact on autism very strongly, such as stressors from the environment. Parents being older also links to ASD and parents' age links with socioeconomic status, which has been associated with autism. Higher socioeconomic status links to autism, which tends to be the opposite of other learning disorders. Though it has been suggested that the rise in autism is down to diagnosis and as parental education and income increase perhaps proper diagnosis of ASD increases too. In addition higher socioeconomic status might mean working in technical fields as it correlates positively with careers that need specialised education. Wen and Wen (2014) conclude that there is evidence for the 'extreme male brain' explanation and its underpinning idea that autism stems from excess testosterone prenatally. They suggest that brain scanning of those with autism to look more at neuronal functioning would be a useful next step.

Evaluation

You can see in Wen and Wen's discussion the problem of looking for causation when there are so many variables that affect one another. Excess testosterone might well be the underlying cause and might lead to 'extreme male brain' as well as difficulty with theory of mind. The other factors, such as socioeconomic status, parental education and age of parents, might well relate to one another but are hard to pin down as a 'cause' of autism. This section of your course discusses 'explanations' rather than causes because explaining a disorder can be very helpful and understanding can help in dealing with something. However, an explanation is not necessarily a cause. Autism might mean lack of theory of mind, but that might not be the cause of the disorder; it might just be one of the features.

Evaluation of the extreme male brain explanation of autism

Strengths

- Baron-Cohen (2002) presents a great deal of evidence, not all of which is presented in this section, to show that autism relates to having an extreme male brain. He uses evidence from questionnaires and evidence from size of brain regions. The amount of evidence is persuasive.
- A strength of having explanations – and this applies to both the extreme male brain theory and the theory of mind – is that they help in practical ways, not just in helping someone to understand someone with autism, but also in developing ways to help.

Weaknesses

- A problem is in comparing explanations with causes. There is evidence relating different factors to autism, such as what is different in males compared with females is more different in those with autism. However, there is very little evidence showing that testosterone levels *cause* the male brain extremes that are found in autism.
- There is evidence against the extreme male brain theory. Falter *et al.* (2007) did not find evidence to support the extreme male brain theory when they looked at different aspects of the theory, though there was some supporting evidence. They did not find the difference in finger length that was supposed to measure prenatal testosterone levels related to the ability in certain tasks such as mental rotation.

STUDY HINT

Theory of mind is about cognitive processing and difficulties and links to empathy. The extreme male brain theory relates autism to lack of empathy, which is a 'female brain' trait. The two theories do not oppose one other. You could list some similarities and differences ready for a question asking you to compare two explanations of autism.

Progress check 4.21

Explain why it might be said that a problem with both theory of mind and extreme male brain as explanations of autism is that they are just 'explanations' – the cause of autism is not yet known.

Therapies for helping people with autism

Therapies regarding autism tend to be focused on behavioural, developmental and educational goals and are interventions that often involve the whole family. There is no single therapy that works for every child and there is no cure for autism. Therapies are interventions that can help to improve skills in those with ASD. Interventions tend to focus on communication skills, social interaction skills, cognitive and academic skills. Medication can be used to treat symptoms related to autism, such as depression or problems sleeping, so is not given as a therapy in this section. Occupational therapy and speech therapy are often used.

Ospina *et al.* (2008) reviewed therapies to look for effectiveness and their review can help to identify two therapies to focus on in this section. You are asked to look at therapies and in this section two are looked at in depth, but others are mentioned and you can expand your understanding of those if you wish. The therapies Ospina *et al.* (2008) looked at were 'behavioural and developmental interventions'. They looked at trials using the same intervention in their meta-analysis, focusing on quite a few interventions, and 101 studies were included, of which 55 were randomised controlled trials and 32 were controlled clinical trials, so there were controls built in much of the time. Therapies included Applied Behaviour Analysis (ABA) interventions, communication-focused interventions, environmental modification programmes and social skills development interventions, among others. For ABA there was evidence of effectiveness and Lovaas therapy was seen as effective (Ospina *et al.*, 2008). (Lovaas therapy is covered later in this chapter on page 415.)

Another form of therapy was communication-focused interventions such as Computer Assisted-Instruction or Picture Exchange Communication System (PECS). Another group of therapies for helping people with autism is sound therapy, including Auditory Integration Training (AIT). Sound therapy can be useful for children with problems with auditory processing or sound sensitivity. However, AIT is not officially recommended for autism as there is little evidence of its effectiveness according to the NHS website. Sinha *et al.* (2006) reviewed AIT and sound therapies for ASD using meta-analysis. They concluded that, although they found no 'adverse effects', they could not find enough evidence to support AIT as an intervention. This shows the importance of using studies to look at the effectiveness of therapies. Ospina *et al.* (2008) did find studies looking at AIT and it does seem to be researched, but as it is not 'recommended' it is not chosen here as a therapy to consider in depth.

Ospina *et al.* (2008) distinguished between ABA and contemporary ABA. Contemporary ABA includes Pivotal Response Training and CBT. When ABA brings in naturalistic aspects and developmental issues it is called 'contemporary ABA'. ABA is chosen as one therapy in this section and contemporary ABA is the second therapy chosen. It is thought to be different enough from ABA to be seen as separate. One contemporary ABA programme is Pivotal Response Training (PRT), which is the one looked at in this book.

> **STUDY HINT**
> When answering questions about therapies, such as for autism, or two explanations, be sure you write about *different* therapies or explanations. Theory of mind is different enough from the extreme male brain theory, but you need to be sure to present them as clearly separate. Also with ABA and PRT you must present them as clearly separate. In psychology explanations can overlap, as can therapies.

Applied Behaviour Analysis (ABA)

One therapy for autism is Applied Behaviour Analysis (ABA), which focuses on play and social behaviour, communication and living skills. ABA is widely used and aims to improve communication and social skills. The idea is to consider what are seen as challenging behaviours and teach more appropriate forms of communication, including social and self-help skills. ABA is a form of therapy that includes Token Economy features, which involve setting out behaviours that are to be encouraged and rewarding them with something the child wants and appreciates. ABA principles use Skinner's ideas about operant conditioning.

Year One link: Recall the principles of operant conditioning which you covered in learning theories as ABA rests on these principles.

The focus is on what happens before the behaviour – the antecedent – and what happens afterwards – the consequence (ABC). The idea is to identify behaviour that needs to change, look at what happens beforehand and intervene to change that, thus changing the behaviour.

Operant conditioning principles and ABC learning

An ABA programme focuses on:

- modifying events that come before a behaviour to manipulate the behaviour itself, such as increasing the likelihood of a behaviour occurring by giving prompts or offering motivation
- modifying consequences to decrease the likelihood of behaviour and to increase other behaviours, such as using reinforcement and shaping
- one-to-one focus on behaviour giving rewards for what is required, giving intensive intervention.

The process involves:

- choosing a behaviour such as a skill deficit
- identifying goals and objectives
- finding a way to measure the behaviour
- getting a baseline measure to show the situation at the start of the therapy
- designing and implementing interventions
- measuring the effectiveness of the interventions
- evaluating the interventions and planning 'next steps'.

> **STUDY HINT**
> You could use the example of Applied Behaviour Analysis (ABA) to show how operant conditioning principles are used in practice when you are discussing or evaluating operant conditioning. When a theory has a practical application, it is useful, which is a strength.

ABA focuses on socially significant behaviours, which refers to reading, academic skills, social skills, communication and living skills. The aim is to support those with autism to increase behaviours such as social interactions and to learn new skills such as communication skills

Discrete trial training

Discrete trial training means breaking a required behaviour or skill up into component parts and working on those before building up to the target behaviour or skill. This approach is good for teaching play, movement skills, daily living skills and communication skills.

> **STUDY HINT**
> In learning theories you covered shaping, which refers to arriving at a required behaviour gradually, step by step. Discrete trial training also focuses on shaping behaviours or skills.

Autism and behaviour therapy

ABA and autism, effects on siblings: Cebula (2012)

Cebula was interested in the impact of autism on siblings and in particular the effects of ABA not so much on the child with autism but on siblings and family members. Parents of children with autism report more stress than parents of typically developing children. However, Smith *et al.* (2000, cited in Cebula, 2012) found that mothers of a child with autism reported less stress during the intervention. This suggests that programmes like ABA help families as well as children with autism. Remington *et al.* (2007, cited in Cebula, 2012) also reported that parents of children with autism who were undergoing behavioural intervention compared with parents of typically developing children did not report higher levels of stress, anxiety or depression, showing that the programme itself is not found to add additional stress. These findings suggest that ABA is effective in helping parents.

Cebula wanted to see how siblings fared when ABA was being used for a child in the family with autism. Cebula (2012) looked at 132 families; 45 of the families included a child diagnosed as having ASD where families were using ABA. These 45 were the 'ABA' group. A group of 26 of the families had had ABA in the past and were the 'Post-ABA' group, while 61 were control families, none of whom had had ABA. Data were gathered using scales and questionnaires.

Cebula thought that ABA would help siblings in terms of their relationship with the child with autism in the family. This was not the finding, however. It was found using data from parents, siblings and teachers that the ABA group siblings did not get higher scores in terms of behavioural adjustment, self-concept or when measuring their relationship with the child with autism compared

with the other groups. There was some evidence of more positive interactions between the sibling and the child with autism in the ABA group and fewer negative interactions between them according to parents. This is some evidence for the effectiveness of ABA. On the whole, parents thought that ABA was effective for the child with autism, though looking at the effectiveness of ABA for the child with autism was not the aim of the study. Issues in how the ABA programme affected siblings of a child with autism seemed to be practical ones, such as the ABA programme meaning less time for the siblings to spend together and perhaps an impact on family finances.

Progress check 4.22

Cebula (2012) did not aim to look at the effectiveness of ABA for the child with autism, but the study did show that the programme was effective. Explain two ways that Cebula (2012) showed ABA to be effective.

Behavioural intervention for eating difficulties in children with autism: Gale *et al.* (2010)

Gale *et al.* (2010) carried out interviews and direct observations with three children with autism to look at acceptance of food and mouth clean (mouth empty of food), refusal to eat and other behaviours at mealtimes, such as crying and pushing the spoon away. These were disruptive behaviours at mealtimes for the children. It was thought the unwanted behaviours were being maintained by how the family were responding and ABA seemed a good choice as a therapy. Intervention for all three participants included presenting the food on a spoon for 30 seconds and (unless the food was accepted) ending the meal after 20 presentations. The 30-second presentations continued no matter what the response of the child, as far as that was possible. It was found that acceptance of the food and mouth clean increased and disruptive behaviour decreased, which is evidence of the effectiveness of ABA.

Gale *et al.* reported that assessments using interviewing before the intervention helped to identify what the targets would be for the intervention. For example, they found out for one child that there were various consequences around his eating behaviour. Sometimes he was allowed a video, sometimes food was removed and sometimes he was allowed to leave the situation. Sometimes these measures worked, sometimes they did not. They also reported assessments using direct observation, which also helped to see antecedent, behaviour and consequences. The intervention for all three children was planned to suit their individual situations. The assessments showed that what happened during mealtimes for each child was not consistent. For example, positive reinforcement was used but not consistently applied. The treatment planned was clear and implemented exactly. Positive reinforcers were selected beforehand to suit each child. For example, whenever food was accepted during the 30-second presentation the spoon was removed and the chosen reward(s) presented for 10 seconds. There was follow-up for two of the children at around five months after the intervention and it was found that at that stage parents no longer saw eating as a problem, suggesting that the therapy had been effective and remained effective even after some time.

Gale et al. suggested that the effectiveness of the interview and observation to assess the situation before the intervention was an important part of the therapy. They focused on needing to know the 'ABC' (antecedent, behaviour, consequence) of the unwanted behaviour before planning the intervention.

Effectiveness of therapies for children with ASD: Warren et al. (2011)

Warren et al. (2011) wrote a comparative effectiveness review focusing on therapies for children aged two to twelve years old with ASD. They reviewed studies from 2000 to 2010 published in English that had relevance to treatment for ASD. They included 159 studies, of which 13 were good-quality studies, 56 were 'fair' and 90 were 'poor'.

Warren et al. suggested that antipsychotic drugs improved challenging behaviour but were harmful and no medical interventions helped with social or communication issues in children with ASD. They found evidence supported behavioural and developmental intervention including the Lovaas model, as Ospina et al. (2008) also found. The researchers found that early intensive intervention in under two year olds was 'promising'. They found that parent training was useful and CBT too for helping with social skills and managing challenging behaviour.

Overall Warren et al. (2011) felt there were not enough consistent data to claim effectiveness of interventions, which suggests more studies are required to show reliability in findings. It seems that Warren et al. (2011) found some evidence to support ABA, in that the Lovaas model is ABA (and some evidence to support the use of CBT in some areas), even though there was not enough evidence for them to draw firm conclusions.

Table 4.14 Some peer-reviewed literature findings about the effectiveness of ABA (Terdal, 2013)

Article	Content/findings
Lovaas (1987)	Compared 19 children who had 40 hours of ABA a week for two years with a comparison group who did not have the intervention. Found 9 of the 19 were in school with minimal support compared with 1 of 40 in the comparison group.
McEachin et al. (1993)	Follow-up of Lovaas's 1987 study looking at long-term progress of the 38 children and found that the experimental group had maintained its improvement over the comparison group.
Cohen et al. (2006)	Replication of Lovaas's 1987 study. Compared 21 children on an intensive ABA programme with 21 in special schools classes. The ABA group had higher IQ and adaptive behaviour scores and 6 of them were in school without help, 11 others were in school with some help, compared with 1 child in the comparison group.

Year One link: Recall ideas about peer review and its function.

> **Explore**
> You can find YouTube material about ABA. Here is a link to one video:
> **www.youtube.com/watch?v=iyCx-OLzgJw**

Evaluation of ABA

Strengths

- Gale et al. (2012) showed that interview and observation were useful in finding out about a situation and in planning an intervention. They also found that individual interventions were needed, in that rewards needed to suit the individual. They also found that the intervention to help with eating behaviours was effective, even after four or five months. A study using empirical data and showing effectiveness is a strength for a therapy.
- Weiss states that the effectiveness of 'early intensive behavioural intervention' has been shown by many studies (e.g. Perry et al., 1995, cited in Weiss). However, intensity is important and strengths might relate to intensive use of ABA, involving 30 to 40 hours of intervention a week, so it is not just that ABA principles are effective, but the intensity and focus used.
- Parents and the child's family can be involved in the therapy and can continue with it. They also

come to understand more about the antecedents and consequences of behaviours so can use ABA ideas in other areas of the child's life. Cebula (2012) found ABA was effective and may have reduced parental stress or at least did not add to it. However, it is important that a careful analysis of the behaviour to be changed, including antecedents and consequences, is carried out and parents might not be in the best position to do that. Therefore, although parents can be involved, therapists are needed at least at the start to set up the programme.

Weaknesses

- A limitation is that the child might need the prompt in the situation so moving the behaviour to get similar responses to different stimuli might be difficult. For example, Gale et al. (2012) found that feeding from a spoon improved with rewards, though there is no evidence that there was generalisation to all feeding. This is a standard problem with behaviourist training in that the learning can be specifically focusing on one piece of learning.
- A related limitation is again an issue with generalisability. Learning might not be generalised to other situations, which limits the value of the ABA approach. This is similar to the limitation above that suggests that generalising to similar situations might not occur. However, this limitation is about generalising beyond even similar situations. It means that most behaviours would have to be shaped, which would be difficult, if not impossible.
- Another criticism is that ABA limits the child to what they are taught and does not let them make choices. A child is pushed towards 'acceptable' ways of behaving, which is possibly unethical and unacceptable.
- A possible limitation is the effect of such a programme on family finances, which can impact on others in the family as well as the child with autism.
- Warren et al. (2011) claim there is some evidence to suggest that therapy like ABA, which is behaviour-oriented, is effective, but not enough data have been gathered to show reliability in findings.

Explore
You can find Warren et al.'s (2011) review using this link if you would like to know more:
www.effectivehealthcare.ahrq.gov/ehc/products/106/656/CER26_Autism_Report_04-14-2011.pdf

Progress check 4.23
What are two limitations of ABA as a therapy for children with autism?

Contemporary ABA – Pivotal Response Training (PRT)

Contemporary ABA (Prizant and Wetherby, 1998) is not the separate trial approach that ABA involves; instead it adds more approaches to ABA, so is called 'contemporary ABA'. Contemporary ABA still focuses on analysing environmental factors that tend to produce certain behaviours, but differs from ABA in that the child has more control of the activities and there is more spontaneity in teacher/child interactions. Interactions are not as structured and this is why this approach is seen as 'natural'. Adults respond to all the child's communications, whether vocal or gestures.

It is hard to discuss a general approach to therapy so one therapy that fits into the contemporary ABA pattern, Pivotal Response Training (PRT), is covered here. PRT was developed to move on from controlled structured and adult-directed ABA. PRT aimed to help the child to generalise beyond ABA training situations to other events and situations. PRT also aimed to help the child not to be dependent on the prompt that they received in ABA and, therefore, might need in another situation. These focuses help to address two criticisms of ABA.

PRT focuses on teaching specific pivotal behaviours. These are motivation, responding to many cues rather than one at a time, self-management and initiating behaviour themselves. The idea is to help the child to become more autonomous so they can learn on their own and generalise their skills.

PRT includes:
- clear uninterrupted instruction
- mixing new tasks with those already mastered
- use of natural reinforcers
- using many cues not one
- child choice of activities
- reinforcement of child attempts
- use of naturally occurring teaching opportunities.

PRT programmes tend to involve 25 hours or more a week, as intensive training is found to be effective, as shown by studies looking at ABA interventions. PRT is described as a lifestyle change as it needs to be used consistently and within the family.

Kroegel et al. (1987) turned to more naturalistic approaches than traditional ABA allowed, focusing on natural language procedures. They thought that focusing on pivotal responses would make intervention more effective and efficient and would also mean improvement in other areas. Where ABA targets one behaviour at a time, PRT focuses on pivotal issues for the child, such as motivation, self-management, responding to cues and initiating social interactions. The idea was that building these skills would enable the child to improve in other areas, including behavioural areas not specifically focused on. This shows how contemporary ABA and PRT differ from traditional ABA. PRT strategies include child choice and variation in the task as well as rewards for attempts that include natural reinforcers. The child chooses the activities and what will be used in the intervention. Natural reinforcers include giving the child the toy the child is asking for, not a sweet as a reward. Parents are also involved.

Evidence for the effectiveness of PRT

- Simpson (2005) claimed that PRT was one of the evidence-based treatments for autism.
- Weiss and Harris (2001) also consider PRT a useful treatment of social skills for those with autism.
- Mohammadzaheri *et al.* (2014) carried out a randomised clinical trial comparison between PRT and structured ABA in children with autism. The structured approach is what in this section is called 'ABA' or 'traditional' ABA and PRT is a naturalistic approach based on ABA (contemporary ABA). Two groups of children were used, matched for age, sex and vocabulary use. The PRT approach was 'significantly more effective in improving targeted and untargeted areas after three months of intervention'. The researchers felt that PRT was better than structured ABA because it involved preferred toys and chosen preferred activities rather than artificial tasks. Also the skills were taught in natural play situations which may have kept the child more interested, which in itself led to more communication and so helped those skills. Koegel and Koegel (2011, cited in Mohammadzaheri *et al.*, 2014) found when motivational skills are focused on (such as the child wanting to play and communicate) there are improvements, such as in vocabulary. Structured ABA can help in care situations, such as feeding, as was shown earlier.

Explore

You can read Mohammadzaheri *et al.* (2014) using this link if you would like to know more:

www.autismspeaks.org/sites/default/files/docs/koegel_prt_rancomized_controlled_trial_of_prt.pdf

Voos *et al.* (2013) looked at the use of PRT to improve social motivation in those with autism and used two case studies to look at neural changes around social motivation using fMRI. Baseline measures were noted, looking at neural response to social stimuli (response to human movement), as well as baseline measures looking at social communication, adaptive behaviour and eye tracking. These measures were taken before treatment and after four months of PRT.

Voos *et al.* reported that both children 'showed striking gains' in behavioural measures and also increased activity in brain regions that are known to relate to social stimuli in typically developing children. The findings suggest that PRT can affect neural systems. Brain regions affected were, in one child, the left fusiform gyrus and left dorsolateral prefrontal cortex, and in the other child, the right posterior superior temporal sulcus and the left ventrolateral prefrontal cortex. The researchers thought that the neural effects centred around perception of human motion, which is important in social interactions, and the task they used involved this perception.

Voos *et al.* (2013) felt that their study showed that targeting pivotal behaviours was a successful therapy for children with ASD. Though the two children showed differences, as expected in children with ASD, there was some overlap in the neural mechanisms involved in response to movement.

Ventola *et al.* (2015) looked at ten pre-school aged children with ASD and used fMRI to look at brain responses in a human movement perception task. They took measures before PRT and after 16 weeks of treatment. Like Voos *et al.* (2013), Ventola *et al.* (2015) found that the neural systems were malleable and changed through the use of PRT. Also after treatment the neural systems that relate to social perception in the children with ASD were similar to those of typically developing children. There were interesting findings relating to whether children showed hypoactivation (reduced activation) relative to the typically developing children or hyperactivation (enhanced activation) relative to the typically developing children. The researchers found that the children who showed hypoactivation increased activation in the brain related to the reward system (ventral striatum and putamen), whereas those showing hyperactivation had decreased brain activity in areas regulating flow of stimulation (thalamus, amygdala and hippocampus).

Ventola *et al.* suggest that the individual child needs treatment tailored to them, given these differences in brain activity.

Management of children with ASD: Myers *et al.* (2007)

Myers *et al.* (2007) said that the goals of treatment in ASD are to help a child to gain independence and to help with quality of life. This is done by keeping to a minimum the effects of the ASD, achieving learning and socialising and reducing unwanted behaviours. Educating families is another goal, focusing on avoiding medical problems as well as using interventions. Myers *et al.* (2007) gave the figures for ASD as around 6.5 per cent per 1,000 people. The core features of ASD are problems with social turn taking and communication and restricted and repetitive behaviour, and these are the features focused on in interventions.

Interventions tend to be 'educational', which means focusing on learning, and ABA fits into that category. Myers *et al.* (2007) explained that contemporary ABA takes ideas from developmental and cognitive psychology. These ideas include addressing attention skills as cognitive psychology would suggest, using imitation as social learning theory suggests, engaging in symbolic play to help social skills and focusing on theory of mind, again a cognitive contribution. Alongside these ideas behavioural techniques are employed. Myers *et al.* (2007) listed what they found gives effective intervention:

- Starting intervention as soon as possible.
- Using intensive intervention, at least 25 hours a week and 12 months a year.
- Using a systematic planned intervention with appropriate educational activities.
- Having one-to-one interaction if possible and a low student–teacher ratio.
- Including parents in the training.
- Including opportunities for peer interaction.
- Measuring and documenting so that the programme can be tailored to the child and adjusted as necessary.
- Having clear structure and minimal distractions with a predictable routine.
- Using strategies to promote generalisation of skills.
- Focusing on communication and social skills, including self-management and initiation.
- Including cognitive skills like symbolic play and taking the view of another.

Myers *et al.* (2007) say that ABA-based intervention in children who experience intervention early enables them to make gains in IQ, language, academic performance and behaviour change as well as in their social behaviour (e.g. Cohen *et al.*, 2006, cited in Myers *et al.*, 2007). Myers *et al.* (2007) mention ABA such as Lovaas's work, including discrete trial training, but they also suggest that this sort of training has problems with generalisability and might not represent adult–child interactions, so lacks validity. They explain that this is why ABA was modified to include naturalistic behavioural interventions such as Pivotal Response Training, and that this 'contemporary' ABA is likely to mean generalising of skills (Schreibman and Ingersoll, 2005, cited in Myers *et al.*, 2007).

Explore
Myers *et al.* (2007) discuss many therapies for autism, including medication and complementary and alternative medicine. You can read Myers *et al.*'s (2007) article using this link:
http://pediatrics.aappublications.org/content/120/5/1162.full.pdf+html

Table 4.15 Some peer-reviewed literature findings about the effectiveness of contemporary ABA (Terdal, 2013)

Article	Content/findings
Dawson *et al.* (2010)	Carried out a randomised controlled trial of the Early Start Denver Model looking at 48 children with autism between 18 and 39 months old, who either had the Early Start intervention or other community providers. The ones on the Early Start intervention showed IQ improvements and improvements in adaptive behaviour.
Dawson (2011)	Reviewed 27 studies done since 2010 focusing on behavioural interventions and found they are effective for language, cognitive ability, social skills and adaptive behaviour, as well as reducing anxiety and aggression.

Explore
You can find Terdal (2013) and a list of evidence for the effectiveness of ABA as a treatment using this link:
https://olis.leg.state.or.us/liz/2013R1/Downloads/CommitteeMeetingDocument/13979

STUDY HINT
You could look at the issue of using ABA for autism as a key question for society. ABA has been said to involve control over the child, which has negative ethical implications. However, ABA has been shown to be effective to such an extent that court cases have been brought in the USA where ABA has been denied to a child. For example, in the State of California (2011) the insurance department has said that ABA is a medically necessary treatment for those with autism. A civil action in the USA (2012) found that ABA coverage had to be provided, which makes ABA provision an issue for society here.

Issues and debates

ABA has been said to use psychology as a form of social control because the intervention for the child is planned and structured with required behaviour rewarded and the child's input, at least in standard ABA, is not discussed. In contemporary ABA there is focus on more naturalistic interventions, which might go some way to helping give the child the right to participate as well as to be protected. Social control is one of the issues and debates in your course.

Explore
The following link is to a YouTube video about PRT, which might help in understanding the value of PRT, as opposed to traditional ABA:
www.youtube.com/watch?v=9VdPL8GhPfY

Progress check 4.24

Explain two ways that ABA and PRT differ and two ways in which they are similar.

Evaluation of contemporary ABA – Pivotal Response Training (PRT)

Strengths

- There is a lot of evidence to support the effectiveness of PRT, including evidence using fMRI scanning to show that brain activity changes as a result of PRT (Voos *et al.*, 2013 and Ventola *et al.*, 2015).
- When compared with structured ABA, the PRT approach was 'significantly more effective in improving targeted and untargeted areas after three months of intervention', according to Mohammadzaheri *et al.* (2011). The researchers felt that PRT was better than structured ABA because it involved preferred toys and chosen preferred activities rather than artificial tasks. The skills were taught in natural play situations, which may have kept the child more interested, which in itself led to more communication and so helped those skills.
- PRT targets motivational skills and other 'pivotal' skills with the hope that there can be generalisation to many behaviours and activities, so it addressed weaknesses of structured ABA, such as that each behaviour has to be individually 'trained'.

Weaknesses

- Children with ASD are individuals and need to have training tailored to them. For example, Ventola *et al.* (2015) found that PRT can change brain functioning when looking at perception of biological movement, which is evidence for PRT, but they found differences in such changes in different children. There were differences in changes in brain functioning between hypoactive children and hyperactive children, for example; Voos *et al.* (2013) also found differences in the changes in brain functioning. This suggests that any programme of intervention, such as PRT (or ABA) needs to be fully tailored to each individual and perhaps neural activity needs to give information about what intervention is best. This is a weakness as 'one intervention fits all' would be cheaper and easier in terms of staff training and setting up the intervention.
- It is noticeable that studies tend to involve relatively low numbers of children, such as two case studies used by Voos *et al.* (2013) and ten children in Ventola *et al.* (2015). It is understandable that numbers are low; however, because it is known that ASD varies so much between individuals it is hard to draw conclusions about all children with ASD from studies with such small numbers. Voos *et al.* (2013) comment about this weakness in evaluating PRT. Studies with more children and studies with different age and ability levels would be welcomed when evaluating PRT.

Test yourself

Robert, aged four years old, is a child with autism. He lives with his family and has one sister. His family has sought out what they think is the best intervention for Robert, but they are not sure what treatment to go with. All treatments offered involve more than 25 hours a week of intervention and so will be intensive.

Evaluate two or more treatments for Robert so that the parents can more easily make a choice. You must make reference to the context in your answer. **(12 marks)**

> **STUDY HINT**
>
> When you have a source in an exam question, as there is in the question about Robert and his family, be sure to focus your answer on the source when asked to. You will know if you need to make reference to a source as the question will use the words 'you must make reference to the context in your answer'. If there are 12 marks available you then know that 4 marks are for knowledge and understanding, 4 marks are for applying the material to the source and 4 marks are for evaluation and comment.

Summary

- For the content section in your course you need to know about attachment, deprivation and privation, including the work of Bowlby and Ainsworth.
- You need to know about deprivation and how negative effects can be reduced, and about privation, and whether negative effects can be reversed.
- You have to cover research into day care, including advantages and disadvantages for the child and what makes good- and poor-quality day care.
- Cross-cultural research into attachment types, nature–nurture issues and issues about universality must be covered and linked to what is required in the method part of this chapter.
- Autism is studied as well, including features, two explanations (one biological and one other) and therapies to help children with autism.
- Individual differences are important in child psychology, as in other topic areas, and you need to understand the impact of individual differences on the content, such as on attachments, day care and autism.
- Developmental psychology, as in other topic areas, should also to be noted, though child psychology *is* developmental psychology, so focusing on how day care, autism or attachments can affect a child's development is what you have been doing in any case.

Methods in child psychology

Methodology is about research methods used and design decisions taken when studying any area in psychology. Child psychology involves using many different research methods. In this section only some areas of methodology are considered.

You need to cover questionnaire, interview and observation as research methods in child psychology. All the issues related to these three research methods should be familiar to you, though you need to focus on the methods as used in child psychology. This chapter focuses on relating the methods to child psychology and reviewing the main features of the methods.

Year One link: In Year One you covered all the method material required in child psychology except for the focus on the ethics of researching with children. Draw on your learning of observation, questionnaire and interview, as well as issues when analysing data. Descriptive statistics and inferential statistics will be familiar to you, as well as using thematic analysis for qualitative data.

You also need to know about cross-cultural designs, longitudinal designs, cross-sectional designs and meta-analysis as a means of analysing data. All four of these aspects of method in psychology are explained in Chapter Two when methods in clinical psychology were covered. They will be reviewed here, with a focus on child psychology.

You need to cover descriptive statistics, inferential statistics and analysis of qualitative data using thematic analysis and grounded theory. Again, all of these are covered in Chapter Two, which looks at methods in clinical psychology, and will be reviewed here briefly.

A final section with regard to methods in child psychology is a focus on the ethics of researching with children, including the rights of the child, such as the need to balance their participation rights with their protection rights.

Observation as a research method in child psychology

You have learned about naturalistic observations and structured observations as research methods when looking at learning theories in Year One. This section reviews features of observations and also considers how they are used in child psychology.

Summary of the naturalistic observation research method

Observations are naturalistic if they take place in the participants' natural setting, without the situation being set up. They can be overt and open, covert and secret, participant observations with the observer taking a role, or non-participant observations with the observer not taking a role. They can gather qualitative data if a story of what is happening is recorded, or they can gather quantitative data by recording actions using tallying. Inter-observer reliability means that more than one observer uses the same categories and participants, so that results can be checked to make sure they correspond.

Year One link: You should already know the terminology when explaining observations as a research method, as you covered both structured and naturalistic observations when you looked at learning theories.

Table 4.16 Key terms used in observations as a research method

Term relating to observations	Explanation
Naturalistic observation	A naturalistic observation takes place in the participant's natural setting and is not set up. It involves everyday and natural behaviour.
Structured observation	This is where a situation is set up and then what happens in that situation is observed. This can be because the behaviour rarely happens naturally and so is hard to study, or because such behaviour is hard to replicate in a natural setting. By structuring the behaviour there can be repetition of observations.
Overt observation	When the participants know the observation is taking place.
Covert observation	When the participants do not know that the observation is taking place.
Non-participant observation	The observer does not have a role in the situation that is being observed; they are 'non-participant'.
Participant observation	The observer has a role in the situation and is the observer as well.
Qualitative data	Refers to words, stories, pictures, photographs, notes, diaries and other such data where there is richness.
Quantitative data	Refers to numbers such as percentages, number of 'yes' and 'no' answers, or measurements like height.
Tallying	This is done when observing in order to get quantitative data and involves counting the number of times a behaviour occurs.

Progress check 4.25
A researcher has gathered information from children by asking them to explain what they like about their classroom. Explain what type of data is being gathered.

Naturalistic observations in child psychology

Parten (1932) carried out naturalistic observations when looking at play and found categories of types of play, according to a child's age. She observed free play sessions to gather her data. Many other features of child development, such as language development, are studied using naturalistic observations. This is because the child in his or her natural setting will show natural behaviour, which is what the researcher wants to study. This is the 'research' side of child psychology, and naturalistic observations are extremely useful to child psychologists too in helping them to understand 'real' behaviour, and thus to help children develop appropriate behaviour. This is because there is little interference with the child's usual behaviour, making data valid. Children who are having problems at school are observed in the classroom, for example, to see what triggers certain behaviour patterns. From this observation, **interventions** can be suggested to help the child in some way. Naturalistic observations may take place when children are with their peers, as well as in the home.

Because behaviour happens in an environment, it is important to have an understanding of that environment. Naturalistic observations can help to see how often abnormal or deviant behaviour occurs, and time sampling can be employed. In **time sampling**, chunks of time are allocated and the observer can record what behaviour occurs during each chunk, to help build a detailed picture of a child's behaviour. Patterson (1982) recorded detail about parent–child interactions in this way, in order to understand what led to a particular behaviour.

Definitions

Intervention means planning an activity or a therapy, gathering data beforehand, then gathering data afterwards to see the effect the intervention has had.

Time sampling in an observation is a recording of what is happening at specific time intervals.

Studies in child psychology using naturalistic observation

Dodge et al. (1983)

Dodge *et al.* (1983) used naturalistic observation to study friendships (or the lack of them) in what they called 'rejected' children. Dodge *et al.* observed how peers played together, looking at popular, rejected, neglected, average and 'controversial' boys involved in free play. They in fact observed videos of the episodes of play and found that attempts at entering into peer group play were affected by the group the child was in (e.g. neglected or rejected). The differences were in the way they tried to gain entry into play and how successful their attempt was.

Pepler and Craig (1995)

Pepler and Craig (1995) discussed naturalistic observations of children and they used audio visual recording. Their aim was to observe aggression without the children changing their behaviour because of being watched. They used video cameras and wireless microphones to look at how peers interacted together, looking at both aggressive and non-aggressive children. The main strength of using naturalistic observations and remote observing is that there is **ecological validity** and **external validity**. Pepler and Craig mention structured observations, mentioning laboratory observational studies and contrived play group situations (citing Dodge *et al., 1990*) and explain that naturalistic observations can lead to more validity. External validity means what is observed represents children's everyday interactions and activities and remotely observing can give better external validity than using structured observation.

Explore
You can find the Pepler and Craig study using this link if you would like to read more about how the observation was carried out:
http://psycserver.psyc.queensu.ca/craigw/Pepler_Craig_1995.pdf

Definitions

Ecological validity means the data represent the natural setting, such as a naturalistic observation gathering data from children in their natural setting, perhaps at home going about their everyday life. A naturalistic observation has to study real life data in a way that represents it sufficiently to generalise the findings beyond that study. A structured observation could set a situation up enough that it represented real life interactions and so it could have external validity, but it would not have ecological validity.

External validity means how far findings can be generalised to other situations, which relies on the study being enough about real life behaviour that the findings can be generalised.

Slatcher and Trentacosta (2011)

Slatcher and Trentacosta (2011) carried out a naturalistic observation to look at links between depression in parents and the everyday behaviour of pre-school children. The researchers wanted to look at everyday behaviours and emotional language of young children and to look at how parents dealt with parent–child conflict in families where parents were depressed.

The researchers did the observation over one day and then one year later repeated the observation. The study took place on a Saturday or a Sunday. They used 35 families with children who were younger than school age. The sample consisted of 21 girls and 14 boys. They used an Electronically Activated Recorder (EAR) to gather the data so they gathered sounds while participants went about their daily lives. They found that they could associate a lot of problem behaviours in the children with parental depression. Behaviours that were cited included crying, watching TV and 'acting mad'.

> ### STUDY HINT
> In 'Psychological skills – methods' online you will be able to review the methods that you have covered throughout your course, including naturalistic observation as a research method. Slatcher and Trentacosta (2011) is given as an example of a naturalistic observation. Remember you can use your knowledge and understanding in different parts of your course.

> ## Explore
> You can find the study by Slatcher and Trentacosta (2011) using this link if you would like to know more. For example, you can read the introduction to their study to find out more about the effects of negative emotionality (depression) on people.
> www.ncbi.nlm.nih.gov/pmc/articles/PMC3387524/

Slatcher and Trentacosta (2011) suggest strengths and limitations of their research, which helps with considering strengths and weaknesses of using naturalistic observations.

Strengths

- Slatcher and Trentacosta (2011) collected ecologically valid rich data because they deliberately collected data directly from the child with no adults to interfere with everyday behaviour.
- They felt the strengths of their study were that their data were more independent than using a questionnaire and also were more generalisable than using a structured observation.

- Slatcher and Trentacosta (2011) felt by getting data directly from the children and not relying on parental reports they had valid data.
- They felt their data were easy and inexpensive to collect and that using the recorder was something other researchers could copy.

Limitations

- A difficulty was that Slatcher and Trentacosta's method took a lot of time and work because they gathered data throughout the day. This meant they had quite a small sample because it was not easy to use the recorder all day with a lot of children.
- The data were rich and detailed qualitative data, so they could not use statistical testing easily.
- They could not record interactions between the parents and the child easily nor record parental 'expressiveness' and a child's 'negative emotionality' because they only recorded sound. As they wanted to look at parental depression and its effect on a child's everyday life, this meant data were missing.
- A child could only wear the recording device for a day because of the short battery life and because of having to ask the family to get the child to wear the device for more than one day. They did a replication, however, a year later, which helped with reliability. They also used more than one rater when coding the data, finding very high reliability, which helped.
- They used children with a wide age range and as children's cognitive and emotional development is fast in the pre-school years, using different ages may have meant not much comparability between the children.
- The researchers did not check that the children were biologically related to the parents and they did not ask whether brothers and sisters were present. If they had used a larger sample these variables might have been controlled for.

> ### STUDY HINT
> Terms used in this section, such as reliability and generalisability, are reviewed in 'Psychological skills – methods' online if you need to check up on their meaning. They are often referred to when looking at studies and hopefully you have seen the method ideas you have covered in your course being used in psychology, so you can see their relevance.

Year One link: Slatcher and Trentacosta's (2011) evaluation of their study uses evaluation issues you covered in Year One. They are ecological validity, reliability, generalisability and the value of qualitative data. Remind yourself of the meaning of these terms if you need to, as they are central in your course.

Progress check 4.26

Evaluate Slatcher and Trentacosta's (2011) study in terms of both ecological and external validity.

Campos et al. (2009)

Campos *et al.* (2009) used naturalistic observation to study families where both parents worked. They studied them after work and school and were interested in uncovering everyday patterns of interaction. The researchers wanted to find out what opportunities there were for interactions between parents and children in dual-earner families. They studied 30 such families, observing them and video-recording in the home, covering two weekday afternoons and evenings. They looked at the behaviour of family members towards a parent coming home from work and they looked at how close the family members got to one another through the evening. They found that women tended to come home earlier than men and were greeted more positively as well as being told more about the family members' day's events. Men came home later and did get positive behaviour from family members but there tended to be no acknowledgement of the men as they came back from work because family members were doing other things. Mothers spent more time with children during the evenings and fathers spent more time alone. Couples rarely spent time with the children together.

Using recordings as data

Notice that all four studies given as examples here used recordings to gather the data. Three used video recordings and one used a recorder that was sound-activated. Having the data recorded meant there could be inter-observer reliability checked, as the recordings could be examined any number of times. It also meant less difficulty with taking notes at the time and other practical issues. As Pepler and Craig (1995) point out, recording everyday activities means external validity is more likely than an observer being part of the situation and so possibly affecting it.

Progress check 4.27

Using one research study, explain how the naturalistic observation took place.

Table 4.17 Brief summary of studies using naturalistic observations

Study	Summary
Dodge (1983)	Looked at type of child (e.g. neglected or rejected) to see how they tried to move into a friendship group.
Pepler and Craig (1995)	Looked at aggressive and non-aggressive children and wanted to observe natural behaviour, including between peers.
Slatcher and Trentacosta (2011)	Looked at children of parents with depression to see how the child was affected in their everyday life. They used an Electronically Activated Recorder (EAR).
Campos et al. (2009)	Studied family patterns where both parents worked to look at parent–child interactions and differences between the parents.

Progress check 4.28

Practise learning the data collection tools used or modified in the studies referred to in this section about naturalistic observation by completing the table below.

Name of study	Data collection tool used/ modified	Initials of the data collection tool
Dodge *et al.* (1983)		
Pepler and Craig (1995)		
Slatcher and Trentacosta (2011)		
Campos *et al.* (2009)		

Structured observations in child psychology

In the applied side of child psychology, structured observations are used to gather evidence about a child's deviant or inappropriate behaviour. The teacher, researcher or psychologist (or someone else depending on the aims) decides which situations will be observed and may set up a situation. Then the observer records certain information about the child's behaviour in that structured situation – the antecedent, the behaviour and the consequence. This is called ABC (A: antecedent, B: behaviour, C: consequence). The purpose is to find out what sets off the behaviour (the antecedent), then to observe the actual behaviour, and finally to see what happens to or for the child as a result of the behaviour (the consequence). Problems in behaviour may have arisen at any of these stages. For example, the child may have been rewarded for their inappropriate behaviour (the consequence) and a structured situation can reveal this. Structured observations can be used for research purposes too.

> **STUDY HINT**
>
> When describing a research method it is useful to explain an example, as this helps to illustrate your understanding. An example needs more than just a name — always write something about the aim and/or what was found.

Studies in child psychology using structured observation

Ainsworth's strange situation procedure

In the 1970s Mary Ainsworth, working on the academic side of child psychology to develop theory, carried out a special kind of structured observation called the 'strange situation' task. This is explained in detail in the content section of this application (page 377). Use what you learn there to explain and evaluate structured observations.

Ponitz *et al.* (2009)

Ponitz *et al.* (2009) carried out a study of 343 three to four year olds in the USA using a sample from a five-year longitudinal study on social and academic development. They used children on two sites, Oregon and Michigan. They collected data from parents, teachers and the children. Parents completed questionnaires and also rated temperament, which was about attention focusing and control. Teachers gave data about how the child related with others and about how they controlled their behaviour.

Children were measured on maths, literacy and reading. There was also a structured observation to measure their control over their behaviour. Children were given 20 commands relating to a Head-Toes-Knees-Shoulders (HTKS) task. The HTKS task had shown both reliability and validity previously. Commands included 'touch your toes' and involved children responding 'against' the command. An example of a trial going 'against' the command condition was if they were told to 'touch your toes' they had to touch their heads. The commands were given in the same planned order for all children though there were two forms of the task and there was counterbalancing of the two forms.

Parent ratings of the child's focusing of their attention and the child's control over their behaviour as well as teacher ratings of behavioural control in class both correlated positively with the HTKS task score and this was taken to show construct validity. The researchers found that including tasks like this one for children to practise controlling their behaviour related to academic achievement. The more behavioural regulation in the autumn, the stronger the achievement levels in the spring and also better ratings of classroom regulation (p<.01), although gains were in maths, not in language or literacy.

In this study focus was on how this was a structured observation rather than on other issues with the study, such as their analysis of how representative the sample was.

> **STUDY HINT**
>
> When you come across a study using a particular methodology issue — for example, Ponitz *et al.* (2009) used counterbalancing — make a note so that when you are revising you have examples of 'doing psychology'.

Progress check 4.29

Ponitz *et al.* (2009) found links between academic achievement and behavioural regulation at p<.01. Explain what p<.01 means in this context.

Ponitz *et al.* (2009) used a Heads-Toes-Knees-Shoulders task, where children had to go against the command, to show behavioural control in young children.

Methodology issues in your course illustrated by Ponitz *et al.* (2009)

Construct validity refers to how far a test measures what it claims to measure, so in the case of Ponitz *et al.* (2009) how far the structured task represented control over behaviour, which they called 'behavioural regulation'. As there were other sources of data that showed the same findings for a child, the task was said to have construct validity.

> **STUDY HINT**
> Three types of validity have been mentioned in the section on observations. You also need to know about predictive validity, so remind yourself about that type of validity and the others. The more you use terms and check your understanding, the more you will remember definitions and examples.

Roberts (2001)

Roberts (2001) discussed structured observation of parent–child interaction to recreate conditions so that parent and child can be observed as if in their natural setting. The purpose was to look at dysfunctional parent–child interactions in order to modify them and this study had a clinical purpose; it was not only about research. The study used three situations: a free play situation, one with parent-directed play and one with parent-directed chores.

Roberts suggested that the free-play sessions did seem to represent a real life situation enough to have merit when used in clinical practice. A clinician could see parental control and negativity when a child was playing, which was useful and could be targeted using interventions. It was in parent-directed play that child deviance could be observed. Parent instructions, child compliance and parent reinforcement of compliance could all be observed in parent-directed play. Parent training could modify responses as it could in free play situations. However, with regard to parent-directed play, Roberts felt the structured element did not represent real life enough to be useful. Parent-directed chores did seem to show sufficient links to real life to be useful for a clinician to observe and develop strategies to help. Both the free play structure and the parent-directed chores structure seemed to be valid, but not the parent-directed play situation.

In Roberts (2001) there had not been test-retest reliability, which he saw as a limitation. Roberts felt that structured observations (excluding the parent-directed play) were better than interview or questionnaire at uncovering actual parent–child interactions so that dysfunctional interactions could be addressed.

> **STUDY HINT**
> If you are comparing the use of observations, interviews and questionnaires and considering research methods in child psychology, you could use Roberts (2001) as an example of saying that observations are better. Studies are summarised here to show examples of method, so that you can refer to them in your exam.

Johnson *et al.* (2009)

Johnson *et al.* (2009) looked at a parent training programme for children with pervasive developmental disorders (PDD). They used what can be called a structured observation to obtain data before the programme and the same 'structured' observation to obtain data after the programme, to look at the effectiveness of the programme. This is an example of using a structured observation to obtain before and after data and is about the training programme rather than the observational data being done as research alone.

The researchers used 12 children aged from four years to thirteen years old, all with PDD. This was a pilot study in preparation for a large-scale study. The Standardised Observational Analogue Procedure (SOAP) was used and involved more than one procedure. The data were collected by videoing the behaviour in each of the conditions and there was inter-rater reliability in the coding of the observations. There was a free-play condition with some structure because parents had to use three very desirable toys, three with medium desirability and three neutral toys. There was a social attention condition where children had four neutral toys and parents had to pretend to be busy. There was a high demand condition where parents had to issue one of ten commands every minute and do what they did at home to get compliance from the child. Also there was a tangible restriction condition where parents played with the child using a highly desirable toy for one minute and then the parent was told (using a 'bug in the ear' device) to remove the toy.

The researchers pointed out that this was not an experiment because the parent was told to do what they would typically do in response to the child's behaviour. The researchers felt that they were using naturalistic observation because of the natural element of the study, though the situations were set up and they called the procedure 'Standardised Observation Analogue Procedure' so it can be argued this is a structured observation.

> **Explore**
> Pervasive developmental disorders (PDD) include autism, Asperger syndrome and others. In child psychology you need to know about autism. Explore more about PDD using the following link:
> **www.webmd.com/brain/autism/development-disorder**

Evaluation of Johnson et al. (2009)

The researchers felt they were using naturalistic observation because parents were responding to their child as they normally would, although there was structure in the 'Standardised Observation Analogue Procedure'. The researchers argued this was not an experiment because of the element of naturalness in the behaviour. Here Johnson et al. (2009) is used as an example of a structured observation but you can see there are issues in attributing research method to a study and you need to be able to discuss such issues.

> **STUDY HINT**
>
> Johnson et al. (2009) discuss their research method and explain why it is not an experiment (because there is too much of an element of measuring natural behaviour); they feel it is a naturalistic experiment. However, their method is called 'standardised' and there is clearly some structure (e.g. in the commands given to the parents), so it is suggested here as a standardised observation. If it is difficult to confirm a study is representative of a particular research method, you must explain such a claim.

Li et al. (2013) – an example of an observation

Li et al. (2013) used observations of children to look at high- versus low-quality day care to look at cognitive, language and pre-academic development linked to the quality of day care experienced. Li et al. (2013) is one of the contemporary studies in child psychology in your course and you can use it as an example of the use of observations in child psychology (page 465).

> **Progress check 4.30**
>
> Explain one example of a structured observation in child psychology.

> **STUDY HINT**
>
> It is useful to know other examples of a structured observation in child psychology; however, you will know a lot about the use of the strange situation procedure, so you will be able to give more information about that. If you need to give detail it is probably worth using the strange situation as your example.

Table 4.18 Studies using structured observations

Study	Summary
Ainsworth (1970s)	Used the strange situation procedure (SSP) to look at attachment types, looking at mother–child reunions.
Ponitz et al. (2009)	Looked at children controlling their behaviour and used the Heads-Toes-Knees-Shoulders task (HTKS). They linked behavioural control to academic success.
Roberts (2001)	Set up three tasks: free play, parent-directed play and parent-directed chores, so that clinicians could observe parent and child and suggest intervention.
Johnson et al. (2009)	Naturalistic to an extent but set up tasks such as playing with a desirable toy – like Roberts (2001) this was to see parent-child interaction to plan intervention. They used the Standardised Observational Analogue Procedure (SOAP).

> **Progress check 4.31**
>
> Practise learning the data collection tools used (even though often modified) in the studies used in this section about structured observation by completing the table below.
>
> | Name of study | Data collection tool used/modified | Initials of the data collection tool |
> |---|---|---|
> | Ainsworth (1970s) | | |
> | Ponitz et al. (2009) | | |
> | Johnson et al. (2009) | | |

Evaluating observations in child psychology

Strengths of naturalistic observations

- Naturalistic observations are carried out in a natural setting, with the aim of observing children doing what they normally do and interacting with others as they usually would. This means they have validity – more so than experiments or surveys.
- If time sampling is used carefully, with tallying, prepared categories and more than one observer, the data can have reliability since inter-observer reliability can be checked.
- If video or sound recording is used this can help with validity as disruption is at a minimum.

Weaknesses of naturalistic observations

- Children can be influenced by being observed and they may display different behaviour from normal, which means data will not be valid.
- Similarly, there can be **observer drift** – observers tend to move away from what they planned to observe, and bias can be introduced, again meaning that the observations lack validity.
- Reliability can be a problem, as an observation often cannot be repeated because it is a particular time, day, situation and set of children and observers. If those circumstances are not exactly repeated, then data cannot be tested for reliability.

Definition

Observer drift is when an observer intends to observe certain behaviours but can, during the observation, start to look at something different.

Strengths of structured observations

- Structured situations are set up and documented in enough detail that they can be replicated and so tested for reliability.
- The point of the structured observation is to provide evidence, for example, for a child's deviant behaviour and what might trigger it, which means the situation must be carefully noted and the antecedent, behaviour and consequence clearly visible and able to be recorded.
- Careful noting of the situation means that reliability is more likely than for naturalistic observations. Structured observations can be efficient, because the behaviour to be observed might either not occur again or not occur for a long time, making it difficult to observe in any other way.
- Structured observations are time and cost effective.

Weaknesses of structured observations

- Structured observations are set-up situations that are not natural, so they can be said to lack validity.
- They may not have been correctly set up, so may not represent reality.
- There is the chance of demand characteristics occurring – that the subjects know that the situation has been structured (set up) and will behave as they think they should. This too will affect validity. (Adults may show demand characteristics but very young children are likely to be less aware so are less likely to.)

STUDY HINT
When looking at Slatcher and Trentacosta (2011) strengths and limitations of their naturalistic observation were considered. In the content section strengths and limitations of the strange situation procedure are given, some of which can be applied when evaluating structured observations. The 'Psychological skills – methods' section online reviews the method in your course and you will find both naturalistic and structured observations covered there too, including strengths and weaknesses. You have come across material about observations often in your course so draw everything together ready to discuss observations as a research method.

Year One link: You covered strengths and weaknesses of both naturalistic and structured observations when you studied learning theories so use your notes to remind yourself.

Progress check 4.32

Compare naturalistic and structured observations in terms of validity and reliability.

STUDY HINT
Use the answers to progress checks to help in understanding.

Usefulness of observations in child psychology

Observations are extremely useful in all areas of psychology. Practising psychologists (such as educational psychologists, clinical psychologists and forensic psychologists) work in similar ways. They are called upon in a certain situation, usually when a change in behaviour is required. Their first aim is to study the situation, which they do by observing. Such observation has to be as natural as possible to have validity. Having gathered evidence by observing, the psychologist then plans an intervention and, finally, evaluates the intervention. Evidence is also likely to be gathered by interview and perhaps by using **psychometric testing**. Observation is an important method, because it involves the individual directly, whereas interviewing others does not. Psychometric testing also tends to be artificial, even though it can be useful.

Explanation

Psychometric testing involves psychological measurement involving objective measures such as IQ tests or personality tests. Questionnaires can be used, often using a Likert-type scale.

Roberts (2001) considered structured observation as a method to help a clinician to understand parent–child interactions and to formulate strategies to help. Johnson *et al.* (2009) looked at a specific standardised set of observations to gather data before and after a programme of intervention to help parents and children when a child has a pervasive developmental disorder. Both these examples show that observations are not only used to gather data about child development but also to help with their development in a clinical setting.

> **STUDY HINT**
> There are naturalistic and structured observations. Be ready to answer questions about either one or the other, but if a question asks you to focus on 'observations' you can bring in both naturalistic and structured (though be sure to identify which one you are discussing in any point).

Test yourself

1 Assess differences between structured and naturalistic observations using examples from child psychology. **(8 marks)**
2 To what extent is observation as a research method valid when it comes to researching with children? **(16 marks)**

Questionnaire and interview as research methods in child psychology

In social psychology in your course you covered the use of questionnaires as a research method, including gathering both qualitative and quantitative data, using open and closed questions, and considering issues of social desirability and demand characteristics.

> **STUDY HINT**
> When discussing a research method you will need to talk about it 'as a research method' as is done in this section. That is because there can be ambiguity otherwise. A question may ask 'Evaluate questionnaires used in child psychology' or 'Evaluate questionnaires as a research method used in child psychology', and the two have quite different meanings. Make sure when writing about research methods that you are being very clear.

In social psychology you also covered the use of interviewing as a research method, including three types of interview: semi-structured, structured and unstructured. Issues of social desirability and demand characteristics can crop up in interviewing too. Interviews can use both open and closed questions and can gather both qualitative and quantitative data. Table 4.19 will help you revise how interviewing and questionnaires are used as a research method by explaining the key terms.

Table 4.19 Key terms used in questionnaire and interview research methods

Key term	Explanation
Qualitative data	Refers to words, stories, pictures, photographs, notes, diaries and other such data where there is richness.
Quantitative data	Refers to numbers such as percentages, number of 'yes' and 'no' answers, or measurements like height.
Questionnaire	A research method that uses a set list of questions and items to find out about something specific. There are likely to be standardised instructions at the start to help with ethics and to make sure all participants are told the same thing in order to avoid bias. Data can be gathered by post or by the researcher, or questionnaires can be left for people to complete. A questionnaire asks for personal data and tends to use both open and closed questions to gather both qualitative and quantitative data.
Interview	A research method carried out by an individual either face to face or over the telephone. In a structured interview specific questions are asked, while an unstructured interview has much less of a focus on specific questions. Qualitative data are focused on, though quantitative data can be gathered as well.
Structured interview	An interview where there is a clear idea of what is to be covered by the person responding. Questions tend to be standard and the same for everyone, which means data are reliable because there is replication.
Semi-structured interview	An interview that has some standardised questions that everyone is asked, but there is some room to explore participants' replies in more detail and to ask spontaneous questions. This can help with validity and should retain reliability for the most part.
Unstructured interview	An interview where there is a research question and a focus, although the respondent can lead the interview by how they discuss the issues of interest. This type of interview is more likely to have validity than the other two but can be hard to test for reliability.
Open questions	Questions that gather qualitative data and ask for ideas, attitudes, emotions or judgements from people. The answer given can vary because the respondent is not forced to choose from a limited choice of answers.
Closed questions	Fixed answer questions where the respondent is limited by the choice of answer offered. Closed questions gather quantitative data.
Social desirability	Refers to the possibility that a respondent will reply according to what they think is expected according to social norms. If a respondent does this then the data are not valid.
Demand characteristics	Where the respondent has worked out what is required by the researcher and answers accordingly. If a respondent does this then the data are not valid.

You also need to know about sampling in this section on questionnaire and interview. In Year One you covered four sampling techniques. Table 4.20 reviews those four and adds one more, **snowball sampling**.

Table 4.20 Sampling techniques in psychology

Sampling technique	Explanation
Opportunity/ convenience sampling	A researcher selects participants according to who is available at the time they want to gather the data. This is not likely to be a fully representative sample because the people available at one time are likely to have similarities – for example, being in town on a Wednesday afternoon.
Random sampling	Everyone in the chosen population has the opportunity of being chosen, so this is a sampling technique that should get a sample representative of the target population.
Snowball sampling	Refers to finding one participant who then introduces the researcher(s) to others and the size of the sample grows like a snowball. There will be bias in the sampling because of having to make choices, but in a sensitive area of research this type of sampling can be ethical and might be all that can be done.
Stratified sampling	A sample where there are categories or strata that the researcher is particularly interested in and needs in the sample, such as a particular gender, social situation or ethnicity. Using stratified sampling can ensure that there is the right number of people from the groups in the sample.
Volunteer or self-selected sampling	A sample where people answer an advertisement or put themselves forward in some other way. In a postal questionnaire, those who return the questionnaire select themselves and in that sense are volunteers.

Year One link: You covered four of the sampling techniques in Table 4.20 when you looked at social psychology, though snowball sampling is new to you. Recall what you learned about sampling, including issues like target population and sampling frame.

You will now look at some studies that used questionnaires and some that used interviews so that you have a better idea how these two research methods are used in child psychology. You can also use these studies, and those using observation that were covered earlier in this chapter, to learn more about what child psychology is about.

Child psychology studies that use questionnaires

Heflinger *et al.* (2014)

Heflinger *et al.* (2014) developed a questionnaire and in order to make sure it had validity, they used interviews and focus groups to check the items being used. The focus of the study was on stigma and a child's mental health. The focus was on what adults with children with mental health issues thought about attitudes to child mental health in the area where they lived. First the questionnaire was developed based on previous work in the area, then focus groups and interviews with adults with children with mental health issues took place to validate the items on the questionnaire. The result was a 45-item questionnaire that adults could self-administer to measure what they thought about attitudes about child mental health, known as the Attitudes about Child Mental Health Questionnaire (ACMHQ).

The aim of the questionnaire was to look at attitudes to child mental health in a rural community so that is where the data were gathered. The researchers wanted to find out about the extent of stigma around child mental health in rural communities, from the viewpoint of adults with children with mental health issues. The questionnaire was used over six weeks with 185 parents. When parents went to the clinic that was being used, which was a large paediatric clinic, serving several counties, they were given a package containing the questionnaire and told that participation was voluntary. Privacy was protected as there was no information collected that could identify anyone.

The researchers found some general stereotypes, some points about child dangerousness or incompetence and ideas about discrimination and devaluing the child in the community. These were three subscales. There were some interesting findings, including how the more familiar someone was with mental health problems, the less they thought about or talked about child dangerousness and/or incompetency. There was also mention of teachers and community disapproval, such as 'many teachers treat children with mental health issues unfairly'.

Limitations of the study

The researchers pointed out that the questionnaire respondents were mainly female and white and from a rural community and they suggest further studies are needed in more diverse populations. Construct validity of the questionnaire also needs to be tested more. However, overall the researchers felt that the questionnaire did uncover stigma in the situation they were investigating and was a useful method.

Esbjørn et al. (2013)

Esbjørn et al. (2013) focused on using a 30-item questionnaire for children including young people looking at **metacognitions** and relation to anxiety symptoms. The researchers point out that questionnaires designed for adults are not likely to suit children as they are still in the process of developing skills. The researchers' aim was to find a psychometric assessment tool that suited children when measuring metacognitions and anxiety. They wanted to uncover an early signal of anxiety disorders developing so that interventions would be possible to help the child.

The questionnaire Esbjørn et al. (2013) focused on is the Metacognitions Questionnaire for Children (MCQ-C$_{30}$). They used 974 children and adolescents aged nine to seventeen years old. Metacognitions are thoughts about thought, and in particular monitoring of thoughts that include personal goals as well as thoughts about cognitive tasks that can achieve personal goals. Thoughts might include 'my worrying is dangerous for me' when looking at metacognitions and anxiety disorders, which is the focus of this study.

Data were gathered by children completing a self-report questionnaire in school hours in their school. As well as the Metacognitions Questionnaire for Children (30-item) to find out about their metacognitions, the participants also completed the Penn State Worry Questionnaire for Children (14-item) to find out about their worrying and the Screen for Child Anxiety Related Emotional Disorders (Revised) (69-item) to look at their anxiety. The researchers found the MCQ-C$_{30}$ was useful for looking at metacognitions in relation to generalised anxiety and OCD. The researchers recommend research that looks at metacognitions in children with a view to predicting possible generalised anxiety disorder and OCD.

Definition
Metacognitions are thoughts about thinking and are about focusing, for example, on thinking around goals and actions, including about cognitive processes that can achieve goals and skills required for controlling thoughts.

Limitations

The sample was not a clinical sample, meaning the children and young people who took part did not suffer from

generalised anxiety disorders or OCD. It would be interesting to see if the findings are replicated in a clinical sample involving children with mental disorders. Esbjørn et al. (2013) felt too that it would be useful to measure depression. Also the results could not be generalised to children under the age of nine years because the sample started at that age.

Duckworth and Seligman (2005)

Duckworth and Seligman (2005) looked at the effect of self-discipline on final grades in school and they collected self-report data using a questionnaire. They studied 140 students, measured their self-discipline using a questionnaire but also used parent and teacher reports (also using questionnaires), school attendance and test scores. They also used an IQ test. They found the self-discipline measured in the autumn at school accounted for twice as much of the variance in final grades as IQ, school attendance, hours spent doing homework, hours spent watching television and a few other variables. The researchers claimed that final scores very much depended on self-discipline as well as other factors. Duckworth and Seligman (2005) felt that using many methods and many sources helped them to measure self-discipline and they found good reliability between measures. The conclusion was that if a student falls short of their intellectual potential this could be down to their lack of self-discipline – which could relate to a failure to defer gratification.

Limitations

The researchers suggest that self-discipline was measured well, including by more than one means, but IQ might not have been so well-measured so might not have truly shown the effect from IQ. Self-discipline is not often measured so the researchers could not see if the sample showed 'normal' performance with regard to self-discipline.

Explore
You can access Duckworth and Seligman's (2005) study at: http://citeseerx.ist.psu.edu/viewdoc/download?doi=10.1.1.368.8509&rep=rep1&type=pdf

Progress check 4.33
Explain why in Duckworth and Seligman's (2005) study on self-discipline and academic achievement, a questionnaire was a useful data collection tool.

STUDY HINT
When answering a question about a method in child psychology aim to bring in something specific about the method using children or at least refer to a study that uses children or young people.

Gagnon-Oosterwaal *et al.* (2012)

Gagnon-Oosterwaal *et al.* (2012) used questionnaires to gather self-report data to find out about the long-term impact of problems before a child was adopted together with a questionnaire to gather information from mothers. Gagnon-Oosterwaal *et al.* (2012) is one of the contemporary studies in child psychology in your course and is covered in detail later in this chapter (page 461), so you can use what is done in this study when talking about the use of questionnaires in child psychology. Gagnon-Oosterwaal *et al.* (2012) focus on internationally adopted children. There have been quite a lot of studies on internationally adopted children in recent years, because they are institutionalised in one country and then adopted into another country with a new culture, so the effects of both institutionalisation and change of culture are of interest. There are issues, too, about the child's autonomy in regard to the choice of making such a move, as well as issues around children 'being bought'.

Table 4.21 Studies using questionnaires

Study	Summary
Heflinger *et al.* (2014)	Looked at attitudes to child mental health in a rural community. They developed the Attitudes about Child Mental Health Questionnaire (ACMHQ).
Esbjørn *et al.* (2013)	Looked at how children think about their thinking (metacognition) and how that relates to developing anxiety or OCD. They used the Metacognitions Questionnaire for Children (MCQ-C$_{30}$). They also used the Penn State Worry Questionnaire for Children (14-item) and the Screen for Child Anxiety Related Emotional Disorders (Revised) (69-item).
Duckworth and Seligman (2005)	Looked at the effect of self-discipline, identified through self-report data, on academic achievement.
Gagnon-Oosterwaal *et al.* (2012)	Looked at the long-term impact on an adopted child from their early pre-adoption experiences.

Progress check 4.34

Practise learning the data collection tools used (even though often modified) in the studies used in this section about questionnaires by completing the table below.

Name of study	Data collection tool used/ modified	Initials of the data collection tool
Heflinger *et al.* (2014)		
Esbjørn *et al.* (2013)		

Evaluation of using questionnaires in child psychology

Strengths

- Esbjørn *et al.* (2013) found the links between metacognitions, general anxiety disorder and OCD seemed to have validity and supported their questionnaire. Heflinger *et al.* (2014) found that there were attitudes to children with mental health issues that showed stigma, such as teachers treating children with mental health issues 'unfairly', so their questionnaire too gathered data to suit their research question. Duckworth and Seligman (2005) found that self-discipline did go with good grades in school. The questionnaires appeared to have given data that suited the research question and showed enough reliability and validity to make them worth using. For example, Duckworth and Seligman compared data from different sources and found the results from the questionnaire were supported.

- The brief overview of studies given here does not cover all the ways in which the researchers worked hard to make sure their questionnaires were fit for purpose. For example, one study used 185 parents and another had 974 families involved so there were large samples, which helps with generalising. Items were considered carefully and a the questionnaire that was developed was because there was no suitable existing questionnaire to use. A strength of the studies is that they developed a new data collection tool for a special purpose and it could be used again.

- Ethics were quite carefully considered. The reports mentioned the relevant institution review board approving the studies and also how privacy was protected. In some cases, such as when obtaining self-report data, the children or young people were asked for data directly so they had participation rights.

Limitations

- Limitations tended to focus on the sample, which in Heflinger *et al.* (2014) were female, white and in rural communities. Heflinger *et al.* suggest a wider sample is needed before generalising their findings beyond the characteristics in their sample. Esbjørn *et al.* (2013) only asked children aged nine years and over so could not generalise to children below that age. They could not know whether their questionnaire would suit the lower age range. Esbjørn *et al.* (2013) also did not use a clinical sample and thought that using participants with, for example, generalised anxiety disorder to look at their metacognitions, would have been useful. Perhaps they could not generalise from a non-clinical to a clinical sample. (A clinical sample refers to people with the disorder(s) of interest.)

- Limitations also focused on construct validity, which means questioning whether what was being asked represented what it was said it represented. Heflinger *et al.* (2014) questioned whether they were measuring attitudes to child mental health in a rural community, which is what their aim was. They asked parents of children with mental health issues, which perhaps was not enough as that would measure what parents think the attitudes of others are. Duckworth and Seligman (2005) felt they had measured self-discipline well, though they used more than a questionnaire because they gathered data by other means too. Perhaps using a questionnaire is helpful but using multiple methods and different sources can help to demonstrate validity.
- Duckworth and Seligman had no baseline measure for self-discipline to measure their findings against, which is a limitation. A difficulty of putting forward a new questionnaire to measure something new is that it is hard to show reliability and validity and there are often no previous data to help to strengthen the findings.

STUDY HINT

For strengths and weaknesses of questionnaires as a research method you can use what you learned about questionnaires in social psychology in Year One of your course. The 'Psychological skills – methods' section online summarises the method covered in your course and you can find an overview of strengths and weaknesses of questionnaires there. What is provided here is a focus on the use of questionnaires specifically in child psychology.

Progress check 4.35

Explain why the sampling in a study is so important for generalisability and why being able to generalise findings is important too.

Usefulness of questionnaires in child psychology

You can use what you know about the usefulness of questionnaires as a research method in psychology to consider how useful they are in child psychology. The examples given above which describe how researchers have used questionnaires illustrate their usefulness. For example, Heflinger *et al.* (2014) left packages for the possible participants at the clinic they were attending. The packages included information about the study. The usefulness of using this procedure is that individuals had the choice of whether to take part, which was ethical, and also for the researchers they could maintain a lower profile and not affect the data if the questionnaires were filled in without the researchers present.

Questionnaires are not necessarily a cheap and quick research method because they take a long time to produce and need to be explained to participants. Transcribing the data takes a long time and coding needs more than one person and is likely to be very time-consuming. However, getting the participant to complete a questionnaire has a simplicity that can be valuable in terms of not influencing the answers given and enabling them to choose whether to take part or not. Items in one questionnaire can focus on the same issue and reliability can be tested because if someone responds in the same way to similar questions that suggests the data are reliable.

However, validity might be more in doubt. Construct validity can be a problem as an item on a questionnaire might not measure what it claims to measure. Parents asked about attitudes to child mental health might have answered about their own attitudes, for example, or what they had experienced about the attitudes of others (Heflinger *et al.,* 2014).

Studies in child psychology using interviews

Staal *et al.* (2011)

Staal *et al.* (2011) were interested in finding a way of looking at parenting and developmental problems in young children and focused on a structured interview that child health care workers could use to assess problems in toddlers. The focus was to uncover the need for parental support. They used a structured interview called Structured Problem Analysis of Raising Kids (SPARK) and adapted and expanded it. The SPARK looks at 16 areas from physical health to family issues. Staal *et al.* (2011) used children aged 18 months and the study involved 1,140 families in the Netherlands. They found that the SPARK was useful and uncovered 4.5 per cent of toddlers and parents needing intensive help. They found 2.9 per cent were at high risk and 16.5 per cent were at increased risk of parenting and developmental problems. The researchers altered the SPARK to suit subject areas relevant to 18-month-old children and they included asking parents to assess the severity of any problem as well as the child health care worker. The child health care worker made an overall risk assessment. The structured interview had set items such as parents assessing seriousness of their concern using a 5-point Likert scale. Respondents were also asked to elaborate on any concerns. The child health care worker administered the interview and after all the areas were covered he or she discussed with the parents the amount and content of care needed. The interview took place in the home and there was an observational element in that the child health care worker observed interaction between the parent and child and also observed living environment and development and growth of the child.

Limitations

It was found that completing the SPARK was quite time-consuming, taking about 37 minutes, and in a clinic this time would not be available, so that is a drawback to the SPARK being used for all toddlers to check development issues. The SPARK did not uncover child maltreatment (though it was intended for general use rather than specifically maltreatment). Using the child health care workers gave some validity as they were experts in the area of study, but otherwise validity was not checked.

Venta et al. (2014)

Venta et al. (2014) were interested in how attachment quality might affect well-being of adolescents and were interested in how to capture relevant data. They used the Child Attachment Interview (CAI) as a way of uncovering links between attachment relationships and adolescents with problems related to adolescence. Their focus was to see the relevance of using the CAI. Venta et al. (2014) looked at adolescents with psychiatric disorder in the USA to look at the inter-rater reliability of the CAI and at the subscales in the CAI when adolescents were the participants. Venta et al. used 194 young people aged 12 to 17 from an in-patient unit for adolescents with psychiatric disorders. Of these, 39 per cent had major depressive disorder, 25 per cent had OCD and 22 per cent had Oppositional Defiance Disorder (ODD).

The CAI works by assessing the adolescent's way of mentally representing their attachment relationships. There are 17 questions and focus is on times of conflict, hurt and distress, because that is when the young person might call on their attachment figure as a secure base. The children tell their stories and are prompted by the interviewer to make sure they talk about their emotions. The interview is videotaped and transcribed and the coding is done by a trained person.

The parents gave consent and then the young people gave assent in person and the study was approved by the institutional review board. The interview was done in a naturalistic setting in that the participants were in-patients in a psychiatric unit. The researchers found 30.4 per cent secure attachments, 38.1 per cent dismissing, 14.4 per cent preoccupied and 17 per cent disorganised. There was some validity because this split in attachment types was similar to the validation study relating to this interview schedule. Venta et al. (2014) felt that the CAI was a useful tool for studying adolescents and attachment relationships.

Explore

Venta et al. (2014) is available online if you would like to read more. Here is the link:

www.uh.edu/class/psychology/clinical-psych/research/dpl/publications/_files/venta-schmuli-goetz-sharp-2014.pdf

STUDY HINT

Both Venta et al. (2014) and Staal et al. (2011) used interviews with a main purpose of developing ways of collecting data that suited the purpose of interest. In both cases the suggestion is that there was not a suitable data collection tool and so one needed to be developed. It is interesting that ways of collecting data are the focus of a study as much as what is found out and this emphasises the importance of data collection tools being reliable and valid – and available. When reading about studies try to compare them in some way and think about them together, as is done here when considering how both studies focus on developing a useful data collection tool, as that will help your evaluation skills.

Leyfer et al. (2006)

Leyfer et al. (2006) looked at using interviewing when looking at children with autism. The focus was to look for other psychiatric disorders that might go along with autism (co-morbidity). The focus of the study was on the interview itself and how to do the interviewing. For example, interviewers had information about the various psychiatric disorders to be looked at and had to relay some information to the interviewee at certain stages before continuing with the interviewing.

Leyfer et al. (2006) modified the Kiddie Schedules for Affective Disorders and Schizophrenia (KSADS) and called their new interview schedule the Autism co-morbidity Interview-Present and Lifetime version (ACI-PL). The study involved piloting the new interview, using two different samples. One sample was from a longitudinal study looking at language and social functioning and the other study used participants taking part in a scanning study for males with autism.

The families volunteered to take part in the study and there were 109 children in the study with ages from five to seventeen years – their parents gave the data. The children all had a diagnosis of autism. The interview had one section each for each disorder and the researchers listed quite a few disorders because they were looking for co-morbidity in those with autism. Each section started with an introduction about the disorder and then some screening questions to ask about features that characterised the disorder in the child with autism.

Leyfer et al. (2006) gave the example of depression, which is generally characterised by low mood and loss of interest, whereas in those with autism the symptoms seem to be temper outbursts and more agitation. The interviewer gave information about the likely symptoms that someone with autism might show for each disorder before asking the questions in the schedule, which meant the interview was interviewer led. The interview had probes too, that were laid down, to get more information. There was a clear structure to the interview, which was called a semi-structured interview as there was room for the interviewer to adjust the interview according to symptoms shown.

The study found that 72 per cent of the children had at least one psychiatric disorder alongside the autism, though the sample included relatively high-functioning children, which might affect generalisability. Many of the children in the study met the criteria for more than one psychiatric disorder as well as autism. The researchers felt that the Autism co-morbidity Interview had successfully identified co-morbidity, which should help researchers to study links between autism and other disorders, since they appear so often together.

Limitations

The researchers did not find reliability and validity in the Autism co-morbidity Interview for all diagnoses and they found the results only in high-functioning individuals. They pointed out that the information came from a parent, not from the child or a teacher. Information from many sources helps validity and reliability. The sample consisted of just males too, all able to use language, and all high-functioning, which affects generalisability.

> ### Explore
> You can look at the article by Leyfer *et al.* (2006) online if you want to know more. Here is the link:
> www.bu.edu/autism/files/2010/03/2006-Leyfer-et-al-co-morbid-disorders1.pdf

Table 4.22 Studies using interviewing

Study	Summary
Staal *et al.* (2011)	Looked at parenting and developmental problems for a child to see when support was needed in a specific situation. They modified the Structured Problem Analysis of Raising Kids (SPARK).
Venta *et al.* (2014)	Looked at adolescents and their well-being to uncover any effect(s) from their attachment experiences. They used the Child Attachment Interview (CAI).
Leyfer *et al.* (2006)	Looked at children with autism focusing on other psychiatric disorders they had as well (co-morbidity). They modified the Kiddie Schedules for Affective Disorders and Schizophrenia (KSADS).

Progress check 4.36

Practise learning the data collection tools used (even though often modified) in the studies used in this section about interviews by completing the table below.

Name of study	Data collection tool used/ modified	Initials of the data collection tool
Staal *et al.* (2011)		
Venta *et al.* (2014)		
Leyfer *et al.* (2006)		

Evaluation of using interviews in child psychology

Strengths

- Validity: There can be validity because interviews tend to be face to face and are often carried out by a professional in the field, who is able to check the questions and data for validity. For example, Staal *et al.* (2011) said their interview schedule was not fully checked for validity, but the child health care workers agreed the schedule, which helped with its validity. Venta *et al.* (2014) thought there was some validity in their study because the split in attachment types that the CAI uncovered was similar to the validation study of the CAI. Also Venta *et al.* (2014) used the adolescents' natural setting, although as this was a residential psychiatric unit, it does seem strange to call this their natural setting.
- Replicability: Interview schedules are used by researchers – they do not always develop their own. For example, Venta *et al.* (2014) used the CAI and was able to compare the attachment types found with those found in the validation study for the CAI. Often interview schedules are adapted rather than used completely in the same way, as you have seen in the studies used here. Clearly interview schedules are replicable, which helps to build a body of knowledge, although adapting them to suit individual purposes does question their replicability to an extent.

Weaknesses

In studies in psychology the researchers give limitations in the discussion part of their report. It is useful to use such limitations to discuss weaknesses of using interviews in child psychology.

- Practical issues with the use of the interview schedule: For example, Staal *et al.* (2011) found completing the SPARK to assess young children with regard to developmental and parenting needs took a long time and would not fit into the standard time allocated for child health care workers. As clinic time would not be enough to use the interview schedule, this meant in practical terms its use was limited. They found that the SPARK did not uncover maltreatment and, although it was not intended to, the importance of finding out about maltreatment is clear.

- Limited sample: Often with interviewing a limited sample is used and the sample can be a special one. For example, Leyfer *et al.* (2006) used parents of children with autism but the children were all high-functioning, used language and were male, so generalising to all children with autism would not be possible. In Leyfer *et al.* (2006) parents were interviewed but the child was not, which Leyfer *et al.* (2006) saw as a limitation. There might be more validity about co-morbidity in children with autism if the children gave the data. The researchers did use two samples, however, so there was some opportunity to check reliability and validity.

> **STUDY HINT**
> When evaluating the use of interviews in child psychology you can bring in what you learned about evaluation of interviews as a research method in social psychology. General evaluation issues are useful, such as how a structured interview can give less validity than an unstructured one but might offer more reliability. Try to match the points to studies in child psychology that use interviewing, for example, Staal *et al.* (2011) used a structured interview.

Progress check 4.37

Explain one way in which interviews are a valid research method in child psychology and one way they are perhaps not.

Usefulness of using interviews in child psychology

As you have seen, interviews gather qualitative in-depth and detailed data about a specific situation and are useful in child psychology in practice. Structured interviews tend to be easier to repeat and so can show reliability, while semi-structured or unstructured interviews can be more valid because the interviewer can explore the interviewee's responses, which does not limit the data so much.

All three studies used in this section that relate interviewing to child psychology are intended to help the children/young people they focus on. Staal *et al.* (2011) try to see what they can identify as problems in development in a family dealing with child development issues, for example. The idea is to help with such problems and to put support in place to prevent problems from developing or to improve the situation. Having a tool to uncover issues that

might lead to future problems would be beneficial. Venta *et al.* (2014) want to see what attachment issues might underpin adolescents with problems and such information can be useful in predicting problems and perhaps in suggesting how to improve things for young people. Leyfer *et al.* (2006) were interested in finding a way to identify psychiatric disorders that can accompany autism. Information in this area is useful to enable treatment planning and to add to the body of knowledge about psychiatric disorders that can accompany autism.

You can see that very young children with developmental issues are the focus of one study, adolescents with difficulties are the focus of the second study, and children with autism are the focus of the third study. In all cases the underlying aim is to uncover knowledge using the interview so that it can be used to help support the child or young person and those in the future, as well as to hopefully prevent problems occurring.

Test yourself

To what extent are interviews as a research method in child psychology reliable? **(2 marks)**

> **STUDY HINT**
> 'Test yourself' questions tend to be broad ones so you can bring in a lot of your understanding. They tend to use 'evaluate', 'assess', or 'to what extent' because these command words (injunctions) require some knowledge and understanding (AO1) and some evaluation, comment, analysis and assessment, including ending with a conclusion and making a judgement (AO3). Be sure to show knowledge and understanding of the required area and also make comments throughout.

Ethics of using observation, interview and questionnaire in child psychology

Observation, interview and questionnaire, and indeed other research methods used in child psychology, have largely the same ethical issues, but there are some differences. We begin by looking at how observations are evaluated in ethical terms because there can be differences compared with interviews and questionnaires.

Ethics of using observation as a research method in child psychology

An important point about naturalistic observations used in research is that, if the behaviour being observed takes place in a public place, where someone would expect to be observed, then it is not unethical to make such observations. This is as long as other relevant ethical guidelines are adhered to, such as confidentiality. Only if the observation takes place where someone would not expect to be observed do ethical questions start to arise.

Year One link: In social psychology you studied the British Psychological Society (BPS) Code of Ethics and Conduct (2009) as well as issues of risk management. When discussing studies or research methods be ready to talk about ethics. As observation relates to human behaviour, just the ethics of using humans in research are discussed here. You covered ethical issues regarding animals when you studied learning theories, so you can review that area too.

Ethical issues in psychology include:
- informed consent
- deceit
- debriefing
- the right to withdraw
- competence
- privacy
- confidentiality.

Observations can involve deceit if they are covert but not if they are overt. With covert observations, debriefing can help – for example, after a full debrief the participants can be given the right to withdraw their data, which helps make a study ethical. In some covert observations, however, there is no right to withdraw from the study, as the participant could not know about the study. This raises questions about the ethics of such observations.

You will look at the United Nations Convention of the Rights of the Child (1989), which holds that children (up to aged 18 years) must be given the right to participate and must also be protected. Children should be asked when a study of them is to take place and they must give their informed consent as well as having the right to withdraw and the right to privacy, just as adults have those rights. More about the ethics of researching with children is discussed later in the method section of this chapter.

Structured observations may not involve fully informed consent because, if participants knew about them, they might perform differently. So in a structured observation there is likely to be deceit, lack of informed consent and no right to withdraw. Again, a full debrief is needed. All these issues require competence on the part of the researcher, as there is likely to be some breach of ethical guidelines in all cases. Structured observations are likely to be known

about in general by the participants, such as if parents and child are in a setting being observed with the purpose of there being a clinical intervention. However, some might not be known about, such as if using a structured task in a playgroup setting, like the Heads-Toes-Knees-Shoulders task (Ponitz et al., 2009).

It is likely that there are ethical issues involved in both naturalistic and structured observations. Johnson et al. (2009) discussed ethics in their study and explained that the study was approved by the various university review boards involved. The Institutional Review Boards dictated the informed consent processes that were required, which involved someone explaining the study in person to the participants and an informed consent document being signed. All families received a copy of the informed consent document. Ponitz et al. (2009) simply mention that parents of all children as well as the teachers provided written informed consent before they took part in the study. It was noticeable that the studies do not mention obtaining the consent of the children and also do not go into detail about ethics beyond a consideration of consent. However, that does not mean that ethical issues such as right to withdraw were not considered.

Progress check 4.38

In research what are two ethical issues that can be difficult to adhere to when using an observation research method?

STUDY HINT

This section on observations assumes you have already studied both naturalistic and structured observations, so does not go into great detail about what is involved in each.

Ethics of using interview or questionnaire as a research method in child psychology

Interviews and questionnaires must follow the same ethical guidance as all research methods in psychology, including child psychology. The main difference is about the vulnerability of children and young people so there is even more emphasis on ethical issues. The idea of 'do no harm' must be in the forefront of a researcher's mind at all times and perhaps especially when researching with children and young people.

Again, the UNCRC (1989) is referred to in this section and must be considered in relation to using interview and questionnaire when researching in the area of child psychology.

The power relationship

An issue with researching with children and young people is the power relationship. Children (and parents) are likely to see the researcher(s) as having the power in a research or clinical situation. It is important to acknowledge possible issues with power relationships, such as being sure that the child understands what the study is about and that they can withdraw at any time. The child needs to know, for example, that if they withdraw from research there will be no adverse consequences. The information must be in a language level that the child can understand, such as using visual aids. A parent is also in a power position and it is the child who must give the consent, though there are issues around parental consent too. These guidelines focus on children aged 16 years and under.

Research with children and comparisons to research with adults

Punch (2002), well-known for ethnographic work with children in Bolivia, wrote an article about researching with children and compared it to researching with adults. Her ideas are not just about ethics, though they involve ethical issues. She discusses how working with children differs from working with adults. She suggests that the way children are viewed affects how they are listened to and mentions the power imbalance between researchers (adults) and children. Her ideas link to what was said above about the ethics of working with children, including power issues, as adults tend to have the power. In addition, adults see children as different, which affects how they are researched. Punch says that research with children is different because of:

- the need not to impose the researcher's own perceptions
- the need to be aware of the way child participants might lie or exaggerate to please the researcher
- the focus on clarity of language to make sure there is understanding
- the way research takes place usually in an adult-controlled setting and situation
- issues with adults building rapport with children
- issues in analysis where adults might misinterpret the data from children
- the need to tailor research methods to those preferred by the child so that sources and techniques are familiar.

Explore
You can read Punch's (2002) article on researching with children and how it is different from researching with adults using this link:
www.dreamscanbe.org/Reasearch%20Page%20Docs/Punch%20-%20research%20with%20children.pdf

Ethical issues in a clinical setting

There are different ethical guidelines for practitioners. In your Year One course you looked at the BPS Code of Ethics and Conduct (2009). For practitioners guidelines related to contracting, consent, confidentiality, keeping records, supervision and working with other professionals apply in addition to the guidelines for researchers. The British Psychological Society (BPS) has a number of documents relating to ethical guidelines for practitioners and the titles of some of these indicate both the range of issues dealt with and the importance attached to practising in an ethical way.

Some guidelines for practitioners published by the BPS:
- Challenging behaviour: a unified approach (2007)
- Childhood ASD (autistic spectrum disorder) (2006)
- Child protection portfolio (2007)
- Generic professional practice guidelines (2008)
- Learning disability: definitions and contexts (2000)
- Psychologists as expert witnesses (2010)

Explore
You can look at the BPS documents listed above using the internet. For example guidance for chartered psychologists working with children and young people with autistic spectrum disorders can be found at:
www.bps.org.uk/sites/default/files/documents/autistic_spectrum_disorder-guidance_for_chartered_psychologists_working_with_children_and_young_people.pdf

In a clinical setting, if ethical guidelines relating to that setting are not adhered to then a psychologist faces criticism from the BPS and his or her peers. Chartered psychologists must, as part of their continuing professional development, keep a log and ethics is part of that log. Psychologists usually work for institutions such as the NHS or the prison service and those institutions will also demand a high level of ethical conduct. Members of the public can complain to the BPS if they feel they have not been treated in an ethical manner by a psychologist, and complaints are followed up.

Special ethical issues that apply when studying children

An important point about studying children is that the tendency is to ask parents or guardians for consent on the child's behalf and to explain to adults what will happen. Children's rights are an issue of interest, however, and researchers are now encouraged to ask children for permission and to explain to a child what a study will entail, as well as offering the right to withdraw. It is increasingly expected that the child is treated as the participant, and in some cases as the researcher, to give them their participation and protection rights. There is a need to pay special attention to ethics where children are too young to give consent, such as in the strange situation (page 377).

The BPS Code of Human Research Ethics (2010) has a section on special safeguards for vulnerable populations, including children (and young people) up to the age of 16, though the UNCRC goes up to 18 years old. Children must be given 'ample opportunity' (p. 31) to understand what the research is about, what will happen and any likely outcomes. Children should give informed consent 'to the extent their capabilities allow'. The BPS document agrees that if children are too young to give consent then someone must do that on their behalf, paying attention to any preferences the child expresses.

Explore

You can access the BPS Code of Human Research Ethics (2010) at:
www.bps.org.uk/sites/default/files/documents/code_of_human_research_ethics.pdf

Progress check 4.39

Why are issues of informed consent and right to withdraw particularly important when researching with children?

Summary of evaluation of observation, questionnaire and interview in child psychology with regard to ethics

- Observations of people in a public place are considered ethical.
- Covert observations do not have informed consent or the right to withdraw and they involve deceit – a debrief must put these issues right.
- Overt observations involve informed consent, the right to withdraw and no deceit – a debrief is still needed.
- Questionnaires and interviews must pay attention to issues of privacy, confidentiality, informed consent, right to withdraw, deceit and researcher competence, just as all research methods do.
- The United Nations Convention of the Rights of the Child (UNCRC) (1989) has led to focus on a child having the right to participate in research and having the right to be protected (with other rights), and more about ethics of researching with children and young

people is considered when the UNCRC is discussed later in this chapter (page 448).
- In a clinical setting there are very clear BPS guidelines and sanctions if these guidelines are not adhered to.
- There is an issue with regard to children's rights and children's participation.
- There are special guidelines for vulnerable people, including children up to 16 years old (BPS Code of Human Research Ethics, 2010). An important issue is to make sure that consent from the children is obtained and is informed, which means they must have understood the research and the implications. Also right to withdraw must have no negative consequences and the child must understand that.

STUDY HINT

When answering a question about method in a specific topic area, including about ethics, be sure to give examples that focus on research in that area, not on use of the method in general.

Test yourself

A semi-structured interview was carried out with parents of children with autism to ask about other psychiatric disorders they may show symptoms of. The interviewer outlined the symptoms of a disorder and then asked the parent some questions about the symptoms and whether the child displayed any of the symptoms. Disorders focused on were OCD, generalised anxiety disorder and major depression. The children were all aged seven, male and high functioning.

(Adapted from Leyfer et al., 2006).

Discuss ethical issues when carrying out this study. You must make reference to the context in your answer. **(8 marks)**

STUDY HINT

When the command word is 'discuss' and you have 8 marks and a source to relate your answer to, there will be 4 marks for knowledge and understanding and 4 marks for applying what you know (such as about ethics) to the source.

Cross-cultural, longitudinal and cross-sectional designs and meta-analysis

In clinical psychology you cover four specific ways of doing research: cross-cultural, longitudinal and cross-sectional designs and meta-analysis. These four issues are covered here by giving one example for each from child psychology.

You can draw on your understanding of the issues from your study of clinical psychology (Chapter Two) and the review of methods in your course (online). Longitudinal, cross-sectional and meta-analysis are in your course within the topic of cross-cultural design, but they are used in child psychology outside a cross-cultural focus too, so they are explained separately in this section.

Cross-cultural research focusing on attachment types as well as nature–nurture issues involved and issues of universality were examined in the content part of this chapter when you looked at attachment, deprivation and privation. You can use what is given here about cross-cultural research, nature–nurture issues, universality and meta-analysis to understand about issues relating to attachment types and vice versa.

Cross-cultural approach

Research methods that use a cross-cultural approach include studies using the strange situation procedure developed by Ainsworth, and ethnography.

Using the strange situation procedure

Mary Ainsworth's work, which is explained in the content section of this chapter (page 377), takes a cross-cultural approach to understanding child psychology. Her research procedure, known as the strange situation procedure, is used in different cultures to draw conclusions about varying cultural practices and she used different cultures herself when drawing up her attachment styles. Other researchers have used her method as well, and have continued to compare different cultures.

Cross-cultural approaches refer to when something is carried out in different cultures and then comparisons are drawn. Van IJzendoorn and Kroonenberg (1988) is the classic study in child psychology in your course and is a meta-analysis looking at studies that used the strange situation to find out about attachment styles. Cassibba *et al.* (2013), one of the contemporary studies in child psychology in your course, also uses the strange situation procedure. As the strange situation procedure is explained elsewhere in this chapter it is not covered in detail here.

Ethnography

Although your course requires you to study a set procedure for comparing different cultures (the 'strange situation'), some cross-cultural studies are ethnographic. Ethnography links with anthropology and means using different research methods, with researchers immersing themselves in a different culture or sub culture, to learn about it thoroughly. Comparisons can be made between such in-depth studies to look at similarities and differences between cultures. Using ethnography does not lead to ease of comparison, however, because the data are in-depth and detailed about one culture and likely to be sufficiently different from results of ethnographic work in another culture not to be easily compared. 'Culture' can refer to a sub culture and a narrow field of research, such as Corsaro's (1985 and 1994) ethnographic work looking at friendship patterns in young children.

Explore

Research some ethnographic studies and read about practices in different cultures. If possible, find out about child care practices so that you have an example of how cross-cultural studies are used. One example is the Mundurucú culture from South America and a study carried out by Yolanda and Robert Murphy. They wrote a book called *Women of the Forest* (1974) and you can read some reviews of their book to give you an idea of what their study was about and what they found.

Explore

LeVine (2007) has written an article exploring ethnographic studies of childhood. You can access the article using this link to find out more about the ethnographic research method and findings of studies:
http://ashforddocs.com/140429-PSY104/W-02/gaskins.pdf

You can look more at research in child psychology using ethnography; however, it does come close to being research in sociology and anthropology, rather than focusing on psychology, so no more is explained here. It is interesting, however, to note that there is a large body of research using ethnographic methods looking at children and childhood.

Explore

Tisdall and Punch (2012) have published an article about children's relationships in different cultures. It has a strong sociological basis; however, it is interesting as it refers to the UNCRC and also takes a cross-cultural approach:
www.research.ed.ac.uk/portal/files/5457511/Tisdall_and_Punch_2012_Not_so_new_children_S_Geographies_10_3_.pdf

Studies using the cross-cultural design

Three cross-cultural studies are provided in the content and studies sections of this chapter, so no additional studies are provided here.

- Ainsworth and Bell (1970) – Ainsworth's work is discussed in the content section of this chapter, including her studies using the strange situation procedure to compare cultures to devise a list of attachment styles/types.

- Van IJzendoorn and Kroonenberg (1988) is the classic study for child psychology in your course and is detailed later in this chapter (page 452)
- Cassibba *et al.* (2013) is one of the contemporary studies for child psychology in your course and is detailed later in this chapter (page 456).

Nature–nurture issues in cross-cultural studies

There is a nature–nurture issue when drawing conclusions from cross-cultural studies. If the same procedures are used in different cultures and the same results are found, then this suggests that what is found is due to nature, is biological, is a universal law and shows **universality**. If different results are found, then it seems that what is found is because of nurture and comes from different cultural practices.

Definition

Universality refers to some behaviour or characteristic that is found in all cultures where it has been studied and so is thought to be due to nature and so is universal in human behaviour. For example, it could be claimed that children who do not form attachments at a young age find it hard to form adult relationships. If this is the case no matter what the culture, then it might be concluded that strong attachments at a young age are the building blocks of firm adult relationships, and that this is a universal law of behaviour. Bowlby considered issues like this, and his work is explained in the Content section in this chapter.

Issues and debates

Nature–nurture is one of the issues and debates in your course and is discussed in Chapter Seven. You can use cross-cultural research and ideas when discussing the nature–nurture debate as they are one way of studying the issue.

Emic–etic distinction

A problem with using the same procedure(s) in different cultures is that when drawing conclusions between the two cultures based on the data collection tool(s) used it is hard to be sure that what is being compared is the same. Aiming to develop a theory between cultures, as is done in attachment research relating to attachment styles, is **etic analysis**. **Emic analysis** focuses on the culture itself to find out more about it as a distinctive culture with its own meaning. The strange situation procedure is etic analysis when it is used to look at similarities and differences between cultures. Ethnographic research is more likely to be emic analysis as the aim is to uncover information about a specific culture.

Research in a culture that is different from that of the researchers might mean immersion in the culture if conclusions are going to have validity and meaning.

Definitions

Emic analysis is when research focuses on specifics in one culture intending to use the meanings of that culture.

Etic analysis is aiming to use the same procedure(s) across different cultures in order to develop a theory.

STUDY HINT

It is helpful to use the correct terms when describing psychology research, so try to learn all the terms provided in the Glossary, such as 'emic analysis' and 'etic analysis'.
It is worth developing ways to help you to learn such terms.
If you can remember 'T' for 'theory', then you might be able to remember 'etic' as 'theory interlacing cultures' and 'emic' can be remembered as 'mainly in a culture'.

Progress check 4.40

Complete the table to define 'emic', 'etic' and 'ethnography'.

Term	Definition
Emic	
Etic	
Ethnography	

Evaluating cross-cultural procedures

Strengths

- In cross-cultural studies where the procedures are kept the same, any differences in behaviour should be because of the cultural differences (nurture) and any similarities in behaviour should be because of natural similarities (nature).

- There is likely to be reliability as well, because the procedures are carefully documented so that they can be repeated in the different cultures.
- For ethnographic cross-cultural studies, the strengths are the same as for case studies.
- A main strength is validity because the whole process of what is being studied is covered and data should be about 'real life' and there is no reductionism, because the whole situation is covered. A strength of using a structured observation procedure like the strange situation is that there would be replicability because of the clear and strong structure.

Weaknesses

- There are problems when using the same procedures in different cultures, because the way a procedure is understood is part of the findings and it might differ between cultures.
- If the understanding of what is required in the study causes differences in findings, then this means that such differences are because of the study rather than because of either nature or nurture, and the validity of the findings is questioned.
- If standard procedures are set up, such as the strange situation procedure, to compare behaviour in different cultures, then they are not likely to be valid because, by being standardised and by behaviour being made measurable, it is likely that such behaviour is not then 'real life'.
- Ethnographic cross-cultural studies have the same weaknesses as case studies, in that they are hard to generalise from and difficult to repeat.
- Another weakness in making cross-cultural comparisons is that there are differences that are likely to affect the data and they are hard to control for. For example, what is being measured is likely to differ between cultures so making a comparison is difficult.
- Participants will be different in different cultures. For example, some might want to please the researcher, which would bias the data, while some might want to hamper the research, also biasing the findings.

> **STUDY HINT**
> You looked at the case study as a research method when you looked at clinical psychology, so you should be familiar with the strengths of focusing in depth and using detail to gather qualitative data. A main strength of the case study is its validity and a main weakness is its generalisability. Ethnographic cross-cultural studies have the same strengths and weaknesses as case studies.

Test yourself

Explain why cross-cultural research is carried out in child psychology. **(6 marks)**

Longitudinal design as a method in child psychology

A study that looks at participants over a length of time, documenting changes over that period, is known as a longitudinal study. As with cross-cultural studies, longitudinal studies can involve using the same procedures but over time to measure changes, or they can involve a more ethnographic or case study approach to gather data.

> **STUDY HINT**
> You looked at longitudinal design in Chapter Two, so you can refer to the material there for more information. Methods are reviewed in 'Psychological skills — methods' online, which provides another source of information about longitudinal studies.

There are quite a few well-known longitudinal studies of children, in which children born at a certain time were thoroughly researched over a long period to document changes. These include Growing up in Australia; a study in Bristol called the Avon Longitudinal Study of Children and Parents; and the Early Childhood Longitudinal Program in the USA. These are often government-funded programmes, and many studies then draw their data from these large programmes. The Longitudinal Studies Centre at Essex University was established in 1999. The Effective Provision of Pre-school Education (EPPE) project in the UK and the National Institute of Child Health and Human Development (NICHD) study in the USA are both longitudinal studies looking at day care, and these are described in the content section of this chapter.

> **Explore**
> You can investigate the work of the Longitudinal Studies Centre at Essex University using this link:
> **www.understandingsociety.ac.uk/**

Studies using a longitudinal approach

Nakahara et al. (2010)

Nakahara et al. (2010) used a longitudinal observation to look at children on a waiting list for day care outside the home and to see if their needs were judged by actual care needs and being from a disadvantaged family. The study was done in Nepal.

They found that high caste, low household weekly income and father being absent from home were issues that associated with the child being admitted into day care early. However, the mother working and the lack of available child care support were not related to early admission. The researchers felt that caste/ethnicity accounted for the prioritisation, whereas the most need and the most deprivation should be the main priorities. Possibly places should be reserved for low-caste groups.

Seventeen day care centres were used (though in the end two were excluded) and data were collected from 2003 to 2006. Fifteen day care centres were recruited into the study and written informed consent was obtained. A lot of data were obtained about the family, using questionnaires. The researchers measured the time a child waited from the waiting list to the day care place, though the time itself was not the measure – it was the order of admission that was recorded. The actual time would depend on when children left the day school, so if a place became available, the order of admission was used. Early admission was characterised as the shortest to the median length of time. After some drop out and some not admitted into a day care centre, with one excluded because of insufficient data, 161 children remained for analysis.

The study was longitudinal in the sense that the researchers collected a lot of data early on and then gathered data again about the actual admission order for the child. This meant they could see which factors predicted early admission. The researchers mentioned that similar studies used cross-sectional design and looked at characteristics of children on the waiting list or getting a place to estimate priority for admission, rather than being able to see when children got a place to see actual prioritisation, so a longitudinal approach was better. They found that the privileged caste/ethnic group were prioritised and disadvantaged groups suffered discrimination. Priority was given to low income families where the father was absent; however, there were other issues to be taken into account, such as children who were malnourished and those needing child care support.

Evaluation

Nakahara et al. (2010) used all of the public day care centres in the city of Pokhara but they did not use private day care facilities, which might affect the generalisability of their findings. Also the participants were only from Pokhara city and not from the whole country, again affecting generalisability. However, Nakahara et al. (2010) felt that there were similar Hindu values across the country, which means probably marginalised groups had similar problems across the country.

Sosinsky et al. (2007)

Sosinsky et al. (2007) used the NICHD (National Institute of Child Health and Human Development) Study of Early Child Care and Youth Development data to look at differences in child care quality in centres. They used indicators of quality – caregiver wages and turnover, child/staff ratio, caregiver education and professionalism and positive caregiving – and compared these in different day care centres separating those that were for-profit and those that were not-for-profit. They compared the data from infancy to pre-school age. The NICHD had already collected the data longitudinally and Sosinsky et al. (2007) used secondary data because they used the data that had already been collected. The NICHD Study on Early Child Care and Youth Development collected data from more than 1,300 children and their families (at the start) and gathered data from when the children were infants to when they were 15 years old, collecting the data in four phases. This makes the study longitudinal.

> **STUDY HINT**
> It is useful to make notes when you see an example of a method issue you need to know about. Many of the studies in this child psychology method section collected their own data (primary data) but Sosinsky et al. (2007) used secondary data so you can use their study as an example of such use.

The findings of Sosinsky et al. (2007) were that non-profit-making centres had higher caregiver wages and education at most ages, with better staff–child ratios, better turnover of staff (they stayed longer), better caregiver professionalism and better positive caregiving. There were differences in type of day care, such as quality being higher in non-profit centres with no religious affiliation, medium quality when non-profit centres had religious affiliation and lower quality in for-profit chains.

Evaluation

The sample did not represent the whole of the USA and could not be said to represent all the different sectors that were considered. The researchers also point out that the NICHD study did not gather data using the experimental method, so there could be no cause-and-effect conclusions drawn about the differences in the quality of care between the sectors. They also point out that the data were gathered in the early 1990s and there have been changes in day care provision since that time.

Siraj-Blatchford *et al.* (2008)

Siraj-Blatchford *et al.* (2008) discuss the Effective Provision of Pre-school Education (EPPE) research programme and how it continues to inform improvements for young children in day care. The research programme relates to the Foundation Stage for young children and this study follows on from the EPPE programme beginnings. Siraj-Blatchford *et al.* (2008) draw on the findings from the EPPE programme, including case studies gathering qualitative data as evidence, and they say that practitioners respond well to training when it includes teaching and learning in practice, which is what the case studies focused on.

The aim of the case studies was to identify 'good' and 'excellent' centres by identifying variables that explained children's progress and development in pre-school environments. Twelve good and excellent centres were chosen and used as case studies to gather in-depth qualitative data. The qualitative data could add to the quantitative analysis using triangulation. The qualitative data and some of the quantitative data has been used to inform good practice to improve early years educational practice.

Siraj-Blatchford *et al.* (2008) argued that it was the case study evidence that was very effective in implementing early years educational policy with practitioners, because it provided a detailed account of teaching contexts and also examples of good and excellent practice.

The researchers cite the EPPE project aims and findings. The aims were to look at pre-schools and they found that pre-school education has a positive impact in reducing the effects of social disadvantage and giving children a better start. There was a great deal of data gathered as part of the EPPE project and it was seen as a longitudinal project. The researchers, who were Kathy Sylva, Edward Meluish, Pam Sammons, Iram Siraj-Blatchford and Brenda Taggart, called it the 'first major European longitudinal study of a national sample of young children's development between the ages of three and seven years' (p. 1). Children were assessed when they joined the study at three to four years old and they were assessed again when they started school, making the study longitudinal.

The longitudinal approach: validity, reliability and generalisability

Generalisability

Longitudinal studies follow individuals over time and often this means the sample is rather small or if not small, focused on particular issues. Some large-scale studies are undertaken, often involving government funding, but if the study is in a normal research budget it is likely that the sample and focus is narrow.

Validity

Longitudinal studies have validity in that the same individuals are tested over time and so it is likely that data are 'real life' data, especially as they tend to be in a specific context or culture. For example, Nakahara *et al.* (2010) used only Pokhara city in Nepal and only public day care provision. However, a measure can be repeated over time and still not measure what it claims to measure so validity can be in doubt. It is not so much the longitudinal nature of a study that makes it valid but how the data are gathered.

Reliability

As longitudinal studies tend to mean a measure is repeated over time it could be said that results have reliability. However, things change over time and results are likely to be affected by that, so the repeat of a measure is not the same as it was the time before. Reliability might be hard to test. It is not so much the longitudinal nature of a study that makes it reliable but the measures that are undertaken to gather the data.

STUDY HINT
Make notes about the reliability, validity or generalisability of a research method. It is not the particular designs — longitudinal, cross-sectional and cross-cultural — that are not in themselves valid or reliable, it is the data collection tools that must be examined to look for reliability and validity.

Longitudinal, cross-sectional and cross-cultural designs are not really research methods as such nor are they data collection tools. The three designs are ways of carrying out a study but they do not directly collect data. List a) three research methods and b) three data collection tools to help you to differentiate.

Table 4.23 Three studies using a longitudinal design

Study	Longitudinal element in the study
Nakahara *et al.* (2010) in Nepal	Gathered a lot of data from children going onto waiting lists for a day care place and then measured how long it was before the child got a place. This was to see whether children in need (and what the need was) were prioritised.
Sosinsky *et al.* (2007) in the USA	Used the NICHD (National Institute of Child Health and Human Development) Study of Early Child Care and Youth Development data to look at differences in child care quality in different types of centre. The Study of Early Child Care and Youth Development had four phases and followed children from infancy to aged 15.
Siraj-Blatchford *et al.* (2008) in the UK	Used the EPPE findings. The EPPE programme followed three to four year olds from when they joined the programme to when they were seven. The aim was to look at what made good day care. This study verified that the 12 case studies used in the EPPE project were still being used in training and useful because they showed good and excellent practice.

Progress check 4.42

Explain problems with generalising results when using longitudinal research, referring to one of the three studies used here.

Evaluation of longitudinal ways of studying children

Strengths

- Longitudinal studies compare the same people over a period of time, which means controlling participant variables such as gender, temperament and IQ.
- They are a good way of studying development because, if the procedures are controlled, only the age changes, so cause-and-effect conclusions can more easily be drawn than if different people are used.
- They are useful for looking at the development of some behaviour or characteristic because they can track development over time.

Weaknesses

- Even though the same people are used in the study, there will be many factors affecting the individuals' development, making it hard to draw conclusions about one feature that might cause any changes.
- There is often quite a high drop-out rate as people move away or no longer wish to take part.
- Those who do not drop out may have something in common that makes them a biased sample, such as having the same sort of family or being more confident about taking part.
- Longitudinal research takes a long time and can be expensive, partly because of the time it takes. There might be just a small group of participants, which makes generalising hard.

Progress check 4.43

What are the advantages of using a longitudinal design in a study?

Progress check 4.44

Decide whether the following studies are examples of a longitudinal study, a cross-cultural study, a structured observation, a naturalistic observation or an ethnographic study.

Example of a study	Research method
Children's behaviour in the playground was watched by two observers, tallying behaviour according to whether it was aggressive or not.	
A culture in Africa was studied by someone who lived with them for a year and made detailed notes from many different activities and sources.	
A task involving play materials was carried out in three different countries to see whether young children understood someone else's point of view, in order to discover if the findings were the same in each country.	
Ten children aged from six months to six years were studied by observing them and interviewing their parents periodically, to see how their language patterns developed.	

Cross-sectional design as a method in child psychology

The opposite of a longitudinal design is a cross-sectional one. Instead of following participants over time, different groups of participants are studied at one time, to look at development relating to some characteristic or behaviour. For a cross-sectional design the different groups must differ in the important characteristic but must be the same with regard to other characteristics so that comparisons can be made. For example, if you wanted to look at reasoning ability of three year olds compared with six year olds you would want gender to be matched, as well as early experiences and whether the children had attended day care and so on. If other variables are controlled for and one variable is different, any differences found can be said to be down to that one variable. However, cause and effect cannot be claimed, because such studies describe a situation rather than explain it. For example, it could be claimed that six year olds have better reasoning than three year olds from a cross-sectional study, but it might not be claimed that age is what caused the different reasoning ability.

A cross-sectional design means a study takes place at one moment in time and variables tend not to be manipulated, though they are measured. Different variables can be looked at using a cross-sectional design, such as the impact of age and gender on a behaviour or characteristic. Cross-sectional research tends to be observational in that the two groups are observed, data are gathered and then comparisons made. However, data could be gathered by questionnaire, for example, or interview, and still compared between the groups considering the variable of interest.

> ### Progress check 4.45
>
> What is the main difference between a longitudinal and cross-sectional design in research?

Studies using cross-sectional design in child psychology

Piškur *et al.* (2015)

Piškur *et al.* (2015) looked at issues parents had around helping their school-aged child with a physical disability participate in activities. The study also considered whether the issues related to the child's physical abilities, the parents' perception of their own health, the family socioeconomic status or the family type. Piškur *et al.* (2015) used 146 Dutch participants (84.9 per cent mothers) and used questionnaires to gather the data. The questionnaires were sent out by post with a stamped addressed envelope for a reply and also an information letter and informed consent form. They used the Family Needs Inventory – Paediatric Rehabilitation and the General Health Questionnaire and others. There was a response rate of

27 per cent. Parents' view of needs included focus on rules and fees, issues around leisure time and focus on aids and adaptations. All the needs correlated with parents' view of their own general health. There were also needs that showed a negative correlation to the family socioeconomic status, including 'emotional and mental support' and 'day care and school'.

The study aimed to describe the issues, which suits a cross-sectional design. A snapshot of parents' views about their needs regarding their child with a physical disability participating in activities was taken, which was surveying parents for their views at one moment in time – a cross-sectional design.

Limitations

Parents were selected from the database of the Dutch association of people with a physical disability (BOSK) and those not members of the BOSK would not have taken part. The sample may not represent all parents with a child with a physical disability in the Netherlands. A response rate of 27 per cent might affect how representative the sample was, as those with very high needs or very few needs might not have responded. As a cross-sectional study, cause-and-effect conclusions cannot be drawn. One of the questionnaires was designed for parents with children with cerebral palsy so it might not have suited parents of children with other physical disabilities.

Söderström *et al.* (2013)

Söderström *et al.* (2013) carried out a study to look at how the quality of the outdoor environment in a day care centre affected a child's health. The researchers assessed the environment using the Outdoor Play Environmental Categories (OPEC) tool and they also noted time spent outdoors as well as physical activity measured using a pedometer. They used nine day care centres in Sweden and covered children from three years old to around six years old.

They measured health by using body mass index, waist size, cortisol in saliva and how long the child slept through the night. Parents rated the well-being and health of their child too, using a questionnaire.

Söderström *et al.* (2013) found that a high-quality outdoor environment in a day care centre is associated with health aspects in children, such as them sleeping longer at night, having a leaner body, better well-being and higher saliva cortisol levels mid-morning. The study data were collected at one moment in time across the different day schools so it was not a longitudinal design. This makes it cross-sectional.

Strengths and limitations

The researchers felt they had not covered day school centres in very low socioeconomic areas where the outdoor environment might not be as good. The researchers said such day schools either did not wish to take part or there were language problems. They used participant observations and said that was very important as they were able to check time spent indoors and outdoors and could communicate with both children and staff to clarify issues they needed clarifying. They did not include air quality, which perhaps they should have as it could have an effect.

STUDY HINT

Note that Piškur *et al.* (2015) and Söderström *et al.* (2013) used questionnaires so you can use them as examples when discussing questionnaires as well as when discussing cross-sectional research. Söderström *et al.* (2013) also included participant observation so you can use their study as an example of that research method too.

Söderström *et al.* (2013) suggest that use of outdoor play areas in day care centres relate to a child's health.

Explore

If you would like to know more about the importance of outdoor space for children you could look at this link:
www.sciencedirect.com/science/article/pii/S1877042815000580

Kover *et al.* (2013)

Kover *et al.* (2013) looked at boys with autistic spectrum disorder and focused on their receptive language (words heard or read) and their expressive language (speaking words). The study used a cross-sectional design with age as a variable, as well as nonverbal understanding, receptive and expressive vocabulary as variables. They used 49 boys aged 4 to 11 years old, as well as 80 'typically developing' boys aged 2 to 11 years old.

The researchers used the Peabody Picture Vocabulary Test to assess receptive language and found it was a weakness for boys with autistic spectrum disorder (ASD) compared to the controls, relative to age and nonverbal understanding. They measured expressive language using

the Expressive Vocabulary Test and found expressive language increased more slowly in boys with ASD.

Kover *et al.* (2013) felt that nonverbal cognition accounted for the differences. The researchers explained that the cross-sectional developmental approach let them use age as a variable and let them measure both receptive and expressive language ability. They could also use a control group, measured across ages using the same tests, as a baseline measure for typical development.

Limitations

The researchers point out that they did not measure different types of vocabulary such as mental state or abstract words, which may have affected the findings. They also found that many of the typically developing boys had higher receptive than expressive vocabulary scores, which may have affected the comparisons with the ASD boys. Their sample of typically developing boys did not match the samples that standardised the two tests used.

Explore

If you would like to know more about the Peabody Picture Vocabulary Test you could use this link:
http://scsu568.wikispaces.com/file/view/PPVT-IV_training_10–08_258864_7.pdf
You can access the study by Kover *et al.* using this link:
www.ncbi.nlm.nih.gov/pmc/articles/PMC3797266/

Table 4.24 Three studies using a cross-sectional design

Study	Their use of cross-sectional design
Piškur *et al.* (2015)	Gathered data from parents of children with a physical disability to find out what the needs were when considering the child taking part more in activities. They gathered the data at one moment in time with a wide range of families and disabilities in order to describe what needs there were.
Söderström *et al.* (2013)	Used children aged from three years to six years old and measured their outdoor play against their health to find out if outdoor play in a day care centre related to a healthier child. They could compare the different ages and gathered data at one moment in time. The study aimed to describe outdoor play use and health issues.
Kover *et al.* (2013)	Used boys with autistic spectrum disorder and a control group of typically developing boys and both groups included a range of ages. They gathered data about receptive and expressive vocabulary and nonverbal cognition across all the ages in both groups and so could compare the development of language ability over time. They gathered the data at one moment in time. The study aimed to describe the vocabulary ability of children with autistic spectrum disorder.

Progress check 4.46

Kover et al. (2013) used two standardised tests, one to measure receptive vocabulary ability and one to measure expressive vocabulary ability. Explain what 'standardised' means in this context.

Evaluation of using a cross-sectional design in child psychology

Strengths

- A strength is that a study can be done gathering data at one moment in time, unlike a longitudinal design where data are gathered more than once over a period of time.
- A cross-sectional design is therefore quicker and more manageable than a longitudinal design.
- A cross-sectional design is good for describing variables and data can be used to generate hypotheses.
- Data only have to be collected once, which perhaps has ethical value and also is more convenient and cheaper than using a longitudinal design.

Weaknesses

- A limitation is that it is very hard to find people where all variables except those of interest are the same.
- A particular group can be affected by experiences of that particular group, such as growing up in a particular period of history (this is called a 'cohort effect'), whereas the other group had different experiences, so there are differences between the groups other than the variable of interest. The problem of cohort effects and differences between the two samples is a problem of validity.
- It is hard to be sure that what is being measured is what is claimed to be measured.
- Cause-and-effect conclusions cannot be drawn using a cross-sectional design as variables are not controlled – they are only measured at the moment in time.
- Not collecting data about a variable that turns out to be important can be a problem, whereas in longitudinal designs variables can be introduced through the study.

Test yourself

Explain why the longitudinal research method might be used in child psychology compared with cross-sectional research. **(6 marks)**

Meta-analysis as a technique in child psychology

The classic study in child psychology in your course is van IJzendoorn and Kroonenberg (1988). It is a meta-analysis which you can use as an example study and as a way of learning what a meta-analysis actually is. The contemporary study in child psychology in your course, Cassibba et al. (2013), is also a meta-analysis. Both studies focus on attachments and cross-cultural studies looking at attachments, so both illustrate the cross-cultural design in psychology as well as what a meta-analysis is. Both studies used the strange situation procedure (a structured observation), so they can help to illustrate that procedure as well. They are explained in detail in a later section of this chapter (pages 452 and 456).

Meta-analysis is explained below, but further examples are not given as you already have two that you can use, as described above. In Chapter Two you studied meta-analysis in the method section and it is reviewed in 'Psychological skills – methods' on the accompanying website.

Explanation of meta-analysis

Meta-analysis is a way of analysing data rather than collecting data. Data are already collected and findings from separate studies are brought together in a meta-analysis and then analysed as if they were collected in one study. This can help to give an overview of results in one area of study. The aim is to find patterns by merging data from different studies. Care must be taken when considering which studies to include in a meta-analysis as the data must be collected in a similar way for them to be comparable.

Meta-analysis in a search for universality

Meta-analysis can use studies from different cultures and look at the data to see what is consistent across all cultures and what is different between cultures. When something is found consistently across all cultures, such as the secure attachment type, then it is said to be universal. More about this is discussed when the cross-cultural design is discussed and nature–nurture issues looked at. These issues are also discussed more in the classic study for child psychology later in this chapter, as well as in the content section where cross-cultural issues and attachment types, including universality of attachment types, are looked at.

Evaluation of meta-analysis as a technique in child psychology

Strengths

- By combining results from different studies, a meta-analysis has more power because the sample size is larger and there are more data.
- Results can be generalised to a larger population because of the larger and wider sample.
- Because more data are used there is likely to be more precision in the analysis.
- If findings from one of the studies are inconsistent, it can help to know that when assessing those findings. It is a way of testing reliability of those findings.

Weaknesses

- When a meta-analysis is done using some small studies it is not the same as carrying out one study with a large sample, because the studies will have design differences and other differences that a large study would not have.
- Only studies that have sound methodology should be included in a meta-analysis. This is **best evidence synthesis**.
- There can also be **publication bias**, which means that studies where results are not significant or where the results go against what is expected are less likely to be published. This can bias the findings of a meta-analysis, which is likely to use only studies that have been published.

Definitions

Best evidence synthesis refers to how a meta-analysis must only include studies that have sound methodology, so that just the 'best evidence' is pulled together into the overall analysis.

Publication bias in a meta-analysis means the analysis will only use studies that come up in a search and they will be published studies. Studies that do not have significant results or that go against expectations are less likely to be published so there can be a bias in a meta-analysis.

> **STUDY HINT**
> You will be evaluating one meta-analysis because you will evaluate the classic study in child psychology in your course. Use these evaluation points when evaluating meta-analysis as a technique.

Progress check 4.47

What is meant by publication bias in relation to meta-analysis as a technique?

The UNCRC (1989) and children's participation and protection rights

Ethical issues when using observation, questionnaire or interview in child psychology have already been mentioned and you have looked at the ethics of researching with children as well as issues around power. This section ends the discussion on ethics and researching with children and young people by looking specifically at the United Nations Convention on the Rights of the Child (UNCRC) (1989) and in particular its focus on participation and protection rights.

The United Nations Convention on the Rights of the Child

In 1989 governments across the world adopted the UNCRC to show they would all give children the same rights. Children were to be seen as human beings with rights of their own and not passive. The rights focused on what a child needs to survive and develop, reaching their potential. The UNCRC is also called the CRC. There are 54 articles setting out children's rights and explaining how adults and governments can allow children their rights. The USA has not ratified the convention, though it has its own focus on children's rights. Somalia has not had a government so could not ratify the convention. In the UK the convention came into law in 1992. Table 4.25 gives a brief overview of some of the Articles.

Table 4.25 Overview of the Articles of the UNCRC (1989)

Article	Brief explanation
Article 1	A child is defined as everyone under the age of 18.
Article 2	The CRC applies to all children whatever their ethnicity or status.
Article 3	The top priority must always be the child's best interests.
Article 5	Governments must respect the rights of parents to provide guidance.
Article 12	Every child has the right to express their views, feelings and wishes.
Article 16	Every child has the right to privacy.
Article 23	A child with a disability has the right to live a full and decent life.
Article 36	Governments must protect children from all forms of exploitation.
Article 42	Children and adults must know about the Convention and their rights.

Four principles of the UNCRC

There are four general principles that are fundamental to children's rights – the four 'P's:

- participation (in decisions made about them)
- protection (from harm)
- provision (of services and all that children need)
- privacy (and confidentiality, at all times).

Provision is important, but when researching with children in psychology, protection and participation rights are very important. Privacy is one of the ethical guidelines in psychology so must also be covered.

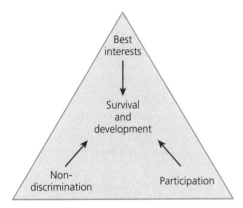

The four main principles of the United Nations Convention on the Rights of the Child

Protection rights

Article 4 is about keeping the child safe from harm. Ethics in psychology, both when researching and when working in practice, have as their main focus the requirement to 'do no harm' and guidelines like the BPS Code of Ethics and Conduct (2009) have a strong focus on protecting participants from harm, both adults and children.

A main focus on ethics when using animals in experiments is around not causing undue distress. Children are treated as vulnerable when it comes to researching with them and special attention has to be paid; for example, when obtaining informed consent from a child it is important to use language they understand. When giving the right to withdraw, children must understand fully that they can withdraw from a study without penalty. The CRC has laid down the right of the child to be protected, but in psychological research this would be the case any way.

In the CRC protection rights include children not being taken out of the country illegally (Article 11) and children being protected from all forms of violence (Article 19). Any form of discipline involving violence is unacceptable, for example. Children deprived of a family environment (Article 20) have a right to special care and children who are adopted or fostered have the right to care and protection (Article 21). Refugee children have to be protected (Article 22) and there is protection too against child labour (Article 32), though they can do work in the home that is safe and appropriate to their age and help out in a family business if this is safe and appropriate. Article 36 holds that children should be protected from any activity that takes advantage of them or harms their development. You can see that some of these points can relate to research with children and so the researcher must be aware of the protection rights of the child. Research is likely to require permission from an ethical body, such as a university review board, and they will be aware of the rights of the child.

Progress check 4.48

Using one UNCRC (1989) Article, explain children's right to protection in terms of doing research with them.

STUDY HINT
Learning a few of the Articles of the UNCRC (1989) can help to give evidence to your arguments about the UNCRC and researching with children.

Participation rights

Protection rights were taken into account in research before the CRC came into being, but participation rights were not always part of ethical guidelines when researching *with* children. Under the CRC the child has the right to be protected (Article 4) and the views of the child must be respected (Article 12). The child has the right to freedom of expression (Article 13) and that includes sharing information in any way they choose. Article 13 specifies that this can be by talking, drawing or writing. The child has the right to privacy too (Article 16), which is included in ethical guidelines in any case.

Progress check 4.49

Using two UNCRC (1989) Articles, explain children's right to participation in terms of doing research with them.

Historically, children, like adults, were objects of research in psychology. Research was done 'on' them as if there was no interaction. Then participants became subjects, which at least gave them some status in the research, but they were still 'subjected' to the research. Then the term 'participants' was introduced to show that they had a full part in the research. Children (and adults) should 'participate' in research and they have that right. Research is *with* the child, not *on* the child, and children are seen as social actors in the research. Participants can still be 'subjects' if, for example, covert observation is carried out where those observed are unaware, and there can be 'objects' for research, such as the brain. On the whole, though, people taking part in research now are seen as 'participants'.

More recently in research with children there has been focus on them as 'researchers' in the study, which gives them more participation rights, such as deciding how to give their information as data. There is focus on 'hearing the voice of the child', which means the child must give data themselves rather than data being given for them, for example, by parents. A study mentioned in this method section is Leyfer *et al.* (2006), who looked at co-morbidity in children with autism (looking to see if they had other psychiatric disorders as well). The parents gave the data rather than the children, which might be seen as a difficulty. However, it is fair to say that for the most part it is still the case that parents give consent for children and young people to take part in research and parents and teachers often give the data too. The idea of the child as the researcher is a new one.

Explore
You can look more at the idea of research being done by children using this link:
http://eprints.ncrm.ac.uk/87/1/
MethodsReviewPaperNCRM-003.pdf

A way of giving participation rights is for children to be the researchers.

Explore
You can explore more about ethics with human participants at the link below, which takes you to a diagram where you can click on the issues in the diagram to learn more:
http://researchskills.epigeum.com/courses/researchskills/4/course_files/html/et2_1_10.html

The European Union Agency for Fundamental Rights describes how child participation in research is dealt with in different countries according to the rules and practices of each country. It is noticeable, however, that often the comment against 'role of children' is 'not applicable' (such as in Austria), which suggests research does not involve full child participation. In Bulgaria it is said that when the child is over 14 his or her consent is required and in Croatia over 14 means the child consents while under 14 means the parent consents. In Croatia children between seven and fourteen have to be informed about consent, according to their age. In Cyprus and in Lithuania the child's opinion should be respected and in Denmark it is said that the child must receive information orally. Finland requires the child to have power over decision-making and taking part in research must be voluntary. The UK uses 'Gillick competence', which means the child has to give consent if there is enough understanding there about what is proposed. You can see there is a wide variety of practice given here and this is just a sample of what is in the document.

Explore
You can look at the European Union Agency for Fundamental Rights document using this link:
http://fra.europa.eu/en/theme/rights-child/child-participation-in-research

Protection rights versus participation rights

Taking the CRC into account, one issue that arises is that children must be able to participate fully in any research they feature in and yet they must also be protected. These two 'rights' can oppose one another. Power and Smith (2009) explain that when the child participants are vulnerable and the area of research is sensitive, participation rights can be compromised. What tends to happen is strong gatekeeping and some children are then prevented from participating in research, which is against their participant rights. If children are seen as social actors who can decide whether to participate or not in research that can help to balance their participation rights and their right to be protected. According to Power and Smith (2009) this means that children must be told about any piece of research in detail so they can make the decision about whether to participate or not.

In relation to researching with children, decisions around choosing a sample need to take into account the possible results of a study as well. If a child does not take part (perhaps because their parents have not given consent), that means they do not have the right to participate, because of being protected. However, if findings can be used to help the child and others, it might help to justify the research taking place. There is the right to be properly researched as well as the right to participate directly.

Abebe and Bessell (2014) discuss the ethics of researching with children and argue against the idea that participation rights mean that *all* children have the right to be researched, as Alderson (2012, cited in Abebe and Bessell, 2014) implies. Abebe and Bessell say rather that all children involved in research have to have their rights respected, which is what they call 'the right to be properly researched'. This is perhaps a more manageable aim.

Progress check 4.50

Distinguish between Alderson's (2012) view about the participation rights of the child in research and Abebe and Bessell's (2014) view.

Test yourself

Evaluate the ethics of researching with children, including children's rights and the UNCRC (1989). **(20 marks)**

Data analysis

You need to know about data analysis as part of methods for child psychology, including quantitative data using descriptive statistics and inferential statistics. You also need to know about analysis of qualitative data, using both thematic analysis and grounded theory.

You covered all the issues around data analysis that are required for child psychology when you considered them in the context of clinical psychology in Chapter Two.

(W) The 'Psychological skills – methods' section online also covers data analysis, so it is not explained here. Remember, however, that you need to know and understand data analysis in the context of child psychology and could be asked about them in the child psychology section of your examination.

Year One link: All the issues around data analysis that you need to know were covered in Year One so review them for this application. The only exception is the use of grounded theory for qualitative data, which is covered in Chapter Two of this book.

Progress check 4.51

Name a) four inferential tests that you must know about; b) two ways of analysing qualitative data; and c) three levels of measurement.

Test yourself

Explain why inferential testing is useful when analysing results in psychology. **(4 marks)**

Summary

- You have to cover method in child psychology, much of which you have covered in other parts of your course. However, you need to be able to relate a method to its use in child psychology.
- Observation must be studied, including gathering qualitative and quantitative data and tallying, as well as types of observation – participant, non-participant, covert and overt.
- Questionnaire and interview are required, again including gathering both qualitative and quantitative data as well as issues around the use of questionnaires and interview, including semi-structured, structured and unstructured interviewing. Sampling, open and closed questions, social desirability and demand characteristics are required.
- You must study cross-cultural research, including the strange situation procedure and nature–nurture issues when drawing conclusions about universality of

attachment types. Here the content and studies you have covered will be useful as the classic study involves the strange situation procedure and the content section considers issues of attachment and universality. Meta-analysis is also required as well as longitudinal and cross-sectional designs – again you have covered these.
- The ethics of researching with children, including the UNCRC (1989) and participation and protection rights issues, are required.
- The data analysis part of method in child psychology in your course is not new to you because you covered it in Year One, except for grounded theory and qualitative data, which you looked at in clinical psychology in your course. You need to know about descriptive and inferential statistics when analysing quantitative data, and analysis of qualitative data, including thematic analysis and grounded theory.

Studies in child psychology

In child psychology in your course you need to learn about one classic study and one contemporary study from a list of three. The classic study you need to know about is van IJzendoorn and Kroonenberg (1988). You can then choose one other study from Cassibba *et al.* (2013), Gagnon-Oosterwaal *et al.* (2012) or Li *et al.* (2013). All four studies are covered here for your interest.

Van IJzendoorn and Kroonenberg (1988) used meta-analysis to look at the universality of attachment types and Cassibba *et al.* (2013) did the same, but focusing on Italian attachment types as opposed to a USA baseline measure of attachment types, taken from Ainsworth's Baltimore study. Those two studies are given here first and they relate to one another. Gagnon-Oosterwaal *et al.* (2012) is about international adoptees, which is a key question explained on the accompanying website, so is of interest. Li *et al.* (2013) looked at high- and low-quality day care so suits the other key question (explained in this chapter) as well as helping your focus on poor- and good-quality day care and advantages and disadvantages for the child.

Cross-cultural attachment patterns: van IJzendoorn and Kroonenberg (1988)

Van IJzendoorn and Kroonenberg (1988) looked at nearly 2,000 studies using the strange situation procedure with data gathered across eight countries. The aim was to carry out cross-cultural analysis to look for differences between cultures and within cultures.

Aims

Van IJzendoorn and Kroonenberg (1988) wished to use a large database using data from the strange situation procedure and thus get a 'global distribution' regarding child attachment types. They wanted to put together data from the same countries so that the focus on individual samples, which might individually have bias, was lessened.

Background

Van IJzendoorn and Kroonenberg (1988) suggested that studies showed differences of attachment classifications across cultures and they cited Ainsworth (1977) and Sagi and Kewkowicz (1987) among others as showing such differences. They suggested that in Germany (Grossmann *et al.*, 1985, cited in van IJzendoorn and Kroonenberg, 1988), Japan (Miyake *et al.*, 1985, cited in van IJzendoorn and Kroonenberg, 1988) and Israel (Sagi *et al.*, 1985, cited in van IJzendoorn and Kroonenberg, 1988) there are large differences in the distribution of attachment types compared with the US 'standard' of the time. The US standard came from Ainsworth's Baltimore study of attachment types, which found about 20 per cent avoidant, 70 per cent secure and 10 per cent ambivalent resistant. Van IJzendoorn and Kroonenberg (1988) suggest that Germany showed a relatively high percentage of Type A (avoidant) attachments and Japan and Israel found a relatively high percentage of Type C (ambivalent resistant) attachments.

Van IJzendoorn and Kroonenberg (1988) suggested that in studies using the strange situation procedure sample sizes tended to be low so there could be a sampling error, which means it is not easy to generalise with confidence from the studies to the finding about a whole country or culture. Van IJzendoorn and Kroonenberg (1988) suggested that studies need to be replicated if their findings are to be generalised and held as a norm for that country. Within a country there can be different cultural norms, for example, and van IJzendoorn and Kroonenberg (1988) suggested that the assumption was that between countries there will be large cross-cultural differences but within countries more similarity in attachment types. They pointed out that the 'American norm' had not been tested using a wide range of American and non-American samples.

Method

Database

A meta-analysis was used and a search carried out to find suitable studies. Sagi and Connell had gathered together a multinational data set, which was used as well as using a search for 'attachment'. Criteria used by van IJzendoorn and Kroonenberg (1988) included the following:

- Only studies of infant–mother attachment using the strange situation procedure and giving ABC classifications were included.
- Special samples such as Down's syndrome children were not included or studies where the sample size was less than N=35.
- Studies with overlapping samples were not included – some samples were used in more than one study.
- Studies had to involve children under the age of two.

Using these decisions van IJzendoorn and Kroonenberg (1988) included 32 samples from 8 countries, which meant 1,990 strange situations.

Progress check 4.52

Explain two decisions that van IJzendoorn and Kroonenberg (1988) made when choosing samples for use in their meta-analysis.

Ainsworth's attachment types are focused on in this study. Type A is avoidant, Type B is secure and Type C is ambivalent/resistant, while Type D was added later. In 1988, van IJzendoorn and Kroonenberg used just the main three types.

Results

In all but one of the studies it was Type B, which is secure attachment, that was the one found most frequently. The exception is Grossmann et al. (1985, reported as 1981 in the table of results).

Table 4.26 shows *some* of the studies van IJzendoorn and Kroonenberg (1988) used, the number of participants and the ABC distribution (frequency in the sample fitting into that type).

Table 4.26 Some studies used by van IJzendoorn and Kroonenberg (1988)

Study	Number in the sample (N)	Attachment type distribution		
		Type A	Type B	Type C
Germany				
Beller and Pohl (1986)	40	7	31	2
Grossmann et al. (1981)*	46	24	16	6
Great Britain				
Smith and Noble (1987)	72	16	54	2
Netherlands				
Goossens (1986)	136	33	98	5
van IJzendoorn (1986b)	39	14	21	4
Sweden				
Lamb et al. (1982)	51	11	38	2
Israel				
Sagi and Lewkowicz (1985)	36	1	29	6
Japan				
Takahashi (1986)	60	0	41	19
China				
Li-Repac (1982)	36	9	18	9
USA				
Ainsworth et al. (1978)	105	22	70	13
Main (1983)	40	11	25	4

*This is the only one not to have secure attachment as the most common

Differences from the expected distribution

In general there are fewer Type C attachments and more Type A attachments in the Western European countries. In Israel and Japan there are more Type C and fewer Type A attachments. In the China study Type B is not as frequent as was expected. Some individual studies have attachment type distribution different from what was expected, such as Grossmann *et al.* in Germany having more Type A attachments.

Variations between and within cultures

Van IJzendoorn and Kroonenberg (1988) found that between countries, between individual samples and between continents, there were significant differences. When looking at attachment types using studies in Germany there are significant differences in the distribution between the findings, and there are differences within Japan and the USA as well. Differences between studies in Israel are only just significant and the same for the Netherlands. Differences between non-US and US samples are very small. The conclusion here is that there are between-culture and within-culture differences.

Van IJzendoorn and Kroonenberg (1988) point out that the variation within countries is nearly one and a half times the variation between countries, which is an important finding when it comes to claiming universality of attachment types. In Germany and the USA the differences within the country are particularly large, whereas in the Netherlands and Japan they are much smaller. It is Israel and Japan that make the most difference in the variations between countries and between continents, and the Western European countries have similar distributions regarding types of attachment.

Similarities and differences between the individual samples

Van IJzendoorn and Kroonenberg (1988) looked at the individual studies and found similarities across countries that were greater than similarities within a country. For example in Japan the Tokyo sample (Durrett *et al.*, 1984, cited in van IJzendoorn and Kroonenberg, 1988) was more similar to two US samples than it was to the Japanese sample from Saporo (Takahashi, 1986, cited in van IJzendoorn and Kroonenberg, 1988).

Progress check 4.53

Explain two results of van IJzendoorn and Kroonenberg's (1988) meta-analysis.

Discussion

- The conclusion was that differences within a country were 'quite considerable' (p. 153). As it is often the same researcher working within one country it is unlikely that the differences in distribution of attachment types come from different procedures between the studies.
- Van IJzendoorn and Kroonenberg (1988) found that when all the USA studies were put together the overall distribution did match Ainsworth *et al.*'s (1978) study, which does give a norm of sorts, even though separate studies had different findings regarding the distribution.
- The researchers went on to say that there are different samples in the 18 US studies they used, such as Easterbrook and Lamb (1979) having a middle-class sample with mainly professional families compared with other studies having samples of people with low socioeconomic status. They suggest that there might be effects of stress. Therefore, even though overall the US samples together seemed to match a global pattern for attachments, separately there were quite large differences.
- Some of the US samples matched samples in other countries more than they matched other US samples, such as Owen *et al.* (1984) having a sample more like a study done in an Israeli city (Sagi *et al.*, 1985).

- The overall conclusion was that it does not seem justified to conclude that an individual sample represents the country the study was done in or represents a particular sub-culture. There are 'outlier' findings and replications are necessary before cross-cultural conclusions can be drawn.
- The overall conclusion was that the secure attachment type (Type B) was the modal one (the one found most often). However, data collected by means other than the strange situation procedure would be required to validate the claim that a secure attachment is dominant in all countries.
- It seems that there are more Type A attachments in Western European countries and more Type C attachments in Israel and Japan, with the US being in the middle regarding Type A and Type C attachment distribution.
- It seems that the strange situation procedure is valid in other countries. This is because the US samples taken together seem to produce a norm with regard to distribution of the three types. The US 'norm' does not differ from the global samples taken together either (with the US samples not included). Therefore, on this global level there does seem to be a norm, Type B is the most common, and the distribution shown by the US samples together does seem to show a 'norm'.
- Possibly the media are a reason for the overall distribution of attachment types being similar globally (such as Type B predominating). Perhaps media images of child rearing in the Western world have spread and have affected child-rearing practices. What is needed is more data from 'less Western-oriented' cultures to test out this idea.

Year One link: You looked at social learning theory and Bandura's ideas about observational learning when you studied learning theories in your course. Van IJzendoorn and Kroonenberg (1988) are referring to observational learning when they discuss the possibility that media images have affected child-rearing practices, leading to similarity in distribution of attachment types.

Evaluation of van IJzendoorn and Kroonenberg (1988)

Strengths

- The meta-analysis chose studies carefully by using only those with samples of children up to two years old, all using the strange situation procedure and all with a sample size of more than 35. The strange situation procedure is a carefully controlled procedure with clear steps and clear instructions about what to look for, so there is control in what they chose to include in their meta-analysis, which should make the study results comparable.
- For many of the countries (five) they had two or more studies (though for China, Great Britain and Sweden, there was just one study), so they could compare within countries as well as between countries. This helped them to show that there are within-country differences in attachment type distribution as well as between-country differences. They used 32 studies across 8 countries, so the breadth of studies to help them to look for universality in attachment types is a strength.

Weaknesses

- In three countries they had just one study so could not look at findings within those countries and for Israel and Japan they just had two studies. Two studies would not perhaps give a sufficient sample to make comparisons from. For the US, Germany and the Netherlands, perhaps, they had enough studies within the country to draw comparisons, but this was just three out of eight of the countries. Van IJzendoorn and Kroonenberg (1988) said that there was quite a bit of variation within a country, such as in the USA, so it can be assumed that to give a 'country' distribution of attachment type a lot of studies would be needed. The researchers do say that replications are required.
- Possibly using the strange situation procedure was a weakness as it was developed in the 'Western' world and may only apply to Western cultures. Van IJzendoorn and Kroonenberg (1988) said that studies in non-Western countries would be useful to test the universality of attachment types using the strange situation. They also said that findings coming from data other than using the strange situation would add to claims of validity.
- The study had a large sample, which suggests findings were generalisable; however, 27 of the studies used focused on **individualist cultures** and just five were in **collectivist cultures**, so the studies may not have represented all countries. As van IJzendoorn and Kroonenberg say, studies should be done in non-Western countries to find out more about universality of attachment types.

Definitions

Individualist cultures are those that place more importance on the needs of the individual over the needs of the group as a whole.

Collectivist cultures are those that emphasise the needs of the whole group over the needs and wishes of the individuals in the group.

Progress check 4.54

Why is it possible that using the strange situation procedure for their meta-analysis was a problem?

Attachment types in Italy: Cassibba *et al.* (2013)

Cassibba *et al.* (2013), in a team that included van IJzendoorn, carried out a meta-analysis of studies using the strange situation procedure to look at 'attachment the Italian way', which is the title of their study. Their study spanned 1990 to 2009 and their aim was to test the universality hypothesis of attachment. They were also interested in looking at cultural specifics in attachment, focusing on participants in Italy alone.

Aims

Cassibba *et al.* (2013) wanted to see if attachment studies in Italy showed the same distribution of adult and child attachment classifications found globally or to see if attachment patterns in Italy were different. Questions asked by Cassibba *et al.* (2013):

- Are attachment types mainly secure?
- Are there fewer unresolved attachment types?
- Are the three attachment types (A, B and C) differently distributed in different cultures?
- Are there gender differences in attachment types?

STUDY HINT

Recall from reading about attachments in the content section of this chapter that in infants Ainsworth found three main types: Type A – Insecure Avoidant, Type B – Secure and Type C – Insecure Ambivalent/Resistant. Also recall that Type D was 'detached' and added as a fourth type. Cassibba *et al.* (2013) used ABC and ABCD in their study.

Background

Cassibba *et al.* (2013) mentioned the value of having the strange situation because of its replicability. Also they used studies using the Adult Attachment Interview (AAI)

to measure adults' feelings about attachment. Part of the reason for seeing Italy as different is that women's status is low in Italy compared with other industrialised societies (Wilkinson and Pickett, 2009, cited in Cassibba *et al.*, 2013). Also Italy has a combination of individualism and collectivism in its focus. Attachment theory supposedly shows that humans have an innate tendency to form attachments, however, this universality, according to Cassibba *et al.* (2013), does not mean there are not also cultural differences in patterns of attachment.

Issues and debates

Cassibba *et al.* refer to nature–nurture issues when they explain that the formation of attachment is an instinct but features of such attachments can differ according to your culture. Nature–nurture and culture are issues and debates in your course. Cassibba *et al.* (2013) used similar data when making comparisons, as did van IJzendoorn and Kroonenberg in their 1988 meta-analysis. They both used studies that used the strange situation procedure too. You can compare them to look at how the development of psychology has changed over time, another issue and debate in your course.

Van IJzendoorn and Sagi-Schwartz (2008, cited in Cassibba *et al.*, 2013) explained how, in all cultures that have been studied, a secure attachment is the dominant type, which is evidence for universality in attachment type. Secure, avoidant and ambivalent attachments in children are found in all cultures studied, and secure, dismissing and preoccupied attachment patterns in adults are also found in all cultures studied.

Progress check 4.55

When Cassibba *et al.* commented about the universality of attachment types, they talked about secure attachment being the dominant type in 'all cultures that have been studied'. Why did they say this and not that secure attachment is the dominant type universally (i.e. in all cultures)?

Year One link: You looked at psychology as a science, at gathering empirical data, and at falsification when you learned about learning theories.

Issues and debates

The progress checks related to Cassibba *et al.* (2013) give arguments about the nature–nurture debate in psychology, the idea of psychology as a science and how psychological understanding has changed over time. These are three issues and debates for your course so you can make a note that this area of study is useful when discussing those issues and debates.

Table 4.27 shows attachment types in adults, which may help your understanding of Cassibba *et al.* (2013).

Table 4.27 Adult attachment types

Adult attachment type (romantic relationships)	Explanation
Secure (Secure autonomous – F type)	A secure attachment style goes with a secure attachment in the child, and includes feelings such as not worrying about being alone and finding it relatively easy to get emotionally close to people.
Anxious-preoccupied (Preoccupied – E type)	An anxious-preoccupied style goes with anxious-ambivalent in children and includes feelings such as worrying that others do not value the person as much as they value others and looking for high levels of approval and intimacy from partners.
Dismissive-avoidant (Dismissing – D type)	A dismissive-avoidant style goes with avoidant attachment in the child, as does fearful-avoidant. A dismissive-avoidant style in the adult accompanies feelings of being comfortable without close relationships and preferring to be independent.
Fearful-avoidant	Fearful-avoidant means being discomfort in getting close to others and finding it hard to trust them. They tend to see themselves as unworthy of having close relationships and uncomfortable showing affection.

Adult attachment types in relation to attitudes towards self and others

Alongside the evidence for universality in attachments there is also evidence for cultural differences, suggesting an element of 'nurture' affecting attachment type. For example, in Israel there are almost no examples of avoidant attachments and more ambivalent attachments than in other cultures (Sagi *et al.,* 1997, cited in Cassibba *et al.,* 2013).

Cassibba *et al.* (2013) expected to find more secure attachments than other types. However, they thought they would also find cultural variations in attachment types given differences in Italian culture. Italy is high in individualism compared with the USA, but it also has elements of collectivism, more than is found in the USA, so there are cultural differences that might give differences in attachment patterns. In Italy 80 per cent of the population is Catholic, which may lead to fewer unresolved attachment types as religion possibly offers a resolution of trauma for people, according to Cassibba *et al.* (2013). They also felt mental ill health would affect the 'normal' patterns of attachment for both adults and infants. A final focus was on gender as Italy has a strong gender differentiation.

Method

The method was meta-analysis, which was the same method used by the classic study for child psychology in your course, van IJzendoorn and Kroonenberg (1988). Cassibba *et al.* (2013) searched for 'strange situation procedure', 'attachment' and 'Italian' to find studies. They also used the tables of content of all Italian psychology journals and books. They included unpublished dissertations and conference papers to try to avoid the 'file drawer' problem. They used only Italian samples, only studies that used the strange situation procedure and studies reporting either ABC or ABCD types. They also used studies looking at adult attachment using only those that used the AAI or the AICA to get their data. The AAI is the Adult Attachment Interview and the AICA is the Attachment Interview for Child and Adolescence. Adult attachment types were in the three categories – Type D (dismissing), Type E (preoccupied) or Type F (secure) – or in four categories, where Type U was added (unresolved/disorganised). They chose 17 studies (which meant 627 participants) using the strange situation procedure and 50 studies (which meant 2,258 participants) using the AAI with Italian samples.

Table 4.28 shows infant and adult attachment types to help you understand Cassibba et al.'s (2013) meta-analysis.

Table 4.28 Infant and adult attachment types

Attachment type	Explanation	Attachment type	Explanation
Child		**Adult**	
A	Avoidant	D	Dismissing
B	Secure	E	Preoccupied
C	Ambivalent/ resistant	F	Secure
D	Detached	U	Unresolved

> **STUDY HINT**
> There is value in using standardised measures in studies so that meta-analyses can be carried out, Cassibba et al. (2013) depended on the reliability of the strange situation procedure and of the Adult Attachment Interview (or the AICA).

Results

Cassibba et al. (2013) used the same analysis techniques as van IJzendoorn and Kroonenberg (1988), the classic study for your course. Table 4.29 shows percentage distributions of three attachment types for infants in the Italian sample compared with the American norm. The results table shows similarity in the attachment types for the non-clinical Italian sample and the US norm percentages. There are more 'avoidant' types and fewer 'secure' types but in general there is similarity.

Table 4.29 Percentage distributions of three attachment types: Cassibba et al. (2013)

	Number of participants	Type A – Avoidant	Type B – Secure	Type C – Ambivalent/ resistant
*American norm	1,584	21%	67%	12%
Overall non-clinical Italian sample	419	33%	53%	14%

*The American norm came from 21 samples often used as the norm for other meta-analyses (van IJzendoorn et al., 1992, cited in Cassibba et al., 2013).

Year One link: Chi squared tests were done to look for significance. Attachment type is a category so gives nominal data. Each participant is in only one group so the design is independent groups. Remember how to choose an inferential test as this will help your learning.

Cassibba et al. (2013) also looked at gender, age and non-clinical versus clinical samples. A clinical sample is one where there are mental health issues and a non-clinical sample is 'typical' people without mental health issues. They also looked at clinical/at risk as opposed to non-clinical samples using the AAI, also including looking at gender and age (adult versus adolescent).

Child attachment results

Non-clinical

The largest percentage of non-clinical children were in the secure attachment group, as expected from other studies, including van IJzendoorn and Kroonenberg (1988). It was noticeable that Italian children were more avoidant (Type A) than in the US sample. Table 4.30 gives the results for the non-clinical Italian sample.

Table 4.30 Italian non-clinical sample: Cassibba et al. (2013)

Italian non-clinical sample (N = 262)	Type A	Type B	Type C	Type D
Includes Type D	28%	44%	6%	22%

Clinical

Clinical/at risk Italian children had fewer secure attachment types and more insecure attachment types compared with the US non-clinical sample. Also the D category was over-represented in the Italian clinical/at risk sample. The Italian clinical/at risk sample compared with the US clinical sample had more in the avoidant type ($\chi^2 = 44.9$ which was significant at p<.001, N=1299). Table 4.31 gives the results for the clinical Italian sample.

Table 4.31 Italian clinical sample: Cassibba et al. (2013)

Italian clinical sample (N = 208)	Type A	Type B	Type C	Type D
Three types only	40%	32%	28%	–

Maternal clinical/at risk compared with child clinical/at risk

When the Italian clinical/at risk children were separated into maternal versus child risk factors the split of attachment types differed from the norm by quite a lot. When there were maternal risk factors the secure attachment type (Type B) was no longer the largest. When there were child risk factors the distribution matched the 'norm' more closely and Type B was again the highest percentage. Table 4.32 gives the results for the clinical/at risk Italian sample divided by child and maternal risk factors.

Table 4.32 Results for the clinical/at risk Italian sample divided by child and maternal risk factors: Cassibba *et al.* (2013)

Italian clinical/at risk sample	Type A	Type B	Type C	Type D
Maternal risk factors	43%	27%	30%	–
Child risk factors	36%	40%	24%	–

Comparing the clinical/at risk and non-clinical Italian samples

There was a significant difference between the non-clinical and clinical/at risk groups. The clinical/at risk children were not so often securely attached (32 per cent for the clinical/at risk children compared with 44 per cent for the non-clinical sample; 27 per cent compared with 44 per cent if Type D is included) and were more often ambivalent (28 per cent for the clinical/at risk children compared with 14 per cent for the non-clinical sample using just ABC).

Progress check 4.56

Using the figures for the child attachment results explain the overall conclusion that in the Italian samples there were more 'avoidant' attachment types than in the US sample.

Adult attachment results

Non-clinical Italian mothers

Italian non-clinical mothers had secure (Type F) as the most frequent category when using the AAI classification. When three categories were used the non-clinical Italian mothers did not differ from the norm but when the U type was included there was a difference from the norm with fewer being in the U category. Table 4.33 gives the results for the non-clinical Italian mothers.

Table 4.33 Results for the non-clinical Italian mothers: Cassibba *et al.* (2013), compared with the US norm

Italian non-clinical mothers	Type D	Type E	Type F	Type U
Three types only	22%	19%	59%	–
Includes Type D (N = 301)	19%	11%	60%	10%
US norm	23%	19%	58%	–
Includes Type D (N = 700)	16%	9%	56%	18%

Non-clinical Italian fathers

There were slightly more dismissing fathers but the figures were not that different from the norm.

Table 4.34 gives the results for the non-clinical Italian fathers.

Table 4.34 Results for the non-clinical Italian fathers: Cassibba *et al.* (2013)

Italian non-clinical fathers	Type D	Type E	Type F	Type U
Three types only	35%	19%	46%	–

Non-clinical Italian adolescents

For the Italian adolescents, both when using the three types and when including the U type, there were differences from the norm. For example, the U type was quite a lot lower than the US sample. More were 'dismissing' in the Italian sample. Table 4.35 gives the results for the non-clinical Italian adolescents.

Table 4.35 Results for the non-clinical Italian adolescents: Cassibba *et al.* (2013)

Italian non-clinical adolescents	Type D	Type E	Type F	Type U
Three types only	27%	12%	61%	–
Includes Type D (N = 301)	24%	10%	62%	4%

Combining all clinical samples (adults)

When combining all the clinical Italian samples the figures were all 'strongly divergent from the norms', according to Cassibba *et al.* (2013). There were fewer secure-autonomous types and more dismissing and preoccupied types than in the 'norm'. Table 4.36 gives the results for all the clinical Italian samples (adults).

Table 4.36 Results for all the clinical Italian samples (adults): Cassibba *et al.* (2013)

Italian non-clinical adults	Type D	Type E	Type F	Type U
Three types only	35%	27%	38%	–
Includes Type D	27%	15%	25%	33%

All the Italian samples, clinical and non-clinical

There were more D and E types and fewer F types in the Italian clinical/at risk samples.

Summary and gender differences

The study looked at other Italian samples as well as the results reported here. Overall the Italian samples were different in attachment types compared with the US norms, as has been shown so far. They also looked at gender, comparing the non-clinical mothers and non-clinical fathers using the AAI data. They found a significant difference ($\chi^2 = 13.2$, which was significant at p<.01, N = 743).

Discussion

The interest in universality of attachment types justified the use of the Italian sample as Italy presents a Western individualised culture but has strong family ties and features strong independence. It also has a significantly Catholic population. These features of its culture are different enough from a US sample norm that if infant attachment types found using the strange situation procedure or adult attachment types found using the AAI compared with the US norm then it could be claimed that there is universality in attachment types. A further reason for this meta-analysis was that knowing more about Italian attachment patterns gave insights so that clinicians could help individuals.

- The majority of non-clinical Italian infants were in the secure attachment category (53 per cent), as were the majority of non-clinical Italian adults (60 per cent).
- Using the three types of classification for both infants and adults the distribution of attachment types was very similar to those in the US norm that was being used.
- The conclusion is that there is universality in attachment types.
- However, Cassibba et al. (2013) also found differences between cultures, which suggests attachment types have some environmental basis. There was a higher percentage of avoidant attachment types in the Italian clinical and non-clinical samples than in the US norms. Cassibba et al. (2013) suggested that individual differences come from cultural differences in child rearing and this can account for there being more avoidant attachment in Italian mothers. Italian mothers see child development taking place naturally, whereas US mothers focus on promoting their child's development. Italian mothers focus on stimulating independence more than US mothers do. Italian mothers expect a high level of 'social maturity' (e.g. Bornstein et al., 2008, cited in Cassibba et al., 2013). Promoting early autonomy may lead to more avoidant attachments.
- With regard to the adult attachment distribution in the Italian sample there was a high percentage of dismissing types in both clinical and non-clinical samples and a high percentage of unresolved types in general. However, there was a low percentage of unresolved types in the Italian adolescents. Cassibba et al. (2013) pointed out that religion played a role in 'cognitive and emotional coping processes'.

- There seemed not to be gender differences in attachment types. In the Italian samples there seemed to be more fathers in the 'dismissing' category, which may link to the differences in gender roles in Italy (Wilkinson and Pickett, 2009, cited in Cassibba et al., 2013). Males may have 'dominant status', which may lead to a more 'dismissive stance when it comes to relationships'.
- This means it can be said that there are cultural differences in attachment types and they are not all about 'universality'.

Issues and debates

Cassibba et al.'s (2013) findings show evidence for nature being involved in attachment types, and also for nurture. This is a useful study to use when discussing the issue of nature-nurture in your course. You could use this study to show cultural similarities and cultural differences too.

The overall conclusion is that this meta-analysis has shown avoidant attachments are more common in the Italian studies, which may relate to a mothering style that promotes early independence. There may be a similar issue with father–infant attachment types but this area needs more research. The 'U' type in adults, which represented unresolved loss, was found much less in the Italian adolescent samples than in the US sample (though higher when non-clinical Italian adults were considered), which needs more investigation and might be because of cultural factors such as religious differences. There were universal trends in attachment types as well as cultural effects. They found in the children that secure attachment was the largest type, as was found in other studies, and this seems to be universal.

Evaluation

Strengths of Cassibba et al. (2013)

- The US norm distribution that was used was worked out in 1992 and was very similar to Ainsworth et al.'s (1978) distribution, so is seen as the norm to measure other studies against. This is a strength because if studies use the same norm then their conclusions are more comparable and the US norm seems to be reliable if it is similar to Ainsworth's original Baltimore study and van IJzendoorn et al. (1992) using 21 studies.
- Cassibba et al. (2013) generated a lot of variables to consider, all stemming from perceived cultural differences between Italy and the US, and they analysed their data separately using the different variables. They found differences too, such as non-clinical Italian mothers have a much lower percentage (22 per cent) in the dismissing category regarding adult attachment

types than non-clinical Italian fathers (35 per cent). Without separating using these variables the differences would not have been teased out.

Weaknesses of Cassibba *et al.* (2013)

- It is not easy to draw conclusions from a large number of studies that have quite a few differences and this is a problem with using meta-analysis. Cassibba *et al.* included studies that used the strange situation procedure and not other studies, which helped them to draw comparisons. They also used studies using the AAI or the AICA, which again helped with comparisons. However, sampling in each study is likely to be different, the researchers are likely to be different and there may be different decisions about how to record the interviews or the observations. In meta-analysis there are sure to be differences between the studies that are being compared directly.
- Although many variables were chosen, such as clinical versus non-clinical and mothers versus fathers, there were unexplained differences in the data. For example, the Italian adolescent samples had fewer unresolved attachment types in the adults compared with the US norm but the clinical Italian sample (adults) had a high percentage in the unresolved loss category. This sort of issue needs more research to explain it. However, it does show that there are cultural differences, even if in general attachment types are thought to be universal for both child and adult attachment types.

> **STUDY HINT**
> You can use strengths and weaknesses of meta-analysis when evaluating Cassibba *et al.* (2013), though note they did include unpublished dissertations and conference papers to try to avoid the 'file drawer' problem.

Progress check 4.57

Summarise the findings of Cassibba *et al.* (2013).

Problems before adoption in seven-year-old international adoptees: Gagnon-Oosterwaal et al. (2012)

Gagnon-Oosterwaal *et al.* (2012) wanted to look at the long-term effects of problems for children before being adopted. They measured what they called '**externalising**' and '**internalising**' **symptoms**.

Definitions

Internalising symptoms refer to withdrawal, physical symptoms and anxiety and depression.
Externalising symptoms refer to aggressive or defiant behaviour.

Data were gathered using self-report data from school-aged children (seven years old) and mothers' reports were used as well. The study used 95 adopted children and their mothers, with the child's health and developmental status assessed soon after they were adopted. The self-reports of the adopted children were compared to the self-report data from non-adopted peers. Adopted children reported more phobias than their peers. For externalising symptoms there was a significant correlation between the mother's report and the child's data, and symptoms using the self-report data also related to psychosocial deprivation and nutritional deprivation on arrival. The conclusion is that the perception of psychological adjustment of the adopted children is important as is the long-term effect of early pre-adoption problems.

Aims

The main aim was to collect data from adopted children and their mothers about behaviour problems as well as collecting nutritional data and information about deprivation. The focus was on the development of international adoptees and their psychological adjustment. The researchers aimed to look at behaviour problems in seven-year-old internationally adopted children and considered the 'impact of pre-adoption adversity' (p. 650). They aimed to use self-report measures focusing on 'seven specific externalising and internalising disorders' (p. 650).

Background

The focus was on **international adoptees**, which means children who are adopted into a new country, so adopted 'across countries'.

Definition

International adoptees are children who were adopted into one country from another, such as a baby in Korea being adopted by a family in the USA.

Gagnon-Oosterwaal *et al.* (2012) claimed that internationally adopted children often suffer from deprivation before being adopted, such as living in an institution and not having sufficient stimulation or stable care-giving so that they could form attachments. The researchers said, for example, that there are delays in cognitive and social development as well as physical delays (e.g. Miller, 2000, cited in Gagnon-Oosterwaal *et al.,* 2012). MacLean (2003, cited in Gagnon-Oosterwaal *et al.,* 2012) suggests that early deprivation can have lasting effects on a child's intellectual, physical and social development. Studies have shown that international adoptees compared with non-adopted children show more externalising and more internalising problems (e.g. Ames, 1997, cited in Gagnon-Oosterwaal *et al.,* 2012).

> **STUDY HINT**
> Link the ideas of lack of stimulation in an institution and lack of stable care-giving to what you learned about deprivation and attachments in the content section of this chapter.

It is possible that the age of adoption makes a difference to the effects of any pre-adoption deprivation, but Juffer and van IJzendoorn (2005, cited in Gagnon-Oosterwaal *et al.,* 2012) did not find evidence that the age of adoption related to the effect of early risk factors. However, there are studies that show that children adopted later do have more behaviour problems (e.g. Hawk and McCall, 2010, cited in Gagnon-Oosterwaal *et al.,* 2012).

Gagnon-Oosterwaal *et al.* (2012) suggest that most studies looking at behaviour problems and international adoptees rely on parents' assessments. Parents who adopted children internationally might be different from those who had not adopted children and so reports from parents might emphasise certain aspects of an adopted child's development, such as behaviour problems. Partly it is because ways of collecting reliable self-report data from children about their emotional and behavioural problems have not been available that parent data have been relied upon.

Wiik *et al.* (2011) looked at internationally adopted children aged 8 to 11, one group from an institution and one adopted from foster care, as well as a group of non-adopted children. The findings were that externalising problems were found more often in internationally adopted children than in non-adopted peers. This finding came from both the parents and the children themselves. Parents of children internationally adopted reported more internalising problems than parents of non-adopted children, but only the children who were adopted from an institution reported more internalising problems. This showed that it was not being adopted that gave the child's view of themselves as having internalising problems; it was adoption from an institution.

Hypotheses

- 'Children adopted from foreign countries would report more behaviour problems than their non-adopted peers' (p. 650).
- The researchers wanted to look at the self-report data and mothers' reports to see if there was a relationship.
- They also looked at relationships between behaviour problems (self-reported) and their 'health, developmental status and age' when the child arrived at their adoptive family.

Progress check 4.58

When looking at externalising versus internalising problems, why might mothers' and children's reports not correspond?

Method

The measures taken are explained below.

Health and developmental status on arrival

Medical data, including neurological signs (such as evidence of disorders), were used as well as other measures, including height and weight. The researchers used the Bayley Scales of Infant Development to assess children's developmental status.

Dominic Interactive to get self-report data

The Dominic Interactive (DI) is a pictorial questionnaire gathering self-report data assessing internalising and externalising symptoms in children aged 6 to 11. There are 94 items displayed by computer, each one illustrated by one or more pictures with a voice-over question. Children click a 'yes' or 'no' button to show whether they feel, think or act like Dominic, who features in all the pictures. Questions relate to symptoms of disorders using the DSM-IV-TR. Disorders include major depressive disorder, generalised anxiety disorder, separation anxiety disorder, specific phobias, attention deficit disorder, oppositional defiance disorder and conduct disorder. The Dominic Interactive runs for 15 minutes, so considers the participants' attention span.

> **STUDY HINT**
> You can relate what you know about the DSM and disorders to Gagnon-Oosterwaal *et al.*'s (2012) comments about the Dominic Interactive measure.

Child Behaviour Checklist

The study also used the Child Behaviour Checklist for the mothers to give their data. The checklist is a questionnaire with 118 items that assess child behaviour problems. The parent uses a three-point rating scale for each item. The choice of responses is 'not true', 'sometimes true' and 'very true'. A total score can be calculated based on three sub-scales. These are:

- internalising problems (withdrawn/depressed; anxious/depressed; physical complaints)
- externalising problems (rule-breaking behaviour; aggressive behaviour)
- other problems (thought problems, social problems, attention problems).

> **STUDY HINT**
> The Child Behaviour Checklist is a questionnaire so you can use this study as an example of questionnaire use in child psychology.

Results

Self-report data

Table 4.37 shows the percentages of self-reported behaviour problems in internationally adopted and non-adopted children. You can see that with regard to internalising symptoms the main difference between internationally adopted children and non-adopted children is in specific phobias. For generalised anxiety and depression the non-adopted children report themselves as 'higher' and for separation anxiety there is not much in it. With regard to externalising symptoms, oppositional and conduct disorders come out higher for international adoptees, with ADHD being higher in the non-adopted children.

- Analysis showed no gender differences.
- A Chi squared analysis was done to look for differences in the externalising disorders and there was no difference ($\chi^2=1.05$, N=136).
- There tended to be more internalising problems in the internationally adopted children ($\chi^2=3.23$, N=136), though this was only significant at p=.07.
- There were significantly more specific phobia symptoms in the adopted children (p=.0001). The number of children presenting specific phobia was higher in the adopted children ($\chi^2=9.79$, p=.002).

Table 4.37 Percentages of self-reported behaviour problems in internationally adopted and non-adopted children: Gagnon-Oosterwaal *et al.* (2012)

Behaviour problems	Internationally adopted children (N=95)	Non-adopted children (N=41)
Internalising symptoms	43.2%	28.6%
Specific phobia	32.6%	7.3%
Separation anxiety	22.1%	17.1%
Generalised anxiety	10.5%	17.1%
Depression	6.3%	12.2%
Externalising symptoms	30.5%	22.0%
Opposition	22.1%	12.2%
ADHD	10.5%	17.1%
Conduct disorder	13.7%	7.3%

> **Progress check 4.59**
> In the results for Gagnon-Oosterwaal *et al.* (2012) the Chi squared result is given, often with the level of significance. One level of significance is p.002, when saying that adopted children have more specific phobia. What does p.002 mean in this situation?

Year One link: Levels of significance are given in this study, such as p<.05. You have covered levels of significance in cognitive psychology in your course and method issues are reviewed in the 'Psychological skills – methods' section online.

> **STUDY HINT**
> The progress check asks about levels of significance, which you should know about. However, it is not easy to remember everything you have learned and you may not yet be entirely confident about statistics. The more you read about an issue (like levels of significance) the easier to understand it becomes, so don't be put off as there is a lot more to the course than statistical testing!

Table 4.38 Correlations between internationally adopted children's health and developmental status on arrival and self-reported behavioural problems at school: Gagnon-Oosterwaal *et al.* (2012)

Children's condition	Internalising symptoms				Externalising symptoms		
	MDD	GAD	SAD	SPh	ADHD	ODD	CD
Neurological signs							
Small head circumference							.27**
Weight/height ratio	−.21*			−.23*			−.28**
Height/age ratio							−.22*
Developmental status							
Age at arrival							

MDD = major depressive disorder; GAD = generalised anxiety disorder; SAD = separation anxiety disorder; SPh = specific phobia; ADHD = attention deficit hyperactivity disorder; ODD = oppositional defiant diso rder; CD = conduct disorder.
*p<.05 **p<.01

Correlation between mothers' and children's reports

A significant correlation was found between the data from the mothers and the child self-report data for externalising problems (p.001) but not for internalising problems.

Child health and developmental status at arrival compared with behavioural problems

Table 4.38 shows correlations between internationally adopted children's health and developmental status on arrival and self-reported behavioural problems at school. Only the significant correlations are shown.

Significant correlations were found in some of the comparisons. Children's self-reports of behaviour problems at school age correlated with their condition when they arrived at their adoptive family. Specific phobia, depression and conduct disorders correlated with low weight to height ratio. Conduct disorders correlated with low height/age ratio and small head circumference.

Progress check 4.60

Explain two correlations relating to health and developmental status on arrival and self-reported behaviour problems in school age.

Discussion

- Like Juffer and van IJzendoorn (2005), Gagnon-Oosterwaal *et al.* (2012) found that most of the internationally adopted children were 'well-adjusted'.

- Unlike Wiik *et al.* (2011), Gagnon-Oosterwaal *et al.* (2012) did not find more internalising, externalising and ADHD symptoms in the internationally adopted sample compared with the non-adopted children. It is suggested that the sample reported here was younger and also had not spent as long in institutions as in Wiik *et al.*'s study, which may account for the different findings.

- Gagnon-Oosterwaal *et al.* reported that many of their adopted sample were girls adopted from China and adoptees from China tend not to show high levels of behaviour problems (p. 655).

- A main finding is that the adopted children reported more symptoms of specific phobia than the non-adopted children. Gagnon-Oosterwaal *et al.* (2012) explained that low-responsiveness in 'parenting' in an institution could result in stress, which might explain this finding about specific phobia, an anxiety disorder. However, adopted parents may over-protect and over-protective parenting and parenting control has been associated with anxiety in childhood, especially specific phobia (Beesdo, 2009, cited in Gagnon-Oosterwaal *et al.*, 2012).

- Health status on arrival for adoption related to behaviour problems in school, including head circumference and height/age ratio negatively relating to conduct disorders.

- An issue is that pre-adoption environment is just one factor that might affect an adopted child's self-report on their behaviour problems. Their post-adoption environment may affect their self-evaluation more, such as the effects of recent events.

- The mothers' reports and child reports only matched for externalising symptoms but this might be because they were observable and so mothers could report on them.

A child's private feelings might be harder for a mother to know about. This suggests that using the self-report data as well as parent information was useful.

Evaluation

Strengths

- A strength was in managing to collect self-report data from the children about their behavioural and emotional problems, which gave an insight into their perception of their 'psychological adjustment' (p. 657). Gagnon-Oosterwaal et al. (2012) claimed that theirs was the first study to do this, which is a strength. There was validity in asking the children. For example, though the mothers' reports matched the self-report data in externalising symptoms, they did not match in internalising symptoms, which suggests child data have validity and mother's data are not sufficient.
- A strength was the longitudinal design in that the researchers gathered developmental status and health information when the children arrived for adoption and then collected the self-report and mothers' report data later. The data focused on individuals and so could be fairly compared and related.

> **STUDY HINT**
> Gagnon-Oosterwaal et al. (2012) used a longitudinal design so you can use the study as an example.

Weaknesses

- The comparison group had 41 children in the sample compared with the 95 in the adopted children sample. There were limited data, therefore, when comparing the two groups. Also the sample was an opportunity/convenience sample for the comparison group rather than a representative sample. This can affect comparisons as well and can also affect generalisability of the findings.
- The Dominic Interactive did not cover all of the DSM criteria of the disorders, such as not getting data about duration of the symptoms, so the findings are not about diagnosing the disorder as such. When assessing symptoms using self-report data there may not be reliability or validity.

> **Explore**
> You can find Gagnon-Oosterwaal et al. (2012) using this link if you would like to know more:
> http://lemondeestailleurs.ca/Notre_parole/documents/ reAdoptionAdversityandSelfReportedBehavior JFChicoine6January2012_000.pdf

> **STUDY HINT**
> You may have noticed that when giving strengths and limitations of studies in psychology it is often the sample that is seen as a limitation so that generalisability of the findings is queried. If you need to evaluate a study, look for issues about generalisability as a starting point, though avoid statements like 'the sample was too small', as a small sample by itself does not make a study's findings lack generalisability.

> **Progress check 4.61**
> Give two of Gagnon-Oosterwaal et al.'s (2012) findings.

Timing of high-quality day care: Li et al. (2013)

Li et al. (2013) drew on the data from the SECCYD, which is the longitudinal study run by the National Institute of Child Health and Human Development. The SECCYD is explained in the content section of this chapter (page 394).

> **STUDY HINT**
> Recall information about the NICHD SECCYD longitudinal study to help you to understand Li et al. (2013).

In biological psychology in your course one of the contemporary studies you could have chosen was Li et al. (2013) and their study of heroin addiction. The study for child psychology is also called Li et al. (2013) but it is a different study. Be sure to make it clear which study you are referring to as they cover very different areas.

Li et al. (2013) wanted to look at the effects of high- versus low-quality day care when a child was an infant or toddler and again at pre-school age. The focus was on cognitive, language and pre-academic ability to see if such abilities related to high-quality care, both as an infant/toddler and later at pre-school age. Li et al. (2013) found that high-quality care did improve skills, more so if experienced at both ages and less so if experienced in just one of those stages. Children who experienced low-quality day care in both the stages had the lowest cognitive, language and pre-academic skills. They found that high-quality care at the infant/toddler age was related to better memory when ready to start school and high-quality care at pre-school age related to better language and pre-academic skills.

Aims

Li et al. (2013) were interested in the effects of high- and low-quality day care on children in two age groups, infant/toddler and pre-school (at 54 months old). They wanted to look at any effects on cognitive, language and pre-academic skills in those two age groups according to whether day care was high- or low-quality. An important aim was to look at the combination of quality of day care and whether high- or low-quality care at either of the periods made a difference. For example, they wanted to know whether high-quality day care at the infant/toddler stage would affect cognitive, language and pre-academic skills enough to mean that those skills were still good after pre-school, even if the child had low-quality day care in the pre-school period.

Background

Li *et al.* (2013) began by stating that there had been a growth in day care in the US (National Center for Educational Statistics, 2010, cited in Li *et al.*, 2013). There is evidence that cognitive and academic outcomes are improved by high-quality day care in the first five years. They pointed out that so far the focus had not been on the different ages/stages of day care, such as infant/toddler and pre-school to see if high-quality day care has different effects in those two age ranges.

It is recognised that the first three years are important for language and attention development (e.g. Nelson and Sheridan, 2011, cited in Li *et al.*, 2013). The NICHD Early Child Care Research Network (2000) held that when care givers are warm and responsive and a child is in a stimulating environment that helps with the development of skills. Clarke-Stewart *et al.* (2000, cited in Li *et al.*, 2013) found that high-quality day care in the first three years related to higher scores regarding cognitive and pre-academic skills. Ludwig and Miller (2007, cited in Li *et al.* 2013) and others have found that high-quality day care from ages three to five years, which are the pre-school years, helps cognitive and pre-academic skills. These findings suggest that both before the age of three and in the pre-school years, high-quality day care has been shown to have positive effects regarding cognitive and pre-academic skills.

> **STUDY HINT**
> You can use Li *et al.* (2013) when discussing the effects of poor- and good-quality day care on children, as well as the advantages and disadvantages of day care for the child.

Li *et al.*'s discussion about day care links to the key question discussed later in this chapter, about what issues parents should take into account when making decisions about day care for their child.

Li *et al.* (2013) suggested that what was missing was an examination of how the timing of quality day care affects cognitive, language and pre-academic skills. It would be interesting to look at how infant/toddler quality day care affected such skills, to look at how care affects the skills at the pre-school ages and to see how the combination of the care at both ages has an effect.

Focusing on the timing of high-quality care they drew on a model that 'explains how skill begets skill' (Cunha *et al.*, 2010, cited in Li *et al.*, 2013, p. 1441). The idea was that skills developed early enhance skills developed later; there is a connection, which can be called 'complementarity'. Brooks-Gunn *et al.* (1994, cited in Li *et al.*, 2013) suggest that the effects of interventions in the early years, which have been shown to decline over time, are lost because the intervention ends. The positive effects could have continued if the intervention had continued. This suggests that what happens in the early years may affect learning later but only perhaps if the high-quality care continues, so there was a need to look at the effects of high-quality care over time.

> **Progress check 4.62**
> What do Li *et al.* (2013) mean by complementarity?

Hypotheses

- Hypothesis 1: High-quality infant/toddler day care improves cognitive outcomes at 24 months of age. However, at 54 months such children would not have higher cognitive, language and pre-academic scores unless they had high-quality care in the pre-school period as well. At 54 months they would not have higher scores than children who had low-quality care at the infant/toddler age and low-quality care at pre-school age too.
- Hypothesis 2: High-quality care in the pre-school years would improve cognitive, language and pre-academic outcomes at 54 months of age. If children had high-quality rather than low-quality care in the infant/toddler ages then they would also have better outcomes at 54 months than those who had low-quality infant/toddler care. The combination of high-quality care in the infant/toddler ages and high-quality care in the pre-school years would be what would give the best outcomes regarding cognitive, language and pre-academic skills.
- Hypothesis 3: High-quality care at *both* infant/toddler and pre-school ages leads to the best outcomes regarding

language, cognitive and pre-academic skills and is better than any other quality of care combination during the two periods of interest.

Progress check 4.63

Explain Hypothesis 1 in your own words.

Year One link: Remind yourself about alternate and null hypotheses and how in an experiment the alternate hypothesis is called the 'experimental hypothesis'. Li *et al.* (2013) did not do an experiment so their hypotheses are alternate hypotheses.

Method

Participants

The study recruited 1,364 families with newborn babies in 1991 from many different US states and an attempt was made to include families of different ethnicity, race and socioeconomic status. Teenage mothers, children with disabilities, families leaving the area within three years and mothers without good spoken English were excluded.

The NICHD SECCYD was a longitudinal study starting one month after the child's birth and using observations, interviews, questionnaires and child assessments to gather data. Data were gathered so that high-quality infant/toddler and pre-school day care could be looked at with many variables taken into account. The data from the SECCYD have been used by many researchers and Li *et al.* (2013) also used the data, which was, therefore, secondary data.

> **STUDY HINT**
> You looked at primary and secondary data in clinical psychology (Chapter Two) and it is reviewed in 'Psychological skills - methods' (online). You can use Li *et al.* (2013) as an example of the use of secondary data as well as an example of using longitudinal methods.

Progress check 4.64

Why it is said that Li *et al.* (2013) used secondary data? Give one limitation of using secondary data.

Procedures

Day care quality

The Observational Record of the Care-giving Environment (ORCE) gave measurements of quality of care at 6, 15, 24, 36 and 54 months and that was the data used by Li *et al.* (2013). A score of 3.0 using averaged ORCE scores was chosen as the cut-off point between low- and high-quality day care, using 6, 15 and 24 months for infant/toddler care and 36 and 54 months for pre-school care. A score higher than 3.0 meant sensitive caring with cognitive stimulation (Vandell *et al.* 2010, cited in Li *et al.*, 2013).

Child outcomes

At 24 months:

● The Bayley Mental Developmental Index scores measured outcomes at 24 months and is a test that measured cognitive developmental status, which links with IQ score, so was used as a measure of IQ.

At 54 months:

● The Woodcock-Johnson Memory for Sentences measured short-term memory in the 54-month-old children.
● Two tests measured language at 54 months.
● Learning and identification skills were measured using the Woodcock-Johnson Letter-Word Identification.
● Skills in analysing and solving maths problems were measured using the Woodcock-Johnson Applied Problems.

Li *et al.* (2013) found that the best outcomes regarding cognitive, language and pre-academic skills are if a child has high-quality early and pre-school day care rather than high-quality in just one of the periods.

Other variables

Child race, gender, birth order, temperament, maternal attitudes to child-rearing, maternal age and educational level and paternal educational level were all considered. They measured at 1 month and at 24 months child health, maternal separation anxiety, maternal depression, maternal employment status and family income needs. It was interesting that child temperament was taken into account to consider individual differences.

Analysis

In order to analyse the data, groups were developed and then some matching took place with the aim to control for confounding variables such as the 'other variables' listed above.

1 First there was division into day care quality:
   - Infant/toddler high-quality care regardless of pre-school quality was 'early high'.
   - Infant/toddler low-quality care regardless of pre-school quality was 'early low'.
   - Pre-school care that was high-quality regardless of infant/toddler care was 'late high'.
   - Pre-school care that was low-quality regardless of infant/toddler care was 'late low'.
2 Then to test the effects of the different combinations of care, there was division:
   - Low-quality care at both infant/toddler and pre-school ages was 'low-low'.
   - High-quality care at infant/toddler age with low-quality pre-school care was 'high-low'.
   - Low-quality care at infant/toddler age with high-quality pre-school care was 'low-high'.
   - High-quality care at infant/toddler age with high-quality pre-school care was 'high-high'.

Progress check 4.65

Explain what Li et al. (2013) meant by 'high-low' and 'early high' in their categories.

3 The researchers then sorted out groups to test to enable contrasts to be made looking at the difference in quality of care at the two different ages (24 months and 54 months).

Hypothesis 1

Children at 54 months with just high-quality early care but not high-quality late care will not have higher scores regarding improvements in the skills of interest compared with those having low-quality care at both ages. Also high-quality care at the infant/toddler stage will have improved cognitive outcomes at 24 months.
   - The hypothesis needs to look at 'early high' compared with 'early low' at 24 months and 'high-low' compared with 'low-low' at 54 months.

It is worth spending a little while sorting out the groups in Li et al. (2013) to make sure they are clear. When

there is a hyphen this gives the early quality care first and the later care second. For example, high-low means the early care was high-quality and the later care was low-quality. When there is no hyphen the first word indicates whether the care is early (infant/toddler) or late (pre-school age) and the second word shows the quality. For example, 'early high' means infant/toddler care was of high quality.

Hypothesis 2

Children who have high-quality pre-school day care will do better if they also had high-quality toddler/infant day care compared with if they had low-quality toddler/infant day care. The combination of high-quality at both ages is better than if just the pre-school day care quality is high. Also high-quality care in the pre-school years will improve cognitive language and pre-academic outcomes at 54 months.
   - The hypothesis needs to look at 'late high' compared with 'late low' at 54 months and 'high-high' compared with 'low-high' at 54 months.

Hypothesis 3

High-quality care at *both* infant/toddler and pre-school ages leads to the best outcomes regarding language, cognitive and pre-academic skills and is better than any other quality of care combination during the two periods of interest.
   - This hypothesis needs to look at 'high-high' *compared with* 'low-low' children, 'high-high' *compared with* 'high-low' children and 'high-high' *compared with* 'low-high' children (all at 54 months).
4 This means seven contrasts have to be considered but in fact this is just six as one of the contrasts ('high-high *compared with* low-high' children at 54 months) is required for two of the hypotheses. Li et al. (2013) looked at 'other variables' to see what the likelihood would be of a child being in the different groups.
5 For each of the contrasts (where one group is compared with another group, such as 'high-low' children compared with 'low-low' children), individuals were matched as far as possible using the 'other variables' in a bid to iron out bias from family situation, temperament and other such factors.

Results

Li et al. (2013) took into account many variables, such as maternal depression and ethnicity, but only gender and number of children in each group are given here, as well as the scores arrived at for the different groups for the different measures. Table 4.39 shows some of the scores and variables in Li et al. (2013).

Table 4.39 Scores* and variables: Li *et al.* (2013)

Variable	Infant/toddler		Pre-school		Both stages			
	Early low	Early high	Late low	Late high	Low-low	High-low	Low-high	High-high
Cognitive development at 24 months	0.02	0.32	0.09	0.23	−0.04	0.34	0.15	0.39
Memory for sentences at 54 months	–	–	−0.05	0.27	−0.11	0.19	0.05	0.29
Language comprehension at 54 months	–	–	−0.14	0.36	−0.17	0.10	0.12	0.48
Letter word identification at 54 months	–	–	−0.10	0.35	−0.17	0.10	0.14	0.48
Applied problems at 54 months	–	–	−0.11	0.30	0.19	0.06	0.10	0.43
Sample size (N)	475	412	511	474	251	162	139	186
Gender % male	50%	49%	48%	48%	51%	43%	44%	51%

*Scores are means (and % male as well as number of children in each group)

Progress check 4.66

Table 4.39 gives the scores and some variables relating to gender. What percentage of the children with high-quality care in the pre-school period were female?

Control variables

Li *et al.* (2013) found differences between the groups on certain variables such as mean family income-to-needs at one month being 3.88 for the 'high-high' group and being 2.66 for the 'low-low' group, which is a significant difference (p<.001). However, Li *et al.* (2013) did careful matching on variables and felt they had reduced bias that might come from 'other variables'. They felt that they had succeeded in controlling the variables of interest enough that they could use their findings to relate them to high-quality day care and the effects of it, focusing on two time periods. Table 4.40 shows standardised mean differences after matching.

Table 4.40 Standardised mean differences matched sample: Li *et al.* (2013)

Variable	H1: Quality of infant/toddler care		H2: Quality of pre-school care		H3: Quality of infant and pre-school care		
Age measured	Early high vs Early low 24 months	High-low vs Low-low 54 months	Late high vs Late low 54 months	High-high vs Low-high 54 months	High-high vs Low-low 54 months	High-high vs High-low 54 months	High-high vs Low-high 54 months
Cognitive	0.28***	–	–	–	–	–	–
Memory	–	0.20*	0.05	0.10	0.16	−0.06	0.10
Language	–	0.08	0.19***	0.10	0.35***	0.21**	0.10
Reading	–	0.09	0.28***	0.20*	0.17*	0.17	0.20*
Maths	–	0.17	0.22***	0.16	0.28***	0.15	0.16

*p<.01 **p<.05 ***p<.001

Progress check 4.67

Using the information in Table 4.40 identify two groups that showed a significant difference of p<.001 in one of the measures.

Hypothesis 1

The first part of Hypothesis 1 was that quality of infant/toddler care related to child cognitive outcomes at 24 months. A significant positive association was found. After adjusting for the 'other variables', results showed that high-quality infant/toddler care and not low-quality infant/toddler care gave a 0.28 cognitive score (standardised mean difference) at 24 months. This finding is shown in column one scores in Table 4.40.

The second part of Hypothesis 1 was that the positive effect of high-quality care shown at 24 months would be lost if there was not also high-quality care at the pre-school age. The idea that early gains from high-quality infant/toddler day care are lost if there is no subsequent high-quality pre-school day care is confirmed by the data except for the 'memory' category. At 54 months the memory performance of the high-low group was 0.20 compared with the low-low group, which was significant at p.05. So memory gains from high-quality infant/toddler day care continued in the pre-school years even though the pre-school care was not high quality. The other three measures – language, reading and maths – did not show significant differences according to whether there was high-quality infant/toddler care or not, which was what Hypothesis 1 predicted. This finding is shown in column two scores in Table 4.40.

Hypothesis 2

Hypothesis 2 stated that children who have high-quality pre-school day care will do better in cognitive and academic outcomes. Also Hypothesis 2 said that children who have high-quality pre-school day care do better if they also have infant/toddler high-quality care than if they had infant/toddler low-quality care.

When considering high-quality versus low-quality pre-school day care and comparing the scores, it was found that memory outcomes at 54 months do not support the hypothesis that those in high-quality pre-school day care do better than those in low-quality pre-school day care. However, in language (0.19 difference), reading (0.28 difference) and maths (0.22 difference) the first part of Hypothesis 2 is supported and all three figures are significant at p.001. This finding is shown in column three scores in Table 4.40.

The second part of Hypothesis 2 is not supported for memory (0.10 difference) and language (0.10 difference), but is supported for reading (0.20 difference, significant at p.05) and partly for maths (0.16 difference, significant at p.10). This finding is shown in column four scores in Table 4.40.

Hypothesis 3

Hypothesis 3 holds that the best outcomes are when both periods of time (infant/toddler and pre-school) involve high-quality day care, which is better than any other combination.

The findings suggest that the best positive effects shown from day care are in the high-high group compared with the low-low group, which goes with the prediction. In language (0.35 difference) and maths (0.28 difference) there was a significant difference in the high-high group compared with the low-low group, but when looking at the other combinations there was not much significance.

Discussion

Hypothesis 1: testing the effects of quality of care in the infant/toddler period

At 24 months high-quality care in the infant/toddler period was positively related to higher cognitive development scores than when quality of care was low in that period. High-quality care in the infant/toddler period was also positively related to better memory scores at 54 months than low-quality care was.

Hypothesis 2: testing the effects of quality of care in the pre-school period

Children having high-quality care in the pre-school period had higher language, reading and maths scores at 54 months of age. Those who had high-quality infant/toddler day care as well as high-quality pre-school day care scored better on reading (and to an extent maths) than those with low-quality infant/toddler day care, even though they had high-quality pre-school day care.

Hypothesis 3: testing the combination of quality of care in the two periods

Those who did best on the measures used were the children who experienced high-quality day care both when in the infant/toddler period and when in the pre-school period. This was compared with those who did not have high-quality care in either period. Those who had one experience of high-quality care, either in the infant/ toddler period or in the pre-school period seemed to do as well as each other, although infant/toddler high-quality care seemed to help memory at 54 months and pre-school high-quality care (in the absence of high-quality early care) seemed to help with language, reading and maths.

General findings

- Li *et al.* (2013) were interested in the timing of the development of certain skills and felt that their finding about memory being helped by early high-quality care went with findings of others that cognitive functions develop early.
- An important finding, however, was that early high-quality care is more helpful if it is followed by pre-school high-quality care too. There is the suggestion that early good quality care does not protect a child against later experiences.
- Li *et al.* (2013) provide evidence for high-quality day care being needed through the early years up to school age and they support others, such as Pianta *et al.* (2009, cited in Li *et al.*, 2013), who said that low child/adult ratios and skilled caregivers are needed throughout the early years to support the need for high-quality day care.
- If there is not enough funding for high-quality day care for the infant/toddler period and the pre-school period, then it would be more beneficial to support the pre-school period.

> **STUDY HINT**
> Li *et al.*'s (2013) study might seem rather academic and focused on the development of a child's skills. However, the researchers also made it clear that the study had practical applications too, as it could be used to provide evidence of where funding for early years care should be directed.

Evaluation

Strengths

- Li *et al.* (2013) mention that children having high-quality day care and those having low-quality day care are likely to come from family backgrounds that are different, such as having families with a higher income or families with 'more child-centred beliefs'. The SECCYD observed children in day care and so the families were self-selected in that the children were in the particular type of day care observed. Li *et al.* (2013) acknowledged this issue and took steps to match the children in the comparison groups regarding the 'other variables' they identified. This meant confounding variables were controlled for. They used weighting in the matching to make the comparison groups as similar as possible regarding 'other variables'. Note that this matching also gave limitations when concluding from the findings.
- They were able to use a large sample and the numbers in each of their groups were quite large. The sample came from different US states and was a wide one in many respects. There was some generalisability because of this and the size of the study, as well as the different ways data were collected in the study. There were a lot of data from different sources, which helps generalisability.

Weaknesses

- Although there was matching to cater for the effects of other variables that go along with whether a child receives good-quality day care, Li *et al.* (2013) thought that generalising the findings was still in doubt because only the variables that were measured and controlled for in the samples were considered. Li *et al.* (2013) point out that the NICHD SECCYD does not use a representative sample, as they found out when they tried to match their comparison groups. Sample characteristics are likely to limit generalisability.

> **STUDY HINT**
> You can use Li *et al.* (2013) as an example of a longitudinal study or of day care effectiveness when evaluating the NICHD SECCYD.

- Li *et al.* (2013) point out that they could only consider variables that were observed and were observable. Other variables like selection bias could not be controlled in Li *et al.*'s (2013) use of the SECCYD data.
- Li *et al.* (2013) put the quality of care into categories (high and low quality), which meant losing the variation of types of day care. This meant there was a lack of validity as different day care provision was put into 'high' or 'low' on the basis of scoring.
- Although there was a lot of careful matching, different children were in each group and although one of the variables used for matching was temperament, there are likely to be individual differences in the children that were not controlled for.

In your course you have to learn about van IJzendoorn and Kroonenberg (1988) and one contemporary study from a choice of Cassibba *et al.* (2013), Gagnon-Oosterwaal *et al.* (2012) and Li *et al.* (2013).

1 Compare two of these studies with regard to their procedure. **(8 marks)**

2 To what extent do two of these studies contribute to what is known about child development? **(16 marks)**

Summary

- You have to learn about the classic study in child psychology in your course, which is van IJzendoorn and Kroonenberg (1988), and their meta-analysis of studies using the strange situation to look for cross-cultural patterns of attachment.
- You need to study one of three contemporary studies given in your course in child psychology. One study is Cassibba *et al.* (2013), who looked at attachment the Italian way, using meta-analysis and also considering cross-cultural patterns of attachment. The second study is Gagnon-Oosterwaal *et al.* (2012), who looked at international adoptees. This study links to one of the key questions in your course. The third study is Li *et al.* (2013), who looked at the timing of high-quality day care for children and their development. This study also links to the key question found on the accompanying website.

Key question in child psychology

For your study of child psychology, as in other topic areas in your course, you need to prepare one key question that relates to what you have studied, is a question for society, and can be explained or answered using concepts, theories and/or research from child psychology.

Two key questions for society are suggested for your course, but you may choose any key question. The two key questions suggested are:

- What issues should parents take into account when deciding about day care for their child?
- Is international adoption good or bad for a child?

The content section of this chapter has explained and discussed these issues and they are also considered in the studies section as Li *et al.* (2013) (page 461) focused on day care and Gagnon-Oosterwaal *et al.* (2012) (page 465) focused on international adoption.

 The key question of whether international adoption is good or bad for the child can be found on the website accompanying this book.

What issues should parents take into account when deciding about day care for their child?

Outlining the key question

> **Explore**
> You can find out quite a lot about the pros and cons of day care using the internet. Here is a link to get you started: www.theguardian.com/lifeandstyle/2010/oct/02/nurseries-childcare-pre-school-cortisol

Day care is any form of care for a child where the parents or family of the child are not involved, but which is daily rather than overnight. In the USA it tends to be called 'child care' but is called day care in this chapter. It is a form of deprivation because the child is separated from its attachment figure, so detrimental effects might be expected.

The US Census says 16 per cent of children under one year old are enrolled in child care centres, 26 per cent of children aged 1 to 2 years and 33 per cent of children under 5 are cared for by non-relatives. In Canada it is said that over 70 per cent of children are in a child care arrangement, which is a high figure (figures from the Hanen Centre).

In England, 78 per cent of all families with children aged 0 to 14 years said they used child care when asked about their 'recent term-time week' and this figure includes all children up to the age of 15. In England 63 per cent of families had used day care and early years provision and the parents with children aged 3 to 4 years were the ones most likely to have used formal child care. These English figures are from a 2012–13 UK Department for Education survey of 6,393 parents with children aged under 15 (see link below).

Clearly day care is an issue for society as it affects a great many children and if there are issues around day care that are negative it would be useful for a society to take steps to put them right. If there are positive aspects of day care then it would be good to build on good practice to enhance children's development. There are different types of day care and parents have to choose what they feel is best. For example, day care centres may seem impersonal and childminders might seem to offer more of a 'home' experience. Another factor is the quality of the day care, with day care centres sometimes providing more resources to offer more stimulation. There are of course other considerations, such as cost and convenience, but this key question focuses on a parent choosing day care, taking the advantages and disadvantages of day care for the child into account. It was interesting that the survey of parents in England referred to here (2014) found that '58% of parents rated the overall quality of local child care provision as very or fairly good' (p. 13). This suggests that parents do look for quality of day care. In the survey 39 per cent said they had too little information about child care in their area, which suggests parents do wish to know what to take into account when choosing day care for their children. 'What issues should parents take into account when deciding about day care for their child?' is therefore a key question for society and for parents.

Explore

 An article published in 2010 looks at some of the issues covered in this section:
www.reuters.com/article/2010/05/14/us-daycare-usa-idUSTRE64D0LT20100514

Explore

You can find statistics and information about early years child care using the government website, including survey data from providers and parents. Here is a link to the parent data (2012–13, published January 2014):
www.gov.uk/government/uploads/system/uploads/attachment_data/file/275992/SFR06-2014_Childcare_and_Early_Years_Survey_of_Parents_2012-13_final.pdf

STUDY HINT

You will cover a key question in each of the topic areas in your course. You may find it helpful to take your notes for the key question in each chapter and bring them together for revision, so that you have a 'template' for learning about each key question. The template should include knowing what the question is and why it is a key question for society as well as concepts, theories and research to explain and inform the question.

Using concepts, theories and/or research from child psychology to explain the key question

STUDY HINT

When discussing a key question you may find yourself 'changing' the wording of the question slightly, such as when discussing advantages and disadvantages of day care or discussing good- and poor-quality day care. Always keep the actual wording of the key question in mind when making notes and preparing for the exam, perhaps by writing it down and referring to it often when making notes, to keep yourself on track. Similarly, when writing about your key question, refer to it periodically to keep yourself on track.

An important issue for a parent is whether the child will benefit from being in day care. Studies suggest that day care can help the child so a parent can choose day care not only to suit their situation but also because their child will benefit. The EPPE study in the UK (page 397) showed that day care improved intellectual development as well as social/behavioural development. However, other studies point to disadvantages, such as if a child is there too long, or if the quality of the day care is inadequate (e.g. the NICHD SECCYD study, page 394). For example, the SECCYD study found that children had fewer behaviour problems when younger if they had attended day care, but they found more behavioural problems at the age of four and a half years. The children in day care did, however, develop good language and cognitive development skills.

A parent might think about how long to leave their child in day care. In the first year of life up to twenty hours is enough according to Belsky, who found that too long in day care could be detrimental under the age of one year. So the age of the child might affect the parent's decision-making. The EPPE study found that full-time day care did not have better outcomes than part-time day care so a parent might take this into account and choose part-time day care if they are choosing day care to help the child.

Explore

There is an article about day care and Belsky's ideas that you might find interesting as it raises questions about day care that might suit this key question. You can access it using this link:
www.theatlantic.com/past/docs/issues/88aug/babe.htm

Another important issue is the quality of the day care. There is evidence that high–quality day care is better for a child. Good-quality day care involves a child being asked questions and encouraged, staff showing a positive attitude and having physical contact with the child as well as reading books to them and engaging with them. There should be a low staff–child ratio, which means a child gets good attention from the caregiver in the day care setting and staff should be well-qualified and knowledgeable about child development. These are things that a parent can look for when choosing day care for their child. Li *et al.* (2013) found that high-quality day care helped at the infant/toddler stage (which helped memory) and at the pre-school stage (which helped language, maths and reading skills). Low-quality day care at either period did not have the same effects.

The age of the child when accessing the day care is another consideration. Li *et al.* (2013) found that high-quality day care in the infant/toddler period led to better short-term memory skills and the improvement lasted up to the end of the pre-school period, even if the child during the pre-school years had lower-quality day care. This suggests that early day care can be good for memory skills no matter what the later quality of day care is. They also found that high-quality pre-school care related to higher cognitive, language and pre-academic skills, so high-quality later care is also recommended. Li *et al.* (2013), using the SECCYD data, found that the best day care experiences regarding cognitive, language and pre-academic skills came when both the infant/toddler and pre-school periods involved high-quality day care.

Parents could look out for day care provision where parental involvement is encouraged. The EPPE study found that good-quality day care involved the parents a lot so that would be a way of making a decision about which day care provision to choose.

Parents might choose regulated day care. The SECCYD found that the more of the recommended standards such as adult–child ratio and staff education level were met, the more positive the care giving. This might mean parents choose regulated day care provision where standards should be met and are checked.

Another issue a parent could take into account is whether they can plan the day care sufficiently to alleviate any separation distress. Deprivation is the term used when a child has been separated from its caregiver. It has been shown that deprivation in early infancy can lead to mental health problems in adulthood as well as other problem behaviour, though day care should not include sufficient separation to lead to such problems. Negative effects can be reduced by explaining the need for the separation to the child if he/she is old enough, or by preparing the child for the separation. Robertson filmed a child in hospital and showed how very upsetting the experience was and he and his wife then fostered children while they were separated from their mothers, showing that with planning and

preparation a child could be much less upset and distressed by the experience. If a parent can plan for the separation, such as introducing the child to the day care setting a few times before leaving them there, that might help them in practical ways when making the choice.

Some parents might be choosing day care for children with special needs. Booth and Kelly (2002) used the NICHD data and found that day care was not any better than children cared for by their mothers at home, though it was not thought to be harmful either. Booth and Kelly did find that children with special needs over one year old when they started day care were better in managing their own behaviour than children with special needs who started day care earlier. Again, there is a question over day care in the first year, using the SECCYD data.

> **STUDY HINT**
>
> Most of the information given here can be backed by evidence given earlier in this chapter. Be sure to give evidence for statements that you make and note that not all of the evidence is repeated here. You can bring in new material too: Booth and Kelly (2002) is not a study given elsewhere in this chapter. You must stick to what is in child psychology in your course but you can bring in evidence for a key question if it helps that key question.

Parents could consider the temperament of the child as that can affect their decision. Belsky and Pluess (2011) found that children with the 'difficult' temperament of 'negative emotionality', if they experienced low-quality day care, were more likely to show externalising behaviour (aggression and so on) than those who experienced high-quality day care. This compared their externalising behaviour with children with less difficult temperaments. This means that choosing high-quality day care is particularly important if a child has a 'difficult' temperament.

> **STUDY HINT**
>
> When you are learning the content for your course, keep your key question in mind and make notes as you learn so that you have prepared an explanation for your key question using concepts, theories and/or research that you have covered.

Progress check 4.68

Explain two points that parents might take into account when choosing day care for their child.

Progress check 4.69

Give two pieces of evidence that suggest that international adoption is good for a child.

Test yourself

With regard to one key question for society, assess how far child psychology can help to answer and inform that question. **(20 marks)**

Summary

- You need to cover one key question for society where concepts, theories and research from child psychology can help to inform the key question.
- One example in your course asks what issues parents should take into account when deciding about day care for their child. The other example asks whether international adoption is good or bad for a child. You can, however, choose your own key question.

Practical investigation in child psychology

You must carry out a questionnaire, interview or observation that focuses on an area that is relevant to what you have covered in this chapter on child psychology. You will devise your own practical and must plan it so that the experience helps you to learn and enables you to answer questions about your practical.

What you need to do for the practical investigation

Your practical investigation must gather quantitative data, though it can gather qualitative data as well or you can convert qualitative data into quantitative data for analysis. In the questionnaire outlined as an example practical investigation on the accompanying website only quantitative data are gathered.

Your must use the relevant test for your practical. In the questionnaire chosen for this book, found on the website, which focuses on a relationship, a correlation test is required and Spearman's is the one chosen.

Your investigation must include a research question/hypothesis, research method, sampling, ethical considerations, data collection tools, data analysis, results and discussion. You should also look at the strengths and weaknesses of the practical and describe possible improvements.

 These features of a practical investigation are described briefly in the worked-through example on the website accompanying this book.

Test yourself

You will have done a practical investigation in child psychology using a questionnaire, an interview or an observation. Evaluate your practical investigation in child psychology in terms of reliability, validity and generalisability. **(16 marks)**

Summary

- You have to carry out a practical investigation using either a questionnaire, an interview or an observation.
- Your practical must cover an area you have studied in child psychology for your course.
- You can collect qualitative data, but for analysis purposes you need quantitative data, so either collect that as well or convert your qualitative data into quantitative data, perhaps using content analysis.
- You need to know about the hypothesis/research question, sampling, ethical considerations and data collection tools.
- You also need to focus on data analysis and the results of your practical investigation.
- As part of the results you need to use the relevant inferential test from the four you have covered in your course, so be sure that your practical investigation will suit one of the tests.
- You need to be ready to discuss your practical investigation, including giving strengths and weaknesses and, importantly, being able to consider possible improvements.

Chapter Five: Health psychology

General overview

Health psychology is an application in psychology, which means that theories and studies are applied to issues of concern to society and the individual. It includes views on health from different areas in psychology, including biological, social and cognitive psychology. In your study of health psychology you will focus on substance abuse and you need to know about issues around drug-taking such as addiction, tolerance and withdrawal. You will look at biological and learning factors when explaining substance misuse. Health psychology is also about promoting good health, and the specification requires you to consider two ways of treating drug addiction as well as an 'antidrug' campaign. You will look in depth at three drugs — heroin, alcohol and nicotine — including their effects and how they work.

You are required to know two studies in detail as well as one key question in the area you are studying, and you will also carry out a practical investigation as in other topic areas you have studied. The methodology section of this chapter considers how animals and humans are used to study drugs, and asks you to know about the ethics of using animal experiments and of using humans to study drugs. You will also look at cross-cultural research related to drug misuse. Health psychology is a large field and can include such topics as stress, sleep, beliefs about health and attitudes to health, but your course looks only at the topic of substance misuse.

Health psychology studies issues such as what health professionals recommend in the way of prevention of ill health and how patients and professionals interact, such as focusing on listening and hearing skills. There is focus on how patients deal with illness and when someone might go for professional advice about their health. Health psychologists focus on responses to illness and public health concerns as well as health provision. They also consider health risk behaviours, which are those that damage someone's health, such as smoking and poor diet. They focus on psychological theories and how findings from studies can be put into practice to help changes in health-related behaviours. You can see that health psychology covers a wide range of issues and behaviours. Your course focuses on just one area of concern, substance misuse, including heroin, alcohol and nicotine as examples. You need to know, however, that health psychology covers many more areas.

Health psychology is about promoting good health. It focuses on biological issues such as, with reference to substance abuse, addiction, tolerance and dependence. It focuses on cognitive processes that affect health behaviours, such as issues around self-belief and modifying health beliefs. It also focuses on social factors such as the impact of others on health-related behaviours and interactions between health professionals and patients, including how to improve such interactions, always focusing on improving health.

> ### Explore
> You can use the internet to look at what a health psychologist's job is like. This will help you to understand what health psychology covers, though you will only be doing some of what it entails. Here is a link to help:
> www.nhscareers.nhs.uk/explore-by-career/psychological-therapies/careers-in-psychological-therapies/psychologist/health-psychologist/

There are antidrugs campaigns that show how serious the issue is for society.

> ### STUDY HINT
> Progress check answers can be found on the website accompanying this book.

Study of interest

Madruga *et al.* (2012) carried out a study in Brazil looking at early life experiences, focusing on exposure to violence, and how this related to substance misuse in adulthood. From previous research they conclude that early experiences relate to later substance misuse and there might be a role for depression. Madruga *et al.* (2012) used a national alcohol survey with 1,880 Brazilian participants aged from 20 to 60 years to look at early exposure to violence and later use of psychoactive substances. They used random sampling from all Brazilian households. They found that nearly 20 per cent of the sample had witnessed violence during childhood or adolescence and more than 8 per cent said they had been victims of violence. Madruga *et al.* (2012) found a statistically significant link between alcohol or illegal substance misuse in adulthood and early exposure to violence. They also looked at depression and found depression explained some of the link between alcohol dependence and the early experience of violence but they did not find a statistically significant association between illegal substance misuse and depression. The conclusion was that there seemed to be a link between 'adverse' early life experiences and 'susceptibility to substance misuse' in adulthood, which might link partly to depression. They suggest that intervening when children are exposed to violence is a necessary focus to prevent later substance misuse and problems with alcohol.

STUDY HINT

Madruga *et al.* (2012), after cluster sampling, used random sampling from the chosen Brazilian households and their sample should, therefore, be representative of the population. You could make a note that you can use this study as an example of random sampling when discussing sampling techniques.

STUDY HINT

In health psychology you will look at explanations for substance misuse not only from biological psychology but also from learning theories. When an explanation draws on how learning affects behaviour it links to how our experiences explain our development. Madruga *et al.* (2012) suggest that early exposure to violence affects later substance misuse and their study, therefore, is about development. You need to be able to discuss health psychology in relation to both individual differences and developmental psychology and Madruga *et al.* (2012) can be useful in that respect.

Progress check 5.1

State how two areas you have covered in your course relate to health psychology.

Summary of learning objectives

Content

You need to know about issues relating to taking drugs, including addiction, tolerance, physical and psychological dependency and withdrawal. Then you need to know about two explanations of drug addiction. The three drugs you need to focus on are alcohol, heroin and nicotine. One explanation should be biological and should include the mode of action – you need to know one biological explanation for each of the three drugs. The other explanation should be a learning one and again you need one learning explanation for each of the three drugs. You can use the same explanation for more than one of the three drugs. As well as explanations, you need two treatments for each of the three drugs, though a treatment can apply to more than one drug. One learning treatment must be aversion therapy. Finally, you need to learn about one antidrug campaign and the psychological strategies behind it.

Individual differences and developmental psychology

All topic areas in your course involve you considering two special issues in psychology and these are individual differences and developmental psychology. In each topic area you will find reference to where these issues are within the content or the key question. You need to be able to make links between these two issues and areas that reflect them. Each issue has its own symbol in this textbook to alert you to these links. Individual differences refers to how people might be inherently different, such as in their personality or intelligence. Gender too can give individual differences and other genetic or biological differences can do that too. Developmental psychology is an area of study focusing on how we develop from before birth to adolescence and also beyond and into old age.

Year One link: Year One topic areas consider both individual differences and developmental issues in the content sections. Year Two applications do the same.

Individual differences

In health psychology the link that must be learned about is:

- how biological and social factors in drug misuse can include effects dependent on the individual such as personality.

Developmental psychology

In health psychology the link that must be learned about is:

- how social interactions during development can lead to drug misuse, including learning.

Method

You will be used to learning about method in each topic area. Health psychology has method for you to cover. The main methods for health psychology are how animals and humans are used in the study of drugs. You need to know about the use of animal experiments to study drugs and the ethics of using animals to study drugs. You also need to know two research methods that use humans to study drugs, and the ethics of using human participants to study drugs. You have to cover cross-cultural research, including nature–nurture issues, related to drug misuse.

Year One link: The use of and ethics of using animals in experiments to gather data was covered in learning theories in your course.

As with other topic areas in health psychology you need to know how data are analysed in psychology. You need to know about analysis of quantitative data using measures of central tendency, frequency tables, measures of dispersion (range and standard deviation) as well as analysis of quantitative data using inferential statistics. Issues relating to inferential statistics include the four tests in your course (Chi squared, Mann Whitney U, Wilcoxon and Spearman's) as well as issues of statistical significance, levels of measurement and critical and observed values. Analysis of qualitative data is required including thematic analysis and the use of grounded theory. All of this material except grounded theory has been covered before in Year One of your course – and reviewed in clinical psychology too. Grounded theory was covered in clinical psychology (page 172).

Year One link: Analysis of quantitative data using descriptive and inferential statistics and analysis of qualitative data using thematic analysis has all been covered in Year One, so be sure to revise the material for Year Two studies.

STUDY HINT

There are some terms in this section but most should not be new to you if you have already covered health psychology, so they are not defined here. Use the Glossary to check on their meaning if you need to.

Studies

The classic study you need in health psychology is Olds and Milner (1954), which is about the effects of electrical stimulation of the brain, focusing on biological psychology.

You will choose one contemporary study from three, all of which are covered in this chapter. The three are:

- Mundt *et al.* (2012), a study that looks at alcohol use in adolescents and the effects of peers.
- Dixit *et al.* (2012), a study that focuses on biosocial causes for alcohol and risk behaviour.
- Pengpid *et al.* (2013), a study that looks at alcohol problems and an intervention.

Key question

You have a choice of key question to study. The course suggests that, focusing on how health psychology can help to explain or deal with such an issue, you choose from looking at how to encourage stopping smoking or to what extent government intervention in health-related behaviour is appropriate, compared with freedom of choice. However, you can choose any issue.

Practical investigation within health psychology

You have to carry out one practical research exercise within health psychology and there is a choice about using a questionnaire, interview or content analysis. You will do that within your learning, so it is hard to foresee in this book what you will have done.

A practical investigation in health psychology is provided in the online material using a content analysis and focusing on drug-related references in pop songs with the idea that people are influenced by the media through social learning so such learning might affect behaviour.

You need to gather data relevant to topics you have studied in health psychology and your practical investigation must be ethical throughout. You will also write up some of what is needed in a psychology report – the research question and hypothesis, sampling and data collection tools as part of the method, data analysis, results and discussion. The data have to be quantitative for analysis though can involve qualitative data as well, and you need to use an inferential test when analysing your data. You also have to consider strengths and weaknesses of your practice investigation and possible improvements.

Year One link: You will have looked at questionnaire and interview as research methods in social psychology and at content analysis in your Year One study of learning theories. Your practical will focus on issues you have studied in health psychology but the research methods are the same.

Issues and debates

The 11 issues and debates chosen for your course are: ethics; practical issues in research design; reductionism; comparing explanations; psychology as a science; culture and gender; nature–nurture; how psychology has developed over time; issues of social control; using psychology in society; and issues around socially sensitive research.

Chapter Seven in this book looks at issues and debates in detail so they are not covered in this chapter.

> **STUDY HINT**
> The issues and debates appear for your course in each topic area for Year One and Year Two, in the same order, in the specification. For each topic area in the specification there are examples against each of the issues and debates to show how material from that topic area can illustrate the issues or debate. You can use the specification for ideas relevant to each of the issues and debates.

> **STUDY HINT**
> Make the summary of learning objectives into a checklist. Table 5.1 gives a suggested list. However, you could add detail, which would help your learning.

Table 5.1 What you need to know for health psychology

You need to know about:	
How health psychology can be understood using biological, social and cognitive psychology and that it is about promoting good health	The use of animals in laboratory experiments to study drugs and the ethics of using animals to study drugs
Addiction, tolerance, physical and psychological dependency and withdrawal as issues in drug-taking	The use of humans to study drugs, including two research methods. Also the ethics of using humans to study drugs
One biological explanation including mode of action each for alcohol, nicotine and heroin	The use of cross-cultural research in health psychology related to drug misuse, including nature–nurture issues
One learning explanation each for alcohol, nicotine and heroin (one explanation can suit more than one drug)	Analysis of quantitative data, including descriptive and inferential statistics (the four tests from Year One) and related issues
Two treatments each for alcohol, nicotine and heroin. One treatment can suit more than one drug and one treatment must be aversion therapy	Analysis of qualitative data using thematic analysis and grounded theory
One antidrug campaign and the psychological strategies behind it	The classic study in child psychology is Olds and Milner (1954) and their study of brain regions
Individual differences relating to content you have covered in health psychology, including how biological and social factors in drug misuse can depend on differences between individuals, such as personality	One contemporary study from a choice of three: Mundt *et al.* (2012), Dixit *et al.* (2012) or Pengpid *et al.* (2013)
Developmental psychology linked to health psychology, including how social interactions, including learning, can lead to drug misuse	One key question that can be explained using concepts, theories and/or research from health psychology in your course, and the concepts, theories and research in question
One practical investigation focusing on an area of health psychology in your course and using either an observation, a questionnaire or a content analysis as the research method	Issues and debates (see Chapter Seven for more detail)

An introduction to health psychology

Health psychologists are interested in factors that achieve good health – not only physical aspects but also having social support, a healthy lifestyle and interests.

You need to know in general about health psychology, not just about substance misuse. This is so that you have an overview of what health psychology is about and some information has already been covered at the start of this chapter.

Your course asks you to know that health psychology understands health from a biological, social and cognitive viewpoint. Health seems obviously biological, given the medical focus; however, there are also social and cultural aspects to health psychology, such as looking at problems with relationships that affect health, and there are psychological aspects too, such as the consequences of stress. Cognition features when health psychology looks at what people believe as that can affect health behaviours, such as what people believe about the risks of smoking or drinking alcohol.

Biomedical model

The medical model is something you have probably come across if you have already studied clinical psychology. The medical model when considering mental illness refers to treating mental ill health like physical ill health – as a problem with biology where someone has 'symptoms' and there is 'treatment' that hopefully leads to a 'cure' for a 'patient'. The medical model assumes a physical problem and psychological issues are treated as physical ones – to be treated and 'cured'. An example might be to treat schizophrenia with antipsychotic medication that affects either dopamine or glutamate functioning in the belief that problems with such functioning are what are causing

the symptoms. In health psychology a medical model of health would focus on physical issues about health and ill health, such as the mode of action of heroin in the brain. Biological factors are important for health psychology; however, it is thought that they tend not to work alone, without psychological and social factors having an effect as well. A medical model alone is not usually used as the main explanation for health problems. In health psychology the biomedical model does have importance, such as when asking what causes an illness or how it should be treated.

Biopsychosocial model

Health psychology tends to see the person as having complexity, with illness not being caused by one factor. Gatchel (2004) discusses how the biomedical model is **reductionist** in focusing only on biological factors. Reductionist means focusing on parts of a situation or behaviour and this is a problem as it can mean the whole behaviour is not learned about. This is a problem with the medical model. Gatchel (2004) points to the focus on **biopsychosocial** aspects of health, which takes a more **holistic** view of health. Health concerns interactions between biological, psychological and social factors rather than being about biological aspects only.

The biopsychosocial model was developed by Engel in 1977 and aimed to pull together psychological (focusing on the mind), social (focusing on the environment) and biological (genes, medical problems).

Biology: problems with brain and body, such as brain damage or virus

Psychological: issues around learned behaviour, beliefs, stress, feeling pain and coping

Social: issues affecting health, such as class, employment and race

The biopsychosocial model of health and illness as Engel saw it (1977)

Schneiderman *et al.* (2005) focuses on **stressors** and how they affect mood, behaviour and health, showing that there is a clear interaction between psychosocial stressors and biological disease. Schneiderman *et al.* (2005) point out that stress relates to disease depending on the number of stressors, their nature and how long they last.

How stress relates to disease also depends on an individual's biology, such as their genes, on their psychosocial resources such as support, and on coping mechanisms they have learned. It can be seen by this range of factors that biological, social and cognitive/ psychological factors affect someone's health.

Year One link: You learned about reductionism (and holism) when looking at learning theories and psychology as science, so recall what you learned about knowledge coming from a reductionist viewpoint there.

Year One link: You have covered biological, cognitive and social psychology and can draw on your understanding of their main focus and how they can be applied to understanding health.

Explanation
Reductionist means breaking something down into parts to study it and believing that by putting together the knowledge about the parts there can be knowledge of the behaviour. An **holistic** view means the belief that looking at parts to understand something will not be successful in understanding it fully because the 'whole is more than the sum of the parts'.

Definition
Stressors are things in the environment or inside someone that can cause stress, such as noise in the environment or a trauma for an individual.

Illness is seen as a combination of biological factors, such as genes, and social factors, such as family relationships and social support. Cognitive and behavioural factors like stress and beliefs are also investigated. Cognitive – behavioural therapy, for example, focuses on negative automatic thoughts and helping someone to change these to more helpful thinking patterns. Depression and anxiety in particular are linked to what could be called faulty thinking patterns. This means that they are faulty for that individual, because certain thought patterns can lead to negative emotions.

Health as a continuum

Health is not really something you have (e.g. good health) or don't have (e.g. poor health). Sometimes someone is healthier than at other times and some people might have reasonable health but behave in a way that is likely to lead to poor health

(such as in their eating or exercise habits, or smoking and drinking). Health psychology is involved before ill health begins, such as looking at people's beliefs about eating, exercise, smoking and drinking alcohol, as well as when ill health might start to develop, looking at, for example, seeking help. Health psychology also looks at how someone adapts to illness, the resulting behaviour change and the impact of social support, as well as perception of pain.

Health psychologists are interested in how health issues affect individuals as well, such as how one person finds a lump and goes to the doctor where another person does not, or two people have a heart attack and one has another later, but the other does not. The health psychologist is interested in factors affecting such differences, such as thoughts, feelings, expectations, learning, social norms, peer pressure, coping and social support.

Explore
You can find a lot more about health psychology, the biomedical and the biopsychosocial model using the internet. Here is a link to help you to start:
www.zeepedia.com/read.php?introduction_to_health_ psychology_the_background_to_biomedical_model_health_ psychology&b=89&c=4

Health promotion

Health promotion is of great interest because not only is it good for someone to be healthy, but it is also cost-effective for a society to promote good health. It is cheaper to prevent health problems than to treat them. For example, health psychologists are involved in antismoking campaigns and promoting good diets. They also help to promote good health by working with individuals on behaviour change. Some are involved with giving advice to a wider audience, such as institutions and workplaces.

Promoting good health requires clear communication and education. Health psychologists work with doctors and other health professionals to help them to communicate clearly with their patients and clients, and to ensure that there is understanding of what is needed to achieve and maintain good health. For example, it has been found that a patient in a doctor's consulting room will not remember much of what is said, so it is important for a doctor to ensure that there is good understanding, for example, by repeating the main points and questioning the patient. Promotional campaigns are also about education and communication.

You also need to know that health psychology is about promoting good health, which is why in your course you are asked to learn about one antidrug campaign. As has been shown, health psychology is very interested in prevention of ill health. A government too will be interested in preventing ill health because it is costly in terms of health care as well as lost days of work and for economic reasons. Governments, charities and other bodies put together health campaigns such as focusing on getting help for strokes very quickly and focusing on avoiding heart problems. At a global level the World Health Organization has particular 'days' focusing on different health issues. There is World TB day, 24 March, and World No Tobacco Day, 31 May, as well as World Health Day, 7 April. In your course you need to look at one health promotion campaign and it must be an antidrug campaign.

Health promotion is focused on in many ways, both general ones, such as campaigns promoting visiting your GP, and more focused ones, such as promoting smoking cessation.

> ### Explore
> You can read about an antidrug campaign in Canada using this link: www.cbc.ca/news/politics/anti-drug-campaign-a-hit-with-parents-and-teens-health-canada-says-1.2934672

> ### Explore
> Using this link you can find information about designing your own health campaign, which is about cancer risk and can focus on lifestyle factors in cancer, such as smoking. You could look at the information offered to find out about promotions and campaigns and perhaps design your own campaign to learn more. http://publications.cancerresearchuk.org/downloads/product/YSLPCH07.pdf

The work of the health psychologist

Health psychologists work with health professionals such as doctors, dentists, nurses, occupational therapists and dieticians. They may carry out clinical work themselves, such as therapy or counselling, or they may undertake research. They are often involved in health promotion campaigns and their role is as much about prevention as cure. When

carrying out research, health psychologists use research methods such as experiments, longitudinal studies, cross-sectional studies and case studies. They research any issue that might impact upon how health issues affect an individual.

It is important to note that work in the area of substance misuse is only one part of what a health psychologist might be involved in – they may also look at social support, emotional state, living conditions and diseases such as heart problems, perhaps considering genetic factors. They are interested in factors that lead to certain health problems and in how such factors can be reduced. One example would be to see how more social support could be put in place for a particular section of the population, such as the elderly. This demonstrates evidence for the biopsychosocial model in that, when considering help for an individual, the health psychologist will consider genetic background and medical features. They might also evaluate behavioural features, such as whether someone smokes, and social factors, such as social class or whether there is social support available.

> **Biomedical model**
> • Physical and biological aspects of health
> • Such as prescription drug abuse and brain effects

> **Biopsychosocial model**
> • Biological, social and psychological aspects of health
> • Such as stressors, like plane noise, affecting health

> **Health as a continuum**
> • Health from high-level wellness to premature death and between
> • From awareness, education and growth to signs, symptoms and disability

> **Health promotion and health campaigning**
> • Prevention of ill health using promotion of health
> • Such as eating no more than six grams of salt a day

Some underpinning ideas within health psychology

Progress check 5.2
Explain health psychology using two key elements.

Content in health psychology

This section is about substance misuse. It looks at issues around drug-taking (withdrawal, addiction, physical and psychological dependency and tolerance). Then three drugs, heroin, nicotine and alcohol, are used to look at explanations and treatments. You need to study two explanations for each of the three drugs (one biological explanation that includes the mode of action and one other), two ways of treating each of the three drugs, including aversion therapy, and one antidrug campaign.

Issues around drug-taking

In this section you need to look at issues around drug-taking, including addiction, physical and psychological dependency, tolerance and withdrawal. These are explained in general; however, when using examples it is useful to focus on heroin, nicotine and alcohol as they are the three drugs you have to focus on when considering explanations and treatments.

Tolerance

Tolerance means that as a **recreational drug** is taken increasingly over a period of time, more of it will be needed to obtain the feelings that were produced at first. The same dose of drug will not produce the same feeling of euphoria. This is the case with many drugs, including heroin. Tolerance goes with being physically dependent on a drug because, when people need increasing amounts to get the same high, they are likely to become physically dependent on the drug. A stage may be reached where tolerance works to the extent that no amount of the drug will achieve the resulting high, and at this point the individual will continue taking the drug simply to delay withdrawal symptoms. Tolerance is linked to addiction, which is physical dependence because, when a plateau is reached and more of the drug does not change its effects, then the person is addicted and needs the drug for normal functioning.

Explanations

A **recreational drug** is a chemical substance that is taken for feelings of euphoria and well-being that it produces. Heroin, nicotine and alcohol are recreational drugs. If they or other drugs are used for medical reasons, they are not then 'recreational'.

Tolerance, referring to drug-taking, is when people need increasing amounts of a drug to get the same high. It refers to a lowering of the response to a drug when the body adapts to the drug.

Tolerance has biological underpinning such as there might be reduced receptor response, which is receptor desensitisation, and tolerance relates to neural changes at the synapse. There are different biological mechanisms that produce tolerance. Pharmacokinetic (metabolic) tolerance refers to a decreased amount of the substance reaching the target perhaps because there are more enzymes breaking the drug down (through enzyme induction) and this leads to the drug having less of an effect. Pharmacokinetic tolerance is more likely to apply to drugs taken orally.

Pharmacodynamic tolerance refers to cells having a decreased response to the same dose of a drug (or more of the drug being required to give the same response) from, for example, a reduced receptor response due to receptor desensitisation. Or there may be reasons for changes in the action potential. There can be increased receptor firing rate. Pharmacodynamic tolerance works in different ways but always focusing on working at the cell level. Neural changes come from frequent drug use. There may be a depletion in neurotransmitters, changes in the number of receptors or receptor desensitisation.

Examples of tolerance

- A useful example is morphine. Though morphine is not a recreational drug heroin is converted to morphine in the brain, so this example of tolerance suits heroin. Morphine binds to opiate receptors, which affects production of an enzyme that releases chemicals to maintain the firing of the impulses. When morphine causes the opiate receptor to be activated a lot over time, the enzyme adapts such that morphine stops causing changes in the firing of the impulses. This means the effect of a dose of morphine lessens.

> ### Explore
> You can find out more about morphine and tolerance using this link. The material is complex but interesting. There is a main practical reason for finding out about how tolerance to morphine develops, because knowing more about how the drug works can help to develop more long-term pain-killing drugs. Tolerance is not helpful of course when it arises in painkillers. Here is the link: www.ncbi.nlm.nih.gov/pmc/articles/PMC2628209/

Year One link: In biological psychology you learned about synaptic transmission and the effects of recreational drugs at the synapse. Recall what you learned there, to help your learning of this section.

- Nicotine use quickly leads to tolerance. The body produces more acetylcholine receptors if nicotine is used over a long period, and this gives tolerance even only a few days after exposure to the drug. It is not the case that more and more nicotine is needed to give the effect so much as a plateau is reached quickly and the reaction to the nicotine is fixed. Therefore, at first smokers will need more and more nicotine to get the effects – relaxation, lowering of anxiety, higher levels of concentration and mild euphoria. This means smokers usually start to increase their use of cigarettes in a short time. They rise to a high level of consumption and then have to keep to that to get the results they want. This means that nicotine is addictive.

- When alcohol is drunk the liver produces more of an enzyme that breaks down the potentially harmful parts of alcohol, such as ethanol. This will remove those substances from the body. The liver keeps producing more and more of the enzyme as alcohol is drunk and this means quicker metabolising of the alcohol so less goes into the central nervous system and this means there is tolerance, called 'metabolic tolerance'.
- Alcohol is a GABA agonist and drinking excess alcohol affects inhibitory GABA receptors so postsynaptic cells have to adapt as there is too much inhibition. This adaptation can lead to the withdrawal symptoms that are found in alcoholics and addicts.

Year One link: In biological psychology you learned about pre and postsynaptic cells, how neurotransmitters work at the synapse, including inhibitory effects, receptor firing and action potential. Recall how neurotransmitters work and the synapse to help your understanding of tolerance and other issues related to drug use.

Progress check 5.3
Give three ways of explaining pharmacodynamic tolerance.

Physical dependency

People can be physically or psychologically dependent on a drug, or both. **Physical dependency** means that the body becomes used to functioning with the drug in its system and so 'needs' it for what is then normal functioning of the brain and body. Physical dependency is present if withdrawal symptoms begin when the drug is no longer taken.

Definition

Physical dependency refers to when the body has got used to a drug and if the person stops taking the drug there will be withdrawal symptoms. Someone physically dependent on a drug needs the drug to function normally.

Physical dependency versus addiction

Tolerance and physical dependency refer to physiological changes whereas addiction is a type of behaviour, so physical dependency/tolerance and addiction differ. Addiction is about stopping the use of a drug and goes with not meeting family and work obligations as well as with tolerance and withdrawal. Physical dependency is about the tolerance and withdrawal and needing the drug for normal physical functioning; addiction is where behaviour regarding family and work come in. Addiction tends to include physical dependency but the two are not the same. Someone can be physically dependent on a drug and yet not addicted to it as behaviours related to addiction (and compulsions) are not found. Physical dependence means without the drug there will be signs of withdrawal and tolerance can be found too. Physical dependency is about physical changes in the brain. Addiction is more than that.

Examples of physical dependency

- One aspect of physical dependency when it comes to heroin is that the brains of heroin users tend to produce fewer endorphins and so addicted people will rely on heroin for their pleasure and reduction of pain experiences more than someone who does not use heroin. Physical dependence means that, when the drug is stopped, there will be withdrawal symptoms, which are also physical. Heroin rapidly develops tolerance; therefore, someone can quickly become physically dependent on it.
- Physical dependency regarding nicotine shows different mechanisms from physical dependency on heroin. An increased production of acetylcholine brought about by nicotine causes rapid physiological dependence, just as tolerance is reached quickly. Nicotine is addictive and the brain (and the peripheral nervous system) changes to the extent that nicotine is needed for normal physical functioning.
- Studies using rats or mice to study physical dependence on alcohol use 10 per cent ethanol solution. Kampov-Polevoy *et al.* (2006) found that when rats self-administered ethanol for six weeks there was a significant reduction ($p<.05$) in 'bicuculline-induced seizure thresholds' during alcohol withdrawal. When the alcohol was not drunk after the six weeks there was increased anxiety. Physical dependency was measured by bicuculline-induced seizures and could be found after only six weeks.

> **STUDY HINT**
> You can use examples like Kampov-Polevoy *et al.* (2006) when you discuss the use of animals in lab experiments to study drugs, which is one of the methods you need to cover in health psychology.

Explore

You can find out more about recreational drugs using the 'drugabuse' government website. Here is a link to information on heroin: www.drugabuse.gov/publications/drugfacts/heroin

Psychological dependency

Psychological dependency means a drug takes on great importance in someone's life in a way that makes the cravings hard to resist. The drug is important not just physically but also for the person's mental state. Addiction is likely to include both physical and psychological dependency. Psychological dependency refers to the compulsive seeking of the drug and the cravings. Psychological dependency is about satisfying the need for the drug and this desire is the main motivation in someone's life.

Definition

Psychological dependency means a drug is very important in someone's life and there is an emotional preoccupation with the drug and its effects, as well as a craving for it.

Examples of psychological dependency

- Heroin is often taken by people with living difficulties, no social support, problems with employment and with low self-esteem, so psychological dependence is likely to occur because the feelings of pleasure and dulling of the senses are something such people might seek.
- With regard to nicotine the individual will become used to the oral stimulation and without it would need to substitute something else, such as eating more (though that could be linked to physical issues as well). Nicotine involves a stimulant that leads to craving for the drug – which is as much a psychological element as a physical one. If smoking gives a reward, such as feeling calmer, then the behaviour is likely to be repeated to repeat the reward. If the effect after a puff of cigarette smoke is quick, this is believed to act as a strong reinforcer for taking the drug again. This links to operant conditioning and the power of reward as a reinforcer of behaviour.
- Regarding alcohol, surgery has been used to alleviate alcohol craving with reduced relapse rates and improvement in the person's quality of life,

and this has been treatment specifically targeted at psychological dependence (Wu *et al.*, 2010). This suggests that psychological dependence has physiological underpinnings. Wu *et al.* (2010) found that ablating the nucleus accumbens **bilaterally** using **stereotactic surgery** led to nine cases not showing relapse at the time of the report. Relapse occurred in three cases of the 12 patients treated. Relapse was 16.7 per cent of the 12 at six months and 25 per cent within 12 months. The patients' memory quotient and intelligence quotient was significantly improved six months after compared with before the operation. Their cravings were reduced too and there was a decrease in depression.

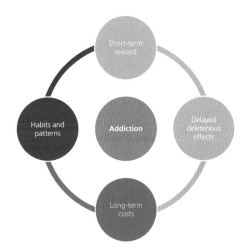

Addiction relates to being rewarded by the euphoria from a drug with short-term reward, followed by long-term costs involving habits and patterns, including cravings and psychological dependence.

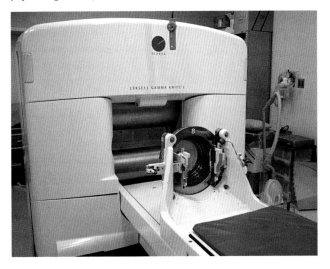

Stereotactic brain surgery can help with psychological dependence on alcohol.

Explanation

Stereotactic surgery refers to using an instrument that holds the head in a fixed position to use something like an electrode to cause damage (lesions or ablations) in the brain to 'fix' some aspect of functioning. **Bilaterally** means on both sides of the brain.

Year One link: When covering the requirements for biological psychology in your course you are likely to have looked at lesions and ablations. Lesions are damage to the brain such as cuts, and ablations refer to damage to the brain by removing some part. Lesions and ablations can occur naturally, can be used as treatments, or can be used in research. Check your understanding of these terms.

Progress check 5.4

Explain two features of psychological dependence.

Addiction

Addiction is when the person needs the drug for normal physical and psychological functioning. Addiction means being extremely involved with the drug and taking it compulsively, together with an obsession with securing a supply of the drug and also someone being very likely to relapse after withdrawal. Someone can be physically dependent on a drug without being addicted; however, addiction is likely to include physical dependence. There are addictions like gambling, which do not relate to physical dependency or drug use. Addiction is the behavioural part of drug misuse, referring to the repeated compulsive seeking out of the drug even though social and physical consequences of doing so can be very negative for the individual. People are physically dependent on food and water and someone taking medication might need it to avoid withdrawal symptoms, but for these examples there does not have to be addiction. There is not likely to be the behaviour that goes with addiction, such as the obsessive looking for the drug even though doing so has negative consequences for the individual.

Explanation

Addiction refers to how much the drug takes over the person, and someone addicted to a drug depends a great deal on it, with the drug controlling their behaviour. Someone addicted will put the drug before other things in their life; it pervades their life.

Explore

You can read more about physical versus psychological addiction using this link: www.psychologytoday.com/blog/all-about-addiction/201007/physical-addiction-or-psychological-addiction-is-there-real

Addiction symptoms

- There is tolerance and the user has needed more of the drug to reach the state of euphoria they reached with less of the substance at first.
- There is both physical and psychological dependency on the drug.
- The individual uses more of the drug than they intend to and finds it hard to cut down.
- They are anxious when they think they may not be able to get access to the drug and they carry on using it even when such use is causing them problems.
- They feel guilty about taking the drug and have no interest in activities they used to enjoy.
- They may lie or act secretly and the drug-taking interferes with their work and family/social responsibilities.

Progress check 5.5

Explain two features of addiction that differentiate addiction from drug dependency.

STUDY HINT

You need to know about addiction, tolerance, physical dependence, psychological dependence and withdrawal. Be ready to write about these together, as effects of drug-taking, and be ready to write about them separately as features of drug-taking. Make sure you have enough material in your notes. You can add to an answer by using examples.

Withdrawal

Withdrawal refers to physical symptoms that come when a drug that has been taken for a while is stopped. Every drug is different when it comes to withdrawal symptoms. Withdrawal symptoms arise because when a drug affects brain processing, such as neurotransmitter functioning, those effects are likely to affect other areas of brain processing as well. For example, if a drug suppresses noradrenaline, which is a neurotransmitter, then you stop taking the drug, that is going to cause a surge of adrenaline as the neurotransmitter is released. Some drugs give a lot of physical withdrawal symptoms, some give fewer such symptoms. Some give emotional withdrawal symptoms like anxiety.

Emotional withdrawal symptoms include anxiety, headaches, social isolation, depression and poor concentration. Irritability and insomnia can be seen as emotional withdrawal symptoms.

Physical withdrawal symptoms include sweating, tremor, sickness, palpitations, chest tightening and breathing difficulties and racing heart.

Examples of withdrawal symptoms

- For example, if heroin is taken (in a sustained way) for only three days, withdrawal symptoms can occur when it is stopped. These tend to start about six hours after last using the drug, although this depends on how much tolerance there is and the quantity of the last dose. Withdrawal symptoms regarding heroin include sweating, anxiety, depression, sensitivity in the genital area, a feeling of heaviness, cramps in the limbs, tears, insomnia, chills and muscle aching. There might also be sickness and diarrhoea. Some users also have what can be called 'itchy blood', which leads to compulsive scratching. Withdrawal symptoms quickly disappear when heroin is taken again, which can lead to a cycle of taking the drug, trying to stop, then taking it again to reduce the physical symptoms of withdrawal. At this stage feelings of euphoria have disappeared because of tolerance.
- Withdrawal symptoms of nicotine include a desire for oral gratification (such as eating), anxiety, poor concentration and memory problems. There may also be depression and sleeping problems as well as an increased appetite. Withdrawal can give headaches as well and is almost the reverse of the effects of nicotine. For example, while nicotine relaxes a user, a withdrawal symptom is anxiety.
- Alcohol and tranquilisers have the most dangerous withdrawal symptoms. Stopping alcohol intake can lead to stroke, seizure or heart attack in some people. There can also be hallucinations. Alcohol withdrawal symptoms can start just two hours after the last drink and go on for weeks. Withdrawal can give mild anxiety and shaking but can lead to seizures and delirium tremens (DTs), which means confusion, rapid heart rate and fever. The death rate from DTs is between 1 per cent and 5 per cent of those who exhibit the symptoms. Also alcohol withdrawal symptoms can get worse quickly so medical attention is recommended.

Explore
There is a document about alcohol withdrawal giving advice. You could read it to help in understanding alcohol withdrawal. Here is the link: www.alcohollearningcentre.org.uk/_library/coping_with_alcohol_withdrawal.pdf

Test yourself
Assess issues around drug-taking, including tolerance and withdrawal. **(12 marks)**

STUDY HINT
When deciding how to answer a question in your course, consider the injunction carefully. Your specification has an Appendix at the end that tells you what each injunction requires. 'Assess', for example, requires careful consideration of the factors involved in the question, identification of the most important and also a judgement and conclusion.

Explanations of drug abuse

You need to look at explanations of drug abuse focusing on heroin, nicotine and alcohol. You have to cover one biological explanation for each of the three drugs and for each this means including mode of action. You also have to cover one learning explanation for each of the three drugs. You can use one explanation for more than one of the drugs, such as operant conditioning, which can apply to all three drugs as an explanation of their misuse. However, biological explanations will differ because the three drugs work in different ways, which means they have different modes of action. First, each of the drugs is looked at with regard to one biological explanation including their mode of action. Then learning explanations are looked at.

Substance abuse/misuse is when a **drug** – defined as a mind-altering substance – is used in such a way that the individual's physical and mental health are affected. The use of the drug is called 'misuse' or 'abuse' when it interferes with a person's social situation and responsibilities.

Explanation
Drug is a mind-altering substance and is chemical in make-up. **Substance abuse/misuse** means a drug is used in a way that affects someone's mental and physical health. The drug is used in amounts or in ways that are harmful to someone or to others. If the drug is a prescription drug, then the use of the drug is not how it was intended so this is misuse or abuse.

Taking a drug is not the same as misusing or abusing a drug. Alcohol is a drug, but not everyone who drinks alcohol is thought of as a drug abuser – at least not in most societies. It is when someone is addicted to a substance that it becomes substance misuse – when the individual does not necessarily want to take the drug but feels he/she must. Addiction/dependence is defined earlier in this chapter.

Substance misuse has a social and economic cost, because individuals who abuse drugs need to be treated, which costs money. A society will want to reduce the number of people addicted to drugs, so it will put together campaigns to minimise such behaviour and to improve health, and such campaigns are expensive. 'Drugs' in these contexts usually refer to recreational drugs but may also include prescribed drugs such as tranquillisers and sleeping pills, as people can become addicted to these.

'Misused' drugs include alcohol, heroin, cocaine and cannabis as well as glue and aerosols. Smoking cigarettes or drinking a lot of coffee can also come under the heading of substance abuse, as can the eating disorder bulimia nervosa, because it involves the misuse of food. In your course you are required to focus on three drugs, heroin, nicotine and alcohol.

People are not likely to start taking a recreational drug for a reason other than some form of pleasure – they start using the drug and like the resultant feelings. They might use the drug because of a reaction from friends or others, so the reason for starting to take a drug is not likely to be biological. A biological explanation, however, might reveal why someone keeps taking the drug, even if at some level they wish to stop. The brain seems to have an agenda of its own when someone who has started taking an addictive drug wants to stop, and this is the biological agenda. For example, cocaine is an addictive drug. The euphoric effect individuals receive from it influences them to try it again, and also changes the structure and function of the brain. The brain continues to change as the drug is taken in terms of biochemical structure, memory processes and in control over motor skills, until the person is addicted.

Biological explanations of substance misuse

In this section a biological explanation for heroin is considered first, then nicotine and finally alcohol.

Firstly, the general biological explanation that is used in this section, the effects of drugs on neuronal transmission, is outlined.

Year One link: Recall what you learned about drugs and neuronal transmission when studying biological psychology. Recall features of neurons like reuptake and synaptic transmission.

Drugs and neuronal transmission – a biochemical explanation

Drugs are chemicals and they work in the brain to provide a pleasure reaction and, for some drugs, an addiction

reaction. Prescribed drugs such as tranquillisers and antischizophrenic drugs work in the same basic way. The drug acts like other neurotransmitters (which are chemicals) – when released by an electrical impulse, the neurotransmitter crosses a synaptic gap to fit with receptors of another neuron. Recreational drugs, like other drugs, work at the receptor of a neuron. Drugs can also prevent reuptake of a neurotransmitter, which means the neural transmission is blocked.

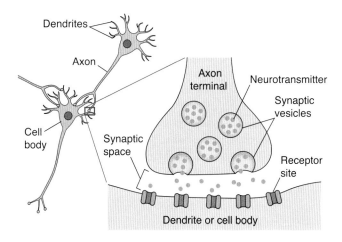

Synaptic transmission between neurons

For example, heroin works in the brain like morphine and acts on opioid receptors. In some mice it acts on mu-opioid receptors and, in others, on delta-opioid receptors. Heroin activity is able to cause changes at the receptors. It is the mu-opioid gene that is thought to be responsible for addiction, though other genes could also be implicated. A genetic explanation for substance misuse is another biological explanation though it does link to neurotransmitter functioning as an explanation. There is more discussion of this point later in the section on heroin.

> **STUDY HINT**
> There were slightly different findings from two studies using mice. Use such evidence when evaluating animal laboratory studies and whether findings from them can apply to humans. If there are differences in different types of mice, there could easily be differences between mice and humans.

Different drugs work in different ways, but both the dopamine and serotonin systems in the brain are involved in drug misuse and addiction – these neurotransmitters are linked to pleasure and positive emotions. Cocaine, for example, directly stimulates the dopamine receptors and this would give pleasurable feelings by increasing the availability of dopamine messages. However, opioids (e.g. heroin) slow down all brain activity, including the reuptake of neurotransmitters, so dopamine messages stay active for longer. This means that it is as rewarding as increasing dopamine activity, but in a different way.

Some people do not become addicted and others do. This might be because of the individual's particular dopamine system, which could link with a genetic explanation. Some people might be more prone to addiction than others. There is currently research looking for an 'addictive gene'. It is possible that the deficient dopamine system leads the person to seek more pleasure and to be susceptible to substance misuse in order to seek pleasure (Blum *et al.*, 1996). This is known as the reward deficiency syndrome.

In a different explanation, it is argued that it is the serotonin system that might lead a person to want more of a drug after starting to use it. Some addictive drugs increase activity in the serotonin system, which leads the person to want more. Some people might have a deficiency in the serotonin system, again linking to a genetic explanation. This is known as the serotonin deficiency hypothesis. A further theory looks at endorphin deficiency, because drugs also stimulate endorphin receptors, endorphin being the brain's own pleasure and pain-reducing neurotransmitter. Both heroin and alcohol increase endorphin arousal so perhaps people with endorphin deficiency are more likely to become addicted. These three explanations all link to the idea of drugs working at the synapse.

Heroin addiction – a neurotransmitter explanation

Issues about heroin have been explained previously in this chapter, when looking at physical and psychological dependence, tolerance and withdrawal. This section reiterates how heroin works at the synapse (the **mode of action**), which is a biological explanation.

Definition
Mode of action refers to how drugs work and focuses on biological and biochemical explanations.

Heroin is an opiate, which acts as a depressant and analgesic (painkiller) in the central nervous system. It is produced from morphine, which comes from the opium or Asian poppy (*Papaver somniferum*). It is in powder form, often white, and is usually injected – although recently with fears about the safety of needles it is sometimes smoked or snorted. In 2004 Afghanistan produced about 87 per cent of the world's supply of raw opium but by 2011 Mexico had taken some of the trade and was the second largest opium producer.

Mode of action

Heroin acts at the opioid receptor sites in the brain. When injected it travels through the bloodstream quickly into the brain, and it reaches the brain just as quickly if smoked, though not as quickly if snorted. It changes the action of dopamine in the reward pathways of the brain, releasing more dopamine than usual, hence the resulting 'high'. Heroin is converted into morphine in the brain by enzymes, and morphine works at the opioid receptors at the synapse. The morphine binds (fits) to receptors in certain areas of the brain and reduces the inhibitory (preventing) effect of GABA (gamma-aminobutyric acid) on dopaminergic neurons. **Dopaminergic neurons** are those that release dopamine. So GABA is not inhibiting the dopamine neurons. The result is more dopamine activity and the release of dopamine into the synaptic cleft. The dopaminergic reward pathways are stimulated, this leads to feelings of euphoria and the high that is reported by heroin users. The areas of the brain where the receptors are affected include part of the cerebral cortex, the VTA, the nucleus accumbens, thalamus, spinal cord and brain stem. These are areas within the reward pathways (the VTA, nucleus accumbens and cortex) and within the pain pathway (the thalamus, brain stem and spinal cord). When the pain pathway is stimulated morphine acts as a pain killer but it is the reward pathways that are of interest when looking at the mode of action of heroin.

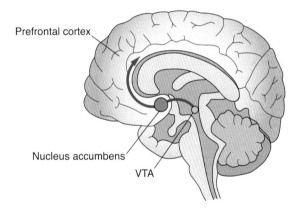

Prefrontal cortex

Nucleus accumbens

VTA

Heroin works on the reward pathways in the brain

Definition
Dopaminergic neurons – neurons that release the neurotransmitter dopamine at the terminal buttons.

STUDY HINT
Review what you learned in clinical psychology about dopamine as you are likely to have covered the dopamine hypothesis to explain schizophrenia so will know about dopaminergic neurons.

Year One link: Review synaptic transmission, including the role of inhibitory neurotransmitters, which you are likely to have covered in biological psychology in your course.

Progress check 5.6

Explain the mode of action of heroin at the synapse.

Short-term effects of taking heroin include pleasure feelings as well as a reduction of pain, which occur because of neurotransmitter functioning at the opioid receptor sites. There is a 'rush', which includes a dry mouth, heavy limbs, flushing of the skin and possibly feelings of sickness and severe itching. In addition, there is a sense of relaxation and drowsiness, as well as a slowing of mental functions, breathing and heart rate. The rush happens at around seven seconds after injection or within a few minutes if heroin is snorted or smoked. Long-term effects come after chronic (persistent) use. There will be psychological and physical dependence, as well as tolerance. Cravings for the effects of heroin develop and, if it is not used regularly, there will be withdrawal symptoms.

Evidence relating to a neurotransmitter explanation for heroin misuse

- Evidence for mu-opioid and GABA mechanisms explaining the effects of heroin

Selecki et al. (2006) carried out a study on rats to look at the role of opioid and GABA mechanisms in heroin usage. They used rats that were trained to distinguish heroin from saline and then used substitution tests to see which substances rats would accept as a heroin substitute. Heroin and morphine led to lever-pressing for heroin and muscimol, which is a GABA reuptake inhibitor, partly worked as a substitution. However, tiagabin, which is a GABA reuptake inhibitor, vigabatrin, an inhibitor of GABA transaminase, and baclofen, a $GABA_B$ receptor antagonist, did not substitute for heroin. Naltrexone and naloxone, both opioid receptor antagonists, blocked the heroin effects (depending on the dose). There were some other findings as well and they backed up the significance of mu-opioid mechanisms being involved in heroin usage and that inhibiting GABA reuptake can decrease the effects of heroin. Stimulating GABA receptors or inhibiting GABA transaminase would not have the same effect. The study shows that neurotransmitter functioning can explain the effects of heroin and there is specific functioning, which, if known, can help to target drugs for the treatment of heroin.

- Rats self-administer heroin if it reaches the brain's pleasure centre

Rats will press a bar to receive heroin that goes directly to the nucleus accumbens and the rat will keep pressing the lever to get the heroin because it gets a reward and feels good. This explanation is a learning explanation and will be looked at later; however, it does show that the reward that heroin gives is in the brain, in regions like the nucleus accumbens. If the needle that takes the heroin to the rat's brain is placed near the nucleus accumbens but not in it, then the rat does not self-administer the heroin. This is evidence for an explanation for heroin misuse that focuses on brain processing.

- Prefrontal cortex functioning differences in drug abusers versus controls

A difficulty in getting evidence for neurotransmitter functioning as an explanation for heroin addiction is that often studies look at people taking more than one drug, which is a frequent occurrence, and so it is hard to look at the effects of heroin alone. Fishbein et al. (2007) in Russia found heroin addicts who did not take other drugs and considered three comparison groups in their study. They used alcoholics, addicts who used both alcohol and heroin, and non-abusers. They measured executive cognitive functioning, which is shown by activation of the prefrontal cortex and looked at visual pattern recognition, problem solving, decision-making, cognitive flexibility and the changing of a response. They found that heroin addicts were similar to alcoholics and people addicted to both heroin and alcohol regarding neurocognitive deficits compared to controls. Heroin addicts showed more risky decision-making and took longer to make a decision than the other groups. Fishbein et al. (2007) concluded that there were differences in executive cognitive functioning both between users and controls and also between the different drug types. This has implications for drug therapy to treat heroin abuse and suggests it must be targeted at problem areas such as the prefrontal cortex. This is evidence for brain functioning being implicated in heroin addiction though looking more at the brain regions than the actual neurotransmitter transmission processes involved.

- Individual differences, possibly genetic, in brain functioning

There might be individual differences in how much people enjoy a substance; some might get more pleasure than others. Some people can use reason not to use heroin more than others. There might be genetic differences in individuals that lead some into addiction but not others. The neurotransmitter explanation can be a successful explanation; however, there is still room for individual differences in drug-taking. Selecki *et al.* (2006) used rats but Li *et al.* (2014) used the genotype of humans and found that GABA$_A$ receptor genes had a role but there were different variants. This suggests that individuals with specific GABA$_A$ gene variants might be more affected than others, giving evidence for the suggestion that there are individual differences in brain processing linked to heroin addiction. Li *et al.* (2014) look at alcohol addiction as well as heroin addiction so their study is explained below (page 497).

Explore

If you would like to know more about neurotransmitter functioning including related to heroin addiction (and other drugs), here is a link: **https://books.google.co.uk/ books?id=felzn3Ntd-cC&pg=PA22&dq=neurotransmitter+ explanation+for+heroin+addiction&hl=en&sa=X&ei=57u bVcDIJMyf7gbAhJ2gAg&ved=0CDMQ6AEwAA#v=onepage- &q=neurotransmitter%20explanation%20for%20heroin%20 addiction&f=false**

STUDY HINT

When you offer evidence for an explanation, treatment or theory, you are evaluating as you are using the evidence either to say it supports the explanation (for example) or to show there is another explanation or to offer evidence against the explanation.

Progress check 5.7

Explain one piece of evidence that supports the neurotransmitter functioning explanation for heroin addiction and one piece of evidence that suggests an alternative biological explanation.

Evaluation of the neurotransmitter explanation for heroin addiction

Strengths

- There is evidence from Li *et al.* (2014) using humans to show that GABA$_A$ receptor genes have a role in heroin addiction even though in human genotypes there are variants in different individuals, so there are individual differences in heroin addiction perhaps because of having the different genotypes. This suggests that genes have a role; however, the findings also support the neurotransmitter explanation for heroin addiction. Using humans gives the findings credibility and generalisability, though often the sample is 'Western'

and there are other genotypes of course so generalising might be limited to specific genotypes.

- Fishbein *et al.* (2007) concluded that there were differences in executive cognitive functioning both between users and controls and also between the different drug types, and also used humans as participants, which is a strength when generalising. They also used controls and different groups (alcoholics, those addicted to both alcohol and heroin, and heroin addicts) so their study had credible findings.

- Selecki *et al.* (2006) carried out a study on rats to look at the role of opioid and GABA mechanisms in heroin usage. The findings backed up the significance of mu-opioid mechanisms being involved in heroin usage and that inhibiting GABA reuptake can decrease the effects of heroin. This study is evidence for GABA being involved in heroin addiction; however, there can be issues with generalising from animal studies to say the findings apply to humans.

Weaknesses

- Studies tend to use mice or rats that are trained to self-administer heroin and then their brain functioning is examined. A difficulty is in generalising from animals to humans because addiction involves psychological dependence, for example, as well as physical dependence, and there can be factors such as low social support and low self-esteem that go with heroin addiction in humans. These differences might be sufficient to discount findings from animal studies when looking at human functioning.

- It is not easy to separate biological explanations. A genetic explanation seems different from a neurotransmitter explanation but it might be that different gene variants cause differences in neurotransmitter functioning that relate to individual differences in addiction, so the biological explanations are not separate. Similarly, looking at different brain regions for an explanation of addiction, such as the regions in the reward pathways, can seem like a different biological explanation. However, activity in the reward pathways takes place by means of neurotransmitter functioning. This suggests that there is more to addiction than neurotransmitter functioning alone, and gene variants as well as brain regions are involved in explaining drug addiction.

Nicotine addiction – a neurotransmitter explanation

This section focuses on nicotine, taken in to the body through smoking. Earlier in this section you will have read about tolerance, physical and psychological dependence and withdrawal related to nicotine so you will know something about how the drug works. Withdrawal symptoms include craving, depression, sleep problems, increased appetite and cognitive problems, such as memory and attention problems.

Nicotine comes from the dried leaves and stems of tobacco plants, and is in the nightshade family of plants. Cigarette tobacco contains varying amounts of nicotine, from 15 to 25 mg per cigarette, so smoking does not give nicotine poisoning in its fullest form, though nicotine is a toxin and extremely poisonous. Nicotine is also an insecticide, and is a very harmful drug. A US government website (www. drugabuse.gov) says that 85 per cent of people who want to give up smoking and try on their own do not succeed within a week of trying and there are nearly 35 million people each year who want to give up.

Mode of action

Nicotine is a powerfully addictive drug that affects both the central nervous system and the peripheral nervous system. The central nervous system is the brain and spinal cord, and the peripheral nervous system includes other areas such as those where messages about the alarm reaction and fight or flight messages are located. The peripheral nervous system has two types of neurons: those for sensory information and those for movement.

When smoked, nicotine enters the lungs and is quickly absorbed through the lungs and then passed across cell membranes. Chewing tobacco or gum allows absorption by means of a different route, through mucous membranes. After being absorbed, nicotine enters the blood. If nicotine is injected it is absorbed and reaches the brain in about one minute. Because smoking takes nicotine directly to the lungs, however, it can enter the blood almost as quickly as by injection and might even get to the brain more quickly than if injected. Nicotine affects other areas as well as the brain, but this takes longer and the brain 'feels' the effect first. As the effects reach other areas of the body after a longer time, it is possible for someone to still feel the effects of nicotine after 24 hours.

Nicotine works at nicotinic receptors in the central nervous system and also in the peripheral nervous system. It inhibits the function of specific acetylcholine receptors, known as nicotinic acetylcholine receptors because they interact with nicotine. Nicotine is a nicotinic acetylcholine receptor agonist. Acetylcholine is a neurotransmitter, and nicotine stimulates the acetylcholine receptor then blocks it. This has the effect of getting in the way of signalling ability. Acetylcholine levels rise because nicotine has disabled the receptors, and so acetylcholine is in the synaptic gap, not being picked up, and levels of the

neurotransmitter norepinephrine (noradrenaline) also rise, which leads to better memory ability. Anxiety is reduced because of higher levels of endorphins.

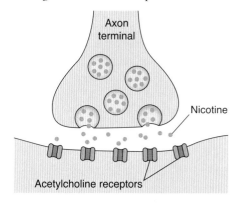

Nicotine works at the synapse by stimulating and then blocking acetylcholine receptors releasing acetylcholine into the synaptic gap.

Blood with nicotine in it when it reaches the brain stimulates the release of different neurotransmitters, not just acetylcholine, but also serotonin, dopamine and others. It is the acetylcholine that seems to help with concentration and memory as well as alertness, which also comes from norepinephrine. Positive effects of smoking come from dopamine and effects in the brain's reward systems.

The effects of nicotine poisoning are a burning feeling in the mouth, salivation, sickness, stomach pains and diarrhoea. The individual can feel agitated, have a headache, and feel dizzy, confused and weak. There can be a lack of coordination and an increase in blood pressure. The heart may be affected and there can be convulsions. Nicotine is a toxin (it is poisonous), and there is no antidote.

However, cigarette smoking does not include enough nicotine for there to be direct poisoning. A low dose of nicotine, such as from cigarette smoking, can help with relaxation and can cause mild euphoria. It can also help to improve attention and problem-solving skills. Dopamine levels increase with nicotine, which causes the same changes in the reward pathways as those associated with using heroin, such as increased pleasure. Increased levels of norepinephrine improve memory ability and raised levels of endorphins decrease anxiety. Some ingredients in cigarettes can have an effect in the brain. One example is how it seems that the smoke itself can lead to a decreased level of monoamine oxidase (MAO), which is an enzyme that works to break down dopamine. This can help to explain the high dopamine levels that come from smoking cigarettes and might explain why people carry on smoking – to get the resulting reward.

Nicotine also seems to affect how other recreational drugs affect the brain and body. In addition, cigarettes themselves cause harm: from inhaling burning plant and from the insufficient burning of some of the constituents of the cigarette and plant, some of which are carcinogenic (can lead to cancer). The lungs become coated in tar, which reduces lung efficiency.

Evidence relating to a neurotransmitter explanation for nicotine addiction

- Certain substances acting in the brain can help to prevent nicotine withdrawal symptoms

Thakre *et al.* (2013) suggest that the neurobehavioural mechanisms underlying how nicotine works are not clear. They looked at nicotine withdrawal in mice and at the influence of neurosteroid allopreganolone (ALLO). They injected nicotine over ten days four times a day and then there was withdrawal. They found severe physical signs, anxiety and movement problems in the mice. However, the mice that were given neurosteroid allopreganolone or progesterone beforehand did not show the same withdrawal symptoms. There is more to the findings, however; briefly, from their study, there is a suggestion that there could be injections to help with nicotine withdrawal symptoms (in humans) and possibly with nicotine addiction. Their findings suggest that nicotine addiction (and withdrawal symptoms) comes from brain processing.

- Stopping smoking affects the hypothalamus, which is a known area for weight gain

Geha *et al.* (2013) looked at how stopping smoking can lead to weight gain and used smokers compared to non-smokers to see the effect on brain response to food in brain regions associated with weight change in non-smokers. fMRI was used to find brain regions associated with weight change in non-smokers using BMI and the brain's response to a milk shake. This part of the study used 27 non-smokers, five of whom were male. Then 16 (three men) returned after a year for another BMI measure and the change in BMI was checked against the brain regions measured before by the fMRI to highlight brain regions relating to weight change. Then for the second part of the study 11 smokers were assessed for brain response to a milk shake compared with a control solution and they used the smokers and a control group as a comparison. So they had a measure of brain response to a milk shake in smokers and non-smokers and brain response to a control solution in smokers and non-smokers as well as knowledge of brain regions associated with weight gain from the first part of the study. In the

16 non-smokers in the first part of the study brain regions related to weight change were the midbrain, hypothalamus, thalamus and ventral striatum and it was in the hypothalamus that the smokers had the greater response to a milk shake compared with non-smokers. They concluded that smokers displayed a different brain response to food in the hypothalamus compared to non-smokers and this is an area related to weight change in non-smokers so it does seem that smoking affects areas related to weight change. This is evidence for smoking affecting brain processing, which supports the neurotransmitter explanation for nicotine addiction even though focusing on brain regions, because processing in brain regions takes place using neurotransmitter functioning.

Year One link: In your course in biological psychology you look at fMRI as a research method and you can use Geha *et al.* (2013) as an example of a study using fMRI scanning.

Explore

The study by Geha *et al.* (2013) looking at hypothalamic response to food in smokers can be found using this link: http://ajcn.nutrition.org/content/97/1/15.full.pdf+html

- GABA, glutamate and sensitisation to stress – relating to nicotine addiction

Yu *et al.* (2010) focus on GABA and glutamate and nicotine self-administration. They consider how in rats self-administering nicotine affects hypothalamo-pituitary-adrenal (HPA) responses to stress, though the actual effects are not clear. Their study can be related to Geha *et al.* (2013) and their discovery of links between smoking and the hypothalamus (and weight gain). Nicotine self-administration in rats affects responsiveness to norepinephrine when there is stress, so there is some link to neurotransmitter functioning. Yu *et al.* (2010) found that a glutamate receptor antagonist blocked the enhanced adrenocorticotropic hormone and conticosterone that comes with shock in rats self-administering nicotine. There is a greater reduction in GABA when rats self-administer nicotine and this disinhibits CRF (corticotropin-releasing factor) neurons. This disinhibition goes with enhanced glutamate input, which relates to how sensitised someone using nicotine is to stress. Smoking seems to be a stressor that sensitises the HPA to stress. This is evidence for nicotine working at the neurotransmitter level and this being an explanation for nicotine addiction.

- A genetic link to smoking – an alternative biological explanation

Shields (1963) looked at 42 identical twin pairs reared apart. Only nine of the 42 twin pairs were different with regard to smoking – they either both smoked or neither smoked. Stitzel *et al.* (2000) suggest from animal studies that the number of nicotinic receptors, how they are distributed and issues such as tolerance all relate to genes. Gilbert and Gilbert (1995) suggest that between 28 per cent and 85 per cent of differences in smoking behaviour are down to inherited factors. This is a wide percentage; however, it does give evidence for there being a heritability factor in nicotine addiction. There is evidence for starting smoking and continuing with smoking both coming from inherited factors (e.g. True *et al.*, 1997). What is given here is evidence for an inherited component in smoking. This can be seen as a different biological explanation though in fact does not contradict the idea that nicotine addiction relates to neurotransmitter functioning as it is that functioning that can be affected by genotype.

Progress check 5.8

Briefly explain the mode of action of nicotine referring to one neurotransmitter.

Evaluation of the neurotransmitter explanation for nicotine addiction

Strengths

- There is evidence for glutamate receptors and neurotransmitter functioning related to norepinephrine being related to nicotine addiction (and stress), as Yu *et al.* (2010) suggest, using rats in their study. Yu *et al.* (2010) also found a role for GABA. When

studies find evidence like this, then that supports the claim – in this case that nicotine addiction can be explained by neurotransmitter functioning. Stitzel *et al.* (2000) suggest from animal studies that the number of nicotinic receptors, how they are distributed and issues such as tolerance all relate to genes as well as to nicotine addiction. This again is evidence for the neurotransmitter explanation even though the study also suggests genetic factors are important.

- The studies using rats are well-controlled and carefully carried out, giving credibility to the findings. Using animals in laboratory experiments can help to rule out confounding variables, for example, even though there can then be issues with generalisability. As animals have such similar brain functioning with regard to neurotransmitter functioning, findings do appear to have generalisability. They do have nicotinergic receptors, for example, as do humans.

Weaknesses

- As was suggested when giving weaknesses of the neurotransmitter explanation for heroin addiction, using animal studies to find out about human addiction might not be credible. This is because, although there are similarities between human and rat brains with regard to neurotransmitter functioning, there are also differences in brain functioning. Humans have executive cognitive functioning in the prefrontal cortex, for example, that is not the same as such functioning in rats. There is cognitive and executive functioning in the prefrontal cortex of rats (e.g. Dalley *et al.*, 2004); however, in rats there appear to be differences from humans with regard to prefrontal cortex functioning (e.g. Brown and Bowman, 2002, cited in Dalley *et al.*, 2004).

- A weakness is that there are other biological explanations, again as with the neurotransmitter explanation for heroin addiction. Gilbert and Gilbert (1995) suggest that between 28 per cent and 85 per cent of differences in smoking behaviour are down to inherited factors. This is a wide percentage; however, it does give evidence for there being a heritability factor in nicotine addiction. There is evidence for starting smoking and continuing with smoking both coming from inherited factors (e.g. True *et al.*, 1997). This does not mean the neurotransmitter explanation does not still stand; however, it does suggest that there might be more to it and more to be understood when considering nicotine addiction, such as someone's genetic make-up.

Progress check 5.9

Explain one strength and one weakness of the neurotransmitter explanation for nicotine addiction.

Alcohol addiction – a neurotransmitter explanation

As with nicotine and heroin, neurotransmitter functioning can explain alcohol addiction and is a biological explanation. You need to know about the mode of action of alcohol so it makes sense to use neurotransmitter functioning as the biological explanation, though genes also have a role.

Mode of action

Alcohol, like heroin, is said to affect receptor sites in the brain, specifically dopamine receptors. It could be claimed that all drug misuse can be explained by the effects of the drug in the brain relating to there being more dopamine produced and specifically in the brain's reward pathways. It is in the reward pathways, which dopamine affects, that the 'high' from a drug is felt. Olds and Milner (1954), the classic study for your course (page 583), puts forward evidence for there being a reward system in the brain.

The role of glutamate and GABA

Weiner *et al.* (1997) pointed out that neurotransmitters can act on different receptors in different ways and produce different effects. A neuron does not produce many neurotransmitters but there can be many receptors, so the process is complex. Alcohol works to reduce glutamate activity at the NMDA glutamate receptor and increases the inhibiting effect of GABA at the $GABA_A$ receptor, thus reducing brain activity in general. Columbo and Grant (1992) showed that NMDA receptor antagonists can lead to behaviour and reactions that seem like alcohol-related ones, which is evidence for NMDA receptors (which are glutamate receptors) being affected by alcohol. Alcohol inhibits glutamate activity in the brain, in particular in the striatum, which contains the nucleus accumbens (Carboni *et al.*, 1993, cited in Gilpin and Koob). This is

one reason for alcohol being seen as a depressant. Alcohol also relates to other neurotransmitters, serotonin (5-HT) and dopamine.

> **STUDY HINT**
> It is useful in psychology to think of 'depression' as 'reduced brain activity' as well as having all the other meanings associated with it. Alcohol as a depressant refers to it reducing brain activity by increasing neurotransmitter functioning that inhibits activity and reducing neurotransmitter functioning that is 'excitory'.

> **STUDY HINT**
> When you looked at Carlsson *et al.* (1999), the study you have to cover focusing on schizophrenia in your course, you will have learned about NMDA glutamate receptor antagonists so you can use that understanding when considering a neurotransmitter explanation for alcohol addiction.

Progress check 5.10

How does the neurotransmitter functioning evidence for the effects of alcohol show that it is a depressant?

The role of dopamine

Dopamine relates to movement and also to motivation, with the role of pursuing pleasure. When it comes to alcohol misuse, dopamine has been shown to have a role. Dopamine relates to the reward pathways in the brain and alcohol works in the reward pathways, such as giving pleasure. There is some evidence that some people have fewer dopamine receptors in the reward pathways and also have low amounts of dopamine. These issues with dopamine come about because of their genes.

● Di Chiara (1995) – the dopamine reward pathways gives motivation for taking the drug or rewards learning

Di Chiara (1995) discussed the role of dopamine in drug and alcohol dependence. Di Chiara explains that drugs act in the same way as all reinforcers in that they activate certain brain pathways that relate to motivation. These pathways relate to the motivation for taking the drug, and to learning and acquiring behaviour, because there is then motivation to learn that behaviour because the reward pathways are stimulated by it. Recreational drugs stimulate the transmission of dopamine in particular in the ventral striatum. Di Chiara, however, claims that not all recreational drugs work in the dopamine pathways as the motivation to take the drug, just those that are psychostimulants. Recreational drugs, however, do stimulate dopamine transmission. This might relate to learning to take the drug if not to the motivation to take the drug. Di Chiara found that withdrawal from drugs of abuse led to less dopamine activity in the pathways and seemed to stop behaviour related to getting the reinforcement from the drug. It was felt that it was learning that was affected by the reward pathways rather than motivation to take the drug. Withdrawal, which means stopping the stimulation of dopamine, would lead to loss of that learning. Di Chiara is discussing the neuroscience aspect of motivation to take a recreational drug coming from brain stimulation and is also discussing the learning aspect of drug-taking. People can learn that taking the drug is rewarding, with the reward coming from the dopamine in the reward pathways, and this is not the same explanation as saying that the drug is 'biologically' rewarding in the brain.

> **STUDY HINT**
> Di Chiara (1995) brings in both biological psychology and learning theories when considering explanations for alcohol misuse and the misuse of other drugs. When you are learning material make notes about such links, as they help with understanding the material.

- Tupala and Tiihonen (2004) and how treatment with a prescribed drug giving dopamine might 'replace' the dopamine release by alcohol

Tupala and Tiihonen (2004) considered dopamine and alcoholism and the neurobiological basis of ethanol abuse. Like Di Chiara (1995) they accept that substance abuse links to the reward pathways in the brain, which is rewarding because of dopamine. Tupala and Tiihonen (2004) review studies using animals and those using humans to look at the role of dopamine in alcohol abuse. They suggest that the dopamine system is affected by alcohol. Studies show that dopamine pathway receptor density and function are lower in certain types of alcoholics, such as those with certain dopamine receptor functioning that might come from genes. The researchers suggest that a treatment for these alcoholics might be prescribing drugs to increase activity in the dopamine pathway. By increasing such activity this could reduce the craving for alcohol and reduce the high that alcohol gives. This would help to prevent the individual from taking alcohol again (relapse) in that alcohol would not be needed to help the craving (which would be reduced by the prescribed drug) or to get the high (which would no longer be achieved because of the prescribed drug).

> **STUDY HINT**
> Di Chiara thought that substance misuse might be because the reward pathways in the brain gave rewards (through dopamine activity) for drug-taking behaviour and that this might be learned behaviour. Tupala and Tiihonen (2004) also referred to learning when discussing alcohol misuse and again the learning is related to dopamine released in the reward pathways because of the alcohol. Both studies (and Olds and Milner, 1954, your classic study) link learning theory to neurobiological functioning. You can use these examples to argue that biological and learning explanations for drug misuse might not be as separate as they might seem.

- Noble (1996) looked at dopamine in the reward pathways in the brain and genetic issues in dopamine receptors and dopamine presence

Noble (1996), as with other papers focusing on dopamine and alcoholism, starts by confirming that drug misuse comes about by reinforcement and this reinforcement comes about through dopamine acting in the reward pathways of the brain. Noble (1996) confirms too that regarding genes and alcoholism, there are reduced dopamine levels and reduced numbers of D2 dopamine receptors in animals that prefer alcohol, which suggests a genetic explanation for alcoholism in humans. Some people (and animals) have genes that give the dopamine receptor differences. Tupala and Tiihonen (2004) agree with this finding. Noble explains that when dopamine is stimulated by dopamine receptor agonists, alcohol consumption reduces, whereas antagonists (decreasing dopamine levels) increase alcohol consumption. Again Tupala and Tiihonen (2004) agreed with this finding and suggested a drug to boost dopamine at the synapse to decrease alcohol consumption. Noble (1996) suggests that animal studies show that the DRD2 gene (DRD2 is the D2 dopamine receptor) and areas around it relate to alcoholism.

Brain scanning shows lowered dopamine in alcoholics, which adds evidence to the claim that the DRD2 gene, which affects dopamine activity in the reward pathways, is for some people an explanation for alcoholism. Treating people with alcoholism with a dopamine receptor agonist reduces alcohol drinking. Also treating people in that way helped alcoholics carrying the DRD2 A1 allele (relates to genes) more than it helped those who did not carry that gene.

Year One link: Recall what 'agonists' and 'antagonists' do with regard to neurotransmitter functioning, which you covered in biological psychology.

STUDY HINT
To help you to remember the difference between agonists and antagonists, you could remember 'anti' as being 'against' so 'anti-agonists' go against the signal.

Explore
You can find out more about alcohol and how it works in the brain using this link and there is more information on the internet too if you would like to know more. **http://pubs. niaaa.nih.gov/publications/arh24-1/12-16.pdf**

Progress check 5.11
How does a dopamine explanation for alcohol misuse fit with a genetic explanation?

Evidence relating to a biological explanation for alcohol misuse focusing on neurotransmitters

- $GABA_A$ receptor genes have a role in alcohol dependence

Li *et al.* (2014) looked at GABA as an inhibitory neurotransmitter in the brain of mammals. GABA receptors are involved in substance abuse, as you will have seen when reading about heroin. Li *et al.* (2014) carried out a meta-analysis of $GABA_A$ receptor genes using 4,739 people who were dependent on alcohol, opioids or methamphetamine, with 4,924 controls. They also used other cases involving people with alcohol dependence and more controls. They found significant associations between variants of the $GABA_A$ receptor genes and alcohol dependence (*GABRA2*) and associations between *GABRAG2* and both alcohol and heroin dependence. They used genotype data to uncover the findings. This means relating alcohol and heroin addiction (separately) to the genotype of individuals involved and comparing with controls to look for gene differences. Their conclusion regarding alcohol misuse was that five $GABA_A$ receptor genes were implicated (with best evidence for *GABRA2*). This is evidence for genetic involvement in alcoholism. Many clinical drugs target $GABA_A$ receptors, such as benzodiazepines and barbiturates, and GABA is known to be an inhibitory neurotransmitter, so the evidence

that GABA is involved in alcohol dependence confirms a role for neurotransmission in alcohol addiction (and probably in other substance misuse).

- Study of twins showed a genetic link to alcohol and smoking

Maes *et al.* (1999) looked at 1,412 MZ and DZ twin pairs and found genetic influence in smoking and in drinking alcohol. If there is a genetic link to alcohol addiction this does not mean a neurotransmitter explanation is wrong, just that there is more to it. There can be a neurotransmitter explanation that can be explained by looking at genes.

- Studies linking alcohol to glutamate functioning

Alcohol suppressed the transmission of signals using glutamate in the central nucleus of the amygdala according to Roberto *et al.* (2004b). Lovinger *et al.* (1989) found that alcohol affected glutamate transmission as well, seemingly by altering how NMDA receptors function. Blednov and Harris (2008) found that a specific type of glutamate receptor (mGluR5) was affected by alcohol. There is more evidence; however, these three studies support the idea of alcohol affecting glutamate transmission.

STUDY HINT
There are quite a few studies given to support the neurotransmitter functioning explanation for alcohol addiction here. Some studies demonstrate the link between alcohol and neurotransmitter functioning and some go into the explanation more. An example of demonstrating a link is how alcohol can suppress the transmission of signals that use glutamate. An example of giving an explanation is how people with a certain genetic make-up might turn to alcohol to change their neurotransmitter functioning to avoid 'depression'. Be sure to discuss the 'explanation' when asked to and not just the 'facts'.

Evaluation of the neurotransmitter explanation for alcohol addiction

Strengths

- There is a lot of evidence that neurotransmitter functioning, particularly in the brain's reward system, relates to drug misuse, including alcoholism. Columbo and Grant (1992) showed that NMDA receptor antagonists can lead to behaviour and reactions that seem like alcohol-related ones. Noble (1996) confirmed that there are reduced dopamine levels and reduced numbers of D2 dopamine receptors in animals that prefer alcohol, which suggests a neurotransmitter explanation for alcoholism in humans as well as a genetic one.

- Studies are often animal laboratory experiments with strong controls and careful testing, which means cause-and-effect conclusions can often be drawn and conclusions have credibility.
- Studies using humans often support animal studies, again lending credibility to findings. For example, Noble (1996) used animals studies as evidence and then showed also that brain scanning in humans shows lowered dopamine in alcoholics, which adds evidence to the claim that the DRD2 gene, which affects dopamine activity in the reward pathways, is for some people an explanation for alcoholism. Treating people with alcoholism with a dopamine receptor agonist reduces alcohol drinking, again giving evidence for dopamine having a role in alcoholism. There are different research methods here, showing similar findings, which adds reliability and credibility to the findings.

Weaknesses

- The use of animal laboratory experiments can be seen as a strength; however, there is the criticism that humans are not the same as animals in their brain functioning and so evidence for an explanation from animal studies might not be generalisable to humans.
- Neurotransmitter functioning as an explanation for alcohol misuse does not seem to be separate from genetic or learning explanations. Genes can affect neurotransmitter functioning, as seen when looking at the DRD2 gene and how dopamine transmission is affected and how it links to people who use/misuse alcohol. Also the reward system in the brain rewards the individual in a positive way, which seems to lead to more of the behaviour that gives the reward. This relates to operant conditioning principles. Alternatively the person might turn to alcohol to avoid negative feelings from not having dopamine in the reward system and this is negative reinforcement. It is hard to separate neurotransmitter, genetic and learning explanations as they all seem to link.

Other evidence regarding biological explanations for drug misuse

What has been said about a pleasure centre in the brain when looking at drug misuse such as alcoholism seems to apply to many drugs. Also there has been mention of the role of the mu-opioid gene in substance misuse. These two areas are briefly considered here to add evidence to what is explained when considering neurotransmitter functioning as a biological explanation for heroin, nicotine and alcohol misuse.

A pleasure centre in the brain?

The idea of the brain having reward pathways as a pleasure centre has been referred to when discussing substance misuse in this section. Research by Olds and Milner (1954), which is the classic study for health psychology in your course (page 583), suggested that there are pleasure circuits in the brain, linked to areas for motivation. The researchers experimented on rats and found that they would press a lever to get an electrical stimulation to the septal areas of the brain. This evidence supports the idea of substance misuse being linked to getting a 'high' from the pleasure centre in the brain, which is the reward pathways.

The mu-opiod gene and substance abuse

Another biological reason for addiction to a substance or substances might be that it is genetic and this idea has been suggested when evidence for neurotransmitter functioning as an explanation for substance misuse is considered. In 2002 reports from a team in Florida (Schinka et al.) stated that a gene had been found for addiction. This is the mu-opioid gene (which fits with the study using mice explained when looking at the neuronal transmission biological theory for heroin misuse). This gene seems to give an increased risk of abusing drugs, including alcohol and nicotine. This is possibly a gene implicated in drug use in general, not just one particular drug. There may be other genes too, with which the mu-opioid gene might work.

Family and twin studies have also been brought into the evidence when looking at neurotransmitter functioning as an explanation for drug misuse and they also suggest that there is a genetic basis for the risk of drug dependency. There might be specific genes for the risk of specific drugs – such as alcohol or cocaine. Laboratory studies have reinforced this work, and mice without the mu-opioid receptor did not drink alcohol even after they had been trained to drink it in other circumstances. Schinka et al. (2002) found that alcoholics lacked a form of the mu-opioid gene, when compared with the non-alcoholics in the study. It was because some of the alcoholics also used other substances that the researchers could not conclude that this gene was implicated in alcohol misuse only.

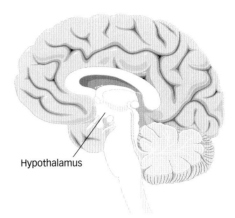

The human brain, showing that the hypothalamus is in the centre, near the area for emotions and where a pleasure centre is likely to be.

Year One link: Review your learning about genes when you covered biological psychology.

STUDY HINT
You could draw up a table with all the studies listed and a brief account of the evidence they offer in your own words, similar to Table 5.2. This would help with your learning and revision of the neurotransmitter explanation for alcohol addiction. You could do the same for heroin and nicotine.

General points about drug misuse and neurotransmitter functioning

You have looked at how neurotransmitter functioning can explain heroin, nicotine and alcohol abuse. The evaluation points when considering this explanation for each of the drugs are similar, such as the strength of using controlled animal experiments and the weakness of this meaning a possible lack of generalisability. It is useful to end this section about biological explanations for drug misuse by looking at some general issues to help understanding.

Table 5.2 Some of the studies given as evidence for neurotransmitter functioning being an explanation for alcohol misuse

Name of study	Explanation regarding neurotransmitters and alcohol
Weiner et al. (1997)	Alcohol works to reduce glutamate activity at the NMDA glutamate receptor and increases the inhibiting effect of GABA at the GABA$_A$ receptor, thus reducing brain activity in general.
Columbo and Grant (1992)	NMDA receptor antagonists can lead to behaviour and reactions that seem like alcohol-related ones, which is evidence for NMDA receptors (which are glutamate receptors) being affected by alcohol.
Carboni et al. (1993, cited in Gilpin and Koob)	Alcohol inhibits glutamate activity in the brain, in particular in the striatum, which contains the nucleus accumbens.
Tupala and Tiihonen (2004)	Say that studies show that dopamine pathway receptor density and function are lower in certain types of alcoholics, such as those with certain dopamine receptor functioning that might come from genes. The researchers suggest that a treatment for these alcoholics might be prescribing drugs to increase activity in the dopamine pathway.
Noble (1996)	Explains that when dopamine is stimulated by dopamine receptor agonists, alcohol consumption reduces whereas antagonists (decreasing dopamine levels) increase alcohol consumption.
	Brain scanning shows lowered dopamine in alcoholics, which adds evidence to the claim that the DRD2 gene, which affects dopamine activity in the reward pathways, is for some people an explanation for alcoholism.
Li et al. (2014)	Found significant associations between variants of the GABA$_A$ receptor genes and alcohol dependence (GABRA2) and associations between GABRAG2 and both alcohol and heroin dependence.
Roberto et al. (2004b)	Alcohol suppressed the transmission of signals using glutamate in the central nucleus of the amygdala.
Lovinger et al. (1989)	Found that alcohol affected glutamate transmission as well, seemingly by altering how NMDA receptors function.
Blednov and Harris (2008)	Found that a specific type of glutamate receptors (mGluR5) were affected by alcohol.

Table 5.3 Some neurotransmitters, functions affected and some drugs that affect them – related to your course

Neurotransmitter	Functions the neurotransmitter affects	Drugs that affect the neurotransmitter
Dopamine	Pleasure, movement, attention, memory, reward	Cocaine, methamphetamine. Most recreational drugs increase dopamine in the reward pathways.
Serotonin	Mood, sleep, appetite, sexual desire	Ecstasy, LSD, cocaine
Norepinephrine	Movement, sleep, mood, memory, sensory processing, anxiety	Cocaine, methamphetamine, amphetamine
Opioids	Painkillers, sedation, mood, bodily functioning	Heroin and morphine
Acetylcholine	Memory, arousal, attention, mood	Nicotine
GABA	Slows neuronal activity, anxiety, memory	Alcohol

The general idea of how a 'high' is achieved, relating to the reward pathways in the brain and dopamine in that system, is generally accepted to apply to all recreational drugs. The general idea about neurotransmitter functioning affecting the effects of a drug and also affecting issues like addiction, tolerance and withdrawal is also generally accepted.

Progress check 5.12

In the table below write the name of the drug to show which of the following statements apply to heroin addiction, which apply to nicotine addiction and which apply to alcohol addiction.

Statement about a type of addiction	Write 'heroin', 'nicotine' or 'alcohol' to show which each statement applies to
Individuals with specific GABA$_A$ gene variants might be more likely to show addiction than others.	
There can be decreased level of monoamine oxidase (MAO), which is an enzyme that works to break down dopamine. This can help to explain the high dopamine.	
There can be effects on GABA so that it increases its inhibiting effect on brain activity as well as effects on glutamate so that there is a decrease in glutamate – both effects leading to lower brain activity.	
This drug stimulates the acetylcholine receptor, then blocks it, which affects signalling ability. Acetylcholine levels rise.	
There can be a gene that means fewer dopamine receptors and less dopamine in the reward pathways in the brain.	
GABA is not inhibiting the dopamine neurons, so there is more dopamine released into the synaptic cleft, which leads to feelings of euphoria.	

Test yourself

Compare nicotine, heroin and alcohol in terms of biological aspects regarding their misuse. **(12 marks)**

Learning explanations of substance misuse

Another way to explain substance misuse is to say that it is a learned behaviour. You are required to know one learning explanation for heroin, nicotine and alcohol.

Learning theories are classical conditioning, operant conditioning and social learning theory. In this section, the three theories are considered to show how they can relate to the three substances because they are specific theories that explain behaviour rather than being targeted at certain drugs. You do not have to use the same learning explanation for each substance. Classical conditioning is considered most in this section as one learning explanation for all three drugs. Operant conditioning and social learning explanations are touched upon so that you can use those if you prefer, perhaps adding more material to add depth. Also, reviewing operant conditioning and social learning explanations for drug misuse can be helpful in revising those two learning theories. Learning theories are useful when explaining human behaviour and it is good to review them to get used to using them when applying psychology to behaviour.

Having looked at biological explanations for heroin, nicotine and alcohol, you now need to look at learning explanations, one for each drug. Although the biological explanation chosen in this chapter for all three drugs was neurotransmitter functioning, you do not have to use the same explanation for each drug as long as you study one biological and one learning explanation for each of them. Here classical conditioning is used for all three drugs as it helps to add depth and detail.

Classical conditioning and substance misuse

An explanation of substance misuse from the learning approach is using the principles of classical conditioning. Classical conditioning suggests that feelings can come from stimuli that are paired. So, if substance misuse gives pleasure, which will be an automatic response because it is biological, then anything associated with the substance misuse will also give pleasure. For example, drug equipment such as syringes or even the place associated by the individual with substance misuse can trigger the pleasure response (Childress *et al.*, 1994). This conditioning makes a relapse after successful treatment a possibility because, when individuals are exposed to objects or people that were linked to the substance misuse, they might experience the pleasure feelings again and trigger a desire to abuse the drug once more.

Cues related to drug abuse can become associated with the response to the drug and can trigger a response in the body themselves.

Linking conditioning to biology

In biological psychology you may have studied van den Oever *et al.* (2008), who showed that cues present when rats become addicted to heroin and then reintroduced after extinction can lead to changes in the brain that might relate to relapse. You can use this sort of evidence when discussing conditioning. Van den Oever *et al.* (2008) use biological explanations when looking at what is considered to be learning from the environment, which is interesting. This helps to show that it is not that learning and environmental explanations for substance misuse are different from biological explanations. It is more the focus that is different as environmental influences, or biological changes, can be focused on though one can cause the other.

Year One link: Review what you learned about classical conditioning in the learning approach, including Pavlov's (1927) work.

Conditioning explanations of taking drugs

Pavlov (1927, cited in Smart *et al.*, 1983) suggested that drug-taking can be explained using conditioning. The unconditioned stimulus is the drug and the unconditioned response is the effect of the drug in the brain. The conditioned stimulus is one or more of the cues and procedures that go with taking the drugs, which can then give the conditioned response, the pleasure response.

Progress check 5.13

Draw a diagram using classical conditioning principles to show how cues might become associated with drug-taking.

Classical conditioning and tolerance

Siegel *et al.* (1982, cited in Ricker, 2012) carried out a study looking at how rats can be classically conditioned to develop heroin tolerance. The idea was that the situation where addicts take a drug can be a conditioned stimulus and a conditioned response can be the tolerance response in the brain and body. This refers to the situational-specificity of tolerance. The body is signalled by the cues to go into a state where any lethal effect of the drug is countered, and this is what tolerance is – this is why more and more of a drug is needed because of tolerance. Siegel (2001, cited in Ricker, 2012) used a case study to explain tolerance. This case study was about a man who needed morphine injections to control his pain. He usually had his injections in his bedroom. He moved into the living room after staying in his bedroom for a month and needed his injection while he was there. The injection led to signs of overdose and he died a few hours later. Siegel used this case study to show that cues in the bedroom had set the man's body up to prepare for the morphine and to signal its arrival, so the body could counter the effects of the morphine. Without the cues, because he was in the living room, the man's body was not prepared by the cues and this led to 'overdose'.

Year One link: Recall learning about classical conditioning in learning theories.

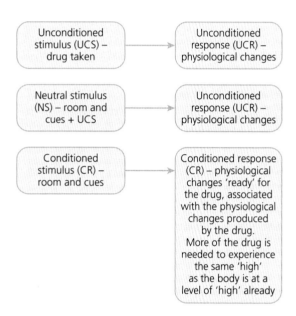

Classical conditioning principles to explain tolerance

Siegel *et al.* (1982) gave rats heroin injections in a specific room with other rats present. They also had sugar injections in a different room in which there were no other rats but there was a machine that generated 'white noise'. This was to ensure no cues were present. There was another group of rats that had their heroin injections in the room with 'white noise' and their sugar injections in the room where the other rats were. There was also a third group of rats who had sugar injections in both rooms. After 30 days the rats were given a large dose of heroin. There was a 'different' condition where rats were given the large dose of heroin in the room they usually had sugar injections in. There was a 'same' condition where the large dose of heroin was given in the room they usually had heroin in. There was a 'control' condition where the rats that had had just sugar injections had the large dose of heroin. Almost all of the control rats died after the large dose and had no tolerance. Around 64 per cent of the rats in the 'different' condition died compared with 32 per cent of the rats in the 'same' condition. Siegel *et al.* concluded that the rats that had had heroin injections

in the first part of the study and were in the 'same' conditions when they had the large dose of heroin had developed tolerance to the heroin and the tolerance was associated with cues in the room.

Explore
You can read an article by Siegel about Pavlovian conditioning and drug overdose, using this link: **http://people.whitman. edu/~herbrawt/classes/390/Siegel.pdf**

Progress check 5.14

Using Siegel *et al.*'s (1982) experiment give one experimental hypothesis from the study. State whether your hypothesis is directional or non-directional.

Year One link: You could revisit your learning about experimental hypotheses and issues around direction. You covered this material when you looked at inferential statistics, probably in cognitive psychology.

 The issues are reviewed in the 'Psychological skills – methods' section online.

Tolerance and learning – biological evidence

There is an argument that tolerance is a form of learning (Cohen, 1965, cited in Smart *et al.*, 1983). It was found that an inhibitor of protein synthesis slowed the development of tolerance and also slowed the acquisition of some responses, so there might be a mechanism in the brain that relates to the development both of tolerance and of learned responses. Ginsburg and Cox (1972, cited in Smart *et al.*, 1983) found that there are inhibitors that can slow the development of tolerance to morphine, linking to heroin use. There is other evidence too that seems to link the development of tolerance to acquiring learned responses, such as electrical stimulation of the frontal cortex slowing tolerance to morphine as a pain killer and also slowing learning. It is thought, therefore, that tolerance and learning are linked.

Therapies for drug addiction, related to classical conditioning

If a therapy works then the principles behind the therapy might show what has led to the problem. In the case of addiction if classical conditioning principles can be used to eliminate the addiction, perhaps this is evidence for classical conditioning principles explaining how the addiction came about.

Cue exposure therapy

Cue exposure therapy relates to classical conditioning principles. The cues that relate to being addicted to drugs, such as smells, sights, people and places, are thought to act as conditioned stimuli, according to classical conditioning principles. If the cues are present for an addict but the drug is not, repeatedly exposing the addict to the cues without the drug should lead to extinction of the association. Price *et al.* (2010, cited in Peters and De Vries, 2014) used 'extinction-based behavioural therapy' to reduce addicts' response to cues. A difficulty is that it is not clear how or why cues act as conditioned reinforcers with regard to relapse, relating to biological processing (Di Ciano and Everitt, 2014, cited in Peters and De Vries, 2014), though this does not take away from any success of the therapy.

Aversion therapy

Aversion therapy relates to classical conditioning principles. In aversion therapy an unwanted experience is associated with the drug that is being misused, to discourage the taking of that drug. The chosen drug might be taken because of a pleasant experience. Replacing that pleasant experience with an unpleasant one can be successful. Alcohol is a good example where aversion therapy can work. For example, a different drug, one that causes a bad feeling of sickness, for example, could be paired with alcohol. Instead of the feeling obtained from alcohol, the person would then experience the sickness, which should lead to stopping drinking alcohol.

STUDY HINT
You need to know two treatments each for heroin, nicotine and alcohol though a treatment can cover more than one drug. One of the treatments must be aversion therapy so you can use what is explained here when discussing aversion therapy. You can use cue exposure therapy as a treatment too, and cognitive-behavioural therapy is mentioned in this section as well. Make notes about treatments ready for the section that follows on treatments for drug misuse.

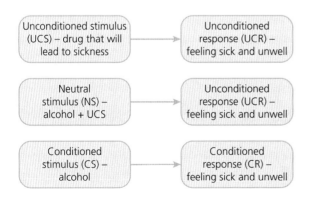

How aversion therapy can work for alcohol addiction

Second-order conditioning

It is worth noting that cues in the environment, which are what become the conditioned stimulus associated with drug-taking responses such as the 'high' feeling, can lead to craving and drug-seeking instead of the physiological response itself. This is **second-order conditioning** and is a step away from the direct association between the stimulus and the original response. Second-order conditioning is where the response is related to the original threatening response but is part of it, such as emotions relating to it. The craving and desire for a drug can be the response from cues rather than the physiological response from the drug itself. The craving is likely to lead to the drug-taking so second-order conditioning can help to explain drug addiction.

Explanation

Second-order conditioning refers to conditioned responses that are not the actual response under consideration, such as, with regard to drug-taking, the release of dopamine. Second-order conditioning refers to emotions and behaviour that goes with that response, such as craving a drug or feeling the fear related to an incident in the past rather than reliving the event.

Heroin, nicotine and alcohol addiction – classical conditioning principles

In what has been said about classical conditioning explaining drug addiction, heroin was used as an example to show how tolerance can be explained by classical conditioning principles and alcohol was used as an example of how aversion therapy can work to help someone to overcome alcohol addiction. Smoking and using nicotine in that way can also be explained using classical conditioning ideas related to cues in the environment linking to nicotine addiction.

Heroin addiction

Siegel *et al.* (1982) (page 501) showed how in rats heroin-taking included tolerance, and tolerance came from cues in the environment triggering physiological reactions that prepared the body for the heroin and so muted its effect. Without those cues, rats 'felt' the effects of heroin more. This is evidence for heroin-taking being related to cues in the environment which act as conditional stimuli giving the conditioned response of tolerance. Also heroin addicts can be 'cued' by what is normally around them when they are taking the drug into feeling the desire to take the drug. The feeling the drug gives will be triggered by the cues around. This comes from classical conditioning principles. The heroin is an unconditioned stimulus that gives a feeling of pleasure (or avoidance of withdrawal) and the feelings are the physiological response that is the unconditioned response. The neutral stimuli are the cues around as they do not at first trigger the heroin-related response. When a neutral stimulus (one of the cues perhaps, like the room 'feel') is associated with the unconditioned stimulus, which is the heroin-taking, then that will give a conditioned response, which is the physiological response to the drug. Evidence for a classical conditioning explanation for heroin addiction is that if someone can either get away from the cues or experience the cues without the heroin effects for a while, the cues can be 'de-conditioned' and the association can be extinguished. If this therapy works, then it suggests that the explanation it is based on has merit.

- Peters and De Vries (2014)

  Peters and De Vries (2014) took up the idea that new stimuli paired with addictive drugs can bring about use of those drugs. They say that the link between stimuli and drugs has been found for cocaine and alcohol though not for heroin, and their study focuses on seeing if heroin is used when cues are present, thus testing the classical conditioning explanation for heroin use. Twenty-four male rats were exposed to an audiovisual cue and a heroin infusion. Food and water were readily available and the study was approved by the animal care committee at the University of Amsterdam. Just five pairings of the cue with the heroin led to the cue being associated with the heroin, and this was measured by lever pressing for heroin. Over two days the association extinguished but there was spontaneous recovery three weeks later.

Explore
You can find the abstract of the Peters and De Vries (2014) study using this link: **www.ncbi.nlm.nih.gov/pubmed/24026484**

Progress check 5.15

In Peters and De Vries' (2014) study what is the independent variable and what is the dependent variable? As a reminder, the IV is what the experimenters manipulate and the DV is what they measure.

Evaluation of classical conditioning as an explanation for heroin addiction

Strengths

- The classical conditioning explanation of heroin addiction has led to cue exposure therapy and Marissen *et al.* (2006, cited in Peters and De Vries, 2014) found that in heroin a bias in attention towards heroin-related cues can be reduced using extinction principles, which is evidence that such therapy can work. This suggests that classical conditioning can be a useful explanation for heroin abuse, a conclusion drawn because a therapy based on the theory can be useful.

- Even though extinction principles can mean less attention to cues related to drug use, Marissen *et al.* (2007, cited in Peters and De Vries, 2014) found that the therapies were not effective in preventing relapse, so there is some question about the success of therapy based on classical conditioning, which raises some questions about classical conditioning as an explanation for heroin misuse. However, Peters and De Vries (2014) suggested that relapse can be explained using classical conditioning principles because relapse shows spontaneous recovery. Overall there seems to be some helpful therapy derived from classical conditioning and some helpful explanations, so it seems to be a useful explanation for drug misuse.

- Both Siegel *et al.* (1982) and Peters and De Vries (2014) use rats to show heroin-related behaviour and both find evidence of cues being associated with heroin addiction. There are strengths in using rats, such as the careful controls that can be put in place with regard to isolating variables for study so that there are no confounding variables. Even so there is the related weakness of using animals in laboratory experiments and then wanting to draw conclusions about humans, which might not be helpful generalising, as well as issues around ethics.

Issues and debates

Siegel *et al.* in 1982 and Peters and De Vries in 2014 used rats to show classical conditioning principles help to explain heroin misuse. You could use this as an example of how perhaps psychology has not changed over time, though Peters and De Vries (2014) talk more about looking for brain changes in response to cues that can help to explain heroin addiction. One of the issues and debates in your course focuses on the development of psychology over time.

Siegel *et al.* (1982) and Peters and De Vries (2014) used rats in their studies and you can use them as examples when discussing ethical issues around using animals in laboratory experiments. Ethics is one of the issues and debates in your course. Another issue and debate in your course relates to practical issues in research design, which can also be illustrated using studies of rats.

Weaknesses

- There is evidence that relapse in drug addicts can relate to cues in the environment that 'remind' the addict that the drug is rewarding and then lead to craving and relapse. However, Peters and De Vries (2014) point out that this association between cues and drug misuse in humans is rather anecdotal and they use Drummond (2000) and Sinha and Li (2007) as evidence for this claim. Evidence tends to come from rats (Fuchs *et al.*, 2008, cited in Peters and De Vries, 2014). It might be claimed that generalising from rats and their drug-related behaviour is not possible as humans have cravings and problem-solving abilities that are likely to differ from rats given brain differences.

- It is hard to separate operant and classical conditioning in the suggested classical conditioning explanation of drug misuse. This is because the cues are thought to be associated with the drug by linking to the pleasure received from taking the drug. If a cue is associated with reward and means behaviour is repeated, that suits an operant conditioning explanation using positive reinforcement. Though as the reward, which is the pleasure response from taking the drug, is an involuntary response in the brain, and the cue not presented deliberately to obtain the reward, classical conditioning seems a more suitable explanation than operant conditioning.

- Marissen *et al.* (2006, cited in Peters and De Vries, 2014) suggest that other forms of cognitive-behavioural therapy (CBT) can be useful in reducing relapse from heroin-related cues, which suggests perhaps more to drug addiction than classical conditioning principles. CBT involves looking at unhelpful thinking, for example, and how thoughts affect behaviour.

Progress check 5.16

Explain briefly the classical conditioning explanation of drug misuse and briefly how this could be explained using operant conditioning principles.

Nicotine addiction

The rewarding effects of smoking are strong possibly because nicotine reaches the brain very quickly, in about 20 seconds, and the stimulation of nicotinic receptors gives feelings of pleasure through release of dopamine, as you will have read about when considering the neurotransmitter explanation for nicotine addiction. Cues related to smoking cigarettes, such as cigarette packets, matches, the environment where smoking takes place, or other smoking paraphernalia, can be associated with the feelings given by nicotine in the brain. Cues can relate to a strong desire to smoke a cigarette, which is second-order conditioning.

- Drug therapy for nicotine addiction, to show classical conditioning principles

  Nicotine craving can be reduced using classical conditioning principles, which suggests classical conditioning is a useful explanation for nicotine addiction. Smokers can take a drug that reduces craving for nicotine, such as varenicline, which is an agonist at the nicotinic receptors and stimulates them less than nicotine does. The receptors are filled with varenicline so the nicotine itself does not have the same effect. This gives a weaker pleasure response from smoking. This neurotransmitter explanation can be related to classical conditioning because the drug varenicline reduces the experience of the drug thus reducing the desire for the drug. Smoking is the unconditioned stimulus with pleasure response as the unconditioned response and varenicline as an unconditioned stimulus gives reduced pleasure response from smoking as the unconditioned response. Pairing smoking cigarettes with varenicline gives the reduced pleasure response until smoking, giving the reduced pleasure response, is stopped.

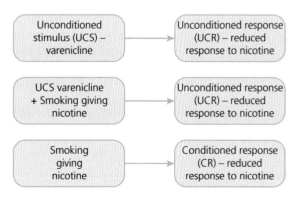

How varenicline can work for nicotine addiction

- Guy and Fletcher (2014)

Guy and Fletcher (2014) discuss conditioning in rats focusing on nicotine exposure at different times during conditioning trials – early, throughout, or late in the trials. They exposed thirsty rats to 13 conditioning sessions. A light or tone was paired with the delivery of water in the sessions. Nicotine was given before either the first or the last of the sessions or throughout the conditioning. Guy and Fletcher (2014) looked at the response, extinction and the reinstatement of responding. Guy and Fletcher (2014) show that nicotine is influenced by stimuli that are related to the rewards that come from nicotine (e.g. Chaudhri et al., 2007) and claim that the conditioned stimuli (the cues) can affect what someone pays attention to as well as reinforcing the smoking of cigarettes more directly. Cues contribute to 'nicotine dependence and relapse' (e.g. Freeman et al., 2012, cited in Guy and Fletcher, 2014, p. 2261). Guy and Fletcher (2014) explain Franklin et al.'s (2011) finding that cues that have been conditioned to be associated with nicotine enhance cravings for nicotine, which can lead to relapse.

Ethical issues

Guy and Fletcher's (2014) study gives detail about how the rats were treated, such as making food available at all times but water only at certain times as it was part of the study. They say that all their procedures were approved by the Centre for Addiction and Mental Health Animal Care Committee and they adhered to Canadian Tri council guidelines referring to how to treat animals in experiments in a humane way. In this book the ethics of studies are not always detailed; however, they are found in the full report. They are referred to quite often so that you can use the study as an example of ethics when discussing ethics.

Procedure

There were different experiments in Guy and Fletcher's (2014) overall study. One experiment focused on administering nicotine at different times during conditioning. The setup involved a rat learning to press a lever on hearing a sound/light in order to get water and there was another lever where there was no response – no water. This was operant conditioning. One condition was where ten rats had saline injections before each conditioning session (the 'control' group). Another condition was where nine rats had nicotine injections throughout, which meant just before every conditioning session (the 'throughout' group). In another condition ten rats received nicotine before the first seven conditioning sessions and saline after that (the 'early' group). A fourth condition was where ten rats had saline injections in the conditioning sessions up to session eight, and then for sessions eight to thirteen they had nicotine injections (the 'late' group). There were also extinction sessions where neither lever gave a reward. Finally, there were more tests where the reward was reinstated. For this part of the study, therefore, there was operant conditioning where rats learned to press a lever for a reward and the classical conditioning involved either saline or nicotine being associated with the learning.

Progress check 5.17

Two ethical principles when using animals in laboratory experiments, according to the Animals (Scientific Procedures) Act (1986) are 1) that animals used for scientific procedures must be cared for according to the best standards and 2) the place where the procedure is carried out must be specified in a personal licence and a project licence. Using these two principles, briefly discuss the study carried out by Guy and Fletcher (2014).

Results and conclusions

Guy and Fletcher (2014) report many findings; however, just some are given here. They found that nicotine injections in the rats that had been exposed to nicotine in the experiment led to reinstatement of the extinguished behaviour, which suggests there was some association with nicotine at exposure and so nicotine could assist in reinstating the behaviour after it had been extinguished. The rats that had nicotine late in the trials were not affected as much as those who had nicotine early or throughout the trial, when it came to looking at their lever-pressing behaviour. They concluded that nicotine interacts with cues that are associated with reward, seemingly to improve motivation to behave in a way to get that reward. There was quite a bit of detail in the study, with only a brief outline given here, but the conclusion was that nicotine works alongside conditioned stimuli, and behaviour is changed. Giving nicotine early when shaping behaviour (in rats) seems to mean more attention paid to the reward stimuli and giving a focus of attention on such stimuli. This suggests that the rewarding effects of nicotine can be associated with other behaviour and that classical learning principles can help to explain such associations.

- Palmatier *et al.* (2013)

    Palmatier *et al.* (2013) have the same conclusion as Guy and Fletcher (2014) in that they suggest that nicotine can increase responding to non-nicotine reinforcers. This effect can depend on the way nicotine increases motivation to behave in certain ways. Nicotine should also increase behaviour in response to stimuli associated through classical conditioning with rewards. It might help to give an everyday example. The idea is that if behaviour is in response to something that has been reinforced by rewards, for example, visiting a certain place because friends are there, which is rewarding, then the smell of the place can become rewarding. The smell would be a cue that became associated with the reward. If someone smoked cigarettes when with the friends, the nicotine should become associated with the smell and vice versa. Nicotine can add to the reward from the cue. The smell may have been associated with a reward for the individual, and nicotine will add to the motivation to get the reward. Nicotine increases responding for primary reinforcers and conditioned reinforcers (e.g. Chaudhri *et al.*, 2006a, cited in Palmatier *et al.*, 2013).

Explore
You can find out more about Palmatier's ideas about smoking and nicotine using this link:
https://huehueteotl.wordpress.com/2008/09/05/its-not-the-nicotine-itself-its-the-cigarette/

Evaluation of classical conditioning as an explanation of nicotine addiction

Strengths

- There is a lot of evidence to show that there are classical conditioning principles involved in nicotine addiction. The response to nicotine, which is an involuntary pleasure response in the brain, can be linked to stimuli in the environment, such as cues related with smoking. What is interesting is that the response can also be linked to stimuli that elicit responses through operant conditioning, so classical and operant conditioning coincide. Evidence comes from Palmatier *et al.* (2013), who cite others such as Chaudhri *et al.* (2006a), and from Guy and Fletcher (2014), who cite others including Chaudhri *et al.* (2006a) as well as Chaudhri *et al.* (2007) and Freeman *et al.* (2012).

- The evidence tends to come from animal laboratory experiments which are carefully controlled so that there are no confounding variables.

STUDY HINT
The strength of studies that use animals in laboratory experiments is that there are careful controls that tend not to be possible when using human participants. This strength is repeated quite often in this chapter, which is about substance misuse, and where studies tend to use animals, such as rats. Be sure to expand on the point fully each time you make it, even though sometimes in this chapter the point is merely summarised.

- As nicotine acts in the brain to give rewards and relaxation, which are involuntary responses to nicotine as a stimulus, this lends itself well to a classical conditioning explanation. Any stimuli associated with nicotine, which is the unconditioned stimulus that leads to the unconditioned response that is the reward, is likely to become a conditioned stimulus leading to the same response. This explanation suits an involuntary response so is a suitable explanation for nicotine addiction.

Weaknesses

- The usual criticism of animal laboratory experiments applies when considering classical conditioning as an explanation for nicotine addiction, in that generalising from such studies to humans with their greater complexity when it comes to motivation and decision-making may lack credibility.

- It could be claimed that operant and classical conditioning principles are hard to separate when considering a classical conditioning explanation for nicotine addiction. The studies given in this section, using rats and linking nicotine to adding rewards so that there is more motivation to repeat a behaviour that is rewarded, look at operant conditioning of behaviours such as pressing a lever to get a reward, and how classical conditioning can explain association between the stimuli giving the reward and nicotine. The difference is about whether the behaviour is voluntary or involuntary, which is important; however, when both are involved then it can be claimed that operant conditioning principles are part of the explanation, which might be seen as a weakness in the classical conditioning explanation.

- A related weakness can be that biological factors need to be involved in the explanation of classical conditioning and nicotine addiction, because the involuntary response in question is a biological one, giving pleasure or relaxation or something similar in the brain. It seems that biological, operant conditioning and classical conditioning principles all have a role in explaining nicotine addiction. This may not be a weakness as classical conditioning principles are still involved; however, it is a weakness in that they seem not to be the only explanation.

Progress check 5.18

Often a strength of an explanation is said to be there being a lot of evidence for that explanation. Explain why having a lot of evidence is a strength.

Alcohol addiction

Classical conditioning principles can explain alcohol addiction, using the same idea as is used when discussing heroin and nicotine addiction. The explanation focuses on the association between a neutral stimulus, such as cues in an environment where alcohol is usually taken, and the conditioned response, which is the feeling alcohol gives. The feelings, as with heroin, can be the pleasure feelings or they might be the feelings of relief at not experiencing withdrawal symptoms. If a therapy based on the explanation works, that can be used as support for the explanation. Aversion therapy can be used to help someone to overcome alcohol addiction because the thought of alcohol can come to bring a feeling of sickness. This suggests that classical conditioning explanations for alcohol use have value.

- Field and Duka (2002)

  Field and Duka (2002) look at drug-related cues and their association with alcohol dependence. They wanted to see whether just any stimuli, if paired with a low dose of alcohol, would give physiological responses in individuals who are social drinkers, such as differences in salivation or skin conductance, as well as differences in craving and how attention is focused. Social drinking is defined as consuming at least 15 units of alcohol a week. The 20 participants, ten of whom were male, consumed two drinks which were different in colour and flavour. The participants were recruited by word of mouth and by poster, and were students and staff at Sussex University. They had £35 as a payment at the end of the experiment. The design of the study was **repeated measures**, using **counterbalancing**. Two types of drink were used. Drinks were given to the participants each day over the days of the study, alternating the order of presenting the drinks, and gathering data such as by use of a questionnaire, physiological measures, and by observation, including of eye gaze. A **double-blind technique** was used, which means the person running the study and the participant were not aware of which condition was which so they did not know what the drinks contained. One of the drinks was tonic water in a green glass with apricot flavouring. The other drink was tonic water with passion fruit flavouring and was in an orange glass. 'CS+' drinks had ethanol added topped up with the flavoured tonic water and 'CS−' drinks just had the tonic water. Field and Duka measured craving for alcohol, amount of salivation and the level of skin conductance in both conditions during the use of the drinks. Afterwards they measured how often the participants directed their attention to the two drinks and what drinks were then chosen. The results were that the participants rated the tastes of the two drinks as comparable, one was not liked more than the other. There were higher rates of craving when the drink had ethanol in it and higher feelings of 'lightheaded' and 'relaxed' after drinking the ethanol drink compared with the tonic water. Skin conductance levels were higher when the drink had the ethanol in it and after conditioning the participants looked more at the ethanol drink than at the tonic water. However, when asked to choose between the two drinks they did not choose the one with ethanol more than the one without. The researchers concluded that cues related to alcohol are quickly associated with its effects, which explained the higher level of looking at the drink with alcohol in it.

Explanation

Double-blind technique means that neither the experimenter or person administering the task(s) nor the participant knows which condition is being used at any one time. **Single-blind technique** means the participants don't know which condition is being used but the researcher does.

Explore
You can read more from Field in an article in *The Psychologist* in 2010 when he writes about how we pay attention, including discussing addiction and anxiety disorders and citing Field and Duka (2002). Here is the link: **https://thepsychologist. bps.org.uk/volume-23/edition-8/cant-take-my-eyes-you**

Explanation

Repeated measures means the participants do all the conditions of a study. **Counterbalancing** means the order conditions are presented in is alternated to avoid order effects, which are fatigue and practice effects.

Year One link: Recall the three experimental/ research designs and issues around counterbalancing and order effects that you learned about in cognitive psychology.

Progress check 5.19

Explain the advantage of using a double-blind technique in an experiment, with regard to conclusions drawn from the results.

- Other evidence that alcohol-related cues are associated with alcohol consumption

Field and Duka (2002) cite other evidence showing that alcoholics shown stimuli associated with alcohol consumption show 'behavioural, cognitive and physiological' responses related to alcohol. They suggest Carter and Tiffany (1999) as a review of the evidence. They cite McCusker and Brown (1995) as finding psychophysiological reactions in the presence of alcohol-related cues and Coffey *et al.* (1999) as finding increased craving for alcohol in the presence of alcohol-related cues. Social drinkers also report more craving for alcohol in the presence of related cues (Willner *et al.*, 1998, cited in Field and Duka, 2002). Field and Duka give quite a bit more

evidence of studies that have found that alcohol-related cues give alcohol-related responses and their evidence is evidence for classical conditioning being an explanation for alcohol use. Field and Duka (2002) conclude 'the evidence suggests that drug cues do act as conditioned incentives and that they do so because of a classical conditioning process' (page 326). Cues can lead people to seek out alcohol and drink it. The term '**cue reactivity**' has been used to cover the idea that cues can lead to alcohol-related responses (Drummond *et al.*, 1995).

Progress check 5.20

List three studies that show that classical conditioning is involved in alcohol addiction.

Definition

Cue reactivity – a term used to cover the reaction of someone addicted to alcohol in response to cues in the environment they associate with alcohol.

Evaluation of classical conditioning as an explanation of alcohol addiction

Strengths

- Aversion therapy works for alcohol addiction in that the pleasurable feelings that come from drinking alcohol are replaced with feelings of nausea and sickness so alcohol is no longer enjoyed. The therapy uses classical conditioning principles and if a therapy works then the underlying principles can be accepted as an explanation. Other aversive stimuli can be used. An issue here is that aversion therapy is not considered appropriate now in the UK. The reason for this is that there are 'more pleasant, less dangerous and less ethically problematic methods of achieving at least as favourable results with less likelihood of treatment dropout' (Raistrick *et al.*, 2006, p. 111). However, having said that, it is found to be effective, such as by Drummond and Glautier (1994, cited in Raistrick *et al.*, 2006).
- Field and Duka's (2002) study used a repeated measures design with careful counterbalancing to control for order effects so participant variables are controlled for. They used a double-blind technique in their experiment as well. As they use the experimental research method with careful controls cause-and-effect conclusions are more easily drawn than in some other methods such as questionnaire or interview. Classical conditioning principles lend themselves well to the experimental method, which Pavlov demonstrated, and experiments have credibility.

- Field and Duka (2002) use an experiment themselves; however, they cite other studies using different methods. For example, they cite McCusker and Brown (1995) as finding psychophysiological reactions in the presence of alcohol-related cues. This means biological evidence confirms their experimental findings. Social drinkers also report more craving for alcohol in the presence of related cues (Willner *et al.*, 1998, cited in Field and Duka, 2002) and this shows that self-report data can also be useful in studying the role of classical conditioning in alcohol misuse. When different methods are used and similar results found, that also adds credibility (and reliability) to the findings.

Weaknesses

- When experiments are used perhaps there is a lack of validity in the findings. Field and Duka (2002) get a variety of evidence from the students, including their rating of the taste of the drinks; however, the situation, such as having to drink the drinks over a period of days and knowing that they were part of a study, may have affected the validity of the results. The double-blind technique would help with validity to an extent; however, there is a lack of ecological validity in that the participants are aware that they are part of a study and may act according to demand characteristics.
- There are other explanations of alcohol misuse, such as the biological explanation, which suggests, for example, that people with a specific gene (DRD2) that means lower dopamine levels in the reward system are more likely to be in the 'addiction' group when considering alcoholics against non-alcoholics. This might be because alcohol gives them more reward in that it lifts their dopamine activity up to the level others may naturally be at. This explanation does not relate to classical conditioning but has evidence for it, and this suggests that classical conditioning may be an explanation for alcohol dependence, but not the only explanation.

Operant conditioning and substance abuse

Detail has been given when looking at classical conditioning and substance abuse, focusing on heroin, nicotine and alcohol. Operant conditioning is also considered as an explanation for substance abuse, including heroin, nicotine and alcohol. It is outlined in this section rather than given in good depth.

Operant conditioning holds that behaviour is repeated if there is a reward and stopped if there is punishment. A reward can be positive (positive reinforcement), such as gaining pleasure, or negative (negative reinforcement), such as removing pain or a problem. Substance misuse can be explained using operant conditioning principles. Drugs can be taken for the reward of pleasurable feelings, which tends to be the case at the start, and drugs can be taken to remove the unpleasant feelings of withdrawal. Withdrawal is explained in more detail earlier in this chapter (page 486) and refers to the symptoms experienced when someone stops taking a drug after having become dependent on it.

After the drug has been taken for a while, it is more likely that negative reinforcement causes the abuse to be continued, because taking the drug removes withdrawal symptoms. There are negative issues about continuing with substance abuse, such as financial and family problems, but the concern about the issues is not as immediate as the reward from taking the drug or from the removal of withdrawal symptoms.

Year One link: Review what you learned about operant conditioning in the learning approach, including Skinner's work and positive and negative reinforcement.

Positive reinforcement – applies to all drugs

Drugs at first seem to be taken because of the euphoria they bring, as discussed when considering neurotransmitter functioning as an explanation for drug misuse and in particular focusing on how dopamine works in the brain's reward pathways. Operant conditioning principles can explain why something is done for a reward and this is called learning through positive reinforcement. Operant conditioning holds that if a behaviour is rewarded it is likely to be repeated and this is behaving because of positive reinforcement. The reward system (the mesolimbic dopamine system) is designed so that food, drink, shelter and sex are reinforcing but drugs can have the same effect, as you saw earlier when considering neurotransmitter functioning and alcohol, so are similarly rewarding. Nicotine, alcohol and heroin are rewarding in this way.

Negative reinforcement – applies to all drugs

Drugs tend to be taken for rewards at the start, for the pleasure they give and perhaps to get the reward of friendship. However, later, stopping the drug will give withdrawal symptoms, as has been explained in this chapter. At that stage someone tends to keep taking the drug to avoid unpleasant withdrawal symptoms. The positive reinforcement may have gone, as tolerance suggests more and more of the drug would be needed to achieve the 'high', which might be hard to provide. However, such is the misery of withdrawal that someone may take the drug to avoid that misery. This then is using the drug because of negative reinforcement. Negative reinforcement is when something unpleasant is avoided by behaviour. The taking of recreational drugs to avoid withdrawal symptoms can apply to all drugs.

Year One link: Recall the difference between positive and negative reinforcement, which you covered when looking at learning theories. Both encourage behaviour.

General points about operant conditioning and drug misuse

Drug addiction can only be rewarding if it gives pleasure. People who get no pleasure from a substance are not likely to become addicted to it. A simple study might be to ask people if they use alcohol and ask them how much they like it and then see if the more they rate it as 'liked' the more they say they use it. This would suggest that people respond to drugs because of them being rewarding, which supports the operant conditioning explanation. You could consider something like this for your practical investigation in health psychology, gathering the self-report data by questionnaire. We respond more to immediate rewards, which a drug can give, and less to delayed rewards, which 'better health' might be an example of. Also with addiction comes the loss of family and friends and that might mean the drug is the main source of reward and so is clung to.

Therapy using operant conditioning principles

There are therapies that use operant conditioning principles, and if they are found to be effective this suggests that operant conditioning principles can explain addiction. One therapy is Community Reinforcement and Family Training (CRAFT) (Meyers and Wolfe, 2004). The idea is to get family and friends to reward positive and healthy behaviours and to remove rewards for unhealthy behaviours.

The rewards have to suit each individual. Similarly, the community reinforcement approach (CRA) covers a wide range of treatments that focus on people in the social environment of the user rewarding being off the drug and not rewarding being on the drug, such as not rewarding being intoxicated. The therapy was developed by Hunt and

Azrin (1973, cited in Raistrick *et al.*, 2006) and was used with in-patients but it has been adapted for use with out-patients as well. Disulfiram, a medical drug, is used with the community reinforcement approach now, and modern versions of a CRA can include disulfiram, training in problem-solving, communication skills and drink-refusal, job finding, muscle relaxation training and motivational counselling. You can see it is a broad package of help and support as well as a therapy using operant conditioning principles. The main focus is on praising and rewarding non-drug-related behaviour and not rewarding drug-related behaviour.

Evaluation of operant conditioning as an explanation for heroin, nicotine and alcohol addiction

Strengths

- Operant conditioning can explain why someone continues to take a drug because of negative reinforcement even though they know that taking it is harmful and even though they don't want to take the drug. It can also explain why someone neglects to eat and drink and neglects themselves, because of the primary drive of taking a drug and getting pleasure in the reward system in the brain. Olds and Milner's (1954) study shows how a recreational drug (in this case heroin) is a primary reinforcer so there is evidence for operant conditioning explanations.
- Therapy like CRA is found to be effective. Raistrick *et al.* (2006) claim that it is one of the top treatments for drug abuse. It does include a package of help and is not just a treatment based on operant conditioning principles; however, the idea of rewarding behaviour

that is not drug-related and not rewarding drug-related behaviour is effective, though the rewards have to suit the individual. If a therapy works then the theory the therapy rests on seems likely to be a suitable explanation of the problem.

Weaknesses

- Learning theories look at one aspect of someone, their actual behaviour, and this is seen as reductionist and, therefore, missing aspects of the individual. When looking at neurotransmitter explanations for drug-taking you have seen that such explanations take learning into account, such as how drugs can be primary reinforcers in the brain; however, there are biological aspects to drug addiction as well. Learning theories take a reductionist view when looking only at behaviour. There are cognitive, social and biological aspects to behaviour that affect such behaviour, and these can be missed. For example, people may take a recreational drug or use alcohol but they may not become addicted. You have seen in what was explained earlier about biological issues and drug addiction that some people have genetic features that might predispose them to alcohol, such as the DRD2 gene.

Progress check 5.21

Explain how positive and negative reinforcement can be explanations for substance misuse.

Social learning and substance abuse

Social learning theory is another learning explanation that suits drug misuse. It is considered here as a general learning theory explanation for substance misuse and can apply to heroin, nicotine and alcohol.

STUDY HINT

If you use a learning theory in a more general sense to explain substance misuse but a question is about a specific drug from heroin, nicotine and alcohol, be sure your answer is explicitly focusing on the drug in question, such as bringing that drug in when you talk about addiction. It is useful to have some information about the three specific drugs for this reason as well as the more general material.

Social learning theory explains that learning takes place by observing role models, particularly those with whom a person identifies and who are similar to them, or who are admired, and then imitating their behaviour.

Year One link: Review your learning about social learning theory when you covered learning theories, including Bandura's studies and social learning principles such as imitation and vicarious reinforcement.

Social learning theory puts forward the idea of **modelling**, which is where behaviour is observed and attended to when watching a model, and then remembered and imitated. Features of modelling include paying attention to a behaviour, remembering it, being able to perform it and being motivated to perform it. There are internal **cognitive processes** at play as well as learning processes, such as motivation and emotional responses and memory. **Identification** with the role model is also a feature of social learning theory. Therefore, if substance misuse is learned through social learning, then the **role model** is likely to be someone similar to the individual and with whom they identify, so that there is motivation to carry out the behaviour, and the observed behaviour is attended to and remembered.

According to social learning theory, children often look up to parents as role models and imitate the behaviour of their parents.

Explanation

Modelling in social learning means watching behaviour and imitating it. For modelling to take place there must be attention paid to issues about the behaviour, there must be retention of what was paid attention to, the behaviour must be reproduced and there must be good motivation to imitate.

Cognitive processes refer to what goes on in the brain from information being input by the senses, through it being processes in some way, to there being an output, such as a memory. Language, thought, problem solving, perception, memory and forgetting are all cognitive processes.

Year One link: Recall what you know about cognitive processes, including memory, from when you covered cognitive psychology. Social learning theory includes cognitive processing.

Explanation

A **role model** is someone a person looks up to and is influenced by, such as parents, teachers or people on television. Social learning theory says these are people who are imitated. **Identification** is the process, in social learning theory, where someone accepts someone else as a role model and imitates them, taking on their values and beliefs.

Progress check 5.22

What are four conditions that are necessary for effective modelling? Use the idea of substance misuse to illustrate your answer.

It is said that parents and peers affect someone's drug misuse, which fits well with social learning theory, as both parents and peers are likely to be role models with whom a person would identify (Baer *et al.*, 1987). **Family studies** show that drug misuse, such as alcohol and smoking, links to the family, which suggests not only a genetic component but also the likelihood of modelling. People who mix with peers who misuse a drug may also get positive reinforcement from misusing the drug, and positive reinforcement is another part of social learning theory, the idea being that there is a reward, such as being part of a group. Akers (1992) has pointed out that television may have a role in promoting substance abuse by providing role models for children. High status people exert a stronger influence on behaviour than low status people (Winett *et al.*, 1989), so it is important that those with high status act responsibly – depending on what is considered 'responsible' in a particular culture.

Explanation

Family studies in psychology look at what runs in families. If a behaviour or characteristic is found in a family there is the assumption that there might be genetic factors underpinning the behaviour, such as alcoholism being found in families. There is also the point that people learn within a family and so might imitate family behaviour.

It is suggested that the social learning of substance misuse depends on the amount of exposure to peers who abuse drugs compared with exposure to peers who do not. It is also affected by the preference of the community towards the particular drug. The frequency of drug use among peers

is important, as well as the age of the individual. Younger adolescents are more susceptible than older adolescents.

An important feature of social learning theory is vicarious learning. For example, at first, smoking seems to be an unpleasant experience. Social learning theory can explain why people continue with it – it is suggested that seeing family and friends enjoying smoking would mean getting a reward vicariously and would lead a person to continue to smoke. **Vicarious reinforcement** suggests that people persist in a behaviour they see rewarded because they expect reward in the future.

Explanation

Vicarious reinforcement means there is no direct reward for a behaviour but someone watching another person being rewarded for a behaviour repeats the behaviour that they have seen rewarded. This is part of social learning theory.

Explore

You can read more about learning theories and addiction using this link. The text looks at classical conditioning, operant conditioning and social learning theories as explanations for addiction.

www.sevencounties.org/poc/view_doc.php?type=doc&id=48409&cn=1408

STUDY HINT

You will have come across the terms associated with social learning when you covered learning theories. Check back over your notes to recall what social learning theory is, and if you kept a glossary of terms, refer to that, as revision.

Progress check 5.23

If a young person sees someone who is smoking a cigarette smiled at and asked to join a social group that the young person would like to join, when the young person starts smoking what could be an explanation?

Evaluation of social learning theory as an explanation of drug misuse

Strengths

- Social learning theory has been developed by Bandura (1977) and also in sociology (e.g. Akers) and has much evidence in many areas of social life. For example, Bandura and others have shown the influence of television and the media on behaviour. Social learning theory has been used to explain many areas of behaviour and has evidence to support it. This adds weight to its use in explaining substance misuse – the amount of evidence in other areas is large, which adds to the reliability of the explanation.

- Social learning has been demonstrated in animals where, for example, monkeys have learned to fear objects that they would not normally fear, just by observing other monkeys showing fear. Therefore, it seems justified to claim that such principles operate in humans too.
- Social learning theory builds on operant conditioning, as it takes reinforcement into account and also incorporates cognitive elements, so it is a theory that has a reasonably complete explanation compared to, for example, classical conditioning.

A girl is likely to imitate her mother's behaviour through principles of social learning – her mother may be a role model, and will smile and give attention, thus reinforcing the behaviour.

Weaknesses

- A study by Ennett *et al.* (1994) found no link between friendship cliques and starting or continuing smoking – only that friendship cliques tended to go against smoking and lead to more 'non-smoking'. There is evidence to suggest, therefore, that peer groups do not lead to substance misuse, but have the opposite effect.
- Mundt *et al.* (2012), one of the contemporary studies in health psychology in your course, found that people show similar alcohol use as their friends not because of peer influence so much as because people choose to be friends with people like them. This goes against a social learning explanation because people are not copying their friends.
- It is hard to show a definite link between observation and learning because there are often many factors involved. For example, it could be argued that family members act as role models because alcohol abuse tends to run in families, but genes are also handed down through families.

Test yourself

With reference to one learning explanation, to what extent can the explanation account for heroin addiction? **(12 marks)**

Comparing the biochemical and classical conditioning explanations of substance misuse

You need to know about two explanations each for heroin, nicotine and alcohol addiction. One must be a biological explanation and one must be a learning explanation. In this chapter the neurotransmitter biological explanation and the classical conditioning learning explanation have been chosen. It is useful to prepare comparison points when you are asked for two different views of some subject matter. Comparing by looking at similarities and differences can help with learning.

It is not the case that biological explanations are right *or* that the classical conditioning explanation is right, as if they cannot both be true. Behavioural reasons may have started the taking of the drug, for example, such as positive reinforcement, which comes from operant conditioning, or social learning theory; however, different theories might explain why someone continues to take the drug. For example, there is the association of cues in the environment with drug-taking and so cues prompt the taking of the drug. Also biological changes occur to maintain the drug-taking. The effects of biological changes on whether a drug leads to addiction can be explained using classical and operant conditioning principles. Those biological changes drive the behaviour to continue substance misuse. Behaviour changes are also needed to overcome the addiction. Drug therapy can be offered, such as when a community reinforcement approach (CRA) uses disulfiram (page 511). Both biological and learning explanations, therefore, are important.

Comparing in terms of validity

- Neurotransmitter explanations are hard to test in terms of **internal validity** because of the difficulty in isolating variables for testing. What happens in the brain is hard to study in real terms, which affects **ecological validity** and **predictive validity**.
- Classical conditioning explanations are easier to study because classical conditioning principles focus on a specific and measurable type of behaviour, involuntary responses, and results might have better internal validity.
- However, as an explanation of a behaviour like drug-taking, classical conditioning is limited in its coverage, which affects the ecological validity of the findings.

- Both neurotransmitter and classical conditioning explanations tend to be studied using experiments because of the need to *isolate* variables to study, and this emphasises the problems with validity.
- Scanning, related to biological explanations, is valid to an extent because the active brain can be measured as it functions, but is done in artificial surroundings using artificial tasks.
- Using animals in laboratory experiments, which both explanations do, is useful for isolating the variables to study them; however, drawing conclusions from animals and relating the conclusions to humans can lack ecological validity.
- Neurotransmitter and classical conditioning explanations for drug misuse do not consider all the aspects of drug-taking, such as the impact of positive and negative reinforcement, the way people imitate others, genetic propensity and the personality of the individual.
- Ecological validity is hard to find when variables must be isolated for study. Internal validity, however, is more easily found as it means there are no **confounding variables**. Using animals in lab experiments means there can be good controls and internal validity is more likely to be found than ecological validity. Predictive validity too is more possible, again because of the controls.

Explanation

Ecological validity refers to something being 'real life' with regard to the setting and situation data are gathered in. This is measuring what is claimed to be measured with regard to the setting and 'ecology' involved and importantly it means that the findings are of use to the individual in the natural setting. **External validity** refers to how far cause and effect findings (coming from a study with internal validity) can be generalised to the target population. **Internal validity** means measuring what it is claimed is being measured with regard to isolating the variable to be studied and 'really' controlling for all other variables so that findings can claim cause and effect because there are no confounding variables. **Confounding variables** are those that are affecting the results of a study as they were not controlled for. **Predictive validity** is measuring what it is claimed is measured such that in the future what is claimed will be found and what is measured can predict something accurately that it should be able to predict.

Year One link: Recall the three different types of validity you need to know in your course. These are predictive, internal and ecological validity. You studied these first in cognitive psychology and they are defined here again to remind you of their meaning.

Comparing in terms of reliability

- Animal studies and scanning have consistently indicated the role of neurotransmitters and receptors in drug use and misuse, so biological explanations appear to have reliability. You looked at a lot of animal studies showing the role of neurotransmitters in drug misuse so you can use those as evidence of the reliability of this explanation.
- In classical conditioning studies too findings consistently show that drug-related cues are associated with the drug and can mean addiction is hard to treat and relapse can occur because of the drug-related cues as well. You have covered studies in this chapter that support the role of cues in relapse, so you can give examples of studies that demonstrate the reliability of the finding that classical conditioning principles can help to explain drug misuse.

Comparing in terms of nature–nurture

- It is worth noting that biological explanations are firmly on the side of a nature explanation, because it is held that receptors react in specific ways according to brain functioning and this applies to all humans. Humans are born with brains that have specific brain functioning.
- Learning theories, however, such as classical conditioning, seem to be firmly in the 'nurture' camp. Classical conditioning theory claims that behaviour such as substance misuse comes from learning from the environment and from experiences, and comes from drug-related cues. Therefore, in the nature–nurture debate, the two explanations can be seen as on opposing sides.
- However, as was seen, the response that is classically conditioned is an involuntary response relating to rewards in the reward pathways in the brain, so biological factors are involved in classical conditioning explanations. The cues involve 'nurture' as they are experienced in our environment, and the resulting response is in our 'nature'.
- Also, classical conditioning can help to explain neurotransmitter functioning (linking it to external cues), which again shows the link between the two. What we experience in the environment outside us, which is our nurture, affects what we experience inside ourselves, which is our nature.

> **STUDY HINT**
>
> Comparing theories (and studies) is quite a difficult skill. One way of doing it is to run through issues such as validity and reliability and to comment on how each theory (or study) fares with regard to these issues. This is done here to illustrate how it might work. Using issues and debates, such as the nature–nurture debate, can also be a way of making a comparison point.

Issues and debates

The nature–nurture debate is one of the issues and debates in your course, which you will be used to making a note of by now, and which you will review at the end of your course. Chapter Seven covers the issues and debates. When you have a biological and a learning explanation, as you do in health psychology in your course, you can consider the two types of explanation in relation to the nature–nurture debate. You could consider how much of our behaviour comes from our nature and how much from our nurture, for example.

Test yourself

Compare one biological and one learning explanation for one drug from heroin, nicotine and alcohol.

(12 marks)

Two ways of treating substance misuse

Having looked at a biological and learning explanation for heroin, nicotine and alcohol, you now need to learn about two treatments for each of the three drugs focused on in health psychology in your course. You can use one treatment to apply to more than one of the three drugs or you can use different treatments for each drug. One of the treatments must be aversion therapy, which has already been brought to this chapter as evidence for classical conditioning being an explanation for drug misuse. The argument was if a therapy based on a theory helps, then the theory is more accepted as an explanation.

- The two treatments for heroin addiction that are focused on are drug treatment (methadone, buprenorphine and naltrexone) and CBT.
- The two treatments for nicotine addiction that are focused on are drug treatment (nicotine replacement therapy, including e-cigarettes and bupropion) and two therapies based on classical conditioning which you can choose one from: varenicline and cue exposure therapy.
- The two treatments for alcohol addiction that are focused on are drug treatment (Diazepam, chlordiazepoxide, chlormethiazole for detoxification and disulfiram for relapse) and one from two therapies based on classical conditioning. You can study both of the therapies based on classical conditioning, which are aversion therapy and cue exposure therapy. You need to know about aversion therapy for your course related to one of the drugs you cover at least, and disulfiram is a drug used in aversion therapy so the treatments link to one another. Another therapy, based on operant conditioning, the community reinforcement approach (CRA), is looked at briefly for your interest as well.

Drug treatment for heroin addiction

Firstly, the therapy is given and then evidence for its effectiveness is discussed, before looking at strengths and weaknesses of the treatment.

Drug treatment involves prescribing heroin, or a substitute that works in the same way. Methadone is a synthetic opiate that blocks the effects of heroin at the synapse and removes withdrawal symptoms. Because use of methadone is enough to take away painful withdrawal symptoms, the individual is helped to give up the drug. One reason for continuing to use heroin is to get rid of withdrawal symptoms (negative reinforcement), so without the withdrawal symptoms, giving up the drug is more likely. There are drug treatments other than methadone, such as buprenorphine. Drugs for heroin use can be opioid receptor antagonists that block the effects of heroin at the synapse. 'Antagonist' means blocking the working of a neurotransmitter by filling the receptor with a drug that does not 'fit' and so does not send a signal, and 'agonist' means activating a signal by filling the receptor with a drug that does suit and so does send a signal. Agonists activate opioid receptors, partial agonists activate opioid receptors too but with a less strong response, and antagonists block the receptor and so stop the rewarding effects of opioids. Heroin is an opioid. Drug therapy is called 'pharmacological' treatments or medications. Drug maintenance programmes, such as using methadone, almost always focus on psychosocial factors as well, such as social support and encouraging the avoidance of people and places linked with the addiction.

> **STUDY HINT**
> You will have come across the terms 'agonist' and 'antagonist' when learning about neurotransmitter functioning and neurotransmitter explanations for drug misuse (e.g. when looking at a neurotransmitter functioning explanation of alcohol abuse) so review your learning there to check your understanding of these terms. You can use your understanding of neurotransmitter functioning to expand on an answer on drug treatment for heroin abuse.

Methadone programmes

Methadone has been used as a treatment since 1964 and is prescribed officially. It is a maintenance programme, which means that it is a way of controlling heroin addiction. Methadone does not affect normal functioning and those taking it are not 'drugged'. It is taken orally and reaches the brain slowly, lowering the 'high' that happens with an injected drug, and prevents withdrawal symptoms for about 24 hours. Methadone also removes cravings for heroin. Someone taking methadone who then takes a normal dose of heroin will not get a feeling of euphoria, so they will be less likely to want to take heroin as well as methadone. Methadone has the brand names Dolophine or Methadose. It is an opioid agonist that acts slowly.

People on the programme have to take methadone once a day and attend a clinic, usually daily, for their prescription. Dosages must be carefully monitored, especially for those who are taking medication for other problems, such as HIV infection. People taking methadone may have problems when coming off the treatment, such as withdrawal symptoms, and methadone use can also create overdose problems.

> ### Explore
> If you would like to know more about methadone maintenance treatment, here is a link that might be of interest: www.cdc.gov/idu/facts/MethadoneFin.pdf

Buprenorphine

Buprenorphine is a treatment being put forward as an alternative to methadone. It has the brand name Subutex. It gives weaker opiate levels than methadone and is less likely to lead to overdose problems. There is also a lower level of physical dependence than with methadone. Buprenorphine is a partial opioid agonist and does not produce the 'high' or dangerous side-effects that heroin can produce. Suboxone is another brand name and is buprenorphine with naloxone, taken orally. Buprenorphine is a drug that can be prescribed without someone attending a specialised treatment clinic, which helps access to it.

Naltrexone

Naltrexone is an opioid antagonist. It has the brand names Depade or Revia. It blocks the action of opioids and is not addictive, nor does it have a sedative effect. It does not result in physical dependence either. There is a long-acting type of naltrexone that can be injected once a month. The brand name is Vivitrol.

> ### Progress check 5.24
> For three drug treatments of heroin state whether they are an agonist, an antagonist or a partial agonist.

Evidence for the effectiveness of drug therapy for heroin use

Year One link: In biological psychology in your course you may have studied the question about how effective drug therapy is for addiction as a key question. If you did, then you can use that material here when considering drug therapy for heroin use.

- Drug treatment is a major way of treating heroin dependence. Blättler et al.'s study (2002) is about whether drug treatment for heroin also affects cocaine use in those who are being treated for heroin. The conclusion is that drug treatment *does* help to reduce cocaine use, as well as heroin use, which is evidence of the success of such an approach.
- Wodak (2005) reported on the success of drug treatment for heroin addiction – methadone and buprenorphine – and reviewed studies to find that, when using such drug treatments, individuals tended to stay on the treatment more than if they were on other treatment programmes.
- The National Institute of Health (1997) found that methadone maintenance treatment is effective in reducing heroin drug use and also helps in a social sense, by reducing crime as well as helping to prevent the spread of HIV/AIDS.
- Studies from Australia, Europe, Asia and the USA have mainly found strong associations between methadone treatment and the reduction in frequency of opioid use, as well as advantages related to HIV.
- Mattick et al. (2009) carried out a review of studies looking at the effectiveness of methadone maintenance for heroin dependence. The aim of the study was to look at the effectiveness of methadone maintenance as a treatment for heroin addiction compared with other treatments, such as detoxification and rehabilitation, or placebo medication. Eleven randomised controlled studies were included in the analysis with 1,969 participants altogether. They found that methadone seemed to be significantly more effective than therapies that did not use drugs in that more people stayed on the treatment and more came off heroin according to self-report data and urine/hair analysis. However, with regard to mortality or criminal activity, methadone was not a more effective treatment. Mattick et al. concluded that methadone therapy was better for keeping patients on a treatment programme and better with regard to decrease in heroin use. When they said 'better' they meant better than treatments that do not use opioid replacement therapy.
- Woody et al. (2008) carried out a clinical trial that compared counselling done together with a short-term programme that used suboxone, with counselling done with an extended suboxone treatment. The short programme lasted two weeks and the extended one lasted 12 weeks. They looked at 154 patients aged 15 to 21. It was the extended suboxone treatment that gave better control over withdrawal symptoms and a

reduction in drug use. The reduction was found again when a long-term follow-up was carried out. There was also better retention on the extended programme. People felt alert on the drug and people showed good daily functioning. This is evidence for the effectiveness of buprenorphine. Suboxone is a drug treatment that includes buprenorphine and naloxone.

- Amato *et al.* (2005) reviewed studies that had a look at the effectiveness of substance maintenance treatments for opioid dependence. They found that methadone maintenance treatment was more effective than methadone detoxification treatment as well as more effective than buprenorphine maintenance treatment. Methadone maintenance treatment was not as effective as injected heroin on its own. High doses of methadone were more effective than low doses. They found methadone maintenance treatment was better than being on a waiting list. Overall they found that methadone maintenance treatment when the dose is right is effective in retaining people on a programme and in stopping heroin use.

- Waal (2013) focused on naltrexone as a treatment of heroin dependence in pregnant women. This is an article about the issue rather than a study. A problem with opioid maintenance treatment (OMT), which is the treatment used for pregnant women (Jones *et al.*, 2011, cited in Waal, 2013), is the effect on the unborn baby, whose body weight and head circumference seem to be affected and neonatal abstinence syndrome (NAS) is found. Opioid maintenance treatment uses methadone. Waal (2013), however, discusses that problems might arise because pregnant women continue with alcohol and nicotine use as well as use of other drugs even while on the OMT programme. Waal (2013) suggests that using buprenorphine as an agonist, as well as focusing on prenatal health services, might bring fewer difficulties. Waal (2013) then considers whether using naltrexone, an opioid antagonist, might be better because this would not lead to NAS in the baby. A problem with using naltrexone is that detoxification must already have occurred before its use and dropping out of the treatment can mean there is relapse to heroin. What would be needed is careful monitoring and, if needed, a return to OMT to avoid relapse to heroin. Waal also points out that not enough is known about naltrexone regarding impact on an unborn child, however it has been used in Western Australia with no apparent problems. The babies are born without NAS (e.g. Kleber *et al.*, 1985, cited in Waal, 2013). A problem is in how to do research when there are not that many pregnant heroin addicts and

also, of course, using anyone to test a drug in this way has ethical implications. Overall, Waal seems to conclude that it is worth investigating the use of naltrexone as a therapy for heroin misuse in pregnant women.

Explore
You can find more out about heroin dependence and medication treatments using this link:
www.betterhealth.vic.gov.au/bhcv2/bhcarticles.nsf/pages/Heroin_dependence_-_medication_treatments

Progress check 5.25
Explain two pieces of evidence that support drug therapy for heroin addiction because of its effectiveness.

Advantages of using drug treatment for heroin dependence – methadone and buprenorphine

- They are taken orally and not injected, which is better as it reduces the risk of diseases that can come from injections.
- They are manufactured carefully unlike street drugs, which may include harmful fillers.
- Heroin effects only last a few hours whereas drug therapy lasts from 24 hours to a few days.
- The addict does not have the problem of having to get their heroin – possibly daily – and so no anxiety that would go with this.
- If an addiction is made stable by drugs then the person can focus on other aspects of their life.
- Drug therapy is less expensive than using heroin so the person would be better off in that way as well.

Advantages of using naltrexone as a treatment for heroin addiction

- Naltrexone gives faster detoxification than methadone.
- It does not cause physical dependence.

Disadvantages of using naltrexone as a treatment for heroin addiction

- Naltrexone does not seem to be as effective as methadone in controlling withdrawal symptoms.
- It does not stop someone wanting to use heroin and it is expensive.
- Naltrexone treatment might just help those who are very committed to coming off heroin.
- It works best as part of a treatment package, such as treatment that includes counselling.

Evaluation of drug treatment for heroin dependence

Strengths

- There is a lot of evidence to show that drug therapy can be effective in treating heroin addiction, with studies showing that methadone means more stay on a treatment programme and more stop using heroin, according to Mattick et al. (2009). Woody et al. (2008) also found drug therapy to be successful, this time looking at buprenorphine and naxolone, which also helped people to come off the drug. However, having an extended drug programme worked better than a short one and also counselling was offered too so perhaps drug therapy can be effective but works well with other therapies alongside.
- Drug therapy that offers replacement for heroin, such as methadone, is better for the person than the heroin. The drugs are manufactured carefully and contain no filler, as well as being cheaper. The individual does not have to worry about where the next amount of heroin is coming from, with the related anxiety.

Weaknesses

- Many patients need treatment for at least two years, and studies suggest that 85 per cent stay on methadone for 12 months. A long treatment has cost implications.
- Randomly assigning or not assigning people to the treatment (or to potentially less effective treatments) is not ethical. Therefore, it is difficult to evaluate the success of methadone maintenance treatment programmes.
- There is both philosophical and political opposition to drug treatment programmes for heroin addiction. Some people object to heroin users being given drugs as treatment, partly because of the withdrawal symptoms when the individual comes off the treatment.
- Politically, a cost–benefit analysis has to be carried out to ensure that the cost of methadone maintenance, or other drug treatment programmes, is worthwhile. In the USA there is said to be a treatment gap (those for whom the treatment is not available) of between 75 per cent and 80 per cent of all addicts (National Institute on Drug Abuse, 2006). The financial cost to the individual, family and society of untreated opiate dependence is extremely high.
- The programmes, even when government-approved, are highly regulated, which makes running them difficult.

Progress check 5.26

Write a short account focusing on two advantages of using drug therapy.

STUDY HINT

When preparing a treatment for one of the drugs you have to cover, be sure you have enough information to describe the treatment, some studies discussing its effectiveness, which can include some showing effectiveness and some showing problems, and then some strengths and weaknesses of the treatment. You could be asked a targeted question, such as about research into its effectiveness.

Cognitive-behavioural therapy for drug addiction

Firstly, the therapy is given and then evidence for its effectiveness is discussed, before looking at strengths and weaknesses of the treatment. Cognitive-behavioural therapy (CBT) helps a patient to consider their expectations and behaviours around drug use.

Cognitive-behavioural therapy (CBT) for drug addiction in general

CBT is a therapy that uses behavioural principles to consider behaviour patterns that are maladaptive for an individual and also looks at the thoughts and emotions around such behaviours. It is used to help to prevent relapse for other drugs, as well as heroin, including nicotine and alcohol, so you can use CBT as a therapy for all three of the drugs you are covering in health psychology in your course.

Year One link: You may have looked at CBT as a therapy for phobias when looking at learning theories in your course. Review the information if you did study CBT earlier in your course.

STUDY HINT

Chapter One, which looks at clinical psychology, uses CBT as a therapy for mental disorders. You may have chosen CBT as one of the therapies for either schizophrenia or your other disorder. You can use material from one place in your course to inform another. However, always focus on the issue being considered, so draw on a therapy in general, but be sure to give a specific focus as well.

CBT works on the assumption that behaviour such as drug addiction relies on learning. CBT focuses on the learning and aims to use different tools to change the learning and to refocus. CBT focuses on drug addiction, not just on stopping taking the drug itself, but on issues surrounding the addiction, including behaviour, feelings and thoughts. CBT is not looking at biological processes such as neurotransmitter functioning, which drug therapy affects. It is considering other aspects of drug addiction.

A main focus is on helping someone to get control over their drug-taking and their lives and developing strategies to cope with such issues. The negative and positive consequences of drug-taking can be explored. Cravings can be focused on, for example, to see how someone might avoid situations where craving the drug might occur.

Beck in the 1960s focused on how irrational or dysfunctional thinking can lead to behaviours that are indeed dysfunctional for someone and Beck pointed out that we have a belief system that is not always useful in affecting our behaviour in a positive way. For example, if we have a core belief that we must be liked by everyone, that would not be helpful as it is unlikely that we can be liked by everyone. CBT would consider how far this is an achievable goal and perhaps suggest someone might aim to be liked about 60 per cent of the time, or whatever they felt was appropriate. A counsellor could consider how reasonable the belief was and how achievable the goal, also how it might be harmful to our self-concept. By breaking a cycle of negative thinking someone can learn new behaviours; for example, with regard to drug dependence like heroin, they can replace behaviour that leads to addiction or continues with the addiction. A network of support can be provided by CBT where the therapist is offering support and encouragement. More positive thought patterns can be encouraged and self-esteem can be boosted. Someone can learn to take gradual steps at their own pace and can practise how to resist peer pressure.

Table 5.4 Types of unhelpful thinking that CBT can focus on

Type of unhelpful thinking	Explanation	Examples
All or nothing thinking	Things are viewed as 'good or bad', for example, or 'right or wrong' with no middle ground.	'He's an idiot' rather than 'some of his behaviour is idiotic'.
Over generalising	Thinking that because something goes wrong it will always go wrong.	'I always burn food.'
Magnification and minimisation	Magnification is when difficulties/shortcomings are exaggerated. Minimisation is when own achievements are made light of.	Magnification: Forgetting a name means 'I am useless at relationships'. Minimisation: Doing well means 'Anyone could do that'.
Jumping to conclusions	Going for a negative interpretation without evidence.	Being alone at break time and thinking 'My colleagues are avoiding me'.
Mind reading	Guessing what someone is thinking without asking or checking.	'You are just saying that to be nice.'
Catastrophising	Tending to magnify and exaggerate bad things in a situation and overestimating problems ahead.	'It is going to be really bad.'
Should, must and ought to	Demands that self, others and the world must be in a certain way.	'I should be a better person.'
Labelling	Attaching a label to one piece of behaviour.	Failing one job interview meaning 'I am a failure'.
Discounting the positive	Dismissing any positive experiences.	'He is just saying that to be nice to me'.

Table 5.5 A tool that CBT can use for finding self-critical thoughts — relating to thinking, feeling and behaviour

Date/time	Situation (what were you doing when you started to feel bad about yourself?)	Feelings (e.g. sad, angry...)	Self-critical thinking (what was going through your mind – exactly?)	Self-defeating behaviour (what did you do as a consequence of your self-critical thoughts?)
	Note down what you were doing	Rate intensity of each feeling from 0–100 (%)	Rate how far you believe each thought/image from 0–100 (%)	Note down what you did

STUDY HINT

In Chapter One, looking at clinical psychology, CBT was suggested as one of the therapies you need to cover for schizophrenia (page 49), as well as for depression (page 71) and OCD (page 85), two of the other mental disorders you need to know about. There was a lot of information in Chapter One relating to CBT so you can find out there more about CBT and how it works, even if you focused on anorexia nervosa.

Explore

You can find out more about CBT as a therapy for substance abuse using this link: www.newbeginningsdrugrehab.org/cognitive-behavioral-drug-therapy/

CBT can help someone with unhelpful thinking by examining it, such as the thought that 'I am no good in social situations'.

Cognitive-behavioural therapy for heroin addiction

There is a question about how far CBT is effective for heroin addiction, however, because heroin addiction is not only about behaving according to core beliefs, it is about addiction to a substance, about getting strong rewards in the reward pathways from the drug, and about miserable withdrawal symptoms if someone stops taking the drug. These are biological aspects of heroin addiction that might be treated better using biological treatments. However, the biological aspects of drug addiction notwithstanding, other aspects of drug-related behaviour, such as emotions, thoughts and social factors, can be addressed to help overcome drug addiction. CBT involves motivational intervention, can include contingency management (CM) (though CM can be seen as a treatment in its own right) and includes relapse prevention (RP).

Evidence for the effectiveness of CBT for heroin addiction

- Fiellin *et al.* (2013) looked at CBT and the use of buprenorphine and naloxone and concluded that adding CBT to drug therapy did not improve the outcomes for patients. The conclusion seems to be that medication, in this case buprenorphine plus naloxone, was not improved by adding CBT. A criticism of this finding, however, is that Fiellin *et al.* (2013) were not looking at a treatment for heroin *addiction* they were looking at treatment using a partial opioid agonist aimed to avoid heroin dependence, which is not the same thing. Relapse avoidance is focused on after detoxification. This argument is found in Shelly, in a blog on the internet (2013), and is worth considering. Considering whether what is under investigation is detoxification or prevention of relapse is a useful evaluation of studies as the two are different. For example, when looking at drug therapy for alcoholism (page 535) it can be seen that different drugs are prescribed to help with detox than are used to prevent relapse, which suggests that treatment to remove the dependence is one thing, whereas treatment to avoid relapse is another. The nature of CBT is to give someone coping strategies and control which would work well after prevention of addiction/dependence, so Fiellin et al.'s (2013) results are not sufficient to show CBT to be effective.

- Rawson et al. (2006) looked at CBT compared with contingency management (CM) for those addicted to drugs. Contingency management is a therapy based on offering direct rewards to people for abstaining from taking a drug and is a behavioural treatment based on operant conditioning principles. It is explained more in the section looking at treatments for alcohol addiction (page 543). Rawson et al. looked at CM, CBT, and at them both combined, to consider their effectiveness. They used 171 people dependent on drugs and their study was a randomised clinical trial. They used either CM, CBT or CM+CBT over 16 weeks. The CM condition involved giving participants vouchers for drug-free urine samples. The CBT condition involved three 90-minute sessions a week. The data were gathered by interview gathering self-report data at the start of the treatment and then again at 17 weeks, 26 weeks and 52 weeks. They found that CM had better retention on the treatment and lower rates of drug use during the study. CBT, however, had similar outcomes over time to CM, just not at the start. When CBT and CM were combined the researchers did not find any improvement compared to their use separately. It seems that CM was useful for reducing drug use and retaining drug users on a treatment programme; however, CBT did reduce drug use and at follow-up did produce similar effects to CM. Rawson et al. (2006) focused on cocaine or methamphetamine addiction rather than heroin addiction; however, they did generalise their conclusions to drug misuse in general. Other reviews, such as McHugh et al., (2010) have taken CM to be part of CBT so it is hard to draw conclusions about the effectiveness of CBT. CBT can be an overarching term covering CM and other interventions, such as motivational interviewing (MI).

Explore
McDuffie (2012) wrote a paper looking at treatment for heroin addiction, which looks at drug therapy, CBT and other therapies and which you could explore to find out more. This paper does not appear to be peer reviewed, which you should consider; however, it raises some useful points. Here is the link: http://opensiuc.lib.siu.edu/cgi/viewcontent.cgi?article=1296&context=gs_rp

Explore
You can access Rawson et al. (2006) using this link if you would like to know more: www.researchgate.net/profile/Karen_Miotto/publication/7327498_A_comparison_of_contingency_management_and_cognitive-behavioral_approaches_for_stimulant-dependent_individuals/links/0fcfd5100bf28a5da5000000.pdf

- McHugh et al. (2010) looked at CBT for substance use disorders. They reviewed evidence supporting the use of CBT and they consider CBT as using different strategies, including operant conditioning strategies, cognitive and motivational aspects and use of tools to build skills. They cite studies that show the effectiveness of CBT for substance abuse, including Dutra et al. (2008) and Magill and Ray (2009). McHugh et al. specifically mention CBT as being effective as a treatment for opioid misuse, as well as other drugs. Rawson et al. (2002) found that 60 per cent of patients having CBT were off drugs at the 52 week follow-up (cited in McHugh et al., 2010), which is evidence that CBT is effective as a therapy for drug misuse.

- McGill and Ray (2009) looked at 53 controlled trials of CBT for adults, focusing on those with alcohol addiction or other drug dependence. They wanted to look at the effectiveness of CBT for drug misuse. McGill and Ray (2009) found a small but significant treatment effect for CBT across the studies they looked at ($p<.005$). Though when they tracked a six-month follow-up finding they found the effect was lower (though still $p<.005$) and at the 12-month follow-up it was lower still, though again still significant ($p<.05$). CBT had the largest effect for marijuana use and also in studies where the control group had 'no treatment'. They found that if there were more female participants the effect of CBT seemed higher. Also as there were more sessions the effectiveness dropped, which is interesting.

Briefly summarise McGill and Ray's (2009) findings.

- Petry and Martin (2002, cited in McHugh *et al.*, 2010) looked at contingency management (CM) for opioid abuse and in 2000 Petry *et al.* looked at contingency management for alcohol dependence. The studies supported the use of CM for these drugs. Research tends to suggest that CM is more effective for heroin and cocaine than it is for nicotine. McHugh *et al.* (2010) take CM to be part of CBT.

- McHugh *et al.* (2010) report that the combination of CBT and CM is the most effective compared with other single interventions according to Rawson *et al.* (2002); however, McHugh *et al.* (2010) say that this evidence comes from just two studies. They say that behavioural therapies in combination are not always found to work well, such as CBT and cue exposure together (Kavanagh *et al.*, 2006, cited in McHugh *et al.*, 2010) or CBT and CM together (Rawson *et al.*, 2002, cited in McHugh *et al.*, 2010). McHugh *et al.* (2010) conclude that CBT covers a lot of behavioural treatments including CM, which is an 'operant learning process'. They felt that an overall conclusion was that CBT was effective, judging from controlled trials, and combining treatments, not just within the CBT 'family' of treatments, such as CBT and CM, but also combining CBT and drug therapy, might give the best outcomes. Finding which combinations are the most effective is a challenge, as is making sure CBT is available as a treatment.

Evaluation of CBT for heroin addiction

Strengths

- CBT has strengths as a therapy, including how the client has control over the therapy. It is short-term, which can be seen as a strength because the client can focus on their issues over a time-limited set of sessions rather than the therapy going on for a very long time. The therapy gives the client control over the issues they want to explore and over the goals they want to achieve. This gives the client power, which is helpful; the therapist works with the client but does not instruct. CBT involves collaboration between the client and the counsellor. CBT involves an element of education, which means the client leaves the sessions with skills and knowledge they can draw on after the sessions end.

- CBT has been shown to be effective, as some studies have shown and as McHugh *et al.* (2010) conclude in their review. McGill and Ray (2009) found using 53 controlled trials that CBT is effective for substance misuse. They found it is still effective at a six-month and a 12-month follow-up, though effectiveness tends to diminish over time.

Weaknesses

- The studies and reviews used in this section to give evidence for the effectiveness of CBT as a therapy for heroin dependence show that there are some differences in how CBT is defined. Sometimes contingency management (CM) is taken to be part of CBT (e.g. McHugh *et al.*, 2010), sometimes CM is covered separately (e.g. Rawson *et al.*, 2006). When CBT is defined widely, to include CM, it is seen as effective, whereas if CM is seen as a separate therapy it can be said to be more effective than CBT (e.g. Rawson *et al.*, 2006). This means it is hard to be definitive about the effectiveness of CBT.

- McHugh *et al.* (2010) suggest that more needs to be done to try therapies in combination for heroin addiction and dependency on other substances. CBT seems to be effective, but can be said to be more effective if combined with CM, and perhaps effective if combined with drug therapy. There are results from studies about combinations of therapies; however, according to McHugh *et al.*, more results are needed to be sure about which is the 'best' combination.

- It is important perhaps to check when saying that CBT is effective (or not effective) whether it is detoxification that is focused on or prevention of relapse. Detox means helping with withdrawal symptoms and coming off a drug and prevention of relapse means helping someone to stay off the drug. Different medication is useful for these different purposes and perhaps CBT is more useful for prevention of relapse than for detoxification.

Progress check 5.28

Which studies have you learned about that focus on heroin specifically when it comes to CBT and its effectiveness and which focus on substance abuse in general? Complete the table:

Study — CBT effectiveness focusing on heroin	Study — CBT effectiveness focusing on substance misuse in general

Drug therapy for nicotine addiction

Firstly, the therapy is given and then evidence for its effectiveness is discussed, before looking at strengths and weaknesses of the treatment. Nicotine replacement therapy is one therapy using drugs to help with nicotine addiction, and e-cigarettes can be put into the category of nicotine replacement. Other drugs such as the antidepressant bupropion can be used. Varenicline tartrate can be used to help with withdrawal symptoms and block the effects of nicotine when someone smokes and can also cause nausea, which can help to prevent smoking for nicotine. In this section nicotine replacement is focused on and bupropion is considered briefly. Varenicline is looked at as part of therapies based on classical conditioning principles.

Nicotine replacement therapy

Nicotine replacement therapy (NRT) does what it says and gives nicotine for those who want to give up smoking cigarettes. E-cigarettes also replace nicotine, though are not included as NRT directly. In this section both NRT and e-cigarettes are covered, focusing on using nicotine as a way of stopping smoking, so they are included as 'drug therapy' as nicotine is a drug. Nicotine acts on the brain to produce effects such as activating the brain's reward pathways and so is seen as a drug.

Nicotine gum, patches, tablets, mouth spray and nasal spray have been used as nicotine replacement therapy to help with nicotine addiction. There is also a tablet that can be taken. Mecamylamine can be used as well. Both nicotine

and mecamylamine fill receptors that nicotine from cigarettes would work on if they were not filled, so possibly using nicotine replacement and mecamylamine would work together to help someone to stop smoking.

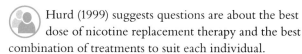 Hurd (1999) suggests questions are about the best dose of nicotine replacement therapy and the best combination of treatments to suit each individual.

Nicotine replacement therapy (NRT) releases nicotine into the bloodstream at a steady rate and at a much lower rate than a cigarette would give. NRT also does not give the tar and carbon monoxide that comes with cigarette smoke. Having NRT helps to control cravings and mood while someone gives up cigarette smoking. There can be side-effects, including skin irritation if patches are used, sleep problems, upset stomach, dizziness and headaches. The side-effects are not usually strong ones, however.

Progress check 5.29

How does nicotine replacement therapy work to help someone to stop smoking?

Evidence about the use of nicotine replacement therapy as a treatment for nicotine addiction

- Alpert *et al.* (2012) found using a survey that NRT is not effective in helping people to stop smoking. Alpert *et al.* found that smokers who used nicotine replacement therapy over the last two years and were non-smokers at the time of the study were no more or less likely to relapse than ex-smokers who were not using NRT.
- Hughes *et al.* (2012) present three reasons to show that Alpert *et al.*'s (2012) study findings were not warranted. Firstly, Hughes *et al.* suggest that Alpert *et al.* were testing people who had used NRT up to two years before their study to see if that use of NRT prevented relapse much later. Hughes *et al.* point out that NRT focuses on when it is being used and after that period relapse is similar between those who had used NRT and controls (e.g. Fagerstrom, 2003, cited in Hughes *et al.*, 2012). NRT helps with stopping smoking in the long term by helping people to stop smoking at the time of using NRT. It is not appropriate to evaluate nicotine replacement therapy years after its use as that is not what it is for. Secondly, Hughes *et al.* (2011, cited in Hughes *et al.*, 2012) say that Alpert *et al.* (2012) give three studies that fail to find NRT to be effective but that there were 12 studies that show that NRT is effective that were not given in Alpert *et al.* (2012). This suggests that there are a lot of studies showing the effectiveness of NRT. Thirdly, Hughes *et al.* (2012)

cite Shiffman et al. (2008) as showing that a problem with studying the effectiveness of NRT is that those smokers who find it hard to quit are the ones using NRT so the sample is a biased one and effectiveness of the therapy might be harder to show in this biased sample.

- Ferguson et al. (2011) look at the value of using education about nicotine replacement therapy in relation to its being used. They used 900 smokers who completed an online survey asking about NRT. They found three main misperceptions about NRT. They found that 93 per cent of smokers did not realise that smoking while wearing nicotine patches would not result in heart attacks, 76 per cent of smokers did not know that nicotine gum is not as addictive as smoking tobacco and 69 per cent did not know that nicotine replacement therapy 'products are not as dangerous as cigarettes'. Importantly, more than 50 per cent of respondents said they would be more likely to use NRT to help them to stop smoking if they had more information about it. Fifty-three per cent of those who thought that NRT caused heart attacks if someone smoked at the same time, 58 per cent of those who thought nicotine gum was as addictive as smoking tobacco and 66 per cent of those who thought NRT products were as dangerous as conventional cigarettes said they would consider using them if they had more information.

- O'Connor et al. (2011) looked at education, as did Ferguson et al. (2011). They felt that people would switch to NRT if they knew the differences between NRT and cigarette smoking in terms of the risks. Their study included 67 adult smokers who were not looking to stop but were given the chance to try oral nicotine products. Participants at the first visit were given information about oral NRT and smoking conventional cigarettes. At the second visit they were given samples of four oral nicotine products to use for a week and at visit three they had a one-week supply of the product they preferred to see if it would help them to stop smoking. O'Connor et al. (2011) found that Commit lozenges were preferred and after a week using one of the nicotine replacement products there was a significant lowering of smoking cigarettes from 11.8 to 8.7 cigarettes a day. The researchers concluded that smokers might be willing to use NRT as an alternative in the short-term as a substitute for smoking but it seems they would continue to smoke though in a reduced form.

- Morphett et al. (2013) in Australia carried out interviews to find out what members of the public thought about what would help someone to stop smoking. They felt that what the public choose is not related to understanding of nicotine addiction so much as focus on individual choice, motivation and willpower, including unassisted quitting being seen as a successful way to stop. If the public is not informed enough about NRT then that is a factor in evaluating its success.

Evaluation of NRT to help with stopping smoking

Strengths

- Hughes et al. (2012) mention 12 studies that show the effectiveness of NRT. However, a search for the studies showed they were hard to pin down. Nonetheless they were mentioned.

- O'Connor et al. (2011) found some reduction in cigarette smoking over a week when using a replacement oral nicotine product though the participants did not give up smoking and the product was just used for one week so this is a limited finding regarding the success of NRT.

Weaknesses

- Nicotine replacement therapy may work when it is being used but is not, according to Hughes et al. (2012), a therapy intended to work in the long term. The aim is to help someone to stop smoking and then there would be therapy to prevent relapse, which NRT is not suitable for.

- One issue raised by Ferguson et al. (2011) is that people do not know enough about NRT (such as nicotine gum) and their misperceptions might mean they do not use NRT even though it might help, so education about NRT is important and lack of such education can limit its effectiveness. Morphett et al. (2013) seem to support the conclusion that there is a lack of information.

- Alpert et al. (2012) found that smokers who used nicotine replacement therapy over the last two years and were non-smokers at the time of the study were no more or less likely to relapse than ex-smokers who were not using NRT. This suggests NRT is not effective.

E-cigarettes

There has been some discussion about e-cigarettes and their health effects, suggesting they may lead people to become addicted to nicotine. They are electronic, battery-operated cigarettes that deliver a spray of nicotine in a similar way to a cigarette but they have lower toxin levels than tobacco cigarettes and so seem to be safer. Possibly e-cigarettes in young people are a way to start smoking and not a way to stop it. As e-cigarettes lead to inhalation of a vapour, this can be called 'vaping'.

Evidence about the use of e-cigarettes as a treatment for nicotine addiction

Overall the findings of studies looking at e-cigarette use as a treatment for nicotine addiction suggest that this is not a successful treatment. Furthermore there is a suggestion that in young people at least using e-cigarettes can lead to smoking conventional cigarettes.

- Wimmer (2015) wrote about e-cigarettes as a 'new challenge' for public health and for schools. He cites the US Department of Health and Human Services in 2014 as saying that almost 90 per cent of the 20 million Americans who have died from tobacco-related problems since 1964 began their addiction before the age of 19 years. Wimmer cites studies between 2011 and 2013 that show that e-cigarette use doubled in school-aged children and young people, including more than 250,000 students who had never smoked before (e.g. Bunnell et al., 2014, cited in Wimmer, 2015). Zhu et al. (2014, cited in Wimmer, 2015) report that from early in 2014 there were around 466 brands and 7,764 flavours of e-cigarettes available in an unregulated industry and a problem is that nicotine levels in e-cigarettes seem to vary (Palazzolo, 2013, cited in Wimmer, 2015). A concern is that e-cigarette use will lead to smoking cigarettes, not to stopping smoking. Bunnell et al. (2014, cited in Wimmer, 2015) found that young people who tried e-cigarettes and had not smoked cigarettes were twice as likely to say they would smoke conventional cigarettes than young people who had never tried e-cigarettes. Nicotine is addictive and can affect adolescent brain development as well as being toxic, according to Schraufnagel et al. (2014, cited in Wimmer, 2015). Schipper et al. (2014) suggests there have been attempts at suicide in those who have ingested e-cigarette liquid and Chatham-Stephens et al. (2014) found a high rise in cases of nicotine poisoning after e-cigarettes have become available (both cited in Wimmer, 2015). There seems to be enough evidence here to suggest that e-cigarettes are harmful, at least to young people, and are not a suitable treatment for nicotine addiction.

- Grana et al. (2014) review the use of e-cigarettes and suggest that criticism of e-cigarettes needs to be kept up to date because they are changing and newer products could be more safe and more effective. However, Grana et al. suggest that e-cigarettes should be restricted where smoking conventional cigarettes is restricted and should have the same restrictions on how they are marketed, which reflects the current uncertainty about their value as a treatment for nicotine addiction. Grana et al. (2014) cite Choi and Forster (2014), who looked at young adults who had not used e-cigarettes from 2010 to 2011 and followed them up later. They found at the time of the follow-up that 21.6 per cent of those who smoked at the time of the follow-up had used an e-cigarette at some time, 11.9 per cent of former smokers said they had used an e-cigarette at some time and 2.9 per cent of non-smokers reported having used an e-cigarette at some time. Those who said at the start that e-cigarettes could help with stopping smoking and were less harmful than smoking cigarettes were more likely to say they had experimented with e-cigarettes. Choi and Forster's (2014, cited in Grana et al., 2014) study gives evidence that e-cigarettes can affect smoking behaviour negatively, in that they relate to more cigarette smoking.

- Grana et al. (2014) reported Adkison et al.'s (2013) finding that in the US, Canada, the UK and Australia e-cigarette users had reduced cigarette smoking per day significantly more than those who did not use e-cigarettes. The results were that e-cigarette users reduced from 20.1 to 16.3 conventional cigarettes per day and those who did not use e-cigarettes reduced from 16.9 a day to 15.0 a day. However, one year later e-cigarette users were no more likely to have given up conventional cigarette smoking than those who did not use e-cigarettes.

- Polosa et al. (2011, cited in Grana et al., 2014) carried out a study in Italy with 40 smokers who were not intending to stop smoking in the next 30 days. The study asked the participants to use e-cigarettes and to use up to four cartridges a day to reduce smoking. Twenty-seven of the participants gave follow-up data at six months. Thirteen of the smokers used both tobacco and e-cigarettes, five kept on smoking conventional cigarettes and nine stopped smoking tobacco but kept on with e-cigarettes. In the 13 who used both types of cigarette, conventional cigarette smoking was reduced by 50 per cent. At 18 and 24 months Polosa et al. (2011) did follow-ups with 23 participants. At 24 months, 18 continued to smoke and 11 had reduced their smoking by 50 per cent or more, on average going from 24 conventional cigarettes to four a day (p=0.003). Five participants had stopped conventional cigarettes at the 24-month follow-up. A problem with Polosa et al.'s study was that there was no control group. The findings of Polosa et al. are rather mixed as e-cigarette use does seem to have had some effect on smoking of conventional cigarettes, but only to an extent. However, this was in a group that did not intend to give up smoking and so drawing conclusions from the participants to people who want to quit is not suitable.

Using e-cigarettes v. using nicotine replacement therapy

- Pokhrel *et al.* (2014) carried out a study looking at 834 daily smokers in Hawaii. They wanted to compare the use of e-cigarettes with the use of NRT. They gathered data about smoking and stopping smoking as well as other data about age, gender and so on. They looked at whether people had ever used an e-cigarette only, whether they had used NRT only or whether they had used both to help them to stop smoking. They found that younger smokers, non-white smokers, high income smokers, those with lower dependence on nicotine, those who had been smoking for less time and those who had tried more often to stop were likely to have tried e-cigarettes but not NRT to help with stopping smoking. They concluded that smokers who used e-cigarettes but not NRT products might be different from smokers using NRT but not e-cigarettes in terms of age, ethnicity or how much they had tried to stop smoking conventional cigarettes.

- Pokhrel *et al.* (2014) confirm the general idea that there is not enough known about health effects of e-cigarettes or how effective they are when stopping smoking so they say that more needs to be known about smokers who are likely to use e-cigarettes.

Evaluation of e-cigarettes as treatment for nicotine addiction

Strengths

- Polosa *et al.* (2011, cited in Grana *et al.*, 2014) suggest some value in using e-cigarettes, in reducing smoking if not in giving up. At 24 months, 18 continued to smoke, 11 had reduced their smoking by 50 per cent or more and five participants had stopped smoking conventional cigarettes.

- Adkison *et al.*'s (2013) study found that e-cigarette users had reduced cigarette smoking per day significantly more than those who did not use e-cigarettes. However, one year later e-cigarette users were no more likely to have given up conventional cigarette smoking than those who did not use e-cigarettes.

Weaknesses

- Bunnell *et al.* (2014) found that e-cigarette use increased three-fold in children and young people from 2011–2013, and this included more than 250,000 young people who had never smoked before, using e-cigarettes in 2013. Chatham-Stephens *et al.* (2014) found a high rise in cases of nicotine poisoning after e-cigarettes have become

available. Both these studies are cited in Wimmer (2015) and they suggest e-cigarettes are harmful.

- Grana *et al.* (2014) cite Choi and Forster (2014), who found at the time of a follow-up that 21.6 per cent of those who smoked at the time of the follow-up had used an e-cigarette at some time, 11.9 per cent of former smokers said they had used an e-cigarette at some time and 2.9 per cent of non-smokers reported having used an e-cigarette at some time. This suggests that use of an e-cigarette links more with smoking than with not smoking.

- Pokhrel *et al.* (2014) confirm the general idea that there is not enough known about health effects of e-cigarettes or how effective they are when stopping smoking.

Evaluation of nicotine replacement therapy and e-cigarettes as treatment for nicotine addiction

Strengths

- A problem in looking at the effectiveness of using NRT including e-cigarettes is that nicotine replacement is not intended as a long-term treatment so should be assessed as a short-term aid for helping with stopping smoking. When considered in this way, as short-term aids, there is some evidence of effectiveness, as Hughes *et al.* (2012) point out, citing Adkison *et al.*'s (2013) study referring to e-cigarette use.

- Another strength is the availability of many different types of NRT to suit individual choice. E-cigarettes too are widely available. There is no need for someone to sign up to a programme, for example – there is an element of choice involved. However, if there is doubt about the effectiveness of NRT and of e-cigarettes then perhaps this is not so much of a strength as it might appear.

- Studies tend to use controls and follow-ups so the findings have some credibility. However, people are lost in the follow-ups (e.g. at 18 and 24 months Polosa *et al.* (2011) did follow-ups with 23 participants out of 40 participants who started the study). Those left might have specific characteristics that affect generalisation of the findings. Also Polosa *et al.* (and other studies) use smokers who do not intend to give up smoking, which again is a biased sample.

Weaknesses

- E-cigarettes and NRT are not effective in the long-term with regard to stopping smoking conventional cigarettes and even though they are not intended for that purpose, this should be noted. Other therapies might be needed for prevention of relapse.

- O'Connor *et al.* (2011) and Ferguson *et al.* (2011) claim that members of the public need to know more about NRT and e-cigarettes as misinformation can prevent their use. A weakness of NRT and e-cigarettes as therapy for nicotine addiction is that people are wary of their use through lack of information so they are not used. Indeed not enough is known about e-cigarettes and their safety.
- E-cigarettes are thought to encourage smoking in young people, which is a worrying finding.
- There might be individual differences in what suits smokers when it comes to stopping smoking. Pokhrel *et al.* (2014) found some such differences as evidence for this idea.

Progress check 5.30

Give the names of two studies that suggest NRT or e-cigarettes are effective for nicotine addiction and the names of two studies that consider the treatment not to be effective.

> **STUDY HINT**
> If you are using nicotine replacement therapy as one treatment for nicotine addiction you can include e-cigarettes as long as you explain that they too give nicotine or you can use e-cigarettes as a therapy in itself. It is not only what the right answer is to a question so much as how you justify and explain your choice of material in your answer.

Other drug therapies for nicotine addiction

There are drug therapies for nicotine addiction other than those that work on replacing the nicotine in the system. Bupropion can help with nicotine addiction by affecting dopamine activity in the brain. Noradrenaline receptors also seem to be important in nicotine addiction so a drug focusing on noradrenaline might be useful. The main therapy in this section is nicotine replacement therapy, including e-cigarettes, but other ideas are given here to extend your understanding and you can look up more about them if you wish.

Bupropion as a treatment for nicotine addiction

Firstly, the therapy is given and then evidence for its effectiveness is discussed, before looking at strengths and weaknesses of the treatment. Bupropion sustained-release (SR) is a non-nicotine drug therapy helpful for stopping smoking and it affects dopamine activity in the reward pathways in the brain. It works in the mesolimbic system

and nucleus accumbens, which were covered earlier in this chapter when discussing neurotransmitter explanations for substance misuse (page 487). Bupropion inhibits the reuptake of dopamine so affects the amount of dopamine in the synapse. It also is a weak noradrenaline reuptake inhibitor. Bupropion was developed as a drug to help with depression and it seems to help people to stop smoking. Bupropion (brand name Zyban) has side-effects including dry mouth, difficulty concentrating, dizziness, headaches, drowsiness and sleep problems, as well as upset stomach. It is thought that about one in five smokers is helped to stop smoking by bupropion, according to Wilkes (2008). Bupropion is given to people who set themselves a target of two weeks to stop smoking and they are given 150 mg once a day of bupropion for six days and then 150 mg twice a day for between seven and nine weeks. Those who stop smoking are then given the rest of the course.

Bupropion works at the dopamine and noradrenaline receptors to prevent reuptake, which leaves more of those neurotransmitters in the synapse. There is no effect on serotonin. Bupropion also affects the stimulant effects of nicotine on the nicotinic receptors, according to Wilkes (2008).

Progress check 5.31

What does 'reuptake' signify when referring to neurotransmitter functioning in the brain?

Evidence for bupropion's effectiveness for nicotine addiction

- Wilkes (2008) considers the use of sustained-release bupropion as a treatment for smoking cessation. Bupropion was only licensed in the UK in 2000 so is relatively recent as a treatment for nicotine addiction. It is licensed for use with people aged 18 years and over. Bupropion affects levels of dopamine, such as in the reward pathways, though it does affect dopamine levels differently in different areas of the brain. Wilkes cites two studies as showing that bupropion is effective for nicotine addiction. Hurt *et al.* (1997) showed that at one year bupropion showed a 23 per cent abstinence rate compared with 12 per cent in a placebo group. Jorenby *et al.* (1999) showed at one year an abstinence rate of 30 per cent for bupropion compared with 16 per cent in a placebo group. Both these findings were significant.

> **Explore**
> You can find a table of results in Wilkes (2008) showing the effectiveness of bupropion using this link:
> www.ncbi.nlm.nih.gov/pmc/articles/PMC2528204/

- Killen *et al.* (2006, cited in Wilkes, 2008) found that treatment using bupropion over 14 weeks, thus extending the treatment, does not improve the rate of stopping smoking over one year compared with a placebo group. The bupropion group showed 33 per cent abstinence compared with 34 per cent for the placebo group. This suggests perhaps that long-term, after the treatment has been stopped, bupropion is not effective. However, there are quite a few studies that show it is effective.
- Wilkes (2008) reports that there are more adverse effects with bupropion than with nicotine replacement therapy, though the rate of stopping the treatment is similar between the two. It seems that about 30 per cent stop using bupropion because of adverse effects, which is quite high and a disadvantage of bupropion.
- Studies that use varenicline and compare it with bupropion and a placebo tend to find that bupropion is effective but varenicline is more effective. Studies include Jorenby *et al.* (2006), which is explained later when the effectiveness of varenicline is looked at (page 531).
- Roddy (2004) suggests that bupropion is as effective if used in conjunction with behavioural therapy as NRT and both NRT and bupropion lead to a 'near doubling' of the stopping smoking rate. Nineteen per cent of smokers who use bupropion to stop smoking achieve long-term abstinence.
- Swan *et al.* (2003) examine Zyban, which is sustained-release bupropion, and its effectiveness in stopping smoking. They carried out a randomised trial in Seattle with a year of follow-up. They used 1,524 adult smokers who wanted to stop smoking and they randomly assigned them to different combinations of bupropion and counselling. Bupropion was given in either 150 mg or 300 mg doses and counselling was given in either brief format or moderate so there were four groups. They measured smoking over the period of a week using self-report data and they gathered the data at three months and at twelve months after the date set to give up smoking. At three months there was more non-smoking in those getting the larger dose of bupropion and at twelve months the higher rate of smoking was in the group with moderate intensity counselling. At three months the higher dose of bupropion was associated with problems with sleeping, difficulty with concentrating, shakiness and stomach problems as well as a lower reported desire to smoke. They found a one year quit rate of between 23.6 per cent and 33.2 per cent for those having a combination of bupropion and moderate counselling. This is evidence that bupropion is effective but perhaps with counselling more than on its own.

Evaluation of using bupropion as a therapy for nicotine addiction

Strengths

- There is evidence for the effectiveness of bupropion for stopping smoking, including the fact that it is recommended by NICE as a treatment. Swan *et al.* (2003) and Roddy (2004) both found that bupropion was effective with behavioural therapy, which is evidence of its usefulness, though perhaps with the comment that counselling alongside the drug therapy is more helpful. Hurt *et al.* (1997) and Jorenby *et al.* (1999) – both cited in Wilkes (2008) – showed that bupropion was more effective than a placebo.
- Drug therapy is tested using randomised trials, which means participants are put randomly into either a 'drug therapy' group or a placebo group. This means there are good controls. A double-blind design can be used as well, where neither the people running the study nor the participants know which group a person is in. Such controls tend to mean findings are credible. There is more than one study that shows bupropion is more effective than a placebo, which suggests findings have reliability too.

Weaknesses

- Varenicline can be successful for stopping smoking. One study showed that 10 per cent of people who had a placebo gave up smoking, 15 per cent of those who had bupropion gave up and 23 per cent of those using varenicline gave up smoking, which is evidence for the success of varenicline and against the usefulness of bupropion. However, buproprion had some success. Also the success of both bupropion and varenicline was limited, which questions the effectiveness of both of these therapies. Jorenby *et al.* (2006) had similar findings, which put varenicline ahead of bupropion when it came to helping smoking cessation (page 531), though bupropion was more effective than the placebo in Jorenby *et al.* (2006), which supports its use.
- If studies show that bupropion and counselling or some behavioural therapy are used alongside each other, this suggests that bupropion alone is not as effective. If therapy uses more than one approach it is hard to show effectiveness of a single therapy. Differences in studies such as whether people who want to quit or people who do not want to quit are used can also mean it is hard to draw conclusions as their motivation is likely to play a part. Examining the effectiveness of a therapy for nicotine addiction is difficult because there are many factors affecting smoking cessation, including individual differences.

- There are negative effects when using bupropion. For example, Wilkes (2008) reports that there are more adverse effects with bupropion than with nicotine replacement therapy. It seems that about 30 per cent stop using bupropion because of adverse effects. Swan *et al.* (2003) found that the higher dose of bupropion was associated with problems with sleeping, difficulty with concentrating, shakiness and stomach problems, though this was as well as a lower reported desire to smoke, which would perhaps help. It does sound as if taking bupropion is unpleasant, which might affect dropout from treatment.
- Being part of a trial can lead to someone feeling more motivated to give up smoking, which can be effective in itself. This might account for some of the smoking cessation in a trial, though of course if the drug treatment group shows more cessation than a placebo group, that difference does seem to be down to the drug. Often in trials looking at drug therapy a placebo group does show a reasonable level of 'effectiveness'.
- The percentage of people giving up smoking after a year when bupropion was the therapy is generally rather low and less than 50 per cent. Although bupropion might be better than a placebo, it could be said to be not very successful. Studies looking at placebo, bupropion and varenicline suggest bupropion is better than placebo but varenicline is better than bupropion, emphasising that the success of bupropion is not that good.

Progress check 5.32

Explain the purpose of using a placebo group in studies, such as those looking at the effectiveness of drug therapy for nicotine addiction.

A treatment focused on blocking noradrenaline – prazosin

Forget *et al.* (2010) write about treatment of nicotine addiction being focused on targeting specific receptors in the brain. Dopamine tends to be the neurotransmitter talked about to explain how nicotine is rewarding. However, Forget *et al.* (2010) suggest that noradrenaline has a large role in nicotine addiction. The focus is on noradrenergic receptors (receptors for noradrenaline) when looking at nicotine addiction and at relapse. Forget *et al.* (2010) used rats and focused on nicotine-induced dopamine release in the nucleus accumbens in rats and on the role of noradrenaline in self-administration of nicotine in rats. They found that self-administration of nicotine in the rats was reduced by a noradrenaline receptor antagonist (prazosin), though the antagonist did not reduce self-administration of food. Antagonists block the receptors so would block noradrenaline messages. Prazosin also reduced

the rats' nicotine cue-related search for nicotine after their addiction had been extinguished. Prazosin seemed to have reduced the response to nicotine-related cues in the environment that might lead to relapse. Prazosin also reduced nicotine-induced dopamine release in the nucleus accumbens. Forget *et al.* (2010) suggest that stimulation of noradrenergic receptors is involved in nicotine taking and in relapse and this might be about activation of the mesolimbic dopamine brain reward system. Blocking noradrenaline at the receptor might be a useful treatment for nicotine addiction.

Progress check 5.33

Why did Forget *et al.* (2010) use both self-administration of food and self-administration of nicotine in their study of rats?

Therapies for nicotine addiction based on classical conditioning

Two different treatments using classical conditioning principles are explained in this section. Firstly, the therapy is given and then evidence for its effectiveness is discussed, before looking at strengths and weaknesses of the treatment. One explanation uses a drug (varenicline) to change the response to smoking cigarettes and the other focuses on exposure to cues without the response to smoking, to change response to the cues. You can use just one of these treatments as they are different treatments. The treatment using varenicline relates well to the principles of aversion therapy, which is a therapy you need to know about in relation to at least one of the drugs you have to cover and which is chosen for alcohol addiction in this chapter. Varenicline has been mentioned when discussing the effectiveness of bupropion so you will already know some studies showing that varenicline is effective, in fact more effective than bupropion and more effective than a placebo as well.

The use of a drug to discourage nicotine addiction – varenicline

Nicotine craving can be reduced using classical conditioning principles. Smokers can take a drug that reduces craving for nicotine, such as varenicline, which is a partial agonist at the nicotinic receptors and stimulates them less than nicotine does. The receptors are filled with varenicline so the nicotine itself does not have the same effect. This gives a weaker pleasure response from smoking. Pairing smoking cigarettes with varenicline gives the reduced pleasure response until smoking, giving the reduced pleasure response, is stopped. The way varenicline is used relates to classical conditioning and is explained earlier when considering classical conditioning as an explanation for nicotine addiction (page 530) so you can use that explanation to explain how the treatment works too. Varenicline was recommended by NICE in 2007 as a treatment for smokers who want to give up smoking cigarettes.

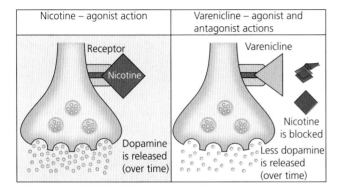

Nicotine – agonist action	Varenicline – agonist and antagonist actions

Varenicline works at the synapse to lower the response to nicotine, which can help in stopping smoking.

Evidence for the effectiveness of varenicline for nicotine addiction

- Jorenby *et al.* (2006) compared varenicline as a treatment for nicotine addiction with a placebo or sustained-release buprorion. In all three conditions there was also brief counselling for smoking cessation. Jorenby *et al.* (2006) used a randomised double-blind placebo-controlled trial, using 14 researcher centres and a 12-week long study as well as a follow-up up to one year after the trial. They enrolled 1,027 adult smokers and 65 per cent completed the study. They measured continuous abstinence from smoking at the end of the treatment (9 to 12 weeks) and also through the one year follow-up period.

Table 5.6 Results of Jorenby *et al.* (2006)

Week the measure was taken in	Percentage abstinent from smoking in the three treatment groups		
	Varenicline	**Placebo**	**Bupropion**
Weeks 9 to 12	43.9%	17.6%	29.8%
Weeks 9 to 24	29.7%	13.2%	20.2%
Weeks 9 to 52	23%	10.3%	14.6%
Treatment discontinued	*10.5%*	*7.3%*	*12.6%*

The most common reason for discontinuing the treatment in the varenicline group was nausea, which occurred in 29.4% of the participants.

Progress check 5.34

Using Table 5.6 and the row for weeks 9 to 52, give the percentage differences between groups with regard to giving up smoking. Give two percentages – the percentage difference between the placebo group and the bupropion group and the percentage difference between the placebo group and the varenicline group. Then summarise what these figures show about the results of this study.

STUDY HINT

Be ready to use numbers in tables to work out calculations. Your exams will have 10 per cent of the questions involving maths of some sort so it is worth practising when you come across tables of results.

- At the weeks 9 to 12 measure, varenicline was compared with the placebo group and was more effective (p<.001) and compared with bupropion it was more effective too (p<.001).
- At the weeks 9 to 24 measure, varenicline was compared with the placebo group and again found to be more effective (p<.001) and compared with bupropion again was more effective (p<.003).
- At the weeks 9 to 52 measure, again varenicline gave more people who had stopped smoking compared with the placebo group (p<.001) and compared with bupropion it was also more effective (p<.004).

The conclusion was that varenicline was much more effective in stopping smoking than bupropion and is a useful therapy. It was said by Jorenby *et al.* (2006) to be effective and safe.

- Oncken *et al.* (2006) focused on four different ways of giving varenicline. They looked at two that were **titrated** doses, which means there was progressive dosing over the first week, and two that were not titrated, which means there was a fixed dosage schedule. They used participants aged 18 years to 65 years and more than one centre. The study used a double-blind technique and was placebo-controlled as well as randomised. Participants were all given varenicline in different doses and patterns, with about 130 participants in each of four groups. There was a 40-week follow-up period. The researchers measured carbon monoxide over four consecutive weeks to confirm smoking cessation and they did this at weeks 4 to 7 and weeks 9 to 12 as well as looking for continuous abstinence for weeks 9 to 52. The results gave a higher continuous quit rate in weeks 9 to 12 for the 1.0 mg group (49.4 per cent) and the 0.5 mg group (44 per cent) compared with the placebo group (11.6 per cent). For weeks 9 to 52 the 1.0 mg group had a higher quit rate (22.4 per cent) as did the 0.5 mg group (18.5 per cent) compared with the placebo group (3.9 per cent). Nausea was found in between 16 per cent and 42 per cent of the participants who had varenicline, though nausea was not reported as much in the groups with titrated dosing. It was concluded that varenicline at both the 1.0 mg and 0.5 mg doses was effective for nicotine addiction.

Definition

Titrated – referring to drug dosage, titrated means dosage is increased over a period as opposed to non-titrated, which means there is a fixed dose throughout.

Progress check 5.35

With reference to the way a study is designed what does 'double-blind' mean and what does 'single-blind' mean?

- Kotz *et al.* (2014) considered varenicline as a treatment compared with nicotine replacement therapy using 1,579 adult smokers who had made at least one attempt to stop smoking using varenicline or NRT. Kotz *et al.* measured self-report data with regard to having stopped smoking. The researchers made adjustments for various other variables, such as the urge to smoke and whether the attempt at stopping was in the first or last half of the year before the study. They found that there was more abstinence in those taking varenicline compared with those using NRT. In fact, those taking varenicline, after adjusting for the various variables, were 1.76 times more likely to quit. There was no difference though in those who started their attempt to stop more than six months before the study compared with those who started to quit in the six months before the study. They concluded that in the short-term varenicline was more effective than NRT but in the long-term there may be no difference between the two. This is evidence for varenicline as a successful way of stopping smoking, at least when compared with NRT.
- Zincir *et al.* (2013) looked at the effectiveness of varenicline, bupropion (extended release) and NRT with regard to nicotine addiction. They used 300 nicotine-addicted patients from a smoking cessation clinic with 251 completing the study. They used randomisation to the conditions. They used a semi-structured clinical interview to get information about people's smoking habits to look at the effectiveness of

the therapies. They also measured carbon monoxide levels. The treatment lasted 12 weeks, whichever condition the participant was in.

Year One link: You looked at randomisation to conditions when you covered cognitive psychology.

Zincir *et al.* (2013) found no significant differences between the group relating to age, gender and education level, which was interesting and suggests perhaps that individual differences do not play a part in the effectiveness of therapies, even though for some therapies it was thought this might be the case. Smoking cessation rates were 54.8 per cent in the NRT group, 57.1 per cent in the bupropion group and 72.3 per cent in the varenicline group, though the number of cigarettes used in a day were a lot lower in the NRT group. The bupropion group and the NRT group showed less depression using a depression measure. 61.8 per cent of those taking part in the study continued the smoking cessation behaviour during the follow-up period (12 weeks). Varenicline was thought to be the best treatment though the lowering of depression found in the bupropion and NRT groups was evidence for their effectiveness to an extent.

Table 5.7 Studies and their findings regarding varenicline

Study	Findings regarding the effectiveness of varenicline for smoking cessation
Jorenby *et al.* (2006)	The conclusion was that varenicline was much more effective in stopping smoking than bupropion and was a useful therapy. It was said to be effective and safe.
Oncken *et al.* (2006)	It was concluded that varenicline at both the 1.0 mg and 0.5 mg doses was effective for nicotine addiction.
Kotz *et al.* (2014)	They concluded that in the short-term varenicline was more effective than NRT but in the long-term there may be no difference between the two. This is evidence for varenicline as a successful way of stopping smoking, at least when compared with NRT.
Zincir *et al.* (2013)	Varenicline was thought to be the best treatment, though the lowering of depression found in the bupropion and NRT groups was evidence for their effectiveness to an extent.

Progress check 5.36

There are studies given to show the effectiveness of varenicline that you can use to discuss the effectiveness of NRT and of bupropion. Explain the effectiveness of NRT and bupropion as shown using two of these studies.

Evaluation of varenicline as a classical conditioning-based therapy for nicotine addiction

Strengths

- There is a lot of evidence to support varenicline as a treatment for nicotine addiction, including Jorenby *et al.* (2006) and Oncken *et al.* (2006). The studies do not consider the link to classical conditioning; however, they do show that the drug is useful with regard to nicotine addiction and stopping smoking.
- As with other treatments considered, a strength is that studies use randomised controlled trials so cause-and-effect conclusions are claimed. Studies do consider issues such as demographics too, such as Zincir *et al.* (2013), who did not find differences depending on age, gender or educational attainment. Controls are carefully done, which gives credibility to findings.

Weaknesses

- Randomised controlled trials often include follow-up, which often goes up to one year; however, it rarely carries on after that time. Even at the one-year follow-up there can be lower numbers stopping smoking than there were earlier in the study. 43.9 per cent went to 23 per cent in Jorenby *et al.* (2006) when the measure was 9 to 52 weeks rather than 9 to 12 weeks, looking at varenicline. This sort of finding suggests that after the one-year period there might be a continuation in the decline in the effectiveness of the therapy.
- Oncken *et al.* (2006) found a 22.4 per cent rate of effectiveness for the 1.0 mg dose of varenicline at the 9 to 52 week measure, which shows effectiveness compared with the placebo, but is still rather low and leaves a 77.6 per cent lack of effectiveness.
- Longitudinal studies, where there is follow-up over a period, give drop out, which studies do report and this is a problem because those who continue on the study may have more motivation or may be different in some way. Having said that, that would apply to a placebo group as well so there is some credibility in the claims about effectiveness. Nonetheless drop out in longitudinal designs are regrettable.

Cue-exposure therapy for nicotine addiction – focusing on classical conditioning principles

Firstly, the therapy is given and then evidence for its effectiveness is discussed, before looking at strengths and weaknesses of the treatment. Cue exposure therapy works on having the cues for smoking present without the smoking, which should lead to extinction of the association between the cues and smoking. Cue exposure therapy is also explained in relation to treating alcohol addiction (page 540).

The idea of cue exposure comes from the classical conditioning explanation of drug addiction, which suggests that cues in the environment are associated with smoking and the pleasure or calming effect of smoking. In classical conditioning it would be said that the cues are conditioned stimuli. Nicotine, coming from smoking cigarettes, is the unconditioned stimulus which gives the unconditioned response of pleasure, as explained earlier (page 505). Cues that are related to smoking for an individual are neutral stimuli at first, such as perhaps meeting up with certain friends, perhaps those who smoke. The friends or meeting place can then become a conditioned stimulus associated with the conditioned response, which is the pleasure. Cue exposure therapy involves classical conditioning principles in reversing the association. The idea is that a smoker is presented with smoking-related cues without smoking or the pleasure that would bring, and so the cues become neutral once more. That would help in not triggering relapse after extinction.

Progress check 5.37

Draw up a classical conditioning diagram to show how nicotine addiction might be triggered by cues in the environment.

Evidence for the effectiveness of cue exposure therapy for nicotine addiction

- Lee *et al.* (2004) found that smokers exposed to smoking-related cues show reaction such as in urges to smoke and cardiovascular measures compared with when they encounter neutral cues. Cue exposure therapy means repeated exposure to cues that a person associates with smoking so that the learned association is extinguished. Lee *et al.* (2004) carried out a pilot study and found that using a virtual environment to show the cues is more effective than other ways of exposing someone to smoking-related cues. The virtual environment they used had a virtual bar and objects in it, including an alcoholic drink, a packet of cigarettes, an ashtray, a lighter, advertising posters and a glass of beer. There was also an avatar that was smoking and the noise and music of a restaurant was simulated. Sixteen adolescent males (in late adolescence) who smoked at least ten cigarettes a day took part in the study where over six sessions the participants were exposed to the virtual bar using different questions and procedures for each session. They found that cue exposure therapy did not show significant reduction in smoking related to all of the variables; however, the craving for cigarettes did gradually reduce over the six sessions. Lee *et al.* concluded that the virtual environment cue exposure therapy (VE-CET) was successful in reducing craving in people with a nicotine addiction.

- Park *et al.* (2014) compared virtual cue exposure therapy with CBT for nicotine dependence. They used 30 male participants with nicotine dependence who underwent four weeks of therapy using either cue exposure therapy or CBT, with 15 in each condition. None of the participants received NRT during the study. The cue exposure therapy used a virtual bar. The CBT therapy used smoking cessation education, focus on withdrawal symptoms, focus on coping mechanisms as well as restructuring thinking. The researchers gathered data about daily cigarette count, level of carbon monoxide, level of dependence, withdrawal symptoms and participant cravings and the measures were taken before the study, after the four weeks of the study, and again at week 12 for a follow-up. They found that the daily smoking count, the carbon monoxide and nicotine dependence had all decreased significantly. These effects carried on throughout the study, including at follow-up. They found similar changes in the cue exposure and the CBT groups so the conclusion was the cue exposure therapy is as good as CBT for nicotine addiction.

- Culbertson *et al.* (2012) looked at a virtual environment cue exposure therapy focusing on nicotine addiction compared with a placebo virtual environment. Participants were randomly assigned to either the therapy or the placebo group and the sample consisted of smokers who were seeking treatment. The participants had CBT twice a week and then either the smoking-related virtual environment or the placebo

virtual environment. They found that the smoking-related virtual environment gave a higher 'quit rate' than the placebo virtual environment (p=.015). The participants who experienced the smoking-related cues also reported smoking significantly fewer cigarettes a day at the end of the treatment compared with the placebo group (p=.034). This gives evidence for the effectiveness of cue exposure therapy for nicotine addiction.

Explore
If you would like to know more about cue exposure therapy for treating nicotine dependence, here is a link to Culbertson *et al.* (2012): www.ncbi.nlm.nih.gov/pmc/articles/PMC4204479/

- Pericot-Valverde *et al.* (2014) point out that cue-induced craving refers to periods of intense craving triggered by smoking-related cues whereas background craving refers to a steady craving for nicotine. These are two different types of craving and the study aimed to look at both types of craving to consider the effectiveness of cue exposure therapy for both types. The researchers used a virtual environment to expose participants to smoking-related cues. They used 48 smokers who were seeking treatment and the virtual environment treatment was given once a week over five weeks. Each individual had their own hierarchy of cues from the easiest to manage virtual environment to the hardest to manage one. Both background and cue-induced craving were measured at each session. They found that the exposure to reduced cue-induced craving was as expected and the virtual environment cue exposure therapy also reduced background craving. The craving was more and more reduced as the five sessions progressed.

Explore
You can read a review of the progress in cue exposure therapy for the treatment of addictions using this link if you want to know more: http://benthamopen.com/contents/pdf/TOADDJ/TOADDJ-3-92.pdf. The review has a table of studies that you can use to get more evidence when looking at treatments for addiction.

Evaluation of cue exposure therapy for nicotine addiction

Strengths

- As you can see, the studies reported here all find that cue exposure therapy is effective for nicotine addiction and all use the virtual environment approach to expose smokers to cues. Park *et al.* (2014) and Culbertson *et al.* (2014) both found that virtual environment cue exposure therapy was effective for nicotine addiction.

- As with other studies looking at the effectiveness of therapies regarding substance misuse and dependence, these studies tend to use controls, randomisation and a placebo so there is a strong focus on controls and cause-and-effect conclusions can be claimed, giving credibility to the findings. As can happen with such studies, there can be credibility and reliability; however, validity can be an issue.

Weaknesses

- The studies used smokers who wanted to give up and it was noticeable that for other therapies for nicotine addiction given earlier, such as studies looking at nicotine replacement therapy, studies tended to use smokers who did not intend to stop. NRT was not found to be that effective and yet cue exposure therapy (CET) is found to be effective. Perhaps that is because using smokers who want to quit means it is more likely that a therapy will be effective. Having said that, studies do use placebo conditions, so possibly it makes little difference to the effectiveness which type of participant is used, just making a difference to the generalisability.
- A virtual environment is used to expose the smoker to smoking-related cues and in some studies there is no matching to individual recognition of the cues. Pericot-Valverde *et al.* (2014) did create for each individual their own hierarchy but still used a virtual environment. There might be a lack of ecological validity if a virtual environment is used and if each individual does not relate to the smoking-related cues that can affect validity as well. In some studies (such as Lee *et al.*, 2004) the virtual environment is based on a questionnaire, so there is an attempt to match it to reality; however, there is perhaps a difficulty with validity.

Test yourself

Evaluate one treatment for nicotine addiction focusing on the validity of the evidence for and against the treatment. **(12 marks)**

Drug therapy for alcohol addiction

Firstly, the therapy is given and then evidence for its effectiveness is discussed, before looking at strengths and weaknesses of the treatment. Drugs can be used to treat alcohol addiction both in the detoxification stage and to prevent relapse.

Drug therapy for alcohol misuse – for detoxification

Firstly, drug use in the detox stage is explored.

- Mark *et al.* (2003, cited in Raistrick *et al.*, 2006) found that out of 1,388 doctors specialising in substance misuse in the USA 13 per cent of those with alcohol problems were given naltrexone, 9 per cent were given disulfiram, 46 per cent were given antidepressants and 11 per cent were given benzodiazepines. This shows that drug therapy is used for alcohol misuse.
- With regard to antidepressants, SSRIs (selected serotonin reuptake inhibitors) were prescribed and seen to be safe and effective, though Garbutt *et al.* (1999, cited in Raistrick *et al.*, 2006) thought such drugs should only be used when a disorder like depression was present as well.
- Drug therapy is often not used for uncomplicated alcohol withdrawal; however, if it is used then Librium is the usual choice according to Duncan and Taylor (1996, cited in Raistrick *et al.*, 2006).
- Diazepam is used too though it tends to be more habit-forming than chlordiazepoxide, which is used and is as effective as benzodiazepines and less habit-forming. Chlordiazepoxide is given at the rate of about 100–200 mg a day and is the drug of choice for an uncomplicated detoxification (Raistrick *et al.*, 2006).
- Chlormethiazole can be used to prevent alcohol delirium but it is habit-forming.

Drug therapy for alcohol misuse – disulfiram for relapse prevention

Medication is also used to prevent relapse when it comes to treating alcohol addiction. Some drugs are used so that they make taking alcohol unpleasant, and this relates to aversion therapy, which is explained as a therapy for alcohol addiction next.

- Disulfiram is used and the brand name is Antabuse, which you may have heard of. Disulfiram is called a 'sensitising agent' because it sensitises people to alcohol, and there are other such drugs.
- Sensitising drugs work because they change the person's view about taking alcohol. Someone through operant conditioning principles might know that alcohol will relieve withdrawal symptoms or will give pleasure when drinking in a pub with friends. If the individual then takes a sensitising agent they will learn that the consequences of drinking are bad, because of the effects of the sensitising agent, and their expectations will have been changed by the sensitising agent. With the drug

they have the expectation that drinking alcohol will have unpleasant consequences, so expectations have changed. This is the way the drug works to prevent relapse.

- Aversion therapy is explained later as a separate therapy (page 537), though disulfiram (Antabuse) has been the drug chosen to give the unpleasant response that alcohol can be paired with, so disulfiram is both a drug therapy and a classical conditioning-based therapy.

> **STUDY HINT**
> Be sure to say clearly when using a therapy for drug addiction exactly what therapy you are using and in what way you are explaining and discussing it.

How disulfiram works

Disulfiram inhibits the liver enzymes that break down acetaldehyde, which leaves more acetaldehyde available. Acetaldehyde is toxic and the raised levels of acetaldehyde by disulfiram bring about nausea, sweating, headache and vomiting when someone drinks. This is because of the disulfiram-ethanol reaction.

People react differently to acetaldehyde so some people may not have a reaction when disulfiram is prescribed in a standard dose. It should also be prescribed carefully as it can impact on cardiac failure and lead to high blood pressure (Raistrick et al., 2006).

> **STUDY HINT**
> Alcohol is ethanol, in case you were wondering about the difference. Ethanol is the alcohol content of alcoholic drinks and it is produced by yeasts fermenting sugar. It is a psychoactive drug. When talking about alcohol probably it is ethanol that should be referred to. It is ethanol that is used in animal laboratory experiments focusing on the effectiveness of treatments for alcohol addiction.

Progress check 5.38

Why do you think it is suggested that there are different drug treatments for detoxification than there are for prevention of relapse?

Evidence for the effectiveness of drug therapy as a treatment for alcohol dependence

Raistrick et al. (2006) wrote a review of the effectiveness of treatment for alcohol problems and the evidence presented in the review is given here as evidence for drug therapy as a treatment for alcohol issues.

- Wines et al. (2004) found that 24 months after detoxification that may have included medication,

19.9 per cent of people had suicidal thoughts and 6.9 per cent made suicide attempts, which suggests that detoxification must be followed up with support. These are rather negative findings.

- Hughes and Cook (1997) looked at 24 trials where disulfiram was used orally and 14 where it was implanted and concluded that method problems in the trials made it hard to interpret the data. It seemed, however, that the evidence does not support implanted disulfiram but does support disulfiram as an effective therapy if taken orally.
- Fuller and Roth (1979) at a six-month follow-up found that 42 per cent of people who drink alcohol who had disulfiram managed to give up alcohol, with just 17 per cent of a group who were given vitamins doing so.
- Chick et al. (1992) found disulfiram helped in giving more days of abstinence from alcohol and in giving less alcohol consumed.
- Heather (1993b) found that supervision of disulfiram made a large difference. Unsupervised disulfiram led to about 20 per cent of the days being 'abstinent' from alcohol, whereas supervised disulfiram with social support gave 100 per cent days of not taking alcohol. Measures were taken at the three to six months follow-up.
- Fuller and Gordis (2004) claim that disulfiram has a clear role for treating alcohol addiction.

> **STUDY HINT**
> You are likely to get questions in your exams that ask you to 'use research evidence' and that is why studies are so important. For each statement you make, such as disulfiram is effective for treating alcohol addiction, you need evidence for the claim, such as giving Fuller and Gordis (2004) as an example. When revising prepare such evidence.

> ### Explore
> You can find out more about disulfiram and prevention of relapse in alcohol abuse using this link:
> www.robertjmeyersphd.com/pdf/Does%20Disulfiram%20 Help%20to%20Prevent%20Relapse%20in%20Alcohol%20 Abuse.pdf

Evaluation of drug therapy for alcohol addiction

Strengths

- There is a lot of evidence that disulfiram is successful with regard to preventing relapse. Chick et al. (1992) found disulfiram helped in giving more days of abstinence from alcohol and in giving less alcohol consumed and Fuller and Roth (1979) at a six-month follow-up found that 42 per cent of people who drink alcohol who had disulfiram managed to give up alcohol with just 17 per cent of a group who were given vitamins doing so.

- Evidence tends to come from randomised controlled trials, such as Fuller and Roth (1979), who used disulfiram or vitamins with the groups being otherwise comparable. This means cause-and-effect conclusions are easier to draw and conclusions are credible.

Weaknesses

- Some evidence for disulfiram helping to prevent relapse with regard to alcohol addiction is rather negative. Heather (1993b) found that it was when disulfiram was given and supervised that there was better protection from relapse. Unsupervised prescribing did lead to some prevention of relapse but not to the extent that a supervised programme achieved. This suggests that support is a main element in drug therapy, not just the therapy alone.
- The drugs used are habit-forming, which is a disadvantage. Diazepam is more habit-forming than chlordiazepoxide, which is used and is as effective and less habit-forming than benzodiazepines– although chlordiazepoxide is itself habit-forming. Although such drugs may help with detoxification, there would then need to be careful management of coming off those drugs themselves.

STUDY HINT
In this chapter quite often a strength of a treatment is said to be the amount of evidence for that treatment. On its own that is not a very strong point so be sure to give some examples of the evidence to back up your point.

Progress check 5.39

What does it mean to say that different drugs are used for detoxification than for prevention of relapse?

Aversion therapy for alcohol addiction

Your course asks you to cover two treatments each for three drugs: heroin, nicotine and alcohol. You also must cover aversion therapy and in this section aversion therapy is paired with alcohol addiction, where it fits because drinking alcohol can be associated with nausea rather than pleasure, which is aversion therapy. For example, disulfiram works to give nausea as a response if someone using disulfiram drinks alcohol. This is aversion therapy. The drug is given to avoid the pleasure response in a biological way and once someone has experienced the unpleasant biological consequences of drinking while

taking disulfiram they are likely to avoid drinking, which is aversion therapy based on classical conditioning principles. Cue exposure therapy is similar to aversion therapy as it relies on classical conditioning principles, as does varenicline as a treatment for nicotine addiction.

Raistrick *et al.* (2006), who reviewed the effectiveness of treatments for alcohol addiction, suggest that aversion therapy is not used currently and they offer cue dependency as a treatment that links to aversion therapy but is different. In this section aversion therapy is reviewed, because it was explained earlier when looking at the classical conditioning explanation for alcohol misuse (page 503). Disulfiram was discussed as a drug therapy, with evidence for its effectiveness. Disulfiram is a drug used in aversion therapy so it could be said that aversion therapy is still used. Then cue dependency is explained to show how it links to classical conditioning principles, though the principles of cue exposure therapy are not given in a lot of detail as they are given for nicotine addiction (page 533). Community reinforcement approach (CRA) is a therapy based on operant conditioning principles, and is also briefly outlined in this section as extra information you can use in evaluation of therapies for alcohol dependence. CRA was explained earlier when operant conditioning principles were offered as an explanation for alcohol misuse (page 511).

Aversion therapy

You can see how aversion therapy works by looking again at how classical conditioning principles can explain alcohol addiction. If a therapy that rests on a theory helps a problem, then it is assumed that this is evidence for the theory being a successful explanation of the problem. Aversion therapy can be explained in fact using disulfiram (Antabuse) as an example, and other drugs that cause nausea can also be used.

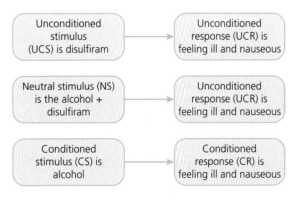

Aversion therapy as a treatment for alcohol addiction

The idea is to condition someone to experience an unpleasant response to something that started out as neutral. A response that is an unpleasant experience is associated automatically to a certain stimulus. Some drugs make people feel unwell. Then a neutral stimulus is paired with the original stimulus and the automatic response appears to be triggered by the neutral stimulus, now conditioned to give that response. For example, the drug that makes someone feel unwell could be paired with a bell sound as a neutral stimulus, and the bell sound would soon make that person feel unwell.

With alcoholism, aversion therapy is a bit different because the alcohol has automatically been giving a pleasure response. The aim is to replace that pleasure response with an unpleasant response. It could be said, therefore, that the alcohol is not a neutral stimulus in the process, though the procedure works in the same way. The association with something bringing an unpleasant experience will change the response that alcohol usually brings. Aversion therapy can work with smoking in the same way, and indeed with other behaviours. It has been used to 'treat' what are seen as deviant behaviours, though that is now a controversial idea and aversion therapy is not relied upon as a treatment.

Aversion therapy could involve **overt sensitisation**, which means using drugs to produce the unpleasant experience, usually nausea. This is overt and the person would know how the therapy works. There is also **covert sensitisation**, which involves the person visualising something unpleasant to help them to associate an unpleasant experience with alcohol.

Explanation

Overt sensitisation in relation to aversion therapy means something is given directly to the person to produce the unpleasant experience, which is generally a drug to make people feel nauseous. **Covert sensitisation** refers to someone using imagery to think about something unpleasant associated with alcohol.

Antabuse, which is involved in overt sensitisation, is a drug used to treat alcohol addiction for some time and of course this is disulfiram, which has already been discussed as a treatment for alcohol addiction. Disulfiram interferes with how the body metabolises alcohol. The body metabolises alcohol by turning it into acetaldehyde, which is toxic and is normally dealt with by the body by breaking it down into harmless acetic acid. Antabuse prevents the body from breaking down the acetaldehyde, which then builds up and causes unpleasant symptoms such as nausea, vertigo, headache, anxiety and feeling weak. The idea is that someone will associate these symptoms with alcohol and so will then not drink alcohol.

Explore
There is quite a bit about aversion therapy on the internet so you can look up more about it. Here is a link to start with: www.the-alcoholism-guide.org/aversion-therapy.html

Covert sensitisation is seen as more ethical because the client is involving their own imagination to pair something very unpleasant with either the alcohol or the craving for the alcohol. In fact they can also imagine something pleasant as a result of not drinking, which is a more positive approach. Virtual reality can be used to help the person's imagination.

Progress check 5.40

In this example of how covert sensitisation works to help to prevent relapse to alcohol drinking, complete the diagram by filling in the brackets to show how aversion therapy is being used.

In order to prevent relapse to alcohol Aldo has been advised to use covert sensitisation. He has to use a virtual reality scenario which he accesses online to visualise himself in a bar wanting a drink when he experiences something very unpleasant, a situation that he chooses. He has to do this once a day for a week. The therapist explains that alcohol gives a reward in that it is pleasurable and craving a drink is linked to that reward. The idea is to replace the reward with the unpleasant experience that comes from the imagined bad experience.

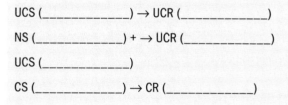

UCS (_____) → UCR (_____)

NS (_____) + → UCR (_____)

UCS (_____)

CS (_____) → CR (_____)

Evidence for the effectiveness of aversion therapy for alcohol addiction

- Choi and Lee (2015) look at covert sensitisation, which is imagery-based aversive treatment for substance abuse. Choi and Lee use virtual reality to help with covert sensitisation and the focus is on reducing alcohol craving in heavy social drinkers. They used self-report questionnaire data to measure reduction in cravings as well as an association test and eye-tracking. They used 20 heavy social drinkers and 20 light drinkers and the virtual covert sensitisation was administered for ten minutes to each participant and then the measures were repeated again. The researchers only used the covert sensitisation once and yet their findings were that there was change in the self-report craving so it was concluded that virtual covert sensitisation seemed to be effective to reduce craving in those with alcohol addiction. Choi and Lee say that aversion therapy has dehumanising effects and so is not thought of as a proper therapy to use and so covert sensitisation is preferred and successful (Kearney, 2006, cited in Choi and Lee, 2015). Kraft and Kraft (2005, cited in Choi and Lee, 2015) say that one of the best points of using covert sensitisation is that it pairs the aversive stimulus with the craving for the behaviour so focuses on what needs to be reduced – which is the craving if it is relapse prevention that is being targeted. A difficulty with the findings of Choi and Lee (2015) was that they found no difference between the heavy social drinkers and the light drinkers in the success of the therapy, though this might simply be because the covert sensitisation with one episode was not enough to separate types of drinker.

Explore
You can find Kraft and Kraft (2005) using this link if you would like to know more about covert sensitisation: www.londonhypnotherapyuk.com/covert-sensitisation-for-alcoholism.asp

- Kraft and Kraft (2005) discuss six case studies where maladaptive behaviour is treated using covert sensitisation. They use it for alcoholism and also for cigarette smoking and chocolate addiction. It is the craving that is focused on rather than the behaviour itself. They claim that after just a few sessions the craving is paired with something unpleasant and is 'treated'. Kraft and Kraft use hypnosis whereas virtual reality assisting someone's imagination is perhaps more usual and gives the power to the client. It is interesting that the case of alcoholism that they report needed a 'booster' after a period of time and also that Kraft and Kraft say not all patients respond to this treatment, though they claim 90 per cent do respond. They also comment that covert sensitisation requires total abstinence from alcohol and if someone wants to drink socially that would need systematic desensitisation. The references that Kraft and Kraft use in their paper are old ones, ranging from 1843 to 1970, which suggests that therapy has moved on since then, though their paper is written in 2005.

Year One link: You covered systematic desensitisation as a therapy for phobias that you looked at in learning theories. It is another therapy based on classical conditioning principles where relaxation is the response that replaces fear.

Evaluation of aversion therapy to treat alcohol addiction

Strengths

- Studies have shown disulfiram to work as a treatment for alcohol dependence, as was shown earlier when it was treated as a drug therapy. For example, Chick et al. (1992) found disulfiram helped in giving more days of abstinence from alcohol and in giving less alcohol consumed and Fuller and Roth (1979) at a six-month follow-up found that 42 per cent of people who drink alcohol who had disulfiram managed to give up alcohol, with just 17 per cent of a group who were given vitamins doing so. However, although disulfiram has a useful role in treating alcohol addiction, it is not seen as part of aversion therapy; it is used as a drug therapy to help with alcoholism.
- Covert sensitisation is more ethical than overt sensitisation because there is no directly unpleasant response; there is an imagined situation which the person is in charge of.

Issues and debates

The way psychology is used in social control is an issue and debate in your course and aversion therapy – and other therapies for substance misuse – can be discussed in terms of how the therapist has power over a client. Covert sensitisation perhaps gives power to the client in that they use their own imagination in the therapy.

- Virtual reality can help with realism and there can be ecological validity if the virtual situation is real enough, which is a strength. Bordnick et al. (2008, cited in Choi and Lee, 2015) found covert sensitisation using virtual reality was useful for helping patients to imagine the required experiences and was helpful in improving their concentration.

Weaknesses

- A problem with alcohol addiction is that the person has to keep taking the drug because without it drinking alcohol will not give unpleasant symptoms, and associating the symptoms with alcohol is not likely to last if not re-conditioned. Watson and Rayner's (1920) study of Little Albert showed that classical conditioning has to be repeated for the effect to last, for example. Kraft and Kraft (2005) report having to 're-condition' someone after a while, when they used hypnosis as a form of covert sensitisation.

Year One link: Watson and Rayner's (1920) study is the classic study for learning theories in your course.

- A problem is that there is no direct impact on how someone withdraws from taking alcohol; aversion therapy focuses more on prevention of relapse. The person when coming off the drug is still going to have cravings for the drug so aversion therapy using Antabuse is often paired with other treatment, or covert sensitisation is used to focus on the cravings specifically. Other treatments can involve drugs to help with withdrawal symptoms, as was discussed earlier when looking at drug therapy for alcohol addiction.
- There are ethical issues with using aversion therapy because the individual experiences unpleasant symptoms and also the therapy focuses on negative ideas rather than positive reasons for avoiding relapse.
- Covert sensitisation is not as unethical as overt sensitisation because there are no direct unpleasant symptoms; however, it does rely on the person's imagination so might not be suitable for everyone. In order to overcome this difficulty virtual environments have been used to help someone's imagination. This can also enhance ecological validity. Riva *et al.* (1999, cited in Choi and Lee, 2015) have suggested that virtual reality can be effective in treatment and not just in studies.

Progress check 5.41

Explain one strength and one weakness of using aversion therapy to treat alcoholism.

Cue exposure for alcohol addiction

Firstly, the therapy is given and then evidence for its effectiveness is discussed before looking at strengths and weaknesses. You need to know two therapies for alcohol addiction and one therapy you need when considering treatment for alcoholism is aversion therapy, so you might not need to look at cue exposure therapy for alcohol as well. It is given here as an alternative treatment and to help your learning. Cue exposure therapy is not explained in depth here because it was covered earlier as a therapy for nicotine addiction (page 533).

Cues related to drinking alcohol can trigger relapse.

Cue exposure therapy

Cue exposure is relatively new and is based on classical conditioning theory. If cues lead to drug misuse, and those cues are then presented without the pleasure response from the drug, then according to classical conditioning principles, the cues stop being associated with the drug, which helps someone to stop using the drug.

> **STUDY HINT**
>
> Be sure you have enough information about a treatment to describe it in some detail. When using a therapy based on classical conditioning principles it is useful to be able to draw a diagram to show how the therapy works. You can use cue exposure therapy for any substance misuse and it is used in this chapter for nicotine and alcohol misuse so you can use what was given for nicotine addiction to describe how the treatment works for alcohol addiction.

Evidence for cue exposure therapy for alcohol addiction

- Drummond *et al.* (1995, cited in Raistrick *et al.*, 2006, a review of treatments for drug addiction) give evidence for the success of cue exposure as a therapy for drug misuse.
- Studies by Goddard and Abrams (1993, cited in Raistrick *et al.*, 2006) and Drummond and Glautier (1994, cited in Raistrick *et al.*, 2006) give evidence that using cue exposure can lead to abstinence.
- Drummond and Glautier (1994, cited in Raistrick *et al.*, 2006) used 35 men who were very dependent on alcohol and used either cue exposure or a relaxation treatment as a control. The therapies were used after detoxification (detox). The researchers carried out a follow-up up to six months after the treatment and the cue exposure gave better outcomes than the relaxation control treatment. The outcomes measured were time to relapse into heavy drinking and a measure of total alcohol consumption. This is evidence for the effectiveness of cue exposure therapy.
- Sitharthan *et al.* (1997, cited in Raistrick *et al.*, 2006) compared cue exposure that was delivered over six sessions of 90 minutes with cognitive-behavioural therapy (CBT) and homework. They used alcohol users that were not addicted and aimed to achieve moderate drinking in the participants. The cue exposure group drank less often and drank less quantity of alcohol at a six-month follow-up than those given CBT homework.
- Conklin and Tiffany (2000) carry out a meta-analysis using studies to look at the effectiveness of cue exposure treatment for addiction and find that there is no consistent evidence for effectiveness. Also they

comment that cue exposure treatments do not use procedures from animal studies that explain how extinction works, whereas they should. Conklin and Tiffany conclude that there is little evidence for the effectiveness of cue exposure therapy in preventing relapse and they cite various researchers as evidence for this claim, including Franken *et al.* (1999). Though they conclude as well that many researchers feel that there is merit in cue exposure therapy if the right cues are chosen, the right number of sessions are used and psychotherapy is involved as well. Conklin and Tiffany (2000) claim that if extinction is seen as new learning rather than 'unlearning', in that a new conditioned stimulus gives the conditioned response rather than the response being 'extinguished', then extinction is about learning abstinence, which is a more useful way of seeing the therapy. Animal studies show that features of extinction include the renewal effect, spontaneous recovery, reinstatement and failure to extinguish important cues, all of which are important in cue exposure therapy but are not focused on sufficiently. Conklin and Tiffany comment that animal laboratory studies give careful controls whereas in humans conditioning is far from controlled and can vary a lot between people and between drugs. Therefore, using findings from animal studies to inform a therapy such as cue exposure therapy should perhaps be done cautiously.

> ## Explore
> You can look at Conklin and Tiffany's (2000) paper on cue exposure addiction treatments if you would like to know more, including about animal studies. Here is the link: **http://gettingstronger.org/wp-content/uploads/2010/12/Conklin-2002-Cue-Exposure-and-Addiction.pdf**

Evaluation of cue exposure as a treatment for alcohol addiction

Strengths

- Classical conditioning principles are used in other therapies as well as cue exposure therapy, such as systematic desensitisation and covert sensitisation. Animal studies, starting from Pavlov's work, have supported classical conditioning as an explanation of learning, including extinction. Cue exposure therapy rests on a strong underpinning theory, which adds weight to it as a treatment.
- Sitharthan *et al.* (1997, cited in Raistrick *et al.*, 2006) found cue exposure was more effective for reducing alcohol intake than CBT and Drummond *et al.* (1995, cited in Raistrick *et al.*, 2006) also found cue exposure an effective therapy for alcohol addiction.

There is evidence for the therapy and it rests on strong theoretical underpinning.

- The therapy can give power to the client rather than a therapist having power over the client as might be the case if drug therapy is being used. The client can identify cues to focus on, for example, and can understand the principles behind the therapy, which gives them some power. This suggests that cue exposure therapy is an ethical one.

Weaknesses

- Cue exposure, based on classical conditioning principles, does take its understanding of addiction behaviour from animal studies and, as Conklin and Tiffany (2000) explain, controlled animal laboratory experiments where cues are strictly controlled might not match human drug-related behaviour enough to be useful.
- A problem with cue exposure therapy is that it does not address the pleasure that alcohol brings, it simply focuses on 'de-conditioning' the cues related to the alcohol use. It is possible that the pleasure response, relating to the reward pathways in the brain, is strong and might be stronger than the power of cues when it comes to drinking alcohol.

> ## Progress check 5.42
> Explain one strength and one weakness of drawing on animal laboratory studies to develop a therapy for human behaviour such as addiction.

A community reinforcement approach (CRA) as a treatment for alcohol addiction

Firstly, the therapy is given and then evidence for its effectiveness is discussed before considering evaluation of the therapy. CRA was referred to when operant conditioning principles were offered as an explanation for alcohol misuse.

CRA

CRA is a treatment based on operant conditioning principles, which was outlined earlier when looking at operant conditioning as an explanation for substance misuse (page 511). The idea is to give rewards for positive behaviours and to remove rewards for negative behaviours, such as those related to alcohol addiction. The rewards are tailored to the individual. Disulfiram can be used with CRA, as well as training in communication skills and refusing a drink. Community reinforcement approach is a broad therapy.

A family sports day can be rewarding and such rewards are emphasised in the community reinforcement approach (CRA) to treating alcohol addiction, with no such rewards for drug misuse.

Evidence for CRA

- Myers and Miller (2001) say that CRA can be as good as CBT and is similar to CBT (cited in Raistrick et al., 2006); however, they claim that the therapy is behavioural with strong operant conditioning principles and so is a separate treatment.
- Raistrick et al. (2006) in their review say that CRA is one of the most successful treatment programmes, which is evidence that operant conditioning principles are found in drug addiction if it is agreed that when a treatment works for an addiction, then its underlying theory is an explanation for the addiction.
- Hunt and Azrin (1973, cited in Raistrick et al., 2006) found that compared with using Alcoholics Anonymous and some alcohol education, CRA meant at a six-month follow-up those having the therapy were drinking on 14 per cent of the days on average, compared with 79 per cent in the controls.
- Azrin (1976, Raistrick et al., 2006) evaluated the CRA and the use of disulfiram and at the six-month follow-up found that those having CRA had fewer than 1 per cent drinking days a month compared with 55 per cent in a control group that had a standard programme as treatment and not CRA.
- Miller and Meyers (1999) claim that CRA is a successful treatment and can work with other drugs as well as alcohol. They cite Smith et al. (1998) as finding that CRA resulted in 'significantly improved outcomes' during the one year follow-up period when it was used with homeless people with alcohol addiction. It was found that the group having CRA hardly used alcohol during the one year follow-up, whereas the group that

had standard care, the control group, were drinking on about 40 per cent of the days during the one-year follow-up and had high levels of intoxication.

Explore

Miller and Meyers's (1999) paper on CRA can be found using this link if you would like to know more:

http://pubs.niaaa.nih.gov/publications/arh23-2/116-121.pdf

Evaluation of CRA for drug addiction

Strengths

- There is evidence for the success of CRA, such as Smith et al. (1998, cited in Miller and Meyers, 1999), who found much better resistance to alcohol in a CRA group than in one that had standard care. Azrin (1976, cited in Raistrick et al., 2006) found the same in that those on the CRA programme (with disulfiram) had 1 per cent drinking days a month when checked after six months compared with 55 per cent of days drinking for a group that had standard care.
- The treatment rests on operant conditioning principles, which have a lot of evidence to support them, such as Skinner's experiments with rats and pigeons and also evidence focusing on token economy programmes, which are similar in the theory they use. Rewarding required behaviour using positive reinforcement has been shown to work, such as Peirce et al. (2006), showing how prizes helped people with heroin addiction to stop taking the drug. When a therapy rests on strong theory, that can be used as evidence for the effectiveness of the therapy, at least to an extent.

Weaknesses

- CRA uses motivational and communication training as well as disulfiram so it is a broad therapy that uses a lot of different approaches within it. It is hard to show which part of CRA is effective or whether all the parts go together to give the effectiveness.
- Also it relies on everyone around the individual being part of the therapy and rewarding the required behaviour (giving up the alcohol) rather than unrequired behaviour (any behaviour related to alcohol). This might be more possible in institutions or specific places like hostels for the homeless (e.g. Smith et al., 1998), where CRA is implemented, and not so easy in everyday family life.

Progress check 5.43

Explain two features of CRA related to principles of operant conditioning.

Token economy for drug misuse

You may have looked at token economy as a therapy in your course, and token economy can be used for drug misuse as well. It is briefly explained here so that you can use it when discussing operant conditioning and its usefulness, and to offer an alternative to the treatments that have been given in this section. It is not written with a focus on one of the three drugs of interest in health psychology on your course, just in general, so you can see how it works as a therapy in general. Contingency management (CM), which uses operant conditioning principles, is a form of token economy that is mentioned when considering CBT for heroin so it is useful to review contingency management here as a treatment for drug addiction.

Token economy programmes (TEPs) are used for treating drug use. TEPs work on the principle that behaviour is repeated for a reward. Rewards can take the form of positive or negative reinforcement.

Elements needed for a token economy programme

- Clear identification of what will be used as tokens: points, counters, stickers and so on. Tokens have to be given immediately and must 'buy' something desirable.
- Clear identification of the behaviour or behaviours to be rewarded.
- Clear identification of what the tokens can buy: outings, food, television, privileges, etc.
- An agreed and clear time and place for exchanging the rewards.
- A system for recording behaviour.
- Consistent application of the programme by staff.
- A system for changing the rewards to shape behaviour, so that rewards are gradually given less frequently or for different behaviours, all of which must be clear to staff and those on the programme.

Explore
Find out about a token economy programme. For example, the Salvation Army hostels sometimes use these to promote required behaviour. They may take points away for undesired behaviour as well as rewarding required behaviour. Here is a link to a site that gives some ideas about behaviour therapy to treat alcohol addiction: **http://alcoholrehab.com/drug-addiction-treatment/behavior-therapy/**

Contingency management therapy

One type of token economy programme in current use is contingency management (CM) therapy. This uses a voucher system where participants earn points if they test negative for drugs. They may exchange their points for items that encourage healthy living. The idea is to reinforce positively not using drugs with rewards that encourage healthy behaviour. One reason for this is that rehabilitation programmes for drug users aim to stop substance misuse but also to help to lower criminal activity and the associated issues with HIV/AIDS infection. A healthier lifestyle and not misusing drugs help to achieve these aims. Voucher-based reinforcement (VBR) involves giving a patient a voucher for each drug-free urine sample given. The voucher can be exchanged for food or other goods/services. The more drug-free urine samples, the higher the value of the vouchers. CM was referred to when CBT was considered as a therapy for heroin addiction (page 522) because CM was used as a comparison treatment to evaluate CBT, so you can find out more about CM there.

STUDY HINT
Contingency management can be used for heroin addiction as well. Stanger and Budney (2010) work on the principle that the reward for taking a drug is quite quick and is either the euphoria from taking the drug or the avoidance of unpleasant withdrawal symptoms. The idea is that the rewards from not taking the drug, such as having better health, take longer so offering vouchers for not taking the drug can offer quicker reward and so can offer competition for reward. Although sometimes different treatments are offered for the different drugs, a treatment often covers more than one of the three drugs in your course.

STUDY HINT
Token economy can be used for mental disorders as well, so you could review your learning of clinical psychology to see where token economy has been mentioned, as you could have used it as a therapy for schizophrenia, for example.

Explore
You can read more about contingency management interventions using this link: www.drugabuse.gov/publications/principles-drug-addiction-treatment-research-based-guide-third-edition/evidence-based-approaches-to-drug-addiction-treatment/behavioral-0

Year One link: Recall your learning about operant conditioning in learning theories as token economy is based on operant conditioning principles.

Evaluation of token economy programmes

Advantages

- A token economy programme suits everyone and focuses on praise. There is no strong punishment involved, so it is ethical in that regard.
- There is evidence that contingency management programmes (rewards) work to reduce substance misuse. Peirce *et al.* (2006) carried out a study in the USA involving six community-based settings with a methadone maintenance programme for heroin users. A control group underwent the usual treatment and another group had the chance to win prizes in a draw for 12 weeks. They were entered into the draw if they submitted negative samples (heroin- and alcohol-free) and the more they abstained from using the drugs, the more draws they were entered into. It was found that continuous abstinence was twice as likely for the group with the chance to win prizes than for the control group. The conclusion was that such prize-based programmes worked in reducing substance misuse, alongside a methadone maintenance programme.

Disadvantages

- It can be costly to provide the rewards, train staff and manage the programme.
- Some staff find such a programme impractical, time-consuming and difficult to carry out effectively.
- Staff can neglect the rights of the individual by withholding essentials such as food and comfort.
- Staff who are not trained properly might inadvertently reward inappropriate behaviour, thus encouraging negative behaviour.

Issues and debates

One issue and debate you need to cover is the issue of psychology being used as a form of social control. It can be argued that token economy can be used as a form of social control because the staff and people administering the programme have control over what the rewards are, when to give them out, and so on. You can use therapy when discussing psychology used in social control.

Progress check 5.44

Explain two strengths of using token economy as a therapy for drug misuse.

Test yourself

1 Compare two treatments for alcohol addiction focusing on their underlying theoretical bases. **(12 marks)**
2 Evaluate two treatments for addiction regarding one drug from heroin, nicotine and alcohol. **(16 marks)**

One antidrug campaign and the psychological strategies behind it

In this section you are required to look at one campaign that has encouraged people not to use recreational drugs. As nicotine has been chosen in this textbook as one of the substances to cover, an antismoking campaign is chosen here, but you may choose a different drugs campaign. One of the two key questions focused on in health psychology in your course asks how to encourage the cessation of smoking, so you can link the antidrug campaign considered here with that key question.

Antismoking legislation and policies

Laws against smoking have been established in many countries in recent times, such as the law passed in 2007 in England banning smoking in any public place, including pubs and clubs. Previous laws included banning cigarette advertising and placing strong health warnings on cigarette packets. There are also government policies and funding to discourage smoking. For example, funding has been given to encourage women to give up smoking in pregnancy. Smoke-free legislation in England is part of the Health Act 2006 and in Scotland legislation is similar (2006), with Wales and Northern Ireland having an April 2007 Act. In the EU 17 countries have smoke-free laws with Ireland, Greece, Bulgaria, Malta, Spain, the UK and Hungary all having a complete ban on smoking in enclosed public places and public transport.

Explore

You can find out more about 'smoke-free England' using this link: **www.smokefreeengland.co.uk/**.

You can also use the internet to explore regulations about smoking in other regions and countries, such as using this link to see EU policy: **http://ec.europa.eu/health/tobacco/smoke-free_environments/index_en.htm**

Explore

ASH (Action on Smoking and Health) gives key dates in the history of anti-tobacco campaigning, which you can access using this link: www.ash.org.uk/files/documents/ASH_741.pdf

A specific antismoking campaign – the 'Toxic Cycle Health Harms' campaign, December 2013

In 2008 the British Heart Foundation instigated an antismoking campaign that included what they call a 'hard-hitting' campaign, showing the harm that smoking can do by using strong images intended to shock people into quitting. The British Heart Foundation claims that 'stopping smoking is the single most important thing a person can do to avoid a heart attack'. On 29 December 2013 Public Health England launched a campaign with a similar message, focusing on the physical damage smoking can cause. Public Health England had a three-year strategy and the campaign launched in December 2013 was the second year of that strategy. The campaign focused on 'making the invisible visible' by focusing on the harm caused by smoking involving the whole body, including heart, brain, lungs and blood. The campaign emphasised how every cigarette thickened the blood, put toxins into the body and increased the chance of stroke or heart attack.

The December 2013 antismoking campaign focused on the harm smoking does to the body; however, there was also a message of hope. The harm was meant to encourage people to stop smoking and the hope was to give them a way of stopping smoking using support from Smokefree. Smokers could order free support in a Quit Kit, there was a Smokefree app, text and emails could be used and there was information on how to use local NHS Stop Smoking Services. More than 75 per cent of pharmacies in England had Quit Cards which promoted the Smokefree products to help people to stop smoking.

The campaign used television for six weeks and also radio and online advertising. Posters were available for partners in the campaign, as well as the Quit Cards and a PR toolkit. There was a TV advertisement showing a man inhaling on a cigarette and then cutting to show smoke going into the lungs with toxins in the bloodstream turning the blood black. A voice-over explains the damage and says 'if you could see the damage you'd stop'.

Explore

You can read about the campaign using this link if you would like to know more:

http://psnc.org.uk/halton-st-helens-and-knowsley-lpc/wp-content/uploads/sites/45/2013/12/FINAL-Comms-Toolkit-NHS-Health-Harms-111213.pdf. You can see the advertisement that went with the campaign using this link. Also there is a document from Public Health England (2014) about the campaign, which you can access using this link:

http://psnc.org.uk/halton-st-helens-and-knowsley-lpc/wp-content/uploads/sites/45/2013/12/FINAL-Comms-Toolkit-NHS-Health-Harms-111213.pdf

The results of the campaign can be found on the internet using the first link in the Explore box above and here are some of them:

- The advertising achieved 87 per cent awareness.
- 84 per cent of those seeing the advert agreed it was targeted at people like them.
- 40 per cent of people who saw the advert said they were more likely to quit.
- 68 per cent said 'these ads made me think that every cigarette is harmful'.
- 87 per cent believed that cigarettes cause heart attacks and stroke.
- 30 per cent of people who saw the campaign took action, such as ordering a Quit Kit or talking about smoking with family and friends.

The Smokefree website to support the campaign

The related website (www.nhs.uk/smokefree) gives a great deal of information, including advice about 'why quit', covering health, family and financial reasons, and videos of people who had stopped, with their stories as encouragement, such as 'find out how Brendan did it'. There is also a link to local stop smoking services, giving information on what to expect, why it helps and how to find a local stop smoking service. The website discusses treatments too, including varenicline, bupropion and NRT, all of which you have covered in this chapter.

Explore

You can use the website to find out a lot of information about smoking and nicotine addiction, which you might find helpful when covering explanations and treatments for nicotine as well as this campaign. The website is: **www.nhs.uk/smokefree**.

Psychological strategies behind the Toxic Cycle Health Harms campaign

There are different theories in psychology that can be used to explain how the Toxic Cycle Health Harms campaign (December 2013) might be effective. One is social learning theory, another is operant conditioning.

Health promotion and social learning theory

Social learning theory suggests that learning comes from observing others, in particular significant others who are role models, and imitating their behaviour, particularly perhaps if it is reinforced. Bandura's studies in the 1960s showed that children who watched aggression tended to behave more aggressively than those who did not watch aggression. The way social learning works is explained earlier in this chapter (page 512).

Year One link: Recall what you learned about social learning when you looked at learning theories, including three of Bandura's studies that you covered, and which give evidence for observational learning.

From social learning principles comes the idea that people copy what they see on television and that is one of the bases for advertising. A television campaign about stopping smoking would intend to give images and ideas to someone that they would then use in their behaviour, just as the children in Bandura's studies imitated what they saw. The Toxic Cycle Health Harms advert shows a man smoking outside his workplace and then shows the harm the cigarette is doing to his body. The idea is to show the man wanting to stop smoking so that others who identify with him will stop smoking too. In the campaign it was said that 84 per cent of those seeing the advert agreed it was targeted at people like them, which is what would be wanted. The advert, therefore, reached the required people and social learning theory holds that people imitate people like them, so if people identify themselves with the advert that should help them to stop. Also the man smoking was

not rewarded for his behaviour, so there would be no vicarious reinforcement and no imitating because of that, quite the opposite.

Health promotion and social cognitive theory

Bandura himself moved on from social learning to consider social cognitive theory and he has written about health promotion from the view of social cognitive theory (1998). Social cognitive theory focuses on **self-efficacy**, which refers to people's belief in their ability to achieve in certain areas in their life. Social cognitive theory also draws on goals, expectations and perceived difficulties in the environment to explain health promotion. The important point is that health promotion must focus on changing the practices of social systems as well as changing the habits of individuals. An issue with the Toxic Cycle Health Harms campaign is that it appeals to each individual to realise that every cigarette does harm to them physically and it is not focusing on changing social systems or people's habits when within a social system. From this point of view, social cognitive theory would suggest focusing on people's beliefs that together they can achieve social change perhaps more than focusing on changing the habits of each individual. These ideas suggest that the Toxic Cycle Health Harms campaign will not be as effective as is desired.

Bandura suggests, however, that there is a role for informing individuals about how their lifestyle affects their health, which the Toxic Cycle Health Harms campaign does. However, it is not enough to do that to change habits. Self-efficacy theory suggests that if people believe they can change, even under difficult circumstances, that will help the change to happen, so along with the 'fear' campaign there must be the idea that it is possible for the person to change their behaviour, which is the 'hope' part of the campaign. Though Bandura's ideas suggest the 'fear' campaign will not effect change, the 'hope' campaign might affect beliefs enough to cause change.

Having said that, Bandura suggests that the best way to bring about change is for success to be quick and for there to be immediate rewards for behaviour leading to the change. The campaign discussed here gave out a lot of information to help change; however, this would not reward the individual directly and so might not actually bring about the change.

One way that might persuade someone to make a change in their health behaviour is to use social models, which is where Bandura is referring to his social learning ideas. Seeing someone similar to oneself achieve success can raise someone's belief that they too can change. The campaign did find that 84 per cent of people identified with the man in the TV advert, which goes some way to achieving change in a viewer.

Social persuasion can also help, and the voice-over on the TV advert might help with that, although people rely on physical and emotional responses and if they feel stress then that might undermine their belief in their ability to make the change. Bandura says that positive mood enhances self-efficacy, whereas seeing the physical damage smoking can do gives a negative image so again the campaign does not fit Bandura's ideas.

Explore
You can access Bandura's paper (1998) on health promotion seen from the view of social cognitive theory using this link if you would like to know more:
http://exordio.qfb.umich.mx/archivos%20pdf%20de%20trabajo%20umsnh/aphilosofia/2007/NEUROPSICOLOGIA/BanHealthPro.pdf

Definition

Self-efficacy refers to someone's belief about how far they can succeed in certain situations and self-efficacy plays a role in how someone approaches a situation.

Table 5.8 Summary of how the campaign fits in with social cognitive theory

The Toxic Cycle campaign suits social cognitive theory ideas	The Toxic Cycle campaign does not suit social cognitive theory ideas
There was a 'hope' campaign as well as a 'fear' campaign, which shows there was focus on the possibility of change. Self-efficacy is boosted in situations where change is believed to be possible.	The campaign focuses on changing the behaviour of each individual by focusing on effects on their health, whereas change tends to come from the belief that social systems can be changed, such as smoking habits of a society.
Eighty-four per cent of those seeing the TV advert said they felt it was aimed at them, which goes some way towards them identifying with the man in the advert and so accepting that the very unpleasant physical changes would apply to them too. The campaign used an 'ordinary' man outside his workplace and an 'ordinary' male voice as the voice-over giving the message.	Focusing on fear is not positive and does not give people the belief that they can make the change. Without the belief, the change is not likely to occur according to social cognitive theory. Also, if people feel stress and negative emotions that interferes with their self-efficacy and beliefs about their ability to change. The campaign was stressful and negative so unlikely to be successful.
The voice-over message was clear and gave an easy-to-understand message so it might work as a form of social persuasion.	The campaign does not offer any quick rewards to someone for making the change so that goes against the likelihood of change.

Progress check 5.46

Explain one way in which the Toxic Cycle Health Harms campaign makes choices that are supported by social cognitive theory and one way in which the campaign does not go along with the theory.

Health promotion and operant conditioning

- Operant conditioning suggests that people do again what they are rewarded for doing and avoid doing something when there is no reward.
- Positive reinforcement holds that rewards encourage behaviour and this would suggest that an antismoking campaign should include rewards to encourage someone to stop smoking. The Toxic Cycle Health Harms campaign did not include rewards directly.
- Negative reinforcement suggests that people avoid doing something that has had negative consequences. This concept might help to explain this campaign as the negative consequences of smoking are clearly illustrated in a graphic way so the idea is that someone will stop smoking to avoid these negative consequences.
- These are 'covert' consequences in that they are shown rather than experienced, which might affect whether someone will change their behaviour through negative reinforcement.

Health promotion and classical conditioning

Perhaps classical conditioning principles can help to explain the strategies of the Toxic Cycle Health Harms campaign. Smoking nicotine gives the stimulus that leads to the physiological responses that are focused on in the campaign, including the TV advert and the posters. If someone associated smoking with being sociable and having fun, they might come to associate nicotine and the physiological response with having fun. The campaign wants to replace that association and go back to the association between nicotine and the very harmful physical consequences of nicotine.

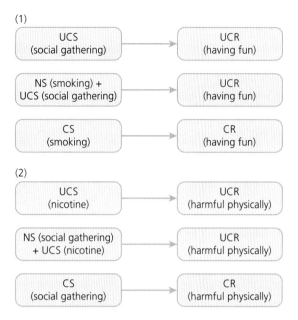

(1)

UCS (social gathering)	→	UCR (having fun)
NS (smoking) + UCS (social gathering)	→	UCR (having fun)
CS (smoking)	→	CR (having fun)

(2)

UCS (nicotine)	→	UCR (harmful physically)
NS (social gathering) + UCS (nicotine)	→	UCR (harmful physically)
CS (social gathering)	→	CR (harmful physically)

How the advertisement might aim to associate nicotine with the physical harm in someone's mind and change from it being associated with having fun.

It is known that nicotine is harmful physically so it is the second example in the above diagram that fits with classical conditioning ideas. However, this is about changing the association for the individual and how they understand the consequences. This is about how the individual focuses on their learning and getting them to focus on the physical damage response rather than the pleasure response. This is not completely about classical conditioning as it depends on focus on involuntary responses as well as the conditioning of neutral stimuli to engender an involuntary response.

Health promotion and the health belief model

Becker (1974) developed the health belief model to understand how people would respond to and use prevention programmes focusing on ill health and disease. The health belief model focuses on how people have individual beliefs about a disease and how to avoid it. They consider seriousness, how susceptible they might be, what the benefits of accepting prevention techniques are and what the barriers are. Self-efficacy, which was discussed earlier, can also be part of the health belief model.

With these ideas in mind the Toxic Cycle Health Harms campaign can be assessed. It targets people's beliefs about ill health by very clearly giving the message that smoking cigarettes harms health. This is shown to be serious and the campaign aims to indicate that anyone smoking a cigarette is susceptible. The benefits of stopping smoking are not really outlined because the fear is the message

and there is not much focus on how quickly the physical damage could be put right if someone stopped smoking. The barriers are not really considered either, such as social pressures to smoke if others smoke around the individual or the difficulty of giving up the habit side of smoking. The campaign gives a strong message about the harm smoking does to the body without addressing the other parts of the health belief model.

Health promotion and the theory of reasoned action

Fishbein and Ajzen (1975) developed the theory of reasoned action, which looks at attitudes, beliefs, intentions about behaviour and how they can predict whether someone will use a prevention service. Fishbein (2008) has written about a reasoned action approach to health promotion. The integrative model, which relates to the reasoned action approach, sets about explaining someone's health-related behaviour, which is important when considering how to set up an effective health campaign where change in behaviour is the goal.

> ### Explore
> You can access Fishbein's (2008) article about reasoned action and health promotion using this link if you would like to know more: www.ncbi.nlm.nih.gov/pmc/articles/PMC2603050/

The integrative model suggests that what someone intends to do relates to their attitudes, self-efficacy and pressure from others. When considering the value of a health campaign issues that need to be covered are someone's intention and attitude, in this case towards smoking, as well as how they perceive norms around smoking. Their self-efficacy is important as well as how much control they believe they have over their behaviour (Fishbein, 2008). If there is readiness to engage in the behaviour, such as to give up smoking, then that is the biggest predictor of action and the evaluation of the Toxic Cycle Health Harms campaign claimed that 40 per cent of people who saw the advert said they were more likely to quit, which gives figures focusing on their intention to quit perhaps. Although Fishbein (2008) goes through factors that affect whether someone takes action about a health-related issue, he also says that very little is known about what influences someone to accept or reject an argument or some information, such as the information in the campaign being discussed in this section. Fishbein suggests that Bandura's ideas about how to increase self-efficacy and how this can increase the likelihood of change in behaviour are the only ideas that tell us how to change behaviour or beliefs about health, including smoking.

Evidence for the effectiveness of health campaigns like the Toxic Cycle Health Harms campaign

Snyder and Hamilton (2002, in a book chapter) discuss how separate case studies looking at campaigns and studying their effectiveness do not give an overall picture of how effective health campaigns are, whereas a meta-analysis of studies looking at the effectiveness of such programmes can be useful. Snyder *et al.* (cited in Snyder and Hamilton, 2002) suggest that campaigns promoting new behaviour are more successful than those focusing on prevention, which suggests that the campaign being looked at here is not likely to be successful because it is about stopping smoking and there have been other campaigns before it.

Snyder and Hamilton put forward some hypotheses about what would make a successful campaign and then test them. Here the ideas are listed with possible consequences for the campaign being discussed and then the findings of Snyder and Hamilton's meta-analysis are added and discussed.

- 'Having some enforcement message such as a change in the law about seat belts will mean a more successful campaign.' The campaign being focused on here has no enforcement message, suggesting lack of success. It was hard for Snyder and Hamilton (2002) to judge whether having an enforcement message was necessary as some campaigns had one and others did not, so they had to be analysed separately. If there was new information and an enforcement message, that seemed to make a campaign more effective, but not if the enforcement message went with old information.
- 'Campaigns that have at least one message giving new information will be more successful.' The campaign being focused on here might have some new information for some people, who might not have realised how harmful smoking is, so for some at least it might be successful. New information was important for the success of a campaign according to Snyder and Hamilton's (2002) meta-analysis.
- 'Campaigns that promote a service that helps a health behaviour are more successful than those not promoting a service but just promoting health behaviour.' The campaign being focused on here does promote a service and this is the 'hope' part of the message, which should make for more success. However, Snyder and Hamilton did not find an effect with regard to promotion of a service because they found a lot of successful campaigns that did not promote a service. It seems that whether or not a service is promoted does not affect the success of the campaign.

- 'Using role models helps a campaign.' The campaign being focused on here does not use a role model as such, which might affect its success with regard to helping people to stop smoking. However, Snyder and Hamilton found that, contrary to what was expected given social learning theory findings, the effect of having a role model was not found.
- More people exposed to the campaign means more success and this campaign was well-promoted with wide TV and radio coverage as well as posters and engagement of shops like pharmacies, so should be successful to that extent. Snyder and Hamilton did find that reach, which means how far the campaign spreads, is important with regard to effectiveness.
- It seems that campaigns that last a reasonable time do better than short or long campaigns and this one lasted quite a short time, which maybe questions its likelihood of success. However, Snyder and Hamilton (2002) did find that some short campaigns lasting a month or so were successful, as were others that lasted a year. So perhaps the length of the campaign is not as important as was first thought.

Table 5.9 Features of a campaign that can affect its success according to Snyder and Hamilton (2002)

Features of a campaign that affect its success
Whether there is an enforcement message and, if it is a new message, the campaign is then more effective.
Whether there is new information and, if there is, then the campaign is more successful.
Whether the campaign promotes a service (like Smokefree) does not affect its success; one that does not promote a service would seem to be just as effective (or not).
Using a role model is thought to lead to a more successful campaign but Snyder and Hamilton found that it made no difference and could in fact lead to less success.
The larger the reach of a campaign, which means it reaches more people, the more likely it is to be successful.
The length of the campaign does not seem to affect success as there are very successful, very short campaigns and very successful ones that have lasted a year.

Progress check 5.47

Evaluate the Toxic Cycle Health Harms campaign using Snyder and Hamilton's (2002) ideas and findings.

Evaluation of the Toxic Cycle Health Harms campaign

Strengths

- The campaign had a website, Smokefree, which was a good source of information, along with posters and other forms of advertising aimed at reaching as many people as possible. As part of their campaign there was a short advertisement about smoking and heart disease, to catch people's imagination. Many different media were used, which is a strength, as more people are likely to be reached that way than by using just one medium. When there is good reach, as Snyder and Hamilton (2002) suggest, that is more likely to give a successful campaign.

- It is claimed that antismoking campaigns are generally effective. For example, in the USA, it has been said that smoking has fallen by half because of antismoking campaigns (Mechanic et al., 2005). A public health document (2000) commenting on an antismoking campaign in Scotland concluded that the campaign was cost-effective, although the conclusion added that this assumed that the figures for cessation were accurate and that the reduction in smoking was as a result of Smokeline (the campaign at the time). The Toxic Cycle Health Harms campaign launched in December 2013 had promising results too. There was an estimate that during the campaign 172,051 Smokefree products were ordered and 420,091 Quit Cards were distributed by 75 per cent of pharmacies across England. All this is evidence that such campaigns work and to some extent at least, with regard to reach, the Toxic Cycle Health Harms campaign was successful too.

- Hafsted et al. (1997) report an evaluation study of Norwegian media campaigns against smoking, and it was found using a questionnaire that smokers reacted more emotionally to the campaigns than non-smokers, and that women reacted more strongly than men. Those who reacted positively to the campaign were those more likely to give up smoking. These conclusions suggest that the Toxic Cycle Health Harms campaign would work.

- Some studies have used meta-analysis, drawing on a number of studies looking at individual campaigns, such as Snyder and Hamilton (2002). This gives the advantage of using a lot of participants and different types of campaign to show what is effective and what might be less effective. Using case studies of specific campaigns to look at their effectiveness and then using meta-analysis to draw together the findings is a method that should lead to reliability and generalisability.

Weaknesses

- The campaign-related website is very informative; however, this suits only someone who has already accessed the website and who is, therefore, probably already on their way towards giving up.

- A campaign may not be successful if there is advertising or another campaign working against it and it might be more successful if other social factors support it. For example, banning the advertising of cigarettes, banning cigarette smoking in public areas and on public transport, and smoking becoming perhaps more socially undesirable might work alongside a particular antismoking campaign like the one used here. It is unlikely to be just that campaign that is succeeding in stopping people smoking. The number of variables that are found to be important when considering a self-efficacy explanation for changing behaviour or a health belief or reasoned action explanation suggest that one campaign alone will not be enough to change behaviour.

- This particular campaign seemed to miss out on what psychology might suggest is good in a campaign to change behaviour such as smoking. Bandura in his ideas about self-efficacy suggested that behaviour change required a reward and that was not focused on in the Toxic Cycle Health Harms campaign TV advert, although it is there on the website, such as the story from someone who says he quit smoking for his daughter, which can be seen as a reward. The campaign was stressful and negative, which Bandura felt would not change behaviour.

Test yourself

1. Describe one antidrug campaign. **(6 marks)**
2. Assess the psychological strategies behind one antidrug campaign. **(16 marks)**

Summary

- Issues around drug-taking include withdrawal, addiction, physical and psychological dependence and tolerance.
- One biological explanation for heroin addiction is a neurotransmitter explanation focusing on how heroin acts on the opioid receptors in the brain. A biological explanation for nicotine addiction is also a neurotransmitter explanation focusing on nicotinic receptors. There is also a neurotransmitter, thus biological, explanation of alcohol addiction, focusing on the reward pathways in the brain and dopamine giving the pleasure alcohol can bring.
- Classical conditioning is a learning theory that can explain heroin addiction, nicotine addiction and alcohol addiction.
- Operant conditioning and social learning can also be used to explain drug misuse.
- Two treatments for heroin addiction are drug treatment and CBT.
- Two treatments for nicotine addiction are drug treatment and either varenicline or cue exposure, both of which use classical conditioning principles.
- Two treatments for alcohol addiction are drug treatment and one from two therapies based on classical conditioning, which are aversion therapy and cue exposure therapy.
- Aversion therapy links to disulfiram, which is Antabuse.
- The community reinforcement approach (CRA) is a therapy based on operant conditioning principles used for alcohol addiction.
- One antidrug campaign is the antismoking campaign from Public Health England, released in December 2013, called Toxic Cycle Health Harms campaign and it rests on various psychological strategies, including ideas about self-efficacy, the health belief model, reasoned action, operant conditioning, social learning and classical conditioning.

Methods in health psychology

For methods in health psychology in your course you need to look at the use of animal lab experiments to study drugs and the ethics involved. You also have to cover two research methods using human participants to study drugs and again you need to look at the ethics involved. The classic study for your course is Olds and Milner (1954) (page 583) so you will have covered one animal laboratory experiment related to drugs when studying health psychology in your course,

though they focused mainly on the reward pathways in the brain rather than looking at drugs directly. The three contemporary studies in health psychology all look at alcohol. These are found in the next section in this chapter. Mundt *et al.* (2012) (page 587) use data from a longitudinal study involving questionnaire and interview. Dixit *et al.* (2012) (page 592) used structured interviewing to find out about alcohol use and Pengpid *et al.* (2013) (page 596) carried out an intervention focusing on alcohol and had an experimental and control group in a randomised controlled trial. You can see that a range of methods to study drugs in humans, as well as one study using animal laboratory experiments, will have been covered in this chapter. Animal laboratory experiments are looked at first in this section, including ethics involved, and then two research methods using human participants, and ethics involved, are covered. The two research methods involving humans are randomised controlled trials to look at the effectiveness of therapies for drug-related problems, and interviewing. Pengpid *et al.* (2013) used a randomised controlled trial and both Dixit *et al.* (2012) and Mundt *et al.* (2012) used interviewing (and Mundt *et al.*, 2012, used questionnaire too). After those two main research methods, questionnaires and PET scanning are also covered, to give you a choice of research methods to focus on.

Animal laboratory studies focusing on drugs

In this section, animal laboratory studies – including those looking at drugs – are outlined as a research method.

Year One link: Review what you have learned about animal laboratory studies when looking at the learning approach, including the ethics of using animals, as laid out in the Animals (Scientific Procedures) Act 1986.

Features of animal laboratory studies

Laboratory studies using animals are laboratory *experiments*. Ethology is the research method where animals in their own environment are observed and studied but, in the study of drugs, experiments are used to test the effects of different drugs, so ethology is not suitable. Animal experiments involve observing an animal's behaviour, but there will have been manipulation of an independent variable, and it is the experimental method that is being discussed here, not the observational research method.

An animal experiment will have an independent variable (IV) that is manipulated to see the effect on a dependent variable (DV). There are strong controls, such as the environment, duration of the study, biochemical factors, gender, age, type of animal and whatever variables are important for a particular study. The aim is to control all variables except the independent variable, so that it can be shown that a change in the IV has caused any change in the DV. This means laboratory experiments can show a cause-and-effect relationship.

Progress check 5.48

Olds and Milner (1954), the classic study in health psychology in your course, used electrical stimulation to different brain regions in rats to see which brain region led to a lot of pressing for stimulation, and they then concluded that the brain regions that led to a lot of pressing for stimulation were those where the rat was being rewarded by the stimulation. Give the IV and the DV for Olds and Milner's (1954) study. You may not have covered Olds and Milner's study yet but the information here should be enough.

STUDY HINT
You need to be able to respond to material in an exam using your understanding of methodology, such as identifying an IV and a DV or giving the experimental hypothesis. It is a good idea to practise doing this when you are learning studies.

STUDY HINT
The progress checks in this chapter (and in the book) are there to suggest ways you may be assessed in your course so use what is asked and practise answering similar questions to help your learning.

Table 5.10 Summary of the features of animal laboratory experiments

Animal laboratory experiments
● Strong controls such as environment, care, type of animal, and state of animal (such as hunger and thirst).
● Manipulation of one feature, which is the independent variable (IV).
● Measurement of change in another variable (the dependent variable), as a result of manipulation of the IV.
● Cause-and-effect conclusions are able to be drawn (to a large extent).
● Scientific procedures are often used, requiring scientific equipment.

Using animals instead of humans has some effect on how a laboratory experiment is run because animals have to be fed, housed, looked after and handled in ways that

humans do not. Such issues have to be incorporated into the study. Studies cannot last too long and they must be suitable for the species – animals are only able to act and react in certain ways. The animal also has to have the right features, such as biochemistry or brain structure, depending on what knowledge is sought. Part of a description of animal laboratory experiments, therefore, needs to include features such as preparing appropriate housing, feeding and care routines, planning the necessary controls and how they will be put into place.

On the whole, there can be more control with animals in laboratory experiments than with humans. The study would be scientific in drawing a hypothesis from a theory, controlling all variables except the IV, and often using scientific equipment to measure the DV.

Progress check 5.49

What does it mean to say 'cause-and-effect conclusions are found'?

STUDY HINT
When you are studying, it is worth stopping each time you come across something you do not understanding and looking it up. The internet is really useful, of course. For example, you might come across a term you are now familiar with, such as 'dependent variable' or 'cause and effect' but might not be completely sure what is meant. Stop to look it up as that will help your understanding and your learning and it does not take long. Then make a note so you can check if you are still not sure about that term on another occasion.

Numbers and types of animals used

Figures for animals used in laboratory experiments in psychology are hard to find because the data tend to show overall animal testing numbers, not just use of animals in psychology studies. Home Office figures in the UK in 2013 showed 4.2 million scientific procedures started in Great Britain, and figures had been rising up to then, so the number may be greater than that now. Around 2.02 million of that larger figure involved animals in procedures that were not about genetic modification (GM) or harmful genetic mutation (HM). A graph from the Home Office (2013) document suggests that the highest figure not counting specially protected species and breeding to produce GM and HM animals was in 1995, with that peak nearly being reached again in 2009, and the 2013 figure being below it, but not by much. Taking into account all use of animals the figure has risen for most years from 1995 and in 2013 was 52 per cent higher than in 1995. Dogs, non-human primates, cats and horses are specially protected species and their use has declined. Mice, fish and rats were the most commonly used in 2013 with 75 per cent of all procedures being done on mice, 12 per cent on fish and 6 per cent on rats. Other species include guinea pigs, sheep, rabbits and others.

Explore
Find out about animal experiments to get an idea of which animals are used a lot and whether particular animals are preferred for particular studies. Here is a link to a Home Office document that gives annual statistics of procedures on living animals in Great Britain in 2013, though this will not only be studies in psychology.
www.gov.uk/government/uploads/system/uploads/attachment_data/file/327854/spanimals13.pdf

Dogs, non-human primates, cats and horses are specially protected species when looking at animal laboratory experiments.

Different animals are chosen for different purposes. Insects, for example, do not have a brain structure at all similar to that of humans, whereas mice and humans share many characteristics. The size of mice is useful, they are low cost and they have fast reproduction rates. Genetically modified mice can be bred to suit whatever purpose is required. Other types of animals are used in experiments, such as rhesus monkeys, as explained in one example later in this section.

Year One link: Review what you learned about the numbers and types of animals used in laboratory studies when you studied the learning approach.

Animal experiments for research into drugs

In this section three examples of animal laboratory experiments are given, two using monkeys and one using

mice. Then a list of animal laboratory experiments used in this chapter is given so that you can look at more examples and at evaluation points as well.

1 The link between cocaine/heroin use and renal disease

Experiments have used animals to help to understand the prevalence of renal disease in heroin and cocaine users. Renal disease occurs when the kidneys fail to function properly. In the laboratory experiments, mice are given either heroin or cocaine in various doses and then their renal function is tested. Animal studies have shown that renal disease is linked more to cocaine use than to heroin, which could point to the drug itself being implicated in renal disease (rather than taking any drug).

Explore
Look up some of the many other animal laboratory experiments that are used to study the effects of drugs. You have studied heroin, nicotine and alcohol in this chapter; however, you could look at studies that consider other recreational drugs.

Studies other than animal experiments have also investigated the link between heroin/cocaine and renal disease. For example, it was concluded with regard to heroin (Jaffe and Kimmel, 2006) that economic conditions, behavioural practices and culture were factors more likely to relate to renal disease than heroin use itself, partly because renal disease in heroin users is not as common as it once was. If heroin caused the renal disease then there would still be the same level of link, and there is not. Their findings support the animal experiments that found more of a link between cocaine and renal disease than heroin and renal disease. Animal studies can be used in this way to back up studies of humans.

STUDY HINT
Link Jaffe and Kimmel's findings (2006) with the biopsychosocial model of health. They considered biological factors (use of heroin), social factors (socioeconomic conditions and culture) and behavioural factors (lifestyle), and drew the conclusion that the use of heroin was not the prime cause of renal disease in heroin users. You will have looked at the biopsychosocial model probably when looking at schizophrenia in clinical psychology and it is discussed in Chapter One (page 164). Be ready to link material in your course where possible as it will help your learning.

Evaluation

Strengths

- The human study cited reinforces the conclusions from the animal studies, which tends to give reliability to the conclusion that it is likely that cocaine affects renal function more than heroin does. Animal studies can be used to back up human studies. They can add credibility as well as reliability because of their scientific nature.
- The animal studies are evidence for a biological explanation – that taking drugs into the body affects physical aspects of the body. This is possibly the case for some drugs more than others. Controls regarding biological aspects make animal studies useful in this way.
- An advantage of using mice is that such studies would not be possible with humans because you could not inject humans with cocaine or heroin and then test their renal function in such controlled conditions.

Weaknesses

- There are differences in brain structure between mice and humans, so conclusions about the effects of drugs on the brain and behaviour might not be generalisable.
- The human study shows how important it is to look at factors other than the drug-taking, because it seems that although taking heroin correlated with renal disease, there were other factors. Psychosocial factors are not studied using animals.
- The human study is evidence for the biopsychosocial model, which suggests that with complex human behaviour there are complex causes affecting such behaviour.

STUDY HINT

When giving strengths and weaknesses here about animal laboratory experiments there is not much expansion on a point. This is because the strength of animal experiments being their controls, enabling cause-and-effect conclusions, and the weakness of the difficulty in generalising to humans from animals, have both been explained earlier in this chapter when explanations for drug misuse were covered. In an answer be sure to expand a strength or weakness so that the point is fully made and backed up.

---

2 Looking at drugs as reinforcers

Meisch (2001) considered animal laboratory experiments into oral self-administration of drugs (taking it themselves by mouth). For example, rhesus monkeys were given the opportunity to take drugs so that researchers could see whether drugs are reinforcing. Here 'reinforcing' refers to the drug being taken as a reward, which would link to factors like addiction. Drugs used included barbiturates, opioids, stimulants and ethanol (alcohol). Animal laboratory experiments showed that drugs of this kind become reinforcers if they are taken by mouth, which means that the animal will choose to take the drug as a reward, so it will get pleasure from taking the drug.

There are problems in animal experiments like this because the study has to take the taste into account (which the animal may not like). The delay before the drug starts to work also has to be considered, as it has to be clear that it is the effect of the drug that is the reinforcer rather than anything else. Animal studies have shown that monkeys will choose to take in more drug solution than water, which is taken to show that they choose the drug as a reward.

Progress check 5.50

When a researcher discusses how a delay before a drug starts to work or the taste of the drug has to be taken account of in a study, what is the term for these types of variable – those that have to be controlled for in a study so that they do not become confounding variables?

Evaluation

Strengths

- Monkeys share many of the genes of humans, so generalising from monkeys may be a reasonable thing to do.
- Humans can become addicted to certain drugs, which appear to be taken for their reward value, so the findings of the study of monkeys fit with known human behaviour, which gives them reliability.

Weaknesses

- Rhesus monkeys are not human, so generalising from what acts as a reinforcer for monkeys to humans might not be reasonable.
- Ethical issues about using animals might be raised, though if the guidelines for using animals are adhered to, then such experiments are generally allowed.

3 Testing the properties of amphetamines in reducing cocaine addiction

The researchers Czoty *et al.* at Wake Forest University School of Medicine in California have found that amphetamines can reduce in monkeys, for up to a month, the behaviour of obtaining cocaine for reward. According to an article written by the researchers in 2008, amphetamine seems to mimic cocaine, but without leading to drug abuse. This means that cocaine addiction could be treated in the same way as nicotine and heroin addiction – by prescribing a replacement drug.

The monkey was taught to press levers to get food or an injection of cocaine as a reward. The number of times the monkey had to press the lever to receive cocaine was increased until it was too much for the monkey to keep pressing. At this stage the cocaine was removed and the monkey was treated by injection (intravenously) with an amphetamine for 24 hours a day. A week later the monkey was offered the possibility of getting cocaine again and the researchers found a large decrease in the number of times the monkey responded. They tried different doses of amphetamine and found a moderate dose was the most effective. Cocaine use over the month was reduced by about 60 per cent.

Evaluation

You can make the same points for the study on cocaine as the reinforcer study above:

- Monkeys are not humans so it is hard to generalise, but they do share many genes with humans, so perhaps some generalisation is possible.
- Human behaviour shows that cocaine is reinforcing, which suggests the study findings can be generalised.
- There are ethical issues you could discuss, such as asking how many monkeys were used (the researchers should use a restricted number) and how the animals were cared for (a licence is required, and caging should be suitable).

You have come across a lot of studies using animals in laboratory experiments in the course of reading this chapter. Table 5.11 summarises nine studies and gives page numbers so that you can use them as examples in a discussion about the use of animal laboratory experiments to study drugs. Also use the evaluation of such studies, as that will enable you to evaluate the research method in general as well.

Table 5.11 Nine studies using laboratory experiments with animals that have been used in this chapter in the content and studies sections in relation to research into heroin, nicotine and alcohol

Name of study	Drug focused on	Brief summary	Page number
Kampov-Polevoy et al. (2006)	Alcohol	When rats self-administered ethanol for six weeks there was a reduction in seizures as withdrawal symptoms, suggesting seizures are withdrawal symptoms in alcohol addiction. This is about physical dependency.	484
Selecki et al. (2006)	Heroin	They carried out a study on rats to look at the role of opioid and GABA mechanisms in heroin usage, showing the role of neurotransmitters.	491
Thakre et al. (2013)	Nicotine	They injected mice and found substances that linked to nicotine withdrawal symptoms, showing nicotine addiction relates to brain processing.	493
Yu et al. (2010)	Nicotine	They used rats self-administering nicotine which affected responsiveness to norepinephrine, showing a link with neurotransmitter functioning	494
Noble (1996)	Alcohol	The review confirmed reduced D2 (dopamine) receptors in animals that preferred alcohol suggesting a genetic explanation for alcohol addiction.	496
Olds and Milner (1954)	Pleasure centre so relates to all	They used rats to show the pleasure centre in the brain is in the septal area and other areas too but not in other specific areas.	583
Siegel et al. (1982)	Heroin	They used rats to show classical conditioning can be used to develop tolerance, and without cues associated with heroin a dose that was too large meant the rats died.	501
Peters and De Vries (2014)	Heroin	They used rats to show five pairings of a cue with heroin led to the cue being associated with heroin and after extinction there was spontaneous recovery. Supports the classical conditioning explanation.	504
Guy and Fletcher (2014)	Nicotine	They show, using rats, how nicotine can be a cue itself that can become associated with reward.	506

You could use the studies in Table 5.11 as examples of animal laboratory experiments and use any evaluation points that were noted in the relevant part of the chapter as well.

> **STUDY HINT**
> Review the studies in Table 5.11 by reading about them in the chapter or by recalling each one. You can choose some and make notes about their aims, procedures, results and conclusions as well as strengths and weaknesses and then you will have studies to use as examples when discussing animal laboratory experiments in the study of drugs.

> **STUDY HINT**
> When making notes about a study you could use a template to help with revision. You could have one large box and inside it the subheadings: Title; Aims/hypotheses; Brief background; Procedure; Sampling; Ethics; Data collection tools. Then another box underneath with the subheadings: Data analysis; Results; Conclusions; Discussion. Finally, a third box with the subheadings: Strengths; Weaknesses; Improving on the study. If you can fit all this onto two sides of A4 you can file all of the studies in some sort of order (by topic perhaps or by method), ready for revision.

> **Explore**
> You can look at some of the arguments about whether animals should be used in research by accessing this link: **www.yourgenome.org/debates/should-animals-be-used-in-research**.

Ethics of using animals to study drugs

The Animals (Scientific Procedures) Act 1986 in your course forms part of learning theories, so it is covered there. Here is a brief review:

- The Animals (Scientific Procedures) Act 1986 regulates the use of animals in studies like lab experiments, including regulations about procedures that may cause pain, suffering or distress. Procedures that might cause lasting harm also come under the Act and the 'protected animals' referred to are any living vertebrae other than man, and any living cephalopod.
- Animals bred and supplied for scientific procedures, which includes animals in laboratory experiments, must be cared for following the best standards and licences must be obtained for the procedures as well as the premises and the researchers.

> **Explore**
> More about the Animals (Scientific Procedures) Act 1986 can be found using this link: **www.gov.uk/research-and-testing-using-animals#animals-scientific-procedures-act-1986**.

- The Animal Welfare Act 2006 gives information about the duty to ensure animal welfare and to make arrangements that an animal's needs are met. Though the provisions of the Animal Welfare Act 2006 tend to come in only when someone does not have a licence under the Animals (Scientific Procedures) Act 1986, so the Animal Welfare Act 2006 is not the one focused on when considering animal lab experiments.
- Guiding principles used in animal testing involve the Three Rs (3Rs), which are replacement, reduction and refinement. Replacement is the idea that non-animal methods are preferred if the same scientific aims can be achieved that way. Reduction means keeping the number of animals used to a minimum, including either using fewer animals or getting more information from the animals used. Refinement means minimising pain, suffering or distress and attending to the animal's welfare by using procedures that do this as much as possible.

Evaluation of animal laboratory experiments – practical and ethical issues

You are required to evaluate animal laboratory experiments, both as a research method and in terms of how useful experiments are in learning about the effects of drugs. In this section experiments are evaluated with regard to practical and ethical issues, as well as how useful they are in learning about drugs.

Year One link: You will have evaluated the use of animal laboratory experiments when you studied this research method in learning theories. Recall what you learned there as you can use the material again here. However, when using any examples remember to focus on research looking at drugs as that is the focus you need in health psychology.

Evaluation focusing on practical issues

Strengths

- Animals are relatively small and usually easy to handle, which means some procedures are more feasible.
- Some animals have short gestation periods and reproductive cycles so generations and genes can be studied more easily than with humans.
- Some animals, such as mice, have a similar brain structure to humans so there is value in studying animals and relating results to humans.
- Some procedures are not suitable for humans but they can be done on animals (ethical guidelines allowing).

- There can be stronger control over the environment than for humans, which means that findings of studies are more likely to be objective.

Weaknesses

- The brains of animals are not exactly the same as those of humans, so relating the results from animals to humans may not be accurate. Furthermore, animals' genetic structure is not the same as that of humans, again making generalisation difficult.
- Human behaviour is complex, so isolating variables – especially in animals – will not address that complexity. This is about reductionism.
- There is a lack of credibility when using animals and concluding about humans because of differences in genes and brain functioning.

Evaluation focusing on ethical issues

Strengths

- Procedures can be carried out on animals that cannot be done on humans – there are ethical reasons for using animals rather than humans.
- Pro-speciesism puts forward the view that we must do all we can to protect our own species, so using animals is one way of discovery that does not harm humans and which also benefits them.
- The knowledge found can sometimes benefit animals as well, which makes a study more ethical.
- There are strong guidelines that have to be followed when using animals in laboratory experiments, so there are safeguards that make such studies ethical, to an extent at least.

> **STUDY HINT**
> Remember to make each point very clearly when discussing strengths and weaknesses.

Weaknesses

- Many animals feel pain and become distressed during experiments, although there are guidelines to avoid unwanted discomfort, as explained in the Animals (Scientific Procedures) Act 1986.
- Some people believe that animals should not be treated as objects. They argue that humans are animals and there is an obligation to treat non-human animals well. This is the opposite view to pro-speciesism

> **Explore**
> You can read about substitutes that can be used instead of animals in drug research using this link:
> www.ncbi.nlm.nih.gov/pmc/articles/PMC3224398/

Year One link: You learned about the ethics of using animals in research, such as research looking at drug misuse, when you covered learning theories. Recall that material for this section in health psychology.

(w) The 'Psychological skills – methods' section online reviews the use of animals in laboratory experiments.

Progress check 5.51

Give three issues that the Animals (Scientific Procedures) Act 1986 regulates in animal laboratory experiments.

Evaluation of animal laboratory experiments – validity, generalisability, reliability, objectivity/subjectivity and credibility

You can evaluate animal laboratory experiments used to research drugs in the same way as you would evaluate them in general, by looking at practical and ethical issues as well as issues of validity, generalisability, reliability, objectivity/subjectivity and credibility.

> **Explore**
> Find out about the various organisations that are against using animals in experiments at all. There are a relatively large number of people in the UK who would like to liberate all animals from being used in this way. Here is a link for you to start with, though of course this is a very sensitive area so only research what you want to read about:
> www.animalaid.org.uk/h/n/CAMPAIGNS/experiments/ALL/

> **STUDY HINT**
> In your course you need to consider issues of validity, reliability, credibility, generalisability, objectivity and subjectivity (and ethics) and it is a good idea when evaluating to consider these issues so that you are ready to answer questions relating specifically to them. You could choose a few animal laboratory experiments in health psychology and evaluate them using these issues, as practice.

Validity

The validity of using findings from animal studies to apply to humans can be argued either way. Validity can be claimed or not. If an animal experiment is being used to test the effects of a drug, this is not a valid study because the effects of a drug on an animal will not necessarily be the same as the effects on a human being. However, neuronal transmission takes place in the same way in the brain of mammals as in humans, so it may be possible to generalise from the brains of animals to the brains of humans.

Year One link: Review the process of neuronal or synaptic transmission from your learning of biological psychology. It has been argued that the recreational drugs you will be studying in this chapter work by neuronal transmission, so it is useful to remind yourself about the process.

Internal validity

Internal validity is about the controls in a study and about having no confounding variables that caused the results. Animal laboratory experiments are very carefully controlled, as you have seen. In fact that is why animals are used in such studies, because control over the environment and perhaps genes is possible. There might be uncontrolled variables; however, the researchers will do all they can to avoid any confounding variables and will raise questions about any possible causes for the results. For example, Olds and Milner (1954) suggested that the rats might have pressed for electronic stimulation to alleviate pain rather than to get reward, but they did not think that was the case, given their observations of the animals. Animal laboratory studies are likely to have internal validity when it comes to using them to study drugs.

Ecological validity

Animal laboratory studies are used in drug research to look at brain functioning rather than to look at behaviour in a natural situation and setting. They do not represent the animal's natural setting of course, and they do, not represent a human's natural setting either; however, for what they are used for, ecological validity is not the focus in the main. The stimulation a drug gives to the reward pathways in the brain, for example, is probably validly represented. When animal lab experiments are used to study the effect of environmental cues on drug-taking, including on brain processing, it could be argued that the cues are artificially introduced into the situation (e.g. Siegel et al., 1982) (page 501) and so there is no ecological validity. However, Pavlov (1927) developed the idea of classical conditioning by using cues in a laboratory and Watson and Rayner (1920) showed that artificial cues instilled a fear in a young baby, so there might be some validity in the claim that cues can be studied by isolating them. Nevertheless, environmental cues studied using a virtual environment and humans might give more ecological validity (e.g. Bordnick et al., 2008, cited in Choi and Lee, 2015) (page 539).

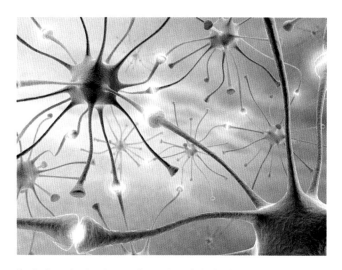

Brain functioning in rats has a lot of similarities with brain functioning in humans and in this area of study there might be validity in using data from animals.

Year One link: You have looked at Pavlov (1927) and Watson and Raynor (1920) when studying learning theories.

Predictive validity

Animal lab experiments using drugs predict issues such as drugs having a rewarding effect on the reward pathways in the brain and drugs affecting certain brain regions. They also predict that cues can lead to relapse and they predict tolerance. Their predictions relate well to what is seen in humans who take such drugs. For example, the relationship between cues and relapse can be found in animals (e.g. van den Oever et al., 2008, found in your Year One studies) and cue exposure therapy, based on such findings in rats, is found to work in humans (e.g. Bordnick et al., 2008, cited in Choi and Lee, 2015) (page 539).

Progress check 5.52

Suggest why studies using virtual reality to help to expose those with drug addiction to cues when using cue exposure therapy might or might not be a valid procedure.

Generalisability

Animals are different from humans, so to claim that findings from animals are true of humans may not be safe. One example is the drug thalidomide, which was tested on rabbits and found to be safe but was far from safe when given to pregnant humans. This suggests that any drug, including recreational drugs, might have a different effect on humans than on animals. Amphetamines have been shown to have a different effect on humans than on rats. However, Deneau et al. (1969, cited in Di Chiara and

Imperato, 1988) showed that drugs that are rewarding for humans are also rewarding for animals. It is the activation of the mesolimbic dopaminergic system that gives the pleasure effect. Di Chiara and Imperato (1988) tested amphetamine, cocaine, opiates, alcohol and nicotine and found all were rewarding for rats. As these drugs are known to be rewarding for humans too, perhaps using animals in lab experiments to test the effects of such drugs does mean results are generalisable to humans, so animal studies are relevant in this type of research.

Explore

You can read Di Chiara and Imperato (1988) using this link if you would like to know more:

www.ncbi.nlm.nih.gov/pmc/articles/PMC281732/pdf/pnas00293-0337.pdf

STUDY HINT

In this book there have been suggestions for links to studies, as there is here, giving a link to Di Chiara and Imperato (1988). You can make notes from studies about how a report is written, including abstract, introduction, method, results, discussion and references. You need to know about report-writing.

Reliability

Animal studies tend to be reliable because of the strong controls in the experimental situation, where more can be controlled than with a study using humans. Variables that might be controlled are the type of animal, size, age, gender, environment, what the animal has eaten, how thirsty it is, its body weight, and whether it is in a crowded situation. With such control and a well-documented procedure, it is possible to repeat the study and to show that the findings are reliable. Usually a study is repeated as a matter of course and findings are not published from just one study on one animal. Also a lot of animals studies will focus on similar areas of study when it comes to the study of drugs (and in other areas), because researchers build on previous studies. When studies are given in this chapter quite often a comment is made about how the study builds on previous understanding in the area. For example, Di Chiara and Imperato (1988) cited Deneau et al. (1969) as showing that drugs that are rewarding for humans are also rewarding for animals, and there are other references to previous studies in their research. When Di Chiara and Imperato (1988) also found that drugs rewarding for humans are rewarding for animals that was showing reliability with regard to Deneau et al.'s (1969) work 20 years earlier. When Di Chiara (1995) (page 495) and Tupala and Tiihonen (2004) (page 496) accept that substance abuse links to the reward

pathways in the brain, which is rewarding because of dopamine, they are showing that the earlier findings were reliable.

Objectivity/subjectivity

Science involves objectivity because it is important to get cause-and-effect conclusions and to do that no variables other than the IV and DV must change and there must be no bias in recording data or in how a study is set up. Objectivity means there is no bias and a study is not affected by experimenter effects or by data being interpreted. A section on the accompanying website related to this chapter suggests a content analysis that you can do as a practical investigation and you can see when you read that section how hard it was to decide the meaning of song lyrics, which is what the content analysis is about. It was hard to remain objective. For example, one song – Can't Feel My Face by The Weekend – could have been all about a drug or all about a woman. It was decided that the lyrics were not about a drug, but this involved subjective interpretation. Animal laboratory experiments have objectivity as what is measured tends to be done 'scientifically', such as using number of lever presses. Experiments follow scientific procedures so you would expect them to be objective and for there not to be subjectivity. Olds and Milner (1954) measured the lever presses that gave the rat electrical stimulation and they carefully placed the electrode into specific brain regions. Both these measures were objective. Olds and Milner's (1954) study is detailed later in this chapter (page 583).

Scientific credibility

Scientific credibility refers to how far data are reliable and verifiable and relies on the scientific nature of the research, and importantly refers to how far using scientific methods is a way of getting reliable information about the world. The findings of research have to be trustworthy and this can be about subjective factors, such as the reputation of the researcher; however, it is mainly based on reliability and objectivity in the way the study is carried out, as well as whether findings that are reliable and objective do represent 'real life'. Animal laboratory experiments have been shown to be reliable and objective, as is argued here, and so they have scientific credibility in the sense of using scientific method. There is just some doubt about the other part of scientific credibility, which is about whether findings are a reliable source of information about the world. This doubt is because they are animal studies and even though it has been argued that rats have the same brain regions, reward pathways and neurotransmitter functioning as humans, it might be claimed that the differences between animals and humans, such as around decision-making and problem-solving, might mean such studies lack credibility when findings are applied to humans.

Progress check 5.53

Complete the table by filling in the term or the explanation as appropriate:

Term	Explanation
	In an experiment confounding variables do not cause the results, they are down to the independent variable being studied.
Generalisability	
Reliability	Results are found consistently each time the study (or a similar study) is carried out.
	Results are affected by someone's own opinion or feelings rather than being objectively measured as 'fact'.
Scientific credibility	

Test yourself

Evaluate animal laboratory experiments as a way of researching the effects of drugs in terms of practical and ethical issues. **(16 marks)**

Using humans to look at the effects of drugs

You need to know two research methods, using humans, which look at the effects of drugs. This section considers four research methods related to drug misuse and recreational drugs. You are required to study only two such methods and two main ones are given here, but two more are briefly covered as well to help your choice and to assist with reviewing methodology in your course.

There are four studies that you can focus on in depth in health psychology in your course. One is Olds and Milner (1954), the classic study, and this is an example of an animal laboratory experiment that has been used to discuss the effect of drugs in the brain. Olds and Milner (1954) was used in the section in this chapter focusing on using animal laboratory studies as a method to study drugs.

The other three studies, of which you will choose to look at one in detail, use different research methods and humans as participants, so they can be used in this section

to show the use of research methods with humans to study drugs. The two main research methods given here involving humans are randomised controlled trials to look at the effectiveness of therapies for drug-related problems, and interviewing. Pengpid *et al.* (2013) used a randomised controlled trial and both Dixit *et al.* (2012) and Mundt *et al.* (2012) used interviewing (and Mundt *et al.*, 2012, used questionnaire too).

Randomised controlled trials as a research method using human participants to study drugs

You will have studied randomised controlled trials (RCTs) through your course; for example, if you studied depression in clinical psychology and chose Williams *et al.* (2013) you would have covered a randomised controlled trial comparing internet CBT with or without cognitive bias modification as a treatment for depression. Looking at Williams *et al.* (2013) helps in understanding the randomised controlled trial as a research method; however, in this section the focus is on using it as a research method to study drugs. Pengpid *et al.* (2013) in health psychology in your course looked at the effectiveness of a brief intervention focusing on alcohol and used randomised controlled trials. Their study is explained in some detail later in this chapter (page 596).

Randomised controlled trials

Randomised controlled trials are often used to look at the effectiveness of therapy. The idea is that one group has the therapy and the control group does not. Participants are randomly allocated to the **treatment group** or **control group** and that is where the 'randomised' element comes into it. **Placebo controlled trials** are like randomised controlled trials but they involve a treatment group and a group that gets a placebo so it is like being in the treatment group. What is good about a randomised controlled trial is that it gives scientific evidence in the form of cause-and-effect conclusions. This is because whether someone is in the treatment or the control group is randomised to avoid bias and difference in the two groups. The two groups must be statistically equal. If all else is controlled, which it should be, then any change in what is being treated can be said to be caused by the treatment in question. Often randomised controlled trials are done in a clinical setting and they can be called 'clinical trials', though the randomised controlled trial method is used in other areas too – for example, in educational attainment. Therefore, here they are called 'randomised controlled trials'. A randomised controlled trial can help to show effectiveness of a treatment as well as side-effects as the control group will not get the side-effects or the success that can be attributed to the treatment.

One problem with randomised controlled trials is that one group, the treatment group, gets the treatment and hopefully benefits and the other group, the control group, does not get the treatment and so does not benefit. This has ethical implications. One solution is to have the control group on a waiting list so that they get the treatment at the end of the trial, just a little later. This helps with ethics. In this situation the control group can be called the 'wait list group'. Another way would be to give the treatment group the treatment being measured and the other group the standard treatment, which is the one that was used before the new one being tested was produced. That is not as unethical as not giving the control group treatment at all.

Progress check 5.54

Explain a main ethical issue with using randomised controlled trials.

Explanation

Randomised controlled trials are where there are different groups that are formed using randomisation so that the groups are equal in terms of characteristics. There is a **treatment group** and a **control group**, for example. One group gets the treatment or variable of interest and the other group does not. **Placebo controlled trials** are where one group gets the treatment and the other gets a **placebo** treatment. A **placebo** will be a dummy treatment like giving a sugar pill where the treatment group gets medication.

Reasons for using randomised controlled trials

- A difficulty with giving someone treatment and then assessing the effect(s) of the treatment is that people can improve just by being on a treatment programme no matter what the treatment is. This is the **placebo effect**. One group has the treatment and another group does not have the treatment but has a placebo treatment, like a sugar pill, but not knowing theirs is not the actual treatment. If all else is kept the same, this can help to overcome the placebo effect. When the participants do not know whether they are in a treatment or a placebo group this is called a single-blind technique. When neither the person running the experiment nor the participant knows which group they are in this is a double-blind technique. Using a blind technique helps to avoid the placebo effect. There can also be an **open trial**, which means the participant and the researcher running the study know which group the participant is in. A trial might have to be open for ethical reasons or because the treatment will be obvious, such as surgery.

Explanation

A **placebo effect** is the term for participants responding to being in a treatment group by improving anyway purely because of being in the group. A **placebo** is a substance or a treatment that is not the treatment being looked at but seems to be the treatment; the participant cannot tell the difference. In an **open trial** both the person running the study and the researcher know which group the participant is in.

> **STUDY HINT**
> When learning about method issues there are often a lot of terms involved. By this time in your course you probably know a lot of them, but it is worth having the research method as a heading, such as in the middle of an A4 sheet of paper, and then putting all the terms around the research method with a definition of each so that you have a diagram to remind you about the research method. You could add one or two examples of the use of the method and, if there is room, strengths and weaknesses and then you have a revision sheet. You could file the revision sheets in alphabetical order by research method and review them often to help your learning.

- Using a randomised controlled trial should help to show something about the effectiveness of a treatment that just observing the effects of a treatment or using a questionnaire to find out about the effectiveness might not pick out. Having the control group as a comparison group makes a difference and can mean just small effects can be uncovered.
- Using randomised controlled trials means having quite a few participants being tested using the treatment, which helps to uncover effects as well. Using case studies might help to see some effect but to look at effectiveness the effects on more people need to be considered.

Progress check 5.55

Why is a double-blind technique better than single-blind?

Pengpid *et al.* (2013)

Pengpid *et al.* (2013) used a randomised controlled trial with six- and twelve-month follow-ups to look at the effectiveness of a brief intervention looking at alcohol consumption. The researchers gathered data at six and twelve months about alcohol consumption and compared the treatment group with the control group. They could also compare the alcohol consumption of the treatment group at the start, at six months and at twelve months after the brief intervention, again to see its effectiveness. They wanted to look at alcohol consumption over time as well as the effectiveness of a brief treatment involving some counselling.

The researchers screened out-patients for alcohol problems at the hospital that was chosen and identified medium risk drinkers, who would be the participants in the study. These participants were randomly allocated to either the experimental condition, where the brief intervention was used, or the control condition, where a health education leaflet was handed out. The brief intervention consisted of one brief counselling session and lasted 20 minutes. If the intervention was found to be effective, then the control group would be offered a delayed brief alcohol intervention; however, it was not found to be effective so this did not happen.

Randomisation was done using generated random numbers. The hospital staff and the out-patients would know whether they were in the intervention or the control group, but those collecting the data and assessing the outcomes were blind to the status of each participant. This means they did not know which condition each patient was in. This was an open trial in the sense that the participants had to know whether they were experiencing the brief intervention or not, but there was some blinding in that the person doing the analysis did not know which group each participant was in.

All the clients visiting out-patients were screened for alcohol problems and randomised into either the intervention or the control group. Two hundred and eighty participants were recruited. Research assistant 1 asked for consent from all patients visiting the hospital out-patients department regarding taking part in the study, which at first was responding to the initial questionnaire. Research assistant 2 scored the results of the initial questionnaire, which gave the screening score. Medium risk drinkers could then be included in the study. People with a score of 20 and over were referred on. Research assistant 2 also carried out the randomisation and the intervention for all participants. Assessments were done by Research assistant 1, who did not know which condition the participants were in. The study made at least six attempts by telephone and letter to contact a participant to avoid drop out at the two follow-ups. If someone missed the six-month follow-up they would be contacted again for the twelve-month follow-up. These measures were to avoid drop out as much as possible. Each time participants turned up at the two follow-up sessions and completed them they were given 40 South African Rands for transport. Ethical approval for the study was obtained from a Research and Ethics Committee and from the hospital itself.

The study found no difference between the group having the brief intervention and the control group. It was thought that as both groups had the leaflet that was successful as there was evidence of a drop in alcohol consumption over time; however, the brief intervention was thought not to have been effective. The results of the study might have come from the participants being in a study as well as them all having the leaflet, but the results were not due to the brief intervention as the successful results (the improvement in alcohol intake) were found in both the control and the treatment group.

Progress check 5.56

What evidence is there that this study was carried out ethically?

Evaluation of Pengpid *et al.* (2013)

Strengths

- Pengpid *et al.* (2013) carried out an experimental study with careful controls, including using an experimental and a control group. They collected baseline data and then carried out two follow-ups to look for reduction in alcohol use following the intervention they put into place. Randomised controlled trials are seen as leading to cause-and-effect conclusions because of the careful controls and they have credibility because of that.
- The use of a single-blind technique so that the researcher doing the assessment did not know which condition a participant was in helped with the controls in the design and with the ability to draw cause-and-effect conclusions from the findings.
- The researchers took a lot of trouble to avoid drop out as much as possible, such as using both telephone and letter reminders and going back to a participant six times to try to engage them in the follow-ups. They achieved about 70 per cent of participants going through to the twelve-month follow-up, which is not bad as longitudinal designs do suffer from drop out and it can bias the results.

Weaknesses

- The careful use of an intervention and a control group seems to have been compromised because the health education leaflet that the control group had and the screening they underwent at baseline and at the two follow-up times meant that they did experience a form of intervention. Though they did not get the additional brief intervention they did not receive 'no treatment' and that might have been why the control group and the experimental group both showed reductions in alcohol use over the time of the study. Pengpid *et al.* (2013) acknowledge this limitation.
- Pengpid *et al.* (2013) acknowledge their use of self-report data and how such data might not be valid. They mention that use of self-report data is generally accepted and that this acceptance is particularly so in effectiveness

studies, but they also comment that they have not tested the validity of self-report data in South Africa, which suggests they think there might be cultural issues in how valid self-report data are.

Explore
You can find Pengpid *et al.* (2013) using this link if you would like to know more: www.biomedcentral.com/1471-2458/13/644

STUDY HINT
Pengpid *et al.* (2013) is explained in more detail later in this chapter because it is one of the contemporary studies for health psychology in your course. You can look at the study in more detail if you wish (page 596).

George *et al.* (2009)

George *et al.* (2009) carried out a placebo controlled trial looking at nicotine use and stopping smoking in those with schizophrenia. This study is chosen here because it focuses on smoking nicotine and also because it links to schizophrenia, which you cover in clinical psychology in your course, so it might be a useful study in that topic area as well as here for health psychology. Also it is freely available online, so you can explore it more if you wish to.

STUDY HINT
You can use George *et al.* (2009) when discussing issues around nicotine as well as when talking about schizophrenia. George *et al.* (2009) compare sustained-release bupropion with nicotine replacement therapy, both of which were used as treatments for nicotine addiction in this chapter so you can also use the study when discussing treatments of nicotine addiction.

George *et al.* (2009) emphasised that people with schizophrenia smoke between 58 per cent and 88 per cent more than the general population and find it harder to stop smoking, so this is an important area of study. George *et al.* (2009) set up two conditions. One condition was using sustained-release bupropion with a transdermal nicotine patch and the other condition was using a transdermal nicotine patch and a placebo. The aim was to look at people with schizophrenia in these two conditions to see how many would stop smoking and to see the effectiveness of the combination therapy as opposed to the single therapy. The combination therapy was the bupropion with nicotine replacement therapy, and the single therapy was just the nicotine replacement therapy. An important part of the study was the use of

a placebo so that the participants did not know whether they were taking bupropion or the placebo. This kept all the conditions in the two groups the same so if there were differences they would be down to the difference in the two groups.

George *et al.* (2009) used a ten-week randomised placebo controlled trial with a double-blind technique so that not only did the participants not know which group they were in but neither did the people running the study. This was all to control for any bias and to make sure cause-and-effect conclusions could be drawn. They measured the stopping smoking by the participant stopping continuously for the four weeks before the measure was taken and they measured smoking again at the six-month follow-up looking again for abstinence. They found that the 29 smokers in the combined treatment group were more likely to stop smoking (27.6 per cent of them stopped) compared with the 29 smokers in the single treatment with placebo group (13.4 per cent of them stopped). At the six-month follow-up four out of 29 (13.8 per cent) in the treatment group compared with none out of 29 (0 per cent) in the control group had stopped. The bupropion and nicotine patches were more effective than the nicotine patches alone. They found some side-effects in the combination therapy, such as poor concentration and insomnia, but they said these were 'modest', which supports the idea that using bupropion and the nicotine patch might be a suitable treatment for those with schizophrenia to help with stopping smoking.

Progress check 5.57
Explain the phrase 'ten-week randomised placebo controlled trial with a double-blind technique'.

Evaluation of George *et al.* (2009)

Strengths
- The study's findings were similar to other studies also using people with schizophrenia, which gives reliability. Fatemi *et al.* (2005), Evins *et al.* (2001) and Evins *et al.* (2005) are all cited by George *et al.* (2009) as having similar findings. George *et al.* (2009) take this as meaning the combination they used would be a safe clinical treatment to help with stopping smoking for people with schizophrenia. Having other studies back up their findings gives reliability as the findings are consistent.
- By using a placebo and a double-blind technique their study controlled for variables and cause-and-effect conclusions could be claimed.

Weaknesses

- However, there was relapse to smoking over the six months before follow-up as even in the treatment group, which was successful for 27.6 per cent, just 13.8 per cent had still stopped at the six-month point. This suggests that giving the treatment for a longer period should be tested.
- George *et al.* (2009) suggest that there was a small sample size, which was a limitation. There were 29 in each group, which might be considered small and might affect generalisation. Another issue with generalising that the researchers point out is that they chose participants who were motivated to stop smoking so perhaps the findings would not apply to those who were not so keen to stop smoking.

Explore

You can access George *et al.* (2009) using this link if you would like to know more: www.ncbi.nlm.nih.gov/pmc/articles/PMC2693008/

Evaluation of randomised controlled trials as a research method using human participants to study drugs

Strengths

- They are a way of setting up an experiment so that there is an experimental group that has the treatment and a control group that does not. All other variables are kept the same, including participant variables, which is why participants are randomly allocated to groups. This means cause-and-effect conclusions can be drawn.
- Giving a treatment in this way is not the same as testing something experimentally and so 'experimenting on someone', which might be seen as unethical. This is because giving a treatment should be ethical, though it could be argued that randomised controlled trials are not ethical if the effects of the treatment are not sufficiently known about.

Weaknesses

- If a treatment does not work or is dangerous it should not be offered in any case and is unlikely to be used if it is likely to be risky for the participant unless there has been a lot of testing beforehand, such as on animals. This means the treatment is expected to work at least to an extent. Therefore, a problem with using randomised controlled trials is that the control group is deprived of the treatment. This is a possible weakness but usually the control group is a wait list group, which means they are waiting for the treatment in any case and will be getting it.

- Another weakness is the placebo effect. If the design of the randomised controlled trial is an open trial, that means the participants know whether they are in the treatment group or not and those in the treatment group might improve because they expect to, and this might have nothing to do with the actual treatment. A single- or double-blind technique is generally used where possible for this reason.

Progress check 5.58

Briefly suggest a randomised controlled trial that could be set up to measure the effectiveness of methadone treatment for young heroin addicts.

STUDY HINT

Be ready to answer questions asking you to offer ideas for improving a study as well as to design a study of your own using a certain research method. It is useful to practise this skill. As well as noting evaluation points regarding studies it might be useful to add two 'improvement' ideas to get in the habit of doing that. You could improve by changing the research method or changing the type of data (such as gathering qualitative as well as quantitative if only quantitative measures are being taken).

Interviewing as a research method using human participants to study drugs

One research method that uses human participants to study drug behaviour and the effects of drug usage is interviewing. Interviews can be structured, semi-structured or unstructured. They usually involve gathering qualitative rather than quantitative data, although some interviews gather both sorts. Qualitative data involve attitudes, opinions and comment, and quantitative data are numbers such as scores, percentages and the number of 'yes' or 'no' answers

Dixit *et al.* (2012)

Dixit *et al.* (2012) is one of the contemporary studies in health psychology in your course and is explained in detail later in this chapter (page 592). They used interviewing to look at the prevalence of alcohol in Northern India and factors that related to alcohol use. The study used structured interviewing with a schedule that had been prepared and piloted. The schedule was divided into three sections, the first asking for personal data about the family and the participant, the second asking about use of alcohol and the third section asking about patterns of alcohol use. They used 'current alcohol use' to mean someone had used alcohol in the last month and they used 'ever user' to mean someone had used alcohol at least sometime in their lifetime. Dixit et al. (2012) call their study an interview though they do also mention 'questionnaire'. They used a structured interview because the questions were administered by a researcher, but the written down answers were then called a 'questionnaire'.

Evaluation of Dixit et al. (2012)

Strengths

- By using a structured interview the researchers asked everyone the same questions and so could compare the data.
- They piloted the schedule so they had checked that the interview schedule would be understood in the same way by all the participants and that it would cover the data required to answer their research question.

Weaknesses

- A structured interview means that the interview could not stray from the schedule so could not explore areas that the respondent was talking about. This means that data are likely to lack validity because the data given are limited by what is asked.
- They used self-report data and there might have been social desirability so the measure was open to some interpretation and bias.

Progress check 5.59

Dixit et al. (2012) used self-report data and there might have been social desirability in their answers about their alcohol use. What is the difficulty with using self-report data and risking social desirability in the answers to the interview?

Palepu et al. (2010)

Palepu et al. (2010) used interviewing to look at addiction treatment and attainable stable housing. Palepu et al. (2010) used data from the Vancouver Injection Drug Study (VIDUS). They looked at stable housing during the follow-up period of the study and considered the variable of stable housing against addiction treatment. The participants were recruited by 'self-referral and street outreach', which involved posters in the community, referrals from the community organisations and word of mouth, and they were eligible for the study if they had injected illegal drugs over the six months beforehand, at least once, lived in the region in question, and provided written informed consent.

At the start of the study and every six months the participants completed a questionnaire where data were collected by an interviewer. This was a semi-structured questionnaire. Not much is said about the role of the interviewer but as the questionnaire is semi-structured (which is explained in Tyndall et al., 2003, who used data from the VIDUS study too), the interviewer will be exploring some of the responses. The questionnaire used asked for demographic data, housing status, diagnoses of mental health, drug use and drug treatment. Analysis included looking at stable housing and then looking at the other variables in relation to stable housing. They found that if the participant was enrolled in addiction treatment that was negatively associated with being in stable housing, this suggests that addicts access treatment when they are vulnerable and other needs are more important than finding stable housing. They concluded that 'addiction treatment exposure may have been a marker of life instability'. The addicts who were the participants were using drugs frequently, often daily, and they were using crack cocaine and injection heroin, which was negatively associated with being in stable housing. They suggest addiction treatment should be linked to 'supportive housing services' to support this vulnerable population. As limitations, Palepu et al. suggest that their study only collected data on the addiction treatment the participants accessed during the study, which would be care for drug addicts taking the drug rather than being some way through a planned programme. Also the participants were heavy drug users who might not be housed because of their addiction. They used a non-random sample so the generalisability of the findings is in doubt.

Explore

You can read Palepu et al. (2010) using this link if you would like to know more: http://journals.plos.org/plosone/article?id=10.1371/ journal.pone.0011697. More about the method and the Vancouver Injection Drug Study (VIDUS) can be found in Tyndall et al. (2003) and here is the link to that study: www.cmdr.ubc.ca/trainingprogram/papers/MEDI%20 580A%20papers/Medi580-Celia-Oct4.pdf

Progress check 5.60

In Palepu et al.'s (2010) study they thought that addicts on a longer-term addiction treatment programme and who were using drugs less regularly might not have had the same problems with lack of stable housing. Explain what they may have meant by this comment.

Evaluation of Palepu et al. (2010)

Strengths

- There is mention of the participants all giving written informed consent and the study being passed by the relevant ethics committee, which is a strength with regard to the ethics of the study.

- Having an interviewer administer the questionnaire means there can be some explanations given about the questions so they should be similarly understood by each respondent, and so data are comparable.

Weaknesses

- The study just uses those currently injecting drugs and on treatment programmes, which limits the generalisability, as the researchers say.
- Housing of this particular group might be a problem because of their current heavy drug use rather than about those on addiction treatment programmes in general. This affects generalisability, as has been said, but it also affects conclusions drawn about the need to link housing associations with addiction treatment clinics, because it might be only this group that are having difficulty with stable housing.
- A semi-structured interview method has the strength of having data that are comparable because a lot of the same questions are asked and this is a questionnaire administered by an interviewer so data can be compared. However, there is possibly the weakness that the particular interviewer affects the responses in some way and if different interviewers are used, as this is a longitudinal design, this might give bias to the data.

STUDY HINT
Palepu *et al.* (2010) call their research method an interviewer administered questionnaire and they say the method was reported elsewhere. When the reference for 'elsewhere' is researched, the research method is called a 'semi-structured interview'. You can use studies as examples of a research method but be sure to fit your answer to a question; in other words explain why it is an 'interview' in this study if using this study as an example of an interview.

Evaluation of interviewing as a research method using humans to study drugs

Strengths

- Interviewing can be in-depth, so data are likely to be more valid than questionnaires because different issues can be explored (depending on the type of interview).
- Interviewing can gain valid data because participants can use their own wording and are not as restricted as they are with questionnaires (such as unstructured interviewing).

Weaknesses

- Interviewers may influence responses by the way they dress, or their age or gender. This would affect

reliability, as another interviewer might get different results.

- The data have to be analysed, which can be subjective as there may be a lot of qualitative data to be put into themes, and these can come from the researcher's preconceived ideas rather than from the data. If analysis is subjective another researcher might analyse the results differently, so there would not be reliability.

Progress check 5.61

Often a study will mention that the method used is interviewing and then they use the term 'questionnaire' for the data collection tool. Dixit *et al.* (2012) and Palepu *et al.* (2010) both used 'questionnaire' as a term when they say their method is interviewing. Explain why this might not be a problem and why they might be using both terms when talking about their research method.

Questionnaires to study the effect of drugs

Questionnaires are used to study the effects of drugs and to look at substance misuse. Participants are asked questions, for example, about their smoking habits, their family and friendships. Questionnaires tend to involve both open and closed questions: open questions gather qualitative data and closed questions gather quantitative data. Questionnaires can be administered to groups or individuals, and they can be posted or issued face to face. They often involve Likert-type questions that involve ranked data, such as whether someone strongly agrees, agrees, disagrees or strongly disagrees with certain statements. Other question types are also chosen, such as yes/no questions or circling factors that apply to the individual. With a questionnaire a pilot study is often carried out to check that the questions are appropriate and that it measures what it is supposed to.

Mundt *et al.* (2012)

Mundt *et al.* (2012) used a questionnaire to find out about demographic characteristics of the students, education and occupation of parents, risk behaviours including alcohol use, self-esteem, health status, extracurricular activities at school and friendships. The students also looked at the school register and had to name their five best male and five best female friends. The data come from the National Longitudinal Study of Adolescent Health (Add Health).

Then after about a year the next questionnaire took place with 14,738 students taking part. Similar data were gathered as in the first questionnaire, including frequency of alcohol consumption over the past year. The students looked at the school register and had to name their five best male and five best female friends as they had had to do in the first questionnaire.

Students had to answer the question 'how often did you consume alcohol in the past year' and were given the option of responses of 'never' through to 'more than once a week'. The students had to name their five best male friends and their five best female friends from the school register to give information about their social networks and they did this in the first questionnaire and after about a year in the second questionnaire. Students were asked 'on a scale of 1 to 5, how often do you and your family have fun together?'

Progress check 5.62

When the questions were repeated in the second questionnaire/wave, the same question was asked about five male friends and five female friends. Why was the question repeated exactly?

Mundt *et al.* (2012) found that friends were chosen because of similarities, including similarity in alcohol consumption. They did not find that alcohol consumption came from peer influence. Not only was choice of friends based on alcohol consumption, it was also based on age, gender and race/ethnicity.

Evaluation of Mundt *et al.* (2012)

Strengths

- Mundt *et al.* (2012) used very large samples, which added strength to their findings in that their findings are generalisable. The original sample came from stratified sampling, then there was random sampling. These two techniques should have achieved a representative sample to help generalisability.
- The researchers claim that as there was 'computer-assisted' data entry this helped to protect confidentiality, which showed good ethics.

Weaknesses

- The participants could only give five best male and five best female friends, which limited their choice to ten friends. It could be said too that some had to find five friends to nominate, which meant they went beyond their closer friends. This way of gathering the data could have given some bias to the data. Mundt *et al.* (2012) acknowledge this point in their discussion.
- Similarly, the study narrowed choice of friendships to just those in the school and did not cover friendships outside the school, which again limited the data. This

point was also acknowledged by Mundt *et al.* (2012) in their discussion.

- Alcohol use in the study relied on self-report data. The researchers themselves felt that this was 'a valid measure' and it is accepted as a valid measure.
- The researchers point out that those who were not in the follow-up part of the study (Wave 2) did show some differences from those who took part in the follow-up, as it seemed to an extent 'heavier' drinkers were in the group that was not in the follow-up, which could have affected the findings.
- The figure for the parental alcohol consumption was lower than national surveys find. Their figure was 40 per cent compared with between 60 per cent and 70 per cent of adults being alcohol drinkers according to national surveys. This perhaps affects generalisability of the findings as possibly parents may not have declared their drinking.

STUDY HINT

These evaluation points do draw on more information about the study than is given here, but the study is given in good detail later in the chapter and the evaluation points are there too, so you will be able to look at this study more if you decide to use it as an example of the research method.

Evaluation of questionnaire as a research method using humans to study drugs

Strengths

- They can be reliable because the same clear questions are set for everyone, with the same instructions.
- There should be no bias, such as response set, because of careful planning and the use of a pilot study. With no bias, if the study were to be carried out again, the same results would be found, making the results reliable.

Weaknesses

- The fixed questions can limit validity because people must answer what is asked and may miss important areas of enquiry.
- There can be social desirability if people answer how they think they are supposed to answer. Therefore, answers would not be valid because they are not 'real life' answers about genuine beliefs and behaviour.

Progress check 5.63

Explain the term 'social desirability'.

PET scanning

PET (positron emission tomography) scanning has been used to study drug use and the effects of drugs. Because drugs affect the brain, scanning can be useful to get a picture of what happens in the brain when drugs are taken. PET scanning involves a radioactive tracer that is taken into the body by adding it to a solution such as glucose, sometimes by injection. Glucose is taken up by the body and the tracer goes along with it. By looking at the progress of the tracer, which provides small positively charged positrons, a PET scanner can pick up 'hot spots' and follow blood flow to see which parts of the brain are active.

Year One link: You looked at PET scanning as one scanning method in biological psychology so recall what you learned there.

Scott et al. (2004)

A study (Scott *et al.*, 2004) using PET scanning on humans showed that smoking cigarettes stimulates the brain to produce opioids, which act in the brain to increase positive emotions and relieve pain symptoms. Morphine and heroin also affect the brain in the same way. The researchers studied the opioid system in the brain – PET scans are able to show opioid receptor activity. The researchers managed to find a way for human participants to smoke while in a PET scanner. Six healthy male participants stopped smoking for at least ten hours before the study began and, during the scan, they each smoked first a cigarette with practically no nicotine and then a 'normal' cigarette. The researchers also asked the men how they were feeling at certain times during the study.

The scan picked up significant differences in opioid flow when the participant smoked the low-nicotine cigarette compared to the normal one. There was increased opioid activity when the men smoked the normal cigarette. The scans also showed that, after the normal cigarette, the men had fewer cravings and it was noted from the scan that the brain regions for memory, emotion and pleasure were less active. The men reported feeling more relaxed and less alert, which matches the scan findings. The same activity was not found in the low-nicotine cigarettes. The findings

suggest that nicotine binds to the opioid receptors just as morphine and heroin do.

Evaluation of Scott *et al.* (2004)

Strengths

- This study uses PET scanning, which gives data that can be checked by more than one person so reliability can be obtained.
- The same participants were those who smoked low-nicotine and normal nicotine cigarettes, which would control for participant variables.

Weaknesses

- The study took place in unfamiliar surroundings, which may have affected the ecological validity of the findings.
- The task was unnatural as, presumably, the smokers usually smoked a particular brand and type of cigarette, whereas in this study the choice of cigarette was prescribed, so the task itself lacked validity.

Year One link: You will have learned about participant variables in cognitive psychology in your course, so you can refer to your notes to remind yourself about what these are.

Progress check 5.64
Explain what is meant by participant variables in a study.

Evaluation of PET scanning as a research method using humans to study drugs

Strengths

- PET is a relatively non-invasive way of studying brain activity, so it is reasonably ethical given the choices of ways of studying the brain (such as lesioning).
- There tends to be reliability because the scans do not require analysis as such: they are pictures and can be repeated exactly. If carried out again, you would expect the same results.

Weaknesses

- Even though they are reasonably ethical, having to have an injection of a radioactive tracer can still be distressing.
- Although brain activity can be seen relatively clearly, it is difficult to pinpoint an exact area of the brain, so the findings can be limited. To an extent they are valid because they are 'real' pictures from a 'real' working brain, but the area covered is large, whereas the brain area affected may well be tiny.

Progress check 5.65

Olds and Milner (1954) used electrodes placed carefully in the brains of rats to send an electrical stimulus to a specific brain region. They then watched lever pressing for the stimulus to be sent, and concluded that the more lever pressing the more pleasure for the rat so the area being stimulated was in the reward pathways of the brain. Scott *et al.* (2004) used human participants and PET scanning of them smoking either a nicotine-filled cigarette or a low-nicotine one. They used smokers and non-smokers and found differences in opioid flow in the brain depending on the nicotine present. Referring to their methodology, explain one strength of each study compared with the other.

Year One link: Three of the research methods chosen here are the three that you studied in Year One of your course. You covered interviews and questionnaires in social psychology and PET scanning in biological psychology.

Studies in this chapter using human participants to study drugs

Table 5.12 gives a list of some of the studies used in this chapter. You could choose some of these and consider the research method used to help in discussing two research methods using humans to study drugs.

Table 5.12 Nine studies using human participants that have been used in this chapter in the content section in relation to research into heroin, nicotine and alcohol

Name of study	Drug focused on	Brief summary	Page number
Fishbein *et al.* (2007)	Heroin	Looked at brain differences in alcoholics, people addicted to alcohol and heroin, and non-abusers and found heroin addicts showed more risky decision-making related to activation of the prefrontal cortex. Used experimental method comparing different groups using cognitive tasks.	490
Li *et al.* (2014)	Heroin (and alcohol, see below)	Used humans to show that $GABA_A$ receptor genes have a role in heroin addiction even though in human genotypes there are variants in different individuals so there are individual differences in heroin addiction, perhaps because of having different genotypes. Compared different genes to find gene differences in those with addiction and those without.	491
Geha *et al.* (2013)	Nicotine	Compared smokers with non-smokers and found that smokers showed a different brain response to food in the hypothalamus compared with non-smokers. They concluded that smoking relates to weight change. Used fMRI scanning and BMI measures in smokers and non-smokers and made comparisons. An experimental and a control group.	493
Shields (1963)	Nicotine	Used a twin study to show that mainly either both twins smoked or neither twin smoked, showing a genetic link.	494
Li *et al.* (2014)	Alcohol	A meta-analysis looking at $GABA_A$ receptor genes and alcohol dependence as well as heroin dependence, as seen above. Used genotype research, which compares people with characteristics (such as addiction) with those without to look for gene differences.	497

Cont.... Table 5.12 Nine studies using human participants that have been used in this chapter in the content section in relation to research into heroin, nicotine and alcohol

Name of study	Drug focused on	Brief summary	Page number
Maes *et al.* (1999)	Alcohol	Used MZ and DZ twins and found a genetic link in alcoholism. This was a twin study. If MZ twins are more similar than DZ twins a characteristic (like alcoholism) might be down to genes.	497
Field and Duka (2002)	Alcohol	Showed social drinkers reacted to cues related to alcohol such as feeling more relaxed and having higher rates of craving. They used an experiment and gathered data by observation, questionnaire and physiological measures.	508
Mundt *et al.* (2012)	Alcohol	Found that friends tend to choose others like them (including in their alcohol-related behaviour) rather than people being influenced to drink alcohol by peers. They used questionnaires to gather data from the young people as well as interviews with parents.	587 (studies section)
Mattick *et al.* (2009)	Heroin	Found that methadone was better than a non-drug-related therapy and more people stayed on the treatment, with more people on the methadone programme coming off heroin. This was a review of studies and they looked at 11 randomised controlled trials.	517

Progress check 5.66

In the list of studies given there were some that used experiments. Identify the ones that used an independent groups design, which means different participants were in the different groups.

Test yourself

Using two research methods using human participants to study drugs, assess which of the two gives more valid data and which gives more reliable data and give your arguments. **(16 marks)**

Ethics of using human participants to study drugs

So far in this methods section for health psychology in your course you have had to cover the use of animal laboratory experiments to study drugs and also the ethics involved, and you have had to cover the use of two research methods (though four were offered) using human participants to study drugs. You also need to look at the ethics involved in using human participants to study drugs.

You covered ethics when doing research in psychology with humans when you covered social psychology and

you had to cover the British Psychological Society's Code of Ethics and Conduct (2009) as well as issues around risk management. In clinical psychology you looked at the Health and Care Professions Council (HCPC) guidelines for clinical practitioners and you can see by the research methods given in this section, such as randomised controlled trials to look at the effectiveness of therapy for drug addiction, that health psychology and clinical psychology come close together when it comes to therapies.

Here ethical issues when using humans to study drugs are reviewed only briefly because you can use the information in other parts of your course.

Year One link: You studied the ethics of using human participants in research in psychology when you looked at social psychology, including covering the BPS Code of Ethics and Conduct (2009).

The BPS Code of Ethics and Conduct (2009)

There are four ethical principles in the Code. These are respect, competence, responsibility and integrity. Table 5.13 summarises these four principles and includes other ethical guidelines that are within the principles and with which you will be familiar.

Table 5.13 The four ethical principles, with some detail, of the BPS Code of Ethics and Conduct (2009)

Ethical principle	Some explanation	Guidelines covered as part of the principle
Respect	This is about the dignity and worth of all people, with focus on their rights, including privacy and self-determination. All people should be respected no matter what their race, gender and so on. Practices must not be unfair or prejudiced. All clients must know all about the study so that consent is informed and such consent must be given. Deception must be avoided unless necessary but deception must be disclosed as soon as feasible.	• Privacy and confidentiality • Informed consent • Deception
Competence	High standards of competence in professional work must be maintained and psychologists must work within their limits. There must be ethical decision-making and adherence to the professional code. Alternative courses of action must be considered and actions must be justified on ethical grounds. A psychologist must monitor their own competence but importantly also the competence of others and must challenge – including reporting to the Health and Care Professions Council.	• Competence
Responsibility	This is about the avoidance of harm and prevention of misuse of contributions to society. Psychologists should avoid harming clients but also take into account individual differences, which may conflict. Consider alternative courses of action. Psychologists must also be aware of potential risks – this is about risk that goes beyond risk in their normal lifestyles. Psychologists must give the right to withdraw at any time and ensure that no payment puts this right at risk. Research participants should be debriefed at the end of their participation so that they know what the research was about and to check no harm has been done.	• Right to withdraw • Debriefing
Integrity	Psychologists must value honesty, accuracy and clarity as well as fairness. This is integrity. This is about boundaries and not abusing relationships as well as recognising conflicts of interest and inequality of power.	

Explore
You can access the BPS Code of Ethics and Conduct (2009) using this link if you would like to know more: **www.bps.org.uk/system/files/documents/code_of_ethics_and_conduct.pdf**

STUDY HINT
When discussing ethical issues in using human participants when studying drugs, be sure to use as examples studies that are looking at drugs in some way. For example, when discussing ethics you might be tempted to discuss Milgram's work; however, this is not about using humans to study drugs, so would not be relevant.

The rights of human participants

The National Institute of Justice in the USA (2010) lists the recommended rights of human participants and these can apply to other countries as well, even if not in legal terms. These rights are:

- The right to give voluntary, informed consent.
- The right to be respected and treated as 'autonomous agents'.
- The right to withdraw from a study at any time.
- The right to maintain their own integrity and not to do what they do not want to do.
- The right to be protected from physical, mental and emotional harm.
- The right to have information about the research.
- The right to privacy and to well-being.

You can see that these rights match the ethical principles in the BPS Code (2009), including issues of informed consent, respect, right to withdraw, integrity, protection, information and privacy.

People being interviewed on the street, perhaps about their alcohol drinking habits, have rights that must be adhered to.

The Nuremberg Code

Ethical principles for using humans in studies come from the Nuremberg Code, which was established by the Allies after the Nuremberg Trials. In 1947 German doctors who had conducted terrible experiments on prisoners in concentration camps were prosecuted in the Nuremberg Trials. The Nuremberg Code was the first document giving the idea that 'voluntary consent of the human subject is absolutely essential' and also participants had to be informed of any risks in being involved in an experiment. You can see where the emphasis on getting informed consent comes from and why it is so important.

Clinical/randomised controlled trials

Clinical trials in particular have to have health authority/ethics committee approval, though all research studies have to have ethics committee approval, and the relevant committee will depend on where the research is taking place. Studying drugs involves randomised controlled trials, as has been explained, and these are clinical trials when they involve looking at the effectiveness of treatment for addiction, such as George et al. (2009) (page 563).

Seven principles for ethical research to protect participants

Emanuel, Abdoler and Stunkel write about research ethics and how to treat people who participate in research. Their paper is published by the National Institute of Health (NIH), an American body. The seven principles they suggest are briefly explained here:

1 Social value: The study should have social value, such as helping the researcher in improving health or well-being of others. Benefit might be in information. Research is unethical if neither the participant nor society can benefit. Helping students to learn is about social value.

2 Scientific validity: Research should produce useful results and these results must be able to be taken seriously. This means a hypothesis, a control, controlled variables and so on, as well as a study lasting long enough for findings to be firm enough. Good research must be able to be reproduced and reliable.

3 Fair participant selection: Research should be fair to participants; for example, in a randomised controlled trial where a treatment is expected to be effective, all participants should have access to the treatment.

4 Favourable risk–benefit ratio: This is about cost–benefit analysis. The riskier the study the more it must benefit and the risks and burdens must be as low as possible.

5 Independent review: An independent review by people not connected to the research must be undertaken to make sure the study is ethical and that people will be treated fairly.

6 Informed consent: There are four parts to informed consent. These are about competence of the participant, meaning they understand what they are agreeing to. The researcher must disclose everything. The participant must understand and then, fourthly, they must give consent voluntarily.

7 Respect for participants: Participants must be able to withdraw from the study at any time, any information about them must be kept confidential, their well-being must be checked through the study and the results must be shared with them.

> ## Explore
> You can access the paper by Emanuel, Abdoler and Stunkel using this link if you would like to know more:
> http://bioethics.nih.gov/education/FNIH_BioethicsBrochure_WEB.PDF

> ## STUDY HINT
> When ethics are summarised here they are not especially focused on research into drugs, so be sure to make your answer focused on that area of research if you are asked about it. One way of doing this is to only use examples from research into drugs.

The ethics of some of the studies in this section to use as evidence

When discussing ethics be sure to use examples to illustrate the points. As this section is about ethics of doing research to study drugs, your examples and focus must be on this area of research. The ethics of some of the studies used in this section are summarised here; however, you can use other studies and examples of other research methods.

Pengpid et al. (2013) and their ethics

Pengpid et al. (2013) paid attention to ethics in that they made provision for the control group to get the brief intervention if it was effective, which was being fair to the participants and treating them with respect. Consent was asked for as well, though whether this was informed consent was not mentioned and Pengpid et al. (2013) would want the control group not to know about the brief intervention the treatment group had so probably informed consent was not obtained. If someone had a high score for alcoholism in the study, they were referred on for help, which again is about respect and integrity.

Pengpid *et al.* (2013) rewarded their participants but did this to pay for their travel, which should not have put pressure on them to remain in the study, though it might have done. Pengpid *et al.* obtained ethical approval from the Medunsa Research and Ethics Committee and they cite the project number. The hospital also gave approval for the study.

George *et al.* (2009) and their ethics

George *et al.* (2009) controlled their study carefully and had a treatment group who had bupropion as well as nicotine patches and a control group who had a placebo and nicotine patches. There was deceit because the control group participants did not know they had the placebo. Avoiding deceit is one of the guidelines within the ethical principles of respect, so perhaps George *et al.*'s (2009) study had some ethical issues. However, written informed consent was obtained from all the participants and the Yale School of Medicine's Human Investigation Committee approved the procedure, which adheres to ethical principles and guidance. There was protection of harm to participants too, such as excluding people having a history of seizures from the study, as well as those with psychiatric instability.

Dixit *et al.* (2012) and their ethics

Each participant gave verbal informed consent and when a participant was aged 15–18 years, parents also gave consent. There was an explanation for each individual about the reason for the interview and what would be involved and it was explained that confidentiality would be maintained. Only people involved in the study saw the responses, which were kept securely.

Palepu *et al.* (2010) and their ethics

The participants were recruited by 'self-referral and street outreach', which involved posters in the community, referrals from the community organisations and word of mouth. This shows that participants were able to volunteer for the programme in the sense of having to respond to a poster or go along to the study on being told about it. In this way they self-selected themselves. This is a fair way of recruiting participants. However, they were drug addicts and vulnerable so if a community organisation asked them to take part perhaps they would have found it hard to refuse. This may mean they did not feel they could withdraw. The University of British Columbia/Providence Health Care Research Ethics Board approved the study.

Progress check 5.67

Four studies are covered with regard to their ethics. Using the four studies complete the table below. The studies are Pengpid *et al.* (2013), Dixit *et al.* (2012), George *et al.* (2009) and Palepu *et al.* (2010). Just use each study once.

Ethical principle/ guideline	Example of a study giving evidence for or against this guideline/ principle
Informed consent	
Right to withdraw	
Respect (using fair practices)	
Confidentiality	

Test yourself

1 Compare two research methods using humans to study the effects of drugs in terms of reliability, validity and objectivity. **(12 marks)**
2 To what extent can studies using human participants to study drugs be ethical? **(8 marks)**

The use of cross-cultural research, including nature–nurture issues, to study drug misuse

Cross-cultural research methods are studied in clinical psychology for your course and you may well have already covered that section. Chapter Two of this book covers cross-cultural research as a method.

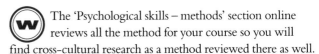 The 'Psychological skills – methods' section online reviews all the method for your course so you will find cross-cultural research as a method reviewed there as well.

In this section the focus is on cross-cultural research to study drug misuse. The research method is reviewed first here and then examples of its use to study drug misuse are given so that you have examples. Cross-cultural research can be about nature–nurture so that issue is also covered here.

Firstly, some ideas about the effect of culture and **subculture** on drug use are discussed, to show that culture is a variable that is considered. Terms are considered too, to help to set the scene for cross-cultural research. Then the cross-cultural research method with its links to the nature–nurture debate is briefly reviewed to explain it. After that cross-cultural research used to study drug misuse is considered.

Culture as a variable in drug addiction

Assumptions about drug use in different subcultures and societies

Adrian (2002) comments that research looking at drug misuse has a different focus depending on the society being looked at. When it focuses on **minority 'primitive' communities** research sees drugs as being about **social integration**. When research into drug misuse focuses on subcultural groups within a **mainstream society**, drug use tends to be seen as being about **social disorganisation**. It seems in mainstream societies that drugs are seen as being problematic and representing the problematic status of **minority groups**. Adrian (2002) reports on a content analysis of the abstracts (summaries) of studies and of studies themselves in the US National Institute of Alcohol and Alcoholism database. Adrian says 44 abstracts were looked at in the content analysis and 40 actual reports. Adrian (2002) found that neither the abstracts nor the reports showed that there was more drug use or drug associated problems in minority **ethnocultural** subgroups compared with mainstream society so there seem to be implicit assumptions about ethnicity, societies and addiction that should be noted. '**Ethnicity**' refers to common traditions and ancestry and '**race**' refers to physical characteristics and biology, though they can be taken to mean the same thing.

STUDY HINT

If you discuss minority society and mainstream society and want to look up more about these issues, you could use the term 'majority world' because it refers in fact to minority groups in a way and 'minority world' refers to what are called 'developed countries'. These terms make the point that it could be claimed that 'minority' societies make up most of the world. This shows how you need to explain terms that you use, like 'minority', as there can be more than one meaning.

Explanation

Minority 'primitive' communities refers to communities with less culture and society in the sense of not having developed in the same way as more developed communities, but having a more simple way of life. **Mainstream society** refers to more typical and conventional groups which are taken as the norm.

Explanation

Social integration refers to members of a society participating together in something and working together to achieve social rules and social relations, bringing cohesion. **Social disorganisation** refers to a community made up of differences often according to place because where someone lives shapes their behaviour, including their behaviour related to using illegal substances.

Explanation

Subculture refers to a culture within a culture in that it has different values, beliefs and traditions from the culture it belongs to. A **minority group** is a group in a society that is not as important as the main group in that society, and a minority group tends to be different racially or ethnically with different cultural values and traditions from the main group. **Ethnocultural** refers to an ethnic group with a specific culture. **Ethnicity** means a group of people with common social, cultural or ancestral experiences. **Race** has to do with biology and ethnicity is to do with culture.

Impact of culture affects approach to treatment for drug addiction

Abbott and Chase (2008) consider the impact of culture on the approach to treatment. Culture refers to the patterns of beliefs and behaviour that guide the worldview of someone in a society. Abbott and Chase say that most cultural groups have abused alcohol and other drugs at some time and there are codes of behaviour in cultural groups about the approach in that culture to alcohol and other drugs. Culture can provide expectations about drug use and problems that might come with drug use. Abbott and Chase (2008) suggest that in periods of rapid change in a culture drug use might be found more, especially if there is an incoming culture that knows more about drugs or uses them more or differently. An example is the North American Indians who had no exposure to alcohol before the whites arrived. It is thought that alcohol use and substance misuse go with loss of culture, with people who are in two cultures turning less to substance misuse if they are comfortable with the cultural values of both cultures (e.g. May, 1982, cited in Abbott and Chase, 2008).

Abbott and Chase (2008) say that DSM-IV can illustrate the importance of culture in respect of drug dependence because it mentions the need to consider culture and there is a mention of culture-bound syndromes as well as a requirement for an overall cultural assessment for diagnosis and care. Abbott and Chase underline the need to consider cultural reference groups for a person, their involvement with their culture and cultural factors that might affect development, as well as language issues. Finding out about these issues can help to see if someone identifies with their 'host culture', which is the culture they are living within but might not be the culture they 'feel' associated with. These are issues that impact on drug-taking and need to be considered when diagnosing and when planning treatment. Their conclusion is that culture is an important aspect of issues like drug abuse and should be considered because it will impact on the success of a treatment.

North American Indians were introduced to alcohol by whites. The more comfortable someone feels in two cultures they belong to the less they might turn to substance abuse. Drugs use links with cultural issues.

Explore
You can access the article by Abbott and Chase (2008) using this link if you would like to know more:
www.psychiatrictimes.com/articles/culture-and-substance-abuse-impact-culture-affects-approach-treatment

Cross-cultural research as a research method

Cross-cultural research refers to studies that are done in different cultures and societies, and done in the same way so that results in the different cultures can be compared. If similarities in results are found between different cultures that suggests what is being studied is universal. If there are differences it suggests what is being studied is affected by culture. What is universal tends to be seen as part of human nature and what is different between cultures tends to be seen as being given by environment and culture. This is the nature–nurture issue. It is hard to see what about us comes from our nature and biology, and what comes from our nurture and the influence of our environment. Cross-cultural studies can help to uncover what in humans is 'nature' and what is 'nurture', by uncovering universal laws about behaviour, and that is its value for psychology.

A consideration is that what is found in all cultures studied might be universal because it suits social living and helps to hold a society together rather than it being in human nature.

Issues and debates
The nature–nurture debate is one of those covered in your course and is discussed in Chapter Seven where issues and debates are looked at. Cross-cultural research can help to inform the nature–nurture debate so you can use the material considered here about substance abuse when considering the debate.

> **STUDY HINT**
> You covered the cross-cultural research method in clinical psychology and more is found in Chapter Two where methods in clinical psychology are covered.
>
> The 'Psychological skills – methods' section online reviews all the methodology in your course and the cross-cultural research method is reviewed there.

The use of cross-cultural research in relation to drug misuse

1 Room et al. (1996): The diagnosis and assessment of substance use disorders in different cultures

Room et al. (1996) used nine cultures to look at whether criteria for the diagnosis of substance use disorders were applicable in different cultures. They found language to be an issue in that ways used to diagnose the disorders in the different cultures were found in some form though not in single words. In assessing substance use disorders, items that were hard to 'translate' included those about self-consciousness relating to feelings and those that related to causes for behaviour. Some criteria used in assessment, such as time spent finding the drug and using the drug, and tolerance for the drug, were not so easy to use in other cultures (other than the USA). Also Room et al. found that clinicians used different thresholds for diagnosis. They said that clinicians were more likely to make a diagnosis of drug dependency than alcohol dependency even though there were similar behaviours assessed and this was the case in most cultures. Room et al. concluded that attitudes of a society to drug misuse and alcohol misuse affected the diagnoses.

> **STUDY HINT**
> In clinical psychology you looked at reliability and validity of diagnosis. You could use material about the diagnosis of substance misuse when discussing such issues, such as suggesting that culture affects diagnosis. However, be sure to discuss mental health disorders when discussing diagnosis in clinical psychology and discuss substance misuse when using material in health psychology.

Room *et al.* (1996) report on their study where nine cultures and eight languages were studied. Data for alcohol and one other drug were collected so that they could compare diagnosis for the two. The data meant they could compare across the cultures but also within each culture. The researchers asked respondents (experts, professionals and lay people) about their own ways of describing behaviour as well as about diagnostic terms. They asked about severity too, such as looking at how alcoholism was described but also at how severe drinking alcohol would be for 'alcoholism' to be diagnosed. Their interest was in the meanings used in diagnosis and different meanings perhaps being used between (and within) cultures. For example, they wondered when someone would be seen as intoxicated and when this would be seen as 'acute intoxication' according to ICD-10. Also what would be seen as 'normal' drug use and what would be seen as harmful and drug 'abuse'. Countries involved in the study were Turkey, Greece, India, USA, Nigeria, Romania, Mexico, Spain and South Korea with one city in each. The researchers wanted a wide range of language groups and of cultural patterns of drinking and drug use. Data were gathered by interview asking about what people living in each society thought about the concepts used to diagnose alcohol and drug disorders. The interview was semi-structured with mostly open-ended questions gathering qualitative data. The interview schedule included optional probes to follow up on answers so detailed information was gathered.

STUDY HINT
Room *et al.* (1996) used semi-structured interviewing so you can use the study as an example of using the interview method using humans to study drugs.

Each centre chosen for the study, in all nine countries, interviewed at least 20 people asking about concepts and terms for alcohol and 20 people asking about other drugs too. There were also focus groups with between seven and ten participants in each, to discuss issues around diagnosis of alcohol and drug misuse. The focus group involved various professionals and also someone who used alcohol or drugs and a family member. All nine sites did at least two focus groups. Questionnaires were also used, with rating scales, to find out about alcohol and drug-related issues such as from social workers and health workers.

The results of the study suggest that there are validity and reliability issues in the diagnosis of substance use disorders. A main point is that diagnosis assessment tools tend to require translation. Respondents might reply the same way another time, which seems like reliability; however, the issue is what the respondent understands by what is being asked and whether that represents their 'real life' issues, which is about validity. They found that they could use the diagnosis tools to compare alcohol and drug use and misuse across cultures but one of the difficulties is that what is being asked about can be a subjective state and is less easily measured because subjective states are hard to find out about if concepts are fixed. 'There are cultural differences in ways of thinking about subjective states' (page 217). If a culture is used to the 'modern self' that can stand outside itself and describe and evaluate what is being felt, that fits the diagnosis instrument, but that might not suit all cultures. Also English terms can be hard to translate in different languages, such as 'tolerance' and 'withdrawal', and that might affect the validity of diagnosis. For example, in Korea 'hangover' means having alcohol in the system in the morning whereas in Bangalore respondents talk about problems with tolerance and cutting down their drinking when talking about a small dose of alcohol from a Mediterranean wine culture viewpoint.

Evaluation of Room *et al.* (1996) as a cross-cultural study

Strengths

- The data are gathered using many means, including interview, focus groups and self-ratings, so there can be triangulation, which means data gathered by different means can be compared to check for reliability and validity. Not only are many methods used but also many different groups, including experts, health workers, addicts and family members, so the data have detail and breadth.
- Using nine countries gave a good comparison regarding diagnosis of substance use disorders because there were many differences between the countries, not only eight different languages, but different cultural issues around alcohol and drug misuse, such as how 'hangover' is defined and viewed. Using nine countries means generalisability is more able to be claimed though cultural differences that were found suggest that diagnosis of alcohol and drug use disorder is different in different cultures so generalising even from nine countries to 'all countries' is not what was intended.
- The same procedure is used in all nine countries to enable cross-cultural comparisons to be made and care is taken, such as training the interviewers to use the semi-structured interview and the probes, so that the procedure is the same as far as possible.

Weaknesses

- Room *et al.* point out that on some sites data were not collected in the same way as in other sites, because of issues such as getting the focus groups together with the same personnel represented. The data were supposed to be collected simultaneously and there were difficulties with that.
- A problem with making comparisons was that, apart from alcohol, which was involved in the study in all countries, the 'other drug' varied and that meant making comparisons was difficult. The 'other drug' was chosen by the different locations because in reality different drugs were common in the different countries. Also Room *et al.* felt that asking about just one other drug as well as alcohol would be more manageable. They found, however, that they had to focus most on alcohol when drawing conclusions from their data.
- An issue was that covering nine countries meant less depth of data. Room *et al.* give the example of an in-depth study in Korea looking at alcohol and the meaning of hangover and withdrawal and differences between the two, using ethnography as a method. They use the example to show that their study lacked that sort of detail and they cite Taipale (1979) as having done such a study. They also comment, however, that their approach allowed for comparisons that a more detailed study would not allow.
- Room *et al.* comment that their study relied on psychiatrists and professionals and they say many of these would have had their training in the UK or the USA so their perceptions regarding diagnosis would be influenced by their training and not just by their culture. This means that concepts in the cultures might be affected by things in common in the training of the professionals involved.
- Another possible limitation is that the data were interpreted by the interviewers and those running the focus groups. There was training; however, the concepts and ideas had to be translated, for example, which could affect the data.

> **STUDY HINT**
> You can use the strengths and weaknesses of Room *et al.* (1996) when evaluating the cross-cultural research method as many of the issues apply and also you can use the study to give examples, which will show understanding of the issues.

Progress check 5.68

Room *et al.*'s (1996) study brings up issues with using a cross-cultural research method. They mention validity and reliability. Explain what they felt were reliability and validity issues in their study.

2 Deng *et al.* (2001): Drug-using offenders in Taiwan and the USA

Deng *et al.* (2001) use data from national surveys of drug-using offenders in the USA and in Taiwan to compare the differences in drug use in offenders focusing on different variables. The variables chosen are **demographic characteristics**, drug use, drug treatment patterns, childhood experiences and criminal histories.

Definition

Demographic characteristics – characteristics of a population or sample, such as age, gender, education and occupation.

Deng *et al.* found that American drug users who are offenders have more complex issues regarding the consequences and use of drugs. Social constructionism better explains drug-using offenders in Taiwan.

> **STUDY HINT**
> Luhrmann's finding about the differences in the voices that are heard and related to schizophrenia are discussed in Chapter One (page 29), when clinical psychology and schizophrenia are covered.

American drug-using offenders reported earlier drug and criminal involvement with more prior arrests and committing more crimes that were not drug-related. American drug-using offenders also had more family problems and used a variety of different drugs as well as being involved in different treatment programmes. These were differences between American and Taiwanese drug-using offenders. The differences led the researchers to suggest different actions in the two cultures to help to reduce drug misuse. They suggested in the USA focusing on 'troubled teens' and families and they suggested that in Taiwan focus should be on treatment instead of imprisonment. It seems that the cultural differences were enough to suggest different courses of action and knowing the differences helped to inform the different courses of action. This underlines the usefulness of the cross-cultural research method and cross-cultural studies.

How the data were gathered

The US data came from the 1991 Survey of Inmates of State Correctional Facilities and the data from Taiwan came from the 1999 Survey of Drug Offenders. Both surveys gathered data on childhood histories, drug and alcohol use, criminal involvement and treatment before imprisonment so comparisons could be made. However, the same survey was not used and it was not in the same year either, so that might affect comparisons. Nevertheless, because the same data were gathered Deng *et al.* (2001) felt they could generalise the findings about the different social and cultural contexts. It is interesting that Room *et al.* (1996) felt that terms might have different meanings and spent time looking at translation of terms like 'hangover', whereas Deng *et al.* (2001) felt that data about treatment and childhood histories could be compared despite possible differences in understanding, such as about 'treatment'. Deng *et al.*, however, carried out a two-year longitudinal study in Taiwan to look at the effectiveness of treatment for drug addiction in prison and it was data from structured interviews before release that were used in this cross-cultural study. So possibly there was some depth in the data as they were obtained using interviewing. For the US data too interviews were used, so again there was some depth to the data.

Models explaining drugs and crime

Deng *et al.* (2001) outline three models that can explain how drugs relate to crime. One model is the criminal model, which means drug addiction does not lead to crime, it is more that lack of social ties and stability can lead to a deviant lifestyle such as drug misuse and crime. A second model is the medical model. This links drug use to crime directly, such as suggesting that some substances lead to more impulsive and aggressive behaviour because of their effects on the brain. It is the addiction that leads to criminal behaviour. A third model is the social constructionist model. This looks at how drug culture is 'constructed' in a society, such as meanings and tensions, such as tensions between a dominant group in society and other groups and subcultures. For example, 'drug wars' are about groups seen by a dominant group as a threat.

Results of Deng et al. (2001)

Table 5.14 shows some differences between the Taiwanese and American drug-using offenders with regard to demographic data – to show differences in their experiences. You can see that the differences are very noticeable and the cross-cultural study of Deng *et al.* is useful for giving that information alone.

Table 5.14 Sociodemographic characteristics and family backgrounds for the American and Taiwanese participants in Deng *et al.*'s (2001) study (adapted from Deng *et al.*, 2001)

Sociodemographic characteristics	US sample of drug-using offenders (N = 1480)	Taiwan sample of drug-using offenders (N = 700)
Mean age in years	31.2	33.0
Married	19.8%	29.4%
Education (college or higher)	15.3%	3.4%
Mean number of children	2.6	1.0
Living arrangements while growing up	Mother only 41.1% Father only 3.4% Both parents 40.6% Grandparents 9.3% Other 5.6%	Mother only 18.1% Father only 13.6% Both parents 63.8% Grandparents 2.9% Other 1.6%
Unemployed in the month before arrest	41.2%	15.1%
Parents abused alcohol or drugs	71%	4.2%
Ever physically/ sexually abused	15.6%	4.2%

Progress check 5.69

Draw a graph to show the distribution of living arrangements for drug-using offenders in Taiwan compared with those in the USA according to Deng *et al.* (2001).

Table 5.15 shows drug use patterns for the participants in Deng *et al.* (2001) to highlight cultural differences.

Table 5.15 Drug use patterns for drug-using offenders in the USA and Taiwan (adapted from Deng *et al.*, 2001)

Drug use pattern	US (N = 1480)	Taiwan (N = 700)
Mean number of illegal drugs taken	3.3	1.6
Mean age in years of first drug use	17.2	25.7
Taking drugs daily or almost daily	73.1%	59.7%
Main source of drugs	Bought from a dealer you know = 51.6%	Bought/given by a friend or acquaintance = 63%
Ever used heroin	31.9%	58.4%
Ever used cocaine	59.9%	1.3%

Table 5.16 shows the treatment history for the drug-using offenders in Taiwan and those in the USA, to compare the data. The results clearly show the differences in treatment between the two groups.

Table 5.16 Treatment history for the Taiwan and US samples (adapted from Deng et al., 2001)

Drug treatment	US (N = 1480)	Taiwan (N = 700)
Non-prison-based drug user treatment attended		
In-patient	41.3%	13.4%
Individual counselling	35.8%	7%
Group counselling	49.1%	–
General drug education	31.7%	–
Religious admonishment	–	1.1%
Mean time (days) until relapse after attending in-patient drug abuse treatment programme	126.6	6.5

The tables in this section show the many differences between the US and Taiwan samples relating to drug use. These differences alone show the value of cross-cultural studies because without them such data would not be known.

Conclusions

Deng et al. (2001) explain how in Taiwan the government launched the 'war on drugs' in 1993 after martial law was lifted in the 1980s, bringing more street crime and environmental issues. The 'war on drugs' led to more arrests and led to the government being seen as doing something about the problems. That is why Deng et al. concluded that in Taiwan the issues around drug use and offending related to social constructionism and how drug use was seen in Taiwan. In the USA, however, a similar connection was not found. It was thought that drug use came from family relationships and conditioning during upbringing. These different conclusions led Deng et al. to propose different solutions in the two countries.

Progress check 5.70

Deng et al. felt that social constructionism could explain experiences with drug use in Taiwan. What do they mean by social constructionism in this context?

Evaluation of Deng et al. (2001)

Strengths

- The two ways of gathering data both used survey data and gathered data about similar issues around sociodemographic data and treatment experienced, for example. This means comparisons could be made. Both sets of data gathering used drug-using offenders. There was enough similarity in the data gathered to make the comparisons, even though the procedure was not exactly the same.
- Deng et al. bring in background information about Taiwanese and US society and policy to help to put the data into context, which helps to understand some of the differences, such as the different understanding of domestic violence. This helps in understanding the comparisons drawn and the differences in the data gathered between the cultures.
- It is interesting that the study focuses on two cultures but uses a cross-cultural study to consider the impact of different environmental issues on the two samples rather than looking at nature–nurture. Cross-cultural studies are said to be useful for getting information about universals in behaviour, and it could be said that drug-taking and crime appear to be universal, or at least found in the two societies. However, the focus is on environmental influences in the two cultures and how knowing about them can help to plan effective treatments. A strength of the study is in its focus on using the data and applying the findings to helping the individuals and groups concerned.

Weaknesses

- The data were the drug users' retrospective recall of their drug use before being arrested, which may mean underreporting.
- Also there were differences in the two cultures where the data were gathered, which of course is the point of cross-cultural research; however, such differences make it hard to draw cause-and-effect conclusions. Deng et al. see their study as exploratory, showing differences and giving ideas for further study.

- Differences in some areas such as domestic violence would be interpreted by the drug-using offenders in different ways in the different cultures so comparing the figures needs to take account of different understanding of the concepts. In Taiwan domestic violence was only classified as a criminal offence in 1998, for example. This means the drug users may not see themselves as being victims of such violence.

3 Gullo *et al.* (2011): British and Australian young adults and substance abuse

Gullo *et al.* (2011) looked at data from young adults in Britain, where 183 participants were used, and Australia, where 271 young adults were involved. They measured the one-factor and two-factor models of impulsivity to see how they related to substance misuse. The idea was that drug-taking might come from the reward it brings and that is what gives the motivation, or drug-taking might come from impulsivity, where someone cannot prevent being impulsive even if such behaviour has negative consequences. Gullo *et al.* look at whether it is the reward that a drug brings or impulsivity around drug-taking that someone cannot stop which 'causes' drug misuse. The two-factor model is one that predicts that both reward and impulsivity are present in substance misuse. Gullo *et al.* want to test this idea and they want to see if the model is found in both Britain and Australia so that they can suggest it has 'cross-cultural consistency'.

In Britain and in Australia the participants were students. In both cultures psychology students got course credit for taking part and non-psychology participants had a small payment. Standard measures were used. Reward drive was measured using the BAS-D scale asking about the pursuit of goals and the BAS-RR scale, which asked about positive responses to reward. Reward drive was also measured using the BAS-FS scale, which asks about fun seeking, such as asking about trying something new if thinking it will be fun. Rash impulsiveness was measured using the TPQ-NS, which asks about novelty seeking behaviours, and BAS-FS to show rash impulsiveness in someone. The AUDIT was used to find out about alcohol consumption. ASSIST was used to find out about alcohol, smoking and substance abuse. The main idea was to measure what someone is like regarding behaving for a reward, what they are like regarding behaving impulsively, and what their substance use is. Then the researchers could see if the substance use related to reward, impulsivity or both (or neither). Also, being a study done in two cultures, there could be cross-cultural comparisons.

STUDY HINT

Pengpid *et al.* (2013), which is one of the contemporary studies in health psychology in your course and is explained in a later section in this chapter (page 596), also uses the AUDIT to find out about alcohol consumption. A lot of studies use standardised scales because they have already been shown to have reliability and also because then data using them can be compared because the same items are used. A cross-cultural study using the same scales will give good comparison possibilities between the cultures.

Conclusions

Gullo *et al.* (2011) found that the results were very similar between the British and Australian samples, which shows consistency in personality and drug misuse between the cultures. This suggests perhaps that the personality factors are universal and found in all cultures, which is a nature explanation. However, Britain and Australia do share many cultural characteristics so generalising to 'all cultures' would be problematic. They found that rash impulsiveness predicted hazardous substance use but reward drive was not so much associated with alcohol and illegal drug use.

Evaluation of Gullo *et al.* (2011)

Strengths

- Gullo *et al.*'s findings were consistent with other studies that also found that rash impulsiveness predicts illegal substance use more than reward drive does. They cite Loxton *et al.* (2008) and Johnson *et al.* (2003) as finding just rash impulsiveness as a predictor of the problematic use of alcohol or illegal drugs, which goes with their own finding that rash impulsiveness is the most significant predictor compared with reward drive.
- They used standardised scales, which have been shown to be reliable, which is a strength. Also they used the same scales and measures in the different countries so comparing the data was possible.

Weaknesses

- A limitation is that the data come from self-report, which may have given social desirability. The researchers cite Reynolds *et al.* (2006) as suggesting that self-report data can have bias from lack of insight someone might have into their own personality. Gullo *et al.* (2011) suggest that a study measuring actual behaviour driven by impulsivity would have more validity.

- Gullo *et al.* recruited mostly a female sample and they were non-clinical substance users so the findings would not generalise to all substances users. There tend to be more male than female substance users, according to Gullo *et al.* (2011), for example.

Summary of what was found in the three cross-cultural studies used here

- Room *et al.* suggest that diagnosis might not be valid between cultures and this might be because of different understanding of terms like tolerance and hangover. There might be reliability because these terms would be translated consistently, but how the translation interprets the terms might not represent the same reality. This means if comparing diagnoses between cultures consistency might be found that shows reliability in the findings but not validity.
- Deng *et al.* suggest that there are many factors between drug-using offenders in the USA and Taiwan that are different. These are environmental factors like family characteristics and drug-related experiences, and there are also differences in what is offered and taken up in the way of treatments. Cross-cultural comparisons help to show such differences and suggest that different cultures need to use different means to address drug-taking.
- Gullo *et al.* (2011) found that rash impulsivity was more of a personality factor relating to the use of hazardous substances than a reward drive, though a reward drive was related to alcohol and illegal substance use, just

not as much. Their findings in Britain and Australia using a similar sample and the same measures were very similar to one another, which suggests they might be uncovering universality in personality traits that relate to substance misuse. They think perhaps that people with an impulsive temperament might be those to target when it comes to early intervention regarding substance misuse.

Progress check 5.71

Match the issues in the table below with the three cross-cultural studies on drug misuse that are used here.

Issue	Study that involves this issue
Targeting temperament, such as impulsivity, can help in early prevention of substance misuse and this might apply cross-culturally, possibly showing nature issues involved in drug misuse.	
Considering treatment for drug-using offenders is likely to require considering a lot of cultural issues around family and social structures in a specific country. In the USA focusing on family issues early on can be useful; in Taiwan focusing on how drug use is seen in the society can be useful.	
Using diagnosis tools in different countries might seem to have reliability but because concepts and terms are hard to translate in different cultures, there might not be validity.	
Generalisability is difficult because the sample was limited by being mainly female and not being diagnosed drug abusers.	

Test yourself

Evaluate nature–nurture issues related to drug misuse as shown by cross-cultural studies. **(12 marks)**

Data analysis

You need to know about data analysis. This includes with regard to quantitative data using descriptive statistics and inferential statistics and all the issues involved therein. Also you need to know about analysis of qualitative data, using both thematic analysis and grounded theory.

Year One link: All the issues around data analysis that you need to know about were covered in Year One so review them for this application. The only exception is the use of grounded theory for qualitative data.

You covered all the issues around data analysis that you need here in health psychology in clinical psychology too, so you can review this by referring to Chapter Two. Remember, however, that you do need to know and understand such issues in health psychology and could be asked about them in the health psychology section of your examination.

 The 'Psychological skills – methods' section online reviews all you need regarding data analysis.

Progress check 5.72

Show your understanding of analysis of quantitative data. To do this sort the terms in the table here into an order and put them under the headings in the 'answer' table.

nominal	p<.01	mode
mean	interval	p>.05
p<.05	median	ordinal

Answer table:

Levels of significance	Levels of measurement	Measures of central tendency

Test yourself

Assess the difference between analysis of qualitative data and analysis of quantitative data in terms of the results obtained. **(8 marks)**

Summary

- Animal laboratory studies are used to study drug misuse and abuse. There are practical issues around their use. Rats tend to be used often and the focus is on areas like the pleasure centre, which is thought to be where the pleasure from drugs 'works' as a reward.
- Ethics when carrying out animal laboratory studies are very important and the Animals (Scientific Procedures) Act 1986 must be adhered to.
- There are many different research methods used using human participants to study drugs and two of them are randomised controlled trials and interviewing.
- Other research methods include questionnaires and PET scanning.
- Ethics when using human participants to look at drugs are very important, as they are in all research, and the British Psychological Society's Code of Ethics and Conduct (2009) is an important document giving four main principles.
- The four main principles surrounding ethics in psychology are respect, competence, responsibility and integrity.

- Cross-cultural studies can help to consider the impact of environment and culture on substance misuse, as well as possibly suggesting any universal issues surrounding substance misuse, possibly such as having an impulsive temperament.
- Cross-cultural studies can help with the nature–nurture debate as they are a way of separating nurture from nature. If different cultures are different in their environments and influences, but similarities are found with regard to substance misuse, then those similarities might be down to nature.
- The data analysis part of method in health psychology in your course is not new to you; you will cover it in Year One, except for grounded theory and qualitative data, which you will cover in clinical psychology in your course. You need to know about descriptive and inferential statistics when analysing quantitative data, and analysis of qualitative data, including thematic analysis and grounded theory.

Studies in health psychology

You need to cover the classic study in health psychology in your course, which is Olds and Milner (1954), as well as one contemporary study from a list of three. The studies are Mundt *et al.* (2012), Dixit *et al.* (2012) and Pengpid *et al.* (2013). The classic study and all of the contemporary studies are covered in this section.

Olds and Milner (1954)

Olds and Milner's study was done a long time ago but is still a classic study because of its findings about the reward pathways in the brain, not that it was called that then.

> **STUDY HINT**
> You have looked at the brain's reward pathways in this chapter when considering the mode of action of recreational drugs.

Olds and Milner (1954) focused on positive reinforcement, which relates to learning theories regarding explaining behaviour; however, the study is about how positive reinforcement comes from within the brain rather than focusing on environmental stimuli and the effects of reinforcers. The researchers use rats and electrical stimulation of brain regions to show how reward relates to brain functioning.

Year One link: Recall what you learned in the learning theories topic in your course about the ethics of using animals in experiments. Olds and Milner's study can be distressing when considering what happens to the rats. It is worth considering how they dealt with ethics. Of course, this was in 1954, and the Act that you study was developed in 1986.

Aim

The aim was to see which structures were active when a rat was pressing a lever for electrical stimulation of the brain and to look at different structures to see whether stimulating them was rewarding. This was to see if there were brain areas for reward.

Method

The electrical stimulation was administered through electrodes implanted in such a way that they did not interfere with 'normal' functioning in the rats. There were 15 male hooded rats and a Skinner box was used in the experiment.

Year One link: Recall how Skinner used what was called a 'Skinner box' when working with rats and pigeons to explore principles of operant conditioning. For example, a rat in a box without stimulation, just a lever that gives food when a red light is on and not when a green light is on, can be trained to press the lever only when the red light is on. You covered operant conditioning in learning theories as well as in this chapter when looking at explanations for drug misuse.

In Olds and Milner's (1954) study the Skinner box delivered an electrical current to the brain when the rat pressed the lever and the rats were given electrical stimulation to the brain for a total of between twelve and six hours. This was the acquisition phase. Then around one and a half hours of extinction was given, which means a lever-press (response) gave no stimulation.

Year One link: Recall the principles of operant conditioning and the idea of extinction from classical conditioning.

Each rat was given a percentage score, which was the proportion of time the rat was responding by pressing the lever during the whole of the acquisition phase. The score showed whether the simulation was positively reinforcing, negatively reinforcing or had a neutral reinforcing effect. Each rat also had a percentage score giving the proportion of time the rat pressed the lever in the extinction phase.

After the acquisition and extinction phases the rat's brain was examined to see which structure in the brain had been stimulated, which means that area had been active.

The electrical stimulation took place at the tip of the needle, which was inserted under anaesthetic into the rat's brain into specific areas. There were different areas studied, so different rats were stimulated in different brain areas. The study took place four days after the needle/electrode was inserted. After the four days there was an hour of pre-testing and then the rat was put into the Skinner box and the study began, one rat at a time. The voltage of the electrical current was set at what seemed to be just enough to produce a response in a resting animal. Each day the rat spent three and a half hours in the box and this gave three hours of acquisition time and half an hour of extinction time. This went on for four days. At this stage of the study, however, Olds and Milner noted that there did not seem to be much difference in the daily results so they reduced the study to three days and then, again observing there weren't differences between the days, reduced the study to two days. This explains why some rats (the early ones) had twelve hours of acquisition time and some had nine or six hours of acquisition time. Rats were not deprived of food or water at all and the only reinforcement they had was the electrical stimulation.

> **STUDY HINT**
> You may not think that Olds and Milner's study was ethical given their treatment of the rats. However, they did reduce the number of days the experiment lasted for when they realised there was no need to keep repeating the study for four days. This decision helped to minimise distress, which is one of the ethical requirements when using animals in experiments. You can use studies in this way to show examples of ethical issues.

A rat in a Skinner box pressing a lever

The lever in the Skinner box operated a switch so that when it was pressed the rat received the electrical stimulation to the brain via the electrode, which had been carefully placed into a specific brain region. The stimulation lasted as long as the lever was pressed down, though sometimes there was a time switch to stop the stimulation after a certain length of time even if the rat kept the lever depressed.

> **STUDY HINT**
> Olds and Milner (1954) used animals in a laboratory experiment so you can use the study when discussing this research method as well as when discussing the ethics of using animals in lab studies in research.

The recorded scores all used just six hours of acquisition because early rats had twelve hours and later ones had six, and the scores had to be comparable. The score was the percentage of the time spent pressing the lever compared with the overall acquisition time. The score for the rats when there was no stimulation, which was the extinction period, was also calculated to give a baseline measure.

If the percentage of acquisition time lever pressing is above the baseline, which means there is more pressing of the lever if there is stimulation, that is reward. If the percentage of acquisition time lever pressing is below the baseline, which is when the rat avoids pressing the lever more than those who press the bar but get no stimulation, that is punishment. The rat is avoiding the stimulation and presses the lever less than in the extinction period.

The researchers used a 30-second period of the rat pressing the lever at least once in that period as a 'period of responding' and it was recorded as such. Thirty seconds or more without responding was counted as a 'period of no response'.

Results

Table 5.17 shows for each of the 15 animals the percentage of acquisition time responding and the percentage of extinction time responding. Then in the results section the scores are related to the brain region being stimulated. This is to find out about which regions of the brain are the ones where electrical stimulation is rewarding for the rat.

Table 5.17 The animal number, the percentage of acquisition time responding and the percentage of extinction time responding

Number of the animal	Percentage acquisition time responding	Percentage extinction time responding
32	75%	18%
34	92%	6%
M-1	85%	21%
M-4	88%	13%
40	6%	3%
41	4%	4%
31	37%	9%
82	36%	10%
36	11%	14%
3	0%	4%
A-5	71%	9%
6	0%	31%
11	0%	21%
17	2%	1%
9	77%	81%

You can see that the individual rats responded quite differently from one another. For example, rat No. 9 pressed the lever 77 per cent of the time during the acquisition time but 81 per cent during the extinction phase. In contrast rat No. 32 pressed the lever 75 per cent of the time during acquisition, similar to rat No. 9, but rat No. 32 pressed the lever just 18 per cent of the time during extinction. What is not in Table 5.17 is the region of the brain that was stimulated. Information about the scores and which area of the brain was stimulated can be found next.

The position of the electrode

The electrode was put in different places in the rats' brains and the researchers could look at the percentage of time spent responding to get the electrical stimulation and see the effect of the different brain regions.

Central portion of the forebrain

Olds and Milner (1954) found that the highest scores were from the central portion of the forebrain. There were four acquisition stores when the electrode was placed beneath the corpus callosum and between the two lateral ventricles. The scores ranged from 75 per cent to 92 per cent. This was the septal area of the brain. All four rats that responded a lot with the electrode in the septal area scored less than 22 per cent in the extinction phase. The researchers concluded that the stimulation in the septal area represents a primary reward.

Away from the septal area

The researchers found that as the electrode was moved away from the septal area of the brain the acquisition scores dropped sharply to 4–6 per cent responding for the stimulation during the acquisition phase.

The cingulate cortex

In the cingulate cortex there was an acquisition score of 37 per cent and an extinction score of 9 per cent, which suggests the stimulation of this area was rewarding.

The thalamus area

Regarding the thalamus area there was a 36 per cent score with the electrode in the cingulate cortex, an 11 per cent score relating to the hippocampus, a 71 per cent score with the electrode in the mammillo-thalamic tract, and a 0 per cent score if the electrode was in the medical lemniscus. The 0 per cent score means negative reinforcement, in that the electric stimulation was avoided by the rat.

Mid-brain

In the mid-brain electrodes gave two scores of 0 per cent, with the extinction rates for the two rats being 21 per cent and 31 per cent. The 0 per cent suggests a negative effect as the rats pressed the lever much more for 'no stimulation'

in the extinction phase, so they appeared to avoid pressing the lever when it gave stimulation. Deep in the medial posterior tegmentum gave a 2 per cent acquisition score and a 1 per cent extinction score so was judged to be neutral.

Between the red nucleus and posterior commissure

When the electrode was between the red nucleus and the posterior commissure there was an acquisition score of 77 per cent and an extinction score of 81 per cent, which shows reward from the stimulation but a high extinction score too, which the researchers said was hard to interpret.

Progress check 5.73

Explain the results of Olds and Milner with reference to two brain regions.

Behavioural data

Olds and Milner (1954) also looked at the behaviour of the rats when the electrodes were placed in a position that was judged to be rewarding. This was when the acquisition scores were high.

Rat 32

Rat 32 gave just over 3,000 responses in the 12-hour acquisition phase and when there was electrical stimulation the response rate was 285 responses per hour. With the current off, the response rate was nearly 0. Rat 32 was the lowest scoring rat with the electrode in the septal area.

Rat 34

Rat 34 was the highest scoring rat with the electrode in the septal area and gave over 7,500 responses over the 12-hour acquisition period. The response rate when there was stimulation was 742 responses per hour and again almost 0 responses during extinction.

Rat A-5

Rat A-5 was discussed to show a rat's pattern regarding one day of responding. The rat pressed at a rate of 1,920 responses per hour, which was one response every two seconds. During the acquisition phase in the first period of the day, the rat responded regularly and stopped quickly when the stimulation stopped (extinction). The rat started pressing again when the stimulation returned. Rat A-5 spent nearly three-quarters of the acquisition time responding and after extinction, if a current was given, was quick to start pressing again.

Discussion

Olds and Milner (1954) concluded that electrical stimulation of the brain, especially in the septal area, leads to behaviour that fits an explanation that the rat is rewarding itself. The rat stops pressing when there is no reward. With electrical stimulation in other areas of the brain the stimulation can be negatively reinforcing or neutral – the stimulation then does not act as a primary reward.

Areas that are rewarding include the septal area and also to an extent the mammillo-thalamic tract and cingulate cortex. The researchers concluded that a 'system of structures' (page 425) seemed to give a reward system in the brain. They called the 'system of structures' 'reinforcing structures' (page 425).

They considered the idea that the electrode caused pain that the stimulation reduced. They felt though that they would have observed pain in the animals and they saw no evidence of that. During the study the rats were not aggressive, they ate and slept well. The experimenters felt that the rats were pursuing a positive stimulus and not escaping a negative one.

Olds and Milner felt they had found evidence for a primary reinforcing effect that did not relate to the basic drives of hunger, thirst and so on. They felt they had found reinforcing structures in the brain relating to the physiological mechanisms of reward. They thought they had found a system in the brain that is there 'to produce a rewarding effect on behaviour' (page 426).

Olds and Milner (1954) summarise their findings. They say they found many places in the lower centres of the brain where electrical stimulation is rewarding and that these places go 'as far back as the tegmentum and as far forward as the septal area' (page 426). They felt they had also found sites where the animal would avoid stimulation and areas that were 'neutral'. The electrode in the septal area was the one most likely to be rewarding for the animal.

Progress check 5.74

Olds and Milner (1954) claim they had found evidence for a primary reinforcing effect that did not relate to the basic drives. What did they mean by this?

Explore

If you would like to know more about Olds and Milner's (1954) study and ideas about stimulating 'happiness' there is a BBC news article you can access using this link: http://news.bbc.co.uk/1/hi/programmes/happiness_formula/4762941.stm

Evaluation

Strengths

- This is an animal study with careful controls, such as how the electrode is placed and where the electrical

stimulation is felt, at the tip of the needle only. Using different brain regions when placing the electrode enabled the researchers to draw firm conclusions about the brain area and the behaviour relating to getting a reward. Using humans in this way would not be ethically possible. Using animals in laboratory experiments with strong controls can be seen as a strength in this sort of study.

- There was some reliability in that more than one rat was stimulated in the septal area and the rats with the electrode in that area showed similar percentages when it came to lever pressing for a reward.

- Olds and Milner did adhere to ethics to an extent, even though there are those who do not agree with any animal experiments so might not call ethics a strength of this study. As soon as they saw that there was no need to keep repeating the study, they cut down on the number of days the trials were done over, from four days to two days. They also made sure the rats could have food and water when they liked. They observed the rats to see if there was distress and they waited for a few days after the electrode was inserted before they began the actual experiment. They, therefore, stuck to some of the guidelines (though the Animals (Scientific Procedures) Act was in 1986, after their study). They used a minimum number of animals (15 rats) and gave them some care. They also used anaesthetic, which is a requirement.

Weaknesses

- When animals are used in a study and findings are related to humans, there are issues around generalising. Olds and Milner (1954) found that rats will press a lever to get electrical stimulation to some brain areas and not to others, so it seems as if there is a reward system in the brain. However, human brains, though having similarities in functioning and regions, have differences such as in the executive cognitive functioning in the prefrontal cortex and so the motivation of a human is likely to be different.

- Olds and Milner (1954) say they don't think the rats were pressing for stimulation to avoid pain from the electrode, because of their observations; however, they realise that this might be an alternative explanation. Even though they took care with where the electrode was delivering the shock to and eliminated stimuli other than the stimulation, there might be alternative explanations for their findings.

- It is hard not to think of the difficulties with the ethics of this study, even though the way they ran the study was to an extent ethical, as has been argued here. The rats were 'sacrificed', which is how they describe it, and they could perhaps have used fewer rats (for example, they used more than one focusing on the septal area). However, repetition did give reliability. There are strengths in the ethics of their study too.

> **STUDY HINT**
> If using ethics as a weakness of a study or a strength, make sure you give examples of the point you make. Saying that a study is ethical or not ethical is not enough on its own. As you see with Olds and Milner (1954) their ethics can be praised or criticised.

Year One link: You learned about the ethics of using animals in laboratory experiments in psychology when you covered learning theories (and again in this chapter).

Progress check 5.75

List two strengths and two weaknesses of Olds and Milner (1954).

Mundt *et al.* (2012)

Mundt *et al.* (2012) thought it was important to look at peer influence on alcohol use. The aim of the study was to look at adolescent friendships and alcohol use. They used data from a longitudinal study of American students aged from 12 to 16, which is seventh grade to eleventh grade in the USA. They found more friendships between two students sharing the same frequency of alcohol use than between two students similar in many ways but not sharing the same frequency of alcohol use. They concluded selection of friends relates to alcohol use among adolescents. They suggest that intervention to help with adolescent alcohol abuse could be based on adolescent social networks. Adolescent social networks help them to see what characteristics to judge themselves and others on, and help them to make friends they see as being like them. Mundt *et al.* (2012) found that adolescent alcohol use did not come from peer influence alone, but from choosing friends similar to themselves, including similar in alcohol use.

Aims

Mundt *et al.* (2012) were interested in alcohol use in adolescents. They knew from previous studies that children and young people are affected with regard to their alcohol use by the alcohol use of their peers and friends. They also knew that children and young people choose their friends using characteristics that are seen as important and which they see as being similar

in themselves and in their friends. What is difficult is studying the relative contribution with regard to alcohol use of either peer influence or selection of friends. There have been studies using actor-based modelling, which looks at small steps when it comes to deciding whether to stay with friendships or change alcohol use.

- Mundt *et al.* (2012) aimed to use actor-based modelling to study the co-evolution of alcohol use from peer influence and friendship selection.
- They wanted to see if adolescents choose friends with similar alcohol use.
- They wanted to see whether adolescents change their alcohol use in response to the alcohol use of their friends.

Background

According to Mundt *et al.* (2012) 25 per cent of all adolescents start drinking alcohol by the age of 13 and they found that drinking by the age of 14 relates to being dependent on alcohol as an adult. Grunbaum *et al.* (2005, cited in Mundt *et al.*, 2012) says early alcohol use relates to other risky behaviours in adolescents, such as academic underperformance and cocaine use. Ennett *et al.* (2008, cited in Mundt *et al.*, 2012) found that adolescents and their friends showed significant similarities in their alcohol use. This link in alcohol use between friends could be explained by peer *influence* and behaviour spreading through knowing others. Using these ideas friends' behaviour would get more similar over time. Another explanation is that people make friends with others like them and this explains the similarities between friends, as people *select* others like them as friends.

If the **influence explanation** is accepted, interventions to help prevent alcohol abuse could focus on peer-to-peer interactions and if one member of the group stops alcohol use, others may be influenced to do the same.

If the **selection explanation** is accepted then intervention could focus on social network characteristics – what adolescents use to judge themselves similar and to make friends.

Explanation
The **influence explanation** for alcohol abuse being found in peer groups and friendship groups is that the members of the group influence one another and so their behaviour (including their alcohol use) becomes similar. The **selection explanation** for alcohol abuse being found in peer groups and friendship groups is that people choose friends like themselves and so members of friendship groups have similarities (including their alcohol use) not because they influence one another but because they have got together because of being similar.

Mundt *et al.* (2012) explain that studies looking at adolescents, friendships and alcohol use need to separate the idea of *influence* from *selection*. The question is 'Is the similarity in alcohol use that is found in friendship groups down to the influence of the people in the group or down to the way people select people similar to themselves when making friends?' Mundt *et al.* (2012) say that both influence and selection are involved but it is not possible to find out the relative contribution of each when it comes to studying alcohol use in adolescents in relation to their friendship groups.

A problem when looking at alcohol use is that either it has to be assumed that friendship networks stay the same and alcohol use is studied, or alcohol use is assumed to stay the same while friendship network changes are studied. What happens in real life is that network ties change and alcohol use changes – they evolve together. It is this complexity in social behaviour that is hard to capture and study.

Mundt *et al.* (2012) focus on a new analytic approach to try to capture and study the co-evolving relationship between friendship networks and alcohol use. They talk about stochastic actor-based modelling and reference this to, among others, Ripley *et al.* (2011). **Stochastic actor-based modelling** can look at an adolescent's selection of friends based on alcohol use and also at the change in alcohol use and behaviour of the adolescent at the same time. The model suggests that people choose their friendships and their behaviours in small steps, one step at a time (called a 'micro-step'). At each **micro-step** a person uses characteristics a social network is using to make decisions as to whether it is better for them as an individual to change a friend (a 'network-tie') or to change a behaviour. This is how co-evolution of friendships and alcohol use can be studied.

Explanation

Stochastic actor-based modelling refers to a way of unpicking the two variables of friendship choice and alcohol use in such a way that their co-evolution can be studied in an individual. This is from Mundt *et al.* (2012). **Stochastic** is used by researchers when variables are unpredictable and it is the opposite of deterministic. A **micro-step** refers to measuring very small decisions that an individual or 'actor' makes, suggesting that at each micro-step the individual chooses whether to abandon a friendship or stop the use of alcohol.

Explore

You can find out more about stochastic actor-based modelling using this link if you would like to know more: www.stats.ox.ac.uk/~snijders/siena/SnijdersSteglichVdBunt2009.pdf

Mundt *et al.* (2012) explain that the actor-based model can look at both selection, which means people choose friends that are similar in characteristics, and influence, which means people are influenced by their friendship groups. They cite Mercken *et al.* (2012) and their study using actor-based modelling. A sample of 1,204 12-year-olds in Finland over 30 months were studied to look at how far the children were *influenced* by friends based on alcohol use or *selected* their friends accordingly. They found that influence was found in the younger children and selection was more likely as the children got older, though they found both influence and selection. Burk *et al.* (2012, cited in Mundt *et al.*, 2012) studied different age groups in Sweden over two years and found that selection based on alcohol was strongest in early adolescence with both influence and selection being linked to alcohol use in the older young people. Mundt *et al.* (2012) explain that their study looks at alcohol use behaviour in young people aged 12 to 16 in the USA, using a large sample.

Research questions and hypothesis

The study gives the following research questions:

1. Do adolescents select friends with similar alcohol use?
2. Do adolescents adjust their alcohol use according to the alcohol use of their friends?

Their hypothesis is that both selection and influence effects will be found in the network model of adolescent alcohol consumption.

Progress check 5.76

Describe the two explanations that can explain why adolescents show similarities in friendship groups with regard to alcohol use.

Methods

The data come from the National Longitudinal Study of Adolescent Health (Add Health). This longitudinal study used stratified sampling using high schools and middle schools in the USA to make sure they represented funding, racial composition and other factors.

STUDY HINT

The National Longitudinal Study of Adolescent Health that Mundt *et al.* (2012) get their data from used stratified sampling, which is one of the four sampling techniques you need to know about in your course. You could make a note and use this study as an example when writing about this sampling technique. You can also use evaluation points relating to stratified sampling when evaluating Mundt *et al.* (2012).

A survey of all the 12- to 16-year-olds in the 132 schools that were chosen was carried out. Then a random sample was taken using the 90,118 students who completed the questionnaire in their school, giving 20,745 students. An interview was carried out in the homes of these randomly selected students and there was also a parent survey.

> **STUDY HINT**
> After the stratified sampling to get the schools, random sampling was used to reduce the number of students responding to the in-school survey. So Mundt et al. (2012) gives an example of random sampling too.

First part of the survey: Wave 1

Data gathered in the first part of the survey included demographic characteristics of the students, education and occupation of parents, risk behaviours including alcohol use, self-esteem, health status, extracurricular activities at school and friendships. The students also looked at the school register and had to name their five best male and five best female friends.

Second part of the survey: Wave 2

Then after about a year the next part of the survey took place with 14,738 students taking part. Similar data were gathered as in the first part of the survey, including frequency of alcohol consumption over the past year. The students looked at the school register and had to name their five best male and five best female friends as they had had to do in the first part of the survey.

> ### Progress check 5.77
> What was a main question/item asked to find out about friendship both at Wave 1 and at Wave 2, and which meant friendships could be compared over time — and which also makes Mundt et al. (2012) a longitudinal study?

Add Health sampling

Another part of the study used all the students at 14 schools and they were used for the in-home survey at the same time as Wave 1 took place. This meant all the peer structures in the school could be examined because all the students from a school were included.

Analysis of friendship ties

The study reported here used 2,563 students from the Add Health sampling where all the students were used from 14 schools. Just those who were named by at least one friend or named at least one friend were included in the sample for analysis. Mundt et al. (2012) used a system to find out the proportion of the friendship ties that remained in both

the data-gathering waves out of the total number of ties. The number of new ties and the number of friendship ties that no longer existed are used as well as the number of ties that remained constant across the two waves of data gathering. The stochastic actor-based model analysis requires a proportion of 0.20 or more for the school to be included in the analysis, as this indicates at least an element of stability in the friendship networks in that school.

Measures included

Alcohol use

Students had to answer the question 'how often did you consume alcohol in the past year?' and were given the option of responses of 'never' through to 'more than once a week'.

> **STUDY HINT**
> When measuring alcohol use the survey used closed questions to find out about frequency of alcohol use. You can use this study as an example of use of closed questions and as an example of a use of a questionnaire.

Social networks

The students had to name their five best male friends and their five best female friends from the school register to give information about their social networks and they did this in the first part of the survey and after about a year.

Family bonding

Students were asked 'on a scale of 1 to 5, how often do you and your family have fun together?' and in the interview parents were asked how often they drank alcohol in the past year.

> ### Progress check 5.78
> From Mundt et al.'s study give two examples of questions/items that could have given quantitative data.

Statistical analysis

Stochastic actor-based modelling was used to look at the co-evolution of friendship ties and alcohol use in the period from the first part of the survey (Wave 1) to the second part about a year later (Wave 2). This modelling assumes that change takes place using micro-steps and decisions are based on the information present at the time each micro-step is taken. The modelling includes various factors to look at one student as an example at each micro-step. In the micro-step of interest the student might change a friendship, and also there is allowance for a random influence occurring. The student might change their alcohol use in the micro-step. The modelling can control for age, gender, race, parental drinking and family bonding as well. The calculations are all done using a statistical program.

Friendship network evolution

The model includes the evolution of friendship networks for an individual, looking at preferred choices of friendships based on current friendships and on friend attributes. The alcohol-related variables that go with preferred choice of friends include:

- the effect of the adolescent's alcohol use on the number of friends that are chosen (this was called 'alcohol use ego')
- the effect of the adolescent's alcohol use on how much they are chosen as a friend by others (this was called 'friend alcohol use')
- the effect of choosing a friend with similar alcohol consumption levels (this was called 'alcohol use similarity').

The study also looked at **reciprocity**, which means the likelihood of someone being friends with a person who has nominated them as friend, and density, which means how many friends there are in a network. They also looked at whether friends of friends are friends, which they called '**transitive triplets**', as well as looking at three-person friendships (which they referred to as '**3-cycles**'). They considered popularity too.

Progress check 5.79

Using three terms that Mundt *et al.* (2012) used in their study complete this table.

Explanation	Term
Three-person friendships	
When friends are friends of friends	
When someone nominates as a friend someone who has nominated them as a friend too	

Explanation

Reciprocity refers to when someone is a friend of someone who has also nominated them as a friend. **Transitive triplets** is when friends of friends are friends. **3-cycles** is when there is a three-person friendship network.

Alcohol use behaviour evolution

The model looked at variables that could affect alcohol use behaviour. One main variable was the tendency to change

alcohol use based on the alcohol use of immediate friends, which is the 'influence' explanation.

Results

The analysis used 2,563 students aged 12 to 16 in Wave 1 and there were 51 per cent boys and 49 per cent girls. The mean age was 15.8 years. Thirty-nine per cent of the sample were from minority groups. Forty-four per cent of the parents 'reported drinking alcohol in the past year' (p. 5). Seventy per cent of the adolescents reported having fun with their family quite a bit or very much, so strong family bonding was reported.

The analysis used 2,299 students in Wave 2, which was 89.3 per cent of the original sample and it was interesting that students who did not complete Wave 2 were more likely to use alcohol weekly than those who went through into Wave 2. There were 50 per cent of the students reporting no alcohol use in the past year at Wave 1 and 54 per cent reporting no alcohol use in the past year at Wave 2, a small difference. Overall there did not seem to be much difference in reported alcohol use in Wave 2 compared with Wave 1.

Progress check 5.80

Complete the following table using Mundt *et al.*'s (2012) findings.

Statement	Percentage found by Mundt *et al.* (2012)
Difference in percentage reporting no alcohol use in Wave 1 compared to those reporting no alcohol use in Wave 2	
Percentage of those starting Wave 1 found to be in Wave 2	
Percentage of boys in the sample in Wave 1	
Percentage of adolescents reporting family bonding	

STUDY HINT

You can use Mundt *et al.* (2012) as an example of using longitudinal data, which you have to know about. You can see that the loss of participants from Wave 1 to the following year when Wave 2 took place could have led to bias in the results because those who dropped out seemed to be more heavy alcohol users. It is useful to note this sort of information as it will help you to evaluate the longitudinal design in studies.

Friendship network evolution

Friendship selection was related to similarity in alcohol consumption (p<.001). Issues that controlled friendship choices included reciprocity (p<.001), transitive triplets (p<.001), 3-cycles (p<.012) and popularity (p<.001). It was found that the probability of being chosen as a friend by others related with increased alcohol use (p<.006).

> **STUDY HINT**
> You can see that the significance of the finding that friendship selection was related to similarity in alcohol consumption was p<.001. Recall from Year One that this means that the probability of the result being due to chance is less than 1 in 1,000, which is a strongly significant result. You can use findings like those of Mundt *et al.* (2012) to illustrate method features in your course like levels of significance, and this will help your learning.

> **Progress check 5.81**
> Mundt *et al.* (2012) found that the probability of being chosen as a friend by others related with increased alcohol use (p<.006). In this finding what does 'p<.006' mean?

Adolescents are more likely to say they are friends with someone who drinks similarly to themselves. This seems to show the similarity explanation rather than the influence explanation, which suggests adolescents adjust their drinking behaviour because of peer influence rather than because of choice of friends. Mundt *et al.* (2012) found that friendship evolution relates to reciprocity, transitivity, age, race and alcohol use similarity.

Alcohol use behaviour evolution

They found that more frequent drinking by close friends did not relate to increase in drinking alcohol (p=.139). The model does not support the influence explanation, which suggests adolescents adjust their drinking behaviour according to peer influence. Family bonding seemed to protect from alcohol use (p. 809) and the frequency of parental alcohol consumption did not relate to the adolescent's alcohol consumption.

Discussion

The study focused on whether adolescents were likely to change their alcohol intake because of being influenced by their peers or whether their alcohol intake matched that of their friends because they chose friends that were similar to them. Mundt *et al.* (2012) found that friends were chosen because of similarities, including similarity in alcohol consumption. They did not find that alcohol consumption

came from peer influence. Not only was choice of friends based on alcohol consumption, but it was also based on age, gender and race/ethnicity. Burk *et al.* (2012) found that selection of friends is an important factor in explaining similarity in alcohol use between friends, and Mundt *et al.* (2012) found the same. A strength of Mundt *et al.* (2012) is the use of actor-based modelling to separate the variables of friendship choice and alcohol consumption when considering the selection explanation and the influence explanation. Mundt *et al.* (2012) found that it was not peer influence that led to the similar alcohol consumption but the selection of friends that show similarities including in alcohol consumption that led to the similarity in alcohol use found between friends.

Mundt *et al.* (2012) reported some differences in findings from their study and others, including Burk *et al.* (2012), but thought that the differences might come from the different age groups chosen in the different studies. Studies had tended to show that selection of friends explained alcohol use between friends more than peer influence and also that peer influence reduced with age, so Mundt *et al.* (2012), using older children in their age range, may have found more of an effect for selection than influence because they used older adolescents as well.

Mundt *et al.* (2012) point out a practical application of their findings in suggesting that strengthening family bonding and having family fun can protect against adolescents' use of alcohol. They also wondered whether focusing on social networks and friendship groups of adolescents might modify alcohol use and abuse.

> **Explore**
> You can find Mundt *et al.* (2012) using this link if you would like to know more: **www.biomedcentral.com/1471-2431/12/115**

Evaluation

Strengths

- Mundt *et al.* (2012) claim that they were the first to use actor-based modelling to separate peer influence as an explanation for similarity in alcohol use between friends and friend selection as an explanation. They say that their 'innovative methodology' is a strength, not only the modelling but also bringing in many variables around friendships. They aim to look at co-evolution of variables, which is hard to do, and they claim success because of their statistical analysis choices.
- Mundt *et al.* (2012) used very large samples, which added strength to their findings in that they are generalisable. The original sample came from stratified

sampling, then there was random sampling. These two techniques should have achieved a representative sample to help generalisability.

- The researchers claim that as there was 'computer-assisted' data entry this helped to protect confidentiality, which showed good ethics.

Weaknesses

- The participants could only give five best male and five best female friends, which limited their choice to ten friends. It could be said too that some had to find five friends to nominate, which meant they went beyond their closer friends. This way of gathering the data could have given some bias to the data. Mundt *et al.* (2012) acknowledge this point in their discussion.

- Similarly, the study narrowed choice of friendships to just those in the school and did not cover friendships outside the school, which again limited the data. This point was also acknowledged by Mundt *et al.* (2012) in their discussion.

- Alcohol use in the study relied on self-report data. The researchers themselves felt that this was 'a valid measure' and it is accepted as a valid measure. Cohrs *et al.* (2012) looking at ratings of prejudice found that self-report data matched peer-report data rather well, which supports the use of self-report data. However, possibly adolescents might report alcohol use, or the opposite, focusing on looking good. This is a possible weakness or indeed could be seen as a strength as the researchers feel the data were valid.

- The researchers point out that those who were not in the follow-up part of the study (Wave 2) did show some differences from those who took part in the follow-up, as it seemed to an extent 'heavier' drinkers were in the group that was not in the follow-up, which could have affected the findings.

- The figure for the parental alcohol consumption was lower than national surveys find. Their figure was 40 per cent compared with between 60 per cent and 70 per cent of adults being alcohol drinkers according to national surveys. This perhaps affects generalisability of the findings as possibly parents may not have declared their drinking.

Progress check 5.82

Explain one strength of Mundt *et al.* (2012).

Dixit et al. (2012)

Dixit *et al.* (2012) look at alcohol risk behaviour and biological explanations for such behaviour. They claim that alcohol misuse is found in all societies and that there is a World Health Organization (WHO) claim that alcohol relates to 2.5 million deaths every year. Alcohol links to social issues such as violence and child abuse, as well as absenteeism in the workplace so it is a topic worthy of study. Dixit *et al.* surveyed 848 people aged 15 years old and over and covering both urban and rural communities. Households were used by going door-to-door with a survey. This was a cross-sectional study, gathering the data at one time, rather than being longitudinal as Mundt *et al.*'s (2012) study was. There was a 13.4 per cent use of alcohol with 5.07 per cent of the sample using alcohol at the time of the survey and 8.37 per cent of the survey having used alcohol at some time in their lives. Alcohol use was associated with age, sex, socioeconomic status, religion, caste, occupation, living rurally and parental alcohol use. Dixit *et al.* concluded that health promotion and health education, focusing on the most vulnerable in the population, could help to change alcohol behaviour and related illness patterns.

Aims

Given the importance of alcohol abuse with regard to links to illness and to social factors too, Dixit *et al.* (2012) want to look at the prevalence of alcohol use in urban and rural areas in a district in Northern India and to look at which variables relate to alcohol use.

Background

Dixit *et al.* (2012) claim that it is in the nature of humans to seek pleasure. They do not link this idea to the reward pathways in the brain; however, evidence for such reward pathways (page 495) could be evidence for their claim. The researchers say that in India drinking has turned into a social event and they cite Gupta and Saxena (2003) as evidence for this claim. They cite WHO (2000) figures of alcohol consumption saying that alcohol use is increasing in developing countries with 47 per cent of developing countries moving towards higher alcohol consumption and 35 per cent of developed countries having increased their consumption too. In 2005 in India it was estimated that there were 62.5 million people using alcohol and 17.4 per cent of them were dependent on alcohol (Ray *et al.*, 2000, cited in Dixit *et al.*, 2012). The WHO suggest that there are 76.3 million people in the world who have alcohol disorders. These figures, and knowing that alcohol use can affect health and can have social consequences, suggest that alcohol use is an important issue for society. Dixit *et al.* (2012) suggest that knowing about the prevalence of alcohol use in urban and rural areas in a district of Northern India, the Aligahr District, is a useful endeavour and is the aim of their study.

Method

Participants

Dixit *et al.* (2012) calculated the required sample size to be 385. They increased the sample to 424 to allow for some non-response. They used two areas, 424 individuals in both areas, so 848 overall.

Sampling

The study involved all the villages and areas in two health training centres, urban and rural, with households chosen from both centres. The sample included people in each household aged 15 or older who consented to be interviewed, choosing just two individuals from each household so that there was a spread of respondents. The study picked every tenth household on the list and continued until the required number of participants was achieved. This was done in both areas.

Data-collection tool

The study used structured interviewing with a schedule that had been prepared and piloted. The schedule was divided into three sections, the first asking for personal data about the family and the participant, the second asking about use of alcohol and the third section asking about patterns of alcohol use. They used 'current alcohol use' to mean someone used alcohol in the last month and they used 'ever user' to mean someone had used alcohol at least some time in their lifetime.

Dixit *et al.* (2012) call their study an interview though they do also mention 'questionnaire'. They used a structured interview because the questions were administered by a researcher; however, the written down answers were then called a 'questionnaire'.

Ethics

Each participant gave verbal informed consent and when a participant was aged 15–18 years, parents also gave consent. There was an explanation for each individual about the reason for the interview and what would be involved and it was explained that confidentiality would be maintained. Only people involved in the study saw the responses, which were kept securely.

> **STUDY HINT**
> You can use Dixit *et al.* (2012) in your course when asked about interview or questionnaire use, as examples are useful. Also they discuss the ethics of their study, such as issues of informed consent, confidentiality and data protection, so the study can be used as an example when discussing such issues. When revising method you could draw up a table listing the research methods you need to know about (and possibly adding rows for issues, such as 'structured interview' and 'unstructured interview') and put in studies that exemplify the method/issue.

Data analysis

The study used a Chi squared analysis, with two-tailed values and $p < .05$ was chosen as a suitable level of significance.

Year One link: Recall the meaning of 'two-tailed' and '$p < .05$' as well as what the Chi squared test involves. You looked at this test in learning theories and covered issues around significance in cognitive and biological psychology as well.

> ### Progress check 5.83
> Dixit *et al.* (2012) used Chi squared analysis. You can work out from this which research design they used in the analysis and what level of measurement was used. What was the design and what was the level of measurement?

Results

Dixit *et al.* (2012) found 13.4 per cent prevalence of alcohol in their study and this figure included both 'ever user' and 'current alcohol user'. Forty-three of the participants (5.07 per cent) were current alcohol users and 71 (8.37 per cent) were 'ever users' of alcohol. Seven hundred and thirty-four (86.6 per cent) said they had never used alcohol.

Table 5.18 Use of alcohol and risk factors relating to age, marital status and occupation (numbers of respondents out of 848) (adapted from Dixit et al., 2012)

Variable	Alcohol use – yes	Alcohol use – no
Age group		
15–25	6	224
26–40	71	308
41–60	17	119
>60	20	83
Total	114	734
Marital status		
Married	91	531
Unmarried	15	163
Widowed/divorced/living alone	8	40
Total	114	734
Occupation		
Unemployed	27	471
Unskilled	32	121
Semi-skilled	30	86
Clerical/shop/farm	22	38
Professional/semi-professional	3	18
Total	114	734

Table 5.19 Use of alcohol and risk factors relating to education, religion, parental alcohol use, socioeconomic status, caste and rural v. urban living (numbers are numbers of respondents out of 848) (adapted from Dixit et al., 2012)

Variable	Alcohol use – yes	Alcohol use – no
Education		
Illiterate	46	345
Up to high school	56	297
Intermediate/diploma/graduate	12	80
Above graduate	–	12
Religion		
Hindu	97	267
Muslim	17	467
Parental alcohol use		
Yes	107	507
No	7	227
Socioeconomic status		
Lower	99	604
Upper	15	130
Gender		
Male	114	330
Female	–	404
Rural–urban		
Rural	72	352
Urban	42	382
Caste		
General	43	401
Specific	71	333

The largest age group in the survey covered 26 to 40 years and most of those were illiterate or had education up to high school.

Low socioeconomic group associated with alcohol use, as did Hindu religion and certain castes. Married individuals showed more alcohol use, though this was not a statistically significant finding. Alcohol use significantly linked to parental alcohol use and only males were alcohol users. Living in a rural setting significantly related to alcohol use, as did being unemployed or a skilled or unskilled labourer compared with professions or being well paid.

Table 5.20 Chi squared results for the different variables

Variable looking at difference between yes/no responses to alcohol use	Chi squared result	df	Level of significance/result
Age group	14.457	1	p<0.0001
Marital status	5.33	2	p>0.05
Occupation	77.3	4	p<0.001
Education	5.4	3	p>0.05
Religion	95.6	1	p<0.001
Parental alcohol use	30.3	1	P<0.001
Socioeconomic status	1.93	1	p<0.001
Gender	–	–	–
Rural-urban	9.1	1	p<0.01
Caste	11.3	1	p<0.001

Progress check 5.84

What does it mean to say the Chi squared result gave a finding of 1) p>0.05, 2) p<0.01, 3) p<0.001

It was found that 55.5 per cent of those in rural areas and 85.7 per cent of those in urban areas started using alcohol between the ages of 21 and 25 years and nobody started under the age of 15 years. People said most that peer pressure was the reason for their alcohol use, with 86.1 per cent of those who used alcohol saying it was because of peer pressure.

> **STUDY HINT**
> If you read Mundt et al. (2012) you will see that they suggest it is not so much peer pressure that leads to alcohol use as who people choose as friends. Adolescents choose as friends people like them, and that is why friends show similar alcohol usage. It is useful to use the studies to inform one another in this way. However, you only have to study one contemporary study so if you are choosing Dixit et al. (2012) you do not have to study Mundt et al. (2012) as well.

Other reasons for alcohol use, besides peer pressure, were given as curiosity (68 per cent), social acceptance (25 per cent), unemployment (2.8 per cent), health benefit (2.8 per cent) and anxiety and stress (1.4 per cent).

Discussion

Dixit et al. (2012) suggest that their figure for current alcohol use (5.07 per cent) was low compared with national figures, which reported figures of 9.6 per cent according to two Family Health Surveys and 13.4 per cent among 15- to 49-year-olds. They felt that as there was a high number of Muslims in their study (57 per cent) and Muslims are not allowed to drink alcohol for religious reasons, this could have affected their findings. Social class strongly predicted alcohol use as other studies have also found (e.g. D'Costa et al., 2012, cited in Dixit et al., 2012). Parental alcohol use and also gender were strong predictors of alcohol use in the study, with only males saying they used alcohol. The finding that alcohol use went by caste confirmed what was found in another study in Tirupati as well (Kumar and Prabhu, 2006, cited in Dixit et al., 2012). D'Costa et al., 2012, cited in Dixit et al., 2012) found that those who are unemployed or low paid workers use alcohol more and Dixit et al. found the same. Studies also confirmed Dixit et al.'s findings that those who were illiterate or less educated as well as those in rural areas were people who used alcohol more than people more educated or in urban areas. They also found that alcohol use tended to increase with age and Dhupdale et al. (2006), in Goa, found the same up to age 40 years old.

Dixit et al. (2012) concluded that they found alcohol risk behaviour and some significant differences in those using alcohol compared with those not using alcohol, such as those in rural areas, specific castes, unemployed or low paid and male being those more likely to be using alcohol. The researchers suggest targeting these more vulnerable groups and establishing centres to help people to reduce or give up alcohol use. They felt that education about alcohol in schools and having media anti-alcohol campaigns would also be useful, as well as increasing people's knowledge about alcohol through education programmes.

Evaluation

Strengths

- The discussion shows that many of Dixit et al.'s (2012) findings were confirmed by other studies, which adds weight to the findings and shows reliability. When more than one study shows very similar findings then that is like repeating a study and then data, if similar, are said to be reliable. This adds to the credibility of the findings as well.

- Ethics are carefully followed with some detail in the study, including giving full information about the study and its purpose, to get informed consent and also including maintaining confidentiality.
- The study included a lot of variables from employment through marital status to religion and caste, so the researchers were able to test each issue to see if there was a significant difference in those who used alcohol and those who did not. They used variables shown to be significant in other studies too, which helped to give weight to the results when they showed similar findings.

Weaknesses

- They used self-report data, which have been claimed to be valid, such as by Mundt *et al.* (2012) and also Cohrs *et al.* (2012), which was a study in social psychology that you might have chosen. However, individuals could have given incorrect data such as because of social desirability. None of those who were Muslim said they used alcohol and they are not allowed to because of their religion. Of course there is no way of knowing whether they did or had used alcohol, but it is a possibility and, being interviewed in their home, they would not have said so. Any of the questions may have been answered according to socially desirable norms.

Year One link: You looked at self-report data when considering interview and questionnaire as research methods in social psychology.

> **STUDY HINT**
>
> If you did not look at Cohrs *et al.* (2012) in social psychology, the reference to their study here is that they gathered self-report data about someone's prejudiced attitudes by giving them a questionnaire. They also gave the individual a questionnaire to give to a friend or peer, so that peer-report data were gathered about that individual's prejudice. When they correlated the peer-report data and self-report data they found a match and concluded that self-report data do have validity. You can use Cohrs *et al.* (2012) as evidence for the validity of self-report data (though of course they only looked at prejudice).

- The researchers seem to have felt strongly about alcohol use and, from their conclusions, would like to put in place interventions to help to reduce alcohol use or stop it, because of the health issues it brings. They may have conveyed their ideas either through the questions or through their manner as interviewers, so there may have been demand characteristics in the responses, where respondents replied as they felt was wanted.

Pengpid *et al.* (2013)

Pengpid *et al.* (2013) studied alcohol issues, as did Mundt *et al.* (2012) and Dixit *et al.* (2012), the other two contemporary studies in health psychology in your course. Pengpid *et al.* were interested in treatment for alcohol problems and the study focused on South Africa. They chose to look at out-patient clinics where a high rate of alcohol use and substance abuse was found. Large hospital out-patient clinics are a good place to deliver interventions because of the large numbers that pass through the hospital every year. Pengpid *et al.*'s study is a randomised controlled trial where there was screening for alcohol misuse and a brief intervention delivered, aiming to reduce alcohol intake in hospitals in South Africa.

The researchers published a protocol for their study (in 2012) and a report including the results (2013). The study including results is used here.

The study used a brief alcohol intervention to reduce alcohol use in problem drinkers and they also did a six-month and twelve-month follow-up. The participants were those called 'medium risk drinkers' and they were randomly allocated to either an experimental or a control group. The brief intervention was one counselling session with a focus on education about the risks of alcohol consumption and the control group were given a health education leaflet. They found that out of 1,419 people who agreed to take part 392 when screened for alcohol use had a score that put them into the medium risk category and made them eligible to be participants in the study. Of the 392, 282 attended the twelve-month follow-up and the screening scores were significantly affected ($p<.01$) in those participants – time seemed to have affected alcohol use. However, the changes found had been for all participants. When the study considered the experimental group against the control group, it was found that the brief intervention at twelve months was not found to have significantly affected the alcohol use ($p<0.804$). The conclusion was that the alcohol screening itself may have affected the follow-up scores and the health education leaflet may have been effective in causing reduction in drinking too. The brief intervention was not found to have made a difference by itself.

Aim

The aim of the study was to contribute to government policy about brief alcohol interventions by evaluating the intervention used in the study, in order to consider its use more widely, aiming for reduction in alcohol use.

Pengpid *et al.* (2013) aimed to consider Screening and Brief Intervention (SBI) for alcohol problems. They wanted to use a randomised controlled trial to evaluate SBI in hospital out-patients with a view to getting evidence for its effectiveness.

Background

Pengpid *et al.* (2012) start their study by giving figures for alcohol use in Africa, which is high. Fifty-five per cent of men and 30 per cent of women in Africa, including South Africa, consume alcohol, with the annual consumption for each drinker being 16.6 litres of absolute alcohol, which Pengpid *et al.* (2012) say is the highest level for any region worldwide (Rehm *et al.*, 2003, cited in Pengpid *et al.*, 2012). In Africa in the year 2000 the African region was the second worst regarding alcohol abuse, with high rates of binge drinking and dependence on alcohol. Rehm *et al.* (2003, cited in Pengpid *et al.*, 2012) give the figures of 1 per cent for all deaths in women and 4 per cent for all deaths in men in the African region being due to alcohol. The figures for South Africa were 10.7 per cent for men and 3.1 per cent for women having death attributable to alcohol (Schneider *et al.*, 2007, cited in Pengpid *et al.*, 2012). It was clear from these figures that alcohol use is something the South Africa government would want to address.

Pengpid *et al.* (2011) looked at a sample of 1,532 people (56.4 per cent male and 43.6 per cent female) who were out-patients in a South Africa hospital and found 41.2 per cent of men and 18.3 per cent of women were 'hazardous' drinkers and 3.6 per cent of men and 1.4 per cent of women reached a level of alcohol use that could be diagnosed as dependence.

Pengpid *et al.* (2013) cite Kaner *et al.* (2007) as looking at randomised controlled trials in non-health care settings and finding that hazardous and harmful drinkers who had five to ten minutes of structured advice and a self-help booklet reduced their consumption of alcohol by about 25 per cent compared with controls. Pengpid *et al.* (2013) wanted to look at the effectiveness of a Screening and Brief Intervention programme for out-patients with alcohol use issues.

Objectives

They have four main objectives:

1. To measure alcohol consumption in the out-patients at the chosen hospital.
2. To describe drinking patterns in the out-patients and to identify medium risk alcohol users needing intervention.
3. To measure the drinking of medium risk alcohol users at the start of the trial and compare their alcohol consumption then, at six months and at twelve months after the brief intervention, to measure the effectiveness of the intervention.
4. To compare the alcohol consumption at six months and at twelve months of the experimental group and the control group.

Hypotheses

1. 'Out-patient medium risk drinkers in the intervention group reduce drinking much more than those in the control group' (page 2).
2. 'The drinking patterns of patients in the intervention group will continuously reduce over a twelve-month assessment period' (page 2).

Progress check 5.85

For the two hypotheses given, say in each case whether they are directional or non-directional and why you made your choice.

Method

Design

The study used a randomised controlled trial with six- and twelve-month follow-ups to look at the effectiveness of a brief intervention, considering alcohol consumption at six and twelve months, comparing the experimental group with the control group. They could also compare the alcohol consumption of the experimental group at the start, at six months and at twelve months after the brief intervention, again to see its effectiveness.

Participants and population

The study took place in a hospital in Gauteng, South Africa.

The researchers screened out-patients for alcohol problems at the hospital that was chosen and identified medium risk drinkers, who would be the participants in the study. These participants were randomly allocated to either the experimental condition, where the brief intervention was used, or the control condition, where a health education leaflet was handed out. The brief intervention consisted of one brief counselling session. If the intervention was found to be effective, then the control group would be offered a delayed brief alcohol intervention; however, it was not found to be effective.

Year One link: Recall what is meant by randomisation from your studies in cognitive psychology. Also recall any other studies you have looked at that used randomised controlled trial as the design.

Sampling

Out-patients who were 18 years old and older were included as long as there was no mental impairment, and as long as they came out as medium risk drinkers when screened. Medium risk means scoring between 8 and 19 for men and 7 and 19 for women using a questionnaire. Someone with a score of 20 or more on the questionnaire was thought to be dependent on alcohol (probably) and so was not included and those scoring less than 8 for men and 7 for women were also not included, as well as those with mental impairment, pregnant women and anyone having treatment for alcohol use. Randomisation was done using generated random numbers.

Blinding

The hospital staff and the out-patients would know whether they were in the intervention or the control group; however, those collecting the data and assessing the outcomes were blind to the status of each participant. This means they did not know which condition each patient was in.

Procedure

All the clients visiting out-patients were screened for alcohol problems and randomised into either the intervention or the control group. Sampling took place during all hours of the out-patients department being open and for four months. Two hundred and eighty participants were recruited. Research assistant 1 asked for consent from all patients visiting the hospital out-patients department regarding taking part in the study, which was responding to the initial questionnaire. Research assistant 2 scored the results of the initial questionnaire, which gave the screening score. Medium risk drinkers could then be included in the study and participants chosen as explained in the sampling section above. People with a score of 20 and over were referred. Research assistant 2 also carried out the randomisation and the intervention for all participants. Assessments were done by Research assistant 1, who did not know which condition the participants were in. The study made at least six attempts by telephone and letter to contact a participant to avoid drop out at the two follow-ups. If someone missed the six-month follow-up they

would be contacted again for the twelve-month follow-up. These measures were to avoid drop out as much as possible. Participants were given 40 South African Rands each time for transport for turning up at the two follow-up sessions and completing them. Ethical approval for the study was obtained from a Research and Ethics Committee and from the hospital itself.

Progress check 5.86

Why did Pengpid *et al.* (2013) in their design focus so much on drop out at the six- and twelve-month follow-ups?

Interventions

The control group

The control group were given a health education leaflet on responsible drinking. If the study had found effectiveness for the brief intervention it would have been offered to the control group but effectiveness was not found.

The experimental group

The experimental group had personalised feedback on the screening questionnaire results as well as the health education leaflet. They had a 20-minute one-session intervention where they received advice and brief counselling about reducing excessive drinking. The brief counselling covered:

1. Identifying any alcohol-related problems that had shown up in the feedback about the screening questionnaire.
2. Introducing the 'sensible drinking' leaflet, emphasising sensible limits and ensuring the person knew they were in the medium risk group.
3. Working through problem-solving ideas in a manual and emphasising the value of reading the rest of the manual.
4. Describing drink diary cards as a strategy.
5. Identifying a helper.
6. Mentioning the two follow-up sessions.

Measures

- A questionnaire designed by the researchers was used to gather information about age, gender, education level, marital status, income and residential status.
- The screening questionnaire was the ten-item AUDIT that assesses alcohol use, including consumption level, symptoms of alcohol addiction and problems with alcohol use. AUDIT stands for Alcohol Use Disorders Identification Test. The responses use a 4-point Likert scale and so the

maximum score is 40. Scores of 8 to 19 for men and 7 to 19 for women were taken to indicate medium risk drinking. Participants were asked about their alcohol consumption over the past six months.

- The AUDIT questionnaire was reused at six and twelve months so that the alcohol use could be compared from the baseline measure, which was the initial score, and then the six-month score and the twelve-month score.

Explore

You can access a manual about the AUDIT questionnaire using this link if you would like to know more: **www.talkingalcohol.com/files/pdfs/WHO_audit.pdf.**

Data analysis

Descriptive statistics were used to show the results, including means, standard deviations and percentages. The Mann Whitney U and Chi squared tests were used to look for differences between the groups. Other statistical analyses were carried out too.

Sample size calculation

The calculated sample size needed for the study was 284, with 142 in the experimental group and 142 in the control group, and with this sample size there was at least an 80 per cent possibility of finding change between the groups. In the event the study used 196 in each of the groups at the start. There were 109 at the six-month follow-up in the control group and 129 in the experimental group at that time. There were 139 at the twelve-month follow-up in the control group and 143 in the experimental group. In the end 139 (70.9 per cent) participants' data were analysed in the control group and 143 (73 per cent) in the intervention group.

STUDY HINT

It might be tempting when evaluating a study to consider sample size as a problem for generalising the results; however, it is hard to know without working it out what sample size will suit a particular study. Aim to avoid saying in evaluation that there was a small sample size and so results were not generalisable. Contemporary studies (and earlier ones) tend to calculate the sample size required to give a reasonable chance of drawing conclusions about difference or relationship between variables. You could, if a study has a small sample, suggest that it might be a problem and it might affect generalisability (such as Olds and Milner just using 15 rats), but avoid making strong statements about sample size unless you are specific.

Results

The effect of drop out

The researchers first studied the drop out from the study. Data from 139 (70.9 per cent) participants were analysed in the control group and 143 (73 per cent) in the intervention group. They found that drop out did not relate to gender, age, education, marital status, household income, or place of residence. They felt that drop out did not skew the results because they concluded that drop out was not affected by particular variables.

Participant characteristics

They found that the randomisation to groups had done its job in that the two groups did not differ by gender, age, education, household income or place of residence. There was some inequality between the groups, however. Participants in the intervention group were more often never married and also scored higher on the overall AUDIT. Overall the study had 72.4 per cent men and the participants had an average age of 35.6 years. With regard to the medium risk drinking category, 81.8 per cent of the sample used was in the hazardous drinking category, with an AUDIT score of 7 to 15. 18.4 per cent were harmful drinkers with an AUDIT score of 16 to 19.

Alcohol use outcomes

The alcohol use outcomes were reported for both the control and the intervention groups giving the AUDIT total score at baseline, six months and twelve months. The researchers also reported the baseline, six-month and twelve-month heavy episodic drinking score for specific items on the AUDIT, again giving baseline, six-month and twelve-month scores. They reported the number and percentage showing harmful alcohol use as well (which was defined using an AUDIT score of 16 to 19).

Table 5.21 Alcohol use outcomes at baseline, six months and twelve months

Variables	Time	Control group	Intervention group
AUDIT total score Scores give the mean with standard deviation in brackets	Baseline	11.3 (3.4)	12.7 (3.4)
	6 months	6.3 (4.6)	7.0 (4.5)
	12 months	7.3 (6.8)	7.2 (5.8)
Heavy episodic drinking score Scores give the mean with standard deviation in brackets	Baseline	1.9 (0.8)	1.9 (0.8)
	6 months	0.9 (1.1)	1.1 (1.0)
	12 months	1.1 (1.3)	1.1 (1.4)
Harmful alcohol use (AUDIT score of 16 to 19) Scores are number of participants with % in brackets	Baseline	29 (14.8%)	43 (21.9%)
	6 months	5 (4.6%)	5 (3.9%)
	12 months	24 (17.3%)	12 (8.4%)

Table 5.21 shows that the baseline measures were a lot higher than the follow-up scores, in both groups, so it seems that there was an effect from the study. This effect might be because of the attention of the study, or because of the leaflet which was given to all participants. Mainly there is not much difference in the scores at six months compared with twelve months, the difference occurs by the six-month follow-up, although the percentage of participants with a high AUDIT score (16 to 19) did go down at the six-month measure and then went up at twelve months. Those in the intervention group with the high AUDIT score had a reduced score at the twelve-month follow-up compared with the control group. It was found that there seemed to be some reduction in harmful drinking in the intervention group; however, there was no statistically significant intervention effect.

Progress check 5.87

Using Table 5.21 showing Pengpid *et al.*'s (2013) findings, complete the following table.

Statement/question	Answer
Regarding the heavy episodic drinking score what is the difference in the intervention group between their baseline mean score and their mean score at the twelve-month follow-up?	
Regarding the AUDIT total score explain how far the control group and intervention group differed in respect of the mean scores at the six-month and twelve-month follow-ups.	

STUDY HINT
Pengpid *et al.* (2013) found that the brief intervention intended to help with reducing alcohol consumption was not significantly effective. You may have found in your practical investigations that your studies did not show a statistical difference or relationship. You can see that studies in psychology do not always give a significant result; it is not that it is wrong to get a result that is not significant.

Discussion

Pengpid *et al.* (2013) mention that self-report data suggest that screening and providing a health education leaflet can reduce the alcohol use in medium risk people attending the out-patients department at a hospital in South Africa. Kaner *et al.* (2007, cited in Pengpid *et al.*, 2013) found similar reduction in alcohol consumption for the same reasons in the primary care setting.

Alcohol use declined in both groups from baseline to the six- and twelve-month follow-up in both groups, but there was no significant effect from the intervention. In Taiwan a similar study was done and at twelve months there was an intervention effect (Tsai *et al.*, 2009, cited in Pengpid *et al.*, 2013). Findings from the Taiwan study and others suggest that there are benefits from brief interventions to heavy alcohol users admitted to hospital wards. Pengpid *et al.* (2013), however, feel they found that health education can help out-patients reduce their alcohol consumption, rather than the intervention itself.

Pengpid et al. (2013) consider their finding that there was significant reduction in alcohol use in medium use drinkers for both the control and the intervention groups. They offer explanations for this finding, one explanation being that it was the effect of the screening itself and the follow-up that helped to reduce alcohol intake as well as the leaflet. These are the features of the study that the two groups have in common. McCambridge and Kypri (2011, cited in Pengpid et al., 2013) found that just answering questions about drinking seems to change subsequent behaviour. This means that the control group experiences some of the features that help people to stop drinking, just not the actual brief intervention, and this might have meant the consequences of the brief intervention were underestimated.

Limitations

There was a problem with losing some participants at the follow-ups. Also the two groups did differ to an extent even though there was randomisation to groups. Participants in the experimental group were less likely to be married and also scored higher on the AUDIT than those in the control group. The internal validity of the study might have been affected by these differences between the groups and other variables that were not controlled for.

Year One link: You need to know about internal validity, predictive validity and ecological validity and you covered these in cognitive psychology.

Another issue is that the data are gathered using self-report, which Pengpid et al. (2013) suggest is valid and is accepted as such. Mundt et al. (2012) (page 587) also claim that self-report data are accepted as valid, as you may have seen if you read that study. Pengpid et al. (2013) point out that the acceptance of the validity of self-report data tends to come from studies looking at the effectiveness of treatments, such as Noknoy et al. (2010, cited in Pengpid et al., 2013), which adds to the claim that Pengpid et al.'s study's self-report approach has validity. However, they add that they cannot claim that self-report data have validity in South Africa.

Explore
You can access Pengpid et al.'s (2013) study, including the results, using this link: **www.biomedcentral.com/content/pdf/1471-2458-13-644.pdf**

Evaluation

Strengths
- Pengpid et al. (2013) carried out an experimental study with careful controls, including using an experimental

and a control group. They collected baseline data and then carried out two follow-ups to look for reduction in alcohol use following the intervention they put into place. Randomised controlled trials are seen as leading to cause-and-effect conclusions because of the careful controls and they have credibility because of that.
- The use of a single-blind technique so that the researcher doing the assessment did not know which condition a participant was in helped with the controls in the design and with the ability to draw cause-and-effect conclusions from the findings.
- The researchers took a lot of trouble to avoid drop out as much as possible, such as using both telephone calls and letters and going back to a participant six times to try to engage them in the follow-ups. They achieved about 70 per cent of participants going through to the twelve-month follow-up, which is not bad as longitudinal designs do suffer from drop out and it can bias the results.

Weaknesses
- The careful use of an intervention and a control group seems to have been compromised because the health education leaflet that the control group had and the screening they underwent at baseline and at the two follow-up times meant that they did experience a form of intervention. Though they did not get the additional brief intervention they did not receive 'no treatment' and that might have been why the control group and the experimental group both showed reductions in alcohol use over the time of the study. Pengpid et al. (2013) acknowledge this limitation.
- Pengpid et al. (2013) acknowledge their use of self-report data and how such data might not be valid. They mention that use of self-report data is generally accepted and that this acceptance is particularly so in effectiveness studies; however, they also comment that they have not tested the validity of self-report data in South Africa, which suggests they think there might be cultural issues in how valid self-report data are.

Test yourself

You will have studied one of the studies in the list given here. Using one of these studies assess the suitability of the research method used for the purpose(s) of the study. **(16 marks)**

List of studies:
- Mundt et al. (2012)
- Dixit et al. (2012)
- Pengpid et al. (2013)

Summary

- The classic study in health psychology in your course is Olds and Milner (1954) and you need to know this study in good detail. You can be asked about sections of the study, such as the discussion element, the results or the procedure.
- There are three contemporary studies in health psychology in your course and you need to study one of them. All three look at alcohol use.
- One study is Mundt *et al.* (2012), who look at the similarity in alcohol use between friends. They are interested in whether this is because of peer pressure or whether adolescents choose their friends because of having characteristics similar to them.
- One study is Dixit *et al.* (2012), who look at the prevalence of alcohol use and variables associated with alcohol use such as gender, marital status, religion and caste. Their study is done in Northern India.
- One study is Pengpid *et al.* (2013), who look at a brief intervention regarding alcohol use to see if it is effective. Their study is done in South Africa. They found that the intervention itself did not mean a lowering of alcohol use after a year; however, they found that the screening carried out as part of the study and the health education leaflet provided to both the experimental and the control groups may have been effective because alcohol use did indeed reduce.

Key question in health psychology

For your study of health psychology you must prepare one key question. The focus must be on a key question for society and you need to know why it is a question for society as well as how your studies of health psychology can help to inform the key question for society. In your course there are two examples of key questions; however, you can choose your own. You will have covered one key question for each topic area in your course so you will be familiar with what is required here in health psychology. The examples in your course are 'How can the cessation of smoking be encouraged?' and 'Government intervention in health behaviours versus freedom of choice: to what extent is government intervention appropriate?' One of these two examples of key questions is covered in this chapter. The other is found on the website accompanying this book.

How can the cessation of smoking be encouraged?

In this chapter nicotine addiction has been considered quite often. Though the contemporary studies in your course focus on alcoholism and the classic study, Olds and Milner (1954), is about stimulation of the brain's reward pathways, you have seen a lot of studies focusing on nicotine addiction. You have looked at two explanations for nicotine addiction, including neurotransmitter functioning and classical conditioning. You have also looked at two treatments for addiction including drug therapy, including nicotine replacement therapy and e-cigarettes, and cue exposure therapy. All the material you have covered in these areas will have given you material to use when answering a question about how to encourage stopping smoking. A most useful part of the chapter when considering this key question is the material focusing on one antismoking campaign, the Toxic Cycle Health Harms campaign. This is because when focusing on the campaign there was an examination of ideas around how to encourage stopping smoking. Firstly, in this part of the chapter the key question is explained, focusing on why it is a key question for society, and then concepts, research and theories that have been covered in this chapter are used to help to inform the key question.

Describing the key question

Society benefits if people stop smoking, mainly in terms of health gains as well as gains in work hours lost to illness and disease because smoking relates to poor health.

Nicotine addiction is a problem for society, which is why cessation of smoking is something that society would encourage. The antismoking campaign launched in December 2013, called 'Toxic Cycle Health Harms', was focused on getting people to stop smoking, which shows the importance for society of stopping smoking. There are benefits for the individual if they stop smoking, both health benefits because they feel fitter and function better, and also financial benefits because smoking is costly. There are also benefits for society, which is what this section is about.

Benefits for society if people stop smoking

Many internet websites focus on helping the individual to stop smoking and they do not explain the benefits for society. However, clearly there are benefits for society. One negative might be lost revenue from taxes on cigarettes but the saved costs in health care for people who smoke would be very large. As evidence for the financial cost to society Action on Smoking and Health (ASH, 2015) report that in 2013–2014 the government received £9.5 billion in tax revenue from smoking. In 2012–2013 they spent £87.7 million on stopping smoking and £58.1 million on medication for stopping smoking. Those figures suggest that the income from taxes is very large, but adding in the cost to the health service would change the figures considerably.

ASH (2015) smoking statistics

ASH published figures in January 2015 about smoking. Regarding adults they say about 10 million smoke cigarettes in Great Britain, which is about one-tenth of the whole population. They say 22 per cent of adult men in Great Britain smoke and 17 per cent of adult women, showing a gender difference. In 1974, however, 51 per cent of men and 41 per cent of women smoked, showing a large drop in the number of people smoking over that period. The age group with the highest rate of smoking is the 25 to 34 age group, of which 25 per cent smoke, and the lowest rate of smoking is in the 60+ age group where 11 per cent smoke. Fifty-eight per cent of adults say they have never smoked. These figures show that smoking is an issue for society because so many in the population smoke but as figures of those smoking in Great Britain have fallen by a large number, perhaps it is not the problem it was.

One factor that might emphasise how smoking is a problem for society and how to get people to stop is that smoking rates are higher in poor people. In 2013, according to ASH (2015) 14 per cent of adults in managerial jobs smoked compared with 29 per cent for people in manual and routine jobs. Showing that large numbers of people smoke and that

there is an imbalance in the type of people who smoke means society will see the stopping of smoking as a key question.

Smoking is widely accepted as being linked to a lot of health problems, including heart attack, stroke and lung damage as well as cancer. Health is a large cost to society in the UK, so any reduction in demands on health services can benefit society. ASH (2015) suggest that every year more than 100,000 smokers die from health problems that are smoking related. Smoking accounts for more than a third of deaths from respiratory problems, a quarter of cancer deaths and about one-seventh of heart-related diseases. These are high figures and show clearly the cost to society in financial terms. Cost in emotional and personal terms are there too. The NHS Smokefree website has stories from people who have stopped smoking and they help to show the personal cost of smoking.

Young people are smokers too, again a problem for society. ASH (2015) say that two-thirds of smokers start before they are 18 years old and up to one half of those who start smoking then carry on to become regular smokers.

Around two-thirds of smokers start before they are 18 years old and between two-thirds and a half of those turn smoking into a regular habit.

Costs to the individual

An individual is a member of society and costs to the individual affect society. For example, if an individual is not well due to smoking-related issues and misses work, these are lost days for the society and they come at a cost. For the individual costs of smoking include higher life insurance rates and different pension offers (though these can rise because of a shortened life expectancy). Smoking itself costs money and a packet of cigarettes costs a lot of money.

Someone who smokes 20 cigarettes a day might pay out over £100 a week on cigarettes alone. Some figures claim that health is so much affected by smoking that one pack of cigarettes a day for a year can cost someone 55 days off their life. Individual costs of smoking also involve health issues, as has been shown, not only health problems from the nicotine and tar, which people tend to know about, but also from other substances found in cigarettes. Passive smoking affects people as well, including children, as is now more widely known. Again this is about health risks and costs to society in terms of health problems.

It can be seen from all this evidence that a key question for society is how the stopping of smoking can be encouraged.

STUDY HINT

Be sure to focus on how the cessation of smoking can be encouraged and how this is an issue for society, rather than thinking about 'issues with smoking' and using material in a way that relates to this more general area. It is useful to keep re-reading a question in an exam, to make sure your focus is exactly on the question as that is how you will get marks.

Explaining the key question using concepts, theories and/or research drawn from health psychology in your course

- In this chapter nicotine addiction has been discussed, looking both at the neurotransmitter explanation and the classical conditioning explanation. The rewarding effects of smoking are strong possibly because nicotine reaches the brain very quickly, in about 20 seconds, and the stimulation of nicotinic receptors gives feelings of pleasure through release of dopamine, as you will have read about when considering the neurotransmitter explanation for nicotine addiction. The pleasure response to smoking needs to be addressed if society is to encourage people to stop smoking and that can be done using nicotine replacement therapy, which can add nicotine into the bloodstream more slowly, helping with the nicotine activity that leads to pleasure being experienced but in a more safe way, such as avoiding the tar and giving a weaker response at the synapse.
- Cues related to smoking cigarettes, such as cigarette packets, matches, the environment where smoking takes place, or other drug paraphernalia, can be associated with the feelings given by nicotine in the brain. Cues can relate to a strong desire to smoke a cigarette, which is second-order conditioning. One way of encouraging cessation of smoking is to use therapies. One therapy works on having

the cues for smoking present without the smoking, which should lead to extinction of the association between the cues and smoking. This is cue exposure therapy and is a way of society encouraging smoking cessation.
- Nicotine craving can be reduced using classical conditioning principles. Smokers can take a drug that reduces craving for nicotine, such as varenicline, which is a partial agonist at the nicotinic receptors and stimulates them less than nicotine does. The receptors are filled with varenicline so the nicotine itself does not have the same effect. This gives a weaker pleasure response from smoking. Pairing smoking cigarettes with varenicline gives the reduced pleasure response until smoking, giving the reduced pleasure response, is stopped.
- However, using drugs to help people to stop smoking tends to mean side-effects of depression, such as if using varenicline or buproprion. Varenicline can also cause nausea. If side-effects stop someone from continuing with a therapy then that is a problem with the therapy and will affect cessation of smoking, which is something society requires.
- Society uses antismoking campaigns such as the one explained and evaluated in this chapter (page 545). In the Toxic Cycle Health Harms campaign, many different media were used, including TV, radio, an internet website and posters, which is a strength, as more people are likely to be reached that way than by using just one medium. When there is good reach, as Snyder and Hamilton (2002) suggest, that is more likely to give a successful campaign. This is one way that society can encourage smoking cessation, by using campaigns that are well-focused and successful. The Toxic Cycle Health Harms campaign, launched in December 2013, had some good results, such as 40 per cent of people watching the TV advert saying they would like to stop smoking.
- If an antismoking campaign contains new information and has a wide reach then the campaign, according to Snyder and Hamilton's (2012) meta-analysis, is more likely to be successful. An enforcement message is possibly more effective so society could consider how far to go with regard to prosecuting smoking. There is a smoking ban in public places, most workplaces and on public transport already. Bandura (1998) focusing on self-efficacy thought reward was better than punishment or a negative message; however, Snyder and Hamilton found that people paid more attention to a campaign with enforcement behind it.
- Culbertson et al. (2012) found using cue exposure therapy and a virtual environment to help to expose someone to cues that the smoking-related virtual

environment gave a higher 'quit rate' than the placebo virtual environment (p=.015). This suggests that cue exposure is a successful therapy and is a way that society can encourage smoking cessation.

- Park *et al.* (2014) compared virtual cue exposure therapy with CBT for nicotine dependence and found both were effective so there are therapies that society can use to encourage smoking cessation.
- However, offering free therapy for smokers is still an expensive option for society so campaigns might be more efficient as they reach more people at one time compared with individual therapy.
- Bandura's ideas about social learning suggest that role models on television and in other media would be useful in not smoking as they would model 'non-smoking' behaviour. However, this has been done for some time and still there are a lot of smokers in society. The figures for smoking have dropped a lot though, and this drop can be said to relate to the banning of advertising of cigarettes as well as the stopping of smoking on television so that it has not been modelled. Perhaps social learning ideas have contributed to the cessation of smoking and that would continue. Snyder and Hamilton (2002), perhaps surprisingly, found that using a role model or not did not change how effective a health campaign was, which goes against Bandura's ideas about social learning.
- One way to change behaviour seems to be positive or negative reinforcement. People do again what they are rewarded for and avoid behaving in a way that has unpleasant consequences. Society could use those principles to encourage people to stop smoking, which is where the idea of enforcement might come in. Rewards are there for people who smoke as nicotine can be rewarding. Perhaps that is a place to start and society can come up with a plan to give direct rewards for not smoking and more negative consequences for smoking so people would give up smoking to avoid those consequences.

STUDY HINT
There is a lot covered in health psychology in your course that can contribute to a discussion about how society might encourage the stopping of smoking and just some of the ideas are covered here. Draw up a diagram showing all the ideas and how they relate to the key question so that you are prepared to answer questions about it.

Progress check 5.88

Give three pieces of evidence that can answer the key question 'how can the cessation of smoking be encouraged?'.

STUDY HINT
The second key question suggested for health psychology in your course is asking to what extent government intervention in health behaviours is appropriate. This key question is considered on the website accompanying this book.

Progress check 5.89

Explain using one piece of evidence an argument that government should not interfere with health behaviour and it should be the individual's free choice.

Progress check 5.90

List two theories, two concepts and two studies that are used in the explanation of how psychology concepts, theories and research can inform the key question of 'Government intervention in health behaviours versus freedom of choice: to what extent is government intervention appropriate?'.

STUDY HINT
In each topic area you have covered one key question for society and have been asked to use concepts, theories and/ or research that you have studied to explain the key question. Make sure you understand what a theory is, what a concept is and what 'research' is so that you can answer questions on these issues separately if asked to.

Test yourself

Using a key question for society that you have studied, assess the contribution of psychology that you have covered in health psychology to your key question. **(16 marks)**

Summary
- You need to cover one key question for society where concepts, theories and research from health psychology can help to inform the key question.
- One example in your course is asking 'How can the cessation of smoking be encouraged?'.
- The other example is asking 'Government intervention in health behaviours versus freedom of choice: to what extent is government intervention appropriate?'.
- Both these examples are provided, either in the book or online; however, you can choose your own key question.

Practical investigation in health psychology

In your course for each topic area you have carried out one practical investigation and in health psychology you need to do the same. You have the choice of using questionnaire, interview or content analysis. You need to gather quantitative data because of the analysis that is required, though you can gather qualitative data as well or turn qualitative data into quantitative data for the purpose of analysis. You need to carry out the relevant statistical test for your practical, from the four tests in your course (Wilcoxon, Mann Whitney U, Spearman's and Chi squared). You need to include your research question/hypothesis, the research method, sampling, ethical considerations, data–collection tools, data analysis, results and discussion when writing up your practical and when preparing for the examination. Also consider strengths, weaknesses and possible improvements of/for your practical. In your course two examples are suggested: content analysis of pop music/television programmes, such as looking for references to drugs; content analysis of newspaper articles/news, such as comparing references to alcohol and nicotine.

Drug addiction can only be rewarding if it gives pleasure. People who get no pleasure from a substance are not likely to become addicted to it. A simple study might be to ask people if they use alcohol and ask them how much they like it and then see if the more they rate it as 'liked' the more they say they use it. This would generate a correlation for analysis. You could consider something like this for your practical investigation in health psychology, gathering the self-report data by questionnaire.

However, you will have done your own practical investigation, which is what you need to focus on when preparing for your examination. You will be doing your own practical and will need to know about it from start to finish. That sort of information is not possible here as the experiences will help you to learn and also to answer questions about your practical.

What you need to do for the practical investigation

Your practical investigation must gather quantitative data though it can gather qualitative data as well or convert qualitative data into quantitative data for analysis.

In the content analysis outlined online quantitative data are gathered, with some qualitative data in the form of quotes to illustrate the categories. You must use the relevant test for your practical. In the content analysis outlined online, which focuses on references to drugs in popular songs, a Chi squared test is used because the data are nominal, being in categories. You need to include a research question/hypothesis, research method, sampling, ethical considerations, data collection tools, data analysis, results and discussion. Also look at strengths and weaknesses of the practical and possible improvements. These features of a practical investigation are given in the practical outlined online, though not in detail.

> **STUDY HINT**
> When preparing for the examination, both when revising your practical investigations and when revising method in general, or studies, be ready to offer possible improvements. Your course assesses your understanding of 'possible improvements'.

Test yourself

You will have done a practical investigation in health psychology using either a questionnaire, an interview or a content analysis. Evaluate your practical investigation in health psychology in terms of reliability, validity, generalisability and subjectivity/objectivity. **(16 marks)**

Summary

- You have to carry out a practical investigation using either a questionnaire, an interview or a content analysis.
- Your practical must cover some area you have studied in health psychology for your course.
- You can collect qualitative data; however, for analysis purposes you need quantitative data so either collect that as well or convert your qualitative data into quantitative data, perhaps using content analysis.
- You need to know about the hypothesis/research question, sampling, ethical considerations and data collection tools.

- You also need to focus on data analysis and the results of your practical investigation.
- As part of the results you need to use the relevant inferential test from the four you have covered in your course so be sure that your practical investigation will suit one of the tests.
- You need to be ready to discuss your practical investigation, including giving strengths and weaknesses and, importantly, being able to consider possible improvements.

Chapter Six: Psychological skills – review of studies

Psychological skills is Topic Nine in your course and can be seen as a revision topic. There are three sections to this topic, covered in the online Appendix and Chapters Six and Seven of this book, as shown in Table 6.1.

Table 6.1 Psychological skills section and chapter related to it

Section	Chapter
1 Review of method material	Online material
2 Review of studies	Chapter Six
3 Issues and debates	Chapter Seven

What 'review of studies' means in your course

Section Two of Psychological skills asks you to draw on and compare studies from the classic study section throughout the specification and to review these classic studies synoptically, in terms of issues and debates. You need to be able to use principles of understanding, evaluation and synopticity on unseen material. Table 6.2 gives the specification requirements for this section and Table 6.3 gives the issues and debates, which you must be able to use when discussing the classic studies you have learned about.

Table 6.2 Specification requirements for Section Two of Psychological skills

Specification requirements for Section Two of Psychological skills
Draw on and compare studies from the classic study section throughout the qualification
Review synoptically the classic studies of psychology in terms of issues and debates
Use principles of understanding, evaluation and synopticity on unseen material

Table 6.3 Issues and debates

Issues and debates required for the A level course
Ethical issues in research (animal and human)
Practical issues in the design and implementation of research
Reductionism in the explanation of behaviour
Comparisons of ways of explaining behaviour using different themes
Psychology as a science
Cultural and gender issues in psychological research
The role of both nature and nurture in psychology
An understanding of how psychological understanding has developed over time
The use of psychology in social control
The use of psychological knowledge in society
Issues related to socially sensitive research

Using the classic studies to illustrate these issues and debates will help you to understand them fully and will also help you compare them. In addition, understanding, evaluating and considering the classic studies will also help you do the same for an unseen study.

Research in psychology can be in socially sensitive areas, can be in cultures different from that of the researcher and will have ethical implications.

Format of this chapter:
- The classic studies are outlined to remind you about them.
- Each classic study is considered with regard to the issues and debates to illustrate and inform.
- Comparisons are made between the classic studies.
- Two unseen studies are used to show how your learning about the classic studies, method issues and issues and debates will be of help.

The classic studies: an overview

The classic studies for your course are listed in Table 6.4. Although the classic studies for the options in Year Two are listed here, they are not considered in this chapter because you may not have studied them. You will, however, have studied one of them (from a choice of criminological psychology, child psychology and health psychology) so for the classic study in your chosen option, work through what has been done here using the five classic studies for the other topic areas, so that you are prepared to use the 'option' classic study in this section.

> **STUDY HINT**
> If questions are in a synoptic area of the course this means that any question can be asked. This chapter reviews some of the areas of importance regarding the classic studies and addresses issues in unseen studies, but you need to be able to respond to whatever is asked. Your course has given you the skills to do that and practising with different studies will also help.

> **STUDY HINT**
> Re-read your notes for each classic study so that you have sufficient detail for this section of Psychological skills.

Social psychology: Sherif *et al.* (1954/1961)

Sherif carried out research into the effect of groups on attitudes and behaviour.

Aims

The aims of the Robbers Cave study were to use a field experiment to produce group norms and to measure their effects on the perceptions and judgements of those involved. The researchers wanted to see how in-group behaviour developed to include related out-group hostility and to see how such friction could be reduced.

Procedure

Participants

The participants were 22 boys, aged 11 years, who did not know each other before the study. The boys were matched as far as possible. In order to produce 'natural' groups, participants were not informed that they were part of a study and were kept unaware of the aims of the camp.

Data collection

One important feature of the study was the range of data collection methods:
- Observation: a participant observer was allocated to each group for 12 hours a day.

Table 6.4 Classic studies for the A level course

Topic area	Classic study (those in italics are the studies you were able to choose from)
Social psychology	Sherif *et al.* (1954/1961), the study of boys in a Summer Camp, the formation of prejudice and the reduction of prejudice.
Cognitive psychology	Baddeley (1966b), the study of how memory is encoded in long-term memory.
Biological psychology	Raine *et al.* (1997), the study of brain differences between people pleading not guilty by reason of insanity to murder and a control group.
Learning theories	Watson and Rayner (1920), the study of how a phobia could be conditioned in a small boy using classical conditioning principles.
Clinical psychology	Rosenhan (1973), the study of people pretending to have schizophrenia symptoms being admitted into a hospital and what happened to them.
Criminological psychology	*Loftus and Palmer (1974), the study of how changing a verb in a question can make people judge the speed of a car differently.*
Child psychology	*Van IJzendoorn and Kroonenberg (1988), a meta-analysis of studies using the strange situation to look at how and whether attachment type differs in different cultures.*
Health psychology	*Olds and Milner (1954), the study of stimulation of brain areas to study brain functioning.*

- Sociometric analysis: issues such as friendship patterns were noted and studied.
- Experiment: the boys had to collect beans and estimate how many each boy had collected.
- Tape recordings: adjectives and phrases used to refer to their own group members and to out-group members were examined.

Three stages of the study

Stage 1: in-group formation

The two groups were kept apart for one week to help the formation of group norms and relations. Status positions and roles in the groups were studied. There is much detail about how hierarchies within each group developed. The measurements were thought to be both valid and reliable because different data collection methods produced similar results.

Stage 2: inter-group relations, the friction phase

After the first week, the two groups were told about one another and a tournament was set up with competitive activities. As soon as they heard about each other, the two groups became hostile. The aim behind the competition was to make one group frustrated because of the other group, to see if negative attitudes developed. Adjectives and phrases were recorded to see if they were derogatory and behaviour was observed as previously. The researchers introduced the 'collecting beans' experiment. The boys had to collect beans and then judge how many each boy had collected. This was to see if the boys overestimated the abilities of the in-group members and minimised the abilities of the out-group members.

Stage 3: inter-group relations, the integration phase

The researchers wanted to achieve harmony between the two groups, which they did by introducing superordinate goals (the resources and energies of either group were not adequate for the attainment of the goal; the groups had to work together).

Results

Stage 1: in-group formation

Near the end of Stage 1 the boys gave themselves names – the Rattlers and the Eagles. The groups developed similarly; they had been matched carefully, so this might be expected. The Rattlers discussed the existence of the other group frequently, once they knew about them. For example, they said 'they had better not be in our swimming hole'. It seemed that the very existence of the out-group led to hostility.

Stage 2: inter-group relations, the friction phase

As soon as the groups found out about each other they wanted to compete at baseball, so they had naturally moved themselves on to Stage 2. The Rattlers were excited and discussed issues such as protecting their flag. The Eagles were not as keen as the Rattlers, but they made comments such as 'we will beat them'. When the two groups first came into contact, there was some name calling. It was found that there were clearly negative attitudes towards the out-group members.

Stage 3: inter-group relations, the integration phase

During the initial contacts in this stage, hostility between the two groups remained. There were comments such as 'ladies first' and when they watched a film together, they sat in their own groups. In this stage, the need to work together was set up with situations where there were superordinate goals:

- First, the staff turned off the valve to the water supply and placed two large boulders over it. The boys were told that vandals had damaged the system in the past. The boys worked together to restore the system. When the water came through they rejoiced in common.
- The second goal was to get a movie by chipping in to pay for it. They agreed eventually that both groups should contribute equally, even though one group had fewer members than the other group. There was cooperation between the two groups.
- The third goal involved all the boys going on a trip to Cedar Lake, which required transport. As they were about to leave, the truck 'developed' a problem and they had to use the tug-of-war rope to pull it to try to get it started.

Table 6.5 Friendships compared between the end of Stage 2 and the end of Stage 3: Sherif *et al.* (1954/1961)

	Rattlers	Eagles
Out-group friendship choices at end of Stage 2	6.4%	7.5%
Out-group friendship choices at end of Stage 3	36.4%	23.2%

Table 6.6 Friendship choices of in-group and out-group members at the end of Stage 3: Sherif *et al.* (1954/1961)

	Rattlers	Eagles
In-group choices of friends	63.6%	76.8%
Out-group choices of friends	36.4%	23.2%

At the end of Stage 3, friendship choices were still found more within the in-groups but had also increased between the groups.

It was noticeable how friendships differed between Stage 2 and Stage 3. More out-group members were chosen as friends by the end of Stage 3, which is evidence that friction was reduced.

Conclusions

The hypotheses put forward at the start of the study were largely confirmed. The conclusions include the following:

- Picking matched participants ruled out home background or individual factors that would explain the attitudes and behaviour of the boys.
- Leader–follower relations developed as a result of having to solve problems through combined action; as group structure stabilised, an in-group formed.
- When two groups meet in competition and in frustrating situations, in-group solidarity and cooperation increases and inter-group hostility is strong.
- Because of the various means of collection, the data were considered valid.
- Contact between two groups is not enough to reduce hostility.
- When groups needed to work together, exchanged tools, shared responsibilities and agreed how to solve problems, friction was reduced. One example of working towards a superordinate goal was not sufficient, however; they needed to cooperate more than once.

Explore
You can look more at the Robbers Cave study using this YouTube link:
www.youtube.com/watch?v=6QGNxRGgBwM

Evaluation of the Robbers Cave study, Sherif et al. (1954/1961)

Strengths

- There were controls, such as the careful sampling and the briefing of observers so that they followed the same procedures; this meant cause-and-effect conclusions could be drawn more justifiably than when observing naturally occurring groups
- There were several data collection methods and the findings agreed, so validity was claimed – for example, observations showed derogatory behaviour and recordings found derogatory remarks against the out-group.

Weaknesses

- It was unethical in the sense that consent was not obtained, there was no right to withdraw and parents could not visit, so there was no check on the boys' welfare.

- It was hard to generalise to other situations because the sample was restricted to boys with a specific background.

Progress check 6.1
Why did Sherif et al. (1954/1961) claim that their findings had validity?

Study of interest showing the current relevance of Sherif et al.'s work

Ward and Berno (2011) discuss the issue of tourism, which is seen as important in a society. They mention social exchange theory, which is the idea that there are costs and benefits around tourism and if the benefits outweigh the costs tourism is welcomed. Benefits include financial benefits for a society (and for individuals). Tourism is also important because it enables inter-group contact in providing a good opportunity for people from different cultures to mix. Ward and Berno (2011) discuss how competition and threat predict attitudes between groups, which is what realistic group conflict theory predicts. Ward and Berno suggest that integrated threat theory can be useful in explaining intergroup conflict, as it focuses on four threats:

- realistic threat
- symbolic threat
- negative stereotypes
- intergroup anxiety.

Ward and Berno (2011) suggest that contact alone can help to reduce prejudice but it is better when there are other factors too, such as equal status and cooperative contact. This is similar to Sherif et al.'s ideas about working towards superordinate goals. Ward and Berno test the idea that positive attitudes to tourism go along with frequent and satisfying contact with tourists, low perception of threat and low levels of intergroup anxiety. Ward and Berno's research shows that Sherif et al.'s work on realistic group conflict theory is built on in more recent research and that it can have relevance to today's society, such as focusing on the important economic benefits of tourism in a society.

Tourism can help a society's economy and can also help in other ways, such as reducing prejudice, because contact with other cultures is increased.

> **STUDY HINT**
>
> Perhaps tourism does not seem especially relevant to psychology at first glance, but you can see that it does relate to prejudiced attitudes and to society, in terms of economics as well as harmony among people. Such links help to show that psychology is relevant for many aspects of society.

Cognitive psychology: Baddeley (1966b)

Baddeley (1966b) knew from previous studies that in short-term memory (STM) words that sounded alike (acoustic similarity) were less well recalled and it was thought that STM used acoustic coding. He wanted to see if long-term memory (LTM) also used acoustic coding. Baddeley had found in the same year, in a different study looking at STM, that when words sounded alike there was 72.5 per cent lower recall, but when words were similar in meaning (semantic similarity) there was just 6.3 per cent lower recall. Baddeley thought this related to how in STM there was 'sounding out' to help recall, which might explain why in STM, words that sound alike were harder to recall. Baddeley wanted to look at acoustic and semantic coding in LTM (which means the recalling had to last longer than 30 seconds).

Aims

The aim was to see if LTM used acoustic coding or semantic coding and to see if words with acoustic similarity were harder to recall than those with semantic similarity. The question was whether STM and LTM had the same coding systems.

Procedure

Baddeley (1966b) used three experiments, because Experiment I was done in a way that meant the participants might be using STM. He used Experiment II to test the idea that STM had been involved, found it was, and so Experiment III was devised to prevent the use of STM. This meant that his findings suited his aim as all were about LTM.

Participants

Experiment I

There were four conditions (acoustic similarity and control list, semantic similarity and control list) and an independent groups design. About 20 participants were in each group and a hearing test made sure the words could be heard (three participants in Condition A did not do the test because of hearing issues). The participants were young servicemen. When the recall of the list after 20 minutes was compared with the earlier recalls of the list, this was a repeated measures design.

Participants – Experiment II

This time participants were housewives from a subjects panel kept by the university; again they were tested in groups of 20. This time six participants failed the hearing test.

Participants – Experiment III

Males and females from the university subjects panel were used, with around 15 people in each condition.

Materials

For his experiments Baddeley (1966b) used four ten-word lists. List A had ten words that sounded like, List B had words that matched List A but did not sound alike. List C had ten words with similar meaning and List D had words that matched List C but not with similar meaning. Lists B and D were control lists.

Experiment I

Words were presented using a tape recording at three-second intervals and different participants did the four different lists. After the list was seen, participants had 40 seconds to recall the list in the right order and they learned and recalled the list four times. After 20 minutes doing something else each participant was tested again, again requiring words in the right order.

Experiment II

This time the control lists were not used, just List A (sound-alike words) and List C (words with similar meaning). This time there were three conditions alongside using either List A or List C. For both List A and List C in Condition

X, Experiment I procedure was followed. In Condition Y there was an interference task between each presentation of the list and each test. Condition Z had an interference task as in Condition Y but this time between the test and the next presentation (as a control). The interference task presented eight numbers at one-second intervals and the participant had to write down the eight numbers in the right order in eight seconds. There were six trials of this interference task in both Condition Y and Condition Z. Test-retest (the wait for 20 minutes) was kept the same as in Experiment I and for all three conditions in Experiment II.

Experiment III

Experiment III used all four lists again as in Experiment I, using the interference task between hearing the words and recalling them, as in Experiment II (Condition Y). This was to remove the effects of STM on the findings – to remove rehearsal. This time words were presented visually, visible for three seconds. Between showing the words and recall the same interference task was used as in Experiment II (showing eight numbers and writing them down and doing this six times). This time after the four trials (as in Experiment I) there was a 15-minute wait before the final recall.

Results

Experiment I

Experiment I involved analysis of the first set of four recalls, using a Mann Whitney U test and analysis of the four recalls against the recall 20 minutes later, using a Wilcoxon.

When the words sounded alike (List A) and recall (in the right order) was compared with the control list (List B), it was clear that the control list was better recalled – though after the 20-minute break there was no real difference in recall.

When the words had similar meaning (List C) and recall (in the right order) was compared with the control list (List D), it was clear that recall was very similar throughout. The four trials showed recall getting better for both the semantically similar list and the control list. In Experiment I it was the acoustically similar list that gave the worst recall. The acoustically similar list showed less forgetting after the 20 minutes; however, there was less learning in the other three conditions. It seemed that in that first learning (the four trials) there was some STM involved, shown by the problems with the words sounding alike. Experiment II was done to remove the STM element.

Experiment II

Acoustic similarity

In the condition where there was acoustic similarity, for all three conditions there was similar recall in the four

trials. In Condition Z, where there was an interference task between the test and the next task, there was more forgetting after the 20-minute break but other than that the conditions showed the same results. Acoustic similarity no longer led to poorer recall in the four trials. When STM was blocked by interference acoustic similarity was no longer a problem. This suggests that it was the rehearsing in STM that caused the problems in Experiment I in recall of the order of words, which supports what was known about STM (that coding is acoustic).

Semantic similarity

With regard to the semantically similar list, there was a statistically significant difference (p<.001) between the condition with no interference and the condition with interference between hearing the words and recalling them. In the conditions where there was no interference or interference was after the recall there was forgetting in the 20-minute period but there was no forgetting in the condition with the interference between hearing the words and recalling them. Experiment II had shown sufficient differences from Experiment I to lead to Experiment III being carried out, using interference to block rehearsal but this time using the control lists too.

Experiment III

Acoustic similarity

The acoustically similar list compared with its control list showed no differences and little forgetting for the 15-minute break before the final recall.

Semantic similarity

The semantically similar list showed a large difference in learning over the four trials compared with its control (neither the semantically similar list nor the control showed forgetting over the 15-minute period after the four trials). Between the semantically similar list and the control list at Trial Four – the end of the trials – there was a significantly higher learning score for the control list (List D) than for the list of semantically similar words (p<.005).

Conclusions

Once STM was not involved, it was the semantically similar list that showed less learning compared with its control list and with the acoustically similar list and its control list. Recall after the 15 minutes was similar in all conditions but semantic similarity affected the learning phase (the four trials). It was the acoustically similar list that gave problems in Experiment I and the semantically similar list gave problems in Experiment III. The difference between Experiment I and Experiment III was that STM was involved in Experiment I. With just LTM involved it seems that semantic coding gives problems, and so LTM and STM are shown to be different in coding, which was the aim of the study.

Progress check 6.2

Why was the Mann Whitney U test used to look for differences between recalls using the first four recalls for each participant and then the Wilcoxon used to look for difference between those first four recalls and the one after a 20-minute break?

Evaluation of Baddeley (1966b)

Strengths

- Baddeley's (1966b) study used careful controls and an experimental design, such as controlling for the time a stimulus was available for. This means the study can show cause-and-effect conclusions because of controls over extraneous variables.

- The study used different conditions and three experiments as part of the main study, with the result that within the main study Baddeley (1966b) had replications and could claim reliability. Reliability is required if a study is to add to a body of knowledge.

Weaknesses

- The study can be said to lack ecological validity as it used lists of words and adjectives to test coding of STM and LTM and these are not naturalistic tasks. Steyvers and Hemmer (2012) explain how when they used pictures of scenes to look at reconstructive memory they had different results from other studies that had not had such realism.

- The study reduced memory to how well the order of lists of ten words each is recalled when lists have certain conditions (such as the list of words being acoustically similar). This links to the weakness of the study not having valid findings. Reductionism can help with reliability and experimental findings but lacks a holistic look at something, so may not be relevant to everyday life.

Explore

You can hear more from Baddeley about his work in memory looking at LTM, using this link:

www.youtube.com/watch?v=7yvWlpQYQbM

STUDY HINT

In the summary of the classic studies in this part of Chapter Six, detail is given according to what will be useful when reviewing the studies. The focus is on what is relevant to issues and debates, for example, or useful method detail for comparing classic studies.

Study of interest showing the current relevance of Baddeley's work

Rönnberg et al. (2011) looked at hearing loss and memory systems in hearing aid users. This was a study done in Sweden on older people who had dementia and the focus was on hearing and cognitive and memory functions. The researchers cite evidence that cognitive decline accompanies hearing loss in old age. The researchers suggested that both cognitive decline and hearing loss might go with general sensory decline rather than them having a stronger relationship with one another. Lehrl et al. (2005, cited in Rönnberg et al., 2011) found, using a control group, that a hearing aid improved working memory (for two to three months). They found that people with issues in both episodic and semantic long-term memory had more hearing loss, but there was no link between hearing loss and short-term memory. Age correlated with episodic LTM more than with STM or semantic LTM. Episodic and semantic LTM performance related to hearing loss. The conclusion was that hearing loss and decline in episodic memory went together but STM is unrelated to hearing loss. This work shows that there is current interest in memory and that an LTM/STM split is still acknowledged, with episodic and semantic memory still being seen as separate too.

As they get older someone might find it harder to remember episodes in their life such as riding a bike when they were young — and they might experience loss of hearing. Hearing loss and episodic memory difficulties go together in someone older.

Biological psychology: Raine et al. (1997)

Raine *et al.* (1997) used PET scanning results for people pleading not guilty by reason of insanity (NGRI) and PET scans for controls to see if there were differences in brain functioning in those pleading NGRI.

Aims

The aim was to see if brain dysfunction related to violent behaviour and Raine *et al.* (1997) thought that those who showed serious violence would show dysfunction in specific brain areas. The areas they thought would show dysfunction included the prefrontal cortex, angular gyrus, amygdala, hippocampus, thalamus and corpus callosum. They also listed areas they thought would not show dysfunction. Raine *et al.* felt that studies using animals might not have findings generalisable to humans and brain scanning studies tended to have small samples. Their aim was to use brain scanning to look at the areas of interest and to use a large, more generalisable sample. They had done a study (Raine *et al.*, 1994) using 22 people pleading NGRI and 22 controls and found some support for there being prefrontal dysfunction in the 'murderers'. This 1997 study was to build on that finding.

Procedure

Participants

A total of 41 'murderers' and 41 controls were used with matching done – the average age was about 32 years old. The 41 murderers had the scan to either look for evidence of incompetency to stand trial or, if already found guilty, to look for evidence of diminished capacity. In the main sample there were people with a history of brain damage, substance abuse, schizophrenia and epilepsy and the control group was put together to match these (and other) issues.

PET scanning procedure

A radioactive tracer was injected after the brain activity was recorded and each participant was scanned while doing a test that increased glucose metabolism in the frontal lobes. The PET scan took place after the tracer had had time to be taken up into the blood stream. Areas of the brain were measured using the slices the PET scan produced and glucose values for each area of interest were looked at, compared with other areas. They also used a box technique to focus on brain areas.

Results

Raine *et al.* (1997) focused on the brain areas they were interested in.

- The murderers had lower glucose metabolism than controls in some prefrontal areas, showing different activity levels in the murderers compared with the controls in certain areas in the prefrontal cortex. This was also the case in the parietal lobe, such as in the left angular gyrus.
- There were no significant differences between the murderers and controls in lateral temporal lobe glucose metabolism.
- In the occipital lobe the murderers had higher glucose metabolism than the controls.
- They had lower glucose metabolism in the corpus callosum than the controls and there were other differences too.

They looked at other variables they had not been able to control. This included handedness, which showed no significant effect (there was some effect for left-handed murderers), ethnicity, which gave no significant differences, and head injury, which showed lower activity in the corpus callosum, which might have affected the conclusions about that brain area.

Conclusions

The researchers looked at how the biological deficits that they found translate into violence.

- Prefrontal deficits can result in impulsivity and loss of self-control, as well as emotionality and an inability to modify behaviour. This inability to modify can result in aggression.
- The posterior parietal cortex seems to be linked to cognitive functioning, in relation to forming abstract concepts and in relation to input from the senses. For example, reductions in glucose metabolism in the left angular gyrus have been correlated with reduced verbal ability. Cognitive dysfunction could mean educational and occupational failure, which may lead to crime and violence.
- A dysfunction in the corpus callosum may explain hemisphere differences because the corpus callosum links the two hemispheres. The right hemisphere has

been said to generate negative effects in humans and may be, in the murderers, less regulated by the left hemisphere. Studies of rats reinforce this idea.

- Socially inappropriate behaviour found in violent individuals might come from the posterial parietal cortex, amygdala and medial temporal lobe, including the hippocampus, and there seem to be differences in glucose activity in these areas in murderers. These areas link to recognition systems. Misunderstanding social situations might lead to violent behaviour, for example.

Findings show that neural processes underlying violence are complex and that there is no single mechanism in the brain that causes violence.

There were brain areas that appear to be relevant to violent behaviour that were not measured in the study, such as the hypothalamus, so the findings were not thought to be a complete account of brain mechanisms and aggression. The researchers felt that they could conclude that, overall, murderers pleading not guilty by reason of insanity seem to have different brain functioning from controls. They also felt that the brain structures they measured and the findings of the study did show that certain brain areas did link to aggression, especially as the brain areas were chosen from the findings of other studies in the first place. The findings show that murderers pleading not guilty by reason of insanity have statistically significant differences in glucose metabolism in certain brain areas compared to a control group (p. 505). The conclusion was that reduced activity in the prefrontal, parietal and callosal areas in the brain, as well as some abnormal asymmetry between left and right hemispheres in the amygdala, thalamus and medical temporal lobe, including the hippocampus, may lead to violence in this group of people.

Explore

This YouTube video link will help you to summarise Raine *et al.* (1997):

www.youtube.com/watch?v=liBa2uqXyjw

Evaluation of Raine *et al.* (1997)

Strengths

- PET scanning is an objective technique and the results can be interpreted by more than one researcher; it is a scientific method and is likely to give reliable findings.
- It was the largest sample size (up to 1997) for PET scanning and large enough for useful comparison with the control group and for generalisation to murderers pleading not guilty by reason of insanity.

Weaknesses

- It is hard to generalise beyond murderers pleading not guilty by reason of insanity as there were no violent criminals in the control group.
- It does not show biological causes for violence because environment can cause brain differences.

Progress check 6.3

What was the purpose of a control group in Raine *et al.* (1997)?

Study of interest showing the current relevance of Raine *et al.*'s work

Hanlon *et al.* (2013) studied violence, looking at two types of violence. They explain that impulsive violence that is emotional (affective/impulsive) and instrumental violence that is done in a more calculated way (predatory/instrumental) are different forms of violence. Hanlon *et al.* say that previous research has shown that offenders committing affective/impulsive homicide show lower executive functions (such as decision-making) and different brain activity in certain regions when compared with predatory/instrumental homicide offenders. They cite Raine *et al.* (1998) as showing that affective/impulsive murderers showed less bilateral prefrontal activation compared with controls and with predatory/instrumental murderers.

Hanlon *et al.* (2013) divided 77 murderers into two groups representing the two types of violence (affective/impulsive or predatory/instrumental). They then compared the two groups using a great many tests looking at IQ, memory, attention and decision-making. They did not use brain scanning but drew conclusions from the various tests. They found that affective/impulsive murderers tended to be undereducated and possibly had neuro-developmental disorders such as learning disorder. They also had issues with substance misuse. The researchers found problems in attention and a slow rate of information processing as well as problems with verbal memory. With regard to predatory/instrumental murderers they found they tended to have average IQ though possibly more psychiatric disorders than the other type of murderer. Predatory/instrumental murderers also showed high rates of drug misuse but not as high as in the other type of murderers.

Hanlon *et al.* explained that the differences they found using testing matched differences regarding actual brain activity differences in the two groups. They point out that attentional dysfunction and problems with information processing and with executive functioning relate to the differences in prefrontal activity that were shown in other studies. They found significant differences between murderers classified as affective/impulsive and those classified as predatory/impulsive with the affective/impulsive group having lower IQ. It was interesting that Hanlon *et al.* report that only one of their participants was found not guilty by reason of insanity. They cite Raine *et al.* (1998) and Gilligan and Lennings (2010, 2012) and explain that their participants were confined to forensic hospitals, being found not guilty by reason of insanity or incompetent to stand trial. Hanlon *et al.* reported that all of their participants were considered fit to stand trial and all were incarcerated in county jails or state prisons. They felt that because of this their sample was more representative as a sample of murderers.

STUDY HINT

Hanlon *et al.* (2013) use tests to find out about information processing, IQ and other features of the brain, whereas Raine *et al.* (1997) used scanning to 'see' the brain more directly. You can use these two studies to show how different research methods have different strengths and weaknesses. For example, Hanlon *et al.* gathered a great deal of information but they were not able to show the brain in action; they had to make assumptions about brain functioning. Raine *et al.* showed show brain functioning, but they did not have as much information about the abilities and differences in their participants.

Learning theories: Watson and Rayner (1920)

Watson and Rayner (1920) wanted to use the principles of classical conditioning to see if a fear could be instilled in a young baby. They called the baby 'Little Albert'. They felt that instinctive emotions in humans had a limited range and that there could be an element of learning in emotions, including fears.

Aims

Watson and Rayner wanted to see if striking a bar loudly if paired with something liked would then give a fear response instead of a liking response. They wanted to see if any fear that was learned would be generalised to other similar items. The researchers also wanted to see the effect of time on conditioning, such as how long it would last.

Procedure and results

This was a single case experiment and was more of a demonstration really. They did not gather rich and detailed information about Little Albert so it was not a case study. The procedures and results occurred together because the results were a recording of what happened in response to a sequence of procedures.

Participant

The participant was a baby aged about 11 months, whose mother was a wet-nurse at the hospital where the study took place. Ethics were considered in that Watson and Rayner chose a healthy and well-developed, seemingly rather unemotional child, and they thought that for these reasons the study would do him relatively little harm.

What they did

Watson and Rayner at the start filmed Little Albert's reactions to a white rat, cotton wool, a rabbit and other stimuli to make sure he had no fear. They banged a hammer against a metal bar and found a fear response. Then they set about pairing an 'unfeared' object with the fear response (achieved by the noise from the metal bar).

What they found

They found Albert liked the white rat and reached out for it. When he reached out to the rat they banged the metal bar and he fell forward and jumped. He touched the rat so they banged the bar again. He started to whimper. This was evidence that his fear response to the metal bar being hit (the noise) had transferred to the rat, which was the neutral stimulus. There was then a series of procedures including presenting the rat and banging the bar, and they also made sure they gave him blocks to play with, without a noise, so they did not condition him to fear all toys.

Watson and Rayner, once Little Albert had shown fear to the rat, looked to see if he would generalise his fear to other similar objects, while still being happy playing with blocks. They also tested to see how long the conditioning of the fear to the white rat would last, and found it lasted five days.

They found that a rabbit gave some fear and a dog made Albert turn away and cry. Then they paired the rat with the sound again to give fear (the conditioning was repeated), and that gave more of a reaction to the rabbit. All the time in between different conditions they presented blocks and Little Albert was happy to play with the blocks.

Watson and Rayner then moved the study to different surroundings to see the effect of being in a different place and they concluded Albert did indeed transfer his fear to different surroundings (as well as the different objects).

Conclusions

Watson and Rayner (1920) concluded that a conditioned fear response could be given to a small child after just a few pairings of the neutral stimulus with the unconditioned stimulus. They found they had to repeat the pairings though. They also found that the fear could be transferred to other similar objects, which they called 'generalising'. They found too that the conditioning lasted some time – at least days. They also found that the fear response could be transferred to a different setting.

What happened to Little Albert?

After a lot of investigation a team of researchers felt they had tracked Little Albert down and that he was a young boy called Douglas. It was often thought that Little Albert might have had problems later because his fear response had not been extinguished, but it was found that Douglas sadly died at the age of six years old. However, later a different child was said to be Little Albert, so there is still doubt.

Evaluation of Watson and Rayner (1920)

Strengths

- The experiment was well-designed and controlled; for example, the independent variable each time was clear and the dependent variable (the behaviour) was measured and recorded carefully.
- The study showed that Pavlov's ideas about classical conditioning (from his work with dogs) could be said to be true of humans.

Weaknesses

- It was not ethical because Albert was distressed throughout and even though he was distressed the study continued for weeks.
- The setting was a laboratory and, therefore, artificial; the study lacked ecological validity and perhaps validity with regard to the task.

Explore

You can investigate Watson and Rayner's (1920) study using this YouTube link:
www.youtube.com/watch?v=9hBfnXACsOI

Progress check 6.4

Explain two weaknesses of Watson and Rayner's (1920) study of Little Albert.

Study of interest showing the current relevance of Watson and Rayner's work

Schweckendiek et al. (2011) looked at classical conditioning as being central in starting and maintaining phobias. They point out that neuronal functioning behind fear conditioning is known about but the study of neuronal functioning in patients with specific phobias has not been studied. This shows how Watson and Rayner's ideas about phobias being learned through classical conditioning still holds, but that now there is focus on brain activity and brain functioning that relates to such conditioning.

Schweckendiek et al. (2011) used fMRI scanning to look at conditioned responses in 15 people with specific phobias, looking at brain activity in reaction to a phobia-relevant stimulus and a non-phobia-relevant stimulus. There was a control group of 14 healthy participants. The study used either pictures of spiders, 'highly aversive' scenes or household items.

The study found higher levels of activity in the medial prefrontal cortex, anterior cingulate cortex, amygdala, insula and thalamus when the phobia-related conditioned stimulus was introduced. Those with spider phobia showed higher activity in the amygdala when the conditioned stimulus was phobia-related than when it was not. There was no difference between those with a phobia and controls in the condition when the stimulus was non-phobia-related.

The conclusion was that the amygdala is involved in fear processing and that a learned phobia results in a greater than usual activity in the 'fear network' in the brain. In general those with a phobia were not different in their brain activity from the controls; it was just when a phobia-related conditioned stimulus was used that there was more activity in the specific brain areas. This suggests a phobia does not come from brain differences but that there are differences in brain functioning when a phobia has been conditioned in someone.

STUDY HINT

The study of interest here shows how psychology has developed over time, which links to the issues and debates section of your course. It uses fMRI scanning, which links to biological psychology in your course. There is a control group as well, showing methodological features of studies. Use information when you come across it to illustrate other areas of psychology you have learned about.

Clinical psychology: Rosenhan (1973)

Rosenhan (1973) used pseudo-patients (people who presented themselves at a hospital with symptoms of hearing voices) who were then admitted, even though they were not telling the truth about what they were hearing. Rosenhan wanted to look at diagnosis of mental disorders and he wanted to see what would happen if someone was diagnosed with schizophrenia.

Aims

Rosenhan wanted to see if eight people who gained admission into twelve different hospitals would be found out as being sane. One of the eight was himself. He also wanted to know what it would be like to be seen as insane and to be in a hospital.

Procedure

The pseudo-patients went to 12 different hospitals in different states in the USA and said they had been hearing voices saying things like 'empty' or 'thud'. Apart from that, the pseudo-patients were 'themselves' and just answered questions normally, though changing some information and their names to protect their identity.

The patients were given medication that they did not swallow and they behaved sanely (they wanted to get out of the hospital).

After the main study Rosenhan carried out another study. He let it be known in some institutions that over the next three months there would be some pseudo-patients arriving (of course they never did).

Results

All except one patient was admitted with a diagnosis of schizophrenia in remission and nothing in the hospital records suggests that the hospital knew there was a problem about the authenticity of the patients. The patients were kept in hospital for between 7 and 52 days. Rosenhan emphasised that these were not bad hospitals and there was nothing to observe in the patients that would show themselves to have schizophrenia. They behaved in a sane manner and visitors and other patients felt the patients were 'not crazy'. In fact, because of the note-taking, the other patients thought the pseudo-patients were journalists or a professor, whereas the staff saw the note-taking as part of the 'illness'.

In the second part of the study where other hospitals were told pseudo-patients would arrive, at least one member of staff judged 41 out of 193 patients admitted for psychiatric treatment to be pseudo-patients. There were in fact no such patients; Rosenhan said there would be some but there were not.

Rosenhan felt that once diagnosed the individual could not get rid of the label and once in hospital with a diagnosis the staff interpreted behaviours and events according to the label. For example, with regard to the note-taking, one patient had a comment in their notes saying 'engages in writing behaviour' as though that were abnormal.

When a pseudo-patient asked when they would be discharged, such contact was avoided and members of staff tended to ignore patients. However, a student at Stanford University asked staff for help and had no problem with getting help. It was thought that mental health issues are avoided by people. In a study looking at helping behaviour relating to psychiatrists in the hospital, nurses in the hospital or staff at the university, it was found that 100 per cent of the staff at the university stopped to talk on being asked for help. Only 4 per cent of the psychiatrists stopped to help when being asked a question in the hospital and just 0.5 per cent of the nurses. It was found that 71 per cent of the psychiatrists and 88 per cent of the nurses moved on with their head averted.

Conclusions

Rosenhan concluded that the sane and insane cannot be separated in a psychiatric hospital and also in such hospitals special meaning is given to behaviour. He felt that the study showed that using labels when diagnosing someone is not helpful.

Progress check 6.5

What did Rosenhan's (1973) study find out about being sane in insane places?

Evaluation of Rosenhan (1973)
Strengths

- There were 12 different hospitals in different places and they were carefully chosen. With the same things being found this gives generalisability of the findings.
- The study had validity because the pseudo-patients, after their first complaint about hearing voices, were themselves and the hospital setting was real.

Weaknesses

- The pseudo-patients did say they heard voices, which is a symptom of schizophrenia, which reduces the validity of the study as the patients did lie and say they heard voices in their heads.

- The study took place in 1973, which was more than 40 years ago. Things changed because of Rosenhan's work and today the impact of labelling when diagnosing is well known, partly thanks to Rosenhan. It might be hard to draw the conclusion now that such institutions cannot recognise the insane.

Explore

You can explore Rosenhan's (1973) study using this YouTube link:

www.youtube.com/watch?v=BZRVEVqvmbg

Study of interest showing the current relevance of Rosenhan's work

Dickens *et al.* (2011), working in the UK, looked at labelling of patients in the secure psychiatric services to see what terminology is used about such patients. They mention various terms used for people accessing mental health services, including 'patient', 'service user', 'people affected by mental illness' and 'survivor'. The researchers found that the people using the services had not been asked for their views. The researchers asked 100 people questions about which term(s) they preferred. The participants were randomly selected though there was some stratification in the sample to make sure both males and females were represented. The order of the terms was counterbalanced when questions were asked to minimise response bias and respondents ranked the terms in order of preference as well as giving some qualitative data about term usage. In the sample, 51 of the respondents were judged by 'responsible clinicians' not to have the capacity to consent and were, therefore, excluded.

Of those replying to the questionnaire, 42 per cent said they preferred to be known as a 'patient', 20 per cent preferred 'client', 17 per cent preferred 'service user' and 2 per cent liked to be called a 'consumer'. The preference for a certain label was not affected by gender, age, diagnosis, ethnicity, security level or length of stay. There was no term that the majority liked, but 'patient' was preferred by the largest group. There was some interesting qualitative data, such as one male saying 'I think I'm a prisoner', which perhaps relates to Rosenhan's (1973) findings. Another male said 'patient is more familiar, more acceptable. Not necessarily the best way to describe us but it is well understood'.

The researchers concluded that there was no need to avoid the term 'patient' from the findings of their study. The study showed that the people in the hospitals (there were three used in the study) did feel labelled, judging from the qualitative data. Unlike Rosenhan's participants of course, these participants could not leave so there were differences. However, this study shows that there is still interest in labels used and in how people 'receive' the labels used.

STUDY HINT

Dickens *et al.* (2011) is useful for a number of methodological issues. They use random sampling and some stratification in the sampling too. They use counterbalancing to avoid response bias, which is interesting, and they include qualitative data to add depth to their data, which is about labels and so is about the feelings of those the labels are applied to. They also used clinicians to check ethics and found they had to exclude a lot of respondents who were judged as not having the capacity to consent. Use such examples when discussing such issues.

Test yourself

To what extent can two classic studies in your course be used to show the value of psychology for society? **(12 marks)**

Using classic studies to inform issues and debates in psychology

The 11 issues and debates are now considered singularly to examine how the five classic studies – from social psychology, cognitive psychology, biological psychology, learning theories and clinical psychology – can be used to illustrate them.

Each is considered in order, with the five studies related to them in so far as that is possible. This approach will also help you to compare the five classic studies. You can draw on the chosen classic study from your optional application if you wish.

Chapter Seven considers issues and debates in more detail, including explaining what each one is about. For each of the 11 issues and debates there is a brief recap of what the issue and debate is about and then a focus on how the classic studies relate to it.

Ethical issues in research (animal and human)

Ethical issues in your course with regard to researching with humans focus on the four ethical principles in the BPS Code of Ethics and Conduct (2009), which include respect, responsibility, integrity and competence.

Risk management must be considered when undertaking research in psychology.

Ethical issues with regard to animals focus on the Animals (Scientific Procedures) Act 1986. The five classic studies featured in this chapter do not include animals as participants so such issues are not considered. If you are discussing Watson and Rayner (1920) you could briefly consider the animals they used in the experiment, but it was not an animal study.

Table 6.7 The five classic studies linked to ethical issues in research (animal and human)

Ethical issues in research (animal and human)				
Sherif *et al.* (1954/1961)	**Baddeley (1966b)**	**Raine *et al.* (1997)**	**Watson and Rayner (1920)**	**Rosenhan (1973)**
The parents were asked not to visit the boys, which might have been seen as unethical. It was not clear that the boys were asked for informed consent, which would be required now, considering the focus on research being *with* the child not researching *on* the child.	Adults were involved so fewer ethical issues than Sherif *et al.*, who used children, where special rules apply.	The experimental group were having the PET scan anyway to help their case so that was ethical to an extent.	There was some harm to Little Albert as he was clearly upset and distressed when hearing the loud noise.	Rosenhan's study was about ethics in a way, being focused on the harm diagnosis can do. So the aims were ethical.
Some boys were allowed to go home, because they were homesick, so they were taken care of.	Participants in part were in the subject 'pool' at the university, which they had presumably volunteered for.	Findings showed brain dysfunctioning, so perhaps that supported their case.	They did not have the chance to extinguish the fear but his mother was given the right to withdraw him from the study, which was good.	Rosenhan was one of the participants and he did not ask others to do what he would not do. He obtained fully informed consent too.
There was responsibility in that there was confidentiality.	There was competence in that the university was involved.	Controls were matched to an extent, such as six having schizophrenia.	They chose a baby they thought would not be too upset by the study.	He limited the number of people he used and he had volunteers — all quite ethical.
	There is no suggestion that confidentiality was broken.	It is assumed that all gave informed consent but it is not known as there might have been some impairment for some.	They took care to let him play happily with blocks alongside the conditioning and they took breaks between the phases.	He deceived the hospital staff, which was not ethical.
				There was a second part where staff doubted the patients' sanity, which may have caused harm.

Progress check 6.6

Choose two of the four ethical principles (respect, responsibility, integrity and competence) and for each explain how one classic study illustrates that principle.

Practical issues in the design and implementation of research

- Practical issues in research, both in design and implementation, are found in all research methods, as you will have found in your studies.

- For example, to get reliability careful controls are necessary, but for results to be valid, there has to be real-life focus, which is hard if there are careful controls. Often a balance is required and this can mean practical problems.
- Working with participants can give practical issues in implementing research, such as order effects if using a repeated measures design.
- Other practical issues include ensuring there are no confounding variables when aiming for cause-and-effect conclusions.
- The five classic studies looked at in this section include mostly experiments and Rosenhan's case study.

Questionnaires or interviews are not used, for example, and neither is a longitudinal or cross-cultural design. Practical issues are limited to those in these five classic studies in this section.
- Ethical issues are not considered in this section.

Reductionism in the explanation of behaviour

- Reductionism refers to the way studies tend to take parts of a behaviour or attitude and then study that part rather than a whole situation.

Table 6.8 The five classic studies linked to practical issues in the design and implementation of research

Practical issues in the design and implementation of research				
Sherif *et al.* (1954/1961)	**Baddeley (1966b)**	**Raine *et al.* (1997)**	**Watson and Rayner (1920)**	**Rosenhan (1973)**
The sample involved matching the boys carefully, not only the boys chosen but also when splitting them into two groups for the study.	Baddeley wanted to claim cause-and-effect conclusions from his experiments so had to avoid any confounding variables. He found one, in that STM was involved in his first experiment though he wanted to study LTM. He had to carry out another experiment to take account of this confounding variable.	They had to match the control group to the experimental group so that comparison in brain functioning could be made. Matching on all variables is hard, if not impossible.	Watson and Rayner were unable to continue studying Little Albert because his mother moved away, which was a practical issue for them.	It was important that the eight pseudo-patients reported hearing voices in the same way so that the findings could be put together and so Rosenhan stuck to people he knew and were keen on the study.
It is hard (if not impossible) when matching to be sure that all the required variables are considered.	He could not be sure that in the different groups there were no individual differences between the participants.	They gave the participants a task so they were all doing the same thing, but the brain is active in all individuals and some might have felt more stress perhaps. There might have been differences other than the 'violence' in the 'murderers'.	They had to be sure he was not conditioned to be afraid to play at all so they made sure he played with blocks and was not made afraid then.	However, they then behaved as themselves, with consequent individual differences that may have affected the findings.
The boys made decisions during the study, such as when setting up competitions, so they were active in the study. This might mean the study is not replicable because if done again things would be different as the situation would differ.			Watson and Rayner had to be sure Little Albert was safe as he was a baby, such as putting him on a mat to play.	On the other hand being themselves was what patients would do, so perhaps that was a strength.
			He had limited mobility too so they had to bring the rat and other animals to him.	

- Holism refers to a whole situation, including interactions between people and all decision-making.
- It is hard to study a 'whole' human pattern of behaviour and so, in order to introduce controls, for example, parts of behaviour are broken down to be studied. This 'breaking down' is reductionism.

Explore
You can use this link to look more at reductionism:
www.youtube.com/watch?v=6P4QpZJbI9A

- Reductionism is the idea that it is possible to study something by looking at its parts whereas holism is the idea that this is not a good way to study something because the 'whole is more than the sum of the parts'.
- **Parsimony** is a scientific idea that the simplest way of explaining something is the best.

Definition
Parsimony is the idea in science that complex things should be explained in as simple a way as possible.

Table 6.9 The five classic studies linked to reductionism in the explanation of behaviour

Reductionism in the explanation of behaviour				
Sherif *et al.* (1954/1961)	**Baddeley (1966b)**	**Raine *et al.* (1997)**	**Watson and Rayner (1920)**	**Rosenhan (1973)**
This study reduced the rise of prejudice to bring about competition over resources and the reduction of prejudice to bring about working together in cooperation.	This was a lab experiment and very clearly controlled, which suggests a reductionist approach.	Raine *et al.* reduced violent behaviour to brain functioning and dysfunctioning rather than taking into account the whole situation, including environmental triggers.	Watson and Rayner were looking at classical conditioning, which reduces learning of reflexive responses, saying they come from a stimulus in the environment.	Rosenhan reduced the complexity of schizophrenia to hearing words like 'thud' in one's head, whereas there are other symptoms too and also issues around social functioning.
It is hard to focus on prejudice in a complete social situation, however, as breaking it down to study it can miss important interactions and inter-relationships. The boys were in a social situation, which partly addresses the criticism of reductionism. This was a field experiment/study so in a way is less reductionist than a laboratory experiment.	There were four conditions with four lists and some matching of the lists so that there were control conditions as well as experimental conditions.	PET scanning also is reductionist in that though slices of the brain are imaged and the brain is active (glucose uptake), just that processing at the time is studied, not all processing and not processing in real life situations (a lab is unnatural, as is a scan).	This removed focus on any brain functioning and also did not consider operant conditioning or social learning as explanations.	However, this was enough to get the diagnosis 'schizophrenia in remission' (for all but one of the participants) so even though it seems reductionist it does seem to suit real-life diagnosis of schizophrenia, which makes it more holistic.
	This reduced memory to the learning of a list of ten words and recalling them in order. This was not a very natural thing to do perhaps. Though it clearly was about memory and has practical applications (helps with revision perhaps), which is a real-life application.	The 'murderers' were surely in a social situation at the time of the 'incident'.	Behaviour, including phobias, was reduced to single instances of learning.	Staff perhaps reduced behaviour to symptoms, such as 'writing behaviour', which underlines how diagnosis is 'scientific' being about parts of a whole mental disorder.
			However, they did let the child play with blocks without instilling fear, acknowledging that learning has some complexity, though still focusing on classical conditioning.	

Progress check 6.7

Explain one study from the classic studies being used in this section that might focus more on an holistic view than a reductionist one.

Comparisons of ways of explaining behaviour using different themes

- Themes in psychology can be ideas, categories, concepts or theories. A theme is an idea (a fairly central idea) that can be thought of as separate from other ideas in a body of knowledge. 'Theme' is quite hard to define.
- For example, in cognitive psychology the different memory theories can be said to have different themes with the influence of schemas being one theme in memory and information processing being another.
- Gender, culture and personality can be thought of as themes that might affect obedience in social psychology.
- Learning theories have themes such as the idea of stimulus–response learning or observational learning.

Table 6.10 The five classic studies linked to comparisons of ways of explaining behaviour using different themes

Comparisons of ways of explaining behaviour using different themes				
Sherif et al. (1954/1961)	**Baddeley (1966b)**	**Raine et al. (1997)**	**Watson and Rayner (1920)**	**Rosenhan (1973)**
A theme in this study is that prejudice relates to us being in groups and this can link to social identity theory because the boys formed an in group and an out group as soon as they knew about one another.	Memory is split into many different parts and themes are formed. For example, the idea of memory being processing of information and split into stores such as STM and LTM could be one theme.	Raine et al. took the view that violence and aggression in our behaviour can be explained by looking at brain functioning and dysfunctioning, which is one theme to explain human behaviour.	Watson and Rayner used the underpinning idea that classical conditioning gives associations between stimuli and responses such that learning takes place.	Rosenhan's study was not an experiment, unlike the other classic studies. In a way he was considering the theme of diagnosis and labelling, so he was working within a theme. He wanted to see if a label would stick in a mental hospital and even though it was an untrue label (though brought about by lying of course) it would be hard to get away from when normal behaviour was displayed.
Sherif focused on the theme of conflict in prejudice – not only about being in groups but about there being conflict, such as competition over scarce resources.	There being episodic and semantic memory fits with LTM but could be seen as a different theme around what is being memorised rather than how it is done.	Another theme would be how we learn behaviour, and Watson and Rayner perhaps focused on this other theme in their study on classical conditioning and the role of the environment.	They thought that this underpinning idea might account for how humans learn phobias as fear is an innate response, such as the startle response to a loud noise.	His theme was the medical model and how understanding of behaviour was within a context. In the context of a hospital all behaviour was interpreted according to the diagnosis.
Even when showing how to reduce prejudice the theme was 'groups', making one large group that had a common goal out of smaller groups.	Baddeley focused on one theme, the LTM and STM split, and he continued to work on STM so focused on the theme that short-term memory is different and separate.	Raine et al. did not look at neuronal transmission that might underpin brain dysfunctioning and it can be seen as a different biological theme.	They went about conditioning a fear to a neutral stimulus in a baby and they succeeded, giving evidence for that idea underpinning learning.	

- Biological psychology has themes such as neurotransmitter functioning and brain structures as well as the role of genes and evolution.
- Clinical psychology has the theme of diagnosis of mental health issues and perhaps the medical model can be seen as a theme running through clinical psychology.

Psychology as a science

- One aspect of psychology being a science is reductionism, so the discussion under that heading can help when discussing psychology as a science.
- Science takes a theory, puts forward a hypothesis that the theory would predict, sets about getting data to support the hypothesis and then according to what is found either accepts, rejects or amends the theory.
- If psychology is a science then it must be using this scientific approach to studying mind and behaviour.

Experiments do just that – a hypothesis is derived and then tested against reality in some way. To that extent psychology is science.

- However, some studies have a research question and a focus rather than a hypothesis, such as Lavarenne et al.'s (2013) case study (page 158), which showed how group support can act as an ego boundary for someone. Also Vallentine et al. (2010) (page 162), where they used interviewing to see how successful explaining someone's condition was to them when they were offenders in a psychiatric unit, is not really focusing on a hypothesis and testing the data in the same way as explained here.

Explore
You can hear more about psychology and science using this YouTube link:
www.youtube.com/watch?v=1sCSnRRzHEs

Table 6.11 The five classic studies linked to psychology as a science

Psychology as a science				
Sherif *et al.* (1954/1961)	**Baddeley (1966b)**	**Raine *et al.* (1997)**	**Watson and Rayner (1920)**	**Rosenhan (1973)**
A field experiment takes a scientific approach to gathering data, in this case to look at causes of prejudice and ways to reduce prejudice. However, elements of the study were not 'experiment'.	A lab experiment that took a scientific approach by using very careful controls, such as the timing the words were heard for (or seen for).	Also an experiment though the scanning took place where the evidence was gathered for their plea of NGRI.	Their study had clear controls in that they obtained baseline measures by making sure Little Albert was not scared of a dog, rabbit, white rat and so on, and that he was scared of the noise of the metal bar.	This was not an experiment in the sense of generating a hypothesis and testing against reality using controls so that cause-and-effect conclusions could be drawn.
There were careful controls, such as matching the boys in the two groups to make the groups 'equal' with regard to individual differences.	Controls included the setting as well, which was an artificial laboratory setting as this controlled for situational variables.	There was perhaps lack of control to this extent in that the scanning was likely to have been stressful, which would have affected brain functioning and dysfunctioning.	Then they paired the noise with the neutral stimulus (first, the rat) to link it to a fear response.	There were controls such as what the pseudo-patients said when they presented themselves at the hospital and when they were told to then just be themselves.
There was testing against reality by setting up a realistic situation for the boys.	Participant variables were also controlled as some participants were excluded because of hearing difficulties.	However, there were careful controls in matching the control group and in having a control group for a baseline measure.	This was carefully controlled, including allowing him to play with blocks without the noise. This was experimental in method.	However, data were qualitative and the investigation was more like separate specific case studies, so not scientific in some ways.

Cultural and gender issues in psychological research

- Cultural issues relate to how being part of a different culture with different norms and customs might affect

someone's behaviour and attitudes. Cultural issues are part of our nurture as they come from our interactions with our environment.
- Gender issues are similar in that they relate to how being male or female might affect someone's behaviour and attitudes and gender attitudes tend to arise within

a culture. Gender behaviour then comes from our nurture, though it can be said that genes can dictate sex differences, which would be down to nature.

- Not all of psychology has culture and/or gender issues and the way this is found out is by, for example, doing cross-cultural studies. How memory works is not thought to be affected by culture or gender, for instance.

- Some human processing is thought to be universal and so not affected by culture. It might be affected by gender because, seemingly unlike culture, gender has biological aspects as well as environmental ones.

Table 6.12 The five classic studies linked to cultural and gender issues in psychological research

Cultural and gender issues in psychological research				
Sherif et al. (1954/1961)	**Baddeley (1966b)**	**Raine et al. (1997)**	**Watson and Rayner (1920)**	**Rosenhan (1973)**
It could be argued that the findings applied only to the USA where the study took place and Summer Camps like the one in the study are frequently used.	Culture is not generally considered an issue in memory. It is generally thought that memory processing is the same for all humans, as it relates to brain processing and humans share brain structure with one another.	Raine et al. did not show gender differences in their findings, and gender differences were not expected in that they focused on brain areas such as the prefrontal cortex relating to aggression/lack of planning.	It was not thought that Little Albert being a boy had any bearing on the learning of the phobia.	Rosenhan used both males and females in his study looking at what it was like to be sane in 'insane' places.
They are less frequently used in other cultures so possibly generalising from such a specific setting is not appropriate.	Gender too is not thought to be an issue in memory. Baddeley, for example, used both males and females in Experiment III and did not report gender differences.	Culture too was not thought to relate to Raine's work on brain dysfunction and violence and aggression.	Classical conditioning is not thought to be different depending on gender.	He did not report gender differences in the findings and both males and females found it hard to be released from the hospital.
Similarly the participants were all boys so perhaps generalising to say prejudice would be formed and reduced in the same way in girls is not appropriate.		In general biological processing such as brain functioning does not focus on cultural differences; it focuses on nature.	Classical conditioning principles are not thought to apply differently according to culture either, though what is learned can be culturally specific.	It could be the case that the study represented mental health attitudes and procedures in the USA rather than in different cultures.
				However, the DSM, which is used in America but also in other places, is not so different from the ICD, which is used worldwide.

Progress check 6.8

Explain one example of the effects of culture on mind and behaviour as shown in one of the classic studies used in this section.

The role of both nature and nurture in psychology

When the role of culture and gender was discussed above, it was said that cultural effects on behaviour will come from nurture, whereas gender behaviour is likely to be learned through experiences in the environment. However, there are aspects of gender that are biologically given.

Our nature is in our biology, including what has evolved in humans, each person's genotype and also general aspects of biological functioning, such as neurotransmitter functioning and brain structure and functioning.

Our nurture is what affects us from our environment even before birth and phenotype is what we take from our genotype and our experiences together.

Explore

A YouTube video about twins looks at nature-nurture, which you might find useful:

www.youtube.com/watch?v=bRKbZtpBcgI

Table 6.13 The five classic studies linked to the role of both nature and nurture in psychology

The role of both nature and nurture in psychology				
Sherif *et al.* (1954/1961)	**Baddeley (1966b)**	**Raine *et al.* (1997)**	**Watson and Rayner (1920)**	**Rosenhan (1973)**
The study of prejudice tends to focus on our nurture, such as how some cultures are multicultural in their outlook and others take an assimilation view. Those more multicultural are less prejudiced.	What we remember, such as episodes in our lives or what we have learned and experienced, might come from our nurture and be individual.	Raine too looked at brain processing and our biology, making the assumption that prefrontal lobe functioning, for example, is the same for everyone and if there is dysfunction for an individual that can lead to violence and aggression.	There is the assumption that all humans (and animals in fact) learn through classical conditioning principles, associating things in the environment with reflexes like the fear response. So this is in our nature.	Rosenhan focused on diagnosis and how the situation of the hospital meant that understanding of the behaviour of the pseudo-patients came from a particular way of seeing the world.
Sherif *et al.* focused on how the formation of groups and competition over resources led to prejudice, which is also about nurture in that our experiences of groups might lead to prejudicial attitudes.	However, Baddeley looked at memory as a process which all humans use and as such this would link to our biology and our nature. For example, evidence suggests that our STM relates to hippocampal functioning or temporal lobe functioning, as Schmolck *et al.* (2002) suggest. These are brain areas common to all, so about nature not nurture.	Such violence would not, therefore, come from the situation but from brain dysfunctioning — part of someone's nature not their nurture.	Though what we learn and associate does depend on our nurture and what we encounter in the way of stimulus and response association.	Diagnosis is done within a culture and we learn how we react to mental disorders, for example. This is through our nurture not our nature.
Though perhaps the tendency to favour our in-group and to fight over scarce resources is an innate tendency, Sherif does not look at that aspect of prejudice.		If the dysfunctioning was from environmental influences such as an accident, this would not really be about nurture as such as it is not about how the environment influences our behaviour directly, more about the environment affecting our nature/biology.	Little Albert had the startle response to the noise because of his nature. However, the actual fear, which related to the pet rat, was through his experiences and his nurture.	Rosenhan's study is not about nature, unless we say that symptoms of schizophrenia come from someone's nature; it is how they are then interpreted, understood and dealt with that is down to nurture.

Progress check 6.9

Using the classic studies being looked at in this chapter, give one example of where nature is involved and one example of nurture being involved.

An understanding of how psychological understanding has developed over time

- When studying psychology it is useful and interesting to see how psychology has developed over time. It is by developing over time that a body of knowledge can be built, for example.

- Research methods have developed over time though the classic studies are largely older ones (except perhaps for Raine *et al.*) and so they tend not to use newer, more modern data collection techniques, for example.

- Raine *et al.* is perhaps an exception, using PET scanning to get images of an active brain at work. Using scanning in research is a relatively new approach.

- When writing up a report in psychology it is necessary to present background to the study and that is a review of the literature that underpins the study. The idea is to draw on what is already known so that a body of knowledge is built. This shows psychology developing over time.

Table 6.14 The five classic studies linked to an understanding of how psychological understanding has developed over time

Understanding of how psychological understanding has developed over time				
Sherif et al. (1954/1961)	**Baddeley (1966b)**	**Raine et al. (1997)**	**Watson and Rayner (1920)**	**Rosenhan (1973)**
Sherif et al. worked in social psychology in the 1960s when it was a very popular and rather new area so there was not much for them to go on.	In the 1960s cognitive psychology was new. There was focus on memory models and Baddeley was working in the same area so not really drawing on older understanding, more building a current body of knowledge.	Raine et al. (1997) build on a previous study in 1994.	Watson and Rayner were working at the same time as Pavlov so working in what was a current area of research.	Rosenhan's study has stood the test of time and is still used to show the dangers of labelling through diagnosis.
Tajfel, working at a similar time, put forward the idea of social identity theory. Sherif gave the theory of realistic conflict.	Baddeley then moved on to develop the working memory model, looking more into STM, and he has continued to build his working memory model, developing it over time.	They also used other evidence for the parts of the brain they chose to study, using parts of the brain previously linked to aggression and violence, like the prefrontal lobes and the amygdala.	However, classical conditioning is still of interest today as an underpinning idea for treatments for phobias, such as systematic desensitisation.	It has practical relevance to those working in the field of mental health and to clinicians diagnosing using one of the classification systems.
What was new was the focus on groups and interactions. Adorno et al. (1950) had linked prejudice with personality and situation became a focus of interest in the 1960s.	Ideas from Baddeley's understanding of memory have helped in society, and being able to apply knowledge in psychology tends to move a field of research forward.	This means psychology in the area of study of brain functioning has built up over time.	Treatments have developed over time. CBT incorporates behavioural aspects of therapy, including replacing a fear response with a relaxation response.	Diagnosis does not rest on just one symptom (e.g. hearing 'thud' in one's head), for example.
		However, until PET scanning was available the active brain was unknown.		
		fMRI is beginning to take over from PET scanning, and is likely to become more commonly used than PET scanning in the future.		

The use of psychology in social control

- Social control refers to regulating the behaviour of others to try to gain obedience and compliance in relation to social rules and norms.
- The question in this issue and debate is whether and how far psychology is used in social control.
- If behaviour is controlled by social systems then that might mean that we are regulated by society and not in a conscious way. This might be related to ideas of conditioning and social learning.
- The understanding about mind and behaviour that psychology brings might be used consciously to enable society to control people, and this is an issue of interest because there are ethical and moral implications.

Explore

You can explore more about social control by using this YouTube link. This information is linked to sociology, so is not directly about psychology but it gives some background to the idea of social control.

www.youtube.com/watch?v=haXJl_dl91g

Table 6.15 The five classic studies linked to the use of psychology in social control

The use of psychology in social control				
Sherif et al. (1954/1961)	**Baddeley (1966b)**	**Raine et al. (1997)**	**Watson and Rayner (1920)**	**Rosenhan (1973)**
How prejudice might occur and how it might be resolved can link to issues of social control. Controlling prejudice can help in society, because it can help to avoid violence that might come from hostility. Hostility can come from competition over resources, as Sherif et al. found.	How memory works is not related directly to control in a society. However, knowing about issues like the acoustic nature of STM might help others, for example, treating those with dementia so that they have time to process sound.	If the brain regions related to violence are known about then in theory violence can be more easily controlled.	Classical conditioning is about developing an association between a stimulus and a response and that association can be engineered by others.	Being in a hospital unable to get out is about being controlled and Rosenhan found that once the pseudo-patients had said a rather simple thing — hearing something in their head — they were diagnosed with schizophrenia in remission and kept in the hospital.
Sherif also suggested a solution — the use of overarching goals. This solution can help to control people in society.	Another use is for revision and learning, being sure to focus on the semantic nature of LTM. This is not likely to be about social control as such as learning is for the individual; however, it could be said that control is about understanding.	Though changing someone's brain structure is unlikely in a society, it is possible that neurotransmitter functioning could be altered.	Watson and Rayner controlled Little Albert's fear, for example.	It took an average of 19 days for them to get out.
		Raine et al. looked more at the brain regions, but knowing about the brain can lead to the development of ideas about controlling aggression in society.	Classical conditioning principles can be used to associate a fear response (or other reflex) to any stimulus apparently, judging by the findings of this study. For example, advertising uses classical conditioning principles.	They were treated according to the diagnosis, not according to their subsequent normal behaviour.
				The diagnosis itself gave a label and the label was a form of social control.

Progress check 6.10

From the classic studies used in this section, give two examples of social control.

The use of psychological knowledge in society

- In your course for each topic area you will have studied concepts, theories and studies to explain a key question in society and possibly to offer solutions. This is about the use of psychological knowledge in society.

- Psychology is the study of mind and behaviour and can be helpful for individuals, such as offering treatments for issues like mental disorders.
- However, it very often helps society as well. Helping individuals helps the society they are in; for example, ill health in a society costs money, as does not controlling violence or not having an educated workforce. It is therefore of benefit to society as a whole to help the individuals that make up that society.

STUDY HINT

You can draw on the key questions that you covered in the topic areas in your course to understand more about the use of psychological knowledge in society.

Table 6.16 The five classic studies linked to the use of psychological knowledge in society

The use of psychological knowledge in society				
Sherif *et al.* (1954/1961)	Baddeley (1966b)	Raine *et al.* (1997)	Watson and Rayner (1920)	Rosenhan (1973)
Prejudice can be a problem for society as it can lead to violence, such as race riots.	Studies that show how memory works can help people with memory problems, such as those with dementia.	The more that is known about what causes violence, including which brain regions are implicated, the more violence in a society can be reduced perhaps.	Advertising has benefitted from realising that pairing something liked, such as a beautiful person, with a product will lead to the person liking the product.	It is useful for society to realise the extent to which labelling guides how we see others and Rosenhan found that if someone is seen as having a mental disorder (like schizophrenia) that guides how others see them. For example, 'writing behaviour' becomes a symptom.
In-group favouritism can lead to violence, which costs society in terms of policing, for example.	If it is known that STM uses acoustic coding and that rehearsal helps with putting memories into LTM then that is useful for society.	Raine *et al.* suggested that those guilty of violence were guilty because of differences in brain functioning, which might be about blame or lack of blame. Issues of responsibility are useful for a society to know about.	Watson and Rayner showed that such principles could work with humans when they conditioned Little Albert to be scared of a pet rat.	He also warned society that deciding who is 'sane' and who is 'insane' is not straightforward.
Conflict over resources can be costly for a society.	Helping people with memory problems can help a society with regard to its workforce as well as helping individuals.		Society can benefit from knowing how associations are made.	
Sherif showed that prejudice can be reduced by requiring people to work towards superordinate goals. His research helped society to understand such issues as how to reduce prejudice.	Giving people with memory problems time to rehearse in itself can be useful.		People may be seen as being manipulated by such conditioning as their free will seems to be bypassed.	

Issues related to socially sensitive research

- Research in psychology can be socially sensitive. This means research can have implications for those being researched or for other individuals to whom the findings of research are generalised.
- Sensitive topics are where there is risk or where the findings are threatening for someone.
- Research can be socially sensitive if it involves loss of confidentiality, for example, or can lead people to experience stigma or labelling.
- Socially sensitive research is any research which poses a threat to those involved in it.

Explore

You can hear more about socially sensitive research using this YouTube link:

www.youtube.com/watch?v=PM_hoZW6k-E

Table 6.17 The five classic studies linked to issues related to socially sensitive research

Issues related to socially sensitive research				
Sherif et al. (1954/1961)	**Baddeley (1966b)**	**Raine et al. (1997)**	**Watson and Rayner (1920)**	**Rosenhan (1973)**
Prejudice can be seen as a socially sensitive topic in psychology. If it is found that a particular personality is more likely to be prejudiced (such as the right wing authoritarian personality as Cohrs et al. (2012) suggest), then that can pose a threat to those individuals.	Memory is not really socially sensitive as a topic in psychology.	If people pleading not guilty by reason of insanity are not seen as responsible for their actions because of different brain functioning, this might pose a threat to others or to the people themselves, if scanning does not show that result.	Classical conditioning principles can be used by people to condition other people to have a phobia, for example, or can condition other reflex responses.	The area of mental health and mental disorders is socially sensitive as individuals may have their liberty restricted, for example, according to what is known about their mental health.
Sherif showed that prejudice comes more from the situation, such as competition over resources, which is less threatening to each individual. Prejudice and discrimination pose a threat to individuals so knowing more about reducing prejudice is useful.	Some memory studies might need sensitivity, such as Sebastián and Hernández-Gil (2012), who looked at older people having a much shorter digit span, which might be upsetting for them to know about.	Knowing more about how the brain works can be helpful to individuals but is an area that seems to be a sensitive one. This relates to finding out about responsibility for one's actions, which may be a sensitive area.	This gives power to one person over another, which means there is a threat to someone.	The participants in Rosenhan's study had their liberty restricted and were labelled mentally ill when they were not, which is an illustration of how people can be threatened in some way. This signals social sensitivity as it links to social rules.
	Baddeley found out that LTM had a semantic basis and STM an acoustic basis, which on the face of it does not seem to be a threat to individuals or wider society.		Little Albert was caused distress and fear in the study, which suggests the research was socially sensitive. Conditioning can lead to distress for society's members.	

Test yourself

Using two classic studies in your course, assess how far psychology involves social sensitivity. (**12 marks**)

Comparing the classic studies

Having looked at the 11 issues and debates in relation to the five classic studies, you should now be able to compare the classic studies. You could compare them with respect to how they illustrate each issue and debate, which in a way is done for you in this chapter. You could compare them with regard to their ethics, for example, or how far they illustrate psychology as a science. You could compare them with regard to their methodology or their areas of research. You could compare them with regard to their usefulness for society.

There are many different ways you could be asked to compare the classic studies. In this section just some of these ways are illustrated. Your exam will aim to

test you on material you have not necessarily prepared, so be ready to use your all of your knowledge and understanding to inform answers you may not have thought of beforehand.

What follows aims to give you some comparison points and also to help you plan how you will answer questions about classic studies. Remember as well to prepare to use the classic study in the option you chose. In this next section the comparisons relate to methodology.

Comparing studies according to their methodology

Methodology covers a lot of different issues, as you will know.

 The 'Psychological skills – methods' section online goes through the method issues in your course and you can refer to that section or the glossary if a methodological issue is mentioned here that you need to know more about.

One way of comparing studies is thinking about how they are reported, because there is a sequence in the reporting that can help to structure comparisons.

Studies can be compared in terms of the following:

- The background material that gives rise to the research question, which means comparing them in terms of the area of research, which might work if their focus is similar.
- The aims can be compared, perhaps focusing on the research question, as that can lead to comparisons about the chosen research methods and design.
- The method can be compared, first, in terms of their sampling techniques and participants.
- The method can also be compared in terms of the materials used, the design of the study (including the main research method) and also the procedure and what was done.
- The results can be compared either in themselves or in terms of the analysis that was undertaken, such as using percentages, inferential statistics or thematic analysis.
- Their conclusions can be compared either in terms of the actual conclusions in their chosen research area or in terms of strengths and limitations of the studies.

Here, method issues are considered first, including, the research methods and the design of the study, then the choice of data collection tools and, finally, sampling issues and participants. Then evaluation points are considered in terms of strengths and limitations, including comparing the classic studies in terms of validity, reliability and generalisability. You could consider objectivity/subjectivity and credibility as well, although because these ideas are found within the issue of psychology as a science, they are not considered here.

> **STUDY HINT**
> If you are comparing studies you will have a list of issues that can inform any comparison of general methodological issues. This list will be useful for making comparison points if you are presented with novel studies in your exam and asked to make comparison points. For example, research method, data collection tools and sampling decisions are three useful areas to focus on.

Aim, area of interest and research question	Research method and design – and reliability	Sampling and participants – and generalisability
Data collection methods and types of data – and validity	Analysis procedures and results	Issues and debates in psychology, such as how far the study is 'scientific'

Method issues that can be used when comparing studies

> **STUDY HINT**
> When asked to consider a study in psychology, it is worth looking at evaluation points – the main ones are validity, reliability, generalisability, objectivity/subjectivity and credibility; ethics is another. If you cannot think of how to comment on a study, run through these evaluation features as they might help you to get started on an answer.

Research method choice

Experiment

Sherif *et al.* (1954/1961) (in the main), Baddeley (1966b), Raine *et al.* (1997) and Watson and Rayner (1920) all used experiments. Baddeley (1966b) and Watson and Rayner (1920) used an artificial setting which was not natural to the participants. Though it could be argued that in Watson and Rayner's case the hospital was Little Albert's home, the two places the study took place in were not really his normal setting. Raine *et al.* (1997) went to where the PET scanning took place, which was not a place they set up but on the other hand was not natural for the participants either. Sherif *et al.* carried out a field experiment/ study where the boys were in a Summer Camp, which was a realistic setting for them – though still not their natural environment as such. Sherif *et al.*'s field study, though experimental in a way because groups were set up and an experiment took place (to do with counting beans), had elements that were not experimental – such as using a lot of observation and letting the boys have a say in the competitions that were set up.

- These four studies have in common the use of the experimental method and the use of a setting that was not really the participants' natural setting, although Sherif *et al.*'s study was more than just an experiment and was a field study. Rosenhan's study was more like a set of case studies, so was different, though Watson and Rayner also used a single case and a set up procedure, and there were similarities between Rosenhan's and Watson and Rayner's studies.

> **STUDY HINT**
> In what is written here about research methods and the five studies, first, the research method of each is considered. Though the five studies are considered they are not at this stage always directly compared. You need to be sure to make explicit comparisons, as shown in the bullet point(s) after the examination of each method point.

Non-experimental

As has been said, Sherif *et al.*'s Robbers Cave study had elements that were non-experimental. They used a field study that involved an experiment but also involved more qualitative data, such as noting down the names the boys used to refer to one another. Experiments gather quantitative data. Raine *et al.* measured brain areas and brain activity, which is quantitative and Baddeley's DV was the number of words recalled out of a list of ten words and they had to be recalled in the right order. Watson and Rayner used careful controls in their study, but their data tended to have a qualitative element, such as recording crying, reaching out or falling over. Rosenhan's study set up a situation in which eight participants, used in 12 hospitals, presented themselves at a hospital with their script; after which they had to behave normally and there was no script. Data were qualitative in being about their experiences.

- Three of the studies gather qualitative data in some way, which makes them non-experimental to that extent. These are Rosenhan (1973), Watson and Rayner (1920) and Sherif *et al.* (1954/1961).

Progress check 6.11

Which two studies can be said to be experimental in nature and can also be said to be non-experimental, and why?

STUDY HINT

You will find that studies often do not fit into research methods very well. For example, though Milgram did experiments he also gathered qualitative data concerning the reactions of the participants to the orders they received. In psychology be ready to offer arguments to make points as it is not often that you can make clear statements about methodology in a particular study.

Explore

You can access Watson and Rayner's report on their study with Little Albert using this link:

http://psychclassics.yorku.ca/Watson/emotion.htm

You can see that it is called an experimental test. Read the study in full to see what comparisons you can make with one or more of the other classic studies used in your course.

Study design

Raine *et al.* (1997) used an independent groups design and one of the groups was a control group where there was quite a bit of matching to make the comparison suitable. Sherif *et al.* (1954/1961) also used an independent groups design as the two groups of boys were different, although they too used careful matching to make comparisons between the two groups meaningful. Watson and Rayner (1920) used a single case design and Rosenhan (1973) used a case study approach in a way, with eight people in twelve different hospitals writing up their experiences. Baddeley (1966b) used an independent groups design in that one person just learned one of the four lists. However, when Baddeley compared the learning over the four trials and the recall at each trial with the recall after 15 or 20 minutes, that was a repeated measures design as the same person was being compared. None of the studies was longitudinal, though it could be argued that Little Albert was studied over quite a while to see how long the conditioning lasted, so there was an element of the study being done over time. Baddeley used control lists to give baseline measures and Raine *et al.* used a control group as a baseline measure. The other three studies did not use controls in that sense.

- Only Baddeley used a repeated measures design (as part of the study), while Raine *et al.* and Sherif *et al.* used independent groups (with the participants being well-matched). Watson and Rayner used a single case design and Rosenhan used one person in each hospital as well, though eight people overall.
- Raine *et al.* (1997) and Baddeley (1966b) used control groups to get baseline data; the others did not.
- Though Watson and Rayner studied Little Albert over a little while to see how long conditioning would last, so there was an element of a longitudinal design, none of the studies used a fully longitudinal design.

STUDY HINT

You can see that it is not easy to make categorical claims about studies. Someone might say that Watson and Rayner did use a longitudinal design, while another person might think the study did not last long enough for that. You do not need to make such decisions, just be sure to present the arguments. If you are asked to 'evaluate', 'assess', 'explain' or respond to a question 'to what extent ...?' then you need to come to a judgement. You can, however, say that having looked at the arguments it is hard to decide.

Data collection tools

None of the studies used a questionnaire or an interview. Sherif *et al.* used participant observation as well as an experiment, tape recordings and analysis of friendship groups. Raine *et al.* used PET scanning, though none of the others used scanning, and Baddeley used recall of a list of words (in the right order) as his data. Watson and Rayner made careful notes and films to show Little Albert's reaction to the various conditions he was put into. Rosenhan's participants made notes and wrote things down to indicate what happened to them in each of the hospitals. The data collection tools are all different and the different means of collecting data reflect the differences in their research questions, as does the differences in their use of research method and the designs of their studies.

- The data collection tools are all different, some gathering qualitative data and some gathering quantitative data, for example. The differences reflect the different research questions and areas of study.

Participants and sampling issues

Sherif *et al.* used 11-year-old boys and started with 22 of them, whereas Rosenhan used eight colleagues in his study. Baddeley carried out three experiments within his main study, two with four conditions and one with two conditions. In each condition he tended to have about 20 participants. The three experiments had different participants, the first one having young servicemen, the second having housewives and the third having both males and females from a subject pool. Raine *et al.* used 'murderers' in their experimental condition, or at least people pleading not guilty by reason of insanity (NGRI) and took 41 people who happened to be going to have a PET scan as part of their defence. Then Raine *et al.* put together a control group, matching the control group with the experimental group in various ways. Watson and Rayner chose a baby who did not have a phobia and made sure he was calm and placid, unlikely to be too upset by the procedures. With regard to sampling, Rosenhan was asking quite a bit of his participants so he used colleagues, himself and people he knew. Watson and Rayner had to be careful regarding ethics and chose a child they thought would be suitable. Raine *et al.* used the people who were pleading NGRI and having PET scanning. So sampling was not random and not that planned, to an extent. They tended to take volunteers and people who were available. Sherif *et al.* also did not use random sampling; they had to take those who were willing and whose parents were willing.

- All five classic studies used different types of sample and did not use random sampling, but had to take who they could get to an extent.

> **STUDY HINT**
> You have learned about different sampling techniques but you can see that not all studies are able to use sampling techniques clearly. However, Dickens *et al.* (2011) used random sampling as well as some stratification to get their sample of respondents for their questions. You can use these examples when discussing such issues. (Though Dickens *et al.* had to have a lot of their respondents excluded because of not being judged competent to consent to the study, so the random sampling was affected by that decision.)

Evaluation issues relating to method
Validity

Qualitative data tend to be more valid because they are detailed and have depth so might be more about the real life of the participant than the possibly more artificial quantitative data. For example, Baddeley's data, which were number of words out of ten recalled in order, can be said not to represent short-term or long-term memory so can be said to be not valid. However, recall of words in order is about memory so to that extent there is validity. Generally data from experiments like Baddeley's are seen as not valid. Raine *et al.*, however, used PET scans of brains in action and controlled what the participants were doing at the time of the scan too, so that the scans could be compared. Though experimental, Raine *et al.*'s study used scans of people's brains in action so to an extent the data are valid. It could be claimed that the stress of the situation (e.g. being scanned) might affect the brain functioning, though, which leads to accusations of lack of validity in the findings. Sherif *et al.* used many different ways of collecting data and allowed the boys to make decisions about their groups. The data from the different methods matched so there was validity claimed. The situation was reasonably natural, again supporting the likelihood that the data were valid. Rosenhan studied the artificially set-up situation where someone was wrongly diagnosed with schizophrenia and admitted to hospital, which suggests a lack of validity. However, they were in real hospitals and once there acted normally so the findings do seem to have validity. Watson and Rayner, like Rosenhan, used an artificial situation in instilling a phobia in a small boy, although the way it was done could be said to be as it might occur in real life so there was an element of validity. Watson and Rayner were present and filming, so the baby might have been stressed by that situation rather than by the fear he had learned. Then again, he did play happily with blocks, which suggests the crying was because of fear.

- There is doubt about the validity of many of the classic studies. However, Rosenhan seemed to be able to claim some validity in his findings, as did Sherif *et al.* The other three studied might be said not to have validity because of issues such as the participants feeling stress which affected the data (Raine *et al.* and Watson and Rayner) or because the study was very artificial (Baddeley).

> **Progress check 6.12**
> Explain, using at least two of the classic studies considered here, how stress in a study situation can affect data and findings.

Reliability

Experiments tend to be reliable because they are well set up with controls and detail and so can be replicated. Raine *et al.*'s study was clearly set up, including using a control group and the findings seem to be reliable. Even if stress due to the situation caused differences in brain activity that would affect validity but not reliability as the same stress might occur again, giving the same findings. Baddeley's work was replicable and reliable. Indeed his three experiments within the main study supported one another and showed reliability. Sherif *et al.*'s field study was hard to replicate as it involved a lot of personnel and a lot of effort so it is hard to test for reliability. Having said that, the different ways of gathering data, showing the same findings, were a way of giving the study reliability. Rosenhan did repeat his procedure because eight participants went separately into twelve hospitals so his study had reliability. Also in a second part to the study hospitals who were told that some pseudo-patients might arrive thought they identified pseudo-patients when there were none, which backs up Rosenhan's main finding that 'sanity' is not identified in a mental health hospital and gives the finding reliability. Watson and Rayner also did their own replications to some extent, as they used many variations of the conditioning, including a dog, a rabbit, fur and so on, always giving a fear response, so their findings seemed to have reliability.

- Watson and Rayner (1920), Baddeley (1966b) and Rosenhan (1973) did replications within their study and showed that their findings were reliable. Sherif *et al.*'s (1954/1961) study was not easily replicated, although they used different data gathering methods and data matched so it was said the data were reliable. Raine *et al.* (1997) had a replicable study and so data could be tested for reliability. All the studies seemed to be able to claim reliability.

Generalisability

Watson and Rayner (1920) used one baby in their study and it is hard to generalise from one participant to say that everyone can be conditioned using classical conditioning principles to have a phobia. Rosenhan (1973) used eight different people who were all treated in a similar way, so perhaps the findings were generalisable to others with schizophrenia. However, the eight people did not have schizophrenia, which might limit the generalisability. Also the study was done in one culture with a specific view of mental disorders, which might limit the generalisability to other cultures. Baddeley (1966b) used a variety of different people in his three experiments so his findings are reasonably likely to be generalisable, although as he used different samples in the three experiments that might raise

questions about the generalisability. Raine *et al.* (1997) claimed that at that time theirs was the largest sample for such a study and they claimed generalisability. Sherif *et al.* (1954/1961) used just boys so perhaps the results are not generalisable to girls or adults – or to different situations other than different groups in a Summer Camp.

- All five studies have problems with generalisability, though some of the studies have more generalisable findings than others, depending on the sample used and the situation.

Progress check 6.13

Which of these features of a study is the most important when considering its generalisability?

a How objective the study is.
b The research design used.
c How data are collected.
d The sample used, including the sampling technique.

> **STUDY HINT**
> Use the section comparing five classic studies in your course to review your understanding of validity, reliability and generalisability.

Test yourself

Compare three classic studies in your course in terms of their generalisability. **(8 marks)**

Focus on unseen studies

In the exam you need to be ready to apply your knowledge and understanding, as well as your evaluation skills, to studies that you have not seen before and this section will to help you to practise doing that. Your learning about the classic studies, method issues and issues and debates can help you when focusing on unseen studies.

It is not possible to know what might be on your exam paper with regard to unseen studies, so we have chosen two studies that are different from the five classic studies, so that other issues can be discussed. For each, the study is briefly presented before issues around understanding the study, evaluating it and synoptic issues are examined.

Unseen Study One

The first choice is a study looking at the effectiveness of a ten-week selective desensitisation programme focusing on reducing anxiety that comes from technophobia (fear of computers). The study is chosen because it focuses on a phobia, it has a practical application (fearing computers can affect educational achievements), it uses a control group as a baseline and it focuses on material you have covered (systematic desensitisation to help a phobia). The study was done by Brosnan and Thorpe in 2006.

Outline of the study

Eight North American students were found to be suffering from technophobia and the study used eight matched non-anxious controls. The eight students had volunteered to take part in a Technophobia Reduction Programme (TRP) and controls were matched for age, sex, ethnicity and academic level.

All participants at the start of the study completed a questionnaire to find out about their phobic beliefs and coping. They also completed another assessment using items from DSM-IV criteria for anxiety. This meant that all participants had a phobic beliefs score and a level of anxiety score before the treatment. Both assessments focused on fear of computers (technophobia).

The TRP followed systematic desensitisation principles, with each person developing their own hierarchy of imagined scenes through to high anxiety situations and then learning to relax at each stage of the hierarchy.

At the end of the programme the two measures were again taken to get a phobic belief score and an anxiety score for all participants. All participants were 'fully debriefed'. The controls had no intervention but the measures were taken before the TRP (which just the treatment group underwent) and afterwards too. At the end of the study, faculty members gathered qualitative data reflecting experiences of the treatment.

Progress check 6.14

What was the purpose of the control group?

Table 6.18 shows some of the mean scores (with standard deviation in brackets) from Brosnan and Thorpe (2006).

Table 6.18 Effectiveness of a ten-week selective desensitisation programme focusing on reducing anxiety that comes from technophobia: Brosnan and Thorpe (2006)

Measure	Technophobes	Controls
Anxiety at the start	19.4 (13.5)	54.0 (26.8)
Coping at the start	50.2 (17.7)	66.7 (17.6)
Anxiety at the end	44.3 (21.2)	55.9 (25.4)
Coping at the end	64.3 (21.3)	63.4 (11.3)

Both qualitative and quantitative data led to the conclusion that using a systematic desensitisation programme helped with a phobia of computers.

Technophobia is fear of computers and systematic desensitisation can help to reduce anxiety and improve coping with such a fear.

Understanding the study

The first thing you need to do is to understand the study.

- This is a study of the effectiveness of a treatment and as is common in such studies it uses a treatment group and a control group.
- The control group is matched with the treatment group, undertakes the same measures before and after the treatment and the only difference is that they undertake no treatment.
- You have studied systematic desensitisation as a treatment for phobias so you should understand the treatment that was received.
- The questionnaire asking about their phobia and the questions about anxiety both gave a score, which meant both the treatment and the control group had two scores at the start of the treatment and two scores at the end.
- The control group gave a baseline measure, so that it would be known what people without the phobia would score on the measures used.
- The study was done in North America and students were used, which might be important when drawing conclusions, and there were just eight people with the phobia.
- There are both qualitative and quantitative data, which means descriptive statistics can be used to display the data (such as the mean score, which is the one reported), but also some comments are available for the reader to judge the success of the programme.
- This is an independent groups design as there is a treatment and a control group.

Progress check 6.15

What is the value of the qualitative data?

Evaluating the study

Validity

Having the qualitative data helps to add validity as it comprises statements directly from the participants saying how helpful the programme of treatment was. The quantitative data backs this up, again adding to validity.

Reliability

The control group is carefully planned and having the baseline scores both at the start and the end help with interpreting the quantitative data. The control group's scores remain similar before and after so that suggests reliability, and the treatment group scores at the end of the programme are similar to the control group scores, again suggesting reliability. However, having just eight people in each condition does perhaps suggest that repeating the study to test for reliability would be useful.

Progress check 6.16

What is meant when it is said that data are reliable?

Generalisability

It is not easy to get people with a specific phobia and just eight people were in the treatment group, which is worth noting when it comes to thinking about the generalisability of the study. Also the treatment group consisted of students, who might have more fear of computers or perhaps think they have a fear of computers, so perhaps the results can only be generalised to students who have a fear of computers. The study was done in North America. There might be cultural differences there with regard to use of computers and to do with the programme. The students might be familiar with the idea of gradual desensitisation, for example, and it might suit their understanding of fear and anxiety, which might not be the case in other cultures.

Synoptic issues relating to the study

In your course synoptic issues focusing on psychology concern having a broad focus and looking at wider issues. In your course 11 issues and debates are listed to illustrate synopticity in psychology, and the methodological issues discussed in this chapter also take a synoptic view.

Overview of psychology as covered in your course

- Methodology is seen as very important because we need to know that study findings are worth building upon. Therefore, evaluation issues like the validity, reliability and generalisability of study findings are also important when considering psychology, which is the study of mind and behaviour.

- The issue of psychology as science links to methodology issues because science is given a status that non-science does not have. Scientific method – having a theory, deriving a hypothesis, testing against data and then accepting the theory or rejecting or amending it – is given credence in our culture. This is about credibility of data and gathering empirical evidence as well as focusing on falsifiability (which means focusing on testing something that can be found to be false, otherwise there is no value in testing it).

- Nature and nurture are important focuses as well, as it is acknowledged that people are partly their nature (biology) and partly their nurture (their experiences and environment). Psychology focuses both on brain functioning and biology and on environmental influences. Environmental influences include culture and gender, which both involve learned norms. Gender has a biological aspect too.

- The uses of psychological understanding are important to researchers. Psychology can be studied for the sake of understanding mind and behaviour, but often it is studied to the purpose of improving lives, which can involve helping society as well as individuals.

- Psychological knowledge itself, such as all the theories and themes, and how they fit together, builds a body of knowledge and has value.

There are 11 issues and debates in your course, and just five synoptic areas here, but the 11 issues and debates can be fitted into these five areas, as Table 6.19 shows.

Table 6.19 Main synoptic areas and how the 11 issues and debates fit into them

Five main synoptic areas	Issues and debates required for the A level course
Methodology	Ethical issues in research (animal and human)
	Practical issues in the design and implementation of research
Psychology as a science	Reductionism in the explanation of behaviour
	Psychology as a science
Nature and nurture	Cultural and gender issues in psychological research
	The role of both nature and nurture in psychology
Emphasis on the use of psychology for society and for the individual	The use of psychology in social control
	The use of psychological knowledge in society
	Issues related to socially sensitive research
Building a body of knowledge in psychology	An understanding of how psychological understanding has developed over time
	Comparisons of ways of explaining behaviour using different themes

Issues and debates are examined more closely in Chapter Seven and the five main synoptic areas discussed here are used to sort the issues and debates into a different order. The idea is that seeing them in a different order can help you to understand them. This means that Chapter Seven will help your review of the studies explained here in Chapter Six.

Progress check 6.17

What is the importance of the nature–nurture debate in psychology?

Unseen Study One and synoptic issues

1 Methodological issues relating to Unseen Study One have been discussed.

2 The issue of psychology as a science can be seen in this study. There is a strong focus on science, including having a control group as well as a treatment group so that there is a baseline measure to set any improvements against. There is objectivity – for example, the qualitative data are gathered by a Faculty member, not by the researchers. Empirical data (data gathered directly by means of senses) are gathered using the two measures outlined to get a measure of anxiety and of phobic beliefs. The idea that the programme reduces anxiety and increases beliefs about coping can be falsified. The programme might not have improved the scores. Science requires that what is tested can be falsified. There is a theory which the treatment rests on: the idea of systematic desensitisation coming from conditioning principles. Science has a theory from which an idea is derived and then tested against reality, which is what this study does. The study supports the idea that psychology is a science. However, the gathering of qualitative data goes some way to looking at the experience of the whole person rather than reducing the treatment to steps in a hierarchy, so there is an element of going beyond science. Science tends to take a reductionist view.

3 There is no explanation of how the technophobia might have come about but it is unlikely to be from someone's nature and much more likely to be about nurture. Though it might be more about low self-esteem and fear about trying something unfamiliar than about actual computers; low self-esteem might link to temperament, which can be in our nature. Systematic desensitisation assumes that a phobia comes from associating something with something else that naturally gave a fear response. The idea then is to replace the association of computers (in this case) with a fear response with a relaxation response instead. The conditioning of the phobia is

assumed to be environmentally caused, as in the case of Little Albert.

4 Another synoptic point raised in this section about psychology is that it aims to be useful for the individual and/or society. The researchers in Unseen Study One point out at the start of their report that a fear of computers can be disabling for some people, particularly if it affects their education. The participants in this study are students and the assumption is that if they do not get over their fear of computers that will affect their future. This study illustrates how psychology focuses on areas of study that will be of use.

5 Finally, a synoptic focus in psychology is about the desire to build a body of knowledge and to consider what themes are to be studied and what theories are accepted at any one moment in time. Pavlov started the idea of classical conditioning in the 1920s and Watson and Rayner worked in the same time period. From classical conditioning came the idea of using systematic desensitisation to help with reduction of phobias. In 2006 Brosnan and Thorpe carried out a study to see if a programme based on systematic desensitisation would be effective for what can be seen as a 'modern' phobia, a fear of computers. The study shows how psychology has developed over time, perhaps by accepting that qualitative data have value, and contributes to the body of knowledge built in the area of phobias.

STUDY HINT
The analysis of Unseen Study One has hopefully given you an idea of how to make sense of an unseen study, including how to evaluate it and understand it from the view of synoptic issues in psychology. You will need to do the same with studies in your exam, so practise this type of analysis and be ready for any questions drawing on the whole of your course.

Progress check 6.18

Explain one synoptic issue that is illustrated by Unseen Study One.

Unseen Study Two

Unseen Study Two is chosen because it involves qualitative data as well as quantitative data and also because it focuses on a comparatively new issue, internet use and addiction. The study was done in Finland, which offers a perspective on a different culture. The data come from the adolescents themselves, including their feelings about their internet use, which suggests some validity in the findings. There seems to be a clear practical use for this area of study, which links well to synoptic issues. Alongside the collection of qualitative data is the statistical analysis of quantitative data, which shows how in many new studies more than one research method is used, as was the case with Unseen Study One.

Outline of the study

Sinkkonen *et al.* (2013) looked at internet use in 475 adolescents in Finland combining qualitative and quantitative research. Internet addiction (IAD) is measured by how much time is spent on the internet, how preoccupied someone is with it, how much they feel the need to use it, whether they keep trying to stop using it and whether it can mean they stop social relationships. There are other features of internet addiction too.

Adolescents were recruited through university student counsellors who were asked to offer questionnaires to students aged 15 to 19 and to let students complete questionnaires during student counselling lessons. The questionnaire asked about background information, internet use, choice of profession, decision-making related to career choice and self-image. The questionnaire used Likert-type and open-ended questions.

Internet use was measured using the Internet Addiction Test translated into Finnish. A score of 30 or below on the test meant normal internet use, 31 to 49 as a score meant mild over-use and a score of between 50 and 79 meant a moderate addiction to the internet. A score of 80 or more meant a serious addiction.

The results showed that just six students (1.3 per cent) were shown as having serious internet problems, 109 (22.9 per cent) were moderately addicted and 75.8 per cent of total participants had average internet use. The groups were reorganised into moderate or serious over-users (115 students), mild over-users (292 students) and those with normal use (68 of the students). It was found using a Chi squared test that females had more mild internet use than males and males had more moderate over-use than females (p=.033).

Progress check 6.19

In Unseen Study Two what percentages (go to two significant figures) were moderate or serious over-users, what percentage were mild over-users and what percentage had normal usage. Draw up a table to display these figures.

STUDY HINT

Be ready to do calculations in an exam when asked about an unseen study — not just percentages but other calculations as well focusing on both descriptive and inferential statistics.

There were data on the reasons for using the internet and a large percentage said it was for fun (62.3 per cent of those with mild over-use). Others mentioned social reasons (66.4 per cent of those with mild over-use) and some mentioned seeking information (50 per cent of those with mild over-use).

Respondents were asked to describe the harm they experienced because of their internet use using the open questions in the questionnaire. The most common harm was that it was very time-consuming. Social disadvantages were also seen as a 'harm' and social withdrawal could be seen. Some kind of harm was mentioned by 214 students (7.4 per cent of normal users, 62.2 per cent of mild over-users and 30.4 per cent of moderate or serious over-users).

The researchers concluded that the more the internet was used the less the user perceived its harmful effects, which seems to be like any other addiction, showing tolerance so more of a 'dose' gives a weaker effect. They felt there was evidence of internet addiction, which showed similar issues to other forms of addiction.

Understanding the study

The study used questionnaire data involving Likert-type questions, such as giving statements and the respondents having to indicate their answer using a scale of: strongly agree, agree, don't know, disagree and strongly disagree. This gave quantitative data. The questionnaire also used open questions to get qualitative data about reasons for internet use and ideas about harm they saw in their internet use. There was a separate test that gave each respondent an internet use score. The score was used to categorise respondents into three main categories – normal use of the internet, mild over-use and moderate to severe use.

Progress check 6.20

Likert-type scales give ratings such as 'strongly agree'. What level of measurement is being used?

There was a large sample and both males and females were used, with a significant difference in gender and internet use, with males having more moderate over-use and females having more mild usage. The sample was of a particular age range (15 to 19 year olds) and consisted of Finnish adolescents in school/university. The sample was a volunteer/ self-selected sample in that only those willing to complete the questionnaire would have taken part. The researchers themselves did not know much about how the sampling was done. They gave instructions about how to administer the questionnaire but were not there to check who responded and who did not, so there might have been sample bias.

Progress check 6.21

What are some advantages of using a volunteer/self-selected sample?

The results showed a wide variety of internet use with very few of the adolescents showing severe internet addiction. They did, however, indicate that they saw harm in their internet use, though the closer they were to severe usage the less they saw the harm. The researchers felt they had found out that the users did see the internet as doing harm and that internet use for some did match what was expected of other addictions.

> **STUDY HINT**
>
> When trying to understand an unseen study go through the same features of a study as were listed earlier when thinking of how a report is written up. Consider the aim(s) of the study, the participants and sampling. Look at the procedure and the materials used to gather the data. Consider the design if appropriate and also the results and how analysis took place. Finally, consider the conclusions and possibly strengths and limitations with the study as well as whether there are practical applications. You could make yourself a checklist.

Evaluating the study

Validity

The study asked the young people directly about their internet use, including asking open questions to get qualitative data with richness and detail. Data gathered in this way should be valid. However, a questionnaire can show social desirability. Perhaps the young people had someone with them when they were completing the questionnaire and they wanted to 'look good', which would mean data would not be valid.

Reliability

To show reliability the study would need to be repeated. It was replicable because standardised questionnaires were used and the procedure for giving out the questionnaires is quite well detailed. Until the study is repeated reliability cannot be claimed. The researchers merged the different groups as measured by the Internet Addiction Test into different groups, which might have affected how findings were summarised and presented, possibly affecting reliability. However, the way they did the merging was given in the study, which does give replicability.

Generalisability

The sample was adolescents only so the findings are generalisable only to that age group. Also they were a Finnish sample and the internet is used widely in Finland as the population can be very spread out (if not located in the city). There might be cultural differences with internet use that meant that the findings can only be generalised within Finland. Also the researchers were not sure who had refused to take part and whether that meant the sample had bias, which raises questions about generalisability.

Synoptic issues relating to the study

1 Methodological issues relating to Unseen Study Two have been discussed to an extent when explaining the study and when evaluating the study; for example, discussing the sampling used. This study gives an example of using a Likert-type scale as well as demonstrating the use of open-ended questions on a questionnaire. There is use of a Chi squared test as well, so this study is useful as an example of that. Percentages are used to display the data. A volunteer and self-selected sample is used. Unseen Study Two covers issues you have learned about in your course.

2 The issue of psychology as a science can be seen in this study to an extent, though the data are gathered by means of questionnaire and test and there are no controls as there are in experiments. The questionnaires are standardised ones, which helps with finding out whether data are reliable and also helps to show a scientific approach to research because the questionnaires would have included a pilot study when they were first used and some reliability would be built in. There is credibility in asking the young people directly about their actual internet use and also their reasons for using the internet and their ideas about harm it might do. There is less science in how the respondents were recruited and the researchers themselves say the uncertainty of their sample is a weakness. They also felt they should have asked about using the internet via smartphones, which they did not do. So there were elements of the study that were not scientific. There may be a lack of objectivity in how the sample was recruited; there might also be an element of subjectivity in the responses if there was social desirability.

3 There is no suggestion in this study that internet addiction is anything but something learned through the widespread availability of the internet. Addiction has been talked about in terms of it being inherited, but this study does not focus on that element of addiction and it is not really about nurture either. The study is more a description of the amount of internet use, the reasons the users gave for using the internet and ideas about harm that might arise from using the internet.

The study is not really looking for explanations in terms of nature or nurture.

4   The research clearly has use for the individual if they see that their internet use is scored as either moderate or severe over-use. Internet addiction is a disorder and if someone realises their usage is enough to fit into the 'symptoms' of that disorder they may decide to seek help. Society can also benefit from studies considering reasons for internet use and over-use and the harm that can be caused, because if individuals experience harm this may lead to a cost to society. For example, if school work suffers because of internet use that has implications for the future workforce.

Knowing more about internet addiction can be beneficial for society as it can bring harm to the user, such as social withdrawal.

5   Finally, a synoptic focus in psychology is about the desire to build a body of knowledge and to consider what themes are to be studied and what theories are accepted at any one moment in time. The outline of the study here does not go into detail about the theory behind the study but in the study itself there is information about internet addiction and there is some mention here of the features of internet addiction. The study uses what is known about internet addiction, including a measure of internet addiction, so is building a body of knowledge about this area. The internet is still comparatively new and so there will not be a body of knowledge about it going back a long way, which means it is not easy to show the development of psychology over time, except perhaps to show that as society and technology change, so psychology brings in new areas of research in response to such changes.

Test yourself

Find a study using the internet. For example, put 'dementia research study' into a search engine and look at any scholarly articles suggested. You might see one by Prince *et al.* (2003) about diagnosis of dementia in developing countries. Or use a different focus such as 'brain functioning research study', where you might find Davidson *et al.* (2003), who looked at brain and immune function changes that come from mindfulness meditation.

1   Using a study you have found write about the participants and the sampling technique. **(4 marks)**
2   Evaluate a study you have found in terms of validity and reliability. **(4 marks)**
3   To what extent does the study you have found show that psychology is a science? **(8 marks)**

Summary

- When reviewing studies in your course, focus on the classic studies. These include four classic studies from Year One which looked at foundations of psychology and covered social, cognitive and biological psychology as well as learning theories. There is also a classic study in clinical psychology. These five are the main classic studies — the final one is the classic study from the application that is chosen from criminological, child and health psychology.
- The four classic studies from your Year One learning are Sherif *et al.* (1954/1961) from social psychology, Baddeley (1966b) from cognitive psychology, Raine *et al.* (1997) from biological psychology and Watson and Rayner (1920) from learning theories.
- The classic study in clinical psychology is Rosenhan (1973).
- Criminological, child and health psychology, which you will study one of, each have one classic study.
- You need to draw on the classic studies and to compare them.
- You also need to review them synoptically using the 11 issues and debates for your course.
- Finally, you need to be able to understand, evaluate and review synoptically any unseen studies you are presented with in an examination.

Chapter Seven: Psychological skills – issues and debates

Psychological skills is Topic Nine in your course and can be seen as a revision topic. There are three sections to this topic, covered in the online Appendix and in Chapters Six and Seven of this book, as shown in Table 7.1.

Table 7.1 Psychological skills sections and related chapters

Section	Chapter
1 Review of method material	(W) Online material
2 Review of studies	Chapter Six
3 Issues and debates	Chapter Seven

What 'issues and debates' mean in your course

Psychological skills is a topic area at the end of your course which will help you to revise for your A level exams. The online Appendix goes through the method requirements and Chapter Six reviews the classic studies you covered in Year One and in clinical psychology. These two sections will help with your revision of this topic.

In section three of Psychological skills you will cover 11 issues and debates and relate the material in your course to these issues and debates. The aim of this section is to draw together your knowledge and understanding of what you have learned in your course and to consider it within the wider picture of psychology. Table 7.2 lists the issues and debates that are covered in this section.

Table 7.2 Issues and debates in the A level course

Issues and debates in the A level course	
1	Ethical issues in research (animal and human)
2	Practical issues in the design and implementation of research
3	Reductionism in the explanation of behaviour
4	Comparisons of ways of explaining behaviour using different themes
5	Psychology as a science
6	Cultural and gender issues in psychological research
7	The role of both nature and nurture in psychology
8	An understanding of how psychological understanding has developed over time
9	The use of psychology in social control
10	The use of psychological knowledge in society
11	Issues related to socially sensitive research

In this chapter, the 11 issues and debates are presented in five areas, though they are still covered separately. The five areas are shown in Table 7.3.

Table 7.3 The five areas of the issues and debates

Five main synoptic areas	Issues and debates in the A level course
Methodology	• Ethical issues in research (animal and human) • Practical issues in the design and implementation of research
Psychology as a science	• Reductionism in the explanation of behaviour • Psychology as a science
Nature and nurture	• Cultural and gender issues in psychological research • The role of both nature and nurture in psychology
Emphasis on the use of psychology for society and for the individual	• The use of psychology in social control • The use of psychological knowledge in society • Issues related to socially sensitive research
Building a body of knowledge in psychology	• An understanding of how psychological understanding has developed over time • Comparisons of ways of explaining behaviour using different themes

Methodology

Method has such importance in psychology, because what we know, or think we know, must be backed by evidence that can be trusted. Findings from studies must be acceptable and accepted before they can be used. Studying method in psychology is about finding information to answer research questions and understanding how useful that information is.

Few conclusions can be drawn from seeing a young woman using her phone while standing by a pushchair. We don't even know that this is the child's mother, though we would probably assume it is. There is more to gathering data in psychology than one observation.

When carrying out studies in psychology there are practical and also ethical issues to consider.

Ethical issues in research (animal and human)

Research in psychology must follow ethical guidelines and in the UK the British Psychological Society (BPS) guidelines are followed. Different countries have different guidelines but the basic requirement, which is to protect participants, is the same.

Here is a summary of the ethical principles and guidelines you have covered in your course:

- Social psychology: you have looked at the four ethical principles of respect, responsibility, integrity and competence in the BPS Code of Ethics and Conduct (2009). Issues include giving the right to withdraw, getting informed consent as far as possible, not deceiving participants (as far as possible), giving a full debrief and taking care to maintain confidentiality and privacy.
- Social psychology: you have looked at the management of risk, which is an important element in planning and carrying out a study in psychology.

- Learning theories: you have covered ethical principles when using animals in research in psychology, focusing on the Animals (Scientific Procedures) Act 1986. These principles include a licence requirement; the researcher, the research project, the place the study takes place in and where the animals are kept all require licences. Other issues include the caging of animals and how they are kept, endangered species and choosing suitable species and what is being done to the animal. A cost–benefit analysis can help in deciding whether a study using animals should go ahead. The cost to the animals must be less than the benefits from the research and the study needs to be sound, because the results must be credible and acceptable.
- Clinical psychology: you have covered the Health and Care Professions Council guidelines. The HCPC is the body that governs practising psychologists and has the power to take their title away if there is wrong-doing.
- Criminological psychology: if you chose this option, you will have revisited the BPS Code of Ethics and Conduct (2009) as well as the HCPC principles for undertaking formulation and intervention with offenders.
- Child psychology: if you chose this option, you will have looked at the ethics of researching with children, including the United Nations Convention on the Rights of the Child (1989) and participation and protection rights. The research must be *with* children, not *on* children; they are participants, not subjects or objects of study and they can be fellow researchers.
- Health psychology: if you chose this option, you will have covered the ethics of using both animals and humans in research in psychology to study drugs.

Table 7.4 summarises the ethics that must be studied in your course (italics means there is a choice).

Table 7.4 Ethics that must be studied in your course (italics means there is a choice)

Topic area	Ethics that must be studied
Social psychology	• BPS Code of Ethics and Conduct (2009) • Risk management
Learning theories	• Animals (Scientific Procedures) Act 1986
Clinical psychology	• HCPC guidelines for psychologists
Criminological psychology	• *BPS Code of Ethics and Conduct (2009)* • *HCPC guidelines for psychologists*
Child psychology	• *Ethics when researching with children* • *UNCRC (1989) and protection/participation rights*
Health psychology	• *Ethics when using animals and humans to study drugs*

Explaining the ethics of using humans in research in psychology

Although your course focuses on the BPS Code of Ethics and Conduct (2009), you can find out more about using humans in research in psychology by looking at the Code of Human Research Ethics (2014). You will see that the underpinning ideas about working ethically with people do not change.

> ### Explore
> You can access the BPS Code of Human Research Ethics (2014) using this link: **www.bps.org.uk/system/files/ Public%20files/code_of_human_research_ethics_ dec_2014_inf180_web.pdf**

Table 7.5 summarises the key ethical issues that you need to consider when researching in psychology.

Table 7.5 Key ethical issues of research in psychology

BPS Code of Ethics and Conduct main principles	Key ethical issues of research in psychology	
Integrity	Getting informed or valid consent	Offering a debrief
Respect	Giving the right to withdraw	Avoiding deceit
Responsibility	Maintaining privacy	Protecting people from harm, including offering dignity
Competence	Maintaining confidentiality	Maximising benefit and minimising harm
	Allowing independence	Maintaining transparency
	Safeguarding children	Safeguarding people who lack capacity and/or are dependent on others

> **STUDY HINT**
> If you are evaluating a study you should focus on the ethics of the study. You can do this by working through the issues in Table 7.5.

> ### Explore
> You can access an informative section on ethics and frequently asked questions on the BPS website using this link: **www.bps.org.uk/what-we-do/ethics-standards/ethics-qa/ ethics-qa**

Research requiring special focus on ethics

It is important to adhere to ethics when carrying out research in psychology and to work in an institution where there is an ethics committee. Certain types of research must be reviewed by members of the ethics committee, including:

- research with vulnerable groups
- research involving sensitive topics
- research where permission must be given from someone else (a gatekeeper)
- research requiring deception and where fully informed consent cannot be obtained at the start
- research involving access to confidential information or records
- research that would cause stress or anxiety (or pain)
- research where an intervention is intrusive, such as requiring an injection
- research where assessment might reveal problems the person is not aware of (such as a mental disorder).

Four studies to discuss ethics of using humans in research in psychology

The classic studies are discussed in Chapter Six, including focus on ethical issues. Four studies from different topic areas are provided here, so that you can use evidence when considering this issue in relation to what you have covered in your course. You can, of course, choose other studies. It is hard to prepare for the Psychological skills part of your course because there is such a wide variety of questions that can be asked. You can use what is given here as a guide to the sort of preparation you need to do.

1 Milgram's (1963) research (see page 651) still leads to discussions about its ethics, including issues of not properly giving the right to withdraw, not getting informed consent, not preventing harm and distress, but giving a full and careful debrief. You will have studied Milgram's work in social psychology when looking at obedience.

2 Schmolck et al. (2002) studied people with brain damage. They looked at the damage and problems they had with the assumption that the specific damage caused the problems. Schmolck et al. researched vulnerable people, so needed to take special care with getting informed consent and giving the right to withdraw. The study does not explain in detail how consent was obtained from the patients. The eight controls were volunteers and they could be informed about the testing. Schmolck et al. used initials for the

case study patients, which helped with confidentiality. This study is one of three contemporary studies in cognitive psychology and you may have chosen one of the other two. However, you will have looked at Henry Molaison (HM) as a case study of someone with brain damage, and you can apply the ideas here to the study of HM.

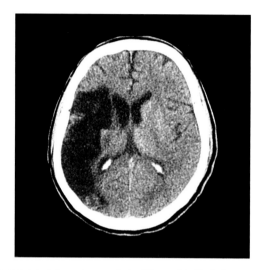

Brain damage (shown here using a CT scan) is likely to cause problems in behaviour and/or processing information and ethics must be carefully adhered to if such people are participants in a psychology study.

3 Bastian *et al.* (2011) asked students to play either a violent or a non-violent video game and then to rate themselves (and others) with regard to their own humanity. Playing the violent video game affected how they saw themselves, which suggests that there was an element of harm done. The students had to take part in the studies as part of their course, which meant they did not give informed consent and did not have the right to withdraw. Students at university often have to sign up to be participants in studies in psychology, which means they are not treated the same as other participants and this may be an ethical issue in such studies. This is one of the contemporary studies in learning theories and you may have chosen Capafóns *et al.* (1998) or Becker *et al.* (2002), both of which have ethical issues so you could prepare your chosen contemporary issue instead.

4 Williams *et al.* (2013) used phone interviews to consider the success of CBT with another imagery-based technique, focusing on depression. They mention in the study that informed consent was gained from all participants. They also explain that although they used a control group whose members did not get the treatment, they made sure that the control group was just a 'wait list' group and that those in the control group had the treatment soon after the end of the study. Ethically it

is hard to have a treatment group and a control group if the control group has to have no treatment, so using a wait list group who will get the treatment soon after the study has ended is a way of having a suitable control group and still treating them ethically. You may not have studied Williams *et al.* either because you did not choose to cover depression as your 'optional' disorder alongside schizophrenia, or because you chose the other contemporary study for depression. You can use that study to discuss ethical issues.

Explaining the ethics of using animals in research in psychology

In your course the focus is on using animals in experiments rather than studying animals in their natural environment.

The British Psychological Society (BPS) has produced a document called 'Guidelines for Psychologists Working with Animals', which covers important issues such as what animals are used, whether efforts have been made to use alternatives, how many animals are used, what is to be done to the animals, how the animals are obtained, how they are cared for and how they are disposed of.

The American Psychological Association (APA) provides this list of guidelines for psychologists researching with animals using the experimental method:

- Comply with regulations and professional standards.
- Be sure those handling animals and caring for them have competence to do so.
- Minimise discomfort, distress and pain.
- Look for alternative methods before using painful or stressful procedures and be sure the results are of sufficient benefit to warrant the 'cost' to the animal.

You can see that the APA and the BPS have similar standards. The ethics of using animals in experiments are clearly laid down in order to protect the animal(s) as far as possible.

Research requiring special focus on ethics

- Some research cannot be done with humans or in any other way, such as using a computer simulation; for example, research into brain functioning which is carried out with the purpose of improving the lives of individuals, such as those with mental disorders such as depression. Drug treatment can be developed from knowledge from animal studies. Using the three Rs can help to make research using animals more ethical: *reduction* in the number of animals used and sharing information with other researchers; *refinement* so that procedures are less invasive perhaps or living conditions for the animals are better; *replacement* by using computer models or human volunteers so animals are not used. Research looking at brain functioning is special because it is going to involve painful procedures and damage to the animals, which to some people is unacceptable.
- Studies that require endangered species are special because they are protected. Endangered species, however, are not used for research in psychology.
- In some special cases, animals are used for research, yet the findings are to be applied to humans. Using a cost–benefit analysis, possibly such studies should not be carried out; the benefits are dubious as generalising from the study is not useful. There would have to be a special case for using animals that do not represent humans – unless the animals were being studied for their own sakes, which is not what is under discussion in your course.

Explore
You can look at the article by Baumans (2004) if you want to know more. Here is the link: www.nature.com/gt/journal/v11/n1s/full/3302371a.html

STUDY HINT
Make a list of issues from the Animals (Scientific Procedures) Act 1986, so that you can work through them if asked about the use of animals in research in psychology.

Four studies to discuss ethics of using animals in research in psychology

The use of animal research in social and cognitive psychology is not appropriate as they focus on human interactions. In both biological psychology and learning theories you have looked at animal experiments. In clinical psychology the contemporary studies do not involve animals, because they are about mental disorders in people. However, animal studies have been used, for example, to give evidence for the dopamine and glutamate hypotheses with regard to schizophrenia.

1 You studied Pavlov's (1927) work with dogs when you looked at classical conditioning in learning theories. Pavlov and his colleagues used apparatus to catch the dogs' saliva, which was invasive. He was working at a time when there was less focus on ethics than there is today. The Cruelty to Animals Act (1876) in the UK was the first legislation in the world to protect animals in science and by the 1900s there was legislation to protect animals in other countries too. The laws in Pavlov's time were not as detailed as they are now. In the UK from 1876, and in Australia from 1883, scientists using animals had to be licensed. Pavlov used evolution ideas to say that findings from animals could be generalised to humans and were justifiable using a cost–benefit analysis. Pavlov's work is set out in a series of lectures and he does not discuss the ethics of using dogs in his work.

2 One of the contemporary studies in biological psychology is van den Oever et al. (2008), who used rats to look at the effects of cues when the rat became addicted to heroin. The focus was on the cues that were there when the addiction was introduced, and then reintroduced after the addiction had been extinguished. The aim was to find out whether the reintroduction of the cues would make changes in the rat's brain. The rats were given a heroin addiction by letting them 'nose-poke' for heroin, which they 'liked', and then the addiction was extinguished (there was no heroin for them to nose-poke). Cues were then reintroduced and the rat's brain studied. The rat was almost certainly harmed. The researchers thought that they could develop an injection therapy to replace 'depression' (lowering) in a substance in the brain and could apply the idea to humans so that they would not relapse when encountering cues after an addiction to heroin had

been extinguished. The researchers felt the benefits outweighed the costs and their study would have passed an ethics committee. If you have covered one of the other contemporary studies in biological psychology, you could still use van den Oever *et al.* as an example of an animal experiment.

3 You studied Skinner's work when you looked at operant conditioning principles in learning theories. Skinner used pigeons and rats to see whether rewarding (or punishing) their behaviour increased (or decreased) the likelihood of it happening again. In a study of 'superstition' in pigeons (1948), he used eight pigeons, which is a low number and might therefore be seen to adhere to the requirement of not using a lot of animals in a study. However, he starved the pigeons to an extent, which could be against the guidelines. He believed that his findings could be applied to humans, and therefore there were benefits to humans in his work.

4 Carlsson *et al.* (1999/2000) is the study you will cover when looking at schizophrenia. It is a review of what is known about neurotransmitter functioning related to schizophrenia and focuses on the glutamate hypothesis, though also acknowledging that dopamine has a role in schizophrenia. Carlsson *et al.* used evidence from animal studies as well as from studies using humans. For example, they cite studies using rodents to show that NMDA antagonists are psychostimulants, meaning they stimulate behaviour and activity. A difficulty is that it is hard to 'see' psychotic behaviour in animals; what is observed is erratic behaviour, which might not be the same as psychotic behaviour in humans. However, there is thought to be sufficient similarity in neurotransmitter functioning between humans and animals for results from animal experiments to be used to help explain psychosis in humans.

STUDY HINT
When you studied learning theories you looked at the use of animals in experiments, including the ethics of using animals. Use what you learned, including the names of people making points about animal use. This section is a review section and would be improved by use of evidence.

Explore
You can access a YouTube video on animal experiments in psychology by using this link or you can use the internet to explore more: www.youtube.com/watch?v=p1cpzLBeRC8

STUDY HINT
You might think that animals should not be used in studies in psychology at all, and you would not be alone in thinking that. If possible, try to give a balanced account and conclusion if asked about the ethics of using animals in experiments in psychology.

Progress check 7.2
When considering the use of animals in experiments in psychology, what does it mean to say a cost–benefit analysis is required?

Test yourself
To what extent is it better in ethical terms to use animals rather than humans in studies in psychology?
(20 marks)

Practical issues in the design and implementation of research

Ethics should come first in the planning of any research study and university ethics committees are set up for that purpose.

Practical issues are important too when planning and carrying out a study. It is not always easy to separate practical and ethical issues as all practical decisions have to be ethical ones. However, practical issues are looked at separately in this section.

A number of steps must be taken when carrying out a study in psychology. To help you understand what a study involves, Table 7.6 links these steps (Robson, 2002) to the relevant sections of a psychology report.

Table 7.6 Steps involved in carrying out research

Report sections	Steps involved in carrying out research
Title	(these come later)
Abstract	
Introduction	• Examine the area of interest to find a focus for a study. • Develop one or more research questions. • Choose a research design and then choose a method that suits the design and the research question(s).
Method – sampling	• Work out how the study will run in practice, including finding out enough information so that appropriate decisions can be made. • Make notes throughout as it is important to be able to discuss decision-making and to log the process and progress. • Collect the data and then prepare it for analysis (for example, prepare a transcript).
Method – design	
Method – materials/ apparatus	
Method – procedure	
Results	• Analyse and interpret the data.
Discussion	• Report and disseminate the findings.
Referencing	(this is a separate but important part of writing a report)

STUDY HINT

You can use the format of a psychology report to think about method in psychology because it gives you a template for how research takes place. If you are stuck on an exam question on method, look back at report writing as it can trigger ideas.

Working out how the study will run in practice

Practical issues tend to be considered once the research question(s) have been set out and the research method(s) have been chosen. A research method arises from the research area and the research question, though a few choices and practical issues may influence that part of the decision-making too.

Practical issues focus on the method, which involves design decisions, including variables to be measured, sampling to find the participants, and the materials and procedures that are required to gather the data.

Design decisions

Design decisions depend on the research question(s).

• If a research question is exploratory because not much is known about the area of interest, a case study might be suitable, with in-depth and detailed qualitative data which can be analysed to look for themes. Perhaps a more focused study can then take place.

• If a research question focuses on description of an area of interest, observation or questionnaire might be appropriate.

• If a research question requires explanation of an area of interest, an experiment might be suitable as it can generate cause-and-effect conclusions. Quantitative data might be preferred as analysis can show statistical significance in any conclusions drawn.

• If a research question is about improving something for someone, a treatment might be considered and a treatment and control group design might be chosen.

Explore

You can find out more about exploratory, descriptive and explanatory research using this link: **http://isites.harvard. edu/fs/docs/icb.topic851950.files/Research%20Methods_ Some%20Notes.pdf**. The focus is on business rather than psychology but the examples might be helpful in explaining more about research.

Design decisions include how to operationalise variables, because what is to be studied has to be made measurable.

Progress check 7.3

Assuming that research in psychology can be exploratory, descriptive or explanatory, which of these aims would be more likely to require qualitative data and which quantitative data?

Variables

Design decisions will include variables, including variables to be measured and variables to be controlled. An exploratory study tends to look for themes that will reveal variables of interest and an explanatory study tends to require controlled variables so that cause-and-effect conclusions can be drawn. In a study where quantitative data are to be gathered, the variables of interest have to be measurable, which involves making practical decisions. The data that are to be gathered (whether quantitative or qualitative) have to be available and able to be gathered.

Progress check 7.4

What are the practical issues relating to variables when planning and implementing a study?

Choosing a participant for a street interview can be difficult and there will be others around, which might be distracting.

STUDY HINT

Use this chapter for revision purposes. For example, when reading about variables and design decisions involving variables, write down as many 'variable' terms as you can — situational, participant, extraneous, confounding, independent and dependent are all types of variable. You can do this in other areas, such as when reading about sampling, write down four sampling techniques.

Sampling to find participants

Some participants are more easily found than others. For example, if you are studying memory, you might not need to worry about gender; however, if you are looking at the effectiveness of a treatment for a specific phobia, you need people with that phobia, which is not so easy. Random sampling might be the least biased and the most representative of the target population but it is not easy to do as the people need to be available and known about in order for them to be there to be chosen. Consider the issues you learned about when looking at the four sampling techniques. Opportunity sampling is fairly straightforward but even then the 'right' people have to be available. For example, finding someone with a specific phobia is not likely to happen in an opportunity sample unless you go to a clinic where that phobia is treated.

Materials required to gather the data

There are a lot of practical decisions involved in preparing materials to gather the required data and in deciding how the data will be gathered. You might need a recording device if you are using the observation method or you might need blank paper and pencils if you are doing a memory study and recording the number of letters recalled. Such decisions are practical ones.

Data collection tools

Questionnaires might need to be prepared if that is the design, or interview schedules written. Other apparatus might be needed, such as a suitable story being written if carrying out a study based on Bartlett's (1932) War of the Ghosts story. Your practical investigations involve preparing data collection tools so you can draw on your own experiences when considering such issues.

Avoiding bias

Many of the practical issues when preparing materials for a study will be about avoiding bias. You need to consider demand characteristics in a study and aim to avoid them by not making the purpose of the study obvious (which is not easy when you need to get informed consent from participants).

Progress check 7.5

Why is it important to make decisions that will avoid bias in a study?

Collecting the data and preparing it for analysis

Decisions about collecting the data are often made when thinking about the required materials but there can be other practical decisions to make. These include deciding for an observation whether it will be participant or non-participant, overt or covert and, depending on such decisions, where you would position yourself as the observer and how you would take notes or do tallying. There are also decisions to make about preparing the data for analysis; for example, how the analysis will take place, whether you can use inferential testing and how you can display the data.

Four studies to discuss practical issues in the design and implementation of research

You need to be ready to discuss the 11 issues and debates in your course. When looking at practical issues in the design and implementation of research you can draw on studies you have learned about. Four studies are provided here and you can, of course, choose other studies. The classic studies are linked to the issues and debates in Chapter Six and you can make use of these when discussing issues and debates.

1 Burger (2009) was one of the contemporary studies in social psychology. He undertook a replication of Milgram's work and therefore had to follow Milgram's ideas. Burger used the same verbal prods and the same generator, as well as the same idea of the 'victim' being a confederate. When a replication is carried out, decisions are often already made. If you have not chosen Burger's study, you could consider practical issues in the design and implementation of a different study.

> **Explore**
> You can access Burger's study using this link:
> www.apa.org/pubs/journals/releases/amp-64-1-1.pdf

2 Steyvers and Hemmer (2012) was one of the contemporary studies in cognitive psychology. Their idea was to look at the use of schemas in remembering but to make sure there was ecological validity in the findings of their study. They felt that studies that had found that people remember what they expect to find in the situation they are put into (even if it is not in what they saw) do not have valid findings. This is because the studies involved an unusual scenario, such as a skull in an office, or they found that people remembered books in the office they were tested in when there weren't any. Steyvers and Hemmer thought that remembering something odd or remembering something 'not there' were both features of using an artificial environment in laboratory experiments. They were criticising the idea that valid findings could come from artificially set-up studies. They felt that their practical decisions could retain the experimental nature of a study but have a situation that had more ecological validity. They used pictures of 'everyday' scenes, including a dining room and a hotel room. They asked some people what they saw in the pictures so they knew what was likely to be remembered. Then they asked people to remember what was in the scenes. They found that people

remembered the scenes rather well and did not draw on schema to 'recall' what was not there – at least not often. Steyvers and Hemmer showed that practical decisions about studies could affect results because they could lead to artificiality that meant findings were not valid and so not useful in explaining human behaviour and processing (such as memory).

3 Lavarenne et al. (2013) is suggested as an example of a case study in your course, but you may have used a different study as your example. Lavarenne et al. choose to report on one session of a group of people with psychosis who met regularly to support one another. The session is quite short and they probably chose to report on just one session because the case study entailed a great deal of detail about the session and using more than one session would have been a lot less practicable. They looked at why the group seemed to be successful and at the role of the group for the members. They, therefore, had to gather data about what happened in the group and they needed a great deal of detail in order to understand group interactions and group dynamics. If a lot of qualitative in-depth and detailed data are to be gathered it makes sense to limit the duration of the data-gathering part of the study.

4 Pavlov's (1927) study of classical conditioning using dogs required careful manipulation of variables and controls. He needed to have a clear unconditioned stimulus and unconditioned response. Then he needed to have a separate and identifiable neutral stimulus (like a bell sound) to pair with the unconditioned stimulus. He needed an unconditioned/conditioned response that he could measure. His decisions had to be very carefully made, such as keeping the dog isolated so that features of the study such as footsteps would not be confounding variables. Although studies in your course tend not to be animal studies, animal studies are often as relevant as human studies in the issues and debates.

> **STUDY HINT**
> In this chapter, examples of different studies (and later theories) are provided to illustrate the issues and debates and help you with your revision. However, you can use just a few studies to illustrate quite a lot of the issues and debates if you wish.

Progress check 7.6

From two of the studies used here, explain two practical decisions (one from each study) that were made and the reasons for them.

Explain the importance of addressing practical issues when designing and implementing research in psychology. **(12 marks)**

Psychology as a science

The focus on science in psychology relates to what is studied and the method of research used (that is how psychology is 'done' as much as what it is). The question is to what extent are those scientific.

The issues include empiricism, **reductionism**, hypothesis testing and falsification. These are covered in the learning theories part of your course and are therefore not covered in depth here.

Reductionism in the explanation of behaviour

Reductionism relates to psychology as a science but is a separate issue in your course so is covered separately here. The opposite of reductionism is **holism** and is therefore considered here as well.

Definitions

Holism – the view that parts of something can never add up to the whole thing because the whole is more than its constituent parts. The parts are in relation to one another.

Reductionism – the idea of breaking down a complex phenomenon into simpler components.

Explanation

Reductionism has become a criticism in psychology because explanations of parts of complex behaviour or processing have meant that the whole complexity has been missed. However, 'reductionist' in itself is not a criticism, more a statement. We can say that a study is 'reductionist' meaning it is scientific and useful in terms of giving reliable, objective and credible results.

> **STUDY HINT**
> When writing about something as 'reductionist' (meaning as a limitation), do not assume that this is a criticism in itself. Explain the point, because reductionism can be useful in science. Always explain a point fully, for example, saying that results of a study 'lack reliability'. You need to explain what this means.

A problem with a reductionist approach is that results can then lack validity; if parts of something are studied then results might not represent reality, as reality is likely to be more complex.

Four studies from your course that show a reductionist approach

Using studies as examples can be a good way of showing knowledge and understanding of a point as well as evaluating it. It can also help to show what you have learned and understood in your course.

1 Bandura and others worked in the 1960s to look at how children copied what they saw, and from this the idea of observational learning developed. Bandura *et al.* (1961) let children watch an adult being 'aggressive' to a Bobo doll (which is a plastic tall toy that can be hit and will right itself). This was breaking 'aggression' down to specific actions (and words) relating to a doll. The result was that imitative aggression could be observed and recorded, the study could be replicated to show reliability and observers could objectively record the imitative acts. However, the reduction of aggression to this operationalised set of actions and words did mean that there was a lack of validity in the results. The question was, was this really aggression with the humanity and complexity aggression might usually entail? You studied Bandura's work in learning theories.

Reducing 'aggression' to counting hammer aggression against a Bobo doll is perhaps not taking account of a 'whole' aggressive situation.

2 In the early 1900s, Pavlov discovered that learning can be through classical conditioning where we associate something in the environment with a stimulus that gives a reflex response and then that environmental occurrence will give the reflex response on its own. This theory can be used to understand and treat phobias as well as being used in other ways in society, such as in advertising. Pavlov studied single reflex behaviours in dogs in order to demonstrate the principles of

classical conditioning. He reduced behaviour to these reflexive behaviours, such as salivating. What he found had practical application for humans, and the theory of classical conditioning does appear to come from reliable, objective and credible findings. In this case reductionism seems to have given useful results. You studied Pavlov's work in learning theories.

3 Milgram's work in the 1960s and 1970s looked at obedience to authority figures and he studied such obedience in a laboratory setting. He reduced obedience to one example, giving what was thought to be an electric shock to someone each time they made a mistake. This helps to show how far people would go to obey someone in authority; however, there is a lack of validity in that people knew they were part of a study and in real life they might have had something else to go on, not just what the experiment allowed them to know. You studied Milgram's work when in social psychology.

4 Another area that shows reductionism in its approach is cognitive psychology. Steyvers and Hemmer (2012) showed people pictures of scenes they were used to, such as a hotel bedroom and a dining room. The aim was to try to bring ecological validity into studies looking at how we use schemas when remembering. However, they were reducing real-life settings to two-dimensional pictures and it could be argued that this is not a valid thing to do as in real life when recalling situations and settings, there would be emotions involved and people would have been interacting with their environment, not just relying on vision, for example.

Progress check 7.7

Explain why taking a reductionist approach when doing research in psychology is likely to mean that findings lack validity.

A study to show a more holistic approach

There are some areas where a more holistic view is taken. It can be useful, when discussing reductionism, to have an example of a study that is less reductionist.

Lavarenne *et al.* (2013) looked at how a group for people with psychosis successfully supported them, using the whole session and making careful and complete notes about what was going on, thus gathering qualitative data. They did not reduce the group situation or behaviour into parts, such as looking at every instance of negativity. Lavarenne *et al.* is an example of a case study in clinical psychology.

STUDY HINT
You could prepare a study that takes a more holistic view of behaviour and processing, so that you have evidence that not all research in psychology takes a reductionist view. In your course many studies do reduce whole situations to parts in order to study them. Case studies tend to be more holistic and as you need to cover a case study in clinical psychology, use that as an example of a study that is not reductionist.

Psychology as a science

In order to consider psychology as a science it is useful to think about what science is. You could be asked questions about science as well as psychology so it is worth noting what makes something 'a science'. Then you can present an argument about psychology being a science (or not).

Scientific method

Scientific method consists of having a theory, developing a hypothesis from the theory, testing it against reality and then from the findings either accepting, rejecting or modifying the theory. That modified or accepted theory is then used to give another hypothesis, which is then tested against reality... and so on. Defining the terms in a scientific cycle of enquiry helps to explain the scientific method.

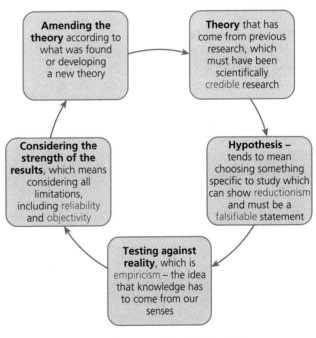

How a scientific cycle of enquiry might look (including some of the terms)

Explanation

John Locke is a name linked to **empiricism** in terms of learning about and understanding the world. Science needs to gather empirical evidence.

Karl Popper put forward the argument that we need to be looking to **falsify** hypotheses, not looking to 'prove' them 'true'. For example, if we wanted to check that all houses have doors, we could look at a great many houses and find they have doors, which seems like proof. However, we might find a house without a door (perhaps people get in and out of the house through a window). We cannot prove that 'all houses have doors' because we could not check 'all houses'. However, we could show that 'all houses do not have doors' if we found one without a door. Science should look to falsify because knowledge about 'what is' can never be proved. This is why you should not use 'prove' or 'proof' when writing a psychology answer or essay.

If we know that all live animals breathe, and that dogs are animals, we know for sure that live dogs breathe. We don't need to look at any live dogs to make sure they are breathing. Science does not use **rational** arguments though once something is 'known' then logical deductions can be made from that knowledge perhaps. For example, to know the truth of 'all live dogs breathe' we had to learn about breathing and animals or at least to categorise those things.

Definitions

Empiricism is the idea that knowledge can only come through our senses — from sight, sound, taste, smell and touch.
Falsification is the idea that we cannot prove anything 'true', we can only show something is not true.
Rationalism is the opposite of empiricism and means we can only know things through reasoning about them.

> **STUDY HINT**
> In learning theories you covered psychology as a science, including empiricism, falsification, reductionism and hypothesis testing so you can use this material in revision.

Explanation

Testing hypotheses gives reliable and objective results, which is called experimental method. Though there are other ways of gathering data in psychology, from the point of view of 'doing science', experiments have a special place because of the **controls** and careful testing that can then lead to reliable, objective and scientifically credible results.

Reductionism has already been considered in this section. Science uses a reductionist approach to develop knowledge and understanding about the world in order to reduce its complexity and formulate hypotheses for testing.

Definitions

Controls are necessary so that the testing of a hypothesis is focused on the statement of what a theory predicts without allowing other variables to have an effect on the results.
Replicability refers to how much a study can be repeated. Replicability is required in science because findings have to be reliable and reliability can only be found by replicating studies.
Testing hypotheses means developing statements of what a theory predicts might happen and then finding a way of testing them.

Progress check 7.8

How can results be reliable and yet not be valid?

> **Explore**
> You can access a discussion about psychology and science using this link or you can use the internet to find out more: http://blogs.scientificamerican.com/the-curious-wavefunction/is-psychology-a-e2809creale2809d-science-does-it-really-matter/

Four studies in psychology that show a scientific approach

If you are discussing psychology as a science, you need to discuss what science is and then use examples from psychology to show that those examples fit a definition of 'science'. Choose studies from your course that suit this 'doing science' definition of psychology. You can use the studies that were used to demonstrate reductionism because taking a reductionist approach to research and being 'scientific' go together.

1   Williams *et al.* (2013) looked at treatments for depression and used a randomised controlled trial. This is a scientific way of gathering data because there were two or more groups. One group had the treatment, the other group waited and acted as a control. The groups were matched. There was nothing different between the two groups except that one had the treatment and one did not so the effectiveness of the treatment could then be studied. There were a lot of controls, which makes randomised controlled trials scientific. For example, the way people were allocated to the groups was done randomly to avoid bias in the samples. Williams *et al.* were studying the combination of an imagery-based therapy to change cognitive bias in those with depression and CBT and they found the combination therapy was effective for depression. If you did not choose depression as your 'other' mental disorder or

you did not choose to study Williams *et al.*, consider the study you did choose for your 'other' disorder (other than schizophrenia) as it would almost certainly have a scientific approach.

2 In Carlsson *et al.* (1999/2000) studies were reported that were scientific. For example, animal studies were reported where neurotransmitter functioning was studied (such as in rodents), and animal experiments will have very careful controls and hypotheses where the independent variable is all that varies and the dependent variable is all that can be affected by the manipulation of the independent variable. You have studied Carlsson *et al.* as part of your learning about schizophrenia in clinical psychology.

3 Raine *et al.* (1997), the classic study in biological psychology in your course, is scientifically carried out. There is a carefully matched control group, for example, and careful measuring of brain differences.

4 Milgram's (1963) study had a lot of careful controls, including the situation itself. Each participant went through exactly the same procedure each time. There were 40 participants in this version of the study and so it can be claimed that there were 40 replications as each participant was tested alone. Controls included the verbal prods that were used.

A study that is less scientific in its approach

When considering psychology as a science, it is useful to have some ideas about how psychology is not a science. The classic study in clinical psychology is an appropriate example here.

> **STUDY HINT**
> Studies other than the classic studies are given as examples in this chapter. However, you can, of course, draw on the classic studies, which are discussed in Chapter Six. Use whatever material from your course that you feel helps to illustrate your argument in an answer.

One study that you have covered that is not as scientific as the four chosen here is Rosenhan's (1973) study of the experience of being labelled as having schizophrenia. Rosenhan's participants did all present (separately) themselves to a hospital saying they heard something like 'thud' or 'hollow' in their head (which was reducing the symptoms of schizophrenia to a single common symptom). However, after that, the participants all behaved 'as themselves' and there were no controls in the study and no attempt at reducing behaviour to parts. The participants aimed for accuracy in their recording of what happened to them so there was objectivity in a way. The

results did come from empirical data. However, there was not a hypothesis as such. Results were found to be reliable in that the situation was repeated 12 times by eight people so there was perhaps an element of science. However, data were qualitative in the main, this was not an experiment and there were no careful controls put in place.

> **Progress check 7.9**
> Explain two ways in which Rosenhan's (1973) study can be said to be 'not scientific' and two ways it can be said to be 'scientific'.

The scientific subject matter of psychology

One argument for psychology being a science is its subject matter.

The subject matter of psychology is scientific

When psychology looks at biological aspects of the mind and behaviour, it is in scientific territory. Psychology uses evidence from scanning, for example, as do other sciences. Cognitive psychology looks at how the brain processes information; not only are models developed about issues such as memory, but also brain structures and functioning are studied for evidence for those models. Classical conditioning, which you studied in learning theories, focuses on how associations can be related to innate reflexes, which are about our biology. Clinical psychology looks at mental health and mental disorders. Biological explanations, such as the dopamine and glutamate hypotheses to explain schizophrenia, feature in clinical psychology. Drug therapy involves chemicals and can also be said to be scientific. Health psychology too involves a lot of 'biology' and 'chemistry' when the focus is on substance misuse.

The subject matter of psychology is not so scientific

There are areas in psychology that do not seem so scientific. Social psychology focuses on obedience and prejudice, both of which are complex behaviours or attitudes that involve looking at how people interact. Some theories aim for a scientific explanation, such as social impact theory. However, it could be argued that the complexity of human behaviour and attitudes defies scientific study. Some learning theories such as social learning theory can also be said to involve interactions between people, which makes a scientific reductionist approach difficult – because data are likely to lack validity if a scientific approach is taken. When clinical psychology studies the effectiveness of therapies a scientific approach can be used, such as using randomised controlled trials. However, there are elements of treatments and therapies that are hard to study except by gathering in-depth, detailed qualitative data from the people involved.

> **STUDY HINT**
> Although reductionism and psychology as a science are two issues and debates in your course, they do link because science uses a reductionist approach. You can draw on different areas when discussing issues and debates.

Why does it matter whether psychology is a science?

It is worth asking why the question about whether psychology is a science is important. If you can see the importance of an issue in psychology, it might help you to learn about the issue.

As you approach the end of your course, you will have seen how interesting a lot of psychology is and even if you have not enjoyed all of it, you will hopefully have found areas that interest you. For example, knowing more about depression, OCD or anorexia nervosa can be both useful and interesting, and learning about how we favour our in group at the expense of the out group is useful for understanding why we like some people more than others. It is also interesting to see how people repeat behaviour that is rewarded as it helps us to understand our own behaviour and to know how to interact with others.

Hopefully, you have not only enjoyed learning about studies in psychology, but you have also understood the value of these studies.

An example might help. You might feel you 'know' that we are more likely to be friends with someone who we judge to be attractive. You might guess that females (of student age) are likely to want to be friends with an attractive male more than an attractive female and that males (of student age) are more likely to want to be friends with an attractive female than with an attractive male. However, that 'knowledge' is better if it is backed by a carefully designed study so that the results are reliable, valid and generalisable, as well as objective and 'scientific'. If you were talking with a friend about what would make someone willing to be friends with someone they don't know on Facebook, what would you say would be important factors? Wang *et al.* (2010) studied whether an 'unattractive' photo, an 'attractive' photo or no photo

would affect someone's willingness to be friends with someone they don't know on Facebook. Their study is summarised here. Wang *et al.* use a lot of scientific elements in their design, such as careful controls over variables and using an independent groups design to avoid order effects. The idea is that an element of 'science' leads to more credible findings.

Study of interest

Wang *et al.* (2010) looked at Facebook friendships and what makes someone willing to start a friendship online. Their focus was on the importance of seeing a photo when it comes to starting online friendships. The researchers wanted to see the effect of displaying visual cues. The experiment involved six conditions: no photo; attractive photo; unattractive photo; all three of these conditions involving both male and female profile owners. They used an opportunity/convenience sample of college students in the USA. The students were given credits relating to their course for participating voluntarily, and 350 students out of 474 asked completed an online questionnaire. All of the participants had to have a Facebook account. They were randomly put into one of the six conditions. There was an online consent form to take care of ethical issues, accessed using a URL that was posted on the course website, and the online questionnaire could be accessed at any time by the participant.

The procedure was that the person would be exposed to someone's profile (a fictitious profile) and they would then be asked to measure their willingness to be friends with this person. Each person saw one profile, either male or female, and either without a photo, with an attractive photo or with an unattractive photo. The willingness to be a friend of the 'person' was measured using a Likert-type scale of four items, focusing not only on whether they would be friends but whether they would interact with them more online (e.g. would they write on the profile owner's wall). The independent variable was the condition the person was exposed to (there were six conditions) and the main dependent variable was whether they were willing to start a friendship. The study found that physical attractiveness was the most important visual cue that predicted willingness to start an online friendship and both males and females were more willing to start a friendship with the opposite sex 'attractive' person. There were other findings too, such as females being more cautious about becoming friends with people they did not know.

STUDY HINT
Wang *et al.* (2010) used opportunity sampling in taking the students at the university and then used volunteer sampling because only those who accessed and completed the questionnaire took part. They explained careful control over the independent variable and had a clearly measurable dependent variable. They used Likert-type questions to measure the dependent variable. These method issues all come up in your course and you can use this study to illustrate them.

Progress check 7.10

What made Wang *et al.*'s (2010) study scientific?

Test yourself

To what extent can research in psychology be called 'scientific'? **(20 marks)**

Nature and nurture

Psychology is the study of mind and behaviour. Indeed, some people define psychology as the scientific study of mind and behaviour. Part of the discussion about understanding mind and behaviour concerns what comes from nature and what comes from environmental influences. This is called the **nature–nurture debate** and it is a common debate in psychology.

Definition

Nature–nurture debate – refers to how much of behaviour, feelings and thoughts are from nature (inherited through genes) and how much is down to the influence of surroundings and environment (the result of nurture).

Cultural and gender issues in psychological research

Culture can be seen as shared meanings within a society. Clearly culture relates to nurture, which is why it is considered as an issue in this section.

Culture as an issue in psychology

In social psychology you will have considered how culture might affect interactions between people, when looking at both obedience and prejudice. There is mention of cultural issues in memory, and learning theories can help to explain differences between cultures.

If a characteristic or behaviour is found in all cultures (where it has been studied), it can be called 'universal' ('found in all cultures') and can mean the characteristic or behaviour has genetic underpinning. If a characteristic or behaviour is different between cultures then it would seem it is not genetically driven but learned from the environment.

Culture and obedience

Studies looking at obedience tend to consistently show the importance of a situation on whether people obey or not and that is the main finding no matter which culture a study is carried out in. As findings are similar in all cultures where such studies have taken place, it seems that in certain situations, such as when people are agents in a society, there will be obedience. Such situations occur in all cultures so there appear to be no cultural differences in obedience.

Study of interest

Blass (2012) reviewed studies done in the USA and those done in other countries and arrived at an average percentage of obedience in the USA of 60.94 per cent and an average percentage of obedience in other countries of 65.94 per cent, two very similar figures. There was a large variation of obedience levels found in the studies, but the average figures were very similar, and very similar to Milgram's result in his basic study. Blass suggests that even if obedience had been found to differ between cultures, there were other differences such as age and gender of the participants, as well as differences in the procedures, that could have caused any differences in obedience. Blass concludes that the similarity in findings in the different cultures showed that people have a powerful tendency to obey authority and this may be 'one of the universals of social behaviour' (Blass, 2012, p. 203).

It could be claimed that having people in an agentic state in a society is a useful survival trait; if everyone was making their own decision (being autonomous), it would be hard to have order and without order a society would perhaps not function. At least this is one theory. The idea backs the claim that obedience in response to certain situations is found universally, so it could be down to human nature.

However, just because something is found in all cultures might not mean it is innate in people. It might just mean that the behaviour helps people to live socially and so all societies display such behaviour.

Culture and prejudice

There have been studies looking at prejudice that do show some cultural differences, unlike research into obedience.

On the one hand, it is suggested that attitudes such as right-wing authoritarianism and social dominance orientation are stable across cultures so are possibly universal. Cohrs *et al.* (2012) found data in Germany, Adorno *et al.* (1950) in the USA and Duckitt and Sibley (2010) in Australia and all found evidence of authoritarian attitude linking to prejudice. Pettigrew (1998) looked at whether factors that affect prejudice differed in different countries (Netherlands, UK, France and West Germany) and found that there were universals relating to what affects prejudice.

On the other hand, there are studies that show cultural effects on prejudicial attitudes. For example, Guimond *et al.* (2013) found that multiculturalism as an alternative to assimilation became popular in the 1970s, and accepting other cultures was seen as a positive feature, thus prejudice was reduced. Multiculturalism supports diversity and is categorised as high in pro-diversity. Assimilation means absorbing other cultures into one set of norms and beliefs; multiculturalism means living with different norms and beliefs in one country. Assimilation as a way of seeing how society can fulfil its needs links to prejudiced attitudes, whereas multiculturalism is more positive in terms of how groups interact with one another. This suggests that there are cultural effects when it comes to prejudice in a society and prejudice depends on attitudes towards other cultures in a society. Guimond *et al.* (2013) cite Becker *et al.* (2012), who looked at data from 21 cultural groups and found that there were effects of cultural norms with regard to prejudice that were over and above personal beliefs and attitudes.

Progress check 7.11

Explain two pieces of evidence that show that prejudicial attitudes are affected by culture.

Explore
You can explore the idea of culture in psychology using the internet. Here is a link to a YouTube video that might be a place to start:
www.youtube.com/watch?v=JgPPuWDx4wg

Culture and memory

There is little in your course that suggests that memory is affected by culture except the fact that memory is not like a tape recorder; it relies on schemas that we have learned through interacting with our environment (this is the reconstructive model of memory). The way memory is reconstructed using schemas is thought to be the case across all cultures so is universal in itself, which means culture might affect what our memories are, but the way memory works is not affected by culture.

However, Sebastián and Hernández-Gil (2012), one of the contemporary studies in cognitive psychology in your course, thought that culture affected memory when they suggested that English speakers had one digit more in their memory span than Spanish speakers. The researchers thought that this was because of the syllables in the words for numbers in the Spanish language, so this could be said to be about culture.

Culture and learning norms and beliefs

Learning theories can explain the importance of culture in learning, for example, focusing on social learning, which suggests people copy what they see, including what others do – for example, children use parents and teachers at school as role models. Thus a society can pass down norms and beliefs and culture can be seen to affect behaviour (as well as attitudes). Social learning theory can help to explain differences between cultures because children would be observing different behaviours, attitudes and reactions and would imitate them. Operant conditioning can help to explain differences too if different responses are rewarded in different cultures and if we agree that we repeat behaviour that is rewarded, as Skinner predicted.

STUDY HINT
Discussion about culture often refers to different countries or societies. In psychology 'culture' can also refer to sub-cultures which are groups of people with different socioeconomic status, or specific sub-cultures such as certain religious groups. You can discuss sub-cultures when talking about culture as an issue in psychology.

Four studies that look at cultural issues in psychology

1 Sebastián and Hernández-Gil (2012) looked at differences in digit span using English-speaking participants and Spanish-speaking participants. They put the difference down to language, which is an aspect of a culture. They thought that digit span in short-term memory was universal (even though language can affect digit span) because encoding in short-term memory is auditory and we use words to sound things out in order to remember in short-term memory. So language affected digit span; however, the process of coding in short-term memory was not thought to be different between cultures. Sebastián and Hernández-Gil (2012) is one of the contemporary studies in cognitive psychology in your course.

2 Guimond et al. (2013) found differences in prejudicial attitudes in societies with a multicultural approach and societies choosing assimilation. It was found that multiculturalism means less prejudice. If you have not covered this study, you will have used other studies to look at culture and prejudice in social psychology, so you can use these here.

3 Blass (2012) carried out a review of studies that looked at obedience, including studies done in the USA and in other cultures. There were some cultural differences in the percentages of obedience; however, they could be due to differences in the way the studies were carried out. Blass worked out an average percentage obedience of 60.94 per cent from studies carried out in the USA and 65.94 per cent from those done in other countries. These figures are very similar and Blass concluded that the similarity in findings in the different cultures showed that people have a powerful tendency to obey authority and this may be 'one of the universals of social behaviour' (Blass, 2012, p. 203). This was not a study, it was a review; however, it reviews studies and the findings are useful. If you have not covered the work of Blass in social psychology, you will have looked at culture and obedience so you can use those studies here.

4 Pettigrew (1998) looked at whether factors that affect prejudice differed in different countries (Netherlands, UK, France and West Germany) and found that there were universals relating to what affects prejudice. This suggests that what leads to prejudice is perhaps universal and that there might be something genetic that affects the way humans interact. If you have not covered Pettigrew (1998) in social psychology, you might prefer to use an example of your own.

STUDY HINT
In this chapter there is a tendency to provide four examples of studies relating to issues and debates in your course. However, there is no requirement to know about four studies. You will, however, need to be able to use research in any question relating to issues and debates so it is wise to prepare some studies and some evidence.

Cross-cultural studies

In clinical, child and health psychology, you will have looked at cross-cultural studies as a way of researching. In cross-cultural studies research is carried out in the same way in different cultures and if there are different results in different cultures, that shows a culture effect in what is being researched.

STUDY HINT
You can use strengths and limitations of using a cross-cultural research method when discussing culture as one of the issues and debates in your course. Review the evaluation of cross-cultural methods when you considered them in clinical psychology (page 148).

Progress check 7.12

Explain why, if you were carrying out a study, you would aim to control for cultural differences between the participants.

Gender as an issue in psychology

Just as culture can be seen as a variable in participants that should be controlled in case it affects findings, so gender is such a variable.

Definitions

Biological sex – this comes from the sex chromosomes (X and Y chromosomes) and is determined by our genes.

Gender – refers to more than our biological sex; it refers to feelings, attitudes and behaviours that a culture assigns to the biological sexes.

Explanation

Gender can be seen as something learned in a culture and can be related to 'nurture'. However, gender can link to biological sex, which comes from genes, so there is an element of 'nature' when considering gender as an issue in psychology.

Gender and biological sex

Biological sex comes from the sex chromosomes (X and Y) and is determined by our genes. **Gender** encompasses more than biological sex; it includes a society's gender behaviour traditions and norms. Gender relates to behaviour or characteristics that are associated with a certain biological sex, though in some cultures there could be more than two genders (e.g. so gender is more than biological sex).

Gender involves the nature–nurture debate as biological sex is genetically given, with evolutionary factors related to gender being passed down through genes. As gender is more than what is biologically given, including learned behaviours and norms, there is a 'nurture' as well as a 'nature' element.

> ### Explore
> You can access a YouTube video on the psychology of gender or use the internet to find out more:
> www.youtube.com/watch?v=56kn_laaF7c
> www.simplypsychology.org/gender-biology.html

> ### STUDY HINT
> A good way of learning and revising is to use key terms and their definitions to remind you of what you have covered. You could make a list of all the bold key terms in this chapter. Then make sure you can define them all. Finally, sort them into an order that would help you to explain what psychology is to a friend. This will give you an overview of your course.

Four studies that relate to gender in your course

1. Bandura's experiments using the Bobo doll found gender differences in imitative aggression and other types of aggression. For example, boys were more likely to copy a male model and boys showed more physical aggression than girls. These findings suggest that gender is an important variable when it comes to carrying out studies and it should be controlled for accordingly. You will have studied Bandura's work in learning theories in your course and he puts forward the idea of social learning.

2. Wang et al. (2010) showed gender differences in willingness to befriend someone on Facebook having seen their profile and depending on whether they were male or female as well as whether there was a photo and how attractive it was. Although this study is not part of your course, you can use evidence such as this when discussing issues and debates. However, the psychological skills part of your course is partly revision and also synoptic, so you would be expected to draw on material in your course for the most part.

3. Kilham and Mann (1974) studied obedience, both when participants were ordering pain to be administered to someone else and when they had to do it. They used university students. They found gender differences in obedience: when actually giving the shocks, obedience was 40 per cent for males and 16 per cent for females, a large difference; when ordering someone else to administer the shocks they found 68 per cent obedience for males and 40 per cent for the female participants. You will have looked at gender differences in obedience and found that not many studies show gender differences, so it is likely that you covered Kilham and Mann (1974) as an example. If you did not, use the evidence you learned about when examining the effects of gender on obedience.

4. Brendgen et al. (2005), which is one of the contemporary studies in biological psychology in your course, looked at identical and non-identical twins, focusing on their physical and social aggression. They found in general that physical aggression has a genetic basis but social aggression (such as name-calling) does not. Brendgen et al. also considered gender differences in the two types of aggression. Gender is a variable that is considered frequently in psychology because it is seen as having such an effect on behaviour and someone's attitudes and characteristics. Brendgen et al. looked at gender and physical and social aggression and found no gender differences; neither did they find that the relative contributions of genes and the environment differed according to gender.

Summary of the four studies

- Bandura found gender differences in imitation of aggression depending on whether the aggression was displayed by a male or a female model and depending on what type of aggression was being considered.
- Kilham and Mann (1974) showed there were gender differences in obedience, though in general studies have not found gender differences in obedience.
- Wang et al. (2010) found clear gender differences in who people said they were willing to be friends with, such as showing that female students were more likely to say they were willing to be friends with an attractive male than an attractive female.
- Brendgen et al. (2005) found no differences between boys and girls when they looked at genetic and environmental contributions relating to physical and social aggression.

It seems that some issues show gender differences and some do not. However, it seems confirmed that gender is a variable of interest, as is culture, in research in psychology.

Progress check 7.13

Explain some evidence that shows gender is an important variable in psychology.

The role of both nature and nurture in psychology

The discussion about gender and culture has explained a lot about the nature–nurture debate, and here is a brief summary of how gender and culture have been shown to link to nature and nurture. In cognitive psychology, you have covered enough to be able to discuss that both nature and nurture affect memory. In biological psychology, you have looked at both genetic explanations for aggression and at the role of the environment in aggression. In clinical psychology, there is discussion about schizophrenia, with a possible genetic explanation as schizophrenia can run in families. In biological psychology, you have looked at twin studies, which as a research method is probably the most well-known way of looking at nature and nurture and their relative effects on behaviour and processing.

Culture and gender and the nature–nurture debate

The discussion about culture shows how issues of both nature and nurture are involved when considering the effects of culture on behaviour and attitudes.

- *Nature*: Obedience was thought to be due to the situation and that was largely the finding in all cultures where obedience has been studied, so perhaps obedience is in our nature.
- *Nurture*: Prejudice, however, was shown to an extent to be affected by culture, so prejudice can be affected by the environment.

The discussion about gender shows how issues of both nature and nurture are involved when considering the effects of gender on behaviour and attitudes.

- *Nature*: The discussion about gender shows that for some behaviours and characteristics, such as obedience, there seem to be no gender differences, again supporting the idea that it might be down to nature.
- *Nurture*: Yet for other behaviours and characteristics, such as imitation of what is observed, there are gender differences, which suggests some behaviour comes from nurture.

It is not easy to draw firm conclusions about the effects of gender on behaviour. For example, though Milgram did not find gender differences in obedience, once the qualitative data from his work were examined, there did seem to be gender differences, at least in the reaction to 'having' to obey, if not in the actual obedience.

Memory and the nature–nurture debate

In cognitive psychology, you can find evidence of the influence of both nature and nurture on human behaviour and processing.

- *Nature*: Cognitive psychology considers the way the brain processes information and the focus in your course is on memory. Animals are used to study how memory works, such as looking at brain activity and their memory for mazes, for example. Case studies of patients with brain damage (for example, Henry Molaison) are used to look at the match between brain damage and problems with processing, assuming that one causes the other. The focus on brain structures and functioning, which is focusing on biology, appears to be a focus on nature. For example, it is assumed that brain structure and functioning in animals is similar enough to human brain structure and functioning to learn from animal studies. This idea seems to rest on the idea of evolution, where humans and animals are seen to have similarities, and survival of the fittest happens through genes. People have the same brain regions, such as the prefrontal lobe, amygdala and hippocampus, and such brain regions appear to have the same function in different people, as shown by case studies of people with similar brain damage and similar problems with functioning (for example, Schmolck *et al.*, 2002).
- *Nurture*: Models of memory show that what we remember is influenced by nurture. The main example of this is reconstructive memory, which suggests we use schema that we have developed through interacting with our environment, to reconstruct memories.

Aggression and the nature–nurture debate

Aggression is focused on in biological psychology where emphasis tends to be on biology and therefore on 'nature'. Aggression also features in learning theories, where, for example, Bandura showed that aggression can be learned by observing aggression.

- *Nature:* Aggression is a main focus in biological psychology in your course. You looked at an evolutionary explanation for aggression, which focused on genes and a survival advantage for aggressive behaviour, such as protecting young and so protecting genes. If aggression is a survival trait, then it is down to our genes and in our 'nature'. You also looked at brain structures and aggression, finding out that the limbic system, for example, is where emotional focusing takes place. Structures such as the limbic system and prefrontal lobe (which focuses on decision-making and controlling behaviour, and therefore damage to it might lead to aggression) are in everyone and genetically given, so therefore link to nature.

- *Nurture*: In the 1960s, Bandura showed the role of nurture in developing behaviour such as aggression as he found that children copied aggressive actions when they observed them. Skinner also showed the role of learning in putting forward the idea of operant conditioning. People repeat behaviour they are rewarded for. Even if someone is not rewarded for being aggressive (and they might be, because it might get them what they want), they might be rewarded by attention even if that attention is meant to be punishment for being aggressive. Social learning and operant conditioning both show that behaviour can come from environmental influences or nurture.

Schizophrenia and the nature–nurture debate

- *Nature*: Gottesman and Shields (1966) used information from twins to see if there are genetic factors in the development of schizophrenia. They looked at situations where one twin had schizophrenia or a psychosis. Then they considered how often the other twin also had schizophrenia or a psychosis. If twins both share a characteristic, such as schizophrenia, there is evidence that it comes from nature. If more identical twins share that characteristic than non-identical twins, that is even more evidence for genes having a role in the characteristic because identical twins share 100 per cent of their genes and non-identical twins share just 50 per cent of their genes. Gottesman and Shields found that for identical (MZ) twins both shared schizophrenia 42 per cent of the time whereas it was just 9 per cent for non-identical (DZ) twins. Tiwari *et al.* (2010) reported on a meta-analysis of twin studies by Sullivan *et al.* (2003), which suggests there is 81 per cent heritability relating to schizophrenia and Tiwari *et al.* (2010) also cite Lichtenstein *et al.* (2009) as giving the heritability figure as about 64 per cent. These two figures are higher than Gottesman and Shields found. The studies do tend to show that there is a genetic element to schizophrenia.
- *Nurture*: Gottesman and Shields's findings suggest that there is indeed a genetic (nature) element to schizophrenia. However, the results also put

schizophrenia down to environmental factors (nurture) if the highest concordance rate (in MZ twins) is only 42 per cent. The other two studies cited give figures of 81 per cent and 64 per cent. No studies show that schizophrenia is 100 per cent inherited (if it was, both MZ twins would always have it), so there seems to be a role for the environment in causing schizophrenia.

You may not have looked at a genetic explanation for schizophrenia, though other biological explanations, such as neurotransmitter functioning, can also be used to discuss elements of nature when explaining schizophrenia. You will have looked at a twin study in biological psychology, which you could use to discuss the nature–nurture debate.

> **STUDY HINT**
>
> If you read through the evidence here relating to genes and schizophrenia, you will see that there are rarely any categorical statements made. For example, instead of saying that 'as twin studies do not find a 100 per cent concordance rate environment must have a role in the development of schizophrenia', the text says 'there seems to be a role'. In psychology, a conclusion is rarely definite so it is useful to make cautious claims. This links with the idea of not being able to prove anything, as Popper explained when discussing falsification (page 652).

> **Explore**
>
> You can access a short YouTube video to help explain the nature–nurture debate. Here is the link: www.youtube.com/watch?v=P-D33oWiOEg

> **Progress check 7.14**
>
> Give two pieces of evidence that show there is a role for nature in a behaviour or characteristic and two pieces of evidence that show there is a role for nurture.

Twin studies and the nature–nurture debate

In biological psychology, you looked at twin studies as a research method. As you have seen in this section, twin studies are a useful way of studying the nature–nurture debate when considering explanations of schizophrenia. They are in a way a natural experiment because MZ twins share 100 per cent of their genes, thereby controlling for environment (they share their environment too, largely), and DZ twins just share 50 per cent of their genes but again share their environment. Differences between MZ and DZ twins can show what behaviour and characteristics come from nature.

Four studies that relate to the nature–nurture debate in your course

These four studies are reviewed here to help your revision.

1 Bandura's work shows that aggression comes from what is seen in the environment. He showed that children imitate aggression that they see.

2 Gottesman and Shields (1966) showed that schizophrenia was shared in 42 per cent of the identical twins studied and just 9 per cent of the non-identical twins, which suggests a role for genes in schizophrenia, which is 'nature'. However, it seems that there is still a role for environmental influences (nurture) as the percentage for identical twins was not 100 per cent.

3 Brendgen *et al.* (2005), which is one of the contemporary studies in biological psychology, used MZ and DZ twins to look at genetic and environmental influences on both physical and social aggression. They found that teacher ratings of the twins' physical and social aggression put about 63 per cent of physical aggression down to genes and 37 per cent down to non-shared environment. For social aggression, about 20 per cent was due to genes, 20 per cent due to shared environment and 60 per cent due to non-shared environment. These figures support the conclusion that physical aggression has a genetic basis but social aggression is much less down to genes.

4 Tiwari *et al.* (2010) reported on a meta-analysis of twin studies by Sullivan *et al.* (2003), which suggests there is 81 per cent heritability with regard to schizophrenia and Tiwari *et al.* (2010) also cite Lichtenstein *et al.* (2009) as giving the heritability figure as about 64 per cent. Tiwari *et al.*'s study is a review which brings together findings from studies that have looked at heritability and schizophrenia. If you have not covered this review, use a different study when discussing the contribution of nature and nurture to behaviour or a characteristic. You could use Bandura's three studies separately, giving more detail.

Test yourself

Assess why psychology is interested in both nature and nurture when trying to understand human behaviour and characteristics. **(20 marks)**

Emphasis on the use of psychology for society and for the individual

Three of the 11 issues and debates in your course form a group that focuses on social issues in psychology. These issues relate to the use of psychology in social control, the use of psychological knowledge in society and socially sensitive research.

Understanding from psychology can help with control in a society, though individuals might 'suffer' from being controlled. There are other ways in which psychology can help society too. In each of your topic areas, you have studied a key question for society that psychology can help to answer, and these all focus on how psychology can shed light on issues society wishes or needs to know more about. Some of what psychology focuses on is socially sensitive. Socially sensitive research affects the individual but is linked with the issues that relate to society as it is often society's reaction to certain topics that makes them 'socially sensitive'.

The use of psychology in social control

Some of what you have studied fits into the idea that psychology is about social control. **Social control** refers to the regulation of the behaviour of individuals for the sake of society. Individuals might be the target of social control because they need to conform to social rules and norms and/or because they can then be more productive for society.

> ### Definition
> **Social control** refers to the way people are regulated for the society's sake.

For example, whenever treatments and therapies are considered, there is an element of someone (usually someone with power in a society) giving treatment to someone else (usually someone with less power). Many people welcome the treatment they get, as studies show when they ask people.

One of the Unseen Studies in Chapter Six (page 634) considered treatment for fear of computers (Brosnan and Thorpe, 2006). After the therapy, a faculty member asked those who took part what they felt about the therapy and the qualitative data gathered showed that it was appreciated and had worked. The participants reported less anxiety. However, there is discussion about the power a therapist has in the situation and moral and ethical issues related to the use (and possible abuse) of that power. Hardesty (2005) suggests that in a therapeutic or counselling relationship emotions are shaped by the therapist; the therapist guides the situation and has the power.

Another area you have studied that can be seen to be about social control is Milgram's work on obedience. Milgram found that if orders are given over the phone there is less obedience, so in order to control people, orders should perhaps be face-to-face.

The role of the police is to maintain social order, which is about social control. Results of studies in psychology can inform society how to maintain social control.

Perhaps any psychological knowledge can be used as a form of social control. For example, in relation to memory, if it is known that leading questions affect recall, leading questions could be asked in court to manipulate someone's testimony. Of course, psychological knowledge can also help in such situations, as a judge would be on the lookout for leading questions. However, this does show that knowledge gained in psychology might be used as a form of control.

Another example relates to knowing more about how to reduce prejudice, such as setting up superordinate goals (Sherif et al., 1954/1961). A society could work on setting up such goals in order to reduce prejudice. However, this is not bad social control – such knowledge could be used for good or for bad.

Operant conditioning is another example where knowledge could be used for good or for bad for an individual. We would expect in a society that rewarded behaviour is desired behaviour and that benefits the individual as well because they 'fit in'; however, shaping behaviour using rewards can be seen as social control.

STUDY HINT
Go through the topics you have covered and consider them in terms of social control so that you have a list of areas you can use in an exam question. Some ideas are given in this part of the chapter to get you started.

Clinical psychology is considered in this section as therapy can be seen as social control, including both drug therapy and psychotherapy.

Drug therapy

Drug therapy has been seen as a form of social control. You need to study two treatments for schizophrenia and two treatments for your other chosen disorder and, in both cases, one of the treatments must be 'biological'. It is likely, therefore, that you will have covered drug therapy.

Elovich and Drucker (2008) published a paper in the *Harm Reduction Journal* and discussed issues around state control and drug use for medical conditions. Although this was a specific situation in Russia, there are some interesting points about social control and drug use.

Explore
You can access Elovich and Drucker's (2008) article using the following link: www.biomedcentral.com/content/pdf/1477-7517-5-23.pdf. It highlights a specific issue in a specific country at a specific time. However, it does raise some issues about social control that you might find of interest.

Mental disorders are frequently controlled by the use of drugs. An example is clozapine, which is an atypical antipsychotic used in schizophrenia. It can improve delusions and hallucinations and seems to be helpful if someone does not respond well to other drugs, but its side-effects can be serious, such as lowered white blood cell count. Another example is the use of SSRIs for depression, such as Prozac. Drugs are used to regulate neurotransmitter functioning to help with the disorder.

Smith (2012) published an account of what he calls 'inappropriate prescribing', which relates to the issue of social control as it is about how writing a prescription and using drug treatment seems to be the first choice but might not be the best choice. Smith points to APA clinical treatment guidelines, which aim to address concerns about over-prescribing.

Explore
You can read Smith's (2012) article on 'inappropriate prescribing' using this link: www.apa.org/monitor/2012/06/prescribing.aspx.

In theory, someone has the choice of whether or not to take drugs for their mental disorder. However, given the acceptance of the medical model in a society, it is possibly unlikely that an individual would not accept medical advice. There is an issue of power and a doctor is likely to be seen by an individual as having power so when they suggest a treatment, it is likely that the treatment would be accepted. Disadvantages of drug therapy for the individual are the side-effects that come from taking the drugs. However, drugs can be inexpensive for society if the alternative is hospital care, for example. Drugs help to control mental disorders and can be said to help to control behaviour that society does not want, so drug therapy is seen as a form of social control.

Systematic desensitisation

In learning theories you studied two treatments for phobias, one of which was systematic desensitisation. You can argue that as in other therapies the therapist has power and the person with the phobia is likely to defer to the therapist, which means there can be a form of control. However, systematic desensitisation asks the person with the phobia to set up the hierarchy going from the least feared example of the phobia to the most feared, so it is the person with the phobia who has that power. Also, they can dictate the pace of the therapy, waiting until they can successfully relax in response to one level of their hierarchy (such as a picture of the feared object) before moving to the next stage. This therapy is praised for giving control to the individual. Nevertheless the therapist is the person in the position of power in the situation. There is an element of social control in systematic desensitisation but perhaps not as much as in other therapies.

> **STUDY HINT**
> You learned about systematic desensitisation as a therapy for phobias when you studied learning theories. Use what you learned then to add evidence to the review here.

Aversion therapy

If you studied aversion therapy as a treatment for phobias in learning theories, you will know that in that therapy the therapist does indeed have control over the situation. The person with the phobia is made to face their fear and to stick with it until it subsides, not because the person is no longer afraid, but because the reaction cannot be maintained by the body. On the plus side this can work, which is good for the individual. However, from the point of view of society there could be abuse of the therapy because it could be used to stop behaviour that society does not want even if the individual does not want to be treated. Thus aversion therapy can be seen and used as a form of social control.

> **Explore**
> Raymond (1956) wrote about a 'case of fetishism treated by aversion therapy' and you can access the report if you wish to using this link: www.ncbi.nlm.nih.gov/pmc/articles/pmc2035612/pdf/brmedj03176-0026.pdf It is an interesting case, partly because it shows you what was being thought in 1956 and you can use the ideas when considering how psychology has developed over time (which is another issue and debate in your course). You might find some of the ideas shocking, perhaps because this is about another era.

The place the therapy takes place in

If you have studied criminological psychology, you will have looked at a CBT treatment and a biological treatment for offenders. The same arguments about social control apply as in clinical psychology. Also, it is important to note that offenders will not have the same freedom when it comes to agreeing to treatment as people who are not in the prison system. There might theoretically be some choice, but offenders, even if they had the choice, are likely not to feel able to refuse treatment. The same might be said of those in hospital. Rosenhan's participants in his 1973 study mentioned that they were given drugs for their 'schizophrenia' but did not take them and, interestingly, they found drugs hidden by other patients so clearly others were not taking them either. However, the fact that the drugs were hidden away shows that the patients had not overtly refused to take them, which suggests that there is a power imbalance in a therapy situation.

> **Explore**
> You can read what Szasz has to say about 'the myth of mental illness' using this link: http://psychclassics.yorku.ca/Szasz/myth.htm. Szasz suggests that a diagnosis itself is a form of social control. He sees what is called 'mental illness' as being about problems in living and it would follow that such 'problems' should be addressed as such and not as illnesses.

> **Explore**
> On the internet you can read an account from the mother of someone with mental health issues who has been imprisoned. The mother talks about how prisons are not the places for people with mental health issues and she mentions some of the issues her daughter has. There are issues in this story about social control, not only issues where social control is not a good thing (the imprisonment will not help), but also where it might be a good thing (such as the idea that her daughter was functioning better with drugs). Here is the link: www.psychologytoday.com/blog/all-in-the-family/201402/prison-or-treatment-people-mental-illness

Social control through obedience to authority

Through studies such as Milgram's, psychology has found out about which situations are likely to improve obedience to authority. For example, orders were obeyed less if they were given by an 'ordinary man', so perhaps wearing uniform is the way police can gain obedience. Orders were obeyed more if the person giving the orders was in the room, so again this might give advice to society about how to obtain and maintain social order. Orders were obeyed more if the setting had prestige, so having civic buildings such as law courts might mean more obedience.

There is an implication in the issue of social control discussed here that social control is 'bad'. In fact, whether social control is benevolent or less benevolent is a different issue from how the psychology is used. The moral element of using what is known about how to get someone to obey goes beyond the psychological knowledge that is used. In some situations, you might say that society needs control, such as over rioting, which has costs for a society. In other situations, you might say that social control goes against individual freedom and is wrong. There might be differences in what is seen as good and bad about social control depending on cultural norms and beliefs. In an answer about the use of psychology in social control, it would be better to stick to how psychology informs social control rather than going into detail about what is right and wrong about such control.

Ross et al. (1977) carried out experiments to look at biasing effects of someone being a 'questioner' and someone else being the 'answerer'. It was found that the questioner has more power in a situation than the one giving the answers. The questioner can show their knowledge in writing the questions and are rated superior to those doing the answering. This sort of study can help to show that power in a situation, and social roles, are about social control.

Four studies relating to psychology being used in social control and the use of therapy

1. Geddes et al. (2003), cited in the WHO Report (2005), carried out a review and found that using drug treatment for depression showed a relapse rate of 18 per cent compared with 41 per cent for a placebo group. Also, the treatment seemed to last up to three years. This seems to support the claim that drug therapy is effective for the individual and if the relapse rate is low, it sounds as if people are being helped. This study suggests that drug therapy is not focusing on social control but on helping individuals. You may not have covered this review in your course, but you will have looked at evidence for the effectiveness of drug therapy so you can draw on your own evidence.

2. Rosenhan (1973) found that when the participants of his study (including himself) went to a hospital and said they heard something in their head like 'thud', they were all but one diagnosed as having schizophrenia in remission and they stayed in the hospital on average for 19 days. They were prescribed medication (though they did not take it), which suggests there was an attempt to control their 'symptoms'.

3. Pavlov (1927) showed that conditioning can occur by manipulating a situation so that a neutral stimulus is associated with an unconditioned response so that it becomes a conditioned stimulus to a conditioned response. This suggests that behaviour can be manipulated so that, for example, a product becomes a conditioned stimulus that gives the conditioned response of 'pleasure' if the product is associated with an unconditioned stimulus that brings pleasure. Such manipulation could be used as a form of social control, for example, brain washing.

4. Watson and Rayner (1920) conditioned a fear in a young baby. They had control over the situation, the baby had no power and the baby's mother might have looked up to the researchers and accepted that they knew what they were doing. Their study did not show social control but it did show control over the young boy and

it demonstrates, as Pavlov's studies demonstrate, that classical conditioning can involve manipulation. Watson and Rayner's study was important because it showed that classical conditioning principles worked in humans.

STUDY HINT

If you have chosen to look at OCD as a disorder in clinical psychology, you may have chosen Masellis *et al.* (2003) as your study. Masellis *et al.* (2003) found that treatment for OCD tends to focus on the compulsions as they are the behaviours resulting from the obsessions. However, focusing on the obsessions would be more beneficial according to Masellis *et al.* (2003). This suggests that psychology can help in studying the effectiveness of treatments and can help to remove the element of social control. You could use this study if you have covered it.

Progress check 7.16

Suggest a study that might be done to help you to find out whether a treatment was a form of social control or a help to the individual.

The use of psychological knowledge in society

The use of psychology in social control links to the use of psychological knowledge in society.

STUDY HINT

You can use ideas about social control in society as examples of the use of psychological knowledge in society; for example, how understanding of prejudice or obedience can be used in society to inform social control.

For each topic area in your course, you have considered a key question about the use of psychology in society. In this part of the chapter, one key question is chosen and reviewed for each topic area. Topics Six, Seven and Eight are excluded here as they are the options in your course so you will only have covered one of those.

STUDY HINT

Some of the key questions you may have covered in your course are briefly discussed here to show how psychology can be used to help with the issues the question raises. However, you will have looked at key questions in more detail, so use these discussions to revise for your key questions. You can also use other key questions for society as examples of how psychology is used in society.

For this issue and debate, you can use any contribution that psychology has made to society. You could work through the content you have covered and pick out areas where you have looked at psychology contributing to society.

Table 7.7 gives a list of some of the topics you have covered in your course. You could use the list to think about where each area has contributed to society.

Table 7.7 Topics you have covered in your course

Social psychology	Cognitive psychology	Biological psychology	Learning theories	Clinical psychology
Obedience	Multi-store model of memory	Neurotransmitter functioning	Classical conditioning	Diagnosis of mental disorders
Agency theory	Working memory	How recreational drugs work	Operant conditioning	DSM and ICD
Social impact theory	Episodic and semantic memory	Brain functioning and aggression	Shaping behaviour	Features and explanations – schizophrenia
Prejudice	Reconstructive memory	Theory of natural selection	Social learning	Features and explanations – depression, OCD or anorexia nervosa
Social identity theory	Digit span as part of short-term memory	Freud's ideas about aggression (to counter biological arguments)	Vicarious learning	Two treatments for depression or schizophrenia
Realistic group conflict theory	Brain damage related to memory loss	Hormones, including aggression	Phobias – acquisition, maintenance, treatment	Two treatments for depression, OCD or anorexia nervosa

Social psychology: key question for society

How can prejudice and anti-social crowd behaviour be reduced?

This is just one example in social psychology of how psychology is used to inform society. Knowing about how to engender obedience can be useful for society (page 664).

Understanding factors relating to obedience can help to control behaviour in society and understanding how prejudice and hostility can result in competition over resources can help to prevent behaviour such as rioting.

How can psychology be used to inform this issue for society?

Society benefits financially and economically from reducing prejudice and controlling unruly crowd behaviour.

Social identity theory can help to explain how hostility forms towards an out group through in group favouritism. When an out group is easily identifiable, there is likely to be prejudice because someone's in group is what they identify with in order to protect their self-esteem.

Crowds might turn to rioting simply because of hostility towards an out group. However, realistic group conflict theory suggests that prejudice is more than out group hostility; there is an element of conflict over resources that leads to prejudice and discrimination. Sherif *et al.* (1954/1961) show how two groups of boys turn against one another as soon as they learn of each other's existence, which supports social identity theory.

However, the study also shows that when competition between the two groups is introduced there is actual prejudice, such as name calling and wanting to win. Society can learn to focus people onto the country or culture as one large group as that would prevent out group hostility. Also, society can take special care when resources are scarce to make sure they are shared out fairly because competition over resources leads to prejudice.

Sherif *et al.* (1954/1961) go further to show how to reduce prejudice. This is done by creating goals that everyone has to work together to achieve. This reduces prejudice – perhaps by creating a larger in group and by reducing competition.

Progress check 7.17

Using one study from social psychology, explain the use of psychology for society.

Cognitive psychology: key question for society

How can psychologists' understanding of memory help patients with dementia?

In places like the hairdresser's, it helps to know how to help people with dementia; for example, not having music on when talking with the person, so as not to overload them with information to process.

How can psychology be used to inform this issue for society?

The number of people with dementia in the UK is growing, which is a concern for society. As with most issues for society, this is about cost of healthcare for such individuals – as well as, of course, the cost to the individual in terms of problems with living with dementia.

Cognitive psychology offers a lot of information about how memory works, not only using models but also in terms of brain functioning that relates to memory processes. Episodic memory can be affected in dementia, which means there are problems with remembering what is happening, both in the past and in the present. This can affect everyday functioning. Episodic memory is less affected the further back in the past the memories go. It could be useful to know this, so that the person with dementia is not contradicted and can live in the past.

Someone with dementia might forget something they have just been told because it was not encoded. A way to help is to cue memories as much as possible. For example, rather than asking 'What did you do today?', which is a very general question, someone can ask 'Did you go for a walk today?', which is more specific and gives the person cues to help them to remember. Using pictures and colours as well

as words can help to recover memories as well, such as using a picture of someone in the family when asking about them.

Short-term memory can be a problem. Sebastián and Hernández-Gil (2012) showed that healthy older people and people with dementia had a shorter digit span than younger people. In fact, their digit span was closer to that of a six or seven year old. This was not just people with dementia but the finding does suggest that things should be written down for those with dementia, for example, labelling keys. Colour-coding can also help.

Working memory shows that someone would have difficulty doing two tasks if they were using the same type of processing. People with dementia, who need to concentrate on incoming information as they have difficulty processing information especially concerning memory, find it even harder to process information using the same type of processing. For example, if you are speaking to someone with dementia, make sure there are no other sources of sound, as it is better if a person with dementia is just processing one message at a time.

If someone is trying to remember something in short-term memory they use rehearsal, which is repeating using silent speech. This can use up the articulatory loop, which the working memory model says is part of the phonological loop. This is from Baddeley and Hitch's (1974) working memory model. Talking to someone with dementia when they are trying to encode information in long-term memory will mean dual processing is taking place, possibly using the same type of processing. This should be avoided.

The idea of memory being reconstructive, as Bartlett suggested in 1932, can be useful in understanding dementia as well. If memories are reconstructed using prior experiences and schemas, then someone with dementia who seems to be saying something that does not make sense, might be using mixed schemas and muddled episodic memories, so it is best to listen carefully, ask limited questions, but try to follow the thought processes of the individual.

Steyvers and Hemmer (2012) cite evidence that people with amnesia can be helped by having prior knowledge of what they are trying to recall. Those with prior knowledge draw on it when recalling and if there is damage to semantic memory, the effect of having prior knowledge is missing. If that prior knowledge can be displayed or explained it might help someone with a poor semantic memory.

Explore
You can read more about how behavioural and psychological issues for those with dementia might be helped by using this link: www.alzheimers.org.uk/site/scripts/documents_info. php?documentID=77&pageNumber=6

Biological psychology: key question for society

How effective is drug therapy for treating addictions?

How can psychology be used to inform this issue for society?

Treating addiction is important for a society for reasons of productivity and cost. People in a society who need treatment often do not work so they are not productive and they cost society money. This seems a bit heartless because a society is likely to want its citizens to be happy; however, when considering how psychology is used in society (even though there is an element of helping individuals, such as by offering treatment if it is needed), there is also focus on financial and practical issues.

An important issue is how effective drug therapy is. For example, buprenorphine is an opiate and used as a substitute for heroin. There are important side-effects, such as headache, sickness and slow breathing. Side-effects must be considered when considering effectiveness.

Buprenorphine produces euphoria as does any opioid but it does act in a different way from heroin and methadone and has less effect, so taken in low doses, it does not have the withdrawal symptoms that heroin has.

Li *et al.* (2013), which is one of the contemporary studies in your course in biological psychology, showed that cues for heroin link to activation and connectivity between certain brain areas (the limbic system and prefrontal cortex), which suggests that cues themselves affect brain functioning. This means that drug therapy, involving using a substitute to help with withdrawal symptoms and addiction, might not be enough if the conditioned cues around the addict are not addressed.

Van den Oever *et al.* (2008), another of the contemporary studies in your course, agreed with Li *et al.* that cues that come with heroin addiction are a problem. Van den Oever *et al.* showed that animals that experience cues they associate with heroin addiction have changes in their brain from the experience of the cues. The changes are at the synapses and the researchers found that injections could affect those synaptic changes and prevent the synaptic depression that seemed to lead to relapse. Van den Oever *et al.* suggest that injections for heroin addicts, to prevent that synaptic depression, might help with relapse from exposure to cues. This is a different form of drug therapy from using substitute drugs, which is an interesting avenue of research.

Learning theories: key question for society

Can anorexia nervosa be caused by cultural images such as 'size-zero' models?

How can psychology be used to inform this issue for society?

Anorexia nervosa is an eating disorder characterised by being extremely underweight (about 15 per cent lower than it should be) and refusing to eat properly, if at all. Sufferers tend to see themselves as fat even when they are painfully thin. Anorexia usually starts in the teenage years. Girls stop menstruating because their bodies 'shut down'. Boys also suffer from anorexia, but less so than girls, although the rate of anorexia in boys is rising. Around 10 to 15 per cent of those wanting treatment for anorexia or bulimia (another eating disorder) are male.

Social learning theory suggests that people imitate role models, especially celebrities and people with prestige. However, the National Association of Anorexia Nervosa and Associated Disorders states that only about 5 per cent of women in the US match the size shown in advertising as the ideal.

Bandura carried out studies in the 1960s where he showed that children copied acts of aggression they observed adults carrying out. He found that there were gender differences in the aggression displayed and also that there was a tendency for a child to copy their own gender more. Such findings can be applied to suggest that young girls might imitate female adults and if female models and celebrities are seen to be thin, then young girls might, through social learning, want to be thin.

Social learning theory suggests people also learn by vicarious reinforcement. This means that if people see being thin as being rewarded, perhaps by praise or by association when a celebrity wins an award, then that could lead to the behaviour or characteristic being imitated.

Anorexia can also be explained by operant conditioning, because of the rewards for being thin and the negative reinforcement against being fat. If peers tease fat children, then to avoid being teased, they will stop eating in order to be thin. If peers are envious of thin children, they will do what they can to become thin, including not eating. It could be said that the current focus on an 'obesity crisis' will lead to an increased desire to be thin in order to avoid the criticism of being obese. This would be an example of negative reinforcement.

Cross-cultural differences in levels of anorexia tend to support the explanation for anorexia given by the learning approach because different types of behaviour and social norms are likely to be modelled in different countries. Therefore, if there is less emphasis in another culture on being thin, then fewer people will try to be thin. Becker *et al.* (2002), which is one of the contemporary studies in learning theories in your course, showed that adolescent girls in Fiji in the late 1990s, before TV was introduced, did not seem to focus on diet and weight, whereas some years later after TV had been introduced for a while, Becker *et al.* found focus on dieting and weight in the same-age girls in Fiji. This did not prove that what they observed led directly to behaviour and attitudes around weight, but it did show an association.

Progress check 7.19

Using the following terms, complete the paragraph: *role models, observational learning, vicarious learning, imitate, positive reinforcement, social learning theory.*

Bandura used _____ to explain how people _____ behaviour that they observe. This can also be called _____. People do not imitate everyone, they imitate in particular _____. Learning can take place using _____, which means watching someone else being rewarded for their behaviour and so reproducing it to get rewarded. This links to operant conditioning, which explains the idea of _____ – we repeat behaviour we have been rewarded for.

Clinical psychology: key question for society

What are the issues around mental health in the workplace?

It is interesting to see how much of what is discussed here can relate to how society can use psychological understanding to inform social control.

How can psychology be used to inform this issue for society?

Stress in the workplace can lead to depression and psychology can inform society about how to help with depression, such as offering treatment. Drug therapy uses selective serotonin reuptake inhibitors (SSRIs), which seem to be effective. They work at the synapse, preventing the reuptake of serotonin and thus leaving more serotonin for use at the synapse. It is thought that low levels of serotonin are an explanation for depression. If depression can be controlled that benefits society as there is likely to be more productivity, which helps the economy, and fewer health costs.

Social isolation can be a factor in depression and in schizophrenia. If someone cannot work because of a mental disorder, they will be more socially isolated, which can worsen the situation. Society can focus on offering support at work rather than them not being able to work, as that can help to maintain productivity and can also help the individual.

Cognitive-behavioural therapy has been shown to be effective in depression and anxiety, both of which can be found in the workplace. For example, a 2008 study (Kuyken *et al.*) reported that a group-based form of CBT (mindfulness based cognitive therapy – MBCT) is at least as successful in treating depression as medication such as Prozac, even in the long term. It was better at preventing relapse, offered a more effective change in quality of life, and was more cost-effective. Such therapy could be offered in the workplace and an employee could be given the time to attend sessions. This might be cost-effective for society in the long run as well as supporting the individual.

Explore
You can read more about issues of mental health in the workplace using this link: www.theguardian.com/society/2014/sep/10/mental-health-workplace-employers

Four studies relating to the use of psychological knowledge in society

Different studies involve different issues relating to how psychological knowledge can be used in society. Here are some ideas:

1 Bandura's work in the 1960s is useful as social learning can explain a lot of behaviour. Classical conditioning shows how an association is formed with something that naturally gives a response, so natural behaviours such as fears can be explained. Pavlov's studies are useful in explaining classical conditioning. Operant conditioning shows that people repeat what they are rewarded for doing and stop when they are punished, and Skinner's work gives evidence for operant conditioning. However, Bandura goes a step further, because he accepts the idea of reward and punishment in explaining behaviour, but he also points out that people observe and imitate behaviour. This means not all behaviour has to be reinforced; social learning can take place anywhere and does not require reinforcement as such.

STUDY HINT

There are a few studies that can be useful in many situations. If you cannot remember a theory or study in an exam, think about some central theories and studies, such as social learning theory and Bandura's studies, to see if they would be helpful. Often you will find they are.

2 Van den Oever *et al.* (2008) used rats to show that cues that are linked to heroin addiction, when reintroduced after extinction of the addiction, give changes in the brain. This is a useful study when discussing the use of psychology for society, as the researchers state in their discussion that their aim is to develop a treatment for heroin-users, which is helping society as well as individuals. Van den Oever *et al.* felt that what they found, which was a lowered level of substance in the brain, could lead to injecting the substance in humans. This could mean avoiding brain changes that might come in humans who had overcome an addiction to heroin when they encountered cues in the environment that they had associated with their heroin addiction. If you have not covered van den Oever *et al.* in your course, you can choose a different study to use in this issue and debate.

3 Sherif *et al.* (1954/1961) is the classic study you covered in social psychology in your course. Sherif *et al.* focus on explaining prejudice, which is useful for society, and also on reducing prejudice, so there is a clear practical application coming from their work.

4 Pavlov's studies (1927) are useful when considering psychology being useful for society. Classical conditioning can be used to develop treatments for phobias, such as systematic desensitisation, which you covered in learning theories.

Test yourself

Assess ways in which psychological knowledge can be used in society. **(20 marks)**

STUDY HINT

Exam questions will use 'injunctions', which are words that tell you what to do in the question. 'Assess' requires you to give consideration to factors that apply to what the question is about and to come to a judgement, and possibly a conclusion. It is worth studying the list of injunctions your course will use so that you know what a question is asking for.

Issues related to socially sensitive research

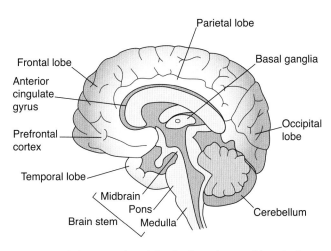

In research it has been found that brain regions and functioning have a role in behaviour, emotions and thinking. If the brain affects such issues, that might absolve people of responsibility, which is a socially sensitive idea.

What is socially sensitive research?

Socially sensitive research is research that has negative implications for the participants and/or for the group they represent, beyond the study itself.

Implications in research include focusing on the participants, those close to them, those in any group represented in the study and also the researchers themselves. If people are affected by the results of a study beyond being affected by the study itself, which would be about the ethics of the study, then that makes the research socially sensitive. Research is socially sensitive if there is the potential for a lot of lives to be affected by the findings, and also if there are effects on psychology itself, and on the psychologists doing the study.

There are areas of research that affect people in a more serious way than others. For example, if research is private or stressful, or if the findings of research lead to stigma, these are likely to affect others negatively. These are the research areas that are seen as 'socially sensitive'.

Sensitivity can also arise because people might be treated differently as a result of the way research findings are interpreted or how they are reported in the media.

Although socially sensitive research can give findings that are a threat to others and upsetting, it is research that should be done. This is because such research is likely to relate to people that are seen as having low status in a society, for example, or where people might be the subject of media reports or targeted because of the findings. Research that is socially sensitive can help people in a society to understand areas of sensitivity; for example, what it is like to experience abuse. The issue in psychology is making sure that such research is handled carefully.

Progress check 7.20
Explain what is meant by socially sensitive research.

Specific issues of socially sensitive research

Attention of the media and general public

Socially sensitive research is likely to attract media attention and the attention of the general public. This must be taken into account when planning and carrying out a study and making decisions about the ethics.

How the research question is formulated

Sieber and Stanley (1988) wrote about 'ethical and professional dimensions of socially sensitive research'. They discuss aspects of research that lead to ethical concerns, including the setting up of the research question. They say that even posing a particular question can have social implications and they give an example about a research question focusing on genes and people exhibiting violent behaviour. Just asking a question about such an area gives rise to some assumptions. A similar example that Sieber and Stanley (1988) give is asking a question about racial differences in intelligence.

How research is conducted and how participants are treated

Ethics for treating participants in psychology focus a lot on doing no harm. A major issue in research that is socially sensitive is maintaining confidentiality in order to do no harm. Privacy is important and it can be argued that the type of research that is socially sensitive is done in areas people are likely to want to keep private, such as the use of recreational (and illegal) drugs. Issues can also arise during a study. Researchers have a duty of care and if a young person reveals something during a study that suggests they, or someone else, might come to harm, the researcher has to breach confidentiality. The researcher may have to make a judgement about the likely harm and the wish to maintain confidentiality and privacy.

Context and place of the research

Another issue according to Sieber and Stanley (1988) is the context the research is carried out in. For example, if research takes place in a specific setting, any findings might affect that setting negatively. If the institution has power over the participants, they may be affected by any 'fallout'. An example is if research finds that there is not much stress in a company, the company might then not put in place counselling to support those who are feeling stress in their workplace.

Interpretation and application of research findings

Research findings and how they are used can go beyond what the researcher intended, perhaps especially in socially sensitive research. It might be obvious that findings about obedience would be applied to real-life settings, such as giving ideas as to how to get people to obey (by having police present in uniform, for example). However, it might not have been so clear that a defence for brutality of soldiers might be that it was the situation that led to the obedience, not their personality. This was a defence used for soldiers who attacked prisoners at Abu Ghraib. It could be argued that this defence was entirely justifiable. The point here is that findings in psychology are used in society and that use is often in a socially sensitive area, which researchers must take into account as far as they can.

Some research is very helpful for individuals and society, for example, research into eyewitness testimony. If you studied criminological psychology, you will have seen that eyewitness memory is unreliable, which has led to courts not wanting to convict on eyewitness evidence alone. McCosker *et al.* (2001) thought that socially sensitive research is important and should be carried out but there must be safeguards, such as careful interviewing and having counsellors on hand to recognise stress in participants and possibly to stop the interview.

Progress check 7.21

Explain two parts of research where social sensitivity can be an issue.

Examples of socially sensitive areas of research

Looking for explanations of anorexia nervosa

Anorexia nervosa, with its emphasis on females and on young people 'starving themselves' and having misperception of body shape as a symptom, is an area of sensitivity. People with anorexia nervosa, and their families, may feel that they are being blamed. Crisafulli *et al.* (2008) considered attitudes to anorexia nervosa to see if people judged the illness differently if they read

about a biological or genetic cause or if they read about a sociocultural explanation. They found that people who read the biological or genetic explanation tended to blame people with the illness less than if they read that social and cultural reasons caused the illness. The results were not that strong, but the researchers felt they had at least given some indication that if people think something has a biological cause they are less likely to blame the individual. Interestingly, this study would be useful when discussing the use of psychology in society because from this it would follow that society should make available findings that relate mental disorders to biological underpinnings as then people are thought to be less to blame.

Studying the brains of murderers: Raine *et al.* (1997)

Studying the brains of murderers to see if there are differences is a socially sensitive area of research. The brains were found to differ from the controls in Raine *et al.* (1997) and this can be taken to mean there is no responsibility for the violent actions, which would then not have been planned and deliberate perhaps. There are consequences for the participants and for the wider population. These are not necessarily negative consequences because if someone's biology is to blame, perhaps they will be treated better by society.

Research into prejudice and personality

If it is found that people with a right-wing authoritarian personality are more prejudiced, as Cohrs *et al.* (2012) suggested, then people might turn against those with that personality or the behaviour that personality relates to. Alternatively, prejudice can be engendered, such as forming an in group with resulting out group hostility, as shown in Tajfel's (1979) work on social identity theory. Though studies might be done to help reduce prejudice, their findings can be used in a different way. Similarly, Guimond *et al.* (2013) found multicultural approaches to other cultures in a country led to less prejudice than countries using an assimilation approach, so those with an assimilation approach might be criticised or ostracised by societies that wish to reduce prejudice.

Diagnosis of mental disorders

The diagnosis of mental disorders is a sensitive area because of the importance of reliable and valid diagnosis. Treatment follows diagnosis, so if the diagnosis is wrong, treatment will be wrong as well. Diagnosis is not always seen as valid; for example, if there are cultural issues that affect diagnosis, then diagnosis is not something scientific, universal and accurate. If someone is diagnosed incorrectly, and if diagnosis leads to labelling, that can cause someone a lot of difficulties. Rosenhan (1973) found that people who presented at a hospital with a basic symptom of schizophrenia were quickly diagnosed as having schizophrenia in remission (all but one) and were put on medication. The study showed that the diagnosis led to labelling because although the participants then behaved normally, the staff treated them as mentally ill; for example, when a participant took notes this was called 'writing behaviour'. Rosenhan's research was socially sensitive as it showed that the staff in a mental hospital did not recognise good mental health in the 'patients'. In a second part to the study, Rosenhan told staff in hospitals that there would be more pseudo-patients presenting themselves and these were 'recognised'. This was in spite of Rosenhan not sending in any other 'sane' pseudo-patients. It seemed clear that 'sanity' and 'insanity' were not easy to diagnose. The study had important implications for such hospitals.

Four studies relating to socially sensitive research

1 Rosenhan (1973) showed that hospitals labelled people mentally unwell and did not recognise good mental health in people once they were labelled or diagnosed as having a mental disorder. This is a socially sensitive finding for society because if those in such hospitals are in fact well, then that is something society needs to address. Rosenhan's study is the classic study in clinical psychology in your course.

2 Raine *et al.* (1997) found that people pleading not guilty by reason of insanity (NGRI) to murder had brain differences compared with a control group. There are social implications in the findings of the study, which were taken to mean that people are not to blame for any violence because their brain structure and functioning are the cause. Raine *et al.* (1997) is the classic study in biological psychology in your course.

3 Guimond *et al.* (2013) found that multiculturalism led to less prejudice than assimilation, which is a socially sensitive result because it might put pressure on countries using an assimilation approach to change to a multicultural one. If you have not covered Guimond *et al.* (2013), you can choose a different piece of research for your study of prejudice.

4 Pavlov's research had the potential to be socially sensitive because it can explain phobias and also can lead to treatment for such phobias. This can be seen as a positive outcome. However, classical conditioning can be used as evaluative conditioning. This means people can be shown something that gives a pleasure response and then something else can be paired with the initial image, thereby giving a pleasure response. Advertisers can use this idea. They can show a picture of a celebrity to get a 'pleasure' response and then pair their product with that celebrity, which should lead to liking of the product. This can be harmless, but it could be seen as 'brainwashing' and there is social sensitivity in this area of research.

Test yourself

Using research, assess issues relating to the social sensitivity of research in psychology. **(16 marks)**

Building a body of knowledge in psychology

One way of looking at how psychology has built a body of knowledge is to consider how it has developed over time. Another way is to see how comparisons are used in psychology using different themes.

An understanding of how psychological understanding has developed over time

A brief history of psychology

Wundt was said to have set up the first laboratory in psychology in 1879, which can be seen as the start of psychology. He used introspection to find out more about how memory works. Introspection focuses on us thinking about how we think. Introspection is no longer used in psychology as a means of studying the brain and behaviour.

In the 1890s, Freud studied mental illness and what could be done to improve things for people with such problems. He focused in particular on hysteria, which was where people had physical symptoms but there seemed to be no physical cause. He went on to develop a whole explanation for human development, and his explanation encompassed what could go wrong. His focus on psychoanalysis underpins modern counselling techniques to a large extent. People have developed Freud's ideas and moved on from them. However, the idea that the unconscious guides our thinking and can be the source of mental problems still remains.

Pavlov's work shows that by the early 1900s laboratory work was starting to inform people about behaviour, as well as thinking. Pavlov was not strictly speaking a psychologist, but his theories, being about behaviour, informed psychology. Classical conditioning principles are used in therapies such as systematic desensitisation and so classical conditioning, developed by Pavlov, is still an accepted theory.

In 1924, experimental psychology first took place at Princeton University, the first university to have a psychology department. Others followed and the American Psychological Association (APA) was set up. So about 100 years ago psychology was just beginning. There were some theories being used, but nothing like what there is today. However, the basic idea of using experiments and aiming for scientific understanding still remains.

The idea of behaviourism, which was started by J.B. Watson and developed by Skinner, was an important development in psychology from around 1920 to the 1940s. The important point Watson made was that in order to build a body of knowledge about humans, it was behaviour that should be focused on because behaviour could be observed and studied. This was before research methods such as scanning were possible. The behaviourists wanted to study the brain and behaviour scientifically and to do that they had to be able to collect empirical data.

In the early 1900s, Spearman and others in the UK were working on ideas about general intelligence and, importantly, ideas about statistical procedures that could help scientific understanding of human processes. You have learned about the Spearman's test for correlations, which shows that there was a focus on building a scientific body of knowledge.

By the 1960s, with Skinner's work on operant conditioning and Pavlov's ideas about classical conditioning being accepted, the experimental method was the main one being used. Cognitive psychology became the focus in the 1960s as well, and social psychology was also important from about that time. Computer science was developing too, and the idea that the human brain worked like a computer helped the focus on the brain and information

processing. Bartlett had looked at memory in 1932, but in general the 1960s was a time of many experiments and a lot of knowledge was built up.

Milgram's work on obedience in the 1960s and both social identity theory and realistic group conflict theory (also known as realistic conflict theory) focusing on explaining prejudice were developed in the 1960s and 1970s. In the 1960s, Bandura studied social learning. Bandura's work can perhaps be seen as linking social psychology and learning theories. You can see that at this time experiments were seen as the way to uncover understanding about people and behaviour.

Progress check 7.22

Explain how three studies that were done in the 1960s showed the focus on experiments at the time.

Areas in your course that show how psychology has developed over time

Four areas that show how psychological understanding has developed over time are included here, but there are others you could use.

STUDY HINT

Use Table 7.7 (page 665) to go through the topics you have covered and think about whether you looked at how knowledge in that area developed over time.

The history of neuroimaging

In the 1970s and 1980s MRI scanning using magnets and CT scanning using x-rays were developed. This meant that brain areas could be studied, so a lot was learned about how the brain was formed. PET scanning was developed too, also in the 1970s, using a radioactive tracer, and for the first time it was not just a static image of the brain that could be seen, but brain activity too and brain function could be studied. From the 1990s, fMRI was used and is still the most popular means of neuroimaging.

Neuroimaging was an important development, but so was the development of computers as scanning uses computers to generate the images that are then used as evidence. Currently there is interest in using more than one scanning technique at the same time to then pool the information generated. For example, transcranial magnetic stimulation (TMS) can be used with MRI and can tell the brain (using magnetic field impulses) to think about actions, which is measuring the brain even more directly than asking someone to perform the action.

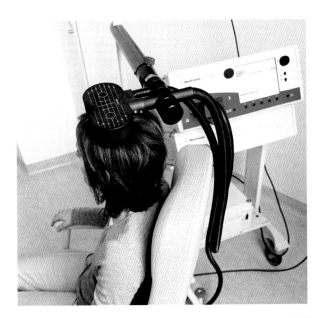

Neuroimaging, such as transcranial magnetic stimulation (TMS), continues to develop.

You have covered PET, CT and fMRI neuroimaging techniques in your course, so you have seen how psychology has developed over time using these techniques.

Progress check 7.23

What is it about CT, PET and fMRI scanning that has developed alongside the ways of measuring brain function?

The growth of the use of qualitative data

Although Freud had gathered qualitative data in his case studies where he aimed to uncover reasons for mental health issues, the focus for a long time was mostly on experimentation, gathering empirical data and focusing on the scientific method (page 651). Although qualitative data were used beforehand, it was not until the 1990s that qualitative data became more accepted as a way of developing understanding in psychology. Grounded theory developed a new way of generating theory, building theory from data rather than using theory to test a hypothesis by means of data. This was not so much to go against science but to show that qualitative data could be used in a scientific way. For example, thematic analysis requires a learning journal to be kept in an attempt to avoid subjectivity in analysis.

Rebbie et al. (2002, cited in Wertz, 2014) say that qualitative research began to appear in professional journals in the 1990s, which in terms of the history of psychology is not that long ago.

Allport in 1942 argued that using personal documents provides valid data and felt that methodological problems that might arise from using qualitative data to build knowledge should be looked at and solved, so that such data had value. Allport felt that researchers in psychology should promote the use of qualitative data and this could be done both with reliability and validity. It took time for this idea to develop and qualitative data only really became more accepted in the 1990s. Glaser and Strauss developed the idea of grounded theory in 1967 so the ideas were there. Currently grounded theory is widely used as a way of doing research. The experimental tradition in psychology, which is still a main focus today, was perhaps hard to compete with.

Explore

You can read Wertz's (2014) paper on qualitative inquiry in the history of psychology using this link: **www.apa.org/pubs/ journals/features/qua-0000007.pdf**

In your course you have looked at qualitative data in research in psychology, including using thematic analysis, content analysis and grounded theory as ways of doing qualitative research. In clinical psychology, you covered a case study and will have seen how case studies tend to use qualitative data.

Progress check 7.24

List three issues in psychology that you have studied relating to the use of qualitative data.

The development of neuroscience and clinical psychology

Although PET scanning meant the active brain could be studied, which was a very important development for psychology, fMRI scanning, which developed in the 1990s, has led to neuroscience moving into new areas. For example, social neuroscience has developed, emphasising that social issues affect how we develop. It is suggested that social isolation links to both depression and schizophrenia. Neuroscience shows that it is not only that social isolation is a factor in depression, but there are physiological changes that come with such isolation. These physiological changes then lead to depression, which adds to the feeling of social isolation and so there is a cycle of depression. The field of neuroscience does not just look at our biology alone, but realises that culture, social interactions and emotions have an effect on the way the brain processes such aspects of living. fMRI brain scanning has been the trigger for these developments because it allows study of the active brain in a way that can give evidence for how brain and life experiences work very closely together. Explanations for schizophrenia have changed over time, though the idea that excess dopamine has something to do with schizophrenia remains, even though issues about glutamate are now implicated too. The DSM has changed over time, with DSM-5 being quite recent. Changes have been affected by social and cultural issues perhaps, as different diagnoses go into the manual and others come out.

Explore

You can access an article on the Association for Psychological Science website which considers how psychological science has changed over 25 years. Here is the link:

www.psychologicalscience.org/index.php/publications/observer/2013/november-13/what-we-know-now-how-psychological-science-has-changed-over-a-quarter-century.html

In your course you will have looked at explanations for schizophrenia and for one other mental disorder, which might have been depression. The explanations might well have explained the diathesis-stress idea that mental disorder can come from underpinning biology and genes, but alongside what is happening in life as well.

The study of genetic influence on brain and behaviour

Darwin had explained how the fittest organisms survive in order to pass on their genes and therefore those genes are the ones inherited. However, the study of genes was not looked at specifically in psychology until fairly recently. Twin studies were carried out, such as Gottesman and Shields in 1966; however, these made deductions based on what a set of twins both did. When what identical twins both did was more similar than what non-identical twins both did (looking at the same behaviour or characteristic), then that behaviour was said to have a strong genetic trait.

When more became known about the human genome, a lot more could be done to see what genes went with what behaviour or characteristic. It was soon realised that it would not be that simple. There were genes that went together, for example, and only with the right combination would a behaviour or characteristic be displayed. The development of knowledge about genetic underpinning of behaviour in humans came about because of method possibilities, as did many developments in psychology. Studies using animals are able to study combinations of genes and to suggest ways in which specific combinations might explain certain features and characteristics of humans.

You may have studied Scott-Van Zeeland et al.'s (2013/2014) work on gene sequencing and its role in anorexia nervosa. Scott-Van Zeeland et al. (2013/2014) is one of the two contemporary studies you need to know if you chose anorexia nervosa as a mental disorder in clinical psychology. The study found gene variants associated with EPHX2, giving susceptibility to anorexia nervosa. This is not a single gene – research now focuses more on variants of genes when looking at the role of genetics in human behaviour. The method involved DNA testing, so such understanding in psychology would not have been possible without DNA testing.

Areas in your course that show how psychology has not changed much over time

You will have noted that some psychological understanding has stood the test of time and appears not to have changed much. When discussing the issue and debate of how psychological understanding has changed over time, you could discuss how it has not changed. However, most of your focus must be on how it has developed over time.

Your study of obedience may have shown you that what is known about the influence of the situation on obedience has not changed over time. Your study of prejudice is also likely to have shown you that similar ideas about prejudice are still held. The use of experiments has not changed over time, the scientific method still being favoured. Some underpinning theories are still used, such as the three learning theories you covered and ideas about how neurotransmitters work.

The study of obedience

In the 1960s and 1970s, Milgram found that it is the situation that leads to obedience rather than personality. In 2009, Burger replicated Milgram's work and he too found that the situation is what leads to obedience. Burger was also working in the USA, so the culture was the same; however, his study took place in 2009, a long time after Milgram's, so it could be argued that the culture had changed. Most studies looking at obedience have found it to be due to the situation.

Burger (2009) is one of the contemporary studies you could have chosen in social psychology and you will have studied Milgram's work.

The study of prejudice

Adorno et al. (1950) suggested the authoritarian personality was what gave prejudice. Cohrs et al. in 2012 looked at personality, right-wing authoritarianism and social dominance orientation and found that the three were connected. Right-wing authoritarianism means thinking society needs rules for there to be order and rules must be obeyed. Social dominance orientation refers to someone thinking they are near the top of a hierarchy and those with social dominance must be obeyed. These are two forms of personality. This suggests that the same traits have been linked to personality from the 1950s to the current day.

Cohrs *et al.* (2012) note that much of the research into prejudice uses self-report data and they question how reliable self-report data are. Therefore, they gave out two questionnaires to their participants. One was to get the participants' views about their own prejudice; the other was given to someone who knew the participant so that peer-report data could be gathered. Cohrs *et al.* found peer-report data matched self-report data sufficiently for reliability (and possibly validity) to be claimed. This was perhaps helping psychology to develop by introducing peer-report as well as self-report data.

Social identity theory, a theory of prejudice, is a theory that has stood the test of time too. Brown (2000) explains what he calls 'past achievements, current problems and future challenges' relating to social identity theory, underlining its usefulness in explaining intergroup relations. Ison and Kent used social identity theory to discuss eating disorders in 2010. They used semi-structured interviews with eight females and used interpretative phenomenological analysis (IPA). They found three themes: one was the shift in social identity in those with eating disorders, the second was about out group influence and the third was about the in group and eating disorders. There are issues in Ison and Kent (2010) that relate to your course. Social identity theory is still used to explain intergroup relationships.

In your course Adorno *et al.* is not a required study. Cohrs *et al.* (2012), however, is a contemporary study in social psychology, so you may have chosen it. You will have covered social identity theory in your study of prejudice. Ison and Kent use qualitative data and semi-structured interviewing to gather the data. These are features of method that you have covered in your course.

Explore

You can read Brown's review of social identity theory using this link: http://onlinelibrary.wiley.com/doi/10.1002/1099-0992(200011/12)30:6%3C745::AID-EJSP24%3E3.0.CO;2-0/pdf

The use of experiments

The experimental method is a constant in psychological understanding over time. However, this does not mean other methods have not been used. The idea of manipulation of an independent variable and measuring the dependent variable to see what changes have come about is the basic experimental method that is used. The idea is to keep all other variables controlled so that cause-and-effect conclusions can be drawn. Steyvers and Hemmer (2012) used the experimental method to look at the effects of prior knowledge and schemas on memory. Bastian *et al.* (2011) used an experimental method to see the effects of playing violent video games on someone's view of their own humanity.

You may not have studied Steyvers and Hemmer (2012) as it is a choice of contemporary study in cognitive psychology in your course. You may not have studied Bastian *et al.* (2011) either as it is a choice of contemporary study in learning theories. However, if you go back through what you covered in your course, you will find examples of reasonably recent experiments that you can use to show that psychological understanding can develop but methods might stay the same.

Progress check 7.25

Explain one area where psychological understanding has developed over time and one area where the same understanding underpins new research.

STUDY HINT

These are just some ideas about how psychological understanding has developed over time. You can bring in other parts of your course as this is a synoptic part of your course. You can use what is suggested here or make your own notes. When you make claims about how psychology has developed, always give evidence for each claim.

Four studies relating to how psychological understanding has developed over time

1 Baddeley (1966b) found differences in the way STM and LTM code memories. He considered the acoustic code of STM. In 1974 Baddeley and Hitch developed the working memory model, which, amongst other features, had a phonological loop consisting of an articulatory loop and an acoustic store. The articulatory loop could be what is used in rehearsal, which is what (according to the multi-store model) moved information from STM to LTM to stop it being forgotten. According to Baddeley, rehearsal is repeating information as if speaking it (even if sub-vocally) and this idea links to STM using acoustic coding.

Sebastián and Hernández-Gil (2012) suggested that the digit span of English speakers is longer than for Spanish speakers because Spanish number words take longer to say (including sub-vocally), which also link to the working memory idea of there being a phonological loop. Carter et al. (1998) carried out a study with people with schizophrenia and found that when their working memory had a lot of processing to do, the prefrontal cortex blood flow was reduced in those with schizophrenia compared with controls. This shows that working memory is still a theory used in recent research. In 2003, Baddeley published a paper called 'Working memory: looking back and looking forward', supporting the idea that the theory is still used and useful.

Explore

You can access Baddeley's paper 'Working memory: looking back and looking forward' (published in 2003) by using this link: http://public.wsu.edu/~fournier/Teaching/psych592/Readings/Baddeley_Review_2003.pdf

2 Sherif et al. (1954/1961) carried out their Robbers Cave study and found that competition gave prejudice and that working together towards a common goal helped to reduce prejudice. Perry (2014) published a paper giving 'the view from the boys'. Perry asks questions about how natural the camp seemed to the boys and how far the role of the researchers in fanning the conflict (such as setting up competition between the groups) led to the findings. One of the findings was that for many of the boys it was the first time they had been to a summer camp so in that respect not natural for them. Two of the boys were paddling a canoe on the lake and saw two snakes – and the man with them in the boat then shot the snakes. The boys called their group the Rattlers because of this incident. Nobody was supposed to be a leader for the boys, but this incident suggests that was not the case. Also, it was difficult for staff to take the data and not join in; for example, they provided the matches for the flag to be burned. Perry says that for both the boys she spoke to, the adults featured a lot in their memories of the study, including in the competitiveness as well as the reconciliation phase; for example, the man in the boat was a member of the Rattlers group. Perry's article shows that Sherif et al.'s study is still important today, but suggests that there are issues about its validity, thus showing how psychological understanding develops over time.

3 Watson and Rayner's (1920) study of Little Albert has been the subject of investigation to find out what happened to 'Albert' and to consider more about the study. Just as Perry (2014) went to find the boys in Sherif et al.'s (1954/1961) Robbers Cave experiment, researchers have looked more at Watson and Rayner's conclusions. Little Albert was identified as a small boy called Douglas who died at the age of six (Beck et al., 2009). It was thought that he might have had health difficulties from the start that may have affected the generalisability of the findings of the study (Fridlund et al. (2012)). Fridlund et al. claimed that Watson knew about Little Albert's condition before selecting him and so from an ethical point of view was wrong to use the boy as his participant.

Power et al. (2014) have done more work on Little Albert's identity and claim he was Albert Barger, who they called 'psychology's lost boy'. If Little Albert is Albert Barger and not Douglas Merritte, then perhaps he did grow up with a fear of furry animals. Of course, Albert Barger's name suits Albert B., which is what the boy was called in the study. There is a lot of detail in the paper written by Power et al. (2014), including a discussion about Douglas being visually impaired and some evidence from film of Little Albert that perhaps he was too. However, Power et al. prepare a lot of evidence to show that Little Albert was Albert Barger, basing their conclusions on his age, his mother's occupation, his name, his body weight at nine months and his medical records. Power et al. say that Albert Barger's niece reported that her uncle had 'an aversion to dogs and to animals in general' (p. 609) and he disliked the sound of barking. However, the family said he had seen a dog killed in an accident so that might have accounted for his fear. Power et al. conclude by saying that Watson and Rayner's study was 'poorly designed and poorly reported'.

You will probably have learned that Little Albert was Douglas Merritte as the case was thoroughly researched before this claim was made. However, as described above, in 2014, other researchers put forward a case for Little Albert being someone else. You can make the claim about the boy being Douglas because that is the current understanding. However, soon perhaps the knowledge provided by Watson and Rayner's study will 'develop' again according to whether this relatively new claim from Power et al. (2014) is accepted.

STUDY HINT
You cannot be aware of all that is known about a study or an area of research in psychology. The Little Albert case shows how hard it is to 'know' psychology, which is the point of this issue and debate.

4 Raine *et al.* (1997) found that people who were pleading not guilty to murder by reason of insanity did have brain differences that were not found in matched controls. Raine had done similar studies beforehand in fact, and has carried on with his research. Psychological understanding develops over time often by the same researcher(s) continuing with their work.

Rocque, Welsh and Raine in 2012 considered modern crime prevention. They wrote a paper focusing on how in criminology there is focus on preventing crime by considering biological risk factors in children. You can see how this builds on Raine's earlier work.

Rocque *et al.* (2012) address the idea of biological crime prevention, which they point out has not yet begun, but does link to what is currently being done in crime prevention programmes to address biology. Biological aspects that relate to crime, according to Rocque *et al.*, include neuropsychological deficits or cognitive deficits in childhood. These include difficulties in planning, problems with controlling inhibitions and problems with selective attention. Another biological aspect that might relate to crime is impulsivity. Even though there are biological aspects suggested linking to the development of criminal behaviour, Rocque *et al.* point out that there are no biological suggestions for crime prevention. Rocque *et al.* suggest that focusing on biology can be an effective way of preventing crime and can be non-discriminatory. The study shows how psychological knowledge develops over time and how a body of knowledge is built – this is because of the existence of earlier knowledge and also because people in the field carry on researching and developing the body of knowledge.

Test yourself

Using research evidence, evaluate how psychological understanding has developed over time. **(20 marks)**

Comparisons of ways of explaining behaviour using different themes

The physicist Kuhn referred to paradigms, which are single theories or ideas about how things work. Psychology tends not to have one paradigm. There are different theories and themes used to explain the brain and behaviour, for example.

What is a 'theme' in psychology?

A 'theme' in this context is hard to define. A useful definition might be that a theme is an idea that recurs in psychology and that seems to have weight. A theme should be a central and a unifying and dominant idea.

What are the approaches in psychology?

An approach in psychology is a way of explaining behaviour and different approaches can offer an explanation for the same behaviour. For example, operant conditioning, which is within the behaviourist approach, offers an explanation for aggression, as does social learning theory, which built on behaviourism. There is also a psychodynamic explanation for aggression, which is Freud's view. The biological approach gives biological explanations for aggression, including an evolution explanation and an explanation looking at neurotransmitter functioning. Another approach is the cognitive approach, which focuses on explaining behaviour by reference to how people process information in the brain. Social psychology considers how people interact with others, including in groups, and it could be said that there is a social approach too.

Table 7.8 shows some approaches in psychology and themes can be found within the approaches.

Table 7.8 Approaches and themes in psychology

Approach/theme	Brief explanation
Behaviourist and 'neo' behaviourist	Psychological knowledge is uncovered by observing behaviour and by rewards and punishments as well as by observational learning.
Biological – neurotransmitter functioning	Neurotransmitter functioning underpins behaviour as well as emotions and thoughts. For example, excess dopamine can be an explanation for schizophrenia and drug therapy can rebalance neurotransmitter functioning.
Biological – genes	Genes influence behaviour and characteristics and environment can interact with genes. Therefore, genes and genetic variants are important when explaining behaviour and characteristics (such as mental disorders).
Biological – evolution	Genes that give characteristics that aid survival are passed on through reproduction and genes that give characteristics that do not aid survival die out. Some of our behaviour and characteristics are survival traits.
Psychodynamic	The unconscious, the id, is powerful in driving our thoughts but we do not know our unconscious. Therefore, we are driven by instincts and thoughts we are not aware of. Our conscience in the form of the superego controls the id; the ego aims to balance the two. Imbalance can explain disorders.
Cognitive	The focus is on the processing of information in the brain, from what is input through the senses, through storage and processing, to an output. Focus is on language, thinking, problem solving, perception and memory.

The approaches offer themes in psychology. One way of understanding the approaches is to compare different ways of explaining behaviour using different themes.

Progress check 7.26

Using the biological, cognitive, behaviourist and psychodynamic approaches, explain one theme from each.

Comparing ways of explaining (and reducing) prejudice using different themes

Social psychology has the overall theme of considering the importance of relationships between people when studying the mind and behaviour. Your study of prejudice illustrates this theme and two main theories of prejudice are offered: social identity theory and realistic group conflict theory.

> **STUDY HINT**
> You will have already learned a lot about the issues and debates. Stop to test yourself at certain points before reading on. For example, you could consider whether social identity theory and realistic group conflict theory seem to be themes and you could make some notes comparing how they explain prejudice.

People at a concert might see themselves as the in group and show favour to their in group (such as when giving someone a job) compared with those who like a different sort of music.

Social identity theory and realistic group conflict theory

Social identity theory

- Social identity theory has the idea that people favour the in group because that enhances their own self-esteem and they can then see themselves as worthwhile, belonging to a 'good' in group. The other side to this idea is that there is hostility towards the out group because other groups have to be 'bad' to help self-esteem.

- Social identity theory can be said to involve themes of in group and out group. If these are themes, they must recur, have weight, be central, unify and have dominance. Social identity theory recurs; for example, Ison and Kent (2010) found a shift in social identity in those with eating disorders (page 677). The idea of out-group hostility can be used to reduce prejudice, such as by forming a larger in group that absorbs the out group, so it has weight. It is unifying in being applied to different areas, such as prejudice and eating disorders, as well as in the workplace, and it has been used since the 1970s so there is some dominance.
- Social identity theory supports the main theme of the social approach, which is that how people interact in groups and between one another has central importance in understanding behaviour.

Realistic group conflict theory

- Realistic group conflict theory has the idea that prejudice comes from competition over resources.
- Realistic group conflict theory has a main theme of conflict and competition between groups affecting how people behave in groups. RCT can be used to explain conflict in today's societies and so the theme recurs.
- It successfully explains prejudice. Sherif *et al.* (1954/1961) showed that the boys in the study turned against one another when they were in competition and yet worked together and liked one another more when they had to work towards superordinate goals.
- It is hard to say that this theory has dominance as social identity theory is also a theory used to explain prejudice. It could be argued that Sherif *et al.*'s study found support for in group and out group behaviour because the boys were against one another as soon as they knew about each other's existence. However, realistic group conflict theory does help to explain how groups can live together harmoniously for a long time and then when there are scarce resources, there tends to be more hostility.
- Brief *et al.* (2005) used realistic group conflict theory to look at 'white' reactions to racial and ethnic diversity in organisations and to consider how far the reactions were affected by the diversity of their experiences in their communities. The idea was to find out if the more interactions between groups in the community, the more acceptance of diversity at work. They found that the more whites lived near to blacks and the more conflict they perceived in their community, the more negative they were towards having ethnic diversity in the workplace. This study supports the realistic group conflict explanation of prejudice.

> **STUDY HINT**
> Look back over your notes about realistic group conflict theory to find evidence for the claims made here. Giving further evidence from what you have learned or ideas of your own will add detail and depth to the arguments.

Summary

It seems that social identity theory has the stronger claim to being a 'theme', but realistic group conflict theory adds to social identity in a way that is useful for society; the element of competition over resources increasing prejudice and conflict appears to have validity. Both are currently used to explain behaviour, as shown in Brief *et al.* (2004) and Ison and Kent (2010). There are ways in which the two theories support one another. Both explain prejudice, both can offer ways of reducing prejudice. This is probably why both theories are still in current use.

> ### Progress check 7.27
> Suggest one way that social identity theory and realistic group conflict theory are the same and one way that they are different when it comes to explaining prejudice.

Comparing ways of explaining memory using different themes

In cognitive psychology, you looked at memory and four theories explaining memory. Here is a brief review of these theories:

- The multi-store model of memory puts forward the idea that there is short-term memory separate from long-term memory. There is emphasis on rehearsal and type of encoding – acoustic or semantic, for example.
- The working memory model examines short-term memory in more detail and puts forward the idea that short-term memory has a phonological loop and a visuospatial sketchpad, as well as an executive control to make decisions. The phonological loop includes an articulatory loop where speech is sounded out.
- Episodic and semantic memory are two ways of looking at long-term memory. Episodic memories are personal memories of episodes in our lives, for example, what we did on our last birthday. Semantic memories are about meaning, such as what 'birthday' means.
- The reconstructive theory of memory focuses on memory accuracy and suggests we use schemas, which are prior information, when making memories. This means our memories are affected by our schemas so are not 'accurate' – they are not laid down as a video would record them.

The following are ways to explain memory using different themes:

- A theory of memory tends to focus on a specific aspect, which can make the theory different. For example, reconstructive memory as a theory looks to explain how memories change over time because of using schemas to guide them and because memory is not a perfect representation of what comes into sensory memory to be coded. The other three theories in your course, however, focus more on the actual coding rather than on any interpretation.

- The idea that short-term memory and long-term memory are separate is upheld by three theories in your course. The multi-store model refers to short-term and long-term memory; the working memory model expands on short-term memory, and the ideas about episodic and semantic memories expand into long-term memory. Thus these three theories can be linked.

- The theories have practical applications, which make them similar, such as how knowledge about working memory can help when working with dementia and understanding of how schemas guide recall can help to understand and use eyewitness memory.

- All the theories focus on information processing and how memory works after the input, in the brain, and then with a resulting output. The cognitive approach is seen as a separate theme. Social psychology focuses on how people behave in groups, biological psychology focuses on biological aspects of behaviour, learning theories look to see how we learn from the environment and cognitive psychology focuses specifically on how we process information in the brain. You can see that cognitive and biological psychology come close in the themes they use (such as case studies of brain damaged patients showing brain regions that inform models of memory in cognitive psychology). The other themes are different.

Summary

- Short- and long-term memory is a theme that has some dominance. Studies still focus on these divisions today. They are central themes; for example, they are used to help people with dementia. If short-term memory

requires rehearsal, which requires the articulatory loop, then someone with dementia can be helped by not having other sound input when they are trying to use their short-term memory.

- The idea of prior knowledge affecting recall can be used when considering eyewitness testimony in court; for example, knowing that such testimony is unlikely to be accurate like a video means there will be interpretation. These ideas are central to our understanding of memory and have dominance.

- All four theories of memory have something to offer when explaining human behaviour, rather than one being the 'best' theory of memory.

Comparing ways of explaining aggression using different themes

In your course you looked at various theories of aggression. Here is a brief review of these theories:

- Aggression can be explained by looking at brain regions, such as the amygdala and the prefrontal cortex. This explanation is within the biological approach.

- Aggression can be explained by ideas around survival of the fittest and evolution. Perhaps aggression in the face of conflict, for example, or to protect one's mate, would be something that led to survival of genes through reproduction. This explanation is within the biological approach.

- Aggression can be explained by Freud's psychodynamic ideas about aggression being an instinct that needs an outlet. Catharsis can help to release instinctive aggressive thoughts from the unconscious.

- Operant conditioning ideas, in the behaviourist approach, can explain aggression by suggesting that it is a response that has been rewarded. For example, if aggression gets attention and attention (even negative attention) is rewarding, aggressive behaviour has then been learned. Operant conditioning is a learning theory.

- Social learning theory suggests that aggression comes from observation of aggression. People copy what they see. Also, if they see aggression being rewarded, which is vicarious reinforcement, then that will mean aggression has been learned. Social learning is a learning theory.

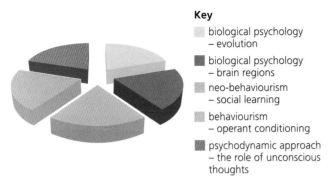

Key

- biological psychology – evolution
- biological psychology – brain regions
- neo-behaviourism – social learning
- behaviourism – operant conditioning
- psychodynamic approach – the role of unconscious thoughts

Five different explanations for aggression, relying on different themes

You can see that explanations of aggression are found in the behaviourist approach, the biological approach and in the psychodynamic approach. The approaches are different themes as they recur, have weight, are central, unify and have dominance. You can see this by using gender as an example as well as aggression. For example, if you were to consider explanations for gender you could give a behaviourist explanation (gender behaviour is reinforced), a social learning explanation (gender behaviour comes from imitating what is observed), a biological explanation (genes dictate our sex) and a psychodynamic explanation (for example, boys identify with fathers to avoid negative emotions about their father).

The three approaches have their own theme(s) which can be applied to aggression. The following are ways to explain aggression using these themes:

- For Freud, using the psychodynamic approach, 'aggression' means a death instinct hidden in the unconscious and needing to be released as the energy in keeping it unconscious needs release.
- The idea of survival of the fittest within the biological approach considers an animal-like instinctive aggression for protecting one's offspring so that genes are passed on. Both Freud's idea and the idea of the fittest genes surviving look at aggression as an instinct.
- Behaviourism and social learning suggest that aggression is learned and refers to violent behaviour or aggressive acts rather than an instinct. Behaviourism and social learning look at how aggression can be nurtured, whereas other theories look at aggression as part of nature. Brain regions being active when someone is aggressive can be seen as an explanation for aggression as an instinct or as a learned behaviour, because this explanation is looking at how aggressive behaviour is carried out.

STUDY HINT

In this section, you can use ideas from other issues and debates. For example, when discussing aggression, you will see a link with nature and nurture. You can take nature and nurture as a theme and use examples here, and you can also use the examples given here when discussing nature and nurture.

Progress check 7.28

Give one strength of having different ways of explaining aggression and one weakness.

Comparing ways of explaining mental disorders using different themes

The approaches listed in Table 7.8 (page 680) can be used when considering explanations for mental disorders, just as they can when considering aggression. You will have covered biological explanations for schizophrenia, one focusing on neurotransmitter functioning and one other. You will have covered a non-biological explanation for schizophrenia too, which might be a social one. For your other chosen disorder, you will have looked at one biological and one non-biological explanation, for example, issues with serotonin related to depression or gene variants linked to anorexia nervosa, which are both biological explanations. OCD tends to come with depression and so serotonin there too can be an issue or another biological focus is that people with OCD seem to show more activity in three brain areas – the basal ganglia, the prefrontal orbital cortex and the cingulate gyrus – as discovered using brain scanning.

Approaches used to explain mental disorders include the cognitive approach, the social approach, behaviourism and learning theories, the psychodynamic approach and various explanations from the biological approach. Clearly these use different themes.

The following are ways to explain mental disorders using different themes:

- The biological approach to explaining schizophrenia focuses on neurotransmitter functioning. It has long been thought that excess dopamine links to schizophrenia and anti-schizophrenic drugs are intended to rebalance neurotransmitter functioning. Another neurotransmitter that is implicated in schizophrenia is glutamate.

- The biological approach also considers genes in schizophrenia, because twin studies suggest a genetic element.
- A social approach to explaining schizophrenia highlights issues like social isolation and difficulties in social functioning.
- A cognitive explanation for OCD is that there is dysfunctional thinking and obsessions are thoughts, which means such an explanation makes sense.
- Compulsions are the behaviours that help to alleviate the anxiety that comes from the thoughts, so there is a behavioural element to OCD too.
- Scott-Van Zeeland et al. (2013/2014) suggested a role for gene variants in anorexia nervosa.
- Social learning theory can help to explain anorexia nervosa as it could come from thin role models and observing them being rewarded.
- The psychodynamic approach explains mental disorders as neuroses arising because of id and superego imbalance and unconscious thinking driving behaviour.

Summary

- The approaches in psychology offer different ways of understanding mental disorders, as has been outlined above. Their explanations suit their themes. Biological psychology focuses on brain regions, neurotransmitter functioning and genes. The psychodynamic approach focuses on the power of the unconscious and social psychology focuses on interactions between people, or the lack of interaction, contributing to mental disorders. The cognitive approach focuses on the way information is processed in the brain, not so much at the neurotransmitter level but in what information is processed and the relationship between thoughts, emotions and behaviour. It is clear that there are fundamental differences in the themes used in the different approaches.
- As with aggression, each explanation tends to take a different view of a mental disorder. A biological explanation sees the disorder as having a biological underpinning and a psychodynamic explanation sees unconscious thoughts as being responsible for a disorder.

> **STUDY HINT**
> When you are comparing ways of explaining behaviour in terms of themes, give examples of studies. For example, when considering the social learning explanation for anorexia nervosa, you can bring in Bandura's work in the 1960s or if you have used it, Becker et al. (2002), who showed that in Fiji the introduction of television gave more focus to dieting and body shape.

Four studies relating to explaining behaviour using different themes

1 Bandura's 1960s work on social learning is so useful when it comes to explaining behaviour because observational learning is a theme in psychology. Bandura showed that children imitated aggression that they watched and he used more than one study to demonstrate his explanation of aggression. His studies can help to explain behaviour other than aggression, such as anorexia nervosa, so it is a study that has a wide application when explaining human behaviour.

2 Lavarenne et al. (2013) is an example of a case study method, so you can use it in clinical psychology in your course. Lavarenne et al. can be used to show how social psychology can explain behaviour. The researchers present a case study of a single session of a support group for people with psychosis and show how the group can work as a substitute for ego boundaries – which are boundaries of 'self'. This shows the value of social groups and links to a main theme of the social approach. You may not have used Lavarenne et al. but you will have studied a case study looking at mental disorders so you can use your own as an example here.

3 Williams et al. (2013) is one of the contemporary studies in clinical psychology relating to depression. Williams et al. focus on cognitive bias in depression and how internet-based CBT as well as imagery to help with cognitive bias can help those with depression. This study is chosen here because it uses a main theme from the cognitive approach, which is the focus on how information is processed in the brain. You may not have used Williams et al. because you did not choose to study depression or you chose the other study for depression in your course (which is Kroenke et al., 2008). However, you can look at any of the studies in clinical psychology (and elsewhere in your course) and you should find it reflects one of the themes covered here or a main theme you can link it to. Use such studies when comparing ways of explaining behaviour using themes.

4 Van den Oever et al. (2008) is one of the contemporary studies in biological psychology relating to mental disorders. The focus is on how the brain changes in response to rats experiencing certain cues in the environment that have meaning for them. Van den Oever et al. focus on the plasticity of the brain and how neurotransmitter functioning can change the brain. The theme here is neurotransmitter functioning. Another theme in this study is the willingness to use animals in experiments and say the findings are true for humans. You may not have covered this study as it is one of the contemporary studies in biological psychology in your course. You can choose a different study that uses biological underpinning ideas about explaining behaviour.

Studies that are used in the 11 issues and debates

Table 7.9 summarises the studies that have been used in this chapter as examples for the 11 issues and debates. This will show you which studies are useful, which should help your revision.

Table 7.9 Studies used in the 11 issues and debates

Study	Issue/ debate
Bastian et al. (2011); Milgram (1963); Schmolck et al. (2002); Williams et al. (2013)	Ethics/humans
Carlsson et al. (1999/2000); Pavlov (1927); Skinner (e.g. 1948); van den Oever et al. (2008)	Ethics/animals
Burger (2009); Lavarenne et al. (2013); Pavlov (1927); Steyvers and Hemmer (2012)	Practical issues in research
Bandura (e.g. 1961); Milgram (1963); Pavlov (1927); Steyvers and Hemmer (2012)	Reductionism
Carlsson et al. (1999/2000); Raine et al. (1997); Milgram (1963); Williams et al. (2013)	Psychology and science
Blass (2012); Guimond et al. (2013); Pettigrew (1998); Sebastián and Hernández-Gil (2012)	Culture
Bandura (e.g. 1961); Brendgen et al. (2005); Kilham and Mann (1974); Wang et al. (2010)	Gender
Bandura (e.g. 1961); Brendgen et al. (2005); Gottesman and Shields (1966); Tiwari et al. (2010)	Nature—nurture
Geddes et al. (2003); Pavlov (1927); Rosenhan (1973); Watson and Rayner (1920)	Social control
Bandura (e.g. 1965); Pavlov (1927); Sherif et al. (1954/1961); van den Oever et al. (2008)	Psychology in society
Guimond et al. (2013); Pavlov (1927); Raine et al. (1997); Rosenhan (1973)	Socially sensitive research
Baddeley (1966b); Raine et al. (1997); Sherif et al. (1954/1961); Watson and Rayner (1920)	Psychology over time
Bandura (e.g. 1961); Lavarenne et al. (2013); van den Oever et al. (2008); Williams et al. (2013)	Using different themes

Table 7.10 shows the studies in alphabetical order and the number of times they are used in this chapter. This shows that one study can be used as an example to more than one issue and debate.

Table 7.10 Studies in alphabetical order and the number of times they are used in this chapter

Study	Number of times used	Study	Number of times used
Baddeley (1966b)	1	Pettigrew (1998)	1
Bandura (e.g. 1961)	5	Raine et al. (1997)	3
Bastian et al. (2011)	1	Rosenhan (1973)	2
Blass (2012)	1	Schmolck et al. (2002)	1
Brendgen et al. (2005)	2	Sebastián and Hernández-Gil (2012)	1
Burger (2009)	1	Sherif et al. (1954/1961)	2
Carlsson et al. (1999/2000)	2	Skinner (1948)	1
Geddes et al. (2003)	1	Steyvers and Hemmer (2012)	2
Gottesman and Shields (1966)	1	Tiwari et al. (2010)	1
Guimond et al. (2013)	2	Van den Oever et al. (2008)	3
Kilham and Mann (1974)	1	Wang et al. (2010)	1
Lavarenne et al. (2013)	2	Watson and Rayner (1920)	2
Milgram (1963)	3	Williams et al. (2013)	3
Pavlov (1927)	6		

STUDY HINT

You can use the list of studies in Table 7.9 to check your knowledge. Note down which are the classic studies and which are the contemporary studies you chose. You could consider learning something about the studies you did not cover in your course. Alternatively, use the table to substitute studies you did cover.

Examples/applications that are used in this chapter

Table 7.11 summarises some of the examples and applications used in this chapter to discuss the various issues and debates. You could practise using one issue in more than one debate to see how you can use your learning in your course efficiently.

Table 7.11 Examples and applications used in this chapter

Example/application	Example/application
Obedience can be obtained using the trappings of authority.	Neurotransmitter functioning can explain mental disorders.
Understanding about the formation and reduction of prejudice can help society.	When labelled with a mental disorder you are treated according to your 'disorder'.
Working memory knowledge can help with dementia.	Schizophrenia has an element of genes in its explanation.
There are biological aspects of aggression, such as brain differences.	There is cognitive bias in depression and focusing on dysfunctional thinking can help.
Identical twins show more similarity for physical aggression than social aggression.	OCD can be seen as a problem with cognitive bias and cognitive processing.
Playing violent video games reduces our view of our own humanity.	Anorexia nervosa may have an element of genetic variance as a cause.
The ethics of using animals in experiments are important.	Social learning can be seen as an explanation for eating disorders.
Protection and participation rights when researching with children are important.	Psychology has many ways of explaining behaviour rather than one single paradigm.
The experimental method is linked to science.	To build a body of knowledge research studies must show no bias.
Gathering qualitative data is a new(ish) method.	Psychology has developed over time.

STUDY HINT

You can use this list of examples and applications and add to it to make your own list of issues you can use in this synoptic section in your course. You will then have some ideas prepared for your exam.

Summary

- There are 11 issues and debates in psychology in your course. You need to bring in examples to discuss, explain and assess them.
- You need to know about the ethics of using humans as participants in research and the ethics of using animals too.
- You need to know about practical issues in the design and implementation of research, which links to your coverage of method throughout the course.
- Nature–nurture is a debate that you must cover. You also need to cover culture and gender, both of which can relate to ideas about nature and nurture.
- You need to consider psychology as a science, including focusing on reductionism. These issues relate to the method you have covered through your course.
- You need to be able to relate what you have learned about psychology to issues in society, including understanding about how psychology can be used as social control and about researching in socially sensitive areas. You also need to know about the use of psychological knowledge in society, which relates to the key questions you covered throughout your course.
- Finally, you need to know how psychological understanding has developed over time and to have a broad understanding of psychology, focusing on comparing ways of explaining behaviour using themes.

3-cycles: when there is a three-person friendship network.

ABC model: a way of looking at behaviour to see its purpose or function for the individual. 'A' is the antecedent (what leads to the behaviour), 'B' is the behaviour and 'C' refers to the consequences of the behaviour (whether they are rewarding or not).

absolute efficacy: when it comes to assessing the effectiveness of a treatment, this looks at whether the treatment is better than nothing.

abstract (of a study): a brief summary of what was done and what is found in a study, given at the start to give readers an overview.

activation mode: the stress response to things in the environment when there is cognitive and somatic anxiety; the activation mode brings increased blood pressure and heart rate.

acute: when a disorder or illness is sudden in onset and is severe.

addiction: refers to how much the drug takes over the person, and someone addicted to a drug depends a great deal on it, with the drug controlling their behaviour. Someone addicted will put the drug before other things in their life; it pervades their life.

affectionless psychopathy: Bowlby's term for what can develop if a child is deprived of attachment; it means showing little concern for others and being unable to form relationships.

aggression: focused on how someone behaves, such as using threatening behaviour or physical assault, but this might not cause harm and might not be against social norms, so is not violence.

agonist: activates the receptor at the site of the receptor so a message is passed on.

allele: an alternative form of a gene; a variant of a gene. One gene can have more than one variant allele.

alternate hypothesis: the statement of what is expected in a study.

altricial species: those where the newly born or hatched young are not very mobile. An example is humans.

ampliative: means a formulation should not just repeat information already known but, by summarising and bringing in theory, should add new understanding of the case.

anaclitic depression: refers to problems with an infant's physical, emotional and social development arising from separation from the primary caregiver.

androgen: a male sex hormone; testosterone is an androgen. Other androgens are dihydrotestosterone (DHT) and androstenedione, less well-known but also important in male development.

anger: an emotion; anger management is about controlling that emotion. It is about how someone feels.

antagonist: blocks the receptor at the site of the receptor and deactivates it.

anti-social behaviour: any behaviour that is seen negatively by others in the sense of harassing them or causing alarm or distress.

anxious avoidant: one of Ainsworth's attachment types; the child is not distressed when the mother leaves and avoids the mother on her return.

anxious resistant: one of Ainsworth's attachment types; the child stays close to the mother without exploring and is very distressed when the mother leaves. The child seeks comfort when the mother returns but might resist comfort offered. There is an element of ambivalence.

application: refers to theories and studies in a specific area of psychology that are used to look at particular issues for an individual or society.

arousal mode: the vigilance response where there is wakefulness and alertness but, without a threat in the environment, there is lowered blood pressure, heart rate and muscle tone.

article: in psychology this refers to a paper published in a journal, often a study that has gathered data. It can be a meta-analysis (which is still a study) or it can be a review of what has been done in a particular area of study.

assessment (in criminological psychology): refers to assessing the risks and needs of an offender.

assumptions: refers to an area of psychology where the underpinning beliefs and ideas support this being a particular area, such as clinical psychology, which focuses on the mental health or mental disorder aspect of humans.

attachment: a warm, continuous loving relationship that connects someone with another person and which begins in infancy. Attachment is a two-way process that relates to how people react when they are hurt or separated from their attachment figures.

atypical antidepressants: drugs that target serotonin as well as other neurotransmitters such as norepinephrine and dopamine.

atypical antipsychotic drugs: used for the treatment of schizophrenia, they include clozapine and newer antipsychotics that cause fewer side-effects.

autistic savants: a special form of autism where there can be outstanding ability in music, art or numbers with no especial need to practice.

autistic spectrum disorder (ASD): refers to a range of conditions that are neurodevelopmental disorders (DSM-5), including Asperger syndrome and autistic disorder.

bar chart: a graph with bars of various lengths that represent scores; useful for displaying categories.

baseline measure: the measure taken at the start, before treatment or intervention takes place. It acts as a comparison so that improvement (or not) can be measured.

best evidence synthesis: how a meta-analysis must only include studies that have sound methodology, so that just the 'best evidence' is pulled together into the overall analysis.

bilaterally: on both sides of the brain.

bimodal: more than one modal score.

biological sex: this comes from the sex chromosomes (X and Y chromosomes) and is determined by our genes.

biomarker: a biological marker that can signal a disease or problem. It is a biological state that can be measured.

biopsychosocial factors: often looked at when studying a mental disorder. Causes of a mental disorder may be biological, social or psychological, but it is common to look at all three under the title 'biopsychosocial'.

biosocial model (of crime): draws on genes, neuropsychology, environment and evolution to explain criminal behaviour and brings in temperament as an innate factor.

bottom-up (in a psychological sense): behaviour or individual components that generate or explain a theory or idea, and which leads to more complex cognitive processing.

case formulation: in criminological psychology, forming a model taking account of an offender's problems, possibly underlying causes and links to theory and research.

case study (in psychology): an in-depth study of a single person or small group. The small group can be a small element of society, like a community, or it can be an event. More than one way of gathering data is usually used, to get the detail that is required.

catastrophe model (of stress): suggests that performance rises with arousal coming from cognitive anxiety without too much somatic anxiety, but with rising cognitive and somatic anxiety, performance starts to fall. If there is a rise then in somatic anxiety, with cognitive anxiety remaining high, that brings a sudden (catastrophic) drop in performance. If arousal drops, performance can lift again, but not back to its original level.

catastrophising: one of a list of unhelpful ways of thinking used in CBT and refers to where a single negative event is blown up into the precursor of disaster.

check-in (in group therapy sessions): refers to everyone saying how things are going for them as an individual before the 'work' starts. This helps to bridge entering a session and the session itself and can help with joining a group together with a common purpose.

chemotherapy: an overall term for drug therapy and drug treatment.

closed questions: also called 'closed-ended' questions, these restrict someone to the answers offered, and they make a choice, which is forced. There is no room for expansion on an answer.

cognitive anxiety: worry about a situation.

cognitive-behavioural therapy (CBT): a form of psychotherapy based on the idea that problems are caused by thinking patterns.

cognitive interview: a questioning technique used by police and forensic psychologists. The aim is to improve testimony so that it is reliable and not affected by how an interview is done, such as by leading questions.

cognitive processes: what goes on in the brain from information being input by the senses, through it being processes in some way, to there being an output, such as a memory. Language, thought, problem solving, perception, memory and forgetting are all cognitive processes.

cognitive triad: a negative view of three issues – of the self, the world and the future.

collectivist cultures: those that emphasise the needs of the whole group over the needs and wishes of the individuals in the group.

co-morbidity: the state of having more than one mental disorder, or more generally, more than one illness or disease.

competence: an ethical principle in psychology and involves all concerned in research having the ability to carry it out in all respects.

component efficacy: when it comes to assessing the effectiveness of a treatment, this looks at which part of a treatment is the most effective.

compulsions (in OCD): the tasks that people do to relieve the obsessions, such as having an obsessional fear about contamination which leads to the compulsion of continual washing of hands.

concordance: agreement, for example, when one twin is found to have the same characteristic as the other twin.

concurrent validity: when the results of two tests done at the same time, and which focus on the same issue, come up with the same results or match. This would seem to suggest that they measure what they claim to measure. One of the tests can then be used to predict the outcome of the other one.

conditions: in a study the independent variable tends to have two or more 'parts' or conditions, such as words in order (one condition) or not (the other condition).

confounding variables: those that affect the results of a study as they were not controlled for.

construct validity: how far the constructs that are being measured (for example, in the case of depression, the number of days the patient has lacked the motivation to go to work) represent that mental disorder.

content analysis: a method of gathering and analysing data. It means looking in detail at some content – which can be newspaper articles, studies, children's books, drawings, stories, films and so on – and analysing that content using particular categories.

control group (in a study): the group not getting the treatment and not exposed to the experimental conditions

control issues: all the issues and variables that need to be kept the same in an experiment so that only the independent and dependent variables are free to vary.

controls: these are necessary so that the testing of a hypothesis is focused on the statement of what a theory predicts without allowing other variables to have an effect on the results.

convergent validity: when two measures of the same construct agree with one another, thus strengthening the validity of the measures.

core schizophrenia spectrum disorders: these come under the spectrum of psychotic disorders, which includes schizophrenia, schizoaffective disorder, delusional disorder, schizotypal personality disorder, schizophreniform disorder, brief psychotic disorder and some other psychoses linked to substance misuse or medical conditions.

cost-benefit analysis (in animal experiments): looking at three features of an experiment using animals (and applies to other research methods too) before accepting it as ethical. There must be a consideration of harm and distress to the animal which must be outweighed by the benefits of the findings of the study, either for humans or for animals or for society. The benefits must be more than the costs to the animals. The third dimension is to consider how good the research is. If it is not good research, such as being neither reliable nor generalisable, then it should not be done as the costs would not be 'worth' it.

counterbalancing: the order conditions are presented in is alternated to avoid order effects, which are fatigue and practice effects.

covariables: these are found in correlations and the idea is that two variables change together, which means they 'co vary' and they are covariables rather than independent and dependent variables, which are found if a difference is looked for.

covert observations: where the participant(s) does not know he or she is being observed.

covert sensitisation: refers to someone using imagery to think about something unpleasant associated with alcohol.

credibility: in the context of psychology, this refers to how believable the data are, considering issues such as objectivity and subjectivity; and competence and

trustworthiness of researchers. Case study data can include some subjectivity perhaps, given researchers are likely to build a relationship with the individual, but if triangulation shows matching data using different sources then it is likely that data are objective.

crime: a behaviour or an action that is an offence and punishable by law.

criminogenic: anything that is likely to cause criminal behaviour, so refers to underlying reasons for a crime.

critical period: something has to develop or be learned by a certain time or it will not develop or be learned at all. Language was said to have a critical period and Bowlby thought attachment might have a critical period.

cross-cultural design: used when researchers want to look at a particular behaviour or pattern of thinking between different cultures. In order to do this, they compare data from the cultures they are interested in. The researchers may not always gather data themselves from the different cultures; they may use data already gathered about one culture and compare it with data from another culture that look at the same thing.

cross-sectional designs: used when a study looks at what development or change has taken place over time and, in order to do so, people of different ages/stages of development are studied at one moment in time.

cue reactivity: a term used to cover the reaction of someone addicted to alcohol in response to cues in the environment they associate with alcohol.

culture: can be defined as the way a group of people share their decisions and behaviour, such as sharing norms in a society.

data collection tool: a way of collecting data, such as a questionnaire, an interview schedule or an observation sheet.

day care: the term for any situation where a child is cared for by someone other than a parent or legal guardian for some or all of a day and where the child tends to be cared for by someone other than immediate family.

deductive thinking: going from a theory to predict what might happen, according to the theory, and then testing the idea against reality to see if it is the case.

delusions: beliefs that are not borne out by reality, such as believing you are being persecuted or you are famous. Delusions are also positive symptoms of schizophrenia.

demand characteristics: these cause bias if they are present in a study. This is when there are characteristics of a study that lead the participant to guess what is required – it is as if a certain response is demanded.

demographic characteristics: characteristics of a population or sample, such as age, gender, education and occupation.

dependent variable (DV): in a hypothesis, this is what is measured and will be the scores in the results.

deprivation: refers to attachments being removed so that the child is deprived of love and care.

descriptive statistics: numbers and graphs used to illustrate results of a study; they include measures of central tendency and measures of dispersion, as well as graphs and distribution pattern (normal and skewed).

determinism: the idea that an action or situation has to occur as it has occurred because of preceding factors and universal laws. Something that is determined, such as our biology, cannot be changed, by definition.

development quotient (DQ): a score that comes from observing physical and mental milestones in young children and is used before IQ can be measured.

diachronic: means a formulation is not just focusing on the past, present or future but spans all those time periods.

Diagnostic and Statistical Manual of Mental Disorders (DSM): a list of mental health disorders, with their symptoms and features, intended to aid diagnosis.

diathesis–stress model: this takes into account both genetic explanations and environmental factors to explain a characteristic. It is about being predisposed towards a characteristic genetically and there perhaps being stress in the environment or some environmental cause to trigger the characteristic.

directional: a hypothesis is directional if it shows which direction the results are expected to go in, such as 'boys will be more aggressive in the playground'.

disordered thinking: when someone finds it hard to put their thoughts into a logical order so they make sense. This is a positive symptom of schizophrenia.

diversity (when discussing people in a society): aiming to value people's differences and to recognise and respect them.

dizygotic (DZ) twins: not identical twins; they share 50 per cent of their genes, the same as other (non-twin) siblings.

dopaminergic: relating to dopamine.

dopaminergic neurons: neurons that release the neurotransmitter dopamine at the terminal buttons.

double-blind technique: neither the experimenter or person administering the task(s) nor the participant knows which condition is being used at any one time.

downward arrow technique: involves the use of taking something important for the client and examining 'what it means' to the client, drilling down until they cannot answer any more about what it means. At that stage they will have reached a core belief.

drug: a mind-altering substance, chemical in make-up.

duration: in relation to the four Ds of diagnosis, this is a fifth D, which refers to the length of time a symptom has lasted; this is important in diagnosing a mental disorder.

dysfunction: problems in functioning.

echolalia: a stage in autism where a child repeats word for word exactly what they have heard.

ecological validity: the data represent the natural setting, such as a naturalistic observation gathering data from children in their natural setting, perhaps at home going about their everyday life. A naturalistic observation has to study real-life data in a way that represents it sufficiently to generalise the findings beyond that study. A structured observation could set a situation up enough so that it represents real-life interactions and so it could have external validity, but it would not have ecological validity.

emic: an approach to studying cultures that looks at a culture from within it, to find out about its norms and ideas.

emic analysis: when research focuses on specifics in one culture intending to use the meanings of that culture.

empirical data: data gathered directly, using touch, sound, smell, taste or sight.

empiricism: the idea that knowledge can only come through our senses – from sight, sound, taste, smell and touch.

encoding specificity principle: the idea that a cue in an environment, which can be a cognitive environment, will be encoded with the memory and so if the cue is reinstated it will assist recall.

engaged theory: involves giving a framework that can move from analysis of empirical data (data from sight, sound and so on) to a theory for understanding the data (about people and social interactions). It is about theories that can offer a framework for understanding the world and engaging with it, sometimes with a view to changing it. Engaged theory does not accept the idea of grounded theory that data can be collected without a theory in mind.

epigenetic: something that comes from genes but is also affected by the environment.

equality: making sure people are treated fairly with no group being favoured over another group; equality includes race, gender, disability, religion, belief, sexual orientation and age.

ethnicity: a group of people with common social, cultural or ancestral experiences.

ethnocultural: an ethnic group with a specific culture.

ethnography: a research method for getting involved in a culture or situation, where the researcher obtains data directly from participants and the researcher immerses themselves in the culture sufficiently for data to be valid.

ethology: the study of animals in their natural setting.

etic: an approach to studying cultures that looks at norms and ideas between cultures.

etic analysis: aims to use the same procedure(s) across different cultures in order to develop a theory.

event sampling: noting down events of interest each time they occur.

evolution: how what is inherited over time changes due to survival of the fittest, which means certain genes survive and others die out.

experimental group: the group getting the treatment of interest and exposed to the independent variable.

experimental hypothesis: the statement of what is expected in a study using the experimental method.

experimenter bias (or researcher bias): characteristics in the researcher that affect the results. These can be features of the researcher such as tone of voice, dress, age or gender. There is also the important form of bias that can come if a researcher manages to convey somehow to participants what results are expected and this information affects the results.

exposure and response prevention (ERP): a therapy for anxiety that is used for OCD, where the patient faces their fears and experiences the fear until it subsides. The patient is encouraged to avoid carrying out the response that is a ritual for them.

external validity: how far findings can be generalised to other situations, which relies on the study being enough about real-life behaviour that the findings can be generalised.

externalising behaviour: when discussing children, this is behaviour such as aggression, delinquency and hyperactivity.

externalising symptoms: aggressive or defiant behaviour.

extralegal factors: those factors that might affect jury decision-making that are not connected to the courtroom, such as biases towards a defendant.

extraneous variables: those that should be controlled for and can affect results in a study. These include situational and participant variables.

eyewitness identification: identifying someone seen.

eyewitness memory: can be recall or recognition of what has been seen.

eyewitness recall: information given by an eyewitness without a prompt.

eyewitness recognition: occurs when given a choice.

falsification: the idea that we cannot prove anything to be 'true', we can only show something is not true.

family studies (in psychology): these look at what runs in families. If a behaviour or characteristic is found in a family, there is the assumption that there might be genetic factors underpinning the behaviour, such as alcoholism being found in families. There is also the point that people learn within a family and so might imitate family behaviour.

fatigue effect: this can affect results and is when someone is more tired in a second condition because of doing the first condition.

features (of a mental health disorder): usually involve statistics about the disorder, or aspects of it, such as how the illness develops or how other factors, such as gender and age, link.

feral: the term for a child that has had no attachment or socialisation from birth or close to their birth.

first-rank symptoms (in schizophrenia): according to Schneider (1959), these include auditory (heard) hallucinations, thought insertion and delusions. These are positive symptoms. (Negative symptoms include withdrawing from usual activities and lacking emotion.)

flashbulb memory: the name given to a memory of a specific and relevant event that is recalled in a lot of detail as if the detail is lit up and in focus.

Four Ds: used to define abnormality: deviance, distress, dysfunction and danger.

frame of reference: a person's way of looking at things, including understanding their own words and how they use them.

frequency (of scores): the number of times each score is found in a set of data.

frequency table: gives the frequency of each score to make it clear and to prepare for a histogram.

functional: when behaviour is said to be functional, it means it serves a purpose, and looking at what function a behaviour fulfils for a person is about seeing what purpose the behaviour has for that individual.

functional analysis: analysing behaviour in terms of its function, which means what it is for and what it achieves for the person. Functional analysis involves looking at what goes before the behaviour, the behaviour itself and the consequences that come from the behaviour.

gender: refers to more than our biological sex; it refers to feelings, attitudes and behaviours that a culture assigns to the biological sexes.

generalisability: when findings can be said to be true of the target population not just the sample used.

glutamatergic: relating to glutamate.

Good Lives Model (GLM) (of offender rehabilitation): refers to taking the offender's personal values and preferences seriously and providing offenders with the skills and opportunities to develop their primary goals. A treatment plan would reflect these aims.

grounded theory: gathering qualitative data without a research question driving the gathering of those data and then using coding to uncover themes and ideas in the data. From those categories, theory can be generated. The theory comes from the data rather than the theory driving the gathering of the data, as happens in a positivist tradition.

hallucinations: a positive symptom of schizophrenia with a focus on seeing (or smelling or hearing) something that is not there.

Health and Care Professions Council (HCPC): the governing body of psychologists since 2008. The HCPC keeps a register of psychologists and social work professionals who meet their standards and they regulate these professions too.

heritability estimate: the percentage of a characteristic that is down to genes, worked out using family and twin studies to look for similarities between them in relation to that characteristic.

heuristics: mental shortcuts coming from cues in an environment, including from people in the environment. Such shortcuts enable people to make judgements quickly and can be useful; however, they can lead to lack of fairness in judgements.

high systematising: being able to use internal rules and planning.

histogram: a way of displaying frequency as a graph so that the spread of scores is visible to help to display data.

holism/holistic: the view that parts of something can never add up to the whole thing because the whole is more than its constituent parts. The parts are in relation to one another.

hospitalism: relates to anaclitic depression and was used in the 1930s to refer to infants in hospital who faded away, probably because of lack of social contact, with some even dying.

hyper: in a medical sense, 'too much'.

hypo: in a medical sense, 'insufficient'.

identification: the process, in social learning theory, where someone accepts someone else as a role model and imitates them, taking on their values and beliefs.

idiographic: looking at specific, subjective and more personal features of people (in psychology). The focus is on the individual. Idiographic can link to individual differences, where laws are not the focus of interest, but individuals are.

imprinting: when certain animals, such as ducks, follow the first moving object they see, usually the mother, though in experiments it can be a rubber glove (Guiton, 1966).

incidence (of disease): when a disease occurs.

independent variable (IV): in a hypothesis, this is what is set up by the researcher(s).

individualised: when applied to a formulation, this means it focuses on an individual offender rather than a 'type'.

individualist cultures: those that place more importance on the needs of the individual than the needs of the group as a whole.

inductive thinking: observing something empirically (using data from the senses) and then developing a model of how things might 'be' from the data gathered.

inferential statistics: the results of tests. In your course, you will use the Mann Whitney U, Wilcoxon, Spearman's and Chi Squared tests. They also include issues around such testing, such as levels of significance and levels of measurement.

influence explanation: members of the group influence one another and so their behaviour (including their alcohol use) becomes similar.

institutionalisation: taking on the norms, social roles and beliefs of an institution.

institutionalised: living in an institution like a hospital or a prison.

instrumental aggression: when someone uses aggression to achieve a goal, such as using threatening behaviour; harm could result but it is not the aim.

integrity: an ethical principle in psychology; refers to honesty and accuracy in all aspects of research, including publishing honest and accurate findings.

intelligence quotient (IQ): a score that comes from written tests that children complete when they are old enough.

internal consistency: questionnaire items that measure the same construct give the same score. If a questionnaire has one question asking about someone's rating of their own well-being and then another question also asking for their opinion about their well-being, the same score should arise from both questions.

internal validity: measuring what is claimed to be measured with regard to isolating the variable to be studied and 'really' controlling for all other variables so that findings can claim cause and effect because there are no confounding variables.

internal working model: a cognitive framework or schemas made up of mental representations of how the world and others are seen.

internalising symptoms: refers to withdrawal, physical symptoms and anxiety and depression.

international adoptees: children adopted into one country from another, such as a baby in Korea being adopted by a family in the USA.

interval/ratio data: real data where the intervals between the numbers are always equal, such as time in seconds.

intervention (in child psychology): planning an activity or a therapy, gathering data beforehand, then gathering data afterwards to see the effect the intervention has had.

intervention (in mental disorder): a treatment or therapy that is designed to affect the outcome for patients.

An intervention sets out to affect the situation, to lead to an improvement in outcome.

interview: a research method where an interviewer asks questions of an interviewee. There are different types of interview, including structured, semi-structured and unstructured interview.

interviewer bias: a type of researcher bias, where something about the researcher affects the results of a study. This can be their dress or way of speaking.

labelling: describing someone using one or more particular terms and often is used to refer to criminal behaviour. A label can be applied by someone to another person, and does not necessarily reflect the nature of the individual being referred to. That is where the idea of labelling as unfair comes from.

learned helplessness: when helplessness is shown following learning even after an unpleasant response to behaviour has stopped.

lesioning: damaging a part of the brain to see the effect on behaviour. This tends to be done using animals but can be carried out with humans, though as part of a surgical procedure to help someone rather than as an experiment.

levels of significance: the levels at which a null hypothesis might be accepted or rejected, which means levels at which the findings of a study might be said to be due to chance. In psychology an accepted level of significance is $p<.05$.

Likert scale: when statements are rated as 'Strongly Agree', 'Agree' and so on. Scores are allocated depending on the number of ways of judging the statement.

line of best fit: the line that has an equal number of scores on either side of it as far as possible, and goes from where the two axes meet through the mean point, aiming to get the scores evenly each side of the line.

longitudinal design: a psychological study that involves studying the same participant or participants over a period of time to make comparisons in the data gathered over that time period.

long-term separation and deprivation: where the attachment figure perhaps does not return, because they have died, or perhaps they do not return for some time and then not fully back into the child's life, such as in divorce.

low empathising: not good at understanding the emotions and feelings of others.

mainstream society: typical and conventional groups which are taken as the norm.

maternal deprivation hypothesis: Bowlby's idea that if an infant does not have a continual attachment with one main attachment figure in their early life then as the child gets older problems will come from having been deprived of the attachment.

mean point: the plot that represents the mean of each set of data.

measure of dispersion: how widely spread a set of scores is; the more similar scores, the lower the measure of dispersion, and the less similar and the larger the spread of scores, the larger the measure of dispersion.

measures of central tendency: the mode, mean and median of a set of scores. The **mode** is the score that appears most often in a set of scores. The **median** is the middle score in a set of scores; if there is no direct middle, the middle is calculated. The **mean** is the average of a set of scores which is found by adding up all the scores and then dividing by the number of scores.

meta-analysis: a study that uses data gathered from a number of other studies (secondary data) which have sufficiently similar research questions that the findings can be compared and conclusions drawn using results from all the studies.

metacognitions: thoughts about thinking and that are about focusing, for example, on thinking around goals and actions, including about cognitive processes that can achieve goals and skills required for controlling thoughts.

methodology: how a study is carried out and issues around doing psychology.

micro-step: measuring very small decisions that an individual or 'actor' makes, suggesting that at each micro-step the individual chooses whether to, for example, abandon a friendship or stop the use of alcohol.

minority group: a group in a society that is not considered to be as important as the main group in that society; a minority group tends to be different racially or ethnically with different cultural values and traditions from the main group.

minority 'primitive' communities: communities with less culture and society in the sense of not having developed in the same way as more developed communities, but having a simpler way of life.

misinformation effect: when incorrect information after an event is somehow incorporated into the memory of the event and affects recall negatively.

mnemonics: special ways of remembering information. An example is Richard Of York Gives Battle In Vain for the colours of the rainbow.

mode of action: how drugs work, focusing on biological and biochemical explanations.

modelling (in social learning): watching behaviour and imitating it. For modelling to take place, there must be attention paid to issues about the behaviour, there must be retention of what was paid attention to, the behaviour must be reproduced and there must be good motivation to imitate.

monoamine oxidase inhibitors (MAOIs): drugs that help to prevent depression and can also treat Parkinson's disease. They inhibit activity of monoamine oxidase enzymes.

monoamines: neurotransmitters that contain an amino group; they come from amino acids such as tryptophan and the thyroid hormones. Neurotransmitters include serotonin, noradrenaline and dopamine.

monotropy: Bowlby's idea that a child has an innate need to have one main attachment figure.

monozygotic (MZ) twins: identical twins; they share 100 per cent of their genes.

morbidity figures: refer to the number of diseases.

mortality figures: refer to the number of deaths.

multimodal: three or more modal scores.

narrative: means a formulation has qualitative elements and is written in clear, accessible language.

naturalistic observation: where the observer observes behaviour in the natural setting of the participants and there is no intervention.

nature: what comes from our biology and what we are born with.

nature–nurture debate: refers to how much of our behaviour, feelings and thoughts are from nature (inherited through genes) and how much are down to the influence of surroundings and environment (the result of nurture).

needs principle: in the RNR model, this focuses on the causes of offending behaviour, which means focusing on criminogenic factors.

negative automatic thoughts: these come from core beliefs from experiences; they are distorted because they do not fit the facts; they are unhelpful because they are hard to change and lead to unwanted feelings, and they are plausible and accepted as facts.

negative correlation: as one score rises, the other falls.

negative reinforcement: encourages behaviour because something unpleasant is avoided in response to the behaviour.

negative symptoms (in schizophrenia): these are the absence of something, usually the absence of normal functioning.

neurogenesis: the making of neurons from cells.

neuroses: mental health issues that fall just outside normal functioning, but the individual is still in touch with reality and knows they are ill.

neurotrophic factors: responsible for the growth of neurons and maintenance of neurons.

nominal data: data in categories and numbers in particular categories.

nomothetic: a tendency to generalise from instances to more general claims, such as is done in science. Empirical data are collected ('empirical' means gathered directly using sense data, sight, sound and so on) and from those data, general laws are derived.

non-directional: a non-directional hypothesis does not give the direction the results will go in; it just states there will be a difference or a relationship.

non-participant observer: has no role and is separate from what is happening.

non-right-handedness: refers to someone who prefers their left hand for writing, sport and so on, or to someone who can use both hands and so has no preference (mixed-handed).

normal distribution: the scores are clustered around a mean that is very similar to the median and mode of the data set.

null hypothesis: the statement that what is expected will not happen and any difference or relationship is due to chance or some other variable, and not the variable that has been manipulated.

nurture: what comes from our experiences and interactions with our environment.

object relations theory: how an infant experiences their family and objects around them and how these affect their later social relationships and interactions.

objectivity: always required in science, it means not affected by personal feelings or opinions, which is why controls are put in place to avoid subjectivity.

observer drift: when an observer intends to observe certain behaviours but can, during the observation, start to look at something different.

obsessions (in OCD): thoughts that are persistent, irrational and unwanted.

offence analysis: the analysis of a crime, including assessment of the offender. It is from the assessment that a formulation can be done.

official bias: the way the criminal justice system looks more at criminal families, which means people from those families are more likely to get caught and prosecuted, not because there is more criminal behaviour in those families but because they are focused on more.

one-tailed: 'directional' when referring to a hypothesis, which means direction of results is predicted in the hypothesis.

open questions (or 'open-ended' questions): these types of questions do not restrict someone; they ask for opinions, attitudes and feelings and allow for expansion on answers.

open trial: when both the person running the study and the researcher know which group the participant is in.

operationalising variables: making variables fully measurable so that what is done in a study is precise, replicable and clear.

opportunity sampling: taking participants who are available at the time the data are being gathered.

order effects: include fatigue effects and practice effects.

ordinal data: data that are ranked in some way, numbers are ranks.

outcome (in relation to a therapy): this is about its effectiveness. Outcome measures look at how far a treatment has been effective (or not).

overt observations: where the participants know they are being observed and that a study is taking place.

overt sensitisation (in relation to aversion therapy): something is given directly to the person to produce the unpleasant experience, which is generally a drug to make people feel nauseous.

paedophilia: when someone experiences an abnormal or unnatural attraction towards children.

paraphilia: abnormal sexual drives that tend to involve dangerous activities and intense sexual arousal to atypical situations or individuals.

participant observer: someone who has a role in what is being observed as well as being the observer.

participant variables: things in the participants that need to be controlled, such as their emotions, age, gender, level of education and occupation (which of these are important may depend on what the study is about).

pathological: behaviour diagnosed as abnormal due to its extreme or excessive nature.

peer-report data: when someone gives data focusing on someone they know, someone who is their peer.

peer reviewed: how a study or a review article is sent to a journal for publication and before being published is reviewed by people in the field to check that it is appropriate for publication.

personal constructs: our way of understanding other people, such as seeing them as mean or generous. One person might look at people as happy or sad, another might see them as rich or poor – we have different ways of understanding the people around us, and these are our personal constructs.

personal data: information about the participant, such as their age, gender and educational experiences; used in questionnaires and interviews to enable analysis relating to such features of the participants.

perspectives: in psychology, these are different approaches to answering questions about why we behave as we do and think the way we do. Perspectives each have a main assumption about such questions and what methods should be used to study such questions. Perspectives included are psychodynamic, behavioural and cognitive.

phenotype: our genetic make-up as well as our environmental influences.

physical dependency: when the body has got used to a drug and if the person stops taking the drug there will be withdrawal symptoms. Someone physically dependent on a drug needs the drug to function normally.

placebo: a substance or a treatment that is not the treatment being looked at but seems to be the treatment – the participant cannot tell the difference.

placebo control: when the control group in a study has the 'treatment' but has actually had either a sugar pill or a 'dummy' treatment in some way.

placebo controlled trials: where one group gets the treatment and the other gets a placebo treatment.

placebo effect: the term for participants responding to being in a treatment group by improving anyway purely because of being in the group.

positive correlation: as one score rises, the other rises too

positive reinforcement: encourages behaviour because something pleasant happens in response to the behaviour.

positive symptoms (in schizophrenia): where there are additions to behaviour and symptoms that can be seen and noted (i.e. the presence of something).

positivism: the methods of the natural sciences. A theory is looked at, a hypothesis comes from the theory and data are gathered accordingly. Then the theory is amended, accepted or rejected depending on the findings of the examination of the hypothesis. This is 'doing science' because the theory comes first.

post-event information (eyewitness reliability): information encountered after an event has occurred; the implications are that it interferes with memory of the event.

practice effect: when someone gets practice from the first condition, which affects their performance on the second condition.

precocial species: those where the young are fairly mobile and mature from the moment they are born or hatch. An example is geese.

predictive validity: when one measure that occurs is intended to measure something later, and when that later measure is done, the two results can be compared to make sure they agree, indicating that there is indeed predictive validity. As with concurrent validity, one of the tests can then be used to predict the other.

pre-trial publicity: media and other coverage of a case before the trial takes place. It is assumed that jury members will have read or heard about a case that has had a lot of publicity (or indeed any case with any publicity can be a problem) and the question is raised about how, in such cases, there can be a fair trial as the jury will be swayed by what they have heard and read.

prevalence of disease: how widespread it is or how frequently it occurs.

primary data: when data are gathered first-hand for the study in question.

privation: when there has been no attachment of the child in the first place so no attachment is taken away; the infant is privated.

prodromal: the early period in schizophrenia, before the onset of psychotic symptoms. In this period, patients still have insight and have not yet experienced a psychotic break with reality.

projective labelling: using a current label or stigma to predict behaviour in the future and say a person will do something bad.

pro-social: in a way that benefits society, being the opposite from anti-social, which means that society does not benefit from the behaviour.

pseudo-patients: the term Rosenhan used for the people in his study who had no mental disorder and yet when placed in an institution they were not 'found out'. They were called 'pseudo-patients' because they were not real patients, but from the point of view of the staff at the relevant hospitals they were patients.

psychological dependency: when a drug is very important in someone's life and there is an emotional preoccupation with the drug and its effects, as well as a craving for it.

psychometric testing: involves psychological measurement involving objective measures, such as IQ tests or personality tests. Questionnaires can be used, often using a Likert-type scale.

psychopathology: refers to the study of either mental illness/distress or those behaviours and experiences that may indicate mental illness or some form of psychological impairment.

psychopathy: 'a personality disorder characterised by a severe affective deficit, lack of respect for the rights of others and the norms of society' (Woodworth and Porter, 2007, cited in Mossière and Dalby, 2008).

psychoses: mental health issues where the individual has lost touch with reality and is not on a continuum with normal mental health.

psychotherapy: a broad term for counselling, psychodynamic therapy and other similar forms of therapy.

psychotogenic: a drug or other agent that produces symptoms similar to psychosis, such as hallucinations.

publication bias: in psychology this refers to the tendency of journals and publications not to publish results that have negative or non-significant results. This might not be deliberate, but might be that such dissertations are not put forward for publication, for example, or it may be that another study is then carried out to look for more significant results by the researchers. In a meta-analysis, it means the analysis will only use studies that come up in a search and they will be published studies. Studies that do not have significant results or that go against expectations are less likely to be published so there can be a bias in a meta-analysis.

Pygmalion effect: refers to the self-fulfilling prophecy, where higher expectations can lead to better performance.

qualitative data: rich, detailed, in-depth data, like a story.

quantitative data: feature numbers, such as miles or age.

race: is about someone's biology and ethnicity is to do with culture.

racial bias: not treating minority group defendants equally; when applied to juror decision-making, it means black defendants being treated 'more harshly' by jurors and juries than white defendants.

racial identity: someone's investment in their own race and culture; also focuses on power differences with regard to race.

random assignment: a participant is put into one of the groups randomly, avoiding bias.

random sampling: when everyone in the target population or sampling frame has the chance of being in the sample.

randomised controlled trials: where there are different groups that are formed using randomisation so that the groups are equal in terms of characteristics. There is a treatment group and a control group, for example. One group gets the treatment or variable of interest and the other group does not.

randomising: in a repeated measures design, using a coin or a similar method to decide which condition is first for each participant. This helps to avoid order effects.

range: a measure of dispersion found in psychology by taking the lowest score from the highest score.

ranked scale items: when someone does some rating in some way, such as rating someone from 1 to 5 on attractiveness or ranking their liking of a group of photographs from 'Most liked' to 'Least liked'.

rationalism: the opposite of empiricism and means we can only know things through reasoning about them.

reactive aggression: when someone is hostile and wants to hit out at someone, perhaps because of a perceived injustice.

recall: to remember and bring something back to awareness – to 're-call' it. Specifically regarding post-event information, recall refers to someone being asked a question without answers to choose from, so memory is relied upon differently in recall than in recognition.

recidivism: refers to someone relapsing into criminal behaviour after having had some treatment and/or been released into the community.

reciprocity: when someone is a friend of someone who has also nominated them as a friend.

recognition: refers to an awareness that something being looked at (or heard, and so on) has been perceived before. Specifically regarding post-event information, recognition refers to someone being asked a question and given a choice for their answer, which includes the right answer.

recreational drug: a chemical substance that is taken for feelings of euphoria and well-being that it produces. Heroin, nicotine and alcohol are recreational drugs. If they or other drugs are used for medical reasons, they are not then 'recreational'.

reductionism/reductionist: the idea of breaking down a complex phenomenon into simpler components.

rehabilitation: preparing someone to become a productive and settled member of a community.

relapse: re-occurrence of something (usually a disorder). For example, in the case of depression, a returning episode of depression after a 'cure' or an improvement.

relative efficacy: when it comes to assessing the effectiveness of a treatment, this looks at whether it is better than other possible treatments.

reliability: when something done again gets the same results, including when a diagnosis is repeated.

remission: when a disorder or illness is not being experienced at a particular time.

repeated measures: when the participants do all the conditions of a study.

repertory grids: these are used in interviews to look at someone's personality and what variables they use to understand people. The theory is that people have personal constructs about others. A repertory grid enables the comparison of people someone knows, and involves thinking about three such people at a time, thinking of a way in which two are the same and one is different, thus finding out how someone thinks about people.

replicability: how much a study can be repeated. Replicability is required in science because findings have to be reliable and reliability can only be found by replicating studies.

research methods: the main ways data are collected in a study, such as using an experiment, a case study, a questionnaire or an interview.

research question: this is what researchers want answering and a piece of research starts with a research question. The research question guides the choice of research method.

researcher bias: see experimenter bias.

respect: an ethical principle in psychology; involves privacy, confidentiality, getting informed consent and giving the right to withdraw.

responsibility: an ethical principle in psychology; doing no harm and avoiding distress, including giving a debrief at the end of research so any harm can be checked and put right.

responsiveness: as applied to parenting, this refers to when a parent responds to a child's needs and signals in a swift, warm and caring way.

responsivity principle: in the RNR model, treatment must match the offender in terms of, for example, their learning style and motivation to change.

retrospective labelling: going back into the past and using a current label or stigma to explain 'retrospectively' someone's past behaviour, such as saying they were always bad (even though that was not said then).

reversible: an important word when discussing the effects of deprivation, separation or privation in child psychology. It means that problems caused can be put right.

review: similar to a study, it is published in a journal but does not gather empirical data in the way a study does. A review considers what is known in an area of research and is useful for seeing what needs to be studied and what conclusions can be drawn about that area of research.

risk principle: in the RNR model, focus on treatment must be at a level that matches the risk the offender poses regarding re-offending.

RNR model (criminological psychology): the risk–needs–responsivity model.

role model: someone a person looks up to and is influenced by, such as parents, teachers or people on television. Social learning theory says these are people who are imitated.

safe haven (or safe base): someone a young child can turn to when afraid and an attachment figure provides that safe haven.

sampling: finding participants for a study who represent the people that a research question focused on. This is if all the people cannot be involved in the study.

sampling frame: getting enough people who fit the target population and who are known about and available so that a sample can be drawn from them using a sampling technique.

scatter diagram: used for correlation data, which means there have to be two scores that are said to vary together and a plot is given for each of the pair of scores.

schemata (or schemas): ways of seeing and understanding the world that come from experiences of the world. Schemata are organised patterns not only of information but of relationships as well. They involve a structure of ideas and a framework for representing the world.

schizotypy: prone to schizophrenia but not necessarily having that diagnosis. Positive schizotypy symptoms include paranoid ideas (ideas of persecution), perceptual aberrations (such as hallucinations) and magic ideation (thinking cause-and-effect thoughts that are not rational).

secondary data: the data used have already been gathered for a different study.

second-order conditioning: conditioned responses that are not the actual response under consideration, such as, with regard to drug-taking, the release of dopamine. Second-order conditioning refers to emotions and behaviour that go with that response, such as craving a drug or feeling the fear related to an incident in the past rather than reliving the event.

secure base: when a young child explores the environment but keeps returning to be reassured and to check that all is well. They return to their attachment figure.

securely attached: one of Ainsworth's attachment types; the child is distressed when their mother leaves and wants comfort from the mother when they return.

selection explanation: people choose friends like themselves and so members of friendship groups have similarities (including their alcohol use) not because they influence one another but because they have got together because of being similar.

selective serotonin reuptake inhibitors (SSRIs): drugs to help with depression that prevent the reuptake of serotonin in the presynaptic neuron.

self-concept: someone's belief about themselves which is formed by responses of others, which can include labels given by society.

self-efficacy: someone's belief about how far they can succeed in certain situations; self-efficacy plays a role in how someone approaches a situation.

self-fulfilling prophecy: this holds that someone is given an untrue label, which then affects their self-esteem or affects them in some other way. It is because of the label and expectations that arise from the label that someone behaves in a certain way and is then given positive feedback. The positive feedback leads to the prediction being fulfilled and someone becomes the label they are given – the false prediction comes true because of the prophecy.

self-identity: the characteristics and qualities that people use to define themselves.

self-report data: when someone completes a questionnaire or is involved in an interview and is giving data about themselves rather than about others. For example, if you are asked about your attitudes to prejudice, you are reporting about yourself.

semi-structured interview: a method that has an interview schedule and topics to cover but the order that topics are covered and the exact wording of questions can vary.

sense check (of data): looking carefully at the data to see the patterns in it, to work out the distribution, for example.

sensitive period: something tends to develop or be learned within a certain time period, and tends to be better developed or learned then, but that period can be extended.

separation anxiety: the worry and fear a child might experience on being away from their attachment figure, which draws them back to safety.

short-term separation and deprivation: where the attachment figure returns after just a short break, such as if the mother is away in hospital for a week.

similarity-leniency relationship: relates to juror decision making where there is more leniency found if characteristics of the juror match those of the defendant, which is about in-group favouritism.

single-blind technique: the participants don't know which condition is being used but the researcher does.

situational variables: things in the situation that need to be controlled, such as heat, light and noise.

skewed distribution: when the mode is quite different from the mean, with skew to the left if the mode is lower and skew to the right if the mode is larger than the mean.

snowball sampling: finding one participant who then introduces the researcher(s) to others and the size of the sample grows like a snowball.

social constructionism: the idea of features and issues in a society being constructed by that society rather than having some external existence. Evidence for social constructionism is found when looking at how features of society can change over time, and mental disorders fit into that category.

social control: the way people are regulated for the society's sake.

social desirability: a form of bias in results. It refers to how people might respond in a study according to what they think is socially desirable, which will affect the responses.

social disorganisation: refers to a community made up of differences often according to place because where someone lives shapes their behaviour, including their behaviour related to using illegal substances.

social integration: refers to members of a society participating together in something and working together to achieve social rules and social relations, bringing cohesion.

somatic: refers to physiology and physical explanations – think of 'soma' as 'body'.

somatic anxiety: the physiological response, such as sweating and increased breathing rate.

standard deviation (of a set of scores): shows how clustered the scores are around the mean: a small standard deviation means clustered closely around the mean; a large standard deviation means scores are spread out.

standardised instructions (in a study): each participant is given the same instructions so they are not affected differently. This acts as a control. Standardised instructions are an opportunity to set out ethics in a study, such as enabling informed consent if enough information is given, and clearly setting out the right to withdraw.

state anxiety: refers to the emotional response to stressors and is the physical arousal from stress; it can affect mental processing as well as physical responses.

stereotactic surgery: using an instrument that holds the head in a fixed position to use something like an electrode to cause damage (lesions or ablations) in the brain to 'fix' some aspect of functioning.

stigma: a reproach or a 'mark of disgrace', and it refers to someone's reputation and their 'label', which affects their self-concept.

stochastic: used by researchers when variables are unpredictable; opposite of deterministic.

stochastic actor-based modelling: a way of unpicking the two variables of friendship choice and alcohol use in such a way that their co-evolution can be studied in an individual (Mundt *et al.*, 2012).

strange situation procedure: Ainsworth's structured observation procedure where a mother and infant interact with a stranger and the focus of importance is the reunion between the mother and infant to see what type of attachment will be exhibited.

stratified sampling: when a sample represents the target population including specific categories being represented in the proportion in which they appear in the target population.

stressors: things in the environment or inside someone that can cause stress, such as noise in the environment or a trauma for an individual.

strong correlation: when the result of a test is close to 1, either negative or positive.

structured interview: has set questions asked in the same order in the same way with no room to vary questions.

structured observation: where a situation is set up, behavioural categories decided upon beforehand, and the observer knows what they are looking at and what they are looking for.

study (in psychology): where researchers take a research question and gather data to consider that research question, drawing conclusions accordingly.

styles of attachment: according to Mary Ainsworth and others, some infants are securely attached, some show an ambivalent-insecure attachment and some have an avoidant-insecure attachment. A fourth type was later added called a disorganised-insecure attachment.

subculture: refers to a culture within a culture, in that it has different values, beliefs and traditions from the culture it belongs to.

subjectivity: a researcher can affect the data by what they choose to record or how they generate themes from qualitative data, which will affect results too.

submicroscopic: unable to be detected with a microscope.

substance abuse/misuse: when a drug is used in a way that affects someone's mental and physical health. The drug is used in amounts or in ways that are harmful to someone or to others. If the drug is a prescription drug and it is not used in the way that it was intended, then this is misuse or abuse.

summative content analysis: looking at some content and counting specific key terms in that content (the key terms are decided beforehand). There are other types of content analysis.

sustained shared thinking: the adult is aware of the child's interests and understanding and the child and adult work together to develop an idea.

symptoms: things that characterise a disorder with regard to how the person thinks, feels or behaves.

synaptic plasticity: how synapses can become weaker or stronger over time depending on activity of neurotransmitters at the synapse.

tallying: involves making a mark each time a score (or behaviour) is found; the number of tally marks is the frequency that score is found.

target-absent: the person to be identified in an experiment looking at eyewitness testimony is not in the line-up, whether a live one or a photo line-up.

target population: all the people the research question is about, such as all four year olds when looking at friendship patterns in that age group.

target-present: the person to be identified in an experiment looking at eyewitness testimony is in the line-up, whether a live one or a photo line-up.

temperament: the innate part of personality, the part that is in our biology.

testable: means a formulation is measurable, so it can be shown to be wrong and be amended.

testing hypotheses: developing statements of what a theory predicts might happen and then finding a way of testing them.

test-retest: if a questionnaire is carried out twice, on different occasions (a test and then a re-test) using the same participants, the same results will be expected if the questionnaire is reliable.

thematic analysis: a way of analysing qualitative data by generating categories. Researchers transcribe (write out) the data and then sort it into patterns and themes.

theory of mind: how children after the age of about three are able to understand that other people have different thoughts from the child, and that others have different 'minds'. People with autism seem to lack a theory of mind.

thought insertion: when someone thinks someone else is putting thoughts into their head. This is a positive symptom of schizophrenia.

time sampling: in an observation, this is recording what is happening at specific time intervals.

titrated: referring to drug dosage, titrated means dosage is increased over a period of time, as opposed to non-titrated, which means there is a fixed dose throughout.

tokenism: a gesture being made in policy and practice to include someone or some people from members of minority groups, which could refer to citizens when considering public administration. The issue is that it is a gesture and not 'true' inclusion.

tolerance: referring to drug-taking, this is when people need increasing amounts of a drug to get the same high. It refers to a lowering of the response to a drug as the body adapts to it.

top-down (in a psychological sense): moving from complex processing or a theory or idea, to explain behaviour and the individual components.

trait anxiety: refers to someone's traits or characteristics that lead to anxiety or the management of anxiety. This is about individual differences.

transitive triplets: when friends of friends are friends.

triangulation: used in the context of psychological research, this refers to using two or more ways of collecting data so that the data can be compared to look for validity and reliability, giving credibility.

two-tailed: 'non-directional' when referring to a hypothesis, which means direction of results is not predicted in the hypothesis.

Type I error: the experimental/alternate hypothesis is wrongly accepted when the null hypothesis should have been accepted.

Type II error: the experimental/alternate hypothesis is wrongly rejected when the null hypothesis should have been rejected.

typical antipsychotic drugs: established drugs that were introduced back in the 1950s when such drug treatments were first used in the treatment of schizophrenia. They include Haldol (haloperidol), Prolixin and Thorazine. These drugs are neuroleptics because they act at the neuron and, though they can be effective, they cause side-effects.

unipolar depression: characterised by lethargy, feelings of despair and hopelessness and loss of interest in usual activities. Unipolar depression is also known as clinical or recurrent depression and is diagnosed as major depressive disorder (MDD).

universal/universality: some behaviour or characteristic that is found in all cultures where it has been studied and so is thought to be due to nature and come from our biology. All cultures have babies babbling and then using language, for example.

unstructured interview: enables the interviewee to guide the course of the interview and gives more data in terms of quantity. Valid data are also more likely.

validity: measuring what is claimed to be measured, including in a diagnosis.

variance (of a set of scores): the square of the standard deviation; this is square rooted to give the standard deviation as squared measures are harder to use.

vicarious reinforcement: there is no direct reward for a behaviour but someone watching another person being rewarded for a behaviour repeats the behaviour that they have seen rewarded. This is part of social learning theory.

violence: when aggression moves to behaviour that does physical harm and goes against social norms. Violence can be planned behaviour.

voir dire: means 'tell the truth' and the truth must be accurate and given honestly. It is about the competence of a jury (as well as other competencies, such as that of a witness). 'Voir dire' means lawyers for the prosecution and defence questioning jurors about their backgrounds and biases, and jurors can be accepted or rejected on that basis.

volunteer sampling: when someone volunteers to be a participant and in that way selects themselves.

wait list controls: the control group in a study that is on a waiting list for the treatment so they can be compared with the treatment group.

weak correlation: when the result of a test is close to 0.

weapon focus: the way a weapon a perpetrator is holding is focused on, taking attention away from other aspects of a situation or event so they are less well recalled and described.

withdrawal: the symptoms that occur when someone stops taking a drug they have been using.

withdrawal symptoms: occur when someone stops taking a drug. These can include sickness, shortness of breath and dizziness. There are likely to be both physical and emotional symptoms.

x axis: the horizontal line on a graph.

XYY syndrome: refers to a male who has an additional Y chromosome so instead of being XY, there is an additional Y. This is sometimes called 47,XYY as there are 47 chromosomes rather than the usual 46.

y axis: the vertical line on a graph.

702   **Index**

Connell (2014) 255–7, 259
Connon (2003) 91
conscientiousness 207–8
consent, informed 319, 327, 436
construct validity 17, **17**, 425, 432
contamination, avoidance of 76
content analysis **2, 4,** 170, 181–3
contingency management 522, 543
controls 652, **652**
    groups 327, 560
    variables 336
convenience sampling 429
conventional content analysis 181
convergent validity 17–18, **18**
Cook & Wilding (1996) 314
Cooper (2005) 42–3
Cooper (2014) 16
Cordioli (2008) 87
core schizophrenic spectrum **26**
cortical arousal 210, 212
counselling 248
counterbalancing 508–9, **509**
Court (2010) 99
covert observation 420, 438
covert sensitisation **538,** 538–40
credibility **157**
    animal studies 559–60
    case studies 157
    criminological studies 326
    primary and secondary data 155
Creutzfeldt-Jakob disease 23
crime and anti-social behaviour 190, **190**
    see also anti-social personality disorder
    addiction to 247
    biological causes 191, 205–18, 231
    biosocial model 207, **207**
    brain damage 191, 194–9, 231
    brain functioning/ structure 191,
        199–203, 231, 608, 614–16
    crowd behaviour 666
    definitions **190,** 190–1
    drug use 577–80
    environmental influences 191
    gender 193–4, 198, 201–5, 214, 217–18,
        221–3
    genetic influences 203–5
    labelling 191, **219,** 219–23, 225,
        231, 290
    nature *vs.* nurture 191
    official bias 220, **220**
    personality 191, 205–18, 231
    PTSD 196–8
    self-fulfilling prophecies 187, 191, 206,
        224, 225–9, 231
    serotonin 215
    as social construct 191
    social influences 219–29
    social learning 229–31, 682–3
    XYY syndrome **203,** 203–5, 231
criminal convictions or cautions 142
criminal personality 208
criminal psychology, generally *see also* crime
    and anti-social behaviour; eyewitness
    testimony; juror decision-making; offenders
    case formulation **184,** 248–56
    case studies in 322–5

cognitive interviews 233–43
    ethical interviews 243–6
    offence analysis **246,** 246–7
    offender profiling 232
    overview 184, 189
    practical investigations 357
criminogenic 246, **246**
Crisafulli (2008) 88, 92, 672
Crisp (1987) 99
critical period 387, **387**
critical values 179–80
cross-cultural studies
    adoption 374, **390,** 390–3, 431
    advantages and disadvantages 440–1
    attachment 360, 381–5, 383, 439, 440,
        447, 452–6, 608
    child psychology 381–5, 439–40
    cultural difference 2, **3,** 143, 148–52
    drug use and abuse 574–81
    emic *vs.* etic approach 149, **149,** 440
    gender and sex 357–659
    generally 2, **3,** 143, 148–52
    nature *vs.* nurture 440, 657
cross-sectional studies
    advantages and disadvantages 445–6
    child psychology 445–7
    generally 2, **3,** 143, 145–8
crowd behaviour 666
crystal-ball thinking 71
cue exposure therapy
    alcohol addiction 540–1
    drug addiction 503–5, 670
    nicotine addiction 533–5, 604–5
cue reactivity 509, **509**
Culbertson (2012) 534–5, 604–5
cultural difference 625 *see also* cross-cultural
    studies
    anorexia nervosa 92–5, 668–9
    attitudes to treatment 21
    culture-bound syndromes 22–3
    drug use and abuse 574–81
    emic approach 149, **149**
    etic approach 149, **149**
    learning theories 656
    memory 665
    mental disorder diagnosis 1–2, 6, 12–13,
        20–3, 575–6
    nature *vs.* nurture 655–7
    non-right-handedness 149–51
    prejudice 656, 672
    schizophrenia 6, 20–2
    spiritual model 20–1
culture 148, **148**
    collectivist cultures 455, **455**
    individualist cultures 455, **455**
    multiculturalism 656
    subculture 573–4, **574**
Curtiss (1977) 386–8
cyproterone acetate (CPA) 265

D

Daftary-Kapur (2014) 312
Dally & Sargant (1966) 98
danger 8–10
Darby & Jeffers (1988) 300
Dare (2001) 97

Darwin, Charles 363–4, 676
DASS Scales 1
data analysis 327–8, 360, 451
data collection 632–3, 648
Davis (2009) 8–9
Davison & Janca (2012) 215
Dawson (2010) 418
day care 359–60, 375, 393, **393**
    advantages and disadvantages 396–7,
        400–1
    behavioural impacts 393–9, 441–3, 442,
        465–73
    cross-sectional studies 445–6
    observational studies 426, 465–72, 474
    parenting decisions 472–5
    quality 426, 465–72
    trends 472–3
deadlock 335
death, impact of loss 365
debriefing 320
deceit 319, 327, 436
deductive thinking 173–4, **174**
Deffenbacher, J. 261, 340–1
deinstitutionalisation 52–4
Delgado (2000) 58–60
delirium tremens 487
delusions 29, **30**
demand characteristics 227, **227,** 428
dementia 667
demographic characteristics 577, **577**
Deneau (1969) 558–9
Deng (2001) 577–80, 581
denial 323–4
Denys (2003) 84
dependency 18–19, 484–6
dependent variables 336
depersonalisation 104
Depo-Provera 267–70
depression *see* bipolar depression;
    unipolar depression
deprivation 359, **359,** 474
    see also day care
    brain functioning 372–4
    definition 365, 386
    maternal deprivation theory 362, 364–8,
        374, 376–7, 380
    reducing negative effects 374–6
    stages 369–70
descriptive statistics 177–8
determinism 212, **212**
development quotients (DQ) 371, **371**
developmental psychology *see also* child
    psychology
    clinical psychology 2
    criminal psychology 187
    disorder diagnosis 11, 16
    health psychology 477–8
    individual difference 359–60
deviance 8–10, 13
Devine (2000) 291, 294
Dhupdale (2006) 595
Di Chiara (1995) 495–6
Di Chiara & Imperato (1988) 559
Di Ciano & Everitt (2014) 503
diabetes 11
diachronic case formulation 251, **251**

diagnosis
    clinical psychology   8–23, 27–8
    criminal psychology   248–9
    cultural influences   20–3, 575–6
    definition   5
    DSM   10–23
    four Ds   8–10, 13
    ICD   23–7
    medical model   20, 27–8
    recovery model   27–8
    sane in insane places   5, 12, 45, 48, 101–8,
        608, 618–22, 624–34, 653, 664, 672–3
    spiritual model   20–1
    vs. case formulation   248–9, 259
Diagnostic and Statistical Manual of Mental
    Disorders (DSM)   1, 5, **8,** 10–23
    compared with ICD   24–7
    cultural influences   20–3
    DSM 5   10–13, 16, 20
    DSM IVR   10–12, 23
    reliability   12, 14–16, 22, 156
    strengths and weaknesses   13–14
    validity   12, 16–23, 156
diathesis-stress model   38–9, **39,** 44, 59, 140
Diaz (1995)   195–9
Diazepam   535, 537
Dickens (2011)   619
Dickerson (2000)   49–50, 52
difference   179
DiGiuseppe & Tafrate (2003)   346
dignity   241
Dimitropoulos (2015)   97
Dion (1972)   299
directed content analysis   182
DISC1 gen   40
discounting the positive   520
disease
    incidence of   23, **23**
    prevalence of   23, **23**
Disner (2011)   66–7
disordered thinking   30, **30**
disorganised children   380–1
disorientated children   380–1
disqualifying the positive   71
dissociative disorders   12, 27 *see also*
    anorexia nervosa
distress   8–10, 77, 319
disulfiram   535–8, 542
diversity   333, **333**
divorce   365, 375
Dixie (2012)   564–5, 592–6
Dixit (2012)   478, 564–5, 573
Dixon (2000)   53
dizygotic twins   37, **37**
DNA pooling   40
Dobash (1996)   264
Dodge (1983)   421, 423
Dodson (2015)   233
Domestic Violence Perpetrator
    Programmes   264–5
dopamine   107, 210, 488–9, 492, 495–6, 500
dopamine hypothesis   6, 33–5, 106–8
dopaminergic   106, **106**
dopaminergic neurons   489, **489**
double-blind technique   318, **318,** 508, **509**
Dougherty (2011)   84–5

Dowden (1999)   347
Dowden & Andrews (2000)   253
downward arrow technique   72, **72**
DR D2 gene   496–7
Drake & Ward (2003)   249
drug addiction   484
    aversion therapy   503
    biological causes   488–91
    CBT for   519–24
    classical conditioning   512–15
    contingency management   522, 543
    criminal behaviour   577–80
    cross-cultural influences   573–4
    cross-cultural studies   574–81
    cue exposure therapy   503–5, 670
    drug treatment   516–19, 668
    individual differences   490–1
    social learning theories   512–14
    symptoms   485–6
    token economy therapy   543–4
    treatment   490, 503–5, 511, 516–24, 543–4
    violence and abuse, influences of   477
    withdrawal symptoms   **69,** 484, 486–7,
        510–11
drug therapy
    anorexia nervosa   91, 98–100
    drug addiction   516–19, 668
    ethics of   48
    evaluation of   46–8, 69–71, 84–5
    OCD   82–5
    schizophrenia   44–8
    side effects   45–6, 48, 69
    social control   662–3
    unipolar depression   68–71
    withdrawal of   69, **69**
    withdrawal symptoms   69, **69**
drugs   **487,** 487–8 *see also* drug addiction
    abuse/misuse, definition   **487,** 487–8
    dependency   18–19, 484–6
    tolerance   483–4
drugs research
    animal studies   553–5
    ethics   554–7, 560–73
    human participant studies   560–73
    interviews   564–6
    PET scans   568–9
    questionnaires   566–8
    randomised controlled trials   152–3,
        560–1, **561**
Drummond (1995)   509, 540
Drummond (2000)   505
Drummond & Glautier (1994)   509, 540
Drury (1996)   51
Duckitt & Sibley (2010)   656
Duckworth & Seligman (2005)   430–2
Duerr (2013)   31
Duncan & Taylor (1996)   535
duration   9, **9**
Dvir (1995)   228–9, 231
dysfunction   8–10, 13, 106, **106**
dysfunctional families   11
dyskinesia   45

E
e-cigarettes   525–8
e-processors   302–3

ear-witness testimony   314
Easterbrook & Lamb (1979)   454
Eating Attitudes Test   92
eating disorders, generally *see also* anorexia
    nervosa
    autism   414–15
    diagnosis   12, 16
Eaton (2000)   42, 44
Eberhardt (2006)   295
echolalia   403, **403**
ecological validity   421, **421,** 514, **515,** 558
Eddy (2004)   87
Eells (2007)   248–9
Effective Provision of Pre-School Education
    (EPPE)
    day care study   393, 397–9
Efran (1974)   298, 303
ego-dystonic homosexuality   12
ego, fragile boundaries   158–61
Eich (1995)   235–6
Eigsti (2011)   390–3
Eisch & Petric (2012)   59–60
Eisle (1997)   96–7
Elboge (2012)   193, 196–8
electroconvulsive therapy   6
Ellason & Ross (1995)   27
Ellis (1962)   49
Elst (2000)   201
Ely (1997)   172
emic approach   149, **149,** 440, **440**
Emor (1992)   269–70
emotion, flatness   30
emotional reasoning   71
empathy   202, 243
empirical data   105, **106,** 207, **207**
empiricism   652, **652**
encoding specificity principle   235, **235**
energy, lack of   30
engaged theory   176, **176**
Engel (1977)   480
Engl (1998)   93–5
enhanced cognitive interviews   236, 272
Ennett (1994)   514, 587
environment
    crime and anti-social behaviour   191
    schizophrenia   42–4
    unipolar depression   59, 61
EPHX2 gene   122–4
epigenetic   385, **385**
episodic memory   667
equality   333, **333**
Erian (1998)   303
Erickson (2014)   286–7, 316, 318, 326, 356
Esbjørn (2013)   430–1
escitalopram   84–5
ESR2 gene   122–3
ethics
    adult-child power relationships   437
    animal studies   368–9, 554–7, 620, 644–6
    BPS Code of Ethics and Conduct   241,
        258, 319, 327, 328, 437–8, 570–1, 642
    case formulation   257
    child psychology studies   360, 435–8,
        448–51
    codes of ethics and conduct   142, 241,
        258, 319, 327